M000308926

Jaguar Series 3 XJ6 and XJ12
Daimler Series 3
Service Manual

Covering: 3.4, 4.2 and 5.3 Litre Engines

Jaguar Cars Limited

Publication Part Numbers

Service Manual Complete AKM 9006 Edition 2
Service Manual Book 14 AKM 9006/15 Edition 2

Brooklands Books Ltd., PO Box 146, Cobham,
Surrey KT11 1LG, England.
E-mail: sales@brooklands-books.com   www.brooklands-books.com

Part Numbers: AKM 9006 Edition 2 and AKM 9006 - 15 Edition 2

Printed and bound in Great Britain by
Marston Book Services Ltd, Oxfordshire

ISBN 9781855204010   Ref: J71WH   1T7/2374

CONTENT

INTRODUCTION

This Service Manual covers the Jaguar Series 3 and Daimler Series 3 range of vehicles. It is primarily designed to assist skilled technicians in the efficient repair and maintenance of Jaguar and Daimler vehicles.

Using the appropriate service tools and carrying out the procedures as detailed will enable the operations to be completed within the time stated in the 'Repair Operation Times'.

The Service Manual has been produced in 13 separate sections; this allows the information to be distributed throughout the specialist areas of the modern service facility.

A table of contents in section 1 lists the major components and systems together with the section and book numbers. The cover of each book depicts graphically and numerically the sections contained within that book. Each section starts with a list of operations in alphabetical order.

The title page of each book carries the part numbers required to order replacement books, binders or complete Service Manuals. This can be done through the normal channels.

Operation Numbering

A master index of numbered operations has been compiled for universal application to all vehicles manufactured by Jaguar Cars Ltd., and therefore, because of the different specifications of various models, continuity of the numbering sequence cannot be maintained throughout this manual.

Each operation described in this manual is allocated a number from the master index and cross-refers with an identical number in the 'Repair Operation Times'. The number consists of six digits arranged in three pairs.

Each operation is laid out in the sequence required to complete the operation in the minimum time, as specified in the 'Repair Operation Times'.

Service Tools

Where performance of an operation requires the use of a service tool, the tool number is quoted under the operation heading and is repeated in, following, the instruction involving its use. A list of all necessary tools is included in section 1, number 99.

References

References to the left- or right-hand side in the manual are made when viewing from the rear. With the engine and gearbox assembly removed the timing cover end of the engine is referred to as the front. A key to abbreviations and symbols is given in section 1, number 01.

REPAIRS AND REPLACEMENTS

When service parts are required it is essential that only genuine Jaguar/Daimler or Unipart replacements are used. Attention is particularly drawn to the following points concerning repairs and the fitting of replacement parts and accessories.

1.   Safety features embodied in the vehicle may be impaired if other than genuine parts are fitted. In certain territories, legislation prohibits the fitting of parts not to the vehicle manufacturer's specification.

2.   Torque wrench setting figures given in this Service Manual must be strictly adhered to.

3.   Locking devices, where specified, must be fitted. If the efficiency of a locking device is impaired during removal it must be replaced.

4.   Owners purchasing accessories while travelling abroad should ensure that the accessory and its fitted location on the vehicle conform to mandatory requirements existing in their country of origin.

5.   The vehicle warranty may be invalidated by the fitting of other than genuine Jaguar/Daimler or Unipart parts. All Jaguar/Daimler and Unipart replacements have the full backing of the factory warranty.

6.   Jaguar/Daimler Dealers are obliged to supply only genuine service parts.

SPECIFICATION

Purchasers are advised that the specification details set out in this Manual apply to a range of vehicles and not to any one. For the specification of a particular vehicle, purchasers should consult their Dealer.

The Manufacturers reserve the right to vary their specifications with or without notice, and at such times and in such manner as they think fit. Major as well as minor changes may be involved in accordance with the Manufacturer's policy of constant product improvement.

Whilst every effort is made to ensure the accuracy of the particulars contained in this Manual, neither the Manufacturer nor the Dealer, by whom this Manual is supplied, shall in any circumstances be held liable for any inaccuracy or the consequences thereof.

JAGUAR

Daimler

Containing
Sections

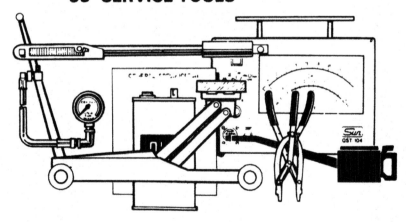

SERIES III
SERVICE MANUAL

STANDARDIZED ABBREVIATIONS AND SYMBOLS IN THIS MANUAL

Abbreviation or Symbol	Term
A	Ampere
A.B.D.C.	After bottom dead centre
a.c.	Alternating current
A.F.	Across flats (bolt/nut size)
Ah	Ampere hour
A.T.D.C.	After top dead centre
Atm	Atmospheres
Auto	Automatic transmission
B.A.	British Association (screw thread)
B.B.D.C.	Before bottom dead centre
B.D.C.	Bottom dead centre
b.h.p	Brake horse-power
b.m.e.p.	Brake mean effective pressure
B.S.	British Standards
B.S.F.	British Standard Fine (screw thread)
B.S.P.	British Standard Pipe (thread)
B.S.W.	British Standard Whitworth (screw thread)
B.T.D.C.	Before top dead centre
C	Centigrade (Celsius)
cm	Centimetres
cm^2	Square centimetres
cm^3	Cubic centimetres
c/min	Cycles per minute
CO	Carbon monoxide
cwt	Hundredweight
d.c.	Direct current
deg.	Degree (angle or temperature)
dia.	Diameter
DIN	Deutsche Industrie Norm (Standard)
E.C.U.	Electronic Control Unit
E.G.R.	Exhaust Gas Recirculation
F	Fahrenheit
F.I.	Fuel Injection
Fig	Figure (illustration)
ft	Feet
ft/min	Feet per minute
g	Grammes (mass)
gal	Imperial gallons
gf	Grammes (force)
h.c.	High compression
hp	Horse-power
h.t.	High tension (electrical)
i.dia.	Internal diameter
i.f.s.	Independent front suspension
in	Inches
in^2	Square Inches
in^3	Cubic inches
inHg	Inches of mercury
kg	Kilogrammes (mass)
kgf/cm^2	Kilogrammes per square centimetre
kgf m	Kilogrammes metres
km	Kilometres
km/h	Kilometres per hour
kPa	Kilopascals
k.p.i.	King pin inclination
kV	Kilovolts
kW	Kilowatts
lb	Pounds (mass)
lbf	Pounds (force)
lbf ft	Pounds feet (torque)
lbf/ft^2	Pounds per square foot
lbf in	Pounds inches (torque)
lbf/in^2	Pounds per square inch
l.c.	Low compression
L.H.	Left-hand

Abbreviation or Symbol	Term
L.H.Stg	Left-hand steering
L.H. Thd.	Left-hand thread
l.t.	Low tension (electrical)
M	Metric (screw thread)
m	Metres
max.	Maximum
MES	Miniature Edison Screw
min.	Minimum
mm	Millimetres
mmHg	Millimetres of mercury
m.p.g.	Miles per gallon
m.p.h.	Miles per hour
N	Newton
Nm	Newton metres
No.	Numbers
Nox	Oxides of nitrogen
N.P.T.F.	American Standard Taper Pipe (thread)
O_2	Oxygen
O/D	Overdrive
o.dia.	Outside diameter
oz	Ounces (mass)
ozf	Ounces (force)
ozf in	Ounces inch (torque)
para.	Paragraph
Part no.	Part numer
PAS	Power assisted steering
pt	Imperial pints
r	Radius
ref.	Reference
rev/min	Revolutions per minute
R.H.	Right-hand
R.H.Stg.	Right-hand steering
S.A.E.	Society of Automotive Engineers
S.C.	Single carburetters
sp. gr.	Specific gravity
Std.	Standard
s.w.g.	Standard wire gauge
Synchro	Synchronizer
	Synchromesh
T.C.	Twin caburetters
T.D.C.	Top dead centre
t.p.i.	Threads per inch
U.N.C.	Unified Coarse (screw thread)
U.N.F.	Unifed Fine (screw thread)
U.K.	United Kingdom
U.S. gal	Gallons (US)
U.S. pt	Pints (US)
V	Volts
W	Watts
1st	First
2nd	Second
3rd	Third
4th	Fourth
5th	Fifth
°	Degree (angle or temperature)
∞	Infinity
/	Minute (angle)
–	Minus (tolerance)
%	Percentage
+	Plus (tolerance)
+ ve	Positive (electrical)
– ve	Negative (electrial)
±	Plus or minus (tolerance)
//	Second (angle)
Ω	Ohms

ENGINE DATA — 3.4 LITRE

General Data

Number of cylinders	6 (in line)	
Bore	83,0 mm	3.2677 in
Stroke	106,0 mm	4.1732 in
Cubic capacity	3441,2 cm³	210 in³

Cylinder Block

Material	Chromium cast iron			
Type of cylinder liner	Dry (used for salvage only)			
Material (liners)	Cast iron			
Liner interference fit	0,064 to 0,0114 mm		0.0025 to 0.0045 in	
Bore diameters after honing: Piston Grade	Maximum	Minimum	Maximum	Minimum
F	82,997 mm	82,989 mm	3.2676 in	3.2673 in
G	83,007 mm	83,000 mm	3.2680 in	3.2677 in
H	83,017 mm	83,010 mm	3.2684 in	3.2681 in

NOTE: 'S' grade pistons are 82,995 to 83,020 mm (3.2675 to 3.2685 in) diameter across bottom of skirt at right angles to gudgeon pins. Honed diameter of bore for these pistons must be 0,018 to 0,133 mm (0.0007 to 0,0013 in) greater than measured diameter of piston at this position.

Outside diameter of liners	86,220 to 86,246 mm	3.3945 to 3.3955 in
Line bore for main bearings	74,08 to 74,09 mm	2.9165 to 2.9170 in

Cylinder Head

Material	Aluminium alloy	
Valve seat angle: Inlet	45°	
Exhaust	45°	

Crankshaft

Material	BS 970–709M 40/T (EN 19 T) or BS 970–605M 36/T (EN 16 T)	
Number of main bearings	7	
Main bearing type	Vandervell VP2C	
Journal diameter	69,855 to 69,842 mm	2.7502 to 2.7497 in
Journal length, over 2,4 mm (0.095 in) radii:		
Front	39,675 ± 0,254 mm	1.562 ± 0.010 in
Centre	34,938 to 34,950 mm	1.3755 to 1.3760 in
Intermediate	30,912 to 31,013 mm	1.217 to 1.221 in
Rear	42,4 mm	1.67 in
Thrust taken	Centre bearing thrust washers	
Thrust washer thickness	2,311 to 2,362 mm or 2,413 to 2,464 mm	0.091 to 0.093 in or 0.095 to 0.097 in
Permissible end-float	0,10 to 0,15 mm	0.004 to 0.006 in
Width of main bearing: Front	34,544 to 34,925 mm	1.360 to 1.375 in
Centre	28,321 to 28,702 mm	1.115 to 1.130 in
Rear	34,544 to 34,925 mm	1.360 to 1.375 in
Intermediate	25,019 to 24,400 mm	0.985 to 1.00 in
Diametrical clearance	0,020 to 0,064 mm	0.0008 to 0.025 in
Crankpins: Diameter	52,987 to 52,974 mm	2.0861 to 2.0865 in
Length	30,142 to 30,193 mm	1.1867 to 1.1887 in
Regrind undersizes	0,51 mm	0.020 in
Minimum diameter for regrind	−0,51 mm	−0.020 in

Connecting Rods

Length between centres	196,85 mm	7.75 in
Big-end bearing type	Vandervell VP2C	
Bore for big-end bearing	56,718 to 56,731 mm	2.2330 to 2.2335 in
Width of big-end bearing	24,38 to 24,77 mm	0.960 to 0.975 in
Big-end diametrical clearance	0,025 to 0,069 mm	0.0010 to 0.0027 in
Big-end side clearance	0,132 to 0,234 mm	0.052 to 0.0092 in
Small-end bush material	Vandervell VP10	
Bore for small-end bush	25,387 to 25,413 mm	0.9995 to 1.0005 in
Width of small-end bush	26,92 to 27,43 mm	1.06 to 1.08 in
Bore diameter of small-end bush	22,231 to 22,235 mm	0.87525 to 0.87540 in

04—1

GENERAL SPECIFICATION

Pistons	Type	Solid skirt	
	Skirt clearance (measured midway down bore across bottom of piston skirt)	0,018 to 0,033 mm	0.0007 to 0.0013 in
Piston Rings	Number of compression rings	2	
	Number of oil control rings	1	
	Top compression ring width	1,562 to 1,588 mm	0.0615 to 0.0625 in
	Second compression ring width	1,961 to 1,986 mm	0.0772 to 0.0782 in
	Oil control ring width	Self expanding ring	
	Top compression ring thickness	3,150 to 3,302 mm	0.124 to 0.130 in
	Second compression ring thickness	3,150 to 3,302 mm	0.124 to 0.130 in
	Side clearance of top compression ring in groove	0,038 to 0,089 mm	0.0015 to 0.0035 in
	Side clearance of second compression ring in groove	0,038 to 0,089 mm	0.0015 to 0.0035 in
	Side clearance of oil control ring in groove	Self expanding ring; groove width	
		4,008 to 4,034 mm	0.1578 to 0.1588 in
	Top compression ring gap in bore	0,33 to 0,46 mm	0.013 to 0.018 in
	Second compression ring gap in bore	0,23 to 0,36 mm	0.009 to 0.014 in
Gudgeon Pins	Type	Fully floating	
	Length	71,882 to 72,263 mm	2.830 to 2.845 in
	Outside diameter: Marked Red	22,228 to 22,230 mm	0.8751 to 0.8752 in
	Marked Green	22,225 to 22,228 mm	0.8750 to 0.8751 in
Camshafts	Number of journals	4 per shaft	
	Number of bearings	4 per shaft (8 half bearings)	
	Type of bearings	White metal steel-backed, Vandervell	
	Journal diameter	25,375 to 25,387 mm	0.999 to 0.9995 in
	Diametrical clearance	0,013 to 0,056 mm	0.0005 to 0.0022 in
	Thrust taken	Front end hafts	
Valves and Valve Springs	Inlet valve material	Silico chrome steel	
	Exhaust valve material	Austenitic steel	
	Inlet valve head diameter	44,32 to 44,58 mm	1.745 to 1.755 in
	Exhaust valve head diameter	41,15 to 41,40 mm	1.620 to 1.630 in
	Valve stem diameter: Inlet and exhaust	7,87 to 7,94 mm	0.310 to 0.3125 in
	Valve lift	9,53 mm	0.375 in
	Inlet valve clearance	0,305 to 0,356 mm	0.012 to 0.014 in
	Exhaust valve clearance	0,305 to 0,356 mm	0.012 to 0.014 in
	Outer valve spring free length	53,42 mm	2.103 in
	Inner valve spring free length	44,04 mm	1.734 in
Valve Guides and Seats	Valve guide material	Cast iron (Brico Alloy 2 or BS. 1452/12)	
	Inlet valve guide length	47,24 mm	1.86 in
	Exhaust valve guide length	49,53 mm	1.95 in
	Outside diameter (both guides)		
	Standard	12,725 to 12,751 mm	0.501 to 0.502 in
	First oversize	12,776 to 12,802 mm	0.503 to 0.504 in
	Second oversize	12,852 to 12,878 mm	0.506 to 0.507 in
	Third oversize	12,979 to 13,005 mm	0.511 to 0.512 in
	Interference fit in cylinder head	0,013 to 0,056 mm	0.0005 to 0.0022 in
	Valve seat material	Sintered iron (Brico AO25/M)	
	Inlet valve seat outside diameter: Standard	47,041 to 47,054 mm	1.852 to 1.8525 in
	Interference fit in cylinder head	0,0762 mm	0.003 in
	Exhaust valve seat outside diameter: Standard	43,066 to 43,078 mm	1.6955 to 1.6960 in
	Interference fit in cylinder head	0,0762 mm	0.003 in
Tappets	Tappet material	Chilled cast iron	
	Outside diameter of tappet	34,895 to 34,905 mm	1.3738 to 1.3742 in
	Tappet guide interference fit	0,185 to 0,221 mm	0.0073 to 0.0087 in
	Diametrical clearance of tappet in guide	0,020 to 0,048 mm	0.0008 to 0.0019 in

04—2

Lubricating System	Oil pump	Hobourn-Eaton rotor-type	
	Oil filter	Full-flow, renewable element or disposable canister	

Timing Chains and Sprockets	Type	Duplex	
	Pitch	9,5 mm	⅜ in
	Number of pitches: Lower chain	82	
	Upper chain	100	
	Crankshaft sprocket: Teeth	21	
	Intermediate sprocket (outer): Teeth	28	
	Intermediate sprocket (inner): Teeth	20	
	Camshaft sprockets: Teeth	30	

4.2 LITRE ENGINE

General Data	Number of cylinders	6 (in line)	
	Bore	92,07 mm	3.625 in
	Stroke	106 mm	4,173 in
	Cubic capacity	4235 cm³	258.43 in³

Cylinder Block	Material (cylinder block)	Chromium cast iron			
	Type of cylinder liner (early cars only)	Interference fit, dry liner			
	Material (liners)	Brivadium			
	Liner interference fit	0,076 to 0,127 mm		0.003 to 0.005 in	
	Bore diameters after honing: Piston Grade	Maximum	Minimum	Maximum	Minimum
	F	92,083 mm	92,075 mm	3.6253 in	3.6250 in
	G	92,093 mm	92,085 mm	3.6257 in	3.6254 in
	H	92,103 mm	92,095 mm	3.6261 in	3.6258 in

NOTE: 'S' grade pistons are 92,080 to 92,105 mm (3.6252 to 3.6262 in) diameter across bottom of skirt at right angles to gudgeon pins. Honed diameter of bore for these pistons must be 0,018 to 0,033 mm (0.0007 to 0.0013 in) greater than measured diameter of piston at this position.

	Outside diameter of liners	95,66 mm max. 95,63 mm min.	3.766 in max. 3.765 in min.
	Line bore for main bearings	74,08 to 74,09 mm	2.9165 to 2.9170 in

Cylinder Head	Material	Aluminium alloy	
	Valve seat angle: Inlet	45°	
	Exhaust	45°	

Crankshaft	Material	En 16, 18 or 111	
	Number of main bearings	7	
	Main bearing type	Vandervell VP2C	
	Journal diameter	69,85 to 69,86 mm	2.7500 to 2.7505 in
	Journal length (over ³⁄₃₂ in radii): Front	39,69 ± 0,254 mm	1.562 ± 0.10 in
	Centre	34,925 $^{+0.025}_{-0.013}$ mm	1.375 $^{+0.001}_{-0.0005}$ in
	Intermediate	30,96 ± 0,051 mm	1.2188 ± 0.002 in
	Rear	42,86 mm	1.6875 in
	Thrust taken	Centre main bearing cap, half washers	
	Thrust washer thickness	2,31 to 2,36 mm	0.091 to 0.093 in
	Permissible end-float	0,10 to 0,15 mm	0.004 to 0.006 in
	Width of main bearing: Front	34,54 to 34,93 mm	1.360 to 1.375 in
	Centre	28,32 to 28,70 mm	1.115 to 1.130 in
	Intermediate	24,81 to 25,40 mm	0.985 to 1.00 in
	Rear	34,54 to 34,93 mm	1.360 to 1.375 in

GENERAL SPECIFICATION

	Diametrical clearance	0,0203 to 0,0635 mm	0.0008 to 0.0025 in
	Crankpins: Diameter	52,984 to 53,00 mm	2.0860 to 2.0866 in
	Length	30,158 to 30,181 mm	1.1873 to 1.1882 in
	Regrind undersize	0,51 mm	0.020 in
	Minimum diameter for regrind	− 0,51 mm	− 0.02 in
Connecting Rods	Length between centres	196,85 mm	7.75 in
	Big-end bearing type	Vandervell VP2C	
	Bore for big-end bearing	56,72 to 56,73 mm	2.2330 to 2.2335 in
	Width of big-end bearing	24,38 to 24,77 mm	0.960 to 0.975 in
	Big-end diametrical clearance	0,025 to 0,069 mm	0.0010 to 0.0027 in
	Big-end side clearance	0,147 to 0,221 mm	0.0058 to 0.0087 in
	Small-end bush material	Vandervell VP10	
	Bore for small-end bush	25,4 ± 0,013 mm	1.0 ± 0.0005 in
	Width of small-end bush	26,92 to 27,43 mm	1.060 to 1.080 in
	Bore diameter of small-end bush	$22,23 ^{+0,0038}_{-0,000}$ mm	$0.87525 ^{+0.00015}_{-0.000}$ in
Pistons	Type	Solid skirt	
	Skirt clearance (measured midway down bore across bottom of piston skirt).	0,018 to 0,033 mm	0.0007 to 0.0013 in
Piston Rings	Number of compression rings	2	
	Number of oil control rings	1	
	Top compression ring width	2 mm nominal	0.0781 in nominal
	Second compression ring width	2 mm nominal	0.0781 in nominal
	Oil control ring width	Self expanding	
	Top compression ring thickness	4,35 to 4,60 mm	0.171 to 0.188 in
	Second compression ring thickness	4,35 to 4,60 mm	0.171 to 0.188 in
	Side clearance of top compression ring in groove	0,038 to 0,089 mm	0.0015 to 0.0035 in
	Side clearance of second compression ring in groove	0,038 to 0,089 mm	0.0015 to 0.0035 in
	Side clearance of oil control ring in groove	Self expanding	
Prior to Vin No. 8L 103481	Top compression ring gap in bore	0,38 to 0,51 mm	0.015 to 0.020 in
	Second compression ring gap in bore	0,23 to 0,35 mm	0.009 to 0.014 in
	Oil control ring gap in bore	0,38 to 1,14 mm	0.015 to 0.045 in
From Vin No. 8L 103481	Top ring	0,38 to 0,51 mm	0.015 to 0.020 in
	2nd ring	0,41 to 0,66 mm	0.016 to 0.026 in
	Oil control ring	0,31 to 0,61 mm	0.012 to 0.024 in
Gudgeon Pins	Type	Fully-floating	
	Length	75,95 to 76,2 mm	2.990 to 3.000 in
	Outside diameter: Marked Red	22,228 to 22,230 mm	0.8751 to 0.8752 in
	Marked Green	22,225 to 22,228 mm	0.8750 to 0.8751 in
Camshafts	Number of journals	4 per shaft	
	Number of bearings	4 per shaft (8 half bearings)	
	Type of bearings	White metal steel-backed, Vandervell	
	Journal diameter	25,387 to 25,375 mm	0.9995 to 0.9990 in
	Diametrical clearance	0,013 to 0,051 mm	0.0005 to 0.002 in
	Thrust taken	Front end of shafts	
Valves and Valve Springs	Inlet valve material	Silico chrome steel	
	Exhaust valve material	Austenitic steel	
	Inlet valve head diameter	47,50 to 47,75 mm	1.870 to 1.880 in
	Exhaust valve head diameter	41,15 to 41,40 mm	1.620 to 1.630 in
	Valve stem diameter: Inlet and exhaust	7,87 to 7,94 mm	0.310 to 0.3125 in
	Valve lift	9,53 mm	0.375 in
	Inlet valve clearance	0,305 to 0,356 mm	0.012 to 0.014 in
	Exhaust valve clearance	0,305 to 0,356 mm	0.012 to 0.014 in
	Outer valve spring free length	49,21 to 50,80	1.938 to 2.00 in
	Inner valve spring free length	42,07 to 43,66 mm	1.656 to 1.719 in

04—4

4 2 litre (cont)

Valve Guides and Seats	Valve guide material	Cast iron (Brico Alloy 2 or BS.1452/12	
	Inlet valve guide length	47,24 mm	1.86 in
	Exhaust valve guide length	49,53 mm	1.95 in
	Outside diameter (both guides):		
	Standard	12,725 to 12,751 mm	0.501 to 0.502 in
	First oversize	12,776 to 12,802 mm	0.503 to 0.504 in
	Second oversize	12,852 to 12,878 mm	0.506 to 0.507 in
	Third oversize	12,979 to 13,005 mm	0.511 to 0.512 in
	Interference fit in cylinder head	0,013 to 0,056 mm	0.0005 to 0.0022 in
	Valve seat material	Sintered iron (Brico AO25/M)	
	Inlet valve seat outside diameter: Standard	47,041 to 47,054 mm	1.852 to 1.8525 in
	Interference fit in cylinder head	0,0762 mm	0.003 in
	Exhaust valve seat outside diameter: Standard	43,066 to 43,078 mm	1.6955 to 1.6960 in
	Interference fit in cylinder head	0,0762 mm	0.003 in
Tappets	Tappet material	Chilled cast iron	
	Outside diameter of tappet	34,895 to 34,905 mm	1.3738 to 1.3742 in
	Tappet guide interference fit	0,185 to 0,221 mm	0.0073 to 0.0087 in
	Diametrical clearance of tappet in guide	0,020 to 0,048 mm	0.0008 to 0.0019 in
Lubricating System	Oil pump	Hobourn-Eaton rotor-type	
	Oil filter	Full-flow, renewable element	
	Min pressure — hot @ 3000 rev/min	2,8 kg/cm^2	40 lb/in^2
Timing Chains and Sprockets	Type	Duplex	
	Pitch	9,5 mm	⅜ in
	Number of pitches: Lower chain	82	
	Upper chain	100	
	Crankshaft sprocket: Teeth	21	
	Intermediate sprocket (outer): Teeth	28	
	Intermediate sprocket (inner): Teeth	20	
	Camshaft sprockets: Teeth	30	

ENGINE DATA — 5.3 LITRE

General Data	Number of cylinders	12	
	Stroke	70 mm	2.756 in
	Bore	90 mm	3.543 in
	Cubic capacity	5343 cm^3	326.0 in^3
	Ignition timing: Initial static setting, to start engine only		
	'A' Emission spec.	9° ± 1° B.T.D.C.	
	'B' Emission spec.	4° ± 1° B.T.D.C.	

GENERAL SPECIFICATION

Cylinder Block			
	Material (cylinder block)	Aluminium alloy	
	Angle of cylinders	60° Vee	
	Type of cylinder liner	Slip fit, wet liner	
	Material (liners)	Cast iron	
	Nominal size of bore after honing:		
	Grade 'A'—Red	89,98 mm	3.543 in
	Grade 'B'—Green	90,01 mm	3.544 in
	Outside diameter of liner—both grades	97,99 mm + 0.02 mm −0,00 mm	3.858 in + 0.001 in −0.00 in
	Main line bore for main bearings	80,429 to 80,434 mm	3.1665 to 3.1667 in

Cylinder Heads			
	Material	Aluminium alloy	
	Valve seat angle: Inlet	44½°	
	Exhaust	44½°	

Crankshaft			
	Material	Manganese molybdenum steel	
	Number of main bearings	7	
	Main bearing type	Vandervell V.P.3	
	Journal diameter	76,218 to 76,231 mm	3.0007 to 3.0012 in)
	Journal length: Front	29,72 to 29,97 mm	1.170 to 1.180 in
	Centre	36,20 to 36,22 mm	1.425 to 1.426 in
	Intermediate	30,43 to 30,53 mm	1.198 to 1.202 in
	Rear	36,20 to 36,22 mm	1.425 to 1.426 in
	Thrust taken	Centre bearing thrust washers	
	Thrust washer thickness	2,57 to 2,62 mm	0.101 to 0.103 in
	Permissible end-float	0,10 to 0,15 mm	0.004 to 0.006 in
	Width of main bearing: Front	24,40 to 24,65 mm	0,963 to 0,973 in
	Centre	30,2 to 30,5 mm	1.190 to 1.200 in
	Intermediate	24,40 to 24,65 mm	0.963 to 0.973 in
	Rear	30,2 to 30,5 mm	1.190 to 1.200 in
	Diametrical clearance: all bearings	0,04 to 0,07 mm	0.0015 to 0.003 in
	Crankpin diameter	58,40 to 58,42 mm	2.2994 to 2.3000 in
	Crankpin length	43,15 to 43,20 mm	1.699 to 1.701 in

Connecting Rods			
	Length between centres	151,4 mm +0,12 mm −0,00 mm	5.96 in +0.005 in −0.000 in
	Big-end bearing material	VP2C	
	Bore for big-end bearing	62,0 mm +0,15 mm −0,00 mm	2.441 in +0.006 in −0.000 in
	Width of big-end bearing	18,3 to 18,5 mm	0.720 to 0.730 in
	Big-end diametrical clearance	0,04 to 0,09 mm	0.0015 to 0.0034 in
	Big-end side clearance	0,17 to 0,33 mm	0.007 to 0.013 in
	Small-end bush material	VP.10	
	Bore for small-end bush	26,98 mm +0,025 mm −0,00 mm	1.062 in +0.001 in −0.000 in.
	Width of small-end bush	26,2 to 26,7 mm	1.03 to 1.05 in
	Bore diameter of small-end bush	23,813 to 23,818 mm	0.9375 to 0.9377 in

Pistons			
	Type	Solid skirt	
	Skirt clearance (measured midway down bore across bottom of piston skirt)	0,03 to 0,04 mm	0.0012 to 0.0017 in

Piston Rings			
	Number of compression rings	2	
	Number of oil control rings	1	
	Top compression ring thickness	3,81 to 4,06 mm	0.150 to 0.160 in
	Second compression ring thickness	3,81 to 4,06 mm	0.150 to 0.160 in
	Oil control ring width	Self expanding	
	Width of oil control ring rails	2,62 ± 0,07 mm	0.103 ± 0.003 in
	Top compression ring width	1,58 to 1,60 mm	0.062 to 0.063 in
	Second compression ring width	1,96 to 1,98 mm	0.077 to 0.078 in
	Side clearance of top compression ring in groove	0,07 mm	0.0029 in
	Side clearance of second compression ring in groove	0,09 mm	0.0034 in
	Side clearance of oil control rings in groove	0,14 to 0,17 mm	0.0055 to 0.0065 in
	Top compression ring gap in bore	0,36 to 0,51 mm	0.014 to 0.020 in
	Second compression ring gap in bore	0,25 to 0,38 mm	0.010 to 0.015 in
	Gap of oil control ring rails in bore	0,38 to 1,14 mm	0.015 to 0.045 in

04—6

Gudgeon Pins	Type	Fully floating	
	Length	79,25 to 79,38 mm	3.120 to 3.125 in
	Outside diameter: Grade 'A' Red	23,81 mm	0.9375 in
	Grade 'B' Green	23,76 mm	0.9373 in

Camshafts	Number of journals	7 per shaft	
	Number of bearings	7 per shaft (14 half bearings)	
	Type of bearings	Aluminium alloy—camshafts run direct in caps and tappet block	
	Journal diameter: All journals	26,93 mm +0.013 mm −0,000 mm	1.0615 in +0.0005 −0.000 in
	Diametrical clearance	0,03 to 0,07 mm.	0.001 to 0.003 in
	Thrust taken	Front end of shafts	

Jackshaft	Number of bearings	3	
	Diametrical clearance in block	0,013 to 0,076 mm	0.0005 to 0.0003 in
	Thrust taken	Front end of shaft	
	Permissible end-float	0,13 mm	0.005 in
	Line bore of front bearing	31,78 to 31,80 mm	1.251 to 1.252 in
	Line bore of centre and rear bearing	30,23 to 30,25 mm	1.190 to 1.191 in

Valves and Valve Springs	Inlet valve material	Silico chrome steel	
	Exhaust valve material	Austenitic steel	
	Inlet valve head diameter (except HE)	41,22 to 41,32 mm	1.623 to 1.627 in
	Inlet valve head diameter HE	41,15 to 41,40 mm	1.620 to 1.630 in
	Exhaust valve head diameter (except HE)	34,5 to 34,6 mm	1.358 to 1.362 in
	Exhaust valve head diameter HE	34,32 to 34,6 mm	1.355 to 1.365 in
	Valve stem diameter: Inlet and exhaust	7,854 to 7,866 mm	0.3092 to 0.3093 in
	Valve lift	9,5 mm	0.375 in
	Inlet valve clearance (except HE)	0,305 to 0,356 mm	0.012 to 0.014 in
	Inlet valve clearance HE	0,254 to 0,305 mm	0.010 to 0.012 in
	Exhaust valve clearance (except HE)	0,305 to 0,356 mm	0.012 to 0.014 in
	Exhaust valve clearance HE	0,254 to 0,305 mm	0.010 to 0.012 in
	Outer valve spring free length	53,4 mm	2.103 in
	Inner valve spring free length	44,0 mm	1.734 in

Valve Guides and Seats	Valve guide material	Cast iron	
	Inlet valve guide length	48,5 mm	1.910 in
	Exhaust valve guide length (except HE)	54,0 mm	2.125 in
	Exhaust valve guide length HE	43.82 mm	1.725 in
	Inlet valve guide outside diameter	As exhaust valve guide	
	Exhaust valve guide outside diameter:		
	Standard	12,75 to 12,72 mm	0.502 to 0.501 in
	First oversize (2 grooves)	12,88 to 12,85 mm	0.507 to 0.506 in
	Second oversize (3 grooves)	13,01 to 12,98 mm	0.512 to 0.511 in
	Inlet valve guide finished bore	7,90 to 7,92 mm	0.311 to 0.312 in
	Exhaust valve guide finished bore	7,90 to 7,92 mm	0.311 to 0.312 in
	Maximum clearance between valve stem and guide ..	0,05 to 0,06 mm	0.0020 to 0.0023 in
	Interference fit in cylinder head	0,05 to 0,15 mm	0.002 to 0.006 in
	Valve seat insert material	Sintered iron	

Service Replacements	Inlet valve seat insert outside diameter (except HE) ..	44,30 mm +0.01/−0,00 mm	1.744 in +0.0005/−0.0000 in
	Inlet valve seat insert HE diameter	42,93 mm +0.01/−0,00 mm	1.6901 in +0.0005/−0.0000 in
	Exhaust valve seat insert outside diameter	38,17 mm +0.01/−0,00 mm	1.503 in +0.0005/−0.0000 in
	Inlet valve seat inside diameter (except HE)	35,56 mm +0.17/−0,00 mm to 39,74 mm +0.25/−0,00 mm	1.400 in +0.003/−0.000 in to 1.565 in +0.010/−0.000 in
	Inlet valve seat inside diameter HE	35,56 mm +0.17/−0,00 mm to 39,95 mm +0.25/−0,00	1.400 +0.0005/−0.0000 in to 1.573 +0.010/−0.000 in
	Exhaust valve seat inside diameter (except HE)	30,1 mm +0.07/−0,00 mm to 33,4 mm +0.12/−0,00 mm	1.185 in +0.003/−0.000 in to 1.315 in +0.005/−0.000 in
	Exhaust valve seat inside diameter HE	30,45 mm +0.07/−0,00 mm to 33,51 mm +0.25/−0,00 mm	1.199 in +0.003/−0.000 in to 1.280 in +0.010/−0.000 in

Tappets and Tappet Guides	Tappet material	Cast iron (chilled)	
	Outside diameter of tappet	34,87 to 34,90 mm	1.373 to 1.374 in
	Diametrical clearance	0,02 to 0,04 mm	0.001 to 0.002 in

04——7

GENERAL SPECIFICATION

Lubricating System	Oil pump	Epicyclic gear type	
	Oil pump gears:		
	Driving gear outside diameter:		
	Diametrical clearance	0,127 to 0,305 mm	0.005 to 0.012 in
	Radial clearance	0,065 to 0,152 mm	0.0025 to 0.006 in
	Driven gear outside diameter:		
	Diametrical clearance	0,178 to 0,254 mm	0.007 to 0.010 in
	Radial clearance	0,09 to 0,13 mm	0.0035 to 0.005 in
	Driven gear internal diameter:		
	Diametrical clearance	0,28 to 0,46 mm	0.011 to 0.018 in
	Radial clearance	0,14 to 0,23 mm	0.0055 to 0.009 in
	Side clearance: driving and driven gear	0,115 to 0,165 mm	0.0045 to 0.0065 in
	Oil filter type	Full flow, disposable canister	
	Oil pressure min. @ 3000 rev/min	2,8 kg/cm^2	40 lb/in^2
Timing Chain and Sprockets	Type of chain	Duplex endless	
	Pitch	9,5 mm	0.375 in
	Number of pitches	180	
	Camshaft sprockets: Number of teeth (each)	42	
	Crankshaft sprocket: Number of teeth	21	
	Jackshaft sprocket: Number of teeth	21	

TORQUE WRENCH SETTINGS

For the Torque wrench settings refer to the front of the relevant section.

04—8

GENERAL SPECIFICATION DATA—6 Cylinder Cars

Engine	See Engine Tuning Data	Section 05
Final Drive Unit	Type	Hypoid with normal differential; Powr Lok differential available as optional extra
	Pre 1982 MY Ratio: Standard	3.31:1 (43/13)
	1982 MY on Alternative	3.07:1 (43/14)
Final Drive Ratios —	3.4L — all cars	3.54:1 (46/13)
1982 MY cars	4.2L — manual transmission cars	3.31:1 (43/13)
	4.2L — automatic transmission cars — not NAS	3.058:1 (52/17) Vin. 326917
	4.2L — automatic transmission cars — NAS only	2.88:1 (49/17) 1982 model year
Automatic Gearbox	Make and type	Borg-Warner Model 66
	Ratios: First gear	2.39:1
	Second gear	1.45:1
	Third gear	1.00:1
	Reverse	2.09:1
	Torque converter	2.3:1 maximum
Manual Gearbox	Type	Five speed with baulk-ring synchromesh on all forward gears
	Ratios: First gear	3.321:1
	Second gear	2.087:1
	Third gear	1.396:1
	Fourth gear	1.0:1
	Fifth gear	0.883:1
	Reverse	3.428:1
Cooling System	Water pump: Type	Centrifugal
	Drive	Belt
	Number of cooling fans	One 12 bladed, driven through Holset coupling
	Cooling system and control	Thermostat
	Auxilary cooling—certain markets	1 or 2 electric fans blowing air through radiator; controlled by a sensor in the radiator
	Thermostat opening temperature	88°C	190°F
	Filler cap: Pressure rating	1,05 kgf/cm²	15 lbf/in²
	Make	A.C. Delco

Fuel Injection Equipment 'A' Emissions—4.2 litre cars for North American and Japanese Markets

Make and type	Lucas/Bosch Jetronic 'L'
Airflow meter reference number	73172A
Extra air valve reference number	73174A
Deceleration valve reference number	54739484A
Electronic control unit reference number	83524A

Fuel Injection Equipment 'B' Emissions—4.2 litre cars for all markets except North America and Japan

Make and type	Lucas/Bosch Jetronic 'L'
Airflow meter reference number	73171A
Extra air valve reference number	73193A
Deceleration valve reference number	54739875
Vacuum switch reference number	175-549A
Electronic control unit reference number	83525A

Fuel System Pumps	Make and type: 3.4 litre carburetter cars	Electrical, two A.C. Delco 'Vega' submerged
	4.2 litre cars	Electrical, Lucas 73175A roller cell pump with integral relief valve and non-return valve

Braking System	Front brakes, make and type	Girling; ventilated discs, bridge-type calipers	
	Rear brakes, make and type	Girling; damped discs, bridge-type calipers incorporating handbrake friction pads	
	Handbrake: Type . . . , ...	Mechanical, operating on rear discs	
	Disc diameter: Front	284 mm	11.18 in
	Rear	263,5 mm	10.375 in
	Disc thickness: Front	24,13 mm	0.95 in
	Rear	12,7 mm	0.50 in
	Master cylinder bore diameter	22,23 mm	0.875 in
	Brake operation	Hydraulic	
	Hydraulic fluid	Castrol/Girling Universal Brake and Clutch Fluid–exceeding specification S.A.E. J.1703/D	
	Main brake friction pad material	Ferodo 2430 slotted	
	Hand brake friction pad material	Mintex M.68/1	
	Servo unit refs.: R.H.D. cars	Girling 64049669	
	L.H.D. cars	Girling 64049668	
Front Suspension	Type	Independent coil spring	
	Castor angle	2¼° ± ¼° positive	
	Camber angle	½° ± ¼° positive	
	Front wheel alignment	1,6 mm to 3,2 mm toe in	$\frac{1}{16}$ in to $\frac{1}{8}$ in toe in
	Dampers	Telescopic, gas filled	
Rear Suspension	Type	Independent coil springs, co-axial with dampers	
	Camber angle	¾° ± ¼° negative	
	Rear wheel alignment	Parallel ± 0,08 mm	Parallel ± $\frac{1}{32}$ in
	Dampers	Telescopic, gas filled	
Power Assisted Steering	Type	Rack and pinion	
	Number of turns lock to lock	2.87	
	Turning circle, wall to wall	12,85 m	42 ft
Electrical Equipment Battery	Make	Lucas, chloride or Delco Remy	
	Voltage	12V	
Alternator	Make and type: All air-conditioned cars	Lucas 25ACR or Motorola 9AR 25 12P	
	Non air-conditioned cars	Lucas 18ACR	
	Nominal voltage	12V	
	Cut-in voltage	13.5V at 2100 rev/min (Motorola 14V at 1050 rev/min)	
	Earth polarity	Negative	
	Maximum output	18ACR	45A
		25ACR	66A
		Motorola	70A
	Maximum operating speed	12 400 rev/min	
	Rotor winding resistance	3.2 ohms (18ACR) at 20°C	
		3.6 ohms (25ACR)	
	Brush spring pressure	9 to 13 ozf	
	Make and type	Lucas A133	
	Maximum output	65A — 6 Cyl. non air cond. cars	
		75A — 6 Cyl. air cond. cars and all 12 Cyl. cars	
	Regulator controlled voltage	13.6-14.4V (measured across battery)	
	Maximum operating speed	15,000 rev/min	
	New brush length	20 mm (0.8 in)	
	Renew at	10 mm (0.4 in)	
	Brush spring pressure	4.7-9.8 oz	
Starter Motor	Make and type	Lucas 3M100 pre-engaged	
	Lock torque at 940 amps	4,01 kgf m	29 lbf ft
	Torque at 1000 rev/min at 535 amps	1,80 kgf m	13 lbf ft
	Light running current	100A at 5 000 to 6 000 rev/min	

Windscreen Wiper Motor	Make and type	Lucas 16W
	Light running speed, rack disconnected (after 60 seconds from cold)	Normal: 46 to 52 rev/min; high: 60 to 70 rev/min
	Light running current (after 60 seconds from cold) ...	Normal: 1.5A; high: 2.0A

GENERAL SPECIFICATION DATA—12 Cylinder Cars

| Engine | See Engine Tuning Data .... | Section 05 |

Final Drive Unit	Type	Hypoid with Powr Lok differential
	Ratio: Standard Non HE	3.07:1 (43/14)
	HE Onwards	2.88:1 (49/17)
	Alternative	3.31:1 (43/13) Australia

Automatic Gearbox	Make and type	General Motors GM 400
	Ratios: First gear	2.48:1
	Second gear	1.48:1
	Third gear	1.00:1
	Reverse	2.07:1
	Torque converter	2.00:1

Cooling System	Water pump: Type	Centrifugal, with two outlets	
	Drive	Belt driven from crankshaft	
	No. of cooling fans	Two (1 12-bladed, belt-driven through Holset coupling, plus 1 4-bladed electrically driven, thermostatically controlled)	
	Cooling system control	2 thermostats	
	Thermostat opening temperature	88°C	190°F
	Thermostat fully open temperature	93.5° to 96°C	200° to 205°F
	Filler cap pressure rating	1,05 kgf/cm²	15 lbf/in²
	Filler cap make	A.C. Delco	

Fuel
Injection Equipment

Make and type:
N.A.S., U.K. and European markets .... Lucas Digital 'P', pressure sensing
Japanese and Australian markets .... Lucas/Bosch Jetronic D

		'A' Emissions N.A.S. only	'A' Emissions Japan only	'B' Emissions U.K./Europe	'D' Emissions Australia only
Injector reference no.		Lucas 73178A	Lucas 73143B	Lucas 73178A	Lucas 73143B
Cold start injector—reference no.		Lucas 73180A	Lucas 73160A	Lucas 73180A	Lucas 73147A
Pressure regulator—reference no.		Lucas 73177A	Lucas 73146A	Lucas 73177A	Lucas 73146A
Throttle switch—reference no.		Lucas type 193SA	Lucas 30625A	Lucas type 193SA	Lucas 30625A
Water temperature sensor—reference no.		Lucas 73170A	Lucas 73142A	Lucas 73170A	Lucas 73142A
Air temperature sensor—reference no.		Lucas 73197A	Lucas 73141A	Lucas 73197A	Lucas 73141A
Thermotime switch—reference no.		Lucas 33704A	Lucas 30491A	Lucas 33704A	Lucas 30491A
Extra air valve—reference no.—all markets		Lucas 73192A			
Deceleration valve—reference no.		Lucas 73156A	—	—	Lucas 73156A
Supplementary air valve—reference no.		—	—	Tecalemit TDA832	—
Full throttle micro-switch—reference no.		Burgess YBFYR1	—	—	—
Electrical control unit—reference no.		Lucas 83622A	Lucas 83477B	Lucas 83632A	Lucas 83546A
E.G.R. control unit—reference no.		—	Lucas 73158B	—	Lucas 73158B
Lambda sensors—reference no.		Lucas 73199A	—	—	—
Pressure sensor—reference no.		—	Lucas 73164A	—	Lucas 73164A
Power resistor—reference no.		Lucas 73196A	—	Lucas 73196A	—
Power amplifier—reference no.		—	Lucas 83486A	—	Lucas 88486A

| Fuel System Pump | Make and type .... | Lucas 73175A — Electrical roller cell pump with integral relief valve and non-return valve. |

Braking System	Front brakes: Make and type	Girling; ventilated discs, bridge-type calipers	
	Rear brakes: Make and type	Girling; damped discs, bridge-type calipers incorporating handbrake friction pads	
	Handbrake: Type	Mechanical, operating on rear discs	
	Disc diameter: Front	284 mm	11.18 in
	Rear	263,5 mm	10.375 in
	Disc thickness: Front	24,13 mm	0.95 in
	Rear	12,7 mm	0.50 in
	Master cylinder bore diameter	22,23 mm	0.875 in
	Brake operation	Hydraulic	
	Hydraulic fluid	Castrol/Girling Universal Brake and Clutch Fluid-exceeding specification S.A.E. J.1703/D	
	Main brake friction pad material	Ferodo 2430 slotted	
	Hand brake friction pad material	Mintex M68/1	
	Servo unit refs.: L.H.D.	Girling 64049668	
	R.H.D.	Girling 64049670	

Front Suspension	Type	Independent, coil spring	
	Castor angle	3½° ± ¼° positive	
	Camber angle	½° ± ¼° positive	
	Front wheel alignment	0 to 1,6 mm toe out	0 to Y_{16} in toe out
	Dampers	Telescopic, gas filled	

Rear Suspension	Type	Independent, coil springs, co-axial with dampers	
	Camber angle	¾° ± ¼° negative	
	Rear wheel alignment	Parallel ± 0,08 mm	Parallel ± Y_{32} in
	Dampers	Telescopic, gas filled	

Power Assisted Steering	Type	Rack and pinion	
	Number of turns lock to lock	2.75	
	Turning circle, wall to wall	13,5 m	44 ft

Electrical Equipment Battery	Make and type	Lucas, chloride or AC Delco	

Alternator	Make and type	Lucas 25ACR or Motorola 9AR2533P	
	Nominal voltage	12V	
	Cut-in voltage	13.5V at 1500 rev/min (Motorola 14V at 1100 rev/min	
	Polarity	Negative earth	
	Maximum output	66A (Motorola 70A)	
	Maximum operating speed	15 000 rev/min	
	Rotor winding resistance	3.6 ohms at 20°C	
	Brush spring pressure	255 to 369 gf	9 to 13 ozf

Starter Motor	Make and type	Lucas M45 pre-engaged	
	Lock torque (at 940 amps)	4,01 kgf m	29 lbf ft
	Torque at 1000 rev/min (at 535 amps)	1,80 kgf m	13 lbf ft
	Light running current	100A at 5000 to 6000 rev/min	

Wiper motor	Make and type	Lucas 16W	
	Light running speed, rack disconnected (after 60 seconds from cold)	Normal: 46 to 52 rev/min, high: 60 to 70 rev/min	
	Light running current (after 60 seconds from cold)	Normal: 1.5A; high: 2.0A	

BULB CHART — 6 cyl. & 12 cyl. cars

	Watts	Lucas Part No.	Unipart No.	Notes
Headlamps				
L.H. Traffic markets				
Tungsten — Outer	60/45	54529739	GLU 136	XJ3.4 Std. only Sealed beam light unit
Tungsten — Inner	50	54529740	GLU 134	XJ3.4 Std. only Sealed beam light unit
Halogen — Outer	60/55	472	GLB 472	H4 base
Halogen — Inner	55	448	GLB 448	H4 base
R.H. Traffic markets				
Normal — Halogen — Outer	60/55	472	GLB 472	H4 base
Normal — Halogen — Inner	55	448	GLB 448	H4 base
France — Halogen — Outer	60/55	476	GLB 476	Yellow bulb H4 base
France — Halogen — Inner	45/40	411	GLB 411	Yellow bulb. The 40 watt filament is not used
*U.S.A. — Tungsten — Outer	37/5/60			Sealed beam light unit
*U.S.A. — Tungsten — Inner	50			Sealed beam light unit
Front Parking Lamp	4	233	GLB 233	Not U.S.A. Headlamp pilot
Front Flasher Lamp	21	382	GLB 382	Not U.S.A.
Front Parking and Flasher Lamp	5/21	380	GLB 380	U.S.A. only
Front Fog Lamp — Cibie	55	—	GLB 212	H4 base
Flasher Repeater	4	233	GLB 233	Not U.S.A.
Front Marker Lamp	4	233	GLB 233	U.S.A. only
Rear Marker Lamp	4	233	GLB 233	U.S.A. only
Rear Door Guard Lamp	5	989	GLB 989	
Stop Lamp	21	382	GLB 382	
Stop Lamp High Mounted (U.S.A. only)	5	989	GLB 989	
Tail Lamp	5	207	GLB 207	
Rear Flasher Lamp	21	382	GLB 382	
Reverse Lamp	21	382	GLB 382	
Plate Illumination Lamp	4	233	GLB 233	
Rear Fog Lamp	21	382	GLB 382	Not U.S.A.
Instrument Illumination	2.2	987	GLB 987	
Warning Light — Cluster	1.2	286	GLB 286	
L.H. Turn Signal	3	504	GLB 504	
Heated Backlight	2.8	650	GLB 650	24 volt bulb
Bulb Failure	2.2	987	GLB 987	
R.H. Turn Signal	3	504	GLB 504	
Catalyst/Oxygen Sensor	2	281	GLB 281	Special markets only
Map Lamp	6	254	GLB 254	
Clock Illumination	2.2	987	GLB 987	
Switch Panel Illumination	1.2	—	GLB 284	
Automatic Selector Illumination	2.2	987	GLB 987	
Cigarette Lighter Illumination	2	—	GLB 288	
Fibre Optic Lamp	6	254	GLB 254	
Interior Lamp	5	989	GLB 989	
Reading Lamp	4	233	GLB 233	
Luggage Boot Lamp	5	239	GLB 239	

*U.S.A. Market differences	HEADLAMP UNIT	MODEL	JAGUAR PART NO.
	Outer	XJ6 & XJ12	C 39638
	Inner	XJ6 & XJ12 L.H. unit	DAC 1826
	Inner	XJ12 R.H. unit	DAC 2131

TYRE DATA

Fitted as complete sets only

Type: 6 cylinder cars . . . .   Dunlop ER70 VR 15 SP Sport or Pirelli Cinturato P5 205/70 VR 15

       12 cylinder cars . . . .   Dunlop 205/70 VR 15 D1 SP Sport Super or Pirelli Cinturato P5 205/70 VR15

                                from Sept. 83   Pirelli Cinturato 215/70 VR 15; Dunlop 215/70 VR 15 D7 Sport Super

PRESSURE:

All Series III 6 cyl. Engined Saloons

	Front	Rear
For speeds above 100 m.p.h. (160 km/h) with driver and two passengers	2.27 bar 2.32 kgf/cm^2 33 lbf/in^2	2.21 bar 2.25 kgf/cm^2 32 lbf/in^2
For speeds above 100 m.p.h. with full load (including luggage) of 410 kg (904 lb)	2.27 bar 2.32 kgf/cm^2 33 lbf/in^2	2.48 bar 2.53 kgf/cm^2 36 lbf/in^2

The above pressures may also be reduced by 0.41 bar; 0.42 kgf/cm^2; (6 lbf/in^2) on the front and rear tyres to obtain maximum comfort, provided the speed does not exceed 100 m.p.h. (160 km/h).

All Series III 12 cyl. Engined Saloons

	Front	Rear
For speeds above 100 m.p.h. (160 km/h) with driver and two passengers	2.48 bar 2.53 kgf/cm^2 36 lbf/in^2	2.21 bar 2.25 kgf/cm^2 32 lbf/in^2
For speeds above 100 m.p.h. with full load (including luggage) of 410 kg (904 lb)	2.48 bar 2.53 kgf/cm^2 36 lbf/in^2	2.48 bar 2.53 kgf/cm^2 36 lbf/in^2

The above pressures may also be reduced by 0.41 bar; 0.42 kgf/cm^2; (6 lbf/in^2) on the front and rear tyres to obtain maximum comfort, provided the speed does not exceed 100 m.p.h. (160 km/h).

Tyre Replacement and Wheel Interchanging
When replacement of tyres is necessary, it is preferable to fit a complete car set. Should either front or rear tyres only show a necessity for replacement, new tyres must be fitted to replace the worn ones. No attempt must be made to interchange tyres from front to rear or vice-versa as tyre wear produces characteristic patterns depending upon their position and if such position is changed after wear has occurred, the performance of the tyre will be adversely affected. It should be remembered that new tyres require to be balanced.

The radial-ply tyres specified above are designed to meet the high-speed performance of which this car is capable.

Only tyres of identical specification as shown under 'TYRE DATA' must be fitted as replacements and, if to different tread pattern, should not be fitted in mixed form.

UNDER NO CIRCUMSTANCES SHOULD CROSS-PLY TYRES BE FITTED.

RECOMMENDED SNOW TYRE

The following information relates to the only snow tyre recommended for Jaguar Cars.

Snow tyres MUST ONLY be fitted in complete sets of four, failure to do so could adversely affect the handling of the car under certain conditions.

Tyre type — Pirelli Winter 190 215/65 R15 M & S
Tyre pressures — Are the same as the standard tyre equipment.
Maximum speed — without snow chains — 190 km/hr (118 m.p.h.)
                 with snow chains — 50 km/hr (30 m.p.h.)

Snow Chains
Rud Kantenspur snow chains may be fitted to the rear wheels only.

NOTE: Always ensure that they are correctly fitted and fully tensioned.

04——14

XK ENGINES

A Emission North America and Japan (1978-80)
B Emission Rest of World
C Emission Canada and Japan 81 on and Australia 1986
D Emission Australia -85 Sweden and Switzerland
E Emission Saudia Arabia

	3.4 Pre 81	3.4 After 81
Ignition timing	8° B.T.D.C.	8° B.T.D.C.
$ = Vac off idle normal run temp	static	$
# = Vac off normal running temp		
! = at 3000 r.p.m.		
& = 700 r.p.m. with vac off		
Valve clearances	0.012 to 0.014 in	0.012 to 0.014 in
Spark plugs — make/type	N12Y	N12Y
— gap	0.025 in	0.035 in
Ignition coil — make Lucas/type	16C6	16C6
Primary resistance @ 20°C (ohms)	1.2 to 1.5	1.2 to 1.5
Output (open circuit) Kv min	25	25
Output at plug Kv min (assuming plug gap and lead to spec)	10	10
Distributor — make/type	45D6	45D6
Rotation of rotor view above	Anticlockwise	Anticlockwise
Points gap	0.015 in	0.015 in
Pick up coil resistance K Ohms	——	——
Firing order	1, 5, 3, 6, 2, 4@	1, 5, 3, 6, 2, 4@
@ — cylinders numbered from rear		
Spark plug lead resistances	Min — Max	
1	8.61 to 20.56K	
2	9.00 to 21.48K	
3	7.24 to 17.34K	
4	6.11 to 14.69K	
5	5.47 to 13.20K	
6	5.13 to 12.30K	
Exhaust emission reading Co	3% max	3% max
HC		
Idle speed	750 r.p.m.	750 r.p.m.
Compression pressure	135 to 150 lbf/in²	135 to 150 lbf/in²
Differential between cylinders	15% maximum	
Carburettor — type	SU HIF7	SU HIF7
— needle	BDW	BDW
— jet	0.100	0.100
— spring	Red	Red
Auto choke — type	TZX 1002	TZX 1002

XK ENGINES

A   Emission North America and Japan (1978-80)
B   Emission Rest of World
C   Emission Canada and Japan 81 on and Australia 1986
D   Emission Australia -85 Sweden and Switzerland
E   Emission Saudia Arabia

	4.2 Emiss A 1979-80	4.2 Emiss A 1982	4.2 Emiss A/D Pre 83	4.2 Emiss A 1983	4.2 Emiss A 1984-
Ignition timing	4° B.T.D.C.	14°B.T.D.C.	8°B.T.D.C.	14°B.T.D.C.	17°B.T.D.C.
$ =Vac off idle normal run temp	at 800 r.p.m.	$	&	&	&
# = Vac off normal running temp					
! = at 3000 r.p.m.					
& = 700 r.p.m. with vac off					
Valve clearances	0.012 to 0.014 in	0.012 to 0.014 in	0.012 to 0.014 in	0.012 to 0.014 in	0.012 to 0.014 in
Spark plugs — make/type	N12Y	N12Y	N12Y	N12Y	N12Y
— gap	0.035 in	0.035 in	0.035 in	0.035 in	0.035 in
Ignition coil — make Lucas/type	16C6	16C6	16C6	32C5	32C5
Primary resistance @ 20°C (ohms)	1.2 to 1.5	1.2 to 1.5	1.2 to 1.5	0.75 to 0.85	0.75 to 0.85
Output (open circuit) Kv min	25	25	25	25	25
Output at plug Kv min (assuming plug gap and lead to spec)	10	10	10	10	10
Ignition coil — Ducellier/type	——	——	——	——	520076A
Primary resistance @ 20°C (ohms)	——	——	——	——	0.8 to 1.0
Ballast resistance @ 20°C (ohms)	——	——	——	——	0.8 to 1.0
Output (open circuit) Kv min					25
Output at plug Kv min (assuming plug gap and lead to spec)					10
Distributor — make/type	45DM6	45DM6	45DM6	45DM6	45DM6
Rotation of rotor view above	Anticlockwise	Anticlockwise	Anticlockwise	Anticlockwise	Anticlockwise
Pick up mod/rot gap	0.008 to 0.014 in	0.008 to 0.014 in	0.008 to 0.014 in	0.008 to 0.014 in	0.008 to 0.014 in
Pick up coil resistance K Ohms	2.2 to 4.8	2.2 to 4.8	2.2 to 4.8	2.2 to 4.8	2.2 to 4.8
Firing order	1, 5, 3, 6, 2, 4@	1, 5, 3, 6, 2, 4@	1, 5, 3, 6, 2, 4@	1, 5, 3, 6, 2, 4@	1. 5, 3, 6, 2, 4@
@ — cylinders numbered from rear					
Spark plug lead resistances	Min — Max				
1	8.61 to 20.56K				
2	9.00 to 21.48K				
3	7.24 to 17.34K				
4	6.11 to 14.69K				
5	5.47 to 13.20K				
6	5.13 to 12.30K				
Exhaust emission reading Co	0.5 to 1.5%	0.5 to 1.5%	0.5 to 1.5%	0.5 to 1.5%	0.5 to 1.5%
HC					
Idle speed	750 r.p.m.	750 ± 50 r.p.m.	750 r.p.m.	800 r.p.m.	800 r.p.m.
Compression pressure	120 to 135 lbf/in²	120 to 135 lbf/in²	120 to 135 lbf/in²	120 to 135 lbf/in²	120 to 135 lbf/in²
Differential between cylinders			15% maximum		
Fuel pressure			35.5 to 38.8 lbf/in²		

XK ENGINES

A   Emission North America and Japan (1978-80)
B   Emission Rest of World
C   Emission Canada and Japan 81 on and Australia 1986
D   Emission Australia -85 Sweden and Switzerland
E   Emission Saudia Arabia

	4.2 Emiss B	4.2 Emiss C 1985-6	4.2 Swiss 1985-6	4.2 Australia 1985
Ignition timing	6° B.T.D.C.	14°B.T.D.C.	4° ± 2	4°B.T.D.C.
$ =Vac off idle normal run temp	$	!	B.T.D.C.$	at 800 r.p.m.
# = Vac off normal running temp				
! = at 3000 r.p.m.				
& = 700 r.p.m. with vac off				
Valve clearances	0.012 to 0.014 in	0.012 to 0.014 in	0.012 to 0.014 in	0.012 to 0.014 in
Spark plugs — make/type	N10Y	N12Y	N12Y	N12Y
— gap	0.035 in	0.035 in	0.035 in	0.035 in
Ignition coil — make Lucas/type	32C5	32C5	32C5	32C5
Primary resistance @ 20°C (ohms)	0.75 to 0.85	0.75 to 0.85	0.75 to 0.85	0.75 to 0.85
Output (open circuit) Kv min	25	25	25	25
Output at plug Kv min (assuming plug gap and lead to spec)	10	10	10	10
Ignition coil — Ducellier/type	520076A	520076A	520076A	520076A
Primary resistance @ 20°C (ohms)	0.8 to 1.0	0.8 to 1.0	0.8 to 1.0	0.8 to 1.0
Ballast resistance @ 20°C (ohms)	0.8 to 1.0	0.8 to 1.0	0.8 to 1.0	0.8 to 1.0
Output (open circuit) Kv min	25	25	25	25
Output at plug Kv min (assuming plug gap and lead to spec)	10	10	10	10
Distributor — make/type	45DM6	45DM6	45DM6	45DM6
Rotation of rotor view above	Anticlockwise	Anticlockwise	Anticlockwise	Anticlockwise
Pick up mod/rot gap	0.008 to 0.014 in	0.008 to 0.014 in	0.008 to 0.014 in	0.008 to 0.014 in
Pick up coil resistance K Ohms	2.2 to 4.8	2.2 to 4.8	2.2 to 4.8	2.2 to 4.8
Firing order	1, 5, 3, 6, 2, 4@	1, 5, 3, 6, 2, 4@	1, 5, 3, 6, 2, 4@	1, 5, 3, 6, 2, 4@
@ — cylinders numbered from rear				
Spark plug lead resistances	Min — Max			
1	8.61 to 20.56K			
2	9.00 to 21.48K			
3	7.24 to 17.34K			
4	6.11 to 14.69K			
5	5.47 to 13.20K			
6	5.13 to 12.30K			
Exhaust emission reading Co	1.25 to 1.75	1.25 to 1.75	0.75 ± 25%	0.5 to 1.0%
HC			300 p.p.m. max	
Idle speed	750 r.p.m.	750 ± 50 r.p.m.	800 ± 100 r.p.m.	800 r.p.m.
Compression pressure	135 to 150 lbf/in²	135 to 150 lbf/in²	135 to 150 lbf/in²	135 to 150 lbf/in²
Differential between cylinders		15% maximum		
Fuel pressure		35.5 to 38.8 lbf/in²		

V12 ENGINES

A   Emission North America and Japan (1978-80)
B   Emission Rest of World
C   Emission Canada and Japan 81 on and Australia 1986
D   Emission Australia -85 Sweden and Switzerland
E   Emission Saudia Arabia

	D Jetronic	
	5.3 A Emiss	5.3 D Emiss
Ignition timing	10° B.T.D.C.	4°B.T.D.C.
$ =Vac off idle normal run temp	Static	Static
at 3000 r.p.m.		
Valve clearances	0.012 to 0.014 in	0.012 to 0.014 in
Spark plugs — make/type	N10Y	N10Y
— gap	0.035 in	0.035 in
Ignition coil — make/type	22C12	22C12
Primary resistance @ 20°C (ohms).	0.9 to 1.1	0.9 to 1.1
Output (open circuit) Kv min	25	25
Output at plug Kv min (assuming plug gap		
and lead to spec)	10	10
Distributor — make/type.	36DE12	36DE12
Rotation of rotor view above	Anticlockwise	Anticlockwise
Pick up mod/rot gap	0.020 to 0.025 in	0.020 to 0.025 in
Pick up coil resistance K Ohms	—	—
Firing order	1A-6B-5A-2B-3A-4B-6A-1B-2A-5B-4A-3B*	
* — cylinders numbered from front		
Spark plug lead resistances	Min — Max	Min — Max
	1A 3.05 to 7.35K	1B 4.00 to 9.66K
	2A 2.09 to 5.04K	2B 2.78 to 6.72K
	3A 2.27 to 5.46K	3B 1.31 to 3.15K
	4A 3.48 to 8.40K	4B 2.00 to 4.83K
	5A 3.13 to 7.56K	5B 3.31 to 7.98K
	6A 3.22 to 7.77K	6B 3.92 to 9.45K
Exhaust emission reading Co	1 to 2%	1 to 2%
Idle speed	750 r.p.m.	750 r.p.m.
HC		
Compression pressure	135 lbf/in²	135 lbf/in²
Differential between cylinders	15% maximum	
Fuel pressure	28.5 to 30.8 lbf/in²	

V12 ENGINES

A Emission North America and Japan (1978-80)
B Emission Rest of World
C Emission Canada and Japan 81 on and Australia 1986
D Emission Australia -85 Sweden and Switzerland
E Emission Saudia Arabia

	P System PI Digital			
	5.3 A Emiss Pre HE	5.3 B Emiss Pre HE 9:1	5.3 B Emiss Pre HE 10:1 to 301612	5.3 B Emiss Pre HE-
Ignition timing . . . . $ = Vac off idle normal run temp . . . . # = Vac off normal running temp . . . . at 3000 r.p.m.	25 to 27° B.T.D.C. #	5°B.T.D.C. Vac on	10°B.T.D.C. #	24°B.T.D.C. #
Valve clearances	0.012 to 0.014 in	0.012 to 0.014 in	0.012 to 0.014 in	0.012 to 0.014 in
Spark plugs — make/type	N10Y	N10Y	N10Y	N10Y
— gap	0.035 in	0.035 in	0.035 in	0.035 in
Ignition coil — make/type	22C12	23C12	23C12	23C12
Primary resistance @ 20°C (ohms)	0.9 to 1.1	0.7 to 0.85	0.7 to 0.85	0.7 to 0.85
Output (open circuit) Kv min	25	25	25	25
Output at plug Kv min (assuming plug gap and lead to spec)	10	10	10	10
Distributor — make/type	36DE12	36DE12	36DE12	36DE12
Rotation of rotor view above	Anticlockwise	Anticlockwise	Anticlockwise	Anticlockwise
Points/pick up mod/rot gap	0.020 to 0.025 in	0.020 to 0.025 in	0.020 to 0.025 in	0.020 to 0.025 in
Pick up coil resistance K Ohms	2.2 to 4.8	2.2 to 4.8	2.2 to 4.8	2.2 to 4.8
Firing order	1A-6B-5A-2B-3A-4B-6A-1B-2A-5B-4A-3B*			
* — cylinders numbered from front				

Spark plug lead resistances . . . .

Min — Max	Min — Max
1A 3.05 to 7.35K	1B 4.00 to 9.66K
2A 2.09 to 5.04K	2B 2.78 to 6.72K
3A 2.27 to 5.46K	3B 1.31 to 3.15K
4A 3.48 to 8.40K	4B 2.00 to 4.83K
5A 3.13 to 7.56K	5B 3.31 to 7.98K
6A 3.22 to 7.77K	6B 3.92 to 9.45K

	5.3 A Emiss Pre HE	5.3 B Emiss Pre HE 9:1	5.3 B Emiss Pre HE 10:1	5.3 B Emiss Pre HE-
Exhaust emission reading Co	1 to 2%	1 to 2%	1 to 2%	1 to 2%
Idle speed	750 r.p.m.	750 r.p.m.	750 r.p.m.	750 r.p.m.
HC				
Compression pressure	135 lbf/in²	135 lbf/in²	150 lbf/in²	165 lbf/in²
Differential between cylinders	15% maximum			
Fuel pressure	35.5 to 38.8 lbf/in²			

V12 ENGINES

A Emission North America and Japan (1978-80)
B Emission Rest of World
C Emission Canada and Japan 81 on and Australia 1986
D Emission Australia -85 Sweden and Switzerland
E Emission Saudia Arabia

	P System PI Digital			
	5.3 A & B Em HE	5.3 A & B Em HE After 7P50275	5.3 Australia 1985	5.3 Switzerland 1985
Ignition timing	18° B.T.D.C.	18°B.T.D.C.	18°B.T.D.C.	18° +0–2 B.T.D.C.
$ =Vac off idle normal run temp	#	#	#	
# = Vac off normal running temp at 3000 r.p.m.				
Valve clearances	0.010 to 0.012 in	0.010 to 0.012 in	0.010 to 0.012 in	0.010 to 0.012 in
Spark plugs — make/type	BN5	RS5C	RS5C	RS5C
— gap	0.025 in	0.025 in	0.025 in	0.025 in
Ignition coil — make/type	35C6x2	35C6x2	35C6x2	35C6x2
Primary resistance @ 20°C (ohms)	0.6 to 0.8	0.6 to 0.8	0.6 to 0.8	0.6 to 0.8
Output (open circuit) Kv min	25	25	25	25
Output at plug Kv min (assuming plug gap and lead to spec)	10	10	10	10
Distributor — make/type	36DM12	36DM12	36DM12	36DM12
Rotation of rotor view above	Anticlockwise	Anticlockwise	Anticlockwise	Anticlockwise
Points/pick up mod/rot gap	0.006 to 0.014 in	0.006 to 0.014 in	0.006 to 0.014 in	0.006 to 0.014 in
Pick up coil resistance K Ohms	2.2 to 4.8	2.2 to 4.8	2.2 to 4.8	2.2 to 4.8
Firing order	1A-6B-5A-2B-3A-4B-6A-1B-2A-5B-4A-3B*			
@ — cylinders numbered from rear				
* — cylinders numbered from front				
Spark plug lead resistances	Min — Max	Min — Max		
	1A 3.05 to 7.35K	1B 4.00 to 9.66K		
	2A 2.09 to 5.04K	2B 2.78 to 6.72K		
	3A 2.27 to 5.46K	3B 1.31 to 3.15K		
	4A 3.48 to 8.40K	4B 2.00 to 4.83K		
	5A 3.13 to 7.56K	5B 3.31 to 7.98K		
	6A 3.22 to 7.77K	6B 3.92 to 9.45K		
Exhaust emission reading Co	1 to 2%	1 to 2%	0.5 to 1%	0.75 ± 0.25%
Idle speed	750 r.p.m.	750 r.p.m.	800 r.p.m.	800 ± 50 r.p.m.
HC				500 p.p.m. max.
Compression pressure	200 to 240 lbf/in²	200 to 240 lbf/in²	200 to 240 lbf/in²	200 to 240 lbf/in²
Differential between cylinders		15% maximum		
Fuel pressure		35.5 to 38.8 lbf/in²		

GENERAL FITTING INSTRUCTIONS

Precautions Against Damage

Always fit covers to protect the wings before commencing work in the engine compartment. Cover the seats and carpets, wear clean overalls and wash your hands or wear gloves before working inside the car.

Avoid spilling hydraulic fluid or battery acid on paintwork. Wash off with water immediately if this occurs.

Use polythene sheets in the boot to protect carpets.

Always use a recommended service tool, or a satisfactory equivalent, where specified.

Protect temporarily exposed screw threads by replacing nuts or fitting plastic caps.

Safety Precautions

Whenever possible use a ramp or pit when working beneath a car, in preference to jacking. Chock the wheels as well as applying the handbrake.

Never rely on a jack alone to support a car. Use axle stands or blocks carefully placed at the jacking points to provide a rigid location.

Ensure that a suitable form of fire extinguisher is conveniently located.

Check that any lifting equipment used has adequate capacity and is fully serviceable.

Inspect power leads of any mains electrical equipment for damage, and check that it is properly earthed.

Disconnect the earth (grounded) terminal of a car battery.

Do not disconnect any pipes in the air conditioning refrigeration system, if fitted, unless trained and instructed to do so. A refrigerant is used which can cause blindness if allowed to contact the eyes.

Ensure that adequate ventilation is provided when volatile de-greasing agents are being used.

CAUTION: Fume extraction equipment must be in operation when trichlorethylene, carbon tetrachloride, methylene chloride, chloroform, or perchlorethylene are used for cleaning purposes.

Do not apply heat in an attempt to free stiff nuts or fittings; as well as causing damage to protective coatings, there is a risk of damage to electronic equipment and brake lines from stray heat.

Do not leave tools, equipment, spilt oil, etc., around or on work area.

Wear protective overalls and use barrier creams when necessary.

Preparation

Before removing a component, clean it and its surrounding area as thoroughly as possible.

Blank off any openings exposed by component removal, using greaseproof paper and masking tape.

Immediately seal fuel, oil or hydraulic lines when separated, using plastic caps or plugs, to prevent loss of fluid and entry of dirt.

Close the open ends of oilways, exposed by component removal, with tapered hardwood plugs or readily visible plastic plugs.

Immediately a component is removed, place it in a suitable container; use a separate container for each component and its associated parts.

Before dismantling a component clean it thoroughly with a recommended cleaning agent; check that the agent is suitable for all materials of component.

Clean the bench and provide marking materials, labels, containers and locking wire before dismantling a component.

Dismantling

Observe scrupulous cleanliness when dismantling components, particularly when brake, fuel or hydraulic system parts or being worked on. A particle of dirt or a cloth fragment could cause a dangerous malfunction if trapped in these systems.

Blow out all tapped holes, crevices, oilways and fluid passages with an air line. Ensure that any 'O' rings used for sealing are correctly replaced or renewed if disturbed.

Mark mating parts to ensure that they are replaced as dismantled. Whenever possible use marking ink, which avoids possibilities of distortion or initiation of cracks, liable if centre-punch or scriber are used.

Wire together mating parts where necessary to prevent accidental interchange (e.g. roller bearing components).

Wire labels onto all parts which are to be renewed, and to parts requiring further inspection before being passed for reassembly; place these parts in separate containers from those containing parts for rebuild.

Do not discard a part due for renewal until after comparing it with a new part, to ensure that its correct replacement has been obtained.

Inspection—General

Never inspect a component for wear or dimensional check unless it is absolutely clean; a slight smear of grease can conceal an incipient failure. When a component is to be checked dimensionally against figures quoted for it, use correct equipment (surface plates, micrometers, dial gauges, etc.) in serviceable condition. Makeshift checking equipment can be dangerous. Reject a component if its dimensions are outside the limits quoted, or if damage is apparent. A part may, however, be refitted if its critical dimension is exactly limit size, and is otherwise satisfactory.

Use Plastigauge 12 Type PG-1 for checking bearing surface clearances.

Directions for its use, and a scale giving bearing clearances in 0,0025 mm (0.0001 in) steps are provided with it.

Ball and Roller Bearings

NEVER REPLACE A BALL OR ROLLER BEARING WITHOUT FIRST ENSURING THAT IT IS IN AS-NEW CONDITION.

Remove all traces of lubricant from a bearing under inspection by washing it in petrol or a suitable de-greaser; maintain absolute cleanliness throughout the operations.

Inspect visually for markings of any form on rolling elements, raceways, outer surface of outer rings or inner surface of inner rings. Reject any bearings found to be marked, since any markings in these areas indicates onset of wear.

Holding the inner race between finger and thumb of one hand, spin the outer race and check that it revolves absolutely smoothly. Repeat, holding the outer race and spinning the inner race.

Rotate the outer ring with a reciprocating motion, while holding the inner ring; feel for any check or obstruction to rotation, and reject the bearing if action is not perfectly smooth.

Lubricate the bearing generously with lubricant appropriate to installation. Inspect shaft and bearing housing for discolouration or other marking suggesting that movement has taken place between bearing and seatings.

If markings are found use Loctite in installation of replacement bearing.

Ensure that the shaft and housing are clean and free from burrs before fitting the bearing.

If one bearing of a pair shows an imperfection it is generally advisable to renew both bearings; an exception could be made only if the faulty bearing had covered a low mileage, and it could be established that damage was confined to it.

When fitting bearing to shaft, apply force only to inner ring of bearing, and only to outer ring when fitting into housing (Fig. 1).

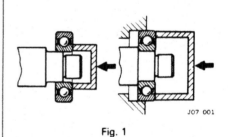

J07 001

Fig. 1

In the case of grease-lubricated bearings (e.g. hub bearings) fill the space between the bearing and outer seal with a recommended grade of grease before fitting the seal.

Always mark components of separable bearings (e.g. taper-roller bearings) in dismantling, to ensure correct reassembly. Never fit new rollers in a used cup.

Oil seals

Always fit new oil seals when rebuilding an assembly. It is not physically possible to replace a seal exactly as it had bedded down.

Carefully examine the seal before fitting to ensure that it is clean and undamaged.

Smear sealing lips with clean grease; pack dust excluder seals with grease, and heavily grease duplex seals in cavity between sealing lips.

Ensure that seal spring, if provided, is correctly fitted.

Place lip of seal towards fluid to be sealed and slide into position on shaft, using fitting sleeve (Fig. 2) when possible to protect sealing lip from damage by sharp corners, threads or splines. If fitting sleeve is not available, use plastic tube or adhesive tape to prevent damage to sealing lip.

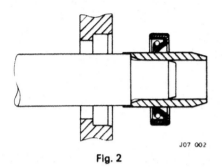

Fig. 2

Grease the outside diameter of the seal, place it square to the housing recess and press it into position, using great care and if possible a 'bell piece' (Fig. 3) to ensure that seal is not tilted. (In some cases it may be preferable to fit the seal to the housing before fitting to the shaft.) Never let the weight of an unsupported shaft rest in a seal.

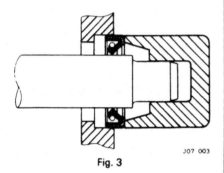

Fig. 3

If correct service tool is not available, use a suitable drift approximately 0,4 mm (0.015 in) smaller than the outside diameter of the seal. Use a hammer VERY GENTLY on the drift if a press is not suitable.

Press or drift a seal in to the depth of housing if the housing is shouldered, or flush with the face of the housing where no shoulder is provided.

NOTE: Most cases of failure or leakage of oil seals are due to careless fitting, and resulting damage to both seals and sealing surfaces. Care in fitting is essential if good results are to be obtained.

Joints and Joint Faces

Always use the correct gaskets where they are specified.

Use jointing compound only when recommended. Otherwise fit joints dry.

When jointing compound is used, apply in a thin uniform film to metal surfaces; take great care to prevent it from entering oilways, pipes or blind tapped holes.

Remove all traces of old jointing materials prior to reassembly. Do not use a tool which could damage joint faces.

Inspect joint faces for scratches or burrs and remove with a fine file or oil-stone; do not allow swarf or dirt to enter tapped holes or enclosed parts. Blow out any pipes, channels or crevices with compressed air, renewing any 'O' rings or seals displaced by air blast.

Flexible Hydraulic Pipes, Hoses

Before removing any brake or power steering hose, clean end fittings and area surrounding them as thoroughly as possible.

Obtain appropriate blanking caps before detaching hose end fittings, so that ports can be immediately covered to exclude dirt.

Clean hose externally and blow through with airline. Examine carefully for cracks, separation of plies, security of end fittings and external damage. Reject any hose found faulty.

When refitting hose, ensure that no unnecessary bends are introduced, and that hose is not twisted before or during tightening of union nuts.

Containers for hydraulic fluid must be kept absolutely clean.

Do not store hydraulic fluid in an unsealed container. It will absorb water, and fluid in this condition would be dangerous to use due to a lowering of its boiling point.

Do not allow hydraulic fluid to be contaminated with mineral oil, or use a container which has previously contained mineral oil.

Do not re-use fluid bled from system. Always use clean brake fluid, or a recommended alternative, to clean hydraulic components.

Fit a blanking cap to a hydraulic union and a plug to its socket after removal to prevent ingress of dirt.

Absolute cleanliness must be observed with hydraulic components at all times.

After any work on hydraulic systems, inspect carefully for leaks underneath the car while a second operator applies maximum pressure to the brakes (engine running) and operates the steering.

Metric Bolt Identification

An ISO metric bolt or screw, made of steel and larger than 6 mm in diameter can be identified by either of the symbols ISO M or M embossed or indented on top of the head (Fig. 4).

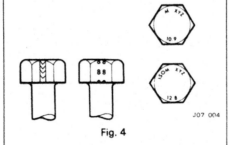

Fig. 4

In addition to marks to identify the manufacture, the head is also marked with symbols to indicate the strength grade e.g. 8.8, 10.9, 12.9, or 14.9, where the first figure gives the minimum tensile strength of the bolt material in tens of kgf/mm².

Zinc plated ISO metric bolts and nuts are chromate passivated, a greenish-khaki to gold-bronze colour.

Metric Nut Identification

A nut with an ISO metric thread is marked on one face (1, Fig. 5) or on one of the flats (2, Fig. 5) of the hexagon with the strength grade symbol 8, 12 or 14. Some nuts with a strength 4, 5 or 6 are also marked and some have the metric symbol M on the flat opposite the strength grade marking.

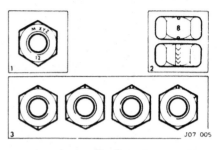

Fig. 5

A clock face system (3, Fig. 5) is used as an alternative method of indicating the strength grade. The external chamfers or a face of the nut is marked in a position relative to the appropriate hour mark on a clock face to indicate the strength grade.

A dot is used to locate the 12 o'clock position and a dash to indicate the strength grade. If the grade is above 12, two dots identify the 12 o'clock position.

Hydraulic Fittings—Metrication

WARNING: Metric and Unified threaded hydraulic parts. Although pipe connections to brake system units incorporate threads of metric form, those for power assisted steering are of U.N.F. type. It is vitally important that these two thread forms are not confused, and careful study should be made of the following notes.

Metric threads and metric sizes are being introduced into motor vehicle manufacture and some duplication of parts must be expected. Although standardization must in the long run be good, it would be wrong not to give warning of the dangers that exist while U.N.F. and metric threaded hydraulic parts continue together in service.

Fitting U.N.F. pipe nuts into metric ports and vice-versa should not happen, but experience of the change from B.S.F. to U.N.F. indicated that there is no certainty in relying upon the difference in thread size when safety is involved.

To provide permanent identification of metric parts is not easy but recognition has been assisted by the following means:

All metric pipe nuts, hose ends, unions and bleed screws are coloured black.

The hexagon area of pipe nuts is indented with the letter 'M'.

Metric and U.N.F. pipe nuts are slightly different in shape.

NOTE: In Figs. 6 to 9, A indicates the metric type and 'B' the U.N.F. type.
The metric female nut is **always** used with a trumpet flared pipe and the metric male nut is **always** used with a convex flared pipe (Fig. 6).

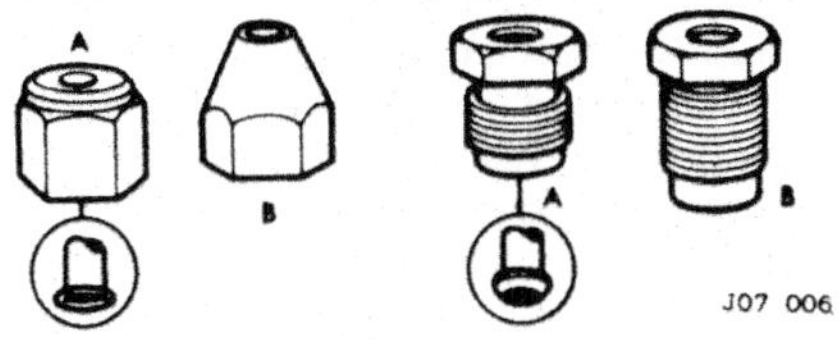

Fig. 6

All metric ports in cylinders and calipers have no counterbores, but unfortunately a few cylinders with U.N.F. threads also have no counterbore. The situation is, all ports with counterbores are U.N.F., but ports not counterbored are most likely to be metric (Fig. 7).

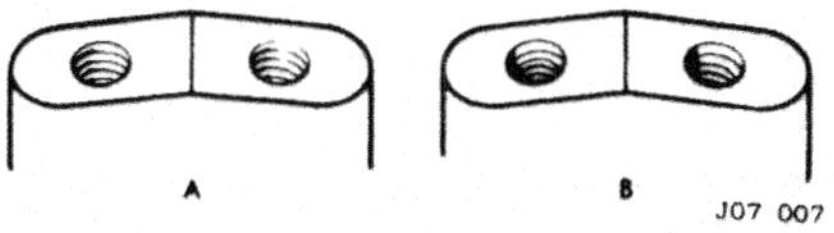

Fig. 7

The colour of the protective plugs in hydraulic ports indicates the size and the type of the threads, but the function of the plugs is protective and not designed as positive identification. In production it is difficult to use the wrong plug but human error must be taken into account. The plug colours and thread sizes are:

	U.N.F.
RED	$\frac{3}{8}$" X 24 U.N.F.
GREEN	$\frac{7}{16}$" X 20 U.N.F.
YELLOW	$\frac{1}{2}$" X 20 U.N.F.
PINK	$\frac{5}{8}$" X 18 U.N.F.
	METRIC
BLACK	10 X 1 mm
GREY	12 X 1 mm
BROWN	14 X 1,5 mm

Hose ends differ slightly between metric and U.N.F. (Fig. 8).

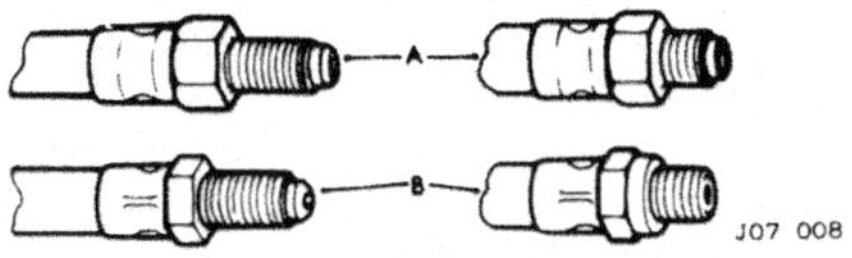

Fig. 8

Gaskets are not used with metric hoses.
The U.N.F. hose is sealed on the cylinder or caliper face by a copper gasket but the metric hose seals against the bottom of the port and there is a gap between faces of the hose end and cylinder (Fig. 9).

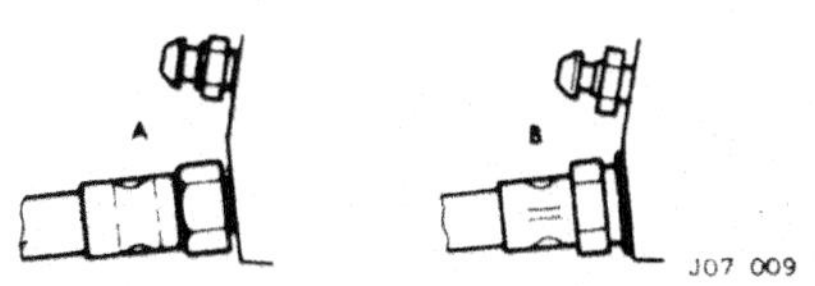

Fig. 9

Pipe sizes for U.N.F. are $\frac{3}{16}$ in, $\frac{1}{4}$ in, and $\frac{5}{16}$ in outside diameter.
Metric pipe sizes are 4,75 mm, 6 mm and 8 mm.
4,75 mm pipe is exactly the same as $\frac{3}{16}$ in pipe.
6 mm pipe is 0.014 in smaller than $\frac{1}{4}$ in pipe.
8 mm pipe is 0.002 in larger than $\frac{5}{16}$ in pipe.
Convex pipe flares are shaped differently for metric sizes and when making pipes for metric equipment, metric pipe flaring tools must be used.

The greatest danger lies with the confusion of 10 mm and $\frac{3}{8}$ in U.N.F. pipe nuts used for $\frac{3}{16}$ in (or 4,75 mm) pipe. The $\frac{3}{8}$ in U.N.F. pipe nut or hose can be screwed into a 10 mm port but is very slack and easily stripped. The thread engagement is very weak and cannot provide an adequate seal. The opposite condition, a 10 mm nut in a $\frac{3}{8}$ in port, is difficult and unlikely to cause trouble. The 10 mm nut will screw in 1½ or two turns and seize. It has a crossed thread 'feel' and it is impossible to force the nut far enough to seal the pipe. With female pipe nuts the position is of course reversed.
The other combinations are so different that there is no danger of confusion.

Keys and Keyways

Remove burrs from edges of keyways with a fine file and clean throroughly before atempting to refit key.
Clean and inspect key closely; keys are suitable for refitting only if indistinguishable from new, as any indentation may indicate the onset of wear.

Split Pins

Fit new split pins throughout when replacing any unit.
Always fit split pins where split pins were originally used. Do not substitute spring washers; there is always a good reason for the use of a split pin.
All split pins should be fitted as shown in Fig. 10 unless otherwise stated.

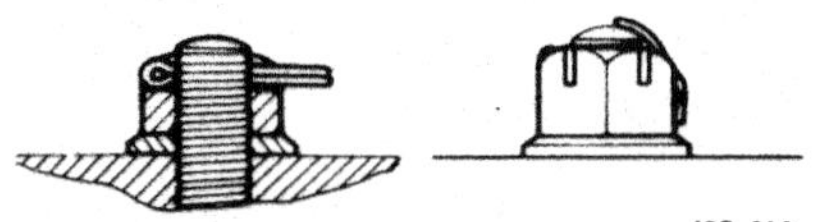

Fig. 10

Tab Washers

Fit new tab washers in all places where they are used. Never replace with a used tab washer.
Ensure that the new tab washer is of the same design as that replaced.

Nuts

When tightening up a slotted or castellated nut **never slacken it back** to insert split pin or locking wire wire except in those recommended cases where this forms part of an adjustment. If difficulty is experienced, alternative washers or nuts should be selected, or washer thickness reduced.

Where self-locking nuts have been removed it is advisable to replace them with new ones of the same type.

NOTE: Where bearing pre-load is involved nuts should be tightened in accordance with special instructions.

Locking Wire

Fit new locking wire of the correct type for all assemblies incorporating it.
Arrange wire so that its tension tends to tighten the bolt heads, or nuts, to which it is fitted.

Screw Threads

Both U.N.F. and Metric threads to ISO standards are used. See below for thread identification.
Damaged threads must always be discarded. Cleaning up threads with a die or tap impairs the strength and closeness of fit of the threads and is not recommended.
Always ensure that replacment bolts are at least equal in strength to those replaced.
Do not allow oil, grease or jointing compound to enter blind threaded holes. The hydraulic action on screwing in the bolt or stud could split the housing.
Always tighten a nut or bolt to the recommended torque figure. Damaged or corroded threads can affect the torque reading.
To check or re-tighten a bolt or screw to a specified torque figure, first slacken a quarter of a turn, then re-tighten to the correct figure.
Always oil thread lightly before tightening to ensure a free running thread, except in the case of self-locking nuts.

Unified Thread Identification

Bolts

A circular recess is stamped in the upper surface of the bolt head (1, Fig. 11).

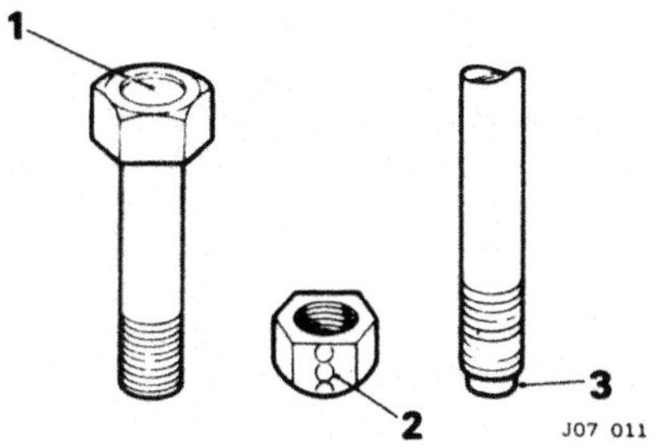

Fig. 11

Nuts

A continuous line of circles is indented on one of the flats of the hexagon, parallel to the axis of the nut (2, Fig. 11).

Studs, Brake Rods, etc.

The component is reduced to the core diameter for a short length at its extremity (3, Fig. 11).

JACKING, LIFTING AND TOWING

JACKING POINT

Four jacking points are provided beneath the body side-members (1, Fig. 1), one in front of each rear wheel and one behind each front wheel. They consist of downward-facing spigots (2, Fig. 1) designed to engage the lifting head of the tool kit jack (3, Fig. 1).

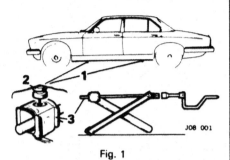

Fig. 1

Ensure that the jack head is fully engaged with spigot before lifting the car, and that wheels on side opposite to that being lifted are chocked, as well as checking handbrake application.

STANDS

When carrying out any work which requires a wheel to be raised (apart from a simple wheel-change) always replace the tool kit jack by a stand engaging the jacking spigot, to provide secure support.

WORKSHOP JACK

Front—one wheel

Place the jack head under the lower spring support pan, interposing a suitable wooden block before raising the wheel. Place a stand in position at the adjacent spigot and remove the jack before working on the car.

Rear—one wheel (Fig. 2)

Place the jack head under the outer fork of the wishbone at the wheel to be raised; interpose a suitable wooden block between the jack head and the wishbone, ensuring that the aluminium alloy hub carrier and its grease nipple will not be contacted by the block as the wheel is raised. Place a stand in position at the adjacent spigot and remove the jack before working on the car.

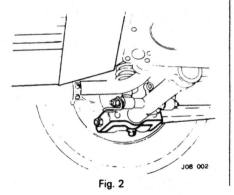

Fig. 2

Front—both wheels (Fig. 3)

Place the jack, with a shallow wooden block on its head, centrally beneath the front cross-member, between the lower wishbones. Raise the car, then lower it on to two stands engaging the front jacking spigots; remove the jack before working on the car.

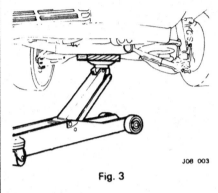

Fig. 3

Rear—both wheels (Fig. 4)

Place the jack head centrally under the plate below the final drive unit and interpose a wooden block between the jack head and plate, the block being shaped to prevent load being applied to the plate flanges. Raise the rear end of the car, then lower on to two stands engaging rear jacking spigots; remove the jack before working on the car.

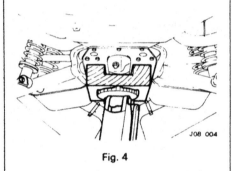

Fig. 4

LIFTING

Locate lifting pads at the four jacking spigots.

TOWING

Two towing eyes are provided on all cars, located adjacent to the front cross-member forward attachments, for use in towing from the front. Tie-down lugs at rear damper lower attachments are NOT suitable for rear towing. When towing an automatic transmission car, it is essential to carry out the following operations:

A. With automatic transmission functioning correctly:

1. Add 1,7 litres (3.0 pints) of correct automatic transmission fluid to the transmission via the underbonnet filler tube.
2. Place the selector lever at 'N'.
3. Check that the ignition key is in place, and turn it to position '1'.
4. Tow the car at a speed not exceeding 48 km/h (30 m.p.h.) for not more than 48 km (30 miles).

5. After completing the tow, remove sufficient fluid from the transmission to restore correct reading on the dipstick.

CAUTION: It must be remembered that steering is no longer power-assisted when the engine is not running, and that the brake servo will become ineffective after a few applications of the brakes. Be prepared, therefore, for relatively heavy steering and the need for increased pressure on the brake pedal. This applies to manual transmission cars as well as to those with automatic transmission.

B. With automatic transmission defective, either tow the car with the rear wheels clear of the ground, or disconnect the propeller shaft at the final drive input flange and firmly secure the rear end of the shaft to one side of the flange. Restrictions on towing distance do not apply when the output shaft of the gearbox is not being turned, but it is still essential that the ignition key is turned to position '1' and the cautionary note above still applies.

Recovery of cars fitted with manual gearbox: Due to the possibility of internal gearbox damage, resulting from inadequate lubrication, it is essential, if the car is to be towed, that either the rear wheels are clear of the ground, or the propeller shaft is disconnected from the final drive input flange. If the propeller shaft is disconnected it must be firmly secured away from the final drive flange. Ensure that the ignition key is in position '1'.

TRANSPORTING

Automatic transmission cars only

CAUTION: When the vehicle is being transported the selector lever must be in 'N' or 'D', never in 'P'. To obviate the possibility of damage to the pawl mechanism, the handbrake should be applied.

RECOMMENDED LUBRICANTS, FLUIDS, CAPACITIES AND DIMENSIONS

Engine Oil—Recommended S.A.E. Viscosity Range/Ambient Temperature Scale

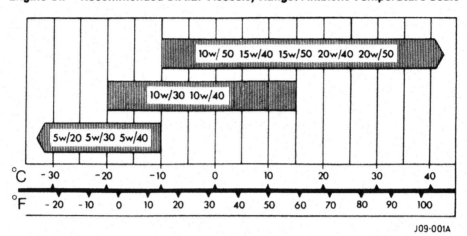

J09-001A

Component—Model	Temperature Range	Specification	S.A.E. Viscosity Rating	Approved Brands Available in U.K. for Temperatures Above −10°C (14°F)
Engine—All Models Distributor—All Models Oil Can—All models	Above −10°C (14°F) −20°C to 10°C (−4°F to 50°F) Below −10°C (14°F)	BLSO OL.02 or MIL-L-2104 B or A.P.1. SE	10W/50, 15W/50, 20W/40, 20W/50 10W/30, 10W/40, 10W/50 5W/20, 5W/30	Unipart Super Multigrade, BP Super Viscostatic, Castrol GTX, Duckhams (15W/50) Hypergrade Motor Oil, Esso Uniflow, Fina Super Grade, Mobiloil Super, Shell Super Oil, Texaco Havoline
Manual Gearbox—6 cyl. —Refill —Top up ONLY	All All	Shell E3766 Hypoid Oil	75W EP 80 W	JRT Part No. RTC 1896
Powr-Lok Differential—All —Initial Fill —Refill	All All	Use only approved brands of fluid specially formulated for Powr-Lok	90 90	Shell Spirax Super 90, Shell Spirax Super 90, BP Gear Oil 1453, BP Limslip Gear Oil 90/1, Castrol G722, Castrol Hypoy LS, Duckhams Hypoid 90 DL, Texaco 3450 Gear Oil, Veedol Multigear Limited Slip S.A.E. 90
Drain and Top-Up —Top-up only if above oil not available Normal Differential—6 cyl. —Refill or top-up	All All	MIL-L-2105 B	EP 90	BP Gear Oil S.A.E. 90 EP, Castrol Hypoy, Duckhams Hypoid 90, Esso Gear Oil GX 90/140, Mobilube HDGO, Shell Spirax HD 90 Texaco Multigear Lubricant EP 90
GM 400 Automatic Transmission—12 cyl.	All	Dexron 2D		BP Autran DX, Castrol TQ Dexron, Esso ATF Dexron, Mobil ATF 220 Dexron, Shell ATF Dexron, Texaco Texamatic Fluid 6673
Borg-Warner Automatic Transmission Model 66 6 cyl.	All	Type G (M2C 33 G)	—	BP Autran G, Castrol TQF, Duckhams Q-Matic, Esso Glide Type G, Fina Purfimatic 33F, Mobil ATF 210, Shell Donax TF, Texaco Texamatic Type G
Power Assisted Steering—All	All	Above Specification or Dexron 2D	—	BP Autran DX, Castrol TQ Dexron, Esso ATF Dexron, Mobil ATF 220 Dexron, Shell ATF Dexron, Texaco Texamatic Fluid 6673
Grease Points—All	All	Multipurpose Lithium Grease, N.L.C.I. Consistency No. 2	—	BP Energrease L8, Castrol LM, Duckhams LB 10, Esso Multipurpose H, Fina Marson HTL2, Mobilgrease MP, Shell Retinax A, Texaco Marfak

09—1

COOLING SYSTEM, CAPACITIES AND DIMENSIONS

COOLING SYSTEM

Additive	Barr's Leak Inhibitor, 1 satchet per car— 6 cylinder models; 2 satchets per car—12 cylinder models.
Anti-freeze	BP Type HS25, Union Carbide UT 184 or I.C.I. 007. If these are not available, anti-freeze conforming to specification B.S. 3150 or 3152 may be used. Concentration—U.K. only 40% S.G. 1.065 All other markets 55% S.G. 1.074

In territories where anti-freeze is unnecessary the cooling system must be filled with a solution of Marston Corrosion Inhibitor Concentrate SQ36.

Always top-up the cooling system with recommended strength of anti-freeze or Corrosion Inhibitor, NEVER with water only.

CAPACITIES

	Litres	Imperial	U.S.
Engine refill (including filter)			
6 cylinder model			
Up to Vin nos. 8L161546; 8A15190; 7M4883	8,25	14.5 pt	17.5 pt
From Vin nos. 8L161546; 8A15190; 7M4883	8,81	15.5 pt	18.7 pt
12 cylinder model	10,8	19 pt	22.8 pt
Automatic transmission unit			
6 cylinder model (from dry)	8,00	14 pt	16.75 pt
12 cylinder model	9,1	16 pt	19.2 pt
Final drive unit	1,6	2.75 pt	3.25 pt
Cooling system, including reservoir and heater or air conditioning:			
6 cylinder model	18,2	32 pt	38.5 pt
12 cylinder model Not HE	21,2	37.5 pt	45 pt
HE	19,5	35 pt	42 pt
Fuel tanks — left and right — per tank	47,7	10.5 gal	12.6 gal
Luggage compartment	0,27 m³	9.55 ft³	9.55 ft³

DIMENSIONS

Wheelbase	2865 mm	112.8 in
Track: Front	1480 mm	58.26 in
Rear	1495 mm	58.86 in
Overall length: European cars	4959 mm	195,25 in
U.S.A. and Canada	5067 mm	199.5 in
Overall width	1770 mm	69.7 in
Overall height	1377 mm	54.2 in
Turning circle: between kerbs	12,2 m	40 ft
Ground clearance: kerb condition	152,4 mm	6 in

09—2

WEIGHTS

U.K. and European Models	XJ 3.4		XJ 4.2 Daimler Sovereign		XJ 5.3 Daimler Sovereign	
	kg	lb	kg	lb	kg	lb
Kerb weight	1766	3902	1830	4044	1930	4265
Gross vehicle weight	2186	4831	2250	4973	2350	6294
*Gross train weight	3453	7631	3517	7773	3617	7994
Maximum permitted front axle load	1055	2332	1085	2398	1170	2580
Maximum permitted rear axle load	1150	2742	1180	2607	1200	2652

Federal Models	XJ 6		XJ 12			
	kg	lb	kg	lb		
Gross vehicle weight rating	2258	4979	2371	5229		
Gross axle weight rating—Front	1074	2370	1170	2580		
Gross axle weight rating—Rear	1183	2609	1201	2649		

* Gross train weight is the gross vehicle weight plus maximum trailer weight.

Maximum permitted luggage compartment load with five passengers is 70 kg (154.3 lb).

FUEL REQUIREMENTS

Only cars with 'S' compression ratio engines require 97 octane fuel.
Cars with 'L' compression ratio engines should use 94 octane fuel.
In U.S.A. use unleaded fuel with minimum octane rating of 87 RON.

In the United Kingdom use '4 STAR' fuel, 98 octane.

If, of necessity, the car has to be operated on lower octane fuel, do not use full throttle otherwise detonation may occur.

RECOMMENDED HYDRAULIC FLUID

Braking System

Castrol-Girling Universal Brake and Clutch fluid. This fluid exceeds S.A.E. J1703/D specification.
NOTE: Check all pipes in the brake system at the start and finish of each winter period for possible corrosion due to salt and grit used on the roads.

MAINTENANCE SUMMARY—UK & Europe—Early Cars (up to VIN 322373)

OPERATION	Interval in Kilometres x 1000 Interval in Miles x 1000	5 3	10 6	20 12
PASSENGER COMPARTMENT				
Fit seat cover, place protective cover on carpets		X	X	X
Drive car on lift (ramp)		X	X	X
Check function of original equipment, i.e. interior and exterior lamps, indicators, horns and warning lights		X	X	X
Check operation of window controls		X	X	X
Check handbrake operation		X	X	X
Check footbrake operation		X	X	X
Check clock is running and set to time		X	X	X
Check windscreen washers and wipers for correct operation and that jets are clear and correctly positioned		X	X	X
Check condition and security of seats and seat belts		X	X	X
Check rear-view mirrors for cracks and crazing		X	X	X
EXTERIOR AND LUGGAGE COMPARTMENT				
Check door locks for correct operation		X	X	X
Check luggage compartment light for correct operation		X	X	X
Check/adjust tyre pressures, including spare		X	X	X
Check that tyres comply with manufacturer's specification		X	X	X
Check tyres for tread depth, visually for cuts in fabric, exposure of ply or cord structure, lumps or bulges		X	X	X
Check tightness of road wheel fastenings and that spare is correctly stowed		X	X	X
Check for fuel leaks at pumps and pipes; ensure that all connections are tight		X	X	X
Check front wheel alignment			X	X
Lubricate all locks and hinges (not steering lock)			X	X
Check, if necessary renew, windscreen wiper blades		X	X	X
Check/adjust headlight alignment		X	X	X
ENGINE COMPARTMENT				
Open bonnet, fit wing covers		X	X	X
Check/top-up engine oil		X		
Top-up carburetter piston dampers (where applicable)		X	X	X
Check/top-up cooling system		X	X	X
Check/top-up windscreen washer reservoir		X	X	X
Check/top-up brake fluid reservoir		X	X	X
Check/top-up clutch fluid reservoir		X	X	X
Check/top-up fluid in power steering reservoir		X	X	X
Check/top-up automatic gearbox fluid			X	X
Check distributor points; adjust or renew (where applicable)			X	X
Clean/adjust spark plugs			X	
Renew spark plugs				X
Lubricate distributor			X	X
Lubricate accelerator control linkage and check operation			X	X
Clean engine breather filter				X
Renew fuel filter				X
Clean A.E.D. unit filter (where applicable)		X	X	X
Renew air cleaner element and seal				X
Check/adjust torque of cylinder head nuts (not V12 engine)				X
Check/adjust torque of exhaust manifold nuts (not V12 engine)				X
Check/adjust ignition timing and distributor characteristics using electronic equipment			X	X
Check/adjust carburetter idle speed (where applicable)			X	X
Check/adjust driving bolts		X	X	X
Check/top-up battery electrolyte; clean and grease terminals		X	X	X
Check cooling and heating systems for leaks		X	X	X
Check visually hydraulic pipes and unions for chafing, leaks and corrosion		X	X	X
Check visually all joints for petrol, oil or air leaks		X	X	X
Check exhaust system for leakage and security		X	X	X

10—1

MAINTENANCE SUMMARY—UK & Europe—Early Cars (up to VIN 322373)

OPERATION	Interval in Kilometres x 1000 Interval in Miles x 1000	5 3	10 6	20 12
UNDERBODY				
Raise ramp		X	X	X
Renew engine oil and filter			X	X
Check/top-up gearbox oil—cars fitted with manual transmission only			X	X
Check/top-up final drive oil			X	
Renew final drive oil				X
Check/adjust clutch push-rod free travel—cars fitted with manual transmission only			X	X
Lubricate clutch linkage			X	X
Lubricate automatic gearbox exposed selector linkage			X	X
Lubricate handbrake mechanical linkage and cable			X	X
Lubricate all grease points excluding hubs			X	X
Lubricate all grease points, including hubs				X
Inspect brake pads for wear and discs for condition		X	X	X
Check security of engine and suspension fixings				X
Check exhaust system for leakage and security		X	X	X
Check engine, power assisted steering, gearbox and final drive for oil leaks		X	X	X
Check condition and security of steering unit joints and gaiters		X	X	X
Check cooling and heating system for leaks			X	X
Check visually hydraulic pipes and unions for chafing, leaks and corrosion		X	X	X
Check visually all joints for petrol, oil or air leaks		X	X	X
Lower ramp				
Remove wing covers, close bonnet and check bonnet for correct operation		X	X	X
ROAD OR DYNAMOMETER TEST				
(Clean hands before carrying out following items)				
Ensure that seat cover and protective cover on carpets are in place		X	X	X
Drive car off lift (ramp)		X	X	X
Carry out road/roller test and check function of all instrumentation. Check safety harness inertia reel mechanism		X	X	X
Remove seat cover and protective cover from carpets		X	X	X

ADDITIONAL MAINTENANCE OPERATIONS—ALL VEHICLES

Brake System—Preventive Maintenance

In addition to the periodical inspection of brake components it is advisable as the car ages and as a precution against the effects of wear and deterioration to make a more searching inspection and renew parts as necessary.

It is recommended that:

1. Disc brake pads, hoses and pipes should be examined at intervals no greater than those laid down in the Passport to Service.

2. Brake fluid should be changed completely every 18 months or 30 000 km (18 000 miles) whichever is the sooner.

3. All fluid seals in the hydraulic system should be renewed and all flexible hoses should be examined and renewed if necessary every three years or 60 000 km (36 000 miles) whichever is the sooner. At the same time the working surfaces of the pistons and the bores of the master cylinder, wheel cylinders and other slave cylinders should be examined and new parts fitted where necessary.

Care should be taken to observe the following:

a. At all times use the recommended brake fluid.

b. Never leave fluid in unsealed containers; it absorbs moisture quickly and can be dangerous if used in the braking system in this condition.

c. Fluid drained from the system or used for bleeding is best discarded.

d. The necessity for absolute cleanliness when carrying out any operations on the braking system cannot be over-emphasized.

10—2

MAINTENANCE SUMMARY — UK & Europe — Later Cars (from VIN 322374)

OPERATION	Interval in Kilometres x 1000 Interval in Miles x 1000	1.5 1	12 7.5	24 15
Fit protection kit		×	×	×
Check condition and security of seats and seat belts		×	×	×
Check operation of seat belt warning system		×		
Check footbrake operation		×	×	×
Check operation of lamps		×		
Check operation of horns		×		
Check operation of warning indicators		×		
Check operation of windscreen wipers		×		
Check operation of windscreen washers		×		
Check security of handbrake — release fully after checking		×	×	×
Check rear-view mirrors for security and function		×		
Mark stud to wheel relationship			×	×
Remove front wheels			×	
Remove road wheels — front and rear				×
Check that tyres are of the correct size and type		×	×	×
Check tyre tread depth		×	×	×
Check tyres visually for external lumps, bulges and uneven wear		×	×	×
Check tyres visually for external exposure of ply or cord		×	×	×
Check/adjust tyre pressures		×	×	×
Inspect brake pads for wear and discs for condition			×	×
Adjust front hub bearing end-float				×
Grease hubs				×
Check for oil leaks from steering and fluid leaks from suspension system		×	×	×
Check condition and security of steering unit joints and gaiters		×	×	×
Refit road wheels in original position			×	×
Check tightness of road wheel fastenings		×	×	×
Drain engine oil		×	×	×
Check/top up gearbox oil (manual)		×	×	×
Renew automatic transmission filter 48.000 km (30 000 miles)				48 km
Renew automatic transmission fluid 48.000 km (30 000 miles)				48 km
Grease all points excluding hubs			×	×
Check/top up rear axle/final drive oil		×	×	×
Renew final drive oil 48.000 km (30 000 miles)				48 km
Check visually hydraulic hoses, pipes and unions for chafing, cracks, leaks and corrosion		×	×	×
Check exhaust system for leakage and security		×	×	×
Lubricate handbrake mechanical linkage and cables		×	×	×
Check condition of handbrake pads				×
Lubricate automatic gearbox exposed selector linkage		×	×	×
Check tightness of propshaft coupling bolts		×		×
Check security of accessible engine mountings		×		
Check condition and security of steering unit, joints and gaiters		×	×	×
Check security and condition of suspension fixings		×	×	×
Check steering rack for oil leaks		×	×	×
Check power steering for leaks, hydraulic pipes and unions for chafing, corrosion and security		×	×	×
Check shock absorbers for fluid leaks		×	×	×
Renew engine oil filter element			×	×
Refit engine drain plug		×	×	×
Check for oil leaks — engine and transmission		×	×	×

10—3

MAINTENANCE SUMMARY — UK & Europe — Later Cars

OPERATION	Interval in Kilometres x 1000 Interval in Miles x 1000	1.5 1	12 7.5	24 15
Check/adjust torque of cylinder head nuts/bolts (not V12 engine)		×		
Fill engine with oil		×	×	×
Lubricate accelerator control linkage and pedal pivot		×		
Top up carburetter piston dampers (where applicable)		×	×	×
Renew air cleaner element(s)				×
Check security of accessible engine mountings		×		
Check driving belts; adjust or renew		×		×
Clean and adjust spark plugs			×	
Renew spark plugs				×
Check/top-up battery electrolyte (where applicable)		×	×	×
Clean and grease battery connections		×	×	×
Check/top-up clutch fluid reservoir (where applicable)		×	×	×
Check/top-up brake fluid reservoir		×	×	×
Check brake servo hose(s) for security and condition		×	×	×
Check/top-up windscreen washer reservoir		×		
Check cooling and heater system for leaks and hoses for security and condition		×	×	×
Change coolant ensuring the correct antifreeze concentration 48.000 km (30 000 miles)				48 km
Check/top-up cooling system		×		
Renew fuel filter — 3.4				×
Clean engine breather filter (where applicable)				×
Check crankcase breathing system for leaks, hoses for security and condition		×		×
Clean A.E.D. filter (where applicable)		×	×	×
Check/top-up fluid in power steering reservoir; check security and condition of oil pressure hose at oil filter		×	×	×
Run engine and check for sealing of oil filter; stop engine			×	×
Check/top-up engine oil			×	×
Connect electronic instruments and check underbonnet label data		×		×
Check visually distributor points; adjust or renew (where applicable)		×		
Renew distributor points (where applicable)				×
Lubricate distributor (not cam wiping pad) V12 at 36.000 km (22 500 miles)		×		36 km
Disconnect vacuum pipe, check dwell angle, adjust as necessary		×		×
Check ignition timing (at normal operating temperature on HE models)		×	×	×
Check distributor automatic advance		×		×
Check advance increases as vacuum pipe is reconnected		×		×
Lubricate all locks, hinges and door check mechanisms (not steering lock)		×		×
Check operation of bonnet lock and boot and door locks and lights		×		
Check operation of window controls		×		
Check and if necessary renew windscreen wiper blades			×	×
Check/adjust engine idle speed and carburetter mixture settings (where applicable) stop engine — disconnect instruments		×		×
Check power steering system for leaks, hydraulic pipes and unions for chafing and corrosion		×	×	×
Check for oil leaks from engine and transmission		×	×	×
Check/top-up automatic gearbox fluid		×	×	×
Re-check tension if driving belt has been renewed		×		×
Remove spare wheel		×	×	×
Check that the tyre is the correct size and type		×	×	×
Check tyre tread depth		×	×	×

10——4

MAINTENANCE SUMMARY — UK & Europe — Later Cars

OPERATION	Interval in Kilometres x 1000 Interval in Miles x 1000	1.5 1	12 7.5	24 15
Check tyre visually for external exposure of cord or ply		×	×	×
Check tyre visually for external lumps or bulges		×	×	×
Check/adjust tyre pressure		×	×	×
Renew fuel filter (not 3.4)				×
Refit spare wheel		×	×	×
Check/adjust headlamp alignment		×		×
Check/adjust front wheel alignment		×		×
Carry out road or roller test		×	×	×
Check operation of seat belt inertia mechanism		×	×	×
Ensure cleanliness of controls, door handles, steering wheel, etc		×	×	×
Remove protection kit		×	×	×
Report additional work required		×	×	×

It is further recommended:
At 18 month intervals:
   Change brake fluid

At 60.000 km (37 500 mile) intervals:
   Renew all fluid seals in hydraulic system; examine and renew if necessary all flexible hoses
   Examine working surfaces of master cylinder and calipers. Renew if necessary

OPTIONAL SERVICES

OPERATION	Interval in Kilometres x 1000 Interval in Miles x 1000	12 7.5	24 15
Check operation of lamps			×
Check operation of horns			×
Check operation of warning indicators			×
Check operation of windscreen wipers			×
Check operation of windscreen washers			×
Check operation of window controls		×	×
Check operation of boot lamp			×
Check operation of all door, bonnet and boot locks		×	×
Check sunroof and controls for correct operation (if fitted)			×
Check operation of headlamp wipe/wash (if fitted)			×
Check rear view mirrors for security and function			×
Check/top-up windscreen washer reservoir			×
Check/top-up cooling system		×	×
Lubricate all locks, hinges and door check mechanisms (not steering lock)		×	
Check operation of cruise control (if fitted)			×
Clean aerial mast		×	
Check/adjust headlamp alignment		×	
Check/adjust front wheel alignment		×	

10—5

MAINTENANCE SUMMARY — North American Markets

Service Code Letter	DISTANCE Mileage x 1000													
A	1													
B		7.5		22.5		37.5		52.5		67.5		82.5		97.5
C			15				45				75			
D					30				60				90	

THE PERIOD BETWEEN SERVICES SHOULD NOT EXCEED 12 MONTHS

Maintenance, replacement or repair of the emission control devices and system may be performed by an automotive repair establishment or individual using any automotive part which has been certified by the part manufacturer. Your dealer will supply particulars.

10—6

MAINTENANCE SUMMARY North American Markets

1000 MILES
A INTERVAL

LUBRICATION

Lubricate handbrake mechanical linkage and cables
Renew engine oil and engine oil filter
Check/top-up rear axle oil
Check/top-up brake fluid reservoir
Check/top-up automatic transmission fluid
Check battery condition/clean and grease connections if necessary
Check/top-up cooling system
Check/top-up power steering reservoir
Check/top-up windscreen washer fluid
Lubricate all locks and hinges (not steering lock)
Renew fluid — manual transmission
Check/top-up clutch fluid

ENGINE

Check for oil leaks
Check all driving belts; adjust
Check cooling and heater system for leaks, for hose condition and security
Check security of engine mountings

FUEL AND EXHAUST SYSTEMS

Check fuel system for leaks, pipes and unions for chafing and corrosion
Check exhaust system for leaks and security

TRANSMISSION, BRAKES, STEERING AND SUSPENSION

Check for fluid/oil leaks
Check condition and security of steering unit, joints and gaiters
Check visually brake hydraulic pipes and unions for cracks, chafing, leaks and corrosion
Check suspension component condition and security
Check shock absorbers for leaks and condition
Check/adjust wheel alignment
Check brake servo hoses for security and condition
Check footbrake and handbrake operation

WHEELS AND TYRES

Check that tyres comply with manufacturer's specification
Check tyres for tread depth and visually for external cuts in fabric, exposure of ply or cord structure, lumps or bulges
Check tyres for irregular tread wear; perform necessary alignment/repair
Check and adjust tyre pressure, including spare wheel
Check for damaged/deformed wheel rims
Check tightness of road wheel fastenings

ELECTRICAL

Check/adjust operation of windscreen wipers and washers
Check function of all original equipment: lights, horns, warning indicators, radio, etc.
Check/adjust headlight alignment (refer to state and local requirement)

BODY

Check operation and security of seats and seat belts — front and rear
Check operation of all door, bonnet and boot locks
Check operation of window and sunroof controls
Check/open underbody drains (also during annual rust inspection)

GENERAL
Road Test:

Check vehicle performance, shifting, braking, handling
Check function of all instrumentation
Check function of trip computer
Check function of cruise control
Check function of climate control and ventilation systems

Report Additional Work Required After Road Test:

Check engine for leaks
Check/top-up automatic transmission fluid
Check/top-up brake fluid reservoir
Check/top-up power steering reservoir

10—7

MAINTENANCE SUMMARY North American Markets

**7500 MILES
B INTERVAL**

LUBRICATION

Lubricate all grease points (not wheel hubs or steering rack)
Lubricate handbrake mechanical linkage and cables
Renew engine oil and engine oil filter
Check/top-up rear axle oil
Check/top-up brake fluid reservoir
Check/top-up automatic transmission fluid
Check battery condition/clean and grease connections if necessary
Check/top-up cooling system
Check/top-up power steering reservoir
Check/top-up windscreen washer fluid
Lubricate all locks and hinges (not steering lock)
Renew brake fluid every 18 000 miles or 18 months
Renew coolant every 2 years
Check/top-up clutch fluid

ENGINE

Check for oil leaks
Check all driving belts; adjust/renew as necessary (applicable above 30 000 miles)
Check cooling and heater system for leaks, for hose condition and security

FUEL AND EXHAUST SYSTEMS

Check fuel system for leaks, pipes and unions for chafing and corrosion
Check exhaust system for leaks and security
Renew fuel filter (at 52 500 miles only)

TRANSMISSION, BRAKES, STEERING AND SUSPENSION

Check for fluid/oil leaks
Check condition and security of steering unit, joints and gaiters
Check visually brake hydraulic pipes and unions for cracks, chafing, leaks and corrosion
Check suspension component condition and security
Check shock absorbers for leaks and condition
Inspect brake pads for wear and discs for condition (including handbrake pads)
Check/adjust wheel alignment
Check brake servo hoses for security and condition

WHEELS AND TYRES

Check that tyres comply with manufacturer's specification
Check tyres for tread depth and visually for external cuts in fabric, exposure of ply or cord structure, lumps or bulges
Check tyres for irregular tread wear; perform necessary alignment/repair
Check and adjust tyre pressure, including spare wheel
Check for damaged/deformed wheel rims
Check tightness of road wheel fastenings

ELECTRICAL

Check/adjust operation of windscreen wipers and washers
Check function of all original equipment: lights, horns, warning indicators, radio, etc.
Check wiper blades and arms: renew if necessary
Check/adjust headlight alignment (refer to state and local requirement)

BODY

Check operation and security of seats and seat belts — front and rear
Check operation of all door, bonnet and boot locks
Check operation of window and sunroof controls
Check/open underbody drains (also during annual rust inspection)

GENERAL
Road Test:

Check vehicle performance, shifting, braking, handling
Check function of all instrumentation
Check function of trip computer
Check function of cruise control
Check function of climate control and ventilation systems

Report Additional Work Required After Road Test:

Check engine for leaks
Check/top-up automatic transmission fluid
Check/top-up brake fluid reservoir
Check/top-up power steering reservoir

10—8

MAINTENANCE SUMMARY North American Markets

15 000 MILES
C INTERVAL

LUBRICATION

Lubricate all grease points
Lubricate handbrake mechanical linkage and cables
Lubricate front/rear wheel hubs
Lubricate steering rack (hand operated equipment only)
Renew engine oil and engine oil filter
Renew manual transmission fluid
Check/top-up rear axle oil
Check/top-up brake fluid reservoir
Check/top-up automatic transmission fluid
Check battery condition/clean and grease connections if necessary
Check/top-up cooling system
Check/top-up power steering reservoir
Check/top-up windscreen washer fluid
Lubricate accelerator control linkages and pedal pivot; check operation
Lubricate all locks and hinges (not steering lock)
Renew brake fluid every 18 000 miles or 18 months
Renew coolant every 2 years
Check/top-up clutch fluid

ENGINE

Check for oil leaks
Check all driving belts; adjust/renew as necessary (applicable above 30 000 miles)
Check cooling and heater system for leaks, for hose condition and security

FUEL AND EXHAUST SYSTEMS

Check fuel system for leaks, pipes and unions for chafing and corrosion
Check exhaust system for leaks and security

TRANSMISSION, BRAKES, STEERING AND SUSPENSION

Check for fluid/oil leaks
Check condition and security of steering unit, joints and gaiters
Check visually brake hydraulic pipes and unions for cracks, chafing, leaks and corrosion
Check suspension component condition and security
Check shock absorbers for leaks and condition
Inspect brake pads for wear and discs for condition (including handbrake pads)
Check/adjust front wheel alignment
Check/adjust front hub bearing end float
Check tightness of propeller shaft coupling bolts
Check brake servo hoses for security and condition

WHEELS AND TYRES

Check that tyres comply with manufacturer's specification
Check tyres for tread depth and visually for external cuts in fabric, exposure of ply or cord structure, lumps or bulges
Check tyres for irregular tread wear; perform necessary alignment/repair
Check and adjust tyre pressure, including spare wheel
Check for damaged/deformed wheel rims
Check tightness of road wheel fastenings

ELECTRICAL

Check/adjust operation of windscreen wipers and washers
Check function of all original equipment: lights, horns, warning indicators, radio, etc.
Check wiper blades and arms; renew if necessary
Check/adjust headlight alignment (refer to state and local requirement)

BODY

Check operation and security of seats and seat belts — front and rear
Check operation of all door, bonnet and boot locks
Check operation of window and sunroof controls
Check/open underbody drains (also during annual rust inspection)

GENERAL
Road Test:

Check vehicle performance, shifting, braking, handling
Check function of all instrumentation
Check function of trip computer
Check function of cruise control
Check function of climate control and ventilation systems

Report Additional Work Required After Road Test:

Check engine for leaks
Check/top-up automatic transmission fluid
Check/top-up brake fluid reservoir
Check/top-up power steering reservoir

10——9

MAINTENANCE SUMMARY North American Markets

30 000 MILES
D INTERVAL

LUBRICATION

Lubricate all grease points
Lubricate handbrake mechanical linkage and cables
Lubricate front/rear wheel hubs
Lubricate steering rack (hand operated equipment only)
Renew engine oil and engine oil filter
Renew automatic transmission fluid (and filter GM400) (clean screen BW)
Check/top-up rear axle oil
Check/top-up brake fluid reservoir
Check/top-up manual transmission fluid
Check battery condition/clean and grease connections if necessary
Check/top-up cooling system
Check/top-up power steering reservoir
Check/top-up windscreen washer fluid
Lubricate accelerator control linkage and pedal pivot; check operation
Lubricate distributor
Lubricate all locks and hinges (not steering lock)
Renew brake fluid every 18 000 miles or 18 months
Renew coolant every 2 years
Check/top-up clutch fluid

ENGINE

Check for oil leaks
Renew air cleaner element(s)
Renew spark plugs
Check all driving belts; adjust/renew as necessary (applicable above 30 000 miles)
Check cooling and heater system for leaks, for hose condition and security
Check crankcase breathing and evaporative loss control system

FUEL AND EXHAUST SYSTEMS

Check fuel system for leaks, pipes and unions for chafing and corrosion
Check exhaust system for leaks and security
Renew oxygen sensor(s)

TRANSMISSION, BRAKES, STEERING AND SUSPENSION

Check for fluid/oil leaks
Check condition and security of steering unit, joints and gaiters
Check visually brake hydraulic pipes and unions for cracks, chafing, leaks and corrosion
Check suspension component condition and security
Check shock absorbers for leaks and condition
Inspect brake pads for wear and discs for condition (including handbrake pads)
Check/adjust front wheel alignment
Check/adjust front hub bearing end float
Check tightness of propeller shaft coupling bolts
Check brake servo hoses for security and condition

WHEELS AND TYRES

Check that tyres comply with manufacturer's specification
Check tyres for tread depth and visually for external cuts in fabric, exposure of ply or cord structure, lumps or bulges
Check tyres for irregular tread wear; perform necessary alignment/repair
Check and adjust tyre pressure, including spare wheel
Check for damaged/deformed wheel rims
Check tightness of road wheel fastenings

ELECTRICAL

Check/adjust operation of windscreen wipers and washers
Check function of all original equipment: lights, horns, warning indicators, radio, etc.
Check wiper blades and arms; renew if necessary
Check/adjust headlight alignment (refer to state and local requirement)

BODY

Check operation and security of seats and seat belts — front and rear
Check operation of all door, bonnet and boot locks
Check operation of window and sunroof controls
Check/open underbody drains (also during annual rust inspection)

GENERAL
Road Test:

Check vehicle performance, shifting, braking, handling
Check function of all instrumentation
Check function of trip computer
Check function of cruise control
Check function of climate control and ventilation systems

Report Additional Work Required After Road Test:

Check engine for leaks
Check/top-up automatic transmission fluid
Check/top-up brake fluid reservoir
Check/top-up power steering reservoir

PAGE INTENTIONALLY LEFT BLANK

SERVICE TOOLS — Section 99

All Service Tools listed are available from:

V. L. Churchill and Co. Limited
P.O. Box 3
Daventry
Northamptonshire NN11 4NF

excepting items marked thus:

* available from JRT Parts Division.
† is a Snap-on Tool and is available from a Snap-on Tool retail outlet.
x is a Girling Tool and is available from a Girling Tool retail outlet.
o is a Kent Moore Tool and is available from Kent Moore.

6 Cylinder Engine — Section 12

Tool No.	Description
*C 3993	Valve timing gauge
*C 37851	Lifting eye
18G 55A (38U3)	Piston ring compressor
JD 2B	Timing chain adjusting plate
JD 17B	Oil seal packing presizing tool
JD 6118C	Valve spring compressor
MS 53A	Engine support bracket

12 Cylinder Engine — Section 12

Tool No.	Description
*C 3993	Valve timing gauge
18G 55A (38U3)	Piston ring compressor
JD 17B	Oil seal packing presizing tool
JD 17B-1	Adaptor crankshaft rear oil seal presizing tool
JD 38	Damper setting jig
JD 39	Jackshaft sprocket holder
JD 40	Camshaft sprocket retainer
JD 41	Cylinder liner retainers
JD 50	Timing chain tensioner retainer
JD 6118C	Valve spring compressor
MS 53A	Engine support bracket

Fuel System — Section 19

Tool No.	Description
18G 1267	Replacer — damper assembly retainer
JD 114	Spark plug lead pliers
JD 116	Injector hose fitting tool

Manual Gearbox — Section 37

Tool No.	Description
18G 47-1	Adaptor — remover layshaft cluster bearings
18G 47-5	Adaptor remover/replacer constant pinion bearing
18G 284 AAH	Adaptor — remover — mainshaft — pilot outer bearing outer track
18G 705-1A	Adaptor — remover 5th speed gear
47	Multi-purpose handpress
MS 53A	Engine support bracket
18G 284	Impulse extractor
18G 1205	Propeller shaft flange wrench
†ST 1136	Offset spanner
18G 705	Remover bearing race centre

Automatic Transmission — Borg-Warner Model 66 — Section 44 BW

Tool No.	Description
CBW 1C	Hydraulic pressure test equipment
MS 53A	Engine support bracket
CBW 1C-5	Adaptor — pressure test
CBW 62	Remover — throttle cable mounting seal
CBW 87	End float checking gauge
CBW 547B-75	Tension wrench
18G 681	Torque screwdriver
CBW 547-50-2A	Rear servo adjuster adaptor
18G 702	Replacer — rear clutch piston
18G 1004	Circlip pliers
18G 1016	Clutch spring compressor
18G 1107	Replacer — front clutch piston
CBW 35-65	Bench cradle

Automatic Transmission — GM 400 — Section 44 GM

Tool No.	Description
18G 677-2	Adaptor set
18G 677ZC	Pressure test equipment
18G 1004	Circlip pliers
18G 1004J	Points for 18G 1004
18G 1016	Clutch spring compressor
18G 1295	Compressor piston accumulator control valve
18G 1296	Extractor bolt oil pump
18G 1297	Replacer oil pump and rear extractor oil seals
18G 1298	Forward and intermediate clutch piston replacer seal protector inner
18G 1309	Intermediate clutch inner seal protection sleeve
18G 1310	Band application pin selection gauge
CBW 87	End float checking gauge

Drive Shafts and Propeller Shafts — Section 47

Tool No.	Description
JD 1D	Hub remover
18G 2	Two-legged puller
MS 53A	Engine support bracket

Final Drive — Section 51

Tool No.	Description
18G 120 5	Flange holder
18G 134 (MS 550, 550, SL 550)	Driver handle
SL 550-1	Replacer differential bearing cone
47 (MS 47, SL 14)	Hand press
{ SL 14-3/2 SL 14-3/1	Adaptor/remover differential bearing cone
SL 3	Pinion setting gauge
4 HA	Pinion height setting button
SL 550-9	Adaptor — replacer — drive pinion inner bearing cup
SL 550-8/1	Adaptor — replacer — drive pinion outer bearing cup
{ SL 47-1/1 SL 47-1/2	Pinion bearing cone remover/adaptor
18G 1428A	Rear oil seal replacer
SL 15A	Remover/replacer — drive shaft bearing cone
18G 681 CBW 548	Torque driver
{ SL 47-3/1	Output shaft outer bearing remover
{ SL 47-3/2	Output shaft outer bearing replacer
JD 14	Dummy shaft

{ Items marked thus are sold as sets

Steering — Section 57

Tool No.	Description
JD 10	Power steering test set
JD 10-2	Adaptor — hydraulic pressure test
JD 10-3A	Adaptor — power steering
JD 10-4A	Adaptor — hydraulic pressure test
JD 24	Steering joint taper separator
JD 25B	Rear camber setting links
JD 36A	Steering rack checking fixture
18G 1326	Remover/replacer pulley power steering pump
18G 1466	Steering rack centralising pin

Front Suspension — Section 60

Tool No.	Description
JD 6G	Front coil spring compressor
JD 24	Steering joint taper separator
MS 53A	Engine support bracket
18G 1466	Steering rack centralising pin

Rear Suspension — Section 64

Tool No.	Description
JD 1D	Hub remover
JD 11B	Adaptor dismantler dampers spring unit
JD 13A	Rear hub end-float gauge
JD 14	Rear wishbone pivot dummy shaft
JD 15	Replacer — rear hub master spacer and bearing
JD 16C	Remover/replacer — rear hub outer bearing cone
JD 20A	Bearing remover — main tool
JD 20A-1	Rear hub inner and outer cups remover/replacer adaptor
JD 21	Torque arm bush remover/replacer
JD 25B	Rear camber setting links
47	Multipurpose handpress

Brakes — Section 70

Tool No.	Description
x 64932392	Girling brake piston retraction tool
18G 672	Replacer — disc brake piston seal

Air Conditioning — Section 82

Tool No.	Description
18G 1363	Air conditioning link setting jig
o 10500	Tool kit
o 10418	Hub holding tool
o 10416	Thin walled socket

Electrical — Section 86

Tool No.	Description
18G 1364	Spark plug wrench

Instruments — Section 88

Tool No.	Description
18G 1001	Spanner for fuel tank unit

JAGUAR
Daimler

6 CYLINDER

Containing
Section

12 ENGINE

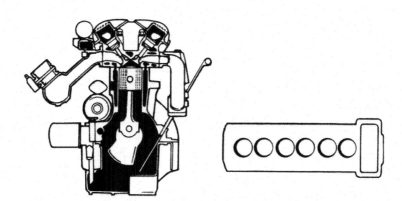

SERIES III
SERVICE MANUAL

INTRODUCTION

This Service Manual covers the Jaguar Series 3 and Daimler Series 3 range of vehicles. It is primarily designed to assist skilled technicians in the efficient repair and maintenance of Jaguar and Daimler vehicles.

Using the appropriate service tools and carrying out the procedures as detailed will enable the operations to be completed within the time stated in the 'Repair Operation Times'.

The Service Manual has been produced in 13 separate sections; this allows the information to be distributed throughout the specialist areas of the modern service facility.

A table of contents in section 1 lists the major components and systems together with the section and book numbers. The cover of each book depicts graphically and numerically the sections contained within that book. Each section starts with a list of operations in alphabetical order.

The title page of each book carries the part numbers required to order replacement books, binders or complete Service Manuals. This can be done through the normal channels.

Operation Numbering

A master index of numbered operations has been compiled for universal application to all vehicles manufactured by Jaguar Cars Ltd., and therefore, because of the different specifications of various models, continuity of the numbering sequence cannot be maintained throughout this manual.

Each operation described in this manual is allocated a number from the master index and cross-refers with an identical number in the 'Repair Operation Times'. The number consists of six digits arranged in three pairs.

Each operation is laid out in the sequence required to complete the operation in the minimum time, as specified in the 'Repair Operation Times'.

Service Tools

Where performance of an operation requires the use of a service tool, the tool number is quoted under the operation heading and is repeated in, following, the instruction involving its use. A list of all necessary tools is included in section 1, number 99.

References

References to the left- or right-hand side in the manual are made when viewing from the rear. With the engine and gearbox assembly removed the timing cover end of the engine is referred to as the front. A key to abbreviations and symbols is given in section 1, number 01.

REPAIRS AND REPLACEMENTS

When service parts are required it is essential that only genuine Jaguar/Daimler or Unipart replacements are used. Attention is particularly drawn to the following points concerning repairs and the fitting of replacement parts and accessories.

1.   Safety features embodied in the vehicle may be impaired if other than genuine parts are fitted. In certain territories, legislation prohibits the fitting of parts not to the vehicle manufacturer's specification.

2.   Torque wrench setting figures given in this Service Manual must be strictly adhered to.

3.   Locking devices, where specified, must be fitted. If the efficiency of a locking device is impaired during removal it must be replaced.

4.   Owners purchasing accessories while travelling abroad should ensure that the accessory and its fitted location on the vehicle conform to mandatory requirements existing in their country of origin.

5.   The vehicle warranty may be invalidated by the fitting of other than genuine Jaguar/Daimler or Unipart parts. All Jaguar/Daimler and Unipart replacements have the full backing of the factory warranty.

6.   Jaguar/Daimler Dealers are obliged to supply only genuine service parts.

SPECIFICATION

Purchasers are advised that the specification details set out in this Manual apply to a range of vehicles and not to any one. For the specification of a particular vehicle, purchasers should consult their Dealer.

The Manufacturers reserve the right to vary their specifications with or without notice, and at such times and in such manner as they think fit. Major as well as minor changes may be involved in accordance with the Manufacturer's policy of constant product improvement.

Whilst every effort is made to ensure the accuracy of the particulars contained in this Manual, neither the Manufacturer nor the Dealer, by whom this Manual is supplied, shall in any circumstances be held liable for any inaccuracy or the consequences thereof.

CONTENTS

TORQUE WRENCH SETTINGS

SECTION 12

NOTE: Set the torque wrench to the mean of the figures quoted unless otherwise specified.

Early cars prior to / Later cars from } Engine 8L137746 — (4.2); 8A14210 — (3.4)

ITEM	DESCRIPTION	TIGHTENING TORQUE		
		Nm	kgf m	lbf ft
ENGINE				
Cam cover (domed nuts) — early cars	¼ in U.N.F. nut	6,7 to 8,1	0,69 to 0,83	5 to 6
— later cars	¼ in U.N.F. nut	9,5 to 11	0,98 to 1,12	7 to 8
Camshaft bearing caps	5/16 in U.N.F. nut	12,2 max.	1,24 max.	9.0 max.
Connecting rod big-end	⅜ in U.N.F. bolt	48,4 to 50,8	4,93 to 5,18	35.7 to 37.5
Crankshaft front end	¾ in U.N.F. bolt	170 to 203	17,29 to 20,73	125 to 150
Cylinder head nuts: check/reset	7/16 in U.N.F. nut	70,5 to 73,2	7,19 to 7,47	52 to 54
initial assembly	7/16 in U.N.F. nut	67,8 to 70,5	6,92 to 7,19	50 to 52
Distributor clamp bolt	¼ in trapped nut	5,7 max.	0,58 max.	4.2 max.
Fan drive assembly securing bolt	⅜ in U.N.F. bolt	40,7 max.	4,15 max.	30 max.
Flywheel	7/16 in U.N.F. bolt	85,9 to 90,4	8,76 to 9,22	63.4 to 66.6
Gemi hose clips (up to No. 16)	4 mm thread	0,34 to 0,68	0,04 to 0,07	0.25 to 0.50
Main bearing caps	½ in U.N.F. bolt	93 to 97,6	9,46 to 9,96	68.4 to 72
Power assisted steering pump to mounting bracket	⅜ in U.N.C. nut	50,2 max.	5,12 max.	37.0 max.
Pulleys to crank damper	5/16 in U.N.F. bolt	16,3 to 20,3	1,66 to 2,07	12 to 15
Sealing cap, CO sampling adaptor	7/16 in U.N.F.	8,5 to 10,2	0,86 to 1,03	6.3 to 7.5
Torque converter	⅜ in U.N.F. bolt	47,5 max.	4,84 max.	35.0 max.
ENGINE MOUNTINGS				
Front mounting bracket to beam	5/16 in U.N.F. nut	19,0 to 24,4	1,94 to 2,48	14 to 18
Rear mounting bracket to body fixing	5/16 in U.N.F. nut	10,8 to 13,6	1,1 to 1,38	8 to 10
	5/16 in U.N.F. bolt	19,0 to 24,4	1,94 to 2,48	14 to 18
	⅜ in U.N.F. bolt	36,7 to 43,4	3,74 to 4,42	27 to 32
Rear mounting peg	½ in U.N.F. nut	33,9 to 40,7	3,46 to 4,14	25 to 30
Rear rubbers	⅜ in U.N.F. nut	36,7 to 43,4	3,74 to 4,42	27 to 32
Strengthening plate assembly to body	M8 setscrew	16,3 to 19,0	1,66 to 1,93	12 to 14
Tie-bolts	½ in U.N.F. nut	33,9 to 40,7	3,46 to 4,14	25 to 30

DESCRIPTION

The 6-cylinder engine fitted to Series III Jaguar and Daimler cars is developed directly from the 3.4 litre unit introduced with the Jaguar XK 120 car in 1948, although superficially very similar, these two engines now have few parts in common and none of the accessories fitted to the current engines are interchangeable with those of the early units. The basic design of the engine has, however, remained unchanged, and the latest units retain chain-driven twin-overhead camshafts, seven main bearings and a stroke of 106 mm (4.173 in) which were incorporated in the first production engines.
Major changes have been made in recent years to the arrangements for fuel supply and the reduction of undesirable emissions, and a redesigned, electronically triggered ignition system is fitted to the 4.2L Series III cars; these items are dealt with fully in the appropriate sections of the manual, but the necessity for the removal of fuel injection and emission control equipment before certain operations can be carried out on the engine will be found to have affected certain of the repair operations in this section, when compared with the instructions for similar operations in earlier publications.

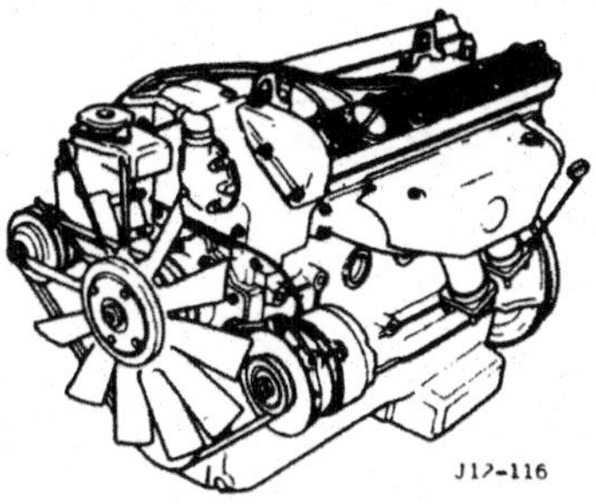

Fig. 1

CYLINDER PRESSURES

Check **12.25.01**

Set the transmission selector at 'P'—automatic transmission cars only.
Run the engine until normal operating temperature is reached. Switch off the engine.
Remove the h.t. cable from the ignition coil.
Remove all sparking plugs.
Fit an approved pressure gauge (1, Fig. 2) at one plug hole and with the throttle held fully open, crank the engine with the starter motor.
Note the highest steady pressure reading achieved and repeat at each plug hole in turn.
The reading taken at each cylinder must not differ from the reading taken at any other cylinder by more than 0,35 kgf/cm² (5 lbf/in²).

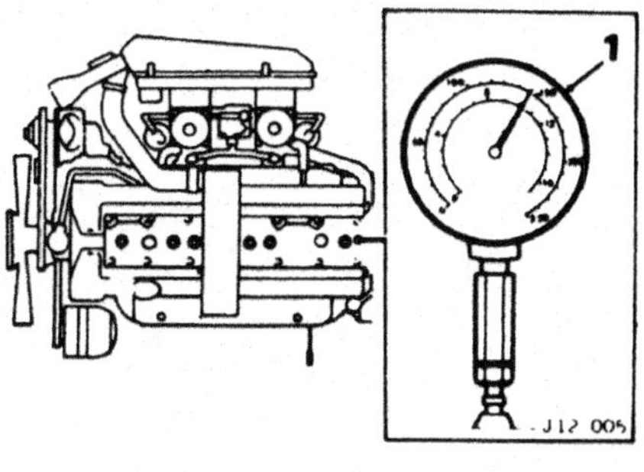

Fig. 2

FAULT FINDING

The location and rectification of faults in the fuel system, emission control and ignition systems is detailed in the sections of the manual dealing with these components; the emission control section includes basic engine checks which are repeated below.

BASIC ENGINE CHECKS

POSSIBLE CAUSE	CHECK AND REMEDIAL ACTION
Low battery condition	Check the battery condition with a hydrometer. Re-charge, clean and secure the terminals, or renew as necessary. (If the battery is serviceable but discharged, trace and rectify the cause of flat battery, e.g. short circuit or insufficient charge from the alternator.)
Start system deficient	If the starter fails to turn the engine briskly, check the engagement circuit and connections. Check and clean the main-starter circuit and connections.
Poor compressions	Check compressions with a proprietary tester. If compressions are low or uneven, check/adjust valve clearances and re-test. If compressions are still unsatisfactory, remove the cylinder head for further examination and rectification. NEVER turn the crankshaft when the head is removed, or the valves and pistons will be damaged when the head is replaced.
Exhaust system leaking or blocked	Check and rectify as necessary.
Faults on areas of the vehicle other than the engine	Check for binding brakes, slipping clutch, etc.
Air leaks at the inlet manifold	Check the inlet manifold/cylinder head joint. Re-make with a new gasket if necessary. Check the manifold tappings for leaks; seal as necessary.
Cooling system blocked or leaking	Flush the system and check for blockage. Check the hoses and connections for security and leakage. Renew as necessary. Check the thermostat, and renew if faulty.
Cylinder head gasket leaking	Check the cylinder block/head joint for signs of leakage. Renew the gasket if necessary.

CAMSHAFT

Remove and refit—Left-hand   **12.13.02**
Right-hand   **12.13.03**

Service tools: Top timing chain adjuster tool JD 2B; valve timing gauge C 3993

Removing

Remove the camshaft covers.
Remove the nuts (1, Fig. 3) securing the breather housing to the front of the cylinder head and withdraw the housing.

Fig. 3

Slacken the nut on the idler sprocket shaft. Knock down the tabs and remove the two camshaft sprocket retaining bolts (1, Fig. 4).
Rotate the engine until the valve timing gauge (1, Fig. 5) can be fitted to the slot in the camshaft, remove the remaining camshaft bolts.
Use service tool JD 2B (2, Fig. 4), turned in a clockwise direction, to slacken the camshaft chain.

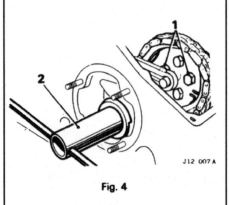

Fig. 4

CAUTION: Do not rotate the engine with the camshafts disconnected.

Slide the sprocket up the support bracket.
NOTE: Mark 'fit' holes in the adjuster plates.
Progressively slacken the camshaft bearing cap nuts, starting with the centre cap and working outwards; lift off the bearing caps. Note the mating marks on each bearing cap (2, Fig. 5).
NOTE: If the same shell bearings are being refitted, note their location to ensure that they are fitted in the original position.
Lift the camshaft from the cylinder head.

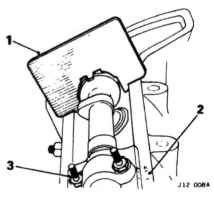

Fig. 5

12—4

Refitting

Fit the camshaft shell bearings.

Fit the camshaft in the bearings so that the keyway in the front flange is uppermost.

Fit the bearing caps to their respective positions and fit 'D' washers, spring washers and nuts

Tighten down the bearing caps evenly, commencing with the centre cap.

Tighten the nuts (3, Fig. 5) to correct torque.

Align camshaft using timing gauge C 3993.

Locate the camshaft sprocket on the camshaft and ensure that the 'fit' holes line up. Fit one bolt on the lock plate.

NOTE: If all the preceding instructions have been followed, valve timing will be correct.

Rotate the engine and fit remaining bolts to the camshaft sprocket. Turn up the tabs.

Using tool JD 2B, tension the top timing chain until slight flexibility remains in the chain on both outer sides of the camshaft sprockets. The chain MUST NOT be dead tight.

Check the tappet adjustment.

Securely tighten the locknut.

Replace the camshaft covers and breather housing.

CAMSHAFT BEARINGS
(Complete set)

Remove and refit   **12.13.13**

Follow the procedure detailed under 'Camshaft—Remove and refit—12.13.02 or 12.13.03 above

CRANKSHAFT DAMPER AND PULLEY

Remove and refit   **12.21.01**

Removing

Remove the central bolt securing the Torquatrol unit and fan to the water pump pulley; collect the washer and remove the unit.

Remove the steering pump belt, compressor belt (on cars fitted with air conditioning only) and alternator belt

Knock back the locking tabs (1, Fig. 6) at the pulley bolts, turning the crankshaft to improve access to the tabs

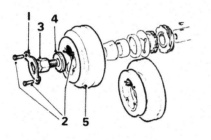

Fig. 6

Remove the four bolts (2, Fig. 6) securing the crankshaft pulley to the torsional damper. Recover the locking ring and remove the outlet pulleys.

Remove the large bolt (3, Fig. 6) securing the torsional damper and recover the large plain washer (4, Fig. 6).

Strike the damper (5, Fig. 6) with a hide mallet and remove it from the crankshaft.

Inspection

Examine the rubber portions of the damper for signs of deterioration and if necessary, fit a new damper.

Examine the pulley and damper grooves for wear. Drive belts must not bottom in the grooves.

Refitting

Reverse the removal operations, fitting new tab washers and tightening the bolts to the correct torque.

Correctly tension the drive belts.

CRANKSHAFT FRONT OIL SEAL

Remove and refit   **12.21.14**

Removing

Remove the crankshaft damper and pulley.

If the cone (1, Fig. 7) has not drawn clear with the torsional damper, prise the slot open and draw it from the crankshaft. Recover the Woodruff key.

Remove the oil sump.

Draw the distance piece from the crankshaft.

Prise the oil seal (2, Fig. 7) from the front timing cover recess, taking great care not to damage the surface of the crankshaft or the oil seal recess

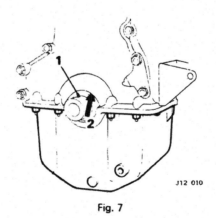

Fig. 7

Refitting

Liberally coat a new oil seal with clean engine oil and locate it in the timing cover recess, open side inwards.

Check the 'O' ring seal in the distance piece, fit distance piece onto crankshaft.

Fit the oil sump.

Fit the Woodruff key in the crankshaft and fit the cone.

Fit the crankshaft damper and pulley.

MAIN BEARINGS

**Remove and refit (set) — Engine
in situ**   **12.21.39**

Removing

Remove the oil pump and pipes (1, Fig. 8).

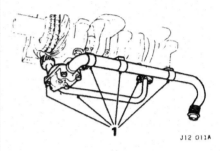

Fig. 8

Withdraw the bolts (1, Fig. 9) securing the rear main bearing cap and discard the washers. Note the corresponding numbers (2, Fig. 9) on the bearing cap and crankcase.

Withdraw the upper half of the bearing shell.

Liberally coat the replacement bearing shells with clean engine oil and locate in the crankcase and bearing cap. Ensure that the lugs on the bearing shell locate correctly.

Secure the bearing cap using bolts and a new flat washer.

Tighten the bolts to the correct torque.

Repeat operations to renew shells on the four intermediate main bearing caps. Continue by removing the bolts securing the centre main bearing cap. Discard the bearing shells and thrust washers.

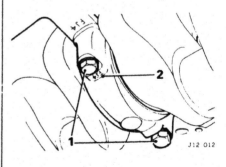

Fig. 9

Liberally coat the replacement bearing shells and two new thrust washers with clean engine oil and locate the shells in the crankcase and bearing cap. Ensure that the lugs on the bearing shell locate correctly.

continued

12—5

Locate the thrust washers (1, Fig 10) on either side of the bearing cap, white metal side outwards, and secure the cap using bolts and new flat washers

Tighten the bolts (2, Fig 10) to the correct torque

Set the crankshaft to T D C. No 6 cylinder (front) firing, and remove distributor cap.

Remove the setscrew and remove the distributor

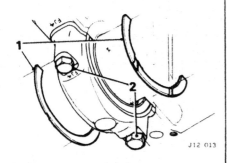

Fig. 10

Remove the bolts (1, Fig 11) securing the front main bearing cap and manoeuvre the cap clear. Discard the bearing shells

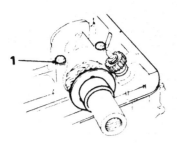

Fig. 11

Refitting

Liberally coat the replacement bearing shells with clean engine oil and locate the shells in the crankcase and bearing cap.

Ensure that the lugs on the bearing shell locate correctly

Secure the bearing cap, using the bolts and new flat washers

Tighten the bolts to the correct torque.

Refit the oil pump and pipes (1, Fig 8)

CAMSHAFT COVERS AND SEALS

Remove and refit   12.29.42

Removing

Disconnect the battery

Disconnect the plug leads.

Cars fitted with air conditioning only

WARNING: On no account must any portion of the air conditioning system be disconnected by anyone other than a qualified refrigeration engineer. Blindness can result if the gas contained within the system comes into contact with the eyes.

Depressurise the fuel system.

Release the inlet and outlet petrol pipe union nuts at the fuel cooler. Plug the inlet petrol pipe to prevent fuel syphon.

On 3.4 litre cars only, detach the hot air duct (1, Fig. 12) early models only.

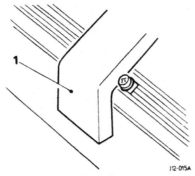

Fig. 12

Remove the 11 nuts and one screw (1, Fig. 13) securing the cover to the head. Remove the cover

Detach the gasket (2, Fig 13) from the cover and prise the cover seal (3, Fig. 13) from the head. Clean the joint surfaces of the cover and head

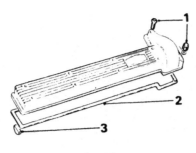

Fig. 13

Refitting

Smear the camshaft cover seal (3, Fig. 13) with sealant and replace it in the head

Fit a new gasket to the head and replace the cover, tighten the attachment nuts and screw, to the figure quoted in the data sheet

Replace the hot air duct on 3 4 litre cars only

Refit the petrol pipes to the fuel cooler and replace the cooler on air-conditioned cars.

Reconnect the plug leads, reconnect the battery

CONNECTING ROD BEARINGS

Remove and refit (set) — Engine in situ   12.17.16

Removing

Remove the oil sump.

Turn the engine until one big-end bearing is at bottom dead centre.

Remove the connecting rod cap, noting that corresponding cylinder numbers on the connecting rod and cap are on the same side (1, Fig. 14).

Lift the connecting rod from the crank pin and withdraw the bearing shells (2, Fig. 14).

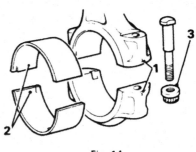

Fig. 14

Inspection

Check the crank pin for signs of overheating, scoring or transfer of bearing metal If the crank pin is suspect in any way, the engine must be removed and the crankshaft rectified, or renewed as necessary

Refitting

Liberally coat the replacement bearing shells with clean engine oil and locate in the connecting rod and cap.

Secure the connecting rod cap, ensuring that the marks coincide.

Tighten the connecting rod nuts (3, Fig. 14) to the correct torque.

Repeat operations to change bearings on the remaining five journals, then replace the oil sump.

TAPPETS

Adjust   12.29.48

Service tool: Valve timing gauge C 3993

CAUTION: If checking valve clearances with the cylinder head removed from the engine, the camshafts must be fitted and checked one at a time. If one camshaft is rotated while the other is in position, fouling is likely between inlet and exhaust valves.

If necessary remove the camshaft covers.
Rotate the camshafts and record the clearance between the back of each cam in turn, and the respective tappet, using a feeler gauge as shown (1, Fig. 15). Clearance to be as detailed in group 05. If adjustment is necessary, proceed with operations below as appropriate.

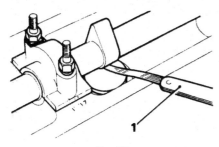

Fig. 15

If the cylinder head is on the engine, before removing the last securing bolt, rotate the engine until the valve timing gauge C 3993 can be located in the front flange of each camshaft (1, Fig 16)

If necessary, disconnect the sprockets from the camshafts

CAUTION: Do not rotate the engine while the camshaft sprockets are disconnected.

When the cylinder head is on the engine and the camshaft sprockets disconnected, ensure that no piston is at T.D.C. otherwise valve/piston fouling could occur.

Remove the camshaft bearing caps (2, Fig. 16) and lift the camshaft clear.

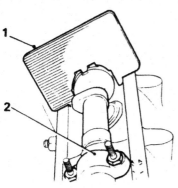

Fig. 16

Remove each tappet, taking careful note of its location. Remove and check the adjusting pad.
NOTE: Subtract the appropriate valve clearance from the dimension obtained above and select suitable adjusting pads which equal this new dimension. Adjusting pads are available rising in 0,03 mm (0.001 in) sizes from 2,16 to 2,79 mm (0.085 to 0.110 in) and are etched on the surface with a letter 'A' to 'Z', each letter indicating an increase in size of 0,03 mm (0.001 in).

Fit selected adjusting pads and fit the tappets.
Fit the camshaft bearing caps and nuts.

NOTE: If the cylinder head is on the engine, locate the camshaft using gauge C 3993 before tightening the bearing cap nuts
Tighten the bearing cap nuts to the correct torque
Connect the camshaft sprockets
Refit the camshaft covers

OIL FILTER ASSEMBLY

Remove and refit   12.60.01

Removing

From beneath the car disconnect the oil pressure switch lead. Separate the filter housing from the pipe to the sump by releasing the two hose clips (1, Fig. 17). Catch any spilled oil.
Release the nut (2, Fig. 17) connecting the camshaft oil feed to the filter housing.
Unscrew and withdraw the four setscrews (3, Fig 17) securing the filter housing to the crankcase casting
Withdraw the filter and housing.
Remove and discard the gasket (4, Fig. 17).
Detach the canister (5, Fig 17) and thoroughly clean the housing

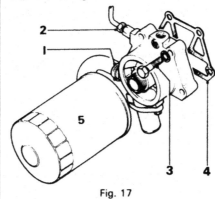

Fig. 17

Refitting

Fit a new gasket and reverse above operations as appropriate
Fit a new canister, smearing the seal with engine oil and screwing the canister into place by hand only.
Run the engine and check for oil leaks.
Check the oil level, and top up as necessary.

OIL PRESSURE SWITCH

Remove and refit   12.60.50

See 88 25 08/2.

OIL PRESSURE RELIEF VALVE

Remove and refit   12.60.56

Removing

From beneath the car, remove the two set bolts (1, Fig 18) securing the relief valve to the filter head and withdraw the cap (2, Fig. 18), spring (3, Fig 18), and valve (4, Fig. 18).
Collect washer (5, Fig 18) from the cap.

Refitting

Fit a new 'O' ring (6, Fig 18) to the valve body and replace in the filter head. Insert the valve and spring, place the washer in the cap and refit to the filter head

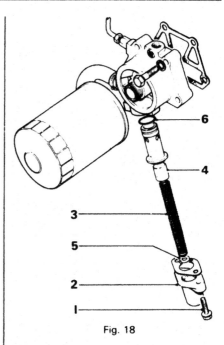

Fig. 18

CAMSHAFT OIL FEED PIPE

Remove and refit   12.60.83

Removing

Remove the union nut (1, Fig. 19) at the oil filter housing.
Remove the banjo bolts (2, Fig. 19) at the rear of each camshaft.
Manoeuvre the oil feed pipe clear
Thoroughly clean out the pipe.

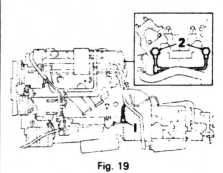

Fig. 19

Refitting

Ensure that the copper seals are in good condition and refit the banjo bolts.

TIMING CHAIN

Adjust   12.65.44

Service tool: Timing chain adjuster tool JD 2B

Release the clip (1, Fig. 20) securing the crankcase breather pipe to the breather.
Remove the dome head nuts (2, Fig. 20) securing the breather housing. Note the position of the clips and brackets fitted.

continued

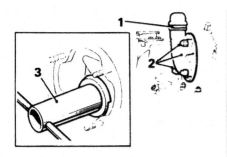

Fig. 20

Withdraw the breather housing and filter gauze.

Slacken the locknut and use tool JD 2B (3, Fig. 20) to tension the top chain. Rotate the tool in an anti-clockwise direction and DO NOT use undue force.

Tighten the locknut and refit the breather housing and all brackets and clips removed.

ENGINE MOUNTING—FRONT SET

Remove and refit   **12.45.04**

Removing

Remove the air cleaner assembly.

Remove the nuts from above and below the rubber mounting pads on both sides of the engine (1, Fig. 21).

Carefully raise the engine, using a trolley jack with a wooden block between the jack head and the sump, to release the weight from the mountings.

NOTE: Avoid fouling the fan and cowl

Remove the bolts (2, Fig. 21) securing the mounting brackets to the engine and withdraw the mounting brackets.

Collect the packing pieces and lift out the rubber mountings.

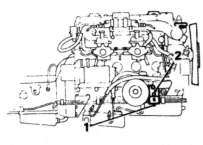

Fig. 21

Refitting

Place replacement mountings in position on the chassis brackets, fitting the insulator between the rubber and the beam on R.H. mountings on 3.4 litre cars only. Replace the spring washers and nuts; tighten the nuts by hand only.

Replace the mounting brackets on the engine, fitting new insulator pads between the brackets and rubber mountings; fit two insulators between the bracket and the rubber mounting on 3.4 litre air-conditioned cars only. Replace the plain washer and Cleveloc nuts, but do not tighten the nuts. Lower the jack.

Tighten the attachment bolts and nuts at the brackets to the correct torque and finally tighten the mounting nuts.

Replace the air cleaner.

ENGINE MOUNTING—REAR SPRING

Remove and refit   **12.45.26**

Service tool: Engine support tool MS 53(A)

Removing

Disconnect the battery.

Position service tool MS 53(A) (1, Fig. 22) across the rear engine lifting eye (2) and set the hook to support the engine.

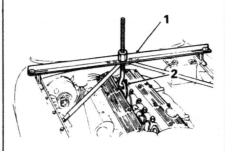

Fig. 22

Jack up the front of the car and place it on two stands.

Disconnect the intermediate exhaust pipe (1, Fig. 23) from the down pipe, remove the sealing olive. Remove the tie plate between the transmission and sump.

Place the jack (2, Fig. 23) with a suitable wooden block under the mounting plate and remove the four setscrews (3, Fig. 23) and washers; lower the jack and remove the rear mounting assembly; collect the spacers and remove the spring.

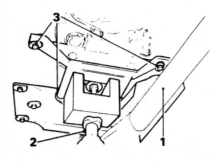

Fig. 23

Refitting

Fit the spring and inner spacers to the mounting assembly and raise it into position on the jack, fit the rear spacers, place washers on the setscrews, insert and tighten.
Lower the jack.

Fit the centre spacer and replace the tie plate. Reconnect the exhaust pipe, using sealant at the joints, remove the car from the stands and remove tool MS 53(A).

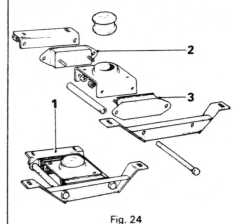

Fig. 24

ENGINE MOUNTING—REAR—FRONT AND REAR RUBBERS

Remove and refit   **12.45.24**
                             12.45.25

Detach the mounting (1, Fig. 24) as above, and dismantle to release the front and rear rubbers (2 and 3, Fig. 24).

CYLINDER HEAD

Remove and refit   **12.29.11**

Service tools: Top timing chain adjuster tool JD 2B; valve timing gauge C 3993

Removing

Depressurize the fuel injection system on 4.2 litre cars and drain the cooling system, retaining the coolant for refill.

Detach the wiring and air-conditioning system pipes (if fitted) from the valance to dash ties, remove the bolts at valances, slacken the bolts at dash and swing the ties across the car. Disconnect the coolant hoses.

WARNING: Do not disconnect any refrigerant hoses. Blindness can result if the gas contained within the system comes into contact with the eyes.

Remove the camshaft covers and seals.

Remove the dome headed nuts securing the breather housing, detach the hose and remove the housing.

Remove the bolt securing dipstick tube from model 66 automatic transmission to the inlet manifold.

12—8

Detach the down-pipes from the exhaust manifolds.

Disconnect and plug the fuel hoses from the fuel cooler, if fitted.

Disconnect the h.t. leads and remove the harness from the head; separate the temperature transmitter lead and detach the earth lead from the manifold.

Remove the air cleaner; detach the air-flow meter hoses and remove the meter; remove the air cleaner and detach the fuel hoses on 3.4 litre cars; disconnect the throttle and kick-down cables.

Disconnect the heater pipes and remove the camshaft oil feed pipes by detaching the banjo bolts at the rear of the head.

Jack up the front of the car and place it on two stands.

Turn the crankshaft until the two camshaft timing notches are below the camshafts, then remove the two accessible bolts (1, Fig. 26) from each camshaft flange; turn the crank through one complete revolution and release the remaining bolts, but leave one bolt in position in each flange.

Slacken the locknut on the idler sprocket shaft.

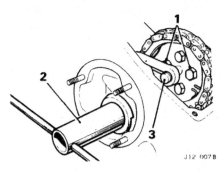

Fig. 26

Use service tool JD 2B (2, Fig. 26) to slacken top timing chain tension by pressing on to serrated adjuster plate and rotating the tool in a clockwise direction.

Remove the remaining bolts.

CAUTION: The engine MUST NOT be rotated while the camshaft sprockets are disconnected and the cylinder head is in place.

Draw the sprockets from the camshafts and slide the sprockets up the support brackets (3, Fig. 26)

NOTE: Mark 'fit' holes in the adjuster plates

Remove the fourteen cylinder head, domed nuts and six nuts securing the front of the cylinder head. Recover the two lifting brackets.

Lower the vehicle from the stands and carefully lift the cylinder head assembly from the cylinder block

NOTE: As the valves in the fully open position protrude below the cylinder head joint face, the cylinder head **must not** be placed joint face downwards directly on a flat surface, support the cylinder head on wooden blocks, one at each end.

Thoroughly clean the joint faces of the cylinder head and block.

Refitting

Fit a new gasket, dry, on the cylinder block ensuring that the side marked 'TOP' is uppermost

Ensure that No. 6 cylinder (front) is at T.D.C. position, with the distributor rotor arm pointing approximately forward along the engine.

Rotate the camshafts until the timing gauge

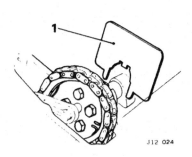

Fig. 27

C 3993 (1, Fig. 27) can be located in the slots in the front flanges.

CAUTION: Ensure that the inlet and exhaust valves do not foul each other.

Lower the cylinder head into position on the cylinder block

Fit the spark plug lead bracket and lifting brackets to appropriate cylinder head studs

Place the washers on the cylinder head studs and fit the fourteen large cylinder head domed nuts

Fit six nuts and washers to secure the forward end of the cylinder head.

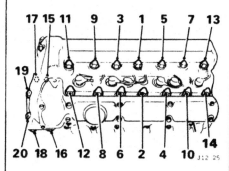

Fig. 28

Tighten the large nuts, in the order shown in Fig. 28, to the correct torque

Fully tighten the six small nuts

CAUTION: Do not rotate the engine or camshaft until the camshaft sprockets have been connected.

Locate the sprockets on the camshaft flanges and ensure that both holes in each flange are in alignment with the 'fit' holes in the adjuster plates

NOTE: If necessary, remove the circlip, disengage the serrations and re-position the adjuster plate as necessary. Refit the circlip

Secure each adjuster plate to the camshaft, using two bolts and lockplates.

Rotate the engine until the remaining holes on each camshaft are accessible and fit the bolts. Turn up the tabs.

Tension the timing chain by using service tool JD 2B rotated in an anti-clockwise direction. See Fig. 29.

NOTE: When correctly tensioned there should be slight flexibility on both outer sides of the chain

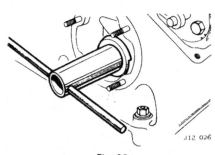

Fig. 29

Securely tighten the locknut.

Ensure that No. 6 cylinder is at T.D.C. firing (with the pointer opposite 'O' on the timing scale) and re-check the position of the camshafts using gauge C 3993.

Reverse the removal operations as appropriate, to complete the reassembly.

Re-check ignition timing as appropriate.

Carry out an exhaust emission check where required by legislation.

CYLINDER HEAD GASKET

Remove and refit   **12.29.02**

Removing

Follow the procedure given for removal of the cylinder head (12.29.11). Check the cylinder head and the faces of the cylinder block and liners for damage that caused, or was the result of, gasket failure, rectify as necessary

OIL SUMP

Remove and refit   **12.60.44**

Removing

Remove the front suspension

Drain engine oil

Remove the two nuts and lock washers securing the oil return pipe

Remove the nuts, bolts and washers securing the transmission oil cooler pipe clips — cars fitted with automatic transmission only

Remove the setscrews and lock washers (1, Fig. 30) and four nuts and lock washers (2, Fig. 30) securing the oil sump.

continued

12—9

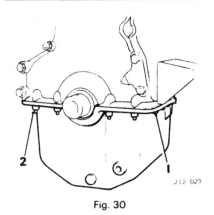

Fig. 30

Remove the four setscrews and washers (1, Fig. 31) securing the intake strainer box. Clean out the sump pan and strainer.

Thoroughly clean all traces of gaskets and seals from the sump, taking great care not to damage the alloy surfaces.

Thoroughly clean the mating surface of the cylinder block

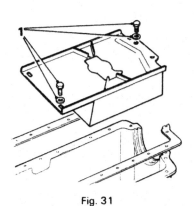

Fig. 31

Refitting

Fit the strainer box and secure using four setscrews and lock washers.

Ensure that the 'O' ring seal is fitted to the oil return pipe.

Lightly coat the new oil seal with grease and locate in groove in the sump. **DO NOT** trim the ends, but press the seal into the groove until the ends are flush.

Lightly grease the new gaskets and locate on the sump.

Offer the sump into position and secure it using twenty-six setscrews — short setscrew at front right-hand corner — four nuts and spring washers.

NOTE:

a. Ensure that the oil return pipe locates in the sump. Secure using two nuts and lock washers

b. Ensure that the front oil seal locates correctly in the groove.

c. Locate the transmission oil cooler pipe brackets on the relevant setscrews — cars fitted with automatic transmission only.

Refit the front suspension.

Pour 8,25 litres (14.5 Imp. pints) of recommended oil into the engine

Run the engine, check the oil level, and adjust as necessary

OIL PICK-UP STRAINER

Remove and refit   12.60.20

Removing

Remove the oil sump.

Remove the four setscrews and spring washers (1, Fig. 31) securing the strainer box.

Clean

Wash the suction strainer gauze in clean paraffin or petrol, and dry thoroughly. Clean out the sump.

Refitting

Secure the strainer box in position, using four setscrews and spring washers.

Refit the oil sump.

OIL PUMP

Remove and refit   12.60.26

Removing

Remove the oil sump.

Detach the suction and delivery pipe clips (1, Fig. 32) from the brackets.

Knock back the tabs and remove the setscrews (2, Fig. 32) securing the delivery pipe.

Pull both pipes from the oil pump.

Knock back the tabs and remove the setscrews (3, Fig. 32) securing the oil pump.

Recover the pipe bracket and drive coupling (4, Fig. 32)

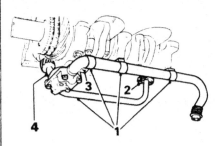

Fig. 32

Refitting

Check the condition of the 'O' ring seals and, if necessary, fit new ones.

Locate the drive coupling on the oil pump and secure the pump using three setscrews, tab washer and pipe bracket. Turn up the tabs.

Fit the delivery pipe on a new gasket, turn up the tabs

Locate the suction pipe and secure the clips to the brackets. Ensure that the pipe intake is on the centre line of the engine

Refit the oil sump.

ENGINE AND GEARBOX ASSEMBLY

Remove and refit   12.37.01

Service tools: Engine support tool MS 53(A); lifting eye C 37851

Removing

Remove the bonnet

Drain the coolant and conserve for refill.

Drain the oil from the engine.

Detach the radiator hoses and remove the radiator and lower cowl.

Remove R.H. harness cover from the inner wing and disconnect the headlamps at the snap connectors

Detach the hoses from the valance to bulkhead ties, remove the bolts to valances and slacken the bolts to bulkhead, swing the ties across the car

Detach the fuel pipes from the cooler (if fitted) and plug them, detach the fuel feed from the carburetters on 3.4 litre cars.

Detach the wiring from the compressor; remove the belt and support the detached compressor alongside the engine. DO NOT SEPARATE REFRIGERANT HOSES FROM THE COMPRESSOR.

Detach the wiring from the alternator.

Disconnect the exhaust down-pipes from the manifolds

Remove the engine earth lead.

Separate the transmission oil cooler from the valance

Remove the air cleaner.

Disconnect the air-flow meter wiring and remove the air-flow meter and bracket on 4.2 litre cars

Disconnect and plug the fuel supply pipe

Remove the power steering pump from the engine (do not disconnect the hoses) and tie to adjacent wheel arch valance.

Disconnect the wiring, hoses, vacuum pipes and throttle cable from the engine

Disconnect the injector harness, earth lead and starter lead

Lift the fresh air intake out of position and remove the heater hose and water valve

Fit engine support tool MS 53(A) and jack up the front of the car, place it on two stands.

Remove rear and intermediate heat shields

Detach the tie from between the sump and transmission

Place the head of the trolley jack under the rear engine mounting and raise it to release the load from the mounting, remove the four bolts and detach the mounting Collect the spacers.

Remove the four bolts securing the propeller shaft to drive flange, disconnect the shaft and speedometer drive from the gearbox, detach the selector control. Lift the car and remove the stands

Detach the front lifting eye from the two R.H. studs and replace with lifting eye C 37851, secured by head nuts on the second row of studs from the front of the engine, engage lifting tackle with eye

Place the trolley jack, with a suitable wooden block on the head, under the gearbox

Remove the securing nuts from both forward engine mountings

Carefully raise the engine on the jack and lifting tackle and move it forward to clear the rack housing, then lower the jack slightly and hoist the engine clear of the body.

Refitting

Lower the engine and gearbox into the car; position the trolley jack under the car with a wooden block on the head

Carefully lower the unit, and locate the gearbox on the trolley jack head; move the unit back (observing clearance of steering rack housing) and align engine to mountings.

Insert the correct packing pieces at the front mountings, fit and tighten the mounting nuts.

Fit engine support tool MS 53(A) and withdraw the lifting tackle.

Remove the lifting eye C 37851 and replace the standard lifting eye.

Remove the jack from under the gearbox, jack up the front of the car and place it on two stands.

Reconnect the speedometer drive, gear selector and propeller shaft.

Raise the rear mounting into position on the jack, insert spacers and secure in position with four bolts.

Fit the sump to the gearbox tie, replace the intermediate and rear heat shields, lower the car from the stands and detach the support tool.

Replace the detached items by reversing the removal sequence; replace or renew the coolant, refill the engine sump and check the fluid levels in power steering and brake reservoirs, and transmission. Bleed the clutch on manual transmission cars.

Replace the bonnet and check emissions where required.

TIMING COVER

Remove and refit   **12.65.01**

Removing

Remove the engine and gearbox assembly.

Remove the gearbox from the engine and place the engine on an approved engine stand.

Remove the cylinder head, using operations from Cylinder head—remove and refit —12 29 11 as appropriate.

Remove the water pump.

Remove the crankcase breather.

Remove the torsional damper (1, Fig. 36), cone (2, Fig. 36) and crankshaft Woodruff key.

Remove the timing gear cover (3, Fig. 36) and recover the timing pointer (4, Fig. 36).

Recover the distance piece (5, Fig. 36) and front oil seal (6, Fig. 36).

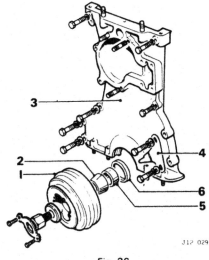

Fig. 36

Refitting

Thoroughly clean all mating faces, taking care not to damage the alloy casting.

Reverse the removal operations, using new gaskets, 'O' rings and seals.

TIMING CHAINS

Remove and refit   **12.65.14**

Removing

Remove the timing cover.

Remove the oil thrower (1, Fig. 37—if fitted) from the crankshaft.

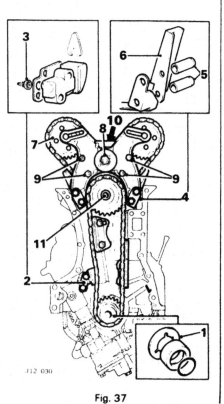

Fig. 37

Remove the setscrews (2, Fig. 37) securing the bottom timing chain tensioner and chain guides. Recover the conical filter (3, Fig. 37) behind tensioner.

Slacken the four setscrews and shakeproof washers (4, Fig. 37) securing the top timing chain assembly. Do not remove the setscrews at this stage.

Withdraw the crankshaft timing sprocket and chain assembly. Recover the distance pieces (5, Fig. 37), top timing chain dampers (6, Fig. 37) and top timing chain retainer.

Disengage the camshaft sprockets (7, Fig. 37) from the top chain.

Remove the nut and serrated washer (8, Fig. 37) from the idler shaft and withdraw the serrated plate, plunger and spring.

Remove the four nuts and serrated washers (9, Fig. 37) securing the front mounting bracket to the rear mounting bracket.

Separate the brackets.

Remove the timing chains from the intermediate and idler sprockets.

Draw the idler shaft (10, Fig. 37), idler sprocket and bush from the rear mounting bracket.

Remove the circlip and press the intermediate shaft from the rear mounting bracket. Recover the intermediate sprockets, bush and shim.

Inspection

Examine the timing chains for signs of damage or wear.

Examine all sprockets for signs of damage or wear.

Examine all dampers and the chain tensioner for signs of damage or excessive wear.

Examine the idler sprocket bush and intermediate sprocket bush for signs of wear.

NOTE: If the timing chains or sprockets show signs of excessive wear or are damaged in any way, all sprockets and the chains should be renewed.

Refitting

Fit the eccentric idler shaft (1, Fig. 38) to the hole in the front mounting bracket.

Fit the spring and plunger (2, Fig. 38) in the bracket and locate the serrated plate (3, Fig. 38) on the shaft. Loosely secure using serrated washer and nut (4, Fig. 38).

Fit the idler sprocket (5, Fig. 38) (21 teeth) to the idler shaft.

Fit the intermediate sprocket (6, Fig. 38), large gear forward, on the intermediate shaft; fit shim in rear mounting bracket, ensuring that the roll-pin engages in the slot, and retain the shaft with the circlip.

Locate the top timing chain (longer) on the small intermediate sprocket, and lower timing chain on the large sprocket.

Loop the top chain beneath the idler sprocket and secure the top mounting bracket to the rear mounting bracket using four nuts and serrated washers (7, Fig. 38).

Fit four long setscrews (8, Fig. 38) and spring washers to the front mounting bracket and fit

continued

12—11

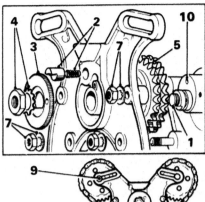

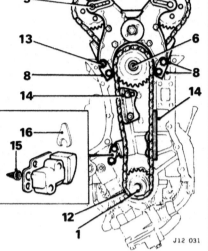

Fig. 38

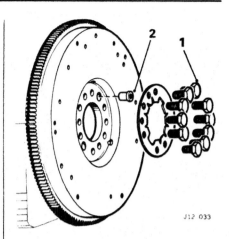

J12 033

Fig. 40

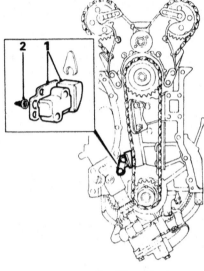

Fig. 39

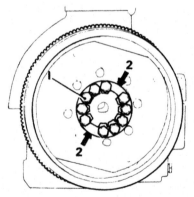

Fig. 41

Position the oil thrower on the crankshaft.
Refit the timing cover.

TIMING CHAIN TENSIONER

Remove and refit   **12.65.28**

Removing

Remove the timing cover.
Remove the setscrews and locking plate securing the tensioner. Recover the tensioner and
shim (1, Fig. 39).
Remove the conical filter (2, Fig. 39) from the
cylinder block.

Refitting

Thoroughly clean the conical filter and fit to the
cylinder block.
Screw the slipper into the tensioner and fit the
distance card supplied with new tensioner or
3,2 mm (0 125 in) slip gauge between the slipper and body.
Locate the tensioner on shims as necessary to
ensure that the slipper runs central on the chain
and secure it using two setscrews and
lockplate.
Slacken the setscrews securing the intermediate damper and set it into light contact with the
chain. Tighten the screws and re-lock.
Remove the slip gauge and tap the chain or
tensioner slipper to release the ratchet.

FLYWHEEL

Remove and refit   **12.53.07**

Removing

Remove the clutch assembly.
Knock down the locking plate tabs and remove
ten bolts (1, Fig 40).

Remove the flywheel from the crankshaft,
using drawbolts through the dowels (2, Fig.
40).

NOTE: On later vehicles dowels are not fitted.

Refitting

Locate the dowels where fitted in the crankshaft and tap them fully home through the
flywheel.
Fit the locking plate and secure the flywheel
using ten bolts. Tighten to the correct torque.
Turn up the tabs.
Refit the clutch assembly.

DRIVE PLATE

Remove and refit   **12.53.13**

Removing

Remove the torque converter.
Knock down the locking plate tabs and remove
ten bolts (1, Fig. 41).
Remove the drive plate from the crankshaft
using drawbolts through the dowels (2, Fig.
41)

NOTE: On later vehicles dowels are not fitted.

Refitting

Locate the dowels where fitted in the crank-
shaft and tap them fully home through the drive
plate.
Fit the locking plate and secure the drive plate,
Fsing ten bolts. Tighten to the correct torque.
Turn up the tabs.
Refit the torque converter.

the dampers, chain support plate and distance
pieces to the setscrews.
Equalize the loops of the top timing chain, and
locate the camshaft sprockets in the loops
(9, Fig. 38).
Rotate the eccentric idler shaft (10, Fig. 38) to
lift the idler sprocket to the highest position
between the camshaft sprockets.
Ensure that the Woodruff key is fitted to the
crankshaft.
Locate the crankshaft sprocket (11, Fig. 38) on
the shaft, but do not slide it fully home at this
stage.
Loop the bottom timing chain (12, Fig. 38)
beneath the crankshaft sprocket, tap the
sprocket fully home and locate the assembly.
Tighten the four setscrews (13, Fig. 38) to
retain the assembly.
Fit the bottom timing chain guides (14, Fig. 38)
but do not tighten the setscrews at this stage.
Fit the conical filter (15, Fig. 38) in the hole in
the cylinder block.
Screw the slipper into the tensioner until the
dimension of 3,2 mm (0.125 in) exists between
slipper and body.
Locate the tensioner on shims as necessary to
ensure that the slipper runs central on the chain
and secure using two setscrews and lockplate.
Place slip gauge or distance card (16, Fig. 38)
supplied with new tensioner between slipper
and body of tensioner to maintain dimension of
3,2 mm (0 125 in) and adjust the intermediate
damper to touch the chain. Tighten the setscrews and turn up tabs of the lockplate.
Remove the slip gauge and top chain or the
tensioner slipper to release the ratchet.

PISTON AND CONNECTING ROD

Remove and refit—engine
set   12.17.01

Service tool: Piston ring clamp 18G 55A

Removing

Remove the engine and gearbox assembly.
Remove the gearbox and place the engine on
an approved engine stand.
Remove the cylinder head.
Remove the oil sump.
Remove the nuts (1, Fig. 42) from the connecting rod bolts.
Remove the connecting rod cap (2, Fig.
42), noting corresponding cylinder numbers (3, Fig.
42) on the connecting rod and cap. Number 1
cylinder at rear of engine.

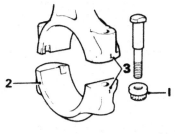

Fig. 42

Remove the connecting rod bolt (4, Fig. 42)
and withdraw the piston and connecting rod
from the top of the cylinder bore.
Repeat operations to remove pistons on each
cylinder, then continue with piston refitting.

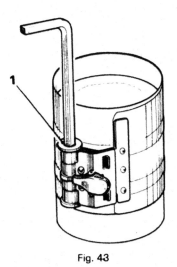

Fig. 43

Refitting

NOTE: If the original pistons and connecting
rods are being fitted, they must be replaced in
the cylinder bore from which they were
removed.

If new pistons and connecting rods are being
fitted they should be stamped with the number
of the bore in which they are to be installed.
Number 1 cylinder is at the rear of the engine. Fit
service tool 18G 55A (1, Fig. 43) to a piston, and
fully compress the piston rings.

Enter the piston into the cylinder bore, ensuring
that stamped 'FRONT' on the piston is towards
the front of the engine.
Fit bearing shells to connecting rod and cap,
liberally coating them with clean engine oil.
Fit cap to connecting rod, ensuring that the
cylinder numbers stamped on each part are on
the same side.
Tighten the connecting rod nuts to the correct
torque.
Repeat for each cylinder in turn.
Refit the oil sump.
Refit the cylinder head.
Refit the engine and gearbox assembly.

PISTON AND CONNECTING ROD

Overhaul   12.17.10

NOTE: Pistons are supplied complete with
gudgeon pins. As pins and pistons are matched
assemblies it is not permissible to interchange
component parts.

Overhaul

Remove the piston and connecting rods.
Remove the circlips.
Push the gudgeon pin out of the piston.
Withdraw the connecting rod.

Refitting

Fit the gudgeon pin (1, Fig. 44) in the piston.

CAUTION: Connecting rods must be refitted
to pistons in such a way that when installed
in the engine the word 'FRONT' on the piston
crown faces the front of the engine and the
chamfer on the big-end eye faces the crank
pin radius.

Align the small-end (2, Fig. 44) with the end of
the gudgeon pin and push the pin home.
Use new circlips (3, Fig. 44) to retain the
gudgeon pin.

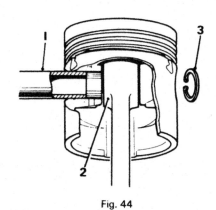

Fig. 44

NOTE: The gudgeon pin is a push fit in the
piston at 20°C (68°F). Fit will vary with
ambient temperature.

Three piston rings are fitted, as follows:

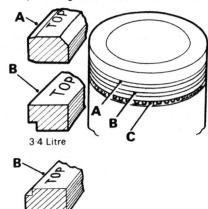

3·4 Litre

4·2 Litre   J12-435

Fig. 45

A. Top ring—compression.
B. Second ring—compression.
C. Bottom ring—oil control.

Both top and second rings have tapered
peripheries and are marked 'TOP' to ensure
correct fitting. In addition, the top ring has a
chrome plated periphery and is also cargraph
coated. This coating is coloured RED and must
not be removed. The bottom ring consists of an
expander sandwiched between two rails.
Check the piston ring gap in the bore. Push the
ring to a point midway down the bore, check
that the ring is square and measure the
gap—see Engine Data.
Fit the bottom ring ensuring that the expander
ends are not overlapping.
Fit the second and top rings ensuring that they
are fitted the correct way up.
Position the rings so that the gaps are staggered around the periphery of the piston.
Check the side clearance of the rings in the
piston groove—see Engine Data.
Check the connecting rods for alignment on a
suitable jig.
Check the bore of the small-end bush—see
Engine Data.

CAUTION: If the small-end bush is worn
beyond acceptable limits, a service
exchange connecting rod must be fitted. It is
NOT advisable to renew the bushes as
specialized equipment is needed to hone the
bushes to finished size. Refit the pistons and
connecting rods.

CYLINDER HEAD

Overhaul   12.29.19

Service tools: Valve spring compressor JD
6118C; valve timing gauge C 3993

Remove the cylinder head.

Dismantling

Remove the inlet and exhaust manifolds from
the cylinder head. Discard the gasket and
thoroughly clean the mating faces, taking great
care not to damage the castings.

continued

12—13

Remove the four bearing caps from each camshaft. Note the mating marks (1, Fig. 46) on each bearing cap.
Lift out the camshafts.
Withdraw the tappets and lay them out in order to ensure the correct replacement.
Remove the adjusting pads from each valve stem, and place them with their respective tappets

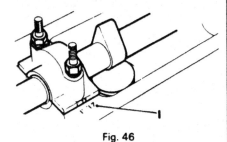

Fig. 46

A 31 mm (1¼ in)
B 31 mm (1¼ in)
C 96 mm (3²⁹⁄₃₂ in)
D 111 mm (4⅜ in)
E 152 mm (6 in)
F 76 mm (3 in)
G 203 in (8 in)

Make up a wooden block to the dimensions given (Fig 47) and use it to support the valves.

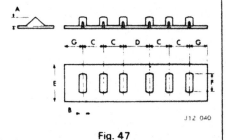

Fig. 47

Compress the valve spring using service tool JD 6118C and extract the cotters, see Fig 48. Remove the collars, valve springs and spring seats Repeat for the remaining five cylinders.

NOTE:
a. Remove the oil seal from the stem of the inlet valves before removing the spring seat.
b. Valves are numbered and must be replaced in original locations, No 1 cylinder being at the flywheel end of the engine.

Remove all traces of carbon from the combustion chambers and deposits from the induction and exhaust ports Great care must be taken to avoid damaging the head, use worn emery cloth and paraffin only

Valve guides
Check the clearance between the valve guide and stem this should be 0,025 to 0,10 mm (0.001 to 0.004 in) When removing a worn guide, care must be taken to identify each individual guide to its bore in the cylinder head. Replacement guides are available in the three following sizes, and have identification grooves machined in the shank as noted below:

Fig. 48

NOTE: Valve guides, when fitted during initial engine assembly, are to the following dimensions and may be fitted in mixed form.

Standard (no identification)
12,73 to 12,75 mm (0.501 to 0.502 in).
1st oversize (one machined groove)
12,78 to 12,80 mm (0.503 to 0.504 in).
2nd oversize (two machined grooves)
12,85 to 12,88 mm (0.506 to 0.507 in).
3rd oversize (three machined grooves)
12,98 to 13,00 mm (0.511 to 0.512 in).

When new guides are to be fitted, they should always be one size larger than the old guide. Standard and 1st oversize valve guides may be replaced in the following manner:
Immerse the head in boiling water for 30 minutes
Using a piloted drift, drive the guide out of the head from the combustion chamber end.
Coat the new valve guide with graphite grease and refit the circlip.
Heat the cylinder head.
Using a piloted drift, drive in the guide (1, Fig 49) from the top until the circlip is seated in the groove

CAUTION: This procedure is not recommended owing to the difficulty of establishing truth with the centre of the valve seat; it should not be attempted unless comprehensive machine shop facilities are available. A replacement cylinder head should be considered as an alternative.

NOTE: If a 2nd oversize guide is to be replaced the cylinder head bore must be reamed to the following dimension
12,95 mm + 0,012 mm—0,005 mm (0.510 + 0.0005 in—0,0002 in)

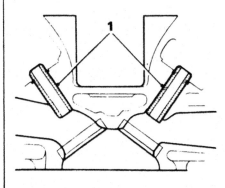

Fig. 49

Valve seats
Examine the valve seats for pitting or excess wear. If the seats are damaged past reclamation by approved refacing procedures, the seat inserts may be replaced.

CAUTION: This procedure is not recommended owing to the difficulty of removing the old valve seat and the risk of damage to the cylinder head; it should not be attempted unless comprehensive machine shop facilities are available. A replacement cylinder head should be considered as an alternative.

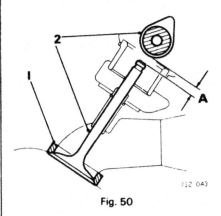

Fig. 50

Remove the inserts by machining, leaving approximately 0,25 mm (0.010 in) of metal which can easily be removed by hand without damaging the cylinder head
Measure the diameter of the insert recess in the cylinder head
Grind down outside diameter of the new insert to a dimension 0,08 mm (0.003 in) larger than the insert recess
Heat the cylinder head for half an hour from cold at a temperature of 150°C (300°F)
Fit the insert (1, Fig 50) ensuring that it beds evenly in the recess
Renew or reface valves as necessary.
Correct valve seat angles are

Inlet	Exhaust
44½ degrees	44½ degrees

Valves
Check the valve stems for distortion or wear, renew the valves with stems worn in excess of 0,08 mm (0.003 in), see section 05 book 1
Using a suitable suction tool, grind the valves into their respective seats
If new valve inserts have been fitted, the clearance 'A' between valve stem and cam (2, Fig 50) must be checked, this should be 8,13 mm (0.320 in) plus the valve clearance The dimension must be taken between the valve stem and the back of the cam Should this dimension not be obtained, metal must be ground from the valve seat of the insert

NOTE: Only suitable grinding equipment should be used

Tappet guides
Examine the tappets and tappet guides for wear The diametrical clearance between the tappet and tappet guide should be 0,02 to 0,05 mm (0 0008 to 0 0019 in)

CAUTION: The following procedure is not recommended owing to the difficulty of removing the old tappet guide and the risk of damage to the cylinder head; it should not be attempted unless comprehensive machine shop facilities are available. A replacement cylinder head should be considered as an alternative.

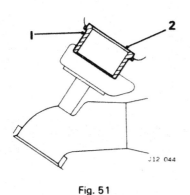

Fig. 51

Remove the old tappet guide (1, Fig. 51) by boring out until the guide collapses. Take great care not to damage the guide bore in the cylinder head.

Carefully measure the diameter of the tappet guide bore at room temperature 20°C (68°F).

Grind down the outside diameter of the replacement tappet guide to a dimension 0,089 mm (0.0035 in) larger than the tappet guide bore diameter measured above.

Grind the same amount from the 'lead-in' at the bottom of the tappet guide. The reduction in diameter from the adjacent diameter should be 0.089 to 0.16 mm (0.0037 to 0.0062 in).

Heat the cylinder head in an oven for half an hour from cold at a temperature of 150°C (300°F).

Fit the tappet guide, ensuring that the lip at the top of the guide beds evenly in the recess in the top of the cylinder head, see 2, Fig. 51.

Allow the cylinder head to cool, then ream the tappet guide bore to the diameter of 34,925 mm + 0,018 mm − 0,000 mm (1.375 in + 0.007 in − 0.000 in).

It is essential that, when reamed, the tappet guide bore is concentric with the valve guide bore.

Adjusting pads

Examine the adjusting pads (1, Fig. 52) for signs of indentation.

Renew, if necessary, with appropriate size when making valve clearances adjustment on reassembly.

Valve springs

Test the valve springs for pressure either by checking against Valve Spring Data or against a new spring.

Reassembling

Examine the valves for pitting, burning or distortion, and reface or renew valves as necessary. Also reface the valve seats in the cylinder head and grind the valves to their respective seats using a suction valve tool. When refacing valves or seat inserts do not remove more metal than is necessary to clean up the facings. Refit the valves in the order removed and place the cylinder head on the wooden blocks.

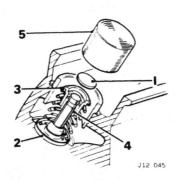

Fig. 52

Refit the valve spring seats (2, Fig. 52) and refit the inlet valve guide oil seals.

Refit the springs and collars (3, Fig. 52).

Compress the springs using service tool JD 6118C and fit the split cotters (4, Fig. 52). Tap the valve stems to ensure that the cotters are seated.

Fit the adjusting pads and tappets (5, Fig. 52) to their respective valves.

CAUTION: Camshafts must not be rotated independently.

Fit the camshaft shell bearings, locate one camshaft and secure the bearing cap nuts working from the centre outwards. Tighten the nuts to the correct torque.

Check the tappet adjustment.

Remove the camshaft fitted previously after checking, and fit the remaining camshaft.

Check the tappet adjustment.

Fit adjustment pads as required and fit camshafts, lining each up using service tool C 3993.

OIL PUMP

Overhaul   **12.60.32**

Dismantling

Remove the oil pump.

Unscrew the four bolts and detach the bottom cover.

Withdraw the inner and outer rotors from the oil pump body.

NOTE: Do not attempt to separate the inner rotor from the shaft.

Inspection

Thoroughly clean all components.

Check that the clearance between the lobes of the inner and outer rotors (1, Fig. 53) does not exceed 0,15 mm (0.006 in).

Check that the clearance between outer rotor and pump body (1, Fig. 54) does not exceed 0,25 mm (0.010 in).

Check that the end-float of the rotors (1, Fig. 55) does not exceed 0,06 mm (0.0025 in).

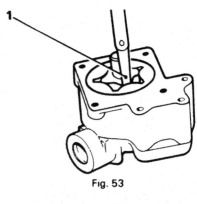

Fig. 53

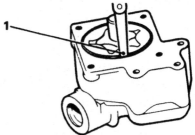

Fig. 54

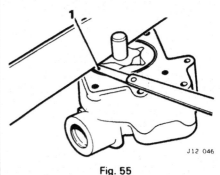

Fig. 55

NOTE: If necessary the outer rotor and/or body may be lapped on a surface plate to rectify.

Examine all components for signs of scoring or wear.

Ensure that the inner rotor is tight on the drive shaft.

NOTE: Inner rotor drive shaft and outer rotor are only available as an assembly.

Renew the 'O' ring seals in the pump body.

Reassembling

Assemble the inner rotor to the body.

Assemble the outer rotor to the body ensuring that the chamfered end is inserted first.

Secure the bottom cover using four bolts and lock washers.

Fit the oil pump.

12—15

ENGINE

Dismantle and reassemble 12.41.05
Deglazing cylinder bores see page 12—21

Service tools: Oil seal pre-sizing tool JD 17B; timing chain adjuster tool JD 2B; piston ring compressor 38 U3; valve timing gauge C 3993.

Drain the engine oil. For plug see item 1, Fig. 56

Remove the torque converter—cars fitted with automatic transmission only.

Remove the clutch assembly—cars fitted with manual transmission only.

Secure the engine to an approved engine stand.

Dismantling

Remove the distributor cap (2, Fig. 56); pull the vacuum pipe from the capsule.

Remove the ignition coil bracket from the engine.

Note the connection and remove the engine cable harness.

Slacken the clips (3, Fig. 56) on the coolant pipes at the front of the engine.

Remove the two screws (4, Fig. 56) securing the hot air duct on 3.4 litre cars only.

Remove the four plain nuts (5, Fig. 56) and spring washers securing the fan and Torquatrol unit to the water pump pulley.

Remove the air-conditioning compressor (6, Fig. 56) and bracket (7, Fig. 56)—cars fitted with air-conditioning only.

Remove the alternator and bracket (8, Fig. 56).

Remove the power assisted steering pump and bracket (9, Fig. 56).

Remove the nut securing the automatic transmission unit filler tube bracket (10, Fig. 56)—cars fitted with automatic transmission only.

Cars fitted with exhaust gas recirculation only

Release the union nut at the E.G.R. system 'Y' piece (11, Fig. 56).

Remove the setscrew at the rear of the cylinder block securing the E.G.R. system supply pipe (12, Fig. 56).

Remove the camshaft oil feed pipe banjo bolts (13, Fig. 56).

Remove the ten dome headed nuts (14, Fig. 56) and two cross-head screws securing each camshaft cover.

Remove the dome headed nuts (1, Fig. 57) securing the crankcase breather.

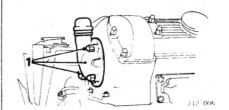

Fig. 57

Slacken the locknut and use tool JD 2B (1, Fig 58) to slacken the top timing chain. Rotate the tool in a clockwise direction.

Knock down the tabs at the camshaft sprockets and remove the two bolts (2, Fig. 58) from each.

Rotate the engine to gain access to the remaining bolts and remove.

CAUTION: Engine MUST NOT be rotated with the camshaft sprockets disconnected and the cylinder head in place.

Draw the sprockets from the camshafts and slide the sprockets up the support brackets.

NOTE: Mark 'fit' holes in the adjuster plates.

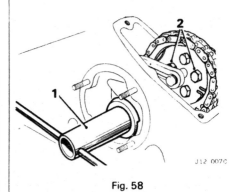

Fig. 58

Remove the fourteen cylinder head domed nuts and six nuts securing the front of the cylinder head working out from the centre.

Recover the two lifting brackets. Lift the h.t. leads clear.

Carefully lift the cylinder head assembly from the cylinder block.

NOTE: As the valves in the fully open position protrude below the cylinder head joint face, the cylinder head MUST NOT be placed joint face downwards directly on a flat surface; support the cylinder head on wooden blocks, one at each end.

Remove and discard the gasket, clean the face of the block.

On the flywheel on manual transmission cars, or the drive plate on automatic transmission cars, tap down the lock plate tabs and remove the bolts. Remove the drive plate/flywheel from the crankshaft using draw-bolts through the dowels

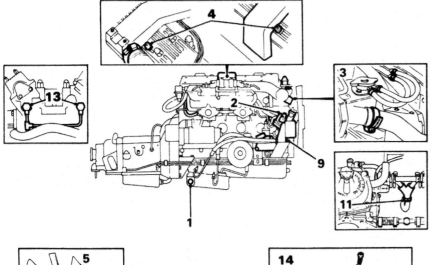

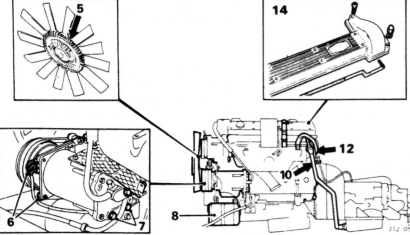

Fig. 56

12—16

Knock back the locking tabs (1, Fig. 59) on the crankshaft pulley bolts.

Remove the four bolts (2, Fig. 59) securing the pulley(s) to the torsional damper. Recover the locking ring and remove the outer pulleys.

Remove the large bolt (3, Fig. 59) securing the

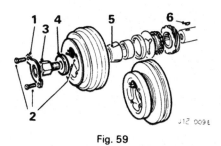

Fig. 59

torsional damper and recover the large plain washer (4, Fig. 59).

Strike the damper with a hide mallet to break the taper, and remove it from the crankshaft.

Remove the cone (5, Fig. 59) and extract the Woodruff key (6, Fig. 59) from the crankshaft.

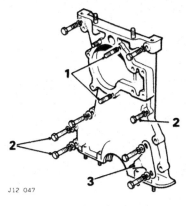

Fig. 60

Remove the bolts, nuts and spring washers (1, Fig. 60) securing the water pump. Remove the water pump and clean all traces of gasket from the mating faces.

Unscrew the oil filter canister from the housing.

Slacken the hose clips on the oil return pipe to the sump.

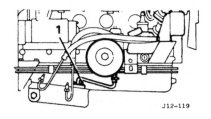

Fig. 61

Remove the four setscrews and spring washers securing the oil filter housing to the cylinder block. Pull the housing from the return pipe and clean all traces of gasket from the mating faces.

Remove the two nuts and shakeproof washers (1, Fig. 61) and lift the return pipe from the oil sump. Check the condition of the 'O' ring seal and renew it if necessary.

Remove the setscrew, plain and spring washers and lift the distributor from the cylinder block.

Twist the dipstick tube from the cylinder block.

Remove the camshaft oil feed pipe banjo bolt.

Slacken the nuts, bolts and washers and draw the transmission oil cooler pipes from the brackets—cars fitted with automatic transmission only.

Remove the four nuts and spring washers, and all setscrews and spring washers securing the oil sump. Note the location of cooler pipe brackets—cars fitted with automatic transmission only.

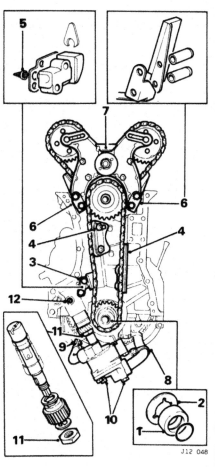

Fig. 62

Remove the setscrews and special washers (2, Fig. 60) and carefully prise the timing chain cover from the engine. Recover the timing pointer (3, Fig. 60).

Remove and discard the gasket and crankshaft oil seal.

Draw the distance piece (1, Fig. 62) from the crankshaft, check the condition of 'O' ring seal, and renew if necessary. Recover the oil thrower (2, Fig. 62) if fitted.

Remove the setscrews securing the lower timing chain tensioner (3, Fig. 62) and chain guides (4, Fig. 62). Recover the conical filter (5, Fig. 62) behind the tensioner.

Slacken the four setscrews and shakeproof washers (6, Fig. 62) securing the upper timing chain assembly. Do not remove the setscrews at this stage.

Withdraw the crankshaft timing gear and chain assembly (7, Fig. 62), carry out the overhaul.

Remove the self locking nuts, bolts and washers and pull the suction pipe (8, Fig. 62) from the oil sump.

Knock down the tabs, remove the self locking nut, washer and bolt, and pull the delivery pipe (9, Fig. 62) from the oil sump.

Knock down the tabs and remove the three bolts (10, Fig. 62) securing the oil pump. Draw the oil pump clear and recover the drive coupling.

Knock down the tab washer and remove the nut (11, Fig. 62) securing the distributor drive gear.

Draw the gear and thrust washer from the shaft; remove the shaft and key.

If necessary, remove the locating grub screw (12, Fig. 62) and drift the distributor drive shaft bush downwards from the cylinder block.

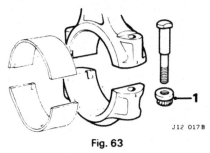

Fig. 63

Remove the special nuts (1, Fig. 63) securing the connecting rod bearing caps; remove the caps together with the shell bearings.

Pass the pistons up through the bores.

Remove the crankshaft rear oil seal assembly cap screws. Remove and discard the oil seal.

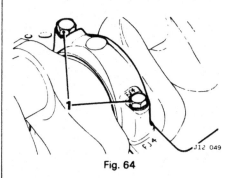

Fig. 64

Remove the main bearing bolts (1, Fig. 64) and washers, noting the position of the oil pipe brackets. Remove the bearing caps.

Remove the two Allen screws securing the lower half of the rear oil seal. Prise out the seal.

Remove the three Allen screws securing the upper half of the rear oil seal. Prise out the seal.

Lift the crankshaft from the cylinder block. Recover the bearing shells.

continued

Inspection

CAUTION: Ensure that all components are scrupulously clean, blow out all oil galleries in the crankcase, crankshaft and camshaft with clean, dry compressed air.

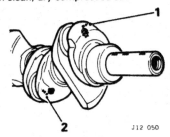

Fig. 65

Early engines prior to engine nos:-

8A15562	All 3.4
8L168437	R o W except
8L147650	UK and Europe

a. Crankshaft. Regrinding of the crankshaft is generally recommended when wear or ovality in excess of 0,08 mm (0.003 in) is found. Grinding may be undertaken to a limit of 0,51 mm (0.020 in). Grinding beyond the limit of 0,51 mm (0.020 in) is not recommended and in such circumstances a new crankshaft must be obtained. Oversizes of journals are stamped in the adjacent web at the forward end of the crankshaft. 1.—Main journal. 2.—Crankpin. See Fig. 65

Later engines from engine nos:

8A15562	All 3.4
8L168437	R o W except
8L147650	UK and Europe

The crankshaft of the above engines are specially hardened and cannot be reground.

b. Cylinder Block. Check the top face of the cylinder block for truth. Check that the main bearing caps have not been filed and that the bearing bores are in alignment. Should the caps show damage or the bearing housing misaligned, the caps must be re-machined and the bearing housings line bored.

Remove the cylinder head studs (1, Fig. 66). Check the area around the studs holes for flatness (2, Fig. 66). Skim any raised areas flush with the joint face to ensure a perfectly flat sur-

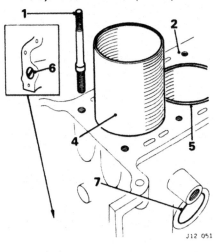

Fig. 66

face. Reboring is normally recommended when the ovality exceeds 0,15 mm (0.006 in). Reboring beyond the limit of 0,51 mm (0.020 in) is not recommended. Oversize pistons are available of this size, see group 05. If the bores will not clean out at 0,51 mm (0.020 in) new liners and standard size pistons should be fitted.

Press out the worn liners (Fig. 67) from below. Before fitting a new liner, lightly smear the cylinder walls with jointing compound to a point halfway down the bore and also smear the top outer surface of the liner (4, Fig. 66). Press in the new liners flush with the top face of the cylinder block (5, Fig. 66). Dry liners are fitted in engine manufacture to early 4.2 litre blocks, but not normally to 3.4 litre blocks.

Bore out and hone the liners to suit the grade of pistons to be fitted. (See piston grades below). See Bore Deglazing page 12—21.

Following reboring, the blanking plugs in the main oil gallery (6, Fig. 66) should be removed and the cylinder block oilways and crankcase interior thoroughly cleaned.

When dry, coat the interior of the crankcase with an oil- and heat-resisting paint.

Check all core plugs (7, Fig. 66) fitted to the cylinder block and renew any which show signs of leaking.

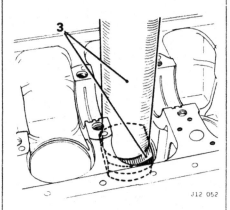

Fig. 67

c. Piston and connecting rod

Piston grades

The following selective grades are available in standard size pistons only. When ordering standard size pistons the identification letter of the selective grade should be clearly stated. Pistons are stamped on the crown with the letter identification and the cylinder block is also stamped on the top face adjacent to the bores.

Grade Identification

Letter	For cylinder bore size	
	3.4 Litre	4.2 Litre
F	82,989 to 82,997 mm (3.2673 to 3.2676 in)	92,075 to 92,0826 mm (3.6250 to 3.6253 in)
G	83,000 to 83,007 mm (3.2677 to 3.2680 in)	92,0852 to 92,0928 mm (3.6254 to 3.6257 in)
H	83,010 to 83,017 mm (3.2681 to 3.2684 in)	92,0953 to 92,1029 mm (3.6258 to 3.6261 in)

'S' pistons are 82,995 to 83,020 mm (3.2675 to 3.2685 in) dia. across bottom of skirt for 3.4 litre engines and 92,080 to 92,105 mm (3.6252 to 3.6262 in) dia. across bottom of skirt for 4.2 litre engines.

Measure exact dimension, at right angles to the gudgeon pin, and hone the bores to 0,018 to 0,033 mm (0.0007 to 0.00013 in) more than this measured dimension when fitting 'S' pistons.

Always use new circlips on assembly.

Gudgeon pins are graded by colour coding (red or green). For identification purposes the colour coding is also indicated on the gudgeon pin hole boss on the pistons.

Oversize pistons

Oversize pistons are available in + 0,51 mm (0.020 in) only.

There are no selective grades in oversize pistons as grading is necessary purely for factory production methods. For reboring the cylinder see the instructions given above.

If connecting rods have been in-use for very high mileage, or if bearing failure has been experienced, it is desirable to renew the rod(s) owing to the possibility of fatigue.

The connecting rods fitted to an engine should not vary one with another by more that 3.5 grammes (2 drams). The alignment should be checked on an approved connecting rod alignment jig.

If alignment is incorrect, an exchange rod should be fitted.

The big-end bearings are of the precision shell type and under no circumstances should they be hand-scraped or the bearing cap filed.

The small-ends are fitted with steel-backed phosphor-bronze bushes which are a press fit in the connecting rod. After fitting, the bush should be bored, reamed and honed to a diameter of 22,225 to 22,23 mm (0.875 to 0.8752 in). Always use new connecting bolts and nuts at overhauls.

Before fitting new big-end bearings, the crankpins must be examined for damage or the transfer of bearing metal.

When a new connecting rod is fitted, although the small-end bush is reamed to the correct dimensions, it may be necessary to hone the bush to achieve the correct gudgeon pin fit.

d. General. Remove the oil suction strainer in the sump and clean thoroughly. Inspect all components for damage.

Reassembling

NOTE: Before refitting the crankshaft the rear oil seal must be offered up and sized correctly. Before fitting the seal halves into the housing grooves, brush a thin coat of red Hermetite into both grooves for 25 mm (1 inch) from the joint face on opposite halves (from leading edge of seal on both)

Carefully tap the new rear oil seal halves (1, Fig. 68) on side face to narrow section and press into the grooves in the seal housings (2, Fig. 68). Use a hammer handle (3, Fig. 68) to roll the seal into the housing until the ends do not protrude. DO NOT cut the ends of the seal. Use a knife or similar tool to ensure that no loose strands are proud.

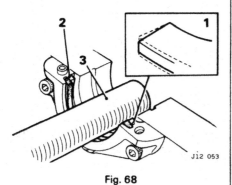

Fig. 68

Assemble the two halves of the seal and secure using two socket head screws (1, Fig. 69).
Fit the rear main bearing cap without bearings and tighten the bolts to torque quoted in data sheet.
Assemble the rear oil seal housing to the cylinder block using three socket head screws.

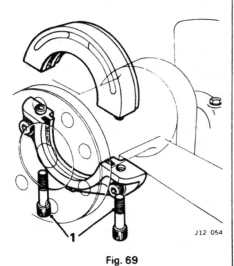

Fig. 69

Smear a small quantity of colloidal graphite around the inside surface of the oil seal and insert the sizing tool JD 17B (1, Fig. 70).
Press the tool inwards and rotate it until 'fully home. Withdraw the tool by pulling and twisting at the same time.
Remove and separate the rear main bearing oil seal housing and remove the rear main bearing cap (2, Fig. 70).
Check the distributor drive shaft bush for wear, and, if necessary, renew it.
Tap the bush in from the bottom of the crankcase ensuring that the locating holes line up.
Fit the locating peg.
Fit the main bearing shells in the cylinder block, lay the crankshaft in position and fit the rear oil seal housing.

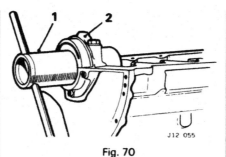

Fig. 70

Fit new thrust washers (1, Fig. 71) to centre main bearing cap, white metal side outwards.
Fit the cap to the cylinder block.
Check the crankshaft end-float which should be 0,10 to 0,15 mm (0.004 to 0.006 in).

NOTE: Thrust washers are supplied in two sizes, standard and 0,10 mm (0.004 in) oversize and should be selected to bring the end-float within required limits. Oversize washers are stamped .004 on the steel face.

Fit the main bearing shells and caps with the numbers on the caps corresponding with the numbers on the cylinder block (2, Fig. 71).
Fit the main bearing bolts, locating the oil pipe brackets as noted, and lock washer and tighten to the correct torque.
Test the crankshaft for free rotation.
Fit the Woodruff key to the inner slot and tap oil pump/distributor drive gear into position.
Fit the pistons and connecting rods to cylinder bores and secure to crankshaft using special nuts. Check the crankshaft for free rotation.

CAUTION: Ensure that the pistons are fitted with 'FRONT' on each crown towards the front of the cylinder block.

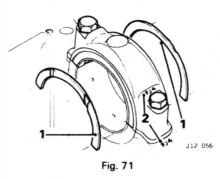

Fig. 71

Turn the crankshaft to accurately set pistons 1 and 6 to T.D.C.
Place the distributor drive shaft in position with the offset slot as shown (1, Fig. 72).
Slightly withdraw the shaft and fit Woodruff key (2, Fig. 72), thrust washer (3, Fig. 72) and drive gear (4, Fig. 72) on shaft.
Maintaining correct slot position, press the shaft into gear, ensuring that the keyway engages correctly.
Fit the pegged tab washer (5, Fig. 72) and secure it with plain nut (6, Fig. 72).
Check the end-float of the shaft. The clearance should be 0,10 to 0,15 mm (0.004 to 0.006 in). If no clearance exists, renew drive gear. In emergency, the thrust washer can be reduced.
Locate the lower timing chain dampers (7, Fig. 72) and loosely fasten.

Fit the Woodruff key to the second slot.
Offer the top and bottom timing chain assembly and chain sprockets (8, Fig. 72) into position and secure using four setscrews and locking washers (9, Fig. 72).
Position the damper in light contact with the chain and secure it.
Screw the slipper of the chain tensioner into the body casting. Fit the slip gauge or distance card (10, Fig. 72) supplied with the new tensioner to maintain a clearance of 3,17 mm (0.125 in) between slipper and body.
Locate the conical filter (11, Fig. 72) in the cylinder block.
Secure the chain tensioner to the cylinder block using two setscrews (12, Fig. 72) and lockwashers. Fit the shims as required to ensure that the slipper runs central on the chain.
Set the adjustable damper (13, Fig. 72) into light contact with the chain and secure it.

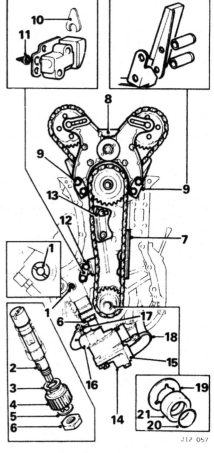

Fig. 72

Remove the slip gauge or distance card, lightly tap to release ratchet.
Locate the coupling on the oil pump (14, Fig. 72) and secure it to the front main bearing cap.
Fit the lockplates and pipe bracket.
Ensure that the 'O' ring seal is fitted in the oil pump suction (15, Fig. 72) and delivery ports (16, Fig. 72).
Use a new gasket and fit the delivery pipe between the oil pump and cylinder block.
Secure the pipe clip (17, Fig. 72).
Fit the oil suction pipe and secure the pipe clips (18, Fig. 72).

continued

12—19

NOTE: Locate the pipe on the main bearing cap brackets so that the intake end is on the centre line of the engine.

Fit the oil thrower (19, Fig. 72) at the timing chain sprocket, if originally fitted.

Use new gaskets smeared with grease and fit the timing cover. Fit the ignition timing pointer. Liberally coat a new front oil seal with engine oil and locate it in the timing cover recess, open side inwards.

Check the 'O' ring seal (20, Fig. 72) in the distance piece (21, Fig. 72) and fit on to the crankshaft.

Use new gaskets smeared with grease and fit the oil sump. Locate the transmission oil cooler pipe brackets on cars fitted with automatic transmission only.

CAUTION: Ensure that the short setscrew is fitted at the front right-hand corner.

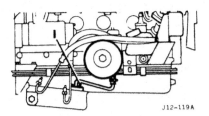

Fig. 73

Fit a new 'O' ring seal on the oil return pipe and secure it to the sump using two plain nuts and spring washers (1, Fig. 73).

Using a new gasket lightly smeared with grease, fit the oil filter housing. Locate the oil return pipe hose, oil feed pipe to camshafts and oil cooler hoses, if fitted.

Secure the housing to the block using four setscrews and shakeproof washers.

Tighten the hose clips and replace the oil pressure transmitter and pedestal.

Smear the seal of the new canister with engine oil and screw it into place by hand only. DO NOT OVERTIGHTEN.

Fit the water pump, omitting the lower right-hand bolt if the car is to Federal emission control specification.

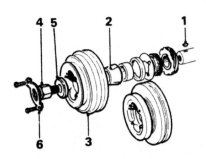

Fig. 74

Fit the Woodruff key (1, Fig. 74) to the forward slot in the crankshaft and fit the damper cone (2, Fig. 74).

Fit the Woodruff key in the damper cone and fit the torsional damper (3, Fig. 74). Secure with the large bolt (4, Fig. 74) and plain washer (5, Fig. 74).

Fit the crankshaft pulley(s) and secure using four setscrews and lockplate (6, Fig. 74).

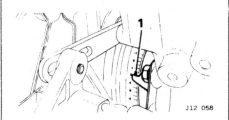

Fig. 75

Accurately set No. 1 and No. 6 pistons at T.D.C. and adjust the position of the ignition timing pointer (1, Fig. 75).

Locate flywheel/drive plate on the crankshaft and tap the dowels through. Secure using ten bolts on the new lockplate.

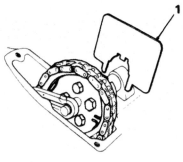

Fig. 76

Fit a new cylinder head gasket, dry, ensuring that the side marked 'TOP' is uppermost.

Check that No. 6 (front) cylinder is at T.D.C. Carefully rotate the camshafts and set with gauge C 3993 (1, Fig. 76).

CAUTION: Ensure that the valves do not foul each other.

Fit the cylinder head, complete with manifolds, to the cylinder block.

CAUTION: The engine MUST NOT be rotated until the camshaft sprockets are connected.

Fit the spark plug lead carrier brackets and lifting eyes to the appropriate studs and fit plain washers to the rest.

Fit and tighten the fourteen large dome headed nuts to the correct torque.

Fit the six nuts and spring washers across the front of the cylinder head.

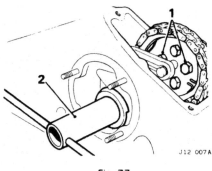

Fig. 77

Locate the camshaft sprockets on the camshafts, remove the circlips and pull the adjuster plates forward to disengage the serrations.

Rotate the adjuster plates until the 'fit' holes line up exactly with the tapped holes in the camshafts.

Fit one bolt at each camshaft.

Rotate the engine to afford access to the remaining holes and fit the bolts (1, Fig. 77). Lock the bolts at both camshafts.

Tension the top timing chain using special tool JD 2B (2, Fig. 77) until there is slight flexibility on the outer sides of the chain. Tighten the locknut.

Complete the reassembly by reversing the early dismantling operations as appropriate.

DEGLAZING CYLINDER BORES

Should it be necessary to deglaze cylinder bores due to excessive oil consumption, the following procedure must be observed. This is the only deglazing method approved by Jaguar Service:

Equipment

a. GBD 89 mm (3.5 in) diameter 80 grit silicon carbide flex hone tool. The Flex Hone Tool is colour coded orange at the hone end of the tool.

b. Variable speed electric drill, which must be capable of running at 750 rev/min unladen.

Method

1. Remove engine and dismantle as per Repair Operation 12.41.05.

   NOTE: It is NOT necessary to dismantle the cylinder head.

2. Position the dismantled cylinder block so that The Flex Hone Tool can be inserted vertically. Tape over water and oil galleries on cylinder block top face.

3. Lubricate each cylinder using clean engine oil.

4. Secure the Flex Hone Tool in drill.

5. The Flex Hone Tool must be revolving when inserted OR removed from each cylinder, and must not be stopped and restarted during the deglazing cycle.

   Using a vertical stroking motion (with flex hone already revolving), hone for 45 seconds at the rate of 2 strokes per second.

   THE DURATION OF HONING TIME AND THE NUMBER OF STROKES PER SECOND MUST BE STRICTLY OBSERVED TO GIVE THE CORRECT BORE FINISH AND CROSS-HATCH SPECIFICATION.

This method has been developed and evaluated on Service cylinder blocks, and when strictly adhered to, will produce the required bore finish.

6. Cleaning:
   a. Remove oil gallery plugs and flush out oilways with suitable cleaning solvent. Replace plugs.
   b. Using soapy water, thoroughly brush cylinder bores AND crankcase.
   c. Brush the bores and crankcase with clean water.
   d. Wipe each bore with clean white cloth/tissue. Wipe all main bearing journals similarly.

   Repeat process until cloth/tissue can be removed clean.

CLEANLINESS CANNOT BE OVERSTRESSED

IMPORTANT

Even though excess oil consumption is diagnosed, IT MAY NOT BE NECESSARY to deglaze cylinder bores.

If there is no measurable bore wear and the cylinder walls have a surface finish as illustrated, it will only be necessary to replace pistons and/or piston rings.

PAGE INTENTIONALLY LEFT BLANK

JAGUAR
Daimler

12 CYLINDER

Containing
Section

12 ENGINE

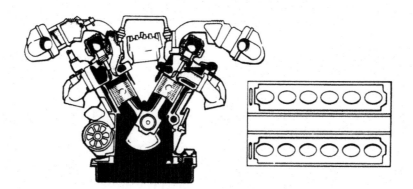

SERIES III
SERVICE MANUAL

INTRODUCTION

This Service Manual covers the Jaguar Series 3 and Daimler Series 3 range of vehicles. It is primarily designed to assist skilled technicians in the efficient repair and maintenance of Jaguar and Daimler vehicles.

Using the appropriate service tools and carrying out the procedures as detailed will enable the operations to be completed within the time stated in the 'Repair Operation Times'.

The Service Manual has been produced in 13 separate sections; this allows the information to be distributed throughout the specialist areas of the modern service facility.

A table of contents in section 1 lists the major components and systems together with the section and book numbers. The cover of each book depicts graphically and numerically the sections contained within that book. Each section starts with a list of operations in alphabetical order.

The title page of each book carries the part numbers required to order replacement books, binders or complete Service Manuals. This can be done through the normal channels.

Operation Numbering

A master index of numbered operations has been compiled for universal application to all vehicles manufactured by Jaguar Cars Ltd., and therefore, because of the different specifications of various models, continuity of the numbering sequence cannot be maintained throughout this manual.

Each operation described in this manual is allocated a number from the master index and cross-refers with an identical number in the 'Repair Operation Times'. The number consists of six digits arranged in three pairs.

Each operation is laid out in the sequence required to complete the operation in the minimum time, as specified in the 'Repair Operation Times'.

Service Tools

Where performance of an operation requires the use of a service tool, the tool number is quoted under the operation heading and is repeated in, following, the instruction involving its use. A list of all necessary tools is included in section 1, number 99.

References

References to the left- or right-hand side in the manual are made when viewing from the rear. With the engine and gearbox assembly removed the timing cover end of the engine is referred to as the front. A key to abbreviations and symbols is given in section 1, number 01.

REPAIRS AND REPLACEMENTS

When service parts are required it is essential that only genuine Jaguar/Daimler or Unipart replacements are used. Attention is particularly drawn to the following points concerning repairs and the fitting of replacement parts and accessories.

1.	Safety features embodied in the vehicle may be impaired if other than genuine parts are fitted. In certain territories, legislation prohibits the fitting of parts not to the vehicle manufacturer's specification.

2.	Torque wrench setting figures given in this Service Manual must be strictly adhered to.

3.	Locking devices, where specified, must be fitted. If the efficiency of a locking device is impaired during removal it must be replaced.

4.	Owners purchasing accessories while travelling abroad should ensure that the accessory and its fitted location on the vehicle conform to mandatory requirements existing in their country of origin.

5.	The vehicle warranty may be invalidated by the fitting of other than genuine Jaguar/Daimler or Unipart parts. All Jaguar/Daimler and Unipart replacements have the full backing of the factory warranty.

6.	Jaguar/Daimler Dealers are obliged to supply only genuine service parts.

SPECIFICATION

Purchasers are advised that the specification details set out in this Manual apply to a range of vehicles and not to any one. For the specification of a particular vehicle, purchasers should consult their Dealer.

The Manufacturers reserve the right to vary their specifications with or without notice, and at such times and in such manner as they think fit. Major as well as minor changes may be involved in accordance with the Manufacturer's policy of constant product improvement.

Whilst every effort is made to ensure the accuracy of the particulars contained in this Manual, neither the Manufacturer nor the Dealer, by whom this Manual is supplied, shall in any circumstances be held liable for any inaccuracy or the consequences thereof.

CONTENTS

TORQUE WRENCH SETTINGS   SECTION 12

ITEM	DESCRIPTION	TIGHTENING TORQUE		
		Nm	kgf m	lbf ft
Main bearings	½ in U.N.F. nut	80,5 to 84,7	8,21 to 8,64	59.4 to 62.5
	⅜ in U.N.F. nut	36,6 to 37,9	3,73 to 3,87	27 to 28
Cylinder head	⁷⁄₁₆ in U.N.F. nut	67 to 70,5	6,8 to 7,19	49.4 to 52
	⅜ in U.N.F. nut	36,6 to 37,9	3,73 to 3,87	27 to 28
Flywheel	⁷⁄₁₆ in U.N.F. nut	85,8 to 90,3	8,75 to 9,2	63.3 to 66.6
Connecting rod big-end	⅜ in U.N.F. nut	54,2 to 55,6	5,53 to 5,66	40 to 41
Crankshaft bolt	¾ in U.N.F. nut	169,5 to 203	17,3 to 20,7	125 to 150
Camshaft cover	¼ in U.N.C. screw	11,25	1,15	8.3
Camshaft cap	⁵⁄₁₆ in U.N.F. nut	12,2	1,25	9
Torque converter	⅜ in U.N.F. bolt	47,45	4,8	38
P.A.S. mounting bracket	⅜ in U.N.F. nut	50,16	5,15	37
Union block to compressor	⅜ in U.N.F. bolt	13,56 to 33,9	1,38 to 3,45	10 to 25
ENGINE MOUNTING				
Rear mounting bracket to body	⁵⁄₁₆ in U.N.F. bolt	19 to 24,4	1,95 to 2,48	14 to 18
Rear mounting bracket to body	¾ in U.N.F. bolt	36,6 to 43,38	3,73 to 4,42	27 to 32
Front bracket to beam	⁵⁄₁₆ in U.N.F. nut	19 to 24,4	1,95 to 2,48	14 to 18
Rear mounting peg	½ in U.N.F. nut	33,9 to 40,67	3,46 to 4,14	25 to 30

12—2

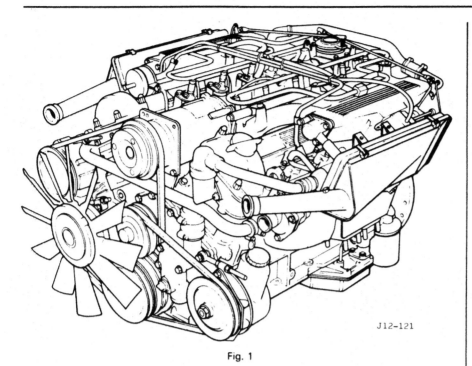

Fig. 1

DESCRIPTION

The V–12 engine fitted to Series III Jaguar XJ12 and Daimler Double-Six cars is the product of many years of improvement and development of the engine originally fitted to the final series of Jaguar E-type cars. In these, it exceeded the high standards of silence and smoothness, combined with high power output, set by the earlier 6-cylinder Jaguar engine. Major alterations during development have been confined to the fuel supply system, the four carburetters of the early engines having been replaced by the Lucas–Bosch Jetronic D fuel injection system which has now been superseded by the Lucas 'Digital' system which provides even closer control of the fuel supply to the engine, enabling improvements to be made in fuel economy and in the elimination of harmful exhaust emissions.

For description of HE Engine see 12—20.

CYLINDER PRESSURES

Check **12.25.01**

Set the transmission selector at 'P'.
Run the engine until normal operating temperature is reached. Switch off engine.
Remove the h.t. cable from the ignition coil.
Remove all spark plugs.
Fit an approved pressure gauge at one plug hole and, with throttle held fully open, crank the engine. Note the highest steady pressure reading achieved and repeat at each plug hole in turn; the pressure noted must be as quoted in the data sheets. The reading taken at each cylinder must not differ from the reading taken at any other cylinder by more than 0,35 kgf/cm² (5 lbf/in²).
Refit the spark plugs.
Refit the h.t. cable to the ignition coil.

TAPPETS

Adjust **12.29.48**

Remove camshaft covers, see 12.29.42, and check that all camshaft bearing nuts (1, Fig. 2) are tight, tighten to correct torque.

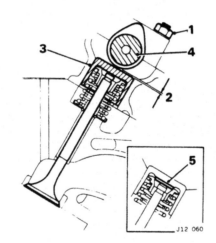

Fig. 2

Check and record the clearance (2, Fig. 2) between each tappet (3, Fig. 2) and heel of each cam (4, Fig. 2). For the correct clearance, see data sheets.
Subtract the appropriate valve clearance from the dimension obtained and select suitable adjusting pads (5, Fig. 2) which equal this new dimension. Adjusting pads are available rising in 0,03 mm (0.001 in) sizes from 2,16 mm to 2,79 mm (0.085 in to 0.110 in) and are etched on the surface with letter 'A' to 'Z' each letter indicating an increase in size of 0,03 mm (0.001 in).
Remove the camshaft and tappets.
Fit adjusting pads, replace the camshaft.

CRANKSHAFT DAMPER AND PULLEY

Remove and refit (engine in situ) **12.21.01**

Removing

Remove the alternator drive belt.
Remove the bolts (1, Fig. 3) securing the pulley to damper, withdraw the pulley.
Remove the crankshaft damper bolt (2, Fig. 3). Strike the damper sharply with a hide mallet to loosen.
Withdraw the damper (3, Fig. 3) and cone (4, Fig. 3), taking care to recover two Woodruff keys (5, Fig. 3) from the cone and from the crankshaft.

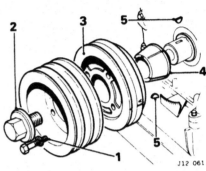

Fig. 3

Refitting

Reverse the removal operations, tighten the bolt to correct torque.

CRANKSHAFT FRONT OIL SEAL

Remove and refit **12.21.14**

Removing

Remove the crankshaft damper and pulley.
Prise the seal (1, Fig. 4) out of the timing cover (2, Fig. 4) and discard it.
Withdraw the distance piece (3, Fig. 4).

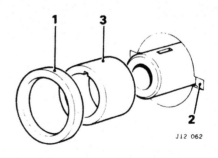

Fig. 4

continued

12—3

Refitting

Ensure that the seal recess in the timing cover is absolutely clean.
Smear the new oil seal with clean engine oil
Position the oil seal squarely in the recess and tap it gently home using a hide mallet.
Refit the distance piece.
Replace the crankshaft damper and pulley

CRANKSHAFT MAIN BEARINGS

Remove and refit (set)   **12.21.39**

It is stressed that this operation should only be carried out if crankshaft damage is not suspected and the failure is due to bearing shell wear.
If upon inspection, journals are found to be damaged, the engine must be removed and the crankshaft renewed.

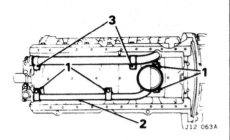

Fig. 5

Removing

Remove the sandwich plate assembly, which entails removal of the front suspension unit and oil sump pan.
Remove four setscrews and washers (1, Fig. 5) securing the suction pipe clips and bracket. Draw the suction pipe (2, Fig. 5) from 'O' ring at elbow.
Remove the two setscrews and washers (3, Fig. 5) securing the crankshaft, undershield and delivery pipe clips. Draw the undershield clear
Remove the bolt and washer and nut and washer securing the oil delivery pipe elbow to oil pump casting

NOTE: Leave the bolt at the outboard fastening in position in the oil pump casting. If the bolt is removed for any reason, it must be replaced in a downward direction.

Draw the oil delivery pipe and elbow downwards from the bore in the crankcase and from the oil pump casting. Remove and discard the gasket.

NOTE: Record the position of the pillar nuts.

Remove the four nuts and washers securing the front main bearing cap. Remove the bearing cap and renew the shells.

Refitting

Fit the bearing cap and tighten the securing nuts. Tighten to correct torque.
Repeat operations on the cap for all main bearings

NOTE: The rear main bearing is secured with four small nuts and washers and two large nuts and washers. Use Sealastik to seal the outer grooves of the bearing cap.

CAUTION: Centre and rear main bearing shells must not be confused with each other; the rear main bearing shell has an oil groove whilst the centre main bearing shell is plain.

Reverse the removal operations, renewing the suction and delivery pipe 'O' ring seals, and cleaning the suction pipe strainer before replacement.

CONNECTING ROD BEARINGS

Remove and refit (set)   **12.17.16**

It is stressed that this operation should only be carried out if crankshaft damage is not suspected and the failure is due to bearing shell wear.
If, upon inspection, journals are found to be damaged, the engine must be removed and the crankshaft renewed.

Removing

Remove the sandwich plate assembly which entails removal of the front suspension unit and oil sump pan.
Remove the four setscrews and washers (1, Fig 6) securing the suction pipe clips and bracket. Draw the suction pipe (2, Fig. 6) from 'O' ring at elbow.
Remove the two setscrews and washers securing the crankshaft, undershield and delivery pipe clips. Draw the undershield clear.
Rotate the crankshaft until the two journals are at bottom dead centre.
Remove the big-end bearing cap nuts from the connecting rods on one journal and renew the shells. DO NOT ROTATE CRANKSHAFT WHILE THE CAPS ARE DETACHED.
Repeat the operation on the other journal
Rotate the crankshaft until two more journals are at bottom dead centre and renew the shells
Repeat for the last pair of journals.

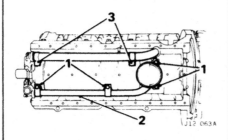

Fig. 6

Refitting

Reverse the removal operations, renewing the suction pipe 'O' ring seal and cleaning the strainer before replacement.
Tighten the bearing cap nuts to correct torque.

CAMSHAFT COVER

Remove and refit   **L.H.**   **12.29.42**
                         R.H.   **12.29.43**

Removing

Disconnect the throttle linkage.
Remove the front and rear inlet manifolds as required. For further details refer to the Manifold and Exhaust Section 30 for 12 cylinder models.
Remove the setscrews (1, Fig. 7), domed head nuts and washers (2, Fig. 7) securing camshaft cover to the tappet block, lift off the cover (3, Fig. 7).

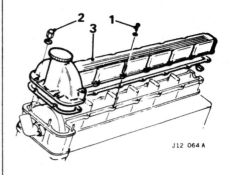

Fig. 7

Refitting

Reverse the operations above; use a new gasket and neoprene sealing plug. Tighten the nuts and bolts by diagonal selection to correct torque

OIL FILTER ASSEMBLY

Remove and refit   **12.60.01**

CAUTION: All cars are fitted with a disposable filter canister; when fitting a new canister, tighten the canister two-thirds of a turn by hand only.

Removing

Remove exhaust front down-pipe; refer to Section 30.
Disconnect the union (1, Fig. 8) on the oil cooler supply pipe.
On the pressure relief valve vent hose (2, Fig. 8), release clip nearest the valve.
Unscrew the filter canister (3, Fig. 8).
Remove the five self-tapping screws retaining the left-hand front heat shield. Remove the four setscrews (4, Fig 8) retaining the filter head

12—4

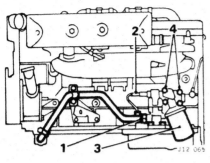

Fig. 8

NOTE: It is not possible to fully withdraw the lower right-hand setscrew.

Carefully break the filter head to cylinder block seal and press the filter head upwards until the by-pass valve stub pipe clears the housing.
Separate the vent pipe from the relief valve and manoeuvre the filter head clear.

Refitting

NOTE: If a new filter assembly complete is being fitted, the canister must first be removed from the head. Check the condition of the 'O' ring seal on the by-pass valve stub pipe, and, if necessary, renew it.

Use a new filter head to cylinder block gasket. Position the setscrew and serrated washer in the lower right-hand fixing hole (1, Fig. 9), and offer the filter head into position.
Press the stub pipe down into the by-pass valve housing and locate the fixing setscrew.
Fit the remaining three setscrews (2, Fig. 9) and serrated washers to secure the filter head.

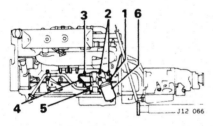

Fig. 9

Replace the clip (3, Fig. 9) on the relief valve vent hose (4, Fig. 9) and secure.
Secure the union nut (5, Fig. 9) on the oil cooler supply pipe.
Place a new gasket on the canister (6, Fig. 9) and screw into position by hand only.
Fit the heat shield. Fit the down pipe.
Run the engine, check the oil level, and top-up as necessary.

OIL COOLER

Remove and refit   **12.60.68**

Removing

Remove the two screws securing the radiator lower grille.
Remove the air conditioning receiver–drier and condenser fixing. Displace units aside.

Disconnect the inlet and outlet pipes from the oil cooler. A backing spanner **must** be used to prevent damage to the end tanks.
Remove the two cross-head screws and washers securing the oil cooler to the support brackets.
Lift the oil cooler from the car and recover spacers.

Refitting

Locate the spacers beneath the oil cooler end tanks; secure the oil cooler to the support brackets using two cross-head screws and plain washers.
Connect the inlet and outlet pipes to the oil cooler. A backing spanner **must** be used to prevent damage to the end tanks.
Start the engine and check for oil leaks at connections. Run the engine until it reaches normal operating temperature. Stop the engine.
Check the oil level after one minute and top-up as necessary.
Refit the radiator lower grille.
Reposition the air conditioning receiver–drier and condenser and secure.

OIL COOLER SUPPLY HOSE

Remove and refit   **12.60.74**

Removing

Remove the two self-tapping screws securing the radiator lower grille.
Release the supply hose union (1, Fig. 10) from the supply pipe.

NOTE: Use a backing spanner to restrain the hose ferrule while releasing the union nut.

Release the supply hose union (2, Fig. 10) from the oil cooler.

NOTE: Use a backing spanner to avoid straining the joint at the end tank.

Cut the strapping and manoeuvre the hose clear towards the rear of the vehicle.

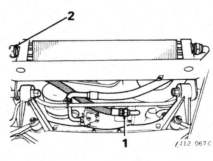

Fig. 10

Refitting

Reverse the removal operations placing the hose into position from the rear of the radiator matrix.
Refit the strapping to secure the hoses.
Run the engine, check the oil level, and top-up as necessary.

OIL COOLER RETURN HOSE

Remove and refit   **12.60.76**

Removing

Remove the two self-tapping screws securing the radiator lower grille.
Release the return hose from the sandwich plate elbow (1, Fig. 11).
Release the return hose union from the oil cooler (2, Fig. 11).

NOTE: Use a backing spanner to avoid straining the joint in the end tank.

Cut the strapping and manoeuvre the hose clear towards the rear of the vehicle.

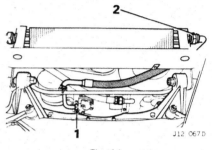

Fig. 11

Refitting

Reverse the removal operations, placing the hose into position from the rear of the radiator matrix.
Refit the strapping to secure the hoses.
Run the engine, check the oil level, and top-up as necessary.

CAMSHAFT

| Remove and refit | L.H. | 12.13.02 |
| | R.H. | 12.13.03 |

Service tools: Sprocket retaining tool JD 40; valve timing gauge C 3993; timing chain tensioner retractor tool JD 50.

Removing

Remove both camshaft covers for L.H. camshaft removal and R.H. camshaft cover for R.H. camshaft removal.
Remove the rubber grommet from the timing cover.

Fig. 12

continued

12—5

Insert the blade of screwdriver JD 50 (1, Fig. 12) through the hole to release the locking catch on the timing chain tensioner.

Using special tool JD 50 lift and retract timing chain tensioner to full extent. The locking catch will engage on the step. Remove the tools.

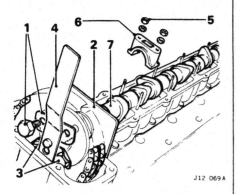

Fig. 13

Bend back the locking tabs and remove the two camshaft sprocket retaining bolts (1, Fig. 13). Rotate the engine until the timing gauge C 3993 (2, Fig. 13) can be inserted in the slot in the camshaft to be removed.

Remove the two bolts (3, Fig. 13) and fit the sprocket retaining tool JD 40 (4, Fig. 13).

CAUTION: Do not rotate the engine while the camshaft is disconnected.

Progressively slacken the camshaft bearing cap nuts (5, Fig. 13) starting with the centre cap and working outwards; lift off the bearing caps (6, Fig 13).

Lift the camshaft (7, Fig. 13) out of the tappet block.

Refitting

Smear the camshaft journals and tappets with clean engine oil.

NOTE: Use gauge C 3993 (2, Fig. 13) to position the camshaft correctly before fitting the bearing caps.

Position the camshaft in the tappet block, refit the bearing caps, washers and nuts.

Progressively tighten the bearing cap nuts, working from the centre outwards, to a torque of 1,2 kgf m (9.0 lbf ft).

Check that the timing gauge is still correctly positioned.

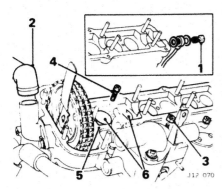

Fig. 14

Engage the camshaft sprocket with the shaft and fit one retaining bolt through 'fit' hole on new tab washer. Turn up the tabs.

Rotate the engine, fit the remaining bolts and tab washer. Turn up the tabs.

Insert screwdriver JD 50 (2, Fig. 12) through the hole in the timing cover and trip the locking catch, refit the rubber grommet.

Refit the camshaft cover(s).

TAPPET BLOCK — L.H.

Remove and refit   **12.13.29**

Removing

Remove the camshaft.

Remove the banjo bolt securing the oil feed pipe to the tappet block (1, Fig. 14).

Disconnect the breather pipe (2, Fig. 14).

Progressively slacken the retaining nuts (3, Fig. 14) and cap screws (4, Fig. 14), working from the centre outwards.

Lift off the tappet block (5, Fig. 14) carefully, retrieve the tappets (6, Fig. 14) and valve adjusting pads.

NOTE: Record from which valve each tappet and pads is removed. Failure to do this will result in incorrect valve adjustment on reassembly.

Refitting

Ensure that mating surfaces of tappet block and cylinder head are clean.

Smear the mating surfaces of the tappet block and cylinder head with Hylomar.

Fit the tappet block, ensuring that dowels are correctly located.

Tighten the retaining nuts and cap screws by diagonal selection, working from the centre outwards.

Lubricate the tappets and adjusting pads with clean engine oil, fit them to their respective valves.

Replace the camshaft.

NOTE: If the tappet block has been renewed, it will be necessary to check valve clearances.

TAPPET BLOCK — R.H.

Remove and refit   **12.13.30**

Removing

Remove the camshaft.

Remove the banjo bolt securing the oil feed pipe to the tappet block (1, Fig 15).

Progressively slacken the retaining nuts (2, Fig. 15) and cap screws (3, Fig. 15), working from centre outwards.

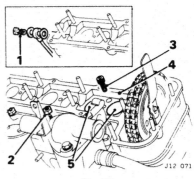

Fig. 15

Lift off tappet block (4, Fig. 15) carefully, retrieve tappets (5, Fig. 15) and valve adjusting pads.

NOTE: Record from which valve each tappet and pads is removed. Failure to do so will result in incorrect valve adjustment upon reassembly.

Refitting

Ensure that the mating surfaces of tappet block and cylinder head are clean.

Smear the mating surfaces of tappet block and cylinder head with Hylomar.

Fit the tappet block ensuring that dowels are correctly located.

Tighten the retaining nuts and cap screws by diagonal selection, working from the centre outwards.

Lubricate the tappets and adjusting pads with clean engine oil, fit them to their respective valves.

Replace the camshaft.

NOTE: If the tappet block has been renewed, it will be necessary to check the valve clearance.

ENGINE MOUNTING—FRONT SET

Remove and refit   **12.45.04**

Removing

Disconnect the battery.

Remove the wing valance stays.

Remove the air cleaners.

Cars not fitted with air conditioning

Slacken the fan relay fixings on the radiator top rail.

Remove the three self-locking nuts and washers securing the fan shield.

Remove the fan shield.

Cars fitted with air conditioning

Remove the four nuts and washers securing the fan and Torquatrol unit to the pulley. Allow the unit to rest forward against the radiator.

All cars

Remove the nuts and spring washers securing the top and bottom of both engine mountings.

78

CAUTION: Air-conditioned cars only. Observe the expansion valve throughout the lift.

Using chains and a spreader, lift the front of the engine sufficiently to free the mountings. Recover the fibre washers.

Refitting

Locate the replacement mountings with the fibre washer on the top surface on front suspension cross-member brackets.
Fit the plain nut and washer to secure each mounting to the brackets on cross-member.
Lower the engine to locate on the mountings.
Fit the plain nuts and spring washers to secure the engine to the mountings.
Remove the chains.

Cars not fitted with air conditioning

Refit the fan shield and secure the relay.

Cars fitted with air conditioning

Fit the fan and Torquatrol unit to the pulley using plain nuts and serrated washers.

All cars

Refit the air cleaners.
Refit the wing valance stays.
Reconnect the battery.

ENGINE MOUNTING — REAR CENTRE

Remove and refit   12.45.08

Follow the relevant procedures detailed under Engine and gearbox assembly — remove and refit, 12 37 01, as necessary.

OIL SUMP PAN

Remove and refit   12.60.44

Removing

Remove the sump plug (1, Fig. 16) and drain the oil into a suitable container.
Remove the power steering pipe to rack distance pieces to gain access to the front sump bolts.
Remove the setscrews (2, Fig. 16) and serrated washers securing the sump pan.
Lower the sump.

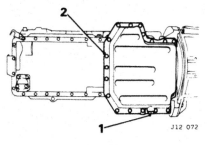

Fig. 16

Refitting

Use a new gasket lightly coated with Hylomar and secure the oil sump pan using setscrews and serrated washers.
Refit power steering pipe to rack distance pieces.

NOTE: Secure the transmission oil cooler pipe clip

OIL PRESSURE RELIEF VALVE

Remove and refit   12.60.56

Removing

Release the clip (1, Fig. 17) on the oil pressure relief valve bleed hose and prise clear.
Slacken the relief valve (2, Fig. 17) and unscrew it from the oil filter head.

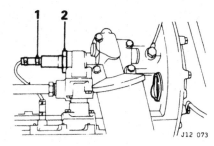

Fig. 17

Refitting

Screw the relief valve into the oil filter head, using a new sealing washer.
Fit the vent hose to the relief valve and secure it with the hose clip.

SANDWICH PLATE ASSEMBLY

Remove and refit   12.60.45

Removing

It is necessary to remove the front suspension unit (1, Fig. 18), for further details refer to Section 60.
Remove the oil sump pan.
Remove the strapping (2, Fig. 18) on oil cooler pipes.
Release the oil cooler suction (3, Fig. 18) and delivery pipe unions (4, Fig. 18) elbow and delivery pipe.
Remove the four setscrews (1, Fig. 19) and serrated washers securing the suction elbow (2, Fig. 19) to the sandwich plate. Carefully break the seal and draw the elbow downwards until the coupling tube is clear.
Release the clips and stay (3, Fig. 19) securing the delivery pipe.
Cut the clip securing the vent pipe hose to the sandwich plate spigot.
Remove the setscrews (4, Fig. 19) and washers securing the sandwich plate. Recover the timing marker (5, Fig. 19) from beneath the front two setscrews.

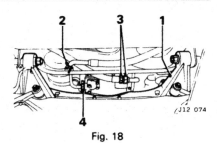

Fig. 18

NOTE: Take careful note of the locations of the setscrews, as several different lengths are used

Remove the four setscrews (6, Fig. 19) securing the baffle plate.
Remove the three setscrews and washers securing the by-pass valve housing to the sandwich plate.
Remove the by-pass valve assembly from the housing; clean, inspect, replace or renew as necessary.
Thoroughly clean all mating faces.
Renew the 'O' ring seals at the by-pass valve housing and spigot.

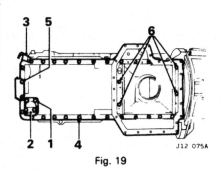

Fig. 19

Refitting

Reverse removal operations, using clean engine oil to lubricate the by-pass valve spigot 'O' ring seal.

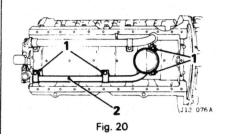

Fig. 20

OIL PICK-UP STRAINER

Remove and refit   12.60.20

Removing

It is necessary to remove the front suspension unit and oil sump pan.
Remove the sandwich plate assembly, and the four setscrews (1, Fig. 20) and serrated washers securing the suction pipe clips and bracket.
Withdraw the suction pipe (2, Fig. 20) from the elbow

continued

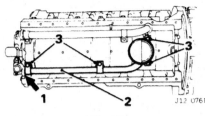

Fig. 21

Clean

Wash the suction strainer in clean paraffin or petrol, and dry it thoroughly

Refitting

Renew 'O' ring seals at the elbow (1, Fig. 21). Offer the suction pipe (2, Fig. 21) into elbow and secure using four setscrews (3, Fig. 21) and serrated washers at the pipe clips and bracket.
Refit the sandwich plate assembly, oil sump pan and front suspension.

CAMSHAFT OIL FEED PIPE

Remove and refit   **12.60.83**

Removing

Drain the coolant.
Remove the banjo connector bolt (1, Fig 22) at the rear of each camshaft.
Remove the four-way banjo connector bolt (2, Fig 22) at the throttle pedestal.
Release the clip from the heater return pipe along engine, and pull hose (3, Fig 22) from pipe
Remove the oil filter canister (4, Fig 22).
Remove the banjo connector bolt at the oil gallery on the crankcase (5, Fig 22).
Manoeuvre the oil pipes clear.
Remove the oil pressure switch from the four-way banjo.

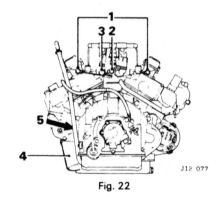

Fig. 22

Refitting

Reverse the removal operations; use new sealing washers where necessary; check the oil level, and top-up as necessary; refill with coolant in accordance with 'cold fill' procedure as detailed in Section 26 for 12 cylinder vehicles.

12—8

DRIVE PLATE

Remove and refit   **12.53.13**

Removing

Remove the gearbox and torque converter as detailed in Section 44 for GM 400 gearbox.
Lift the locking tabs and remove the bolts (1, Fig. 23) securing the drive plate to the crankshaft.
Remove the stiffener plate (2, Fig 23).
Draw the two locating dowels (3, Fig 23) from the drive plate.

CAUTION: If a draw bolt is to be used, turn the crankshaft to react bolt against rear main bearing cap, NOT cylinder block.

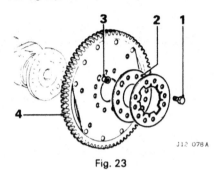

Fig. 23

Remove the drive plate (4, Fig 23)

Refitting

Tap the dowels through the drive plate to locate in the crankshaft flange.
Refit the stiffener plate and lockplate and secure using ten setscrews; tighten to 9,1 kgf m (66 5 lbf ft). Turn up the lock tabs.
Refit the gearbox and torque converter.

CYLINDER HEAD

Remove and refit
R.H. 'A' bank   **12.29.12**
L.H. 'B' bank   **12.29.11**

Service tools: Timing chain tensioner retractor tool JD 50; camshaft sprocket retaining tool JD 40; cylinder liner retaining tool JD 41; valve timing gauge C 3993.

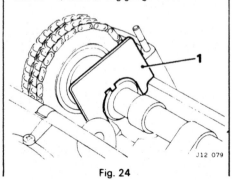

Fig. 24

Removing

Disconnect the battery.
Remove the right-hand induction housing and inlet manifold — right-hand and left-hand cylinder head removal.
Remove the left-hand induction housing and inlet manifold — left-hand cylinder head removal only
Remove the right-hand camshaft cover — right-hand and left-hand cylinder head removal.
Remove the left-hand camshaft cover — left-hand cylinder head removal only.
Remove the battery — adjacent cylinder head removal only.

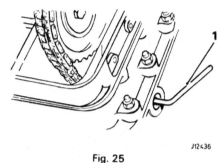

Fig. 25

NOTE: Locate the camshaft of the cylinder head to be removed. If both heads to be removed, locate 'A' bank, right-hand camshaft.
Remove the rubber grommet from the timing cover.
Insert the blade of screwdriver JD 50 (1, Fig. 25) through the hole to release the locking catch on the timing chain tensioner.
Rotate the engine, using the crankshaft damper nut, until valve timing gauge C 3993 (1, Fig. 24) can be fitted in the slot in the camshaft front flange.
Using special tool JD 44 (3, Fig. 25), retract timing chain tensioner to full extent. The locking catch will engage on the step. Remove tools.

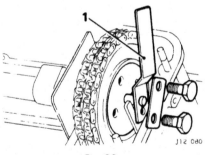

Fig. 26

Disconnect the camshaft sprocket from the camshaft, fit the sprocket retaining tool JD 40 (1, Fig 26)

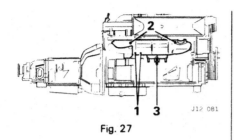

Fig. 27

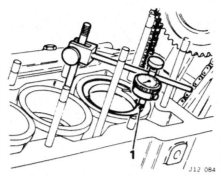

Fig. 30

Rotate the engine until the remaining camshaft sprocket retaining bolts can be fitted, secure the bolts with tab washers (5, Fig. 32).

Refit the camshaft oil supply banjo bolt.

Insert screwdriver JD 50 through the hole in the timing cover (6, Fig. 32) and trip locking catch, refit the rubber grommet.

Refit the exhaust front pipes and heat shields.

Refit the camshaft cover(s) and induction manifolds.

Refill the cooling system.

Reconnect the battery.

Set the ignition timing.

Remove the two self-tapping screws (1, Fig 27) securing the starter solenoid heat shield — right-hand cylinder head only.

Remove the two setscrews (2, Fig. 27) securing the heat shield to the exhaust manifold.

Disconnect the front pipe(s) from the exhaust manifold (3, Fig. 27) and intermediate pipe.

Remove the camshaft oil feed banjo bolts (1, Fig 29)

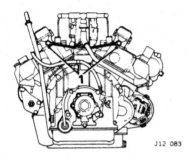

Fig. 29

Displace air conditioning compressor.

Remove the three nuts and washers securing the front of the cylinder head to the timing cover. Move the cable clips from the studs.

Progressively slacken the cylinder head nuts working from the centre outwards.

Lift off the cylinder head(s) and place on blocks of wood. This prevents irreparable damage to the valves which, when open, protrude below the cylinder head face.

CAUTION: Do not rotate the engine until cylinder liner retaining tools JD 41 have been fitted to the cylinder head studs.

NOTE: If the cylinder head has been removed for the purpose of changing the gasket, and neither crankshaft nor camshaft are moved, clean the mating surfaces and fit a new gasket. If either shaft is moved accidentally, or if cylinder head overhaul and/or piston de-carbonization has been carried out, continue by setting valve timing, as detailed below, before fitting the gasket.

Refitting

Right-hand 'A' bank or both banks

Remove the distributor cover.

Attach a suitable clock gauge (1, Fig. 30) to a cylinder head stud.

Rotate the engine and by means of the clock gauge, set number one position 'A' bank at T.D.C. firing stroke. Remove the gauge.

NOTE: The timing mark 'No. 1 cyl.' on the electronic timing rotor will not be pointing directly at the pick-up module but must be approximately 5° from coincidence.

Turn the camshaft until the valve timing gauge C 3993 can be fitted into the slot in the camshaft front flange.

Repeat the last operation on the left-hand cylinder head.

Remove the cylinder liner retaining tools JD 41 from the right-hand cylinder block.

CAUTION: Do not rotate the engine until the cylinder head(s) are fitted.

Ensure that the mating surfaces of the cylinder head and block are clean.

Fit gasket, ensuring that the side marked 'TOP' is uppermost. DO **NOT** use jointing compound or grease.

Fit the right-hand cylinder head and retaining nuts.

Tighten the retaining nuts in the order shown in Fig. 31 to correct torque.

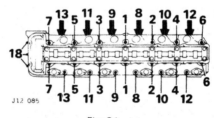

Fig. 31

Tighten the cylinder head to timing cover nuts to correct torque.

Remove the sprocket retaining tool JD 40 (1, Fig. 32) check the alignment of the retaining bolt holes. If the camshaft and sprocket holes are not in alignment, remove the circlip (2, Fig. 32) retaining the camshaft coupling to the sprocket and disengage the coupling from the splines. Press the sprocket on to the camshaft shoulder.

Rotate the coupling (3, Fig. 32) until access to the retaining bolt holes is obtained.

Bolt the coupling to the camshaft on the tab washers.

Refit the circlip and remove the gauge C 3993 (4, Fig. 32).

If left-hand 'B' bank cylinder head has been removed, repeat replacement operations on this head.

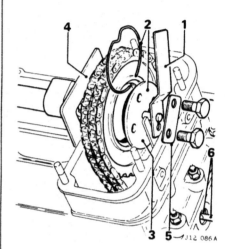

Fig. 32

Refitting

Left-hand 'B' bank only

Rotate the engine until valve timing gauge C 3993 can be fitted to the slot in the front flange of 'A' bank camshaft.

Turn 'B' bank camshaft and fit valve timing gauge C 3993.

If necessary, remove the cylinder liner retaining tools JD 41.

Repeat operations to refit the head, as appropriate.

CYLINDER HEAD GASKET

Remove and refit   L.H.   12.29.02
                          R.H.   12.29.03

Removing

Follow the procedure given for removing relevant cylinder head, see 12.29.11 or 12.29.12. Check the cylinder head and faces of the block and liners for damage that caused, or was the result of, gasket failure, rectify as necessary.

12—9

ENGINE ASSEMBLY

Remove and refit	**12.37.01**

Removing

Pre HE models. For later models see page 12—20.

Remove the bonnet and drain the coolant.

Depressurize the fuel system, and (if fitted) the air conditioning system.

Remove the harness cover from the R.H. inner wing, disconnect the headlamp harness, unclip the harness from the top rail and re-position aside

Disconnect the coil L.T., pick-up module (1, Fig 33) and ballast resistor and re-position aside

Displace the receiver–drier clamps and relays from the top rail location.

Remove the fan cowl to top rail securing nuts, disconnect the thermostat switch harness and re-position all harnesses aside. Remove the top rail securing bolts and remove the top rail assembly

Remove the air cleaner covers and elements (2, Fig. 33).

Remove the air anti-recirculation panel and fan cowl securing nuts.

Remove the lower radiator grille and blanking grommets from the front valance and remove the oil cooler to radiator securing screws.

Carefully displace the condenser assembly over the R.H. wing.

Displace the R.H. top hose and disconnect the top hoses from the thermostat housings.

Disconnect the transmission cooler hoses from the radiator and plug the hoses and radiator.

Disconnect the expansion pipe and heater return hoses from the radiator, displace the engine oil cooler from position and carefully displace radiator forward.

Release the fan belt tension and remove the fan/Torquatrol assembly and fan cowl (3, Fig. 33)

Disconnect the bottom hose and coolant level probe from the radiator; carefully remove the radiator assembly

Remove the battery and displace the L.H. wing stay from the engine compartment.

Disconnect the fuel hoses from the fuel cooler (4, Fig. 33) and plug connections. Disconnect the compressor to fuel cooler hose and plug connections immediately

Displace the fuel cooler from the air cleaner backplate

Release the drive belt from the P.A.S pump (5, Fig. 33), displace the pump from the engine and secure to the adjacent radiator post. Remove the P.A.S. pump bracket from the engine

Disconnect the air conditioning hose (6, Fig. 33) to receiver–drier and condenser assembly, plug all connections and remove from the vehicle

Disconnect the engine and alternator harnesses (7, Fig 33).

Disconnect the fuel feed hoses (8, Fig. 33) from the engine and plug the ends.

Disconnect the brake vacuum hoses from the Reservac pipe, brake servo pipe and manifold one-way valve, then unclip the pipe from the bulkhead clip and displace the brake hose

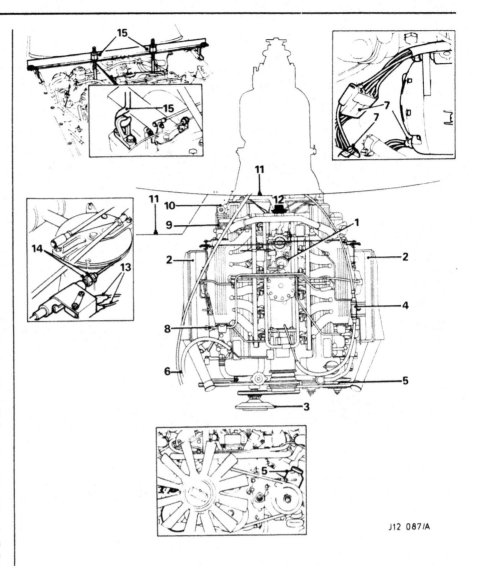

Fig. 33

J12 087/A

assembly and R.H. wing stay from the engine compartment.

Disconnect the vacuum pipes (9, Fig. 33) from the rear of R.H. inlet manifold to prevent damage during engine removal.

Remove the bolt securing the transmission upper dipstick tube (10, Fig. 33) to engine and remove the tube and dipstick assembly.

Disconnect the starter solenoid from the relay and starter feed wire (11, Fig. 33) from the bulkhead connector.

Disconnect and displace the harnesses for the throttle switch, oil pressure switch, coolant temperature sensor, ballast resistor and (where fitted) Econocruise.

Displace the fresh air grille for access and remove the nuts and bolts securing the water valve to the bulkhead. Disconnect the vacuum pipe from the valve, the heater to valve hose and the heater valve to R.H. water rail hose. Remove the water valve assembly.

To prevent damage during engine removal, displace the starter relay from the bulkhead.

Disconnect the E.C.U. vacuum feed pipe from the manifold cross-pipe (12, Fig. 33)

Disconnect the kick-down switch wires (13, Fig. 33) and disconnect the throttle cable (14, Fig. 33) from the engine

Where fitted, disconnect and displace the Econocruise control cable.

Fit the engine support tool MS 53 A to the wing channels and position above the rear engine lifting eyes. Take the weight of the engine on the support hooks (15, Fig. 33).

Raise the vehicle; place on stands.

Remove the steering rack gaiter heat shields (Figs 34 & 34A) and disconnect the down-pipes from the exhaust manifolds.

Fig. 34

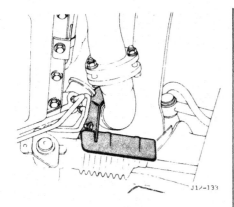

Fig. 34A

Remove the crash bracket (1, Fig. 35), from the rear mounting, using a suitable wooden block with a trolley jack take the weight of the rear mounting. Remove the bolts (2, Fig. 35) securing the mounting and carefully lower the mounting assembly on the jack and remove; collect the spacers.

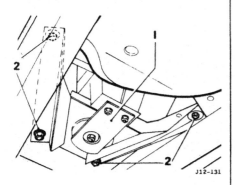

Fig. 35

Remove both the intermediate heat shields (1, Fig. 36) and the rear heat shield (2, Fig. 36). Remove the bolts securing the body cross-member and remove the cross-member.

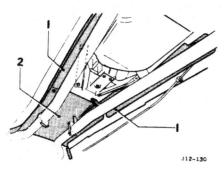

Fig. 36

Remove the nuts and bolts (1, Fig. 37) securing the propeller shaft to the gearbox drive flange and disconnect the propeller shaft.
Disconnect the speedometer cable from the angle drive (2, Fig. 37).
Lower the engine on MS 53 A by undoing tool hook nuts by **10 threads only.**

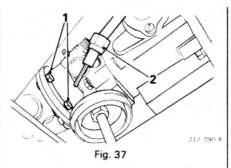

Fig. 37

Remove the bolt securing the selection cable to the gearbox casing (1, Fig. 38), remove the nut securing selection pin to selector lever (2, Fig. 38) and re-position the cable away from the gearbox.

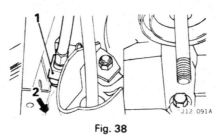

Fig. 38

Disconnect the earth lead (1, Fig. 39), from the body and collect the starred washer.

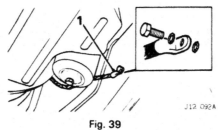

Fig. 39

Lower the vehicle from the stands.
Using a suitable wooden block, take the weight of the transmission unit on a jack, and remove tool MS 53 A.
Attach chains to the engine lifting eyes (Fig. 40).

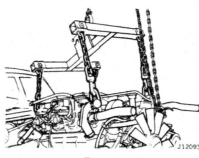

Fig. 40

WARNING: Chains must be of sufficient length to ensure that the distance between the lifting eyes and the hook of the hoist is as follows:

Front lifting eyes to hook 876 mm (34.5 in)
Rear lifting eyes to hook 1041 mm (41 in).

On cars fitted with emission control take care not to damage the thermostatic vacuum switch or pipes.
Undo and remove the upper engine mounting nuts, slacken only the R.H. lower mounting nuts.
Carefully take the weight of the engine with the hoist, simultaneously raising the jack to keep the engine level. Lift only 50 to 70 mm (2 to 3 in).

WARNING: Throughout lift, the rear of the engine must be kept as high as possible until the oil sump is clear of the steering pinion housing.

Carefully lift the engine level, whilst observing the forward corner of the oil sump and steering pinion pipework; bear sideways against the engine to keep clear. The side pressure must be maintained until the engine is clear of the steering pinion assembly and pipework.
On cars fitted with air conditioning take care not to damage the expansion valve or evaporator unions.
Withdraw the engine from the sub-frame, allowing the tilt angle to increase until the drive flange is clear of the bulkhead.

Refitting

Secure the transmission selector cable and speedometer cable against the sides of the transmission tunnel (Fig. 41).

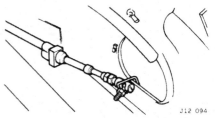

Fig. 41

Ensure that all the hoses within the engine compartment are held back against the valances.

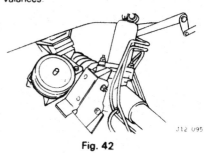

Fig. 42

Ensure that the fibre discs are in position on the front engine mountings (Fig. 42). Hoist the engine on the lifting chains (see WARNING about chain lengths), and position it with the drive flange just forward of the engine compartment bulkhead.
Roll the trolley jack in from the front of the vehicle, to a position beneath the transmission oil pan.

continued

12—11

Lower the engine into the engine compartment, simultaneously easing it to the rear until the trolley jack will support the transmission oil pan

WARNING: Maintain a continual watch on the power steering pump hoses and steering pinion pipes.

Continue lowering and positioning the engine, using both lifting chains and the trolley jack to keep the engine level, until the front mounting brackets locate.

Fit and tighten the engine mounting fixings.

Fit the engine support tool MS 53A across the rear of the engine, and remove the trolley jack and lifting chains.

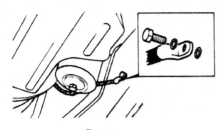

Fig. 43

Working beneath the vehicle, refit the engine earth strap (Fig. 43).

Fit the transmission selector outer cable in the abutment (2, Fig. 44) and secure it using the pinch-bolt.

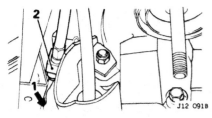

Fig. 44

Refit the transmission selector inner cable to the gearbox selector lever (1, Fig. 44).

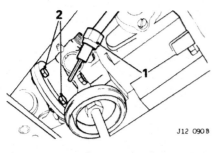

Fig. 45

Reconnect the speedometer cable to the angle drive (1, Fig. 45).

Secure the propeller shaft to the drive flange, using the bolts and new self-locking nuts (2, Fig. 45)

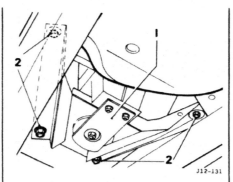

Fig. 46

Refit the body cross-member, offer up the rear mounting spring and plate (2, Fig. 46). Ensure that the spring is correctly located.

Support the mounting plate with a jack and secure

Fit and secure the crash bracket (1, Fig. 46).

Locate the rear heat shield and secure. Fit the intermediate heat shields on either side of the transmission tunnel and secure

Remove the engine support tool MS 53A (1, Fig. 47).

Fit and secure the front exhaust pipes to the exhaust manifolds, using the washers and special nuts

NOTE: Take care not to damage the steering rack gaiters

Refit the rack gaiter and pinion heat shields. Lower the vehicle.

Reconnect the Econocruise control cable (where fitted)

Reconnect the throttle cable (2, Fig. 47) and kick-down switch connections (3, Fig. 47).

Connect the E.C.U. vacuum pipe (4, Fig. 47) to the manifold cross-pipe

Reconnect the starter solenoid to relay and secure the relay to the bulkhead.

Reconnect the starter feed wire to the bulkhead connector. Refit and secure the water valve assembly to the bulkhead.

Reconnect all pipes and hoses; re-position the fresh air grille.

Reconnect the throttle switch, coolant temperature sensor, ballast resistor, and (where fitted) Econocruise, harnesses and secure to the cross-pipe with the plastic ratchet clips.

Refit the transmission upper dipstick tube (5, Fig. 47) to the engine

Reconnect all the vacuum pipes to the manifold (6, Fig. 47).

Refit the R.H. wing stay to the engine compartment, reconnect the brake vacuum hoses to the Reservac pipe, brake servo pipe and manifold one-way valve; clip the pipes to the bulkhead clip. Remove the plugs from the ends of the fuel feed hoses (7, Fig. 47) and reconnect to the engine.

Reconnect the engine and alternator harnesses (8, Fig. 47).

Position the air conditioning receiver–drier to the vehicle, remove all the plugs previously fitted and reconnect the hoses using new 'O' rings

Check alignment of the hoses (9, Fig. 47) before fully tightening them. Displace receiver–drier to allow the fitment of the radiator

Reposition and secure the P.A.S. oil cooler to the front cross-member

Refit the power steering pump and bracket (10, Fig. 47) to the engine; fit and adjust the drive belt

Refit the fuel cooler (11, Fig. 47). Remove the plugs and connect the hose using new 'O' rings. Reconnect all the fuel pipes.

Refit the L.H. wing stay to the engine compartment, refit the battery.

Refit the radiator assembly, connect the bottom hose, heater return hose and coolant level probe.

Refit the fan cowl; do not fully tighten the lower securing nut, to allow final alignment.

Refit the fan and Torquatrol unit (12, Fig. 47) and fan belt, adjust to the correct tension.

Reconnect the transmission oil cooler hoses and top hoses to the radiator.

Reposition the harness to the R.H. top hose.

Refit the engine oil cooler to the radiator, the access grommet and lower radiator grille.

Reposition the receiver–drier assembly to the radiator.

Refit, using new sealing washers, the expansion pipe to the radiator.

Refit the top rail–amplifier assembly to the radiator and body.

Reconnect the thermostat switch harness, align the fan cowl and earth wires, then fully tighten the fan cowl fixings.

Refit the air anti-recirculation panel to the body

Refit the receiver–drier clamps and relays to the top rail

Reconnect the amplifier, ballast resistor, coil and pick-up module (13, Fig. 47) harnesses.

Reconnect the headlamp harness and clip to the radiator top rail, refit the harness cover.

Refit the air cleaners and elements (14, Fig. 47)

Refill the engine with oil and water, the power steering reservoir (15, Fig. 47) with the correct specification fluid, and (if fitted), recharge the air conditioning system

Refit the bonnet.

12—12

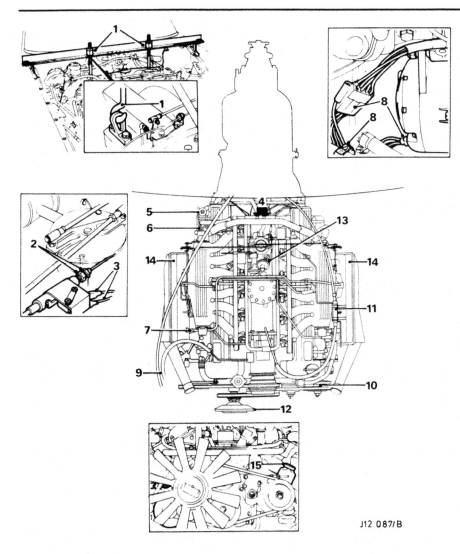

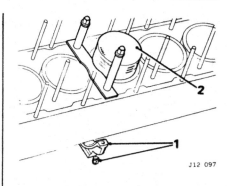

Fig. 48

Fig. 47

CRANKSHAFT

Remove and refit   12.21.33

Follow the procedures detailed under 'Engine
— Dismantle and Reassemble', 12.41.05, as
necessary.

OIL PUMP

Remove and refit   12.60.26

If the oil pump is to be removed, it is necessary
to use procedures from 'Engine — Dismantle
and Reassemble', 12.41.05, that will provide
access. As the work involved is so extensive,
it is recommended that the oil pump is
inspected for wear or damage whenever it is
accessible for other reasons.
The crankshaft **must not** be rotated while the
oil pump is removed.

PISTON AND CONNECTING ROD

Remove and refit   12.17.01

Service tool: Piston ring clamp 18G 55A.

Removing

Remove the engine and gearbox assembly, see
12.37.01.
Remove the cylinder head — 12.29.11/12.
Remove the sump pan and sandwich plate.
Rotate the crankshaft until the bearing cap to
be removed is accessible.
Remove nuts, bearing cap and shell (1, Fig. 48).
Remove any carbon deposit from the top of the
cylinder bore. Push the connecting rod up the
cylinder bore, withdraw the piston (2, Fig. 48)
together with the connecting rod.
Retrieve the remaining bearing shell.

Refitting

Ensure that the cylinder bore, piston and all
bearing surfaces are scrupulously clean.
Coat the piston rings, gudgeon pin, big end
bearing shell and cylinder bore liberally with
clean engine oil.
Ensure that the piston ring gaps are spaced
evenly around the circumference of the piston.
Compress the piston rings with service tool
18G 55A (1, Fig. 49).

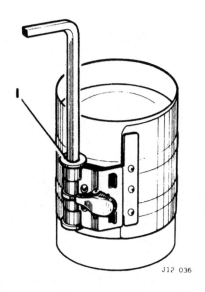

Fig. 49

Enter the piston and connecting rod into the
bore, ensuring that the word stamped 'Front'
on the piston faces the front of the engine.
Push the piston and connecting rod down the
bore, do not use undue force.
Check that the big-end shell bearing tab is correctly located in the connecting rod.
Fit the other half of the big-end bearing shell to
the cap, oil shell and crankshaft journal.
Refit the bearing cap and nuts; tighten the nuts
to the torque quoted in data sheet.
Refit the sandwich plate.
Refit the cylinder head — 'A' right-hand, 'B'
left-hand.
Refit the engine and gearbox assembly.

12—13

TIMING COVER

Remove and refit   **12.65.01**

Removing

Remove the engine and gearbox assembly, see 12.37.01

Remove the cylinder heads, see 12.29.12 and 12.29.11.

Remove the sandwich plate.

Remove the alternator.

Remove the power-assisted steering pump.

Remove the emission control air pump — cars fitted with emission control only.

Remove the air-conditioning compressor and compressor bracket — cars fitted with air conditioning only.

Remove the water pump.

Carefully spread the cone and draw it from the crankshaft.

Remove the bolts, washers and spacers securing the alternator and air pump mounting bracket.

Remove the bolts (1, Fig. 50) and serrated washers securing the timing cover to the cylinder block, noting the relative positions of different length bolts also dowel bolts.

Remove the timing cover (2, Fig. 50) together with the oil seal.

Remove the gaskets (3, Fig. 50) and oil seal (4, Fig. 50) and discard.

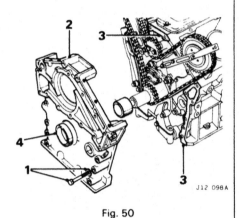

Fig. 50

Refitting

Ensure that the mating surfaces of timing cover and cylinder block are scrupulously clean.

Immerse a new oil seal in clean engine oil and press it into the timing cover.

Smear both sides of each new gasket with a suitable jointing compound and position on the timing cover.

Fit the timing cover, ensuring that the lip on the oil seal is not distorted or damaged.

Fit the bolts and serrated washers; tighten the bolts by diagonal selection.

Reverse the dismantling operations as appropriate.

TIMING CHAIN

Remove and refit   **12.65.12**

Service tool: Jackshaft retaining tool JD 39

Removing

Remove the timing cover, see 12.65.01.

Fit jackshaft retaining tool JD 39.

Disconnect the timing chain from the camshaft and jackshaft sprockets; withdraw the crankshaft sprocket and chain. **Do not rotate the engine.**

Refitting

Reverse the removal operations; check engine timing both statically and by means of a stroboscope.

TIMING CHAIN TENSIONER

Remove and refit   **12.65.28**

Removing

Remove the timing cover, see 12.65.01.

Move the chain tensioner clear of the locating bracket and slide it off the dowel pin.

Refitting

Reverse removal operations.

TIMING CHAIN DAMPERS

Remove and refit   **12.65.50**

Service tool: Timing chain damper setting jig JD 38

Removing

Remove the engine and gearbox assembly, see 12.37.01.

Remove the timing chain, see 12.65.12.

Remove the oil pump, see 12.60.26.

Remove the bolts securing the camshaft sprocket hangers and timing chain dampers to the cylinder block.

Refitting

Fit the camshaft sprocket hangers (1, Fig. 51) and timing chain dampers (2, Fig. 51) to the cylinder block; do not fully tighten the bolts at this stage.

Note the relative position of jackshaft sprocket to jackshaft sprocket retaining tool.

Remove the jackshaft sprocket retaining tool JD 39

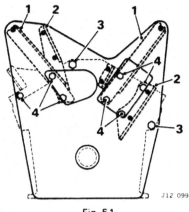

Fig. 51

Position the damper setting jig JD 38 (shown above (Fig. 51)) on the front of the cylinder block; do not overtighten the retaining bolts (3, Fig. 51).

Position the camshaft sprocket hangers and timing chain dampers so that they are in even contact with the locating dowels; tighten the securing bolts (4, Fig. 51).

Remove the damper setting jig JD 38.

Refit the jackshaft sprocket retaining tool JD 39.

Refit the oil pump and timing chain and replace the engine and gearbox assembly.

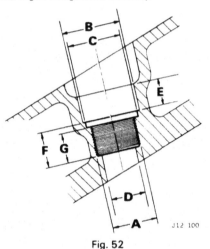

Fig. 52

SPARK PLUG INSERTS PRE HE ONLY

Fitting   **12.29.78**

Remove the cylinder head, see 12.29.10.

Remove the inlet and exhaust valves, see 12.29.18.

Bore out the stripped thread to 19.05 mm (0.750 in) diameter and tap out to 16 UNF—2B—Dimension 'A' (Fig. 52).

Counterbore to 24,13 mm (0.95 in) —Dimension 'B' and dimension 'C' = 22,23 mm (0.875 in).

Dimension 'D' = 14,22 to 14,48 mm (0.560 to 0.570 in).

Dimension 'E' = 10,78 mm (0.425 in).

Dimension 'F' = 15,75 mm (0.575 in).

Dimension 'G' = 11,81 to 11,94 mm (0.465 to 0.470 in).

Fit the screwed insert ensuring that it sits firmly at the bottom of the thread.

12—14

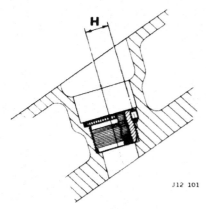

Fig. 53

Drill and ream a 3,17 mm (0.125 in) diameter hole 2,83 mm (0.19 in) deep between the side of the insert and the head. Drive in the locking pin and secure by peening the edge of the insert and the locking pin.
Dimension 'H' = 10,16 mm (0.40 in).

CYLINDER HEAD

Overhaul   **12.29.18**

Service tool: Valve spring compressor J 6118C.

Support valves by means of a wooden block. Compress the valve spring using Service Tool (1, Fig. 54) J 6118C.
Retrieve collars (3, Fig. 54), cotters (4, Fig. 54) and spring retaining plates (5, Fig. 54).
Remove valves (6, Fig. 54) ensuring that they will be refitted in their original guides.

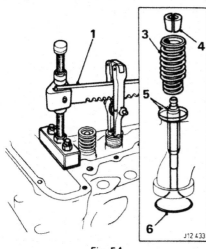

Fig. 54

Remove all traces of carbon from the cylinder head and deposits from the induction and exhaust ports. Great care must be taken to avoid damaging the head; use worn emery cloth and paraffin only.
Check the clearance between the valve guide and stem; this should be 0,025 to 0,10 mm (0.001 to 0.004 in).

Should the guides be worn, proceed as follows:
Immerse the head in boiling water for 30 minutes.
Using a piloted drift, drive the guide out of the head from the combustion chamber end.
Coat the new valve guide with graphite grease and refit the circlip.
Heat the cylinder head.
Using a piloted drift, drive in the guide from the top until the circlip is seated in the groove (1, Fig. 55).

DATA

Replacement guides are available in two sizes and have identification grooves machined in the shank. Sizes are as follows:

First oversize (2 grooves) 12,88 to 12,85 mm (0.507 to 0.506 in) diameter.

Second oversize (3 grooves) 13,00 to 12,98 mm (0.512 to 0.511 in) diameter.

When new guides are to be fitted, they should always be one size larger than the old guide. Cylinder head bores will require reaming as follows:

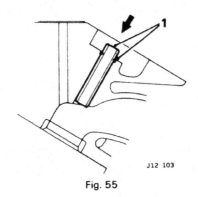

Fig. 55

1st oversize — two grooves
  12,83 mm + 0,012 mm − 0,005 mm
  (0.505 in + 0.0005 in − 0.0002 in).

2nd oversize — three grooves
  12,95 mm + 0,012 mm − 0,005 mm
  (0.510 in + 0.0005 in − 0.0002 in).

Examine the valve seat inserts for pitting or excess wear. If renewal is necessary, proceed as described at items 12 to 16.
Remove the inserts by machining, leaving approximately 0,25 mm (0.010 in) of metal which can easily be removed by hand without damaging the cylinder head.
Measure the diameter of the insert recess in the cylinder head.
Grind down the outside diameter of the new insert to a dimension 0,08 mm (0.003 in) larger than the insert recess.
Heat the cylinder head for half an hour from cold at a temperature of 150°C (300°F).
Fit the insert, ensuring that it beds evenly in the recess.
Renew or reface the valves as necessary.
Correct valve seat angles are:

Inlet	Exhaust
44½ degrees	44½ degrees

Check the valve stems for distortion or wear; renew valves with stems worn in excess of 0,08 mm (0.003 in), see data sheets.
Using a suitable suction tool, grind the valves into their respective seats.

If new valve inserts have been fitted, the clearance between valve stem and cam must be checked, this should be 8,13 mm (0.320 in) plus the valve clearance. The dimension must be taken between the valve stem and the back of the cam. Should this dimension not be obtained, metal must be ground from the valve seat of the insert.

NOTE: Only suitable grinding equipment should be used.

Fit the valves and place the cylinder head on wooden blocks.
Fit the valve spring seats, inlet valve guide oil seals, springs and collars.
Compress the springs using service tool J 6118C insert the split cotters.
Check and adjust valve clearances.
Refit cylinder head.

OIL PUMP

Overhaul   **12.60.32**

Remove the eight bolts and lock washers and detach the pump cover from the gear housing. Mark the drive and driven gear faces (1, Fig. 56) to ensure that when reassembled the gears are replaced in the same position as prior to removal.

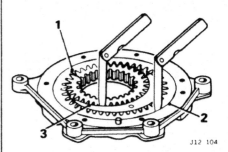

Fig. 56

Remove both gears, wash all parts in clean petrol and dry with compressed air.
Check the condition of all gear teeth and remove any burrs with a fine file.
Refit the driven gear and check the radial clearance between gear and housing.
Checks should not be taken at the six radial flats on the gear.
The clearance should not exceed 0,127 mm (0.005 in), (2, Fig. 56).
Refit the drive gear and check the radial clearance between the gear and crescent.
The clearance should not exceed 0,152 mm (0.006 in), (3, Fig. 56).
Check the gear end-float by placing a straightedge across the joint face of the housing and measuring the clearance between the straightedge and gears.
The figure obtained should not exceed 0.127 mm (0.005 in), (1, Fig. 57).

Reassembly is the reverse of dismantling; ensure that the gears are correctly meshed.
Lubricate the gears with clean engine oil before refitting the pump assembly and check that all surfaces are clean.

12—15

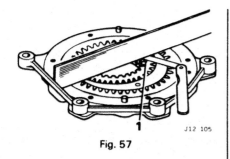

Fig. 57

CAMSHAFT

Overhaul   12.13.26

Check that journal diameters are within limits, see Engine Data.

Ensure that all oil passages are unobstructed; blow through with dry, clean compressed air.

ENGINE

Dismantle and reassemble 12.41.05

NOTE: All instructions, unless otherwise stated, apply to both 'A' bank right-hand and 'B' bank left-hand cylinder head assemblies.

Service tools: Camshaft sprocket retaining tools JD 40; cylinder liner retaining tools JD 41; jack shaft retaining tool JD 39; oil seal pre-sizing tool JD 17B and adaptor JD 17B:1; piston ring clamp 18G 55A; valve timing gauge C 3993; timing chain tensioner retractor tool JD 50.

Dismantling

Drain the lubricating oil sump.

Remove the engine and gearbox, see 12.37.01.

Remove the fuel rails and inlet manifolds.

Remove the exhaust manifolds; refer to Section 30.

Remove the gearbox.

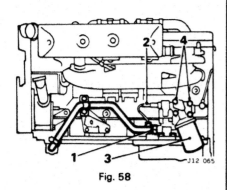

Fig. 58

Remove the hose clip securing the oil pressure relief valve bleed pipe to the top of the sandwich plate (1, Fig. 58).

Remove the setscrews securing the clips (2, Fig. 58) on the oil cooler feed pipe.

Disconnect the oil cooler feed pipe at the pipe union (3, Fig. 58).

Remove the oil filter canister (4, Fig. 58).

Remove the three setscrews (5, Fig. 58) securing by-pass valve union to the sandwich plate.

Remove the four setscrews (6, Fig. 58) securing the filter head to the cylinder block.

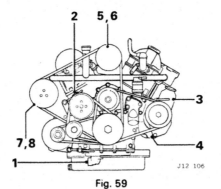

Fig. 59

Release the oil cooler suction pipe union nut (1, Fig. 59).

Slacken the fan belt (2, Fig. 59) and remove the setscrews and nuts securing the fan belt idler pulley assembly. Remove the assembly.

Remove the power steering pump mounting bracket (4, Fig. 59) and adjustment link.

Remove the four setscrews securing the compressor (5, Fig. 59) cars fitted with air-conditioning only.

Remove the compressor mounting bracket (6, Fig. 59) — cars fitted with air conditioning only.

Remove the air pump (7, Fig. 59) (if fitted).

Remove the air pump mounting bracket (8, Fig. 59) and adjustment link.

Release the transmission oil cooler pipe clips and remove the pipes from the engine.

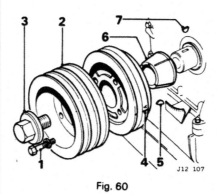

Fig. 60

Remove the four bolts (1, Fig. 60) securing the crankshaft pulley (2, Fig. 60) to the damper; withdraw the pulley.

Remove the damper bolt (3, Fig. 60), strike damper (4, Fig. 60) sharply with a hide mallet; withdraw the damper. Recover the Woodruff key (5, Fig. 60).

Remove the damper cone (6, Fig. 60). Recover the Woodruff key (7, Fig. 60).

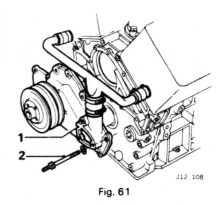

Fig. 61

Remove the setscrews and washers retaining the water inlet spout (1, Fig. 61) to the water pump. Carefully break the seal.

Remove the setscrews, studs (2, Fig. 61) and bolt retaining the water pump. **Carefully** break the seal and remove the water pump and backplate assembly complete with engine cross-pipe.

Remove the distributor and amplifier unit.

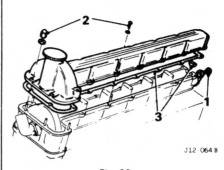

Fig. 62

Remove the banjo bolts (1, Fig. 62) securing the camshaft oil feed pipes to the rear of the tappet blocks and oil gallery. Remove the throttle pedestal, amplifier bracket, heater return pipe and engine cable form.

Remove the alternator and bracket.

Remove the domed head nuts copper washers and setscrews (2, Fig. 62) securing the camshaft covers to the cylinder head; lift off the covers.

Remove and discard the gaskets and neoprene plugs (3, Fig. 62).

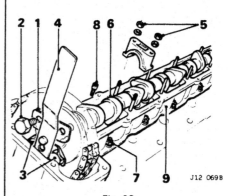

Fig. 63

Bend back the locking tabs (1, Fig. 63) securing the camshaft sprocket retaining bolts.

Remove the two bolts (2, Fig. 63) from each sprocket.

12—16

Use timing chain tensioner retractor tool JD 44 to extend the tensioner to full extent.

Rotate the engine until the remaining bolts (3, Fig. 63) are accessible and remove.

Fit the retaining tool JD 40 (4, Fig. 63) to each sprocket and remove JD 44.

Slacken off the camshaft bearing cap nuts (5, Fig. 63) working from the centre outwards. Remove the camshafts (6, Fig. 63).

Remove the nuts (7, Fig. 63) and capscrews (8, Fig. 63) securing the tappet block to the cylinder head; remove the tappet block (9, Fig. 63) together with the tappets. Note their location.

Retrieve the valve adjusting pads. Note their location.

Progressively slacken the cylinder head nuts, working from the centre outwards. Lift off the cylinder heads and place them on blocks of wood.

Fit the cylinder liner retainers JD 41.

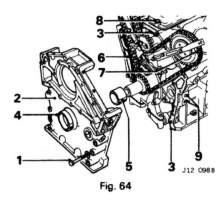

Fig. 64

Remove the bolts (1, Fig. 64) securing the timing cover to the cylinder block, noting the relative positions of long, short and dowelled bolts.

Remove the timing cover (2, Fig. 64), lift off gaskets (3, Fig. 64) and discard them.

Remove the oil seal (4, Fig. 64) from the cover and discard it.

Withdraw the spacer (5, Fig. 64) from the crankshaft.

Move the chain tensioner (6, Fig. 64) clear of locating bracket and slide off dowel pin.

Disengage the timing chain (7, Fig. 64) from sprockets and remove it.

Remove the bolts (8, Fig. 64) securing the jackshaft cover to the cylinder block, lift off cover.

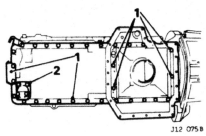

Fig. 65

NOTE: Note the position of the spacing washers and long bolts to assist replacement — non air-conditioned cars only.

Remove the engine mounting brackets (9, Fig. 64), invert the engine and remove the bolts securing the oil sump pan.

NOTE: Note the position of the oil cooler pipe clip.

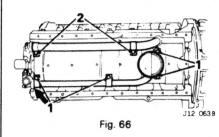

Fig. 66

Remove the bolts (1, Fig. 65) securing the sandwich plate baffle and sandwich plate; recover the crankshaft angle indicator scale. Carefully break the joint and remove all traces of gasket. Remove the suction union elbow (2, Fig. 65) from the sandwich plate.

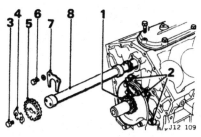

Fig. 67

Remove the four setscrews (1, Fig. 66) and washers securing the suction pipe clips and bracket. Draw the suction pipe from the 'O' ring at the elbow.

Remove the two setscrews (2, Fig. 66) and washers securing the crankshaft undershield and delivery pipe clips. Draw the undershield clear.

Remove the bolt and washer and nut, bolt and washer securing the oil delivery pipe elbow to the oil pump casting. Lift the oil delivery pipe from the crankcase. Remove and discard the gasket.

Withdraw the crankshaft sprocket (1, Fig. 67) and Woodruff key.

Remove the four bolts (2, Fig. 67) securing the oil pump to the cylinder block, withdraw the pump, drive gear and Woodruff key.

Remove the setscrews (3, Fig. 67) and tab washer (4, Fig. 67) securing the sprocket (5, Fig. 67) to the jackshaft; withdraw the sprocket, discard the tab washer.

Remove the bolts (6, Fig. 67) securing the jackshaft locking plate (7, Fig. 67) to cylinder block; lift the plate out of the groove in the jackshaft flange.

Withdraw the jackshaft (8, Fig. 67).

NOTE: Care must be taken to identify the pistons with their respective bores; big-end caps should be fitted to connecting rods immediately after removal.

Remove the nuts securing the connecting rod bearing cap; lift off the cap together with the shell bearing.

Remove the carbon deposit from the top of the bore, push the connecting rod and piston up

the cylinder bore and withdraw.

Repeat the two above operations for the remaining pistons.

Remove the bolts on the locking plate securing the drive plate to the crankshaft.

Lift off the drive plate.

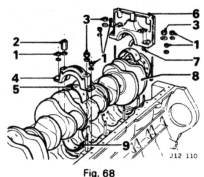

Fig. 68

Remove the small nuts (1, Fig. 68) securing the main bearing caps, starting from the centre bearing.

Remove the pillar nuts (2, Fig. 68) and large nuts (3, Fig. 68) securing the main bearing caps, starting from the centre bearing.

NOTE: Note the location of the pillar nuts to assist replacement.

Lift off the bearing caps (4, Fig. 68) and shell (5, Fig. 68), slide the rear main bearing casting (6, Fig. 68) out of the cylinder block, remove and discard the seals (7, Fig. 68).

Lift the crankshaft (8, Fig. 68) out of the cylinder block, retrieve the upper half of the main bearing shells (9, Fig. 68).

NOTE: If for any reason the cylinder liners are to be removed and re-used, they should be marked 'front' and refitted in their original bores.

Remove cylinder liner retaining tools JD 41.

Position a suitable mandrel between the cylinder liner and the press arbor.

Press out the cylinder liners from below.

CYLINDER LINERS

Checking   12.25.27

Check the bore of the liner and compare the dimension obtained with the dimensions quoted in data sheet.

Bore grade of liner, e.g. 'A' or 'B', is stamped on the top of the liner. When liners are to be renewed; the new liner must be of the same grade as the old one.

Cylinder block — general

Following the engine dismantling operation the crankcase must be thoroughly cleaned.

Check all core plugs and renew any showing signs of corrosion.

Ensure that all galleries are unobstructed. Blow through with dry, clean compressed air.

Check the condition of the studs; renew any showing signs of corrosion.

continued

12—17

Reassembling

CAUTION: Ensure that all components are scrupulously clean, blow out all oil galleries in the crankshaft, camshafts, etc., with dry, clean compressed air.

Smear the shoulders of the cylinder liners with Hylomar and slip them into the cylinder block. Remove excess sealant.

NOTE: Cylinder liners must be fitted dry.

Ensure that liners are correctly seated and fit retaining tools JD 41.

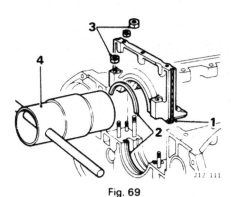

Fig. 69

Seal the grooves (1, Fig. 69) of the rear main bearing casting, with Sealastik.

Fit a new crankshaft rear oil seal (2, Fig. 69), apply one drop of Hermetite into both sealing grooves top and bottom before fitting the seal halves into the grooves.

Fit the main bearing casting to the cylinder block and tighten the retaining nuts (3, Fig. 69).

Pre-size the rear oil seal using service tool JD 17B (4, Fig 69) together with adaptor JD 17B 1.

Remove the rear main bearing casting.

Liberally oil the upper main bearing shells and fit in the cylinder block. Smear the rear oil seal with Dag Colloidal Graphite.

CAUTION: Centre and rear main bearing shells must not be confused with each other; the rear main bearing shell has an oil groove whilst the centre main bearing shell is plain.

Liberally oil the upper main bearing shells and fit in the cylinder block.

Position the crankshaft in the cylinder block.

Fit the bearing shells to the caps; fit the caps, using pillar nuts as noted.

Tighten the securing nuts to the correct torque.

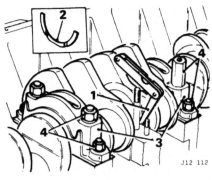

Fig. 70

Check the crankshaft end-float (see 1, Fig. 70). Select thrust washers which will reduce the end-float to 0,10 to 0,15 mm (0.004 to 0.006 in). For sizes of thrust washers available see Engine Data.

Remove the bearing caps and fit the thrust washers selected (2, Fig 70) to groove in block

NOTE: The grooved side of the washers must face outwards

Fit the bearing shells to the caps; oil the shells and crankshaft journals.

Fit crankshaft and main bearings caps.

Remove all traces of oil from the joint faces of the rear main bearing cap and the cylinder block joint face. A small amount of cellulose paint thinners on a soft lint free cloth should be used, taking care to avoid contact with the seal material.

Apply 5,0 mm ($\frac{3}{16}$ in) dia. quantities of the sealant to the bearing cap at the positions marked C, (Fig. 71).

Fit bearing cap, tighten all fixings to specified torque and continue engine rebuild.

To remove old sealant from the joint faces, cellulose paint thinners on a soft lint free cloth should be used.

DO NOT SCRAPE SURFACES TO REMOVE OLD SEALANT

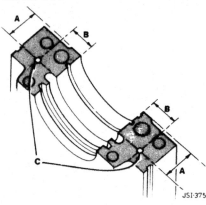

A—32 mm (1.25 in); B—28 mm (1.10 in)

Fig. 71

NOTE: Ensure that the reference marks on the bearing caps face the marks on the cylinder block

Tighten the bearing caps one at a time, working from the centre outwards to the correct torque

Liberally smear the bore of the number one cylinder with clean engine oil

Ensure that the piston ring gaps of number one piston are evenly spaced around the circumference of the piston.

Smear the piston rings with oil and compress using service tool 18G 55A.

Enter the piston and connecting rod into the top of the bore ensuring that 'FRONT' stamped on the piston faces forward. DO NOT use undue force when fitting piston.

Fit the big-end bearing shell to the connecting rod and bearing cap; ensure that the locking tabs on the shells are correctly located.

Oil the shells and crankshaft journal, fit the bearing cap ensuring that it is the correct way round. Tighten the connecting rod nuts to 5,53 to 5,56 kgfm (40 to 41 lbf ft).

Repeat operations to fit the remaining pistons. Check that the engine rotates freely.
Refit the oil pump to the drive gear and secure.

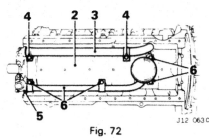

Fig. 72

Use new 'O' ring seals at both ends of the oil delivery pipe (1, Fig. 72).

Locate the crankshaft undershield (2, Fig. 72) on the pillar nuts, and place the oil delivery pipe (3, Fig. 72) into position

Loosely secure the undershield and delivery pipe using two setscrews (4, Fig. 72) and serrated washers.

Use a new 'O' ring seal at the suction elbow (5, Fig 72) and locate the suction pipe.

Secure the suction pipe clips and bracket using four setscrews (6, Fig. 72) and serrated washers Fully tighten all six setscrews securing the undershield.

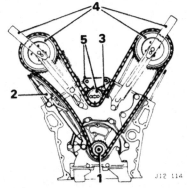

Fig. 73

Refit the drive plate (1, Fig. 73) to the crankshaft, use a new locking plate (2, Fig. 73); tighten the bolts to the correct torque.

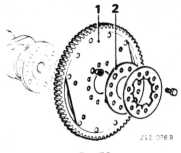

Fig. 74

Refit the crankshaft sprocket (1, Fig. 74).

If a timing chain guide has been renewed, reset all guides, see 12 65 50.

Refit the timing chain tensioner (2, Fig. 74) ensuring that it is fully retracted.

Smear the journals of the jackshaft with clean engine oil and fit the jackshaft

Refit the jackshaft locking plate (3, Fig. 74).

Refit the camshaft sprockets, jackshaft sprocket and chain, use retaining tools JD 40 (4, Fig 74)

12—18

Attach the clock gauge to number one 'A' bank cylinder head stud.

Turn the engine over and by means of the clock gauge set number one 'A' piston at T.D.C. Ensure that the centre punch marks (5, Fig. 74) on the sprocket and jackshaft are at 180° and that the mark on the jackshaft is at the top. Fit jackshaft retaining tool JD 39. Tighten the bolts and turn up the tabs.

Remove jackshaft retaining tool JD 39.

CAUTION: The engine must on no account be rotated until the camshaft sprockets are coupled to the camshafts.

Refit the timing cover, use new crankshaft oil seal and gaskets, tighten the bolts by diagonal selection.

Refit the crankshaft spacer.

If necessary, renew the 'O' ring seal in the oil pump suction elbow.

Fit the sandwich plate to the crankcase, using new gasket, and secure using setscrews and washers. Secure the crankshaft angle indicator scale at the front.

Fit the baffle plate to the sandwich plate.

Fit the oil sump pan, securing the oil cooler pipe bracket as noted.

Fit the suction union elbow to the sandwich plate and secure. Use a new seal.

Remove cylinder liner retaining tools JD 41.

Smear the mating faces of the tappet block and cylinder head with Hylomar.

Refit the tappet block, tighten the nuts and cap screws by diagonal selection, working from the centre outwards.

Refit the camshafts.

Refit the bearing caps, ensuring that the reference marks correspond, tighten the nuts by diagonal selection working from centre outwards to the correct torque.

Adjust the tappets.

Fit the cylinder head gasket with 'TOP' uppermost. Do not use jointing compound or grease. Turn each camshaft until the valve timing gauge C 3993 can be fitted to the slot in the front flange (1, Fig. 76).

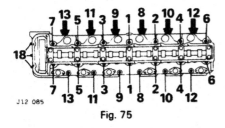

Fig. 75

Refit the cylinder heads, tighten the nuts in the order shown in Fig. 75 to the correct torque. Reconnect the camshaft oil feed pipe.

Remove the retaining tools JD 40 (2, Fig. 76).

Remove the circlip (3, Fig. 76) retaining the camshaft sprocket couplings, press the sprocket on to the camshaft shoulder. Rotate the coupling until the two bolt holes align with the holes in the camshaft.

Refit the couplings to the camshaft sprockets (4, Fig. 76), refit circlip (3, Fig. 76), remove gauge C 3993 (1, Fig. 76).

Bolt the couplings to the camshafts on the tab washers (5, Fig. 76).

Insert screwdriver (6, Fig. 76) through the hole in the timing cover and release the chain tensioner locking catch, refit the rubber grommet.

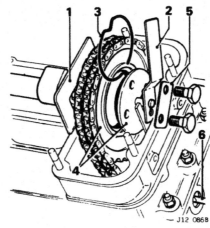

Fig. 76

Rotate the engine until the remaining bolt holes in the coupling are visible.

Fit the remaining bolts, secure all bolts with tab washers.

Use the new camshaft cover gaskets and neoprene sealing plugs.

Refit the camshaft cover, tighten the bolts to the torque quoted in data sheet.

Refit the jackshaft cover.

Replace the alternator and bracket throttle pedestal, distributor, water pump and inlet spout, crankshaft damper and cone, pulleys, starter motor, oil cooler pipes, air pump and compressor (if fitted), fan belt and idler pulley, oil filter head, pipes and canister, automatic transmission and fuel rails.

Tighten all attachments to torque figures quoted in data sheet.

Replace engine and transmission.

Check engine timing by means of a stroboscope.

CRANKSHAFT—GENERAL

NOTE: Due to the extremely hard surface of the crankshaft journals, it is not possible to grind crankshafts satisfactorily.

PISTON AND CONNECTING ROD
Overhaul   12.17.10

NOTE: Pistons are supplied complete with gudgeon pin. As pins and pistons are matched assemblies, it is not permissible to interchange component parts.

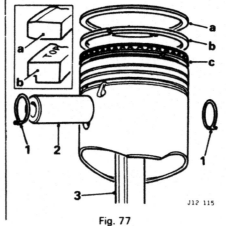

Fig. 77

Remove the circlips (1, Fig. 77).

Push the gudgeon pin (2, Fig. 77) out of the piston.

Withdraw the connecting rod (3, Fig. 77).

Refitting

Fit the gudgeon pin in position.

CAUTION: Connecting rods must be refitted to pistons in such a way that when installed in the engine, the word 'FRONT' on the piston crown faces the front of the engine and the chamfer on the big-end eye faces the crank pin radius.

Align the small-end with the end of the gudgeon pin and push the pin home.

Use new circlips to retain the gudgeon pin.

NOTE: The gudgeon pin is a push fit in the piston at 20°C (60°F). Fit will vary with ambient temperature. Three piston rings are fitted; they are as follows (Fig. 78):

a.   Top ring — compression.
b.   Second ring — compression.
c.   Bottom ring — oil control.

Both top and second rings have tapered peripheries and second rings are marked 'TOP' to ensure correct fitting. In addition, the top ring has a chromium plated periphery and is also cargraph coated. This coating is coloured RED and must not be removed.

The bottom ring consists of an expander sandwiched between two rails.

Check the piston ring gap in the bore. Push the ring to a point midway down the bore, check that the ring is square and measure the gap — see Engine Data.

Fit the bottom ring, ensuring that the expander ends are not overlapping.

Fit the second and top rings, ensuring that they are fitted the correct way up.

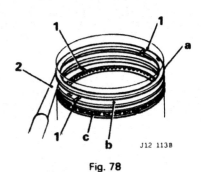

Fig. 78

Position the rings so that the gaps are in the positions shown (1, Fig. 78).

Check the side clearance of the rings in the piston groove (2, Fig. 78)—see Engine Data.

Check the connecting rods for alignment on a suitable jig.

Check the bore of small-end bush — see Engine Data.

CAUTION: If the small-end bush is worn beyond acceptable limits, a service exchange connecting rod must be fitted. It is NOT possible to renew bushes as specialized equipment is needed to hone the bushes to finished size.

12—19

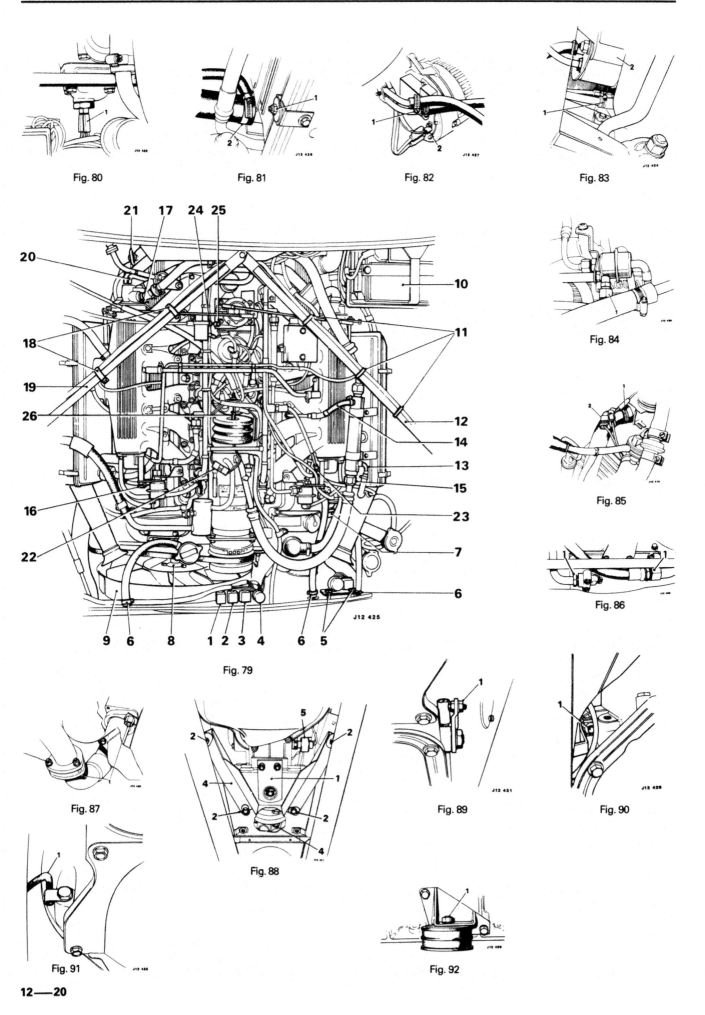

Fig. 80

Fig. 81

Fig. 82

Fig. 83

Fig. 84

Fig. 85

Fig. 86

Fig. 79

Fig. 87

Fig. 88

Fig. 89

Fig. 90

Fig. 91

Fig. 92

12—20

ENGINE ASSEMBLY (V12 HE AIR CONDITIONED AND CRUISE CONTROL)

Renew   12.37.01

Remove bonnet.

Drain coolant and depressurise the air conditioning and fuel systems.

Disconnect head lamp harness block connectors at R.H. inner wing.

Reposition the harness from the radiator top rail to the L.H. side of the vehicle.

Reposition the weather proof cover from the auxiliary coil.

Remove the nuts securing the harness to the auxiliary coil.

Reposition the harness to the engine.

Displace the fuel injection main (1, Fig. 79), pump (2, Fig. 79), cold start relay (3, Fig. 79) and cooling fan relay (4, Fig. 79) from the top rail mounting bracket.

Undo the headlamp/wash wipe relays to the top rail securing screws (5, Fig. 79).

Undo and remove the fan cowl upper securing nuts.

Displace the harness clips and earth leads from the cowl studs.

Disconnect the green/brown harness (coolant temperature switch).

Reposition the harness/relays over the R.H. wing.

Disconnect the thermostatic switch wires (1, Fig. 80).

Disconnect the electric fan motor cooling wires. Swing the harness/relays aside.

Slacken the three coolant hoses to the top rail bleed pipe securing clips (6, Fig. 79).

Disconnect the 3 hoses from bleed pipe.

Remove the bleed pipe to radiator banjo bolt and remove the spacer.

Displace the bleed pipe from retaining clips.

Remove the bleed pipe.

Undo condenser to compressor hose at condenser.

Undo receiver/drier to expansion valve pipe at drier.

Reposition the hose from receiver/drier.

Plug the air conditioning pipes.

Undo and remove top rail securing nuts/bolts (6 off).

Remove top rail auxiliary coil receiver drier and condenser as an assembly.

Remove the air cleaner elements.

Remove the fan cowl lower securing nuts (1, Fig. 81).

Remove the harness clips from the R.H. top hose.

Disconnect both top hoses from the thermostat housing (7, Fig. 79).

Disconnect the transmission cooler hoses at the cooler pipes (1, Fig. 82).

Reposition the transmission hoses through body 'P' clip.

Disconnect the main engine harness multiplug at the lower R.H. inner wing.

Disconnect the warning light wire from the alternator (2, Fig. 82).

Disconnect the heater return pipe hose and the return pipe (1, Fig. 83).

Remove the fan/torquatrol unit (8, Fig. 79).

Displace and remove the fan cowl (9, Fig. 79).

Disconnect the bottom hose from the radiator (2, Fig. 81).

Carefully displace and remove the radiator/hoses assembly.

Remove the battery (10, Fig. 79).

Cut the ratchet straps from the wing stay bar (11, Fig. 79) and reposition the distributor filter/hose to the engine.

Reposition the left hand wing stay bar aside for access (12, Fig. 79).

Disconnect the fuel return (13, Fig. 79) and feed (14, Fig. 79) hoses at the fuel cooler.

Undo the fuel cooler to air box securing screws. Plug the hoses and cooler.

Undo the air conditioning compressor to the fuel cooler union nut at the cooler (15, Fig. 79).

Reposition the fuel cooler over the wing.

Displace the drive belt from the P.A.S. pump.

Reposition the P.A.S. pump (2, Fig. 83) from the engine to the sub frame.

Undo and remove the P.A.S. Cooler securing bolts.

Tie the P.A.S. pump aside to the frame.

Cut and remove the ratchet straps at the engine harnesses.

Disconnect the engine harness multi-plug at the R.H. inner wing.

Disconnect the fuel feed pipe at the regulator union (16, Fig. 79) and (1, Fig. 84).

Disconnect the brake servo vac hoses at the manifold (17, Fig. 79), servo and vac tank.

Remove the servo pipe to the wing stay securing clips (18, Fig. 79).

Remove the servo pipe.

Undo the wing stay to wing securing bolt.

Reposition the wing stay (19, Fig. 79) aside.

Disconnect the vacuum hoses from R.H. rear manifold (air conditioning, gearbox and ignition) (20, Fig.79).

Disconnect water valve heater hose to R.H. water rail at the water valve (1, Fig. 85).

Undo and remove transmission dipstick tube upper securing bolt.

Remove dipstick (21, Fig. 79) and upper tube (to enable lifting hook to locate).

Disconnect starter solenoid wire at the relay red/white.

Disconnect main starter lead from bulkhead terminal post.

Remove ratchet straps securing harness to balance pipe rear of engine.

Disconnect econocruise multi-plug (22, Fig. 79), throttle pot multi-plug and ignition vac timing multi-plug.

Disconnect water temp, air temp and fuel rail heat sink connectors (23, Fig. 79).

Reposition harness aside.

Disconnect full throttle switch connectors (2, Fig. 85) at balance pipe.

Disconnect E.C.U. vac pipe at balance pipe.

Disconnect harness to ignition amplifier connector.

Reposition through 'P' clip at L.H. rear manifold.

Disconnect kickdown switch wires (24, Fig. 79).

Disconnect throttle cable (25, Fig. 79).

Disconnect econocruise cable (26, Fig. 79).

Reposition cable from mounting bracket aside.

Fit Service Tool M.S. 53 across wing channel and locate rear lifting eye.

Raise vehicle on 2 stands.

Undo engine oil cooler pipes at sump (1, Fig. 86) and reposition aside.

Remove L.H. rack gaiter heat shield.

Remove L.H. exhaust down pipe heat shield.

Remove R.H. rack gaiter heatshield.

Disconnect down pipes from manifold (1, Fig. 87).

Remove intermediate heatshields.

Remove gearbox crash bracket (1, Fig. 88).

Take weight of gearbox on jack.

Undo and remove gearbox mounting securing bolts (2, Fig. 88).

Lower jack and remove mounting and spacers spring, etc. (3, Fig. 88).

Remove transmission tunnel heatshield.

Remove transmission tunnel body crossmember.

Disconnect propshaft (4, Fig. 88).

Disconnect speedo transducer multi-plug (5, Fig. 88).

Lower engine on Service Tool MS 53 (10 turns only).

From below:

Disconnect gear lever selector inner (1, Fig. 89) and outer (1, Fig. 90) cables.

Disconnect engine earth lead from body (1, Fig. 91).

Lower vehicle from stands.

Fit wooden block to jack.

Take weight of transmission on jack.

Undo and remove Service Tool MS 53.

Connect lifting hooks to engine.

Undo and remove R.H. engine mounting upper securing nut.

Undo but do not remove R.H. lower securing nut.

Undo and remove L.H. engine mounting upper securing nut (1, Fig. 92).

Clear P.A.S. pipes from L.H. mounting bracket.

Using hoist and jack raise engine from vehicle, ensuring steering rack and bumper are cleared.

Reverse the removal procedure to refit.

PAGE INTENTIONALLY LEFT BLANK

JAGUAR
Daimler

6 CYLINDER

Containing
Sections

17 **EMISSION CONTROL**

19 **FUEL SYSTEM**

26 **COOLING SYSTEM**

30 **MANIFOLD AND EXHAUST SYSTEM**

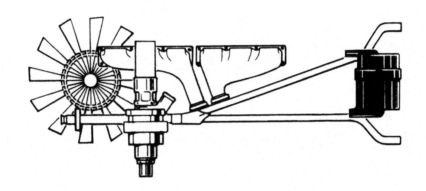

SERIES III
SERVICE MANUAL

INTRODUCTION

This Service Manual covers the Jaguar Series 3 and Daimler Series 3 range of vehicles. It is primarily designed to assist skilled technicians in the efficient repair and maintenance of Jaguar and Daimler vehicles.

Using the appropriate service tools and carrying out the procedures as detailed will enable the operations to be completed within the time stated in the 'Repair Operation Times'.

The Service Manual has been produced in 13 separate sections; this allows the information to be distributed throughout the specialist areas of the modern service facility.

A table of contents in section 1 lists the major components and systems together with the section and book numbers. The cover of each book depicts graphically and numerically the sections contained within that book. Each section starts with a list of operations in alphabetical order.

The title page of each book carries the part numbers required to order replacement books, binders or complete Service Manuals. This can be done through the normal channels.

Operation Numbering

A master index of numbered operations has been compiled for universal application to all vehicles manufactured by Jaguar Cars Ltd., and therefore, because of the different specifications of various models, continuity of the numbering sequence cannot be maintained throughout this manual.

Each operation described in this manual is allocated a number from the master index and cross-refers with an identical number in the 'Repair Operation Times'. The number consists of six digits arranged in three pairs.

Each operation is laid out in the sequence required to complete the operation in the minimum time, as specified in the 'Repair Operation Times'.

Service Tools

Where performance of an operation requires the use of a service tool, the tool number is quoted under the operation heading and is repeated in, following, the instruction involving its use. A list of all necessary tools is included in section 1, number 99.

References

References to the left- or right-hand side in the manual are made when viewing from the rear. With the engine and gearbox assembly removed the timing cover end of the engine is referred to as the front. A key to abbreviations and symbols is given in section 1, number 01.

REPAIRS AND REPLACEMENTS

When service parts are required it is essential that only genuine Jaguar/Daimler or Unipart replacements are used. Attention is particularly drawn to the following points concerning repairs and the fitting of replacement parts and accessories.

1.   Safety features embodied in the vehicle may be impaired if other than genuine parts are fitted. In certain territories, legislation prohibits the fitting of parts not to the vehicle manufacturer's specification.

2.   Torque wrench setting figures given in this Service Manual must be strictly adhered to.

3.   Locking devices, where specified, must be fitted. If the efficiency of a locking device is impaired during removal it must be replaced.

4.   Owners purchasing accessories while travelling abroad should ensure that the accessory and its fitted location on the vehicle conform to mandatory requirements existing in their country of origin.

5.   The vehicle warranty may be invalidated by the fitting of other than genuine Jaguar/Daimler or Unipart parts. All Jaguar/Daimler and Unipart replacements have the full backing of the factory warranty.

6.   Jaguar/Daimler Dealers are obliged to supply only genuine service parts.

SPECIFICATION

Purchasers are advised that the specification details set out in this Manual apply to a range of vehicles and not to any one. For the specification of a particular vehicle, purchasers should consult their Dealer.

The Manufacturers reserve the right to vary their specifications with or without notice, and at such times and in such manner as they think fit. Major as well as minor changes may be involved in accordance with the Manufacturer's policy of constant product improvement.

Whilst every effort is made to ensure the accuracy of the particulars contained in this Manual, neither the Manufacturer nor the Dealer, by whom this Manual is supplied, shall in any circumstances be held liable for any inaccuracy or the consequences thereof.

CONTENTS

EMISSION CONTROL SYSTEM

Description 17.00.00

The emission control system fitted is designed to comply with local legislative requirements. Some or all of the following components may be fitted depending on those requirements. The description that follows refers to cars with an emission control system that complies with North American Federal Specification.

Crankcase breather system

To ensure that piston blow-by gas does not escape from the crankcase to atmosphere, a depression is maintained in the crankcase under all operating conditions. This is achieved by connecting the crankcase breather housing, located at the front of the cylinder head, to the air intake system between the air-flow meter and the throttle housing where a depression exists under all engine operating conditions.

Fuel evaporative loss control

The fuel tank venting is designed to ensure that vapours are vented through the control system even when the car is parked on an inclined surface.

A capacity limited device in the fuel tanks ensures sufficient free volume is available after filling to accommodate fuel which would otherwise be displaced as a result of high temperature rise.

Cars have a fuel tank evaporative loss control system fitted as standard equipment to meet U.S. Federal and Californian requirements.

The system operates as follows:

Interconnected tubing attached to the air vents in both fuel tanks conveys petrol vapour via a sealed storage canister to the throttle body.

The system is completely sealed. However, it is essential that routine maintenance operations detailed in this supplement are carried out by your Dealer at the specified mileage intervals.

Catalytic converters

A catalytic converter is fitted into the exhaust system in order to reduce emissions of carbon monoxide, hydrocarbons, and oxides of nitrogen.

Catalytic converter precautions

1. In order to maintain the efficiency of the emission control system it is essential to use UNLEADED gasoline only; this fuel minimizes spark plug fouling, thereby sustaining engine performance.

2. DO NOT tamper with the engine settings; they have been established to ensure that the vehicle will comply with stringent exhaust emission regulations. Incorrect engine settings could cause unusually high catalytic converter temperatures and thus result in damage to the converter and vehicle. If adjustment to the settings is considered necessary this should be performed by a British Leyland Dealer or other qualified service facility.

3. A correctly tuned engine optimizes exhaust emissions performance and fuel economy and it is recommended that the vehicle is maintained as outlined under **MAINTENANCE SUMMARY** of this manual.

4. DO NOT continue to operate the vehicle if any engine malfunction is evident; malfunctions should be rectified immediately. For instance, misfire, loss of engine performance or engine run-on may lead to unusually high catalytic converter temperature and may result in damage to the converter and car.

5. NEVER leave the vehicle unattended with the engine running.

6. The use of a catalytic converter increases exhaust system temperatures (particularly under engine malfunction), therefore do not operate or park the vehicle in areas where combustible materials such as dry grass or leaves may come into contact with the exhaust system.

7. The vehicle is designed for normal road use. Below are examples of abuse which could damage the catalytic converters and car and may lead to a dangerous condition due to excessively high catalytic converter temperatures:

    a. Competition use
    b. Off roadway use
    c. Excessive engine revolutions
    d. Overloading the vehicle
    e. Excessive towing loads
    f. Switching off the engine and coasting in gear.

8. DO NOT run the engine with either a spark plug lead disconnected or a spark plug removed.

    DO NOT use any device that requires an insert into a spark plug hole in order to generate air pressure (e.g. tyre pump, paint spray attachment, etc.), as this could also result in catalytic converter damage.

9. DO NOT push or tow the vehicle to start it; this could damage the catalytic converters. It is recommended that jumper leads are used.

10. Heavy impact on the converter casing must be avoided as it contains ceramic material which is easily damaged.

Fuel filler caps

Unleaded fuel MUST be used on cataylst-equipped cars, and labels to indicate this are displayed on the fuel gauge and the tank filler caps. The filler caps are designed to accommodate unleaded fuel pump nozzles only. The anti-surge flap prevents leaded fuel from being added to the fuel tanks because it does not open when a leaded fuel pump nozzle is entered into the filler neck up to the position of the restrictor and the pump is switched on.

Misfiring

If the engine misfires, the cause must be immediately rectified to prevent catalytic converter damage.

The emission control system fitted to this engine is designed to keep emissions within legislated limits providing ignition timing and fuel injection settings are correctly maintained and the engine is in sound mechanical condition.

It is essential that routine maintenance operations detailed in this Manual are carried out by your Dealer at the specified mileage intervals.

Exhaust Emission—Testing

In order that exhaust emissions are kept within the legislated limits an idle exhaust emission test MUST be carried out after any unscheduled service operations which might affect the emission control system.

CAUTION: CO content must not exceed 1.5% or be less than 0.5% with the electrical lead to the oxygen sensor disconnected.

It is essential that the equipment used for testing purposes is of the following type:

1. An infra-red CO exhaust gas analyser.

2. Engine and ignition diagnostic equipment.

3. Lucas 'EPITEST' fuel injection diagnostic equipment.

17—2

EXHAUST GAS RECIRCULATION (E.G.R.)

A vacuum operated E.G.R. valve (Fig. 1) meters a proportion of the exhaust gas into the intake system. The exhaust gas is diverted from the rear exhaust manifold and fed via the E.G.R. valve into the rear of the inlet manifold.

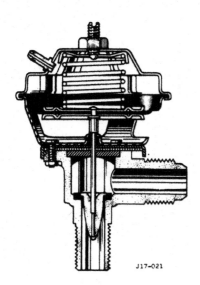

Fig. 1

The vacuum signal 81 mmHg which lifts the valve is obtained from the throttle edge port and is such that no recirculation occurs at idle. The E.G.R. valve has a shaped pintle to give the variation in gas flow required for different engine operating conditions.

THERMAL VACUUM VALVE

With the high rates of E.G.R. required to reduce emission of NO_2 following engine cold starting, it is necessary to inhibit the E.G.R. until the engine is part warm.
A thermal vacuum (Fig. 2) at the rear of water rail senses coolant temperature. The vacuum signal is switched to the E.G.R. valve when its temperature-sensitive bi-metal discs which open the valve on rising temperature (43°C) and close on a falling temperature of 33°C.

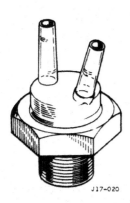

J17-020

Fig. 2

Another throttle edge vacuum port operates the distributor vacuum capsule (6) rotating the base plate and relative to the reluctor. This vacuum port is positioned such, that when the throttle is in the idling or near fully open there is insufficient vacuum to operate the capsule. To delay the operation of the vacuum advance capsule, a delay valve is fitted in the signal pipe between the capsule and the throttle edge port. This valve consists of sintered discs which determines the vacuum delay, and a non-return by-pass valve which allows the vacuum in the distributor capsule to dissipate immediately the signal is removed.

EMISSION CONTROL SYSTEM

Evaporative Loss

Description

Hydrocarbon emissions in the form of fuel vapour are emitted from vehicle fuel tanks (1, Fig. 3).
To prevent these emissions entering the atmosphere the fuel tanks have unvented, sealed filler caps.
The vapour is passed to a vapour storage canister (2, Fig. 3) containing activated charcoal which absorbs the vapours when the vehicle is stationary and desorbs them when the engine is running.
The desorption or purging is obtained by connecting the purge pipe from the canister to a vacuum source via a 3mm restriction located at the junction of the purge pipe and the crankcase breather pipe (3, Fig. 3).
To ensure that piston blow-by gases do not escape from the crankcase a depression is maintained in the crankcase under all operating conditions.

This is achieved by a pipe (with 6mm restriction) connecting the crankcase breather housing (at the front of the cylinder head) to a port in the throttle housing (air cleaner side) upstream of the throttle disc, such that a depression is created in the breather pipe at all times.
The depression is at minimum at closed throttle and maximum at full throttle.

Charcoal canister

The canister is mounted in the R.H. front wheel arch. Filter pads above and below the charcoal prevent the ingress of foreign matter or passage of charcoal into the purge line.
Emissions from the fuel tanks enter at the bottom of the canister and the purging air enters at the top, passing through the charcoal to the purge outlet at the top of the canister to the vacuum source.

Fuel expansion and tank venting

The fuel tanks, mounted in each rear wing, have a 10% expansion volume incorporated, obtained by limiting the amount of fuel into the tank.
A fuel filler tube extends into the tank to the required level.
A 1mm orifice (6, Fig. 3) at the top of the filler neck extension allows the expanding fuel to slowly displace the air from the tank into the venting system via the filler neck and a port in the tanks side panels to vapour separators (4, Fig. 3) in each rear screen pillar.
Condensed vapour drains back to the tanks. Excess vapour is passed to the charcoal canister via a pipe under the floor and a pressure relief valve (5, Fig. 3). The valve controls the flow of vapour.

continued

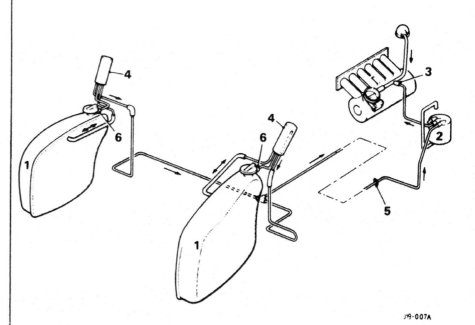

J19-007A

Fig. 3

17—3

When the fuel tanks are full and pressurized, to prevent fuel spillage when the filler cap is released it is necessary to lower the level of the fuel below the filler neck extension.

A domed restriction tank is sealed to the inside of the tank side panel. This tank occupies fuel space during refuelling.

To lower the fuel level fuel is allowed to flow into the restriction tank via a 2,5mm orifice.

Fuel filler cap

Each tank has a lockable fuel filler cap incorporating a pressure blow-off facility. A spring-loaded seal is mounted on the filler neck flap and seats on the filler neck face. No vacuum relief is provided. Incorporated in the filler neck is the leaded fuel restriction.

Pressure relief valve

This valve (5, Fig. 3) controls the transfer of vapour from the vapour separators to the charcoal canister (2, Fig. 3), and prevents the transfer until a pre-set pressure is exceeded.

To allow a flow to the tanks from the canister a vacuum relief is incorporated.

EMISSION TEST AND CHECKS (1979)

3.4 Cars

Anti-run-on valve check

Run engine at idle, switch off ignition, listen for operation of E.G.R. valve two to five seconds after the engine has stopped.

Restart engine and idle.

Disconnect black lead from anti-run-on valve solenoid.

Connect —ve lead from battery to anti-run-on valve solenoid.

Engine should stop immediately connection is made.

Remove lead and replace original black lead. Switch off ignition.

XJ6 Fuel Injection with E.G.R. Valve—Australia—Check E.G.R.

Run engine at idle speed when warm after probe.

Slowly open throttle to 2000 rev/min. Observe movement of E.G.R. valve spindle.

XJ6 Fuel Injection with Catalyst and Oxygen Sensor—U.S.A./Canada/Japan

Remove exhaust manifold sample cap and fit sample pipe to manifold.

Run engine until warm (engine temperature 90). Clamp off extra air valve hose. If idle speed drops, warm up for extra five minutes. Adjust idle speed (750 rev/min) using screw in air distribution block.

Connect exhaust analyser to sample pipe. Read off CO emission.

Reading should be 0.5 to 1.5 %. Adjust screw in air metering unit. Disconnect manifold vacuum pipe from fuel pressure regulator. Blank off pipes.

Observe CO reading. After five seconds reading should increase and after a further few seconds return to original reading.

This indicates correct operation of the oxygen sensor.

XJ6 Fuel Injection—European

Run engine at 2000 rev/min in neutral or 'N' for ten seconds. Close throttle and allow engine to idle for fifteen seconds.

Insert probe into tail pipe or connect sample pipe to manifold. Switch analyser switch to 'T' in Test (Sun-Tester EPA 75).

Read off CO 0.56 to 1.5 %. If incorrect, adjust setting screw in air metering unit to achieve correct CO reading.

XJ6 Fuel Injection with Catalyst and Oxygen Sensor—USA/Canada/Japan

Switch off engine after warm-up. Remove plug from exhaust manifold sample cap and fit sample pipe to manifold. Disconnect oxygen sensor electrical lead.

Run engine at 2000 rev/min for 10 seconds in Neutral or 'N' then close throttle, allow to idle. Connect exhaust analyser to sample pipe, switch to 'T' or Test.

Read off CO 0.5 to 1.5 %. Adjust setting screw in the air metering unit to achieve correct CO reading.

Switch off ignition, remove sample pipe from exhaust manifold. Replace plugs. Restart engine, run at 2000 rev/min, close throttle and allow idle to stabilize. Reconnect oxygen sensor lead.

Insert probe into tail pipe. Read off emission level from analyser.

LUCAS CONSTANT ENERGY IGNITION

A Lucas Constant Energy Ignition System is fitted to XJ 4.2 E.F.I. Models on Series III. The new ignition system operates by maintaining the energy stored in the coil at a constant level, allowing the output voltage to remain constant over a wide range of engine speeds. The power dissipated in both the coil and module compared with equivalent constant dwell systems is greatly reduced.

Constant energy system component description

Amplifier AB 14

The amplifier consists of a solid state electronic module housed in a aluminium case with two pre-wired leads which connect to the low tension terminals on the ignition coil.

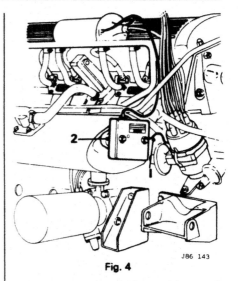

Fig. 4

Connection from the distributor pick-up module is made by an assembly of two leads inside a screening braid which plugs into a socket on the amplifier side (1, Fig. 4). The amplifier mounting is shown in (2, Fig. 4).

Distributor (45 DM)

The distributor incorporates a standard automatic advance system, anti-flash shield (1, Fig. 5), rotor arm, and cover (2, Fig. 5). The previous pick-up and module assembly is replaced by a reluctor and pick-up module (3, Fig. 5). The reluctor is a gear-like component (with as many teeth as there are cylinders) which is mounted on the distributor drive shaft.

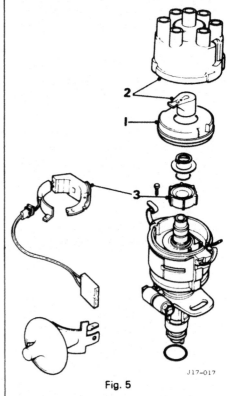

Fig. 5

The pick-up module consists of a winding around a pole-piece attached to a permanent magnet.

The distributor is pre-wired with two leads terminating in a moulded two-pin inhibited connector, which plugs into the amplifier previously described.

During normal service the air gap between the reluctor and the pick-up module does not alter and will only require re-setting if it has been tampered with. If it is necessary to adjust the gap, then it should be set so that the minimum clearance between the pick-up and the reluctor teeth is not less than 0,20 mm (0.008 in). The gap should not be set wider than 0,35 mm (0.014 in) (1, Fig. 6).

The air gap is measured between a reluctor tooth and the pick-up module and should be checked with a plastic feeler gauge. The use of a metal feeler gauge may result in a misleading gauge reading due to the pick-up module contacts being magnetic. However, their use will not affect the electical operation of the pick-up module.

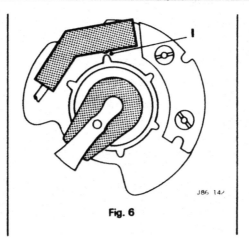

Fig. 6

FAULT FINDING PROCEDURE

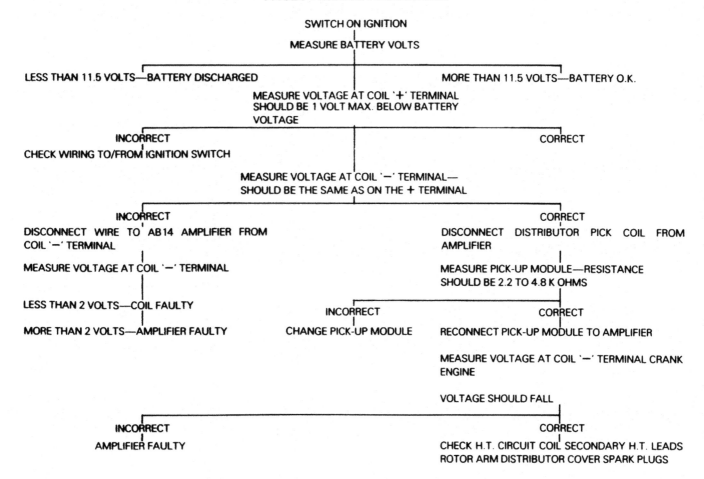

SWITCH ON IGNITION

MEASURE BATTERY VOLTS

LESS THAN 11.5 VOLTS—BATTERY DISCHARGED   MORE THAN 11.5 VOLTS—BATTERY O.K.

MEASURE VOLTAGE AT COIL '+' TERMINAL
SHOULD BE 1 VOLT MAX. BELOW BATTERY
VOLTAGE

INCORRECT   CORRECT
CHECK WIRING TO/FROM IGNITION SWITCH

MEASURE VOLTAGE AT COIL '—' TERMINAL—
SHOULD BE THE SAME AS ON THE + TERMINAL

INCORRECT   CORRECT
DISCONNECT WIRE TO AB14 AMPLIFIER FROM   DISCONNECT DISTRIBUTOR PICK COIL FROM
COIL '—' TERMINAL   AMPLIFIER

MEASURE VOLTAGE AT COIL '—' TERMINAL   MEASURE PICK-UP MODULE—RESISTANCE
                                                   SHOULD BE 2.2 TO 4.8 K OHMS

LESS THAN 2 VOLTS—COIL FAULTY   INCORRECT   CORRECT

MORE THAN 2 VOLTS—AMPLIFIER FAULTY   CHANGE PICK-UP MODULE   RECONNECT PICK-UP MODULE TO AMPLIFIER

                                                   MEASURE VOLTAGE AT COIL '—' TERMINAL CRANK
                                                   ENGINE

                                                   VOLTAGE SHOULD FALL

INCORRECT   CORRECT
AMPLIFIER FAULTY   CHECK H.T. CIRCUIT COIL SECONDARY H.T. LEADS
                                                   ROTOR ARM DISTRIBUTOR COVER SPARK PLUGS

17—5

FAULT FINDING

This chart indicates the possible areas of the cause of the faults. Perform checks and remedial action shown in the order given until the fault is rectified.

Details of the checks and remedial action are given on the respective area charts.

Extra checks shown in brackets refer only to the specific condition shown in brackets after the symptom.

SYMPTOM	POSSIBLE CAUSES IN ORDER OF CHECKING
Will not start (warm engine)	B1, B2, D1, D2, A1, A13, (A5), A5, A3, A6, A7, C1, C2, C3, A20 A8, A18.
Poor or erratic idle (cold engine)	D1, D2, A1, A12, A6, (A5), A3, C4, C6, C3, C5, A10, B4, B3, B6, (A13), E1, E3, E4, E5, A21, A7, A8, A18.
Hestitation or flat spot (cold engine)	D1, D2, A1, A4, (A5), A9, A3, A6, B5, (A13), C4, C6, C3, C5, A15, B4, B3, B6, E1, E3, E4, E5, A7, A8, A18.
Excessive fuel consumption	D3, A4, A5, B5, B4, B3, B6, B8, B7, E1, E3, E4, E5, A21, A7, A19, A8, A18.
Lack of engine braking or high idle speed	A2, A16, A9, A12, A3, A13, A10, C3, B5, A14, B6.
Lack of engine power	D1, D2, A1, A4, A5, A17, A3, B5, A15, A6, C4, C6, C3, C5, B4, B3, B6, E1, E3, E4, E5, A8, A18.
Engine overheating	B7, B8, C4.
Engine cuts out or stalls (at idle)	D1, D2, A1, A7, (A12), (A5), A5, A15, (A3), B4, A6, C4, C6, C3, C5, B6, E1, E3, E4, E5, B3, A8, A18.
Engine misfires	D1, D2, A1, A5, A6, A3, C4, C6, C3, C5, A15, B4, B3, B6, E1, E3, E4, E5, A21, A8, A18.
Fuel smells	D3, A5, E4, E2, E3, E5, A15, A19, A21, A8, A18.
Engine runs on	D1, A12, A16, A10, E4, E3, B7, B8, C3, C5.
Engine knock or pinking	D1, C3, C5, B7, B8.
Arcing at plugs	C4, C6.
Lean running (low CO)	A1, A14, A4, A2, A7, D1, D2, B6, E1, E3, E4, E5, A8, A18.
Rich running (excess CO)	A5, E5, A19, A21, A8, A18.
Backfiring in exhaust	D1, D2, A1, A15, B4, B6, C3, E1, A8, A18.

ELECTRONIC FUEL INJECTION SYSTEM CHECKS

	POSSIBLE CAUSE	CHECK AND REMEDIAL ACTION
A1	Connections	Ensure all connector plugs are securely attached. Ensure electronic control unit (E.C.U.) multi-pin connector is fully made. Ensure all ground connections are clean and tight.
A2	Air leaks	The engine will run weak because air leaking into the manifold is not mo itored by the air-flow metering device. Ensure all hose and pipe connections are secure. Check all joints for leakage and re-make as necessary.
A3	Sticking air flap	Ensure that the air-flow meter flap moves freely. If the flap sticks, the air-flow meter should be replaced.
A4	Throttle switch	Check function of full load switch or vacuum switch.
A5	Cold start system inoperative	Check function of cold start system (see Epitest Section 3).
A6	Triggering system	Check function of triggering system (from coil).
A7	Temperature sensors	Check sensors for open and short circuit.
A8	E.C.U.	As a last resort the E.C.U. should be checked by substitution.
A9	Throttle butterfly adjustment	Reset as per operation.
A10	Throttle by-pass valve	The valve should be suitably adjusted until fault has been rectified and re-check function.
A12	Incorrect idle speed	This should be adjusted by means of the screw on the air distribution block.
A13	Auxiliary air valve inoperative	Test in accordance with operation 19.20.17.
A14	Throttle spindle leaks	Check seals, bearings and spindles for wear. Renew as required.
A15	Air cleaner blocked	Inspect element, and renew as necessary.
A16	Throttle sticking	Lubricate, check for wear and reset.
A17	Throttle inhibited	Check and remove obstructions of free movement of throttle mechanism through total travel. If no obstructions apparent, reset.
A18	Air-flow meter	As a last resort, the air-flow meter should be checked by substitution.
A19	Oxygen sensor	The oxygen sensor should be checked by substitution.
A20	Power resistors	The power resistors should be checked by substitution.
A21	Injector faults	Check function of injectors.

BASIC ENGINE CHECKS

	POSSIBLE CAUSE	CHECK AND REMEDIAL ACTION
B1	Low battery condition	Check battery condition with hydrometer. Re-charge, clean and secure terminals, or renew as necessary. (If battery is serviceable but discharged, trace and rectify cause of flat battery, e.g. short circuit or insufficient charge from alternator.)
B2	Start system deficient	If starter fails to turn engine briskly, check engagement circuit and connections. Check and clean main starter circuit and connections.
B3	Poor compressions	Check compressions with proprietary tester. If compressions are low or uneven, check/adjust valve clearance and re-test. If compressions are still unsatisfactory remove cylinder head for further examination and rectification.
B4	Exhaust system leaking or blocked	Check, and rectify as necessary.
B5	Faults on areas of vehicle other than engine.	Check for binding brakes, slipping clutch, etc.
B6	Air leaks at inlet manifold	Check inlet manifold/cylinder head joint. Re-make with new gasket if necessary. Check manifold tappings for leaks—seal as necessary.
B7	Cooling system blocked or leaking	Flush system and check for blockage. Check hoses and connections for security and leakage. Renew as necessary. Check thermostat, and renew if faulty.
B8	Cylinder head gasket leaking.	Check cylinder block/head joint for signs of leakage. Renew gasket if necessary.

IGNITION SYSTEM CHECKS

	POSSIBLE CAUSE	CHECK AND REMEDIAL ACTION
C4	System deterioration	Check ignition wiring for fraying, chafing and deterioration. Check distributor cap for cracks and tracking and rotor condition. Renew leads, cap or rotor as necessary.
C5	Advance system faults	Disconnect vacuum pipes and check operation of advance mechanism against advance figures, using stroboscopic timing light. Lubricate or renew as necessary. Re-connect vacuum pipes and check operation of advance unit. Renew or secure vacuum pipes if necessary.
C6	Spark plug faults	Remove spark plugs, clean, reset gap and test on proprietary spark plug testing machine. Renew if in doubt.

FUEL SYSTEM CHECKS

	POSSIBLE CAUSE	CHECK AND REMEDIAL ACTION
D1	Insufficient, incorrect or contaminated fuel	Ensure that the fuel tank has an adequate level of the correct grade of fuel. If dirt or water contamination is suspected, drain and flush the fuel tank, flush the system and renew the fuel line filter before filling with clean fuel.
D2	Fuel starvation	Check fuel pressure according to operation 19.45.12. if not satisfactory, check fuel feed pipes for leaks or blockage. Renew connectors if damaged or deteriorated. If contamination of fuel is discovered, flush fuel system and renew line filter. If necessary, renew fuel line filter, pressure regulator or fuel pump to rectify.
D3	Leaking fuel	Check fuel system for leaks and rectify as necessary. Renew any doubtful connectors.

EVAPORATIVE AND CRANKCASE VENTILATION SYSTEM CHECKS

	POSSIBLE CAUSE	CHECK AND REMEDIAL ACTION
E1	Engine oil filter cap loose or leaking	Check cap for security. Renew cap if seal is deteriorated.
E2	Fuel filler cap defective	Check seal for condition—renew if deteriorated. Check filler cap for security—rectify or renew as necessary.
E3	Restrictors missing or blocked	Check and clear or renew as necessary.
E4	Hoses blocked or leaking	Check and clear as necessary. Renew any deteriorated hoses.
E5	Charcoal canister restricted or blocked	Inspect, and renew if necessary.

ENGINE BREATHER FILTER

Remove and refit   **17.10.02**

Removing

Remove the hose clip securing the rubber cover to breather housing and disconnect. Remove the rubber cover and lift out the filter (Fig. 7).

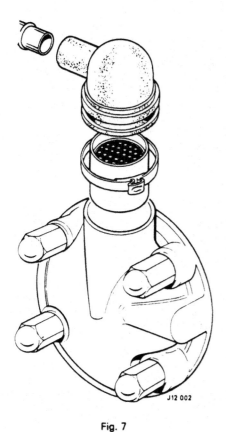

Fig. 7

Refitting

Refitting is a reversal of the above procedure.

ADSORPTION CANISTER

Remove and refit   **17.15.13**

Removing

Remove the front right-hand road wheel. Detach the pipes from the canister (1, Fig. 8). Remove the nut, spring washer, plain washer and bolt (2, Fig. 8) securing the canister clamp to the mounting strap and withdraw the canister (3, Fig. 8).

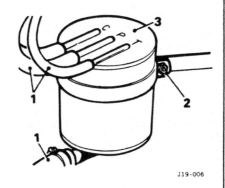

Fig. 8

Refitting

Refitting is a reversal of the above procedure.

CATALYTIC CONVERTER

Remove and refit   **17.50.01**

Removing

Raise the vehicle on a ramp.
Remove the nuts, plain washers and bolts securing the flanges, separate the intermediate pipe from the down-pipe. Ensure that the intermediate pipe is adequately supported.
Remove the nuts and plain washers securing the heatshield and down-pipe to the exhaust manifolds, withdraw the heatshield.
Withdraw down-pipe/catalyst (Fig. 9).

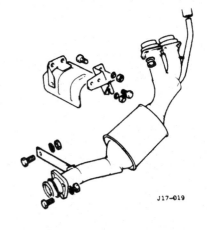

Fig. 9

Refitting

When refitting, first coat all joints with Firegum. Tighten the down-pipe and clamping flange fixings by diagonal selection to avoid distortion.

AIR SWITCHING VALVE VACUUM FEED HOSE

Renew   **17.25.46**

Open the bonnet.
Cut and remove the plastic straps securing the vacuum feed hose.
Disconnect the vacuum feed hose from the air switching valve.
Disconnect the hose from the manifold.
Remove the vacuum hose.
Fit the new vacuum hose to the engine.
Connect the hose to the manifold.
Connect the hose to the air switching valve.
Reposition the hose to its mounting position and secure with plastic straps.
Close the bonnet.

HOSE — FEED PIPE TO AIR CLEANER

Renew   **17.25.45**

Open the bonnet.
Slacken the air cleaner feed pipe to the air cleaner hose securing clips.
Disconnect the hose from the air cleaner.
Remove the hose assembly from the feed pipe.
Remove the hose clips.
Place the hose aside.
Place the new hose to the front.
Fit the hose clips.
Fit the hose assembly to the feed pipe.
Connect the hose to the air cleaner.
Tighten the hose clips.
Close the bonnet.

HOSE — AIR SWITCHING VALVE TO AIR CLEANER FEED PIPE

Renew   **17.25.44**

Open the bonnet.
Slacken the air switching valve to the air cleaner feed pipe hose clips.
Disconnect the hose from the switching valve.
Remove the hose assembly from the air pipe.
Remove the hose clips.
Place the hose aside.
Place the new hose to the front.
Fit the hose clips.
Fit the hose assembly to the air feed pipe.
Connect the hose to the air switching valve.
Tighten the hose clips.
Close the bonnet.

HOSE — CHECK VALVE TO AIR RAIL

Renew   **17.25.43**

Open the bonnet.
Slacken the check valve to air rail hose securing clips.
Disconnect the hose from the air rail.
Remove the hose assembly.
Remove the clips.
Place the hose aside.
Place the new hose to the front.

Fit the hose clips.
Fit the hose assembly to the check valve.
Connect the hose to the air rail.
Tighten the hose clips.
Close the bonnet.

HOSE — AIR RAIL FEED PIPE TO CHECK VALVE

Renew   **17.25.42**

Open the bonnet.
Slacken the air rail feed pipe to check valve hose clips.
Disconnect the hose from the check valve.
Remove the hose assembly from the feed pipe.
Remove the hose clips.
Place the hose aside.
Place the new hose to the front.
Fit the hose clips.
Fit the hose assembly to the feed pipe.
Connect the hose to the check valve.
Tighten the hose clips.
Close the bonnet.

HOSE — AIR SWITCHING VALVE TO AIR RAIL FEED PIPE

Renew   **17.25.41**

Open the bonnet.
Slacken the air switching valve to air rail feed hose securing clips.
Disconnect the hose from the feed pipe.
Remove the hose from air pump.
Remove the hose clips.
Place the hose aside.
Place the new hose to the front.
Fit the hose clips.
Fit the hose to the air pump.
Connect the hose to the feed pipe.
Tighten the hose clip.
Close the bonnet.

THERMAL SWITCH

Renew   **17.25.40**

Open the bonnet.
Remove and refit the pressure cap to the relieve coolant pressure.
Disconnect the switch feed wires.
Undo and remove the switch.
Fit and tighten the new switch.
Connect the switch feed wires.
Close the bonnet.

AIR SWITCHING VALVE

Renew   **17.25.38**

Open the bonnet.
Disconnect the switching valve block connector.
Disconnect the switching valve vacuum hose.
Slacken the air cleaner feed pipe hose securing clip.
Disconnect the hose from valve.
Slacken the air rail feed pipe hose securing clip.
Disconnect the hose from valve.
Undo and remove the switching valve to **lower** air pump securing nuts.
Remove the air switching valve.
Remove and discard the switching valve gasket.
Clean the gasket faces.
Fit the new valve gasket.
Fit the new switching valve.
Fit and tighten the switching valve securing nuts.
Connect the air rail feed pipe hose to the valve.
Tighten the hose clip.
Connect the air cleaner feed pipe hose to the valve.
Tighten the hose clip.
Connect the valve vacuum feed hose.
Connect the valve block connector.
Close the bonnet.

CHECK VALVE/NON RETURN VALVE

Renew   **17.25.21**

Open the bonnet.
Slacken the valve hose securing clips.
Disconnect the air rail feed hose from the valve.
Remove the check valve assembly.
Undo and remove the check valve from the union.
Fit and tighten the check valve to the union.
Fit the check valve assembly to the feed hose.
Connect the air rail feed hose.
Tighten the hose clips.
Close the bonnet.

AIR RAIL — SINGLE

Renew   **17.25.17**

Open the bonnet.
Slacken the air rail feed hose clip.
Disconnect the hose from air rail.
Undo and remove the heat shield to air rail securing nuts.
Remove clamp halves.
Displace the rear plug lead bracket for access.
Remove the heat shield.
Undo the air rail to cylinder head union nuts.
Remove the air rail assembly.
Remove and discard the air rail olives.
Finally remove the union nuts.
Place the air rail aside.
Clean the air rail, seatings and olives.
Place the new air rail to the front.
Fit the air rail union nuts.
Fit the new sealing olives.
Fit and seat the air rail assembly to the head.
Seat the air rail sealing olives.
Tighten the union nuts.
Fit the heat shield to the air rail.

17—10

Fit the heat shield clamps.
Fit and tighten the heat shield securing nuts.
Reposition and secure the plug lead bracket.
Connect the air rail feed hose.
Tighten the hose clip.
Close the bonnet.

AIR PUMP DRIVE BELT

Renew   17.25.15

Open the bonnet.
Undo the link arm adjusting nut.
Slacken the link arm trunnion nut.
Slacken the link arm pivot bolt.
Slacken the pump pivot nut/bolt.
Pivot the pump to the engine.
Release the drive belt from the pulley.
Slacken the power steering pump adjuster link trunnion.
Slacken the adjuster link eye bolt at the power assisted steering pump.
Slacken the power steering pump pivot bolt/nut.
Slacken the adjuster link lock nut.
Pivot the power steering pump towards the engine.
Release the power steering pump from the air pump drive belt pulley.
Reposition the air pump belt from the pulley and into the fan cowl.
Release the drive belt from the fan blades.
Remove the air pump drive belt.
Clean the pulley registers.
Fit the new belt to engine.
Engage the belt over fan blades.
Reposition the air pump belt behind the P.A.S. belt.
Reposition the P.A.S. belt over the pullies.
Tighten the adjusting nut.
Check the tension and tighten the locknut.
Tighten the adjuster link trunnion bolt.
Tighten the adjuster link eye bolt.
Tighten the pump pivot nut/bolt.
Engage the drive belt over the air pump pulley.
Pivot the pump from the engine.
Tighten the link arm adjusting nut to obtain the correct belt tension.
Tighten the lock nut.
Tighten the link arm trunnion nut.
Tighten the link arm pivot bolt.
Tighten the air pump pivot bolt.
Close the bonnet.

AIR PUMP BELT

Tensioning   17.25.13

Open bonnet.
Slacken the air pump pivot nut/bolt.
Slacken the link arm pivot bolt.
Slacken the link arm trunnion nut.
Slacken the link arm locknut.
Tighten the link arm adjusting nut to give the correct belt tensioning.
Tighten the link arm locknut.
Tighten the link arm trunnion nut.
Tighten the link arm pivot bolt.
Tighten the air pump pivot nut/bolt.
Close the bonnet.

AIR PUMP

Renew   17.25.07

Open bonnet.
Disconnect the switching valve block connector and the switching valve vacuum hose.
Slacken the air cleaner feed pipe hose securing clip.
Disconnect the hose from the valve.
Slacken the air rail feed pipe hose securing clip.
Disconnect the hose from the valve.
Manually tension the air pump drive belt and break 'Sticktion' of pump pulley securing bolts.
Undo the link arm adjusting nut.
Slacken the link arm trunnion nut.
Undo and remove the air pump pivot nut only.
Undo the link arm pivot bolt.
Pivot the pump to the engine.
Disconnect the drive belt from the pulley.
Finally remove the pump pulley securing bolts.
Remove the pump pulley.
Finally remove the link arm pivot bolt.
Pivot the link arm aside.
Remove the link arm spacer.
Finally remove the pump pivot bolt.
Remove the air pump assembly.
Undo and remove the air switching valve securing nuts.
Remove the switching valve.
Remove and discard the gasket.
Undo and remove the air switching valve studs.
Place the pump aside.
Clean the gasket faces.
Place the new air pump to front.
Fit and tighten the switching valve studs.
Fit switching valve gasket.
Fit switching valve to pump.
Fit and tighten the switching valve securing nuts.
Fit the pump assembly to engine.
Fit but do not tighten the pump pivot nut/bolt.
Align the pump and link arm and fit the spacer.
Fit but do not tighten the link arm pivot bolt.
Fit the pump pulley to pump.
Fit but do not tighten the pump securing bolts.
Engage the drive belt over the pump pulley.
Pivot the pump from the engine.
Tighten the link arm adjusting nut to obtain the correct belt tension.
Tighten the lock nut.
Tighten the link arm trunnion nut.
Finally tighten the link arm pivot bolt.
Finally tighten the pump pivot bolt/nut.
Manually tension the belt.
Finally tighten the pump pulley securing bolts.
Connect the air rail feed hose to the valve.
Tighten the hose clip.
Connect the air cleaner feed pipe hose to valve.
Tighten the hose clip.
Connect the vacuum feed hose to the valve.
Connect the valve block connector.
Close the bonnet.

PAGE INTENTIONALLY LEFT BLANK

CONTENTS

DATA   19.15.00

Needle type   BDW
Spring   RED
A.E.D. unit type   TZX 1002

Torque figures

All fuel feed hoses 0,20 to 0,23 kgf m (17 to 21 lbf in).

Description   19.15.00

The HIF (Horizontal Integral Floatchamber) carburetter is functionally similar to preceding SU designs and operates on the variable choke/constant depression principle. This instrument has been designed as part of a carburation system which can achieve the precise induction of mixture required to control exhaust emissions to within statutory limits.

The HIF employs the familiar suction chamber/piston assembly together with a single jet-needle fuel metering system.

Main design changes are to be found in the position and layout of the float chamber, the incorporation of a fuel temperature compensating device and the arrangement for mixture setting.

Float chamber design

The float chamber is integral with the main body casting. Access to the chamber is obtained by removing the bottom cover-plate. The moulded float is shaped so that it surrounds the jet tube and is pivoted along a line parallel to the inlet flange. The float is retained by a spindle which screws into the body casting.

Entry of fuel into the float chamber is through a brass tube in the side of the carburetter body via a needle valve assembly.

The jet is pressed into the top of an aluminium tube which is in turn pressed into a plastic moulding. This hollow moulding known as the jet head is open at the lower end allowing fuel to enter the jet tube.

Mixture adjustment

The jet tube is moved in the vertical plane to provide mixture adjustment only.

Fuel temperature compensation

This device alters the jet position in relation to the metering needle to compensate for changes in fuel viscosity which takes place with changes in fuel temperature.

The jet head is attached to a bi-metal blade. This bi-metal blade is immersed in fuel in the float chamber and will move in the vertical plane in response to changes in fuel temperature. The jet will be raised to a weaker position on the jet needle when the fuel temperature rises and will be lowered to a richer position when the temperature falls.

From this it will be seen that once the jet position has been selected by adjusting the mixture screw, alterations of fuel temperature will bring about slight alterations in jet position to compensate for the change in fuel viscosity.

The effect of this device is that driveability is improved over wide ranges of temperature, and exhaust emissions kept within closer limits during cold starting and warm-up period. Temperature compensation also allows carburetters to have the mixture setting pre-set and sealed before a vehicle is delivered.

AIR CLEANER

Remove and refit   19.10.01

Removing

Disconnect the flexible inlet pipe and the air duct flexible pipe (1, Fig. 1).

Pull the vacuum pipe from the flap valve servo motor (3, Fig. 1).

Release the hose clip securing the vent hose to stub pipe on the inner face of the backplate (2, Fig. 1)

Release the toggle clips and withdraw the air

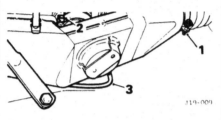

Fig. 1

cleaner cover (1 & 2, Fig. 2).

Lift out the filter element (3, Fig. 2).

Remove the outer pair of nuts and bolts securing the backplate to the carburetter flanges and spacers (4, Fig. 2).

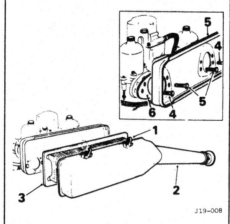

Fig. 2

Support the A.E.D. unit and remove the inner pair of nuts and bolts. Collect spacers (5, Fig. 2).

Move the backplate away from the carburetters and disconnect the vacuum pipe from the temperature sensor unit and the vent hose from the stub.

Lift out the backplate; remove and discard the gaskets (6, Fig. 2).

When refitting, use new gaskets.

RAM TUBE

Remove and refit   19.10.21

Remove the nuts, bolts and washers securing the expansion tank pipe and radiator bleed pipe clips. Retain the cable harness clips (1, Fig. 3).

Remove the setscrews, washers and locknuts securing the fan cowl brackets (2, Fig. 3).

Remove the two self-tapping screws securing the headlamp relay (3, Fig. 3).

Pull the connectors from the headlamp relay and fuse boxes (4 Fig. 3), noting the connections.

Carefully pull the cable harness from the top rail grommet.

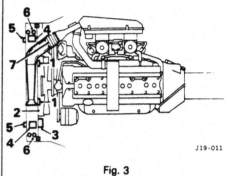

Fig. 3

Cars fitted with air conditioning only

Remove the Phillips head screws, washers and rubber bushes securing the condenser unit (5, Fig. 3). Support the condenser, using suitable padding.

All cars

Remove the six setscrews and two nuts, bolts and washers securing the radiator top rail (6, Fig. 3).

Release the clip securing the flexible inlet pipe. Lift the ram tube and radiator top rail assembly from car.

Release the clips (7, Fig. 3) and remove the fuse boxes from the top rail.

CARBURETTERS—CAR SET

Tune and adjust   19.15.02

NOTE: Carburetter mixture adjustment is pre-set and sealed and should not normally be altered. The only adjustments that should be made are to idle speed setting and throttle controls.

Before making any adjustment to carburetters or throttle controls, check and if necessary rectify, spark plug conditions and gaps, contact breaker gap, ignition timing, distributor centrifugal advance mechanism and compression pressures. Check tappet clearances if compression pressures are uneven.

If satisfactory results are not achieved by carrying out the procedure detailed below it will be necessary to refer to 'Mixture Controls, Adjust and Reset'.

NOTE: The operations may not be undertaken unless suitable CO metering equipment is available for emission testing, and it is a legal

19—2

requirement for cars in the United Kingdom that the tamperproofing seals fitted to the carburetters of these cars may not be removed unless such equipment is provided. Tamperproof seals MUST be renewed after current emission regulations have been met in test.

Remove the air cleaner element.
Unscrew the damper cap of one carburetter (2, Fig. 4).

CAUTION: (Early models only) It is essential that in lifting the cap, the damper retainer clip fitted below it is not displaced from its position in the position rod. If the retainer is inadvertently displaced it must be refitted by pressing fully into the piston rod.

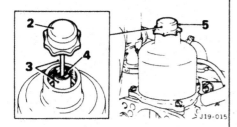

Fig. 4

Carefully withdraw the damper, by raising the cap, until the piston and damper TOGETHER reach the limit of upward travel, and inspect the oil level in the damper retainer (3, Fig. 4).
If the oil is not visible in the retainer, add engine oil (preferably S.A.E. 20) to the recess in the retainer until it is just visible at the bottom of the retainer recess (4, Fig. 4). Move the damper GENTLY up and down to 'pump' any trapped air out of the reservoir.
Replace the cap and tighten firmly by hand.
Repeat on the other carburetter (5, Fig. 4).
Check that the throttle linkage and cable to pedal operate smoothly.
Remove the lids of the tamperproof caps over the slow-running adjusting setscrews (1, Fig. 5). Detach the setscrews, remove the tamperproof seals and replace with new seals. Refit the adjusting screws and screw in until they almost contact the throttle levers. DO NOT close the lid on this operation.

NOTE: If the tamperproof cap is not fitted, unscrew the slow-running adjusting screws until they no longer contact the throttle levers.

Slacken the nuts of the clamp bolts on the throttle operating spindles on both sides of rear carburetter (2, Fig. 5).
Raise the piston in each carburetter with a finger and, using the mirror, inspect to check that both butterfly valves are fully closed and that the over-run valves are correctly seated.
Screw down both of the adjusting screws until they just contact the throttle levers, then screw down another one turn (1, Fig. 5).
Start the engine and run until it reaches normal operating temperature; stop the engine
Check that the mixture pipe from the A.E.D. unit is warm (3, Fig 5).
Start the engine again and using a rubber tube as a 'listening tube', compare the intensity of hiss of air entering each choke. Alter the setting of the adjusting screws until hiss is the same on both carburetters.

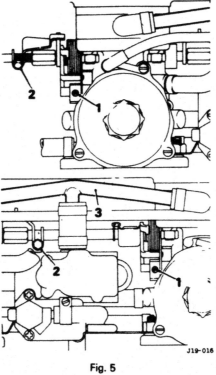

Fig. 5

NOTE: This operation may, if preferred, be carried out using a balance meter to makers' instructions.

Alter the settings of both adjusting screws by the same amount to achieve correct idling speed, i.e. 750 rev/min (1, Fig. 5).
When the correct idling speed is achieved, re-check the balance of the carburetters, alter the settings of the adjusting screws if necessary to secure the correct balance and idling speed.
Stop the engine.
Re-tighten the clamp bolts on the throttle operating rods (2, Fig. 5) to secure the correct opening characteristics on throttle. On automatic transmission cars there should be no backlash between the tongue and upper arm of yoke behind the rear carburetter, or between the tongue and the lower arm of the yoke between carburetters: both butterflies should start to open as soon as throttle cable is moved. On manual transmission cars there should be a gap of up to 0,9 mm (0.036 in) between the tongue and the lower arm of yoke between carburetters, so that the rear butterfly opens by up to 3° before front butterfly starts to open.
There should be no backlash between the tongue and the upper arm of yoke behind the rear carburetter.
Slacken the locknuts on the outer throttle cable and adjust the position of the cable in abutment so that the throttle operating lever rests against the back stop, yet the inner cable is not slack; tighten the locknuts (1, Fig. 6).
Check the operation of the throttle cable; the cable should pick up linkage immediately the pedal is moved (2, Fig. 6).
Slacken the locknut and wind back the operating lever to stop screw (3, Fig. 6).
Press the operating lever (4, Fig. 6) to open the butterfly valves and turn the stop screw (5, Fig. 6) to contact the lever. Tighten the locknut (3, Fig. 6).

Depress the pedal and ensure that the operating lever moves to touch the stop screw with the pedal at the end of its travel.
Adjust the pedal stop so that cable is not under due strain when the pedal is fully depressed.
Check the operation of the kick-down cable on cars fitted with automatic transmission (6, Fig. 6).
Refit the air cleaner element. Check CO emissions, using approved equipmen., and correct if necessary to bring within cu rent requirements.
Secure the lids of the tamperproof caps over the slow-running adjustment setscrews.

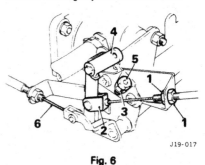

Fig. 6

MIXTURE CONTROL

Adjust and reset   **19.15.06**

NOTE: Do not adjust the mixture control on carburetters until all other possible factors which could cause faulty carburation have been eliminated; control setting has been correctly set and sealed before delivery, and should not require alteration.
Resetting mixture controls necessitates a check of emissions, using an exhaust gas analyser; regulation regarding emissions must be strictly adhered to. Ensure that equipment required for emission check is available before commencing mixture adjustment, and proceed as follows:
If possible, choose a location with an ambient temperature of between 15° and 26°C (60° to 80°F) to carry out the job. Place selector at 'P' on automatic transmission cars.
Remove the air cleaner.
Remove the plugs and sealant from both carburetter jet adjustment screws (1, Fig. 7).
Turn the jet adjusting screws clockwise, if necessary, (to lower jets) until jets are below level of the transverse bridges in the carburetter bores (2, Fig. 7).
Lift one carburetter piston by hand and insert straight-edge approximately 13 mm (0.5 in) wide alongside the needle in a vertical plane (3, Fig. 7). *continued*

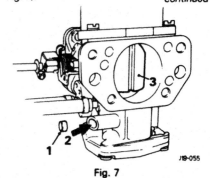

Fig. 7

19—3

Turn the adjusting screw anti-clockwise until the jet just contacts the steel rule. The jet is then accurately positioned level with the carburetter bridge.

Screw in the adjusting screw 3⅔ turns, bringing jet 2,97 mm (0.117 in) below carburetter bridge. This is the datum position at 20°C (68°F) from which final adjustments are to be made.

Repeat on the second carburetter.

Check the oil level in the carburetter piston bores.

Start the engine and run until fully warm, for at least five minutes after thermostat opens.

Run the engine at approximately 2500 rev/min for one minute; stop the engine.

NOTE: Adjustment may now be carried out for three minutes, then engine must be run again for one minute at 2500 rev/min before any further adjustment is made.

This cycle of operations—run for one minute, adjust for three—may be repeated as often as necessary.

Check that the idling speed is 750 rev/min and, if not, adjust to this figure.

Turn each jet adjusting screw clockwise to enrich the mixture or anti-clockwise to weaken, turning each screw by the same small amount until fastest idling speed is indicated.

Turn each screw anti-clockwise, each by the same amount, until engine speed just begins to fall.

Turn each screw clockwise by the same very small amount until maximum speed is regained.

Re-adjust the tickover, if necessary, to 750 rev/min.

Connect a suitable exhaust gas analyser to the vehicle exhaust and allow it to stabilise for at least one minute before checking CO emission. If necessary, adjust the mixture screws further to bring emissions just within current regulation limit.

Seal the mixture setting screws and close the aperture with a red plug.

Refit the air cleaner.

CARBURETTERS—CAR SET

Remove and refit   19.15.11

Removing.

Remove the air cleaner and the A.E.D. unit (1, Fig. 8)

Disconnect the crankcase breather pipes from the carburetters (2, Fig. 8).

Disconnect the fuel pipes from the carburetters, and plug the fuel supply pipe (3, Fig. 8).

Disconnect the vacuum pipe from the rear carburetter (4, Fig. 8)

Release the external circlips from the throttle rod and lower pin in linkage (1, Fig. 9). Withdraw the pin

Disengage the links from the lever on the rod and draw the rod back until its forward end disengages from the nut on the rear carburetter spindle (2, Fig. 9).

Remove the eight nuts and spring washers securing the carburetters to the manifold, and slide the carburetters off the studs (5, Fig. 8).

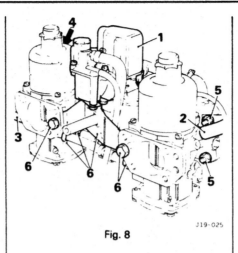

Fig. 8

Discard the flange gaskets but replace two nuts on studs to retain the adaptors and insulating spacers in their original positions.

Release the clips off fuel and vent pipes, remove the A.E.D. bracket and draw the front carburetter with throttle linking rod away from the rear carburetter (6, Fig. 8).

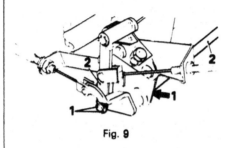

Fig. 9

Refitting

Slide new 'O' clips over the fuel and vent hoses and fit the hoses over the stubs on the carburetters. Do not tighten the clips at this stage.

Engage the rear end of the throttle linking rod with hollow nut on front of the rear carburetter spindle and engage the tongue of clamping bracket with the yoke.

Remove the nuts from manifold studs, place new gaskets in position and offer up carburetter to the studs.

Fit the spring washers and retaining nuts and tighten the nuts by diagonal selection. Ensure that the fuel and vent hoses between the carburetters are not twisted or distorted and secure the 'O' clips retaining them to the stubs.

Move throttle rod forward, engaging its ball-end with the hollow nut on the rear throttle spindle, and the tongue of the clamping bracket with the yoke.

Replace the link pin and circlips.

NOTE: Ensure that the circlips are replaced on the rod and pin. They are not interchangeable.

Check that both of the throttle butterflies are fully closed.

Refit the A.E.D. unit and connect the fuel, breather and vacuum hoses. Tune and adjust the carburetters. Refit the air cleaner.

CARBURETTER

Overhaul   19.15.17

Dismantling

NOTE: Overhaul procedure is given for rear carburetter. Front carburetter differs in fuel supply and vent pipe connections, throttle spindle details and in absence of vacuum take-off stub.

Service tools: Replacer damper assembly retainer (early models only).

Unscrew the cap of the suction chamber, lift until resistance is felt, support the piston (with a finger through the intake) at the top of its travel and pull the cap firmly upwards to release the damper retainer from the piston rod. Remove the damper (1, Fig. 10).

Unscrew the suction chamber retaining screws and remove the identity tag (2, Fig. 10).

Slightly rotate the suction chamber to free it, and lift vertically from the body without tilting (3, Fig. 10).

Remove the spring, lift out the piston and needle assembly and empty the oil from the piston rod (4, Fig. 10).

Mark the lower face of the piston (to locate the

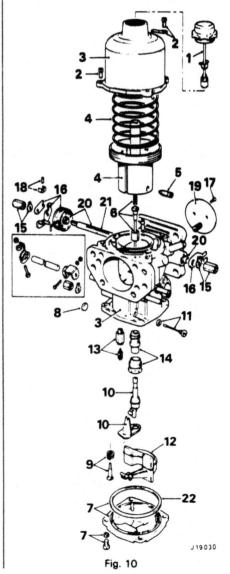

Fig. 10

position of 'V' mark on needle guide for correct reassembly) and remove the needle guide locking screw. Discard the screw (5, Fig. 10).

Withdraw the needle with guide and spring (6, Fig. 10).

Remove the bottom cover-plate retaining screws and the spring washers and detach the cover-plate with the sealing ring (7, Fig. 10).

Only if it is essential, remove the jet adjusting screw, plug and sealing from its counterbore and withdraw screw; and 'O' ring is carried in a groove in its head (8, Fig. 10).

Remove the jet adjusting lever retaining screw. Collect the spring (9, Fig. 10).

Withdraw the jet and adjusting lever together and separate the lever from the jet (10, Fig. 10).

Unscrew and remove the float pivot spindle. Collect washers from between the pin head and carburetter body (11, Fig. 10).

Withdraw the float (12, Fig. 10).

Remove the needle valve and unscrew the valve seat (13, Fig. 10).

Unscrew the jet bearing locking nut and withdraw the jet bearing (14, Fig. 10).

Bend back the lock washer tabs and unscrew the nut retaining the throttle levers and return spring. Note location of levers and spring (15, Fig. 10).

Remove the yoke lever and the return spring (16, Fig. 10).

Remove the throttle disc retaining screws (17, Fig. 10).

Remove the slow-running adjustment grub screw, tamperproof cap, and spring clip (18, Fig. 10).

Close the throttle and mark the position of the throttle disc in relation to the carburetter flange. Do not mark the disc in the vicinity of the over-run valve. Open the throttle and carefully withdraw the disc from the throttle spindle, taking care not to damage the over-run valve (19, Fig. 10).

Withdraw the throttle spindle and remove its seals, noting the way it is fitted in relation to the carburetter body to ensure correct reassembly (20, Fig. 10).

Inspection

Examine the throttle and its bearings in the carburetter body, check for excessive play, and renew parts as necessary (21, Fig. 10).

Examine the float needle and seating for damage and excessive wear; examine the nylon body of the needle for cracks; renew both the needle and the seat if necessary (13, Fig. 10).

Examine all the rubber seals and 'O' rings for damage or deterioration; renew as necessary. The cover-plate sealing ring must be renewed.

Examine the carburetter body for cracks and damage and for security of brass connections and piston key (3, Fig. 10).

Clean inside of the suction chamber and the piston rod guide with fuel or methylated spirit (denatured alcohol) and wipe dry. Abrasives must not be used.

Examine the suction chamber and piston for damage and signs of scoring.

Check that all balls are in piston ball-race (2 rows, 6 per row).

Fit the piston into the suction chamber, without the damper and spring, hold the assembly in a horizontal position and spin the piston. The piston should spin freely in the suction chamber without any tendency to stick.

Reassembling

Fit the new seals to the carburetter body and replace the spindle. Press the seals just inside the spindle housing bosses (1, Fig. 11).

Insert the throttle disc in the spindle, ensuring that it is positioned as previously marked (2, Fig. 11).

Fit two new throttle disc retaining screws. Ensure that the throttle closes correctly before tightening the screws fully, and spread their slotted ends sufficiently to secure. Do not overspread (3, Fig. 11).

Replace the return spring, lever and yoke on throttle spindle (4, Fig. 11).

Fit the new lock washer and replace the nut on throttle spindle. Tighten to 0,43 kgf m (37 lbf in) and secure by bending over tabs (5, Fig. 11).

Replace the slow-running adjusting grub screw, with new spring clip and tamper-proof cover. DO NOT CLOSE LID OF COVER (6, Fig. 11).

Replace the jet bearing and tighten the locking nut 1,38 to 1.65 kgf m (10 to 12 lbf ft) (7, Fig. 11).

Replace the needle valve seat and refit the needle (8, Fig. 11).

Replace the float and spindle with washer and tighten to 0,07 kgf m (6 lbf in) (9, Fig. 11).

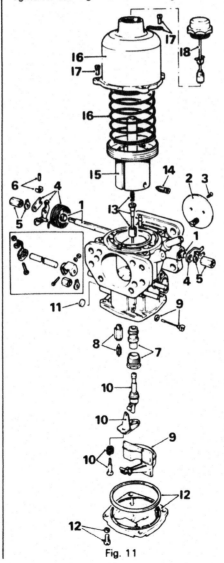

Fig. 11

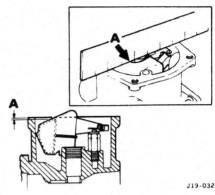

J19-032

Fig. 12

Invert the carburetter so that the needle valve is held on the seat by the weight of the float. Check that the lowest point indicated on float as 'A' in illustration (Fig. 12) is 1,0 ± 0,5 mm (0.04 ± 0.02 in) below the level of the float chamber face. Adjust if necessary by carefully bending the brass arm. Check that the float pivots correctly about the spindle.

Assemble the jet and the adjusting lever and plate in position in body, engaging the forked end of the lever with the reduced diameter of the adjusting screw. Fit the retaining screw and spring, but tighten finger-tight only initially (10, Fig. 11).

Check that the jet head is free to move in the cut-out in the adjusting lever and slides easily in the jet bearing. Fully tighten the retaining screw.

If the adjusting screw has been removed, fit new 'O' ring to it and insert carefully ensuring that its reduced tip diameter engages the slot of the adjusting lever. Screw in until jet is flush with the bridge of the body, then screw in a further 3⅔ turns, to bring jet 3,0 mm (0.117 in) below bridge (11, Fig. 11).

Fit a new sealing ring to the bottom cover-plate and refit as marked. Replace the four retaining screws and spring washers and tighten the screws (12, Fig. 11).

Refit the spring to needle, ensuring that the spring is located in its groove (13, Fig. 11).

Slide the needle guide over the needle (with open end of slot adjacent to the projection in flange) and insert in the piston as previously marked.

Insert NEW needle retaining screw in the piston, position the needle guide flush with the bottom face of the piston and tighten the screw to 0,14 to 0,17 kgf m (12 to 15 lbf in) (14, Fig. 11).

Carefully replace the piston and the needle assembly in the carburetter body (15, Fig. 11).

Replace the spring on the piston, and lower the suction chamber carefully over the spring, avoiding turning the chamber as it compresses the spring (to prevent the spring from twisting the piston) (16, Fig. 11).

Fit the three screws and the identity tag (17, Fig. 11).

Insert the damper piston in bore of the piston rod using tool, press the damper retainer fully into top of rod (early models only) (18, Fig. 11).

Fill the bore of the piston rod with engine oil, preferably S.A.E. 20, up to the bottom of damper retainer and tighten suction chamber cap firmly by hand.

Replace carburetters.

19—5

AUTOMATIC ENRICHMENT DEVICE (A.E.D.)

Remove and refit 19.15.38

Removing

Disconnect the battery, the fuel inlet and over-flow pipe (1, Fig. 13).

Disconnect the air delivery pipe and the mixture delivery pipe (2, Fig. 13).

Remove the bolts and spring washers securing the A.E.D. unit to mounting bracket; lift off the A.E.D. unit (3, Fig. 13).

Refitting

Reverse the above procedure, use new clips on the hot air inlet and mixture delivery pipes.

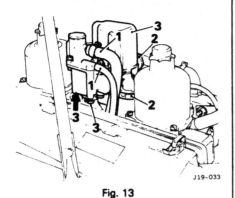

Fig. 13

DIAPHRAGM

Remove and refit 19.15.40

Remove the A.E.D. unit (1, Fig. 14) and invert. Remove the four screws and the spring washers securing the diaphragm cover (2, Fig. 14). Withdraw the cover, spring, diaphragm and locating dowel (3, Fig. 14).

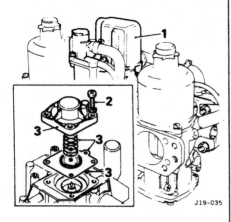

Fig. 14

Refitting

When refitting, ensure that the bore of the locating dowel is clean.

Push the dowel into the hole in the A.E.D. unit.

Locate the diaphragm on the A.E.D. unit.

NOTE: The rivet head must face toward the A.E.D. unit.

Insert the spring in the diaphragm cover.

Position diaphragm cover and spring squarely over the diaphragm, ensuring that the spring is seated in the diaphragm plate.

Push the cover down, ensuring that the locating dowel enters the hole in cover.

Refit the four securing screws and refit the A.E.D. unit.

NEEDLE VALVE

Remove and refit 19.15.42

Removing

Remove the A.E.D. unit.

Carefully prise off the insulation cover (1, Fig. 15).

Remove the three screws and spring washers securing the float chamber cover (2, Fig. 15). Lift off cover (3, Fig. 15).

CAUTION: Do not move cover sideways.

Remove and discard the gasket (4, Fig. 15). Unclip the needle valve from the float arm (5, Fig. 15).

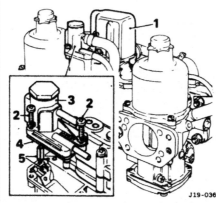

Fig. 15

Refitting

Lift float from the chamber.

Position the needle valve in the recess in the cover.

Clip the needle valve to the float arm by using a steel rule; hold the float against the cover.

Position the new gasket on the A.E.D. body—do not use jointing compound or grease.

Lower the cover on to the A.E.D. unit, ensuring that the float and needle valve are not displaced.

Ensure that the float hinge pin is correctly located before fitting the three securing screws and insulation cover. Refit the A.E.D. unit.

A.E.D. FILTER

Remove, clean and refit 19.15.43

Disconnect the battery. See operation 86.15.20.

16).

Withdraw the filter element, wash it in petrol and dry using clean, dry compressed air (2, Fig. 16).

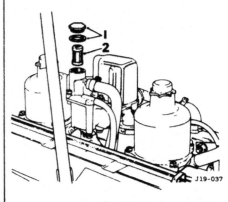

Fig. 16

HOT AIR PICK-UP UNIT

Remove and refit 19.15.44

Slacken the clamping bolt and withdraw the air delivery pipe from the outlet tube (1, Fig,. 17). Remove the bolts securing the pick-up unit to the exhaust manifold, withdraw the pick-up unit together with the air filter (2, Fig. 17).

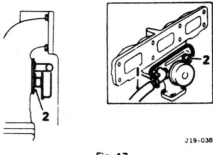

Fig. 17

HOT AIR DELIVERY PIPE

Remove and refit 19.15.45

Slacken the clamping bolt and withdraw the air delivery pipe from the outlet tube.

Remove the nut and bolt securing the pipe clip to the support bracket.

Disconnect the delivery pipe from the A.E.D. unit.

Use a new clip to secure the delivery pipe to the A.E.D. unit when refitted.

HOT AIR FILTER

Remove, clean and refit   19.15.46

Slacken the clamping bolt and move the filter towards the cylinder block to withdraw it (1, Fig. 18).

Wash the filter in petrol and dry with compressed air (2, Fig. 18).

Lightly oil the filter gauze with engine oil and refit.

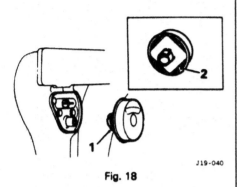

Fig. 18

THROTTLE LINKAGE

Check and adjust   19.20.05

Fully depress the throttle pedal and ensure that the butterfly valve operating lever comes to a position just touching the operating lever stop screw (1, Fig. 19). If the lever does not touch the stop screw, and linkage was initially correctly set up, adjust as follows:

Slacken the locknuts at the outer throttle cable abutment (2, Fig. 19).

Adjust the position of the outer cable in abutment to place the inner cable under light tension but NOT to move throttle operating lever; secure the locknuts (3, Fig. 19).

Re-check adjustment as above.

Slacken locknuts on outer throttle cable and adjust position of cable in abutment so that throttle operating lever rests against back stop, yet inner cable is not slack; tighten locknuts.

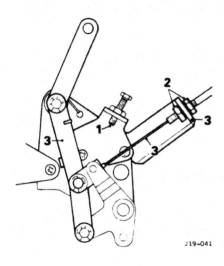

Fig. 19

Depress throttle pedal and ensure that operating lever moves to touch stop screw with pedal at end of its travel. Adjust pedal stop so that cable is not under due strain when pedal is fully depressed.

Check operation of kick-down cable (see 44.30.02—cars fitted with Model 66 automatic transmission only).

THROTTLE OPERATING ROD BUSHES

Remove and refit   19.20.10

Remove the throttle pedal.

Remove the under-scuttle casing.

Prise the spring clips from the steering-column universal joint cover; detach the covers and padding—left-hand-drive cars only.

Remove the split pin at the top end of the operating rod (1, Fig. 20).

Disengage the sleeve and nipple from the rod (2, Fig. 20).

Remove the two self-locking nuts and draw the pedal arm from the stubs—right-hand-drive cars only.

Remove the split pin from the operating rod pivot (3, Fig. 20).

Pull the rod from the pivot. Recover the plain washer (4, Fig. 20).

When refitting, remove worn bushes and fit new ones where necessary (5, Fig. 20).

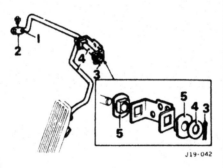

Fig. 20

FUEL PIPE ARRANGEMENT
(Fig. 21)
(Carburetter cars only)

Description   19.40.00

The system utilizes two fuel pump assemblies and draws from two fuel tanks fitted in the rear wings.

When the left-hand tank is selected on the instrument panel switch, voltage is applied to the left-hand fuel pump and fuel is passed via the filter to the two carburetter float chambers.

Selection of the right-hand tank energizes the right-hand fuel pump.

The outlet non-return valve of the inoperative pump prevents fuel passing from one tank to the other.

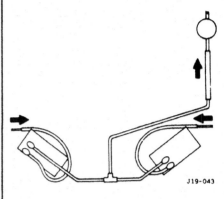

Fig. 21

Separate non-return valves are fitted in the flexible hoses near the tanks.

Air-conditioned cars are equipped with fuel coolers, attached to the hot air duct near the carburetters.

Special precautions detailed below must be taken before working on the fuel cooler.

FUEL COOLER

Remove and refit   19.40.40

WARNING: Exposure to refrigerant gas, which is released if a refrigerant hose is detached from the cooler, can cause blindness. It is therefore essential to depressurize the air-conditioning system before disconnecting a refrigerant hose.

Fire precautions are also essential as fuel may be spilled when fuel hoses are disconnected.

Disconnect the battery.

Depressurize the air-conditioning system.

Disconnect the refrigerant inlet and outlet hoses from the cooler.

Clamp the fuel hoses.

Disconnect the fuel hoses.

Remove the two self-tapping screws and washers securing the fuel cooler. Collect the mounting clips and insulating sleeve.

After refitting, re-charge the air-conditioning system.

19—7

FUEL PUMP

Remove and refit (either side)   19.45.08

Place the car on a ramp, NOT over a pit.
Disconnect the battery.
Remove the rear wheel adjacent to the pump to be removed.
Drain the fuel tank.

WARNING: Take all due precautions against fire and explosion when draining fuel.

Remove the four screws securing the circular cover-plate to the rear vertical wall of the wheel arch. Withdraw the cover along the flexible hose (1, Fig. 22).
Disconnect the electrical leads from the pump (2, Fig. 22).
Release the hose clips and detach the flexible hose from the pump (3, Fig. 22).
Turn the locking flange anti-clockwise to release the pump and withdraw the pump and sealing washers, taking care to avoid damage to the filter as the pump is removed.
Discard the sealing washer (4, Fig. 22).
Remove all sealant from the pump, mounting flange and tank.
When refitting, ensure that the mounting faces of the pump flange and fuel tank are clean, and that the correct pump assembly is being refitted—C45442 is R.H. pump and C45443 is L.H. pump.
Fit new sealing washer and introduce the pump carefully into tank, securing in position with the locking flange.
Refit the flexible hose to the pump outlet pipe and tighten the hose clip screw to not more than 0,07 kgf m (6 lbf in).
Fit the electrical connections and smear the terminals with waterproof grease.
Replace the cover-plate and secure with the four screws.
Make good the sealing around the cover and screw leads by coating with Flintkote or similar protective covering.

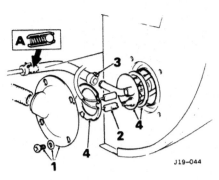

Fig. 22

NOTE: If it is found necessary to detach the forward end of the flexible hose, or to fit a new hose, it is most important that a non-return valve fitted in the forward end of the flexible hose is correctly installed. The purpose of the non-return valve is to prevent fuel from draining into the lower tank when the car is tilted, and therefore the ball must be at rear, or tank, end of fitting, as shown in illustration at 'A'.

NOTE: This type of fuel pump cannot be overhauled and must be renewed if found to be defective.

FUEL TANK

Remove and refit—either   19.55.01

Removing

Drain the fuel tank (1, Fig. 23) and disconnect the battery.
Remove the side section of rear bumper.
Remove the cross-head screws and washers securing the rear quarter fuel tank cover (2, Fig. 23).
Remove the setscrews and nuts, spring and plain washers securing the rear quarter fuel tank cover (3, Fig. 23). Remove the cover.
Remove the self-tapping screw securing the forward end of the luggage compartment side casing. Remove the casing.
Remove the four screws and shakeproof washers securing the flange of the fuel tank filler cap (4, Fig. 23).
Taking care to avoid damaging the paintwork, prise the flange (5, Fig. 23) from the body.
Pull the vent pipe (6, Fig. 23) from the stub where applicable.
Remove the gasket and 'O' ring seal.

NOTE: On carburetter cars fitted with submerged fuel pumps omit above operation and reach up between rear of tank and tail/stop/flasher light units to detach leads from the fuel gauge tank unit. (Submerged pump replaces gauge unit in forward tank aperture.) Detach the leads and flexible hose from pump before withdrawing tank.

Remove the bolt, special washer and shakeproof washer at the side of the luggage boot.
Release the fuel pipe connector at the base of the tank. Separate the connection and push the pipe carefully inwards flush with the panel (8, Fig. 23).
Remove the two bolts, special washers and shakeproof washers in the silencer tunnel and recover wedges (9, Fig. 23).
Release Nyloc nut at the hanger bolt (10, Fig. 23).
Carefully lower the fuel tank, note connections and detach the cables from the tank unit (11, Fig. 23).
On cars with an evaporative control system lower tank until vent pipe (7, Fig. 23) is accessible and detach pipe from stub.

Refitting

On cars with an evaporative control system offer up the tank and attach the vent pipe to stub.

All cars

Lift the tank and connect cables to the tank unit and submerged pump where applicable.
Lift the tank and engage the hanger bolt in bracket; secure with Nyloc nut.
Fit the bolts and special shakeproof washers at the upper and forward location. Do not tighten them at this stage.
Fit the bolt, special and shakeproof washer at the rear location. Fit wedges between the fuel

tank and the side panel. Do not tighten at this stage.
Fit new 'O' ring seal in the fuel tank neck.
Press vent pipe onto filler neck stub, where applicable.
Use new gasket at the petrol filler cap flange

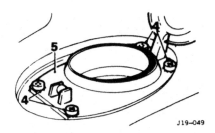

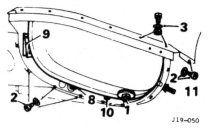

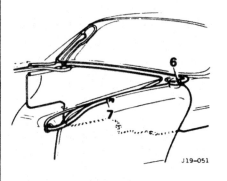

Fig. 23

and secure using the four screws and shakeproof washers.
From beneath, firmly press the fuel tank up to locate on the filler cap flange spigot and tighten the rear mounting bolt on wedges.
Secure the hanger bolt nut. Do not overtighten.
Tighten the remaining two mounting bolts.
Secure the supply pipe union to tank; connect the hose to pump on cars with submerged pumps.
Pour 2 to 3 gallons Imp. (9 to 13 litres) of specified fuel into the tank.
Connect the battery.
Switch on the ignition and select the fuel tank that has been changed.
Check to ensure that there are no leaks at the unions and that the fuel gauge registers. Switch off the ignition.
Fit and secure the rear quarter fuel tank cover and the side section of the rear bumper.

FUEL TANK

Drain 19.55.02

WARNING: Petrol (gasoline) must not be extracted or drained from a vehicle standing over a pit.

Petroleum or gasoline vapour is highly flammable and in confined spaces is also very explosive and toxic.

When petrol/gasoline evaporates it produces 150 times its own volume in vapour, which when diluted with air becomes an ignitable mixture. The vapour is heavier than air, and will always fall to the lowest level and it can readily be distributed throughout a workshop by air currents. Even a small spillage of petrol or gasoline is potentially very dangerous.

Extracting or draining petrol (gasoline) from a vehicle fuel tank must be carried out in a well-ventilated area, preferably outside the workshop. All forms of ignition must be extinguished or removed, any hand lamps used must be flameproof and kept clear of any spillage. The receptacle used to contain the petrol drained or extracted must be more than adequate to receive the full amount to be drained.

Open the fuel tank filler cap.
Place a suitable receptacle beneath the fuel tank drain plug.
Remove the drain plug, allow the fuel to drain.
Check the condition of the sealing washer and replace the plug. Do not overtighten.

FUEL FILLER CAP ASSEMBLY

Remove and refit 19.55.08

Remove the four screws and shakeproof washers (1, Fig. 24) securing the flange of the fuel tank filler cap.
Taking great care to avoid damaging paintwork, prise the flange (2, Fig. 24) from the body.
Pull the vent pipe (3, Fig. 24) from the stub—evaporative loss control cars only.
Remove the gasket and 'O' ring seal.

When refitting use a new gasket and 'O' ring seal.

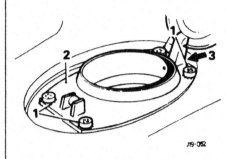

Fig. 24

FUEL FILLER LOCK

Remove and refit 19.55.09

Open the filler cap lid.
Cover the filler hole with rag or adhesive tape.
Remove the screw and washer securing the ward to the lock barrel.
If the key is available, insert it in the lock, and press the barrel from inside to out.
If the key is not available, insert a piece of stiff wire to lift the tumblers and turn the barrel to mid position (1, Fig. 25).
Keep the barrel in this angular position and press from the lid (2, Fig. 25).

When refitting, insert the key in the barrel of the replacement lock and offer into the lid. Remove the key (3, Fig. 25).
Secure the ward to the barrel using the screw and washer (4, Fig. 25).
Test-operate the lock and ensure that the ward turns to a position in line with, and facing, the lid catch. Unlock (5, Fig. 25).
Remove the obstruction from the filler hole and close the lid.

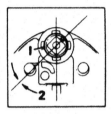
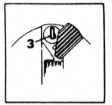
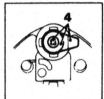

Fig. 25

19—9

PAGE INTENTIONALLY LEFT BLANK

CONTENTS

ELECTRONIC FUEL INJECTION

Description

The electronic fuel injection 'L' system can be divided into two separate systems interconnected only at the injectors.

The systems are:

1. A fuel system delivering to the injectors a constant supply of fuel at the correct pressure.

2. An electronic sensing and control system which monitors engine operating conditions of load, speed, temperature (coolant and induction air) and throttle movement. The control system then produces electrical current pulses of appropriate duration to hold open the injector solenoid valves and allow the correct quantity of fuel to flow through the nozzle for each engine cycle.

As fuel pressure is held cons ant, varying the pulse duration increases or decreases the amount of fuel passed through the injector to comply precisely with engine requirements.

Pulse duration, and therefore fuel quantity, is also modified to provide enrichment during starting and warming-up and at closed throttle, full throttle and while the throttle is actually opening.

All the injectors are simultaneously operated by the Electronic Control Unit (E.C.U.) twice per engine cycle.

The induction system is basically the same as that on a carburetted engine: tuned ram pipe, air cleaner, plenum chamber and induction ports. The air is drawn through a paper-element cleaner to a single throttle butterly valve and to individual ports for each cylinder leading off the plenum chamber. The injectors are positioned at the cylinder head end of each port so that fuel is directed at the back of each inlet valve.

Fuel system

Fuel supply

Fuel is drawn from the tanks (1, Fig. 1) at the rear of the car by a fuel pump (3, Fig. 1) via a solenoid operating change-over valve (2, Fig. 1) to a fuel rail, through an in-line filter (5, Fig. 1) and a pressure regulator (7, Fig. 1). Fuel is controlled so that the pressure drop across the injector nozzle is maintained at a constant 2,5 bars (36.25 lbf/in²). Excess fuel is returned to the tank from which it was drawn via a fuel cooler (4, Fig. 1)—on air conditioned cars only—and a solenoid-operated shut-off valve. The six fuel injectors (8, Fig. 1) are connected to the fuel rail (6, Fig. 1) and are electromechanically operated to inject into each inlet port. Fuel is also supplied to a cold start injector (9, Fig. 1) which is only operated during the starting of a cold engine.

SCHEMATIC DIAGRAM

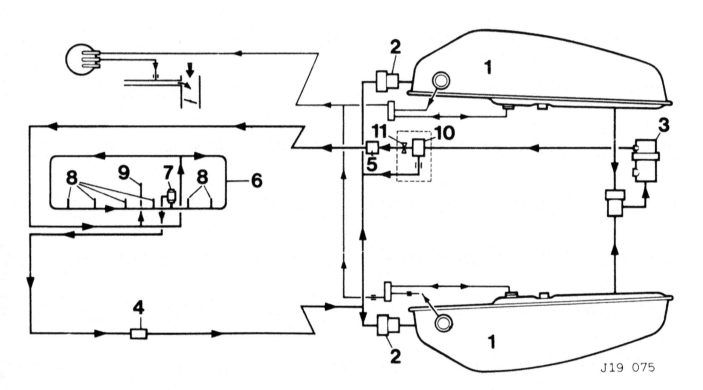

J19 075

Fig. 1

1. Fuel tank	5. Fuel filter	9. Cold start injector
2. Change-over valve	6. Fuel rail	10. Air bleed valve
3. Fuel pump	7. Fuel pressure regulator	11. Non return valve
4. Fuel cooler	8. Injectors	

19—2

ENGINE COMPONENT LOCATION (U.K. AND EUROPEAN)

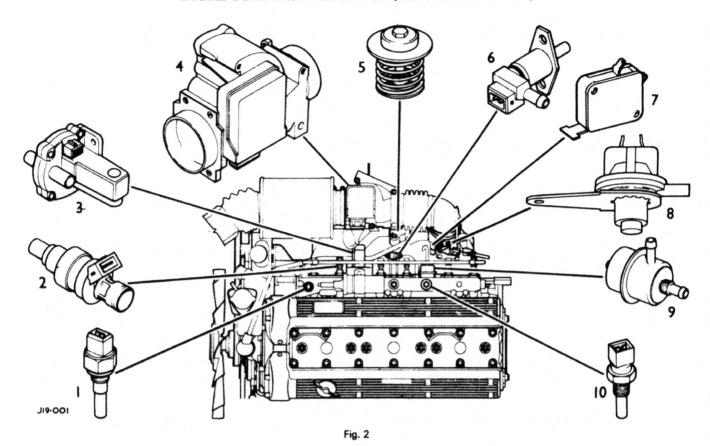

J19-001

Fig. 2

1. Thermotime switch	5. Over-run valve	9. Fuel pressure regulator
2. Fuel injector	6. Cold start injector	10. Water temperature sensor
3. Auxiliary air valve	7. Micro-switch (automatic cars only)	
4. Air-flow meter	8. Vacuum throttle switch	

Air intake system

Air is drawn from the air cleaner through the air meter and throttle into the engine. The air passing through the air meter deflects the flap inside against a spring to a position dependent on the rate of air flow. A potentiometer connected to the flap spindle converts the flap angular position to a voltage. This voltage is transmitted to the E.C.U. as a measure of air flow.

Electronic system

The Electronic Control Unit (E.C.U.) receives information from the sensors placed about the engine. It computes the quantity of fuel required and therefore the time for which the injectors must remain open. An ignition L.T. circuit triggers all injectors simultaneously at every third spark. The injectors open twice per engine cycle, each time delivering half the fuel requirement of each cylinder.

Ballast resistor

In order to open and close the injectors a fairly high current drive is needed, about 1.5 amps per injector. The E.C.U. has an output stage designed to deliver this current, but to protect the output transistors of the E.C.U. from injector faults and short circuits there is a ballast resistor wired in series with each injector. These resistors will limit fault current to a safe value, thus protecting the E.C.U. The ballast resistors for each injector are housed in a single unit which is secured to the right-hand front engine valance by two screws.

Idle speed adjustment

The idle speed adjusting screw is located in the air distribution block and controls air flow to the extra air valve.

Auxiliary air valve

The auxiliary air valve consits of a variable orifice controlled by a bi-metal element. The unit is mounted on the water rail and also responds to coolant temperature. A heater is fitted around the bi-metal element to speed up the bi-metal response. The heater is connected in parallel with the fuel pump and so is energized as long as the engine is running.

Temperature sensors

The temperature sensor of the air being taken into the engine through the inlet manifold, and the temperature of the coolant in the cylinder block are constantly monitored. The information is fed directly to the E.C.U. The air temperature sensor has a small effect on the injector pulse width, and should be looked upon as a trimming rather than a control device. It ensures the fuel supplied is directly related to the weight of air drawn in by the engine. Therefore, as the weight (density) of the air charge increases with falling temperature, so the amount of fuel supplied is also increased to maintain optimum fuel/air ratio.

The coolant temperature sensor has a much greater degree of control although its main effect is concentrated while the engine is initially warming-up. The coolant temperature sensor operates in conjunction with the cold start system and the auxiliary air valve to form a completely automatic equivalent to a carburetter choke.

Flooding protection system

With the ignition switched on, the pump will not operate until the engine is cranked. The system prevents flooding should an injector or injectors become faulty (remain in the open position), and the ignition is left switched on.

19—3

ENGINE COMPONENT LOCATION (FEDERAL)

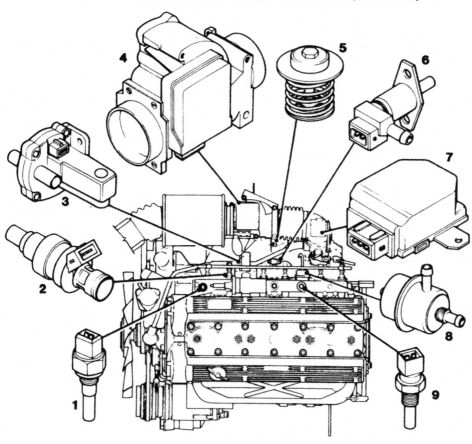

Fig. 3   J19·163

1. Thermotime switch	4. Air-flow meter	7. Throttle switch
2. Fuel injectors	5. Over-run valve	8. Fuel pressure regulator
3. Auxiliary air valve	6. Cold start injector	9. Water temperature sensor

Cranking enrichment

The E.C.U. provides an increased pulse duration during engine cranking in addition to any enrichment due to the coolant temperature sensor or the cold start injectors. The additional signal reduces slightly when cranking stops, but does not fall to normal level for a few seconds. This temporary enrichment sustains the engine during initial running.

Throttle switch (Federal)

The throttle switch mounted on the throttle spindle, signals the position of the throttle to the E.C.U.

In addition to a richer air/fuel mixture during cold starting and warm-up a slight additional amount of fuel is required during idle. The E.C.U. supplies this additional amount of fuel on European cars in response to the closed throttle contact on the throttle switch. This contact is fitted, but not used, on cars to the U.S.A. and certain other countries.

Fuel return valves are situated in the left-hand and right-hand rear wheel arches, in line with the rearmost edge of the tyres. Care must be taken when changing them as they are NOT interchangeable, side for side.

The left-hand valve has a fixing bracket spot-welded to it that prevents it being incorrectly fitted (it would contact the wheel). It has an arrow showing direction of fuel flow (towards the rear).

Vacuum full throttle switch (U.K. and European only)

A vacuum switch is fitted to the throttle cable mounting bracket wired into the full throttle enrichment circuit. This senses inlet manifold depression and switches the fuelling from the generally weak condition required for emission control or minimum fuel consumption to a richer condition necessary for maximum engine power. On cars fitted with an automatic gearbox there is an over-run fuel cut-off micro-switch mounted on one of the throttle body mounting bolts, which is mechanically operated by the throttle mechanism when the throttle is fully closed. The switch is controlled by a circuit incorporated in the E.C.U.

When the engine is over-running with the throttle in the closed position the fuel remains cut off until the engine speed falls to below 1400 rev/min.

The control unit circuit will not re-activate the fuel cut-off function until the engine speed exceeds 1470 rev/min.

Cold start

For cold starting, additional fuel is injected into the inlet manifold by the cold start injector. This is controlled by the cold start relay and Thermotime switch. The Thermotime switch senses coolant temperature, and depending on the temperature it senses, interrupts or completes the ground connection for the relay. When the starter is operated the cold start relay is energized with its circuit completed via the Thermotime switch. The Thermotime switch also limits the length of time for which the relay is energized, to a maximum of 12 seconds under conditions of extreme cold. This enrichment is in addition to that provided by the coolant temperature sensor.

If the coolant temperature is above 35°C the switch does not operate at all, no starting enrichment additional to cranking enrichment being required.

Fuel pressure regulator

The fuel pressure regulator operates to maintain a constant pressure drop across the injector nozzles. It is connected one side to a manifold depression and is operated by a spring-loaded diaphragm. Excess fuel is returned to the tank from which it was drawn via a solenoid-operated shut-off valve.

19—4

FAULT FINDING

It is assumed that the vehicle has sufficient fuel in the tanks, and that purely engine functions, e.g. ignition timing, valve timing, and the ignition as a whole are operating satisfactorily. If necessary, these functions must be checked before the fuel injection system is suspected.

Symptoms	
Will not start*	Difficult cold start
Difficult hot start	Starts but will not run
Misfires and cuts out	Runs rough
Idle speed too fast	Hunting at idle
Low power and top speed	High fuel consumption

* Before proceeding with checks, hold the throttle fully open and attempt a start. If the engine then starts and continues to run, no further action is necessary.

Possible causes in order of checking	
Battery:	Battery depleted, giving insufficient crank speed or inadequate spark. Check battery condition with hydrometer or by battery condition indicator on 'Freedom Battery'. Re-charge, clean and secure terminals, or renew as necessary.
Connections:	Ensure that all connector plugs are securely attached. Pull back rubber boot and ensure that plug is fully home. While replacing boot press cable towards socket. Ensure that Electronic Control Unit (E.C.U.) multi-pin connector is fully made. Ensure that all ground connections are clean and tight.
Ignition System:	Check ignition system as detailed in the Electrical Section.
Fuel System:	Open filler cap of fuel tank being used. Change tank being used. Check for fuel pipe failure (strong smell of fuel) and retention of in-line fuel pressure. Check inertia switch closed. If necessary, clear fuel tank vents or supply pipe.
Cold Start System:	Fault conditions could cause cold start system to be inoperative on a hot engine. If engine is either very hot, or cold, these particualr faults will cause the engine to run very rich. Check cold start system, see 19.22.32.
E.C.U.:	If the E.C.U. is faulty it is possible that injectors will be inoperative. The E.C.U. may also be responsible for any degree of incorrect fuelling. Before suspecting the E.C.U. for fuelling problems, however, all other likely components should be proved good.
Air Leaks:	Ensure that all hose and pipe connections are secure. Engine is, however, likely to start more easily with air leaks if cold, as air leaking augments that through the auxiliary air valve. A leak, or failed air valve is shown up, however, by a very high idle speed when engine is warm and air valve main passage should be closed.
Temperature Sensors:	If either sensor is short-circuited, starting improves with high engine temperature. Engine will run very weak, improving as temperature rises, but still significantly weak when fully hot. If a sensor is open-circuit, or disconnected, engine will run very rich, becoming worse as temperature rises. Engine may not run when fully hot, and will almost certainly not restart if stalled. Effect of air temperature sensor will be less marked than coolant temperature sensor.
Extra Air Distribution Block:	Check opening throttle. If engine immediately starts, unscrew idle speed adjustment, and re-check start with closed throttle. Re-set idle speed when engine hot. Check cold start. Check throttle return springs and linkage for sticking or maladjustment as a sticking throttle may have enforced incorrect idle speed adjustment on a previous occasion.
Throttle Switch:	Check operation of throttle switch. Incorrect function or sequence of switching will give this fault.
Throttle Butterfly:	Check adjustment of the throttle butterfly valve, ensure that return springs are correctly fitted, and throttle not sticking open.
Over-run Valve:	Check operation of over-run valve.
Compression:	Low compressions: a general lack of engine tune could cause this fault. Check engine timing, ignition timing, and function of ignition system complete. If necessary, check valve condition.
Idle Fuel Control Setting:	Check exhaust gas CO level. If necessary, adjust fuelling trim control in air metering unit. **CAUTION: This knob MUST NOT be moved unless correct test equipment and skilled personnel are in attendance to monitor changes made.**
Air Filters:	Remove air filter and check for choked filter element.
Throttle Linkage:	Check throttle linkage adjustment and ensure that throttle butterfly valve can be fully operated.

For further information relating to 'L' electronic fuel injection refer to the 'Lucas Epitest' operating instructions and test procedures.

MAINTENANCE

There is no routine maintenance procedure laid down for the electronic fuel injection system other than that, at all service intervals, the electrical connectors must be checked for security. The fuel filter must be discarded and a replacement component fitted at intervals specified in the Maintenance Summary.

CAUTION

The following instructions must be strictly observed:

Always disconnect the battery before removing any components.

Always depressurize the fuel system before disconnecting any fuel pipes.

When removing fuel system components always clamp fuel pipes approximately 38 mm (1.5 in) from the unit being removed. Do not overtighten clamp.

Ensure that material is available to absorb possible fuel spillage.

When reconnecting electrical components, always ensure that good contact is made by the connector before fitting the rubber cover. Always ensure that ground connections are made to clean bare metal, and are tightly fastened using correct screws and washers.

AIR CLEANER ELEMENT

The air cleaner element is of the paper type and is situated between the air intake trumpet and the air-flow meter.

Remove and refit   19.10.08

To renew the element:

Slacken the clips (1, Fig. 4) securing the inlet and outlet hoses; slide the air cleaner assembly forward until the bracket is clear of the mounting spigots.

Release the spring clips securing front cover (2, Fig. 4) and the Nyloc nut (3, Fig. 4) securing the end-plate, withdraw the end-plate filter element and gasket (4, Fig. 4).

Remove dirt, grease, etc., from the air cleaner casing.

Do not overtighten the Nyloc nut when refitting.

19—6

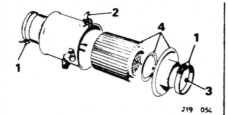

Fig. 4

THROTTLE PEDAL

Remove and refit   19.20.01

Removing

Fold the carpet away from the base of the throttle pedal.

Remove the nuts and washers securing the base of the pedal to the mounting plate (1, Fig. 5).

Pull the base of the pedal away from the mounting plate and disengage the spring from the pedal (2, Fig. 5).

Examine the spring for wear, and renew if necessary (3, Fig. 5).

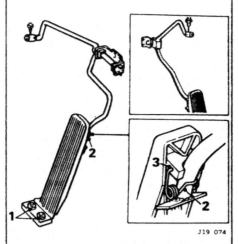

Fig. 5

Refitting

Engage the rod with the pedal. Position the spring on the pedal and push the base of the pedal to locate on the mounting studs, fit nuts and tighten.

THROTTLE SWITCH

U.K. and European Automatic Transmission

Check and adjust   19.22.37

Check that the throttle butterflies are adjusted correctly with 0,05 mm (0.002 in) between valve and housing when closed. See 19.20.11 for full details.

To adjust throttle micro-switch, connect Continuity Tester across switch terminals (1, Fig. 6).

When throttle lever (2, Fig. 6) is held in direction of arrow by spring (3, Fig. 6) contacts are closed, bulb is on.

Pull lever against spring until spigot (4, Fig. 6) contacts the opposite side of slot (5, Fig. 6). Bulb is off.

Slacken screws (6, Fig. 6) to adjust micro-switch as required. Re-tighten screws.

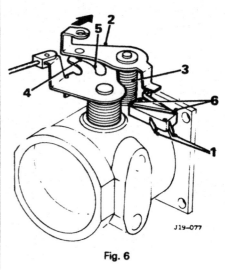

Fig. 6

THROTTLE LINKAGE

Check and adjust   19.20.05

Checking

Ensure that the throttle return springs are correctly secured and that the throttle moves freely and rests against the closed stop when released.

Ensure that the throttle butterfly closed stop screw has not been moved. If it has, check and if necessary, adjust.

Adjusting

Slacken the locknuts at the outer throttle cable abutment (1, Fig. 7).

Adjust the position of the outer cable in abutment to place inner cable under light tension but NOT to move the throttle operating lever. Tighten locknuts.

Re-check adjustment.

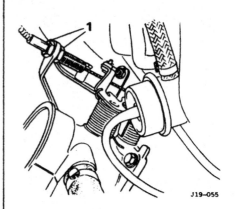

Fig. 7

THROTTLE CABLE

Remove and refit 19.20.06

Removing

Disengage the throttle return spring from the throttle operating lever.

Slacken the locknuts at the outer throttle cable abutment and draw the cable clear.

Remove the 'C' clip securing the cable yoke clevis pin and detach inner cable from the operating lever: temporarily replace clevis pin.

Slacken the locknut on the top surface of footwell.

Remove the under-scuttle casing.

Remove the split pin at the top end of the operating rod (1, Fig. 8).

Disengage the sleeve and nipple from the rod (2, Fig. 8).

Remove the nut (3, Fig. 8) from the cable sheath and draw the cable assembly into the engine compartment. Recover the operating rod abutment plate.

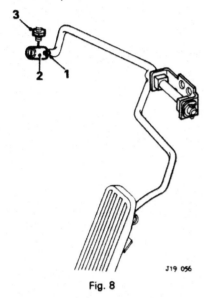

Fig. 8

Refitting

Examine the grommets for wear, and renew as necessary.

Reverse above procedure. Apply sealing compound around thread on top surface of footwell.

THROTTLE BUTTERFLY VALVE

Adjust 19.20.11

Remove the elbow and convolute hose to expose the throttle body.

Slacken the throttle butterfly locknut and stop screw to ensure that the throttle butterfly valve closes fully.

Insert 0,05 mm (0.002 in) feeler gauge between top of valve and housing to hold valve open (Fig. 9).

Set the stop screw to just touch the stop arm and tighten locknut with the feeler in position.

Press the stop arm against the screw and withdraw the feeler.

Seal the threads of the adjusting screws and locknuts using a spot of paint.

Refit the elbow and convolute hose.

Check the throttle linkage adjustment, operation of the throttle switch and the kickdown switch adjustment.

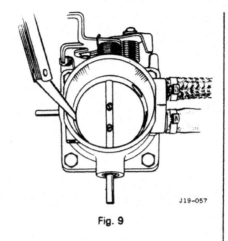

Fig. 9

AUXILIARY AIR VALVE

Description

The auxiliary air valve (Fig. 10) is mounted on the water outlet rail and is controlled by coolant temperature. The valve opens to pass additional air into the inlet manifold under cold start and cold idle conditions.

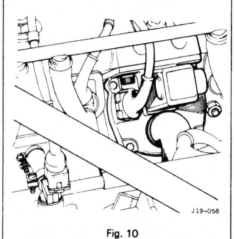

Fig. 10

Remove and refit 19.20.16

Removing

NOTE: This procedure MUST ONLY be carried out on a cold or cool engine.

Disconnect the battery.

Carefully remove the pressure cap from the remote expansion tank to release any cooling system residual pressure. Replace the cap tightly.

Slacken the clips securing the air hoses to the auxiliary air valve. Pull the hoses clear.

Remove the two screws and washers securing the auxiliary air valve to coolant pipe and lift clear.

Clean all traces of gasket from the coolant pipe, taking care not to damage seating area.

Refitting

Refit the air valve by reversing the above procedure.

Coat the new gasket with suitable non-hardening sealing compound.

Check the coolant level at the remote header tank, and if necessary, top-up.

AUXILIARY AIR VALVE

Test 19.20.17

Remove the electrical connector from the auxiliary air valve.

Connect a voltmeter across the terminals of the connector.

Crank the engine: battery voltage should be obtained. If there is no voltage there is a fault in the electrical system: check cables for loose connections or open circuit. When power is reaching the extra air valve, the heating coils resistance should be checked.

Connect an ohmmeter between the terminals of the air valve. A resistance of 33 ohms should be obtained. If there is no resistance the air valve should be replaced.

Remove the extra air valve mounting plate from the water rail.

Place the air valve in cold water, do not let water into the electrical terminals or into the by-pass channel. The blocking plate should fully expose the by-pass orifice.

Immerse the air valve mounting plate in hot water. The blocking plate should gradually close the by-pass orifice.

IDLE SPEED

Adjust 19.20.18

Ensure that the engine is at normal operating temperature.

Check the throttle linkage for correct operation, and that return springs are secure and effective.

Start the engine and run for two to three minutes.

Set the idle speed adjustment screw on air distribution block to achieve 800 rev/min.

NOTE: If it proves impossible to reduce idle speed to specified level carry out the following:

Check ALL pipes and hoses to inlet manifold for security and condition.

Check security of injectors and cold start injectors.

Ensure that all joints and inlet manifold to cylinder head fastenings are tight.

Ensure that throttle butterfly is correctly adjusted.

Check operation of over-run valve.

If the above do not reduce the idle speed, check operation of auxiliary air valve.

OVER-RUN VALVE—Cars fitted with Emission Control

Description

An over-run valve is fitted beneath the air distributor block. The valve is calibrated to open and limit manifold depression under conditions

continued

of closed throttle over-run. This ensures that air is available to maintain a combustible air/fuel ratio under all conditions. Air bleeds into the inlet manifold at 564 mm/Hg 22.2 in/Hg depression.

Test   19.20.21

Slacken the hose clip securing the over-run valve air feed hose to the throttle body and block the hose.

Start the engine; idle speed should remain correct.

If the idle speed is not correct, renew the over-run valve.

Remove and refit   19.20.22

Disconnect the battery.

Remove the air-flow meter.

Slacken the securing clip and disconnect the auxiliary air hose from the air distribution block (1, Fig. 11).

Slacken the clip securing the hose from the throttle butterfly housing.

Remove the three screws securing the air distribution block to the inlet manifold.

Lift the air distribution block from the inlet manifold and disconnect the air hose.

Withdraw the over-run valve (2, Fig. 11).

Reverse the above procedure to refit.

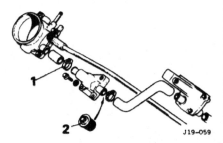

Fig. 11

FUEL CUT-OFF INERTIA SWITCH

Remove and refit   19.22.09

Removing

Disconnect the battery.

Unclip the switch cover at passenger side of fascia.

Disconnect cables from switch and switch from spring clips.

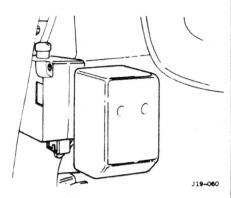

Fig. 12

Refitting

Press switch into spring clips with the ribs towards rear of car and terminals at bottom. Ensuring that the switch is raised in clips to abut on top lip of bracket.

Connect cables and press in plunger at top of switch.

Fit cover and re-connect battery.

OXYGEN SENSOR

Description

The oxygen sensor is located in the exhaust down-pipe. The sensor monitors the oxygen content in the exhaust and sends a proportional signal to the E.C.U., thus maintaining close air/fuel ratio control under all operating conditions.

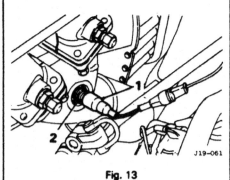

Fig. 13

Remove and refit   19.22.16

Disconnect the battery.

Disconnect the electrical connector on the oxygen sensor and remove (1, Fig. 13).

Clean the sensor sealing face (2, Fig. 13) and fit new oxygen sensor.

Reset the Service Interval Counter.

COOLANT TEMPERATURE SENSOR

Description

The coolant temperature sensor (Fig. 14) is located at the rear of the water rail.

The sensor comprises a temperature-sensitive resistor with a negative temperature coefficient, that is, the electrical resistance decreases with increasing temperature. The sensor provides the E.C.U. with a coolant temperature parameter that controls the injector signal pulse with respect to engine temperature. Practically, the sensor establishes a rich level of fuelling at low temperature, and a weaker level at high temperature. In conjunction with the auxiliary air valve the coolant temperature sensor forms an equivalent to a carburetter automatic choke.

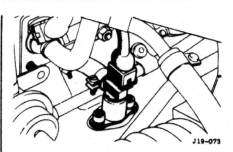

Fig. 14

Remove and refit   19.22.18

NOTE: This procedure MUST ONLY be carried out on a cold or cool engine.

Disconnect the battery and the connector from the coolant temperature sensor.

Carefully remove the pressure cap from the remote header tank to release any cooling system residual pressure. Replace the cap tightly. Ensure that the sealing washer is located on a replacement temperature sensor and coat the threads with suitable sealing compound, then remove the temperature sensor from the water rail and screw the replacement temperature sensor into position.

Refit the electrical connector, re-connect the battery and check the coolant level at the remote header tank. If necessary, top-up.

Test   19.22.19

Disconnect the battery.

Disconnect the cable from the temperature sensor.

Connect a suitable ohmmeter between the terminals; note the resistance reading. The reading is subject to change according to temperature and should closely approximate to the relevant resistance value given in the table.

Disconnect the ohmmeter.

Check the resistance between each terminal in turn and the body of the sensor. A very high resistance reading (open circuit) must be obtained.

Re-connect cable to sensor and re-connect the battery.

Coolant Temperature (°C)	Resistance (kilohms)
−10	9.2
0	5.9
+20	2.5
+40	1.18
+60	0.60
+80	0.325

THERMOTIME SWITCH

Description

The Thermotime switch (Fig. 15) is located at the front of the water rail. The switch comprises a bi-metallic contact opened and closed by coolant temperature and, in addition, auto-excited by a heating element. The switch controls the cold start injector through the cold start relay and is energized by operation of the starter motor. While the start system is in operation a voltage is applied to the bi-metallic switch contact heating element which then tends to open the contact and isolate the relay and injector. The time that this takes depends upon the initial temperature of the bi-metallic element and can be up to eight seconds under conditions of extreme cold. When the engine is warm, or at normal operating temperature, there will be no fuel supplied by the cold start injector.

Fig. 15

Remove and refit   19.22.20

NOTE: This procedure MUST ONLY be carried out on a cool or cold engine.

Disconnect the battery and the connector from the Thermotime switch.
Carefully remove the pressure cap from the remote header tank to release any cooling system residual pressure. Replace the cap tightly.
Ensure that a new sealing washer is located on replacement Thermotime switch and coat the threads with a suitable sealing compound.
Remove the Thermotime switch from the front of the water rail.
Screw replacement Thermotime switch in position.
Refit electrical connector and re-connect battery.
Check coolant level at remote header tank, and top-up if necessary.

Test   19.22.21

Equipment required: Stop watch, ohmmeter, single-pole switch, jump lead for connecting switch to battery and Thermotime switch, and a thermometer.

NOTE: Check coolant temperature with thermometer and note reading before carrying out procedures detailed below. Check rated value of Thermotime switch (stamped on body flat) should be obtained. The test must be carried out with coolant temperature below the operating temperature to ensure correct operation of the switch.

Disconnect the battery earth lead and the electrical connector from the Thermotime switch.
Connect ohmmeter between terminal 'W' and earth. A very low resistance reading (closed circuit) should be obtained.
Connect 12V supply via isolating switch to terminal 'G' of Thermotime switch.

Using stop watch, check time delay between making isolating switch and indication on ohmmeter changing from low to high resistance. Delay must closely approximate to time stated below.
Renew Thermotime switch if necessary and re-connect the battery.

Coolant Temperature	Delay
−20°C	8 seconds
0°C	4½ seconds
+10°C	3½ seconds
+35°C	0 seconds

AIR TEMPERATURE SENSOR
Description

The air temperature sensor is an integral part of the air-flow meter. The sensor provides information to the E.C.U. relating to the ambient air density and temperature thus maintaining an optimum fuel/air ratio.

Test   19.22.23

Disconnect the battery and remove the multi-pin electrical connector from the air-flow meter.
Connect a suitable ohmmeter between terminals 6 and 27 of the air-flow meter.

Ambient Air Temperature (°C)	Resistance (kilohms)
−10	9.2
0	5.0
+20	2.5
+40	1.18
+60	0.60

Note the resistance reading. The reading is subject to change according to the temperature and should closely approximate to the relevant resistance value given in the table above.
Disconnect the ohmmeter.
Re-connect the multi-pin connector and battery.

AIR-FLOW METER
Description

The air-flow meter is located between the air cleaner and the inlet manifold mounted throttle butterfly. The flap in the air-flow meter is opened when the air is drawn into the engine. The E.C.U. uses the flap angle to compute fuel requirements.

Remove and refit   19.22.25

Disconnect the battery.
Slacken the two clips which secure the air-intake hoses on each side of the air-flow meter (1, Fig. 16).
Disconnect the electrical connector from the air-flow meter.
Remove the three screws which secure the air-flow meter to its mounting bracket (2, Fig. 16), remove the air-flow meter and withdraw the air-intake hoses.
After refitting reset idle mixture screw using correct equipment.

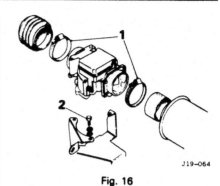

Fig. 16

COLD START SYSTEM
Test   12.22.32

WARNING: This test results in fuel vapour being present in the engine compartment. It is therefore imperative that all due precautions are taken against fire and explosion.

NOTE: The ambient temperature and the engine temperature must be below 35°C in order for the system to work and be testable.

Remove the electrical connector from the cold start injector.
Connect a voltmeter across the terminals of the connector.
Crank the engine: battery voltage should be obtained.
Remove the setscrew and washer securing the cold start injector to the inlet manifold.
Remove the cold start injector.
Arrange a container to collect sprayed fuel, and refit the connector.
Check for fuel leaking past the nozzle.
Crank the engine. The cold start injector should spray fuel out for a few seconds until the Thermotime switch switches off the injector. When the engine is warm the injector should not spray fuel during engine cranking.

ELECTRONIC CONTROL UNIT (E.C.U.)
Description

The E.C.U. is mounted in the luggage compartment against the front bulkhead (Fig. 17). The E.C.U. receives all electrical input signals from the various sensors. This information is used to determine the correct period of time for which the injectors are held open in each engine cycle.

continued

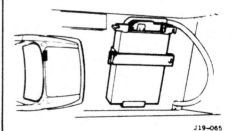

Fig. 17

19—9

Remove and refit   **19.22.34**

Disconnect the battery.

At the forward end of the luggage compartment, remove the E.C.U. cover.

Remove the retainer band and cable clamp clip. Unclip the end cover.

Locate handle on the harness plug and withdraw the plug, lift out the unit.

THROTTLE SWITCH (FEDERAL CARS)

Description

The throttle switch (Fig. 18) is located on the end of the throttle spindle. The switch closes when the throttle nears the wide-open position and provides information to the E.C.U. of fuel quantity required by the injector for maximum power output at full throttle.

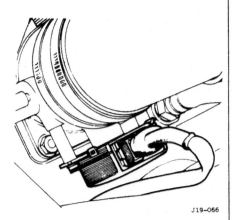

Fig. 18

Remove and refit.   **19.22.36**

Disconnect the battery.

Pull the electrical connector from the throttle switch.

Remove the two screws, plain and shakeproof washers securing the throttle switch and lift the switch from the spindle. Collect spacers. Refit by reversing the above procedure.

Test   **19.22.37**

NOTE: Before commencing the following tests ensure that the throttle butterfly valve and throttle linkage are correctly adjusted.

Disconnect the battery.

Remove the electrical connector from the throttle switch.

Connect a powered test lamp between terminals 3 and 18 of the throttle switch.

Open the throttle; the bulb should light up when the throttle nears the wide open position. If the bulb does not light, replace the throttle switch.

Refit the electrical connector to the switch.

Re-connect the battery.

THROTTLE SWITCH (U.K. and EUROPE)—Manual Gearbox only

A micro-switch actuated by the throttle is fitted to U.K. and European cars. This switch replaces the Federal switch. A full load vacuum switch is also fitted all European cars.

MAIN RELAY/PUMP RELAY/ DIODE UNIT

Description

Three relays, main relay cold start (2, Fig. 19), pump relay (3, Fig. 19), diode unit (1, Fig. 19) are mounted on the engine rear bulkhead next to the vehicle battery. When the ignition key is turned, the main relay is activated, connecting the battery circuit to the ballast resistors and the injectors. The relay also allows current to flow to the E.C.U. and the pump switch on the air-flow meter.

When the engine is cranked for starting, the diode unit is activated and thus energizes the auxiliary air valve, the cold start system and the fuel pump.

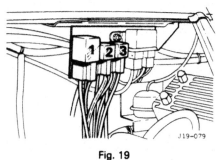

Fig. 19

FUEL LINE FILTER

Remove and refit   **19.25.01**

WARNING: The spilling of fuel is unavoidable during this operation. It is therefore imperative that all due precautions are taken against fire and explosion.

The fuel filter (Fig. 20) is located in the luggage compartment mounted on the right-hand side under the floor.

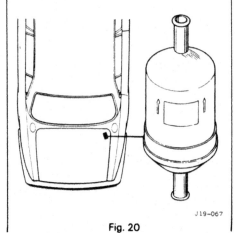

Fig. 20

NOTE: Early Series III cars were built with the fuel filter mounted in the engine compartment on the R.H. valance under the air cleaner.

Disconnect the battery and remove the luggage compartment floor.

Remove the bolt securing the filter and draw the filter clear of the clamp.

Clamp the inlet and outlet pipes.

Slacken the pipe clips on either side of the filter and remove the filter unit.

Fit a new filter, observing the direction of flow denoted by arrows on the filter.

After fitting a new filter check for leakproof joints by running the engine before fitting the luggage compartment floor.

FUEL TANK CHANGE-OVER VALVE

Description

The change-over valve is located in the luggage compartment adjacent to the fuel pump. When energized by the change-over switch, the valve opens the outlet pipe from the right-hand fuel tank. When de-energized, the valve opens the outlet pipe from the left-hand fuel tank.

Remove and refit   **19.40.31**

Disconnect the battery.

Remove the spare wheel.

Clamp the inlet and outlet pipes, release the pipe clips and pull the pipes from the change-over valve.

Disconnect the cable to the valve.

Remove the valve by unscrewing the clamp securing screws.

Refitting

When refitting ensure that the ground lead is secured by one foot of securing clamp.

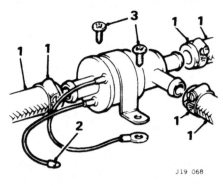

Fig. 21

FUEL TANK CHANGE-OVER VALVE

Test   19.40.32

Depressurize the fuel system and disconnect the battery.

Remove the spare wheel.

Clamp the inlet and outlet pipes, release the pipe clips and pull the pipes from the change-over valve.

Disconnect the cable to the valve.

Push a suitable length of rubber pipe on the centre inlet port of the valve.

Blow through the rubber pipe. Air should flow from the outlet union through the body of the solenoid.

Apply 12V d.c. to the valve cable.

Blow through the rubber pipe. Air should flow from the outlet union towards the opposite side.

If the results are satisfactory, reverse the above procedure.

If the results are not satisfactory, fit new valve.

FUEL COOLER

Remove and refit   19.40.40

Removing

WARNING: Refrigerant gas can cause blindness. It is therefore essential to depressurize the air conditioning system prior to disconnecting refrigerant hose to fuel cooler. See Air Conditioning System.

Depressurize the fuel and air conditioning systems.

Disconnect refrigerant inlet and outlet hoses (1, Fig. 22). Plug hoses.

Clamp the fuel hoses and disconnect (2, Fig. 22).

Remove setscrews, washers and Spire nuts securing the fuel cooler to the compressor (3, Fig. 22).

Refitting

Test systems after refitting.

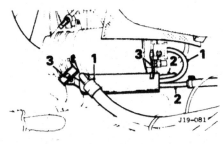

Fig. 22

FUEL RETURN VALVES

Remove and refit   19.40.44

Removing

Depressurize the fuel system.

Place the vehicle on stands and remove the rear wheel(s).

Remove the valve cover (1, Fig. 23).

Remove screws securing valve to body (2, Fig. 23).

Fit hose clamps both sides of the valve and slacken the hose to valve clips (3, Fig. 23).

Disconnect the solenoid cables from the valve and remove valve (4, Fig. 23).

Refitting

Reverse the above procedure, ensuring tight connections. Check for fuel leaks.

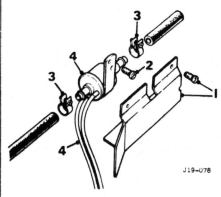

Fig. 23

FUEL PUMP

Description

The fuel pump is located beneath the luggage compartment floor. It is flexibly mounted and secured using noise- and shock-absorbing material. The pump is a roller-type machine delivering a continuous flow of fuel under pressure.

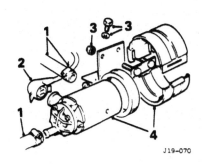

Fig. 24

Remove and refit   19.45.08

Disconnect the battery.

Remove the spare wheel.

Clamp the inlet and outlet pipes, release the clips and pull the pipes from the pump unions (1, Fig. 24).

Remove the electrical connector (2, Fig. 24).

Remove the screws securing the pump mounting bracket (3, Fig 24).

Remove securing nuts from clamp and withdraw the pump (4, Fig. 24).

Reverse above procedure to refit, locating the earth wire on bright metal beneath one securing screw.

FUEL PRESSURE REGULATOR

Description

The fuel pressure regulator is mounted on the inlet manifold and is connected to the fuel rail on one side and inlet manifold depression on the other (Fig. 25). The regulator maintains the correct fuel pressure in the fuel rail.

Remove and refit   19.45.11

Depressurize the fuel system and disconnect the battery.

Remove two setscrews and washers (1, Fig. 25) securing the pressure regulator mounting bracket and carefully pull regulator and brackets upwards. Note orientation of regulator in bracket.

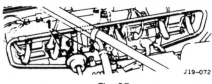

Fig. 25

Clamp inlet and outlet pipes of regulator, release the clips and pull the pipes from the regulator unions.

Remove the nut and washer and release the regulator from the bracket.

When refitting, locate the regulator in the bracket orientated as noted; ensuring that pipes are not kinked or twisted.

Check   19.45.12

Depressurize the fuel system:

Slacken the pipe clip securing the cold start injector supply pipe to the fuel rail and pull the pipe from the rail.

Connect the pressure gauge pipe to the fuel rail and tighten the pipe clip.

CAUTION: The pressure gauge must be checked against an approved standard at regular intervals.

Pull the '−ve' L.T. lead from the ignition coil and switch ignition on.

Check reading on pressure gauge: reading must be 2.55 ± 0.05 kgf/cm² (36.25 ± 0.725 lbf/in²).

NOTE: The pressure reading may drop slowly through either the regulator valve seating or the pump non-return valve. A slow, steady drop is permissible; a rapid fall MUST be investigated.

Operate fuel change-over switch on centre instrument panel.

Re-check the pressure gauge reading.

NOTE: If satisfactory results have been obtained, depressurize the fuel system. Disconnect the pressure gauge. If satisfactory results have not been obtained replace the regulator with a new unit.

FUEL SYSTEM

Depressurize   19.50.02

CAUTION: The fuel system MUST always be depressurized before disconnecting any fuel system component.

Remove the fuel pump relay socket.
Switch on and crank the engine for a few seconds.
Switch the ignition off and re-connect the pump relay socket.

INJECTORS

Description

The six injectors are mounted on the induction ram pipes so that the fuel jet is directed onto the back of each inlet valve. The injectors are solenoid-operated valves which are controlled by the E.C.U.

Remove and refit   19.60.01

Depressurize the fuel system, and then disconnect the battery.
Clamp the fuel inlet pipe adjacent to the fuel rail.
Pull the electrical connector from the injector(s) to be removed.
Remove the two setscrews securing the fuel rail to the inlet manifold.
Release the clips securing the supply rail to the return rail.
Pull the manifold pressure pipe from the inlet manifold.
Remove the six nuts and spring washers securing the injector clamps to the induction ram pipes.
Carefully lift the fuel rail complete with injectors sufficient for injectors to clear the induction ram pipes. Ensure that adequate material is to hand to absorb spilled fuel.
Suitably plug or cover the injector holes in ram pipes to prevent ingress of dirt or foreign matter.
Slacken the pipe clip(s) of injector(s) to be removed.
Note position of electrical sockets and pull injector(s) from fuel rail.
Remove two rubber sealing 'O' rings from ALL injectors.
When refitting the injectors the sealing rings MUST be renewed.

INJECTORS — SET

Injector winding check   19.60.02

Use an ohmmeter to measure the resistance value of each injector winding, which should be 2.4 ohms at 20°C (68°F).
Check for short-circuit to earth on winding by connecting ohmmeter probes between either injector terminal and injector body. Meter should read ∞ (infinity).
If any injector winding is open-circuited or short-circuited, replace the injector.

FUEL RAIL

Remove and refit   19.60.04

Depressurize the fuel system and disconnect the battery.
Pull the manifold pressure pipe from the inlet manifold.
Clamp the fuel pipe adjacent to the supply fuel rail.
Release the clips securing the return fuel rail to the supply rail and the return fuel rail to the regulator outlet hoses and fuel return pipe. Pull the hoses from the rail.
Release the clips securing the supply fuel rail to main fuel rail, cold start injector and regulator inlet hoses. Pull the hoses from the supply rail.
Remove supply and return fuel rails.
Pull electrical connectors from injectors and cold start injector.
Remove the six nuts and spring washers securing the injector clamps to the induction ram pipe.
Carefully lift the fuel rail complete with injectors from the induction ram pipes. Ensure that adequate material is to hand to absorb spilled fuel.
Suitably plug or cover the injector holes in the ram pipes to prevent the ingress of dirt or foreign matter.
Slacken the clips securing the injectors to the fuel rail stubs, pull the injectors from fuel rail.

NOTE: If necessary, transfer clips and insulation to replacement fuel rail.

When refitting fit new 'O' rings to each injector and test for leaks.

COLD START INJECTOR

Description

A cold start injector (Fig. 26) is mounted in the inlet manifold, aligned to spray a finely atomized mist of fuel towards the throttle butterfly valve. The injector is controlled by the cold start relay and the Thermotime switch and is only operative during the first few seconds of a cold engine starting cycle.

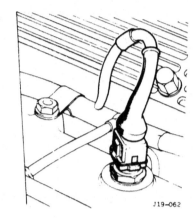

J19-062

Fig. 26

Remove and refit   19.60.06

Depressurize the fuel system and disconnect the battery.
Pull the electrical connector from the injector.
Fit clamp on the supply pipe to the injector, slacken the clips and pull pipe from the injector.
Remove the two setscrews securing the injector to the inlet manifold.
Check the condition of the gasket, and renew as necessary.
To test the system see operation 19.22.32, 'Cold start system — test'.

CONTENTS

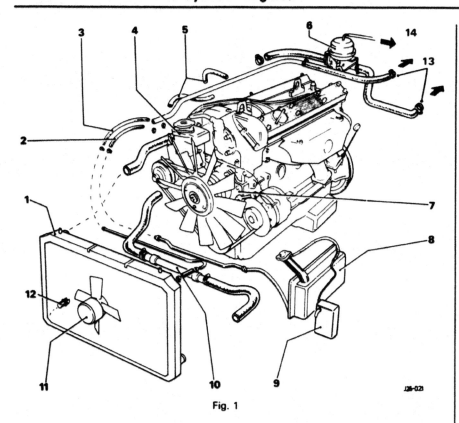

1. Radiator matrix
2. Radiator vent. pipe
3. Expansion pipe
4. Header tank (Thermostat housing)
5. Fuel injection throttle housing heater pipe
6. Water control valve.
7. Water pump
8. Remote header tank
9. Atmospheric tank
10. Transmission oil cooler
11. Single or twin fan
12. Fan thermostat
13. To heater matrix
14. To vaccum control

Fig. 1

COOLING SYSTEM

Description   26.00.00

The cooling system consists of a radiator matrix, A; a water pump, B—belt driven by the engine crankshaft; a header tank, C, and a remote header or expansion tank, D, a thermostatic valve located in the header tank is fitted to ensure a rapid warm-up from cold.

Air-conditioned cars are fitted with either single or twin electric fans, E, mounted in front of the condenser and radiator, in addition to the engine-driven fan. The electric fans are thermostatically controlled and it is possible, in very hot conditions, for them to continue to operate after the engine has been switched off. They will switch off automatically when the coolant temperature drops to 92°C. Under cold start condition coolant is forced by the water pump through the cylinder block, cylinder head, and the induction manifold to the thermostatic valve housing, C. The valve is closed and the coolant is therefore returned via a by-pass drilling, to the water pump suction inlet.

The heater matrix, K, is purged during this period by opening the heater control valve, L, at the matrix inlet and allowing pump suction to remove trapped air. The radiator has a vent pipe, M, through which, during the initial cold filling, the radiator is vented. When engine temperature rises to a predetermined level the thermostatic valve opens and allows hot coolant to flow into the top of the radiator. Full pump suction then draws coolant from the base of the radiator and starts the full cooling circuit; coolant expansion due to the rise in temperature is accommodated by the expansion tank, D, via expansion pipe, N.

Cars fitted with automatic transmission have a cooling tube, O, included in the centre section of the radiator bottom hose.

We use and recommend BP Type H21 or Union Carbide UT184 or Unipart Universal antifreeze which should be used at the specified concentration whenever the cooling system is refilled. For topping-up purposes, only reputable brands of anti-freeze, formulated and approved for 'mixed metal' engines be used.

IMPORTANT NOTE: The concentration of anti-freeze must not be allowed to fall below the recommended strength as sediment may be formed in the cooling system by certain types of anti-freeze at low concentrates.

A 40% solution by volume in the United Kingdom (55%, U.S.A./Canada and all other countries) must be used at all times, either by topping-up or replenishing the cooling system. For maximum corrosion protection, the concentration should never be allowed to fall below 25%. Always top-up with recommended strength of anti-freeze, NEVER WITH WATER ONLY.

In countries where it is unnecessary to use antifreeze, Marston SQ 35 Corrosion Inhibitor must be used in the cooling system in the proportion of 1 part SQ 36 to 24 parts water. CHANGE COOLANT EVERY TWO YEARS. The system should be drained, flushed and refilled with fresh anti-freeze (or Corrosion Inhibitor), mixed with 1 satchet of 'Barrs Leaks'.

An alternative coolant known as CARBUROL FORLIFE is recommended where temperatures below 10°C (14°F) are not encountered. Before Carburol Forlife is used, the coolant already present in the system must be drained out and the system flushed before filling with Carburol Forlife. Once in use the system should be topped-up with Carburol Forlife only, and a label giving this information should be affixed in an appropriate and prominent position.

TORQUE WRENCH SETTINGS

NOTE: Set the torque wrench to the mean of the figures quoted unless otherwise specified.

ITEM	DESCRIPTION	TIGHTENING TORQUE		
		Nm	kgf m	lbf ft
Radiator to front cross-member	⅜ in U.N.F. nut	29,8 to 35,2	3,05 to 3,59	22 to 26
Retainer to radiator cross-member	⁵⁄₁₆ in U.N.F. nut	19 to 24,4	1,94 to 2,48	14 to 18
Fan cowl upper bracket to body	¼ in U.N.F. nut	8,1 to 9,5	0,83 to 0,96	6 to 7
Expansion tank to valance	⁵⁄₁₆ in U.N.F. nut	10,8 to 13,6	1,10 to 1,38	8 to 10
Engine oil cooler pipes	1¹⁄₁₆ in U.N.S. nut	54,3 to 61	5,53 to 6,22	40 to 45
Deflector and bracket to cowl	¼ in U.N.F. bolt	8,1 to 9,5	0,83 to 0,96	6 to 7
Lower bracket to cowl	¼ in U.N.F. nut	6,1 to 7,5	0,62 to 0,76	4.5 to 5.5
Lower cowl bracket to body	¼ in U.N.F. bolt	8,1 to 9,5	0,83 to 0,96	6 to 7

COOLANT

Drain and refill   26.10.01

Draining

With the engine cold, remove the pressure cap at the expansion tank and the sealing cap at the engine header tank. Check the condition of the seals on the pressure caps, renew seals or caps.

Remove the radiator drain plug, and drain the radiator.

Remove the engine block drain plug, and drain the engine block.

Insert a water hose in the remote header tank, and regulate the flow so that the tank remains full with a minimum of overflow. Start the engine and run it at fast idle (about 1000 rev/min) until the water from the drain holes becomes clear. Stop the engine, turn off the tap and allow the system to empty.

Refilling

Refit the radiator and engine drain plugs.

Set the heater control to 'DEF' ('HIGH' non-air conditioned cars only).

Slowly pour the recommended coolant mixture into the engine header tank.

When the header tank is completely full with coolant refit the sealing cap.

Start and run engine at fast idle (1 000 rev/min) for approximately five minutes.

Switch off the engine, carefully remove the pressure cap from expansion tank, and if necessary add coolant to bring level to the base of filler neck. Refit the cap.

NOTE: It is not important if coolant is above this level as excess liquid will be ejected through the vent pipe.

When the engine is cold, remove the header tank cap to check that it is full. If not top it up and run the engine for another five minutes and check the coolant level in the header tank again, after the engine has cooled. If the tank is not full a leak has developed in the system which must be traced and rectified.

TOPPING-UP AND CHECKING COOLANT LEVEL

NOTE: This procedure must only be carried out when the engine is cold.

Remove the pressure cap from expansion tank, and if coolant is below the base of filler neck add specified coolant mixture to correct level. Refit the pressure cap.

EXPANSION TANK

Remove and refit   26.15.01

Removing

Remove the pressure cap and sealing cap.

Remove windscreen washer reservoir and the bracket rear upper securing screw.

Disconnect the expansion pipe from the bottom of the expansion tank and the overflow pipe from the filler neck.

Remove expansion tank securing nut and bolt, carefully displace windscreen reservoir bracket, and lift the tank clear.

Refitting

Carefully displace the windscreen washer reservoir and locate the expansion tank to the inner wing.

Fit and tighten nut and bolt to secure.

Refit the expansion pipe to the bottom of expansion tank and the overflow pipe to the filler neck.

Fit and tighten the windscreen washer reservoir bracket securing screws.

Refit the washer reservoir.

Top-up cooling system.

Refit pressure cap and sealing cap.

FAN/STEERING PUMP BELT TENSION

Check and adjust 26.20.01

Slacken the power steering pump adjuster link trunnion bolt (1, Fig. 2).
Slacken adjuster link eye-bolt (2, Fig. 2) at power-assisted steering pump and pump pivot bolt (3, Fig. 2).
Slacken the adjuster link locknut (4, Fig. 2).

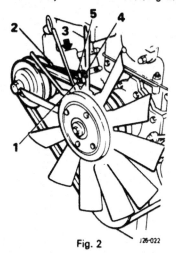

Fig. 2   J26-022

Tighten the adjuster nut (5, Fig. 2), and check the tension. Deflecting force 2,9 kgf (6.4 lbf). Deflection longest run 4,3 mm (0.17 in).
Tighten the locknut.
Tighten the adjuster link trunnion bolt.
Tighten adjuster link eye-bolt and tighten pump pivot bolt nut.

FAN/STEERING PUMP BELT

Remove and refit 26.20.07

Removing

Slacken the power steering pump adjuster link trunnion bolt (1, Fig. 2).
Slacken adjuster link eye-bolt (2, Fig. 2) at power-assisted steering pump.
Slacken the pump pivot bolt nut (3, Fig. 2).
Slacken the adjuster link locknut (4, Fig. 2) and press the pump towards the engine.
Remove the belt.

Refitting

Manoeuvre the belt over the fan blades and pulleys.
Tighten the adjuster nut (5, Fig. 2).
Check the belt tension. Deflecting force 2,9 kgf (6.4 lbf). Deflection on longest run 4,3 mm (0.17 in).
Tighten the locknut, adjuster link trunnion bolt, adjuster link eye-bolt and pump pivot bolt nut.

FAN AND TORQUATROL UNIT

Remove and refit 26.25.19

Removing

Remove the top fan cowl from the top rail and from the main cowl.
Restrain pulley with a suitable spanner, and remove the Torquatrol securing bolt (1, Fig. 3).

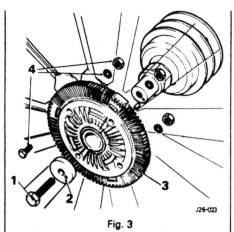

Fig. 3

Remove the pegged washer (2, Fig. 3).
Gently tap Torquatrol unit (3, Fig. 3) forward from pulley spigot and lift unit from car.
Remove nuts and bolts (4, Fig. 3) securing fan assembly.
Remove fan assembly.

Refitting

Locate fan to Torquatrol unit, secure with the nuts and bolts, lightly grease the spigot and offer Torquatrol unit on to pulley.
Secure the Torquatrol unit using the pegged washer and centre bolt.

NOTE: Ensure that the washer locates on pin in pulley spigot before tightening bolt.

Sit the top cowl to the main cowl assembly, and secure to top rail.

FAN MOTOR

Remove and refit 26.25.22

Removing

Remove the radiator lower grille, and unclip the harness from the fan motor mounting cross-beam.
Disconnect the fan motor harness at the block connector.
Remove the cross-beam to body securing bolts, spacers and washers.
Remove the fan motor mounting frame to cross-beam securing nuts and bolts.
Displace the motor for access and remove the mounting frame to cross-beam spacing washers.
Remove the cross-beam and the fan assembly.
Remove the fan blades.
Remove the fan motor securing nuts and bolts.
Remove the fan motor and fan motor mounting rubbers.

Refitting

Fit fan motor and fan mounting rubber to frame, secure with fixing nuts and screws.
Fit and align the fan blades; secure with circlip.
Fit the fan motor assembly to vehicle.
Fit and align the mounting cross-beam.
Fit the spacers and washers to body, fit but do not tighten the cross-beam to body securing bolts.

Fit mounting rubber to cross-beam washers.
Align the mounting frame to cross-beam.
Secure with the fixing nuts and bolts.
Connect the fan motor harness block connector, and clip the harness to the cross-beam.
Tighten the cross-beam securing bolts.
Refit the radiator grille.

FAN MOTOR RELAY

Remove and refit 26.25.31

Removing

Remove the screw securing the relay cover to the wing valance and remove the cover.
Note and disconnect the cables from the relay.
Remove the relay.

Refitting

Identify and re-connect the cables to the relay.
Refit the relay to its mounting position.
Refit the relay cover.
Fit and tighten screw to secure.

THERMOSTATIC SWITCH

Remove and refit 26.25.35

Removing

Drain the radiator, see operation 26.10.01
Jack up vehicle and place two stands.
Note and disconnect the cables from switch.
Remove the switch.

Refitting

Fit and tighten the thermostatic switch.
Identify and connect cable to the switch.
Remove stands, lower the vehicle, and refill the radiator, see operation 26.10.01.

RADIATOR BLOCK

Cars fitted with Air Conditioning
Remove and refit 26.40.04

WARNING: Under no circumstances must any portion of the air conditioning system be disconnected by anyone other than a qualified refrigeration engineer. Blindness can result if the gas contained within the system comes into contact with eyes.

Removing

Drain the coolant from the radiator, see operation 26.10.01.
Disconnect the battery.
Remove the bonnet.
Slacken the clips securing the top hose, bottom hose and expansion pipe to the radiator.
Disconnect the hoses from the radiator.
Unclip the cable harness from the top rail.
Remove the top rail to body and top rail to fan cowl securing nuts/bolts.
Reposition the cowl from top rail.
Remove top rail to air conditioning condenser securing bolts and remove the spacers.
Unclip the receiver/drier from top rail.
Remove the receiver/drier to top rail securing bolts and remove the spacers.
Reposition the top rail from radiator location.
Remove the air cleaner ram pipe.

26—4

Disconnect the coolant level probe.
Displace the radiator to gain access to thermostatic switch.
Note and disconnect cables from switch.
Lift radiator from car, and recover the foam rubber padding.

Refitting

Locate radiator in a position to reconnect the thermostatic switch.
Reposition the radiator into its mounting rubbers and reposition the air conditioning pipes.
Reconnect the coolant level probe.
Refit the air cleaner ram pipe.
Align the top rail to the radiator, and fit but do not tighten the securing nuts and bolts.
Fit the top rail to condenser spacers, and fit but do not tighten the securing nuts and bolts.
Locate the fan cowl to the top rail.
Fit nuts and bolts to secure.
Tighten all the nuts and bolts.
Align the receiver drier with the top rail, fit the spacers and secure the receiver drier with the fixing bolts.
Clip the air conditioning pipe and cable harness to the top rail.
Connect bottom hose, top hose, and the expansion pipe to the radiator.
Tighten hose clips.
Refill the radiator with coolant, see operation 26.10.01.
Reconnect the battery.
Refit the bonnet.

RADIATOR BLOCK
Cars fitted with Heater only
Remove and refit　　　　**26.40.04**

Removing

Drain the coolant from the radiator, see operation 26.10.01.
Disconnect the battery.
Remove the bonnet.
Slacken clips and remove the top hose, bottom hose and expansion pipe from the radiator.
Unclip the cable harness from the top rail.
Remove the top rail to body securing nuts and bolts.
Remove the top rail to fan cowl securing nuts and bolts.
Displace the cowl from the top rail, and the top rail from the radiator location.
Remove the air cleaner ram tube.
Disconnect the coolant level probe, and lift the radiator from car.
Recover the rubber foam padding.

Refitting

Fit radiator to the mounting rubbers, and reconnect the coolant level probe.
Fit and secure the air cleaner ram pipe.
Align the top rail to the radiator.
Fit but do not tighten the securing nuts and bolts.
Secure the fan cowl to top rail, and tighten all securing nuts and bolts.
Reclip the cable harness to the top rail.
Fit and secure bottom hose, top hose and expansion pipe to the radiator.

Refill the radiator with coolant, see operation 26.10.01.
Reconnect the battery.
Refit the bonnet.

THERMOSTAT
Remove and refit　　　　**26.45.01**

Removing

Partially drain the coolant from the radiator.
Disconnect the battery.
Slacken the vent pipe clips and remove the pipe from the filler neck.
Slacken the top hose clips and disconnect the hose from the filler housing.
Slacken water pump to the filler housing clip.
Remove the filler housing securing bolts (1, Fig. 4).

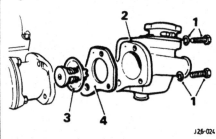

Fig. 4

Displace the engine breather pipe clip bracket and remove the spacing washer.
Carefully break the joint and remove the thermostat housing (2, Fig. 4) from the water pump hose.
Remove the thermostat (3, Fig. 4) from the thermostat housing.
Discard the old gasket (4, Fig. 4) and clean the sealing faces.
Remove all sludge or scale present.

Refitting

Refit the thermostat into the thermostat housing.
Replace the filler housing gasket and fit the filler housing.
Fit the spacing washers and align the engine breather pipe bracket.
Fit and tighten the filler housing securing bolts.
Refit the water pump to filler housing hose, top hose and vent pipe.
Tighten all the clips.
Refill the radiator with coolant, see operation 26.10.01.
Reconnect the battery.

WATER PUMP
Remove and refit　　　　**26.50.01**

Removing

Drain the coolant, see operation 26.10.01.
Remove the fan cowl and the Torquatrol assembly (Fig. 5).

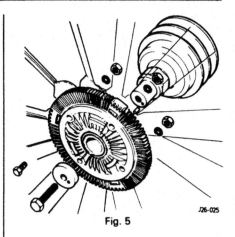

Fig. 5

Release and screw back inner locknut (1, Fig. 6) at the power-assisted steering pump adjuster trunnion.
Slacken the nut of the pivot bolt (2, Fig. 6) and slacken the bolt (3, Fig. 6) securing the adjusting link to the pump.
Slacken the bolt securing the trunnion block (4, Fig. 6) and swing the pump towards the engine.
Remove the belt.
Remove the trunnion bolt and pivot the pump away from the engine.

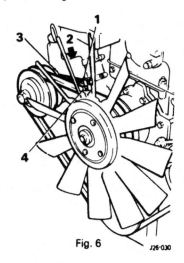

Fig. 6

Cars fitted with heater only

Slacken the alternator adjuster trunnion bolt (1, Fig. 7), remove the alternator adjuster pivot bolt (2, Fig. 7) and slacken the alternator mounting bolt (3, Fig. 7).
Pivot the alternator adjuster from the engine, and release the tension from the belt.

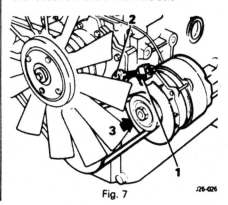

Fig. 7

26—5

Cars fitted with air conditioning

Slacken the two compressor pivot bolts on front and rear flanges.

Slacken the compressor trunnion bolt and remove the adjuster pivot bolt.

Pivot the adjuster from the water pump and release the tension from drive belt.

All cars

Disconnect the oil cooler to water pump hose at the water pump.

Disconnect the throttle housing to water pump hose at the water pump.

Loosen the clips on the heater return pipe and the filler housing hose.

Remove the nuts and bolts securing the water pump.

Disconnect the water pump hose from the pump. Displace the pump from the studs and disconnect from the filler housing. Remove the pump assembly.

Remove and discard the gasket.

Refitting

Fit a new gasket to the timing cover.

Fit the pump to the filler housing.

Locate the pump onto the timing cover, and into the water pipe hose.

Tighten the clips.

Fit and tighten securing the nuts and bolts 'by diagonal selection'.

Connect the throttle housing hose, and oil cooler hose to the water pump.

Cars fitted with air conditioning

Pivot the compressor to tighten the drive belt.

Pivot the adjuster to the water pump and fit the adjuster pivot bolt.

Adjust and check for correct drive belt tension, refer to Drive Belt Tension Data.

Tighten locknut and all bolts.

Cars fitted with heater only

Pivot the alternator and tighten the drive belt.

Pivot the adjuster towards the engine, and refit the adjuster pivot bolt.

Adjust and check for correct drive belt tension, refer to Drive Belt Tension Data.

Tighten the locknut and all the bolts.

All cars

Pivot the power-assisted steering pump towards the engine.

Fit but do not tighten the trunnion bolt.

Refit the drive belt, and adjust the nuts on the links to obtain the correct belt tension, refer to Drive Belt Tension Data.

Retighten all bolts and nuts.

Refit the Torquatrol assembly and fan cowl.

Refill the radiator with coolant, see operation 26.10.01

ADDITIONAL WORK FOR WATER PUMP RENEWAL — FEDERAL VEHICLES

Remove the air pump — 17.25.07.

Release the air conditioning compressor belt tension 82.10.01 and remove the link arm pivot bolt.

Undo and remove the air pump mounting bracket to the timing cover securing bolt.

Displace and remove the bracket spacer.

On removal of water pump securing bolts:-
Remove the air pump mounting bracket.

On refitting of the water pump securing bolts:-
Fit the air pump mounting bracket.

Fit the bracket spacer.

Fit and tighten the bracket securing bolt.

Refit the compressor link arm pivot bolt and re-adjust the belt tension.

Refit the air pump assembly.

DRIVE BELT TENSION DATA

Driving belt for	Deflection force		Deflection	
	kg	lb	mm	in
P.A.S. pump and water pump	2,9	6.4	4,3	0.17
Alternator	1,45	3.2	3,8	0.15
Compressor	2,9	6.4	4,3	0.17

WATER PUMP

Overhaul   26.50.06

Remove water pump, see operation 26.50.01.

Dismantling

Use extractor bolt (⅜" U.N.F. × 2 in).

Slacken the locknut (1, Fig. 8) and remove the bearing lockscrew (2, Fig. 8).

Support the body of the pump on press bed, close around impeller.

Using a suitable mandrel acting against the case of bearing, press the bearing/spindle and impeller assembly (3, Fig. 8) from the body of the pump.

Press the bearing/spindle assembly from impeller (Fig. 9).

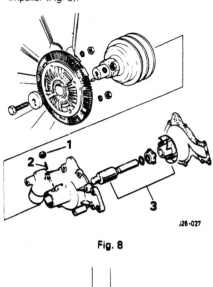

Fig. 8

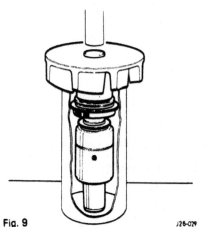

Fig. 9   J26-029

Inspection

Thoroughly clean all parts of the pump except the bearing/spindle assembly in a suitable cleaning solvent.

Inspect the bearing for excessive play and remove any burrs, rust or scale from the shaft using fine emery cloth.

NOTE: Wrap the bearing in a clean cloth to prevent contamination by emery dust.

If signs of wear or corrosion are evident in bearing bore or on the face in front of the impeller, the body of the pump must be replaced.

Reassembling

Align the location hole in the bearing with the tapped hole in the pump body and press the bearing/spindle assembly into the body until the holes coincide.

Fit the bearing lockscrew and secure using the locknut.

Coat the outside of the brass seal housing with a suitable sealing compound, and fit into the recess in the pump body.

Carefully press the impeller onto the spindle until the dimension (A) shown on illustration (Fig. 10) is obtained. A = 0.381 ± 0.07 mm (0.015 ± 0.003 in)

Press pulley onto spindle, taking care to ensure that impeller is not moved from dimensions given above.

Refit the water pump, see operation 26.50.01.

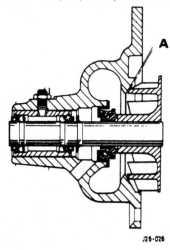

Fig. 10

CONTENTS

KEY TO EXHAUST SYSTEM

1. Catalyst
2. Down-pipe
3. Front silencer
4. Rear intermediate pipe
5. Front intermediate pipe
6. Tail pipe and silencer
7. Exhaust trim

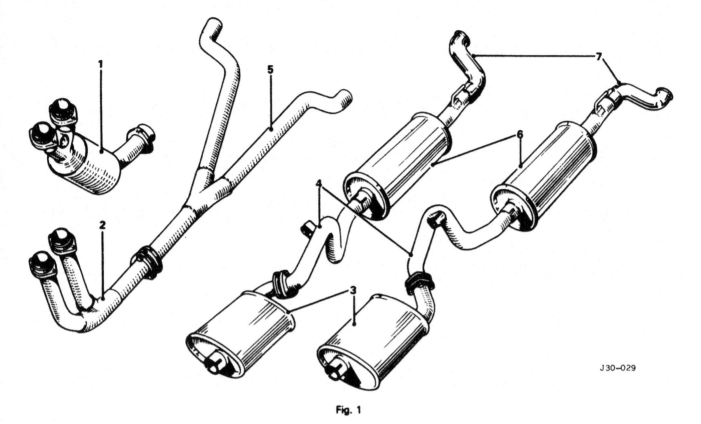

J30–029

Fig. 1

EXHAUST SYSTEM COMPLETE

Remove and refit　　　　**30.10.01**

Removing

In the luggage compartment, remove the two self-locking nuts securing each rear silencer mounting (1, Fig. 2).

Remove the three nuts, bolts and washers securing the down-pipe/intermediate pipe flange (2, Fig. 2).

Release the clamp at the rear of forward silencer assembly (3, Fig. 2).

Separate the intermediate pipe and the forward silencer assemblies from the rear intermediate pipes, taking care to avoid damage to the catalyst unit, if fitted.

Release the clamp at the tail pipe and silencers and from the rear intermediate pipes (4, Fig. 2).

Draw the rear intermediate pipes rearwards from the mounting rubbers and suspension unit (5, Fig. 2).

Remove the screws and separate the trim from the tail pipe and silencers (6, Fig. 2).

Draw the tail pipe and the silencer forwards from the body (7, Fig. 2).

Remove the nuts, bolts and washers securing the heat shield at exhaust manifold/front pipe joint (8, Fig. 2).

Remove the special nuts and plain washers at each exhaust manifold and draw the front pipe downwards. Recover the heat shield brackets.

CAUTION: Take great care to avoid damaging steering rack gaiter.

Check the condition of the mounting rubbers in the rear suspension unit and mounting brackets and renew as necessary.

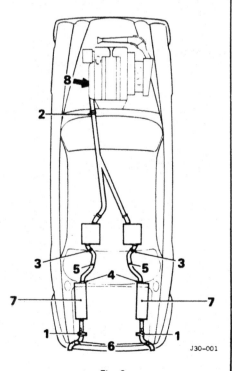

Fig. 2

Refitting

When refitting use Firegum on all joints, assemble the components completely before tightening all clamps and screws.

FRONT PIPE

Remove and refit　　　　**30.10.09**

Removing

Remove the nuts, bolts and washers securing the heat shield at exhaust manifold/front pipe joint (1, Fig. 3).

Remove the special nuts and plain washers at each exhaust manifold (2, Fig. 3).

Beneath the car remove the three nuts, bolts and washers securing front pipe/intermediate pipe flange (3, Fig. 3).

Draw the front pipe downwards and remove.

CAUTION: Take great care to avoid damaging the steering rack gaiter.

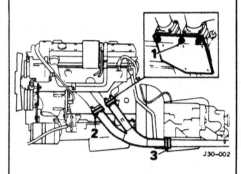

Fig. 3

Refitting

Reverse the above procedure to refit, using new seals. Apply Firegum at front pipe/intermediate pipe joint.

INTERMEDIATE PIPE

Remove and refit　　　　**30.10.11**

Removing

Remove the nuts, bolts and washers securing the flange (1, Fig. 4).

Release the clamp at the front end of both forward silencer and assemblies (2, Fig. 4).

Remove the pipe, taking care to avoid damage to catalyst unit, if fitted (3, Fig. 4).

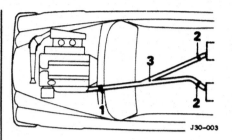

Fig. 4

Refitting

When refitting, use Firegum to seal joint to silencer and front pipe. Use new seal at front pipe/intermediate pipe flange.

SILENCER ASSEMBLY

Remove and refit
　　　　　　Left-hand　　**30.10.15**
　　　　　　Right-hand　**30.10.16**

Removing

Remove the intermediate pipe.
Slacken the clamp and draw the silencer from the rear intermediate pipe (1, Fig. 5).

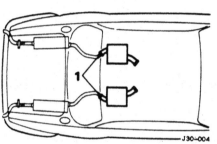

Fig. 5

Refitting

When refitting use Firegum to seal the joints.

TAIL PIPE AND SILENCER

Remove and refit
　Left-hand or Right-hand　**30.10.22**

Removing

Remove the Allen grub screw and separate the trim from tail pipe (1, Fig. 6).

Release the clamp to the rear intermediate pipe and separate (2, Fig. 6).

Draw the tail pipe and silencer forwards down through the tunnel to clear the mounting rubber (3, Fig. 6).

Check the condition of the mounting, and renew as necessary.

continued

30—3

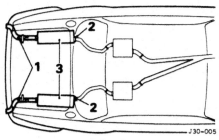

Fig. 6

Refitting

When refitting coat the joint with Firegum.

NOTE: Cars to U.S.A. Federal Specification must have a distance of 38 mm (1.5 in) between top surface of exhaust trim and lower surface of energy absorbing beam.

EXHAUST TRIM

Remove and refit   **30.10.23**

Remove the grub screw using an Allen key and separate trim from tail pipe and silencer (1, Fig. 7).

Use Firegum to seal the joint when refitting.

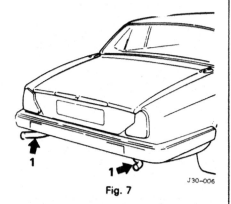

Fig. 7

NOTE: Cars to U.S.A. Federal Specification must have a distance of 38 mm (1.5 in) between the top surface of exhaust trim and lower surface of energy absorbing beam.

REAR INTERMEDIATE PIPE

Remove and refit
    Left-hand   **30.10.24**
    Right-hand   **30.10.25**

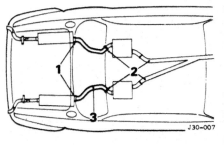

Fig. 8

Release the clamp to the tail pipe and silencer and separate (1, Fig. 8).
Support the intermediate pipe, release the clamp to silencer and separate (2, Fig. 8).
Draw the rear intermediate pipe from the suspension unit (3, Fig. 8).
Check the condition of mounting rubbers, and renew as necessary.

Reverse above procedure to refit. Always use Firegum to seal the joints.

INDUCTION MANIFOLD

Remove and refit   **30.15.02**

Remove the radiator header tank cap and open the radiator drain tap to drain coolant.

NOTE: Conserve coolant if anti-freeze is in use.

Depressurize the fuel system.
Remove the air cleaner and the air-flow meter from the throttle housing.
Remove the servo hose from NR valves, hoses from throttle housing. Disconnect the cables from the air-flow meter throttle switch.
Remove the throttle cable, kick-down cable and service interval counter (if fitted).
Remove the breather pipe and fuel feed pipe from the fuel rail. Remove the thermostat housing.
Remove the ignition amplifier coil and harness.
Remove the distributor cap and H.T. cables.
Remove the connector from the auxiliary air valve cold start injector, coolant temperature sensor, and Thermotime switch.
Remove the F.I. harness, disconnect the fuel hoses from the cold start injector regulator and fuel rail.
Remove the nuts and withdraw the induction manifold.
Clean gasket surfaces.

To refit reverse above procedure. Use new gaskets.

EXHAUST MANIFOLD

Remove and refit   **30.15.10**

Removing

Cars fitted with emission control only
Remove the two cross-head screws and washers securing the hot air duct to the camshaft covers (1, Fig. 9).
Pull the hot air duct from the exhaust manifold heat shield (2, Fig. 9).

Cars to U.S.A. Federal Specification only
Remove the nut, washers, spacer and bolt securing the air delivery pipe clip to the exhaust manifold heat shield (3, Fig. 9).
Pull the air delivery pipe from the air pump outlet elbow (4, Fig. 9).
Slacken the locknuts on the air pump belt

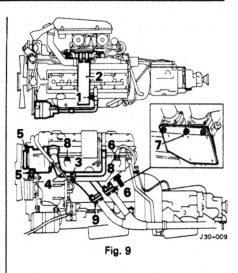

Fig. 9

adjustment, remove the air pump belt from the pulley and draw pump as far as possible away from the cylinder head (5, Fig. 9).
Restrain the adaptor and release the nut securing the E.G.R. pipe.

Rear manifold only on cars with SU carburetters
Slacken the pipe clip and pull hot air pipe from the A.E.D. hot air pick-up unit (6, Fig. 9).

Left-hand-drive cars only
Remove the three 2 B.A. nuts, bolts and washers securing the steering pinion heat shield (7, Fig. 9).

Remove the setscrews/adaptor and washers securing the exhaust manifold heat shield to the exhaust manifolds (8, Fig. 9).

NOTE: Do not mislay the restrictor from the E.G.R. adaptor (fixed orifice system only).

Cars fitted with air conditioning only
Remove the compressor heat shield.

Remove the eight nuts and the washers securing the exhaust manifolds to the exhaust front pipes (9, Fig. 9).
Remove the eight nuts and washers securing each exhaust manifold to the cylinder head.
Remove the three screws securing the hot air pick-up unit to the rear exhaust manifold.
Clean all traces of gaskets from the joint faces.

Refitting

Reverse the above procedures as appropriate, using new gaskets and seals throughout.

NOTE: After loosely securing the exhaust manifolds to the cylinder head, locate the exhaust front pipe on studs before finally tightening manifold nuts.

MOUNTING RUBBER — FRONT

Remove and refit   **30.20.02**

Removing

Reach over the rear suspension unit and release the self-locking nut and bolt securing the rear mounting bracket (1, Fig. 10).
Slide the bracket from the spigot on the rear intermediate pipe and remove.

When refitting locate the replacement mounting rubber in the bracket ring, noting that the brackets are handed (2, Fig. 10).
Smear the bush with soft soap and press into the mounting rubber (3, Fig. 10).
Locate the bush on the spigot and secure using the bolt from below and self-locking nut (4, Fig. 10).

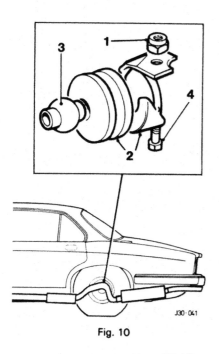

Fig. 10

MOUNTING RUBBER — REAR

Remove and refit   **30.20.04**

Remove the tail pipe and silencer (1, Fig. 11).
In the luggage boot, remove the two self-locking nuts securing the rear mounting (2, Fig. 11).

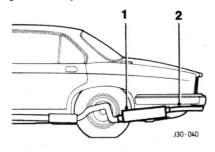

Fig. 11

PAGE INTENTIONALLY LEFT BLANK

JAGUAR
Daimler

12 CYLINDER

Containing
Sections

17 EMISSION CONTROL

19 FUEL SYSTEM

26 COOLING SYSTEM

**30 MANIFOLD AND
EXHAUST SYSTEM**

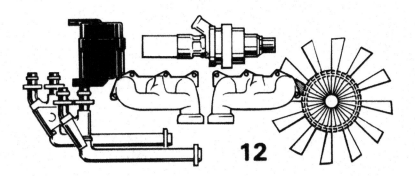

SERIES III
SERVICE MANUAL

INTRODUCTION

This Service Manual covers the Jaguar Series 3 and Daimler Series 3 range of vehicles. It is primarily designed to assist skilled technicians in the efficient repair and maintenance of Jaguar and Daimler vehicles.

Using the appropriate service tools and carrying out the procedures as detailed will enable the operations to be completed within the time stated in the 'Repair Operation Times'.

The Service Manual has been produced in 13 separate sections; this allows the information to be distributed throughout the specialist areas of the modern service facility.

A table of contents in section 1 lists the major components and systems together with the section and book numbers. The cover of each book depicts graphically and numerically the sections contained within that book. Each section starts with a list of operations in alphabetical order.

The title page of each book carries the part numbers required to order replacement books, binders or complete Service Manuals. This can be done through the normal channels.

Operation Numbering

A master index of numbered operations has been compiled for universal application to all vehicles manufactured by Jaguar Cars Ltd., and therefore, because of the different specifications of various models, continuity of the numbering sequence cannot be maintained throughout this manual.

Each operation described in this manual is allocated a number from the master index and cross-refers with an identical number in the 'Repair Operation Times'. The number consists of six digits arranged in three pairs.

Each operation is laid out in the sequence required to complete the operation in the minimum time, as specified in the 'Repair Operation Times'.

Service Tools

Where performance of an operation requires the use of a service tool, the tool number is quoted under the operation heading and is repeated in, following, the instruction involving its use. A list of all necessary tools is included in section 1, number 99.

References

References to the left- or right-hand side in the manual are made when viewing from the rear. With the engine and gearbox assembly removed the timing cover end of the engine is referred to as the front. A key to abbreviations and symbols is given in section 1, number 01.

REPAIRS AND REPLACEMENTS

When service parts are required it is essential that only genuine Jaguar/Daimler or Unipart replacements are used. Attention is particularly drawn to the following points concerning repairs and the fitting of replacement parts and accessories.

1.   Safety features embodied in the vehicle may be impaired if other than genuine parts are fitted. In certain territories, legislation prohibits the fitting of parts not to the vehicle manufacturer's specification.

2.   Torque wrench setting figures given in this Service Manual must be strictly adhered to.

3.   Locking devices, where specified, must be fitted. If the efficiency of a locking device is impaired during removal it must be replaced.

4.   Owners purchasing accessories while travelling abroad should ensure that the accessory and its fitted location on the vehicle conform to mandatory requirements existing in their country of origin.

5.   The vehicle warranty may be invalidated by the fitting of other than genuine Jaguar/Daimler or Unipart parts. All Jaguar/Daimler and Unipart replacements have the full backing of the factory warranty.

6.   Jaguar/Daimler Dealers are obliged to supply only genuine service parts.

SPECIFICATION

Purchasers are advised that the specification details set out in this Manual apply to a range of vehicles and not to any one. For the specification of a particular vehicle, purchasers should consult their Dealer.

The Manufacturers reserve the right to vary their specifications with or without notice, and at such times and in such manner as they think fit. Major as well as minor changes may be involved in accordance with the Manufacturer's policy of constant product improvement.

Whilst every effort is made to ensure the accuracy of the particulars contained in this Manual, neither the Manufacturer nor the Dealer, by whom this Manual is supplied, shall in any circumstances be held liable for any inaccuracy or the consequences thereof.

CONTENTS

EMISSION CONTROL SYSTEM —Evaporative Loss

Description

Hydrocarbon emissions in the form of fuel vapour are emitted from vehicle fuel tanks. To prevent these emissions entering the ambient atmosphere the fuel tanks have unvented, sealed filler caps.

The vapour is passed to a vapour storage canister containing activated charcoal which absorbs the vapours when the vehicle is stationary and desorbs them when the engine is running. The desorption or purging is obtained by connecting the purge pipe from the canister to a vacuum source located at the junction of the pipes between the two throttle housings.

Charcoal canister

The canister is mounted in the R.H. front wheel arch (L.H. for Japan and Australia)*. Filter pads above and below the charcoal prevent the ingress of foreign matter, or passage of charcoal into the purge line.

Emissions from the fuel tanks enter at the bottom of the canister and the purging air enters at the top, passing through the charcoal to the purge outlet at the bottom of the canister to the vacuum source.

  * L.H. 1979 Series III U.S.—Australia— Japan

    R.H. 1980 All cars

Fuel expansion and tank venting

The fuel tanks mounted in each rear wing have a 10% expansion volume incorporated, obtained by limiting the amount of fuel into the tank.

A fuel filler tube extends into the tank to the required level.

A 1mm orifice at the top of the filler neck extension allows the expanding fuel to slowly displace the air from the tank into the venting system via the filler neck and a port in the tanks' side panels to vapour separators in each rear screen pillar.

Condensed vapour drains back to the tanks, excess vapour is passed to the charcoal canister via a pipe under the floor and a pressure relief valve. The valve controls the flow of vapour.

When the fuel tanks are full and pressurized to prevent fuel spillage when the filler cap is released it is necessary to lower the level of the fuel below the filler neck extension.

A domed restriction tank is to the inside of the tank side panel. This tank occupies fuel space during refuelling.

To lower the fuel level, fuel is allowed to flow into the restriction tank via a 2,5 mm orifice.

Fuel filler cap

Each tank has a lockable fuel filler cap incorporating a pressure blow-off facility.

A spring-loaded seal is mounted on the filler neck flap and seats on the filler neck face. No vacuum relief is provided. Incorporated in the filler neck is the 'leaded' fuel restriction.

Pressure relief valve

This valve(s) controls the transfer of vapour from the vapour separators to the charcoal canister and prevents the transfer until a present pressure is exceeded.

To allow a flow to the tanks from the canister a vacuum relief is provided.

EMISSION CHECKS XJ12 FI Digital, U.S.A.

Vacuum advance dump valve check

Remove the throttle edge vacuum pipe from the control port on the dump valve. The idle speed should increase and ignition timing should advance to 24°.

Remove vacuum pipe from 'A' from valve and connect to manifold vacuum idle speed should reduce and ignition should retard 12° from previous check.

XJ12—Japan and Australia

Disconnect E.G.R. solenoid leads. Connect the bulb, ignition on. The bulb should light at idle. Open the throttle 3 mm (⅛ in). Bulb should go out after two seconds and come on again at full throttle.

EMISSION CHECKS

XJ12 Japan and Australia

Remove the cap from the diverter valve (on the car pump).

1. Run the engine at 2000 rev/min in 'N' for 10 seconds.

2. Close the throttle and allow the engine to idle for 15 seconds before probing (not more than two minutes).

3. Insert probe into tail pipe or air distribution pipe.

4. Switch analyser to 'T' or Test (Sun Tester EPA 75).

    Read off CO and HC. Repeat on second tail pipe.

    Readings should be 1 to 2%. If incorrect, adjust setting screw in E.C.U.

XJ12—European Digital—No Catalyst

1. Run the engine at 2000 rev/min in 'N' for 10 seconds.

2. Close the throttle and allow the engine to idle for 15 seconds.

3. Insert probe into tail pipe.

4. Switch analyser to 'T' or Test.

    Disconnect the vacuum pipe from the three-way solenoid valve and the rear of the R.H. inlet manifold. Cap open pipe. Disconnect the earth (black) lead from the two-way solenoid valve located at the front of the R.H. air cleaner.

    Read off CO and HC. 1 to 2%.

    If incorrect, adjust setting screw in E.C.U.

    Replace vacuum pipe and earth lead.

XJ12—U.S.A./Canada, Oxygen Sensors and Catalyst

Repeat 1 to 4 as XJ12 European Cars. Disconnect feedback, disable plug. Connect feedback monitor to socket. If feedback monitor indicates an imbalance, adjust throttle settings at the throttle stops.

Set the E.C.U. idle mixture screw to achieve the correct reading.

To check oxygen sensor function:

Disconnect one injector plug on 'A' bank and observe reading on feedback monitor. Reconnect plug and note return to original reading. Repeat for 'B' bank. Disconnect feedback monitor and reconnect disable plug.

Run engine at 2000 rev/min for 10 seconds close throttle, allow to idle for 15 seconds minimum. Read off CO_2 HC.

Readings should be A and B bank 1 to 2%. If incorrect, adjust setting screw in E.C.U. Remove probe.

Switch off ignition.

XJ12—Australia and Japan

Run engine (after probe).

Slowly open throttle.

Listen for opening of E.G.R. valves (below throttle housings).

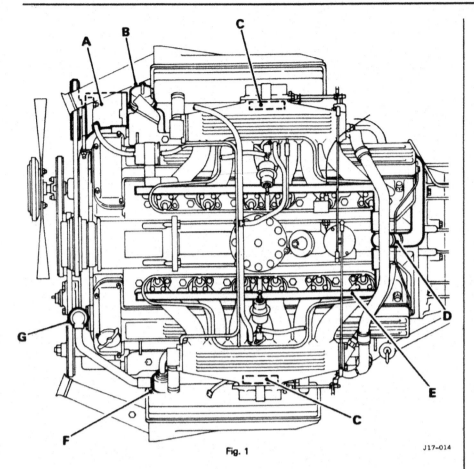

Fig. 1

J17-014

EMISSION CONTROL SYSTEM

Description

The emission control system fitted is designed to comply with the local legislative requirements. Some or all of the following components may be fitted depending on those requirements. The description that follows refers to cars with an emission control system that complies with Australian and Japanese specification.

The system is of the air injection type and comprises the following major components. The components act upon the engine and interact with each other as detailed.

Air injection system

An air delivery pump (A, Fig. 1) supplies air under pressure, air being passed through a diverter valve (B, Fig. 1) and a check valve (D, Fig. 1) through air rails (E, Fig. 1) to the exhaust ports just above the exhaust valve heads.

This air combines with the exhaust gas to continue the oxidization process in the exhaust system. The check valve prevents flow in the air rails when exhaust gas pressure exceeds air supply pressure. The diverter valve operates in response to an abrupt fall in manifold pressure, i.e. sudden closure of the throttle, and diverts secondary air to atmosphere for a period of 2–3 seconds. This reduces the fuel/air ratio which would otherwise be too rich to burn and would pass through the engine to mix with secondary air and become combustible. The next firing cycle would then ignite the mixture, causing a backfire in the exhaust system. The diverter valve is actuated by manifold pressure

via a rubber tube connected to a tapping in the inlet manifold.

Crankcase breather system

To ensure that piston blow-by gas does not escape from the crankcase to atmosphere, a depression is maintained in the crankcase under all operating conditions. This is achieved by connecting the crankcase breather housing (G, Fig. 1) to a chamber (F, Fig. 1) in the left-hand air cleaner backplate; this chamber has two outlets, one of which is connected to the inlet manifold balance pipe and the other to the inlet side of the air cleaner. In the former there is fitted a variable orifice valve that controls the part throttle crankcase ventilation. A depression is maintained in the crankcase at full throttle by the depression on the inlet side of the air cleaner.

Exhaust gas recirculation (E.G.R.) system

Solenoid-operated valves (C, Fig. 1) meter a proportion of exhaust gas into the induction system. The gas is diverted from the exhaust down-pipe at a tapping upstream of the cata-

lytic converters and fed via valves and fixed orifices in the induction system upstream of the throttle butterfly valves.

The signal that operates the E.G.R. valves is determined by the position of the throttle switch, such that there is no recirculation at idle and full throttle.

The E.G.R. valves are further inhibited until engine coolant temperature exceeds 35°C (95°F) and at road speeds in excess of 60 to 65 m.p.h. These functions are controlled by the E.G.R. controller mounted inside the luggage compartment behind the right-hand rear light cluster.

Catalytic converters—Japan only

Fitted into the exhaust system to further reduce carbon monoxide and hydrocarbon emissions.

Unleaded fuel MUST be used on catalyst equipped cars, and labels to indicate this are displayed on the instrument panel and below the filler flap. The filler cap is designed to accommodate unleaded fuel pump nozzles only. Also the anti-surge flap prevents leaded fuel from being added to the fuel tank in that it does not open when a leaded fuel pump nozzle is entered into the filler neck, up to the position of the restrictor and the pump is switched on. The emission control system fitted to this engine is designed to keep emissions within legislated limits providing ignition timing is correctly maintained and the engine is in sound mechanical condition. It is essential that routine maintenance operations detailed in the Handbook and Manual are carried out at the specified mileage intervals.

TESTING

In order that engine emissions are kept within legislated limits an emission test MUST be carried out after completing certain operations. The table below lists examples of the operations, together with the type of emission test required.

CAUTION: CO content MUST NOT exceed 2% or be less than 1% with the air injection system inoperative, i.e. by removing the blanking plug from the diverter valve diaphragm housing. It is essential that the equipment used for testing purposes is of the following type.

1. An infra-red CO exhaust gas analyser.
2. Engine and ignition diagnostic equipment.
3. Lucas EPITEST fuel injection diagnostic equipment Section 2, 'D' system.

OPERATION	EMISSION TEST REQUIRED
Air delivery pump—remove and refit	1. Check that pump delivers air
Crankcase breather, valve, pipe—remove and refit	1. Check filter for obstruction 2. Exhaust gas CO content analysed
Catalytic converters—remove and refit	1. Exhaust gas CO content analysed

continued

17—3

Thermostatic vacuum system

In conjunction with the emission control a thermostatic vacuum system is fitted for cars to Australia.

For ignition timing see 86.35.20.

The various components used in this system are described below:

1. **A distributor is fitted with:**

   A vacuum advance/retard capsule (1C, Fig. 2) for Australia cars.

   A vacuum advance capsule (1A, Fig. 3) for Japan.

2. **Throttle edge ports**

3. **Vacuum supply**

4. **Diverter valve with pressure relief valve (P.R.V.)**

   The P.R.V. incorporated in the diverter valve is controlled by secondary air supply back pressure—(8.2 to 10.5 lbf/in²).

   The P.R.V. provides the safety for the secondary air pump protection.

5. **Carbon canister**

6. **Thermostatic vacuum switch (over temperature)**

   The switch incorporates a wax capsule controlled valve sensing engine coolant temperature.

   The valve advances ignition timing should the coolant temperature exceed 150°C (220°F). At this temperature port 'D' switches from port 'C' to port 'M'.

7. **Thermal vacuum valve**

   The valve, controlled by a bi-metal element sensing engine coolant temperature, provides a signal to the vacuum delay valve by-pass during fully warm engine operation so inhibiting the fast idle system.

8. **Vacuum delay valve (by-pass)**

   The valve delays the rise of the vacuum signal received by the supplementary air valve; flow in the opposite direction is made possible by means of a one-way valve; a by-pass of the restriction is present in order to allow the fast idle function to be inhibited under fully warm conditions.

   The delay valve is controlled by inlet manifold vacuum and engine coolant temperature, without this device the cold fast idle will not function.

9. **Vacuum delay valve (full throttle)**

   The valve delays the fall of the vacuum signal to the supplementary air valve when the inlet vacuum drops towards zero, e.g. when the throttles are fully opened; flow in the opposite direction is made possible by means of a one-way valve.

   The function of the valve is to delay operation of the supplementary air valve during short periods of engine operation at or near wide open throttle.

10. **Supplementary air valve**

    A vacuum operated valve delivers extra air to support cold engine fast idle; the operating vacuum is controlled by a vacuum delay valve.

    The valve is controlled by engine coolant temperature inlet manifold vacuum and delay valve calibrations.

The supplementary air valve increases the rate of engine and catalytic converter warm-up, so reducing the emission of unburnt hydrocarbons.

11. **Ignition retard dump valve**

    The valve senses rising throttle edge vacuum signal and dumps the vacuum retard signal.

    The valve is controlled by throttle edge vacuum signal which enables improvements to be made to part throttle fuel economy.

12. **Over-run valve**

    A spring throttle valve bleeds air into the inlet manifold during engine over-run modes.

    The valve is controlled by spring setting, atmospheric pressure and inlet manifold pressure.

    The over-run valve opens at depression 546 mmHg (19.2 mmHg).

    The function of the valve is to reduce emissions of unburnt hydrocarbons during engine over-run modes.

13. **Restrictor**

Fast idle system—Australia

A vacuum-operated supplementary air valve (10, Fig. 2) supplies the extra air required to support a fast idle of up to 1200 rev/min at coolant temperatures up to 50°C (122°F).

The control system operates as follows:

The operating vacuum source is the inlet manifold, therefore in order to prevent the supplementary air valve (which is normally open) closing (immediately the inlet vacuum builds up following engine starting) a vacuum delay valve (8, Fig. 2) is fitted to the signal pipe.

In order to inhibit the operation of the supplementary air valve, after a hot start, it is necessary to by-pass the vacuum delay valve (8, Fig. 2). This is accomplished by means of a thermal

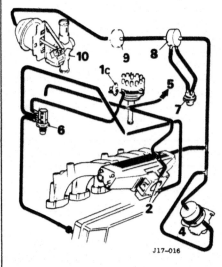

Fig. 2

vacuum valve (7, Fig. 2), sensing engine coolant temperature. The thermal vacuum valve (7, Fig. 2) connects the inlet and outlet ports of a by-pass incorporated in the delay valve (8, Fig. 2).

A second vacuum delay (9, Fig. 2) is placed in the signal pipe between the supplementary air valve and delay valve (8, Fig. 2) with the resistance to flow in the opposite direction to that of valve (8, Fig. 2).

The function of this second valve is to delay the loss of vacuum signal to the supplementary air valve during short periods of engine operations at or near wide open throttle.

Part throttle vacuum ignition retard system—Australia

At idle the ignition timing is controlled by a vacuum operated capsule attached to the ignition distributor (1C, Fig. 2). The vacuum source is a port located downstream of, or in close proximity to, the throttle disc. In the event of the engine overheating the vacuum signal is dumped by means of a thermostatic vacuum switch (6, Fig. 2). The switch is an on/off valve controlled by a wax capsule sensing engine coolant temperature. The valve advances idle ignition timing, hence increasing idle speed, should the engine coolant temperature exceed 104 ± 1.5°C (220°F).

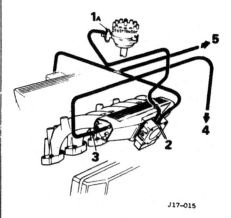

J17–015

Fig. 3

Crankcase breather system

To ensure that piston blow-by gas does not escape from the crankcase to atmosphere, a depression is maintained in the crankcase under all operating conditions. This is achieved by connecting the crankcase breather housing (G, Fig. 1) to a chamber (F, Fig. 1) in the left-hand air cleaner backplate; this chamber has two outlets, one of which is connected to the inlet manifold balance pipe and the other to the inlet side of the air cleaner. In the former there is fitted a variable orifice valve that controls the part throttle crankcase ventilation. A depression is maintained in the crankcase at full throttle by the depression on the inlet side of the air cleaner.

17—4

Exhaust gas recirculation (E.G.R.) system

Solenoid-operated valves (C, Fig. 1) meter a proportion of exhaust gas into the induction system. The gas is diverted from the exhaust down-pipe at a tapping upstream of the catalytic converters and fed via valves and fixed orifices in the induction system upstream of the throttle butterfly valves.

The signal that operates the E.G.R. valves is determined by the position of the throttle switch, such that there is no recirculation at idle and full throttle.

The E.G.R. valves are further inhibited until engine coolant temperature exceeds 35°C (95°F) and at road speeds in excess of 60 to 65 mph. These functions are controlled by the E.G.R. controller mounted inside the luggage compartment behind the right-hand rear light cluster.

Catalytic converters

Fitted into the exhaust system to further reduce carbon monoxide and hydrocarbon emissions. A catalyst/E.G.R. system maintenance indicator is built into the centre switch panel.

Unleaded fuel MUST be used on catalyst equipped cars and labels to indicate this are displayed on the instrument panel and below the filler flap. The filler cap is designed to accommodate unleaded fuel pump nozzles only. Also the anti-surge flap prevents leaded fuel from being added to the fuel tank in that it does not open when a leaded fuel pump nozzle is entered into the filler neck, up to the position of the restrictor and the pump is switched on. The emission control system fitted to this engine is designed to keep emissions within legislated limits providing ignition timing is correctly maintained and that the engine is in sound mechanical condition. It is essential that routine maintenance operations detailed in the Handbook and Manual are carried out at the specified mileage intervals.

TESTING

In order that engine emissions are kept within legislated limits an emission test MUST be carried out after completing certain operations. The table below lists examples of the operations, together with the type of emission test required.

CAUTION: CO content MUST NOT exceed 2% or be less than 1% with the air injection system inoperative, i.e. by removing the blanking plug from the diverter valve diaphragm housing. It is essential that the equipment used for testing purposes is of the following type:

1. An infra-red CO exhaust gas analyser.

2. Engine and ignition diagnostic equipment.

3. Lucas EPITEST fuel injection diagnostic equipment—Section 2
—Section 4

OPERATION	EMISSION TEST REQUIRED
Air delivery pump—remove and refit	*1. Check that pump delivers air
Crankcase breather, valve, pipe—remove and refit	1. Check filter for obstruction 2. Exhaust gas CO content analysed
Catalytic converters—remove and refit	1. Exhaust gas CO content analysed

* Japan and Australia only

Fuel tank evaporative loss control system

An evaporative emission control system is fitted to cars to U.S. Federal and Australian design rule specifications. The system utilizes canister (A, Fig. 4) containing activated charcoal to retain fumes given off the engine crankcase assembly (C, Fig. 4) and the fuel tank (H, Fig. 4) while the engine is at rest.

When the engine is running, a stream of air is drawn through the air pipe (B, Fig. 4) by means of connections to the throttle edge tappings on the inlet manifold throttle bodies (D, Fig. 4) carrying the absorbed fumes into the engine and purging the canister.

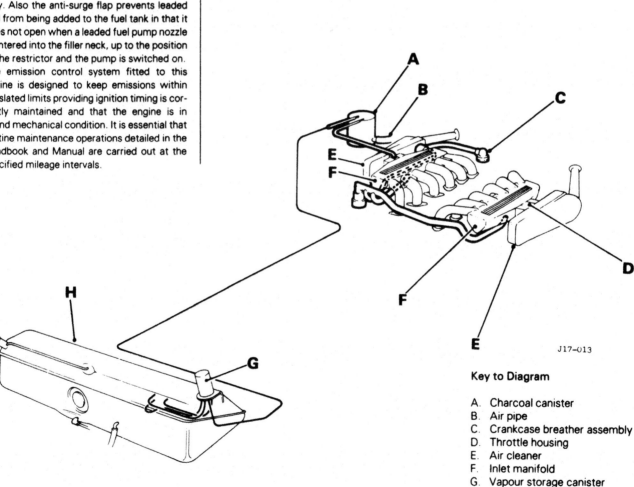

Fig. 4

J17–013

Key to Diagram

A. Charcoal canister
B. Air pipe
C. Crankcase breather assembly
D. Throttle housing
E. Air cleaner
F. Inlet manifold
G. Vapour storage canister
H. Fuel tank

FAULT FINDING

SYMPTOM	CAUSE	CURE
Engine will not start	1. Low battery or poor connections	1. a. Check battery, recharge. Clean and secure terminals. b. Check for short circuit or low charge from alternator.
	2. Start system malfunction	2. Clean and check main starter circuit and connections.
	3. Incorrect or dirty fuel	3. Check grade of fuel. If contamination suspected, drain and flush fuel tank, flush through system, renew fuel filter.
	4. Fuel starvation	4. Check fuel pressure, see 19.50.13. If not satisfactory, check feed pipes for leaks or blockage. Renew connectors if damaged or deteriorated.
	5. Fuel injection equipment electrical connections	5. Ensure that all connector plugs are securely attached. Pull back rubber boot and ensure that plug is fully home. While replacing boot, press cable towards socket. Ensure E.C.U. multi-pin connector is fully made. Check that all ground connections are clean and tight.
	6. Auxiliary air valve inoperative	6. Remove valve and test, see 19.20.17.
	7. Cold start system inoperative	7. Check function of cold start system, see 19.22.32.
	8. Pressure sensor (port of E.C.U. on Digital 'P' System)	8. Ensure manifold pressure pipe is attached to sensor, and is not twisted, kinked or disconnected elsewhere.
	9. Trigger unit (Japan and Australia)	9. Check function of trigger unit, see 19.22.27.
	10. Temperature sensors	10. Check sensor for open and short circuit.
	11. H.T. circuit faults	11. Check for sparking.
	12. Power faults	12. Carry out ignition checks.
	13. L.T. switching fault	13. Check pick-up module.
	14. Ignition timing incorrect	14. Check and adjust as necessary.
	15. E.G.R. valve malfunction (Japan and Australia)	15. Check function of E.G.R. valve on vehicle. If not satisfactory, remove manifold and clean ports. Renew valve if spring is broken, solenoid failed or other fault is obvious.
	16. E.C.U./amplifier	16. As a last resort check by substitution.
Poor or erratic idle	17. Check items 3, 4, 5 and 9 above	17. If trouble still persists, proceed with item 18.
	18. Throttle switch	18. Check function of idle and full load switches, see 19.22.37.
	19. Incorrect idle speed	19. Adjust auxiliary air valve by-pass bleed screw, see 19.20.18.
	20. Check items 8 and 13 above	20. If trouble still persists, proceed with item 21.
	21. Ignition system deterioration	21. Check ignition wiring for fraying chafing and security. Inspect distributor cap for cracks and tracking and rotor condition.

17—6

Fault finding—continued

SYMPTOM	CAUSE	CURE
Poor or erratic idle	22. Spark plug faults	22. Clean, reset and test plugs; renew as necessary.
	23. Check item 14	23. If trouble still persists, proceed with item 24.
	24. Vacuum system faults	24. Check operation of vacuum unit and condition of vacuum pipes. Renew as necessary.
	25. Advance or retard mechanism faults	25. Check operation of advance/retard mechanism. Lubricate or renew as necessary.
	26. Throttle by-pass valves	26. Check and adjust as necessary.
	27. Exhaust system leaking or blocked	27. Check and rectify as necessary.
	28. Incorrect idle mixture. Not to be adjusted on 1980 cars	28. Check CO level, see 17.35.01, and adjust to specified levels using knurled screw on side of E.C.U. Air injection system should be disconnected for this operation.
	29. Poor compressions	29. Check compressions, and rectify as necessary.
	30. Air leaks at inlet manifold	30. Check inlet manifold to cylinder head joint. Remake with new gasket if necessary. Check manifold tappings for leaks.
	31. Check item 6	31. If trouble still persists, proceed with item 32.
	32. Engine oil filler cap loose or leaking	32. Check cap for security. Renew seal if damaged.
	33. Engine breather pipe restrictors missing or blocked	33. Check and clear, or renew as necessary.
	34. Engine breather hoses blocked or leaking	34. Check and clear, or renew as necessary.
	35. Charcoal canister restricted or blocked	35. Inspect, and renew as necessary.
	36. Check items 15, 10 and 9	36. Check in order shown.
Hesitation or flat spot	37. Check items 3, 4, and 5	37. If trouble still persists, proceed with item 38.
	38. Check item 7 with engine cold	38. If trouble still persists, proceed with item 39.
	39. Throttle butterfly	39. Adjust as necessary, see 19.20.04.
	40. Check item 8	40. If trouble still persists, proceed with item 41.
	41. Brakes	41. Check for binding brakes.
	42. Check items, 13, 21, 22, 14, 24 and 25	42. If trouble still persists, proceed with item 43.
	43. Air cleaner blocked	43. Inspect element, and renew as necessary.
	44. Check items 27, 29, 30, 32, 33, 34, 35, 15, 10, 9 and 16	44. Check in the order shown.

continued

Fault finding—continued

SYMPTOM	CAUSE	CURE
Excessive fuel consumption	45. Leaking fuel	45. Check fuel system for leaks, rectify and renew connectors as necessary.
	46. Check items 18, 7, 8, 41, 27, 29 and 30	46. If trouble still persists, proceed with item 47.
	47. Cylinder head gasket leaking	47. Check cylinder head to block joint for signs of leakage. Renew gasket as necessary.
	48. Cooling system blocked or leaking	48. Flush system, check for blockage. Check hoses and connections for security and leaks; renew as necessary. Check functions of thermostats; renew if necessary.
	49. Check items 15, 30, 32, 33, 34. 35, 10 and 16	49. Check in the order shown.
Lack of engine braking or high idle speed	50. Air leaks	50. Any air leak into the manifold will appear as an equivalent throttle opening; correct fuel will then be supplied for that apparant degree of throttle and the engine will run faster. Ensure that all hose and pipe connections are secure. Check all joints for leakage, and remake as necessary.
Lack or engine braking or high idle speed	51. Throttle sticking	51. Lubricate, check for wear and reset, see 19.20.05.
	52. Check items 6, 24, 26, 14, 28 and 41	52. If trouble still persists, proceed with item 53.
	53. Throttle spindle leaks	53. Check seals, bearings and spindles for wear; renew as necessary.
	54. Check item 30	54.
Lack of engine power	55. Check items 3, 4, 5 and 7	55. If trouble still persists, proceed with item 56.
	56. Throttle inhibited	56. Check throttle operation, free off and reset as necessary.
	57. Check items 41, 43, 8, 13, 21, 22, 14, 25, 27, 29, 15, 30, 24, 32, 33, 34, 35, 39 and 16	57. Check in order shown.
Engine overheating	58. Check items 48, 47, 14, 24 and 15	58. Check in order shown.
Engine cut outs or stalls	59. Check items 3, 4, 5, 10, 19, 7, 43, 8, 27, 13, 21, 22, 14, 25, 28, 18, 30, 24, 32, 33, 34, 35, 15, 29 and 16	59. Check in order shown.
Engine misfires	60. Check items 3, 4, 5, 7, 9, 8, 13, 21, 22, 14, 25, 43, 27, 28, 29, 30, 24, 32, 33, 34, 35, 15 and 16	60. Check in order shown.

17—8

Fault finding—continued

SYMPTOM	CAUSE	CURE
Fuel smells	61. Check items 45, 7 and 34	61. If trouble still persists, proceed with item 62.
	62. Fuel filler cap defective	62. Check seal and cap for deterioration; renew as necessary.
	63. Check items 33, 35, 28, 43 and 16	63. Check in the order shown.
Engine runs on	64. Check items 3, 19, 51, 26, 34, 33, 48, 47, 14, 24, 25 and 15	64. Check in the order shown.
Engine knocking or pinking	65. Check items 3, 14, 25, 24, 48, 47 and 15	65. Check in the order shown.
Arcing at plugs	66. Check items 21 and 22	66.
Lean running (low CO)	67. Check items 5, 53, 18, 10, 3, 4, 30, 24, 32, 33, 34 and 35	67. Check in the order shown.
Rich running (excess CO)	68. Check items 7, 28, 35 and 16	68. Check in the order shown.
Backfiring in exhaust	70. Check items 3, 4, 5, 43, 27, 30, 24, 48 and 32	70. If trouble still persists, proceed with item 71.
	71. Diverter valve malfunction	71. Check valve line for condition and security; rectify as necessary. Check that air is dumped on deceleration by disconnecting air outlet pipe at diverter valve and feeling the operation of the valve when the throttle is opened and closed quickly.
	72. Check item 16	72.
Noisy air injection	73. Incorrectly tensioned air pump drive belt	73. Check and adjust drive belt tension; renew belt if necessary.
	74. Relief valve faulty or low pump pressure	74. Check that valve operates at 8.2 to 10.5 lb/in^2. If pump fails to produce enough pressure to lift the valve, check item 73. If satisfactory, renew the pump.
	75. Check item 71 above	75. If trouble still persists, proceed with item 76.
	76. Check valve sticking (Japan and Australia)	76. Check valve operation and hoses for security or blockage. Rectify or renew as necessary.

17—9

ENGINE BREATHER FILTER

Remove and refit   17.10.02

Remove the hose clip securing the rubber cover to the breather housing, and disconnect. Remove the rubber cover.
Lift out the filter.

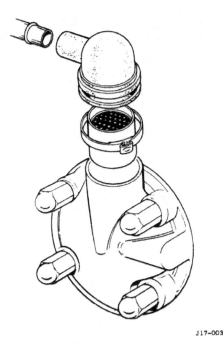

J17-003

Fig. 5

Refitting is a reversal of the above procedure.

ADSORPTION CANISTER

Remove and refit   17.15.13

Remove the front left-hand road wheel.
Note the position of the hoses and remove them from the canister stub pipes (1, Fig. 6).
Remove the screw, nut and washers securing the canister clamp and prise open the clamp and remove the canister (2, Fig. 6).

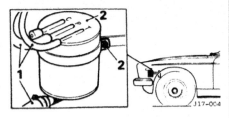

Fig. 6

Refitting is a reversal of the above procedure.

AIR DELIVERY PUMP—Japan and Australia

Remove and refit   17.25.07

NOTE: No servicing or overhaul of the air delivery pump is possible. In the event of failure a service exchange unit must be fitted.

Remove the right-hand air cleaner cover.
Remove the three bolts securing the air pump pulley to the drive shaft (1, Fig. 7).

CAUTION: A screwdriver or wedge MUST NOT be used to prise the pulley off the drive shaft as extensive damage to the filter element will result.

Remove the pump pulley (2, Fig. 7).
Slacken the bolt securing the adjuster rod trunnion to the pump and remove the locknut from the adjuster rod (3, Fig. 7).
Slacken the nut securing the air pump mounting bolt (5, Fig. 7).
Pivot the pump (6, Fig. 7) away from the engine.
Support the pump, remove the mounting nut, flat and spacer washer and bolt (7, Fig. 7).
Disconnect the vacuum hose and secondary air pipe from the diverter valve (8, Fig. 7).
Remove the delivery pump (6, Fig. 7).
Remove the two bolts and washers securing the diverter valve elbow to the air pump, remove the elbow and diverter valve (9, Fig. 7).
Remove and discard the gasket (10, Fig. 7).

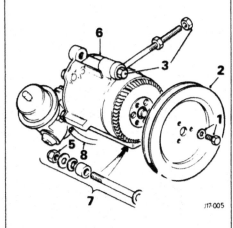

J17-005

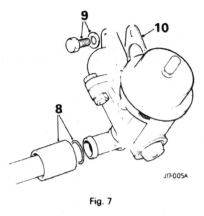

J17-005A

Fig. 7

Reverse the above operations, using a new gasket and sealing ring.
Check the tension of the air/pump/compressor drive belt.

AIR DELIVERY PUMP/ COMPRESSOR DRIVE BELT

Tensioning   17.25.13

Remove the right-hand air cleaner cover.
Slacken the nut securing the air pump mounting belt and the adjusting link securing bolt and locknut (1, Fig. 8).

CAUTION: Ensure that the head of the bolt does not foul pulley.

Adjust the belt tension by means of the adjusting link nut (2, Fig. 8); the correct tension is as follows:
A load of 2,9 kgf (6.4 lbf) must give a total belt deflection of 5,6 mm (0.22 in) when applied at point 'A'.
When the tension is correct, reverse the above procedure.

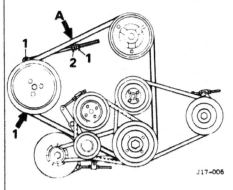

J17-006

Fig. 8

AIR DELIVERY PUMP/ COMPRESSOR DRIVE BELT

Remove and refit   17.25.15

Remove the right-hand air cleaner cover.
Remove the fan drive belt and the power-assisted steering/water pump drive belt (1, Fig. 9).
Slacken the nut securing the air delivery pump mounting bolt (2, Fig. 9).
Slacken the adjusting link securing bolt and locknut (3, Fig. 9).

CAUTION: Ensure that the head of the bolt does not foul the pulley.

Slacken the adjusting link nut and wind along the thread until the belt can be manoeuvred clear (4, Fig. 9).

Fit a new belt and adjust the tension as previously described, then fit and tension the P.A.S. and fan drive belts.

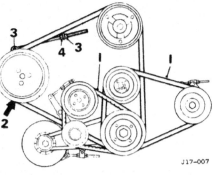

J17-007

Fig. 9

AIR RAIL—D. System
Remove and refit

Left-hand	**17.25.17**
Right-hand	**17.25.18**

Depressurize the fuel system, and disconnect the battery.

Remove the fuel rail and the fuel pressure regulator.

Remove the two screws securing the air rail bracket to the inlet manifold ram tubes (1, Fig. 10).

Remove the earth strap from the rear inlet manifold ram tube—right-hand side only.

Remove the six nuts and serrated washers securing the air rail and manifold stud spacers to the cylinder head (2, Fig. 10).

Release the hose clip securing the air rail to the check valve connecting hose (3, Fig. 10).

Lift out the air rail and disconnect it from the check valve connecting hose (4, Fig. 10).

Remove and discard the rubber sealing rings (5, Fig. 10).

Using new rubber sealing rings refit by reversing the above procedure.

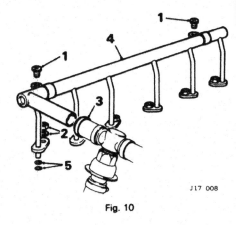

Fig. 10

CHECK VALVE
Remove and refit   **17.25.21**

Release the hose clips securing the air delivery rail hoses to the non-return valve outlet; slide the hoses clear of the valve outlets (1, Fig. 11).

Remove the lower clip securing the hose to the check valve inlet pipe (2, Fig. 11).

Remove the check valve (3, Fig. 11).

Using new hose clips, refit by reversing the above procedure.

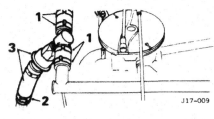

Fig. 11

DIVERTER VALVE
Remove and refit   **17.25.25**

Remove the air cleaner and element.

Disconnect the vacuum hose from the diverter valve stub pipe (1, Fig. 2).

Remove the two bolts, nuts and spring washers securing the diverter valve to the elbow (2, Fig. 12).

Release the air rail pipe from the diverter pipe (3, Fig. 12) and remove the diverter valve (4, Fig. 12).

Remove and discard the diverter valve to elbow gasket (5, Fig. 12).

Remove and discard the air rail pipe sealing ring (6, Fig. 12).

Remove the air rail pipe to diverter valve union from the diverter valve, remove and discard the sealing ring (7, Fig. 12)

When refitting, use a new gasket and sealing rings.

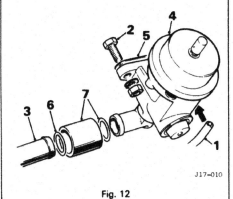

Fig. 12

EXHAUST GAS RECIRCULATION (E.G.R.) VALVE
Remove and refit   **17.45.01**

Remove the air cleaner cover.

Disconnect the E.G.R. valve transfer pipe from the down-pipe take-off (1, Fig. 13).

Remove the electrical connectors from the rear of the E.G.R. valve (2, Fig. 13).

Remove the two bolts and spring washers securing the E.G.R. valve to the elbow (3, Fig. 13).

Remove the E.G.R. valve and gasket (4, Fig. 13).

Remove the transfer pipe from the E.G.R. valve (5, Fig. 13).

When refitting use a new gasket and E.G.R. valve transfer pipe.

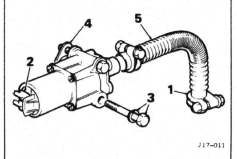

Fig. 13

E.G.R. CONTROL UNIT
Remove and refit   **17.45.07**

Disconnect the battery.

Remove the two nuts and washers securing the right-hand rear light cluster.

Disconnect the earth lead from the light cluster stud.

Remove the light cluster from the housing.

Remove the two nuts and bolts securing the E.G.R. control unit.

Disconnect the block connector and remove the E.G.R. control unit.

When refitting, ensure a good ground on the light cluster earth lead.

E.G.R. VALVE TRANSFER PIPE
Remove and refit   **17.45.11**

Remove the air cleaner cover.

Slacken the nuts securing the E.G.R. valve transfer pipe clamps (1, Fig. 14).

Release the transfer pipe from the E.G.R. valve and the down-pipe take-off.

Clean the E.G.R. valve and the down-pipe take-off connections before refitting, using a new valve transfer pipe.

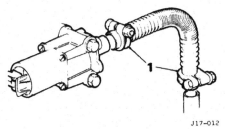

Fig. 14

CATALYTIC CONVERTER
Remove and refit

Left-hand	**17.50.01**
Right-hand	**17.50.03**

Remove the air cleaner element.

Slacken the nut securing the E.G.R. valve transfer pipe clamp at the take-off pipe.

Disconnect the E.G.R. valve transfer pipe from the take-off pipe.

Beneath the car, remove the bolts and spring washers securing the power steering bellows, heat shield, remove the heat shield.

Remove the nuts, plain washers and bolts securing the flanges, separate the intermediate pipe from the down-pipe. Ensure that the intermediate pipe is adequately supported.

Remove the nuts and plain washers securing the heat shield and down-pipe to exhaust manifolds; withdraw the heat shield.

Withdraw the down-pipe/catalyst assembly.

NOTE: This operation will be greatly facilitated if the steering is turned when manoeuvring the assembly clear.

When refitting, coat all joints with Firegum. Tighten the down-pipe and clamping flanges fixing by diagonal selection to avoid distortion.

17—11

PAGE INTENTIONALLY LEFT BLANK

CONTENTS

THE ELECTRONIC FUEL INJECTION SYSTEM

(Digital 'P' Pressure Sensing Type)

Description

The Digital ('P' Pressure Sensing Type) Fuel Injection System is fitted to 5.3 models excluding specified markets.

The electronic fuel injection system is divided into two sub-systems interconnected only at the injectors.

The systems are:

1. The fuel system delivering to the injectors a constant supply of fuel at the correct pressure, 2,5 bar (36 lbf in).

2. The electronic sensing and control system which monitors engine operating conditions of load, speed, temperature (coolant and induction air) and throttle movement. The control system then produces electrical pulses of

appropriate width to hold open the injector solenoid valves and allows the correct quantity of fuel to flow through the nozzle for each engine cycle.

As fuel is held constant, varying the pulse width increases or decreases the amount of fuel passed through the injector to comply with the engine requirements.

Pulse width and therefore fuel quantity is also modified to provide enrichment during starting and warming-up, at closed throttle, full throttle and while the throttle is actually opening.

The injectors are operated by the Electronic Control Unit (E.C.U.) in two groups of six. Each is further broken into two sub-groups of three, although each pair or sub-groups is operated simultaneously to make up the two groups of six twice per engine cycle.

Injection in two groups of six:

A Bank			B Bank		
1A	3A	5A	1B	3B	5B
2A	4A	6A	2B	4B	6B

Firing order:
1A 6B 5A 2B 3A 4B 6A 1B 2A 5B 4A 3B

Cylinders numbered from front of engine.

The induction system is basically the same as that on a carburetted engine: tuned ram pipe, air cleaners, plenum chambers and induction ports. Air is drawn through paper element cleaners to a butterfly valve for each bank and to individual ports for each cylinder leading off the plenum chamber. The injectors are positioned at the cylinder head end of each port so that fuel is directed at the back of each inlet valve.

	A	(1)	(2)	(3)	(4)	(5)	(6)
Front							
	B	(1)	(2)	(3)	(4)	(5)	(6)

(1)	Inlet opens	13 ° B.T.D.C.
(2)	Inlet closes	55° A.B.D.C.
	Ignition with engine at normal operating temperature	
	U.K./Europe	24° B.T.D.C.
	All others	25–27° B.T.D.C.
(4)	Exhaust opens	55° B.B.D.C.
(5)	Exhaust closes	13° A.T.D.C.

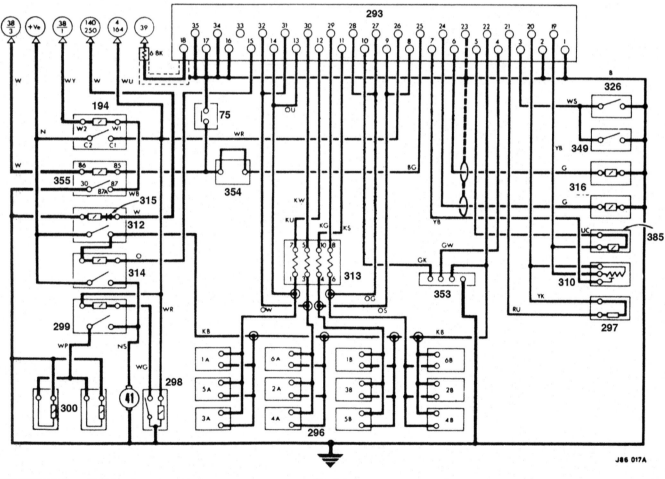

North American — Emission A

Fig. 1

J86 017A

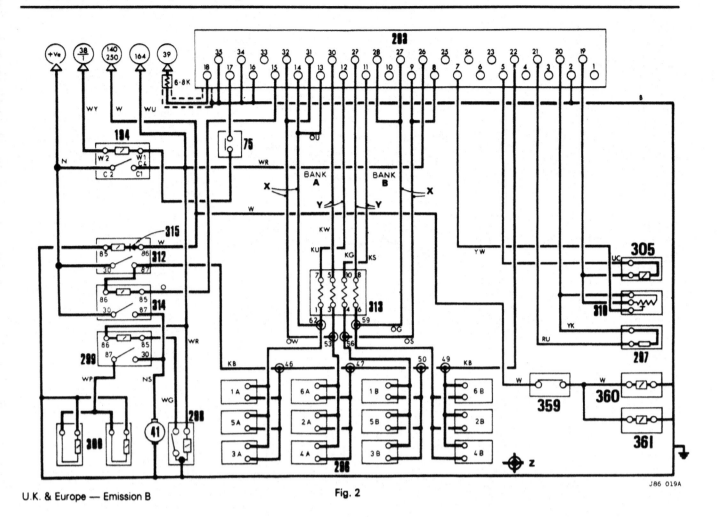

U.K. & Europe — Emission B

Fig. 2

J86 019A

MASTER KEY FOR CIRCUITS EMISSION A AND B

	4.	Starter solenoid	A
	38/1.	Ignition switch pin 1	A
	38/3.	Ignition switch pin 3	A
	39.	Ignition coil	A
	41.	Fuel pump	A
	75.	Start inhibit switch	
	140.	Fuel change-over switch	
	164.	Ballast resistor	
	194.	Starter relay	
	250.	Inertia switch	
A	293.	E.C.U.	
&	297.	Injectors	
B	298.	Air temperature sensor	
	299.	Thermotime switch	
	300.	Cold start relay	
	305.	Cold start injectors	
	310.	Coolant sensor	
	312.	Throttle potentiometer	
	313.	Main relay	
	314.	Power resistors	
	314.	Pump relay	
	315.	Block diode	

A	316.	Oxygen sensors
A	326.	Vacuum switch
A	349.	Micro-switch
A	353.	Feed-back monitor socket
A	354.	Disable socket
	355.	Feedback monitor relay
B	359.	Oil temperature switch
B	360.	Vacuum changeover switch
B	361.	Supplementary air valve
X		Turn on
Y		Hold on
Z		Part of 10 way engine harness

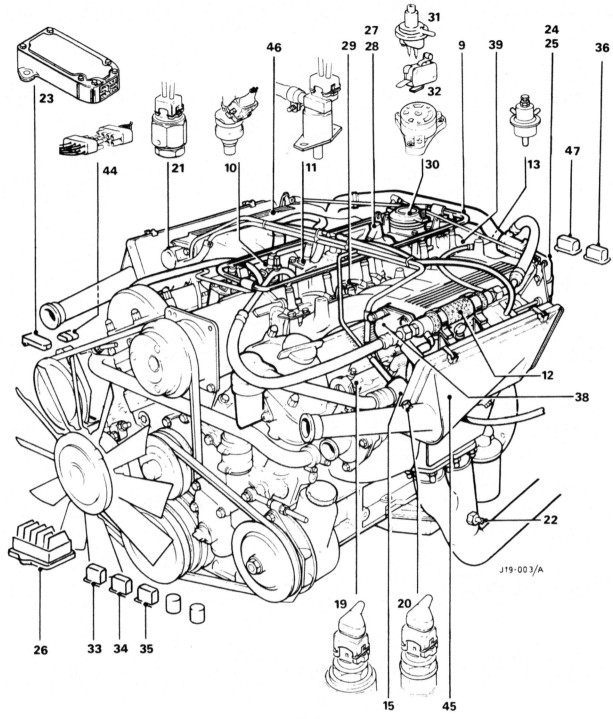

Fig. 3

J19·003/A

KEY TO LOCATIONS DIAGRAMS

1. Fuel tank
2. A–B–C change-over valves
3. Fuel pump
4. Vapour separators
5. Restrictors
6. Air bleed valve
7. Non-return valve
8. Filter — in boot
9. Fuel rail
10. Fuel injectors
11. Cold start injectors (early models only)
12. Fuel cooler
13. Fuel pressure regulators

14. Carbon canister
15. Positive crankcase ventilation (P.C.V.) valve
16. Electronic control unit (E.C.U.)
17. Manifold pressure sensor (in E.C.U.)
18. Idle setting screw (in E.C.U.)
19. Coolant temperature sensor
20. Air temperature sensor
21. Thermotime switch
22. Oxygen sensor
23. Power resistors
24. Auxiliary air valve
25. Idle speed screw

19—5

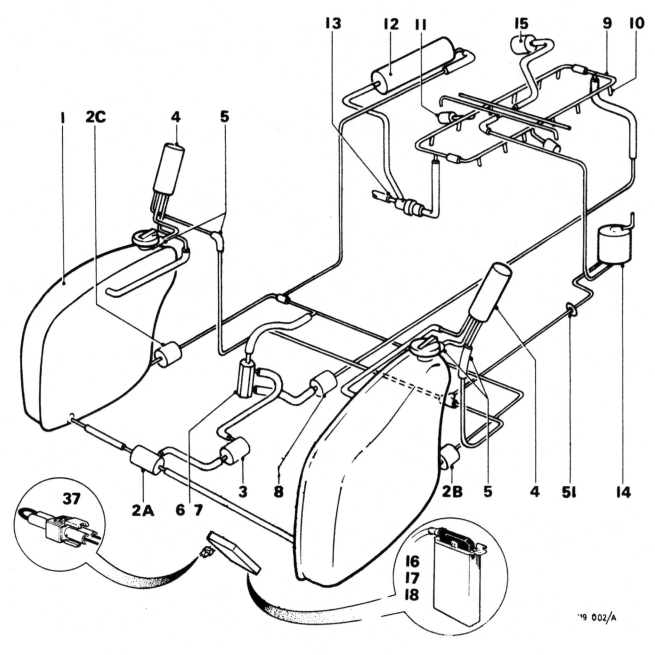

Fig. 4

19 002/A

26. Ignition amplifier	39. Oil temperature switch
27. Ignition coil (speed sensor)	40. Change-over valve (3-way)
28. Ballast resistor	41. Supplementary air valve
29. Distributor and vacuum capsule	42. Vacuum delay valve
30. Throttle potentiometer	43. Vacuum advance dump valve
31. Throttle vacuum switch	44. Sockets (10 4-way sockets)
32. Throttle micro-switch	45. Air cleaner
33. Main relay	46. Inlet manifolds
34. Pump relay	47. Start relay
35. Cold start relay	48. To air-conditioning unit
36. Feedback monitor relay	49. To automatic gearbox
37. Feedback disable socket	50. Brake non-return valve
38. Over-run valve	51. Pressure relief valve

19—6

ELECTRONIC FUEL INJECTION

Electronic control unit (E.C.U.)

PARAMETERS CONTROLLED Stoichiometric (air/fuel) ratio

	PARAMETERS SENSED	SOURCE	RESULT
Primary (Digital)	1. Inlet manifold absolute pressure	Sensor in the E.C.U.	
	2. Engine speed	Ignition coil	
	3. Throttle movement and position	Potentiometer	Triggers injector pulses
	4. 'Closed loop' correction	E.C..U.	
	5. Supply voltage		
Secondary (Analogue)	6. Oxygen partial pressure in exhaust	Oxygen sensors	
	7. Full load	Vacuum switch	Opens 'closed loop'
	8. Engine coolant temperature	Sensor	
	9. Starter signal	Starter relay	Triggers cold start pulses
	10. Intake air temperature	Sensor	

The system contains an integrated circuit for the dedicated fuel injection control chip and an analogue/digital converter for the intake manifold depression signal.

The fuelling information is stored in a (ROM) Read Only Memory (1288-bit words) so that for any combination of manifold pressure and speed the memory gives a number proportional to the amount of fuel required by the engine. The injectors will be energized for a time proportional to the number computed, plus the constant of the proportionality varied according to the secondary parameters.

To ensure a fast opening of the injectors the full battery voltage is applied but, to reduce power dissipation when they are open, drive is maintained via a resistor pack external to the E.C.U.

FUEL SYSTEM

Fuel supply

Fuel from the tank selected by the panel switch is drawn by a fuel pump (3, Fig. 4) via a solenoid-operated over valve (2A, Fig. 4) to a fuel rail (9, Fig. 4) through an in-line filter (8, Fig. 4) and a pressure regulator (13, Fig. 4). Fuel is controlled so that the pressure drop across the injector's nozzle is maintained at a constant 2,5 bar (36 lbf/in²). Excess fuel is returned to the tank from which it was drawn via a fuel cooler (12, Fig. 4) (on air-conditioned cars only) and a solenoid-operated change-over valve (2B, Fig. 4) or (2C, Fig. 4) to the selected tank. The twelve fuel injectors (10, Fig. 3) are connected to the fuel rail (9, Fig. 4) and are electromechanically operated to inject into each inlet port. Fuel is also supplied to two cold start injectors (11, Figs. 3 & 4) which are only operated during the starting of a cold engine. An air bleed valve (6, Fig. 4) allows the fuel supply line

to purge itself of vapour when changing over fuel tanks, i.e. very little fuel in tank.

An orifice in the purge line allows fuel pressure to build up when all the air has been bled to the fuel return line. A non-return valve (7, Fig. 4) in the outlet of the valve prevents the fuel line draining while the vehicle is standing.

Fuel pressure regulator

The fuel pressure regulator (13, Fig. 4) maintains a constant pressure drop across the injector nozzles. It is connected to manifold depression which operates against a spring loaded diaphragm.

Engine load sensing

The driver controls engine power output by varying the throttle opening and therefore the flow of air into the engine. The air flow determines the pressure that exists within the plenum chamber; this pressure therefore is a measure of the demand upon the engine. The pressure is also used to provide the principal control of fuel quantity, being converted by the manifold pressure sensor in the E.C.U. into an electrical signal. This signal varies the width of the injector operating pulse as appropriate. The pressure sensor is fitted with a separate diaphragm system that compensates for ambient barometric variations. The manifold pressure sensor is located in the E.C.U. and connected by a pipe to the inlet manifold balance pipe.

Air intake system

Air is drawn from the air cleaner through the throttles into the engine. A potentiometer connected to the throttle pulley converts the throttle angular position into a voltage which is transmitted to the E.C.U.

The potentiometer must be set initially using the recommended equipment.

A vacuum-operated switch (31, Fig. 3) and a micro-switch (32, Fig. 3) also provides throttle position information to the E.C.U. (see Full Load Fuelling, page 8).

Electronic system

The E.C.U. receives information from sensors placed about the engine. It computes the quantity of fuel required and therefore the time for which the injectors must remain open. The ignition coil L.T. circuit (−ve lead) triggers six injectors (A or B bank) simultaneously at every third spark. The injectors open twice per engine cycle, each time delivering half the fuel requirements of each cylinder. (Figures 1 and 2 show the circuits for U.S.A. and Europe).

Temperature sensors

The temperature of the air taken into the engine through the inlet manifold and the temperature of the coolant in the cylinder block are constantly monitored. The information is fed directly to the E.C.U. The air temperature sensor (20, Fig. 3) has a small effect on the injector pulse width, and should be regarded as a trimming rather than a control device. it ensures that the fuel supplied is directly related to the weight of air drawn in by the engine. Therefore, as the weight (density) of the air charge increases with a falling temperature, so the amount of fuel supplied is also increased to maintain optimum fuel/air raio.

The coolant temperature sensor (19, Fig. 3) has a greater control although it functions mainly while the engine is initially warming-up. The sensor operates in conjunction with the cold start system and the auxiliary air valve to form a completely automatic equivalent of the carburetter choke.

19—7

ELECTRONIC FUEL INJECTION

Flooding protection system

When the ignition is switched on, but the engine is not cranking, the fuel pump will run for two seconds to raise the pressure in the fuel rail; it is then automatically switched off by the E.C.U.

Only after cranking has started is the fuel pump switched on again. Switching control is built into the E.C.U. circuitry. This system prevents flooding if any injectors become faulty (remain open) when the ignition is left on.

Auxiliary air valve

The auxiliary air valve (24, Fig. 3) is controlled by the coolant temperature. To prevent stalling at cold start and cold idle conditions due to the increased drag of the engine, the valve opens to allow the air to by-pass the throttles and so increase the engine speed. In addition to the main coolant temperature regulated air passage, the auxiliary air valve has a by-pass, controlled by an adjusting screw (25, Fig. 3).

Idle speed adjustment

The idle speed adjustment screw (25, Fig. 3) in the auxiliary air valve controls the idle speed by regulating the by-pass air flow.

To balance throttles:
Remove air cleaners.
Close throttles with 0,05 mm (0.002 in) feelers between the throttle discs and the housings.
Set the throttle stop screws.
Adjust idle speed screw (25, Fig. 3) to obtain 750 rev/min.
Adjust idle mixture (in E.C.U.) using equipment shown on page 9.

Cold start system

For cold starting, additional fuel is injected into the inlet manifolds by two cold start injectors (11, Fig. 3). These are controlled by the cold start relay (35, Fig. 3) and the Thermotime switch (21, Fig. 3). The Thermotime switch senses coolant temperature and, depending on what temperature, makes or breaks the ground circuit of the relay. When the starter switch is operated, the cold start relay is energized with its circuit completed via the Thermotime switch, which also limits the time for which the relay is energized, to a maximum of twelve seconds under extreme cold conditions.

The enrichment is in addition to that provided by the coolant temperature sensor.

If the temperature is above the rated value 35°C (95°F) of the Thermotime switch it will not operate at all, no starting enrichment being required.

Cranking enrichment

The E.C.U. increases the pulse width during engine cranking; in addition to any enrichment due to the coolant temperature sensor or the cold start injectors, this increase reduces slightly when cranking stops, but fails to normal after a few seconds.

This temporary enrichment sustains the engine during initial running.

Oxygen sensors — cars to U.S.A.

The oxygen sensors (22, Fig. 3) measure the free oxygen concentration in the exhaust system. Excessive free oxygen over a certain proportion indicates a weak mixture, whereas insufficient free oxygen indicates a rich mixture. A signal is fed to the E.C.U. to compensate for these variations by revising the applied injector pulse width. The oxygen sensors are initially set using the equipment shown on page 9. A service interval counter in conjunction with a warning lamp (see page 9) indicate when the oxygen sensors must be replaced.

Engine speed sensing

This is obtained from a connection to the —ve termial of the ignition coil, which triggers the E.C.U. to produce the time pulses to two groups of six injectors. From this signal an engine speed function is determined to modify the pulse width, already established by the manifold pressure sensor (in the E.C.U.). The E.C.U. divides the trigger pulses to give four outputs to the power resistors (23).

Power resistors

To open the injectors at the speeds required by the engine a fairly high current is needed, about 1.5A per injector. The E.C.U. has an output stage to deliver this current, but to protect the output transistors of the E.C.U. from injector faults and short-circuits a power resistor is wired in series with each three injectors. These resistors (23, Fig. 3) will limit fault current to a safe value, thus protecting the E.C.U. The four power resistors (one for each group of injectors) are housed in a single unit secured to the right side of the engine valance by two screws. To ensure fast opening of the injectors the full battery voltage is applied to them via the 'Turn on' circuit then, to reduce power dissipation, once they are open, drive is maintained via the power resistor unit and the 'Hold on' circuit.

Positive crankcase ventilation (P.C.V.) valve

The P.C.V. valve is a variable orifice valve (in the air cleaner) calibrated such that flow through the valve increases with reducing pressure across the valve to a minimum, at which point any further reduction results in a reduction of gas flow until the valve 'chokes'.

Over-run valve

The over-run (38, Fig. 3) valve fitted to the front of the inlet manifolds bleeds air into these manifolds under engine over-run conditions when the manifolds depression exceeds a pre-determined value. The valve is a pressure-differential-sensitive poppet valve.

Fault diagnosis

Faults in the complete fuel injection system may be diagnosed by using the Lucas EPITEST equipment (Section 4, 'P' Pressure System).

Full load fuelling—cars to U.S.A.

To obtain maximum engine power it is necessary to inhibit the 'closed loop' system and simultaneously increase the fuelling level. This is obtained by using a vacuum-operated electrical switch (31, Fig. 3) sensing inlet manifold depression, and a micro-switch, operated by throttle pulley spindle. These two switches are wired in parallel, so that either or both can signal the need for full load fuelling.

Throttle position switch

The micro-switch (32, Fig. 3) is mounted such that its contacts are closed when the throttle is opened beyond a certain position, this condition has the same effect as the closing of the contacts of the full load vacuum switch. The throttle position switch is required to provide full load fuelling when the vehicle is operating under high speed, full load running conditions and the manifold depression is unable to operate the vacuum switch.

Vacuum switch

The contacts of this switch (31, Fig. 3) are operated by a spring-loaded diaphragm in a chamber. This senses inlet manifold vacuum such that, when the depression falls below a certain value, e.g. when the engine is operating at low speed, with part throttle near full load condition, then the contacts close.

The closing of the contacts causes the fuel system to go 'open loop' and simultaneously introduces a fuel enrichment of 12%.

ELECTRONIC FUEL INJECTION

Lucas EFI Feedback Monitor Unit

Check the ignition timing and idle speed.

Remove the blanking plug from the E.C.U. to expose the idling fuel setting adjuster.

Run the engine until it reaches operating temperature (at least 8 minutes from cold or 2 minutes if hot).

Disconnect the Lambda disable plug from the harness socket (1, Fig. 5) otherwise the Lambda sensors will not function while in Neutral or Park.

Connect EFI Feedback Monitor to the Fuel Setting Diagnostic socket (2, Fig. 5).

Position switch to LOW (for Lucas) Electronic Control Unit (3, Fig. 5).

Slowly turn the Idling Fuel Setting Adjuster in the E.C.U. until:

LAMP 2 in ROW A or B is lit and LAMP 2 or 3 in other ROW is lit.

Fit a new blanking plug to cover the idling fuel setting adjuster.

Disconnect the pressure regulator vacuum pipe and temporarily set off the vacuum take-off on the manifold pipe.

The Feedback Monitor unit indicators should move towards 'RICH', i.e. LAMP 2 to LAMP 1 and LAMP 3 to LAMP 2 or 1.

If the indicators do not change, Lambda sensors and associated circuit are suspect.

Re-connect the pressure regulator vacuum pipe.

GOOD PRACTICE

The following instructions must be strictly observed:

1. Always disconnect the battery before removing any components.

2. Always depressurize the fuel system before disconnecting any fuel pipes (see 19.50.02).

3. When removing fuelling components always clamp fuel pipes approximately 38 mm (1.5 in) from the unit being removed. Do not overtighten clamp.

4. Ensure that a supply of cloth is available to absorb any spillage that may occur.

5. When reconnecting electrical components, always ensure that good contact is made by the connector before fitting covers.

6. Always ensure that ground connections are made to clean, bare metal, and are tightly fastened, using correct screws and washers.

MAINTENANCE

There is no routine maintenance laid down for the electronic fuel injection system other than that at all service intervals, the electrical connections must be checked for security. The fuel filter must be discarded and a replacement fitted at 50 000 miles (80 000 km) intervals, when the air cleaner must also be renewed.

WARNING:

1. **Do not run the engine with the battery disconnected.**

2. **Do not use a high-speed battery charger as a starting aid.**

3. **When using a high-speed battery charger to charge the battery, the battery MUST be disconnected from the vehicle's electrical system.**

4. **Ensure that the battery is connected with correct polarity.**

5. **No battery larger than 12V may be used.**

LUCAS POTENTIOMETER ADJUSTER

Remove the throttle linkage from the engine.

Slacken the potentiometer fixing screws (1, Fig. 6).

Connect the adjuster to the potentiometer (2, Fig. 6).

Connect the potentiometer gauge to the battery (3, Fig. 6).

Move the switch to 'T' (4, Fig. 6).

Adjust by rotating the potentiometer to right or left until CORRECT lamp is lit.

Re-tighten the fixing screws.

Refit the throttle linkage.

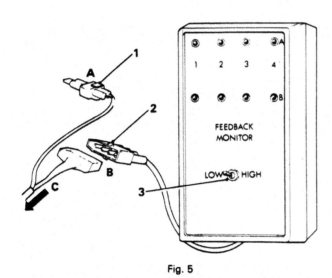

Fig. 5

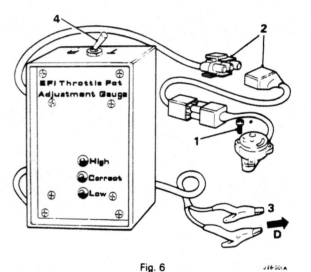

Fig. 6

Key to illustrations (Fig. 7 and Fig. 8)

A.   Double socket.
B.   To E.C.U.
C.   Feedback/monitor socket
D.   To battery

19—9

ELECTRONIC FUELLING INJECTION

Idle fuelling

To obtain good quality engine idling with transmission in Neutral (N) or Park (P) 'closed loop' fuel control is inhibited. This is accomplished by using the 'Start Inhibit Switch' actuated by the transmission lever. The idle fuelling level can be adjusted only when the voltage output from the throttle potentiometer exceeds a predetermined value, i.e. when the throttles are closed.

The adjustment is only effective when the engine is operating in the 'open loop' mode.

Ignition timing (cars to USA)

The ignition timing mechanisms are shown in Section 86. The ignition timing (with the vacuum pipe disconnected) is 25° B.T.D.C., with the engine speed at 3000 rev/min and at normal operating temperature.

Ignition vacuum advance system control

For best fuel economy the engine requires more vacuum advance below 4000 rev/min that can be tolerated above this speed. This control circuit is designed to dump part of the vacuum advance signal to the distributor capsule, at engine speeds above 4000 rev/min road load.

Ignition vacuum dump valve

The dump valve (43, Fig. 7) is used to modify the signal applied to the ignition vacuum advance capsule (29, Fig. 7). This vacuum signal is obtained from the throttle edge tapping and applied to the signal, port 'C', when this signal exceeds 12,5 mmHg (5 inHg) 'A' and 'B' ports are connected; this bleeds air at atmospheric pressure via a restrictor (5, Fig. 7) into the ignition vacuum advance signal hose, thus modifying the signal to the advance capsule.

Ignition vacuum delay valve

The vacuum delay valve (42, Fig. 7) is fitted in the distributor vacuum advance line to ensure that the vacuum is not applied too quickly when the throttle is opened.

Sintered steel restrictors inside the valve allow the signal vacuum at port 'A' of the valve to bleed through to port 'B' at a controlled rate. An umbrella check valve allows an unrestricted flow in the opposite direction.

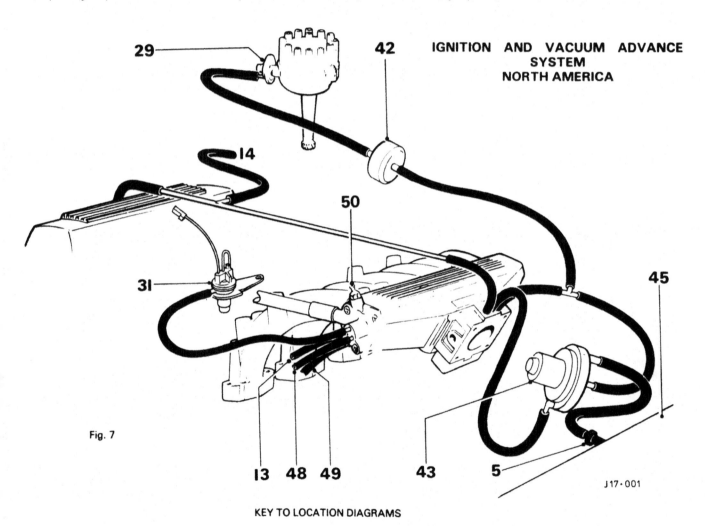

IGNITION AND VACUUM ADVANCE SYSTEM NORTH AMERICA

Fig. 7

J17·001

KEY TO LOCATION DIAGRAMS

5. Restrictors	41. Supplementary air valve
13. Fuel pressure regulator	42. Vacuum delay valve
14. Carbon canister	43. Vacuum advance dump valve
29. Distributor and vacuum capsule	45. Air cleaner
31. Throttle vacuum switch	48. To air-conditioning unit
39. Oil temperatrue switch	49. To automatic gearbox
40. Change-over valve (3-way)	50. Brake non-return valve

19—10

Ignition timing cars to U.K. and Europe

The ignition timing (with the vacuum pipe disconnected) and the engine at normal operating temperature is 24° B.T.D.C. at 3000 rev/min, compression ratio (high 'H').

An oil temperature switch (39, Fig. 8) in the oil system, operates the solenoids of the three way Changeover valve (40, Fig. 8) and the Supplementary air valve (41, Fig. 8) when the oil reaches the operating temperature. This switches the vacuum signal from the throttle edge tapping to the inlet manifold and allows air from the air cleaner (45, Fig. 8) to by-pass the throttle, giving greater fuel economy.

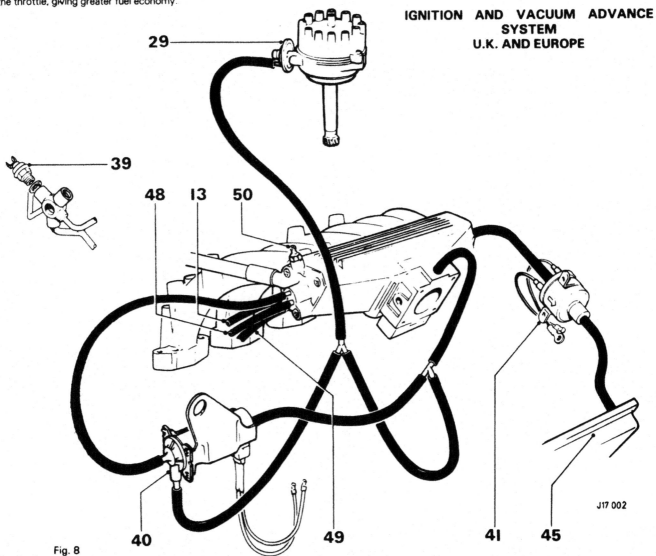

IGNITION AND VACUUM ADVANCE SYSTEM U.K. AND EUROPE

J17 002

Fig. 8

THE ELECTRONIC FUEL INJECTION SYSTEM—'D' SYSTEM

D Pressure Sensing Type

Description

The 'D' Pressure Sensing Type Fuel Injection is fitted to all 5.3 models for the Australian and Japanese markets and other cars prior to the incorporation of the Digital system.

The electronic fuel injection system is divided into two-sub systems interconnected only at the injectors.

The systems are:

1. The fuel system delivering to the injectors a constant supply of fuel at the correct pressure 2,1 bar (3.0 lbf/in).

2. The electronic sensing and control system which monitors engine operating conditions of load, speed, temperature (coolant and induction air) and throttle movement. The control system then produces electrical current pulses of appropriate width to hold open the injector solenoid valves and allows the correct quantity of fuel to flow through the nozzle for each engine cycle.

As fuel pressure is held constant, varying the pulse width increases or decreases the amount of fuel passed through the injector to comply with the engine requirements.

Pulse width and therefore fuel quantity is also modified to provide enrichment during starting and warming-up, at closed throttle, full throttle and while the throttle is actually opening.

The injectors are operated by the Electronic Control Unit (E.C.U.) in two groups of six. Each is further broken down into sub-groups of three, although each pair of sub-groups is operated simultaneously to make up the two groups of six twice per engine cycle.

Injection in two groups of six

| 1A | 3A | 5A | | 1B | 3B | 5B |
| 2B | 4B | 6B | | 2A | 4A | 6A |

Firing order:

| 1A | 6B | 5A | 2B | 3A | 4B | 6A | 1B | 2A |
| 5B | 4A | 3B | | | | | | |

Cylinders numbered from front of engine.

The induction system is basically the same as that on a carburetted engine; tuned ram pipe, air cleaners, plenum chambers and induction ports. Air is drawn through paper element cleaners to a butterfly valve for each bank and to individual ports for each cylinder leading off the plenum chamber. The injectors are positioned at the cylinder head end of each port so that fuel is directed at the back of each inlet valve.

	A	(1)	(2)	(3)	(4)	(5)	(6)
Front							
	B	(1)	(2)	(3)	(4)	(5)	(6)
(1)	Inlet opens					13° B.T.D.C.	
(2)	Inlet closes					55° B.B.D.C.	
(3)	Ignition: Japan					10°	
	Australia					4°	
(4)	Exhaust opens					55° B.B.D.C.	
(5)	Exhaust closes					13° A.T.D.C.	

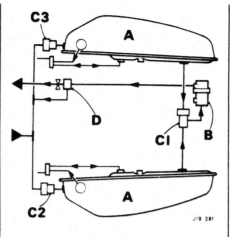

Fig. 9

Key to Diagram
A. Fuel tank
B. Fuel pump
C. Change-over valve
D. Air bleed valve

Fuel system

Fuel is drawn from tanks (A, Fig. 9) by a fuel pump (B, Fig. 9) and fed via a solenoid-operated 3-way change-over valve (C, Fig. 9), air bleed valve (D, Fig. 9), in-line filter (W, Fig. 10) to two fuel rails (Z, Fig. 10).

Two pressure regulators 'N' maintain the pressure at 2,1 kgf/cm² (30 lbf/in²).

Excess fuel is returned to the tank from which it was drawn via fuel cooler (T, Fig. 10) and solenoid-operated valves (H1 and H2, Fig. 9)—mounted under the rear wheel arches.

The 12 injectors (X, Fig. 10) are connected to the fuel rails. They are solenoid-operated and respond to impulses from the E.C.U. via the power amplifier to open and inject fuel into each inlet port.

Fuel is also supplied to two cold start injectors (G, Fig. 10) that are only operated during initial starting of cold engine.

FUEL INJECTION

Electronic system

The main criteria governing the injection of fuel into the engine are manifold depression (engine load) and engine speed.

The driver controls the engine power output by varying the throttle opening and therefore the flow determines the pressure that exists within the plenum chamber, the pressure therefore being a measure of the demand upon the engine. This pressure is used to provide the principal control of fuel quantity being converted by the pressure sensor (A, Fig. 10) into an electrical signal to be passed to the E.C.U. (B, Fig. 10). The signal varies the duration of the injector operating pulse as appropriate.

The pressure sensor is fitted with a separate diaphragm system that compensates for ambient barometric variations.

Engine speed sensing

The trigger unit (C, Fig. 10) fitted within the distributor has two reed switches mounted 180 degrees apart so that they are closed alternately, one each revolution of the crankshaft. Each switch 'triggers' the E.C.U. to produce the timed pulse to a group of six injectors, although the trigger switch itself has no part in determining the pulse length. In addition to this primary function of initiation of injection the trigger unit switching is monitored by the E.C.U. for frequency of operation. From this signal an engine speed function is determined that modifies the pulse width, already established by manifold pressure, to take account of engine speed-dependent resonances in induction and exhaust.

Temperature sensors

The temperature of the air being taken into the engine through the inlet manifold, and the temperature of the coolant in the cylinder block is constantly monitored. The information is fed directly to the E.C.U.

The air temperature sensor (D, Fig. 10) has a small effect on the injector pulse width, and should be looked upon as a trimming rather than a control device. It ensures that the fuel supplied is directly related to the weight of air drawn in by the engine. Therefore, as the weight (density) of the air charge increases with falling temperature, so the amount of fuel supplied is also increased to maintain optimum fuel/air ratio.

The coolant temperature sensor (E, Fig. 10) has a much greater degree of control although its main effect is concentrated while the engine is initially warming-up. The coolant temperature sensor operates in conjunction with the cold start system and the auxiliary air valve (F, Fig. 10) to form a completely automatic equivalent to a carburetter choke.

Cold start system (early models only)

For cold starting additional fuel is injected into the intake manifolds by two cold start injectors (G, Fig. 10). These are controlled by the cold start relay (H, Fig. 10) and Thermotime switch (J, Fig. 10). The Thermotime switch senses coolant temperature and depending on that temperature, interrupts or completes the ground connection for the relay. When the starter is operated the cold start relay is energized with its circuit completed via the Thermotime switch. The Thermotime switch also limits the length of time for which the relay is energized, to a maximum of eight seconds under conditions of extreme cold. This enrichment is in addition to that provided by the coolant temperature sensor. If the coolant temperature is above the rated value of Thermotime switch, the Thermotime switch does not operate at all, no starting enrichment being required.

Cranking enrichment

The E.C.U. provides an increased pulse duration during engine cranking in addition to any enrichment due to the coolant temperature sensor or the cold start injectors. The additional signal reduces slightly when cranking stops, but does not fall to normal level for a few seconds. This temporary enrichment sustains the engine during initial running.

Throttle switch

The throttle switch (K, Fig. 10) is a rotary switch directly coupled to the throttle pulley. It contains sets of contacts that provide information for the E.C.U. regarding the position and movement of the throttle butterfly valves. The operation of these contacts is as follows:

Throttle closed (idle) contacts—These contacts establish a specific, slightly richer, level of fuelling while the throttle is fully closed, and the engine running at idling revolutions. While the throttle is in this position, the exhaust CO level can be varied using the idle mixture control knob on the E.C.U. This knob MUST NOT

be moved unless correct test equipment and skilled personnel are in attendance to monitor changes made.

Throttle movement contacts—Immediately the throttle is opened a series of 20 make and break contacts are put into circuit. If the throttle butterfly is opened quickly a slight delay occurs before the pressure sensor reacts to the change in manifold pressure. This period of delay is overcome by the throttle switch contacts which transmit a series of voltage spikes to the E.C.U. These signals produce an increased pulse duration while the throttle is moving.

Full load enrichment is provided by revising the response curve of the manifold pressure sensor.

Flooding protection system

When the ignition is on but the engine not cranking the fuel pump will run for one to two seconds to raise the pressure in the fuel rail; it is then automatically switched off by the E.C.U.

Only after cranking has started is the fuel pump switched on again. Switching control is built into the E.C.U. circuitry. The system prevents flooding should any injectors become faulty (remain in the open position), and the ignition is left switched on.

Auxiliary air valves

The auxiliary air valve (F, Fig. 10) is controlled by coolant temperature. To prevent stalling at cold start and cold idle conditions due to the increased drag of the engine, the valve opens to allow air to by-pass the throttles and so increase the engine speed. In addition to the main coolant temperature regulated air passage, the auxiliary air valve has a by-pass controlled by an adjusting screw (L, Fig. 10). The screw controls the idle speed by regulatimg the air flow.

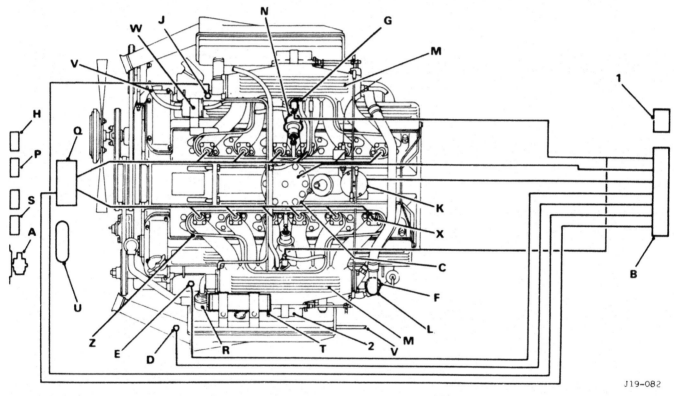

Fig. 10

J19-082

KEY TO LOCATION DIAGRAM (Fig. 10)

A. Manifold pressure sensor
B. Electronic control unit (E.C.U.)
C. Trigger unit (in distributor)
D. Air temperature sensor
E. Coolant tenperature sensor
F. Auxiliary air valve
G. Cold start injector
H. Cold start relay
J. Thermotime switch
K. Throttle switch

L. Idle speed regulating screw
M. Inlet manifolds
N. Fuel pressure regulator
P. Fuel pump relay
Q. Power amplifier
R. Over-run valve
S. Main relay
T. Fuel cooler—on cars fitted with air-conditioning fuel cooler is mounted above compressor

U. Ignition amplifier
V. Fuel feed and return
W. Fuel filter
X. Injector
Z. Fuel rail

1. E.G.R. control unit
2. E.G.R. valve

GOOD PRACTICE

The following instructions must be strictly observed:

1. Always disconnect the battery before removing any components.
2. Always depressurize the fuel system before disconnecting any fuel pipes.
3. When removing fuelling components always clamp fuel pipes approximately 38 mm (1.5 in) from the unit being removed. Do not overtighten clamp.
4. Ensure that rags are available to absorb any spillage that may occur.
5. When reconnecting electrical components always ensure that good contact is made by the connector before fitting the rubber cover. Always ensure that ground connections are made on to clean bare metal, and are tightly fastened using the correct screws and washers.

WARNING

1. **Do not let the engine run without the battery connected.**
2. **Do not use a high-speed battery charger as a starting aid.**
3. **When using a high-speed charger to charge the battery, the battery MUST be disconnected from the rest of the vehicle's electrical system.**
4. **When installing, ensure that battery is connected with correct polarity.**
5. **No battery larger than 12V may be used.**

MAINTENANCE

There is no routine maintenance procedure laid down for the electronic fuel injection system other than that, at all service intervals, the electrical connectors must be checked for security. The fuel filter must be discarded and a replacement component fitted at 12,000 mile (20 000 km) intervals.

AIR CLEANER

Description
The air cleaners are of the paper element type, the back plates of which are fitted to the throttle housings. They are fitted with a short intake tuning tube.

Remove and refit   19.10.01

Removing

Disconnect the battery.
Pull the connector from the air temperature sensor—left-hand air cleaner only (1, Fig. 11).
Release the two toggle clips securing the air cleaner cover, and pull the cover from the backplate (2, Fig. 11).
Remove the cleaner element (3, Fig. 11).

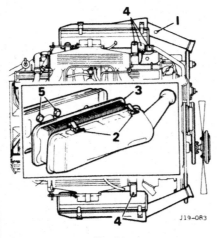

Fig. 11

Release the hose clip and pull the over-run valve air intake pipe from the backplate.
Pull off the crankcase breather pipe and the auxiliary air valve inlet pipes—left-hand air cleaner only (4, Fig. 11).
Remove the four setscrews and washers securing air cleaner backplate to throttle housing (5, Fig. 11).

Refitting

NOTE: If necessary, transfer the components to the replacement air cleaner cover and backplate.

Locate the air cleaner backplate, using a new gasket if necessary, on the throttle housing and secure using the four setscrews and washers.
Fit the over-run valve inlet hose, and tighten the hose clip. Refit the crankcase breather pipes and the auxiliary air valve inlet pipe—left-hand air cleaner only.
Ensure that the air cleaner element seal is in good condition, and locate the air cleaner element.

NOTE: Ensure that the element is correctly orientated, with the metal plate opposite the throttle housing.

Locate the air cleaner cover and secure the two toggle clips.
Fit the connector to the air temperature sensor—left-hand air cleaner only.
Reconnect the battery.

AIR CLEANERS

Renew element   19.10.08

Pull the connector from the air temperature sensor—left-hand air cleaner only.
Release the two toggle clips securing the air cleaner cover, and pull the cover from the backplate (1, Fig. 12).

Remove the air cleaner element (2, Fig. 12).
Ensure that the air cleaner seal is in good condition and locate the air cleaner element.

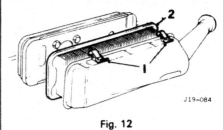

Fig. 12

NOTE: Ensure that the element is correctly orientated, with the metal plate opposite the throttle housing.

Locate the air cleaner cover and secure the two toggle clips.
Fit the connector to the air temperature sensor—left-hand air cleaner only.

THROTTLE PEDAL

Remove and refit   19.20.01

Removing

Fold the carpet away from the base of the throttle pedal.
Remove the nuts and washers securing the base of the pedal to the mounting plate (1, Fig. 13).
Pull the base of the pedal away from the mounting plate and disengage the spring from the pedal (2, Fig. 13).
Examine the spring for wear, and renew if necessary (3, Fig. 13).

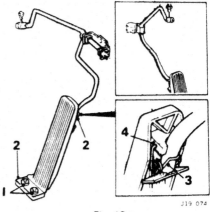

Fig. 13

Refitting

Engage the rod with the pedal. Position the spring on the pedal (4, Fig. 13).
Push the base of the pedal towards the bulkhead and locate on the mounting studs.
Reverse the first two operations.

19—14

THROTTLE LINKAGE

Check and adjust 19.20.05

Check

Ensure that the throttle return springs are correctly secured and the throttle pulley moves freely, resting against the closed stop when released (1, Fig. 14).

Ensure that the throttle butterfly closed stop screw has not been moved. If signs of tampering are present, check, and if necessary adjust (2, Fig. 14).

Ensure that the throttle pulley can be rotated to touch the fully open stop and that the throttle butterfly valve stop arm is touching the throttle housing.

If the conditions of the above operations are not satisfied, proceed with operation 'Adjust'.

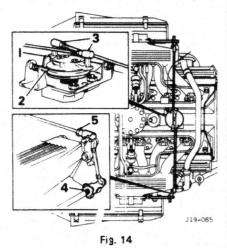

Fig. 14

Adjust

If the throttle butterfly closed stop has been moved, adjust the stop.

Check for worn pivots, damaged rods or linkage and trace of any stiffness. Renew items as necessary.

Release the throttle cross-rods from the throttle pulley (3, Fig. 14).

Slacken the clamps securing lever to rear of the throttle shafts (4, Fig. 14).

With the butterfly valve against the closed stop, bellcrank against the stop, and play in coupling taken up in opening direction, tighten the clamp to the lock lever to the throttle shaft. Repeat for other side of engine.

Offer the cross-rods to ball connectors on the pulley; the rods must locate without moving the pulley or linkage. If adjustment is necessary, continue with operations.

Slacken the locknuts on the cross-rods and adjust the length of the rods to locate the pulley ball connectors while the bellcrank is against the closed stop (5, Fig. 14).

Tighten the locknuts and ensure that the ball joints remain free.

If adjustment is not necessary, slacken the locknut on the throttle pulley fully open stop and wind back the adjustment screw.

Hold the throttle pulley fully open and ensure that both the throttle butterfly stop arms are against the throttle housing.

Set fully open stop to just touch the throttle pulley and tighten the locknut.

Check operations of the throttle switch.

Check the kick-down switch adjustment.

THROTTLE CABLE

Remove and refit 19.20.06

Removing

Disconnect the battery.

Pull the connections from the kick-down switch (1, Fig. 15).

Slacken the locknuts and disconnect the throttle cable (2, Fig. 15).

Beneath the bonnet, slacken the locknut on the top surface of footwell (3, Fig. 15).

Remove the split pin at the top end of the operating rod (4, Fig. 15).

Disengage the sleeve and nipple from the rod (5, Fig. 15).

Remove the nut from the cable sheath (6, Fig. 15) and draw the cable assembly into the engine compartment.

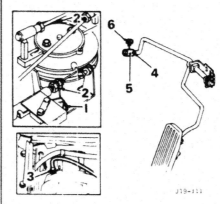

Fig. 15

Refitting

Examine grommets for damage; renew as necessary.

Thread cable through guide bracket and reverse the above operations. Apply sealing compound around the thread on the top surface of footwell.

If the operating rod return spring is fitted, re-secure to the split pin.

Check the throttle linkage adjustment.

Check the kick-down switch adjustment.

THROTTLE BUTTERFLY VALVE

Adjust—both 19.20.11

Adjust

CAUTION: Any adjustment must be carried out on both butterfly valves. It is NOT permitted to adjust one valve only.

Remove both air cleaners.

Slacken the locknut on the throttle butterfly stop screw. Wind back the screw.

Ensure that the throttle butterfly valve closes fully.

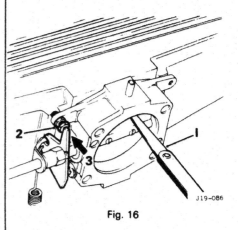

Fig. 16

Insert 0,05 mm (0.002 in) feeler gauge between the top of the valve and the housing to hold the valve open (1, Fig. 16).

Set the stop screw to just touch the stop arm and tighten the locknut with the feeler gauge in position (2, Fig. 16).

Press the stop arm against the stop screw (3, Fig. 14) and withdraw the feeler. Repeat on the other side of the engine.

Seal the threads of the adjusting screws and locknuts using a blob of paint.

Refit the air cleaners.

Check the throttle linkage adjustment.

Check operation of the throttle switch.

Check kick-down switch adjustment.

AUXILIARY AIR VALVE

Description

The auxiliary air valve is located on the left-hand cylinder bank rear coolant pipe.

The valve is controlled by coolant temperature and opens to pass additional air into the inlet manifold under cold start and cold idle positions. A by-pass controlled by the adjusting screw (3, Fig. 17) permits regulation of the hot engine idle speed.

Remove and refit 19.20.16

CAUTION: This procedure MUST ONLY be carried out on a cold or cool engine.

19—15

Disconnect the battery.
Carefully remove the pressure cap from the remote header tank to release any cooling system residual pressure. Replace the cap tightly.
Slacken the clips securing the air hoses to the auxiliary air valve. Pull the hoses clear (1, Fig. 17).

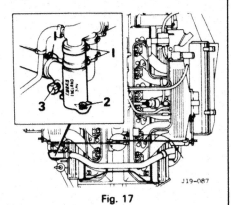

Fig. 17

Remove the two screws and washers securing the auxiliary air valve to the coolant pipe and lift clear (2, Fig. 17).
Clean all traces of gasket from the coolant pipe, taking care not to damage the seating area.
Scribe a line on the adjusting screw and note the number of turns required to fully screw in (3, Fig. 17).

Refitting

Set the replacement screw of the replacement valve to the number of turns open noted in previous operation.
Coat the new gasket with suitable non-hardening sealing compound and locate the valve, orientated correctly, on the coolant pipe.
Secure the valve using two screws and washers.
Fit the air hoses and secure the clips.
Reconnect the battery.
Check the coolant level at the remote header tank, and if necessary, top-up.
Check, and if necessary, adjust idle speed.

AUXILIARY AIR VALVE

Test   **19.20.17**

Remove the auxiliary air valve.
Fully close the adjustment screw.
Immerse the air valve bulb in a container of boiling water and observe valve head through side port. Valve should move smoothly to closed position.
Quickly blow through the side port; no air should pass.
Allow the valve bulb to cool. The valve head should move smoothly back to open the main air passage.

If the valve performance is satisfactory, reset the adjustment screw and refit the valve.
If the valve performance is not satisfactory, fit a replacement component.

IDLE SPEED

Adjust   **19.20.18**

Ensure that the engine is at normal operating temperature.
Check the throttle linkage for correct operation, and that the return springs are secure and effective.
Start the engine and run for two or three minutes.
Set the idle speed adjustment screw to achieve 750 rev/min.

NOTE: If it proves impossible to reduce idle speed to the specified level, proceed as detailed in the following operations.

Check ALL pipes and hoses to the inlet manifolds for security and condition.
Check the security of the injectors and the cold start injectors.
Ensure that all joints are tight, and that inlet manifold to cylinder head fastenings are tight.
Ensure that both throttle butterfly closed stops show no signs of tampering; if they do, adjust throttle butterfly valves.
Check operation of over-run valves.
If the above operations do not reduce the idle speed, check the operation of the auxiliary air valve.

OVER-RUN VALVE—Cars fitted with Emission Control

Description

An over-run valve is fitted in each inlet manifold. The valve is calibrated to open and limit manifold depression under conditions of closed throttle over-run. This ensures that air is available to maintain a combustible air/fuel ratio under all conditions.

OVER-RUN VALVE

Test   **19.20.21**

Slacken the pipe clips at the air filter back plates. Pull the inlet pipes clear.
Block the inlet pipes, start the engine.
If idle speed is now correct, stop the engine and re-connect one valve only.
Start the engine. If the idle speed is still correct, stop the engine and re-connect the second valve.

Start the engine. If the idle speed is too fast, renew relevant valve.

OVER-RUN VALVE

Remove and refit   **19.20.22**

Removing

Slacken the pipe clip securing the air inlet pipe to the over-run valve (1, Fig. 18).
Remove the three screws securing the over-run valves and the fuel pipe brackets to the inlet manifolds. Retrieve the spacer (right-hand side only). Draw the valves from the air pipes and manifolds (2, Fig. 18).

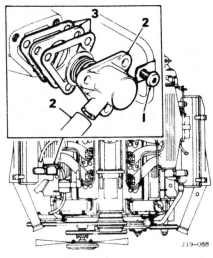

Fig. 18

Refitting

Check the condition of the gaskets and mating surfaces. If necessary, renew the gaskets (3, Fig. 18).
Locate the valves on the air pipes and offer to manifolds. Secure the valves and fuel pipe brackets using three screws and spacer (right-hand side).

FUEL CUT-OFF INERTIA SWITCH

Remove and refit   **19.22.09**

Removing

Disconnect the battery.
Remove the switch cover at passenger side of fascia.
Disconnect cables from switch and remove the switch from the 'A' post.

19—16

Refitting

Secure the switch to the 'A' post.
Connect cables and press in plunger at top of switch.
Fit cover and re-connect battery.

COOLANT TEMPERATURE SENSOR

Description

The coolant temperature sensor is located in the left-hand thermostat housing. The sensor comprises a temperature-sensitive resistor with a negative temperature coefficient; that is, the electrical resistance decreases with increasing temperature. The sensor provides the E.C.U. with a coolant temperature parameter that controls the injector signal pulse with respect to engine temperature. Practically, the sensor establishes a rich level of fuelling at low temperature, and a weaker level at high temperature. In conjunction with the auxiliary air valve the coolant temperature sensor forms an equivalent to a carburetter automatic choke.

COOLANT TEMPERATURE SENSOR

Remove and refit   19.22.18

Removing

NOTE: This procedure MUST ONLY be carried out on a cold or cool engine.

Disconnect the battery.
Pull the connector from the coolant temperature sensor (1, Fig. 19).
Carefully remove the pressure cap from the remote header tank to release any cooling system residual pressure. Replace the cap tightly.

NOTE: The replacement component is prepared at this point, and the transfer made as quickly as possible.

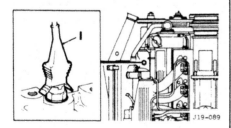

Fig. 19

Ensure that the sealing washer is located on the replacement temperature sensor and coat the threads with suitable sealing compound. Remove the temperature sensor from the thermostat housing.

Refitting

Screw the replacement temperature sensor into position.
Refit the electrical connector.
Reconnect the battery.
Check the coolant level at the remote header tank. If necessary, top-up.

COOLANT TEMPERATURE SENSOR

Test   19.22.19

Disconnect the battery.
Pull the connector from the temperature sensor.
Connect a suitable ohmmeter between the terminals; note the resistance reading. The reading is subject to change according to temperature, and should closely approximate to the relevant resistance value given in the table.
Disconnect the ohmmeter.
Check the resistance between each terminal in turn and body of sensor. A very high resistance reading (open circuit) must be obtained.
Reconnect the cable.
Reconnect the battery.

COOLANT TEMPERATURE (°C)	RESISTANCE (kilohms)
−10	9,2
0	5,9
+10	3,7
+20	2,5
+30	1,7
+40	1,18
+50	0,84
+60	0,60
+70	0,435
+80	0,325
+90	0,250
+100	0,190

THERMOTIME SWITCH

Description

The Thermotime switch is located in the right-hand thermostat housing. The switch comprises a bi-metallic contact opened and closed by coolant temperature and, in addition, auto-excited by a heating element. The switch controls the cold start injectors through the cold start relay and is energized by operation of the starter motor. While the start system is in operation a voltage is applied to the bi-metallic switch contact heating element which then tends to open the contact and isolate the relay and injectors. The length of time that this takes depends upon the initial temperature of the bi-metallic element up to a maximum of eight seconds under conditions of extreme cold. It can be deduced, therefore, that when the engine is warm, or at normal operating temperature, there will be no fuel supplied by the cold start injectors.

THERMOTIME SWITCH

Remove and refit   19.22.20

Removing

NOTE: This procedure MUST ONLY be carried out on a cool or cold engine.

Disconnect the battery.
Pull the connector from the Thermotime switch (1, Fig. 20).
Carefully remove the pressure cap from the remote header tank to release any cooling system residual pressure. Replace the cap tightly.
Ensure that the new sealing washer is located on the replacement Thermotime switch and coat the threads with suitable sealing compound.
Remove the Thermotime switch from the thermostat housing (2, Fig. 20).

Fig. 20

Refitting

Screw the replacement Thermotime switch in position.
Refit the electrical connector.
Reconnect the battery. Check the coolant level at the remote header tank, and top-up if necessary.

THERMOTIME SWITCH

Test   19.22.21

Equipment required: Stop-watch, ohmmeter, single-pole switch, jump lead for connecting switch to battery and Thermotime switch, and a thermometer.

NOTE: Check coolant temperature with thermometer and note reading before carrying out procedures detailed below.
Check rated value of Thermotime switch (stamped on body flat).
Disconnect the battery earth lead.
Pull the electrical connector from the Thermotime switch (1, Fig. 21).

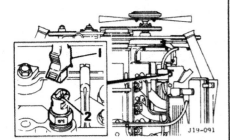

Fig. 21

'A' Coolant temperature higher than switch rated value

Connect the ohmmeter between the terminal 'W' and earth. A very high resistance reading (open circuit) should be obtained (2, Fig. 20).
Renew the switch if a very low resistance reading (short circuit) is obtained.

'B' Coolant temperature lower than switch rated value

Connect the ohmmeter between terminal 'W' and earth. A very low resistance reading (closed circuit) should be obtained.
Connect 12V supply via isolating switch to terminal 'G' of the Thermotime switch (Fig. 22). Using stop-watch, check the time delay between making isolating switch and indication on the ohmmeter changing from low to high resistance. Delay period must closely approximate to the time indicated in table; see the table for specific coolant temperature.

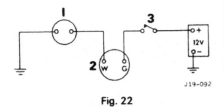

Fig. 22

1. Ohmmeter
2. Thermotime switch
3. Isolating switch and jump leads

COOLANT TEMP.	DELAY 15°C SWITCH	DELAY 35°C SWITCH
−20°C	8 secs.	8 secs.
−10°C	5.7 secs.	6.5 secs.
0°C	3.5 secs.	5 secs.
+10°C	1.2 secs.	3.5 secs.
+15°C	0 secs.	2.7 secs.
+20°C	—	2.0 secs.
+30°C	—	0.5 secs.
+35°C	—	0 secs.

Renew the Thermotime switch if necessary.
Reconnect the Thermotime switch.
Reconnect the battery earth lead.

AIR TEMPERATURE SENSOR

Description

The air temperature sensor is located in the left-hand air cleaner tuned stage. The sensor operates in the same manner as the coolant temperature sensor although through a different resistance range. The information provided by the air temperature sensor, in conjunction with the manifold pressure signal, trims the level of fuelling to take account of ambient air density and temperature.

AIR TEMPERATURE SENSOR

Remove and refit   19.22.22

Removing

Disconnect the battery.
Pull the connector from the air temperature sensor (1, Fig. 23).
Unscrew the sensor from the air cleaner ram pipe.

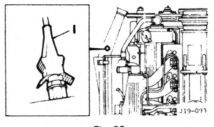

Fig. 23

Refitting

Reverse the above operations.

AIR TEMPERATURE SENSOR

Test   19.22.23

Disconnect the battery.
Pull the connector from the air temperature sensor.
Connect a suitable ohmmeter between the terminals; note the resistance reading. The reading is subject to change according to temperature, and should closely approximate to the relevant resistance value given in the table below.
Disconnect the ohmmeter.
Check the resistance between each terminal in turn and the body of the sensor. A very high resistance reading (open circuit) must be obtained.
Reconnect the cable.
Reconnect the battery.

AMBIENT AIR TEMPERATURE (°C)	RESISTANCE (Ohms)
−10	960
0	640
+10	435
+20	300
+30	210
+40	150
+50	108
+60	80

TRIGGER UNIT

Description

Note:
On later cars fitted with the digital 'P' pressure-sensing fuel injection the pulses are picked up from the h.t. coil.
On early cars fitted with 'D' system fuel injection, a trigger unit is located within the ignition distributor. It consists of two reed switches mounted radially and 180 degrees apart, parallel to the plane of the high tension rotor arm. The rotor arm has a magnet fitted beneath the tail which closes each switch alternately, one each revolution of the crankshaft. The trigger unit switches initiate the start of injection period and also give the E.C.U. an engine speed reference depending upon the frequency at which the successive switches are operated. Small resistors are incorporated in the switch common line and prevent contact damage by limiting the maximum current that can be drawn through the switches.

19—18

TRIGGER UNIT (early models only)

Remove and refit   **19.22.26**

Removing

Disconnect the battery.
Separate one limb of the manifold pressure sensor pipe at tee-piece and secure back from the distributor (1, Fig. 24).

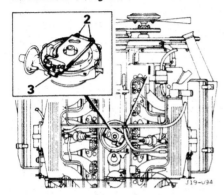

Fig. 24

Ensure that the spark leads are adequately identified and remove the leads from the spark plugs on both banks of cylinders.
Remove the three screws and manoeuvre the distributor cover clear.

Fig. 23

Disconnect the trigger unit at the in-line connector.
Remove the h.t. rotor arm.
Remove four bolts securing the trigger unit platform (2, Fig. 24).
Pull the cable grommet from the distributor body (3, Fig. 24).

Refitting

Reverse the above operations.

TRIGGER UNIT (early models only)

Test   **19.22.27**

Disconnect the cable from the pump relay terminal 85.
Disconnect '−ve' cable at the ignition coil.
Separate the in-line connector to the trigger unit.

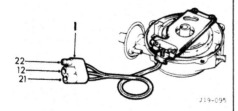

Fig. 25

Connect a suitable ohmmeter between terminals 21 and 12 of distributor side of the in-line connector (1, Fig. 25).
Switch on the ignition and crank the engine. Ohmmeter should show regular, even swing between low resistance (a current-limiting resistor is fitted within the trigger unit), and very high resistance (open circuit).
Transfer the ohmmeter to terminals 22 and 12 (1, Fig. 25). An identical result to that shown in the above operation must be obtained.
If the ohmmeter displays a steady reading during cranking or the swing is uneven or intermittent, the trigger unit must be replaced.
Switch off the ignition.
Reconnect '−ve' cable at the ignition coil.
Reconnect the cable to the pump relay terminal 85.

MANIFOLD PRESSURE SENSOR

Description

The manifold pressure sensor is mounted on the left-hand side of the radiator top rail. The sensor is connected to the inlet manifolds and converts the manifold pressure at any instant into an electrical signal to the E.C.U. The E.C.U. uses this signal (modified by coolant temperature) to determine the duration of operation of the injectors. The sensor is fitted with a diaphragm which serves to relate the manifold pressure level to the existing ambient pressure. This ensures that fuelling is suitable for all atmospheric pressure conditions.

Note:
On cars fitted with the 'P' digital fuel injection system, the manifold pressure sensor is located in the E.C.U., and is not a serviceable unit.

MANIFOLD PRESSURE SENSOR —Early cars fitted with 'D' system fuel injection

Remove and refit   **19.22.29**

Removing

Disconnect the battery.
Pull the electrical connector from the pressure sensor (1, Fig. 26).
Slacken the pipe clip and draw the pressure pipe from sensor (2, Fig. 26).
Remove the bolts and washers securing the pressure sensor bracket to the radiator top rail (3, Fig. 26).
Remove the setscrews and washers securing the pressure sensor to the bracket.

Refitting

Reverse the above operations.

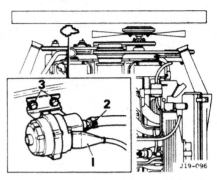

Fig. 26

MANIFOLD PRESSURE SENSOR —Early cars fitted with 'D' system fuel injection

Test   **19.22.28**

Pull the electrical connector from the pressure sensor (1, Fig. 26).
Use a suitable ohmmeter on the pressure sensor terminals and check for resistance readings as follows.
If readings are outside these limits, the pressure sensor must be replaced.
Refit the electrical connector to the pressure sensor.

SENSOR TERMINALS	RESISTANCE (Ohms)
Between 7 and 15	85.5 to 94.5
Between 8 and 10	346.5 to 353.5
Between 7 or 15 and ground	Open circuit (∞)
Between 8 or 10 and ground	Open circuit (∞)

COLD START RELAY (early models only)

Description

The cold start relay is mounted on the radiator top rail. The energizing coil is in series with battery voltage at the starter motor start relay and ground, via the bi-metallic contact of the Thermotime switch. The relay has an internal latching circuit that ensures the contacts remain closed for the full Thermotime delay. The cold start delay is only operated when the starter motor is operated, the ignition switch is 'on' and the Thermotime switch is closed. The single contact applies battery voltage from the pump relay.

19—19

COLD START RELAY

Remove and refit   **19.22.31**

Removing

Early models

Disconnect the battery.
Note the connections and pull the electrical connectors from the cold start relay.
Remove the securing screw.

Later cars

Disconnect the battery.
Remove the cable connector and remove the relay from the clip.

COLD START SYSTEM

Test   **19.22.32**

WARNING: This test results in fuel vapour being present in the engine compartment. It is therefore imperative that all due precautions are taken against fire and explosion.

Remove the two setscrews and washers securing the cold start injectors to the inlet manifolds.
Remove the cold start injectors.
Arrange containers to collect the sprayed fuel.
Disconnect '—ve' terminal from the ignition coil.

NOTE: If the engine is cold (below 15°C), proceed with the following operations.

Switch on the ignition and observe the cold start injectors for fuel leakage. Crank the engine one or two revolutions. Injectors should spray while the engine cranks.

NOTE: Do not operate the starter motor longer than necessary to make this and the following observations.

If the injectors do not spray, carry out the following tests.

a. Crank the engine. Check for battery voltage at the cold start injector supply (white/pink cable).
   If yes: Check all electrical plug and earth connections to the cold start injectors. If satisfactory, the cold start injectors are suspect.
   If no: Proceed to test (b).

b. Crank the engine. Check for battery voltage at terminal 87.
   If yes: Check cables between the cold start relay and the cold start injectors.
   If no: Proceed to test (c).

c. Crank the engine. Check for battery voltage at terminal 30.
   If yes: The cold start relay not energized or contacts faulty; proceed to test (d).
   If no: Check the supply from the pump relay.

d. Crank the engine. Check for battery voltage at terminal 86.

If yes: The cold start relay not energized or contacts faulty. Proceed to test (e). Disconnect the lead at terminal 85.

e. Check for battery voltage at terminal 85.
   If yes. Bridge terminal 85 to earth. The cold start relay should energize—check voltage at terminal 87. If 0V replace the relay; if satisfactory, check cables and connections to the Thermotime switch. If satisfactory, Thermotime switch is suspect.
   If no: Replace the cold start relay.

Replace cold start injectors and all cables and connectors removed.
If the engine is hot (above 15°C), proceed with the following operations.
Crank the engine. Voltage at terminal 87 of the cold start relay must be 0V.
If battery voltage present, disconnect the terminal 85. Crank the engine and re-check voltage at terminal 87.
If the voltage at terminal 87 is 0V, the Thermotime switch is faulty and should be replaced.
If battery voltage is present, replace the cold start relay.
If cold start injectors pass fuel while voltage at terminal 87 is 0V, the injector(s) must be renewed.

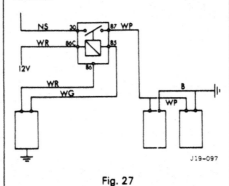

Fig. 27

POWER AMPLIFIER

Description

On early cars fitted with 'D' system fuel injection a power amplifier is fitted and is mounted on the radiator top rail. The amplifier comprises two pairs of transistor switches, each pair controlling six injectors in two groups of three. The amplifier isolates the E.C.U. from the large current drawn, due to six injectors being switched simultaneously.

POWER AMPLIFIER

Remove and refit   **19.22.33**

Removing

Disconnect the battery.
Separate the in-line connectors in the cable harness (1, Fig. 28).

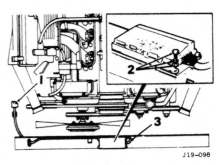

Fig. 28

Remove bolts and washers securing the amplifier to the radiator top rail (2, Fig. 28).
Draw the amplifier cable clear of the radiator top rail grommet (3, Fig. 28).

Refitting

Reverse the above procedure.

POWER RESISTORS

Description

On later cars fitted with 'P' system fuel injection, power resistors are fitted to protect the E.C.U. against the high current required by the injectors, a power resistor is wired in series with groups of three injectors. These resistors will limit the current to a safe value, thus protecting the E.C.U. The four resistors (one for each group of injectors) are housed in a single unit secured to the right-hand side of the engine valance by two nuts and bolts.

POWER RESISTORS

Remove and refit   **19.22.44**

Removing

Disconnect the battery.
Remove the right-hand air cleaner for access.
Remove the nuts and bolts securing the power resistor unit. Retain the spacers. Remove the multi-cable connector from beneath the unit and remove the unit.

Refitting

Reverse the above procedure, ensuring that the cable connector is firmly connected.

THROTTLE SWITCH—Early models fitted with 'D' system fuel injection

Description

The throttle switch is located beneath the throttle pulley. It contains sets of contacts that provide information for the E.C.U. regarding the position and movement of the throttle butterfly valves, thus modifying the fuel quantity delivered by the injectors during idle and change of throttle position.

THROTTLE SWITCH—Early cars

Adjust   19.22.35

Disconnect the battery.
Remove the throttle cross-rods from the throttle pulley.
Pull the electrical connector from the throttle switch.
Remove four nuts and spring washers securing the throttle pulley plate to the throttle pedestal and lift the plate clear. Slacken two screws securing the throttle switch.
Insert a 0,76 mm (0.030 in) feeler gauge between the pulley and the closed throttle stop.
Connect a suitable ohmmeter between terminals 12 and 17 of the throttle switch.
Turn throttle switch slowly until the ohmmeter flicks to very low resistance (short circuit).
Tighten the two fixing screws.
Remove the feeler gauge; ohmmeter should read a very high resistance (open circuit) when pulley is against the closed stop.
Disconnect the ohmmeter.
Locate the pulley plate on the pedestal and secure using four nuts and washers.
Offer the throttle cross-rods to the ball connectors. Ball connectors must fit without moving the throttle bell-cranks.
Adjust the length of the rods if necessary.
NOTE: When tightening the locknuts, ensure the ball joints remain free.
Reconnect the electrical connector to the throttle switch.
Reconnect the battery.

THROTTLE SWITCH—Early cars

Remove and refit   19.22.36

Removing

Disconnect the battery.
Remove the throttle cross-rods from the throttle pulley (1, Fig. 29).
Pull the electrical connector from the throttle switch.

Remove the four nuts and spring washers securing the throttle pulley plate to the throttle pedestal and lift the plate clear (2, Fig. 29).
Remove two screws, plain and shakeproof washer securing the throttle switch and lift the switch from the spindle (3, Fig. 29).

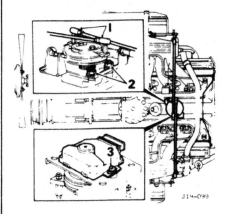

Fig. 29

Refitting

Locate the switch on the spindle with the connector socket facing to rear.
Loosely secure using the two screws, plain and shakeproof washers.
Set up the switch as previously described.

THROTTLE SWITCH (Later cars potentiometer)

On later cars a throttle potentiometer is fitted and the adjustment procedure is as follows. A Lucas potentiometer adjuster gauge is required for this operation.
Remove the throttle pedestal securing nuts and washers.
Tilt the pedestal to one side and slacken the throttle potentiometer fixing screws.
Connect the adjustment gauge supply cables to the battery red to positive, black to negative.
Connect the throttle potentiometer and the adjustment gauge connectors together using the adaptor provided.
Ensure that the switch on the adjustment gauge is in the position marked 'T'.
Slowly rotate the potentiometer body, clockwise or anti-clockwise as required, until the lamp marked 'correct' lights up.
Retighten the potentiometer and refit the throttle pedestal.

Remove and refit   19.22.36

Removing

Disconnect the battery.
Remove the throttle cross-rods from the throttle pulley.
Disconnect the throttle potentiometer in-line cable connector.
Remove the nuts and washers securing the

throttle pulley plate to the throttle pedestal and lift the plate clear.
Remove the potentiometer fixing screws and lift the potentiometer clear.

Refitting

Reverse the above procedure.

THROTTLE SWITCH—Early cars

Test   19.22.37

NOTE: Before commencing the following tests ensure that the throttle butterfly valve and throttle linkage are correctly set.
Disconnect the battery.
Pull the electrical connector from the throttle switch.

Idle position

Connect ohmmeter between the terminals 12/47 and 17 of the switch (Fig. 30). Meter reading must show very low resistance (short circuit). If not, adjust before proceeding.

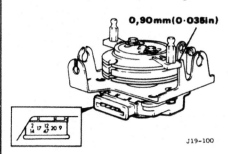

Fig. 30

Temporary enrichment

Connect ohmmeter between the terminals 9 and 12/47 of the switch (Fig. 30).
Observe ohmmeter and turn the throttle pulley by hand. Meter needle should swing regularly between very low resistance (short circuit), and very high resistance (open circuit) ten times.
NOTE: If the meter needle does not swing consistently, or remains steady, replace the throttle switch.

Refit the electrical connector to the switch.
Reconnect the battery.

ELECTRONIC CONTROL UNIT (E.C.U.)

Description

The E.C.U. is mounted in the luggage compartment against the front bulkhead.
The E.C.U. receives all electrical input signals from various sensors. This information is used

19—21

to determine the correct period of time for which the injectors are held open in each engine cycle. A control knob on the E.C.U. adjusts idle CO level and MUST NOT normally be moved.

ELECTRONIC CONTROL UNIT (E.C.U.)

Remove and refit
Early cars   **19.22.34**

Removing

Disconnect the battery.
At the forward end of the luggage compartment, remove the E.C.U. cover (1, Fig. 31).
Remove the retainer band (2, Fig. 31).
Remove the cable clamp clip (3, Fig. 31).
Unclip the end cover (4, Fig. 31).
Locate the handle on the harness plug and withdraw the plug.

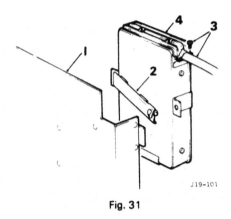

Fig. 31

Refitting

CAUTION: The idle fuelling potentiometer is preset and must not be moved.

Reverse the above operations.
Check idle CO level.

Later cars
Disconnect the battery.
Remove the E.C.U. cover.
Remove the two bolts securing the E.C.U.
Remove the cable harness plug. Disconnect the vacuum pipe.
Withdraw the unit from the boot.

MAIN RELAY

Description

The main relay is mounted on the radiator top rail. The energizing coil is in series with the ignition switch, which, when operated, closes the single set of contacts via the fuel pump cut-off inertia switch. The contacts supply battery voltage to the E.C.U. on early cars, the power amplifier, and to the pump relay. The main relay coil is in series with a diode that prevents operation of the main relay should the battery be connected incorrectly.

MAIN RELAY

Remove and refit   **19.22.38**

Removing

Disconnect the battery.
Pull the electrical connector from the main relay.
Remove the relay.

Refitting

Reverse the above operations.

PUMP RELAY

Description

The pump relay is mounted on the radiator top rail. The energizing coil is in series with battery voltage, supplied by the main relay, and ground via an electronic time delay in the E.C.U. The single contact of the relay applies battery voltage to the in-circuit fuel pump and the cold start system circuitry. Should the ignition switch be turned to 'on' but not to 'Start', the time delay allows the fuel pump to run for one or two seconds before turning it off. When the ignition switch is turned to 'Start' and the engine cranked, the time delay is by-passed. The fuel pump will then run continuously until such time as the ignition is switched off, or the trigger unit pulses cease, indicating that the engine has stopped. This provides a safety back-up to the inertia switch should the engine stop and the ignition be left in the 'on' position due to an accident situation.

PUMP RELAY

Remove and refit   **19.22.39**

Removing

Disconnect the battery.
Pull the electrical connectors from the pump relay.
Remove the relay.

Refitting

Reverse the above operations.

PUMP RELAY

Test   **19.22.40**

Switch on the ignition. The pump should run for one to two seconds, then stop.

NOTE: If the pump does not run, or does not stop, check systematically as follows:

Check that the inertia switch cut-out button is pressed in.
Remove the screws, detach the inertia switch cover, and ensure that both cables are secure.
Pull the connectors from the switch and check continuity across the terminals.
Pull the button out and check for open circuit.
Remove the ohmmeter, replace the connectors, reset the button and refit the cover.
If the inertia switch is satisfactory, ground the pump relay terminal 85, switch on the ignition and check the circuit systematically as detailed below.

a. Check for battery voltage at terminal 86 of the main relay.
   If yes: Proceed to test (b).
   If no: Check the battery supply from the ignition switch via the inertia switch.

b. Check for battery voltage at terminal 87 of the main relay.
   If yes: Proceed to test (c).
   If no: Check for battery voltage at the earth lead and connection from terminal 85 of the main relay. If satisfactory, renew the main relay.

c. Check for battery voltage at terminal 86 of the pump relay.
   If yes: Proceed to test (d).
   If no: Open circuit between terminals 87 of the main relay and 86 of the pump relay. If satisfactory, proceed to test (d).

d. Check for battery voltage at terminal 87 of the pump relay.
   If yes: Proceed to test (e).
   If no: Check for battery voltage at earth lead and connections from terminal 85 of the pump relay. If satisfactory, renew the pump relay.

e. Check for battery voltage at supply lead (NS) and connections to the fuel pump.
   If yes: Faulty pump or earth connections.
   If no: Open circuit between terminal 87 of the pump relay, and supply lead connection to the fuel pump.

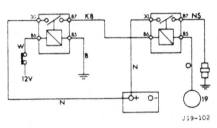

Fig. 32

FUEL MAIN FILTER—Early cars

Remove and refit   **19.25.02**

Removing

Depressurize the fuel system. Clamp the inlet and outlet hoses (1, Fig. 33).
Release the hose clips and pull the hoses from the fuel filter (2, Fig. 33).

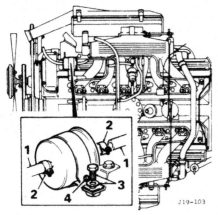

Fig. 33

Remove the bolt and washer securing the filter assembly to the inlet manifold mounting bracket, remove the filter assembly (3, Fig. 33). Remove the screw and Spire nut from the fuel filter clamp, draw the fuel filter clear of the clamp (4, Fig. 33).

Refitting

Reverse the above operations.

FUEL MAIN FILTER—Later cars

Remove and refit   **19.25.02**

Removing

Depressurize the fuel system. Remove the spare wheel.
Clamp the inlet and outlet pipes.
Remove the fuel filter bracket securing bolts.
Release the hose clips and pull the hoses from the filter.

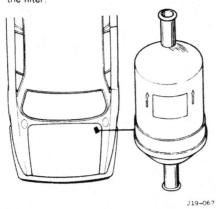

Fig. 34

Slacken the filter bracket clamp screws and remove the filter from the clamp (Fig. 34).

Refitting

Reverse the above operations.

FUEL TANK CHANGE-OVER VALVES

Description

The change-over valve is located in the luggage compartment adjacent to the fuel pump. When energized by the change-over switch, the valve opens the outlet pipe from the right-hand fuel tank.

FUEL TANK CHANGE-OVER VALVES

Remove and refit   **19.40.31**

Removing

Disconnect the battery.
Remove the spare wheel.
Clamp the inlet and outlet pipes (1, Fig. 35).
Release the pipe clips and pull the pipes from the change-over valve (2, Fig. 35).

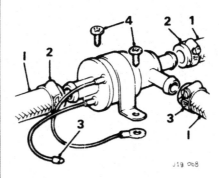

Fig. 35

Disconnect the cable to valve (3, Fig. 35).
Remove the screws securing the valve clamp to boot floor (4, Fig. 35).

Refitting

Reverse the above operations, securing the ground lead beneath one foot of the clamp.

FUEL TANK CHANGE-OVER VALVES

Test   **19.40.32**

Disconnect the battery.
Remove the spare wheel.
Clamp the inlet and outlet pipes.
Release the pipe clips and pull the pipes from the change-over valve.
Disconnect the cable to valve.
Push a suitable length of rubber pipe on to the centre inlet port of valve (1, Fig. 36).
Blow through the rubber pipe. Air should flow from the outlet union through the body of

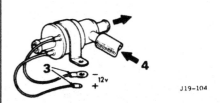

Fig. 36

solenoid (2, Fig. 36).
Apply 12V d.c. to the valve cable. (3, Fig. 36). Blow through the rubber pipe. Air should flow from the outlet union towards the opposite side. (4, Fig. 36).
If results satisfactory, refit the valve.
If results not satisfactory, replace valve.

FUEL COOLER

Remove and refit   **19.40.40**

Removing

WARNING: Refrigerant gas can cause blindness. It is therefore essential to depressurize the air conditioning system prior to disconnecting refrigerant hose to fuel cooler. See operation 82.30.05 of Repair Operations Manual.

Depressurize the fuel system.
Depressurize the air conditioning system.

Disconnect the refrigerant inlet and outlet hoses, and seal with plugs (1, Fig. 37).

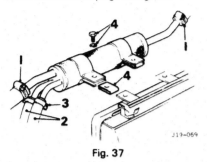

Fig. 37

Clamp the fuel hoses (2, Fig. 37).
Disconnect the fuel hoses (3, Fig. 37).
Remove the two setscrews, washers and Spire nuts securing the fuel cooler to air cleaner brackets (4, Fig. 37).

Refitting

Reverse the above operations.

FUEL RETURN VALVE

Remove and refit   19.40.44

Removing

Depressurize the fuel system.
Jack up the rear of the vehicle.
Remove the rear wheel.
Remove the valve cover screws and remove the cover.
Remove the screws securing the return valve.
Clamp the fuel pipes.
Remove the fuel gauge transmitter cover screws and displace the cover from the body.
Note and disconnect the wires feeding the return valve.
Withdraw the cables through the cover.
Remove the pipes from the valve.
Remove the fuel return valve.

Refitting

Reverse the above procedure.

FUEL PRESSURE REGULATORS
—Early cars

Remove and refit—left-hand or right-hand   19.45.11

Removing

Depressurize the fuel system.
Disconnect the battery.
Remove the setscrews and washers securing the pressure regulator mounting bracket and

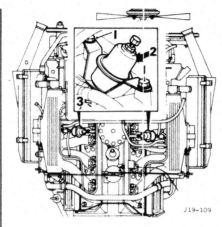

Fig. 38

carefully pull the regulator and bracket upwards. Note orientation of regulator in bracket (1, Fig. 38).
Clamp the inlet and outlet pipes of regulator (2, Fig. 38).
Release the pipe clips and pull the pipes from the regulator unions.
Remove the nut and washer and release the regulator from bracket (3, Fig. 38).

Refitting

Reverse the above procedure.

FUEL PRESSURE REGULATOR
—Later cars

Remove and refit   19.45.11

Removing

Depressurize the fuel system.
Remove the fuel cooler pipe from the fuel pressure regulator, situated below the throttle pedestal.
Remove the regulator securing nut.
Disconnect the regulator pipe from the fuel rail.
Manoeuvre the regulator valve upwards and disconnect the vacuum pipe.
Remove the regulator to fuel rail pipe.
Remove the regulator.

Refitting

Reverse the above procedure.

FUEL PRESSURE REGULATORS

Check and adjust   19.45.12

Check

Depressurize the fuel system.
Slacken the pipe clip securing the left-hand cold start injector supply pipe to the fuel rail and pull the pipe from the rail.
Connect the pressure gauge pipe to the fuel rail and tighten the pipe clip.

CAUTION: Pressure gauge must be checked against an approved standard at regular intervals.

Pull '—ve' lead from the ignition coil and switch the ignition on. Connect terminal 85 of the pump relay to ground.
Check the reading on pressure gauge: reading must be between 2,0 and 2,2 kgf/cm² (28.5 to 30.8 lbf/in²).

NOTE: The pressure reading may slowly drop through either the regulator valve seating or the pump non-return valve. A slow, steady drop is permissible; a rapid fall MUST be investigated.

Operate the fuel change-over switch.
Repeat the operation.
Remove the ground connection to terminal 85 of the pump relay.

NOTE: If satisfactory results have been obtained, depressurize the fuel system, slacken pipe clip and remove pressure gauge from the fuel rail.

Reconnect the cold start injector supply pipe and secure the pipe clip.
Switch the ignition on and check for leaks.
Switch the ignition off.
If satisfactory results have not been obtained, continue with 'Adjust' procedure.

Adjust

NOTE: Fuel pressure should only be adjusted after the complete system has been thoroughly checked.

Remove the setscrews securing both pressure regulators to inlet manifolds.
Clamp the fuel pipe between 'B' bank pressure regulator inlet and fuel rail. Reconnect '—ve' l.t. lead to the ignition coil and start the engine. If 'EPITEST' box fitted, depress 'PUMP' button.
Slacken locknuts at both pressure regulators.
Set the adjuster bolt on 'A' bank regulator to set reading on the pressure gauge to 2,1 kgf/cm² (29.6 lbf/in²). Release clamp at 'B' bank regulator and transfer to 'A' bank pressure regulator inlet.
Set the adjuster bolt on 'B' bank regulator to set reading on pressure gauge to 2,1 kgf/cm² (29.6 lbf/in²). Release the clamp and ensure pressure gauge reading is between 2,0 and 2,2 kgf/cm² (28.5 to 30 lbf/in²).
Restrain the adjuster bolts on each regulator in turn and tighten locknuts.
Switch off the ignition.
Depressurize the fuel system.
Slacken the pipe clip and remove the pressure gauge from the fuel rail.
Reconnect the cold start injector supply pipe and secure the pipe clip. Secure both regulators using two setscrews.
Switch the ignition on and check for leaks.
Switch the ignition off.

19—24

FUEL PUMP

Description

The fuel pump is located beneath the luggage compartment floor. It is flexibly mounted and secured using noise- and shock-absorbing material. This pump is a roller-type machine delivering a continuous flow of fuel.

FUEL PUMP

Remove and refit   19.45.08

Removing

Disconnect the battery.
Remove the spare wheel.

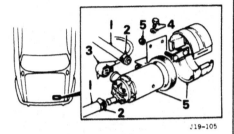

Fig. 39

Clamp the inlet and outlet pipes of the pump (1, Fig. 39).
Release the pipe clips and pull the pipes from the pump unions (2, Fig. 39).
Remove the electrical connector (3, Fig. 39).
Remove the screws securing the pump mounting bracket (4, Fig. 39).
Remove clamp securing nuts and draw the pump from clamp (5, Fig. 39).

Refitting

Reverse the above procedure, ensuring that the pump bracket ground connecting screws are clean, and the ground wire is on bright metal beneath one securing screw.

FUEL SYSTEM

Depressurize   19.50.02

CAUTION: The fuel system MUST always be depressurized before disconnecting any fuelling components.

Pull the cable from terminal 85 of pump relay.
Switch on and crank the engine for a few seconds.
Switch the ignition off and reconnect cable to terminal 85 of pump relay.

Pressure test

Depressurize the fuel system.
Slacken the pipe clip securing the left-hand cold start injector supply pipe to fuel rail and pull the pipe from the rail.
Connect the pressure gauge pipe to the fuel rail and secure the pipe clip.
Pull '−ve' l.t. lead from ignition coil.
Connect the terminal 85 of the pump relay to ground.
Switch on the ignition and check the pressure gauge reading: reading must be between 2,0 and 2,2 kgf/cm² (28.5 and 30.8 lbf/in²).
Operate the fuel tank change-over switch and re-check reading.
If either or both readings are high, check for blockage in return line.
If either or both readings are low, check for blockage or choked filter in supply line or pump suction pipes.
If satisfactory reading cannot be obtained, carry out 'Pressure regulator—adjust' operation, and, if necessary, renew the pressure regulator or fuel pump.
Switch off the ignition, depressurize fuel system and remove pressure gauge.
Switch on the ignition and check for leaks.
Remove ground connection from terminal 85 of the pump relay.
Reconnect l.t. lead at the ignition coil.

INJECTORS

Description

The 12 injectors are mounted one to each induction ram pipe, so that the fuel jet is directed on to the back of each inlet valve.
The injectors are solenoid-operated valves which are controlled by the E.C.U.

INJECTORS—Early cars

Remove and refit   19.60.01

Removing

Depressurize the fuel system.
Disconnect the battery.
Clamp the fuel inlet pipe between the filter and fuel rail (1, Fig. 40).
Pull the electrical connector from the injector(s) to be removed (2, Fig. 40).
Remove two setscrews securing the fuel rail to the inlet manifold.
Release clips securing the supply rail to the return rail.
Pull the manifold pressure pipe from the left-hand inlet manifold.
Remove 12 nuts and spring washers securing injector clamps to induction ram pipes (3, Fig. 40).
Carefully lift the fuel rail complete with the injectors sufficient for the injectors to clear the

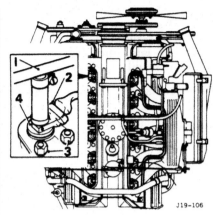

Fig. 40

induction ram pipes. Ensure that adequate rag is to hand to absorb spilled fuel.
Suitably plug or cover the injector holes in ram pipes to prevent ingress of dirt or foreign matter.
Slacken pipe clip(s) of injector(s) to be removed (4, Fig. 40).
Note orientation of electrical sockets, and pull injector(s) from the fuel rail.
Remove two rubber sealing 'O'rings from ALL injectors and discard.
CAUTION: Sealing rings MUST be renewed each time the injectors are removed from the manifold.

Refitting

Locate the new sealing 'O' rings at ALL injectors.
Press replacement injector(s), orientated correctly, on to the fuel rail stub(s).
Secure the pipe clip(s) at replacement injector(s).
Locate the fuel rail complete with injectors into position and secure injector clamps with 12 nuts and spring washers.

INJECTORS

Test   19.60.02

Injector winding

Use ohmmeter to measure the resistance value of each injector winding, which should be 2.4 ohms at 20°C (68°F).
Check for short circuit to earth on winding by connecting the ohmmeter probes between either injector terminal and injector body. Meter should read ∞ (infinity).
If any injector winding is open circuited, or short circuited, replace the injector.

19—25

INJECTORS — Should any vehicle have this type of injector fitted it should be returned to the Dealer to have the later modified rail and injectors fitted

Remove and refit   19.60.01

Removing

Depressurize the fuel system.
Disconnect the battery.
Remove the appropriate fuel rail (Fig. 41).
Disconnect the injector block connector (2, Fig. 41).

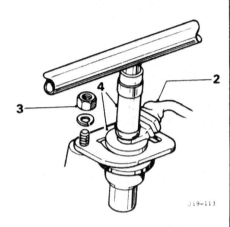

Fig. 41

Remove the injector clamp nuts (3, Fig. 41).
Remove the clamp and the injector (4, Fig. 41).
Remove and discard the injector seal.

Refitting

Reverse the above procedure, fitting a new injector seal.

FUEL RAIL—LEFT HAND AND RIGHT-HAND—Early cars

Remove and refit   19.60.04

Removing

Depressurize the fuel system.
Disconnect the battery.
Pull the manifold pressure pipe from the relevant inlet manifold, and disconnect the throttle switch and cross-rods as necessary (1, Fig. 42).
Clamp the fuel pipe between the filter and supply fuel rail (2, Fig. 42).
Release the clips securing the return fuel rail to the supply rail (3, Fig. 42).
Remove the screws securing the return fuel rail brackets to the over-run valves (4, Fig. 42).
Retrieve the spacer—right-hand side.
Release the clips securing the return fuel rail to the regulator outlet hoses and fuel return pipe. Pull the hoses from the rail (5, Fig. 42).
Release the clips securing supply fuel rail to filter, main fuel rail, cold start injector and regulator inlet hoses. Pull the hoses from the supply rail (6, Fig. 43).

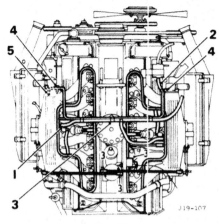

Fig. 42

Remove supply and return fuel rails.
Unclip the cable harness from main fuel rail.
Pull the electrical connectors from injectors and cold start injectors (7, Fig. 43).
Remove 12 nuts and spring washers securing the injector clamps to induction ram pipes (8, Fig. 43).
Carefully lift the main fuel rail complete with injectors from the induction ram pipes. Ensure that adequate rags are to hand to absorb spilled fuel.
Suitably plug or cover injector holes in ram pipes to prevent ingress of dirt or foreign matter.
Slacken the clips securing the injectors to the main fuel rail stubs, pull the injectors from fuel rail.

NOTE: If necessary, transfer the clips and insulation to the replacement fuel rail.

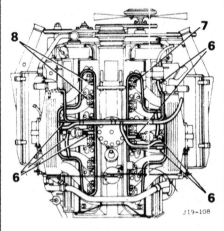

Fig. 43

Refitting

Press the injectors on to the fuel rail stubs; tighten the pipe clips.
Locate new sealing 'O' rings at ALL injectors.
Manoeuvre the fuel rail and injectors into position and secure the injector clamps using 12 nuts and spring washers.
Remove the pipe clamp at filter.
Refit the manifold pressure pipe.
Reconnect the battery.
Switch the ignition on and check for leaks.
Switch the ignition off.

FUEL RAIL — LEFT-HAND AND RIGHT-HAND — Should any vehicle have this rail type fitted it should be returned to the Dealer for the later modified rail to be fitted

Remove and refit   19.60.04

Removing

Depressurize the system.
Disconnect the battery.
Disconnect the relevant throttle rod from the throttle pedestal and swing aside (1, Fig. 44).
Disconnect the throttle kick-down switch (2, Fig. 44).
Disconnect the throttle control cable from the throttle pedestal, and swing the cable to one side—right-hand side (3, Fig. 44).
Disconnect the cross-pipe from the manifold and unclip the cross-pipe from the fuel rail (4, Fig. 44).

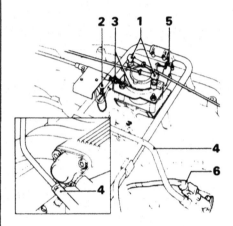

Fig. 44

Slacken the regulator valve hose clip (5, Fig. 44).
Disconnect the cold start injector feed pipe from the fuel rail (6, Fig. 44).
Remove the Econocruise cable harness and the Econocruise pipe from the fuel rail.
Remove the fuel feed pipe—left-hand side.
Remove the fuel return pipe—right-hand side.
Disconnect the fuel rail halves.
Slacken the fuel rail to injector clips and remove the fuel rail from the injectors.

Refitting

Reverse the above operation.

COLD START INJECTOR

Description

A cold start injector is mounted in each inlet manifold, aligned to spray a finely atomised mist of fuel towards the throttle butterfly valve. The injector is controlled by the cold start relay and the Thermotime switch and is only operative during the first few seconds of a cold engine starting cycle.

COLD START INJECTOR (early models only)

Remove and refit   19.60.06

Removing

Depressurize the fuel system.
Disconnect the battery.
Fit clamp on the supply pipe to injector (1, Fig. 45).
Pull the electrical connector from the injector (2, Fig. 45).
Slacken the pipe clips and pull the pipe from injector (3, Fig. 45).

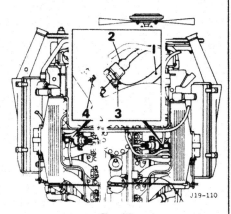

Fig. 45

Remove two setscrews securing the injector to the inlet manifold (4, Fig. 45).
Check condition of the gasket and renew as necessary.

Refitting

Reverse the above operations.

Test

See 'Cold start system—test'.

Initial Fault Diagnosis

Fault conditions in this section can be further divided into three types as follows:
Faults that prevent the engine from starting.
Faults that allow the engine to start, but stop it either immediately or after a short delay.
Faults that allow starting and continued running, but cause incorrect fuelling at some stage of a driving cycle.
Examples of all three classes of fault are given in the 'Symptoms' column of the Initial Diagnosis and Rectification chart, together with a list of possible causes in the order in which they should be checked. This is followed by Procedures for Rectification which details the effect that each possible failure will have upon the engine and its remedy. It is assumed that the vehicle has sufficient fuel in the tanks, and that purely engine functions, e.g. ignition timing, valve timing, and the ignition system as a whole are operating satisfactorily. If necessary, these functions must be checked by following the relevant procedures in the Repair Operations Manual before the fuel injection system is suspected.

INITIAL DIAGNOSIS AND RECTIFICATION

POSSIBLE CAUSES IN ORDER OF CHECKING

	Will not start*	Difficult cold start	Difficult hot start	Starts but will not run	Misfires and cuts out	Runs rough	Idle speed too fast	Hunting at idle	Low power and top speed	High fuel consumption
Battery	A	A	A							
Connections	B	B	B	A	A	A			A	A
Ignition system	C	C	C	B	C	C		D	C	B
Fuel system	D	E	D	C	D	D			D	C
Trigger unit ('D' system only)	E	F	G	E	B	B				
Pressure sensor ('D' system only)	F	G	H	F	E	E		E	E	E
Cold start system	G	D	F	D	F	F		F	F	F
ECU/amplifier	K	J	J	G	H	M		H		H
Air leaks						C				
Temperature sensors	H	H	E	E	G	G		G	G	D
Auxiliary air valve						D				
Throttle switch							H		H	G
Throttle butterfly							J	B	A	J
Overrun valve						E				
Compression	J						L		L	
Idle fuel control setting								C		
Air filters					F					B
Throttle linkage							K	A	B	K

SYMPTOMS

* Before proceeding with checks, hold throttle fully open and attempt a start. If the engine then starts and continues to run, no further action is necessary.

PROCEDURES FOR RECTIFICATION OF CAUSES SHOWN IN TABLE

Battery:
Battery depleted, giving insufficient crank speed or inadequate spark. Check battery condition with hydrometer. Recharge, clean and secure terminals, or renew as necessary.

Connections:
Ensure all connector plugs are securely attached. Pull back rubber boot and ensure plug is fully home. While replacing boot press cable towards socket. Ensure Electronic Control Unit (ECU) multi-pin connector is fully made. Ensure all ground connections are clean and tight.

Ignition System:
Check ignition system as detailed in electrical section of Repair Operations Manual.

Fuel System:
Open filler cap of fuel tank being used. Change tank being used. Check for fuel pipe failure (strong smell of fuel) and retention of in line fuel pressure. Check inertia switch closed. If necessary, clear fuel tank vents or supply pipe.

Trigger Unit:
'D' System
Check operation of reed switches; engine will not run unless both reed switches are satisfactory.

Pressure Sensor:
'D' System
Ensure manifold pressure reference pipe is attached to sensor and is not twisted, kinked or disconnected elsewhere. Engine may start but will run badly.

Cold Start System:
Fault conditions could cause cold start system to be inoperative on a cold engine, or operative on a hot engine. If engine is either very hot, or cold, these particular faults will cause the engine to run very rich. Check cold start system, see 19.22.32.

ECU/Amplifier
Power Resistor:
If either of these components is faulty it is possible that various groups of injectors will be inoperative. This will range from barely detectable, one group, to very rough or no start, two, three or four groups. The ECU may also be responsible for any degree of incorrect fuelling. Before suspecting the ECU for fuelling problems, however, all other likely components should be proved good.

Air Leaks:
Ensure all hose and pipe connections are secure. Engine is, however, likely to start more easily with air leaks if cold, as air leaking augments that through the auxiliary air valve. A leak, or failed air valve is shown up, however, by a very high idle speed when engine is warm and air valve main passage should be closed.

Temperature Sensors:
If either sensor is short circuited, starting improves with higher engine temperature. Engine will run very weak, improving as temperature rises, but still significantly weak when fully hot. If a sensor is open circuit, or disconnected, engine will run very rich, becoming worse as temperature rises. Engine may not run when fully hot, and will almost certainly not restart if stalled. Effect of air temperature sensor will be less marked than coolant temperature sensor.

Auxiliary Air Valve:
Check opening throttle. If engine immediately starts, unscrew idle speed adjustment, and recheck start with closed throttle. Reset idle speed when engine hot. Check cold start. Check throttle return springs and linkage for sticking or maladjustment as a sticking throttle may have enforced incorrect idle speed adjustment on a previous occasion.

Throttle Switch:
Check operation of throttle switch. Incorrect function or sequence of switching will give this fault.

Throttle Butterfly:
Check adjustment of both throttle butterfly valves, ensure return springs correctly fitted, and throttle not sticking open.

Overrun Valve:
Check operation of overrun valve, see 19.20.22.

Compression:
Low compressions; a general lack of engine tune could cause this fault. Check engine timing, ignition timing, and function of ignition system complete. If necessary, check valve condition.

Idle Fuel Control
Setting:
Set butterfly valve, see 19.20.11. Set idle speed adjustment screw, see 19.20.16/17/18 to obtain 750 rev/min with engine fully warm. Remove cap from air injection diverter valve to interrupt air injection. Run engine at 2,000 rev/min for 15 seconds and return to idle speed. Adjust idle potentiometer (see CAUTION) on the electronic control unit to obtain required CO reading (1–2%) at sampling point in the end of each air injection rail. Refit cap to diverter valve and reset idle speed if necessary.
CAUTION: This knob MUST NOT be moved unless correct test equipment and skilled personnel are in attendance to monitor changes made.

Air Filters:
Remove air filters and check for choked filter element.

Throttle Linkage:
Check throttle linkage adjustment and ensure that throttle butterfly valves can be fully operated.

19—28

HOSE LEFT HAND PRESSURE REGULATOR VALVE TO FUEL RAIL

Renew   **19.40.64**

Depressurise the fuel system.
Slacken the unions (1, Fig. 46) at either end of the hose.
Remove the hot start switch (2, Fig. 46), remove the bracket securing screw (3, Fig. 46) and pull the pipe (4, Fig. 46) forward to remove.
Reverse the removal procedure to refit.

NOTE: Torque figures for all pipe unions 20,3 to 27,1 Nm (15 to 20 lbf/ft).

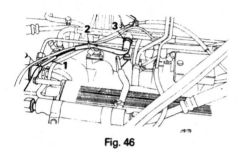

Fig. 46

HOSE FUEL FEED PIPE TO PRESSURE REGULATOR

Renew   **19.40.62**

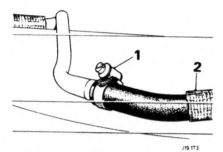

Fig. 47

Depressurise the fuel system.
Remove the R.H. air cleaner box and element.
Slacken the lower clip (1, Fig. 47) securing the hose to the fuel feed pipe, remove the screw retaining the hose clip to the inner wing and pull off the pipe.

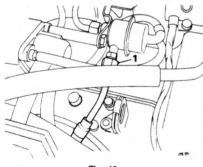

Fig. 48

Slacken the union (1, Fig. 48) at the fuel pressure regulator and remove the hose from the vehicle.
Slide the protective cover (2, Fig. 47) and clip from the hose and fit to the replacement hose.
Reverse the remaining removal procedure to refit.

NOTE: Torque figures for all pipe unions 20,3 to 27,1 Nm (15 to 20 lbf/ft).

NOTE: Torque figure for clip securing hose to fuel feed pipe 1,92 to 2,37 Nm (17 to 21 lbf/ins).

HOSE RIGHT HAND PRESSURE REGULATOR VALVE TO FUEL RAIL

Renew   **19.40.63**

Depressurise the fuel system.
Slacken the unions (1, Fig. 49) at either end of the hose and remove the hose (2, Fig. 49).
Reverse the removal procedure to refit.

NOTE: Torque figures for all pipe unions 20,3 to 27,1 Nm (15 to 20 lbf/ft).

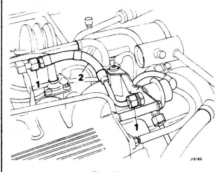

Fig. 49

HOSE PRESSURE REGULATOR VALVE TO FUEL COOLER

Renew   **19.40.78**

Depressurise the fuel system.
Remove the L.H. fuel regulator (1, Fig. 50) and the hot start switch (2, Fig. 50).
Remove the screw (3, Fig. 50) securing the hose bracket to the manifold.
Slacken the clip (4, Fig. 50) securing the hose to the fuel cooler (5, Fig. 50) and manoeuvre the hose (6, Fig. 50) through the manifold.
Reverse the removal procedure to refit.

NOTE: Torque figure for the clips securing the hose to the regulator and the fuel cooler 1,92 to 2,37 Nm (17 to 21 lbf/in).

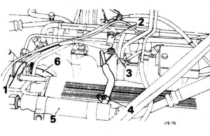

Fig. 50

HOSE FUEL COOLER TO FUEL RETURN PIPE

Renew   **19.40.56**

Depressurise the fuel system.
Remove the L.H. air cleaner element, slacken the clip (1, Fig. 51) securing the hose (2, Fig. 51) to the fuel cooler (3, Fig. 51) and pull the hose clear of the cooler.
Remove the screw securing the pipe supporting clip to the inner wing.
Slacken the clip securing the hose to the return pipe and remove the hose.
Pull the clip off the pipe and fit to the replacement pipe, reverse the remaining procedure to refit the replacement hose.

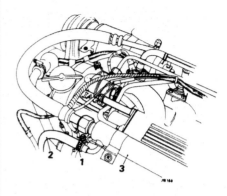

Fig. 51

PRESSURE REGULATOR VALVE VACUUM ELBOW

Renew   **19.45.18**

Disconnect the elbow (1, Fig. 52) from the regulator (2, Fig. 52), pull the elbow off the pipe (3, Fig. 52) and discard.
Fit the replacement elbow to the vacuum pipe ensuring that the 'belled' end is fitted to the pipe and fit the pipe to the regulator.

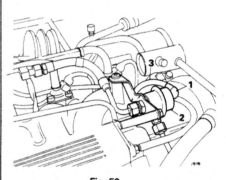

Fig. 52

PRESSURE REGULATOR VALVE VACUUM HOSE

Renew   **19.45.19**

Disconnect the elbow from the regulator and pull the assembly from the manifold.
Remove the elbow and adaptor from the hose.
Reverse the removal procedure ensuring that the 'belled' end is fitted to the pipe and fit the pipe to the regulator.

PRESSURE REGULATOR VALVE LEFT HAND

Renew   **19.45.09**

Depressurise the fuel system.
Disconnect the fuel rail return hose (1, Fig. 53) at the regulator (2, Fig. 53).
Disconnect the vacuum pipe (3, Fig. 53) from the regulator, disconnect the regulator securing bracket (4, Fig. 53) from the manifold, slacken the clip (5, Fig. 53) and pull the regulator (2, Fig. 53) from the fuel cooler hose.

19—29

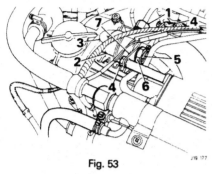

Fig. 53

Slacken the regulator securing nut (6, Fig. 53) and remove the regulator from the bracket (7, Fig. 53) collecting the star washer.

Fit the replacement regulator to the bracket ensuring it is fitted as (Fig. 55) and reverse the remaining procedure to refit.

NOTE: Torque figure for clip securing the hose to the regulator 1,92 to 2,37 Nm (17 to 21 lbf/in).

NOTE: Torque figures for all pipe unions 20,3 to 27,1 Nm (15 to 20 lbf/ft).

PRESSURE REGULATOR VALVE RIGHT HAND

Renew   19.45.10

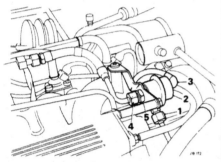

Fig. 54

Depressurise the fuel system.

Disconnect the fuel feed hose (1, Fig. 54) from the regulator (2, Fig. 54), the vacuum hose (3, Fig. 54) and the fuel rail feed hose (4, Fig. 54).

Slacken the regulator securing nut (5, Fig. 54), remove the regulator and collect the nut, star washer and spacer.

Reverse the removal procedure to refit, ensuring that the regulator location peg (1, Fig. 55) is engaged in the hole (2, Fig. 55) in the mounting bracket (3, Fig. 55) and that the hoses are connected to the regulator before finally tightening the securing nut.

NOTE: Torque figures for all pipe unions 20,3 to 27,1 Nm (15 to 20 lbf/ft).

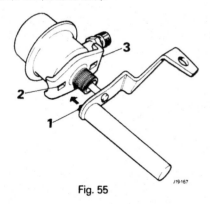

Fig. 55

PRESSURE REGULATOR VALVE ENGINE SET

Renew   19.45.13

Depressurise the fuel system.

Disconnect the fuel rail return hose at the left hand regulator.

Disconnect the vacuum pipe from the regulator, disconnect the regulator securing bracket from the manifold, slacken the clip and pull the regulator from the fuel cooler hose.

Slacken the regulator securing nut and remove the regulator from the bracket collecting the star washer.

Fit the replacement regulator to the bracket ensuring it is fitted as (Fig. 55).

Disconnect the fuel feed hose from the right hand regulator, the vacuum hose and the fuel rail feed hose.

Slacken the regulator securing nut, remove the regulator and collect the nut star washer and spacer.

Reverse the removal procedure to refit, ensuring that the regulator location peg is engaged in the hole in the mounting bracket and that the hoses are connected to the regulator before finally tightening the securing nut.

NOTE: Torque figures for all pipe unions 20,3 to 27,1 Nm (15 to 20 lbf/ft).

NOTE: Torque figures for clip securing the hose to the regulator 1,92 to 2,37 Nm (17 to 21 lbf/ft).

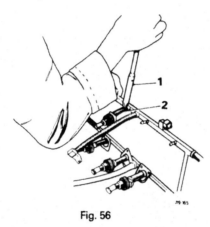

Fig. 56

FUEL INJECTOR

Renew   19.60.15

Remove the fuel rail and injector assembly.

Using a hot soldering iron as (1, Fig. 56) burn through the injector hose (2, Fig. 56), pull the injector and hose down (1, Fig. 57) and remove.

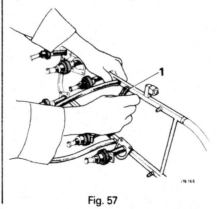

Fig. 57

NOTE: Ensure that a note is made of the position of the individual clamps prior to removal of an injector as each one may differ.

Fit service tool JD 116 (1, Fig. 58) to replacement injector and hose (2, Fig. 58) and push the injector assembly onto the rail (3, Fig. 58) ensuring that the hose is fully seated in the collar (4, Fig. 58). Refit the fuel rail and injector assembly.

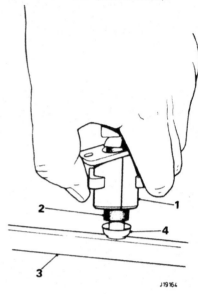

Fig. 58

HOT START SWITCH

Renew   19.22.01

Disconnect the two bullet connectors (1, Fig. 59) and remove the ratchet strap (2, Fig. 59) securing the hot start switch to the fuel rail.

Slacken the switch (3, Fig. 59) and remove.

Reverse the procedure to refit the replacement switch.

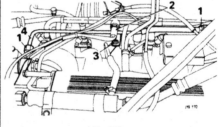

Fig. 59

FUEL SYSTEM

Depressurise   19.50.02

Remove the fuel pump relay and pull the king lead out of the top of the distributor cap.

Crank the engine for 10 seconds.

FUEL RAIL AND INJECTOR ASSEMBLY

Renew   19.60.14

Depressurise the fuel system.

Disconnect the vacuum balance pipes and the fuel feed hose (1, Fig. 48).

Disconnect and remove the throttle rods from the throttle tower and linkage.

19—30

Disconnect the kickdown switch and the throttle inner cable from the pedestal.

Disconnect the throttle return pipe, the fuel temperature switch (3, Fig. 59) and cut the ratchet strap.

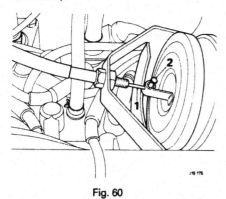

Fig. 60

Disconnect the cruise control cable actuating cable (1, Fig. 60) and collect the nipple (2, Fig. 60). Cut the ratchet straps securing the harnesses to the fuel rail, disconnect the injector connectors (1, Fig. 61), slacken and remove the nuts (2, Fig. 61) and washers securing the injectors to the manifold.

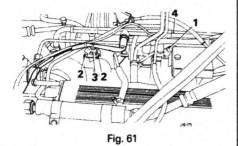

Fig. 61

Displace the injector securing plates (3, Fig. 61) and lift off the fuel rail assembly (4, Fig. 60).

Remove the injector seals from the manifold.

Fit new seals back in the manifold and reverse the remaining procedure to refit the fuel rail and injector assembly.

AUXILIARY AIR VALVE FEED HOSE

Renew 19.20.15

Slacken the clip securing the feed hose elbow to the valve.

Manoeuvre the elbow from the valve, and pull the plastic right angled adaptor (1, Fig. 61) from the elbow (2, Fig. 61) and remove the elbow.

Reverse the removal procedure to refit.

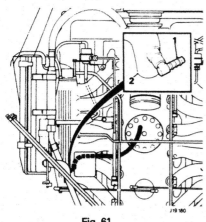

Fig. 61

19—31

PAGE INTENTIONALLY LEFT BLANK

12 CYLINDER COOLING SYSTEM

CONTENTS

COOLING SYSTEM

Description (Fig. 1) 26.00.00
(Not H.E. models)

The cooling system consists of a radiator matrix 'A', a water pump 'B'—belt driven by the engine crankshaft—and a remote coolant header tank 'C'. Two thermostatic valves 'D', are fitted—one to each cylinder bank—to ensure rapid warm-up from cold.

Under cold start conditions coolant is forced by the water pump equally through each cylinder block and cylinder head ('E' and 'F') to the thermostatic valve housings. The valves are closed and coolant is therefore returned via the engine cross-pipe 'G', to the water pump inlet.

During this period the radiator is under pump suction and air is bled by jiggle pins 'H', in each thermostatic valve.

NOTE: When fitting a replacement thermostat the thermostat MUST be fitted with the jiggle pin at the top of the housing.

The engine contains air pockets which have to be purged before effective cooling is possible. The air entrained by the coolant rises to the highest point on each side of the engine, the thermostat housings, then through the jiggle pins to the top of the radiator.

During this phase the Thermotime switch 'J', the coolant temperature sensor 'K' and the auxiliary air valve 'L' function as an automatic choke and warm up the system. Full pump suction draws coolant from the base of the radiator and starts the full cooling circuit.

At this time pump suction also appears at the heater matrix 'M' and the remote header tank, purging both the matrix and the radiator via pipes 'N' and 'P'. The remote header tank carries out an air separation function in addition to providing a reservoir of coolant.

When coolant temperature rises to a predetermined level the thermostatic valves open and allow coolant to flow into the top of the radiator.

A thermostatic switch 'Q' is fitted in the water pump suction inlet elbow. The switch starts the radiator electric cooling fan should the temperature of the coolant leaving the radiator rise above a predetermined level.

A cooling tube coil 'S' is included in the fabrication of the right-hand end tank of the radiator, and is connected in series with the automatic transmission hydraulic fluid circulation.

The radiator is fitted with a bleed tap 'T' through which, during initial cold fill, the radiator is vented.

A drain tap 'U' is located in the base of the right-hand end tank.

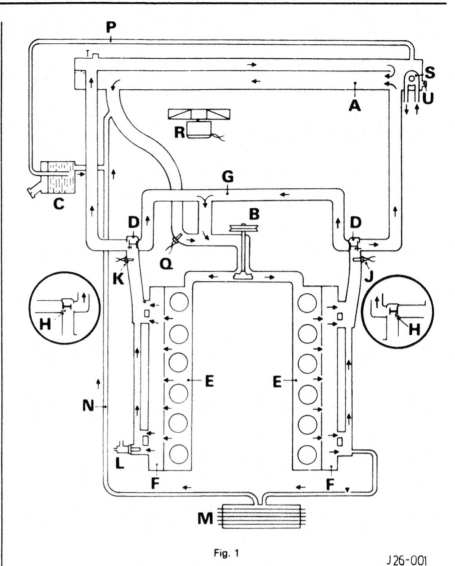

Fig. 1

J 26-001

ANTI-FREEZE

The recommended anti-freeze is BP Type HS 25 or Union Carbide UT 184 anti-freeze (Prestone 2 U.S.A./Canada) or ICI 007 (Unipart Universal), which must be used at all times. This is a specially formulated anti-freeze which is designed to afford the maximum corrosion protection to all metals normally found in engine cooling systems as well as having the normal frost protection properties necessary during winter months. It should not therefore be mixed with other anti-freezes. In places where UNIPART Universal is not available for top-up or replenishment, drain the system, flush and fill with anti-freeze which complies with specification B.S. 3150 or 3152.

A solution of recommended anti-freeze (40% Great Britain; 55% all other countries) must at all times be used either when topping-up or replenishing the cooling system. For maximum corrosion protection, the concentration should never be allowed to fall below 25%. Always top-up with recommended strength of anti-freeze, NEVER WITH WATER ONLY.

Anti-freeze may remain in the cooling system for two years after which the system should be drained, flushed and refilled with fresh anti-freeze mixed with 2 satchets of 'Barrs Leaks'.

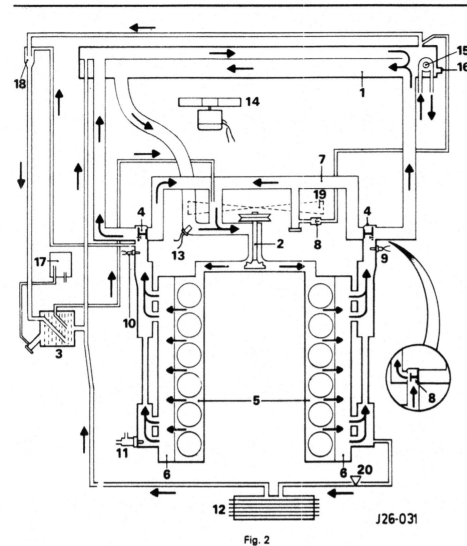

J26-031

Fig. 2

KEY TO 12 CYLINDER H.E. COOLING SYSTEM

1. Radiator matrix
2. Water pump
3. Remote header tank
4. Thermostat
5. Cylinder block
6. Cylinder head
7. Engine cross pipe
8. Jiggle pins
9. Thermotime switch
10. Coolant temperature sensor
11. Auxiliary air valve
12. Heater matrix
13. Thermostatic fan switch
14. Radiator electric cooling fan
15. Automatic transmission fluid cooling tube coil
16. Radiator drain tap
17. Atmospheric catch tank
18. Venting jet
19. Engine driven fan
20. Heater water control valve

TORQUE WRENCH SETTINGS

NOTE: Set the torque wrench to the mean of the figures quoted unless otherwise specified.

ITEM	DESCRIPTION	TIGHTENING TORQUE		
		Nm	kgf m	lbf ft
Radiator to front cross-member	⅜ in U.N.F. nut	29,8 to 35,2	3,05 to 3.59	22 to 26
Retainer to radiator cross-member	⁹⁄₁₆ in U.N.F. nut	19,0 to 24,4	1,94 to 2,48	14 to 18
Fan cowl to body	¼ in U.N.F. nut	6,1 to 7,5	0,62 to 0,76	4.5 to 5.5
Fan cowl fixing bracket to lower cross-member	¼ in U.N.F. nut	8,1 to 9,5	0,83 to 0,96	6 to 7
Expansion tank to valance	⁹⁄₁₆ in U.N.F. nut	10,8 to 13,6	1,10 to 1,38	8 to 10
Mounting bracket to fan motor	6 mm nut	5,4 to 6,8	0,55 to 0,69	4 to 5
Fan mounting to cowl	¼ in U.N.F. nut	8,1 to 9,5	0,83 to 0,96	6 to 7
Fan guard	¼ in U.N.F. nut	6,1 to 7,5	0,62 to 0,76	4.5 to 5.5
Engine oil cooler pipes	1⅟₁₆ in U.N.S. nut	54,3 to 61	5,53 to 6,22	40 to 45

26—3

COOLANT

Drain and refill   26.10.01

NOTE: A topping-up procedure is given at the end of this operation.

CAUTION: Do not remove the pressure cap at the remote header tank unless engine is cold

Draining

Carefully remove the pressure cap (1, Fig. 3) at the remote header tank (and engine filler cap HE models only).
Open the bleed tap (2, Fig. 3) at the left-hand side of the radiator top rail, not HE models.
Place a suitable receptacle beneath the radiator and open drain tap (3, Fig. 3) at right-hand side.

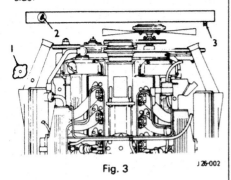

Fig. 3   J26-002

NON HE MODELS

Remove the drain plug from the cylinder block. Insert a water hose in the remote header tank, and regulate the flow so that the tank remains full with a minimum of overflow. Start the engine and run it at a fast idle (about 1000 rev/min) until the water from the drain holes becomes clear. Stop the engine, turn off the tap. Allow the system to empty and replace the drain plug.

HE MODELS ONLY

Open the radiator drain tap. This will only allow approximately 14 litres (25 pints) of coolant to drain without disconnecting any hoses.

ALL MODELS

Check the condition of the seals on the pressure caps, and if necessary, renew the seals or caps.

Refilling (cold fill) NON HE MODELS

WARNING: The following procedure must be carried out exactly as described. Incorrect filling will create air locks within the engine and cause irreparable damage due to resulting hot spots.

Close radiator drain tap at the right-hand side. Ensure that the pressure cap at the remote header tank is removed and the bleed tap is open. Mix the correct proportions of water and anti-freeze (or corrosion inhibitor) in a separate container and SLOWLY add the coolant to the remote header tank filler neck until no more can be added. Wait 1 to 2 minutes, and if necessary add more coolant. Repeat until no more coolant can be added.

Close the bleed tap, fit the pressure cap at the remote header tank.
Set the air conditioner controls to '80' and 'DEF'.
Run the engine at approximately 1 000 rev/min for three minutes. Switch off the engine.
Open the bleed tap. When the air has been purged from the system, remove the pressure cap at the remote header tank and slowly add coolant until it escapes from the bleed tap. Close the bleed tap and refit the pressure cap.

Refilling (cold fill) — HE MODELS ONLY

Close the drain tap and refit any hoses previously removed. Put in the correct amount of antifreeze/corrosion inhibitor, and fill the system with water through the engine filler pipe, until the header tank is full. Replace the cap on the header tank, and continue to fill the system until it is full and has stabilised. Replace the engine filler pipe cap and run the engine for a few minutes to mix the coolant.

Topping-up and generally checking coolant level — NON HE MODELS

CAUTION: This procedure must only be carried out when the engine is cold.

Carefully remove the pressure cap at the remote header tank. If coolant level is sufficient to prevent the addition of more coolant, the system does not require topping-up. Replace the cap.
If coolant is below this level, slacken the bleed tap and SLOWLY add the specified coolant to the remote header tank until coolant escapes from the bleed tap.
Close the bleed tap and refit the pressure cap.

Topping-up and generally checking the coolant level — HE MODELS ONLY

CAUTION: This procedure must only be carried out when the engine is cold.

Remove the cap from the engine filler pipe. If the level is below 7 cm (3 in) from the seal of the neck, top-up with coolant of the correct concentration.

WARNING: If it is necessary to check the coolant level when the engine is hot, use a cloth or gloves and slowly remove the header tank pressure cap first to release the pressure in the system.

REMOTE HEADER TANK

Remove and refit   26.15.01

Removing

Remove the left-hand air cleaner.
Slacken the clip (1, Fig. 4) on the pipe at the top of the remote header tank, remove the pipe and secure, pointing upwards, as high as possible.
Repeat for the pipe (2, Fig. 4) at base of tank.
Pull vent pipe (3, Fig. 4) from the filler neck.
Apply full left-hand steering lock.

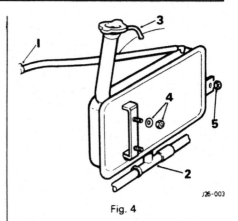

Fig. 4   J26-003

Working beneath the wheel arch, remove the two Nyloc nuts and plain washers (4, Fig. 4) securing the front of the remote header tank. Remove the setscrew, washer and Nyloc nut (5, Fig. 4) securing the rear of the tank. Lift the tank clear.

Refitting

Fit the tank and secure using nuts, washers and setscrews.
Fit the pipes at the base and top of the tank.
Fit the vent pipe to the filler neck.
Refit the left-hand air cleaner.
Carry out the filling procedure previously detailed.

FAN BELT

Adjust   26.20.01

Slacken the bolt (1, Fig. 5) securing the jockey pulley carrier.
Slacken the nut securing the trunnion block (2, Fig. 5).

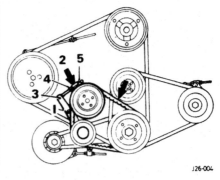

Fig. 5   J26-004

Slacken the nut adjusting the link bolt (3, Fig. 5) and locknut (4, Fig. 5).
Adjust the belt tension by means of the adjusting link nut (5, Fig. 5); correct tension is as follows:
A load of 2,9 kg (6.4 lb) must give a total belt deflection of 3,3 mm (0.13 in) when applied at mid point of belt.
Ensure that all fixings are fully tightened.

FAN BELT

Remove and refit   26.20.07

Slacken the bolt (1, Fig. 5) securing the jockey pulley carrier.

Slacken the nut securing the trunnion block (2, Fig. 5) and the nut securing the adjusting link bolt (3, Fig. 5).

Slacken the adjusting link locknut (4, Fig. 5) until the belt can be removed. Manoeuvre clear.

Fit a new belt to the pulley.

Set the belt tension.

IDLER PULLEY HOUSING

Remove and refit   26.25.15

Removing
Remove the fan belt.
Remove the fan and Torquatrol unit.
Remove the locknut, washers and bolt (1, Fig. 6) securing the adjustment bolt eye to the pulley arm.

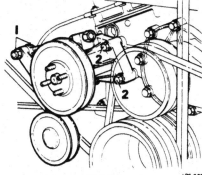

Fig. 6   J26-005

Remove the two setscrews (2, Fig. 6) and washers, and the two nuts and washers securing the idler pulley housing. Remove the housing complete with the jockey pulley and arm.

Refitting
Reverse the above procedure, fit and tighten the fan belt.

JOCKEY PULLEY

Remove and refit   26.25.16

Removing
Remove the right-hand air cleaner.
Wind back the locknut (1, Fig. 7) on the fan belt adjustment bolt.
Slacken the locknut (2, Fig. 7) at the adjustment bolt trunnion.

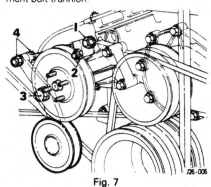

Fig. 7   J26-006

Slacken the jockey pulley pivot bolt (3, Fig. 7). Remove the locknut, washer and bolt (4, Fig. 7) securing the adjustment bolt eye to pulley arm and release the bolt.

Refitting
Reverse the above procedure; ensure that the fan belt is correctly tensioned.

FAN AND TORQUATROL UNIT
Early Cars

Remove and refit   26.25.21

Removing
Remove the setscrews securing the top section of the fan cowl.
Remove the four nuts and washers (1, Fig. 8) securing the fan to the Torquatrol unit.

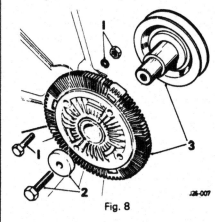

Fig. 8   J26-007

Restrain the pulley and remove the centre bolt (2, Fig. 8) from the Torquatrol unit; recover the special washer.
Gently tap the Torquatrol unit forward from the pulley spigot (3, Fig. 8).
Lift the fan from the cowl.

Refitting
Reverse the above procedure.
Note: When refitting, the special washer locates on the pulley spigot before tightening the bolt.

FAN MOTOR—SINGLE

Remove and refit   26.25.22

Removing
Open the bonnet and disconnect the battery.
Remove the L.H. air cleaner element.
Cut the nylon ties (1, Fig. 9) securing the fan motor harness to the front main harness; disconnect the leads from the fan motor.
Remove the nut (2, Fig. 9) securing the earth lead to the top rail, and disconnect the lead from the stud.
Cut the nylon tie securing the fan motor harness to the mounting frame.
Remove the three inner Nyloc nuts, washers and rubber bushes (3, Fig. 9), securing the fan motor mounting frame to the fan cowl.
Remove the motor and frame from the vehicle.

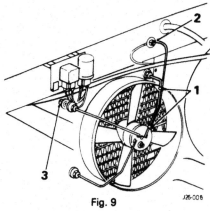

Fig. 9   J26-008

Remove the three Nyloc nuts, washers and rubber bushes, securing the mounting frame to the fan motor.
Prise off the circlip securing the fan to the motor spindle and remove the fan.

Refitting
Fit the fan to the spindle and secure with a new circlip.
Fit the mounting frame to the fan motor.
Fit the fan motor and mounting frame assembly to the fan cowl; ensure that the fan blades do not foul the radiator.
Tighten the inner Nyloc nuts and the outer locknuts.
Connect the earth lead tag to the stud on the top rail and secure with the nut.
Reconnect the leads to the fan motor.
Using new nylon ties secure the fan motor harness to the mounting frame and front harness.
Refit the L.H. air cleaner element.
Reconnect the battery.

FAN MOTOR AND FAN MOTOR RELAY

Test   26.25.25
26.25.29

This test also checks the function of the air-conditioning system and the cooling fan override relay on air-conditioned cars.

A. Cars not fitted with air-conditioning
Pull the connector plug from the thermostatic switch.
Switch on the ignition. DO NOT ROTATE THE ENGINE.
Bridge across the sockets in the plug; the relay should be heard to operate and the fan should start. Remove the bridge.
Switch off the ignition.
Reconnect the thermostatic switch connector.

B. Cars fitted with air conditioning
Ensure that the right-hand air-conditioning switch is set to 'OFF'.
Carry out the operations as for A above.
Switch on ignition. DO NOT ROTATE ENGINE.
Set left-hand air-conditioning control to '65' and right-hand control to 'AUTO'; air-conditioning relay should be heard to operate, the fan should start and compressor clutch should engage.
Switch off the ignition and set the right-hand air-conditioning system control to 'OFF'.

THERMOSTATIC SWITCH

Remove and refit   26.25.35

Removing

Disconnect the battery and drain the coolant. Pull the connector plug from the thermostatic switch.

Use a pair of pliers to withdraw the switch (1, Fig. 10) from the rubber seal (2, Fig. 10).

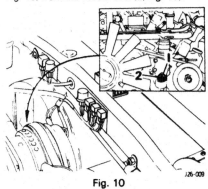

Fig. 10

Remove the rubber seal from the housing.

CAUTION: A new rubber seal MUST be used. Under no circumstances shall a new switch be fitted in an old seal.

Refitting

Fit a new rubber seal into the housing.

WARNING: No lubricant of any description may be used when fitting switch to seal. Use of lubricant will result in ejection of the switch and total loss of coolant.

Press a new switch into the seal; ensure that it is correctly seated.

Refit the electrical connector, reconnect the battery. Refill the cooling system with the correct quantity and specification of coolant.

RADIATOR BLOCK

Remove and refit   26.40.04

Removing

Open the bonnet and disconnect the battery. Remove the bonnet, refer to Section 76 Body.

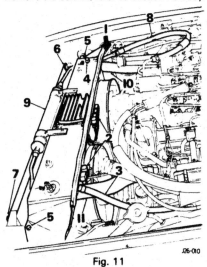

Fig. 11

Remove the fixings securing the relays and sensor: do not disconnect cables.

Drain the coolant.

Where applicable, depressurize the air-conditioning system.

Disconnect the amplifier block connector (1, Fig. 11).

Remove the nuts (2, Fig. 11) securing the fan cowl to the radiator top rail, noting the fitted positions of the earth lead and the line fuse.

Disconnect the hose (3, Fig. 11) from the expansion pipe.

Remove the banjo bolt (4, Fig. 11) securing the expansion pipe to the radiator; note fitted position of the spacer and sealing washers. Discard the sealing washers.

Remove the bolts (5, Fig. 11) securing radiator top rail.

Disconnect the earth leads from the left- and right-hand harnesses.

Remove the bolt and spacer (6, Fig. 11) securing right-hand front stay.

Remove the bolt (7, Fig. 11) securing the left-hand wing valance stay.

Where applicable, disconnect the hoses from the receiver drier unit.

CAUTION: Immediately plug broken connections using dry, clean plugs.

Unclip the condenser hose (8, Fig. 11) from the right-hand wing valance.

Lift off the top rail together with the receiver drier unit (9, Fig. 11).

Disconnect cable from the low coolant level sensor.

Disconnect the right-hand top hose (10, Fig. 11) from the radiator.

On cars fitted with automatic transmission only disconnect the transmission oil cooler hoses. Plug the broken connections.

Disconnect the left-hand top hose (11, Fig. 11) from the radiator.

Disconnect the hose (1, Fig. 12) from the expansion tank 'Tee' piece.

Disconnect the hoses (2, Fig. 12) from the oil cooler.

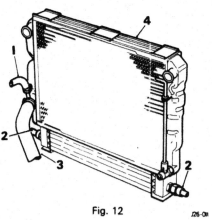

Fig. 12

CAUTION: When carrying out this operation, two spanners must be used, one on the hose union, the other on the oil cooler union.

Disconnect the bottom hose (3, Fig. 12).

Remove the nuts securing the fan cowl to the mounting bracket.

Release the cowl from the brackets.

Lift out the radiator (4, Fig. 12).

Refitting

Reverse the above procedure. Refill the cooling system with the correct quantity and specification of coolant.

RADIATOR DRAIN TAP

Remove and refit   26.40.10

Removing

Drain the coolant.

Pull the split pin (1, Fig. 13) from the fork end of the control rod.

Unscrew the tap (2, Fig. 13) from the radiator block and discard the seals.

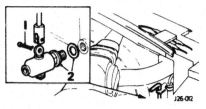

Fig. 13

Refitting

Lightly coat the threads of the tap with non hardening sealing compound, and screw home on new seals to locate beneath the control rod.

Refill the cooling system with the correct quantity and specification of coolant.

THERMOSTAT

Remove and refit
Left-hand   26.45.01
Right-hand   26.45.04

Removing

Partially drain the cooling system.

Disconnect the hose (1, Fig. 14/15) from the thermostat cover.

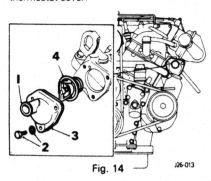

Fig. 14

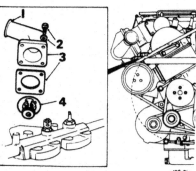

Fig. 15

26—6

Remove the thermostat cover retaining set-screws (2, Fig. 14/15) and lift off the cover (3, Fig. 14/15).
Lift out the thermostat (4, Fig. 14/15).

CAUTION: It is imperative that the correct type of thermostat is used. Thermostats with no jiggle pin prevent correct purging and will inevitably damage the engine.

Refitting
Use a new gasket and avoid distorting the cover by tightening the screws evenly.
Refill the cooling system with the correct quantity and specification of coolant.

THERMOSTAT

Test   26.45.09

Remove the thermostat and clean.
Place the thermostat in a container of water together with a thermometer.
Heat the water and observe if the thermostat operates in accordance with the known temperature rating.

THERMOSTAT HOUSING

Remove and refit
Left-hand   26.45.10

Removing
Remove the air cleaner (1, Fig. 16).
Partially drain the coolant.
Disconnect, the cables from the sensors (2, Fig. 16); the crankcase breather tube from the elbow (3, Fig. 16); the crankcase breather valve pipe (4, Fig. 16) from the water pipe; the top hose (5, Fig. 16) from the thermostat cover, and the cross-pipe hose (6, Fig. 16) from the thermostat housing.

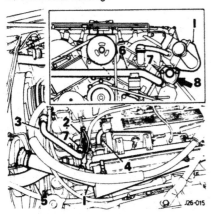

Fig. 16

Remove the bolts (7, Fig. 16) securing the thermostat housing; disconnect the housing from the water rail.
Remove and discard the gasket (8, Fig. 16) and water rail sealing ring.

Refitting
Reverse the above procedure, using a new gasket and sealing ring.

THERMOSTAT HOUSING

Remove and refit
Right-hand   26.45.11

Removing
Partially drain the coolant.
Disconnect the cables from the sensors (1, Fig. 17); the hose (2, Fig. 17) from the thermostat cover, and the cross-pipe hose (3, Fig. 17).

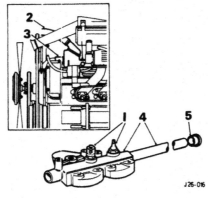

Fig. 17

Remove the bolts securing the thermostat housing; disconnect the housing from water rail (4, Fig. 17).
Remove and discard the gasket and water rail sealing ring (5, Fig. 17).

Refitting
Reverse the above procedure, using a new gasket and sealing ring.

WATER PUMP

Remove and refit   26.50.01
Removing
Remove the radiator block.
Remove the lower bracket fixings of radiator cowl(s), and lay cowl(s) to one side.
Remove the fan and Torquatrol unit.
Remove the fan belt (1, Fig. 18).
Remove the adjuster trunnion bolt (2, Fig. 18).
Remove the two setscrews and washers and two nuts and washers securing the idler pulley housing (3, Fig. 18).
Extract the two studs.
Remove the steering pump belt (4, Fig. 18).

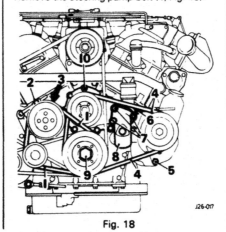

Fig. 18

Air-conditioned cars only—remove the compressor pump belt.
Slacken the steering pump pivot bolts (5, Fig. 18) sufficient to draw the adjustment bolt from the special stud.
Remove the special stud (6, Fig. 18).
Remove the three setscrews and washers (7, Fig. 18) securing the thermostatic switch housing (8, Fig. 18).
Remove housing and bottom hose complete.
Remove the nut (9, Fig. 18) securing the crankshaft pulley and damper assembly.
Tap the damper with a hide mallet to break the taper, and withdraw from the cone.
NOTE: Do not mislay the Woodruff key.
Slacken upper clip on hose to engine cross-pipe.
Remove the special setscrews and washers (10, Fig. 18) securing the water pump; draw the pump out and downwards clear of the cross-pipe hose.

Refitting
Reverse the above procedure.
Always use new gaskets.
Tighten setscrews evenly to avoid distortion.

WATER PUMP PULLEY

Remove and refit   26.50.05

Removing
CAUTION: Irreparable damage to the impeller and water pump body will result if an attempt is made to carry out this operation without removing the water pump from the engine.

Remove the water pump.
Fit the puller to pulley using two $\frac{5}{16}$ in U.N.F. X 2 in long bolts into the tapped holes (1, Fig. 19).
Withdraw the pulley from the pump by screwing in the centre bolt (2, Fig. 19).

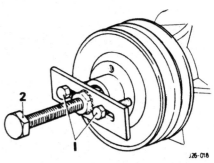

Fig. 19

Refitting
Position the pump on the bed of the hand press.
Locate the pulley on the impeller shaft.
Position a block of wood between the press mandrel and the pulley.
Press the pulley on the shaft until the pulley boss is flush with the end of the shaft.

NOTE: Check that a clearance of 0.635 mm (0.025 in) exists between the impeller blades and sandwich face. Use a puller and press to adjust as necessary.
Refit the water pump to the engine.

26—7

WATER PUMP

Overhaul   26.50.06

Remove the water pump from the engine, and the pulley from the pump.

Dismantling

Fit a puller to the impeller using two $\frac{9}{16}$ in U.N.F. X 2 in long bolts into the tapped holes (1, Fig. 20).
Withdraw the impeller (2, Fig. 20) by turning the centre bolt.

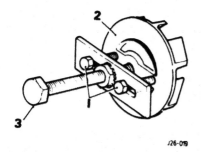

Fig. 20

Slacken the locknut and remove the Allen retaining screw from the water pump body.
Support the water pump body and, using a suitable mandrel, carefully press out the bearing and shaft assembly, from the impeller end to the pulley end.
Carefully tap the seal assembly from the body.
Carefully separate the water pump body and sandwich by supporting the front face of the sandwich and gently tapping the pump body through the impeller orifice on the suction boss.

CAUTION: Under no circumstances must the water pump body and sandwich be prised apart.

Remove all traces of the old gasket from the joint faces and thoroughly clean out the water pump body.

Reassembling

Position the water pump body front face upwards on the press.
Offer the shaft and the bearing assembly, smaller shaft foremost, into the water pump body. Ensure that the location holes in the water pump body and bearing are aligned.
Using a mandrel on the case of the bearing, press the bearing into the body until the location holes line up.
Fit the Allen retaining screw and tighten firmly, using the Allen key only. Fit the locknut and secure.
Fit the seal over impeller end of shaft and drift squarely to seat on the shoulder in the body.
Fit a new gasket, dry, over the ring dowels, assemble sandwich and press firmly together. Place the impeller (1, Fig. 21) on the bed of the press, with the blades uppermost. Locate the shaft to the impeller and press on the shaft to fit.
Press the pulley onto the shaft until the boss of the pulley is flush with the end of the shaft.

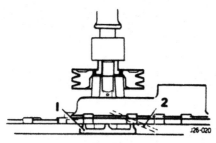

Fig. 21

NOTE: Check that the clearance (2, Fig. 21) of 0,635 mm (0.025 in) exists between the impeller blades and sandwich face. Use a puller and press to adjust as necessary.
Refit the water pump to the engine.

26—8

CONTENTS

30—1

KEY TO EXHAUST SYSTEM

1. Catalyst
2. Front down-pipe
3. Front intermediate pipe
4. Silencer
5. Rear intermediate pipe
6. Silencer and tail pipe
7. Exhaust trim

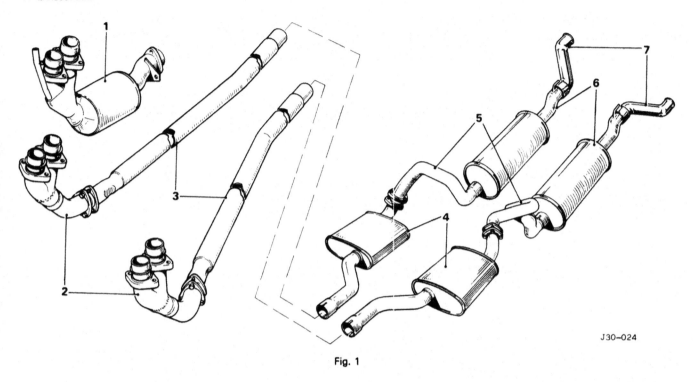

J30–024

Fig. 1

EXHAUST SYSTEM COMPLETE
Remove and refit   30.10.01

It will simplify removal if joints except front pipe/intermediate pipe joints are first heated with a welding torch. Every precaution must be taken when working near petrol and brake piping to prevent damage to components.

Remove air cleaners (1, Fig. 2).

In the luggage compartment, remove the two self-locking nuts securing each of the rear silencer mountings (2, Fig. 2).

Remove the three nuts, bolts and washers securing each of the front pipe/intermediate pipe flanges (3, Fig. 2).

Release the clamp at rear of the forward silencer assembly and separate the intermediate pipe and forward silencer assembly from the rear intermediate pipe (4, Fig. 2).

Release the clamp at the tail pipe and silencer and separate the tail pipe and silencer from the rear intermediate pipe (5, Fig. 2).

Draw the rear intermediate pipe rearwards rom the mounting rubber and suspension unit and separate the trim from the tail pipe and silencer (6, Fig. 2).

Draw the tail pipe and silencer forwards from body (7, Fig. 2).

Remove the eight special nuts and the plain washers at each of the exhaust manifolds and draw the front pipe downwards (8, Fig. 2).

Apply full right steering lock before removing right-hand front pipe — right-hand-drive cars only.

Apply full left steering lock before removing left-hand front pipe — left-hand-drive cars only.

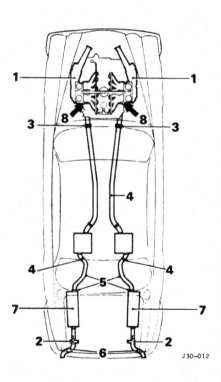

Fig. 2

CAUTION: Take great care to avoid damaging the steering rack gaiter.

Check the condition of the mounting rubbers in the rear suspension unit and mounting brackets, and renew as necessary.

When refitting, first offer the rear intermediate pipe into the rear suspension unit and locate on the mounting.

Position the rear mounting bracket and secure using two self-locking nuts.

Offer the tail pipe and silencer into position and locate in the mounting rubber.

Coat the joints with Firegum, mate up and secure with clamps.

FRONT PIPE
Remove and refit
Left-hand	30.10.09
Right-hand	30.10.10

Remove air cleaner from beneath the car, remove steering rack gaiter heat shield.

Remove the eight special nuts and washers securing the front pipe to the exhaust manifold (1, Fig. 3).

Remove the three nuts, bolts and washers securing flange (2, Fig. 3) and draw the front pipe downwards and remove (3, Fig. 3).

NOTE: Apply right steering lock to align lower steering column universal joint to enable easy removal of the right-hand front pipe—right-hand-drive cars.

Apply left steering lock to ease in removing left-hand front pipe—left-hand-drive cars only.

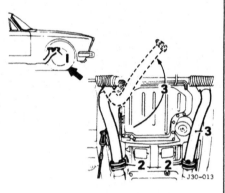

Fig. 3

When refitting, use new sealing rings to intermediate pipes.

INTERMEDIATE PIPE
Remove and refit
Left-hand	30.10.11
Right-hand	30.10.12

Remove the nuts, bolts and washers securing the flange (1, Fig. 4).

Release the clamp at the front of forward silencer and remove the pipe (2, Fig. 4).

When refitting, use Firegum to seal the joint to silencer and new seals to front pipe.

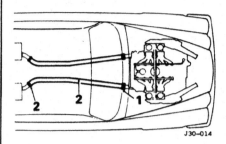

Fig. 4

SILENCER ASSEMBLY
Remove and refit
Left-hand	30.10.15
Right-hand	30.10.16

Disconnect the silencer from the rear intermediate pipe (1, Fig. 5). Slacken the clip securing the silencer assembly to the front intermediate pipe, and withdraw the silencer. When refitting, use Firegum to seal the joints.

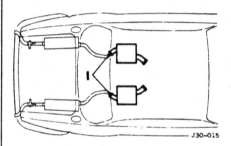

Fig. 5

TAIL PIPE AND SILENCER
Remove and refit
Left-hand	30.10.22
Right-hand	30.10.52

including EXHAUST TRIM

Remove and refit   30.10.23

Remove the Allen grub screw and separate the trim from the tail pipe (1, Fig. 6).

Release the clamp to the rear intermediate pipe and separate (2, Fig. 6).

Draw the tail pipe and silencer forwards down through the tunnel to clear mounting rubber.

Check the condition of the mounting, and renew as necessary.

continued

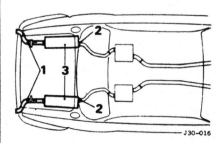

Fig. 6

30—3

When refitting, coat the joint with Firegum, fit the clamp and secure to the rear intermediate pipe.

NOTE: Cars to U.S.A. Federal Specification MUST have a distance of 38 mm (1,5 in) between top surface of exhaust trim and lower surface of energy absorbing beam.

REAR INTERMEDIATE PIPE

Remove and refit
Left-hand	30.10.24
Right-hand	30.10.25

Release the clamp to the tail pipe and silencer, and separate (1, Fig. 7), taking care not to allow pipe to foul the bodywork.
Support the intermediate pipe, release the clamp to silencer and separate (2, Fig. 7).
Draw the rear intermediate pipe from suspension unit (3, Fig. 7).
Check condition of mounting rubber, and renew as necessary.

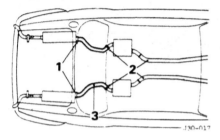

Fig. 7

To refit, reverse the above using Firegum to seal the joints.

INDUCTION MANIFOLD

Remove and refit
Left-hand	30.15.02

Disconnect the battery, remove the air cleaner (1, Fig. 8) and depressurize the fuel system.
Displace wing stay from wing location.
Remove the screws securing the pipe to the over-run valves, retrieve the spacer from the left-hand valve (2, Fig. 8).
Release the hose clip securing the pressure regulator return hose to fuel rail, disconnect hose (3, Fig. 8).
Release the hose clip securing the fuel pipe to fuel rail, disconnect hose (4, Fig. 8).
Disconnect the manifold pressure hose from the manifold (5, Fig. 8).
Disconnect the vacuum hose (6, Fig. 8) from the throttle housing and the electrical connectors from the kickdown switch (7, Fig. 8)—left-hand-drive cars only.
Remove the locknut and disconnect the throttle cable assembly from the throttle pedestal—left-hand-drive cars only (8, Fig. 8).
Release the throttle cross-rod from the bell-crank (9, Fig. 8)

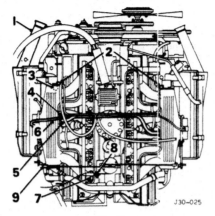

Fig. 8

Remove the plastic clips securing the harness to the fuel rail (1, Fig. 9).
Disconnect the electrical connectors at the injectors and the cold start injector (2, Fig. 9).
Release the hose clip securing brake vacuum hose to the non-return valve, disconnect the hose (3, Fig. 9).
Remove the throttle spring (4, Fig. 9).
Release the hose clip securing the manifold bleed pipe at the rubber elbow, disconnect the pipe from the elbow (5, Fig. 9).
Remove the twelve nuts and serrated washers securing the manifold assembly to the cylinder head (6, Fig. 9).
Remove the two screws securing the air rail clips to the manifold ram tubes (where applicable (7, Fig. 9).
Release the hose clips securing the air rail to the check valve connecting hose, release the air rail from hoses. Remove the air rail and discard the rubber 'O' rings (where applicable) (8, Fig. 9).
Remove the two bolts and the washers securing the E.G.R. valve to throttle housing flange, release the E.G.R. valve, remove and discard the gasket (where applicable).
Remove the six manifold stud spacers (9, Fig. 9).
Remove the induction manifold assembly from the cylinder head, easing aside the air balance pipe and the fuel pipes.
Remove and discard the manifold gaskets.
Plug the inlet ports.
Transfer components to the replacement induction manifold as necessary.

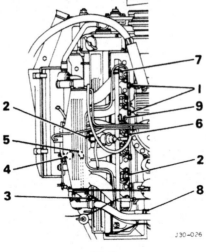

Fig. 9

To refit, reverse above procedure, using new gaskets, hose clips, cable clips and sealing rings and check throttle linkage adjustment.

INDUCTION MANIFOLD

Remove and refit
Right-hand	30.15.03

Disconnect the battery, remove the air cleaner (1, Fig. 10) and depressurize the fuel system.
Remove the screws securing pipe to the over-run valves, retrieve spacer from left-hand valve (2, Fig. 10).
Disconnect the manifold pressure hose from the manifold and 'T' piece (3, Fig. 10).

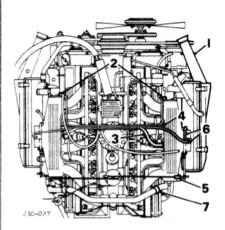

Fig. 10

Release the hose clip securing the fuel pipe to the fuel rail, disconnect hose (4, Fig. 10).
Disconnect the electrical connectors to the kick-down switch—right-hand-drive cars only.
Remove the locknut and disconnect the throttle cable assembly from throttle pedestal—right-hand-drive cars only.
Release the throttle cross-rod from the bell-crank (5, Fig. 10).
Disconnect the vacuum hoses from the throttle housing (6, Fig. 10).
Release the hose clip securing the air balance pipe to the rubber elbow, disconnect pipe from elbow (7, Fig. 10).
Remove the plastic clips securing the harness to the fuel rail (1, Fig. 11).
Disconnect the electrical connectors at the injectors and cold start injector (2, Fig. 11).
Remove the bolt and washer securing the harness earth strap to the manifold ram tube (3, Fig. 11).
Release the hose clip securing brake vacuum hose to the non-return valve, disconnect the hose from the valve (4, Fig. 11).
Disconnect the heater vacuum hose from the manifold stub pipe (5, Fig. 11).
Disconnect the diverter valve vacuum hose from the manifold stub pipe (where applicable) (6, Fig. 11).
Release the hose clip securing the automatic transmission vacuum pipe to the connecting hose, disconnect pipe from hose (7, Fig. 11).

30—4

Remove the throttle return spring (8, Fig. 11). Remove the twelve nuts and serrated washers securing the manifold assembly to the cylinder head (9, Fig. 11).

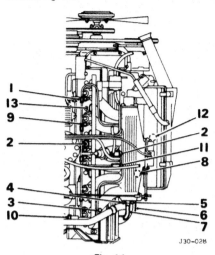

Fig. 11

Release the hose clip securing the air rail to the check valve connecting hose, release the air rail from the hose. Remove the air rail and discard rubber 'O' rings (where applicable) (10, Fig. 11).

Release the hose clip securing the fuel crossover pipe to the fuel rail—disconnect the hose at the fuel rail (11, Fig. 11).

Remove the two bolts and washers securing the E.G.R. valve to the throttle housing flange, release the E.G.R. valve, remove and discard the gasket (where applicable) (12, Fig. 11).

Remove the six manifold stud spacers.

Remove the induction manifold assembly from cylinder head, easing aside air balance pipe and fuel pipe.

Remove and discard manifold gaskets.

Plug inlet ports.

Transfer components to replacement induction manifold as necessary.

To refit, reverse the above procedure, using new gaskets, hose clips, cable clips and sealing rings.

CAUTION: Sealing rings MUST be renewed each time the injectors or air rail are removed from the manifold.

Check throttle linkage adjustment.

EXHAUST MANIFOLD

Remove and refit

Front Left-hand	**30.15.10**
Rear Right-hand	**30.15.11**
Rear Left-hand	**30.15.26**
Pair Left-hand	**30.15.27**
Front Right-hand	**30.15.28**
Pair Right-hand	**30.15.29**

Disconnect and remove the battery.

NOTE: If the manifold to be removed is on the same side as the steering, it is only necessary to disconnect the battery.

Beneath the car, remove the nuts and brass washers from the manifold/front pipe studs (1, Fig. 12).

Remove the three nuts and bolts securing the front pipe to the intermediate pipe (2, Fig. 12).

Free the front pipe and allow it to rest on the front suspension cross-beam.

Remove the inlet manifold (3, Fig. 12).

On R.H. remove the two self-tapping screws securing the starter heat shield to the main heat shield.

Remove the two setscrews and washers securing the heat shield to the exhaust manifolds (where applicable) (4, Fig. 12).

Remove the nuts and spring washers securing the forward exhaust manifold to the cylinder head.

Manoeuvre the manifold clear.

Remove the six nuts and spring washers securing the rear exhaust manifold to the cylinder head.

Manoeuvre the manifold clear.

To refit, use new gaskets, dry and secure exhaust manifolds to cylinder head.

Reverse the above procedure as appropriate, finally fully tightening exhaust manifold front pipe nuts.

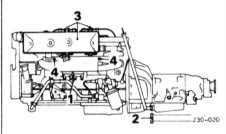

Fig. 12

MOUNTING RUBBER—FRONT

Remove and refit   Either   30.20.02

Remove the rear intermediate pipe; remove the bolts securing the mounting.

Refit by reversing the above.

To refit, locate the replacement mounting rubber in the bracket ring, noting that the brackets are handed (2, Fig. 13).

Smear the bush with soft soap and press into the mounting rubber (3, Fig. 13).

Locate the bush on the spigot and secure, using a bolt from below and self-locking nut.

PAGE INTENTIONALLY LEFT BLANK

JAGUAR
Daimler

**Containing
Sections**

33 CLUTCH

37 MANUAL GEARBOX

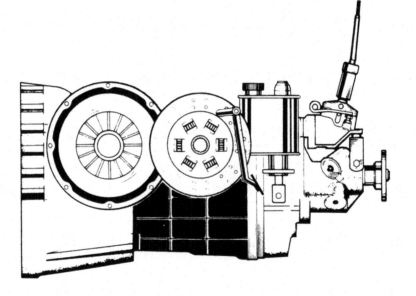

SERIES III
SERVICE MANUAL

INTRODUCTION

This Service Manual covers the Jaguar Series 3 and Daimler Series 3 range of vehicles. It is primarily designed to assist skilled technicians in the efficient repair and maintenance of Jaguar and Daimler vehicles.

Using the appropriate service tools and carrying out the procedures as detailed will enable the operations to be completed within the time stated in the 'Repair Operation Times'.

The Service Manual has been produced in 13 separate sections; this allows the information to be distributed throughout the specialist areas of the modern service facility.

A table of contents in section 1 lists the major components and systems together with the section and book numbers. The cover of each book depicts graphically and numerically the sections contained within that book. Each section starts with a list of operations in alphabetical order.

The title page of each book carries the part numbers required to order replacement books, binders or complete Service Manuals. This can be done through the normal channels.

Operation Numbering

A master index of numbered operations has been compiled for universal application to all vehicles manufactured by Jaguar Cars Ltd., and therefore, because of the different specifications of various models, continuity of the numbering sequence cannot be maintained throughout this manual.

Each operation described in this manual is allocated a number from the master index and cross-refers with an identical number in the 'Repair Operation Times'. The number consists of six digits arranged in three pairs.

Each operation is laid out in the sequence required to complete the operation in the minimum time, as specified in the 'Repair Operation Times'.

Service Tools

Where performance of an operation requires the use of a service tool, the tool number is quoted under the operation heading and is repeated in, following, the instruction involving its use. A list of all necessary tools is included in section 1, number 99.

References

References to the left- or right-hand side in the manual are made when viewing from the rear. With the engine and gearbox assembly removed the timing cover end of the engine is referred to as the front. A key to abbreviations and symbols is given in section 1, number 01.

REPAIRS AND REPLACEMENTS

When service parts are required it is essential that only genuine Jaguar/Daimler or Unipart replacements are used. Attention is particularly drawn to the following points concerning repairs and the fitting of replacement parts and accessories.

1.   Safety features embodied in the vehicle may be impaired if other than genuine parts are fitted. In certain territories, legislation prohibits the fitting of parts not to the vehicle manufacturer's specification.

2.   Torque wrench setting figures given in this Service Manual must be strictly adhered to.

3.   Locking devices, where specified, must be fitted. If the efficiency of a locking device is impaired during removal it must be replaced.

4.   Owners purchasing accessories while travelling abroad should ensure that the accessory and its fitted location on the vehicle conform to mandatory requirements existing in their country of origin.

5.   The vehicle warranty may be invalidated by the fitting of other than genuine Jaguar/Daimler or Unipart parts. All Jaguar/Daimler and Unipart replacements have the full backing of the factory warranty.

6.   Jaguar/Daimler Dealers are obliged to supply only genuine service parts.

SPECIFICATION

Purchasers are advised that the specification details set out in this Manual apply to a range of vehicles and not to any one. For the specification of a particular vehicle, purchasers should consult their Dealer.

The Manufacturers reserve the right to vary their specifications with or without notice, and at such times and in such manner as they think fit. Major as well as minor changes may be involved in accordance with the Manufacturer's policy of constant product improvement.

Whilst every effort is made to ensure the accuracy of the particulars contained in this Manual, neither the Manufacturer nor the Dealer, by whom this Manual is supplied, shall in any circumstances be held liable for any inaccuracy or the consequences thereof.

CONTENTS

TORQUE WRENCH SETTINGS

ITEM	DESCRIPTION	TIGHTENING TORQUE		
		Nm	kgf m	lbf ft
Clutch lever pivot bolt	—	40,7	4,15	30
Bottom cover to bell housing	6 mm setscrew	9,5	0,96	7
Tie plate to bell housing	10 mm setscrew	50,2	5,12	37
Bell housing to gear case	12 mm bolt and setscrew	80	8,16	59
Bell housing to cylinder block	8 mm bolt and dowel bolt	28,5	2,90	21
Cover plate to bell housing	8 mm bolt	20,3	2,07	15
Slave cylinder to bell housing	⅜ in nut	14,9 to 17,6	1,53 to 1,79	11 to 13
Master cylinder to pedal box	⁵⁄₁₆ U.N.F. nut	14,9 to 17,6	1,53 to 1,79	11 to 13
Pedal box to body	⁵⁄₁₆ U.N.F. nut	14,9 to 17,6	1,53 to 1,79	11 to 13
Hydraulic connections	—	8,2 to 9,5	0,87 to 0,96	6.3 to 7

HYDRAULIC SYSTEM

Bleed   33.15.01

WARNING: Only Castrol/Girling Universal Brake Fluid may be used in the clutch hydraulic system. This fluid exceeds S.A.E. J1703/D

Bleeding

Attach one end of a tube (1, Fig. 1) to the slave cylinder bleed nipple.

Partially fill a clean container with hydraulic fluid and immerse the other end of the bleed tube in the fluid.

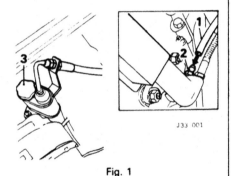

Fig. 1

Slacken the bleed nipple (2, Fig. 1) and pump the clutch pedal firmly up and down, pausing between each stroke.

CAUTION: The fluid should be topped up after every three pedal strokes.

Pump the clutch pedal until the fluid issuing from the bleed tube is free from air bubbles; tighten the bleed nipple.

Top up the reservoir (3, Fig. 1) and apply working pressure to the clutch pedal for two or three minutes then examine the system for leaks.

WARNING: Do not use fluid bled from system for topping up purposes as this will contain air. If fluid has been in use for some time it should be discarded. Fresh fluid bled from system may be used after allowing it to stand for a few hours to allow air bubbles to disperse.

FLUID HOSE

Remove and refit—R.H.D. only   33.15.13

Removing

Remove the nut securing the hose clip to the bell housing bolt.

Release the union nut (1, Fig. 2) securing the hose to the master cylinder pipe.

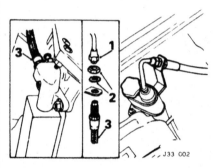

Fig. 2

Restrain the hose union at the bracket and remove the locknut and shakeproof washer (2, Fig. 2).

Unscrew the hose (3, Fig. 2) from the slave cylinder; plug or tape broken connections to prevent the ingress of dirt.

Refitting

CAUTION: Take great care to ensure that unions are not overtightened when refitting a flexible hose.

Connect the hose to the slave cylinder and ensuring that hose is not kinked or twisted, locate the other end in the bracket (1, Fig. 3).

Fit the shakeproof washer and locknut (2, Fig. 3); connect the master cylinder pipe (3, Fig. 3).

Remove the filler cap from the fluid reservoir and top up fluid to the correct level.

WARNING: Only Castrol/Girling Universal Brake Fluid may be used in the clutch hydraulic system. This fluid exceeds S.A.E. J1703/D.

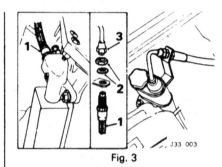

Fig. 3

Attach one end of a bleed tube (1, Fig. 4) to the slave cylinder bleed nipple.

Partially fill a clean container with hydraulic fluid and immerse the other end of the bleed tube in the fluid.

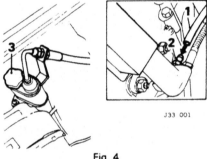

Fig. 4

Slacken the bleed nipple (2, Fig. 4) and pump the clutch pedal firmly up and down, pausing between each stroke.

CAUTION: The fluid should be topped up after every three pedal strokes.

Pump the clutch pedal until the fluid issuing from the bleed tube is free from air bubbles; tighten bleed nipple.

Top up the reservoir (3, Fig. 4) and apply working pressure to the clutch pedal for two to three minutes then examine the system for leaks.

WARNING: Do not use fluid bled from system for topping up purposes as this will contain air. If fluid has been in use for some time it should be discarded. Fresh fluid bled from system may be used after allowing it to stand for a few hours to allow air bubbles to disperse.

FLUID HOSE

Remove and refit—L.H.D. only   **33.15.13**

Removing

Remove the banjo bolt and washer (1, Fig. 5) securing the flexible hose (2, Fig. 5) to the master cylinder.

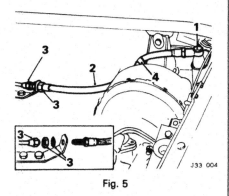

Fig. 5

Disconnect the bundy pipe and hose (3, Fig. 5) at the bracket.
Restrain the hose union and remove the locknut and shakeproof washer also the clip (4, Fig. 5) securing hose to brake servo stud.
Withdraw the hose and plug or tape all broken connections to prevent the ingress of dirt.

Refitting

CAUTION: Take great care to ensure that unions are not overtightened when refitting a flexible hose.

Locate threaded end of hose connector in the bracket and fit the shakeproof washer and locknut (1, Fig. 6).
Connect the bundy pipe (2, Fig. 6) and ensuring that the hose is not kinked or twisted, refit the banjo bolt and washer (3, Fig. 6); fit the clip (4, Fig. 6) to the brake servo mounting stud.

Remove the filler cap from the fluid reservoir and top up fluid to the correct level.

WARNING: Only Castrol/Girling Universal Brake Fluid may be used in the clutch hydraulic system. This fluid exceeds S.A.E. J1703/D.

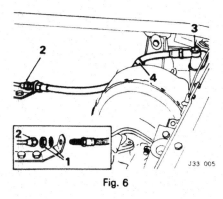

Fig. 6

Attach one end of a bleed tube (1, Fig. 7) to the slave cylinder bleed nipple.

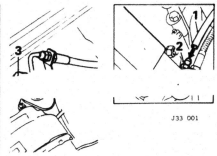

Fig. 7

Partially fill a clean container with hydraulic fluid and immerse the other end of the bleed tube in the fluid.
Slacken the bleed nipple (2, Fig. 7) and pump the clutch pedal slowly up and down, pausing between each stroke.

CAUTION: The fluid should be topped up after every three pedal strokes.

Pump the clutch pedal until the fluid issuing from the bleed tube is free from air bubbles; tighten the bleed nipple.
Top up the reservoir (3, Fig. 7) and apply working pressure to the clutch pedal for two to three minutes then examine the system for leaks.

WARNING: Do not use fluid bled from system for topping up purposes as this will contain air. If fluid has been in use for some time it should be discarded. Fresh fluid bled from system may be used after allowing it to stand for a few hours to allow air bubbles to disperse.

MASTER CYLINDER

Remove and refit   **33.20.01**

Removing

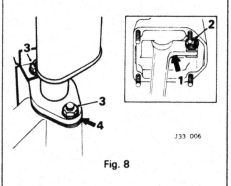

Fig. 8

Remove clevis pin clip (2, Fig. 8); withdraw clevis pin.
Remove the nuts and spring washers (3, Fig. 8) securing the master cylinder to the pedal box.
Lift off the master cylinder and retrieve any shims (4, Fig. 8) that may be fitted.

Refitting

Locate the master cylinder (1, Fig. 9), together with any shims (2, Fig. 9) that were removed, on the mounting studs.

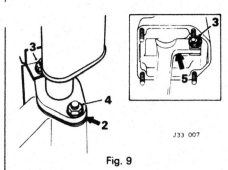

Fig. 9

Connect the master cylinder push-rod to the clutch pedal by means of the clevis pin (3, Fig. 9); refit the clevis clip.

NOTE: Should hole in the clevis not align with hole in pedal, add or subtract shims as necessary until the correct relationship is obtained. (4, Fig. 9). Secure master cylinder with spring washers and nuts.

SLAVE CYLINDER

Remove and refit—R.H.D. only   **33.35.01**

Removing

Remove the setscrews securing slave cylinder cover (1, Fig. 10) to the bell housing.
Slacken the union (3, Fig. 10) but DO NOT attempt to remove the flexible hose. Slide the rubber boot (4, Fig. 10) off the slave cylinder and along the push rod.
Remove the nuts and spring washers (5, Fig. 10) securing the slave cylinder to the bell housing; withdraw the slave cylinder until it can be drawn off the push rod.
Restrain the hose (6, Fig. 10) and screw the cylinder off the union; plug or tape all broken connections to prevent the ingress of dirt.
Release the push-rod from the withdrawal lever.

continued

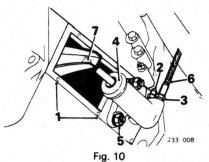

Fig. 10

33—3

Refitting

Restrain the hose (1, Fig. 11) and screw slave cylinder on to union.

Fit push-rod on to the withdrawal lever (2, Fig. 11) and slide the rubber boot (3, Fig. 11) along the rod.

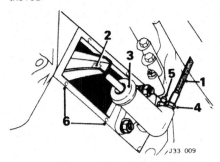

Fig. 11

Position push-rod inside the slave cylinder.

Refit the cylinder and tighten the hose union (4, Fig. 11).

Position the rubber boot on the cylinder.

Ensure that the cover is located correctly and secure it with the four setscrews (6, Fig. 11).

WARNING: Only Castrol/Girling Universal Brake Fluid may be used in the clutch hydraulic system. This fluid exceeds S.A.E. J1703/D.

Attach one end of a bleed tube (1, Fig. 12) to the slave cylinder bleed nipple.

Partially fill a clean container with hydraulic fluid and immerse the other end of the bleed tube in the fluid.

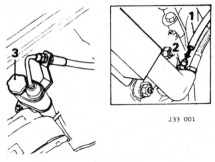

Fig. 12

Slacken the bleed nipple (2, Fig. 12) and pump the clutch pedal firmly up and down, pausing between each stroke.

CAUTION: The fluid should be topped up after every three pedal strokes.

Pump the clutch pedal until the fluid issuing from the bleed tube is free from air bubbles; tighten the bleed nipple.

Top up the reservoir (3, Fig. 12) and apply working pressure to the clutch pedal for two to three minutes then examine the system for leaks.

WARNING: Do not use fluid bled from system for topping up purposes as this will contain air. If fluid has been in use for some time it should be discarded. Fresh fluid bled from the system may be used after allowing it to stand for a few hours to allow air bubbles to disperse.

SLAVE CYLINDER

Remove and refit—L.H.D. only   33.35.01

Removing

Remove the setscrews securing slave cylinder cover to the bell housing (1, Fig. 13).

Slide the rubber boot (2, Fig. 13) off the slave cylinder and along the push-rod.

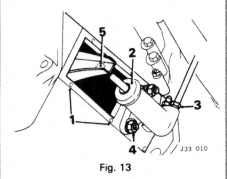

Fig. 13

Disconnect the hydraulic pipe (3, Fig. 13) and plug or tape all broken connections to prevent the ingress of dirt.

Remove the nuts and washers (4, Fig. 13) securing slave cylinder to the bell housing; withdraw cylinder slightly until it can be drawn off the push-rod.

Release the push-rod from the withdrawal lever (5, Fig. 13).

Refitting

Fit the push-rod on to the withdrawal lever (1, Fig. 14), slide rubber boot onto rod.

Position the push-rod inside the cylinder, refit cylinder.

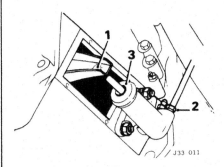

Fig. 14

Reconnect the hydraulic pipe (2, Fig. 14) and position the rubber boot (3, Fig. 14) on the cylinder.

Ensure that the cover is located correctly and secure it with the four setscrews.

WARNING: Only Castrol/Girling Universal Brake Fluid may be used in the clutch hydraulic system. This fluid exceeds S.A.E. J1703/D.

Attach one end of a bleed tube (1, Fig. 15) to the slave cylinder bleed nipple (2, Fig. 15).

Partially fill a clean container with hydraulic fluid and immerse the other end of the bleed tube in the fluid.

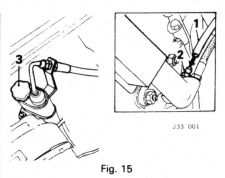

Fig. 15

Slacken the bleed nipple and pump the clutch pedal slowly up and down, pausing between each stroke.

CAUTION: The fluid should be topped up after every three pedal strokes.

Pump the clutch pedal until the fluid issuing from the bleed tube is free from air bubbles; tighten the bleed nipple.

Top up the reservoir (3, Fig. 15) and apply working pressure to the clutch pedal for two to three minutes then examine the system for leaks.

WARNING: Do not use fluid bled from system for topping up purposes as this will contain air. If fluid has been in use for some time it should be discarded. Fresh fluid bled from system may be used after allowing it to stand for a few hours to allow air bubbles to disperse.

CLUTCH ASSEMBLY

Remove and refit   33.10.01

Service tools: Engine support tool MS 53A; Tangye Epco V.1000 transmission hoist; ST 1136 Offset spanner.

Removing

Drive the vehicle onto a ramp and disconnect the battery.

Unscrew the gear knob and withdraw the cigar lighter.

Remove the screws (1, Fig. 16) securing the centre console and raise console (2, Fig. 16) slightly to gain access to the electric window switches.

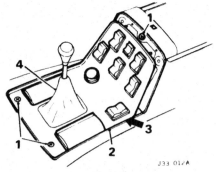

Fig. 16

Disconnect the harnesses at the multi-plug connectors and withdraw the console followed by the gear lever gaiter (4, Fig. 16) and rubber finisher.

Place gear lever in third gear position.

33—4

Position engine support tool MS 53A across engine compartment and attach hook to rear engine lifting eye. Take the engine weight.

Disconnect the exhaust intermediate pipe at the front flange and secure pipe to one side.

Remove screws securing the intermediate heat shield to the body; withdraw heat shield.

Remove bolts securing tie plate to bell housing and sump

Position a suitable ramp jack and wooden block (1, Fig. 17) beneath the rear engine mountings and remove the body cross-member and rear engine mounting securing bolts (2, Fig. 17).

Lower ramp jack and remove the rear engine mounting and body cross-member.

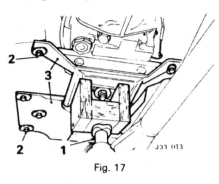

Fig. 17

Disconnect the speedometer cable from the gearbox.

Disconnect the slave cylinder from the gearbox, secure to one side.

Remove nuts, bolts and washers securing the propeller shaft to the gearbox output flange; move shaft away from flange.

Lower rear of engine using MS 53A.

CAUTION: Ensure that engine does. not damage the water valve during this operation.

Remove bolts securing the starter motor to the bell housing (2, Fig. 18); withdraw motor and secure to one side.

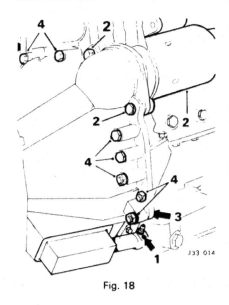

Fig. 18

Remove bolts securing the flywheel cover plate (3, Fig. 18); withdraw plate.

Disconnect reverse light wires from top of gearbox.

Position transmission hoist beneath gearbox and ensure that angle of platform matches that of the gearbox. Secure gearbox to platform.

Remove nuts, bolts and washers securing the bell housing (4, Fig. 18), noting fitted position of earth lead.

Withdraw gearbox and bell housing.

CAUTION: When a suitable hoist is not available, the gearbox may still be removed but care must be taken to ensure that the input shaft is not allowed to take the weight of the gearbox.

Recover foam pad from top of gearbox.

Mark relative positions of clutch cover to flywheel and balance weights to clutch cover (1, Fig. 19).

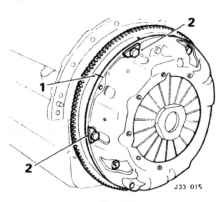

Fig. 19

Remove bolts and spring washers securing clutch cover to flywheel; (2, Fig. 19) withdraw cover together with clutch plate.

Examine flywheel face for scoring. If scoring is found to be excessive, the flywheel must be renewed.

Examine the clutch plates for oil contamination or evidence of slipping.

If oil contamination is evident, crankshaft or gearbox oil seals are suspect and should be examined and if necessary, renewed.

WARNING: Do not use compressed air to remove dust from the clutch assembly. If dust contamination is evident, wash assembly in Gamlen 265 or Rochem Electrosol quick dry solvent.

CAUTION: It is always advisable when renewing the clutch to fit a new release bearing. To do this, proceed as follows:

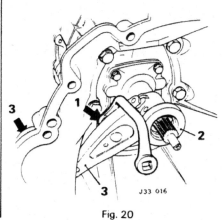

Fig. 20

Using tool ST 1136, remove the pivot bolt (1, Fig. 20) and carefully release withdrawal lever taking care not to bend the spring clip. DO NOT pull lever off the bolt. Slide release bearing (2, Fig. 20) off the input shaft. Remove the shield from over the slave cylinder and disconnect the withdrawal lever (3, Fig. 20) from the push-rod.

Refitting

Smear the input shaft with lithium based grease and fit the release bearing (1, Fig. 21). Refit the pivot bolt (2, Fig. 21).

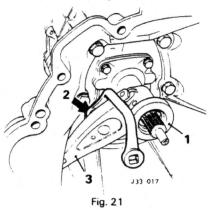

Fig. 21

Engage the lugs of the withdrawal lever in the groove of the release bearing and press withdrawal lever on to the pivot bolt.

Connect the withdrawal lever (3, Fig. 21) to the push-rod but do not fit the cover at this stage.

Position the clutch plate and cover (1, Fig. 22) on the flywheel ensuring that the reference marks made during dismantling are in alignment.

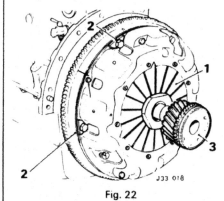

Fig. 22

Fit the balance weights, bolts and washers but do not tighten the bolts (2, Fig. 22) at this stage.

Using a dummy input shaft (3, Fig. 22), align the clutch plate ensuring that the clutch cover is correctly located.

Tighten the securing bolts by diagonal selection to the specified torque figure.

Position the foam pad on top of gearbox casing.

Refit the gearbox and bell housing, reconnect the reverse light switch and tighten the bell housing securing bolts to the specified torque figure.

Refit the starter motor.

continued

Refit the flywheel cover plate and remove the transmission hoist.

Raise engine using MS 53A or a ramp jack and wooden block (1, Fig. 23) positioned under the gearbox and re-connect the propeller shaft.

Refit slave cylinder.

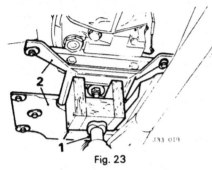

Fig. 23

CAUTION: Always use new self-locking nuts to secure the propeller shaft.

Connect the speedometer drive cable; refit the rear engine mounting and body cross-member (2, Fig. 23).

Refit the heat shield and exhaust intermediate pipe.

CAUTION: Always use a new olive, coated with 'Firegum' when refitting the exhaust pipe.

Refit the tie-plate between the oil sump and the bell housing.

Refit the flexible pipe to the slave cylinder.

Remove the engine support tool MS 53A.

Refit the gear lever gaiter (1, Fig. 24) and centre console (2, Fig. 24), followed by the gear knob (3, Fig. 24).

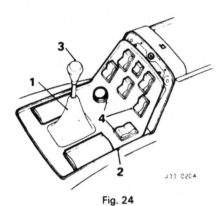

Fig. 24

Reconnect the battery and check operation of electric windows, cigar lighter and electric door locks where fitted (4, Fig. 24).

If the clutch fluid pipes were disconnected:

Remove the filler cap from the fluid reservoir and top up fluid to the correct level.

WARNING: Only Castrol / Girling Universal Brake Fluid may be used in the clutch hydraulic system. This fluid exceeds S.A.E. J1703/D.

Attach one end of a bleed tube (1, Fig. 25) to the slave cylinder bleed nipple.

Partially fill a clean container with hydraulic fluid and immerse the other end of the bleed tube in the fluid.

Slacken the bleed nipple (2, Fig. 25) and pump the clutch pedal slowly up and down, pausing between each stroke.

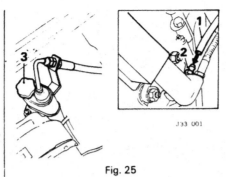

Fig. 25

CAUTION: The fluid should be topped up after every three pedal strokes.

Pump the clutch pedal until the fluid issuing from the bleed tube is free from air bubbles; tighten the bleed nipple.

Top up the reservoir (3, Fig. 25) and apply working pressure to the clutch pedal for two to three minutes then examine the system for leaks.

WARNING: Do not use fluid bled from system for topping up purposes as this will contain air. If fluid has been in use for some time it should be discarded. Fresh fluid bled from system may be used after allowing it to stand for a few hours to allow air bubble to disperse.

MASTER CYLINDER

Overhaul   33.20.07

WARNING: Use only clean brake fluid or Girling cleaning fluid for cleaning. All traces of cleaning fluid must be removed before reassembly. All components should be lubricated with clean brake fluid and assembled using the fingers only.

Dismantling

Remove master cylinder as detailed in operation 33.20.01

Detach rubber boot (1, Fig. 26) from end of barrel and move boot along push-rod.

Depress push-rod and remove circlip (2, Fig. 26)

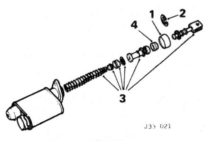

Fig 26

Withdraw push-rod, piston, piston washer, main cup, spring retainer and spring (3, Fig. 26)

Remove secondary cup (4, Fig. 26) from piston

Inspection

Examine cylinder bore for scores.

Thoroughly wash out reservoir and ensure by-pass hole in cylinder bore is clear. Dry using compressed air or lint-free cloth.

Lubricate replacement seals with clean brake fluid.

Reassembling

If necessary, fit end plug on new gasket.

Fit spring retainer (1, Fig. 27) to small end of spring. If necessary, bend over retainer ears to secure.

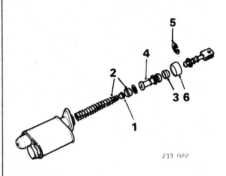

Fig. 27

Insert spring, large end leading, into cylinder bore; follow with main cup (2, Fig. 27), lip foremost. Ensure lip is not damaged on the circlip groove.

Using fingers only, stretch secondary cup (3, Fig. 27) onto piston with small end towards drilled end and groove engaging ridge.

Gently work round cup with fingers to ensure correct bedding.

Insert piston washer into bore, curved edge towards main cup.

Insert piston in bore (4, Fig. 27), drilled end foremost.

Fit rubber boot (5, Fig. 27) to push-rod.

Offer push-rod to piston and press into bore until circlip can be fitted behind push-rod stop ring.

CAUTION: It is important to ensure that circlip is correctly fitted in groove.

Locate rubber boot in groove (6, Fig. 27).

RELEASE BEARING

Remove and refit   33.25.12

To carry out this operation proceed as described in Operation 33.10.01.

SLAVE CYLINDER

Overhaul   33.35.07

Dismantling

Prior to overhaul, the slave cylinder must be removed as detailed in Operation 33.35.01.

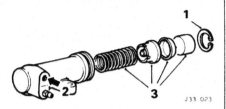

Fig. 28

Remove the circlip (1, Fig. 28) and applying low air pressure (2, Fig. 28) to the inlet port expel the piston, cup, cup filler and spring (3, Fig. 28), discard the cup

Inspecting Components

WARNING: Use only clean brake fluid or Girling cleaning fluid for cleaning. All traces of cleaning fluid must be removed before reassembly. All components should be lubricated with clean brake fluid and assembled using the fingers only.

Examine the piston and slave cylinder bore for signs of scoring. Should scoring be evident, components must be renewed
Examine the spring for signs of distortion and renew it if necessary.
Check that the rubber boot is not distorted or perished.

Reassembling

Press spring, cup filler, a new cup and the piston (3, Fig. 28) into the cylinder; refit the circlip (1, Fig. 28).
Check that piston moves freely and refit the cylinder as detailed in Operation 33.35.01.

PAGE INTENTIONALLY LEFT BLANK

CONTENTS

DESCRIPTION

The five-speed gearbox was introduced on the Jaguar 3.4 and 4.2 and Daimler Sovereign Series III saloons as an option to automatic transmission. The fifth gear, in effect, replaces the overdrive as fitted to the four-speed gearbox on Series II cars. Fifth gear is engaged as a normal gear. Reverse is engaged by lifting the lever and moving it as far as possible to the left then forward.

The gearbox oil capacity (from dry) is 2 litres (3½ pints, 4½ U.S. pints). To check the level, raise the car on a ramp or place it over a pit and remove the filler/level plug on the left-hand side of the box. Oil should reach the bottom of the threaded hole. If additional oil is required, S.A.E. 75W hypoid oil should be used. If this is unobtainable S.A.E. 80W hypoid oil may be used for topping-up.

No routine oil change is required but if a refill is necessary the recommended lubricant is Shell E3766 gearbox oil which is used for the initial factory fill. This oil is available under part number RTC1896. If this oil cannot be obtained it is permissible to use an S.A.E. 75W hypoid oil, but S.A.E. 80W oil should NOT be used as it will impair gear change quality.

The internal gear ratios are given in GENERAL DATA. The gearbox is recognised as the '77 mm' gearbox and is derived from the dimension between the mainshaft and the layshaft.

GENERAL DATA

5 Speed Manual Gearbox

Gearbox type	5 speed with baulk-ring synchromesh on all forward gears.
Ratios	First gear 3.321 :1
	Second gear 2.087 :1
	Third gear 1.396 :1
	Fourth gear 1.00 :1
	Fifth gear 0.883 :1
	Reverse 3.428 :1
Capacity	2 litres (3½ pints, 4½ U.S. pints)

TORQUE WRENCH SETTINGS

ITEM	DESCRIPTION	TIGHTENING TORQUE		
		Nm	kgf m	lbf ft
Clutch lever pivot bolt	12 mm threaded pin	40,6	4,15	30
Bell housing to gearcase	12 mm bolt and setscrew	80	8,16	59
Cover plate to bell housing	8 mm bolt	20,3	2,07	15
5th gear interlock spool retainer to gearbox extension	5 mm setscrew	6,1	0,62	4 5
Output flange to mainshaft	18 mm Nyloc nut	203,4	20,74	150
Dust cap assembly to extension housing	6 mm setscrew	9,5	0,96	7
Extension and centre plate to main case	8 mm bolt	28,5	2,90	21
5th gear selector fork pivot bracket to centre plate	8 mm setscrew	28,5	2,90	21
Front cover to main case	8 mm setscrew	28,5	2,90	21
Interlock spool retainer to main case	6 mm setscrew	9,5	0,96	7
'J' coupling pin to main selector shaft	8 mm threaded pin	20,3	2,07	15
Mounting bracket	8 mm bolt and setscrew	28,5	2,90	21
Drain plug	16 mm	35	3,59	26
Oil pump body to extension	6 mm screw	9,5	0,96	7
Oil inlet access hole blanking	8 mm setscrew	20,3	2,07	15
Propeller shaft to output flange	10 mm bolt	51	5,12	37
Reverse lever mounting pin to centre plate	10 mm threaded pin	28,5	2,90	21
Reverse baulk plate to gearbox extension	6 mm bolt	9,5	0,96	7
Remote control housing to main case rear extension	8 mm setscrew	20,3	2,07	15
Speedometer cable clip to gearbox	6 mm setscrew	9,5	0,96	7
Torsion spring brackets to gearbox extension	6 mm screws	9,5	0,96	7
Torsion spring adjuster locking screw	8 mm setscrew	20,3	2,07	15

37—2

GEAR LEVER BIAS SPRING

Adjust 37.16.01

Service tool: Engine support tool MS 53A

Adjustment

Disconnect the battery, withdraw the cigar lighter and remove the gear lever knob.

Remove the screws securing the centre console, raise the console slightly and disconnect the window and cigar lighter harnesses.

Remove the gear lever gaiter.

Position engine support tool MS 53A so that lifting hook of tool engages with the rear engine lifting eye

Disconnect the intermediate exhaust pipe at the front

Remove the nuts and bolts securing the gearbox crash bracket. Lower the bracket and position a jack and suitably shaped piece of wood beneath the gearbox mounting.

With the mounting supported by the jack, remove the mounting bolts.

Lower the jack and remove mounting. Using tool MS 53A, lower the rear of the engine.

CAUTION: Ensure that heater valve and clutch flexible pipe are not damaged during this operation.

Slacken abutment plate bolts.

Select 1st gear and move the gear lever as far as possible to the left

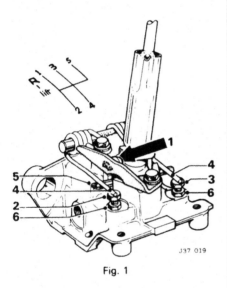

Fig. 1

Check the gap (1, Fig. 1) between the abutment and gear lever pads; the measurement should be 0,35 to 0,75 mm (0.014 to 0.030 in). If this dimension is not obtained, slacken the location bracket securing bolt and adjust position of bracket until clearance is correct. Slacken the locknuts (6, Fig. 1).

Select third gear, i.e., the gear lever will be eight degrees to the right of the vertical.

Adjust screws (2 and 3, Fig. 1) until each spring leg (4, Fig. 1) is approximately 0,5 mm (0.020 in) clear of the cross pin (5, Fig. 1). This will allow radial movement of the lever to take place before contact is made between cross-pin and springs.

Applying a light load, move the lever to the left and position it at the extremity of radial movement

Adjust bolt (3, Fig. 1) until the right-hand spring just touches the cross-pin

Now move the lever to the right and position it at the extremity of radial movement.

Adjust bolt (2, Fig. 1) until the left-hand spring just touches the cross-pin.

Screw both bolts in an equal amount until all radial movement is eliminated.

Return the lever to the neutral position then move it through the gate several times. When released, the lever should return to the 3rd/4th plane

When adjustment is correct, tighten the locknuts (6, Fig. 1). Using tool MS 53A, raise the rear of the engine.

Position a jack and suitably shaped block of wood beneath the gearbox mounting and refit the rear engine mounting and crash bracket. Remove the jack and tool MS 53A.

Connect the intermediate exhaust pipe; coat the olive with 'Firegum' prior to fitting.

Refit the gear lever gaiter, centre console and gear knob. Ensure full movement of gear lever. Reconnect the battery and test electric windows and cigar lighter for correct operation.

GEAR LEVER BIAS SPRING

Remove and refit 37.16.02

Service tool: Engine support tool MS 53A

Removing

Disconnect the battery, withdraw the cigar lighter and remove the gear lever knob.

Remove the screws securing the centre console; raise the console slightly and disconnect the electric window, and cigar lighter harnesses

Remove the gear lever gaiter.

Position engine support tool MS 53A so that lifting eye of tool engages with the rear engine lifting eye

Disconnect the intermediate exhaust pipe at the front

Remove the nuts and bolts securing the gearbox crash bracket. Lower the bracket and position a jack and suitably shaped piece of wood beneath the gearbox casing.

With the gearbox supported by the jack remove the rear engine mounting.

Remove the jack and using tool MS 53A lower the rear of the engine.

CAUTION: Ensure that heater water valve and clutch flexible pipe are not damaged during this operation.

Select 4th gear, remove bias spring securing bolt followed by the spring.

Refitting

Grease the spring and mounting, refit the spring.

Fit and tighten the spring securing bolt.

Select 1st gear and move the gear lever as far as possible to the right.

Check the gap (1, Fig. 1) between the abutment and gear lever pads; the measurement should be 0,35 to 0,75 mm (0.014 to 0.030 in). If this dimension is not obtained, slacken the location bracket securing bolt and adjust position of bracket until clearance is correct. Slacken the locknuts (6, Fig. 1).

Select third gear i.e. the gear lever will be eight degrees to the right of the vertical.

Adjust screws (2 and 3, Fig. 1) until each spring leg (4, Fig. 1) is approximately 0,5 mm (0.020 in) clear of the cross-pin (5, Fig. 1). This will allow radial movement of the lever to take place before contact is made between cross-pin and springs.

Applying a light load, move the lever to the left and position it at the extremity of radial movement.

Adjust bolt (3, Fig. 1) until the right-hand spring just touches the cross-pin.

Now move the lever to the right and position it at the extremity of radial movement.

Adjust bolt (2, Fig. 1) until the left-hand spring just touches the cross-pin.

Screw both bolts in an equal amount until all radial movement is eliminated

Return the lever to the neutral position then move it through the gate several times. When released, the lever should return to the 3rd/4th plane.

When adjustment is correct, tighten the locknuts (6, Fig. 1).

Using tool MS 53A, raise the rear of the engine. Position a jack and suitably shaped block of wood beneath the gearbox casing and refit the rear engine mounting and crash bracket. Remove the jack and tool MS 53A.

Refit the intermediate exhaust pipe; coat the olive with 'Firegum' prior to fitting.

Refit the gear lever gaiter, centre console and gear knob. Ensure full movement of gear lever. Reconnect the battery and test electric windows and cigar lighter for correct operation.

REAR OIL SEAL

Remove and refit 37.23.01

Service tool: Engine support tool MS 53A

Removing

Position engine support tool MS 53A so that lifting hook of tool engages with the rear engine lifting eye

Disconnect the intermediate exhaust pipe and olive

Remove the nuts and bolts securing the gearbox crash bracket. Lower the bracket and position a jack and suitably shaped piece of wood beneath the gearbox mounting.

continued

37—3

Lower the rear engine mounting.

Remove the intermediate heat shield.

Remove the jack followed by the propeller shaft securing bolts; swing shaft to one side.

Remove the output flange securing nut and slide flange off output shaft.

Prise the oil seal out of the gearbox casing.

Refitting

Smear the new oil seal with clean gearbox oil.

Fit the seal ensuring that it is correctly seated.

Refit the output flange; reconnect the propeller shaft.

CAUTION: Always use new self-locking nuts when refitting the propeller shaft.

Support the mounting with a jack and suitably shaped piece of wood; refit the rear engine mounting.

Remove the jack and refit the intermediate heat shield.

Reconnect the intermediate exhaust pipe; coat the olive with 'Firegum' prior to fitting.

Remove tool MS 53A.

Remove the filler/level plug and top up gearbox oil level to the bottom of the filler plug hole; refit the filler plug.

FIRST MOTION SHAFT OIL SEAL

Remove and refit   37.23.06

Service tool: Offset spanner ST 1136

Removing

Prior to renewing the first motion shaft oil seal, it will be necessary to remove the gearbox as detailed in Operation 37.20.01.

Using tool ST 1136, unscrew and remove the clutch pivot bolt, withdrawal lever and release bearing.

CAUTION: Do not pull the withdrawal lever off the pivot bolt prior to removal

Remove the bolts and washers securing the front cover plate to the gearbox, withdraw the plate; discard the gasket.

Remove the oil seal from the front cover.

CAUTION: Ensure that the spacers for the first motion shaft and the layshaft bearings are not intermixed.

Refitting

Smear the replacement oil seal with clean gearbox oil and position the oil seal on the front cover plate with the lip of the seal facing towards the gearbox.

Fit the front cover plate, together with a new gasket, to the gearbox.

Refit the clutch pivot bolt and the release bearing; press the withdrawal lever on to the pivot bolt.

Refit the gearbox to the car, see Operation 37.20.01.

Remove the filler/lever plug and top up gearbox oil level to the bottom of the filler plug hole; refit the filler plug.

SPEEDOMETER DRIVE PINION

Remove and refit   37.25.05

Removing

Remove the bolt and washer (1, Fig. 2) securing the clamp plate (2, Fig. 2) to the gearcase.

On later models with electronic speedometer, disconnect 2 pin connector.

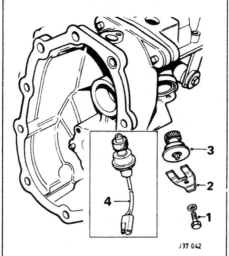

J37 042

Fig. 2

Withdraw the pinion drive, transducer and cable (4, Fig. 2).

Withdraw the speedometer cable followed by the pinion housing (3, Fig. 2) (early models).

Remove the pinion from the housing; discard the 'O' ring and oil seal.

Refitting

Fit the replacement 'O' ring and oil seal, smear both components with clean gearbox oil.

Refit the pinion into the housing.

Refit the pinion housing, speedometer drive cable, drive cable, transducer and (clamp plate early models).

Connect the cable connectors (later models).

REVERSE LIGHT SWITCH

Check and adjust   37.27.02

Disconnect the battery and remove the gear lever knob

Remove the screws securing the centre console slightly and disconnect the electric window and cigar lighter.

Remove the gear lever gaiter.

Connect a test lamp and battery to the switch and select reverse gear (Fig. 3).

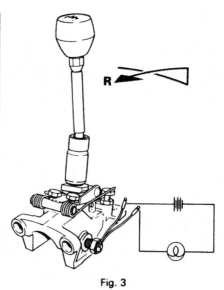

Fig. 3

Slacken the locknut and screw the switch in until the lamp lights.

Screw the switch in a further 180° and tighten the locknut.

Reconnect the battery, switch on the ignition and check that reverse lights are only illuminated when reverse gear is selected. Remove the test lamp and battery.

Switch off the ignition and disconnect the battery.

Refit the gear lever gaiter and centre console.

Reconnect the battery and test the electric windows and cigar lighter for correct operation.

GEARBOX ASSEMBLY

Remove and refit   37.20.01

Service Tools: Engine support tool MS 53A; Tangye Epco V1000 Transmission Hoist; ST 1136 Offset spanner.

Removing

Drive the vehicle onto a ramp and disconnect the battery

Unscrew the gear knob and withdraw the cigar lighter

Remove the screws securing the centre console and raise console slightly to gain access to the electric window.

Disconnect the harnesses at the multi-plug connectors and withdraw the console followed by the gear lever gaiter.

Place gear lever in third gear position.

Position engine support tool MS 53A across engine compartment and attach hook to rear engine lifting eye. Take the engine weight.

Disconnect the exhaust intermediate pipe at the front flange and secure pipe to one side.

Remove screws securing the heat shield to the body, withdraw the shield.

Remove bolts securing tie plate to bell housing and sump

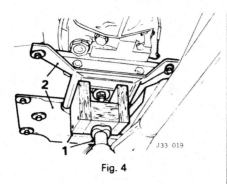

Fig. 4

Position a suitable ramp jack and wooden block (1, Fig. 4) beneath the rear engine mounting and remove the body cross member and rear engine mounting securing bolts.

Lower ramp jack and remove the rear engine mounting and body cross member (2, Fig. 4).

Disconnect the speedometer cable from the gearbox.

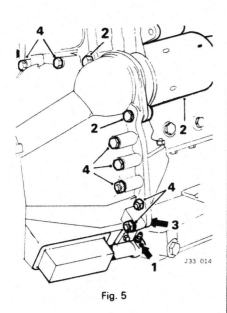

Fig. 5

Disconnect the slave cylinder from the gearbox, secure to one side.

Remove nuts, bolts and washers securing the propeller shaft to the gearbox output flange; move shaft away from flange.

Lower rear of engine using MS 53A.

CAUTION: Ensure that engine does not damage the water valve during this operation.

Remove bolts securing the starter motor to the bell housing (2, Fig. 5); withdraw motor and secure to one side.

Remove bolts securing the flywheel cover plate (3, Fig. 5), withdraw plate.

Disconnect reverse light wires from top of gearbox.

Position transmission hoist beneath gearbox and ensure that angle of platform matches that of the gearbox. Secure gearbox to platform.

Remove nuts, bolts and washers securing the bell housing (4, Fig. 5), noting fitted position of earth lead.

Withdraw gearbox and bell housing.

CAUTION: When a suitable hoist is not available the gearbox may still be removed but care must be taken to ensure that the input shaft is not allowed to take the weight of the gearbox.

Recover foam pad from top of gearbox.

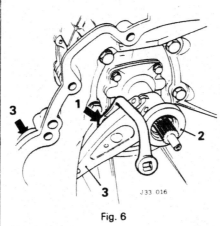

Fig. 6

Using tool ST 1136, remove the pivot bolt (1, Fig. 6) and carefully release withdrawal lever taking care not to bend the spring clip. DO NOT pull the lever off the bolt. Slide release bearing (2, Fig. 6) off the input shaft. Remove the shield from over the slave cylinder and disconnect the withdrawal lever (3, Fig. 6) from the push-rod.

Refitting

Position the bell housing on the gearcase and secure it with six bolts, plain and spring washers.

Smear the input shaft with lithium based grease and fit the release bearing. Refit the pivot bolt.

Engage the lugs of the withdrawal lever in the groove of the release bearing and press withdrawal lever onto pivot bolt.

Position the foam pad on top of gearbox casing.

Refit the gearbox and bell housing, reconnect the reverse light switch and tighten the bell housing securing bolts to the specified torque figure.

Refit the flywheel cover plate and remove the transmission hoist.

Raise engine using MS 53A or a ramp jack and wooden block positioned under the gearbox and reconnect the propeller shaft.

Refit the slave cylinder.

CAUTION: Always use new self-locking nuts to secure the propeller shaft.

Connect the speedometer drive cable; refit the rear engine mounting and body cross member.

Refit the heat shield and exhaust intermediate pipe.

CAUTION: Always use a new olive, coated with 'Firegum' when refitting the exhaust pipe.

Refit the tie-plate between the oil sump and the bell housing.

Refit the slave cylinder.

Remove the engine support tool MS 53A.

Refit the gear lever gaiter and centre console followed by the gear knob. Ensure full movement of the gear lever.

Reconnect the battery and check operation of electric windows, cigar lighter and electric door locks (where fitted).

If the slave cylinder pipes were disconnected remove the filler cap from the clutch fluid reservoir and top up fluid to the correct level.

WARNING: Only Castrol/Girling Universal Brake Fluid may be used in the clutch hydraulic system. This fluid exceeds SAE J1703/D.

Attach one end of a bleed tube to the slave cylinder bleed nipple.

Partially fill a clean container with hydraulic fluid and immerse the other end of the bleed tube in the fluid.

Slacken the bleed nipple and pump the clutch pedal slowly up and down, pausing between each stroke.

CAUTION: The fluid should be topped up after every three pedal strokes.

Pump the clutch pedal until the fluid issuing from the bleed tube is free from air bubbles; tighten the bleed nipple.

Top up the reservoir and apply working pressure to the clutch pedal for two to three minutes then examine the system for leaks.

WARNING: Do not use fluid bled from system for topping up purposes as this will contain air. If fluid has been in use for some time it should be discarded. Fresh fluid bled from system may be used after allowing it to stand for a few hours to allow air bubbles to disperse.

GEARBOX

Overhaul   37.20.04

Service tools: 47, 18G 47-1, 18G 47-5, 18G 284, 18G 284 AAH, 18G 705, 18G 705-1, 18G 1205, ST 1136

Dismantling

Place the gearbox on a bench or gearbox stand, ensuring that the oil is first drained.

Using tool ST 1136, unscrew the clutch withdrawal lever pivot bolt and remove the clutch withdrawal lever complete with the pivot bolt and release bearing slippers.

Remove the bell housing.

Remove the nut and connecting pin linking the selector shaft to the remote control shaft.

Remove the four bolts, spring and plain washers—two top, one either side—securing the remote control housing to the gear-case rear cover.

Remove the nut and plain washer securing the output flange to the mainshaft. Use tool RG 421 or 18G 1205 to prevent shaft rotation. Withdraw the output flange.

continued

Fig. 7

J37 002

Remove the speedometer driven gear and housing. (1, Fig. 7)

Remove the two bolts and spring washers securing the locating boss for the selector rear spool and withdraw the locating boss.

Remove the 10 bolts, spring and plain washers securing the rear cover to the gearcase; withdraw the rear cover.

Remove and discard the gasket.

Withdraw the oil pump drive (1, Fig. 8).

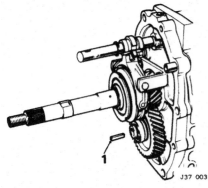

Fig. 8

J37 003

Remove the 2 bolts and spring washers (1, Fig. 9) securing the fifth gear selector fork and bracket (2, Fig. 9).

Remove the circlip (3, Fig. 9) from the selector shaft.

Withdraw the fifth gear selector spool (4, Fig. 9). Note that the longer cam of the spool is fitted towards the bottom of the gearbox.

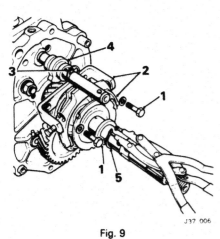

Fig. 9

J37 006

Remove the circlip (5, Fig. 9) retaining the fifth gear synchromesh assembly to the mainshaft (Fig. 10).

Withdraw the synchromesh assembly, fifth gear-driven, and spacer from the mainshaft.

Fig. 10

J37 007

Remove the circlip (1, Fig. 11) retaining the fifth gear-driving, from the layshaft.

Using tool 18G 705 and adaptors 18G 705-1 remove the fifth gear and spacer from the layshaft.

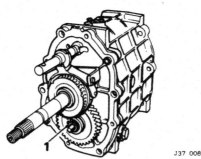

Fig. 11

J37 008

Remove the front cover (1, Fig. 12).

Remove and discard the gasket.

Remove the input shaft selective washer, bearing track, (2, Fig. 12) layshaft selective washer and bearing track (3, Fig. 12) from the gearcase.

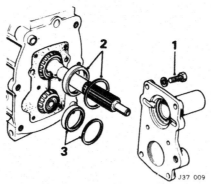

Fig. 12

J37 009

Remove the two bolts and spring washers securing the locating boss for the selector shaft front spool; withdraw the locating boss.

Remove the plug, spring and ball from the centre plate.

Supporting the gearbox on the centre plate withdraw the gear-case.

Remove the input shaft and synchromesh cone.

Withdraw the layshaft cluster.

Support the centre plate complete with gears in protected vice jaws.

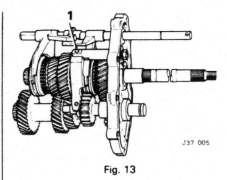

Fig. 13

J37 005

Remove the reverse lever, circlip and pivot pin (1, Fig. 13).

Remove the reverse gear lever and slipper pad. Slide the reverse shaft rearwards and withdraw the reverse gear spacer, mainshaft, selector shaft, selector shaft fork and spool in a forward direction clear of the centre plate. Withdraw the selector fork and spool.

NOTE: The shorter cam of the spool is fitted towards the bottom of the gearbox.

If renewal of the pivot shaft and/or the centre plate is intended, remove the nut and spring washers securing the reverse gear pivot shaft and remove the pivot shaft.

If renewal of the dowels and/or centre plate is intended, remove the centre plate from the vice and extract the two dowels.

Input shaft and front cover

Using tools 47 and adaptors 18G 47-5, remove the external bearing.

Using tools 18G 284 AAH and 18G 284, withdraw the internal bearing track.

Remove and discard the oil seal from the front cover.

Layshaft

Using tools 47 and adaptors 18G 47-1, remove the layshaft bearings.

Mainshaft

Remove the pilot bearing and spacer.

Remove the 3rd and 4th speed synchronizer hub and sleeve (1, Fig. 14).

Remove the 3rd speed gear (2, Fig. 14).

Remove the circlip securing the mainshaft bearing (3, Fig. 14).

Remove the bearing, 1st gear and bush, 1st and 2nd speed hub, sleeve and synchromesh cones, and 2nd gear (4, Fig. 14).

37—6

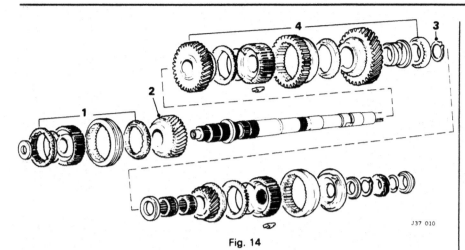

Fig. 14

Rear cover

Remove the oil seal (1, Fig. 15), bearing (2, Fig. 15), oil seal (3, Fig. 15), spacer, and speedometer gear (4, Fig. 15). Remove the oil pump drive, pump cover (5, Fig. 15) and gears (6, Fig. 15).

Thoroughly clean and examine all components; obtain new parts as necessary.

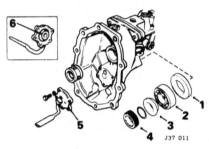

Fig. 15

Layshaft

Fit the bearings to the layshaft.

Mainshaft

Synchromesh assemblies. With the outer sleeve held, a push-through load applied to the outer face of the synchromesh hub should register 8,2–10 kgf m (18–22 lbf ft) to overcome spring detent in either direction.

Checking 1st speed bush end-float. Fit 2nd gear, 1st/2nd speed synchromesh hub and 1st gear bush to the mainshaft.

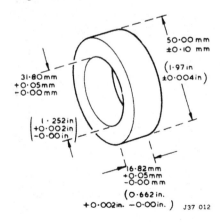

Fig. 16

Manufacture a spacer to the dimensions shown in Fig. 16 and slide the spacer on the mainshaft. This represents a slave bearing.

Using an old circlip and feeler gauges check the clearance existing between the spacer and the circlip, which should be within 0,005 to 0,055 mm (0.0002 to 0.002 in). The first speed bush is available with collars of different thickness. Select a 1st speed bush with a collar which will give the required end-float.

Remove the circlip, spacer, bush, synchromesh hub and 2nd gear from the mainshaft.

Checking 5th gear end-float. Fit the 5th gear assembly to the mainshaft, i.e. front spacer, 5th gear, synchromesh hub, rear plate and spacer. Fit an old circlip and using feeler gauges check the end-float which should be within 0,005 to 0,055 mm (0.0002 to 0.002 in). The rear spacer is available in a range of sizes. Select a rear spacer which will ensure the required clearance.

Remove the circlip spacer and 5th gear assembly.

Assembly

It is important that 1st/2nd synchromesh is assembled correctly with the short splines of inner member towards 2nd gear. Fit 2nd gear baulk ring, which is different to the other three, synchromesh hub and sleeve with the selector fork annulus to the rear of the gearbox, baulk ring 1st gear, selective bush, bearing and a new circlip (Fig. 17). When fitting the circlip care must be taken to ensure that it is not stretched beyond the minimum necessary to pass over the shaft. The internal diameter of an expanded circlip must not exceed 32,30 mm (1.272 in).

Fit 3rd gear, baulk ring, synchromesh hub and sleeve, with the longer boss of synchromesh hub to front of gearbox, to the mainshaft.

Fit the spacer and bearing to front of the mainshaft.

Fit the layshaft bearing track to the centre plate.

Fit the layshaft to the centre plate and fit the fifth gear, spacer and a new circlip. When fitting the circlip care must be taken to ensure that it is not stretched beyond the minimum necessary to obtain entry. The internal diameter of an expanded circlip must not exceed 22,5 mm (0.886 in).

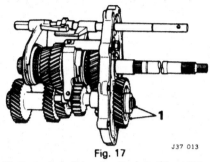

Fig. 17

Fit the mainshaft bearing track to the centre-plate.

Locate the centre plate in protected vice jaws. Take the selector shaft complete with 1st and 2nd selector fork, front spool and 3rd and 4th selector fork and engage both forks in their respective synchromesh sleeves on the mainshaft. Simultaneously engage the selector shaft and mainshaft assemblies in the centre-plate.

Fit the spacer, 5th gear, baulk ring, synchromesh hub and sleeve end-plate, selective spacer, and a new circlip.

CAUTION: WHEN FITTING THE CIRCLIP CARE MUST BE TAKEN TO ENSURE THAT IT IS NOT STRETCHED BEYOND THE MINIMUM NECESSARY TO OBTAIN ENTRY. THE INTERNAL DIAMETER OF AN EXPANDED CIRCLIP MUST NOT EXCEED 27,63 mm (1.088 in). ENSURE THAT THE CIRCLIP IS FULLY SEATED IN THE GROOVE.

Fit the reverse gear with lip for slipper pad to front of box, front and rear spacers and the reverse shaft.

Fit the reverse lever, slipper pad, pivot pin and circlip. If a new reverse gear pivot shaft is to be fitted it is necessary to ensure that its radial location is consistent with reverse pad slipper engagement/clearance.

Radial location is determined on assembly.

Secure with spring washer and nuts, subsequently checking movement of reverse lever and ensuring slipper pad is properly engaged.

Remove the centre-plate and gear assembly from the vice and locate on a suitable stand with the front of the mainshaft uppermost. Ensure that the reverse shaft does not slide out of position.

Fit the centre plate front gasket.

Fit the external bearing and internal bearing track to the input shaft.

Fit the input shaft to the gearcase.

Carefully slide the gearcase and input shaft into position over the gear assemblies. DO NOT USE FORCE. Ensure that the centre plate dowels and selector shaft are engaged in their respective locations.

Fit the layshaft and input shaft front bearing outer tracks.

Using slave bolts and plain washers to prevent damaging the rear face of the centre-plate, evenly draw the gearcase into position on the plate. *continued*

Place a layshaft spacer of nominal thickness 1,02 mm (0.040 in) on the layshaft bearing track, fit the front cover and a new gasket, securing with six bolts.

Using a dial gauge, check layshaft end-float.

Remove the front cover and provisional spacer. The required layshaft end-float is 0,005 to 0,055 mm (0.0002 to 0.002 in). Check the thickness of the provisional spacer. Spacer thickness required is: provisional spacer thickness, plus end-float obtained, minus 0,055 mm (0.002 in).

Again fit the front cover and gasket, this time with the correct spacer arrived at in previous operation.

Check layshaft end-float to ensure it is within the limits specified previously.

Place a ball bearing in the centre of the input shaft. This facilitates checking mainshaft end-float.

Mount a dial gauge on the gearcase with the stylus resting on the ball; zero the gauge.

Check the mainshaft and input shaft combined end-float. Care must be taken when checking dial gauge readings to ensure that end-float only—as distinct from side movement of the input shaft—is recorded. If difficulty is encountered in differentiating between end-float and side movement, remove the front cover and wrap the plain portion of the input shaft below the splines with six turns of masking tape. Refit the front cover and again check end-float ensuring that rise and fall of the input shaft is not restricted by the tape.

Having ascertained end-float, select the spacer required as follows:

End-float minus 0,055 mm (0.002 in) = spacer thickness required.

Fit the spacer thus determined and again check end-float which must be within 0,005 to 0,055 mm (0.0002 to 0.002 in).

Remove the front cover and tape, if used.

Fit the oil seal to the front cover and lubricate the seal lips.

Mask the splines and fit the front cover; remove the spline masking.

Place the gearbox on a bench or stand and remove the slave bolts and washers from the centre-plate.

Fit the 5th gear spool and circlip to the selector shaft.

NOTE: The longer cam of the spool is fitted towards the bottom of the gearbox.

Fit the 5th gear selector fork and bracket.

Renew the selector shaft 'O' ring in the rear cover and fit the oil ring bush.

Fit a new rear gasket to the centre-plate and engage the oil pump shaft in the layshaft.

Fit the oil pump gears and cover to the gearbox rear cover.

Fit the rear cover ensuring that the oil pump drive engages the oil pump.

Fit the selector shaft ball, spring and plug to the centre-plate.

Fit the two spool locating bosses to both the 1st/2nd spool and 5th gear spool.

Fit the speedometer driving gear to the mainshaft ensuring that it engages the flats on the mainshaft.

Fit the spacer and ball race to the mainshaft.

Fit a new rear oil seal, lubricate the seal lip with gearbox oil.

Fit the output flange, washer and nut.

Fit the speedometer driven gear and housing. *

Refit the bell housing.

Refit the clutch pivot bolt.

Assemble the release bearing to the withdrawal lever and press the retaining clip over the head of the pivot bolt.

Fit the remote control housing.

*Later models

Speedo drive pinion for electronic speedometer vehicles.

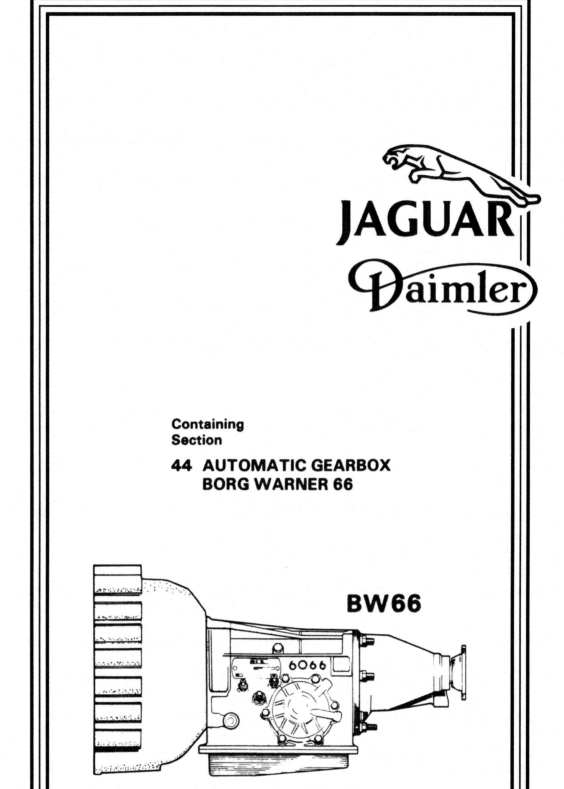

JAGUAR

Daimler

**Containing
Section**

**44 AUTOMATIC GEARBOX
BORG WARNER 66**

BW66

SERIES III
SERVICE MANUAL

INTRODUCTION

This Service Manual covers the Jaguar Series 3 and Daimler Series 3 range of vehicles. It is primarily designed to assist skilled technicians in the efficient repair and maintenance of Jaguar and Daimler vehicles.

Using the appropriate service tools and carrying out the procedures as detailed will enable the operations to be completed within the time stated in the 'Repair Operation Times'.

The Service Manual has been produced in 13 separate sections; this allows the information to be distributed throughout the specialist areas of the modern service facility.

A table of contents in section 1 lists the major components and systems together with the section and book numbers. The cover of each book depicts graphically and numerically the sections contained within that book. Each section starts with a list of operations in alphabetical order.

The title page of each book carries the part numbers required to order replacement books, binders or complete Service Manuals. This can be done through the normal channels.

Operation Numbering

A master index of numbered operations has been compiled for universal application to all vehicles manufactured by Jaguar Cars Ltd., and therefore, because of the different specifications of various models, continuity of the numbering sequence cannot be maintained throughout this manual.

Each operation described in this manual is allocated a number from the master index and cross-refers with an identical number in the 'Repair Operation Times'. The number consists of six digits arranged in three pairs.

Each operation is laid out in the sequence required to complete the operation in the minimum time, as specified in the 'Repair Operation Times'.

Service Tools

Where performance of an operation requires the use of a service tool, the tool number is quoted under the operation heading and is repeated in, following, the instruction involving its use. A list of all necessary tools is included in section 1, number 99.

References

References to the left- or right-hand side in the manual are made when viewing from the rear. With the engine and gearbox assembly removed the timing cover end of the engine is referred to as the front. A key to abbreviations and symbols is given in section 1, number 01.

REPAIRS AND REPLACEMENTS

When service parts are required it is essential that only genuine Jaguar/Daimler or Unipart replacements are used. Attention is particularly drawn to the following points concerning repairs and the fitting of replacement parts and accessories.

1.   Safety features embodied in the vehicle may be impaired if other than genuine parts are fitted. In certain territories, legislation prohibits the fitting of parts not to the vehicle manufacturer's specification.

2.   Torque wrench setting figures given in this Service Manual must be strictly adhered to.

3.   Locking devices, where specified, must be fitted. If the efficiency of a locking device is impaired during removal it must be replaced.

4.   Owners purchasing accessories while travelling abroad should ensure that the accessory and its fitted location on the vehicle conform to mandatory requirements existing in their country of origin.

5.   The vehicle warranty may be invalidated by the fitting of other than genuine Jaguar/Daimler or Unipart parts. All Jaguar/Daimler and Unipart replacements have the full backing of the factory warranty.

6.   Jaguar/Daimler Dealers are obliged to supply only genuine service parts.

SPECIFICATION

Purchasers are advised that the specification details set out in this Manual apply to a range of vehicles and not to any one. For the specification of a particular vehicle, purchasers should consult their Dealer.

The Manufacturers reserve the right to vary their specifications with or without notice, and at such times and in such manner as they think fit. Major as well as minor changes may be involved in accordance with the Manufacturer's policy of constant product improvement.

Whilst every effort is made to ensure the accuracy of the particulars contained in this Manual, neither the Manufacturer nor the Dealer, by whom this Manual is supplied, shall in any circumstances be held liable for any inaccuracy or the consequences thereof.

CONTENTS

44—1

LIST OF COMPONENTS

1. Converter securing bolt
2. Stoneguard
3. Converter housing
4. Rear oil seal
5. Rear extension housing
6. Gasket
7. Transmission case
8. Governor feed, lubrication and return pipes
9. Stoneguard
10. Converter

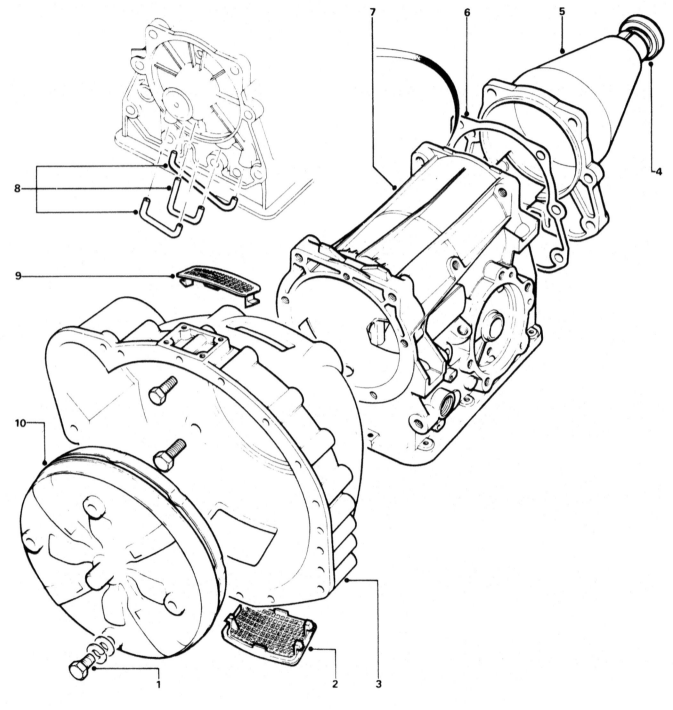

Fig. 1

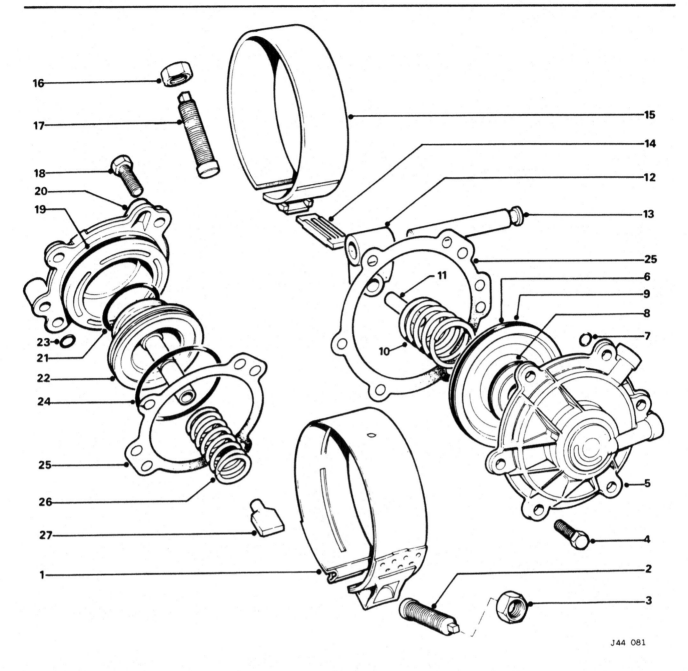

J44 081

Fig. 2

LIST OF COMPONENTS

1. Front brake band
2. Adjusting screw
3. Locknut
4. Cover securing bolt
5. Rear servo cover
6. Piston
7. 'O' ring
8. Piston sealing ring
9. Piston sealing ring

10. Piston return spring
11. Operating rod
12. Fulcrum
13. Fulcrum pin
14. Brake band strut
15. Rear brake band
16. Locknut
17. Adjusting screw
18. Cover securing bolt

19. 'O' ring
20. Front servo cover
21. Piston sealing ring
22. Piston
23. 'O' ring
24. Piston sealing ring
25. Gasket
26. Piston return spring
27. Brake band strut

44—3

DESCRIPTION

TORQUE CONVERTER

The torque converter is of the three-element, single-phase type. The three elements are: impeller, connected to the engine crankshaft; turbine, connected to the gearbox input shaft, and stator, mounted on a one-way clutch on the stator support projecting from the gearbox case. The converter provides torque multiplication of from 1 : 1 to 2.3 : 1 and the speed range during which this multiplication is obtained varies with the accelerator position.

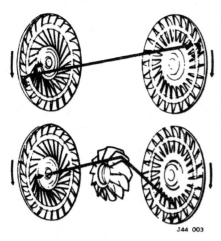

Fig. 3

GEAR SET

The planetary gear set consists of two sun gears, two sets of pinions, a pinion carrier and a ring gear.

Power enters the gear set via the two sun gears, the forward sun gear driving in forward gears, the reverse sun gear driving in reverse gear. The ring gear, attached to the output shaft, is the driven gear. The planet wheels connect driving and driven gears, two sets of planet wheels being used in forward gears and one set in reverse.

The planet carrier locates the planet wheels relative to sun and ring gears, also serving as a reaction member.

CLUTCHES

The gearbox input shaft is connected to the torque converter turbine at the front end and is therefore known as the turbine shaft. The rear end of the shaft is connected to the front and rear clutches; (the clutches are of the multi-disc type operated by hydraulic pressure). Engagement of the front clutch connects the turbine shaft to the forward sun gear. Engagement of the rear clutch connects the turbine shaft to the reverse sun gear.

BRAKE BANDS

The brake bands, operated by hydraulic servos, are used to hold drive train components stationary in order to obtain low, intermediate and reverse gears. The front band is clamped

around the rear clutch outer drum to hold the reverse sun gear stationary. The rear band is clamped around the planet carrier to hold the planet carrier stationary.

ONE-WAY CLUTCH

The one-way clutch is situated between the planet carrier and the gearbox case. Rotation of the planet carrier and the gearbox against engine direction is prevented so providing the reaction member for low gear (drive). Rotation of the planet carrier in engine direction is allowed (free-wheeling) providing smooth changes from low to intermediate and intermediate to low gears.

MECHANICAL POWER FLOWS

Neutral and Park

In neutral the front and rear clutches are off, and no power is transmitted from converter to the gear set. The front and rear bands are also released. In 'P' the rear servo circuit is pressurized while the engine is running, so that the rear band is applied.

First gear ('D') selected

The front clutch is applied, connecting converter to the forward sun gear. The one-way

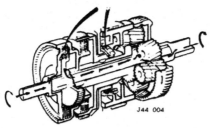

Fig. 4

clutch is in operation, preventing the planet carrier from rotating anti-clockwise. When the vehicle is coasting, the one-way clutch overruns and the gear set free-wheels.

First gear ('1' selected)

The front clutch is applied, connecting converter to forward sun gear. The rear band is applied, holding the planet carrier stationary.

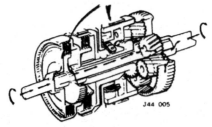

Fig. 5

Planet pinions drive ring gear, and reverse sun gear rotates freely in the opposite direction to the forward sun gear.

Second gear ('D', '2' or '1' selected)

Again the front clutch is applied, connecting converter to forward sun gear. The front band

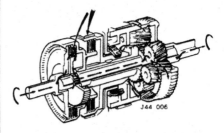

Fig. 6

is applied, holding the reverse sun gear stationary. Combined rotation of planet pinions and carrier drive the ring gear.

Third gear ('D' selected)

Again the front clutch is applied, connecting converter to forward sun gear. The rear clutch is applied, connecting the converter also to the

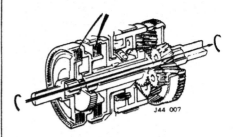

Fig. 7

reverse sun gear; thus both sun gears are locked together and the gear set rotates as a unit, providing a ratio of 1 : 1.

Reverse gear ('R' selected)

The rear clutch is applied, connecting converter to reverse sun gear. The rear band is

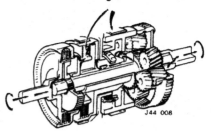

Fig. 8

applied, holding planet carrier stationary. Planet pinions drive ring gear in an opposite direction to engine rotation.

44—4

IDENTIFICATION

The Model 66 Automatic Gearbox was introduced on the Series III 6-cylinder Jaguar and Daimler Cars.

The two initial production transmissions were:

1. 066L transmission for use with the Jaguar XJ6 4.2. This can be identified by the yellow name-plate which will have 'Model 66' and the number 6066 in raised, polished figures.

2. 067H transmission for use with the Jaguar XJ6 3.4. This can be identified by the golden brown name-plate which will have 'Model 66' and the number 6067 in raised, polished figures.

Listed below are some of the improvements and modifications which have been built into this transmission.

CONVERTER

The Model 66 converter turbine hub has an increased spline size to take the larger input shaft.

The stator one-way clutch inner race has a revised profile and increase in hardness.

A Torrington race has been introduced into the impeller side of the stator.

The impeller blades have a rib formed in them to give added strength; this will be introduced into all 11 in torque converters.

Six impeller blades are welded in two places, equally spaced, to the impeller shell, again giving added strength.

The blower ring has been deleted on Model 66 converters, and the converter mounting bosses will be CO_2-welded to the front cover.

PUMP

A groove has been added to the pump/converter bush to improve lubrication of the bush. The groove stops short of the front edge of the bush (oil seal side) to prevent the oil seal being swamped.

A tin/aluminium pump drive gear bush, has also been introduced.

The new stator support will have an increased diameter bush to accommodate the increased diameter input shaft.

A large pump suction tube has been introduced to ensure that the end of the tube is immersed in oil under all conditions.

INPUT SHAFT AND FRONT CLUTCH ASSEMBLY

An increased diameter input shaft is being introduced on the Model 66 transmission.

REAR CLUTCH AND FRONT DRUM ASSEMBLY

To improve the lubrication path to the rear clutch and front band, changes have been made to this assembly. They are:

The rear clutch piston face (clutch plate side) will have four slots at right angles to one another to improve the oil flow from the inside diameter to outside diameter of the clutch pack.

The four wide grooves on the inside diameter of the front drum (steel clutch plate splines area) have been deepened to enable more oil flow around the plates.

Between the outside and inside diameter of the front drum, so that they line up with the four deepened grooves, four holes have been drilled to enable an oil feed to the front band to be maintained.

The rearmost lubrication groove between the three sealing ring grooves of the front drum has been deepened and the holes size increased in order to improve the oil flow.

The lubrication feed hole in the reverse sun gear has been increased in diameter.

ONE-WAY CLUTCH ASSEMBLY

An uprated 1st speed one-way clutch assembly has been introduced which will have 30 sprags instead of the 24 sprags on existing assemblies.

The centre support of the transmission has an increased diameter rear clutch and lubrication drillings.

CARRIER ASSEMBLY

An improved lubrication oil-flow has been achieved by introducing a wider bush into the carrier cover which has opposing helical oil grooves.

Non-crowned, shaved, short pinions have been introduced. In order to improve their durability, these pinions have no identification groove.

OUTPUT SHAFT

The lubrication hole in the output shaft has an increased diameter on Model 66 transmissions.

MAINCASE AND SERVOS

The front clutch and governor feed hole in the rear of the maincase has been increased to 5,0 mm.

The rear servo piston and cover have been strengthened.

OIL-PAN

In order to improve cooling and to ensure that the pump suction pipe is at all times below the fluid level a deep oil-pan is being used on the transmission.

VALVE BLOCK

An adjustable cam bracket is fitted.

A transmission oil filter spacer is being used on the transmission now that a deep oil-pan is employed.

MISCELLANEOUS

A 5 mm spirol pin, secured by a split pin in the transmission cross-shaft is now fitted.

With the deep oil-pan, as fitted to the Model 66, the total fluid capacity, from dry, is approximately 7,9 litres (14 pints; 17 U.S. pints).

CLUTCH AND BAND APPLICATION CHART

A. Front clutch
B. Rear clutch
C. Front band
D. Rear band
E. One-way clutch

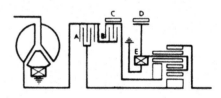

	A	B	C	D	E
1 (first gear)	●			●	
D (first gear)	●				●
2 & D (sec. ge)	●		●		
D (third gear)	●	●			
R (rev. gear)		●		●	

J44 082

44—5

KEY TO COMPONENTS SHOWN ON HYDRAULIC CHARTS

A. Torque converter
B. Front clutch
C. Rear clutch
D. Front servo
E. Rear servo
F. Governor
G. Pump
H. Primary regulator

J. Secondary regulator
K. 2–3 shift valve
L. 1–2 shift valve
M. Servo orifice control valve
N. Manual valve
P. Down-shift valve
Q. Throttle valve
R. Modulator valve

KEY TO HYDRAULIC CHART COLOUR CODE

— Pump pressure
— To torque converter
— Governor line pressure
— Throttle valve
— Pump suction

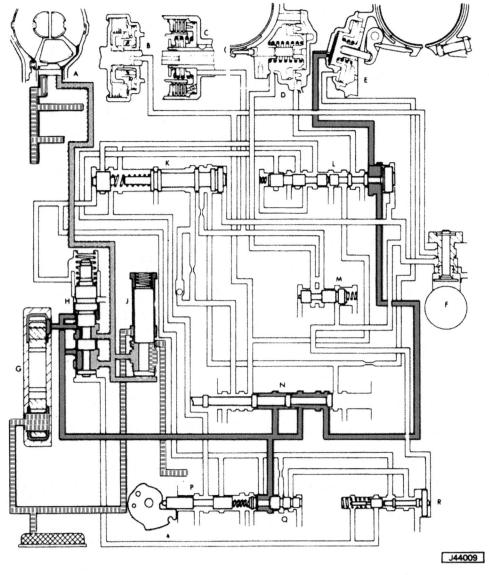

Fig. 9

HYDRAULIC OPERATION IN 'P' (PARK—Fig. 9)

Coupled to the manual valve operating lever is a linkage incorporating a pawl; movement of this lever to the 'Park' position engages the pawl with the toothed outer surface of the ring gear, so locking the output shaft to transmission case. The rear servo is energized in 'P' selection but, as both the front and rear clutches are not energized, drive is impossible and the transmission remains inoperative.

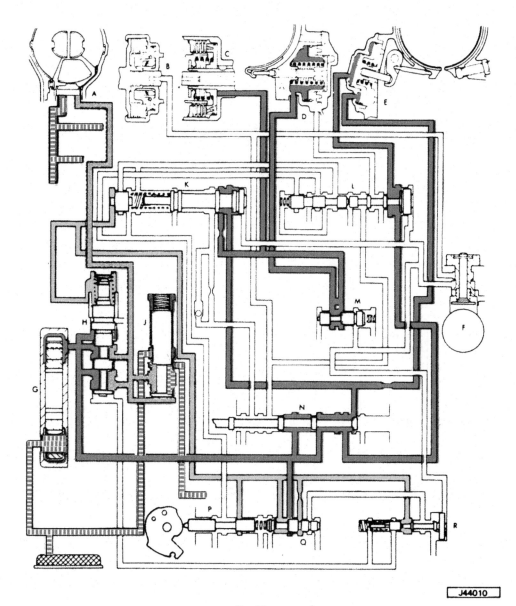

J44010

Fig. 10

HYDRAULIC OPERATION IN 'R' (REVERSE—Fig. 10)

Throttle pressure applied to spring end of primary regulator valve increases line pressure proportional to engine output. Manual valve directs line pressure through 1–2 shift valve to apply rear servo and through 2–3 shift valve to release front servo and apply rear clutch.

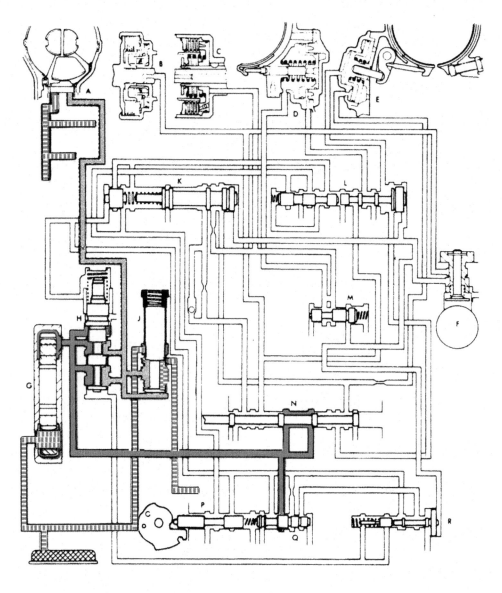

Fig. 11

J44011

HYDRAULIC OPERATION IN 'N' (NEUTRAL—Fig. 11)

With the engine running, the pump supplies fluid to the primary regulator which regulates line pressure.

Spill from the primary regulator supplies the torque converter and lubrication requirements. This supply is regulated by the secondary regulator.

The line pressure supplied to the manual and throttle valves is blocked by a land on the valves so that neither governor, clutches nor servos are energized.

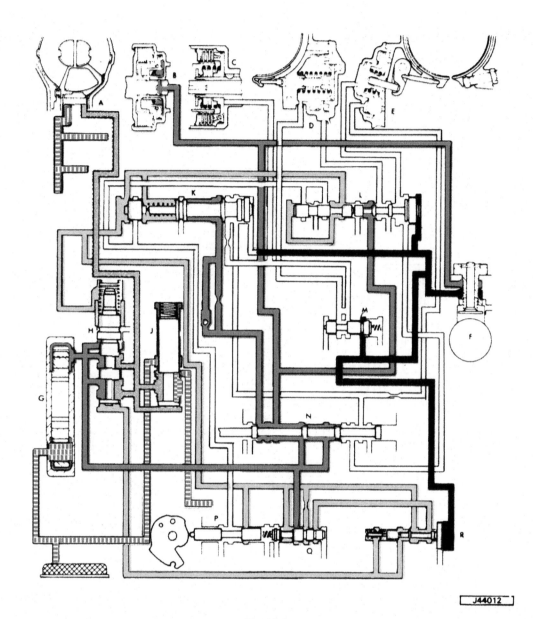

J44012

Fig. 12

HYDRAULIC OPERATION IN 'D' (FIRST GEAR)

Throttle pressure is applied to spring end of primary regulator valve. When throttle valve is in full throttle position, modulator valve plug applies regulated line pressure to other end of primary regulator valve thereby controlling shift quality.

Manual valve directs line pressure to apply front clutch thereby enabling vehicle to move off in first gear.

Manual valve also directs line pressure to governor feed and to 1–2, 2–3 shift valves for subsequent upwards gear-shifts.

44—9

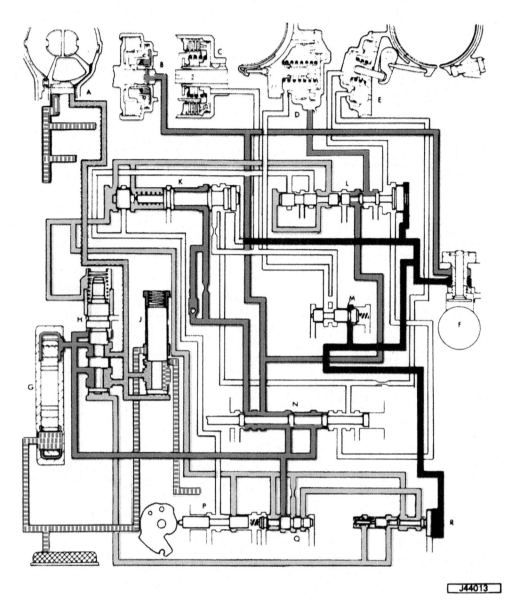

Fig. 13

J44013

HYDRAULIC OPERATION IN 'D' (SECOND GEAR—Fig. 13)

Pressure control by primary regulator valve functions as described in 'D' (First gear).

When governor pressure exceeds throttle pressure, 1–2 shift valve moves and directs line pressure to front servo which applies front brake band. Front clutch being applied, transmission operates in second gear.

When down-shift valve is in forced throttle (kick-down) position, forced throttle pressure acts upon 1–2 and 2–3 shift valves thereby delaying up-shifts or, if governor pressure is low, causes a 2–1 down-shift.

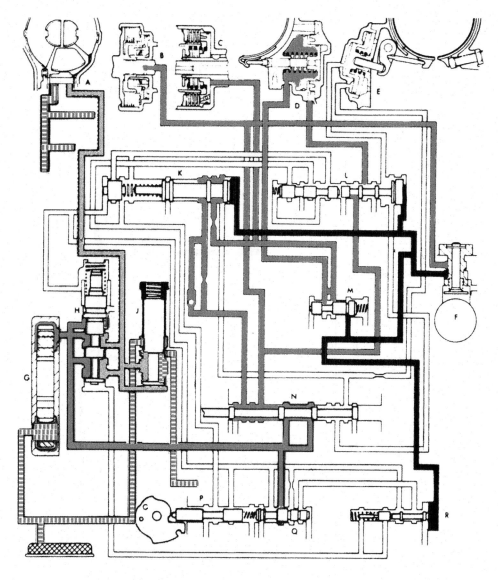

J44014

Fig. 14

HYDRAULIC OPERATION IN 'D' (THIRD GEAR—Fig. 14)

Pressure control by primary regulator valve functions as described in 'D' (First gear).

2–3 shift occurs early at light throttle or late at full throttle depending upon balance between governor and throttle pressure.

When governor pressure exceeds throttle pressure, 2–3 shift valve directs line pressure to rear clutch and also to 'release' side of front servo via servo orifice control valve.

The timed relationship between rear clutch 'apply' and front servo 'release' is dependent on governor pressure which in turn is controlled by road speed. A high governor pressure closes servo orifice control valve so directing front servo 'release' fluid through a restrictor thereby delaying front servo 'release' in relation to rear clutch 'apply'

44—11

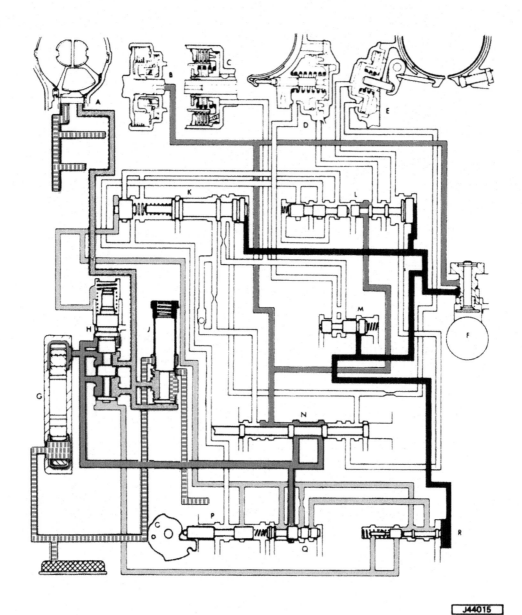

J44015

Fig. 15

HYDRAULIC OPERATION IN '2' (LOW GEAR)—Fig. 15

Pressure control by primary regulator valve functions as described in 'D' (First gear). Front clutch is applied but as engine speed is low, governor pressure causes 1–2 shift valve to remain closed thereby blocking feed from modulator valve.

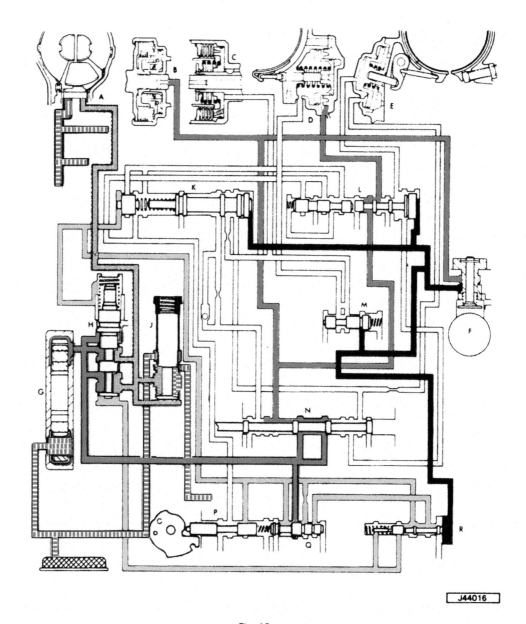

J44016

Fig. 16

HYDRAULIC OPERATION IN '2' (SECOND GEAR)—Fig. 16

Front clutch is still applied and as engine speed increases, governor pressure rises and moves 1–2 shift valve. This allows pressure from manual valve to front servo 'apply'

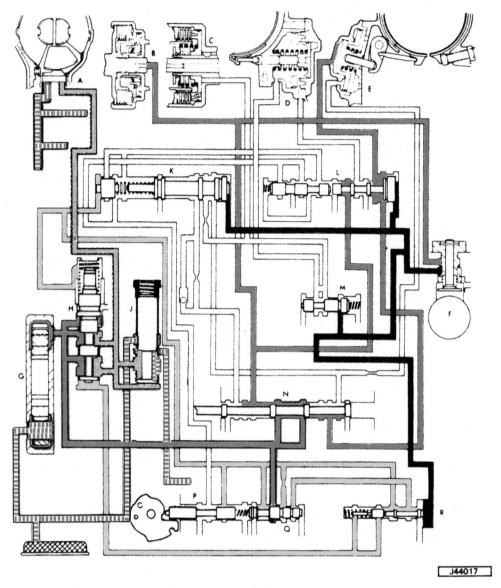

Fig. 17

HYDRAULIC OPERATION IN '1' (LOW GEAR)—Fig. 17

Pressure control by primary regulator valve functions as described in 'D' (First gear). Manual valve directs line pressure to front clutch governor feed and 1–2 shift valve. Pressure is also directed to enlarged end of 1–2 shift valve so opposing governor pressure and hydraulically locking the valve. Rear servo is also applied and no up-shift can occur.

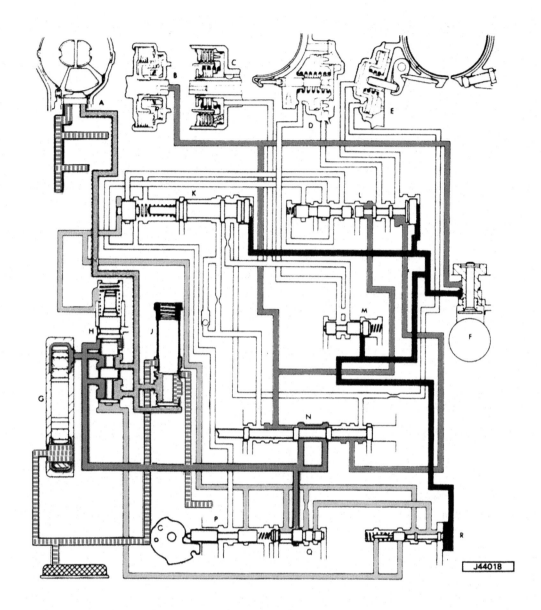

J44018

Fig. 18

HYDRAULIC OPERATION IN '1' (SECOND GEAR)—Fig. 18

When selector lever is moved to position '1' at speed, front servo is released and a down-shift from high to intermediate gear occurs. A further down-shift to low gear occurs when vehicle speed falls sufficiently.

VALVE SPRING IDENTIFICATION

The following spring identification table is given to assist in identifying valve springs when overhaul work is being carried out. When valve block is dismantled, springs should be compared with dimensions given. Any spring which is distorted or coil bound **must** be replaced.

DESCRIPTION	LENGTH		DIAMETER		NUMBER OF COILS	COLOUR
	mm	in	mm	in		
Secondary regulator valve	65,8	2.593	12,2 to 12,4	0.480 to 0.490	23	Blue
Primary regulator valve	74,6	2.94	15,3 to 15,5	0.604 to 0.610	14	Blue
*Servo orifice control valve—Model 65	32,0	1.281	5,0 to 5,3	0.198 to 0.208	17	Yellow
Servo orifice control valve—Model 66	27,5	1.08	5,0 to 5,3	0.198 to 0.208	17	Yellow
2–3 shift valve	40,4	1.59	6,9 to 7,2	0.275 to 0.285	22.5	Yellow
1–2 shift valve	27,7	1.094	5,8 to 6,1	0.230 to 0.240	13	Plain
Downshift valve	20,5	0.807	3,4 to 3,7	0.136 to 0.146	28	Yellow
Modulator valve	27,1	1.069	3,8 to 4,1	0.150 to 0.160	19	Plain
Throttle valve	29,8 to 30,1	1.175 to 1.185	5,8 to 6,1	0.230 to 0.240	18	Green
Dump ball valve	17,7	0.70	5,3 to 5,8	0.210 to 0.230	16	Plain or white

***NOTE:** Should 3–2 kick-down flare-up occur at speeds of approximately 80 km/h (50 m.p.h.) and front band adjustment is correct, the shorter spring (Model 66), should be fitted.

TORQUE WRENCH SETTINGS

SECTION 44

ITEM	DESCRIPTION	Nm	kgf m	lbf ft
Transmission case to converter housing	M10 X 30 (1.5P)	33,89 to 40,67	3,46 to 4,15	25 to 30
	M12 X 30 (1.75P)	54,23 to 67,79	5,53 to 6,90	40 to 50
Oil pan to transmission case	M6 X 15 (1.0P)	7,79	0,80	5.75
Front servo cover	M8 X 25 (1.25P)	17,62 to 24,40	1,80 to 2,48	13 to 18
Rear servo cover	M8 X 25 (1.25P)	17,62 to 24,40	1,80 to 2,48	13 to 18
Oil pump adaptor to oil pump housing	10—24 U.N.C. X 2A X 5/8	3,38	0,35	2.5
	5/16 in—18 U.N.C. 2A X. 7/8	23,04 to 29,82	2,35 to 3,04	17 to 22
Oil pump adaptor to transmission case	M8 X 25 (1.25P)	17,62 to 24,40	1,80 to 2,48	13 to 18
Pressure point on transmission case	1/8 in—27 Dryseal N.P.T.F.	8,13 to 10,84	0,83 to 1,11	6 to 8
Oil pan drain plug	3/8 in—24 X 3/8 in	12,20 to 16,26	1,24 to 1,66	9 to 12
Upper valve body to lower valve body	10—24 U.N.C. 2A X 5/8 in	2,30 to 3,38	0,23 to 0,35	1.7 to 2.5
Lower valve body to upper valve body	10—24 U.N.C. 2A X 15/16	2,30 to 3,38	0,23 to 0,35	1.7 to 2.5
Lower valve body to upper valve body	10—24 U.N.C. 2A X 1 3/8 in	2,30 to 3,38	0,23 to 0,35	1.7 to 2.5
Suction tube assembly to lower valve body	10—24 U.N.C. 2A X 3/8 in	2,30 to 3,38	0,23 to 0,35	1.7 to 2.5
Oil tube plate to lower valve body	10—24 U.N.C. 2A X 5/8 in	2,30 to 3,38	0,23 to 0,35	1.7 to 2.5
	10—24 U.N.C. 2A X 15/16 in	2,30 to 3,38	0,23 to 0,35	1.7 to 2.5
End plate to lower valve body	10—24 U.N.C. 2A X 5/8 in	2,30 to 3,38	0,23 to 0,35	1.7 to 2.5
End plate to upper valve body	10—24 U.N.C. 2A X 3/8 in	2,30 to 3,38	0,23 to 0,35	1.7 to 2.5
Lower valve body to transmission case	1/4 in—20 U.N.C. 2A X 1 1/4 in	6,77 to 10,84	0,69 to 1,11	5 to 8
Lower valve body to cam bracket	No. 10 U.N.F. bolt	2,71 to 4,74	0,27 to 0,48	2 to 3.5
Tube location plate	M5 bolt (0.8P)	2,30 to 2,71	0,23 to 0,27	1.7 to 2.0
Detent spring to lower valve body		2,30 to 2,71	0,23 to 0,27	1.7 to 2.0
Servo adjusting screw locknuts	9/16 in U.N.C. nut	40,67 to 54,23	4,15 to 5,55	30 to 40
Oil cooler connector	1/4 in N.P.T.F.	27,11 to 29,82	2,77 to 3,04	20 to 22
Extension housing to case	7/16 in U.N.F. bolt	54,23 to 67,79	5,55 to 6,90	40 to 50
Extension housing to case	7/16 in U.N.C.	40,67 to 67,79	4,15 to 6,90	30 to 50
Inhibitor switch to main case	No. 10 U.N.C. bolt	5,42 to 6,77	0,55 to 0,69	4 to 5
Park cam plate to main case	M6 bolt (1.0P)	6,77 to 10,84	0,69 to 1,11	5 to 8
Coupling flange nut	M20 nut (1.5P)	98,02 to 117,68	10,0 to 12,0	72,3 to 86,8
Governor retainer	M24 bolt	20,33 to 24,40	2,07 to 2,49	15 to 18
Coupling flange	5/8 in U.N.C. nut	77,57 to 81,34	7,60 to 8,29	55 to 60
Centre support fixing	3/8 in U.N.C. bolt	13,55 to 20,33	1,38 to 2,07	10 to 15
Connector	1/2 in U.N.S. nut	13,55 to 16,26	1,38 to 1,66	10 to 12
Coupling flange	1/2 in U.N.F. bolt	54,23 to 67,79	5,55 to 6,90	40 to 50
Dipstick tube attachment	7/8 in U.N.S. nut	37,96 to 43,38	3,87 to 4,42	28 to 32

GEAR-CHANGE SPEEDS

	LIGHT THROTTLE		FULL THROTTLE		KICK DOWN		DOWN SHIFT	ROLL OUT
	1—2	2—3	1—2	2—3	3—2	3—1	3—2*	2—1
3,4 litre								
k.p.h.	11 to 16	25 to 29	55 to 60	96 to 106	96 to 105	55 to 60	70 to 74	8 to 11
m.p.h.	7 to 10	16 to 18	34 to 38	60 to 66	60 to 65	34 to 37	44 to 46	5 to 7
3.54:1 axle								
4,2 litre								
k.p.h.	13 to 19	21 to 29	66 to 82	117 to 130	101 to 117	40 to 56	51 to 67	8 to 16
m.p.h.	8 to 12	13 to 18	41 to 51	73 to 81	63 to 73	25 to 35	32 to 42	5 to 10
3,31:1 axle								
4,2 litre								
k.p.h.	13 to 19	21 to 30	67 to 85	120 to 134	104 to 120	42 to 59	53 to 69	8 to 16
m.p.h.	8 to 12	13 to 19	42 to 53	75 to 84	65 to 75	26 to 37	33 to 43	5 to 10
3.07:1 axle								
4,2 litre								
k.p.h.	14 to 19	21 to 30	67 to 85	120 to 136	104 to 120	42 to 59	53 to 69	8 to 16
m.p.h.	9 to 12	13 to 19	42 to 53	75 to 85	65 to 75	26 to 37	33 to 43	5 to 10
3.058:1 axle								
4,2 litre								
k.p.h.	14 to 21	22 to 32	72 to 90	128 to 144	110 to 128	45 to 62	56 to 74	8 to 18
m.p.h.	9 to 13	14 to 20	45 to 56	80 to 90	69 to 80	28 to 39	35 to 46	5 to 11
2.88:1 axle								

* Part throttle kick down

NOTE: The figures in these tables are theoretical and actual figures may vary slightly from those quoted due to such factors as tyre wear, pressures, etc.

CAUTION

Ensure that when the downshift cable is disconnected from the throttle linkage the crimp stop gap must be reset to achieve correct gearbox pressures. If there is no crimp fitted to the cable, the gearbox pressures must be reset using the appropriate special equipment.
Failure to carry out the above procedure could lead to a rapid deterioration of gearbox condition.

GENERAL DATA

Gear train end-float	0,21 to 0,73 mm	0.008 to 0.029 in
Pinion end-float	0,25 to 0,51 mm	0.010 to 0.020 in
Minimum clutch plate coning	0,25 mm	0.010 in
Thrust washer sizes: Standard	1,72 mm	0.068 in
Alternative	2,03 mm	0.080 in
Control pressure	4,2 to 6,33 kgf/cm^2	60 to 90 lbf/in^2
Stall speed (normal)	1,950 to 2,100 rev/min	
Cooling capacity of oil cooler up to VIN 352906	2,8 Kw	
from VIN 352906	5,3 Kw	

44—17

ROAD TEST AND FAULT DIAGNOSIS

The following points should be checked before proceeding with the road test.

1. Fluid level.
2. Engine idle speed.
3. Manual lever adjustment.

ROAD TEST

The road speed figures for the tests listed below are to be found under 'GENERAL DATA—GEAR CHANGE SPEEDS'.

Road testing should follow the complete sequence detailed below. Transmission should be at normal working temperature, i.e. after being driven on road or rollers.

1. With brakes applied and engine idling, move selector from:

    'N' to 'R'
    'N' to 'D'
    'N' to '2'
    'N' to '1'

    Engagement should be felt with each selection.
2. Check stall speed.
3. Select 'D', accelerate with minimum throttle opening and check speed of first gear to second gear shift.
4. Continue with minimum throttle and check speed of second gear to third gear shift.
5. Select 'D', accelerate with maximum throttle opening (kick-down) and check speed of first gear to second gear shift.
6. Continue with maximum throttle and check speed of second gear to third gear shift.
7. Check for kick-down shift third gear to second gear.
8. Check for kick-down shift second gear to first gear.
9. Check for kick-down shift third gear to first gear.
10. Check for 'roll-out' down-shift with minimum throttle, second gear to first gear.
11. Check for part throttle down-shift, third gear to second gear.

Should a fault be apparent during road test, first identify the problem from the list printed in the Fault Diagnosis Chart. The reference numbers shown opposite each fault may be translated by reference to the list headed 'TRANSMISSION FAULT KEY'.

TRANSMISSION FAULT KEY

ACTIONS

1	Check fluid level.
2	Check manual selector/adjustment.
3	Reduce engine idle speed.
4	Check down-shift throttle cable/adjustment.
	If pressure cannot be corrected, dismantle and clean valve bodies.
	For low pressure also check strainer, alloy suction pipe, 'O' ring and pump.
5	Check front brake band adjustment.
6	Check rear brake band adjustment.
7	Check front servo seals and fit of pipes.
8	Check rear servo seals and fit of pipe.
9	Examine front clutch, support housing and forward sun gear shaft seals.
10	Check rear clutch feed pipe.
11	Strip valve bodies and clean.
12	Strip governor valve and clean.
13	Examine output shaft rings and governor pressure tube seals.
14	Check front brake band for wear.
15	Check rear brake band for wear.
16	Adjust/examine parking pawl, linkage, and gear.
17	Renew one-way clutch.
18	Examine pump gears and converter nose bush.
19	Strip and examine gear train.
20	Replace torque converter.
21	Examine rear clutch and sealing rings.
22	Test inhibitor switch, circuit, and check for operation.
23	Check one-way clutch (possibly fitted backwards).
24	Ball check valve in forward sun gear shaft faulty, no detriment to performance.

FAULT DIAGNOSIS

STATIONARY TEST FINDINGS	ACTION
Starter will not operate in 'P' or 'N' or operates in all positions	22
Faulty operation of reverse lights	22
Excessive bump on engagement of 'D', '1' and 'R'	3, 4
Drives in 'N' also giving judder or no drive in 'R' depending on degree of front clutch seizure	2, 9

STALL TEST FINDINGS

Stall test shows over 2 100 rev/min (transmission slip), with possible squawk in '1' and 'R'	4
a. only in '1'	9
b. only in 'R'	6, 8, 10, 21, 1!
Stall test shows under 1 300 rev/min (slipping stator)	20

DRIVING TEST FINDINGS

Selection faults

Incorrect selection of all positions except 'P'	2
Parking pawl does not hold vehicle	16

Ratio faults

No drive in 'D', '2', '1' or 'R' but 'P' operates	1, 2, 4
No drive in 'D', '2' or '1'	12, 13, 9
No drive in 'D' 1st ratio	17
No drive in '1' and transmission binding during shift from '1' to 'D'	23
No second ratio	5, 7, 11
No D3 (Reverse indicating rear clutch normal)	11
Drag in 'D'	6
Drag in 'D', '1' and reverse	5
No engine braking in '1' and no drive in reverse ratio	6, 8, 15
Moves off in 2nd ratio in 'D' and '1' and no drive in reverse or engine braking in '1'	11

Shift point faults

Incorrect or erratic 'kick-down' and/or light throttle shift points	4, 12, 13
1–2 shift only incorrect	11
2–3 shifts only incorrect	11
No up-shifts	12, 13
Lack of 'up-shifts' and no reverse ratio	11
Moves off with possible transmission slip	12
Reduced maximum speed in all ratios, more so in 'D', and severe converter overheating	20

Shift quality faults

Bumpy and possibly delayed shifts	4
Slip (engine 'flare-up') shifting into and out of second ratio	5, 7, 11, 14
Slip (engine 'flare-up') on 2–3 and 3–2 shifts*	10, 11, 21

Noise faults

Whining noise from converter area, continuous whenever the engine is running	18
Irregular (possibly grating) noises from gearbox but not in 'D'	19
Whine from converter, for short period following engine starting after vehicle has been standing for, say, not less than 12 hours	24

* See Note on page 44–17.

DOWN-SHIFT CABLE

Remove and refit   **44.15.01**

Service tool: Down-shift cable remover tool CBW 62

Removing

Unscrew the union nut (1, Fig. 19), withdraw the dipstick tube; drain and discard fluid.
Remove the bolts and plain washers (2, Fig. 19) securing oil pan to transmission case.
Lower the oil pan (3, Fig. 19) remove and discard the gasket.

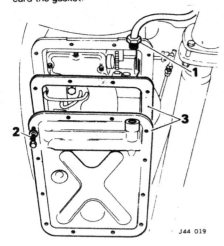

Fig. 19

Disconnect cable from cam.
Position cable remover tool CBW 62 on plastic ferrule, push the tool upwards until the ferrule, together with the cable is pressed out of the transmission case.
Remove the split pin, washer and clevis pin (1, Fig. 20) securing clevis to throttle linkage; discard the split pin.
Slacken the locknut (2, Fig. 20), withdraw down-shift cable.

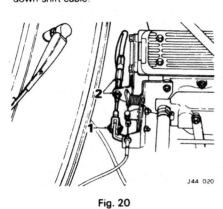

Fig. 20

Refitting

If old cable is being refitted, renew the 'O' ring on ferrule.
Lubricate the ferrule with clean transmission fluid.

CAUTION: Do not lubricate the inner cable.

Press the ferrule into the gearcase; connect cable to cam.
Connect clevis to throttle linkage; use a new split pin.
With the accelerator pedal released and the throttle levers resting on the idle speed screws, adjust the cable until the heel of the down-shift cam just makes contact with the down-shift valve.
With the accelerator pedal depressed, check that the lobe of the cam fully depresses the down-shift valve.
Refit the oil pan, smear the new gasket with grease.
Tighten bolts by diagonal selection to the specified torque figure.

CAUTION: Due to the method of construction it is not possible to completely drain the transmission fluid, and this should be taken into account when the transmission is being refilled.

Fill the transmission to the 'MAX' mark on the dipstick.
Apply the handbrake and select 'P' position.
Run the engine until it reaches normal operating temperature.
With the engine still running, withdraw the dipstick (1, Fig. 21), wipe clean and replace.
Immediately withdraw the dipstick and note the reading on the 'HOT' side of the dipstick (2, Fig. 21).
If necessary, add fluid to bring the level on the dipstick to 'MAX' (3, Fig. 21).

NOTE: The difference between the 'MAX' and 'MIN' marks on the dipstick represents approximately 0,75 litre (1½ pints, 2 U.S. pints).

Carry out the down-shift cable pressure check, see 44.30.03.

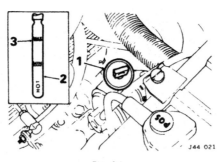

Fig. 21

GEAR SELECTOR CABLE

Remove and refit   **44.15.08**

Removing

This operation requires the removal of the centre console side casing, details of which are to be found in Section 76.

Place the quadrant selector lever in '1'.
Unscrew the gear selector knob (1, Fig. 22).
Remove the four nuts (2, Fig. 22) securing the selector indicator assembly; withdraw the indicator assembly over the selector lever (3, Fig. 22).
Remove the split pin and washer (4, Fig. 22) securing the cable to selector lever; detach the cable (5, Fig. 22).
Unscrew the front locknut (6, Fig. 22) securing the cable to abutment bracket.
Lift the carpet from left-hand side of transmission tunnel.
Remove the screws (7, Fig. 22) securing the cable shroud to the transmission tunnel; withdraw the shroud.
Withdraw the cable from the abutment bracket.

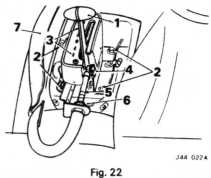

Fig. 22

Remove the screws securing the access panel to the transmission tunnel.
Withdraw the panel; clean off old sealing compound.
Ensure that the gearbox selector lever is in '1'.
Remove the nut securing the selector cable to the gearbox selector lever; detach the cable.
Remove the bolt and spring washer (1, Fig. 23) securing the trunnion block.
Withdraw the cable (2, Fig. 23).

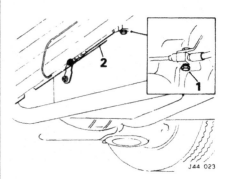

Fig. 23

44—20

Refitting

Refit the cable and position the selector lever in '1'.

Refit the panel, shroud and carpet.

CAUTION: Seal the access panel and the hole in the shroud with a suitable sealing compound.

Fit the front locknut (1, Fig. 24) to the cable but do not tighten at this stage.

Ensure that the gearbox selector and quadrant selector levers are in '1'

Adjust the front (1, Fig. 24) and rear (2, Fig. 24) locknuts until the cable can be connected to the quadrant lever without either quadrant or gearbox lever being disturbed.

Tighten the locknuts, secure the cable with a new split pin (3, Fig. 24).

Refit the selector indicator assembly and gear knob.

Place the selector lever in 'P' and replace the console as detailed in 76.25.01.

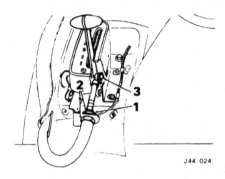

Fig. 24

STARTER INHIBITOR SWITCH

Check and adjust   44.15.18

Adjusting

Disconnect the battery.

Unscrew the gear selector knob (1, Fig. 25). Remove the three screws securing the gear selector surround panel, do not disconnect the window switches. Slightly displace the panel to obtain access to the cigar lighter terminals. Note the fitted position of the cigar lighter terminals, before disconnecting.

Remove four nuts securing the selector indicator assembly and remove the assembly.

Detach the feed cable (2, Fig. 25) from the inhibitor switch.

Connect a test lamp and battery (3, Fig. 25) in series with the switch.

NOTE: Switch is in the earthed position.

Place selector lever (6, Fig. 25) in 'N' position. Slacken the locknuts (5, Fig. 25) securing the switch and adjust the position of the switch until the lamp lights.

Tighten the locknuts, check that the lamp remains on with the lever in 'P' position and is off with the lever in drive position.

Remove the battery and test lamp, reconnect the feed cable to the switch.

Refit the selector indicator assembly.

Reconnect the cigar lighter and refit the gear selector surround panel.

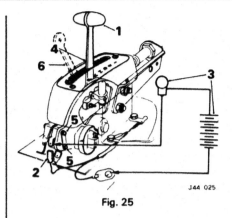

Fig. 25

Refit the gear selector knob and reconnect the battery.

Check operation of the window switches and cigar lighter.

TRANSMISSION UNIT

Remove and refit   44.20.01

Includes:

Torque converter—remove and refit   **44.17.07**

Torque converter housing—remove and refit   **44.17.01**

Service tools: Engine support bracket MS 53A, transmission unit lift.

Removing

Drive the vehicle onto a ramp and disconnect the battery.

Remove the dipstick from the dipstick tube; remove the bolt securing the dipstick tube to the manifold.

Remove the bolts securing the upper fan cowl to the lower fan cowl. Slacken the bolts securing the cowl bracket to the radiator, to facilitate the removal of the top cowl.

Remove and discard the split pin securing the kick-down cable to the throttle bell-crank, withdraw the clevis pin and washer; slacken the locknut and disconnect the cable.

Raise the ramp.

Undo the union nut securing the dipstick tube to the transmission unit sump pan. Remove the dipstick tube, plug the ends to prevent the ingress of dirt. Drain and discard the transmission fluid.

Disconnect the exhaust intermediate pipe from the down-pipe, remove the olive. Remove the exhaust heat shields from the floor pan.

Position the transmission unit lift under the transmission unit, and take the weight. Secure the transmission unit to the lift.

Remove the bolts securing the crash plate to the transmission case studs, undo the nut securing the crash plate to the rear mounting spigot bolt.

Remove the bolts, spacers and washers securing the rear engine mounting to the floor pan.

Remove the bolts securing the propeller shaft tunnel spreader plate to the floor pan.

Chock the front wheels.

Using a ramp jack raise the rear wheels. This will enable the propeller shaft to be rotated and the propeller shaft to output flange fixings removed.

Move the propeller shaft clear of the output flange.

Lower the transmission unit lift to the position required for transmission unit removal; DO NOT REMOVE the transmission unit at this stage.

CAUTION: Take care not to damage the water heater valve.

Position the engine support bracket, MS 53A, and locate the hook to the engine rear lifting eye. Turn the adjusting nut to take the weight of the engine (Fig. 26).

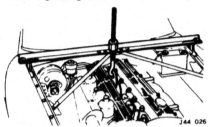

Fig. 26

Lower the ramp jack under rear of car.

Remove the rubber pad from the top of the transmission unit.

Remove the nut securing the selector lever bell-crank to the cross-shaft and remove the bell-crank.

Remove the bolt securing the selector cable trunnion to the mounting bracket.

Remove the bolts securing the tie-plate to the engine sump pan and transmission converter housing front cover-plate and remove the cover-plate.

Rotate the engine until a torque converter securing bolt is accessible; knock back the lock tab and remove the bolt; repeat this procedure for the three remaining torque converter securing bolts.

Remove and discard the tab washers.

Remove the bolt and washer securing the breather pipe clip.

Remove the screw securing the oil cooler pipe clamp plate to the sump bracket.

Disconnect the oil cooler and breather pipes from the transmission casing; plug or tape broken connections to prevent the ingress of dirt.

Disconnect the speedometer cable from the drive pinion (early models).

For later models fitted with electronic speedometer disconnect 2 pin connector only. Disconnect the cables from the starter motor and solenoid.

Ensure that the transmission unit is secured to the unit lift and that the platform is at the correct angle.

Remove the nuts, bolts and washers securing the torque converter housing tp the cylinder block, withdraw the starter motor and spacer. Withdraw the transmission unit lift rearwards and lower.

Remove the torque converter from the input shaft.

Remove the bolts and washers securing the torque converter housing to the transmission case

continued

Refitting

Refit the torque converter housing to the transmission case and tighten the securing bolts to the correct torque.

Refit the torque converter to the input shaft, ensuring that the drive dogs are correctly engaged.

Position and secure the transmission unit onto the transmission unit lift platform.

Position the rubber pad on the top of the transmission unit.

Manoeuvre the unit lift into position and raise to correctly position the transmission unit.

Refit the bolts securing the torque converter housing to the engine; do not tighten until the starter motor and spacer have been fitted.

Align the torque converter to drive plate fixing holes, fit the bolts, with new tab washers; DO NOT tighten until all four bolts are fitted. Bend over the tab washers.

Reconnect the cables to the starter motor and solenoid.

Refit the oil cooler pipes to the transmission unit, and refit clamp plate.

Refit the breather pipe.

Refit the converter front cover, and the tie-plate between the engine sump pan and the converter housing.

Raise the rear of the vehicle, using a ramp jack, to allow the propeller shaft to be refitted to the output flange; secure with the blts and new self-locking nuts.

Refit the gear selector bell-crank to the cross-shaft, fit and tighten the nut to secure.

Align the gear selector lever trunnion to the mounting plate, fit and tighten the bolt to secure.

Reconnect the speedometer cable to the drive pinion, tighten the knurled nut (early models).

On later models connect 2 pin electrical connector.

Raise the unit, refit the propeller shaft tunnel spreader plate, the exhaust heat shield, and the rear engine mounting.

Refit the crash plate, tighten the nuts securing the plate to the transmission case studs and spigot bolt.

Release the transmission unit from the unit lift and lower the lift. Remove the unit lift and engine support bracket MS 53A from the car. Lower and remove the ramp jack from the rear of the car.

Refit the intermediate exhaust pipe, smear the sealing olive with 'Fire Gum'. Fit and tighten the flange bolts.

Refit the dipstick tube to the oil pan and tighten the union nut.

Lower the ramp.

Refit the dipstick tube securing bolt to the manifold.

Refit the upper fan cowl.

Reconnect the kick-down cable, secure using a new split pin and adjust as described in operation 44.30.03.

Refill the transmission—refer to 44.24.02.

Road test the car.

TRANSMISSION ASSEMBLY

NOTE: WHERE ANY BENCHWORK IS UNDERTAKEN CBW-35-65 BENCH CRADLE MUST BE USED.

Overhaul   **44.20.06**

Service tools: Mainshaft end-float gauge

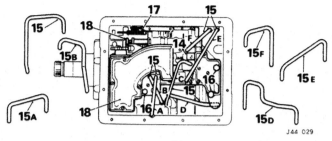

Fig. 28

CBW 87; circlip pliers 18G 1004; clutch spring compressor 18G 1016; torque screwdriver 18G 631; screwdriver bit adaptors CBW 547A-50-2A; torque wrench CBW 547 B-75; rear clutch piston replacer 18G 702; front clutch piston replacer 18G 107; kick-down cable ferrule remover CBW 62; bench cradle CBW-35-65.

CAUTION: Only Gamlen 265 or Rochem Electrosol Quick Dry Solvent should be used for cleaning transmission components.

NOTE: The numbers on the pictures refer to the sequencial numbering on the L.H.S. of the text.

Dismantling

1. Remove the torque converter housing, see 44.17.07.
2. Thoroughly clean the exterior of the gearcase.
3. Remove the dipstick tube and breather assembly; drain the fluid from the gearbox.
4. Invert the transmission.
5. Position the selector lever in 'P' (Park) (Fig. 27).
6. Remove the speedometer driven gear housing together with the driven gear, remove and discard the 'O' ring (Fig. 27).
7. Remove the bolt and plain washer securing the output flange; withdraw the flange (Fig. 27).
8. Note the fitted position of the bolts, stud bolts and spacers. Remove the bolts, stud bolts, plain washers and spacers securing the rear extension housing to the transmission case (Fig. 27).

9. Withdraw the rear extension housing, remove and discard the gasket (Fig. 27).
10. Remove and discard the oil seal (Fig. 27).
11. Slide the speedometer drive gear off the output shaft (Fig. 27).
12. Remove the bolts and spring washers securing the oil pan to the transmission case (Fig. 27).
13. Lift off the oil pan; remove and discard the gasket (Fig. 27).
14. Remove the magnet from the valve block (Fig. 28).
15. Note the fitted positions of the oil tubes (Fig. 28) and using a suitable screwdriver, carefully lever the tubes, with the exception of tube 15D, out of the transmission.
16. Remove the bolts and spring washers securing the valve block (Fig. 28), noting that the shortest bolt is fitted at the front of the valve block.
17. Disconnect the kick-down cable from the cam (Fig. 28).
18. Lift off the valve block (Fig. 28), taking care that the manual valve is not displaced; remove tube 15D as described in operation 15.

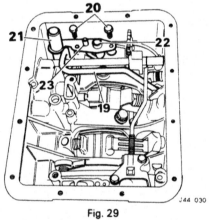

Fig. 29

19. Carefully lever the oil cooler tube from the transmission (Fig. 29).
20. Remove the bolts (Fig. 29) retaining oil tube retaining plate; withdraw the plate.

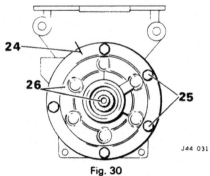

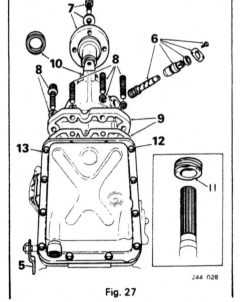

Fig. 27

Fig. 30

21. Using suitable long-nosed pliers, withdraw the pump inlet tube; remove and discard the 'O' ring (Fig. 29).

22. Withdraw the pump outlet pipe (Fig. 29).

23. Withdraw the converter feed tube (Fig. 29).

24. Scribe alignment marks on the transmission case and oil pump (Fig. 30).

25. Remove the bolts and wave washers securing the oil pump to the transmission case (Fig. 30).

26. Support the stator tube and withdraw the oil pump (Fig. 30).

27. Take care when withdrawing the pump that the stator tube is not displaced.

28. Remove and discard the gasket.

29. Remove and discard the bronze thrust washer.

30. Remove the plug and spring washer securing the governor on the output shaft (Fig. 31).

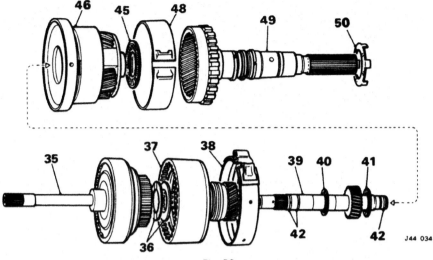

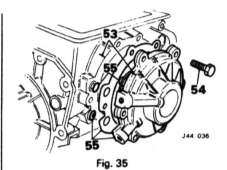

Fig. 33

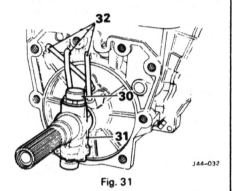

Fig. 31

31. Note the fitted position of the governor; slide the governor off the output shaft (Fig. 31).

32. Carefully lever the governor feed tube, governor return tube and lubrication tube out of the transmission case (Fig. 31).

33. Slacken the locknut and unscrew the front brake band adjuster screw; recover brake band strut (Fig. 32).

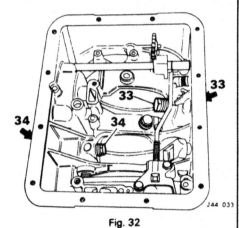

Fig. 32

34. Slacken the locknut and unscrew the rear brake band adjuster screw; recover the brake band strut (Fig. 32).

35. Withdraw the front clutch assembly together with the input shaft (Fig. 33).

36. Remove the steel backing washer and the bronze thrust washer; discard the thrust washer (Fig. 33).

37. Withdraw the rear clutch assembly; remove and discard the sealing rings (Fig. 33).

38. Note the fitted position of the front brake band; compress and withdraw the brake band (Fig. 33).

39. Withdraw the forward sun gear shaft (Fig. 33).

40. Remove the small needle-roller bearing from the input end of the shaft (Fig. 33).

41. Recover the flanged backing washer and large needle-roller bearing from the output end of the shaft (Fig. 33).

NOTE: These components may remain in the sun gear assembly but should still be removed.

42. Remove and discard the two sintered metal sealing rings from the input end and one fibre sealing ring from the output end of the shaft (Fig. 33).

43. Remove the bolts and lock washers securing the centre support.

44. Push the output shaft forwards to displace the centre support and sun gear assembly.

45. Withdraw the centre support and planet carrier from the transmission case; remove the needle-roller bearing from the input end of the planet carrier assembly (Fig. 33).

46. Separate the centre support from the sun-gear assembly (Fig. 33).

47. Pull the output shaft rearwards.

48. Note the fitted position of the rear brake band; compress and withdraw the brake band (Fig. 33).

49. Withdraw the output shaft and ring gear assembly (Fig. 33).

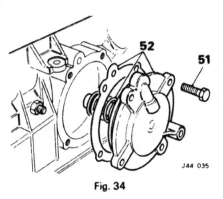

Fig. 34

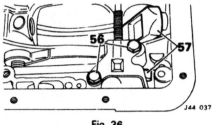

Fig. 36

Fig. 35

50. Remove and discard the bronze thrust washer (Fig. 33).

51. Remove the bolts securing the front servo to transmission case (Fig. 34).

52. Withdraw the front servo, operating rod and spring; remove and discard the gasket (Fig. 34).

53. Scribe alignment marks on the rear servo and transmission case (Fig. 35).

54. Remove the bolts securing the rear servo to the transmission case (Fig. 35).

55. Withdraw the rear servo together with operating rod and spring; remove and discard the 'O' rings and gasket (Fig. 35).

56. Remove the bolts securing the plate retaining parking brake pawl and rear servo operating lever pivot pin; remove the plate (Fig. 36).

57. Withdraw the pivot pin and rear servo operating lever (Fig. 36).

44—23

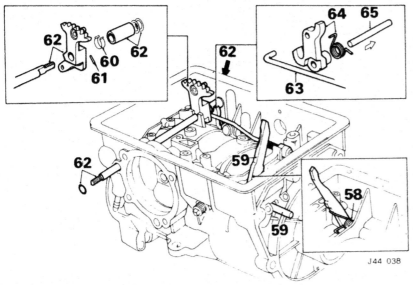

Fig. 37

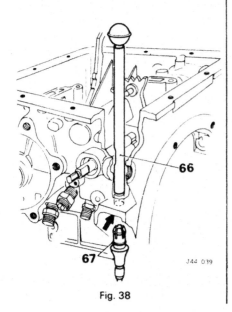

Fig. 38

If it is found necessary to dismantle parking pawl assembly, carry out items 58 to 65 inclusive.

58. Note the fitted position of the parking pawl torsion spring; release the spring from the pawl (Fig. 37).
59. Withdraw the parking pawl pivot pin, collect the pawl and torsion spring (Fig. 37).
60. Release the clip locating manual valve lever (Fig 37).
61. Withdraw the pin locating the manual valve lever (Fig. 37).
62. Withdraw detent shaft, collect manual valve lever, spacer and plain washers, remove and discard 'O' ring and oil seal (Fig. 37).
63. Release parking brake rod assembly from parking pawl (Fig. 37).
64. Note fitted position of parking brake rod operating lever and torsion spring, release spring from lever (Fig. 37).
65. Using suitable punch, drive out operating lever pivot pin, withdraw lever and spring (Fig. 37)

If it is found necessary to remove kick-down cable assembly, carry out items 66 and 67.

66. Using Service tool CBW 62, compress lugs of the cable retaining plug (Fig. 38).
67. Withdraw the kick-down cable assembly; remove and discard the 'O' ring (Fig. 38).

CAUTION: It is not possible to remove retaining plug from the kick-down cable assembly and if lugs are broken, cable assembly must be renewed.

VALVE BLOCK

Overhaul   44-40-04

CAUTION: Ensure that all working surfaces are clean. Use only lint-free cloth and clean transmission fluid for lubricating.

Dismantling

68. Withdraw the manual valve (Fig. 39).
69. Remove the screws securing the suction tube assembly to the lower valve body (Fig. 39).
70. Lift off the tube assembly; remove and discard the gasket (Fig. 39).
71. Remove the six upper valve body securing screws from the lower valve body (Fig. 39).
72. Invert the valve body and remove the four screws securing the upper valve body and cam (Fig. 39) mounting arm; remove the mounting arm (Fig. 39)
73. Extract the down-shift valve and spring (Fig. 39)
74. Lift off the upper valve body (Fig. 39).
75. Remove the screws securing both end plates to the upper valve body, carefully remove the end plates (Fig. 39)
76. Extract the spring, 1-2 shift valve and plunger (Fig. 39)
77. Extract the 2-3 shift valve, spring and plunger (Fig. 39)
78. Remove the eight screws securing the collector plate to the lower valve body; lift off the collector plate (Fig. 39).
79. Slacken, but do not remove the four screws securing the governor line plate (Fig. 39)
80. Hold the separator plate in contact with the valve body, remove the governor line plate securing screws and lift off the governor line plate (Fig. 39)

81. Note the fitted position of the ball valve and carefully slide the separator plate off the valve body (Fig. 39).

CAUTION: The ball valve is spring loaded; ensure that the ball is not displaced during this operation.

82. Remove the ball valve; extract the spring (Fig. 39).
83. Note the fitted position of the check valve (if fitted), remove the valve (Fig. 39).
84. Withdraw the retainer, extract the spring and servo orifice control valve (Fig. 39).
85. Withdraw the retaining pin, extract the plug, modulator valve and spring (Fig. 39).
86. Withdraw the throttle valve spring retainer (Fig. 39).
87. Withdraw the throttle valve retainer (Fig. 39).
88. Extract the spring and throttle valve (Fig. 39).
89. Remove the screw securing the detent spring and roller assembly, detach the assembly, collect the spacer (Fig. 39).

NOTE: The roller arm may be peened to valve body. If so, swing the arm clear of the screws securing the regulator valve retaining plate.

90. Remove the screws securing the regulator valve retaining plate; remove the plate slowly until the spring loading is no longer felt (Fig. 39).
91. Extract the spring, sleeve and primary regulator valve (Fig. 39).
92. Extract the spring and secondary regulator valve (Fig. 39).

Inspection

93. Check the springs with the data shown in spring identification table, see page 44—19; renew springs which are distorted or shorter than the specified length.
94. Check all valves for burrs or scoring. Check that valves move freely in valve bodies.

CAUTION: In the event of valves and/or valve bodies being damaged, valve block assembly must be renewed.

Reassembling

Reverse instructions 68 to 92, ensure that all components are scrupulously clean and that tightening torque figures are adhered to.

CAUTION: A new gasket must be used when refitting the suction tube assembly.

PLANET CARRIER

CAUTION: No overhaul of the planet carrier is possible. In the event of any of the following defects being discovered, the planet carrier assembly must be renewed.

Inspection

95. Check gear teeth for chipping or scoring; light scoring may be disregarded (Fig 40).
96. Check that end-float of gears is not excessive and that gears turn smoothly when spun by hand.
97. Check the bush for scores or evidence of metal transfer (Fig 40)

44—24

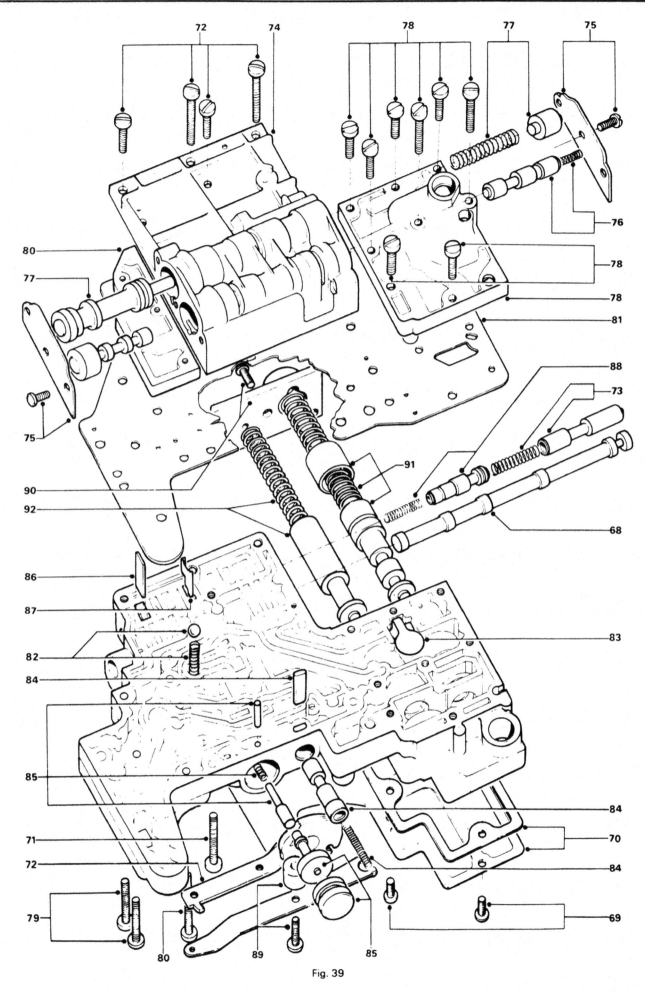

Fig. 39

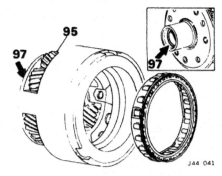

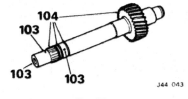

Fig. 42

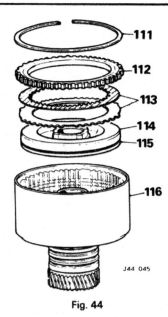

Fig. 40

ONE-WAY CLUTCH

CAUTION: No overhaul of the one-way clutch is possible. In the event of any of the following defects being discovered, the one-way clutch must be renewed.

Dismantling

98. Note the fitted position of the one-way clutch
99. Withdraw the clutch from the planet carrier (Fig. 41).

Inspection

100 Check the sprag faces for flat spots indicating wear (Fig. 41)
101 Check the sprag cage for flat spots indicating wear (Fig. 41).

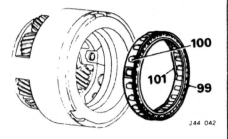

Fig. 41

Reassembling

102. Push the one-way clutch into the planet carrier, ensure that the lip faces outwards and that the clutch is fully seated in the recess.

FORWARD SUN GEAR SHAFT

Inspection

103 Check the drillings in the shaft for obstruction, clear with compressd air only (Fig. 42).
104 Check the splines, sealing ring grooves and gear teeth for burrs or signs of damage, renew if damaged (Fig. 42). Minor burrs may, however, be removed with a very fine abrasive.
105 Examine the large and small needle-roller bearings; renew if either show signs of wear or damage.

REAR CLUTCH

Overhaul

Dismantling

106. Place the rear clutch assembly over the central spindle of the clutch spring compressor 18G 1016 reverse the sun gear down (Fig. 43).
107. Fit spring compressor over spindle (Fig. 43).
108. Compress the spring and remove the snapring (Fig. 43).
109. Slowly release the pressure and remove the compressor.
110. Remove the retainer and spring.
111. Remove the snap-ring retaining pressure plate (Fig. 44).
112. Remove the pressure plate (Fig. 44).
113. Remove the inner and outer clutch plates (Fig. 44).

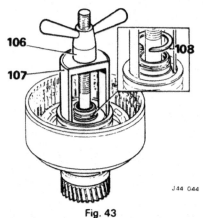

Fig. 43

NOTE: Five outer and five inner clutch plates are fitted.

114. Remove the piston by applying air pressure to the supply hole in the clutch housing pedestal (Fig. 44).
115. Remove and discard the piston seal (Fig. 44).

Inspection

116 Check clutch drum and bearing surfaces for scores or burrs, replace drum if damaged (Fig. 44).
117. Check the fluid passage for obstructions, clear passages with compressed air only.
118. Inspect the piston check valve for free operation.
119. Check the clutch release spring for distortion, renew if distorted.
120. Check the inner clutch plates for flatness and that facings are undamaged.
121. Check that coning on outer clutch plates is not less than 0,25 mm (0.010 in) (Fig. 45).
122. Check the outer clutch plates for scores or burrs, renew if damaged. Minor scores or burrs may, however, be removed with a very fine abrasive.

123. Check needle bearings and bush in clutch housing for signs of wear, scores or evidence of metal transfer. If damaged the clutch hub must be renewed.

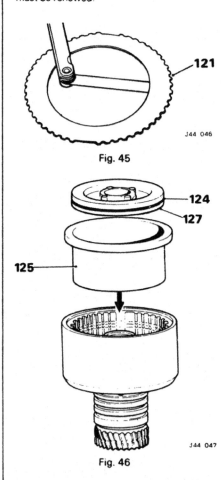

Fig. 44

Fig. 45

Fig. 46

Reassembling

124. Smear the new piston seal with petroleum jelly and fit to the piston (Fig. 46).
125. Position the rear clutch piston replacer tool 18G 702 in the clutch drum (Fig. 46).
126. Lubricate the piston and replacer tool with clean transmission fluid.
127. Install the piston; remove the tool.
128. Reverse operations 106 to 113.

44—26

CAUTION: Outer clutch plates must be assembled with cones facing in same direction.

129. Smear the large needle bearing with petroleum jelly and position it on output end of forward sun gear shaft (Fig. 47).

130. Position the backing washer, flange leading in planet carrier (Fig. 47).

131. Insert the forward sun gear shaft in the planet carrier; fit new fibre sealing ring on output end of shaft (Fig. 47).

132. Position the centre support in the planet carrier (Fig. 47).

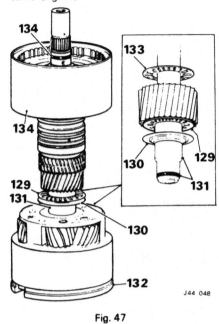

Fig. 47

133. Smear the small needle-roller bearing with petroleum jelly and position it on the forward sun gear shaft (Fig. 47).

134. Position the rear clutch assembly on the forward sun gear shaft; fit new sintered sealing rings on the input end of the shaft (Fig. 47). Ensure that gaps in sealing rings are staggered.

CAUTION: Do not remove the rear clutch assembly and forward sun gear shaft from the planet carrier.

FRONT CLUTCH

Overhaul

Dismantling

135. Remove the snap-ring and withdraw the turbine shaft (Fig. 48).

136. Remove and discard the bronze thrust washer (Fig. 48).

137. Remove the clutch hub (Fig. 48).

138. Remove the inner and outer clutch plates and ring gear (Fig. 48).

NOTE: Four outer and five inner clutch plates are fitted.

139. Remove the snap-ring and diaphragm (Fig. 48).

140. Remove the piston by applying air pressure to the supply hole in the clutch housing pedestal (Fig. 48).

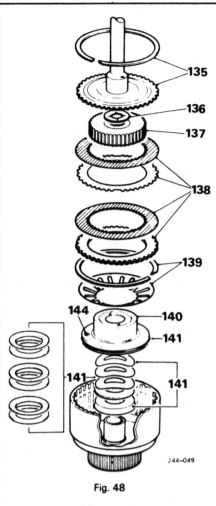

Fig. 48

141. Remove the plain and Belleville washers; remove and discard the seal and 'O' ring (Fig. 48).

NOTE: On later cars, six Belleville washers are used, with no plain washer.

Inspection

142. Check the clutch drum and bearing surfaces for scores or burrs; replace the drum if damaged.

143. Check the fluid passages for obstruction; clear passages with compressed air only.

144. Inspect the piston check valve for free operation (Fig. 48).

145. Check the clutch release diaphragm for cracks or distortion; renew if damaged.

146. Check the inner clutch plates for flatness and that the facings are undamaged.

NOTE: There is no coning on the clutch plates.

147. Check outer clutch plates for flatness, scores or burrs, renew if damaged. Minor scores or burrs may, however, be removed with a very fine abrasive.

148. Check the bush in the turbine shaft for scores or evidence of metal transfer. If damaged, the turbine shaft must be renewed.

Reassembling

149. Smear the new 'O' ring with petroleum jelly and fit to the piston (Fig. 49).

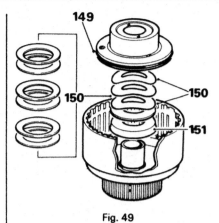

Fig. 49

150. Position the Belleville and plain washers in the piston (Fig. 49), retain the washers with a smear of petroleum jelly.

NOTE: Later cars are fitted with six Belleville washers and no plain washers. Replace these in three opposing pairs, the inner diameters of the washers in each pair being in contact. This washer arrangement may be used to replace the earlier assembly, but if this is done the plain washer originally fitted must be discarded.

151. Soak the new oil seal in clean transmission fluid and insert in the piston (Fig. 49).

NOTE: Open end of seal faces outwards.

152. Position the front clutch piston replacer tool 18G 1107 in the clutch drum (Fig. 50).

153. Lubricate the piston and replacer tool with clean transmission fluid.

154. Install the piston (Fig. 50); remove the tool.

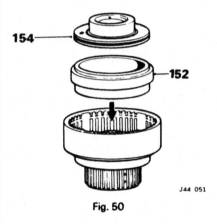

Fig. 50

155. Fit the release diaphragm (Fig. 51).

156. Fit the snap-ring (Fig. 51); ensure that the ring is correctly seated in the groove.

157. Fit the steel backing washer and new bronze thrust washer on the forward sun gear shaft (Fig. 51); ensure that the backing washer is seated correctly.

158. Ensure that the gaps in the sealing rings on the input end of the forward sun gear shaft are staggered (Fig. 51).

159. Check to ensure that the teeth of the rear clutch inner plates are in alignment.

160. Carefully lower the front clutch hub and piston assembly over the shaft and into rear clutch (Fig. 51).

continued

44—27

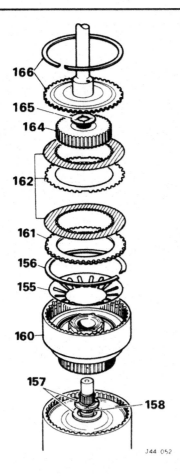

Fig. 51

NOTE: To facilitate engagement of gear with the rear clutch plates, the front clutch should be moved backwards and forwards slightly

161 Fit the ring gear (Fig. 51).
162 Position the inner and outer clutch plates in the clutch drum (Fig 51).

NOTE: For identification purposes, two pairs of teeth at 180° have been omitted on the outer clutch plates.

163 Check to ensure that the teeth of the inner clutch plates are in alignment.
164 Fit the clutch hub, ensure that the hub fully engages all clutch plates (Fig. 51).
165 Position the new bronze thrust washer in the recess in the clutch hub (Fig. 51).
166 Fit the turbine shaft and the snap-ring, ensure that the snap-ring is correctly seated in groove (Fig. 51).

CAUTION: On no account should the front and rear clutch assemblies be separated as damage to the sealing rings on the forward sun gear shaft will result.

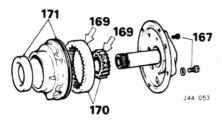

Fig. 52

PUMP

Overhaul

Dismantling

167 Remove the bolts, screw and spring washers securing the pump adaptor to the pump body (Fig. 52).
168 Hold the pump body and using a hide mallet, gently tap the converter tube

CAUTION: Take care that the gears are not displaced when the adaptor and body separate.

169 Mark the mating surfaces of the gears with die marker. **DO NOT** use a punch or scriber (Fig 52).
170 Remove the gears from the pump body (Fig. 52).
171 Remove and discard the 'O' ring and oil seal (Fig. 52).

Inspection

172 Check the bearing surfaces, gears, splines and bushes for damage or wear. Should any component show signs of damage, etc., the oil pump assembly must be renewed.

Reassembling

173 Soak the new oil seal in clean transmission fluid and press carefully into the pump body; ensure that the seal is squarely seated.
174 Soak the new 'O' ring in clean transmission fluid and position in the groove in the periphery of the pump body
175 Reverse operations 167 to 170 ensuring that reference marks on gears, adaptor and body are in alignment.
176 Progressively tighten the bolts to a torque of 35 kgf m (2.5 lbf ft).

FRONT SERVO

Overhaul

Dismantling

177 Remove the piston return spring (Fig. 53)
178 Withdraw the piston from the servo body, remove and discard the 'O' rings (Fig 53).

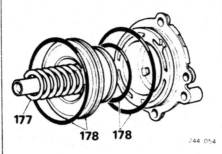

Fig. 53

Inspection

179 Check the return spring for distortion; renew if necessary. Check fluid passage for obstruction, clear the passage with compressed air only

Reassembling

Reverse operations 177 and 178; coat the new 'O' rings with petroleum jelly prior to fitting.

REAR SERVO

Overhaul

Dismantling

180 Withdraw the piston from the servo body; remove and discard the 'O' rings (Fig. 54).

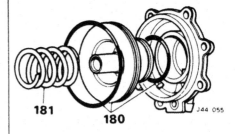

Fig. 54

Inspection

181 Check the return spring removed during operation 55 for distortion; renew, if necessary (Fig. 54).
182 Check the fluid passages for obstruction; clear the passages with compressed air only.

Reassembling

Reverse operation 180, coat the new 'O' rings with petroleum jelly prior to fitting

GOVERNOR

Overhaul

Dismantling

183 Depress the governor weight stem to expose the circlip
184 Remove the circlip and weight, discard the circlip (Fig 55).
185 Withdraw the stem, spring and valve from the governor body (Fig 55).

Inspection

186 Check all components for signs of damage and additionally, check the spring for distortion. In the event of any component being found unsatisfactory, governor assembly must be removed

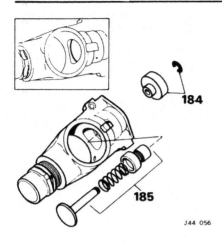

Fig. 55

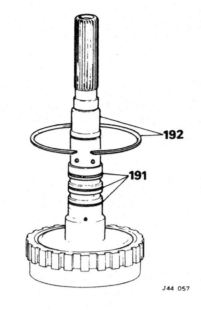

J44 057

Fig. 56

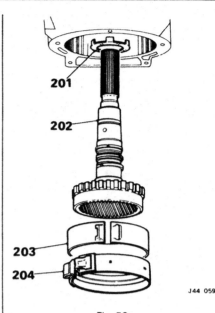

J44 059

Fig. 58

Reassembling

187. Reverse operations 183 to 185; use a new circlip.

188. Check the weight stem for free movement.

CAUTION: If the weight stem shows signs of sticking, the governor assembly must be renewed.

BRAKE BANDS

Inspection

189. Check the front and rear brake bands for damage or distortion.

190. Check the linings for uneven or excess wear.

CAUTION: Bands must be renewed if any of the defects detailed above are apparent or if doubt exists as to their condition.

OUTPUT SHAFT AND RING GEAR

Overhaul

Dismantling

191. Remove and discard the sealing rings from the output shaft (Fig. 56).

192. Remove the snap-ring retaining the output shaft; withdraw the shaft (Fig. 56).

Inspection

193. Check the drillings in the output shaft for obstruction; clear with compressed air only.

194. Check the splines, sealing ring grooves and gear teeth for burrs or signs of damage; renew if damaged. Minor burrs may, however, be removed with a very fine abrasive.

195. Check bush for scores or evidence of metal transfer. Should damage be evident, output shaft must be renewed.

Reassembling

Reverse operations 191 and 192.

CAUTION: Ensure that the gaps in the sealing rings are staggered.

GEAR CASE

Inspection

196. Remove oil cooler return union together with non-return valve assembly (if fitted) (Fig. 57).

197. By means of a piece of thin wire, check the operation of the ball valve. The valve should operate smoothly and seat fully. Check the bush in the gear case for scores, burrs or transfer of metal (Fig. 57).

NOTE: Smear threads of union with Loctite Grade AV before refitting.

198. Reverse operations 56 to 65 as applicable, lightly smearing the manual lever shaft and its bore in the servo housing with lithium-based grease.

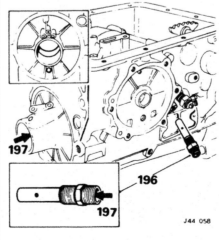

J44 058

Fig. 57

TRANSMISSION ASSEMBLY

Reassembling

199. If the kickdown cable was removed, smear the new 'O' ring with petroleum jelly; position the 'O' ring on retaining plug.

200. Pass the cable into the gearcase and push the retaining plug fully home. Ensure that the lugs of the retaining plug are correctly located in the gearcase.

201. Smear the large bronze thrust washer with petroleum jelly and position the thrust washer, lugs leading, in the gearcase. Ensure that the lugs on the thrust washer are located on the gearcase (Fig. 58).

202. Fit the output shaft and ring gear assembly, taking care that the thrust washer is not displaced (Fig. 58).

203. Position the rear brake band in the gearcase (Fig. 58).

204. Position the front brake band in the gearcase (Fig. 58).

205. Rotate the centre support until the oil holes in outer periphery of support will be in approximate alignment with the oil holes in the transmission case when the clutch assemblies are fitted.

206. Hold the front and rear clutch assemblies firmly together and checking the alignment between the oil holes in the centre support and the gearcase enter the assembly into the gearcase through the rear aperture.

CAUTION: On no account allow clutch assemblies to separate as this will cause damage to the sealing rings on the forward sun gear shaft.

207. Ensure that the planet carrier gears are fully engaged with the output shaft ring gear.

208. Rotate the centre support, ensuring that the alignment of the oil holes is correct, until the securing bolts and lockwashers can be fitted. Tighten the securing bolts evenly.

209. Position the new bronze thrust washer on the oil pump; ensure that the lugs on the washer face towards the pump (Fig. 59).

continued

44—29

NOTE: This thrust washer is selective and determines the amount of gear train end-float. Two thrust washers of different thickness are available and experience has shown that if the thinner of the two washers is selected, the correct end-float is usually obtained. It is recommended therefore that this washer be used.

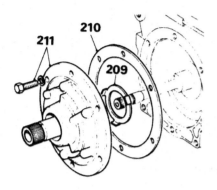

Fig. 59

210. Smear the new oil pump gasket with grease, position the gasket on the oil pump (Fig. 59).

211. Fit the oil pump ensuring that the stator tube is not displaced. **Do not** tighten the oil pump securing bolts at this stage (Fig. 59).

212. Position the new 'O' ring on the oil pump inlet tube; smear the 'O' ring with clean transmission fluid.

213. Fit the oil pump inlet and outlet tubes; also the converter feed tube. Ensure that the tubes are correctly seated (Fig. 60).

NOTE: The oil pump may be rotated slightly to achieve this.

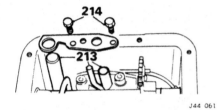

Fig. 60

214. Fit the oil tube retaining plate; tighten the bolts to a torque of 0,24 kgf m (1.75 lbf ft) (Fig. 60).

215. Tighten the oil pump securing bolts by diagonal selection to a torque of 2,63 kgf m (19 lbf ft).

216. Fit the governor feed tube, governor return tube and lubrication tube into the transmission case; ensure that the tubes are correctly seated (Fig. 61).

CAUTION: Do not use undue force when pushing the tubes into the oil holes.

217. Slide governor onto the output shaft, fit the plug and spring washer, ensure that the plug enters BLIND hole in output shaft. Tighten the plug to 2,28 kgf m (16.5 lbf ft) (Fig. 61).

218. Slide the speedometer drive gear onto the output shaft (Fig. 62).

219. Coat the new oil seal with clean transmission fluid; press the seal into the recess in the extension case. Ensure that the seal is correctly seated (Fig. 62).

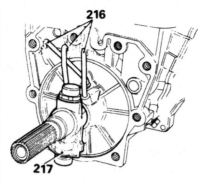

Fig. 61

220. Smear the new extension case gasket with grease, position the gasket on the extension case ensuring that the holes in the gasket and case are in alignment (Fig. 62).

221. Fit the extension case ensuring that the splines of the output shaft do not damage the oil seal and that the extension case does not foul the oil pipes (Fig. 62).

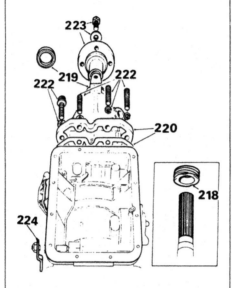

Fig. 62

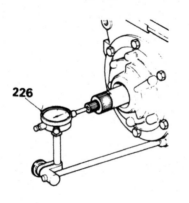

Fig. 63

222. Fit the bolts, stud bolts, washers and spacers (Fig. 62). Tighten the bolts by diagonal selection to a torque of 5,88 kgf m (42.5 lbf ft).

223. Slide the output flange onto the output shaft, fit the plain washer and nut. Do not tighten the nut at this stage (Fig. 62).

224. Move the selector lever until the parking pawl engages with the ring gear (Fig. 62).

225. Tighten the output flange securing bolt to a torque of 5,53 to 6,90 kgf m (40 to 50 lbf ft).

226. Assemble end-float gauge CBW 87 to the gearcase with the stylus contacting the end of the turbine shaft (Fig. 63).

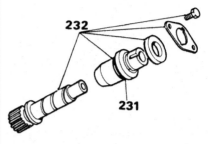

Fig. 64

227. Insert a suitable lever between the front clutch and the front of the gearcase. Ease the gear train to the rear of the gearcase and zero end-float gauge.

228. Insert the lever between the ring gear and rear clutch; ease the gear train to the front of the gearcase.

229. Note the reading on the gauge which should be between 0,20 mm and 0,73 mm (0.008 and 0.029 in).

CAUTION: If end-float exceeds 0,73 mm (0.029 in), reverse operations 217 to 225 and 209 to 215. Fit alternative thrust washer and repeat operations 209 to 215 and 217 to 229.

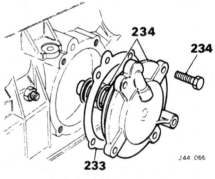

Fig. 65

230. Remove end-float gauge.

231. Smear the new 'O' ring with petroleum jelly, position the 'O' ring in the groove in the speedometer driven gear shaft (Fig. 64).

232. Fit the speedometer driven gear; ensure that the driven gear meshes with the drive gear, do not overtighten the securing bolts (Fig. 64).

233. Smear the new front servo gasket with grease, position the gasket on the servo body (Fig. 65).

234. Fit the front servo and spring (Fig. 65). Tighten the bolts by diagonal selection to a torque of 2,63 kgf m (19 lbf ft).

235. Position the front brake band strut in the gearcase. Ensure the spigot on the strut is located in the detent in the servo rod and that the brake band is correctly positioned (Fig. 66).

236. Screw in the front brake band adjusting screw until contact is made with the brake band. Do not tighten the locknut at this stage (Fig. 66).

44—30

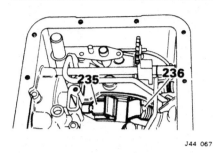

Fig. 66

237. Smear the new 'O' rings with clean transmission oil; position the 'O' rings in the rear servo body oil holes (Fig. 67).

238. Smear the new rear servo gasket with grease; position the gasket on the servo body (Fig. 67).

239. Position the servo operating rod and spring in the servo (Fig. 67).

240. Fit the servo assembly ensuring that the operating rod is located in the detent in the operating lever. Do not tighten the securing bolts at this stage (Fig. 67).

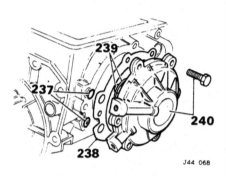

Fig. 67

241. Position the rear brake band strut in the gearcase; ensure that the brake band is correctly positioned (Fig. 68).

242. Screw in the rear brake band adjusting screw until contact is made with the brake band. Do not overtighten the locknut at this stage (Fig. 68).

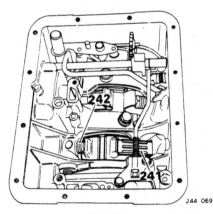

Fig. 68

243. Tighten rear servo securing bolts by diagonal selection to a torque of 2,63 kgf m (19 lbf ft).

244. Fit tube 15D; do not use undue force.

245. Position the valve block in the transmission case, ensure that the spigot on the detent lever is located in the groove in the manual valve and that the valve body fits on the oil tubes (Fig. 69).

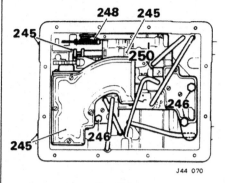

Fig. 69

246. Fit the valve block securing bolts noting that the shortest bolt is fitted at the front of the valve block (Fig. 69).

247. Tighten the valve block securing bolts to a torque of 0,93 kgf m (6.75 lbf ft).

248. Connect the kick-down cable to the cam (Fig. 69).

249. Fit the oil tubes; see operation 15. Do not use undue force when fitting the tubes.

250. Position the magnet on the valve block in the position shown.

251. Smear the new oil pan gasket with grease; position the gasket on the gearcase.

252. Fit the oil pan; tighten the bolts by diagonal selection to a torque of 0,80 kgf m (5.75 lbf ft).

253. Reverse operations 1, 3 and 4, but do not fill the gearbox with fluid.

254. Tighten the front and rear brake band adjusting screws to a torque of 0,7 kgf m (5 lbf ft), and then back off the screws three-quarters of a turn.

255. Tighten each adjusting screw locknut to a torque of 4,8 kgf m (35 lbf ft).

CAUTION: Ensure the screws do not move during this operation.

REAR EXTENSION HOUSING

Remove and refit   44.20.15

Service tool: Torque wrench CBW 547 B-75; engine support tool MS 53A

Removing

Disconnect the battery.

Position service tool MS 53A across rear engine lifting eye and set the hook to support the engine.

Remove the nut at the centre of the mounting and recover the plain washer. Remove the nuts and washers securing the forward end of the tie-plate to the rear of the transmission casing.

Remove the fastenings securing the heat shield. Locate the jack to support the mounting plate and release the four setscrews and washers.

Lower the jack and remove the mounting plate. Recover the spring washers, spacers and rubber rings.

Remove the screws securing the intermediate heat shield; withdraw the shield.

Remove the screws securing the rear heat shield to the rear engine mounting support plate. Remove the six bolts and special washers securing the rear engine mounting support plate to the floor pan.

Remove the bolts and special washers securing the rear engine mounting support plate to the transmission tunnel.

Remove the self-locking nuts and bolts securing the propeller shaft to the gearbox output flange; swing the propeller shaft to one side.

NOTE: This operation will be greatly facilitated if one rear wheel (both wheels if 'Powr-Lok' differential is fitted) is raised and the gear selector placed in 'N' (Neutral), thereby enabling the propeller shaft to be rotated.

WARNING: Chock both front wheels to prevent the vehicle moving

Using engine support tool lower the rear of the engine slightly.

CAUTION: Ensure that the engine does not foul the heater water valve.

Place the selector lever in 'P' (Park).

Remove the bolt and plain washer (1, Fig. 70) securing the gearbox output flange; withdraw the flange.

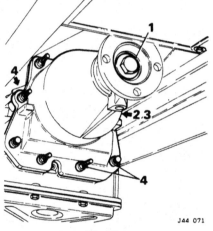

Fig. 70

Disconnect the speedometer right-angle drive (early models).

On later models slacken knurled nut securing transducer and withdraw from speedometer drive retaining plate.

Remove the bolts (2, Fig. 70) securing the speedometer drive retaining plate; withdraw the plate.

Withdraw the speedometer driven gear (3, Fig. 70); remove and discard the 'O' ring.

Remove the bolt securing the selector cable trunnion to the mounting bracket.

Note the fitted position of the stud bolts, bolts and nuts (4, Fig. 70). Remove these fixings, withdraw the trunnion mounting bracket and remove two further stud bolts and spacers.

Withdraw the rear extension; remove and discard the gasket.

Prise the oil seal out of the rear extension housing; discard the oil seal.

continued

44—31

Refitting

Lightly score the oil seal recess in the rear extension housing.

Smear the new oil seal with clean transmission fluid and gently tap the seal into the recess. Ensure that the seal is fully seated.

Using a new gasket, refit the extension housing. Tighten the fixing to the specified torque figure. Refit the selector cable, reconnect the speedometer cable transducer using a new 'O' ring on the speedometer driven gear.

Refit the output flange.

Refit the rear engine mounting after replacing any rubber rings which are damaged.

Run the engine until it reaches normal operating temperature.

With the engine still running, withdraw the dipstick, wipe it clean and replace it.

Immediately withdraw the dipstick and note the reading on the 'HOT' side of the dipstick. If necessary, add fluid to bring the level on the dipstick to 'MAX'.

NOTE: The difference between the 'MAX' and 'MIN' marks on the dipstick represents approximately 0,75 litre (1½ pints, 2 U.S. pints).

REAR EXTENSION HOUSING OIL SEAL

Remove and refit　　　**44.20.18**

Removing

WARNING: Chock both front wheels to prevent the vehicle moving.

Service tool: Torque wrench CBW 547 B-75; engine support tool MS 53A

Disconnect the battery.
Position service tool MS 53 (A) across the rear engine lifting eye and set the hook to support the engine.
Remove the nut at the centre of the mounting and recover the plain washer. Remove the nuts and washers securing the forward end of the tie-plate to the rear of the transmission casing.
Remove the fastenings securing the heat shield. Locate the jack to support the mounting plate and release the four setscrews and washers.
Lower the jack and remove the mounting plate. Recover the spring washers, spacers and rubber rings.
Remove the locknuts from the bolts securing the forward and rear brackets of the mounting, and recover the spacing tubes.
Remove the locknuts securing the mounting rubbers to centre bracket.
Remove the screw securing the intermediate heat shield; withdraw the shield.
Remove the screws securing the rear heat shield to the rear engine mounting support plate.
Remove the six bolts and special washers securing the rear engine mounting support plate to the floor pan.

Remove the bolts and special washers securing the rear engine mounting support plate to the transmission tunnel.
Remove the self-locking nuts and bolts securing the propeller shaft to the gearbox output flange; swing the propeller shaft to one side.

NOTE: This operation will be greatly facilitated if one rear wheel (both wheels if 'Powr-Lok' differential is fitted) is raised and the gear selector placed in 'N' (Neutral), thereby enabling the propeller shaft to be rotated.

Using engine support tool, lower rear of engine slightly.

CAUTION: Ensure that the engine does not foul the heater water valve.

Place the selector lever in 'P' (Park).
Remove the bolt and plain washer (1, Fig. 71) securing the gearbox output flange (2, Fig. 71); withdraw the flange.
Prise the oil seal (3, Fig. 71) out of the rear extension housing, discard the seal.

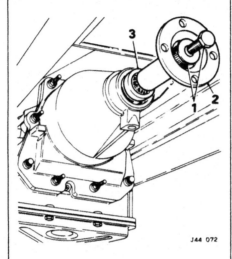

J44 072

Fig. 71

Refitting

Lightly score the oil seal recess in the rear extension housing.
Smear the new oil seal with clean transmission fluid and gently tap the seal into the recess. Ensure that the seal is fully seated.

GOVERNOR

Remove and refit　　　**44.22.01**

Removing

Prior to carrying out the following operation, the rear extension will have to be removed, see operation 44.20.15.
Slide the speedometer drive gear off the output shaft.
Position the selector lever in 'N' (Neutral). If necessary, rotate the output shaft to gain access to the governor securing plug.

Note the fitted position of the governor and remove the plug and spring washer (1, Fig. 72) securing the governor to the output shaft.
Slide the governor (2, Fig. 72) off the output shaft.

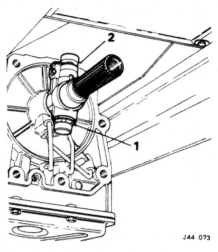

J44 073

Fig. 72

Refitting

Slide the governor onto the output shaft, noting the location of the blind hole in the shaft.
Fit the governor securing plug and spring washer, ensure that the domed end of the plug enters the blind hole in the output shaft. Tighten the plug to the specified torque.
Slide the speedometer drive gear onto the output shaft.
Refit the rear extension housing.

CAUTION: Always fit a new rear seal.

LUBRICATION SYSTEM

Drain and refill　　　**44.24.02**

CAUTION: Due to the method of construction, it is not possible to completely drain the transmission fluid, and this should be taken into account when the transmission is being filled. As it should only be necessary to carry out the following operations preparatory to carrying out work on the transmission which will involve removal of oil pan, the following procedure should be followed.

Draining

Unscrew the union nut, withdraw the dipstick tube (1, Fig. 73), drain and discard the fluid.
Remove the bolts and plain washers (2, Fig. 73) securing the oil pan to the transmission case.
Lower the oil pan, remove and discard the gasket (3, Fig. 73).
Allow the fluid to drain and using a new gasket coated with grease, refit the oil pan.
Tighten the securing bolts by diagonal selection and reconnect the dipstick tube.
Refill the transmission with fluid to the 'MAX' mark on the dipstick.

Apply the handbrake and select 'P' position.
Run the engine until it reaches normal operating temperature.

With the engine still running, withdraw the dipstick (1, Fig. 74), wipe it clean and replace it. Immediately withdraw the dipstick and note the reading on the 'HOT' side of the dipstick. If necessary, add fluid to bring the level on the dipstick to 'MAX'.

NOTE: The difference between the 'MAX' (3, Fig. 74) and 'MIN' (2, Fig. 74) marks on the dipstick represents approximately 0,75 litre (1½ pints, 2 U.S. pints).

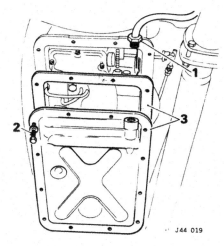

Fig. 73

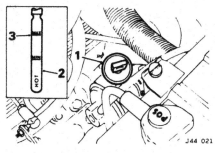

Fig. 74

OIL PAN

Remove and refit   **44.24.04**
Including filter
Remove and refit   **44.24.07**

Removing

Unscrew the union nut (1, Fig. 73), withdraw the dipstick tube; drain and discard the fluid. Remove the bolts and plain washers (2, Fig. 73) securing the oil pan to the transmission case. Lower the oil pan, remove and discard gasket (3, Fig. 73).

NOTE: If the filter is to be removed, carry out the following:

Remove the screws (1, Fig. 75) securing the suction tube to the valve block.
Lower the suction tube (2, Fig. 75), remove and discard the gasket, extract the filter.

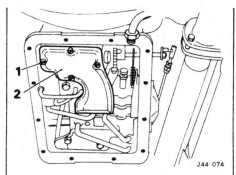

Fig. 75

Smear a new gasket with clean transmission fluid, refit the filter and suction tube.

Having refitted the filter, proceed as follows: smear a new gasket with grease and refit the oil pan.

Tighten the bolts by diagonal selection and refit the dipstick tube.

Fill the transmission with fluid to the 'MAX' marks on the dipstick.

Apply the handbrake and select 'P' position. Run the engine until it reaches normal operating temperature.

With the engine still running, withdraw the dipstick, wipe it clean and replace it.

Immediately withdraw the dipstick and note the reading on the 'HOT' side of the dipstick. If necessary, add fluid to bring the level on the dipstick to 'MAX'.

NOTE: The difference between the 'MAX' and 'MIN' marks on the dipstick represents approximately 0,75 litre (1½ pints, 2 U.S. pints).

DOWN-SHIFT CABLE

Pressure check and adjust   44.30.03

Service tools: Pressure gauge CBW 1C; gearbox adaptor CBW 1C-5.

Check engine tune, i.e. cylinder compressions, spark plugs, ignition timing, carburetters.
Using a suitable Allen key, remove the blanking plug (1, Fig. 76) from the gearcase.

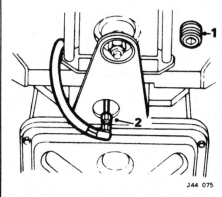

Fig. 76

CAUTION: On later cars, a bracket is fitted between the gearbox and the rear mounting. Access to the blanking plug is through the hole in the bracket and under no circumstances may the bracket be removed.

Connect the pressure gauge to the gearbox, using appropriate adaptor.

CAUTION: Do not overtighten adaptor.

Taking care to ensure that the hose is kept clear of the exhaust system, route the hose around the outside of the car and into the passenger's window.

Run the engine until it reaches normal operating temperature.

Chock the wheels and apply hand- and foot-brakes.

Select 'D'; pressure gauge should read 3,85 to 5,3 kgf/cm² (55 to 75 lbf/in²) at idling speed.

Increase engine speed by 500 rev/min, gauge should read 5,3 to 8,1 kgf/cm² (75 to 115 lbf/in²). There must be a difference of 1,4 to 1,76 kgf/cm² (20 to 25 lbf/in²) in the two readings taken. The lower figure must not exceed 5,3 kgf/cm² (75 lbf/in²).

If above readings are not obtained, proceed as follows:

WARNING: Engine must be switched off and selector lever in 'N' before carrying out adjustment.

Slacken the locknut (1, Fig. 77) on the down-shift cable. By means of abutment nut (2, Fig. 77) on the outer cable, adjust the length of the cable to alter the pressure.

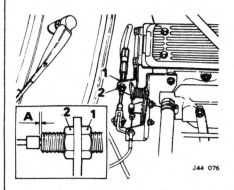

Fig. 77

NOTE: Increasing the length of the cable causes an increase in pressure; decreasing the length of the cable causes a decrease in pressure. The ferrule crimped on the inner cable should be approximately 0,4 mm (0.010 in) from the threaded portion of the outer cable (dimension 'A' Fig. 77).

When the pressure is correct, tighten the locknut.

Remove the pressure gauge and adaptor, refit the blanking plug and, if necessary, top-up the transmission fluid.

CAUTION: Do not overtighten the plug.

Road-test the car as detailed on page 44.13.

44—33

FRONT BRAKE BAND

Adjust   44.30.07

Service tools: Torque wrench CBW 547 B-75; adaptor CBW 547-50-2A

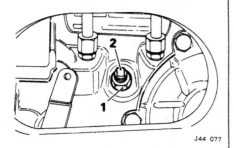

Fig. 78

Remove the self-locking nut securing the selector lever to the selector shaft; withdraw the lever.

Slacken the locknut (1, Fig. 78) securing the brake band adjuster screw.

Slacken the adjuster screw (2, Fig. 78) two or three turns.

Using torque wrench CBW 547 B-75, suitable ⅜ in drive straight extension and adaptor CBW 547-50-2A, tighten the brake band adjuster screw to a torque of 0,80 kgf m (5 lbf ft) and then back off the screw two and one half flats.

Tighten the locknut to a torque of 4,8 kgf m (35 lbf ft).

CAUTION: Ensure the adjuster screw does not turn during this operation.

REAR BRAKE BAND

Adjust   44.30.10

Service tools: Torque wrench CBW 547 B-75; adaptor CBW 547A-50-2A

Slacken the locknut (1, Fig. 79) securing the brake band adjuster screw.

Slacken the adjuster screw (2, Fig. 79) two or three turns.

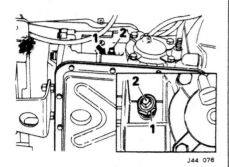

Fig. 79

Using torque wrench CBW 547 B-75 and adaptor CBW 547A-50-2A, tighten the brake band adjuster screw to a torque of 0,80 kgf m (5 lbf ft) and then back off the screw two and one half flats.

Tighten the locknut to a torque of 4,8 kgf m (35 lbf ft).

CAUTION: Ensure that the adjuster screw does not turn during this operation.

STALL SPEED

Test   44.30.13

The results of this test indicate the condition of the gearbox and converter.

Stall speed is maximum engine revolutions recorded whilst driving the impeller against the stationary turbine. Stall speed will vary with both engine and transmission conditions, so before attempting a stall speed check, engine condition must be determined. Engine and transmission must be at normal operating temperature before commencing check.

- Apply handbrake.
  Apply footbrake.
  Start engine.
  Select 'D'.
  Fully depress accelerator.
  Note tachometer reading.

CAUTION: To avoid overheating of transmission do not stall for more than 10 seconds at a time or for a total of one minute in any half-hour period.

Rev/min	Condition indicated
Under 1300	Stator free wheel slip
1950 to 2100	Normal
Over 2,500	Clutch slip

FRONT SERVO

Remove and refit   44.34.07

Service tools: Torque wrench CBW 547 B-75; adaptor CBW 547A-50-2A

Removing

Position the selector lever in 'P'

Remove bolts (1, Fig. 80) securing the servo to the transmission case.

Withdraw the servo (2, Fig. 80) together with the push-rod and spring.

Remove and discard the gasket (3, Fig. 80).

NOTE: If the front servo is to be overhauled, carry out operation 44.20.06, instructions 177 to 179.

Refitting

Smear a new gasket with grease, position the gasket on the servo body.

Position the brake band strut in the transmis-

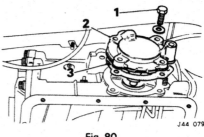

Fig. 80

sion case, ensuring that the strut is correctly located on the brake band.

Insert the servo push-rod and spring in the transmission, ensuring that the spigot on the brake band strut is located in the hole in the push-rod.

Position the servo on the transmission case, ensuring that the push-rod and spring are correctly located.

Fit and tighten the servo securing bolts by diagonal selection to the specified torque figure.

Top up the transmission fluid to the 'MAX' mark on the dipstick.

Run the engine until until it reaches normal operating temperature.

With the engine still running, withdraw the dipstick (1, Fig. 81), wipe it clean and replace it.

Immediately withdraw the dipstick and note the reading on the 'HOT' (2, Fig. 81) side of the dipstick. If necessary, add fluid to bring the level on the dipstick to 'MAX' (3, Fig. 81).

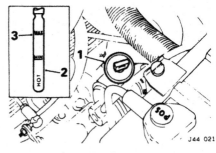

Fig. 81

NOTE: The difference between the 'MAX' (3, Fig. 81) and 'MIN' marks on the dipstick represents approximately 0,75 litre (1½ pints, 2 U.S. pints).

Remove the self-locking nut securing the selector lever to the selector shaft; withdraw the lever.

Slacken the locknut securing the brake band adjuster screw.

Slacken the adjuster screw two or three turns.

Using torque wrench CBW 547 B-75, suitable ⅜ in drive straight extension and adaptor CBW 547A-50-2A, tighten the brake band adjuster screw to a torque of 0,80 kgf m (5 lbf ft) and then back off the screw three-quarters of a turn.

Tighten the locknut to a torque of 4,8 kgf m (35 lbf ft).

CAUTION: Ensure the adjuster screw does not turn during this operation.

44—34

REAR SERVO

Remove and refit   44.34.13

Service tools: Torque wrench CBW 547 B-75;
adaptor CBW 547A-50-2A

Removing

Remove nuts, bolt and washers securing intermediate exhaust pipe to front pipe.

Separate the intermediate pipe from the front
pipe; remove the sealing olive.

Remove the screws and special washers
securing the left-hand heat shield to the body;
withdraw the heat shield.

Remove the self-locking nut securing the selector lever to the selector shaft; withdraw the
lever and selector cable assembly. Mark the
relative position of rear servo body (1, Fig.82)
to transmission case.

Remove the bolts (2, Fig. 82) securing the
servo to the transmission case, withdraw the
servo, push-rod and spring.

Remove and discard the gasket and two 'O'
rings (3, Fig. 82).

NOTE: If the rear servo is to be overhauled,
carry out operation 44.20.06, items 180 to
182.

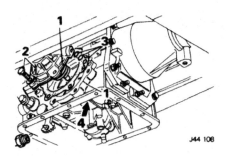

Fig. 82

Refitting

Smear new 'O' rings with clean transmission
fluid, position an 'O' ring in each recess in the
servo body.

Smear a new gasket with grease, position the
gasket on the servo body.

Refit the selector lever to the shaft.

Refit the left-hand heat shield, smear sealing
olive with 'Firegum' before refitting.

Top up the transmission with fluid to the 'MAX'
mark on the dipstick.

Run the engine until it reaches normal operating temperature.

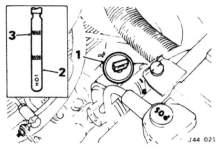

Fig. 83

With engine still running, withdraw the dipstick
(1, Fig. 83), wipe it clean and replace it.
Immediately withdraw the dipstick and note
the reading on the 'HOT' side of the dipstick
(2, Fig. 83). If necessary, add fluid to bring the
level on the dipstick to 'MAX' (3, Fig. 83).

NOTE: The difference between the 'MAX and
'MIN' marks on the dipstick represents approximately 0,75 litre (1½ pints, 2 U.S. pints).

Slacken the locknut securing brake band adjuster screw.

Slacken the adjuster screw two or three turns.
Using torque wrench CBW 547 B-75, and
adaptor CBW 547A-50-2A, tighten the brake
band adjuster screw to a torque of 0,80 kgf m (5
lbf ft) and then back off the screw three-quarters
of a turn. Tighten the locknut to a torque of 4,8
kgf m (35 lbf ft).

CAUTION: Ensure that adjuster screw does
not turn during this operation.

VALVE BLOCK

Remove and refit   44.40.01

Service tool: Torque wrench CBW 547 B-75

Removing

Position the selector lever in 'P' (Park).
Unscrew the union nut (1, Fig. 84), withdraw
the dipstick tube; drain and discard the fluid.

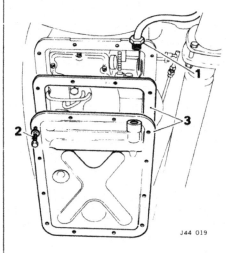

Fig. 84

Remove the bolts and plain washers (2, Fig. 84)
securing the oil pan to the transmission case.
Lower the oil pan (3, Fig. 84), remove and discard the gasket.

Disconnect the kick-down cable from the cam.
Note the fitted position of the oil tubes (see
operation 44.20.06, item 15) and using a suitable screwdriver, lever tubes out of the
transmission.

Note the fitted position of the magnet; withdraw the magnet.

Remove the bolts securing the valve block to
the transmission, noting that the shortest bolt
is fitted at the front.

Pull the valve block downwards, ensuring that
the manual valve is not displaced

**CAUTION: Extreme care must be taken to
ensure that the action of removal does not
damage the converter feed, pump feed or
pump outlet pipes.**

NOTE: If the valve block is to be overhauled,
carry out operation 44.20.06, items 68 to 94.

Refitting

Ensure that the converter feed, pump feed and
pump outlet pipes are not damaged; push each
pipe upwards to ensure correct location is
maintained.

Locate the valve block in the transmission case
ensuring that the tubes are correctly located in
the valve block.

NOTE: The valve block may be tapped gently
with a hide mallet to ensure correct location is
obtained.

Ensure that the spigot on the detent lever
engages with the groove machined in the manual valve.

Refit the valve block securing bolts, ensuring
that the shortest bolt is fitted at the front.

Reconnect the kick-down cable to the cam.

Smear a new oil pan gasket with grease and
refit the oil pan. Tighten the securing bolts by
diagonal selection.

Refit the dipstick tube and fill the transmission
with fluid to the 'MAX' mark on the dipstick.

Run the engine until it reaches normal operating temperature.

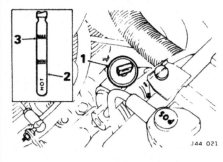

Fig. 85

With the engine still running, withdraw the dipstick (1, Fig. 85), wipe it clean and replace it.
Immediately withdraw the dipstick and note
the reading on the 'HOT' side of the dipstick
(2, Fig. 85). If necessary, add fluid to bring the
level on the dipstick to 'MAX' (3, Fig. 85).

NOTE: The difference between the 'MAX' and
'MIN' marks on the dipstick represents approximately 0,75 litre (1½ pints, 2 US pints).

44—35

PAGE INTENTIONALLY LEFT BLANK

JAGUAR
Daimler

**Containing
Section**

**44 AUTOMATIC GEARBOX
GM 400**

GM 400

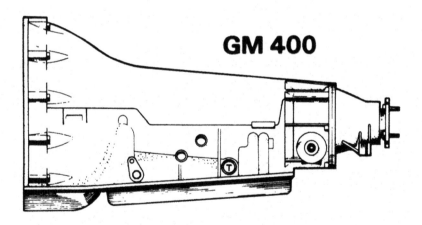

SERIES III
SERVICE MANUAL

INTRODUCTION

This Service Manual covers the Jaguar Series 3 and Daimler Series 3 range of vehicles. It is primarily designed to assist skilled technicians in the efficient repair and maintenance of Jaguar and Daimler vehicles.

Using the appropriate service tools and carrying out the procedures as detailed will enable the operations to be completed within the time stated in the 'Repair Operation Times'.

The Service Manual has been produced in 13 separate sections; this allows the information to be distributed throughout the specialist areas of the modern service facility.

A table of contents in section 1 lists the major components and systems together with the section and book numbers. The cover of each book depicts graphically and numerically the sections contained within that book. Each section starts with a list of operations in alphabetical order.

The title page of each book carries the part numbers required to order replacement books, binders or complete Service Manuals. This can be done through the normal channels.

Operation Numbering

A master index of numbered operations has been compiled for universal application to all vehicles manufactured by Jaguar Cars Ltd., and therefore, because of the different specifications of various models, continuity of the numbering sequence cannot be maintained throughout this manual.

Each operation described in this manual is allocated a number from the master index and cross-refers with an identical number in the 'Repair Operation Times'. The number consists of six digits arranged in three pairs.

Each operation is laid out in the sequence required to complete the operation in the minimum time, as specified in the 'Repair Operation Times'.

Service Tools

Where performance of an operation requires the use of a service tool, the tool number is quoted under the operation heading and is repeated in, following, the instruction involving its use. A list of all necessary tools is included in section 1, number 99.

References

References to the left- or right-hand side in the manual are made when viewing from the rear. With the engine and gearbox assembly removed the timing cover end of the engine is referred to as the front. A key to abbreviations and symbols is given in section 1, number 01.

REPAIRS AND REPLACEMENTS

When service parts are required it is essential that only genuine Jaguar/Daimler or Unipart replacements are used. Attention is particularly drawn to the following points concerning repairs and the fitting of replacement parts and accessories.

1.   Safety features embodied in the vehicle may be impaired if other than genuine parts are fitted. In certain territories, legislation prohibits the fitting of parts not to the vehicle manufacturer's specification.

2.   Torque wrench setting figures given in this Service Manual must be strictly adhered to.

3.   Locking devices, where specified, must be fitted. If the efficiency of a locking device is impaired during removal it must be replaced.

4.   Owners purchasing accessories while travelling abroad should ensure that the accessory and its fitted location on the vehicle conform to mandatory requirements existing in their country of origin.

5.   The vehicle warranty may be invalidated by the fitting of other than genuine Jaguar/Daimler or Unipart parts. All Jaguar/Daimler and Unipart replacements have the full backing of the factory warranty.

6.   Jaguar/Daimler Dealers are obliged to supply only genuine service parts.

SPECIFICATION

Purchasers are advised that the specification details set out in this Manual apply to a range of vehicles and not to any one. For the specification of a particular vehicle, purchasers should consult their Dealer.

The Manufacturers reserve the right to vary their specifications with or without notice, and at such times and in such manner as they think fit. Major as well as minor changes may be involved in accordance with the Manufacturer's policy of constant product improvement.

Whilst every effort is made to ensure the accuracy of the particulars contained in this Manual, neither the Manufacturer nor the Dealer, by whom this Manual is supplied, shall in any circumstances be held liable for any inaccuracy or the consequences thereof.

CONTENTS

PAGE INTENTIONALLY LEFT BLANK

1. Converter pump
2. Pump assembly
3. Forward clutch
4. Direct clutch
5. Front band
6. Intermediate clutch
7. Intermediate sprag
8. Centre support
9. Low roller clutch
10. Rear band
11. Output carrier and internal gear
12. Output shaft
13. Sun gear
14. Speedometer driven gear
15. Rear internal gear
16. Reaction carrier
17. Sun gear shaft
18. Detent solenoid
19. Main shaft
20. Control valve
21. Filter assembly
22. Manual shaft
23. Stator
24. Turbine
25. Turbine shaft
26. Stator shaft
27. Stator roller clutch

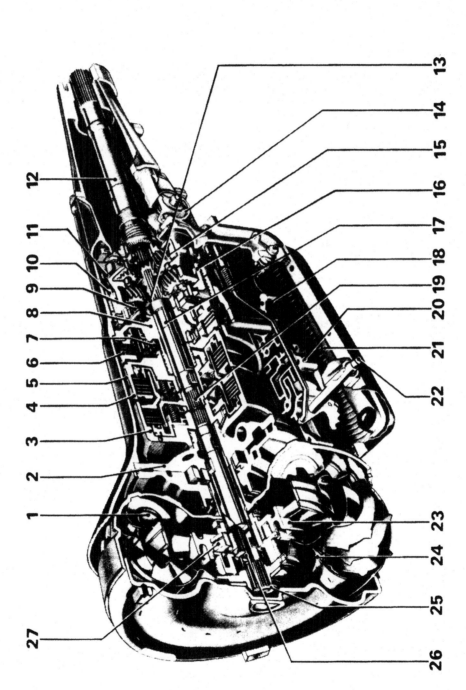

Fig. 1

44—3

DESCRIPTION

The GM 400 Hydramatic transmission is fully automatic and consists of a three-element-type torque converter and a compound epicyclic planetary gear set.

Three multiple disc clutches, two one-way clutches and two brake bands provide the friction elements required to obtain the necessary gear ratios.

The torque converter couples the engine power to the transmission and hydraulically provides additional torque multiplication when the engine and transmission are subjected to high loads.

The compound planetary gear set provides three forward ratios and one reverse. Gear-changing is fully automatic relative to vehicle and engine speed and engine torque input. A vacuum modulator is used to automatically sense engine torque input to the transmission. Engine torque sensed by the modulator is transmitted to the pressure regulator, thus ensuring that the correct gear-shifts are obtained at the relevant throttle positions. Gear or torque ratios of the transmission are as follows:

First 2.48 : 1
Second 1.48 : 1
Third 1.1 : 1
Reverse 2.07 : 1

The gear selection quadrant has six positions 'P', 'R', 'N', 'D', '2', '1'.

An easily recognizable feature on cars fitted with this transmission is the increased length of selector lever travel between 'P' and 'R'.

'P' Park enables the transmission output shaft to be locked, thereby preventing movement of the vehicle, 'P' **must not** be engaged whilst the vehicle is in motion. The engine can be started in this position.

'R' Enables the vehicle to be driven in the reverse direction.

'N' Neutral position, enables the engine to be started and run without driving the transmission.

'D' Drive for all normal driving conditions and maximum economy. It has three gear ratios. Forced down-shifts are available for safe and rapid acceleration by quickly depressing the accelerator pedal to the full throttle position.

'2' '2' has the same starting ratio as 'D' but prevents the transmission changing up from second gear, thereby retaining this gear for acceleration and engine braking. '2' can be selected at any road speed, as there is no safety override.

'1' '1' first gear ratio can be selected at any speed from 'D' or '2' but the transmission will shift to second gear and will remain in this gear until the vehicle speed is reduced sufficiently to allow first gear to be engaged.

GLOSSARY OF TERMS

1 ACCUMULATOR
Controls shift quality by delaying the full drive pressure applied to a clutch or band.

2 MANUAL VALVE
The main line fluid pressure distributing valve, directing fluid to all main components.

3 GOVERNOR ASSEMBLY
Responsible for timing the gear-changes in accordance with output shaft speed.

4 VACUUM MODULATOR VALVE
The vacuum modulator valve, activated by manifold vacuum, senses engine torque. The modulator ensures that the correct gear-shifts are obtained at relevant throttle positions. Pressure from the modulator is applied to the 1–2 shift valve, compensating governor pressure, and to the pressure regulator valve in order to vary line pressure.

Governor pressure directed to the modulator reduces line pressure at high road speeds, when engine torque is minimal, thereby making it unnecessary for high pump output and resulting in a greater fuel economy for the unit.

5 PRESSURE REGULATOR
Controls main line pressure.

6 1–2 SHIFT VALVE
Controls the 1–2 and 2–3 shift patterns.

7 1–2 REGULATOR VALVE
Regulates modulator pressure to a proportional pressure and tends to hold the 1–2 shift valve in the down-shift position.

8 1–2 DETENT VALVE
This valve serves regulated modulator pressure and tends to hold the 1–2 shift valve in the down position shift and provides an area for detent pressure for 2–1 detent changes.

9 2–3 MODULATOR VALVE
This valve is sensitive to modulator pressure and applies a variable force on the 2–3 shift valve; tending to hold the valve in the down position.

10 3–2 VALVE
This prevents modulator pressure from acting on the shift valves after the direct clutch has been applied, thereby preventing a down-shift from third gear should wide throttle openings be used. If detent or modulator pressure rises above 6,5 kgf/cm² (92 lbf/in²) however, this pressure will then be directed to the shift valves to effect a down-shift.

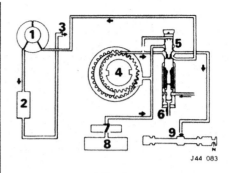

Fig. 2

1. Torque converter
2. Oil cooler
3. Oil to transmission
4. Oil pump
5. Pressure regulator valve
6. From modulator or throttle valve
7. Oil filter
8. Oil sump
9. Manual valve

CAUTION: *Only Gamlen 265 or Rochem Electrical Quick Dry Solvent should be used for cleaning transmission components.*

CLUTCH AND BAND APPLICATION CHART

Selector position		Forward Clutch	Direct Clutch	Front Band	Intermediate		Clutch	Rear Band
					Clutch	Clutch		
Park — Neutral								
Drive	1	●					●	
D	2	●			●	●		
	3	●	●		●			
Intermediate								
2	1st	●					●	
	2nd	●		●	●	●		
Lock-up								
1	1st	●					●	●
Reverse			●					●

CLUTCH PLATE IDENTIFICATION

	Forward Clutch		Direct Clutch		Intermediate Clutch	
	Pressure Plates	Friction Plates	Pressure Plates	Friction Plates	Pressure Plates	Friction Plates
Flat	5	5	5	5	3	—
Waved	—	—	—	—	—	3
Dished	1	—	1	—	—	—

NOTE: The direct clutch has one plate of 2,2 mm (0.091 in) thickness, the other four being of 1,9 mm (0.077 in) thickness.

SHIFT SPEEDS

NOTE: The figures in the following table refer only to the following:

1. All cars with a 3.31:1 final drive ratio.

2. Cars with a final drive ratio of 3.07:1 prior to transmission No. 79ZA2411.

All are pre HE vehicles.

For HE vehicles see page 44—34.

Light Throttle		Full Throttle		Full Throttle Kick-down		Kick-down		Down-shift		Roll Out	
1–2	2–3	1–2	2–3	1–2	2–3	3–2	3–1	Manual 2–1	PTKD* 3–2	3–2	2–1
5–10 m.p.h.	10–20 m.p.h.	45 ± 5 m.p.h.	60 ± 5 m.p.h.	55 ± 5 m.p.h.	85 ± 5 m.p.h.	80 ± 5 m.p.h.	28–35 m.p.h.	13–18 m.p.h.	40–50 m.p.h.	8–12 m.p.h.	3–8 m.p.h.
8–16 km/h	16–32 km/h	72 ± 8 km/h	96 ± 8 km/h	88 ± 8 km/h	136 ± 8 km/h	128 ± 8 km/h	43–56 km/h	21–29 km/h	64–80 km/h	13–19 km/h	5–13 km/h

*PTKD = Part Throttle Kick-down

44—5

AUTOMATIC TRANSMISSION — GM 400

NOTE: The figures in the following table refer only to cars with a final drive ratio of 3.07:1 built from transmission No. 79ZA2411 and are pre HE vehicles — for HE vehicles see page 44—34.

Light Throttle		Full Throttle		Full Throttle Kick-down		Kick-down		Down-shift		Roll Out	
1–2	2–3	1–2	2–3	1–2	2–3	3–2	3–1	Manual 2–1	PTKD* 3–2	3–2	2–1
5–12 m.p.h.	12–20 m.p.h.	40–50 m.p.h.	50–70 m.p.h.	50–60 m.p.h.	80–95 m.p.h.	70–85 m.p.h.	28–38 m.p.h.	13–18 m.p.h.	40–50 m.p.h.	8–12 m.p.h.	3–8 m.p.h.
8–19 km/h	19–32 km/h	64–80 km/h	80–113 km/h	80–96 km/h	129–153 km/h	113–137 km/h	45–62 km/h	21–29 km/h	64–80 km/h	13–19 km/h	5–13 km/h

*PTKD = Part Throttle Kick-down

VALVE SPRING IDENTIFICATION FOR PRE HE VEHICLES

VALVE SPRING IDENTIFICATION CHART				
Function	**Colour**	**Free Length**	**No. of Coils**	**Outside Diameter**
1–2 accumulator valve	Dark Green	1.648 in	12.5	0.480 in
Pressure regulator	Light Blue	3.343 in	13	0.845 in
Front servo piston	Natural	1.129 in	4	1.257 in
Rear accumulator	Yellow	2.230 in	8.5	1.130 in
Governor	Dark Green	0.933 in	9.5	0.316 in
	Red	0.987 in	8.5	0.306 in
1–2 regulator	Pink	0.936 in	13.5	0.241 in
2–3 valve	Red	1.491 in	17.5	0.328 in
2–3 valve	Gold	1.555 in	18.5	0.326 in
3–2 valve	Green	2.017 in	16.5	0.400 in
Front accumulator piston	Natural	2.927 in	8.5	1.260 in
Detent regulator	Green	2.735 in	26.5	0.340 in

For HE vehicles see page 44—34.

TORQUE WRENCH SETTINGS

ITEM	DESCRIPTION	Nm	kgf m	lbf ft
Control valve unit to case	¼ in dia. X 20	10.84	1,1	8
Governor cover to case	5/16 in dia. X 18	24.40	2,49	18
Line pressure plug	⅛ in dia. pipe	13.55	1,38	10
Manual shaft to detent lever	⅜ in dia. X 24	24.40	2,49	18
Parking pawl bracket	5/16 in dia. X 18	24.40	2,49	18
Pump body to cover	5/16 in dia. X 18	24.40	2,49	18
Pump to case	5/16 in dia. X 18	24.40	2,49	18
Rear extension	⅜ in dia. X 16	31.18	3,18	23
Rear servo cover	5/16 in dia. X 18	24.40	2,49	18
Solenoid to case	¼ in dia. X 20	16.26	1,66	12
Speedometer drive shaft nut	¼ in dia. X 28	13.55	1,38	10
Sump	5/16 in dia. X 18	16.26	1,66	12
Vacuum modulation retainer to case	5/16 in dia X 18	24.40	2,49	18

SERVICE TOOLS

18G 677-2	Adaptor Pressure Take-Off
18G 1295	Piston Accumulator Control Valve Compressor
18G 1296	Front Pump Remover Screws
18G 1297	Front Pump and Tailshaft Oil Seal Replacer
18G 1298	Forward and Direct Clutch Piston Replacer Inner and Outer Protection Sleeve
18G 1309	Intermediate Clutch Inner Seal Protection Sleeve
18G 1310	Band Application Pin Selection Gauge
18G 677 ZC	Pressure Test Equipment
18G 1016	Clutch Spring Compressor
18G 1004	Circlip Pliers
18G 1004 J	Circlip Pliers Points
CBW 87	End-float Checking Gauge

TRANSMISSION FLUID LEVEL

Check

Ensure that the transmission is at normal operating temperature by either:

a. Running the vehicle on a rolling road utilizing all the gear positions until fluid reaches a temperature of 80°C, or
b. Conducting a road test of at least 24 km (15 miles).

CAUTION: Engine temperature is no indication of transmission temperature.

Check that the vehicle is on level ground.
Firmly apply the hand- and footbrakes, and run the engine at a maximum speed of 750 rev/min for several minutes. To ensure that the valve block is primed, slowly move the selector lever through all the gear positions.
With the engine still running, engage 'P' (Park) and withdraw the dipstick. Wipe it clean with a lint-free cloth and replace it.
Immediately remove the dipstick again, and note the level indicated on the 'HOT' scale. It should be between the 'MAX' and 'MIN' marks.
Carefully top up the fluid to the correct level, using only a Dexron 2D type fluid. Take care not to overfill.

RECOMMENDED TRANSMISSION FLUID

Dexron 2D type fluid only should be used, which must not be mixed with other transmission fluids.

NOTE: Dexron 2D Fluid is red in colour.

Fluid quantity

Transmission completely dry, but a quantity of fluid still remains in the torque converter; fill with approximately 9,12 litres (16 pints).

Fluid condition

Any moisture in the transmission fluid will cause the transmission seals to swell and will also soften friction material. If this fault is found early, the leak repaired and the fluid changed, no overhaul is needed unless there are obvious defects in the operation of the transmission.

Varnished fluid

This gives the fluid a dark brownish colour. If fluid is varnished through age or overheating, then it will have a pronounced brown colour.
Once varnish starts forming it builds up on all the valves, servos, clutches, etc., and causes sticking and hardening of the seals. Eventually it will clog the filter, and pump pressure will drop. When this happens the torque converter will not fill and there will be insufficient pressure for the clutch or band to hold torque, hence the transmission will not operate.
An evaluation of the degree of varnish will decide whether an overhaul is required or just a fluid change.

Low fluid level

This can result in the pump drawing air along with the fluid, thereby making fluid spongy and compressible due to air bubbles. This can result in delayed engagement or lack of drive, slipping gear-shifts or clutch burn-outs.
Another possible fault is pump wear or governor malfunction indicated by a buzzing noise emanating from the output shaft.

High fluid level

This can cause foaming and overheating of the transmission fluid resulting in the same faults occurring as in low fluid level. Overheating causes rapid oxidation of the fluid, leading to varnish formation.

'D' DRIVE RANGE

Position the selector lever in 'D' and accelerate from rest; check speed of 1–2 and 2–3 shifts.
A part throttle down-shift, 3–2 should be available at road speeds up to approximately 72 km/h (45 m.p.h.) as throttle is opened *progressively*. Care should be taken when checking this that transmission is not 'kicked down'.
At full throttle kick-down, a down-shift into 2nd or 1st gear, depending upon road speed, should occur.
As the vehicle speed decreases, the 3–2 and 2–1 shifts should occur at speeds below 16 km/h (10 m.p.h.).
There is no engine braking in 1st or 2nd gears in this range.
Line pressure at a constant road speed/throttle opening should be 4,3 kgf/cm² (60 lbf/in²).
Line pressure during acceleration should be 7,8 to 10,5 kgf/cm² (110 to 150 lbf/in²).

'2' INTERMEDIATE RANGE

Position the selector in '2' and accelerate the car from rest; check speed of 1–2 shift.

NOTE: At no time should transmission shift into '3'.

At full throttle kick-down, a down-shift into 1st gear, at the appropriate road speed, should occur. As the car speed decreases, transmission should shift from 2 to 1 at the appropriate road speed.

NOTE: The 1–2 shift in the '2' intermediate range is somewhat firmer than in 'D'; this is normal.

Line pressure should remain steady at 10,5 kgf/cm² (150 lbf/in²).

'1' LOW RANGE

Position the selector lever in '1' and accelerate the car from rest; there should be no up-shift from '1' with the selector lever in this position.

NOTE: An up-shift to second gear will occur at an engine speed of approximately 6200 rev/min, but it is not necessary to check this.

'2nd' GEAR—OVERRUN BRAKING

Position the selector lever in 'D' and with vehicle speed at approximately 56 km/h (35 m.p.h.), closed throttle, move the selector lever to '2'. The transmission should immediately shift into '2'. There should also be an increase in engine rev/min coupled with engine braking.

Line pressure should rise from approximately 4,9 kgf/cm² (70 lbf/in²) to approximately 10,5 kgf/cm² (150 lbf/in²) as down-shift occurs.

'1st' GEAR—OVERRUN BRAKING

Position the selector lever in '2' and with vehicle speed at approximately 48 to 64 km/h (30 to 40 m.p.h.), closed throttle, move the selector lever to '1'. A down-shift from '2' to '1' should occur when the vehicle speed falls to between 64 and 32 km/h (40 and 20 m.p.h.). The 2–1 down-shift at closed throttle will be accompanied by an increase in engine rev/min coupled with engine braking.

Line pressure should be approximately 10,5 kgf/cm² (150 lbf/in²) as down-shift occurs.

'R' REVERSE

Position the selector lever in 'R' and check for reverse operation.

GOVERNOR ASSEMBLY

Check

Service tools: Pressure test equipment 18G 677ZC, adaptor set 18G 677-2.

Disconnect the vacuum pipe from the modulator and fit pressure gauge to gearbox, using adaptor 18G 677-2.

CAUTION: Do not overtighten the adaptor.

Taking care to ensure that the hose is kept clear of the exhaust system, route the hose around the outside of the car and into the passenger's window.

Run the engine until transmission fluid reaches a temperature of 80°C or drive the car for at least 24 km (15 miles).

CAUTION: Engine temperature is no indication of transmission temperature.

Support the car on suitable 'wheel-free' equipment and raise the driving wheels clear of the ground.

Start the engine, select 'D', and with the brakes released, check the line pressure at 1000 rev/min; this should be approximately 11 kgf/cm² (150 lbf/in²).

Slowly increase engine speed to 3000 rev/min and check if a line pressure drop of 0,7 kgf/cm² (10 lbf/in²) occurs.

If no pressure drop occurs, inspect the governor for:
1. Sticking valve
2. Sticking weight
3. Restricted orifice in governor valve
4. Scored or cracked bore
5. Restricted feed pipe or filter

STALL SPEED

Test   **44.30.13**

Service tools: Pressure test equipment 18G 677 ZC, pressure take-off adaptor 18G 677-2.

CAUTION: The test MUST NOT last longer than 10 seconds. Always allow the engine to idle for at least two minutes between tests to allow the transmission to cool down. Do not carry out more than six tests without allowing the engine to cool down for at least half an hour.

The results of this test indicate the condition of the transmission and torque converter.

Stall speed is the maximum engine revolutions recorded whilst driving the impeller against the stationary turbine. Stall speed will vary with both engine and transmission conditions, so before attempting a stall speed check, engine condition must be determined. Engine and transmission must be at normal operating temperature before commencing check.

Fit the oil pressure test equipment 18G 677 ZC and the pressure take-off adaptor to the transmission.

Chock the road wheels and firmly apply both foot- and handbrake.

Start the engine and engage 'D'. Apply full throttle and note maximum engine speed and line pressure achieved.

If transmission slip occurs, stop the engine immediately and investigate the cause.

Restart the engine and repeat the above procedure with the selector lever in 'R'.

Data

Stall speed	2100 to 2400 rev/min
Stall pressure in 'D'	9,8 to 9,9 kgf/cm² (145 to 155 lbf/in²)
Stall pressure in 'R'	15,4 to 16,8 kgf/cm² (240 to 260 lbf/in²)

Rev/min	Condition Indicated
Under 1800	Stator slip
1800 to 1900	Poor engine tune
2100 to 2400	Normal
Over 2400	Transmission slip

ROAD TEST

Service tools: Pressure test equipment 18G 677 ZC, pressure take-off adaptor 18G 677-2

Unless the fault is immediately obvious a road test should always be made to establish at first hand, preferably with the customer, what the fault symptoms are and under what conditions they occur. Experience has shown that reports of faults are not reliable and it may even be that the supposed fault is a standard feature. Check all gears, that all shifts occur, and check shift speeds and quality. The part throttle downshift should not be mistaken as being a full throttle kick-down.

Exercise great care that further damage is not done to the transmission during test, particularly if the fault may involve slipping. Try not to let the transmission slip at all; clutches and bands can burn out in seconds.

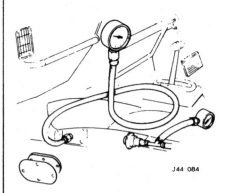

J44 084

Fig. 3

FAULT-FINDING AND DIAGNOSIS

PRELIMINARY FAULT-FINDING PROCEDURE

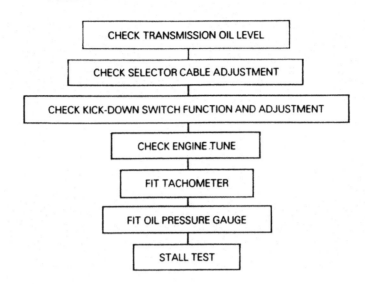

CHECK TRANSMISSION OIL LEVEL

CHECK SELECTOR CABLE ADJUSTMENT

CHECK KICK-DOWN SWITCH FUNCTION AND ADJUSTMENT

CHECK ENGINE TUNE

FIT TACHOMETER

FIT OIL PRESSURE GAUGE

STALL TEST

CAUTION: Total running time for this combination must not exceed 2 minutes

	Check oil pressures in the following manner		
		Oil Pressure	
	Range	kgf/cm²	lbf/in²
1	Neutral—brakes applied—engine at 1000 rev/min	3,8 to 4,9	55 to 70
2	Drive—idle—set engine idle to specifications	4,2 to 5,9	60 to 85
3	Drive—brakes applied—engine at 1000 rev/min	*4,2 to 6,3	*60 to 90
4	2 or 1—brakes applied—engine at 1000 rev/min	9,5 to 11,2	135 to 160
5	Reverse—brakes applied—engine at 1000 rev/min	6,7 to 10,5	95 to 150
6	Drive—brakes applied—engine at 1000 rev/min—down-shift switch activated	6,3 to 7,7	90 to 100
7	Governor check, see below	Drop of 0,7 kgf/cm² or more	Drop of 10 lbf/in² or more
8	Drive—48 km/h (30 m.p.h.)—closed throttle on road, or on hoist	†3,8 to 4,9	†55 to 70

* If high line pressures are experienced, check vacuum and, if necessary, the modulator.
† Vehicle on hoist, driving wheels off ground, selector in drive, brakes released; raise speed to 3000 rev/min, close throttle and read pressure between 2000 and 1200 rev/min.

44—9

PRELIMINARY DIAGNOSTIC CHART
TRANSMISSION MALFUNCTION RELATED TO OIL PRESSURE

MALFUNCTION	1 — NEUTRAL—BRAKES APPLIED 1000 REV/MIN — OIL PRESSURE	2 — DRIVE—IDLE — OIL PRESSURE	3 — DRIVE—BRAKES APPLIED 1000 REV/MIN — OIL PRESSURE	4 — 'I'—BRAKES APPLIED 1000 REV/MIN — OIL PRESSURE	5 — REVERSE—BRAKES APPLIED 1000 REV/MIN — OIL PRESSURE	6 — DRIVE—BRAKES APPLIED 1000 REV/MIN DOWN-SHIFT SWITCH ACTIVATED — OIL PRESSURE	7 — PRESSURE DROP OCCURS WHILE ENGINE REV/MIN INCREASES FROM 1000 to 3000 REV/MIN WHEELS FREE TO MOVE*	8 — DRIVE—48 KM/H (30 M.P.H.) CLOSED THROTTLE — OIL PRESSURE	POSSIBLE CAUSE OF MALFUNCTION
NO 1–2 UP-SHIFT AND/OR DELAYED UP-SHIFT	Normal	Normal	Normal	Normal	Normal	Normal	$0.7\ \text{kgf/cm}^2$ (10 lbf/in²) drop or more	Normal	Malfunction in control valve assembly
	Normal	Normal	Normal	Normal	Normal	Normal	Less than $0.7\ \text{kgf/cm}^2$ (10 lbf/in²) drop	Normal	Malfunction in governor or governor feed system
	Normal	High	High	Normal	Normal	Normal	Drop	High	Malfunction in detent system
	High	High	High	Normal	High	—	—	—	Malfunction in modulator or vacuum feed system to modulator
SLIPPING—REVERSE	Normal	Normal	Normal	Normal	Low	Normal	Drop	Normal	Oil leak in feed system to the direct clutch
SLIPPING—1st GEAR	Normal	Low to Normal	Low to Normal	Low to Normal	Normal	Low to Normal	—	Low to Normal	Oil leak in feed system to the forward clutch
DOWN-SHIFT WITH ZERO THROTTLE AND NO ENGINE BRAKING IN DRIVE	Normal	High	Normal	Normal	Normal	—	—	High	Detent wires switched
NO DETENT DOWN-SHIFTS	Normal	Normal	Normal	Normal	Normal	Low	Normal	Normal	Malfunctions in detent system

* Drive range, vacuum line disconnected from modulator.

NOTE: A dash (—) in the above chart means that the oil pressure reading has no meaning under the test condition.

44—10

LOW LINE PRESSURE

1. **LOW TRANSMISSION OIL LEVEL**

2. **MODULATOR ASSEMBLY** — Carry out 'bellows comparison check'.

3. **FILTER**

   a. Blocked or restricted.
   b. 'O' ring on intake pipe and/or grommet missing or damaged.
   c. Split or leaking intake pipe.
   d. Wrong filter assembly.

4. **PUMP**

   a. Pressure regulator or boost valve stuck.
   b. Gear clearance, damaged, worn. (Pump will become damaged if drive gear is installed backwards, or if converter pilot does not enter crankshaft freely.)
   c. Pump to case gasket wrongly positioned.
   d. Pump body and/or cover machining error or scoring of pump gear pocket.

5. **INTERNAL CIRCUIT LEAKS**

   a. Forward clutch leak. (Pressure normal in neutral and reverse — Pressure low in drive.)
      1. Check pump rings for damage.
      2. Check forward clutch seals for damage.
      3. Check turbine shaft journals for damage.
      4. Check stator shaft bushings for damage.

   b. Direct clutch leak. (Pressure normal in neutral, low, intermediate and drive — Pressure low in reverse.)
      1. Check centre support oil seal rings for damage.
      2. Check direct clutch outer seal for damage.
      3. Check rear servo and front accumulator pistons and rings for damage.

6. **CASE ASSEMBLY**

   a. Porosity in intake bore area.
   b. Check case for intermediate clutch plug leak.
   c. Low line pressure in reverse or '1'. If '1' — reverse check ball missing. This will cause no reverse and no over-run braking in '1'.

HIGH LINE PRESSURE

1. **VACUUM LEAK**

   a. Full leak, vacuum line disconnected.
   b. Partial leak in line from engine to modulator.
   c. Improper engine vacuum.
   d. Vacuum operated accessory leak (hoses, vacuum advance, etc.).

2. **DAMAGED MODULATOR**

   a. Stuck valve.
   b. Water in modulator.
   c. Not operating properly.

3. **DETENT SYSTEM**

   a. Detent switch actuated (plunger stuck) or shorted.
   b. Detent wiring shorted.
   c. Detent solenoid stuck open.
   d. Detent feed orifice in spacer plate blocked.
   e. Detent solenoid loose.
   f. Detent valve bore plug damaged.
   g. Detent regulator valve pin short.

4. **PUMP**

   a. Pressure regulator and/or boost valve stuck.
   b. Pump casting porous.
   c. Pressure boost valve installed backwards.
   d. Pressure boost bushing broken.
   e. Wrong type of pressure regulator valve.

5. **CONTROL VALVE ASSEMBLY**

   a. Control valve to spacer gasket wrongly fitted.
   b. Gaskets installed in reverse order.

BURNED CLUTCH PLATES

1. **FORWARD CLUTCH**

   a. Check ball in clutch housing damaged, stuck or missing.
   b. Clutch piston cracked, seals damaged or missing.
   c. Low line pressure.
   d. Manual valve wrongly fitted.
   e. Restricted oil feed to forward clutch. (Examples: Clutch housing to inner and outer areas not drilled, restricted or porosity in pump.)
   f. Pump cover oil seal rings missing, broken or undersize; ring groove oversize.
   g. Case valve body face not flat or porosity between channels.
   h. Manual valve bent and centre land not properly ground.

2. **INTERMEDIATE CLUTCH**

   a. Constant bleed orifice in centre support blocked.
   b. Rear accumulator piston oil ring, damaged or missing.
   c. 1–2 accumulator valve stuck in control valve assembly.
   d. Intermediate clutch piston seals damaged or missing.
   e. Centre support bolt loose.
   f. Low line pressure.
   g. Intermediate clutch plug in case missing.
   h. Case valve body face not flat or porosity between channels.
   i. Manual valve bent and centre land not properly ground.

3. **DIRECT CLUTCH**

   a. Restricted orifice in vacuum line to modulator (poor vacuum response).
   b. Check ball in direct clutch piston damaged, stuck or missing.
   c. Leaking modulator bellows.
   d. Centre support bolt loose. (Bolt may be tight in support but not holding support tightly to case.)
   e. Centre support oil rings or grooves damaged or missing.
   f. Clutch piston seals damaged or missing.
   g. Front and rear servo pistons and seals damaged.
   h. Manual valve bent and centre land damaged.
   i. Case valve body face not flat or porosity between channels.

continued

j.   Intermediate sprag clutch or roller clutch installed backwards.
k.   3–2 valve, 3–2 spring or 3–2 spacer pin installed in the wrong sequence in 3–2 valve bore.
l.   Incorrect combination of front servo and accumulator parts.
m.   Replace intermediate clutch piston seals.

NOTE: If direct clutch plates and front band are burned, check selector cable adjustment, see 44.30.04.

OIL LEAKS

NOTE: Make sure underside of transmission is clean in order to isolate oil leaks and diagnose them correctly.

1.   **TRANSMISSION OIL PAN LEAKS**

   a.   Attaching bolts not correctly torqued.
   b.   Improperly installed or damaged oil pan gasket.

2.   **CASE EXTENSION LEAK**

   a.   Attaching bolts not correctly torqued.
   b.   If the rear seal is suspected:
      1   Check seal for damage or wrong installation.
      2   Check slip yoke for damage.
      3   If oil is coming out the vent hole in end of the slip yoke, inspect output shaft 'O' ring for damage.
   c.   Extension to case gasket or seal damaged.
   d.   Porous casting.

3.   **CASE LEAK**

   a.   Filler pipe 'O' ring seal damaged or missing.
   b.   Modulator assembly 'O' ring seal damaged.
   c.   Electrical connector 'O' ring seal damaged.
   d.   Governor cover, gasket and bolts damaged or loose; case face damaged or porous.
   e.   Leak at speedometer driven gear housing or seal.
   f.   Manual shaft seal damaged.
   g.   Line pressure tap plug stripped.
   h.   Vent pipe (refer to item 5).
   i.   Porous case, or cracked at pressure plug boss.

4.   **FRONT END LEAK**

   a.   Front seal damaged (check converter neck for nicks, etc., also for pump bushing moved forward), garter spring missing.
   b.   Pump attaching bolts loose. Sealing washers damaged.
   c.   Converter leakage.
   d.   Large 'O' ring pump seal damaged. Also check case bore.
   e.   Porous casting (pump or case).
   f.   Pump drainback hole blocked.

5.   **OIL LEAKS FROM VENT PIPE**

   a.   Transmission overfilled.
   b.   Water in oil.
   c.   Filter 'O' ring damaged or improperly assembled causing oil to foam.
   d.   Foreign material between pump and case or between pump cover and body.
   e.   Case porous, pump face improperly machined.
   f.   Pump wrongly fitted.
   g.   Pump to case gasket faulty.
   h.   Pump breather hole blocked or missing.
   i.   Hole in intake pipe.
   j.   Check ball in forward clutch housing stuck open or missing.
   k.   Drainback hole in case blocked or restricted.
   l.   Inspect turbine shaft bushing journals and stator bushings for scoring or other faults.

6.   **OIL COOLER LINES**

   a.   Connections at cooler loose or stripped.
   b.   Connections at case loose or stripped.

7.   **MODULATOR ASSEMBLY**

   a.   Vacuum diaphragm leaking.

44—12

IMPROPER VACUUM AT MODULATOR

1. **ENGINE**

   a. Engine tune
   b. Loose vacuum fittings.
   c. Vacuum operated accessory leak (hoses, vacuum advance, etc.).
   d. Engine exhaust system restricted.
   e. Faulty exhaust gas recirculation (E.G.R.) valve (if fitted).

2. **VACUUM LINE TO MODULATOR**

   a. Leak.
   b. Loose fitting.
   c. Restricted orifice, or incorrect orifice size.
   d. Carbon build up at modulator vacuum fitting.
   e. Vacuum pipe trapped or collapsed.
   f. Grease in pipe (none or delayed upshift—cold).

MODULATOR ASSEMBLY DIAGNOSTIC PROCEDURE

1. **VACUUM DIAPHRAGM LEAK CHECK**

   Insert a pipe cleaner into the vacuum connector pipe as far as possible and check for the presence of transmission oil. If oil is found, replace the modulator. Transmission oil may be lost through diaphragm and burned in engine.

   NOTE: Fuel or water condensation may settle in the vacuum side of the modulator. If this is found without the presence of oil the modulator should **not** be changed.

2. **ATMOSPHERIC LEAK CHECK**

   Apply a liberal coating of soap solution to the vacuum connector pipe seam, the crimped upper to lower housing seam, and the threaded screw seal. Using a short piece of rubber tubing, apply air pressure to the vacuum pipe by blowing into the tube and observing for bubbles. If bubbles appear, replace the modulator.

   NOTE: Do not use any method other than human lung power for applying air pressure, as pressures over 0,4 kgf/cm^2 (6 lbf/in^2) may damage the modulator.

3. **BELLOWS COMPARISON CHECK**

   Where modulator bellows are suspect, the unit should be checked by substituting a new modulator assembly.

4. **SLEEVE ALIGNMENT CHECK**

   Roll the main body of the modulator on a flat surface and observe the sleeve for concentricity to the cam. If the sleeve is concentric and the plunger is free, the modulator is acceptable.

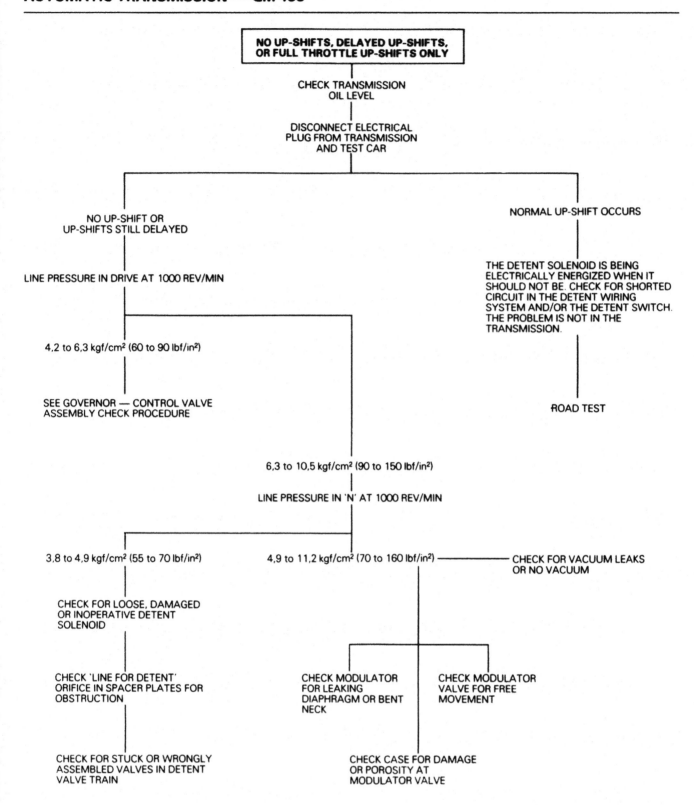

NO UP-SHIFTS, DELAYED UP-SHIFTS, OR FULL THROTTLE UP-SHIFTS ONLY

CHECK TRANSMISSION OIL LEVEL

DISCONNECT ELECTRICAL PLUG FROM TRANSMISSION AND TEST CAR

NO UP-SHIFT OR UP-SHIFTS STILL DELAYED

NORMAL UP-SHIFT OCCURS

LINE PRESSURE IN DRIVE AT 1000 REV/MIN

THE DETENT SOLENOID IS BEING ELECTRICALLY ENERGIZED WHEN IT SHOULD NOT BE. CHECK FOR SHORTED CIRCUIT IN THE DETENT WIRING SYSTEM AND/OR THE DETENT SWITCH. THE PROBLEM IS NOT IN THE TRANSMISSION.

4,2 to 6,3 kgf/cm² (60 to 90 lbf/in²)

SEE GOVERNOR — CONTROL VALVE ASSEMBLY CHECK PROCEDURE

ROAD TEST

6,3 to 10,5 kgf/cm² (90 to 150 lbf/in²)

LINE PRESSURE IN 'N' AT 1000 REV/MIN

3,8 to 4,9 kgf/cm² (55 to 70 lbf/in²)

4,9 to 11,2 kgf/cm² (70 to 160 lbf/in²)

CHECK FOR VACUUM LEAKS OR NO VACUUM

CHECK FOR LOOSE, DAMAGED OR INOPERATIVE DETENT SOLENOID

CHECK 'LINE FOR DETENT' ORIFICE IN SPACER PLATES FOR OBSTRUCTION

CHECK MODULATOR FOR LEAKING DIAPHRAGM OR BENT NECK

CHECK MODULATOR VALVE FOR FREE MOVEMENT

CHECK FOR STUCK OR WRONGLY ASSEMBLED VALVES IN DETENT VALVE TRAIN

CHECK CASE FOR DAMAGE OR POROSITY AT MODULATOR VALVE

44—14

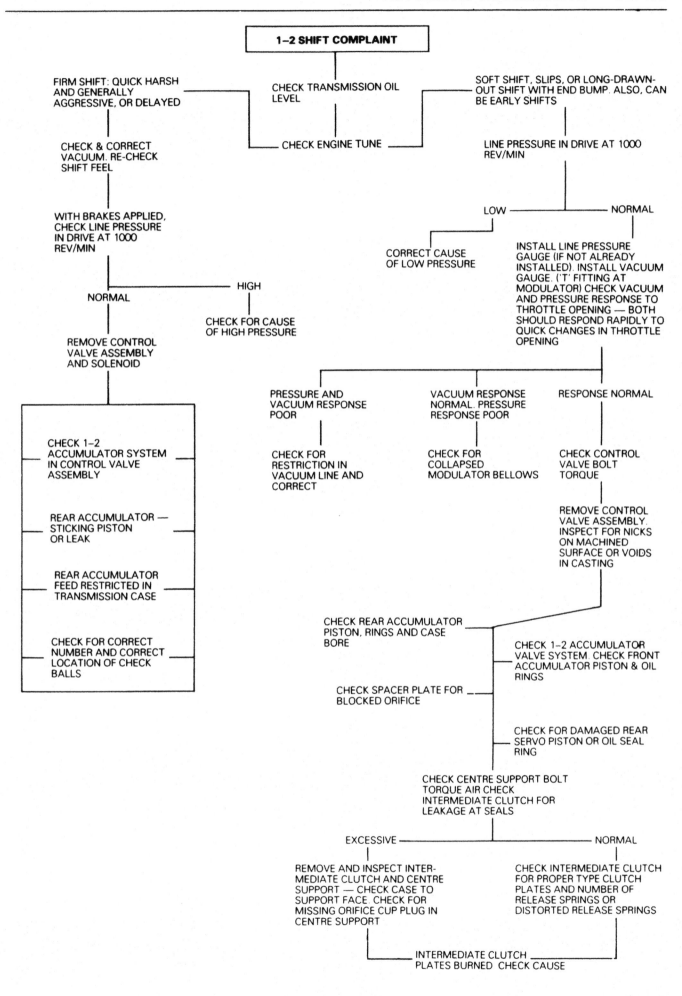

1–2 SHIFT COMPLAINT

FIRM SHIFT: QUICK HARSH AND GENERALLY AGGRESSIVE, OR DELAYED

CHECK TRANSMISSION OIL LEVEL

SOFT SHIFT, SLIPS, OR LONG-DRAWN-OUT SHIFT WITH END BUMP. ALSO, CAN BE EARLY SHIFTS

CHECK & CORRECT VACUUM. RE-CHECK SHIFT FEEL

CHECK ENGINE TUNE

LINE PRESSURE IN DRIVE AT 1000 REV/MIN

WITH BRAKES APPLIED, CHECK LINE PRESSURE IN DRIVE AT 1000 REV/MIN

LOW — NORMAL

NORMAL

HIGH

CORRECT CAUSE OF LOW PRESSURE

INSTALL LINE PRESSURE GAUGE (IF NOT ALREADY INSTALLED). INSTALL VACUUM GAUGE. ('T' FITTING AT MODULATOR) CHECK VACUUM AND PRESSURE RESPONSE TO THROTTLE OPENING — BOTH SHOULD RESPOND RAPIDLY TO QUICK CHANGES IN THROTTLE OPENING

CHECK FOR CAUSE OF HIGH PRESSURE

REMOVE CONTROL VALVE ASSEMBLY AND SOLENOID

CHECK 1–2 ACCUMULATOR SYSTEM IN CONTROL VALVE ASSEMBLY

PRESSURE AND VACUUM RESPONSE POOR

VACUUM RESPONSE NORMAL. PRESSURE RESPONSE POOR

RESPONSE NORMAL

CHECK FOR RESTRICTION IN VACUUM LINE AND CORRECT

CHECK FOR COLLAPSED MODULATOR BELLOWS

CHECK CONTROL VALVE BOLT TORQUE

REAR ACCUMULATOR — STICKING PISTON OR LEAK

REMOVE CONTROL VALVE ASSEMBLY. INSPECT FOR NICKS ON MACHINED SURFACE OR VOIDS IN CASTING

REAR ACCUMULATOR FEED RESTRICTED IN TRANSMISSION CASE

CHECK FOR CORRECT NUMBER AND CORRECT LOCATION OF CHECK BALLS

CHECK REAR ACCUMULATOR PISTON, RINGS AND CASE BORE

CHECK 1–2 ACCUMULATOR VALVE SYSTEM. CHECK FRONT ACCUMULATOR PISTON & OIL RINGS

CHECK SPACER PLATE FOR BLOCKED ORIFICE

CHECK FOR DAMAGED REAR SERVO PISTON OR OIL SEAL RING

CHECK CENTRE SUPPORT BOLT TORQUE AIR CHECK INTERMEDIATE CLUTCH FOR LEAKAGE AT SEALS

EXCESSIVE

NORMAL

REMOVE AND INSPECT INTER-MEDIATE CLUTCH AND CENTRE SUPPORT — CHECK CASE TO SUPPORT FACE. CHECK FOR MISSING ORIFICE CUP PLUG IN CENTRE SUPPORT

CHECK INTERMEDIATE CLUTCH FOR PROPER TYPE CLUTCH PLATES AND NUMBER OF RELEASE SPRINGS OR DISTORTED RELEASE SPRINGS

INTERMEDIATE CLUTCH PLATES BURNED CHECK CAUSE

44—15

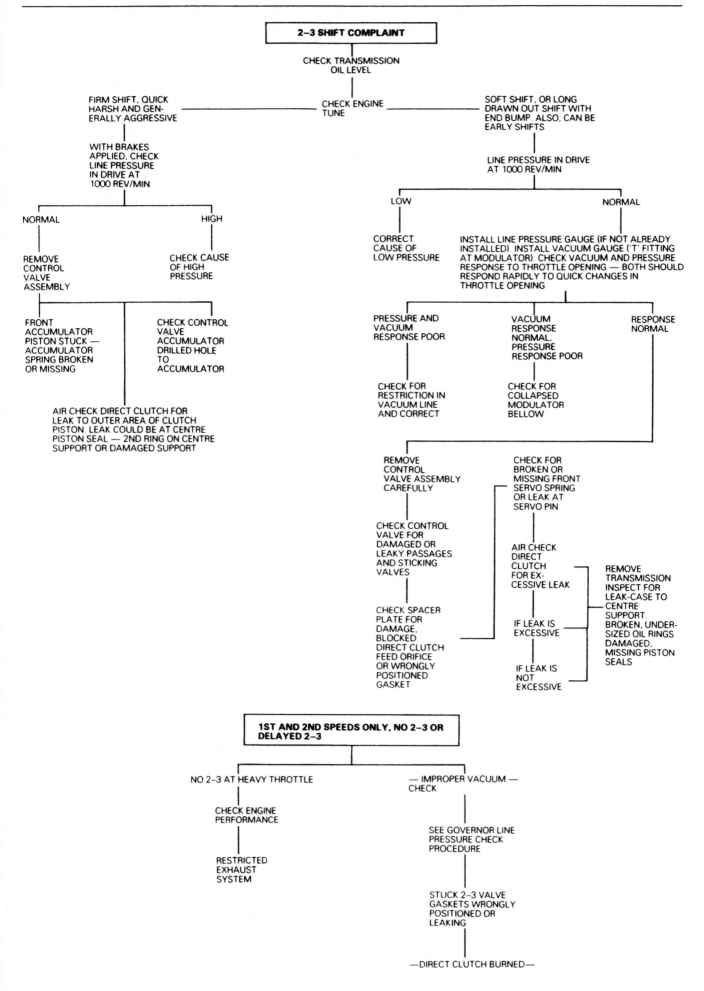

2–3 SHIFT COMPLAINT

CHECK TRANSMISSION OIL LEVEL

CHECK ENGINE TUNE

FIRM SHIFT, QUICK HARSH AND GEN-ERALLY AGGRESSIVE

SOFT SHIFT, OR LONG DRAWN OUT SHIFT WITH END BUMP. ALSO, CAN BE EARLY SHIFTS

WITH BRAKES APPLIED, CHECK LINE PRESSURE IN DRIVE AT 1000 REV/MIN

LINE PRESSURE IN DRIVE AT 1000 REV/MIN

NORMAL

HIGH

LOW

NORMAL

REMOVE CONTROL VALVE ASSEMBLY

CHECK CAUSE OF HIGH PRESSURE

CORRECT CAUSE OF LOW PRESSURE

INSTALL LINE PRESSURE GAUGE (IF NOT ALREADY INSTALLED). INSTALL VACUUM GAUGE ('T' FITTING AT MODULATOR). CHECK VACUUM AND PRESSURE RESPONSE TO THROTTLE OPENING — BOTH SHOULD RESPOND RAPIDLY TO QUICK CHANGES IN THROTTLE OPENING

FRONT ACCUMULATOR PISTON STUCK — ACCUMULATOR SPRING BROKEN OR MISSING

CHECK CONTROL VALVE ACCUMULATOR DRILLED HOLE TO ACCUMULATOR

PRESSURE AND VACUUM RESPONSE POOR

VACUUM RESPONSE NORMAL, PRESSURE RESPONSE POOR

RESPONSE NORMAL

AIR CHECK DIRECT CLUTCH FOR LEAK TO OUTER AREA OF CLUTCH PISTON. LEAK COULD BE AT CENTRE PISTON SEAL — 2ND RING ON CENTRE SUPPORT OR DAMAGED SUPPORT

CHECK FOR RESTRICTION IN VACUUM LINE AND CORRECT

CHECK FOR COLLAPSED MODULATOR BELLOW

REMOVE CONTROL VALVE ASSEMBLY CAREFULLY

CHECK FOR BROKEN OR MISSING FRONT SERVO SPRING OR LEAK AT SERVO PIN

CHECK CONTROL VALVE FOR DAMAGED OR LEAKY PASSAGES AND STICKING VALVES

AIR CHECK DIRECT CLUTCH FOR EX-CESSIVE LEAK

REMOVE TRANSMISSION INSPECT FOR LEAK-CASE TO CENTRE SUPPORT BROKEN, UNDER-SIZED OIL RINGS DAMAGED, MISSING PISTON SEALS

CHECK SPACER PLATE FOR DAMAGE, BLOCKED DIRECT CLUTCH FEED ORIFICE OR WRONGLY POSITIONED GASKET

IF LEAK IS EXCESSIVE

IF LEAK IS NOT EXCESSIVE

1ST AND 2ND SPEEDS ONLY, NO 2–3 OR DELAYED 2–3

NO 2–3 AT HEAVY THROTTLE

— IMPROPER VACUUM — CHECK

CHECK ENGINE PERFORMANCE

SEE GOVERNOR LINE PRESSURE CHECK PROCEDURE

RESTRICTED EXHAUST SYSTEM

STUCK 2–3 VALVE GASKETS WRONGLY POSITIONED OR LEAKING

—DIRECT CLUTCH BURNED—

44—16

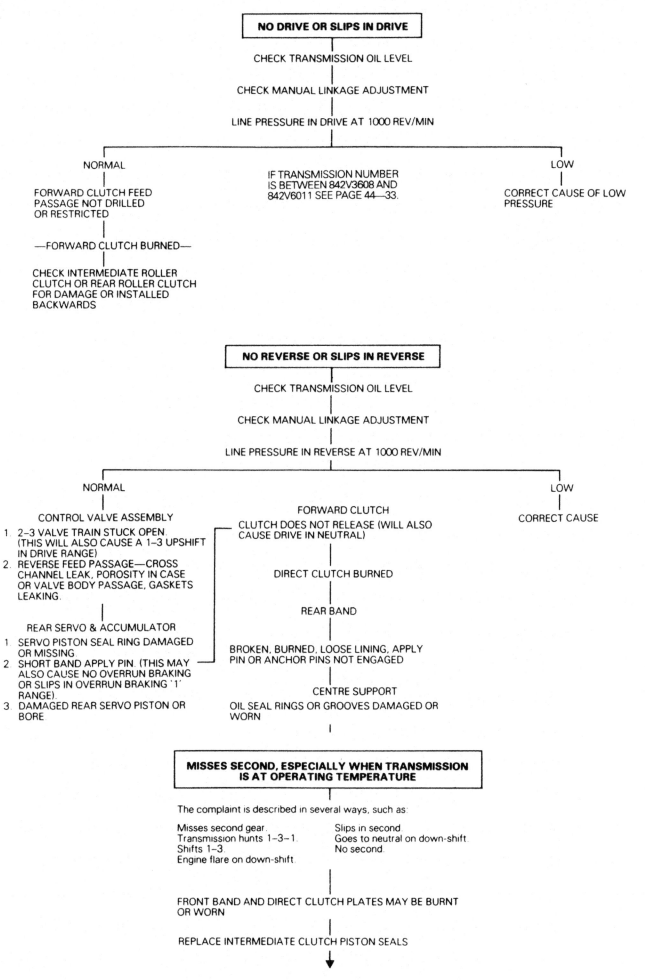

NO DRIVE OR SLIPS IN DRIVE

CHECK TRANSMISSION OIL LEVEL

CHECK MANUAL LINKAGE ADJUSTMENT

LINE PRESSURE IN DRIVE AT 1000 REV/MIN

NORMAL

FORWARD CLUTCH FEED
PASSAGE NOT DRILLED
OR RESTRICTED

—FORWARD CLUTCH BURNED—

CHECK INTERMEDIATE ROLLER
CLUTCH OR REAR ROLLER CLUTCH
FOR DAMAGE OR INSTALLED
BACKWARDS

IF TRANSMISSION NUMBER
IS BETWEEN 842V3608 AND
842V6011 SEE PAGE 44—33.

LOW

CORRECT CAUSE OF LOW
PRESSURE

NO REVERSE OR SLIPS IN REVERSE

CHECK TRANSMISSION OIL LEVEL

CHECK MANUAL LINKAGE ADJUSTMENT

LINE PRESSURE IN REVERSE AT 1000 REV/MIN

NORMAL

CONTROL VALVE ASSEMBLY

1. 2–3 VALVE TRAIN STUCK OPEN.
   (THIS WILL ALSO CAUSE A 1–3 UPSHIFT
   IN DRIVE RANGE)
2. REVERSE FEED PASSAGE—CROSS
   CHANNEL LEAK, POROSITY IN CASE
   OR VALVE BODY PASSAGE, GASKETS
   LEAKING.

REAR SERVO & ACCUMULATOR

1. SERVO PISTON SEAL RING DAMAGED
   OR MISSING.
2. SHORT BAND APPLY PIN. (THIS MAY
   ALSO CAUSE NO OVERRUN BRAKING
   OR SLIPS IN OVERRUN BRAKING '1'
   RANGE).
3. DAMAGED REAR SERVO PISTON OR
   BORE.

FORWARD CLUTCH
CLUTCH DOES NOT RELEASE (WILL ALSO
CAUSE DRIVE IN NEUTRAL)

DIRECT CLUTCH BURNED

REAR BAND

BROKEN, BURNED, LOOSE LINING, APPLY
PIN OR ANCHOR PINS NOT ENGAGED

CENTRE SUPPORT
OIL SEAL RINGS OR GROOVES DAMAGED OR
WORN

LOW

CORRECT CAUSE

**MISSES SECOND, ESPECIALLY WHEN TRANSMISSION
IS AT OPERATING TEMPERATURE**

The complaint is described in several ways, such as:

Misses second gear.
Transmission hunts 1–3–1.
Shifts 1–3.
Engine flare on down-shift.

Slips in second.
Goes to neutral on down-shift.
No second.

FRONT BAND AND DIRECT CLUTCH PLATES MAY BE BURNT
OR WORN

REPLACE INTERMEDIATE CLUTCH PISTON SEALS

44—17

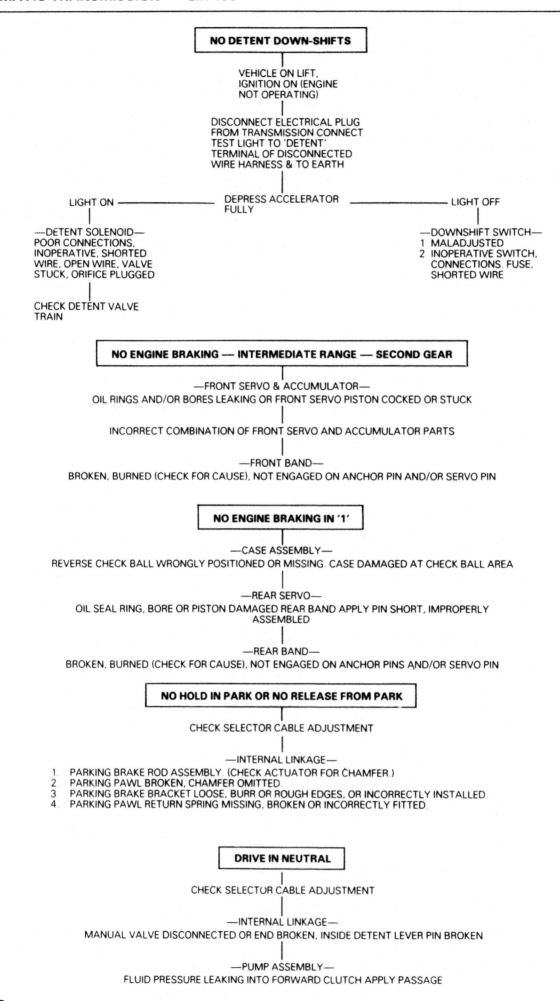

NO DETENT DOWN-SHIFTS

VEHICLE ON LIFT,
IGNITION ON (ENGINE
NOT OPERATING)

DISCONNECT ELECTRICAL PLUG
FROM TRANSMISSION CONNECT
TEST LIGHT TO 'DETENT'
TERMINAL OF DISCONNECTED
WIRE HARNESS & TO EARTH

LIGHT ON —————————— DEPRESS ACCELERATOR —————————— LIGHT OFF
FULLY

—DETENT SOLENOID—
POOR CONNECTIONS,
INOPERATIVE, SHORTED
WIRE, OPEN WIRE, VALVE
STUCK, ORIFICE PLUGGED

—DOWNSHIFT SWITCH—
1 MALADJUSTED
2 INOPERATIVE SWITCH,
CONNECTIONS. FUSE,
SHORTED WIRE

CHECK DETENT VALVE
TRAIN

NO ENGINE BRAKING — INTERMEDIATE RANGE — SECOND GEAR

—FRONT SERVO & ACCUMULATOR—
OIL RINGS AND/OR BORES LEAKING OR FRONT SERVO PISTON COCKED OR STUCK

INCORRECT COMBINATION OF FRONT SERVO AND ACCUMULATOR PARTS

—FRONT BAND—
BROKEN, BURNED (CHECK FOR CAUSE), NOT ENGAGED ON ANCHOR PIN AND/OR SERVO PIN

NO ENGINE BRAKING IN '1'

—CASE ASSEMBLY—
REVERSE CHECK BALL WRONGLY POSITIONED OR MISSING. CASE DAMAGED AT CHECK BALL AREA

—REAR SERVO—
OIL SEAL RING, BORE OR PISTON DAMAGED REAR BAND APPLY PIN SHORT, IMPROPERLY
ASSEMBLED

—REAR BAND—
BROKEN, BURNED (CHECK FOR CAUSE), NOT ENGAGED ON ANCHOR PINS AND/OR SERVO PIN

NO HOLD IN PARK OR NO RELEASE FROM PARK

CHECK SELECTOR CABLE ADJUSTMENT

—INTERNAL LINKAGE—
1. PARKING BRAKE ROD ASSEMBLY. (CHECK ACTUATOR FOR CHAMFER.)
2. PARKING PAWL BROKEN, CHAMFER OMITTED.
3. PARKING BRAKE BRACKET LOOSE, BURR OR ROUGH EDGES, OR INCORRECTLY INSTALLED.
4. PARKING PAWL RETURN SPRING MISSING, BROKEN OR INCORRECTLY FITTED.

DRIVE IN NEUTRAL

CHECK SELECTOR CABLE ADJUSTMENT

—INTERNAL LINKAGE—
MANUAL VALVE DISCONNECTED OR END BROKEN, INSIDE DETENT LEVER PIN BROKEN

—PUMP ASSEMBLY—
FLUID PRESSURE LEAKING INTO FORWARD CLUTCH APPLY PASSAGE

44—18

TRANSMISSION NOISY

CAUTION: BEFORE CHECKING TRANSMISSION FOR WHAT IS BELIEVED TO BE 'TRANSMISSION NOISE', MAKE CERTAIN THE NOISE IS NOT FROM THE WATER PUMP, ALTERNATOR, AIR CONDITIONER, POWER STEERING, ETC. THESE COMPONENTS CAN BE ISOLATED BY REMOVING THE APPROPRIATE DRIVE BELT AND RUNNING THE ENGINE FOR NOT MORE THAN TWO MINUTES AT ONE TIME.

PARK, NEUTRAL AND ALL DRIVE RANGES

DURING ACCELERATION—
ANY GEAR

—PUMP CAVITATION—
OIL LEVEL LOW.
BLOCKED OR RESTRICTED FILTER.
WRONG FILTER.
INTAKE PIPE 'O' RING DAMAGED.
INTAKE PIPE SPLIT, POROSITY IN CASE INTAKE
PIPE BORE.
WATER IN OIL.
POROSITY OR VOIDS IN TRANSMISSION CASE
(PUMP FACE) INTAKE PORT.
PUMP TO CASE GASKET WRONGLY POSITIONED.

—PUMP ASSEMBLY—
GEARS DAMAGED.
DRIVING GEAR ASSEMBLED BACKWARDS.
CRESCENT INTERFERENCE.
BUZZING NOISE — ORIFICE CUP PLUG IN
PRESSURE REGULATOR DAMAGED OR MISSING.
SEAL RINGS DAMAGED OR WORN.

—CONVERTER—
LOOSE BOLTS (CONVERTER TO DRIVE PLATE).
CONVERTER DAMAGE.
CRACKED OR BROKEN DRIVE PLATE.

SQUEAL AT LOW VEHICLE
SPEEDS, ESPECIALLY AT NORMAL
OPERATING TEMPERATURE

SPEEDOMETER DRIVEN GEAR SHAFT SEAL—
SEAL REQUIRES LUBRICATION OR
REPLACEMENT

IF SPEEDOMETER DRIVEN GEAR SHAFT
APPEARS TWISTED, CHECK FOR PRESENCE OF
ENGINE COOLANT IN TRANSMISSION. CHECK
TRANSMISSION COOLER FOR LEAKS.

FIRST, SECOND AND/OR
REVERSE

—PLANETARY GEAR SET—
1. THOROUGHLY CLEAN, DRY & INSPECT CLOSELY THE ROLLER THRUST BEARINGS AND THRUST RACES FOR PITTING OR ROUGH CONDITION.
2. INSPECT GEARS FOR DAMAGE, WEAR, PITTING AND PINIONS FOR TILT.
3. INSPECT FRONT INTERNAL GEAR FOR RING DAMAGE.

44—19

SELECTOR LEVER ASSEMBLY

Overhaul   44.15.05

Removing

NOTE: Prior to carrying out this operation it will be necessary to remove the selector quadrant as detailed in operation 76.25.08.

Remove the nuts (1, Fig. 4) securing the indicator bulb mounting and remove the bulb mounting bracket.

Remove the circlip and circlip washer (2, Fig. 4) from the lever pivot shaft.

Remove the selector lever assembly from the car.

Remove the nuts securing the tension spring (4, Fig. 4) and remove the spring.

Remove the split pin and washers (5, Fig. 4) securing the lever to the cam plate pivot.

Remove the selector lever (6, Fig. 4).

Holding the lever mounting plate in a vice, remove the screws securing the tapped block and illumination bulb bracket (7, Fig. 4) to the cam plate.

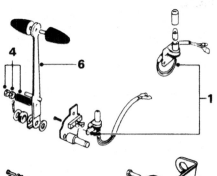

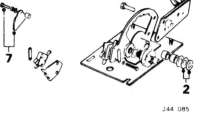

J44 085

Fig. 4

Remove the tension spring screw from the tapped block and remove the block from the cam plate.

Clean all parts.

Refitting

Holding the mounting plate in a vice, refit the tapped block to the cam plate by loosely fitting the tensioning spring screw.

Align the holes of the block with those in the cam plate and fit the illumination bulb bracket without fully tightening the retaining screws.

Tighten the tensioning spring screw.

Tighten the bulb bracket screws.

Secure the tensioning spring screw with two centre dots on the mating surface of the tapped block.

Remove the mounting plate assembly from the vice.

Refit the lever to the mounting plate assembly and secure to the lever pivot with the pivot washer, washer, rubber washer, washer and split pin.

Refit the tensioning spring and spring securing nut. Reset the spring to the correct tension and refit the locknut.

Lubricate the selector lever pivot shaft.

Refit the assembly to the car.

Refit the circlip washer, shim and circlip to the lever pivot.

Refit selector quadrant, see 76.25.08.

STARTER INHIBITOR SWITCH

Check and adjust   44.15.18

Adjusting

Disconnect the battery and unscrew the gear selector knob.

Remove the screws securing the control escutcheon; withdraw the escutcheon slightly to obtain access to the cigar lighter.

Note the fitted position of the cigar lighter and door lock and window switch terminals; detach the terminals and withdraw the escutcheon.

Remove selector indicator assembly.

Detach the feed cable from the inhibitor switch.

Connect a test lamp and battery in series with the switch.

NOTE: Switch is in earthed position. Place the selector lever in 'N' position.

Slacken the locknuts (1, Fig. 5) securing the switch and adjust position of switch until the lamp lights.

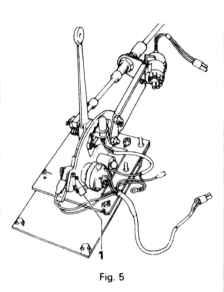

Fig. 5

Tighten the locknuts, check that lamp remains on with lever in 'P' position and is off with lever in drive position.

Remove the battery and test lamp, reconnect feed cable to switch.

Refit the selector indicator.

Refit the terminals to the cigar lighter, and window switches, refit the escutcheon.

Refit the gear selector knob, connect the battery and test the cigar lighter, door and windows switches for correct operation.

REAR EXTENSION HOUSING

Remove and refit   44.20.15

Service tool: MS 53 A, engine support bracket

Removing

1. Drive the vehicle onto a ramp.
2. Remove the transmission dipstick.
3. Unscrew and remove the bolt securing the dipstick upper tube to the lifting eye bracket.
4. Remove the dipstick upper tube.
5. Slacken the wing stay to bulkhead securing bolt.
6. Remove the wing stay to wing securing bolts.
7. Remove the pipe to wing stay clamps.
8. Swing the wing stays away from the wings.
9. Unscrew and remove the handles from the engine lifting hooks—Tool No. MS 53 A.
10. Fit the hooks to the rear lifting eyes.
11. Fit the engine support tool.
12. Fit and tighten the handles to take the weight of the engine.
13. Raise the ramp.
14. Unscrew and remove the nuts/bolts securing the intermediate exhaust pipes, rotating the flanges for access.
15. Disconnect the exhaust pipes and remove the sealing olives.
16. Remove the intermediate heat shields.
17. Remove the rear heat shields.
18. Pull aside the exhaust pipes and secure.
19. Remove the crash bracket bolts.
20. Unscrew and remove the rear mounting centre nut.
21. Remove the spacer and crash bracket.
22. Using a suitable block of wood interposed between the jack head and the gearbox rear mounting, support the mounting plate.
23. Remove the bolts securing the rear mounting.
24. Remove the rear spacers.
25. Lower the jack.
26. Remove the mounting assembly.
27. Remove the wooden block and jack.
28. Unscrew the bolts securing the cross-member.
29. Remove the cross-member.
30. Disconnect the propeller shaft from the transmission and move the shaft clear.
31. Remove the drive flange retaining bolt, and remove the flange.
32. Remove the extension housing bolts, remove the housing and discard the gasket.

Refitting

33. Fit a new gasket to the extension housing.
34. Refit the extension housing to the transmission case, secure with the bolts.
35. Refit the drive flange and tighten retaining bolt, ensure that the propeller shaft bolts are fitted to the flange.
36. Connect the propeller shaft to the transmission drive flange.
37. Position and align the cross-member, fit and tighten the upper securing bolts.
38. Fit and tighten the lower securing bolts.
39. Place the ramp jack under the rear mountings, and locate the wooden block and mounting assembly in position, raise the jack and align the attachment holes.
40. Fit the rear spacers, fit and tighten the securing bolts.
41. Remove the jack and wooden block.
42. Fit the rear mounting spacer.
43. Fit crash bracket.
44. Fit and tighten rear mounting centre nut.
45. Fit and tighten crash bracket bolts.
46. Refit the front heat shields.
47. Untie the exhaust pipes and fit the rear heat shield.
48. Refit the intermediate heat shields.
49. Smear the exhaust sealing olives with 'Firegum', fit the olives, connect and secure the exhaust system.
50. Lower the ramp.
51. Unscrew and remove the support tool hook handles.
52. Remove the support tool, remove the hooks, fit and tighten the handles to the hooks.
53. Refit the dipstick upper tube and secure to the lifting eye bracket.
54. Reposition the wing stays and secure to the wings.
55. Tighten the wing stay/bulkhead attachment and refit the pipe clamps.
56. Fill the transmission unit with fluid and refit the dipstick.

OIL/FLUID PAN

Remove and refit   44.24.04

Service tool: Engine support tool MS 53A

Removing

Raise vehicle on ramp or position over a pit.
Remove the vacuum capsule clamp bolt and clamp, disconnect the capsule and drain the transmission fluid into a suitable container.
Reconnect the capsule, refit the clamp and tighten the securing bolt.
Disconnect the right-hand intermediate exhaust pipe from the down pipe, remove the olive and tie system aside.

Remove the crash bracket assembly, 3 nuts and bolts.
Remove the bolts and spring washers securing the oil pan to the transmission case. Carefully lower the oil pan and allow any oil remaining in the transmission to drain.
Remove and discard the gasket; ensure that all traces of the old gasket are removed from both oil pan and transmission case.

Refitting

Position a new gasket on the oil pan, refit the oil pan.
Tighten the oil pan securing bolts by diagonal selection to the specified torque figure.
Refit the crash bracket.
Reconnect the exhaust system.
Refill the transmission and check for fluid leaks in the vicinity of the vacuum capsule.

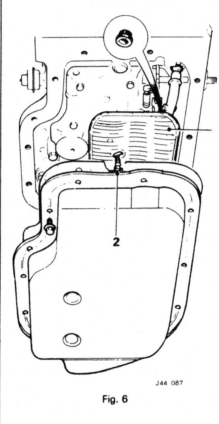

Fig. 6

J44 087

OIL FILTER

Remove and refit   44.24.07

Removing

Prior to carrying out this operation it will be necessary to remove the oil pan as detailed in operation 44.24.04.
Remove the oil filter securing bolt and lower the filter.

Refitting

Fit new filter and tighten the securing bolt.
Refit the oil pan and refill the transmission.

SELECTOR CABLE

Adjust   44.30.04

Disconnect the battery.
Unscrew the gear selector knob.
Remove the screws securing the control escutcheon; withdraw the escutcheon slightly to gain access to the cigar lighter terminals.
Note the fitted position of cigar lighter and door lock switch terminals; detach the terminals.
Disconnect the electric window switch harnesses; withdraw the panel and escutcheon.
Slacken the locknuts (1, Fig. 7) on the outer cable abutment bracket.
Disconnect the cable from the selector lever (2, Fig. 7) below the car.
Position both selector levers in neutral (position 'N') and adjust length of cable by means of the locknuts until cable can be connected to selector lever (2, Fig. 7) without either lever moving.
Tighten the locknuts.

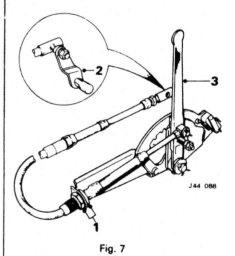

Fig. 7

J44 088

NOTE: A certain amount of free play at the selector lever (3, Fig. 7) should be evident.

Re-connect the electrical harnesses, refit the control escutcheon and switch panel.
Re-connect the battery and test operation of window switches, also the cigar lighter.
Start the engine and check that there is no drive in 'P' or 'N' and that gear engagement is felt in 'D', '2' and '1'.

44—21

KICK-DOWN SWITCH

Check and adjust   44.30.12

Switch on the ignition and check that there is current at the input terminal of the switch (1, Fig. 8) (cable colour—green).
Connect an earthed test lamp (2, Fig. 8) to the output terminal (cable colour—green/white).
Fully depress the throttle pedal.
If the test lamp fails to light, release the throttle pedal and gently depress the switch arm (3, Fig. 8).

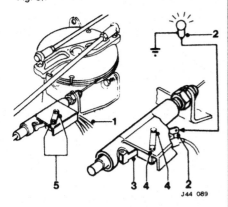

Fig. 8

If the test lamp still does not light, renew the switch (4, Fig. 8).
If, however, the lamp lights when the switch arm is depressed, slacken the securing bolts (5, Fig. 8) and move the switch towards the cable until at full throttle opening the lamp lights.
Tighten the securing bolts and re-check.

BAND APPLY PIN

Selection check   44.30.21

Service tools: 18G 1310, band application pin selection gauge; torque wrench

Remove the fluid pan as detailed in operation 44.24.04; allow the fluid to drain.
Remove the control valve assembly and governor pipes.
Remove the six rear servo cover fixing bolts, remove the cover and gasket.
Remove the rear servo assembly from the transmission case.
Remove the servo accumulator spring.
Fit service tool 18G 1310, band apply selection gauge and gauge pin, secure with two bolts.
Tighten the two bolts, ensure that the gauge pin is free to move up and down in both the tool and the servo pin bore.
Fit a $\frac{9}{16}$ in A.F. socket to the torque wrench.
Apply a torque of 3.46 kgf m (25 lbf ft) to the hexagon nut on the gauge. Identify the land and letter on the gauge pin and select the appropriate size pin.

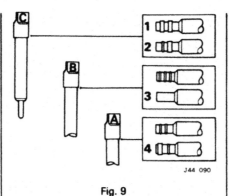

Fig. 9

NOTE: Pins 1, 2, 3 and 4 are fitted on production but are not available as spare part items.
Remove the service tool 18G 1310.
Fit the servo pin as selected in the above check.
Refit the servo accumulator spring and servo assembly.
Refit the servo cover and gasket, secure with the six bolts.
Refit the governor pipes and control valve assembly.
Refit the fluid pan and fill the transmission with fluid.

FRONT UNIT END-FLOAT

Check and adjust   44.30.22

Service tools: CBW 87, 18G 1296

Checking

Remove the gearbox as detailed in operation 44.20.01.
Remove the torque converter.
Remove the front pump attaching bolt and seal.
Attach clock gauge CBW 33; the end-float can now be checked.
Alternatively, CBW 87 can be used, the movement of the turbine shaft being measured with feeler gauges.
Hold the output shaft forward, whilst pushing the turbine shaft rearward to its stop.
Set the dial gauge to zero.
Pull the turbine shaft forward and note the reading obtained.
Correct end-float is 0,076 to 0,610 mm (0.003 to 0.025 in).
The selective washer which controls the end-float is a phenolic resin washer located between the pump cover and the forward clutch housing.
If the end-float is not within the above limits (preferably work to a mean tolerance reading between the above), select a new washer, referring to the chart.

Thickness	Colour
1,52 to 1,63 mm (0.060 to 0.064 in)	Yellow
1,803 to 1,905 mm (0.071 to 0.075 in)	Blue
2,08 to 2,18 mm (0.082 to 0.086 in)	Red
2,36 to 2,46 mm (0.093 to 0.097 in)	Brown
2,64 to 2,74 mm (0.104 to 0.108 in)	Green
2,92 to 3,02 mm (0.015 to 0.119 in)	Black
3,20 to 3,30 mm (0.126 to 0.130 in)	Purple

NOTE: An oil-soaked washer may lead to discolouration. If necessary, measure the washer to ascertain the thickness.
To remove the pump, remove all the locating screws, removing them diagonally opposite each other.
Insert 18G 1296 into the two tapped holes in the pump body.
Apply a gradual equal force on each bolt until the pins force the pump out.
Fit the correct selective washer.
Refit the pump, securing the bolt and seal.
Tighten the locating screws by diagonal selection to avoid distortion.

REAR UNIT END-FLOAT

Check and adjust   44.30.23

Service tool: CBW 87.

Checking

Remove the rear extension, see operation 44.20.19.
Use CBW 87 with the slide bar inserted into the side of the governor holes (governor bolt removed).
Slide the connector on CBW 87 as near the block as possible and extend the dial gauge rod out as far as possible.
Ensure that the indicator stem registers with the end of the output shaft.
Set the gauge to zero.
Move the output shaft to and fro, noting the indicator reading to enable the correct end-float adjusting washer to be used when the transmission is assembled.
The end-float should be between 0,076 and 0,483 mm (0.003 and 0.019 in).
The adjusting washer which controls this end-float is the steel washer with three tabs located between the thrust washer and the rear face of the transmission case. The notches on the tabs serve to identify washer thickness.
Select the correct washer from the table.

44—22

Thickness	Identification Notch
1,981 to 2,083 mm (0.008 to 0.082 in)	None
2,184 to 2,286 mm (0.086 to 0.090 in)	On side of 1 tab
2,358 to 2,489 mm (0.094 to 0.098 in)	On side of 2 tabs
2,591 to 2,692 mm (0.102 to 0.106 in)	On end of 1 tab
2,794 to 2,896 mm (0.110 to 0.114 in)	On end of 2 tabs
2,997 to 3,099 mm (0.118 to 0.122 in)	On end of 3 tabs

SPEEDOMETER DRIVE PINION

Remove and refit   44.38.04

Removing

Raise the vehicle on a ramp.
Slacken the union connecting the speedometer cable angle drive to the pinion.
Disconnect the speedometer cable and place to one side.
Remove the pinion clamp bolt and clamp plate.
Remove the pinion assembly.
Remove the pinion from the housing.
Remove and discard the housing seals.
Clean the pinion and the housing.

Refitting

Refit new seals to the housing.
Lubricate the pinion.
Lubricate the 'O' ring seal.
Refit the pinion to the housing.
Refit the pinion assembly to the gearbox.
Refit the clamp plate and tighten the clamp bolt.
Re-connect the speedometer cable.
Re-tighten the union connecting the speedometer cable angle drive to the pinion.
Lower the vehicle on the ramp.

VALVE BODY ASSEMBLY

Remove and refit   44.40.01

Removing

Prior to carrying out this operation it will be necessary to remove the oil pan and filter.
Reference should therefore be made to operations 44.24.04 and 44.24.07.
Disconnect the pressure switch.
Remove the bolts securing the valve body.
Remove the detent spring.
Remove the valve body assembly.
Remove and discard the gasket.

CAUTION: Front servo components may be displaced after valve block is removed so care must be taken to ensure that they are fitted correctly.

Remove the conical filter.
Remove the oil feed pipes.
Remove the front servo piston assembly.
Slacken and remove the pressure switch.
Place the valve body to one side.
Clean all the relevant parts and faces.

Refitting

Refit and tighten the pressure switch.
Lubricate the front servo piston.
Refit the servo piston assembly.
Refit the oil feed pipes.
Refit the conical oil filter.
Fit a new valve block gasket and refit the valve body assembly.
Align the oil feed pipes.
Align the front servo.
Refit the detent spring.
Refit and tighten valve body securing bolts.
Re-connect the pressure switch.
Refit the oil filter.
Refit the oil pan.

TRANSMISSION ASSEMBLY

Remove and refit   44.20.01

Service tools: MS 53A engine support bracket, Epco V 1000 Unit lift

Removing

1. Drive the vehicle onto a ramp.
2. Remove the transmission dipstick.
3. Unscrew and remove the bolt securing the dipstick upper tube to the lifting eye bracket.
4. Remove the dipstick upper tube.
5. Slacken the wing stay to bulkhead securing bolt
6. Remove the wing stay to wing securing bolts.
7. Remove the pipe to wing stay clamps.
8. Swing the wing stays away from the wings.
9. Unscrew and remove the handles from the engine lifting hooks—Tool No. MS 53A.
10. Fit the hooks to the rear lifting eyes.
11. Fit the engine support tool.
12. Fit and tighten the handles to take the weight of the engine.
13. Raise the ramp.
14. Unscrew and remove the nuts/bolts securing the intermediate exhaust pipes, rotating the flanges for access.
15. Disconnect the exhaust pipes and remove the sealing olives.
16. Remove the intermediate heat shields.
17. Remove the rear heat shield.
18. Pull aside the exhaust pipes and secure.
19. Remove the front heat shields.
20. Unscrew and remove the rear mounting centre nut and crash bracket bolts.
21. Remove the spacer and bracket.
22. Using a suitable block of wood interposed between the jack head and the gearbox rear mounting, support the mounting plate.
23. Remove the bolts securing the rear mounting.
24. Remove the rear spacers.
25. Lower the jack.

26. Remove the mounting assembly.
27. Remove the wooden block and jack.
28. Unscrew the bolts securing the cross-member.
29. Remove the cross-member.
30. Disconnect the propeller shaft from the transmission and move the shaft clear.
31. Working from above the engine compartment, slacken the hooks—10 turns only.
32. From beneath the vehicle, disconnect the speedometer cable from the transmission.
33. Unscrew the nut securing the selector pin to the lever and disconnect the cable.
34. Unscrew the bolt securing the selector cable to the support bracket and move the cable away from the transmission.
35. Disconnect the kick-down solenoid feed-wire and remove the clamp bolt securing the feed wire to the transmission.
36. Disconnect the modulator capsule vacuum tube.
37. Remove the bolt and clamp plate securing the modulator.
38. Place a suitable receptacle under the modulator, withdraw the modulator and partially drain the transmission fluid.
39. Remove and discard the modulator 'O' ring.
40. Unscrew the cooler pipe union nuts from the unions.
41. Unscrew the bolt securing the cooler pipes bracket to the engine sump, remove the spacer.
42. Disconnect and plug the cooler pipes.
43. Unscrew the bolts/nuts securing the converter access cover (and catalysts — where fitted) and remove the cover.
44. Unscrew the bolts securing the converter to the drive plate, turning the drive plate for access.
45. Remove the bolts securing the right-hand rack gaiter heat shield and remove the heat shield (U.S.A. vehicles only).
46. Unscrew the nuts securing the right-hand catalyst (where fitted) and displace the catalyst from the manifold.
47. Remove the engine/transmission securing bolts with the exception of two lower left-hand bolts and lower starter motor securing bolt.
48. Remove the dipstick tube and reposition the tube/vacuum pipe mounting bracket along the vacuum pipe.
49. Utilizing an Epco V 1000 unit lift:
a. Remove the front and rear clamps.
b. Traverse the lift under the transmissions unit.
c. Take the weight of the transmission on the lift.
d. Adjust the tilt angle and side clamps.
e. Tighten the clamps.
f. Fit the chain assembly to the right-hand arm, fit the securing peg and pass the chain over the transmission into the front arm.
g. Tighten the chain adjuster.
50. Remove the remaining bolts securing the engine/transmission and starter motor.
51. Disconnect the transmission unit from the engine, lower the unit (easing the catalyst aside — where fitted) and traverse the transmission/unit lift from beneath the vehicle.

continued

44—23

283

WARNING: Ensure that torque converter does not fall off when removing the transmission.

Extra operations for replacing the transmission assembly

52. Unscrew and remove the rear mounting spigot securing bolts, and remove the mounting.
53. Remove the selector cable mounting collar.
54. Unscrew and remove the cooler pipe unions.
55. Slacken the chain adjuster and release the chain from the front arm.
56. Slacken the clamp wing nuts and release the clamps.
57. Place the transmission unit aside to drain.
58. Fit the replacement transmission unit to the lift.
59. Reposition the clamps and tighten the wing nuts.
60. Refit the chain to the front arm and tighten the chain adjuster.
61. Remove all the blanking plugs from the new transmission unit.
62. Remove the converter strap from the replacement unit and fit to the displaced unit.
63. Fit and tighten the cooler pipe unions to the replacement unit.
64. Fit the selector cable collar.
65. Fit the rear mounting; fit and tighten the securing bolts.
66. Clean the relevant mounting and attachment faces.

Refitting

67. Traverse the transmission/unit lift beneath the vehicle, raise the unit into position (easing aside the catalyst — where fitted) and place the speedometer cable, selector cable, kick-down solenoid feed wire and vacuum pipe into suitable positions.
68. Align the transmission mating flange over the locating dowels.
69. Fit and tighten three lower left-hand transmission/engine securing bolts.
70. Locate the starter motor in position and fit and tighten the securing bolts.
71. Release the unit lift clamps, slacken the chain tensioner and remove the pin from the left-hand arm, release the chain from the front arm and remove the chain assembly.
72. Lower the unit lift and remove from the working area, refit the clamps to the lift.
73. Fit and tighten the remaining engine/transmission securing bolts.
74. Position the dipstick pipe clamp on the torque converter housing and fit the lower dipstick tube.
75. Connect the dipstick tube to the transmission.
76. Pull the vacuum pipe through the bracket.
77. Fit two accessible torque converter/drive plate bolts. Do not tighten.
78. Turn the drive plate, fit two further torque converter/drive plate bolts. Do not tighten.
79. Turn the drive plate, fit and tighten final two torque converter/drive plate and bolts.

80. Turn the drive plate and tighten first four bolts.
81. Fit the torque converter cover-plate (and the strap to the right-hand catalyst — where fitted).
82. Slacken the left-hand nut securing the strap to the cover and swing the strap aside.
83. Remove the blanking plugs from the cooler pipes and connect the pipes to the transmission.
84. Position the cooler pipe mounting bracket, fit the spacer and bolt and secure the bracket to the engine sump.
85. Fit a new 'O' ring to the modulator capsule and fit the modulator to the transmission unit with the clamp plate and bolt.
86. Connect the vacuum pipe to the modulator.
87. Connect the kick-down solenoid feed wire and secure to the transmission with the clamp and bolt.
88. Fit and secure the selector cable bracket to the mounting and connect the cable to the lever. Fit and tighten the selector pin securing nut.
89. Working from above the engine compartment, tighten the hook handles to raise the engine.
90. Working from beneath the vehicle, connect the propeller shaft to the transmission flange.
91. Position and align the cross-member, fit and tighten the upper securing bolts.
92. Fit and tighten the lower securing bolts.
93. Place the ramp jack under the rear mounting, and locate the wooden block and mounting assembly in position, raise the jack and align the attachment holes.
94. Fit the rear spacers, fit and tighten the securing bolts.
95. Remove the jack and wooden block.
96. Fit the rear mounting spacer and crash bracket and secure.
97. Position the right-hand catalyst (where fitted) into the manifold and secure with the nuts.
98. Secure the converter cover strap to the catalyst (where fitted).
99. Refit the rack gaiter heat shield (where fitted).
100. Refit the front heat shields.
101. Untie the exhaust pipes and fit the rear heat shield.
102. Refit the intermediate heat shields.
103. Smear the exhaust sealing olives with 'Firegum', fit the olives, connect and secure the exhaust system.
104. Lower the ramp.
105. Unscrew and remove the support tool hook handles.
106. Remove the support tool, remove the hooks, fit and tighten the handles to the hooks.
107. Refit the dipstick upper tube and secure to the lifting eye bracket.
108. Reposition the wing stays and secure to the wings.
109. Tighten the wing stay/bulkhead attachment and refit the pipe clamps.
110. Fill the transmission unit with fluid and refit the dipstick.

TRANSMISSION ASSEMBLY

Overhaul   44.20.06

NOTE: Before commencing this operation, it is strongly recommended that the following checks are carried out and all readings noted:

Front Unit End-Float Check, see 44.30.22.
Rear Unit End-Float Check, see 44.30.23.
Rear Servo Band Apply Pin Selection Check, see 44.30.21.

CAUTION: Only Gamlen 265 or Rochem Electrical Quick Dry Solvent should be used for cleaning transmission components.

Service tools: 18G 1295 compressor piston accumulator control valve; 18G 1296 front pump remover screws; 18G 1297 front pump and tailshaft oil seal replacer; 18G 1298 forward and direct clutch piston replacer, inner and outer protection sleeve; 18G 1309 intermediate clutch inner seal protection sleeve; 18G 1310 band application pin selection gauge; 18G 677 ZC pressure test equipment; 18G 1016 clutch spring compressor; 18G 1004 circlip pliers; 18G 1004 J circlip plier points.

Dismantling

1. Remove the transmission assembly from the vehicle, see 44.20.01.
2. Thoroughly clean the transmission casing.
3. Remove the torque converter.
4. Invert transmission on to a suitable bench cradle.

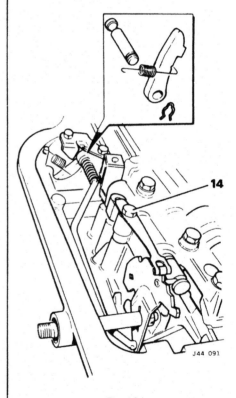

Fig. 10

5. Using a suitable flange retaining tool, undo and remove the drive flange securing bolt and remove the drive flange.

6. Remove the bolt securing the speedometer drive pinion clamp plate.

7. Remove the clamp plate and withdraw the speedometer pinion assembly.

8. Remove the four governor cover-plate securing bolts and remove the cover-plate and gasket.

9. Discard the gasket.

10. Remove the governor assembly.

11. Remove the sump bolts, sump pan and discard the gasket.

12. Remove the bolt securing the oil filter and remove the filter.

13. Remove the oil filter feed pipe.

14. Remove the bolt (Fig. 10) securing the detent spring and roller assembly to the valve block.

15. Remove the retaining bolts and withdraw the valve block with the governor pipes attached.

16. Remove the governor screen assembly from the end of the governor feed pipe, or feed pipe hole in the casing.

17. Remove the governor feed pipes from the valve block. The pipes are interchangeable.

18. Disconnect the detent solenoid wire from the case connector.

19. Depress the tabs on the case connector and remove the connector and 'O' ring. Discard the 'O' ring.

20. Remove the detent solenoid securing bolts and remove the solenoid.

21. Remove the valve block spacer plate from the casing.

22. Remove the six check balls from the transmission casing.

23. Lift the front servo piston assembly from the transmission case (Fig. 11).

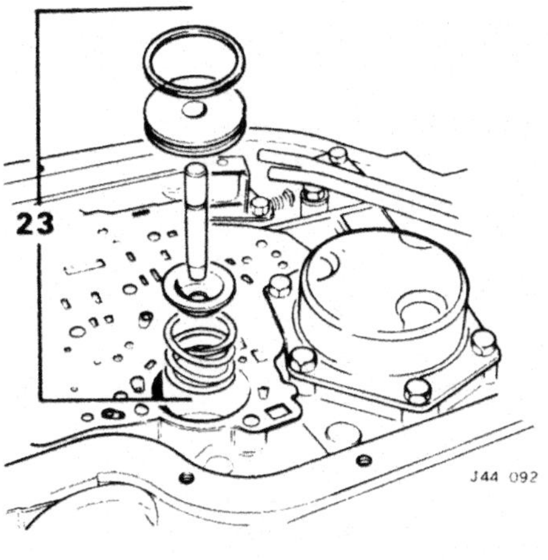

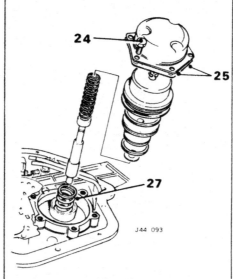

24. Remove the rear servo cover retaining bolts (Fig. 12).

25. Remove the cover and gasket (Fig. 12). Discard the gasket.

26. Remove the rear servo assembly from the transmission case.

27. Remove the rear servo accumulator spring (Fig. 12).

Fig. 12

28. Remove the modulator valve from the case.

29. Undo and remove the six rear extension securing bolts.

30. Remove the rear extension and gasket. Discard the gasket.

31. Turn box over.

32. Undo and remove the front pump securing bolts.

33. Insert service tools 18G 1296 into the two threaded holes in the pump body.

34. Using service tools 18G 1296, extract the pump.

35. Remove the pump assembly and discard the gasket.

36. Remove the service tools 18G 1296 from the pump body.

37. Remove the input shaft and forward clutch assembly.

38. Remove the intermediate one-way clutch assembly.

39. Remove the front band assembly.

40. Remove the intermediate clutch snap-ring.

41. Remove the intermediate clutch backing plate and clutch assembly.

42. Remove the chamfered snap-ring.

43. Undo and remove the centre support retaining peg and remove the centre support/roller clutch assembly.

44. Remove the sun gear shaft.

45. Remove the snap-ring from the bottom groove of the centre support.

46. Remove the rear brake band.

47. Remove the planet carrier assembly.

48. Remove the front internal gear ring.

49. Remove the rear thrust washer.

50. Remove the manual shaft retaining pin.

51. Release the manual shaft from the manual detent lever, remove the lever and shaft.

52. Remove the actuator rod assembly.

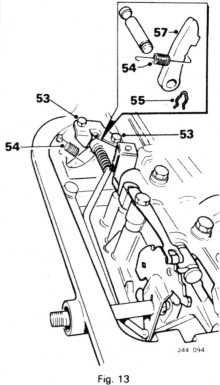

Fig. 13

53. Remove the parking pawl bracket securing bolts (Fig. 13) and remove the bracket.

54. Remove the parking pawl spring (Fig. 13).

55. Remove the spring clip (Fig. 13) securing the parking pawl to the pivot shaft.

56. Press the pivot shaft to displace the plug and remove the plug.

57. Remove the parking pawl (Fig. 13).

58. Remove the pivot shaft.

59. Remove the pressure take-off plug.

60. Remove the filter pick-up seal.

61. Remove the selector shaft seal.

62. Clean and inspect the casing.

Fig. 11

continued

44—25

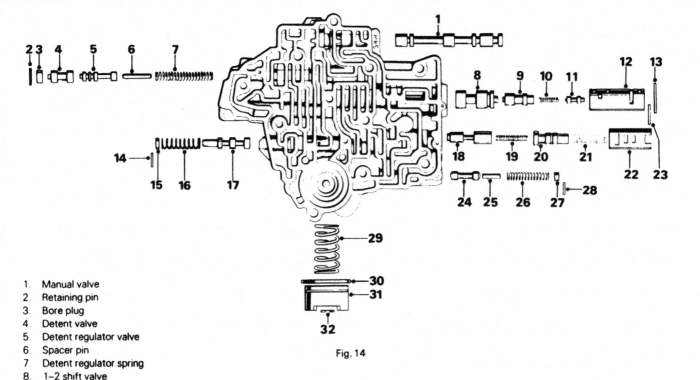

Fig. 14

1. Manual valve
2. Retaining pin
3. Bore plug
4. Detent valve
5. Detent regulator valve
6. Spacer pin
7. Detent regulator spring
8. 1–2 shift valve
9. 1–2 detent valve
10. 1–2 regulator spring
11. 1–2 regulator valve
12. 1–2 modulator bushing
13. Retaining pin
14. Grooved retaining pin
15. Bore plug
16. 1–2 accumulator secondary spring
17. 1–2 accumulator secondary valve
18. 2–3 shift valve
19. 3–2 intermediate spring
20. 2–3 modulator valve
21. 2–3 valve spring
22. 2–3 modulator bushing
23. Retaining pin
24. 3–2 valve
25. Spacer pin
26. 3–2 valve spring
27. Bore plug
28. Retaining pin
29. Accumulator spring
30. Accumulator piston oil ring
31. Accumulator piston
32. 'E'-ring retainer

VALVE BLOCK

CAUTION: During the dismantling procedure carefully identify all valves, bushes and springs, noting their relative positions.

Dismantling—see Figure 14

63. Position the valve block with the gasket face uppermost and the accumulator at the bottom. This position will be used to identify the components.

64. Remove the manual valve (1).

65. Using service tool 18G 1295, compress the accumulator piston (30) and spring (29), remove the 'E' ring retainer (32).

66. Remove the service tool, accumulator piston and spring.

67. Using a pin punch remove the 1–2 modulator bushing retaining pin (13), upper right-hand bore.

68. Remove the 1–2 modulator bushing (12), 1–2 regulator valve (11) and spring (10), 1–2 detent valve (9) and the 1–2 shift valve (8)

NOTE: The 1–2 regulator valve and spring may be inside the 1–2 modulator bushing.

69. Using a pin punch remove the 2–3 modulator bushing retaining pin (23), centre right-hand bore.

70. Remove the 2–3 modulator bushing (22), 2–3 shift valve spring (23), 2–3 modulator valve (20), 3–2 intermediate spring (19) and the 2–3 shift valve (18).

71. Using a pin punch remove the 3–2 valve retaining pin (28), lower right-hand bore.

72. Remove the bore plug (27), 3–2 valve spring (26), spacer (25) and the 3–2 valve (24).

73. Using a pin punch remove the detent valve retaining pin (2), upper left-hand bore.

74. Remove the bore plug (3), detent valve (4), detent regulator valve (5), spacer (6) and detent regulator valve spring (7).

75. Using a pair of long-nosed pliers remove the 1–2 accumulator valve retaining pin (14), lower left-hand bore.

76. Remove the bore plug (15), 1–2 accumulator spring (16) and the accumulator valve (17).

Inspection

77. Wash all components in a clean solvent. Do not allow valves to bump together, as this might cause nicks and burrs.

78. Carefully check all valves and bushings for burrs and damage. Burrs should be removed with a fine stone, taking care not to round off the shoulders of the valves.

79. Check all valves and bushings for free movement in their respective bores.

80. Check the valves housing for cracks and the bores for damage and scoring

NOTE: If any valves or bores are found to be damaged beyond repair, then a new control valve assembly must be fitted.

81. Check all the springs for distortion.

82. Check the front accumulator piston and oil ring for damage; renew as necessary.

44—26

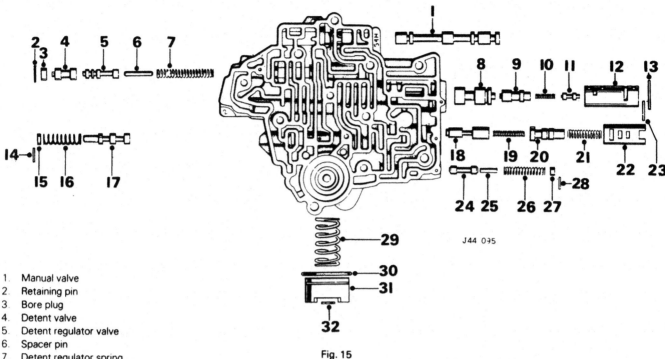

J44 095

Fig. 15

1. Manual valve
2. Retaining pin
3. Bore plug
4. Detent valve
5. Detent regulator valve
6. Spacer pin
7. Detent regulator spring
8. 1–2 shift valve
9. 1–2 detent valve
10. 1–2 regulator spring
11. 1–2 regulator valve
12. 1–2 modulator bushing
13. Retaining pin
14. Grooved retaining pin
15. Bore plug
16. 1–2 accumulator secondary spring
17. 1–2 accumulator secondary valve
18. 2–3 shift valve
19. 3–2 intermediate spring
20. 2–3 modulator valve
21. 2–3 valve spring
22. 2–3 modulator bushing
23. Retaining pin
24. 3–2 valve
25. Spacer pin
26. 3–2 valve spring
27. Bore plug
28. Retaining pin
29. Accumulator spring
30. Accumulator piston oil ring
31. Accumulator piston
32. 'E'-ring retainer

Reassembling

83. Fit the accumulator spring (29) and piston (31) into the valve body.

84. Using service tool 18G 1295, squarely compress the spring and piston.

NOTE: Ensure that the piston pin is correctly aligned with the hole in the piston and the oil seal ring does not foul the lip of the bore when fitting the piston.

85. Fit the 'E' ring retainer (32) and remove the service tool.

86. Fit the 1–2 accumulator valve (17) stem end out in the lower left-hand bore.

87. Fit the 1–2 accumulator secondary spring (16) over the stem.

88. Fit the 1–2 accumulator bore plug (15) to the 1–2 accumulator bore.

89. Turn over control valve assembly and fit the grooved retaining pin (14) from the cast surface side of the body, with grooved end of pin entering the hole last.

90. Tap retaining pin in control valve housing until pin is flush with cast surface. Return control valve assembly to its original position.

91. Fit spacer (6) to detent regulator valve spring (7) and fit spring and spacer into upper left-hand bore; ensure that spring seats correctly.

92. Compress the detent regulator valve spring (7), fit the detent regulator valve (5), stem end last, and detent valve (4), band first.

93. Fit the bore plug (3), hole outermost, and secure with the retaining pin (1), from the cored side of the body.

94. Fit the 3–2 valve (24), bottom right-hand bore.

95. Fit spacer (25) to the 3-2 valve spring (26) and fit the spring and spacer, bottom right-hand bore.

96. Compress the 2–3 valve spring (21), and fit the bore plug, hole end outermost; secure with retaining pin (23), from the cored side of the body.

97. Fit the 3–2 intermediate spring (19) in the open end of the 2–3 shift valve (18), fit valve and spring to the centre right-hand bore. Ensure that the valve seats correctly.

98. Fit the 2–3 modulator valve (20), hole end first, to the 2–3 modulator bushing (22), and fit both parts to the centre right-hand bore.

99. Fit the 2–3 shift valve spring (21) into the 2–3 modulator valve (20), compress the spring and fit the retaining pin (23), from the cored side of the control valve.

100. Fit the 1–2 shift valve (8), stem end outermost ensuring that the valve seats correctly, to the upper right-hand bore.

101. Fit the 1–2 regulator valve (11), large stem first, spring (10), and the 1–2 detent valve (9), hole end first, into the 1–2 bushing (12) and fit all the components to the upper right-hand bore.

102. Compress the bushing against the spring and fit the retaining pin (13) from the cored side of the control valve body.

103. Fit the manual valve (1), with the detent pin groove to the right.

44—27

REAR SERVO ASSEMBLY

Dismantling

104. Remove the rear accumulator piston from the rear servo piston.
105. Remove the 'E' (Fig. 16) ring retaining the rear servo piston to the rear band apply pin.
106. Remove the rear servo piston and seal (Fig. 16) from the band apply pin.
107. Remove the washer, spring and retainer (Fig. 16).

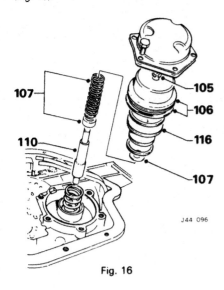

Fig. 16

Inspection

108. Check the freeness of the oil seal rings in the piston grooves. Renew as necessary.
109. Check the fit of the band apply pin in the servo piston.
110. Check the band apply pin (Fig. 16) for cracks and scoring.
111. Check that band apply pin is the correct size as determined by the pin selection check.

Reassembling

112. Fit the spring retainer, cup side towards the band apply servo pin, spring and washer to the servo pin.
113. Fit the servo piston to the pin and secure with the 'E' ring retainer.
114. Renew piston oil seals as necessary.
115. Renew accumulator piston oil seals as necessary.
116. Fit the accumulator piston (Fig. 16) into the bore of the servo piston.

FRONT SERVO ASSEMBLY

Inspection

117. Check the servo pin for damage.
118. Check the piston rand oil seal ring (Fig. 17) for damaged oil ring groove, check that the oil ring is free to move.
119. Check the piston for cracks and porosity.
120. Check the fit of the servo pin (Fig. 17) to the piston.

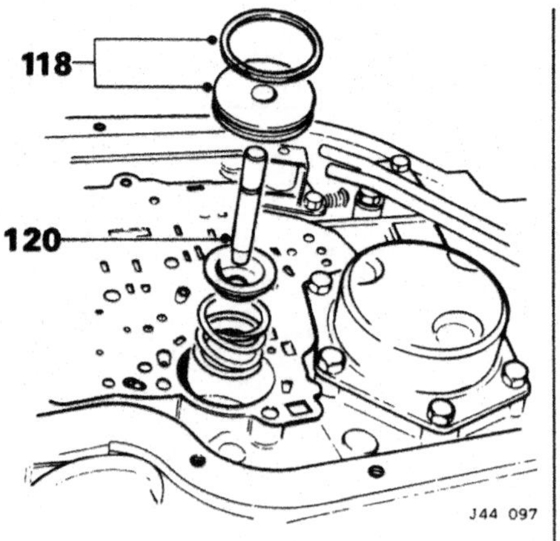

Fig. 17

Reassembling

121. Refit the parts of the front servo; ensure that the tapered end of the servo pin points through the spring and retainer; ensure that the retainer ring is in the servo pin groove.

OIL PUMP

Dismantling

122. Remove the outer seal.
123. Compress the regulator boost valve bushing against the regulator spring and remove the snap-ring (Fig. 18).

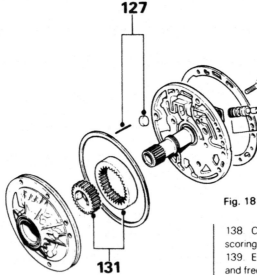

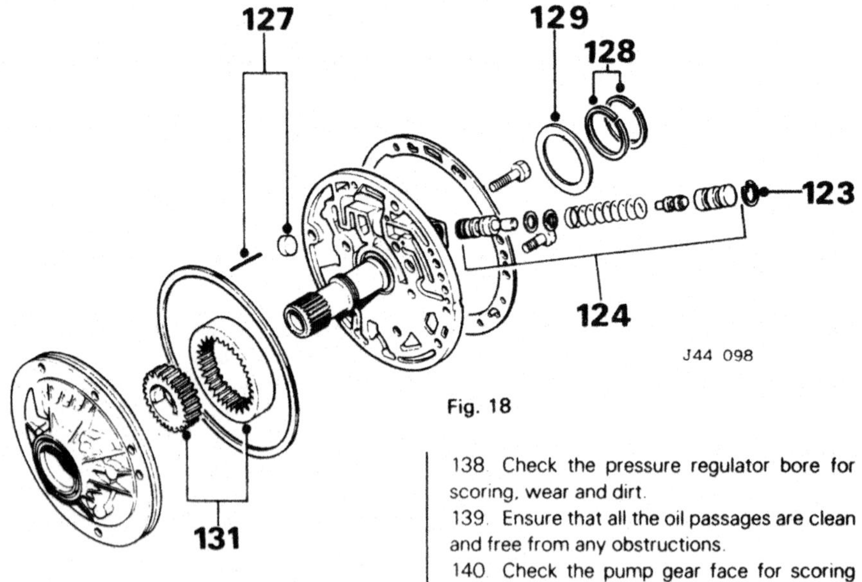

Fig. 18

124. Remove the regulator boost valve bushing, boost valve, pressure regulator spring, spring retainer regulator valve and spacer(s) (Fig. 18).
125. Remove the pump body securing bolts and remove the pump cover from the body.
126. Note **fitted positions** of the oil pump drive and driven gears; it is not necessary to mark tooth to tooth relationship.
127. Remove the retaining pin and bore plug (Fig. 18) from the end of the regulator bore.
128. Remove the two oil rings (Fig. 18) from the pump cover.
129. Remove the pump to forward clutch housing thrust washer (Fig. 18).
130. Remove the front oil seal from the pump body.

Inspection — pump body

131. Check the gears for scoring, chafing and other damage (Fig. 18).
132. Position the pump gears in the pump body, lay a straight-edge over the gears and casing and check the clearance between the gears and the underside of the straight-edge. Clearance should be 0.0008 to 0.0035 in.

CAUTION: Ensure that gears are replaced the correct way round, i.e. lugs on driving gear must face away from torque converter and driven gear should be replaced in the same position as originally fitted.

133. Check the face of the pump body for scores and damage.
134. Ensure that all the oil passages are clean and free from any obstructions.
135. Check the threads in the pump body for damage.
136. Check that the pump body is flat and free from warps.

Inspection — pump cover

137. Check that the pump cover face is of uniform flatness and free from warps.

138. Check the pressure regulator bore for scoring, wear and dirt.
139. Ensure that all the oil passages are clean and free from any obstructions.
140. Check the pump gear face for scoring and damage.
141. Check the stator shaft for damaged splines or scored bushings.
142. Check the oil ring grooves for damage and wear.
143. Check the thrust washer face for wear and damage.
144. Fit the pump cover oil rings into the counterbore of the forward clutch housing and check for correct fit.
145. Ensure that the pressure regulator and boost valve operate freely.
146. Ensure that the air breather hole is free of any obstruction.

44—28

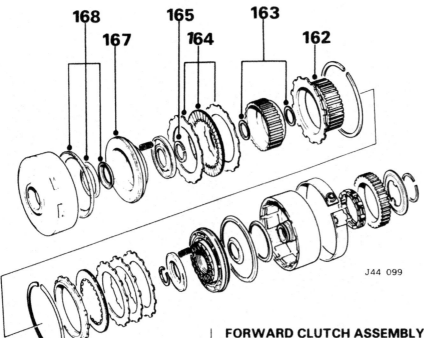

168   165   163
167   164   162

Fig. 19

Reassembling

147. Fit the pump drive and driven gears into the pump body.

CAUTION: Ensure that gears are replaced the correct way round, i.e. lugs on driving gear must face away from torque converter and driven gear should be replaced in the same position as originally fitted.

148. Fit the pressure regulator spacer(s), spring retainer and spring into the pressure regulator bore.

149. Fit the boost valve into the bushing, stem end out, and fit both parts into the pump cover by compressing the bushing against the spring.

150. Fit the retaining snap-ring.

151. Fit the pressure regulator valve from the opposite end of the bore, stem end first.

152. Fit the pressure regulator valve bore plug and retaining pin into the end of the bore.

153. Fit the front unit selective thrust washer over the pump cover delivery sleeve.

NOTE: The correct thickness was determined at the time the Front Unit End-Float Check (see 44.30 22) was carried out.

154. Fit the two oil seal rings to the pump cover.

155. Lubricate the pump gears with transmission fluid and fit the pump cover to the pump body.

156. Fit the pump securing bolts; do not tighten at this stage.

157. Using a suitable Jubilee clip around the pump assembly, tighten to align the pump cover with the pump body.

158. Fully tighten the securing bolts to 2,49 kgf m (18 lbf ft).

159. Fit a new square-cut 'O' ring to the pump.

160. Fit a new pump oil seal, using service tool 18G 1297.

FORWARD CLUTCH ASSEMBLY

Dismantling

161. Carefully secure the turbine shaft in a soft-jawed vice and remove the snap-ring securing the forward clutch housing to the direct clutch hub.

162. Remove the direct clutch hub (Fig. 19).

163. Remove the outer thrust washer, forward clutch hub and inner thrust washer (Fig. 19).

164. Remove the five composition and five steel clutch plates (Fig. 19).

165. Press the input shaft out of the forward clutch drum and using service tool 18G 1016, compress the spring retainer and remove the snap-ring (Fig. 19) securing the forward clutch piston assembly to the housing.

166. Remove the service tool 18G 1016 and withdraw the spring retainer and 16 clutch release springs.

167. Remove the forward clutch piston (Fig. 19) from the forward clutch housing.

168. Remove the seals from the piston (Fig. 19).

169. Remove the centre piston seal from the forward clutch housing and withdraw the clutch housing and turbine shaft from the vice.

Inspection

170. Check the composition-faced and steel clutch plates for signs of burning, scoring and wear.

171. Check the forward clutch hub and direct clutch hub for wear on the splines and thrust faces; ensure that the lubrication holes are not blocked.

172. Check the piston for cracks.

173. Check the clutch housing for wear, scoring and cracks.
Ensure that the oil passages are free from obstruction and that the check ball valve in the rear of the clutch drum is fitted and free to move.

174. Check the turbine shaft for cracks and distortion and the splines for damage.

175. Check the clutch release springs for signs of distortion.

Reassembling

176. Carefully secure the turbine shaft in a soft-jawed vice.

177. Lubricate new inner and outer clutch piston seals (Fig. 20) with new transmission fluid and fit the seals to the forward clutch piston, lips of seals facing away from spring pockets.

178. Fit a new centre piston seal (Fig. 20) to the forward clutch housing, lip facing upwards; lubricate with new transmission fluid.

179. Fit part of service tool 18G 1298 inner seal protector, to the forward clutch hub.

continued

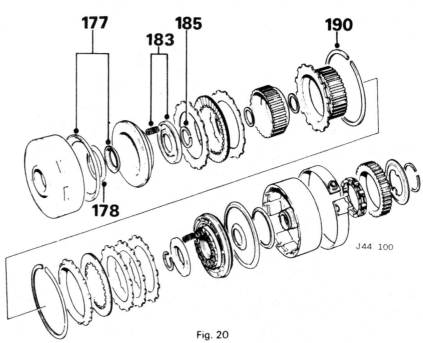

177   185   190
183
178

J44 100

Fig. 20

44—29

180. Fit other part of service tool 18G 1298 outer seal protector, to the clutch piston, and insert assembly in forward clutch housing.

181. Fit the clutch piston by rotating it in a clockwise direction until seated.

182. Remove service tools.

183. Fit the 16 clutch release springs (Fig. 20) to the spring pockets in the clutch piston.

184. Using bench press and service tool 18G 1016 fit the spring retainer, ensuring that retainer does not foul the snap-ring groove. Refit the input shaft.

185. Fit the snap-ring (Fig. 20) and remove the service tools.

186. Ensure that the clutch release springs are correctly seated and are not leaning.

187. Fit the thrust washer to the outside face of the forward clutch hub. The bronze washer is fitted to the side of the hub which faces the forward clutch housing.

188. Fit the forward clutch hub to the forward clutch housing.

189. Fit the dished steel plate to the clutch housing. This should be fitted so that the centre portion of the plate is in contact with the piston.

Fit a steel plate followed by a friction plate. Fit alternate steel and friction plates until a total of five steel plates are in position.

NOTE: Steel plates must be 2,3 mm (0.0915 in) thick.

190. Fit the direct clutch hub in the forward clutch housing and secure with the snap-ring (Fig. 20).

191. Fit the forward clutch housing to the pump delivery sleeve, and applying air to the forward clutch passage in the pump, check operation of forward clutch.

DIRECT CLUTCH AND INTERMEDIATE ROLLER

Dismantling

192. Remove the one-way clutch retainer snap-ring (Fig. 21) and remove the clutch retainer.

Fig. 21

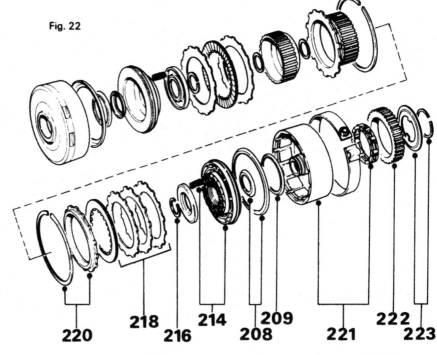

Fig. 22

J44 102

193. Remove the roller outer race and remove the roller assembly (Fig. 21).

194. Remove the snap-ring (Fig. 21) securing the direct clutch backing plate to the clutch housing.

195. Remove the direct clutch backing plate and the six composition and six steel clutch plates (Fig. 21).

196. Using service tool 18G 1016, compress the spring retainer and remove the snap-ring (Fig. 21).

197. Remove the tool, spring retainer and 14 clutch release springs.

198. Remove the direct clutch piston (Fig. 21) from the direct clutch housing.

199. Remove the seals from the piston.

200. Remove the centre piston seal (Fig. 21) from the direct clutch housing.

Inspection

201. Check the one-way clutch for damage, wear or scoring to the locking elements, the cage, drag strip springs and races.

202. Check the direct clutch housing outer race for wear and scoring.

203. Check the direct clutch housing for cracks, wear and blocked oil passages; also check the clutch plate drive lugs for wear.

204. Check the composition-faced and steel clutch plates for signs of wear and burning.

205. Check the back plate for scratches, scoring and other damage.

206. Check the piston for cracks, ensure that the check ball operates freely.

207. Check the springs for wear and distortion.

Reassembling

208. Lubricate new inner and outer clutch piston seals (Fig. 22) with new transmission fluid, fit the seals to the piston, seal lips facing away from spring pockets.

209. Fit a new centre piston seal (Fig. 22) to the direct clutch housing, lip facing upwards, and lubricate with new transmission fluid.

210. Fit part of service tool 18G 1298 forward and direct clutch inner seal protector, over the direct clutch hub.

211. Fit other part of service tool 18G 1298 forward and direct clutch piston outer seal protector to the clutch piston and inset assembly in the direct clutch housing.

212. Fit the clutch piston by rotating it in a clockwise direction.

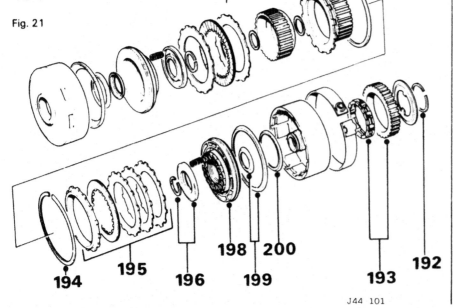

J44 101

213. Remove service tools.

214. Fit the 14 clutch release springs to the spring pockets in the clutch piston (Fig. 22).

215. Using bench press and service tool 18G 1016, fit the spring retainer. Ensure that the retainer does not foul the snap-ring groove.

216. Fit the snap-ring (Fig. 22) and remove the service tools.

217. Ensure that the clutch springs are correctly seated and are not leaning.

218. Lubricate the clutch plates (Fig. 22) with clean transmission fluid. Note that although of the five steel plates, four are 2,0 mm (0.0775 in) and one is 2,3 mm (0.0915 in) thick, there is no special order in which they must be fitted relative to each other.

219. Fit the dished plate followed by a steel plate and then fit alternate friction and steel plates.

220. Fit the direct clutch backing plate and secure with the snap-ring (Fig. 22).

221. Fit the one way clutch assembly to the intermediate clutch inner race (Fig. 22), on the direct clutch housing.

222. Fit the intermediate clutch outer race (Fig. 22). Outer race should not turn in an anti-clockwise direction.

223. Fit the one way clutch retainer and snap-ring (Fig. 22).

224. Fit the direct clutch assembly to the centre support and check operation using compressed air.

PLANET GEAR CARRIER / OUTPUT SHAFT ASSEMBLY

Dismantling

225. Remove the sun gear from the output carrier assembly (Fig. 23).

226. Remove the reaction carrier/output carrier thrust washer (Fig. 23) and the damper ring from around the output carrier.

227. Remove the snap-ring (Fig. 23) securing the output shaft to the output carrier and remove the output shaft.

228. Remove and discard the 'O' ring (Fig. 23) from the output shaft.

229. Remove the thrust bearing and races from the rear internal gear (Fig. 23).

230. Withdraw the rear internal gear and mainshaft from the output carrier (Fig. 23).

231. Remove the thrust bearing and races from the inner face of the rear internal gear.

232. Remove the snap-ring (Fig. 23) from the end of the mainshaft and remove the rear internal gear.

233. Remove the speedometer drive gear.

Inspection

234. Check the splines, 'O' ring grooves, bushes and gear teeth for burrs or signs of damage. Minor burrs can be removed with a very fine abrasive.

235. Check all oil drillings for obstructions and clear only with compressed air.

236. Examine the needle-roller assemblies, and renew if there are any signs of wear or damage.

Reassembling

237. Fit the rear internal gear to the end of the mainshaft that has the snap-ring groove and fit the snap-ring (Fig. 24).

238. Fit the large diameter race, with flanged outer edge facing outwards, to the inner face of the rear internal gear.

239. Fit the thrust bearing to the race (Fig. 24).

240. Fit the small diameter race, with flanged inner edge facing inwards, to the bearing (Fig. 24).

241. Lubricate the pinion gears in the output carrier with new transmission fluid and fit the output carrier to the mainshaft, meshing the pinion gears with the rear internal gear.

242. Insert the assembly and hold the mainshaft in a soft-jawed vice. Be careful not to damage the shaft.

243. Fit the small diameter race, with flanged inner edge facing outwards, to the outer face of the rear internal gear.

244. Fit the thrust bearing to the race.

245. Fit the large diameter race, with flanged outer edge facing inwards, to the bearing.

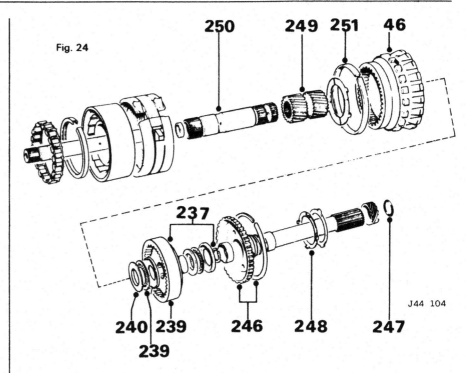

Fig. 24

J44 104

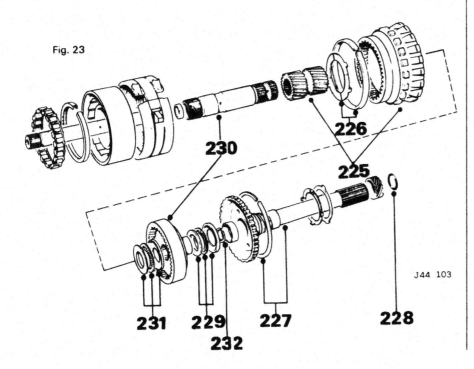

Fig. 23

J44 103

continued

246. Fit the speedometer drive gear. Fit the output shaft into the output carrier and fit the snap-ring (Fig. 24).

247. Fit a new 'O' ring (Fig. 24), to the output shaft.

248. Fit the thrust washer to the output carrier (Fig. 24), engaging the tabs of the washer with the slots in the carrier.

249. Fit the sun gear (Fig. 24), chamfered internal diameter first.

250. Fit the sun gear shaft (Fig. 24), long splined end first.

251. Refit the damper ring round the output carrier.

CENTRE SUPPORT AND INTERMEDIATE CLUTCH

Dismantling

252. Remove the four Teflon oil rings from the centre support.

253. Compress the spring retainer and remove the snap-ring (Fig. 25).

254. Remove the spring retainer and the three intermediate clutch release springs (Fig. 25).

255. Remove the spring guide.

256. Remove the intermediate clutch piston from the centre support (Fig. 25).

257. Remove the seals from the clutch piston.

Inspection

258. Check the roller clutch inner race for wear or damage. Ensure that the lubrication hole is clear.

259. Check bushes for wear, scoring and chafing.

260. Check the oil ring grooves for wear or damage. Check Teflon rings for condition and renew any that are damaged.

261. Using compressed air, check oil passages and clear any obstructions.

262. Check the piston sealing surfaces for scratching and piston seal grooves for damage.

263. Check piston for cracks and seals for wear or damage.

264. Check the springs for distortion.

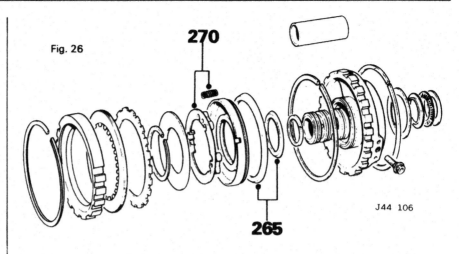

Fig. 26

J44 106

Reassembling

265. Lubricate the new inner and outer clutch piston seals with clean transmission fluid (Fig. 26).

266. Lubricate the seal grooves in the intermediate clutch piston and fit the seals to the piston, with the lips facing away from the spring guide.

267. Fit 18G 1309 intermediate clutch oil seal protector sleeve over the centre support hub, fit the intermediate clutch piston to the centre support. Ensure that it seats fully.

268. Remove service tool 18G 1309.

269. Fit the spring guide.

270. Fit the three clutch release springs, equally spaced in the holes in the spring guide (Fig. 26).

271. Fit the spring retainer and snap-ring.

272. Compress the spring retainer, ensuring that the retainer does not foul in the snap-ring groove; fit snap-ring.

273. Fit the four Teflon oil seal rings to the centre support. Ensure that the ends of the teflon rings overlap correctly.

274. Using compressed air, check the operation of the intermediate clutch. Apply air to the centre oil feed hole to activate the piston.

GEARBOX ASSEMBLY

Reassembling

275. Fit the parking pawl, tooth towards the centre of the transmission case, and fit the parking pawl shaft.

276. Fit the parking pawl shaft retaining clip.

277. Tap the parking pawl shaft plug into position, using a 9,5 mm (0.375 in) diameter rod, until the pawl shaft contacts the case rib.

278. Fit the parking pawl return spring, square end to pawl.

279. Fit the parking pawl bracket and secure with the two bolts.

280. Check the rear brake band for distortion, cracks, damage to the ends of the anchor lugs and apply lugs. Also check the lining for cracks, flaking, burning and looseness.

281. Fit the rear band assembly to the transmission case, locating the band lugs with the anchor pins.

282. Fit the rear unit thrust washer, the correct size having been determined in the Rear Unit End-Float Check, see 44.30.23. Engage the lugs of the washer with the slots in the transmission case.

283. Lubricate the pinion gears in the reaction carrier with clean transmission fluid and fit the reaction carrier to the output carrier; engage the pinion gears with the front internal gear.

284. Fit the large diameter race, flanged outer edge facing outwards, to the sun gear.

285. Fit the thrust bearing to the race.

286. Fit the small diameter race, flanged inner edge facing inwards, to the thrust bearing.

287. Lubricate the reaction carrier to centre support thrust washer with petroleum jelly and fit the washer to the recess in the centre support.

288. Fit the roller clutch to the reaction carrier.

289. Fit the centre support assembly to the roller clutch in the reaction carrier.

NOTE: Ensure that the centre support to reaction carrier thrust washer is correctly positioned before fitting the centre support to the roller clutch in the reaction carrier. With the reaction carrier held, the centre support should only rotate in an anti-clockwise direction.

290. Lubricate and fit the centre support to case snap-ring with the flat face of the ring against the centre support. Ensure that the ring is correctly located in the groove and that the gap is adjacent to the front band anchor pin.

Fig. 25

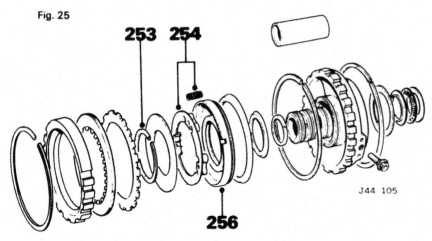

J44 105

291. With the transmission case held vertically, fit the gear unit, centre support and reaction carrier. Align the centre support bolt hole with the hole in the casing.

292. Fit the centre support to case bolt.

293. Check the intermediate clutch plates for scoring, wear and signs of burning.

294. Lubricate the three steel and three composition clutch plates with clean transmission fluid.

295. Fit the clutch plates commencing with a steel plate and alternate composition and steel plates.

296. Fit the intermediate clutch backing plate, flat machined face against clutch plates.

297. Fit the backing plate to case snap-ring, locate the ring gap adjacent to the front band anchor pin.

298. Re-check the Rear Unit End-Float, see 44.30.23.

299. Check the front band for cracks and distortion damage to the ends of the anchor lugs and apply lugs. Also check the lining for cracks, flaking, burning and looseness.

300. Fit the front band, aligning the band anchor hole and the band anchor pin with the apply lug facing the servo hole.

301. Fit the direct clutch housing and intermediate roller assembly. Ensure that the clutch housing hub locates on the bottom of the sun gear shaft and that the splines on the forward end of the sun gear shaft are flush with those in the direct clutch housing.

302. Fit the forward clutch hub to the direct clutch housing thrust washer, to the forward clutch hub.

303. Fit the forward clutch assembly and turbine shaft. Ensure that the end of the mainshaft locates fully in the forward clutch hub. The distance between the forward clutch and pump mounting face should be 25,4 to 31,8 mm (1.0 to 1.250 in).

304. Lubricate the turbine shaft journals and Teflon oil rings on the pump delivery sleeve.

305. Fit a new outer seal.

306. Fit a new gasket to the pump.

307. Fit the pump to the gearbox casing and secure with the bolts.

308. Re-check the Front Unit End-Float, see 44.30.22.

309. Fit a new manual shaft lip seal to the transmission case; use a 19 mm (0.75 in) diameter rod to seat the seal.

310. Fit the actuator rod to the manual detent lever from the side opposite the pin.

311. Fit the actuator rod plunger under the parking bracket and over the parking pawl.

312. Fit the manual shaft to the case, and insert through the detent lever.

313. Fit and tighten the locknut to the manual shaft.

314. Fit the retaining pin.

315. Fit a new extension housing gasket.

316. Check the 'O' ring on the output shaft for nicks and flattening, and renew as required.

317. Fit the extension housing to the case and secure with the six bolts.

318. If required, fit a new extension housing oil seal.

319. Fit the six check balls into their seat pockets in the casing.

320. Using two guide pins in the smaller diameter holes in the valve block casing, fit the control valve housing spacer plate-to-case gasket, 'C' towards case.

321. Fit the control valve spacer plate.

CAUTION: Some overhaul kits contain a solenoid gasket. This gasket MUST NOT be fitted on Jaguar/Daimler transmissions.

322. Fit the detent solenoid assembly, with the connector facing the outer edge of the casing. **Do not** tighten the bolts.

323. Fit the front servo spring and spring retainer to the casing.

324. Fit the retaining ring to the front servo pin and fit the pin to the case, tapered end to contact band.

325. Fit the servo piston to the pin.

326. Fit a new 'O' ring to the solenoid connector.

327. Fit the connector, locate lock tabs to case.

328. Connect the detent solenoid wire to the connector terminal.

329. Lubricate the rear servo inner and outer bores. Fit the rear accumulator spring.

NOTE: Ensure that the rear band apply lug aligns with the servo pin.

330. Fit the rear servo assembly, ensure proper sealing in the bore, and fit the rear servo cover and gasket. Secure with the six bolts.

331. Fit the control valve housing assembly-to-spacer gasket with letters 'VB' towards the valve block.

332. Fit the governor pipes to the control valve assembly.

333. Fit the governor screen assembly, open end first to the feed pipe hole, i.e. the hole nearest the centre of the transmission, in the casing.

334. Fit the control valve assembly and governor pipes to the transmission, carefully align the governor feed pipe with the screen. Ensure that all gaskets and spacers are correctly positioned.

NOTE: Ensure that the manual valve properly locates with the pin on the detent lever. Check that the governor pipes are located correctly.

335. Fit the securing bolts.

336. Remove the two guide pins and fit the detent roller spring assembly and remaining bolts.

337. Tighten the detent solenoid attachment screws.

338. Fit the modulator valve, stem end outermost, into the case.

339. Fit a new 'O' ring to the vacuum modulator.

340. Fit the vacuum modulator to the case.

341. Fit the modulator retainer, curved face inboard, fit and tighten the attachment bolt.

342. Fit the governor to the case.

343. Fit a new gasket, and secure the governor cover to the case with the four bolts.

344. Fit the speedometer driven gear assembly and secure with the clamp bolt.

345. Fit a new 'O' ring to the intake pipe and fit the pipe to a new filter assembly.

346. Fit the filter and pipe assembly to the casing.

347. Fit and tighten the filter retaining bolt.

348. Fit a new gasket to the oil pan and fit the pan to the casing, secure with the attaching bolts.

349. Fit the torque converter to the turbine shaft, fully engage the converter drive hub slots with the pump olive gear lugs.

SLIPPING GEARS OR NO DRIVE ON SOME 1984 BUILT GEARBOXES

Some GM 400 transmissions manufactured during 1984 may exhibit the following faults: Slipping in all gears, loss of drive.

If either of these symptoms is evident then the unit should be dismantled and the forward clutch ring checked to ensure that it is correctly seated. If it is found that the forward clutch snap ring is incorrectly located, or not seated correctly and that some seals have also been dislodged from their seats then the reverse boost valve must be removed from the oil pump and the depth of the bore check, see Fig. 27. If this measurement exceeds 15,8 mm (⅝ in) then the valve should be replaced with Part No. AAU 6640.

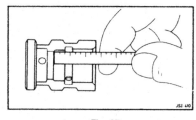

Fig. 27

The suspect transmissions are between Serial Numbers:

842V3608 - 842V6011

HE VEHICLES SHIFT SPEED DATA

NOTE: The figures in the following table refer only to HE cars with a final drive ratio of 2.88:1.

Light Throttle		Full Throttle		Full Throttle and Kick-down		Kick-down		Down-shift		Roll Out	
1–2	2–3	1–2	2–3	1–2	2–3	3–2	3–1	Manual 2–1	PTKD* 3–2	3–2	2–1
5–13 m.p.h.	11–21 m.p.h.	43–53 m.p.h.	60–90 m.p.h.	53–64 m.p.h.	91–101 m.p.h.	80–91 m.p.h.	32–43 m.p.h.	18–25 m.p.h.	43–53 m.p.h.	5–13 m.p.h.	3–9 m.p.h.
8–21 km/h	18–34 km/h	69–85 km/h	96–145 km/h	85–103 km/h	146–163 km/h	129–146 km/h	52–69 km/h	29–40 km/h	69–85 km/h	8–21 km/h	5–14 km/h

* PTKD = Part Throttle Kick-down

NOTE: The figures in the following table refer only to Canadian HE cars with a final drive ratio of 2.88:1.

Light Throttle		Full Throttle		Full Throttle and Kick-down		Kick-down		Down-shift	Roll Out	
1–2	2–3	1–2	2–3	1–2	2–3	3–2	2–1	Manual 2–1	3–2	2–1
7–12 m.p.h.	15–22 m.p.h.	38–48 m.p.h.	67–75 m.p.h.	60–70 m.p.h.	90–100 m.p.h.	80–90 m.p.h.	40–50 m.p.h.	20–30 m.p.h.	8–12 m.p.h.	3–8 m.p.h.
11–19 km/h	24–35 km/h	61–77 km/h	107–120 km/h	96–112 km/h	144–160 km/h	128–144 km/h	64–80 km/h	32–48 km/h	13–19 km/h	5–13 km/h

NOTE: The above figures are theoretical. Actual figures may vary slightly due to such factors as tyre pressures, road conditions etc.

HE VEHICLES VALVE SPRING IDENTIFICATION

VALVE SPRING IDENTIFICATION CHART				
Function	Colour	Free Length	No. of Coils	Outside Diameter
1–2 accumulator valve	Red	1.750 in	12.5	0.470 in
Pressure regulator	Light Blue	3.343 in	13	0.845 in
Front servo piston	Natural	1.129 in	4	1.257 in
Rear accumulator	Yellow	2.230 in	8.5 .	1.130 in
Governor	Dark green	0.933 in	9.5	0.316 in
	Red	0.987 in	8.5	0.306 in
1–2 regulator	Pink	0.936 in	13.5	0.241 in
2–3 valve	Red	1.491 in	17.5	0.328 in
2–3 valve	Gold	1.555 in	18.5	0.326 in
3–2 valve	Yellowy Green	2.500 in	18.5	0.400 in
Front accumulator piston	Pink	2.600 in	8.5	1.260 in
Detent regulator	Green	2.735 in	26.5	0.340 in

44 — 34

JAGUAR
Daimler

Containing Sections

47 PROPELLER AND DRIVE SHAFTS

51 REAR AXLE AND FINAL DRIVE

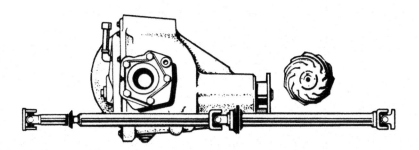

SERIES III
SERVICE MANUAL

INTRODUCTION

This Service Manual covers the Jaguar Series 3 and Daimler Series 3 range of vehicles. It is primarily designed to assist skilled technicians in the efficient repair and maintenance of Jaguar and Daimler vehicles.

Using the appropriate service tools and carrying out the procedures as detailed will enable the operations to be completed within the time stated in the 'Repair Operation Times'.

The Service Manual has been produced in 13 separate sections; this allows the information to be distributed throughout the specialist areas of the modern service facility.

A table of contents in section 1 lists the major components and systems together with the section and book numbers. The cover of each book depicts graphically and numerically the sections contained within that book. Each section starts with a list of operations in alphabetical order.

The title page of each book carries the part numbers required to order replacement books, binders or complete Service Manuals. This can be done through the normal channels.

Operation Numbering

A master index of numbered operations has been compiled for universal application to all vehicles manufactured by Jaguar Cars Ltd., and therefore, because of the different specifications of various models, continuity of the numbering sequence cannot be maintained throughout this manual.

Each operation described in this manual is allocated a number from the master index and cross-refers with an identical number in the 'Repair Operation Times'. The number consists of six digits arranged in three pairs.

Each operation is laid out in the sequence required to complete the operation in the minimum time, as specified in the 'Repair Operation Times'.

Service Tools

Where performance of an operation requires the use of a service tool, the tool number is quoted under the operation heading and is repeated in, following, the instruction involving its use. A list of all necessary tools is included in section 1, number 99.

References

References to the left- or right-hand side in the manual are made when viewing from the rear. With the engine and gearbox assembly removed the timing cover end of the engine is referred to as the front. A key to abbreviations and symbols is given in section 1, number 01.

REPAIRS AND REPLACEMENTS

When service parts are required it is essential that only genuine Jaguar/Daimler or Unipart replacements are used. Attention is particularly drawn to the following points concerning repairs and the fitting of replacement parts and accessories.

1.   Safety features embodied in the vehicle may be impaired if other than genuine parts are fitted. In certain territories, legislation prohibits the fitting of parts not to the vehicle manufacturer's specification.

2.   Torque wrench setting figures given in this Service Manual must be strictly adhered to.

3.   Locking devices, where specified, must be fitted. If the efficiency of a locking device is impaired during removal it must be replaced.

4.   Owners purchasing accessories while travelling abroad should ensure that the accessory and its fitted location on the vehicle conform to mandatory requirements existing in their country of origin.

5.   The vehicle warranty may be invalidated by the fitting of other than genuine Jaguar/Daimler or Unipart parts. All Jaguar/Daimler and Unipart replacements have the full backing of the factory warranty.

6.   Jaguar/Daimler Dealers are obliged to supply only genuine service parts.

SPECIFICATION

Purchasers are advised that the specification details set out in this Manual apply to a range of vehicles and not to any one. For the specification of a particular vehicle, purchasers should consult their Dealer.

The Manufacturers reserve the right to vary their specifications with or without notice, and at such times and in such manner as they think fit. Major as well as minor changes may be involved in accordance with the Manufacturer's policy of constant product improvement.

Whilst every effort is made to ensure the accuracy of the particulars contained in this Manual, neither the Manufacturer nor the Dealer, by whom this Manual is supplied, shall in any circumstances be held liable for any inaccuracy or the consequences thereof.

CONTENTS

TORQUE WRENCH SETTINGS

ITEM	DESCRIPTION	TIGHTENING TORQUE		
		Nm	kgf m	lbf ft
Centre bearing mounting plate to body	$\frac{5}{16}$ in U.N.F. bolts	19 to 24,4	1,94 to 2,48	14 to 18
Centre bearing to mounting plate	$\frac{5}{16}$ in U.N.F. bolts	19 to 24,4	1,94 to 2,48	14 to 18
Drive shaft to drive unit (Cleveloc)	$\frac{7}{16}$ in U.N.F. nut	66,4 to 74,5	6,78 to 7,6	49 to 55
Drive shaft to hub carrier	$\frac{3}{4}$ in U.N.F. nut	136 to 163	13,8 to 16,6	100 to 120
Propeller shaft flange bolts — Automatic gearbox . .	$\frac{3}{8}$ in U.N.F. bolts and nuts	36,7 to 43,4	3,74 to 4,42	27 to 32
— Manual gearbox	10 mm bolts and nuts	50	5,12	37
Rear propeller shaft to centure U.J.		36,8	3,75	27

SERVICE TOOLS

Tool No.	Description
JD1D	Hub remover

DRIVE SHAFTS AND PROPELLER SHAFT

Description

The drive shafts replace the half shafts of a conventional rear axle, and in addition serve as upper transverse members to locate the rear wheels; their inner universal joints are attached to the final drive unit by bolts which also carry the brake discs, but the brakes are not disturbed in drive shaft removal. The outer joints are integral with the hub driving shafts, and the hubs must therefore be separated from the drive shafts before they can be removed.

The propeller shaft is a two universal joint type, at the front end of which is a reverse spline fitting coupled to the gearbox and at the rear a flange bolted to the input drive flange of the final drive unit.

When fitting a propeller shaft it is essential to ensure that the universal joints operate freely; any stiffness, even in a single joint, will initiate propeller shaft vibration.

DRIVE SHAFT

Remove and refit 47.10.01

Service tool: Hub remover JD 1D.
To remove a drive shaft it is necessary to detach the hub and to swing one suspension unit aside to clear the inner joint.

Ensure that car is securely supported on stands before removing the wheel. Release clips (1, Fig. 1) and before removing nut from drive shaft in hub, slide inner shroud along shaft.

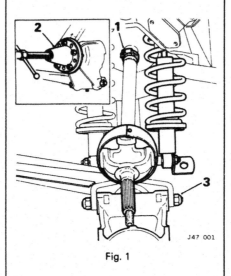

Fig. 1

Remove grease nipple from hub carrier, and using tool JD 1D (2, Fig. 1), withdraw hub from shaft. Allow the hub carrier to pivot about wishbone pin. Before detaching inner joint, release lower end of rear spring/damper unit (3, Fig. 1) and swing aside to clear joint. Collect and retain any camber setting shims fitted between inner joint and brake disc.

Refitting

Replacement drive shafts are supplied without shrouds, oil seal track or spacer; remove these items and transfer them to the new shaft. Seal shroud joints with underseal. Ensure that chamfer on oil seal track clears radius on shaft, and apply Loctite to spline before refitting hub. Tighten all nuts and bolts to the correct torque. Check and if necessary adjust hub bearing end-float and ensure that camber angles of the wheels are correct.

DRIVE SHAFT

Overhaul 47.10.08

Dismantling

Remove drive shaft.
Remove grease nipples (1, Fig. 2), place shaft in vice and remove two opposed circlips (2, Fig. 2).

NOTE: Tap bearings slightly inwards to assist removal of circlips.

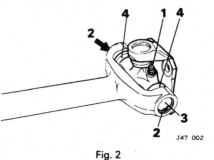

Fig. 2

Tap one bearing inwards to displace opposite bearing (3, Fig. 2).
Trap displaced bearing in vice and remove shaft and joint from bearing.
Replace shaft in vice, displace second bearing by tapping joint spider across and extract second bearing.
Remove two grease seals (4, Fig. 2).
Detach spider, with end section of shaft, from centre section of shaft.
Place end section of shaft in vice and repeat above operations.
Remove spider from end section of shaft.
Repeat above operations on opposite end of shaft.

Inspection

Wash all parts in petrol.
Check splined yoke for wear of splines.
Examine bearing races and spider journals for signs of looseness, load markings, scoring or distortion.

NOTE: Spider or bearings should not be renewed separately, as this will cause premature failure of the replacement.
It is essential that bearing races are a light drive fit in yoke trunnion.

Reassembling

Remove bearing assemblies from one replacement spider; if necessary, retain rollers in housings with petroleum jelly. Leave grease shields in position.

Fit spider to one end section of shaft.

Fit two bearings and circlips in end section trunnions. Use a soft round drift against bearing housings.

Insert spider in trunnions of centre section of shaft.

Fit two bearings and circlips in centre section trunnions.

Fit grease nipple to spider.

Repeat above operations on opposite end of drive shaft.

Grease joints with hand grease gun.

Refit drive shaft.

PROPELLER SHAFT

Remove and refit   47.15.01

Service tools: Engine support tool MS 53A or extension jack.

Removing

To provide access, remove the exhaust heat shield where fitted.

Mark the relationship between the propeller shaft and final drive flanges, and remove the bolts securing the flanges.

Remove the bolts securing the centre bearing support plate, to the centre bearing and body.

Remove the support plate. Collect two spacers with the front bolts.

Using service tool MS 53A or, alternatively, place an extension jack under the gearbox, nut under the oil pan, take the weight off the rear engine mounting.

Separate the exhaust system at the down-pipe and intermediate pipe joints.

On cars equipped with a catalyst, slacken the nut and move the exhaust support stay to one side.

Remove the exhaust strengthening plate from the transmission case; collect two spacers and one washer.

Raise the rear of the engine/gearbox unit to reduce the loading on the mounting spring.

Remove the bolts securing the engine mounting to the tunnel closing plate, and detach the mounting plate. Collect spring, two spacers, two special washers and bump stop rubber.

Mark the relationship between the propeller shaft front flange and gearbox flange. Remove the bolts, turning the shaft to give access to each nut.

Separate the flanges and withdraw the complete propeller shaft rearwards through the transmission tunnel.

Refitting

NOTE: Before refitting the shaft, ensure that all the universal joints operate freely; a tight joint will cause vibration.

Insert the propeller shaft through the rear of the tunnel and line up the front flanges as marked. Fit the bolts through the flanges, fit and tighten the nuts. Refer to torque wrench settings.

Replace the rear engine mounting and strengthening plate and detach the engine support tool or jack.

Replace the rear flange to final drive flange as marked, fit four bolts, fit and tighten the nuts to the correct torque.

Offer up the centre bearing support plate to the centre bearing and body structure. Insert bolts and spacers but do not fully tighten. Move the centre bearing as far as possible to the right-hand side of the tunnel and tighten the bolts.

NOTE: If propeller shaft vibration is experienced, move the centre bearing to the left in small steps until the vibration is eliminated. It is most important that the spacers which control the vertical location of the bearing are replaced as originally installed.

Replace the exhaust stay (catalyst equipped cars) and re-make exhaust flange joint using 'Firegum'.

PROPELLER SHAFT

Overhaul   47.15.10

including:

Propeller shaft — rear — remove and refit   47.15.03

Sliding joint and gaiter — remove and refit   47.15.08

Centre bearing — remove and refit   47.15.33

NOTE: The propeller shaft is supplied as a balanced unit and it is not possible to replace the front or rear shafts separately. Only the sliding joint gaiter, centre bearing, end flanges and spiders of the universal joints can be renewed.

Dismantling

Remove the propeller shaft assembly from the vehicle and place on a workbench.

Clean the assembly and mark the relationship between the centre yoke and the rear shaft.

Rear propeller shaft

To remove the rear propeller shaft, insert a suitable distance piece (e.g. a scrap nut), between the head of the bolt (1, Fig. 3) securing the centre joint yoke to the rear shaft, and the spider of the centre universal joint.

Using an open-ended spanner, unscrew the bolt (1, Fig. 3) from the rear shaft; to separate the shafts, break the Loctite adhesion between the splines and withdraw the rear shaft from the centre yoke.

Centre bearing

Using a suitable puller, remove the centre bearing from the rear propeller shaft. Engage the legs of the puller in the inner reinforcing ring of the rubber mounting.

Universal joints

To overhaul the propeller shaft universal joints, remove the snap-rings from the grooves (2, Fig. 3).

NOTE: If difficulty is encountered, tap the bearing cup (3, Fig. 3) inwards to relieve the pressure on the snap-ring.

Hold the flange yoke and tap the yoke with a soft-faced hammer. The bearing cup should gradually emerge and can be finally removed.

Alternatively, secure the propeller shaft in a vice. Using a suitable soft metal drift, drift down on a bearing cup to displace the opposite cup. Remove the propeller shaft from the vice, hold the displaced cup in the vice and separate from the propeller shaft by pulling and twisting. Repeat the above operations for the opposite bearing cup, and the remaining bearing cups at each end of the shaft.

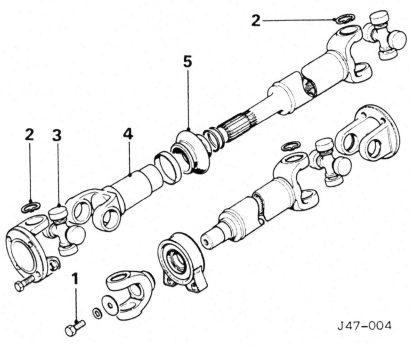

J47–004

Fig. 3

Sliding joint and gaiter

To remove the gaiter from the sliding joint or the front propeller shaft, clean the gaiter and the area of the shaft adjacent to it. Ensure that the arrows are visible on the sleeve yoke and shaft (1, Fig. 4). Cut the metal and rubber rings (2, Fig. 4) securing the gaiter to the yoke and shaft, withdraw the gaiter (5, Fig. 5) along the shaft.

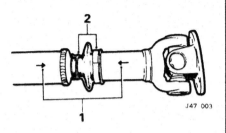

Fig. 4

Partially withdraw the sleeve yoke (4, Fig. 5) from the splined shaft and examine the splines for wear. If there is more than 0,1 mm (0.004 in) circumferential movement measured on the outside diameter of the spline, then the complete propeller shaft assembly must be renewed.

Withdraw the sleeve yoke (4, Fig. 5) from the splines shaft and remove the gaiter (5, Fig. 5).

Inspection

Carefully inspect the internal and external splines of the sliding joint. Ensure that the welch washer in the female spline is secure and leakproof.

Wash all the other components of the propeller shaft assembly in petrol, examine bearing races and spider journals for signs of looseness, load markings, scoring or distortion. Spiders or bearings should not be renewed separately, as this will cause premature failure of the replacement.

It is essential that the bearing cups (3, Fig. 5) are a light drive fit in the yoke trunnions.

Reassembling

Universal joints

Using new universal joint assemblies if necessary, insert the journal cross into the flange, tilting it to engage in the yoke bores.

Ensure that all the needle rollers are in position; fill each bearing cup one-third full of grease of the recommended type.

Fit one of the bearing cups (3, Fig. 5) in the yoke bore, and using a suitable soft metal drift, tap the bearing cup fully home.

Fit a new snap-ring (2, Fig. 5) ensuring it is correctly located in the groove.

Assemble the other spiders and bearing cups, and fit new snap-rings, to retain the bearing cups.

Sliding joint and gaiter

Lubricate the internal and external splines generously with Blended Spline Grease (ref. MNR (A) supplied by Oilene Ltd.), align the arrows and engage the male and female splines.

Ensure that a dimension of less than 185 mm (7.3 in) can be obtained between the yoke joint centre-line and the weld centre-line on the propeller shaft.

Withdraw the shaft and check for complete coverage of the splines by the lubricant.

To prevent damage to the rubber rings and gaiter wrap thin metal or plastic film over the male splines. Pass the two rubber rings over the splines, followed by the smaller end of the gaiter, place the rings over the gaiter.

Remove the protective film from the splines.

Position the metal ring clip on the gaiter, realign the splines and ease the gaiter over the sliding joint. Check that the arrows align (1, Fig. 4) and fit the sleeve yoke to the shaft.

Secure the gaiter clip.

Rear propeller shaft

Coat the splines of the rear propeller shaft with Loctite grade AVV and fit to the centre joint yoke, align the marks previously made.

Fit and tighten the bolt (1, Fig. 5) secure using a new tab washer.

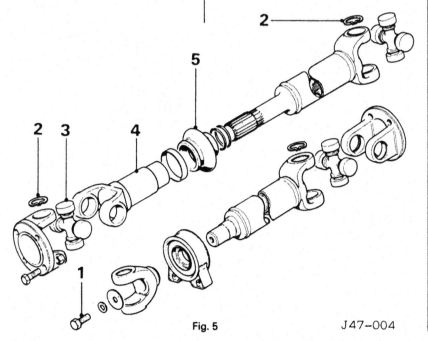

Fig. 5   J47-004

47—4

CONTENTS

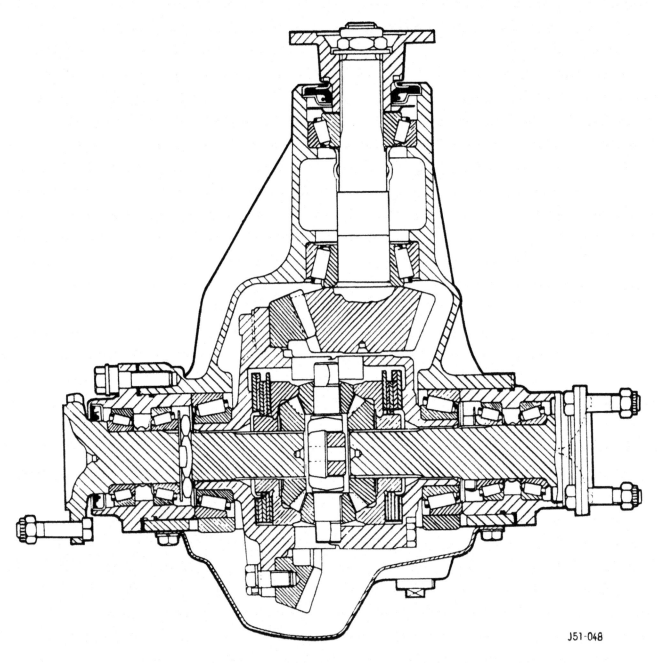

J51-048

CROSS-SECTION OF THE LIMITED SLIP REAR AXLE

TORQUE WRENCH SETTINGS

Item	Spanner Size	Description	Tightening Torque		
			Nm	kgf/m	lbf/ft
Caliper mounting bracket to unit	$\frac{5}{8}$ in AF	$\frac{7}{16}$ in UNC setbolts	81,3 to 93	8,3 to 9,54	60 to 69
Differential bearing caps	$\frac{3}{4}$ in AF	$\frac{1}{2}$ in UNC setbolts	85,4 to 97	8,71 to 9,95	63 to 72
Drive pinion nut	$1\frac{1}{8}$ in AF	$\frac{3}{4}$ in UNF nut	244 to 256	24,92 to 26,34	180 to 190
Drive gear to differential flange	$\frac{6}{8}$ in AF	$\frac{7}{16}$ in UNF setbolts	102 to 118	10,78 to 12,16	77 to 88
Powr-Lok differential case	$\frac{9}{16}$ in AF	$\frac{3}{8}$ in UNC setbolts	58,3 to 67	5,95 to 6,9	43 to 50
Rear cover attachment	$\frac{1}{2}$ in AF	$\frac{5}{16}$ in UNC setbolts	20,5 to 27	2,1 to 2,76	15 to 20
Ring gear attachment	$\frac{11}{16}$ in AF	$\frac{7}{16}$ in UNF Rippbolt	136 to 151	13,8 to 15,46	100 to 111

SERVICE TOOLS

Tool No.	Description
18G 120 5	Flange Holder
18G 134 (MS 550, 550, SL 550)	Adaptor Handle
SL 550-1	Outer Pinion Cup Remover
47 (MS 47, SL 14)	Hand Press
{ SL14-3/2	Differential Side Bearing Remover
{ SL14-3/1	Differential Side Bearing Remover Button
{ SL 3	Clock Gauge Tool
{ 4 HA	Pinion Height Setting Gauge
SL 550-9	Pinion Inner Bearing Cup Replacer
SL 550-8/1	Pinion Outer Bearing Cup Replacer
{ SL 47-1/1	Pinion Head Bearing Remover
{ SL 47-1/2	Pinion Head Bearing Replacer
18G 1428	Rear Oil Seal Replacer
SL 15A	Spanner
18G 681 CBW 548	Torque Driver
{ SL 47-3/1	Output Shaft Outer Bearing Remover
{ SL 47-3/2	Output Shaft Outer Bearing Replacer
JD 14	Dummy Shaft

{ Items marked thus are sold as sets.

DESCRIPTION

The standard transmission unit is a Salisbury 4HU final drive, incorporating a 'Powr-Lok' differential when specified; this is identified by the letters 'PL' on a tab under a cover bolt. A Powr-Lok differential differs from a conventional bevel gear unit by the addition of plate clutches loaded by input torque to oppose rotations of the output shafts relative to the differential cage. Clutch plates are splined to the cage, and their mating discs to the output bevels; the loading between plates and disc increases with input torque due partly to the separating forces of bevels and also to the bevel pinion cross-shafts being carried on ramps instead of being positively located in the cage. Increase in output torque causes the cross-shafts to move 'up' the ramps and, by pressing plates and discs together, to 'lock' the differential; this gives the effect of a differential-less axle at maximum torque without increasing the disadvantages of this type of axle in low-torque conditions. Some low-torque stiffness, to reduce one-wheel spin on ice, is provided by forming the outer plates as Belleville washers to produce compression between plates and discs; if one wheel is held and the propeller shaft is disconnected, a torque of between 5,6 and 9,6 kgf/m (40 to 70 lbf/ft) is required to turn the other wheel.

The final drive unit is rigidly attached to a fabricated sheet steel cross-beam which is flexibly mounted to the body structure by four rubber and metal sandwich mountings. Noises coming from the vicinity of the final drive unit usually originate from incorrect meshing of drive gear and pinion, or from bearings on differential or pinion shafts developing play. Operation procedures for the correction of these noise sources are fully covered in operation 51.25.19, but a noise occurring at low speeds only, under braking, could be caused by loss of pre-load in the output shaft bearings. Bearing inspection involves the removal and renewal of an oil seal before resetting pre-load, and is covered in operation 51.20.04, while if inspection indicates that bearing renewal is advisable this is detailed in operation 51.10.22.

51-3

TO CHECK THE TOOTH CONTACT PATTERN

Sparingly paint eight or ten of the drive gear teeth with a stiff mixture of marking raddle or engineers blue. Move the painted gear teeth in mesh with the pinion until a good impression of the total contact is obtained. The result should conform with the ideal tooth contact pattern (Fig. 1).

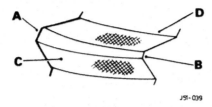

Fig. 1 Ideal tooth contact pattern.

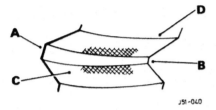

Fig. 2 High tooth contact pattern.

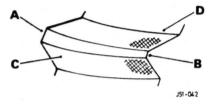

Fig. 3 Low tooth contact pattern.

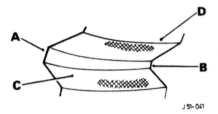

Fig. 4 Toe contact pattern.

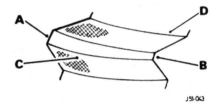

Fig. 5 Heel contact pattern.

A The HEEL is the larger outer end of the tooth.

B The TOE is the small or inner end of the tooth.

C The DRIVE side of the drive gear tooth is convex.

D The COAST side of the drive gear tooth is concave.

51-4

FAULT DIAGNOSIS

TOOTH PATTERN	REMEDY
The ideal tooth bearing impression on the drive and coast sides of the gear teeth is evenly distributed over the working depth of the tooth profile and is located nearer to the toe (small end) than the heel (large end). This type of contact permits the tooth bearing to spread towards the heel under operating conditions when allowance must be made for deflection.	————
In High Tooth Contact it will be observed that the tooth contact is heavy on the drive gear face or addendum. To rectify this condition, move the pinion deeper into mesh, that is, reduce the pinion cone setting distance, by adding shims between the pinion inner bearing cup and the housing and fitting a new collapsible spacer.	Move the drive pinion deeper into mesh. i.e. reduce the pinion cone setting.
In Low Tooth Contact it will be observed that the tooth contact is heavy on the drive gear flank or dedendum. This is the opposite condition from that shown in High Tooth Contact and is therefore corrected by moving the pinion out of mesh, that is, increase the pinion cone setting distance by removing shims from between the pinion inner bearing cup and housing and fitting a new collapsible spacer.	Move the drive pinion out of mesh. i.e. increase the pinion cone setting
Toe Contact occurs when the bearing is concentrated at the small end of the tooth.	Move the drive gear out of mesh, that is, increase backlash, by transferring shims from the drive gear side of the differential to the opposite side.
Heel Contact is indicated by the concentration of the bearing at the large end of the tooth.	Move the drive gear closer into mesh, that is, reduce backlash, by adding shims to the drive gear side of the differential and removing an equal thickness of shims from the opposite side. NOTE: It is most important to remember when making this adjustment to correct a heel contact that sufficient backlash for satisfactory operation must be maintained. If there is insufficient backlash the gears will at least be noisy and have a greatly reduced life, whilst scoring of the tooth profile and breakage may result. Therefore, always maintain a minimum backlash requirement of 0,10 mm. (0.004 in).

51-5

DRIVE PINION SHAFT OIL SEAL

Renew 51.20.01

Service tools: Torque screwdriver 18G 681,
Oil seal replacer 18G 1428.

Detach the four bolts (1, Fig. 6) securing
propeller shaft to final drive flange; support
propeller shaft rear end and clean flange
and nose of final drive.

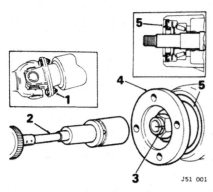

Fig. 6

Accurately measure torque required to turn
flange through backlash, using torque
screwdriver 18G 681 (2, Fig. 6) with a
suitable adaptor and socket.

**NOTE: Set screwdriver initially to 0,057
kgf/m (5 lbf/in) and increase setting
progressively until torque figure is reached
at which flange commences to move.
Flange MUST be turned fully anti-clockwise
through backlash between each check.**

Mark nut and pinion shaft so that in refitting,
nut may be returned to its original position
on shaft (3, Fig. 6).
Unscrew nut and remove washer and place
both washer and nut aside for refitting.
Draw flange (4, Fig. 6) off pinion shaft using
extractor.
Prise oil seal (5, Fig. 6) out of final drive
casing.

Refitting (using original bearings)

Thoroughly clean splines on pinion shaft
and flange. Clean oil seal recess and coat
internally with Welseal liquid sealant. Using
tool No. 18G1428 tap new oil seal squarely
into position with sealing lip facing to rear
(1, Fig. 7).

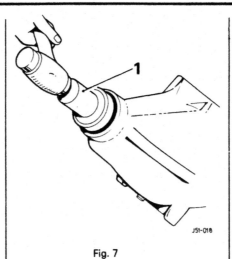

Fig. 7

Smear sealing lip with grease.
Apply grease lightly to outer two thirds of
pinion shaft splines.
Lightly tap flange back on pinion shaft,
using wooden mallet.
Refit washer and nut and tighten nut until it
exactly reaches position previously marked.
Re-check turning torque. Torque required to
turn pinion shaft through backlash should
exceed by 0,7 to 1,4 kgf/m (5 to 10 lbf/in)
the torque recorded earlier. If, however,
torque required to turn pinion shaft exceeds
0,52 kgf/m (45 lbf/in), final drive overhaul,
operation 51.25.19 MUST be carried out.
Lift propeller shaft into position, replace
bolts, fit and tighten nuts to correct torque.
Check oil level in final drive unit and top up if
necessary.
Remove car from ramp and road test.
If final drive is noisy, an overhaul must be
carried out.

FINAL DRIVE REAR COVER GASKET

Renew 51.20.08

Remove the fourteen $\frac{1}{2}$ in AF bolts and
setscrews (1, Fig. 8) securing the bottom
tie-plate to the cross-beam and inner
fulcrum brackets.
Drain the oil from the final drive.
Remove the ten $\frac{1}{2}$ in AF setscrews (1, Fig. 9)
and remove the rear cover (2, Fig. 9) noting
the position of the identification tabs.
Clean off any gasket or sealant from the rear
cover and the hypoid housing.
Smear the rear cover flange with Wellseal
jointing compound and place the gasket on
the casing.
Refit the rear cover and secure with the ten
setscrews, prior to fitting coat the threads of
the bolts with Loctite.
Refill with new oil.

**NOTE: The vehicle must be on level ground
before checking the oil level.**

Replace the bottom tie-plate and tighten the
bolts and setscrews to the correct torque.

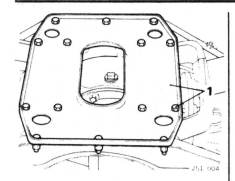

Fig. 8

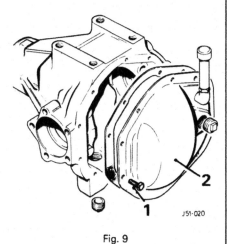

Fig. 9

OUTPUT SHAFT ASSEMBLY (One Side)

Renew 51.10.20

To remove an output shaft it is necessary to detach the inboard end of the drive shaft, the forward attachment of the radius rod, and to remove the brake caliper and disc (1, Fig. 10).

These operations are detailed in Section 70, the Brake System.

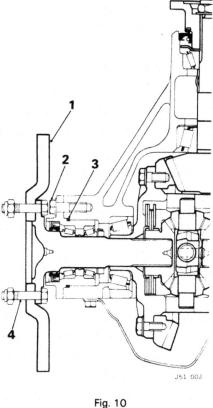

Fig. 10

Cut locking wire and remove five set bolts (2, Fig. 10) securing caliper mounting flange to final drive. Withdraw complete output shaft assembly and discard 'O' ring (3, Fig. 10).

Before fitting, ensure that four bolts (4, Fig. 10) are in position, and that new 'O' ring (3, Fig. 10) is fitted. Lightly oil splines and outside of bearing with final drive oil, insert assembly; fit bolts with spring washers, tighten to 8,4 to 9,66 kgf/m (60 to 69 lbf/ft), tightening the bolt nearest to the input flange first, and wire lock bolt heads together so that wire tension is tending to tighten bolts.

Replace brake caliper and disc as described in Brake System section; check camber angle of rear wheels, and adjust if necessary, refer to Section 64 for the correct procedure.

OUTPUT SHAFT BEARINGS

Renew 51.10.22

Service tools: 47 Press, Torque screwdriver 18G 681, Adaptor, Spanner SL 15A or 15, Output shaft bearing remover/replacer SL 47-3/1, SL 47-3/2.

Remove output shaft assembly incorporating bearing to be removed.

Clean assembly and clamp caliper mounting bracket between suitably protected jaws of vice.

Turn down tabs of lock washer and remove nut (1, Fig. 11) from shaft, using spanner SL 15A (Fig. 12).

Remove and discard lock washer.

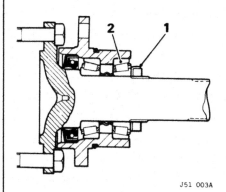

Fig. 11

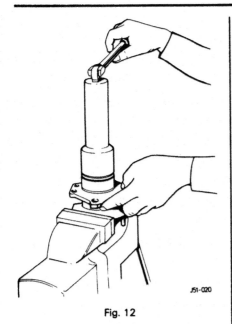

Fig. 12

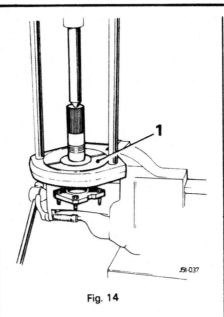

Fig. 14

Withdraw output shaft (1, Fig. 13) from caliper mounting bracket (2, Fig. 13). Collect inner bearing (3, Fig. 13) and·cone. Discard collapsed spacer (4, Fig. 13).

NOTE: If outer bearing remains on shaft and pushes oil seal out of caliper mounting bracket on withdrawal, remove it from shaft using tool SL 47-3/1, 47 (1, Fig. 14).

Prise oil seal from caliper mounting bracket. Collect outer bearing and cone. Discard oil seal.

Using a suitable drift, gently tap bearing cups (5, Fig. 13) out of housing.

Remove caliper mounting bracket from vice and carefully clean internally.

NOTE: When bearings are to be renewed, always replace complete bearings. Never fit new cone and roller assemblies into used cups.

Before fitting, bearings should be lightly greased, but it is most important that at least 4 cc of hypoid oil is added to the cavity between the bearings during assembly, and that the oil seal is lubricated by packing the annular space between its sealing edges with grease. This prevents premature seal or bearing wear before oil flow begins from the axle centre.

Refitting

Press cups of replacement bearings into housing, using suitble press and adaptors to ensure that cups are pressed fully home in housing.

Place roller and cone assembly of outer bearing (already greased) in position.

Press replacement oil seal into position (1, Fig. 15) ensuring that spring-loaded sealing edge is adjacent to bearing. Load seal with grease between sealing edges.

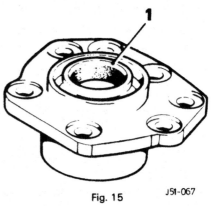

Fig. 15

Clamp caliper mounting bracket between protected jaws of vice.

Check that four special bolts for brake disc are in position in output shaft flange and enter shaft through seal and outer bearing.

Fit new collapsible spacer and fill the space between bearings with Hypoid EP 90 oil before replacing rollers and cone of inner bearing and fitting new lock washer on shaft.

Place nut on shaft, grease face next to washer and tighten finger-tight only.

Using spanner SL15A and a tommy-bar at disc attachment bolts to oppose torque, tighten nut on shaft just sufficiently to almost eliminate play from bearings. Torque required to turn shaft should be 0,14 to 0,28 kgf/m (10 to 20 lbf/in)

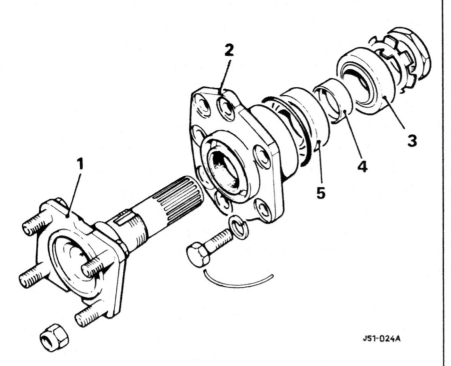

Fig. 13

51-8

Further tighten nut, very slightly (not more than a thirty-second of a turn — about 5 mm ($\frac{3}{16}$ in) at perimeter of nut) and re-check torque required to turn shaft. Continue to tighten nut in very small increments, turning shaft to seat bearings and measuring torque after each increment, until correct figure is reached.

CAUTION: If torque required to turn shaft exceeds by more than 0,28 kgf/m (20 lbf/in) torque recorded in first check, it is necessary to dismantle assembly, discard collapsed spacer and rebuild with new collapsible spacer. It is not permissible to slacken back nut after collapsing spacer as bearing cones are then no longer rigidly clamped.

Turn down tab washers in two places to lock nut and remove assembly from vice. Refit output shaft assembly to final drive unit, see operation 51.10.20.

OUTPUT SHAFT OIL SEAL

Renew   51.20.04

Service tools: 47 Press, torque screwdriver 18G 681, Adaptor, Spanner SL 15A or 15 Output shaft bearing remover/replacer SL 47-3/1, SL 47-3/2.

Remove output shaft assembly.
Clean assembly and clamp caliper mounting bracket between suitably protected jaws of vice.
Turn down tabs of lock washer (1, Fig. 16) and remove nut from shaft, using spanner SL15A (1, Fig. 17).

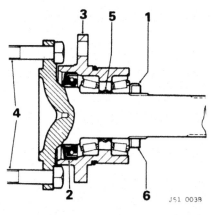

Fig. 16

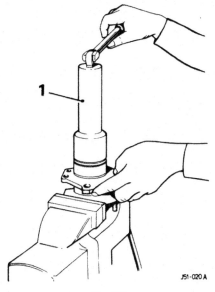

Fig. 17

Remove and discard lock washer.

Withdraw output shaft from caliper mounting bracket. Collect inner bearing and cone and mark for correct reassembly. Discard collapsed spacer.
Prise oil seal from caliper mounting bracket and discard. Collect outer bearing and cone. Remove caliper mounting bracket from vice and thoroughly clean internally.
If outer bearing remains on shaft and pushes oil seal out of caliper mounting bracket on withdrawal, remove it from shaft using tool SL47-3/1, 47 (1, Fig. 18).

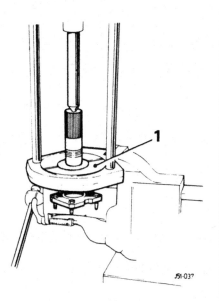

Fig. 18

NOTE: Carefully inspect taper roller bearing components before refitting. If any fault is found in either bearing, replace both complete bearings. Refer to operation 51.10.22, for full details. Never fit new cone and roller assemblies into used cups.

Before fitting, bearings should be lightly greased, but it is most important that at least 4 cc of hypoid oil is added to the cavity between the bearings during assembly, and that the oil seal (2, Fig. 16) is lubricated by packing the annular space between its sealing edges with grease. This prevents premature seal or bearing wear before oil flow begins from the axle centre.

Refitting (using original bearings)

Place roller and cone assembly of outer bearing (already greased) in position.
Press replacement oil seal into position, ensuring that spring-loaded sealing edge is adjacent to bearing. Load seal with grease between sealing edges.
Clamp caliper mounting bracket (3, Fig. 16) between protected jaws of vice.
Check that four special bolts (4, Fig. 16) for brake disc are in position in output shaft flange and enter shaft through seal and fit the outer bearing using tools SL47-3/1, SL47-3/2 (1, Fig. 19).

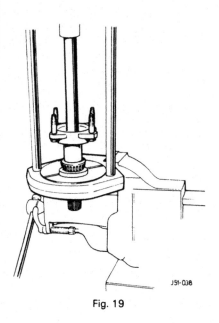

Fig. 19

Smear oil on portion of shaft in contact with seal.

Fit new collapsible spacer (5, Fig. 16) and fill the space between bearings with Hypoid EP 90 oil before replacing rollers and cone of inner bearing and fitting new lock washer on shaft.
Place nut (6, Fig. 16) on shaft, grease face next to washer and tighten finger-tight only.

Using torque screwdriver 18G 681 and adaptor check torque required to turn shaft in caliper mounting bracket against resistance of the oil seal. Record the torque.

51-9

NOTE: Set screwdriver initially to 0,05 kgf/m (4 lbf/in). Setting should then be progressively increased until torque figure is established at the point when shaft commences to turn.

Using spanner SL15A and a tommy-bar at disc attachment bolts to oppose torque, tighten nut on shaft just sufficiently to almost eliminate play from bearings. Repeat torque check. Torque required to turn shaft should be unchanged, if it has increased, slacken nut very slightly and re-check.

Further tighten nut, very slightly (not more than a thirty-second of a turn — about 5 mm ($\frac{3}{16}$ in) at perimeter of nut — and re-check torque required to turn shaft. If this torque exceeds by 0,05 to 0,10 kgf/m (4 to 8 lbf/in) the torque recorded earlier, correct bearing pre-load has been achieved, otherwise continue to tighten nut in very small increments, turning shaft to seat bearings and measuring torque after each increment, until correct figure is reached.

CAUTION: If torque required to turn shaft exceeds by more than 0,10 kgf/m (8 lbf/in) torque recorded initially, it is necessary to dismantle assembly, discard collapsed spacer and rebuild with new collapsible spacer. It is not permissible to slacken back nut after collapsing spacer as bearing cones are then no longer rigidly clamped.

Turn down tab washer in two places to lock nut and remove assembly from vice.

Refit output shaft assembly to final drive unit, refer to operation 51.10.20 for full details.

FINAL DRIVE UNIT

Renew   **51.25.13**

Service tool: Dummy shaft JD 14.

The final drive unit cannot be removed from the vehicle unless it is detached as part of the rear suspension unit, removal of this item is detailed in the rear suspension section.

Drain the oil from the unit to prevent any leakage from the breather, and invert the whole assembly onto a workbench.

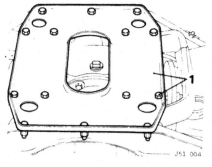

Fig. 20

Remove the fourteen $\frac{1}{2}$ in AF bolts, nuts and setscrews (1, Fig. 20) securing the bottom tie-plate to cross-beam and inner fulcrum brackets.

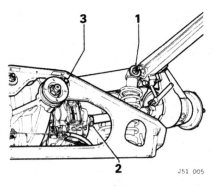

Fig. 21

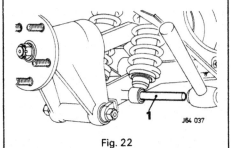

Fig. 22

Remove the $\frac{11}{16}$ in AF nuts and washers (1, Fig. 21) securing the dampers to the wishbone and drift out the retaining pins (1, Fig. 22) recover the spacers and tie-down brackets.

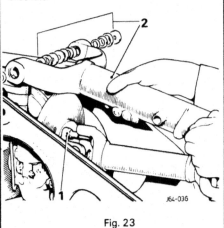

Fig. 23

Slacken the clips (2, Fig. 21) securing the inner universal joint shrouds and slide the shrouds outwards.

Remove the four $\frac{11}{16}$ in AF self locking nuts (1, Fig. 23) either side securing the drive shaft inner universal joint to the brake disc and output flange.

Remove the $\frac{3}{4}$ in AF nut (3, Fig. 21) from the inner wishbone fulcrum shaft and drift out the shaft (1, Fig. 24) collecting the spacers, seals and bearings from the wishbone pivots (2, Fig. 23).

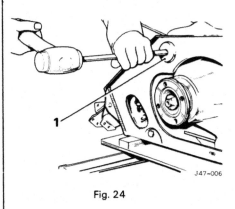

Fig. 24

Remove the drive shaft, hub and wishbone assembly from the rear suspension assembly.

Remove the camber shims from the drive shaft flange studs at the brake disc on both sides.

Remove the spacer tubes from between the lugs of the fulcrum brackets and turn the suspension assembly over on the bench.

Disconnect the brake feed pipes from the calipers, seal the ends of the pipes and the ports in the calipers. Release the brake return springs from the operating levers.

Cut the locking wire and remove the four $\frac{3}{4}$ in AF bolts (1, Fig. 25) securing the final drive to the cross-beam and lift the cross-beam off the unit (Fig. 26).

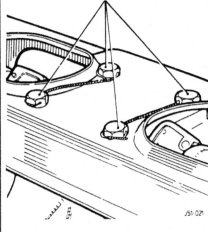

Fig. 25

51-10

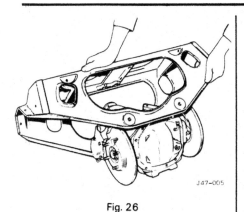

Fig. 26

Invert the unit and remove the locking wires and the $\frac{11}{16}$ in AF setscrews securing the fulcrum brackets to the final drive unit (1, Fig. 27).

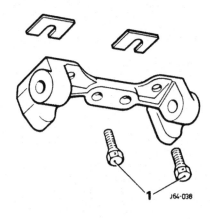

Fig. 27

Remove the brackets, noting the position and number of shims at each attachment point.

Cut the wires from the $\frac{5}{8}$ in AF caliper mounting bolts, remove the bolts and calipers (1, Fig. 28). Remove the brake discs, noting the number of shims between the discs and the flanges.

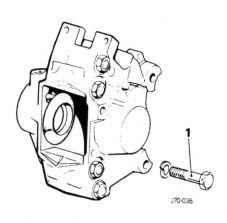

Fig. 28

Replace the shims and disc on one output shaft flange and secure with two nuts. Replace the caliper, tighten the mounting bolts and check the centering and the run out of the disc. The centering tolerance is ±0.25 mm (0.010 in), this can be rectified by transferring shims from one side of the disc to another. The disc run out should not exceed 0.15 mm (0.006 in).
Tighten the caliper bolts to a torque of 6.78 - 7.60 kgf/m 66.4 - 74.5 Nm (49 - 55 lb/ft).
Repeat the above operations on the opposite side. Remove the nuts from both discs.
Place the cross-beam over the final drive, align and replace the bolts and tighten to the correct torque and wire lock 10.4 kgf/m, 101.68 Nm (75 lb/ft). Slacken the brake feed pipes at the centre union, unseal the brake pipes and the ports in the caliper, align and fit the pipes and tighten the unions.
Replace the handbrake lever return springs and invert the assembly on the bench. Position the fulcrum brackets against the final drive unit and locate each bracket loosely with two setscrews. Replace the shims between the fulcrum brackets and the final drive unit.
Tighten the setscrews and wire lock. Refit the camber shims to the drive shaft studs on one side. Fit the drive shaft on to the studs and loosely fit the nuts, and then tighten fully. Replace the spacer tube between the lugs of the fulcrum bracket.
Clean, inspect and grease the lower wishbone bearings, thrust washer etc. Fit new seals and offer up the wishbone fulcrum bracket lugs and locate with dummy shafts.
Tool No. JD14 (1, Fig. 29).

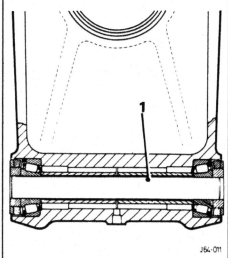

Fig. 29

Take great care not to displace any component during this operation. Drift the dummy shafts from the fulcrum bracket with the fulcrum shaft. Restrain the dummy shafts to prevent spacers or thrust washers dropping out of position.
Tighten the fulcrum shaft nuts to a torque of:

    Inner 61.0 - 67.8 Nm, 6.23 - 6.91 kgf/m (45 - 50 lb/ft).
    Outer 131 - 145 Nm, 13.4 - 14.8 kgf/m (97 - 107 lb/ft).

Reposition the drive shaft shroud and secure it with the clip. Line up the damper lugs with the wishbone bosses and replace the damper shaft, including the spacer and tie down bracket and tighten the nuts to a torque of 43.4 - 48.8 Nm, 4.43 - 4.97 kgf/m (32 - 36 lb/ft).
Replace the wishbone, drive shaft and damper shaft on the opposite side. Replace the bottom tie-plate and tighten the bolts and setscrews.
Replace the rear suspension unit.
Check the rear wheel camber. Bleed the brakes and fill the final drive with oil as necessary.

NOTE: Use Shell Super Spirax 90 or BP Gear Oil 1453 if new gears have been fitted; otherwise use a recommended refill or top up oil as specified in Section 09.

FINAL DRIVE UNIT

Overhaul   51.25.19

Service tools: 18G 1205, 47, SL 47-1/1, 18G 134, SL 550/1, SL 14-3/1, SL 14-3/2, SL 550-1, SL 3, 4HA, SL 550-9, SL 550-8-1, SL 47-1/1, SL 47-1/2, 18G 1428.

Dismantling

Ensure that all lubricant is drained from the unit and support the unit in a vice.

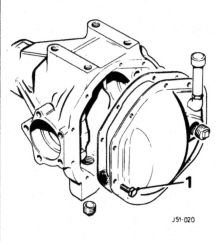

Fig. 30

Remove the ten ½ in AF rear cover securing bolts (1, Fig. 30), the cover and the gasket.
Remove the locking wire and five ⅝ in AF bolts securing the caliper mounting bracket on one side and withdraw the output shaft assembly.
Repeat for the shaft on the other side.
Remove the two ¾ in AF bolts (1, Fig. 31) securing the differential bearing cap, lift out the cap from the differential housing, repeat for the other side.

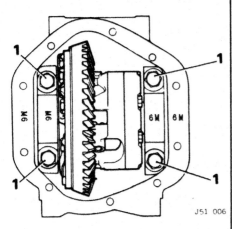

Fig. 31

Using two suitably padded levers, prise out the differential unit.
Using tool 18G 1205 (1, Fig. 32) to hold the drive flange, remove the pinion nut and washer and withdraw the flange (2, Fig. 32).

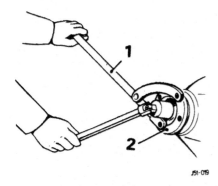

Fig. 32

Using a suitable press extract the pinion from the housing.
Using tool 18G 134 remove the oil seal, oil thrower and outer bearing cone.
Examine the inner and outer bearing cups for wear, if replacement is required extract the outer cup using tools 18G 134 and SL550/1 for inner bearing removal, carefully tap the bearing cone out with a brass punch in the cut-outs provided in the differential casing and carefully collect the shims.

Remove the pinion head bearing using tools 47 (1, Fig. 33), SL 47-1/1 (2, Fig. 33).

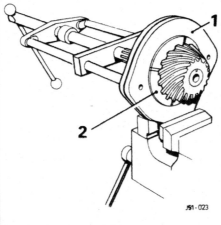

Fig. 33

Remove the differential side bearings using tool Nos. 47 (1, Fig. 34), SL 14-3/2 (2, Fig. 34) and SL 14-3/1 (3, Fig. 34), and collect the shims.

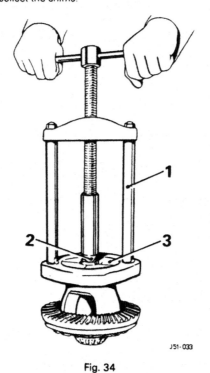

Fig. 34

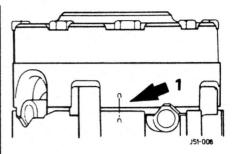

Fig. 35

Powr-Lok only

In the absence of any alignment marks (1, Fig. 35), scribe a line across both halves of differential casing to facilitate reassembly.
Remove the ten 11/16 in AF crown wheel bolts (1, Fig. 36) and remove the crown wheel (2, Fig. 36).

Remove the eight 9/16 in AF bolts (1, Fig. 37), securing both halves of the differential casing (2, Fig. 37).

Remove differential side ring (3, Fig. 37).
Remove pinion side gear and pinion cross-shafts complete with gears (4, Fig. 37).
Separate cross-shafts (5, Fig. 37).
Remove remaining side gear (6, Fig. 37) and ring (7, Fig. 37).

Extract the remaining clutch discs (8, Fig. 37) and plates (9, Fig. 37).

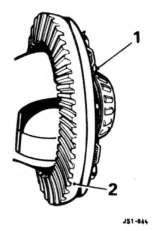

Fig. 36

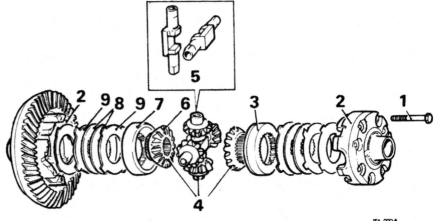

Fig. 37

Reassembling

NOTE: Before commencing assembly, check from reference numbers and letters that pinion and drive gear are a matched pair.

The same serial number must be marked on the pinion end and the outer periphery of the crown wheel (1, Fig. 38), (e.g. 7029). If these requirements are not met the unit must be exchanged.

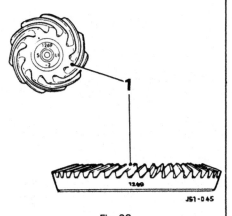

Fig. 38

Powr-Lok only

Prior to reassembly coat all plates and discs with Powr-lok oil.
Refit two Belleville clutch plates (2, Fig. 39) so that convex sides are against differential casing.
Refit clutch plates (4, Fig. 39) and discs (3, Fig. 39) as shown into each half of the casing.
Fit side ring (5, Fig. 39).
Position one side gear into ring recess (6, Fig. 39).
Fit cross-shafts.
Refit pinion mating cross-shafts complete with pinion gears ensuring that ramps on the shafts coincide with the mating ramps in the differential case (7, Fig. 39).
Assemble remaining side gear (6, Fig. 39) and ring (7, Fig. 39).
Offer up right-hand half of differential case (8, Fig. 39) to flange half in accordance with identification marks and position clutch

friction plate tongues so that they align with grooves in differential case.
Assemble right-hand half to flange half of differential case using eight bolts coated with Loctite 275 but do not tighten at this stage (9, Fig. 39).
Tighten eight bolts to a torque of 6,05 to 6,9 kg/m (43 to 50 lb/ft) while drive shafts are in position (1, Fig. 40, 1, Fig. 41). With one drive shaft locked, the torque to turn the other (2, Fig. 41) should be between 40 lb/ft and 70 lb/ft. e.g. hold one shaft in vice soft jaws whilst turning the other.

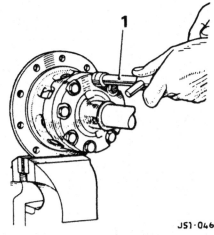

Fig. 40

NOTE: Ensure that prior to assembly the crown wheel mounting face is free from damage or burrs, particularly on the edge; should any burrs be left on the carrier they must be removed with an oil stone prior to fitment of the crown wheel.

Fit the crown wheel to the carrier diametrically using the ten bolts and tab washers, torque up the bolts to 10,78 to 12,4 kgf/m (77 to 88 lb/ft).

Thickness of shims required in the installation of the differential side bearings is determined as follows:

Fit the differential side bearings (1, Fig. 42) using tools 18G 134 (2, Fig. 42) and SL 550-1 (3, Fig. 42) without the shims onto the differential case, making sure that

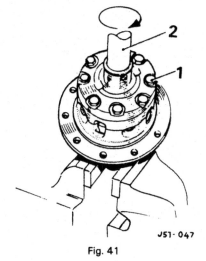

Fig. 41

the bearings and housing are perfectly clean.

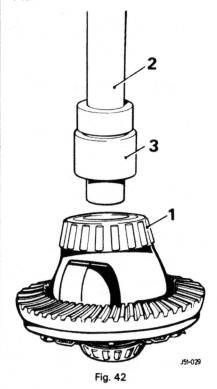

Fig. 42

Place the differential assembly with the bearings in their housing into the differential case without the pinion in position.

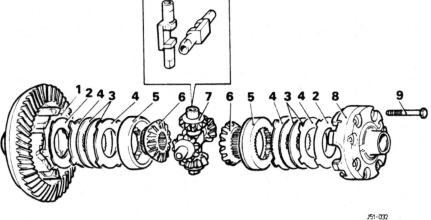

Fig. 39

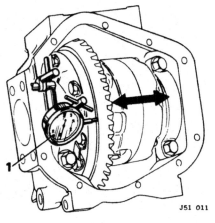

Fig. 43

51-13

Install a dial indicator gauge setting the button against the back face of the crown wheel (1, Fig. 43).

Inserting two levers between housing and the bearing cups, move the differential assembly to one side of the carrier.
Set the dial indicator to zero.
Move the assembly to the other side and record indicator reading, giving total clearance between bearings, as now assembled, and abutment faces of the gear carrier housing.

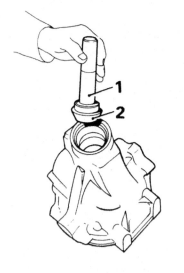

Fig. 44

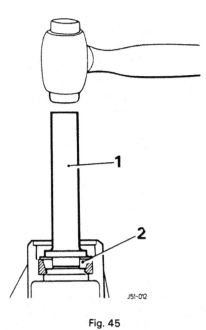

Fig. 45

Remove differential assembly from the gear carrier.
Re-install the pinion outer bearing cup using tools 18G 134 (1, Fig. 44 & 45) and SL 550-9 (2, Fig. 44 & 45).
Fit the inner bearing cup (1, Fig. 46) and shims using tools 18G 134 and SL 550-8 (2, Fig. 46).

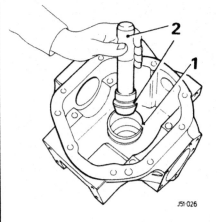

Fig. 46

Press the inner bearing cone onto the pinion using tools 47 (1, Fig. 47), SL 47-1/1 (2, Fig. 47) and SL 47-1/2 (3, Fig. 47).

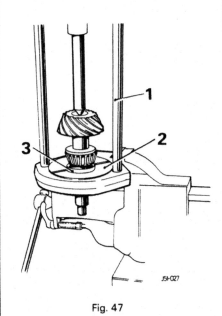

Fig. 47

NOTE: The hypoid drive pinion must be correctly adjusted before attempting further assembly, the greatest care being taken to ensure accuracy.

The correct pinion setting is marked on the ground end of the pinion. The matched assembly serial number is also marked on the periphery of the crown wheel, and care should be taken to keep similarly marked gears and pinions in their matched sets as each pair is lapped together before despatch from the factory. The letter on the left is a production code letter and has no significance relative to assembly or servicing of any axle. The letter and figure on the right refer to the tolerance on offset or pinion drop dimension, which is stamped on the cover facing of the gear carrier housing. The number at the bottom gives the cone setting distance of the pinion and may be Zero (0), Plus (+) or Minus (–) (Fig. 48).

Fig. 48

When correctly adjusted a pinion marked Zero will be at the zero cone setting distance dimension which is 66,67 mm (2.625 in) (i.e. from the centre line of the gear to the face on the small end of the pinion. A pinion marked Plus two (+2) should be adjusted to the nominal (or Zero) cone setting plus 0,0508 mm (0.002 in) and a pinion marked Minus two (–2) to the cone setting distance minus 0,0508 mm (0.002 in). Thus for a pinion marked Minus two (–2) the distance from the centre of the drive gear to the face of the pinion should be 66,619 mm i.e. 66,67 - 0,0508 mm (2.623 in i.e. 2.625 - 0.002 in) and for a pinion marked Plus three (+3) the cone setting distance should be 66,746 mm (2.628 in). Place pinion, together with inner bearing cone, into gear carrier.

A Pinion drop 38,1 mm (1.5 in)
B Zero cone setting 66,67 mm (2.625 in)
C Mounting distance 108,52 mm (4.312 in)
D Centre line to bearing housing 139,57 mm (5.495 in) to 139,83 mm (5.505 in).

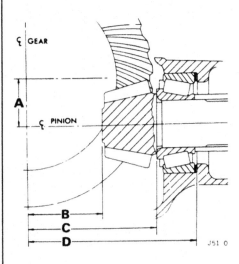

Fig. 49

Turn carrier over and support pinion with a suitable block of wood for convenience before attempting further assembly.

Fit pinion outer bearing cone, companion flange, washer and nut only, omitting the collapsible spacer, oil thrower and oil seal, and tighten nut to remove all backlash.

Check pinion setting distance by means of gauge tool SL3 (1, Fig. 50).

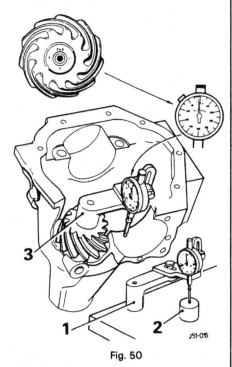

Fig. 50

Adjust bracket carrying dial indicator using 4HA setting block. For differentials with a white painted circle on the rear cover use tool no. SL3-2. (2, Fig. 50) and set dial face to zero.

Check pinion setting by taking a dial indicator reading on the differential bearing bore with the assembly firmly seated on the ground face of the pinion (3, Fig. 50). The correct reading will be the minimum obtained; that is, when the indicator spindle is at the bottom of the bore. Slight movement of the assembly will enable the correct reading to be easily ascertained. The dial indicator shows the deviation of the pinion setting from the zero cone setting and it is important to note the direction of any such deviation as well as the magnitude.

If pinion setting is incorrect it is necessary to dismantle the pinion assembly and remove the pinion inner bearing cup. Add or remove shims as required from the pack locating the bearing cup and re-install the shim pack and bearing cup. Adjusting shims are available in thicknesses of 0,076 mm, 0,127 mm and 0,254 mm (0.003 in, 0.005 in and 0.010 in). Repeat setting operations until satisfactory result is obtained.

Extract pinion shaft from gear carrier far enough to enable the outer bearing cone to be removed from the pinion.

Fit the collapsible spacer to the pinion ensuring that it seats firmly on the machined shoulder on the pinion shaft.

Insert pinion into gear carrier.

Refit the outer bearing cone, oil thrower and using tool 18G 1428 (1, Fig. 51) fit the oil seal. Loctite the splines of the pinion shaft and fit the flange. Fit a new washer, convex face outermost. Fit, but DO NOT tighten the flange retaining nut.

Begin tightening the flange nut, stopping at frequent intervals to check the torque required to turn the pinion, using the string and spring balance, until the required torque is obtained.

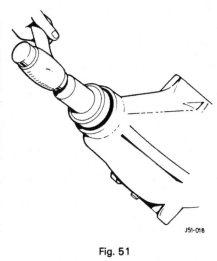

Fig. 51

The flange nut may have to be tightened to as much as 18 kgf/m (130 lbf/ft).

Torque required to turn pinion bearings and oil seal:

Old bearings — 0,20 to 0,28 kgf/m (20 to 25 lbf/in).

New bearings — 0,35 to 0,46 kgf/m (30 to 40 lbf/in).

Note the actual figure required to turn the pinion.

If the above values are exceeded a new collapsible spacer must be fitted. ON NO account must the nut be slackened off and retightened as the collapsed spacer will not then sufficiently clamp the bearing cones.

Place differential assembly complete with side bearings but less shims, in the housing. Ensure that bearings and housing are perfectly clean.

Using the shim pack previously selected, vary the shim thicknesses between each bearing cup and the carrier face to achieve a backlash of 0,15 to 0,25 mm (0.006 to 0.010 in) measured at the outer edge of the ring gear (Fig. 52).

Add an additional 0,07 mm (0.003 in) shim to each pack and carefully note from which side of the differential case the pack was removed.

Remove the bearing cups and cones from the differential case using SL 14-3/2 and SL 14-3/1.

Fit appropriate shim pack to the differential case and refit the bearing cone.

Ensure that the matching shim pack and cone are fitted to the same side of the differential housing that they were removed from.

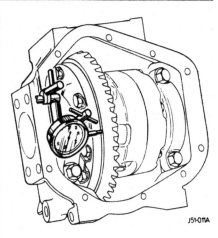

Fig. 52

Lower differential assembly into position lightly tapping the bearings home with a hide hammer.

NOTE: Ensure that gear teeth are led into mesh with those of the pinion. Careless handling at this stage may result in bruising the gear teeth. Removal of the consequent damage can only be partially successful and will result in inferior performance.

When refitting side bearing caps, ensure that position of the numerals marked on gear carrier housing face and side bearing cap coincide (1, Fig. 53).

Tighten cap bolts to a torque of 8,82 to 10,08 kg/m (63 to 72 lb/ft) (2, Fig. 53).

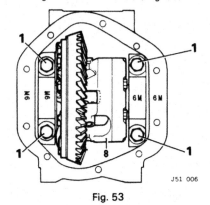

Fig. 53

Mount a dial indicator on gear carrier housing with the button against back face of gear (1, Fig. 54).

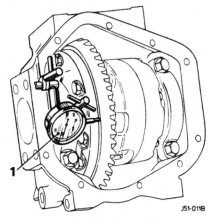

Fig. 54

Turn pinion by hand and check run out on back face of gear. Run out should not exceed 0,13 mm (0.005 in). If run out excessive, strip the assembly and rectify by cleaning the surfaces locating the drive gear. Any burrs on these surfaces must be removed.

Remount dial indicator on gear carrier housing with button tangentially against one of drive gear teeth (1, Fig. 55).

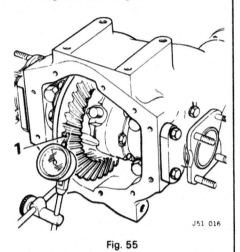

Fig. 55

Move drive gear by hand to check backlash which should be 0,15 to 0,25 mm (0.006 to 0.010 in). If backlash is not to specification, transfer the necessary shims from one side of the differential case to the other to obtain the desired setting. Check backlash in at least four positions of drive gear, ensuring that backlash is always greater than 0,15 mm (0.006 in).

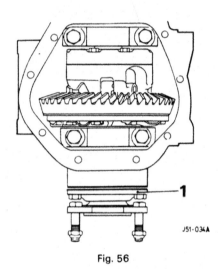

Fig. 56

Check that the torque to turn the input flange is 1,4 to 2,8 kgf/m (10 to 20 lbf/in) additional to the torque measured previously to turn the pinion (page 51-15).

Smear cover flange only with Welseal jointing compound, place gasket on final drive casing, place cover over gasket and insert two bolts to retain, coating threads with Loctite.
Replace remaining eight bolts, coating threads with Loctite and replace the tabs.
Tighten screws by diagonal selection to correct torque 2,1 to 2,8 kgf/m (15 to 20 lbf/ft).

Refit both output shaft assemblies (1, Fig. 56) and torque the bolts to 8,4 to 9,66 kgf/m (60 to 69 lbf/ft), replace the drain plug and refit the drive unit to the cross-member (1, Fig. 57).

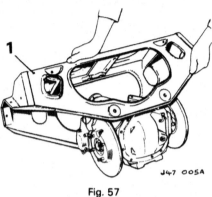

Fig. 57

Secure with bolts (1, Fig. 58) torque and lockwire (2, Fig. 58), ensuring that when lockwired, the wire is tightening the bolts.

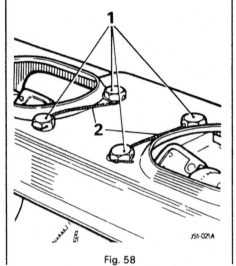

Fig. 58

After refitting the unit to the vehicle fill with new oil.

JAGUAR
Daimler

Containing
Sections

57 STEERING

60 FRONT SUSPENSION

64 REAR SUSPENSION

70 BRAKES

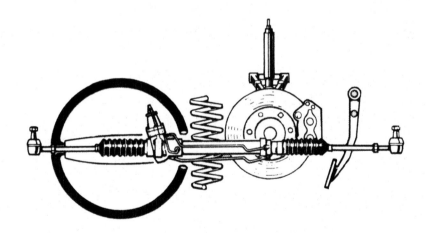

SERIES III
SERVICE MANUAL

INTRODUCTION

This Service Manual covers the Jaguar Series 3 and Daimler Series 3 range of vehicles. It is primarily designed to assist skilled technicians in the efficient repair and maintenance of Jaguar and Daimler vehicles.

Using the appropriate service tools and carrying out the procedures as detailed will enable the operations to be completed within the time stated in the 'Repair Operation Times'.

The Service Manual has been produced in 13 separate sections; this allows the information to be distributed throughout the specialist areas of the modern service facility.

A table of contents in section 1 lists the major components and systems together with the section and book numbers. The cover of each book depicts graphically and numerically the sections contained within that book. Each section starts with a list of operations in alphabetical order.

The title page of each book carries the part numbers required to order replacement books, binders or complete Service Manuals. This can be done through the normal channels.

Operation Numbering

A master index of numbered operations has been compiled for universal application to all vehicles manufactured by Jaguar Cars Ltd., and therefore, because of the different specifications of various models, continuity of the numbering sequence cannot be maintained throughout this manual.

Each operation described in this manual is allocated a number from the master index and cross-refers with an identical number in the 'Repair Operation Times'. The number consists of six digits arranged in three pairs.

Each operation is laid out in the sequence required to complete the operation in the minimum time, as specified in the 'Repair Operation Times'.

Service Tools

Where performance of an operation requires the use of a service tool, the tool number is quoted under the operation heading and is repeated in, following, the instruction involving its use. A list of all necessary tools is included in section 1, number 99.

References

References to the left- or right-hand side in the manual are made when viewing from the rear. With the engine and gearbox assembly removed the timing cover end of the engine is referred to as the front. A key to abbreviations and symbols is given in section 1, number 01.

REPAIRS AND REPLACEMENTS

When service parts are required it is essential that only genuine Jaguar/Daimler or Unipart replacements are used. Attention is particularly drawn to the following points concerning repairs and the fitting of replacement parts and accessories.

1.   Safety features embodied in the vehicle may be impaired if other than genuine parts are fitted. In certain territories, legislation prohibits the fitting of parts not to the vehicle manufacturer's specification.

2.   Torque wrench setting figures given in this Service Manual must be strictly adhered to.

3.   Locking devices, where specified, must be fitted. If the efficiency of a locking device is impaired during removal it must be replaced.

4.   Owners purchasing accessories while travelling abroad should ensure that the accessory and its fitted location on the vehicle conform to mandatory requirements existing in their country of origin.

5.   The vehicle warranty may be invalidated by the fitting of other than genuine Jaguar/Daimler or Unipart parts. All Jaguar/Daimler and Unipart replacements have the full backing of the factory warranty.

6.   Jaguar/Daimler Dealers are obliged to supply only genuine service parts.

SPECIFICATION

Purchasers are advised that the specification details set out in this Manual apply to a range of vehicles and not to any one. For the specification of a particular vehicle, purchasers should consult their Dealer.

The Manufacturers reserve the right to vary their specifications with or without notice, and at such times and in such manner as they think fit. Major as well as minor changes may be involved in accordance with the Manufacturer's policy of constant product improvement.

Whilst every effort is made to ensure the accuracy of the particulars contained in this Manual, neither the Manufacturer nor the Dealer, by whom this Manual is supplied, shall in any circumstances be held liable for any inaccuracy or the consequences thereof.

CONTENTS

DESCRIPTION 57.00.00

All cars are fitted with power-assisted rack and pinion steering gear, movement of the rack by the pinion being assisted by hydraulic pressure acting on a piston carried on an extension of the rack.

Hydraulic pressure is provided by a vane-type pump with integral reservoir, belt-driven from the engine crankshaft; steering assistance is, therefore available only while the engine is running. A control valve, located between steering column and pinion, directs hydraulic pressure to the appropriate side of the piston when the steering wheel is turned. Flow through the control valve is continuous, and when the car is travelling straight a low pressure is applied equally to each side of the piston. When the

steering wheel is turned, a small torsion bar at the base of the steering column allows it to rotate a few degrees before turning the pinions, if the pinion is restrained by the rack. This rotation is used to open and close ports in the control valve so that not only is the pressure directed to one side of the pistons but also, as the torsion bar is twisted, the pressure is increased from about 2,8 kgf/cm² (40 lbf/in²) to a maximum of up to 84,4 kgf/cm² (1200 lbf/in²), the increase in pressure being proportioned to the twist in the torsion bar, and reducing to a minimum when the load in the torsion bar—from the steering wheel becomes zero.

The pressure is prevented from exceeding 84,4 kgf/cm² (1200 lbf/in²) by a flow control valve in the pump which allows some fluid to

circulate internally when this pressure is reached.

Two rigid pipes connect the control valve to the rack cylinder, and two hoses run from pump to control valve. A third rigid pipe, pressed into each end fitting of the rack, balances air pressure in the two gaiters as the rack operates.

Servicing of the steering gear is confined to grease lubrication of the two outer ball-joints and the rack damper pad, topping-up the reservoir and inspection for fluid leaks, hose condition and belt wear. When checking fluid level take great care to ensure that no dirt or scraps of cloth can enter the reservoir since if they should reach the control valve the operation of the system can become affected.

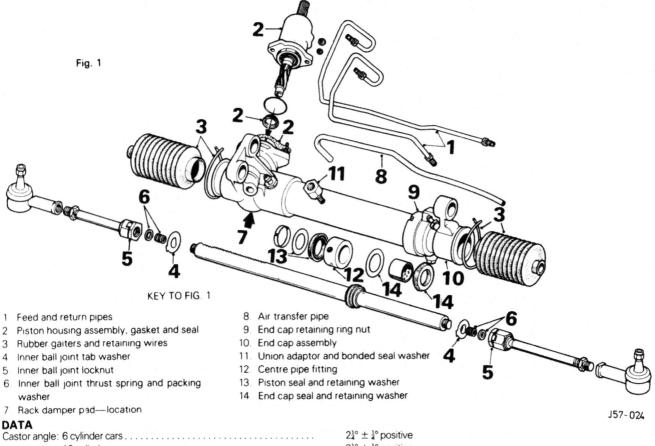

Fig. 1

KEY TO FIG. 1

1 Feed and return pipes
2 Piston housing assembly, gasket and seal
3 Rubber gaiters and retaining wires
4 Inner ball joint tab washer
5 Inner ball joint locknut
6 Inner ball joint thrust spring and packing washer
7 Rack damper pad—location

8. Air transfer pipe
9. End cap retaining ring nut
10. End cap assembly
11. Union adaptor and bonded seal washer
12. Centre pipe fitting
13. Piston seal and retaining washer
14. End cap seal and retaining washer

J57-024

DATA

Castor angle: 6 cylinder cars	$2\frac{1}{4}° \pm \frac{1}{4}°$ positive
12 cylinder cars	$3\frac{1}{2}° \pm \frac{1}{4}°$ positive
Camber angle	$\frac{1}{2}° \pm \frac{1}{4}°$ positive front wheels to be within $\frac{1}{4}°$ of each other
Number of turns of steering wheel, lock to lock	3.36
Total stroke of rack	156,5 mm (6.16 in)

Axial rack load with feed pressure of 2,11 kgf/cm² (30 lbf/in²) and pump flow of 9,45 litres/min (2.08 gal/min) at 71°C is to be 18,1 kg (40 lb) max, 13,6 kg (30 lb) min. Rack to traverse at 6 to 10 pinion rev/min in this test.

From 1983 model year all vehicles (VIN 360146)

Castor angle	$3\frac{1}{2}° \pm \frac{1}{4}°$ positive
Camber angle	$\frac{1}{2}° \pm \frac{1}{4}°$ negative
Front wheel alignment	0 to 3,18 mm (0 to $\frac{1}{8}$ in) toe-in

Power assisted steering racks are now oil filled by the supplier with Shell Spirax EP 80 oil. This has replaced the Shell Retinax 'A' grease fill. Racks to this condition were introduced on Jaguar production at the following VIN 426768.

It is important that when investigating power steering fluid leakage, this lubricating oil is not confused with the hydraulic fluid, as under normal operating conditions a small amount of the oil will be present in the steering rack gaiters. If any oil is lost from the gaiters, then an equal amount to that lost should be added to the gaiter prior to the refitment of the gaiter clips.

It is not necessary under normal circumstances to add oil to the rack during Service, unless a complete overhaul of the rack is undertaken. The total oil capacity of the steering rack is 0,19 litres.

WARNING: It is absolutely essential that the highest standards of cleanliness are maintained in any operations involving access to components in contact with fluid, since steering assistance can be seriously affected by the presence of dirt in the system.

57—2

SYMPTOM AND DIAGNOSIS CHART

SYMPTOM	CAUSE	CURE
External oil leaks from steering rack unit.	Damaged or worn seals. Loose unions. Damaged union sealing washers.	Replace seals. Tighten unions. Replace sealing washers.
Oil leak at pump shaft.	Damaged shaft seal.	Replace shaft seal.
Oil leak at high pressure outlet union.	Loose or damaged union. Damaged pipe end.	Tighten union. Replace pipe.
Oil leak at low pressure inlet connection.	Loose or damaged hose connection.	Remove and refit or renew hose and clip.
Oil overflowing reservoir cap.	Reservoir overfull. Sticking flow control valve (closed).	Reduce level in reservoir. Remove valve, renew and refit.
Oil leak at reservoir edge.	Damaged 'O' ring.	Replace 'O' ring.
Noise from hydraulic system.	Air in system.	Bleed system, see operation 57.15.02.
Noise from pump.	Slack drive belt (squealing). Internal wear and damage.	Adjust drive belt tension, see operation 57.20.01. Overhaul pump, see operation 57.20.20.
Noise from rack (rattling).	Worn rack and pinion gears, see operation 57.10.13. Worn inner ball joints. Universal joint loose.	Adjust rack damper. Replace inner ball joints, see operation 57.55.03. Tighten clamping bolts.
Steering veering to left or right.	Unbalanced tyre pressures. Incorrect tyres fitted. Incorrect geometry. Steering unit out of trim.	Inflate to correct pressure. Fit tyres of correct specification. Reset geometry to correct specification. Replace valve and pinion assembly, see operation 57.10.19.
Heavy steering when driving.	Low tyre pressures. Tightness in steering column. Tightness in steering joints.	Inflate to correct specification. Grease or replace. Grease or renew joints.
Heavy steering when parking.	Low tyre pressures. Tightness in steering column. Tightness in steering joints. Slack drive belt (squealing). Restricted hose. Sticking flow control valve (open). Internal leaks in steering unit.	Inflate to correct specification. Grease or replace. Grease or renew joints. Adjust drive belt tension, see operation 57.20.01. Replace hose. Remove and renew valve. Replace seals.
Steering effort too light.	Valve torsion bar dowel pins worn. Valve torsion bar broken.	Replace valve assembly. Replace valve assembly.

TEST PROCEDURES 57.10.20

Control valve and pinion test

Faults developing in control valve and pinion assembly as indicated in following test or as shown under 'Symptoms and Diagnosis' will necessitate renewal of control valve and pinion. No adjustment or repair is permissible. Check tyres, tyre pressure and steering geometry before testing.

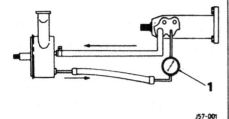

J57-001

Fig. 2

Fit a 7 kgf/cm² (100 lbf/in²) pressure gauge (1, Fig. 2) in feed line from p.a.s. pump, start engine and allow to idle. Gauge should register 2,8 kgf/cm² (40 lbf/in²) approximately.
Turn steering wheel slightly to right or left.

CAUTION: Do not turn steering excessively, as this will produce high pressure resulting in irreparable damage to gauge.

Pressure should increase by an equal amount irrespective of direction of steering wheel rotation. Any unbalance will be indicated by a slight fall in pressure on either side before rising.
Stop and re-start engine and check that steering does not kick to one side.

SYSTEM TESTING 57.15.01

Service Tools: Tap JD 10-2, power steering test set JD 10, JD 10-3A, adaptor power steering JD 10-4A, adaptor hydraulic pressure test/saginaw pump metric thread.

Faults in systems can be caused by inefficiencies in the hydraulic system, see 'Symptom and Diagnosis Chart'.
The following test may be carried out without removing any components from the car.
Before commencing work fluid should be checked for correct level and freedom from froth.

Pump blow off pressure

Fit pressure gauge (1, Fig. 3) reading to 100 kgf/cm² (1500 lbf/in²) in pressure line from pump.
Start engine and allow to run at idling speed.
Turn steering to full lock and continue to increase steering effort until pressure recorded on gauge ceases to rise.
Check that recorded pressure lies between 77,5 kgf/cm² and 84,4 kgf/cm² (1100 and 1200 lbf/in²).

NOTE: If pressure is below 77,5 kgf/cm² (1100 lbf/in²) at tickover, but rises to correct figure with increased engine speed the reason is a defective control valve in pump, or excessive internal leakage in rack and pinion unit. Carry out following test to establish location.

Fit tap JD 10-2 (2, Fig. 3) between pump and pressure gauge (1, Fig. 3), arranging connections as shown, so that pressure gauge is at all times connected to pump, but rack unit can be isolated from it.

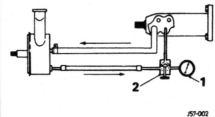

J57-002

Fig. 3

With tap OPEN, start engine and allow to run at idling speed.
Turn steering to full lock.
Check that gauge reading exceeds 77,5 kgf/cm² (1100 lbf/in²).
If pressure does not reach this figure, CLOSE TAP AT ONCE, noting gauge reading as tap reaches 'OFF' position.

CAUTION: Tap must not remain closed for more than 5 seconds when engine is running.

If reading of pressure gauge increases to at least 77,5 kgf/cm² (1100 lbf/in²) when tap is turned off, leaks are confined to steering unit, which must be overhauled—see operation 57.10.07.
If pressure reading exceeds 84,4 kgf/cm² (1200 lbf/in²) remove pump discharge port, withdraw valve assembly located behind it, and inspect a small hemispherical gauze filter carried at its inner extremity, which may be found to be blocked. Clean filter by airline or other means, and replace valve and discharge port.

POWER STEERING SYSTEM

Bleed 7.15.02

Fill the reservoir to the 'full' mark on dipstick, start engine and turn steering wheel from lock to lock a few times to expel any air. Check level and top up if necessary. Use only correct fluid.

FRONT WHEEL ALIGNMENT

Check and adjust 57.65.01

Service Tool: Rack centralising pin 18G 1466.

Check

Inflate tyres to correct pressures.
Set front wheels in straight-ahead position.
Remove grease nipple from rack adjuster pad (1, Fig. 4).

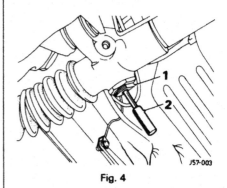

J57-003

Fig. 4

Insert centralizing tool (2, Fig. 4) and adjust position of rack until reduced tip of tool enters locating hole in rack.
Check alignment by using light beam equipment or an approved track setting gauge.

NOTE: As a front wheel alignment check is called for in the Maintenance Summary, very little variation from specified figures for wheel alignment is to be expected; if, however, a discrepancy of as much as 3 mm (⅛ in) from specified limits of 1,6 mm to 1,2 mm (1/16 in to ⅛ in) toe-in is recorded, accidental damage to a steering lever may have occurred and the following check must be carried out, on both levers.

Remove steering levers.
Accurately check dimensions of each lever against those quoted in illustration (Fig. 5).
Reject for scrap and replace any lever with dimensions outside limits quoted.

WARNING: It is absolutely forbidden to attempt to rectify a rejected lever by bending.

If both steering levers are within limits, a discrepancy in alignment figures may be due to distortion of upper or lower wishbones, or end of stub axle carriers (vertical links). Dimensioned drawings of these parts for checking purposes, are given in Group 60.

57—4

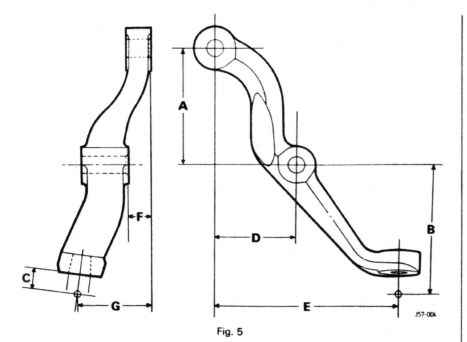

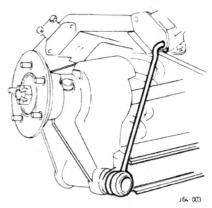

Fig. 5

DIMENSIONS—STEERING LEVER, Fig. 5

'A' 82,5 mm to 82,6 mm (3.248 in to 3.252 in)

'B' 101,85 mm to 102,36 mm (4.01 in to 4.03 in)

'C' 22,23 mm (0.875 in)

'D' 58,93 mm to 59,44 mm (2.32 in to 2.34 in)

'E' 135,38 mm to 135,89 mm (5.33 in to 5.35 in)

'F' 17,78 mm to 18,03 mm (0.70 in to 0.71 in)

'G' 54,36 mm to 54,86 mm (2.14 in to 2.16 in)

Adjust

Slacken locknuts at outer end of each tie-rod.

Release clips securing outer ends of gaiters to tie-rods.

Turn tie-rods by an equal amount until alignment of wheels is correct.

Tighten locknuts to figure quoted while holding track rod end spanner flats.

Re-check alignment.

Ensure that gaiters are not twisted and re-tighten clips.

Remove centralising tool (2, Fig 3) and refit grease nipple.

CASTOR ANGLE/CAMBER ANGLE

Check and adjust   57.65.05

Service Tools: JD 25B Suspension links. Camber and castor angle checking gauges.

CAUTION: Before checking, examine all rubber/steel bushes for deterioration or distortion. Check upper and lower wishbone ball joints for excessive play. Check shock absorbers for leaks and mountings for security.

The two operations require the vehicle to be set up in a mid-laden condition. This can be done as follows:

Ensure that the car is standing on level ground and inflate the tyres to the correct pressure; check that the standing heights are equal on both sides of the car, and the front wheels are in the straight-ahead position.

Make up two front suspension tubes to the dimensions shown (Fig. 6).

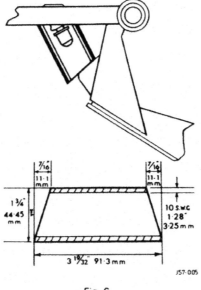

Fig. 6

Compress the front suspension and insert the setting tubes under the upper wishbones, adjacent to the rebound stop rubbers and over the brackets welded to the bottom of the 'turrets'. This locks the front suspension in the mid-laden condition.

Lock the rear suspension in the mid-laden condition using the suspension links, service tools JD 25B.

For each side, compress the suspension, pass the hooked end of service tool JD 25B through the lower hole in the rear mounting and fit the looped end over the rear pivot nut (Fig. 7).

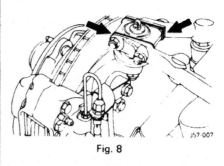

Fig. 7

Castor angle—check and adjust

Using the castor angle checking gauge, check the castor angle. Refer to the Data for correct setting.

To adjust, slacken the two bolts on each side securing the upper wishbone members to the upper ball joints.

Transpose shims, which can now be lifted out, from front to rear or vice versa, to reduce or increase the castor angle respectively (Fig. 8).

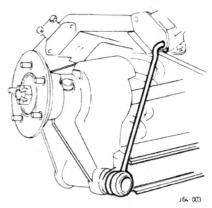

Fig. 8

Transposing one shim 1,6 mm (0.0625 in) thick will alter the castor angle by approximately ¼°.

After adjusting the castor angle to the correct figure, tighten the bolts to the correct torque. Check the front wheel alignment and adjust if necessary.

Camber angle—check and adjust

Using the camber angle checking gauge, check the camber angle. Refer to data for the correct settings.

Rotate the road wheels through 180° and re-check

To adjust, slacken the nuts and bolts securing the upper wishbone inner pivots to the cross member turrets.

Add or remove shims between the pivot shafts and cross member turrets to reduce or increase the camber angle (Fig. 9).

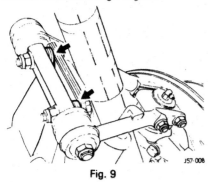

Fig. 9

Shims are available in 0,8 mm ($\frac{1}{32}$ in), 1,6 mm ($\frac{1}{16}$ in) and 3,2 mm ($\frac{1}{8}$ in) thickness. A change of 1,6 mm ($\frac{1}{16}$ in) in shim thickness will alter the camber angle by approximately ¼°.

NOTE: It is necessary to partly withdraw the bolts to change the shims, so only one bolt of a pair should be shimmed at a time. It is important that an equal thickness of shims should be changed on front and rear bolts, otherwise the castor angle will be affected.

Tighten all the bolts and nuts to the correct torque, and re-check the camber angle.
Check the front wheel alignment and adjust if necessary.

STEERING PUMP DRIVE BELT

Adjust   **57.20.01**

6 cylinder models

The steering pump drive belt also drives the coolant pump, and is tensioned by a screw-type adjuster.

Slacken the pump mounting pivot bolt and adjust pivots; reset the adjuster to tension the belt so that a load of 2,9 kg (6 4 lb), applied to its mid-point between crankshaft and steering pump, deflects the belt 4,3 mm (0.17 in) (Fig. 10).

Re-tighten pivot bolts after correcting belt tension.

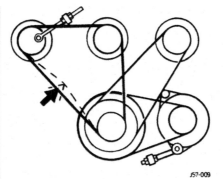

Fig. 10

12 cylinder models

Remove the left-hand air cleaner. Slacken the pump mounting pivot bolt (1, Fig. 11).

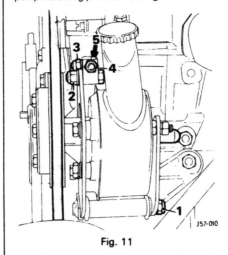

Fig. 11

Slacken the nut securing the adjusting link (2, Fig. 11) and the nut securing the trunnion block (3, Fig. 11).

Unscrew the outer trunnion locknut (4, Fig. 11).

Screw the inner trunnion locknut (5, Fig. 11) outwards to increase the belt tension or inwards, towards the engine, to reduce the tension; correct tension is such that a load of 3 kg (6.4 lb), applied to the belt's mid-point between the crankshaft and the steering pump, deflects the belt 4,0 mm (0.16 in).

Re-tighten all nuts and bolts and re-check the belt tension.

STEERING PUMP DRIVE BELT

Remove and refit   **57.20.02**

6 cylinder models

A damaged belt is most easily removed by cutting it; if it is necessary to remove a complete belt, refer to the fitting instructions below.

Fitting

Slacken pump and adjuster pivots and turn adjuster nut to bring pump towards the engine;

feed the belt past the fan blades (this can be done without removal of the fan cowl), place it over crankshaft, coolant pumps and steering pump pulleys and adjust.

12 cylinder models

Remove the left-hand air cleaner, and fan belt. A damaged belt is most easily removed by cutting it. If it is necessary to remove a complete belt, release and screw back the inner locknut at the pump adjuster trunnion. Slacken the pump pivot bolt, and the nut securing the adjusting link.

Slacken the nut securing the trunnion block, swing the pump towards the engine and remove the belt.

To refit, reverse the above procedure and adjust. Refit the fan belt and left-hand air cleaner.

STEERING PUMP

Remove and refit   **57.20.14**

Remove cover from front of air cleaner on 6 cylinder models, and remove the left-hand air cleaner on 12 cylinder models, to improve access, detach and plug pipes; slacken pivot and trunnion bolts, then remove adjuster rod bolt to pump.

Press pump towards engine, lift belt off pulley, withdraw pivot bolt and lift pump and bracket away from engine. Detach pump from bracket.

POWER STEERING RACK

Adjust pinion clearance   **57.10.13**

Service Tool: Ball joint separator JD 24

The rack should move smoothly through its full travel, and the maximum clearance between rack and pinion should not exceed 0,25 mm (0.01 in).

Clearance is measured from beneath the car by removing the grease nipple (1, Fig. 12) opposite the pinion, and detaching the nearer tie-rod from its steering arm, using tool JD 24. Insert the stem of a dial gauge through the grease nipple hole to contact the back of the rack, and, grasping the tie-rod, pull rack away from pinion; the dial gauge will then indicate clearance. If this is excessive, release locknut (2, Fig. 12) screw in plug (3, Fig. 12) until firm resistance is felt, back off slightly, re-tighten locknut and re-check clearance.

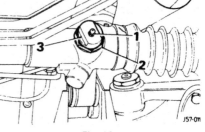

Fig. 12

continued

Move rack through its full travel; if binding occurs at any point, slightly increase clearance and re-check.

When correct minimum clearance is achieved, fully tighten locknut, replace grease nipple, secure tie-rod to steering arm and check wheel alignment.

When greasing the rack damper use **only** Lithium grease N.L.G.I. constituency No. 2.

PINION SEAL

Remove and refit   57.10.23

This seal is accessible from beneath the car; before detaching the internal circlip and retainers which secure it (Fig. 13), thoroughly clean the end of the pinion housing, and detach the lower steering column.

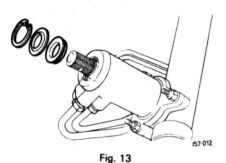

Fig. 13

CAUTION: Do not move road wheels or turn steering wheel while joint is disconnected.

STEERING RACK HOSES

Remove and refit   57.15.21 and 22

Before removing these hoses, ensure that suitable plugs are obtained to close the orifices in pump and rack.

Remove the air cleaner, wipe clean the union nuts and the areas around them and, on L.H.D. cars, remove five clips (1, Fig. 14) securing hoses to cross-beam.

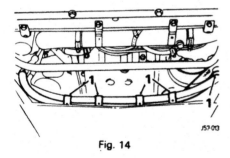

Fig. 14

Detach pipes from pump first, plugging each orifice as the pipe is withdrawn. After refitting pipes, tighten union nuts to figures quoted in Data, top up reservoir and bleed system.

TIE-ROD BALL JOINTS

Remove and refit   Outer 57.55.02
Inner 57.55.03

Service Tool: Ball joint separator JD 24

It is necessary to detach and remove the outer ball joint before the inner joint (which is only supplied complete with its tie-rod) can be removed. The front wheel alignment must be checked after refitting either joint, as it is difficult to ensure that the length of the rod between centres is not altered.

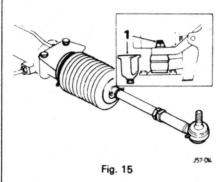

Fig. 15

After separating the outer joint, using tool JD 24 (1, Fig. 15) release the locknut, but do not run it along the thread; unscrew ball-joint from tie-rod and screw on replacement ball-joint up to the locknut; this gives an approximate location before checking wheel alignment.

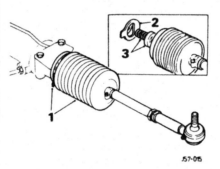

Fig. 16

To remove the inner joint and tie-rod, first detach the gaiter (1, Fig. 16) from the rack housing, knock back tab washers (2, Fig. 16) and unscrew nut securing ball joint to rack bar. Collect washers, spacer and spring (3, Fig. 16), use new tab washers when refitting joint. Coat joint with 60 gm (2 oz) of grease before replacing gaiter.

Check front wheel alignment.

STEERING LEVERS

Remove and refit   57.55.29

Service Tool: Ball-joint separator JD 24

After detaching the ball-joint (1, Fig. 17) by use of tool JD 24, cut the locking wire (2, Fig. 17) and withdraw the two bolts (3, Fig. 17) securing the steering lever to the hub carrier.

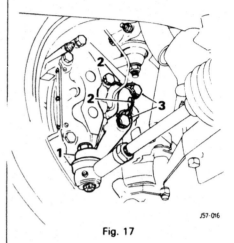

Fig. 17

When withdrawing the lever, inspect carefully for shims which may be fitted between the lever and the lugs on the hub carrier. These shims must be correctly replaced when refitting the lever.

Tighten the set-bolts to the correct torque; renew locking wire and check wheel alignment; adjust if necessary.

STEERING WHEEL

Remove and refit   57.60.01

Removing

Centralise front wheels and mark steering wheel to record its position. Do not turn front wheels again.

Remove three screws securing lower switch cover, and detach cover.

Working from below, remove clamp bolt securing collet adaptor to steering column.

Slacken locknut of grubscrew in collet adaptor and unscrew grub screw two turns.

Withdraw steering wheel, complete with hand locknut, impact rubber, collet adaptor and shaft.

Dismantling

Unscrew two self-tapping screws from lower face of steering wheel boss and lift off padded horn contact.

Unscrew nylon nut from top of steering wheel shaft and remove it carefully. Withdrawing horn contact tube with it.

Remove self-locking nut and plain washer securing steering wheel.

Carefully draw the steering wheel from its splined shaft, collecting both halves of split cone

continued

Reassembling

Clean thoroughly and remove any burrs with a fine file.
Lightly lubricate all enclosed metal parts with engine oil.
Reverse the dismantling procedure operations.

Refitting

Reverse the removal procedure operations, taking care to replace horn contact tube correctly, (enclosing end of contact rod), and to replace wheel in its straight-ahead position, with front wheels still centralised. Tighten grub screw finger tight, tighten its locknut and tighten clamp bolt to the correct torque.

POWER STEERING RACK GAITERS

Remove and refit	57.10.27

It is necessary to remove the outer ball-joint from the tie-rod before a new gaiter can be fitted, when fitting the replacement, clean old grease from the inner joint and smear it with 45 to 55 g (1½ to 2 oz) of recommended grease. Do not omit a check of wheel alignment after replacing the outer ball-joint.

POWER ASSISTED STEERING (P.A.S.) UNIT

Remove and refit	57.10.01

Service Tools: Ball joint separator JD 24, rack centralising tool 18G 1466, checking fixture JD 36A and plugs for pipe connections.

Removing

Slacken filler cap of power steering reservoir and remove pinion heat shield (12 cyl. only) with car over pit or raised on ramp, detach both hoses (1, Fig. 18) from pinion housing; collect escaping fluid in a suitable container and blank off ports and hoses.

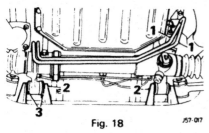

Fig. 18　　　　J57·017

Separate ball-joints from steering arms, using tool JD 24, and release clamp bolt securing joint to pinion shaft; remove three nuts and washers (2, Fig. 18) and withdraw the rack mounting bolts, collecting washers and shims (3, Fig. 18)
Note location of all washers for reassembly, and remove rack downwards.

Refitting

When refitting rack, ensure that single rack lug is shimmed to be central between cross-beam brackets, fitting shims between metal faces of steel/rubber washers and brackets; check that a gap of 2,5 to 3,0 mm (0.10 to 0.12 in) exists between rubber faces of thrust washers and single lug, locate lower steering column coupling onto rack pinion and insert mounting bolts and ensure the bump stops are fitted to the outer edge but do not yet fully tighten nuts.
Remove jubilee clips (4, Fig. 18) securing gaiters to rack housing and pull back both gaiters from rack (1, Fig. 19).

Fig. 19　　　　J57·018

Refit track rod ends.
Locate two attachment brackets of Service tool JD 36A on two large hexagon heads (2, Fig. 19) of lower wishbone fulcrum shafts.
Release locking screw (3, Fig. 19) on forward arm of tool, and move slide until its slot engages with front weld flange of cross-beam. Tighten locking screw.
Lift two couples checking levers (4, Fig. 19) until one or both levers touch rack shaft.
Adjust position of rack, if necessary, to bring both levers into contact.
Tighten nuts of three mounting bolts to secure rack in this position.
Remove checking tool.
Replace gaiters and renew jubilee clips; refit ball joints to steering arms and secure with nyloc nuts. Remove blanking plugs and reconnect both hoses. Refit the pinch bolt and nut to the lower universal joint.
Refit pipe spaces and jubilee clips (12 cyl. only).
Refill system with recommended fluid and bleed, see operation 57.15.02.
Check wheel alignment.

NOTE: (a) It is important that distance between rubber faces of thrust washers and adjacent rack lug should in no case be less than 2,5 mm (0.1 in) to allow adequate 'rack compliance' in either direction.

(b) If a replacement rack unit is to be fitted it may be necessary to detach lower column from upper column at universal joint to obtain correct centralization of steering wheel.

CONTROL VALVE AND PINION

Remove and refit	57.10.19

It is possible to remove this unit without removing the rack, but extreme care must be taken to prevent contaminants from entering the rack housing while the pinion is removed. The car must be placed over a pit, or raised on a ramp.
Remove the lower steering column and prise off the heatshield fitted to the pinion shaft; then thoroughly clean pinion housing and adjacent rack housing before detaching all four pipes (1, Fig. 20) from the pinion housing. Collect fluid and plug apertures.

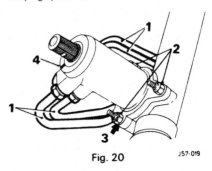

Fig. 20　　　　J57·019

Remove three nuts (2, Fig. 20) attaching pinion housing to rack but before removing housing, release rack adjuster locknut (3, Fig. 20), screw back adjuster one turn and mark position of pinion shaft in relation to housing (4, Fig. 20). Withdraw pinion unit; DO NOT move front wheels, or turn steering column, until unit is replaced.
When refitting, use a new gasket and ensure that relation between pinion shaft and housing is correct before connecting steering column joint.
Reset adjuster plug and bleed system.

UPPER STEERING COLUMN

Remove and refit	57.40.02

Removing

Before removing the column, it is necessary to disconnect the battery and remove steering wheel, speedometer, tachometer and the trim panel below the upper column.
Detach the horn feed from its contact and separate three connections to disconnect switchgear.
Completely withdraw bolt securing universal joint to lower column and slacken the two setscrews screwing the lower end of the column to its mounting strut.
Release upper mountings by working through open adjustment apertures and, supporting column by hand, remove lower setscrews and withdraw column. Collect any packing and record its position. Do not use excessive force in separating joint from lower column.

continued

57—8

Refitting

No repair or adjustment of any description is permitted on upper steering columns. If damage is suspected, remove adjusting clamp, mark its position, remove universal joint and measure overall length of inner column, which must be between 547,74 and 551,04 mm (21. 565 and 21.695 in.) Any column outside these limits must be renewed; renew also in all cases of doubt. If column is to be renewed, refer to electrical section 86 for details of removal and refitting of electrical equipment.

In refitting column, check that an axial clearance of 10 mm (0.375 in) exists at lower universal joint; if less, move upper joint along column to correct it.

Check that direction indicates self-cancel correctly; if not, proceed as follows:

Detach lower switch cover by removing three screws.

Check that lower dogs on fixed portion of switch engage correctly with cutaways on outer (fixed) column, and that a dog on collet adaptor enters slot in movable section of switch.

Turn steering wheel to bring clamp bolt of column adaptor to horizontal, below axis of column; self-cancelling switch will then function correctly.

Remove steering wheel, rotate it to straight ahead position and refit to splined column with minimum of rotation. Refer to Steering Wheel remove and refit, operation 57.60.01.

Refit lower switch cover.

LOWER STEERING COLUMN

Remove and refit   57.40.05

Removing

Place car on ramp and raise ramp.

Remove pinch bolt securing lower universal joint to pinion shaft. Collect heat shield fitted to pinion shaft.

Lower ramp.

Detach lower parcel shelf.

Remove both pinch bolts securing upper universal joint to upper and lower columns.

Release two lower mounting screws of upper column.

Release lower column from upper universal joint.

Raise ramp.

Remove lower universal joint from pinion shaft and withdraw lower column.

Lower ramp.

Refitting

No repairs are permissible. Faulty or damaged columns must be renewed. Reverse above procedure.

Check that upper column and road wheels are centralized before reconnecting splines, and tighten pinch bolt nuts to correct torque. Ensure that a gap of 10 mm (0 375 in) exists between sections of lower universal joint.

CAUTION: Excessive force, which may damage nylon shear plugs, must not be used when withdrawing and refitting columns. Burrs on splines should be removed with a fine file.

STEERING COLUMN ADJUSTING CLAMP

Remove and refit   57.40.07

Removing

Remove steering wheel, see operation 57.60.01.

Remove impact rubber (1, Fig. 21) from steering wheel shaft.

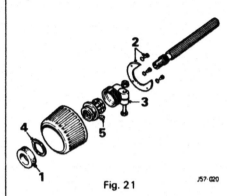

Fig. 21

Remove three small cheese head screws from beneath hand locknut, and collect retaining plate (2, Fig. 21).

Unscrew collet adaptor (3, Fig. 21) completely and remove from shaft.

Remove collet circlip (4, Fig. 21) from within upper side of hand locknut.

Withdraw hand locknut, collecting stop button (5, Fig. 21).

Slide split collet off shaft.

Refitting

Clean thoroughly and inspect all parts; remove any small burrs with a fine file.

Lightly lubricate all enclosed metal parts with engine oil.

Reverse operations for removal.

STEERING COLUMN UNIVERSAL JOINT

Remove and refit   57.40.25

Removing

Detach lower parcel shelf.

Remove both pinch bolts (1, Fig. 22) securing upper universal joint to upper and lower columns.

Remove two lower mounting screws (2, Fig. 22) of upper column.

Remove upper universal joint from upper column, then from lower column.

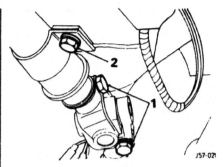

Fig. 22

Refitting

Reverse operations above. Ensure that the two universal joints are correctly aligned with each other, and tighten pinch bolt nuts to correct torque.

NOTE: Lower universal joint is integral with lower steering column and removed with it.

STEERING COLUMN— LOWER—SEAL

Remove and refit   57.40.15

Removing

Remove upper steering column, see operation 57.40.02.

Slacken hose clip (1, Fig. 23) attaching upper sealing sleeve to lower column; remove clip and sleeve.

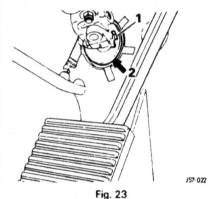

Fig. 23

Remove three setscrews (2, Fig. 23) securing gaiter retainer to bulkhead, slide gaiter, retainer and sealing sleeve up and off lower column.

Refitting

Fit assembly of sealing sleeve, gaiter and retainer over end of lower column, taking care not to damage gaiter or flanged face of sleeve. Insert and tighten three setscrews securing retainer to bulkhead.

Carefully slide second sealing sleeve, flanged end first, over lower column as far as sealing sleeve; replace its hose clip but do not tighten. Move second sealing sleeve approximately 6 mm (0 25 in) towards bulkhead, to pre-load it against first sleeve, secure it with its hose clip in this position.

Refit upper steering column.

STEERING COLUMN LOCK

Remove and refit 57.40.28

Removing

Remove the steering column lower shroud.
Adjust the steering wheel to maximum travel, disconnect the fibre optic strand and remove the ignition switch shroud.
Remove the shear bolts securing the lock assembly and displace the assembly from its mounting position.
Remove the screw securing the lock assembly to the switch, displace the plastic cover and remove the steering column lock.
To fit the new lock reverse the removal procedure.

NOTE: If lock is to be returned to manufacturer under warranty, include key number on material return label.

POWER STEERING RACK

Overhaul

Service Tools: Ball joint separator JD 24 + 2 in long ½ in UNF socket headed (grub) screw. Rack checking fixture JD 36A. Plugs for pipe connections. End housing 'C' nut remover S355. Pinion ring expansion sleeve 606602. Pinion ring compression sleeve 606603 (JD33). Pinion housing seal saver 18G 1259. Rack centralising tool, Jaguar Part No. 12297.

Steering Rack Remove

Slacken the power steering fluid reservoir filler cap. Raise the car and support; detach both the hoses from the pinion housing. Collect the escaping fluid in a suitable container. Blank off all ports and hoses.

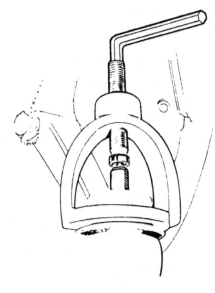

Fig. 25

Separate the ball joints from the steering arms, using Service Tool JD 24 (Fig. 25).

NOTE: It may be necessary to substitute a 2 in long ½ in UNF socket headed (grub) screw, for the existing bolt of JD 24.

Remove the pinch bolt (1, Fig. 26) securing the lower steering column universal joint, to the rack pinion.

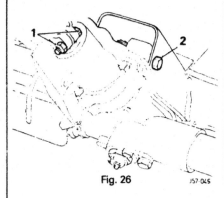

Fig. 26

Remove the bolt, washer and self-locking nut, securing the steering rack top mounting (pinion side of rack assembly) (2, Fig. 26), to the crossmember.
Remove both the rack bottom mounting bolts, washers and nuts, securing the steering rack to the crossmember.

CAUTION: Make a careful record of the number and position of the packing washers for refitting.

Release the steering rack from the crossmember and retrieve the packing washers.

Steering Rack Dismantle

Thoroughly clean the exterior of the steering rack. Remove the blanking plugs from the pinion housing ports and purge any remaining fluid by turning the pinion gently from lock to lock. Centre the pinion gear and note the location of the pinchbolt groove.
Remove the rack mounting rubbers and sleeves. Release the nuts securing the feed pipes to the pinion valve housing and the rack body; remove the pipes from the rack assembly.
Remove the sealing washer from the port in the pinion end rack housing.

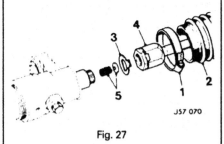

Fig. 27

Make a note of their position and release the two large clips (1, Fig. 27) securing the tie rod gaiters to the pinion and end housings. Pull back the gaiters (2, Fig. 27) to allow access to the inner ball joint assemblies.

NOTE: Do not disturb the outer ball joints, unless replacement is necessary.

If the outer ball joints are to be renewed, measure accurately and record the total length of each tie rod, before releasing the locknuts. This will assist when re-tracking the car.

Knock back the tab washers (3, Fig. 27) securing the inner ball joint assembly locknuts to the rack.

CAUTION: Do not disturb the tab washers between the locknuts and the ball pin housings.

Hold one inner ball joint assembly (4, Fig. 27) with a suitable spanner and release the opposite one. Protect the rack teeth and back of the rack; clamp the rack to enable the other inner ball joint to be released.
Unscrew the tie rod assemblies from the rack. Collect the springs and packing pieces (5, Fig. 27).
Release the locknut securing the rack damper; remove the nut, threaded plug, spring and rack damper pad.

NOTE: If the rack damper adjustment is satisfactory and the rack damper assembly does not require overhauling then remove the two bolts and lift off the plate; remove the 'O' ring, spring and rack damper pad (Fig. 28).

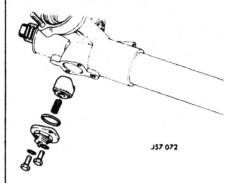

Fig. 28

Pinion Valve and Housing

Remove the three self locking nuts securing the pinion and valve assembly to the pinion end rack housing. Note the relationship of the ports to the rack and remove the complete pinion and valve assembly (1, Fig. 29).

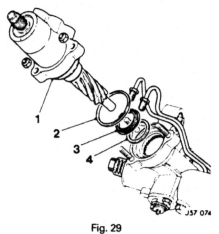

Fig. 29

Remove the sealing ring (2, Fig. 29) the pinion seal (3, Fig. 29) and the backing washer (4, Fig. 29).
Using a suitable mallet gently tap the pinion valve from the pinion valve housing.

Remove the circlip washer and ball bearing race, from the valve assembly, if a replacement is necessary.

NOTE: The pinion valve cannot be dismantled further This item must be replaced as, a complete assembly.

Port Inserts Renew

Tap a suitable thread in the bore of the insert (1, Fig. 30).

Insert a setscrew (2, Fig. 30) with attached nut (3, Fig. 30) and distance piece (4, Fig. 30).

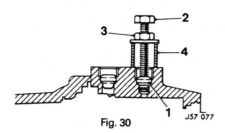

Fig. 30   J57 077

Tighten the nut and withdraw the insert.

Ensure that all swarf and metal particles are completely removed.

Fit a new insert into each port and tap home squarely using a soft mandrel.

End Housing

Release the small hexagon socket grub screw (1, Fig. 31) in the end housing.

Using Service Tool S355, unscrew the ring nut from the end housing (2, Fig. 31). Remove the end housing (3, Fig. 31) from the rack tube.

Remove the air transfer pipe and sealing rings (4, Fig. 31), from both the pinion and end housings.

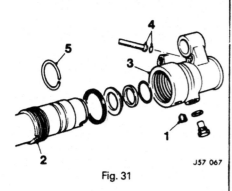

Fig. 31   J57 067

Rack and Inner Sleeve

Remove the hexagon socket grub screw (1, Fig. 32) from the pinion end rack housing and collect the sealing washer (2, Fig. 29).

Remove the rack complete with the inner sleeve (3, Fig. 32) from the bore of the rack tube.

NOTE: Removal of the inner sleeve over the rack teeth will destroy the seal (6, Fig. 32).

Bend up the retaining tabs on the seal cap (4, Fig. 32) and remove the cap from the inner sleeve.

Remove the seal 'O' ring (5, Fig. 32), seal (6, Fig. 32) and split bearing (7, Fig. 32).

Remove the rubber 'O' ring (8, Fig. 32) and nylon washer (9, Fig. 32) from the bottom of the rack tube.

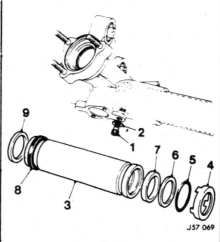

Fig. 32

The piston cannot be removed from the rack but the piston ring (1, Fig. 33) and the backing ring (2, Fig. 33) can be renewed.

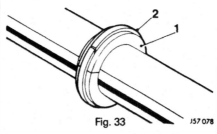

Fig. 33   J57 078

The rack tube cannot be removed from the plain (pinion end) rack housing, but the ring nut (2, Fig. 31) and circlip (5, Fig. 31) can be renewed. Exercise caution, when removing and replacing the circlip over the ground sealing outer diameter of the rack tube.

Renewing Seals

Discard all the old seals, and the inner sleeve seal retaining cap.

Thoroughly clean and inspect each item for surface damage and wear.

For efficient sealing it is essential that all seal surfaces, lead chambers etc., are smooth, with no scratches or score marks.

Re-assembling — Inner Sleeve and Rack Bar

Fit a new backing ring and piston ring to the piston, and ensure that it moves freely in its groove.

Place a new seal retaining cap over the rack teeth, with the three tabs facing away from the piston.

Fit a new split bearing in the recess in the inner sleeve, ensure that it is seated correctly.

To protect the new inner sleeve seal from being damaged by the rack teeth; cover the rack teeth with a piece of suitable plastic adhesive tape, placed lengthways over the teeth.

Carefully slide the seal, with the recessed face towards the piston, over the tape and onto the rack bar.

Remove the tape.

Fit a new 'O' ring in its recess in the inner sleeve, ensure that it seats correctly.

Ensure that the ends of the split bearing are on the opposite side of the rack bar to the teeth and push the inner sleeve along the rack bar. Carefully

push the seal up against the retaining cap and in turn, against the piston.

Ensure that the inner sleeve is square to the piston; continue pushing until the seal is fully home.

Maintain the pressure against the piston and neatly bend the three tangs into the groove on the outside of the inner sleeve, securing the retaining cap.

Apply a smear of silicone to the bore of the new square section sealing ring. Fit the nylon backing washer (9, Fig. 32) and sealing ring (8, Fig. 32) into the bore of the rack tube; slide them all the way down until they contact the pinion end main housing.

Assemble the rack bar, with the inner sleeve still against the piston, into the rack tube bore. Guide the piston ring into the rack tube bore. Continue sliding the rack and inner sleeve assembly into the rack tube bore, until the inner sleeve enters the sealing ring and seats firmly against the pinion end rack housing.

Look into the hexagon socket screw hole and ensure that the retaining shoulder has passed the hole. Fit the sealing washer and socket grub screw (1 & 2, Fig. 32). After tightening, it should fit flush to slightly proud, stake in position.

End Housing

Remove the seal (1, Fig. 34) and 'O' ring (2, Fig. 34) using a suitable sharp instrument.

With a suitable soft metal drift, carefully remove the steel retaining washer (3, Fig. 34).

Fit a new 'O' ring in the recess, pushing a new seal with the groove uppermost, on to the top of the 'O' ring; replace the steel retaining washer with the spigot towards the seal and press home.

Fit a new square section sealing ring (4, Fig. 34) into the end housing; smear the sealing ring bore, with a silicone lubricant, to aid assembly.

Fit new air transfer pipe sealing rings (5, Fig. 34) to the pinion and end housings. Fit the air transfer pipe to the pinion rack housing.

Fit the end housing over the rack bar, taking care to align it, to avoid damaging the end housing seal.

Slide the end housing onto the rack tube with a slightly twisting action. Engage the air transfer pipe in to its port. Align the end housing mounting lug (6, Fig. 34) with the lower cut out of the rack tube. Tighten the 'C' nut using Service Tool S355, to the correct torque.

Refit the hexagon socket, grub screw. Tighten and stake in position.

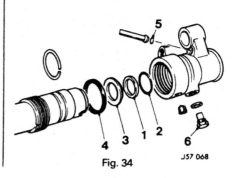

Fig. 34   J57 068

Pinion Valve and Housing

To remove the seals from the pinion, use a sharp knife and cut diagonally, taking care not to damage the groove ends.

Using Service Tool 606602, to expand the seals, fit one in the groove nearest to the ball bearing race. Repeat the procedure for the other three seals.

The rings can then be compressed to their original size by fitting a sleeve over them. Use 606603. If this tool is not available, then recovery will take place naturally if left for about ½ hour.

Fit the washer and 'U' section seal, into the pinion main housing, ensure that the grooves in the seal face upwards and that the seal flange fits snugly in the groove.

Valve Housing

Using suitable circlip pliers remove the circlip (1, Fig. 35). Remove the seal retainer (2, Fig. 35) and the seal (3, Fig. 35).

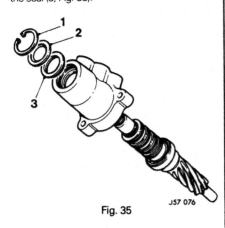

Fig. 35

Fit a new seal, grooved face downwards. Ensure that the flange sits snugly in the recess. Fit the seal retainer, with the rubber side and lip outermost. Fit the circlip, ensure that it is seated fully in the groove.

Smear the seals with a little clean power steering fluid. Fit the taper seal saver 18G 1259 over the serrations on the pinion valve, and enter the pinion valve into the pinion valve housing. Press the ball bearing race fully home.

Refit the rack damper assembly. Ensure that the threaded plug is slack. Remove the grease nipple from the plug, and centralise the rack using Service Tool 18G 1466 (Fig. 36).

Refit the pinion valve assembly to the pinion rack housing, ensure that the coupling groove in the pinion is in the correct position. Fit and tighten the three self-locking nuts.

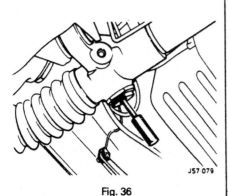

Fig. 36

Adjust the rack damper pad assembly to obtain the correct end float. Tighten the locknut and refit the grease nipple.

Fit a new sealing washer to the port in the pinion end rack housing. Fit and tighten the feed pipes to the pinion valve housing and rack body. Do not overtighten the pipe nuts as irreversible damage could be caused to the pipes.

Tie Rods

Refit the new tab washers to the rack, dished face outermost. Screw on the tie rods. Holding one ball joint and tighten the opposite ball joint (one joint should react against the other). Do not restrain the rack assembly. Secure the tab washers in four places against the spanner flats. Regrease the ball joint areas and replace any lost from the gaiters. Each gaiter should contain 57 gms (2 oz) of grease.

Fit the gaiters and secure with the clips, ensuring that the clips are in their correct position.

Refitting the Steering Rack

Ensure that the steering wheel is set to the straight ahead position and refit the rack.

Fit the lower coupling to the pinion. Ensure that the single rack mounting lug is shimmed so that it is central between the cross-beam brackets. This is achieved by fitting shims between the faces of the steel/rubber washers and the bracket. Check that a gap of 2,5 to 3,0 mm (0.10 to 0.12 in) exists between the face of the rubber thrust washers and the single lug of the rack.

Insert the mounting bolts, fit but do not fully tighten the nuts.

Slacken the clips securing the rubber gaiters to the rack housing, pull the gaiters (1, Fig. 37) clear of the inner ball joint assemblies.

Locate the two attachment brackets of Service Tool JD 36A on the heads of the lower wishbone fulcrum shaft bolts (2, Fig. 37).

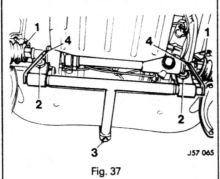

Fig. 37

Release the locking screw (3, Fig. 37) on the forward arm of the tool and position the slide so that the slot engages with the front welded flange of the cross beam. Tighten the lock screw. Rotate the alignment legs (4, Fig. 37) of the tool until one or both rest on the rack shaft.

Adjust the position of the rack if necessary, until both legs are in contact with the rack shaft.

Tighten the nuts of the mounting bolts to secure the rack in this position. Remove Service Tool JD 36A.

Refit the rubber gaiters and secure with the clips. Refit the ball joints to the steering arms and secure with the nyloc nuts.

Remove the blanking plugs and connect both fluid hoses to the pinion housing.

Refit the pinch bolt and nut to the lower universal coupling.

Refill the system with the recommended fluid and carry out the bleed procedure.

Check the front wheel alignment.

NOTE:

(A) It is important that the distance between the rubber faces of the thrust washers and the adjacent rack lug should in no case be less than 2,5 mm (0.1 in). This is to allow adequate 'rack' compliance in either direction.

(B) If a replacement rack unit is to be fitted it may be necessary to detach the lower column from the upper column at the universal joint, to obtain correct centralisation.

PORT INSERTS

Remove and refit   57.10.24

Removing

Tap a suitable thread in bore of seat (1, Fig. 38), and insert a setscrew with attached nut, washer and distance piece.

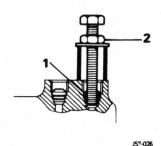

Fig. 38

Tighten nut (2, Fig. 38) and withdraw seat.

Refitting

Insert seat, and tap home squarely with a soft mandrel.

STEERING PUMP

Overhaul   57.20.20

Steering tool: Pulley carrier remover/replacer 18G 326

Dismantling

Absolute cleanliness and extreme care are essential to pump overhaul, which should not be entrusted to inexperienced mechanics; if any doubt exists on the necessity for the replacement of partly worn items they should be replaced, as pump overhaul is not specified in routine maintenance.

After removing pump, detach plugs, drain and discard fluid. Remove three screws and detach pulley, clean out tapped hole in pump shaft and fit reaction screw for Saginaw-approved removal tool, 18G 1326, screwing it fully into shaft. Engage body of extractor with recessed diameter of carrier and remove carrier by tightening extractor screw.

Remove reaction screw before continuing.

Detach pump from mounting bracket, remove adjuster link, thoroughly clear externally, detach outlet union and three studs (1, Fig. 39) and withdraw reservoirs from body. Collect and discard O-rings (2, Fig. 39).

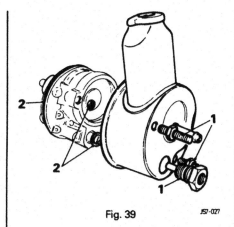

Fig. 39   J57-027

Insert a suitable punch (1, Fig. 40) in hole in rear of pump body and dislodge spring ring. Extract ring with screwdriver (2, Fig. 40) as shown.

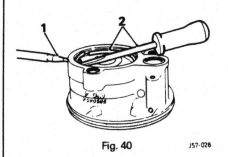

Fig. 40   J57-028

If end-plate (1, Fig. 41) is not ejected by spring (2, Fig. 41), a light tap on the casing will free it. Extract O-ring (3, Fig. 41) and discard; unscrew flow control valve (4, Fig. 41) and tap shaft (5, Fig. 41) lightly through body, carrying rotor assembly with it. Extract second O-ring (6, Fig. 41) and discard it, then carefully separate motor components.

Inspection

Clean all metal parts in solvent; do NOT immerse the new seals. Carefully inspect for wear and damage.

If necessary, light scoring may be removed from thrust and pressure plates by lapping. Reject pump ring and vanes if chatter marks or grooves are present; scuff marks and light uniform wear are acceptable. Check control valve for free movement; remove any burrs and renew valve if at all faulty. Check shaft in bush and measure external diameter of shaft at pully carrier; finally carrier internal diameter MUST provide an interference of 0,025 to 0,066 mm (0.001 to 0.0026 in) with shaft diameter.

continued

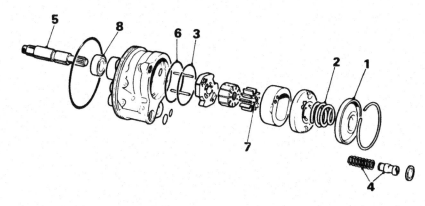

Fig. 41   J57-029

Remove circlip (7, Fig. 41) and withdraw rotor and thrust plate from shaft; finally, extract drive shaft oil seal (8, Fig. 41).

Reassembly

Fit the shaft seal into the casing, smear with petroleum jelly and insert shaft, splined end first. Replace dowel pins (1, Fig. 42) (if withdrawn

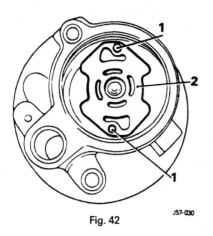

Fig. 42   J57-030

from body) and fit thrust plate (2, Fig. 42) over them, with ports visible. Place counterbored face of rotor (Fig. 43) over splines, press down and fit

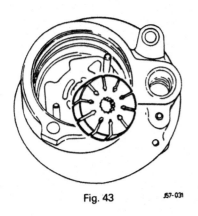

Fig. 43   J57-031

circlip (7, Fig. 41). Slide pump ring (1, Fig. 44) over dowel pins with rotating arrow visible (arrowed

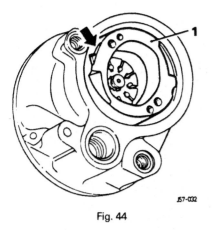

Fig. 44   J57-032

Fig. 44), and place vanes in rotor slots with their radiused edges outmost (Fig. 45).

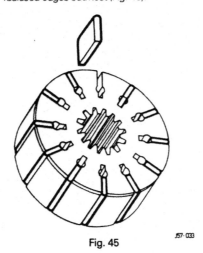

Fig. 45   J57-033

Smear new O-ring for pressure plate with petroleum jelly and insert into inner groove in casing; insert pressure plate (1, Fig. 46) with its spring recess outwards; press firmly into O-ring

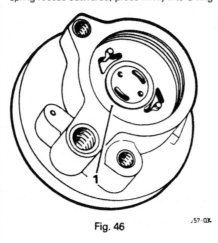

Fig. 46   J57-034

(do not tap) fit second greased O-ring into outer groove, insert spring and place end plate in position with its spring ring on top. Position gap on ring away from extractor hole. Place assembly under a press and depress end plate until spring ring can be sprung into groove (Fig. 47).

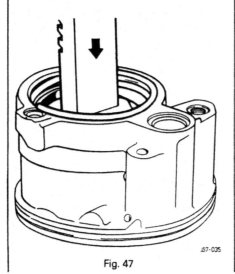

Fig. 47   J57-035

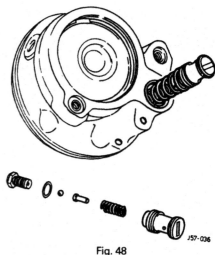

Fig. 48   J57-036

Reassemble control valve details and refit (Fig. 48), replace reservoirs, using new O-rings. Refit pulley carrier to shaft, using tool 18G 1326. Place carrier on tool with its flange adjacent to ⅜ in U.N.C. thread of tool. Screw this threaded stud into tapped hole in pump shaft until it bottoms then, still holding spindle of tool with spanner, screw body of installer down spindle until face of carrier is flush with end of pump shaft. Unscrew tool from pump shaft; (the tapped hole in pump shaft is provided solely to suit installation and removal tools).

After replacing pump test system.

Steering Tie Rod Ends (Track Rod Ends)

Commencing at the Vehicle Identification Numbers listed below, an alternative design of tie rod was introduced. It should be noted that the new tie rod ends are sealed and require no lubrication. A feature of the new tie rod is that there is NO SPRING LOADED FREE MOVEMENT. To avoid any confusion over the identification of these tie rod ends, the old and new types are illustrated below.

Vehicle Identification Number
345390

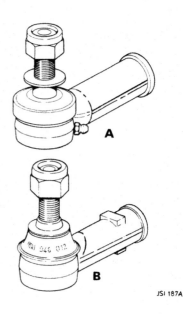

JSI 187A

CONTENTS

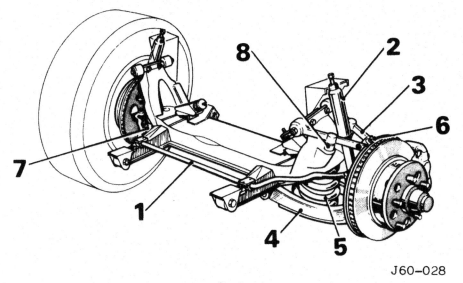

Fig. 1

Key to Fig. 1

1. Anti-roll bar
2. Damper
3. Upper wishbone
4. Lower wishbone
5. Road spring
6. Upper ball joint
7. Lower ball joint
8. Rebound stops

J60—028

Dimension—Lower Wishbone Arm—Fig. 3

A. 225,30 to 225,81 mm (8.87 to 8.89 in)
B. 244,35 to 244,60 mm (9,62 to 9.63 in)
C. 34,67 to 35,18 mm (1.365 to 1.385 in)
D. 5,84 to 6,35 mm (0.23 to 0.25 in)
E. 353,82 to 354,33 mm (13.93 to 13.95 in)
F. 22,86 to 23,37 mm (0.90 to 0.92 in)
G. 26,67 to 27,18 mm (1.05 to 1.07 in)
H. 21,08 to 21,59 mm (0.83 to 0.85 in)

DESCRIPTION

The front suspension is fitted to the car as a complete unit, assembled with anti-roll bar, springs, dampers and steering gear to a fabricated sheet-steel cross-beam which also carries the front engine mountings. The cross-beam is rubber mounted to the body/chassis structure at four points but its removal is not required for most of the operations carried out on the front suspension.

Suspension units are of the coil spring and unequal double wishbone type, the forged steel wishbones being pivoted on inclined inner axes to reduce nose-dip in braking; rubber bushes are used for these inner pivots, the outer ones being formed by the steering ball-joints which are connected by forged steel stub axle carriers, on which the disc brake calipers are mounted. The upper ball joints are sealed units which must be replaced if wear is apparent. Slight wear on the lower joints can be compensated for by the removal of shims. Lubrication nipples are provided on all the ball joints, and it is strongly recommended that grease should only be injected into them with the car's weight removed from its front wheels.

If the front of the car should be accidentally damaged it is most important that castor and camber angles are checked and wheel alignment and ride height measured. If these readings are not to specification the wishbones, hub carriers and steering arms must be removed and dimensionally checked; if any item is not to design dimensions it must be replaced and scrapped.

DIMENSIONAL DATA

The following dimensional drawings are provided to assist in assessing accidental damage. A component suspected of being damaged should be removed from the car, cleaned off and the dimensions checked and compared with those given in the appropriate illustration. Components found to be dimensionally inaccurate, or damaged in any way MUST be replaced, and NO ATTEMPT made to straighten and re-use.

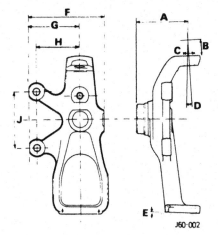

Fig. 2

Dimension—Stub Axle Carrier—Fig. 2

A. 81,7 mm (3.21 in)
B. 25,4 mm (1.0 in)
C. 19,05 mm (0.75 in)
D. 5 degrees
E. 2 degrees
F. 113,9 mm (4.48 in) nominal
G. 51 mm (2.80 in)
H. 59,2 mm (2.33 in) nominal
J. 88,9 mm (3.5 in) nominal

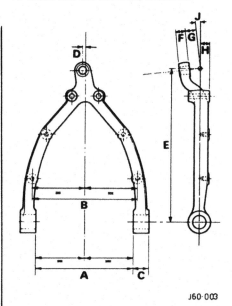

J60-003

Fig. 3

Dimension—Upper Wishbone Arm—Fig. 4

A. 53 mm (2.10 in)
B. 160 mm (6.30 in)
C. 445 mm (1.75 in)

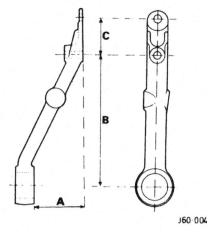

J60-004

Fig. 4

TORQUE WRENCH SETTINGS

ITEM	DESCRIPTION	TIGHTENING TORQUE		
		Nm	kgf m	lbf ft
Stub axle to carrier	5/8 in U.N.F. nut	108 to 122	11,1 to 12,4	80 to 90
Brake disc to hub	7/16 in U.N.F. bolt	40,7 to 54,2	4,2 to 5,54	30 to 40
Lower ball-joint to stub axle carrier	5/16 in U.N.F. bolt	20,3 to 27,1	2,08 to 2,76	15 to 20
Brake caliper to stub axle carrier	M12 Bolt	67,8 to 81,3	6,91 to 8,29	50 to 60
Steering arm to stub axle carrier	M12 Bolt	67,8 to 74,5	6,91 to 7.60	50 to 55
Lower ball-joint to lower wishbone	9/16 in U.N.F. bolt	74,5	7,60	55
Upper ball-joint to stub axle carrier	1/2 in U.N.F. nut	47,0 to 67,8	4,84 to 6,91	35 to 50
Fulcrum shaft upper	1/2 in U.N.F. nut	67,8 to 74,5	6,23 to 7,60	45 to 55
Fulcrum shaft lower	9/16 in U.N.F. slotted nut	43,4 to 67,8	4,43 to 6,91	32 to 50
Upper ball-joint to wishbone	3/8 in U.N.F. nut	35,2 to 43,4	3,60 to 4,42	26 to 32
Upper fulcrum shaft to spring turret	7/16 in U.N.F. nut	66,4 to 74,5	6,78 to 7,60	49 to 55
Clamp and shield to stub axle carrier	1/4 in U.N.F. nut	6,1 to 7,5	0,62 to 0,76	4.5 to 5.5
Spring pan to lower wishbone	3/8 in U.N.F. bolt	36,7 to 43,4	3,74 to 4,42	27 to 32
Damper mounting bracket to wishbone	3/8 in U.N.F. nut	36,7 to 43,4	3,74 to 4,42	27 to 32
Damper upper mounting	3/8 in U.N.F. nut	36,7 to 43,4	3,74 to 4,42	27 to 32
Damper lower mounting	7/16 in U.N.F. nut	54,2 to 74,5	5,54 to 6,23	40 to 45
Bump stop to spring pan	5/16 in U.N.F. nut	10,8 to 13,6	1,10 to 1,38	8 to 10
Rebound stops to upper wishbone	5/16 in U.N.F. setscrew	10,8 to 13,6	1,10 to 1,38	8 to 10
Anti-roll bar bracket to body	3/8 in U.N.F. nut	36,7 to 43,4	3,74 to 4,42	27 to 32
Anti-roll bar to link	3/8 in U.N.F. nut	19,0 to 24,4	1,94 to 2,48	14 to 18
Anti-roll bar link to lower wishbone	3/8 in U.N.F. nut	19,0 to 24,4	1,94 to 2,48	14 to 18
Clamp, cross beam front mounting	1/2 in U.N.F. nut	33,9 to 40,7	3,46 to 4,14	25 to 30
Front mounting bolt	3/4 in U.N.F. nut	129 to 156	13,14 to 15,91	95 to 115
Rear mounting to body	3/8 in U.N.F. bolt	29,8 to 35,2	3,05 to 3,59	22 to 26
Rear mounting to beam	3/8 in U.N.F. nut	19,0 to 24,4	1,94 to 2,48	14 to 18
Wheel nuts	Special nuts	88,0 to 101	8,98 to 10,4	65 to 75

FRONT SUSPENSION RIDING HEIGHT

Check and adjust 60.10.18

Check that car is full of petrol, oil and water, and that tyre pressures are correctly adjusted. Position car with front wheels on slip plates.

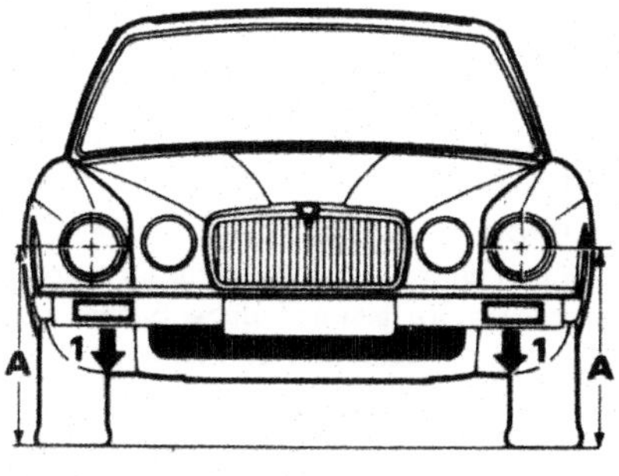

Fig. 5

Press downwards on front bumper as indicated at arrows (1, Fig. 5) to depress car and slowly release. Lift front bumper and slowly release. Measure distance between centre of outer headlight and ground at both sides of car area. Obtain values for dimension 'A', right and left hand. Correct height is 611 mm (24 5/8 in) minimum.

If necessary, fit or remove packing rings beneath springs to achieve this dimension; see operation 60.20.01. Packing rings are 3,18 mm (1/8 in) thick, and vary the riding height by 7,93 mm (5/16 in).

BALL JOINT—LOWER

Adjust 60.15.04

Service tool: Steering joint taper separator JD 24

Jack up front of car and place on stands.
Remove front wheel/s.
Place jack beneath front spring seat pan and raise sufficient to relieve stub axle carrier of spring pressure.
Remove self-locking nut and washer (1, Fig. 6) securing steering tie rod ball-joint.

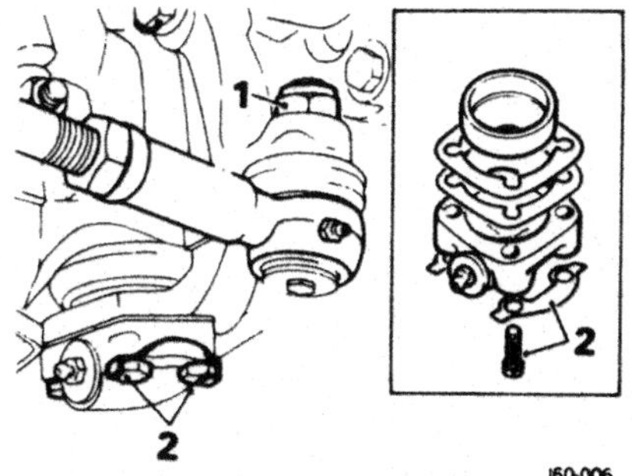

Fig. 6

Separate tie-rod from steering arm using service tool JD 24.
Lift hub and stub axle carrier assembly to reveal any free play in lower ball-joint.
Bend back tab washers, remove four screws (2, Fig. 6) securing ball pin cap to stub axle carrier. Detatch ball pin cap, shims and socket from stub axle carrier.
Clean and examine all parts for wear.

CAUTION: In order to obtain correct adjustment of ball joint it is necessary to shim to correct clearance. Excessive wear on ball pin and sockets must not be adjusted by shims. Worn parts must be renewed.

Remove shims one by one until ball pin is tight in its socket with screws fully tightened.

NOTE: shims are available in 0,05 mm (0.002 in) and 0,10 mm (0.004 in) thicknesses.

Remove screws, ball pin cap, shims and socket.

Add shims to the value of 0,10 mm to 0,15 mm (0.004 in to 0.006 in).
Lightly grease ball pin and socket. Refit socket ball pin cap and new tab washers. Refit and tighten screws (2, Fig.6) to correct torque figure.
When correctly adjusted, hub and stub axle carrier can be pivoted with a very slight drag.
Turn up tab washers and charge joint with correct grease.
Replace nut and washer (1, Fig. 6) refit wheel(s) and lower car.

NOTE: The bolts securing the lower ball pin cap to the stub axle carrier may on some vehicles be in a mixed condition, i.e. the head of the bolts are of different thicknesses 7,94 mm (0.3125 in) and 4,76 mm (0.1875 in).

The bolts with a head thickness of 7,94 mm (0.3125 in) are fitted on production to the inboard holes of the lower ball pin cap.

It is important that if any of these bolts are removed during service, they should be replaced in the correct position.

1. Inboard bolts — head thickness 7,94 mm (0.3125 in)
2. Outboard bolts — head thickness 4,76 mm (0.1875 in)

BALL JOINT—UPPER

Remove and refit   60.15.02

Service tool: Steering joint taper separator
JD 24

The upper wishbone ball joint cannot be dismantled and if worn, the complete assembly must be replaced.

Removing

Jack up car beneath lower wishbone.
Remove road wheel
Tie stub axle carrier to cross member turret to prevent strain on front brake caliper hose.
Remove two nuts, bolts (1, Fig. 7) and plain washers securing ball joint to upper wishbone levers.

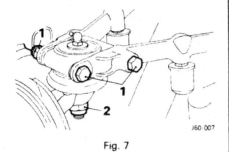

Fig. 7

NOTE: Take careful note of fitted positions of bolts and also positions of packing piece and shims; these control castor angle.

Remove self locking nut (2, Fig. 7) and plain washer securing ball joint to stub axle carrier.
Use taper separator tool JD 24 to extract ball-joint from stub axle carrier.

Refitting

CAUTION: Bolts securing upper ball-joints in upper wishbone must be fitted from front of car towards rear.

Reverse above operations, ensuring that packing piece and shims are positioned as noted.
Fit ball-joint to stub axle carrier before securing to wishbone.
Check castor angle, camber angle and front wheel alignment.

ANTI-ROLL BAR RUBBERS

Remove and refit   60.10.04

Removing—see Fig. 8

Car may be placed on ramp or over pit, but do not jack up front of car.
Remove nuts and setscrews securing anti-roll bar brackets to chassis members; remove keeper plates and remove rubbers from around anti-roll bar

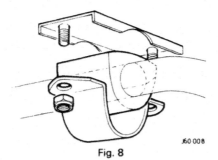

Fig. 8

Refitting

NOTE: Fitting of bushes will be greatly facilitated if a proprietary rubber lubricant or a solution of 12 parts water to one part of liquid soap is used.

Reverse above operations ensuring that each rubber protrudes an equal amount each side of its respective keeper plate; the split in rubbers must face to rear of car.

CAUTION: All nuts and setscrews must be tightened with full weight of car on the suspension; premature failure of rubber bushes may occur if this precaution is not taken.

ANTI-ROLL BAR LINK AND BUSHES

Remove and refit 60.10.02 / 60.10.03

Removing

Jack up front of car and rest on stands.
Remove self locking nut (1, Fig. 9) special washer and rubber pad securing end of anti-roll bar to anti-roll bar link.

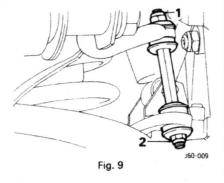

Fig. 9

Remove self-locking nuts (2, Fig. 9) special washer and rubber pad securing anti-roll bar link to anti-roll bar support bracket.
Release upper nut on link at opposite end of anti-roll bar.
Lift link clear and recover two spacer tubes, two rubber pads and special washers.

Refitting

Check conditions of rubber pads, renew if damaged in any way.
Reverse removal operations, but do not fully tighten nuts.
Lower car on to wheels.
Fully tighten self-locking nuts at top and bottom of link, to the correct torque.

ANTI-ROLL BAR

Remove and refit   60.10.01

Removing

Jack up front of car, rest on stands and remove both front wheels.
Remove self locking nut (1, Fig. 10) special washer and rubber pad securing each end of anti-roll bar to anti-roll bar links.

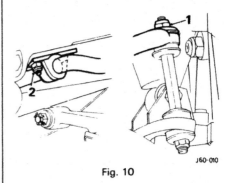

Fig. 10

Remove four self-locking nuts (2, Fig. 10) and setscrews securing keeper plates to sub-frame members.
Detach anti-roll bar and recover split bushes.
Remove nut and release one steering tie-rod ball-joint.
Manoeuvre anti-roll bar clear of car.

Refitting

NOTE: Fitting of bushes will be greatly facilitated if a proprietary rubber lubricant or a solution of 12 parts water to one part of a liquid soap is used.

Manoeuvre anti-roll bar into position across car.
Lubricate bushes and position them on anti-roll bar adjacent to keeper plate locations, split towards rear of car.
Fit keeper plates and loosely secure to sub-frame using four setscrews—from top—and four self-locking nuts.

CAUTION: All nuts and setscrews must be tightened with full weight of car on suspension; premature failure of rubber bushes may occur if this precaution is not taken.

Ensure spacer tube fitted on anti-roll bar link and locate anti-roll bar on link at both sides of car.
Fit rubber pads, special washers and self-locking nuts to anti-roll bar links.
Refit tie-rod ball-joint.
Fit wheels and lower car.
With weight of car on road wheels fully tighten all fastenings.

60—4

FRONT SPRING

Remove and refit   60.20.01

Service tools: Spring compressor tool JD 6F. or JD 6D and adaptor JD 6D-1 with spring locating pegs JD 6E-6.

Removing

Jack up front of car, place on stand and remove road wheel.
Fit spring compressor tool JD 6D with adaptor JD 6D-1 and compress spring sufficiently to relieve load on seat pan fastening.

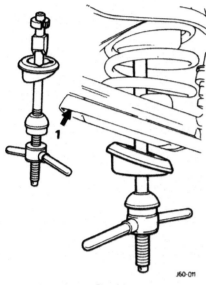

Fig. 11

Remove four setscrews and washers and two nuts, bolts and washers securing spring seat pan to lower wishbone.
Slacken spring compressor tool and remove, together with seat pan, spring and spacers.

NOTE: Record position of packers to assist during replacement.

Refitting

Remove handle nut and adaptors from spring compressor and offer threaded bar up through spring turret.
Secure at top end.
Assemble spring, packing and seat pan as noted in their removal, and lift up into spring turret, retain with handle nut and adaptors of spring compressor.
Fit pilot bolts (1, Fig. 11) to holes nearest centre line of car on forward and rear limbs of wishbone or insert locating pegs JD 6E-6 into tapped holes.

NOTE: A jack may be used beneath lower ball joint to assist with location of spring pan on pilot bolts. Compress spring, locating seat pan on pilot bolts, and tighten until setscrews and nuts, bolts and washers can be fitted in outer location.

Remove pilot bolts and fit two setscrews and washers.
Remove spring compressor.

Fit road wheel and remove stands.
Check front suspension riding height.

WARNING: A maximum of three packers may be fitted in the spring pan and two packers on the cross member.

BUMP STOP

Remove and refit   60.30.10

Removing

Jack up front of car and place on stands.
Remove road wheel.
Remove two plain nuts (1, Fig. 12) and spring washers securing bump stop.

Fig. 12

Manoeuvre bump stop clear through coils of spring, prising coils carefully apart with bar if necessary.

Refitting

Reverse operations for removal. Tighten nuts to correct torque.

REBOUND STOPS

Remove and refit   60.30.14

NOTE: Rebound stops must only be replaced as a pair, uneven loads will be placed on upper wishbone if this is not done.

Removing

Jack up front of car and place stand beneath spring seat pan.
Lower car on to stand.
Remove road wheel.
Unscrew rebound stops (1, Fig. 13) from upper wishbone.

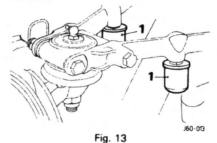

Fig. 13

Refitting

Reverse above operations, tightening stops to correct torque.

FRONT HUB ASSEMBLY

Remove and refit   60.25.01

Removing

Remove road wheel.
Through aperture in disc shield remove five bolts (1, Fig. 14) and washers holding hub assembly to brake disc.

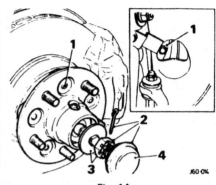

Fig. 14

Remove hub grease cap, extract split pin, and remove nut and washer from stub axle (2, Fig. 14); withdraw hub by hand.

Refitting

Pack hub with specified grease and refit to stub axle.
Fit bearing, nut and washer (3, Fig. 14) to stub axle and tighten nut to give end-float of 0,05 mm to 0,15 mm (0.002 in to 0.006 in).

NOTE: End-float is measured by fitting a dial test indicator with the button against the hub. Fit new split pin.

Refit grease cap (4, Fig. 14). Ensure that vent hole is clear.
Replace road wheel.

FRONT HUB BEARINGS AND GREASE SEAL

Remove and refit   60.25.14

Removing

Remove front hub assembly as detailed above.
Extract grease seal (1, Fig. 15).

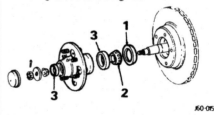

Fig. 15

Withdraw inner bearing race (2, Fig. 15) if necessary
Drift bearing cups (3, Fig. 15) from hub; grooves are provided in the abutment shoulders for this purpose.

continued

60—5

Refitting

Tap replacement cups into position, ensuring that they are seated square to abutments, if bearings have been removed.

Lubricate large bearing race and fit to cup.

Fit new grease seal, using suitable 'bell-piece' and tapping seal squarely into position.

Replace front hub assembly and road wheel.

FRONT HUB STUB AXLE

Remove and refit   60.25.22

Service tool: Steering joint taper separator JD 24

Removing

Jack up front of car and place stand beneath spring seat pan. Lower car to firmly locate on stand and remove road wheel. Remove self-locking nut and washer securing steering tie-rod ball joint (1, Fig. 16).

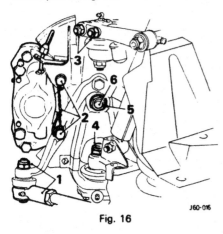

Fig. 16

Separate rod from steering arm using tool JD 24.

Suspend brake caliper by wires or strong cord from damper top mounting to prevent damage to hoses when ball-joints are disconnected.

Break locking wire and remove two bolts and spring washers (2, Fig. 16) securing steering arm and brake caliper to stub axle carrier. Swing caliper aside.

NOTE: Record number of shims fitted between steering arm and brake caliper. Recover large plain washer from between disc shield and caliper.

Remove two nuts, bolts and plain washers (3, Fig. 16) securing upper ball joint to upper wishbone levers.

NOTE: Take careful note of fitted position of bolts and also position of packing piece and shims; these control castor angle.

Remove self-locking nut and washer (4, Fig. 16) and separate lower ball-joint from wishbone, draw assembly from car.

Remove grease cap, split pin and castellated nut securing hub assembly to stub axle; draw assembly clear.

Remove nyloc nut and plain washer (5, Fig. 16) securing stub axle to stub axle carrier.

Support stub axle carrier and drift out stub axle (6, Fig. 16).

Refitting

CAUTION: Bolts securing upper ball joint in upper wishbone must be fitted from front of car towards rear.

Reverse removal operations, ensuring that all shims are correctly replaced.

Tighten bolts and nuts to correct torque figures, wire lock caliper bolts and check wheel alignment castor and camber angles.

FRONT HUB STUB CARRIER

Remove and refit   60.25.23

Service tool: Steering joint taper separator JD 24

Removing

Remove front hub stub axle, see operation 60.25.22.

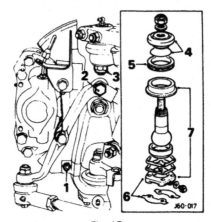

Fig. 17

Remove two nyloc nuts (1, Fig. 17) securing clamps at bottom of disc shields, remove attachment plate and rear disc shield.

Remove bolt (2, Fig. 17) spring and plain washer securing steering arm and forward disc shield to carrier.

Remove self-locking nut and washer (3, Fig. 17) and separate upper ball-joint from stub axle carrier, using separator JD 24.

Remove retaining ring and withdraw rubber gaiter (4, Fig. 17).

Withdraw retainer (5, Fig. 17) from top of ball pin.

Tap back tab washers and unscrew four set-screws securing ball pin cap (6, Fig. 17) to stub axle carrier.

Remove cap, shims, lower ball pin socket, ball pin and spigot (7, Fig. 17).

Refitting

CAUTION: In order to obtain correct adjustment of the ball joint it is necessary to shim to the correct clearance. Excessive wear on ball pin and socket must not be adjusted by shims. Worn parts must be renewed.

Fit spigot, ball pin, socket, shims, ball pin cap and screws. Remove shims one by one until the ball pin is tight in its socket with screws fully tightened.

Remove screws, ball pin cap, shims and socket. Add shims to the value of 0,10 mm to 0,15 mm (0.004 in to 0.006 in).

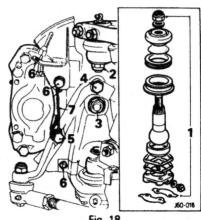

Fig. 18

Lightly grease ball pin and socket (1, Fig. 18). Refit socket, ball pin cap and new tab washers. Refit and tighten screws. Ball pin should now be slightly stiff in socket.

Fit upper ball joint to stub axle carrier and secure using one nyloc nut and washer (2, Fig. 18).

Fit stub axle and secure using new nyloc nut and plain washer (3, Fig. 18).

Assemble forward end of steering arm to its location and loosely secure using one bolt, plain and spring washer (4, Fig. 18).

Fit hub to stub axle.

Locate brake caliper on stub axle to carrier, and secure with long bolt (5, Fig. 18) and spring washer through steering arm. Fit shims removed in dismantling operations between steering arm and caliper.

Locate disc shields and secure using clamps, nyloc nuts (6, Fig. 18) and upper caliper bolt. Fit large plain washer between disc shield and caliper.

Tighten bolts to correct torque.

Fit stub axle carrier to wishbones and steering tie rod, disconnecting wire or cord supporting caliper.

Wire lock brake caliper bolts (7, Fig. 18), and check wheel alignment, castor and camber angles.

FRONT DAMPER

Remove and refit   **60.30.02**

Removing

Beneath bonnet, remove locknut, nut, outer washer, buffer and inner washer from damper front mounting (1, Fig. 19).

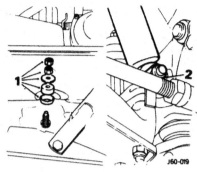

Fig. 19

Jack up front of car and place on stands. Remove road wheel.
Remove self-locking nut and bolt from bottom mounting (2, Fig. 19).
Withdraw damper from car. Collect shaped washer, micron buffer and plain washer from damper stem.

Refitting

Ensure that lower washers and buffer are in place on damper stem and insert stem through hole in wheel arch. Replace nuts and bolt; tighten to correct torque.

WISHBONE UPPER

Remove and refit   **60.35.01**

Removing

Jack up front of car and place stand beneath spring seat pan.
Remove wheel.

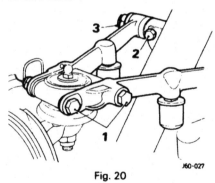

Fig. 20

Remove two nuts, bolts (1, Fig. 20) and plain washers securing upper ball-joint to upper wishbone levers.

NOTE: Take careful note of fitted position of bolts and also position of packing piece and shims, these control castor angle.

Tie stub axle carrier to road spring turret to prevent damage to brake flexible hose.
Remove two bolts (2, Fig. 20), special washers and nyloc nuts securing upper wishbone fulcrum shaft to road spring turret.

NOTE: Take careful note of position of shims as these control camber angle. Manoeuvre wishbone assembly clear of damper unit.

Refitting

Ensure that fulcrum shaft nuts are loose, and not clamping bushes before refitting bolts (2, Fig. 20). Check replacement of shims.
Replace bolts and nuts (1, Fig. 20) with castor shims.
Tighten bolts to specified torques, then replace wheel and lower car BEFORE tightening fulcrum shaft nuts (3, Fig. 20).
Check wheel alignment, castor and camber angles and adjust if necessary.

SUSPENSION UNIT MOUNTING BUSH

Remove and refit   **60.35.06**

NOTE: A worn or damaged bush infers that undue strain has been thrown upon the apparently satisfactory opposite number. Bushes must therefore be changed as a pair.

Removing

Raise front of car by using trolley jack under suspension cross-beam; place stands (1, Fig. 21) under jacking points and lower jack to release load from bushes.
Remove self-locking nut (2, Fig. 21) securing one mounting bolt and drift bolt clear of bush.

NOTE: Record position of plain and special washers, and securing bracket if fitted.

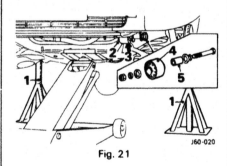

Fig. 21

Slacken clamping nut (3, Fig. 21) and bolt securing relevant mounting bush eye.
Lower jack SLIGHTLY to improve access to bush and tap mounting bush (4, Fig. 21) clear of eye.

Remove sleeve (5, Fig. 21) from mounting bush.
Repeat the removal operations for opposite bush.

Refitting

Reverse the removal operations, tightening nuts to correct torque figures.

SUSPENSION UNIT MOUNTING —REAR

Remove and refit   **60.35.07**

NOTE: A worn or damaged mounting infers that undue strain has been thrown on the apparently satisfactory opposite number. Mountings must therefore be changed as a pair.

Removing

Remove front exhaust pipe, see operation 30.10.09.
Slacken self-locking nuts securing mounting bolts.
Raise front of car and support body on stands (1, Fig. 22).
Remove both front wheels.
Locate trolley jack to support front suspension unit cross-beam.

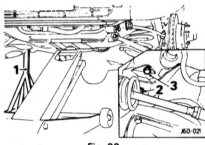

Fig. 22

Remove self-locking nuts and washers (2, Fig. 22) securing suspension unit to mountings.
Carefully lower rear of suspension unit just sufficient to remove two special setscrews and lock washers securing each mounting to body sub-frame (3, Fig. 22).

Refitting

NOTE: Mountings are offset

Position mountings and secure to body sub-frame using special setscrews and lock washers. Tighten to correct torque figure.
Raise rear of suspension unit and secure to mountings using two self locking nuts and plain washers.
Tighten to correct torque figure.
Replace exhaust pipe and front wheels.

FRONT SUSPENSION

Remove and refit   60.35.05

Service tools: Engine support bracket MS.53A; rack centralising tool 18G 1466.

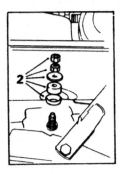

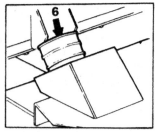

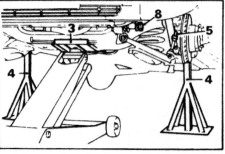

Fig. 23

Removing

Disconnect battery earth lead and remove air cleaner.

Fit engine support bracket MS.53A (1, Fig. 23) to engine front lifting eyes. Adjust links until engine is just supported.

Remove locknut, nut, plain washer, rubber and cup (2, Fig. 23) securing upper end of each damper.

Jack up front of car (3, Fig. 23) place on stands (4, Fig. 23) and remove front wheels.

Remove self-locking nut (5, Fig. 23) securing each anti-roll bar link to anti-roll bar, withdraw cup washers and rubbers.

Turn steering to full lock and cut locking wire at caliper bolts now accessible. Remove bolts securing caliper and steering lever; remove caliper from disc and suspend by wire or cord to avoid damage to hose. Collect shims.

Turn steering to opposite lock and repeat above operation.

Remove nuts securing engine mountings to mounting brackets (6, Fig. 23).

Remove nuts securing cross-beam rear mountings (7, Fig. 23).

Remove steering rack mounting bolts and tie up both ends of rack under engine. Collect packing and rubbers from mountings.

Place trolley jack under centre of cross-beam and raise to take weight of beam.

Remove cross-beam mounting bolts (8, Fig. 23); collect packing washers and towing brackets.

Lower jack and remove cross-beam and suspension units. Transfer to work bench, using adequate lifting tackle.

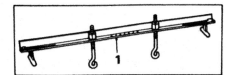

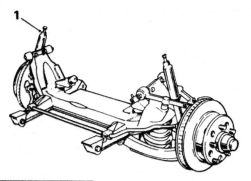

J60-022

Refitting

Reverse removal procedure, fitting front cross-beam mountings first, then jacking up beam to align rear mountings.

Check that towing brackets are in position and all spacers fitted before lowering engine.

Ensure that washers and rubbers are correctly in position on damper stems, and fit upper washers, rubbers and nuts as shown in removal instructions. Connect anti-roll bar links, and replace steering rack; check correct centralization of single lug.

Refit calipers and steering arms with correct shims.

Tighten all bolts and nuts to correct torque figures.

Replace wheels.

Check rack setting, using tool no. 18G 1466, and adjust as necessary. See steering, section 57.

Check wheel alignment, castor and camber angles.

WISHBONE—LOWER

Remove and refit   60.35.02

Service tools. Steering joint taper separator JD 24. Spring compressor JD 6D and adaptor JD 6D-1. Spring plate locating pegs JD 6E-6.

Removing

Remove front suspension unit, see operation 60.35.05 (XJ12 only). Invert unit.

Remove self-locking nut and washer (1, Fig. 24) securing steering tie-rod ball joint. Separate rod from steering arm using tool JD 24.

Remove three bolts, nuts and washers securing steering rack to front suspension cross-member. Remove front spring.

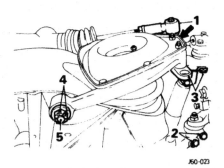

J60-023

Fig. 24

Remove two nuts, bolts and plain washers (2, Fig. 24) securing upper ball-joint to upper wishbone levers.

NOTE: Take careful note of fitted position of bolts and also position of packing piece and shims; these control castor angle.

Remove self-locking nut and washer (3, Fig. 24), and separate lower ball-joint from wishbone. Recover anti-roll bar support bracket and damper unit mounting.

Remove split pin at fulcrum shaft nut (4, Fig. 24) and remove nut and plain washer.

Drift fulcrum shaft (5, Fig. 24) from cross-member and recover two washers.

Refitting

Reverse above operations.

CAUTION: Do not fully tighten fulcrum shaft nut until full weight of car is on suspension.

Fully tighten fulcrum shaft nut to correct torque and fit new split pin.

Check front wheel alignment.

Check castor angle and camber angle.

60—8

WISHBONE—LOWER

Overhaul   60.35.09

Remove lower wishbone, as detailed in operation 60.35.02.

Dismantling

Using a press and suitable mandrel, remove bushes from wishbone arms.

Reassembling

Using a press and suitable mandrel fit new bushes to wishbone arms, ensure each bush is central in arm.

CAUTION: New bushes must be coated with Esso Process Oil 'L' before they are pressed in to wishbone arms.

Refit lower wishbone.

FRONT HUB STUDS

Remove and refit   60.25.29

Removing

Remove front hub, see operation 60.25.01. Using power press and suitable mandrel, press stud/s (1, Fig. 25) from hub.

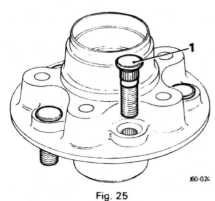

Fig. 25

Refitting

Use power press and suitable mandrel to press stud/s into hub.
Refit front hub.

WISHBONE—UPPER

Overhaul   60.35.08

Remove upper wishbone, see operation 60.35.01

Dismantling

Remove self-locking nut (1, Fig. 26) at each end of fulcrum shaft and recover plain washers and bushes.
Using a press and suitable mandrel, remove bushes (2, Fig. 26) from wishbone arms.

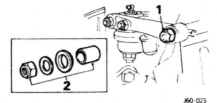

Fig. 26

Reassembling

Using a press and suitable mandrel, fit new bushes to wishbone arms.
Ensure each bush is central in arm.

CAUTION: New bushes must be coated with Esso Process Oil 'L' before they are pressed into wishbone arms.
Assemble wishbone arms to fulcrum shaft, using new bushes, and retain with plain washers and self-locking nuts.

CAUTION: Do not fully tighten at this stage.

Fit upper wishbone.
Tighten to correct torque.

BALL-JOINT—LOWER

Overhaul   60.15.13

Service tool: Steering joint taper separator JD 24.

Removing

Jack up front of car and place stand beneath spring seat pan. Lower car to firmly locate on stand.
Remove road wheel.
Remove self-locking nut and washer securing steering tie-rod ball joint (1, Fig. 27).

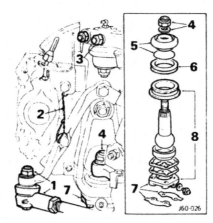

Fig. 27

Separate rod from steering arm using service tool JD 24.
Cut locking wire (2, Fig. 27), withdraw two set bolts and suspend caliper to prevent damage to hose.
Remove two nuts (3, Fig. 27) bolts and plain washers securing upper ball joint to upper wishbone levers

NOTE: Take careful note of fitted position of bolts and also position of packing piece and shims; these control castor angle.

Support hub and stub axle carrier assembly and separate upper ball joint from upper wishbone. Remove self-locking nut (4, Fig. 27) and washer and using service tool JD 24 separate lower ball joint from wishbone, withdraw assembly from car.
Remove retaining ring and withdraw rubber gaiter (5, Fig. 27).
Withdraw retainer (6, Fig. 27) from top of ball pin.
Tap back tab washers (7, Fig. 27) and unscrew four setscrews securing ball pin cap to stub axle carrier.
Remove cap, shims, lower ball pin socket, ball pin and spigot (8, Fig. 27).

Overhaul

Clean and inspect all components.

CAUTION: In order to obtain correct adjustment of ball joint it is necessary to shim to correct clearance. Excessive wear on ball pin and sockets must not be adjusted by shims. Worn parts must be renewed.

Fit spigot, ball pin, socket, shims, ball pin cap and screws. Remove shims one by one until the ball pin is tight in its socket with screws fully tightened.
Remove screws, ball pin cap, shims and socket. Add shims to the value of 0,10 mm to 0,15 mm (0.004 in to 0.006 in).
Lightly grease ball pin and socket. Refit socket, ball pin cap and new tab washers. Refit and tighten screws. Ball pin should now be slightly stiff in socket.

Refitting

CAUTION: Bolts securing upper ball joint in upper wishbone must be fitted from front of car towards rear.

Reverse removal operations, fitting upper ball joint to stub axle carrier before securing it to the wishbone.
Tighten all nuts and bolts to correct torque.
Check front wheel alignment, castor and camber angle.

DAMPER SAFETY   60.37.00

Safety demands, and in certain countries it is a legal requirement, that used shock absorbers must have the gas and oil discharged before final disposal.

It is therefore advisable to complete the following procedure on the disposal of gas filled shock absorbers. The procedure allows the shock absorber to be depressurised and the oil to be disposed of in a proper and orderly manner.

Mark out and centre punch 2 hole positions as illustrated. If access cannot be gained to mark out the upper hole position on the shock absorber, it will be necessary to cut and remove the upper shroud from the piston rod.

Mount the shock absorber vertically in a vice and secure with the lower mounting point uppermost.

Carefully drill a 5 mm hole at the position marked A, nearest to the lower mounting point and allow all gas to escape. Goggles must be worn during the drilling of the shock absorber.

Drill a 5 mm hole at the second position, B, and remove the shock absorber from the vice to allow the oil to drain. This process can be speeded up by carefully working the shock absorber to expel the oil.

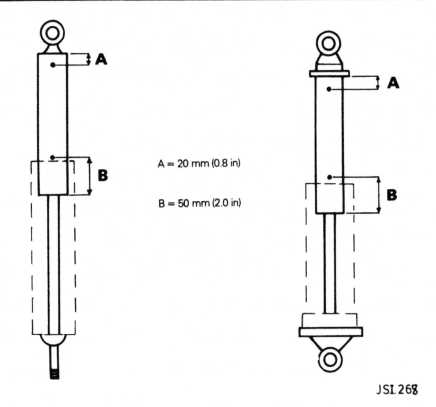

A = 20 mm (0.8 in)

B = 50 mm (2.0 in)

JSI.268

60 — 10

CONTENTS

DESCRIPTION

The complete independent rear suspension system is mounted on a fabricated sheet metal cross-beam (1, Fig. 1) which also carries the final drive unit (2, Fig. 1) and is rubber mounted to the body/chassis structure. Although geometrically similar to a double wishbone system, the upper members are replaced by the drive shafts (3, Fig. 1) and the lower members, (4, Fig. 1) with their inner ends pivoted on the final drive unit, are made torsionally strong to resist drive and braking loads which are partially transmitted by radius rods to the body structure

The wheel hubs (5, Fig. 1) are carried in aluminium alloy castings (6, Fig. 1) which are pivoted to the outer ends of the lower members; brakes are carried inboard, on the final drive unit, and two coil spring and damper units (7, Fig. 1) are fitted on each side of the drive shafts. The lower rear pick-up points of the dampers are connected by plates with the hub carrier pivots; these plates provide the down points for use in transportation of the car.

WARNING: If car is fitted with a Powr-Lok differential, under no circumstance must engine be run with car in gear and one rear wheel off the ground. If it is found necessary to turn transmission with car in gear, both wheels must be raised.

DIMENSIONAL DATA

The dimensional drawing is provided to assist in assessing accidental damage. A component suspected of being damaged should be removed from the car and cleaned off, the dimensions should then be checked and compared with those given in Fig. 2.

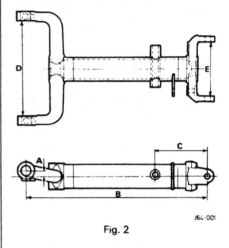

Fig. 2

Dimension

A. 15,75 to 16,26 mm (0.62 to 0.64 in)
B. 519,43 to 519,94 mm (20.45 to 20.47 in)
C. 150,62 to 151,13 mm (5.93 to 5.95 in)
D. 270,05 to 270,31 mm (10.632 to 10.642 in)
E. 155,45 to 155,70 mm (6.12 to 6.13 in)

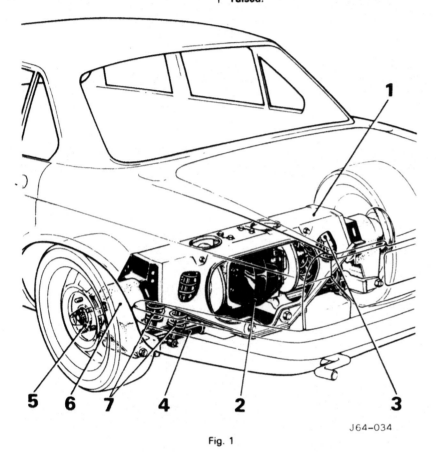

Fig. 1

TORQUE WRENCH SETTINGS

ITEM	DESCRIPTION	TIGHTENING TORQUE		
		Nm	kgf m	lbf ft
Clip, exhaust pipe	⁵⁄₁₆ in U.N.F. nut	14,9 to 17,6	1,53 to 1,79	11 to 13
Bottom tie plate	⁵⁄₁₆ in U.N.F. nuts and bolts	19,0 to 24,4	1,94 to 2,48	14 to 18
Inner fulcrum bracket attachment	⁷⁄₁₆ in U.N.C. bolts	81,3 to 88,0	8,30 to 8,98	60 to 65
Inner fulcrum shaft nuts	½ in U.N.F. nuts	61,0 to 67,8	6,23 to 6,91	45 to 50
Outer fulcrum shaft nuts	⅝ in U.N.F. nuts	131 to 145	13,4 to 14,8	97 to 107
Drive shafts to hub carriers	¾ in U.N.F. nut	136 to 163	13,83 to 16,6	100 to 120
Radius arms to wishbones	½ in U.N.F. bolt	81,3 to 94,4	8,30 to 9,68	60 to 70
Safety straps and radius arms to body	⁷⁄₁₆ in U.N.F. bolt	54,2 to 61,0	5,54 to 6,22	40 to 45
Safety straps to floor panel	⅜ in U.N.F. bolt	37,6 to 43,4	3,74 to 4,42	27 to 32
Damper attachments	⁷⁄₁₆ in U.N.F. nut	43,4 to 48,8	4,43 to 4,97	32 to 36
Mounting brackets to body	⅜ in U.N.F. nut	37,6 to 43,3	3,74 to 4,42	27 to 32
Mounting brackets to beam	⁵⁄₁₆ in U.N.F. nut	19,0 to 24,4	1,94 to 2,48	14 to 18
Bump stops to body	⁵⁄₁₆ in U.N.F. nut	10,8 to 13,6	1,10 to 1,38	8 to 10
Wheel nuts	Special nuts	61,0 to 88,0	6,23 to 8,98	45 to 65

REAR SUSPENSION HEIGHT

Check   64.25.12

Ensure radiator is topped up with coolant.
Ensure engine sump is filled to correct level
with specified lubricant. Ensure tyre pressures
are correct.
Note contents of fuel tanks by switching on
ignition and switching from one tank to
another.

NOTE: Fuel tanks hold a total of 20 Imperial
gallons (24 U.S. gallons or 9.1 litres). Calculate
ballast weights required to represent difference between weight of fuel tank contents and
weight of full tanks. Full fuel tanks total approximately 73 kg (160 lb).

Place ballast weights required in centre of luggage compartment floor. Roll car forward
three lengths on perfectly level surface.

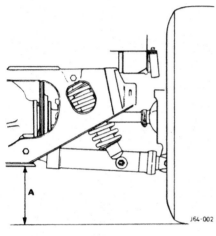

Fig. 3

Measure distance between lower surface of
rear cross member and ground at both sides of
car. (Dimension A in Fig. 3 must be 189 mm
± 6,4 mm (7.45 ± 0.25 in).
If dimension is not correct, check all bushes
and bearing points of rear suspension. If the
cause is not discovered, rear road springs must
be changed. Remove all four springs and
change as complete set.

REAR SUSPENSION CAMBER ANGLE

Check and adjust   64.25.18

Service tool: Setting links JD 25B.

Checking

Set car on level surface.
Ensure tyre pressures correct.
Hook one end of setting link tool (1, Fig. 4)
JD 25B, in lower hole of rear mounting, depress
body until other end of setting link can be slid
over outer wishbone fulcrum nut. Repeat on
other side of car.

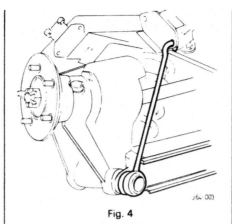

Fig. 4

Set camber gauge (1, Fig. 5) against each rear
tyre and read off camber angle. The correct
reading should be ¾° ± ¼° negative. If these
limits are not met, note deviation and adjust
camber angle.

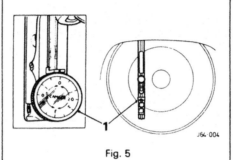

Fig. 5

If result satisfactory remove setting links.
To adjust the camber angle.

Remove setting links.
Jack up rear of car, place stands to support
body and remove road wheel.
Remove lower wishbone outer fulcrum grease
nipple

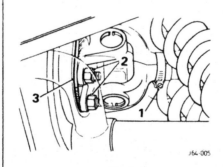

Fig. 6

Release clip (1, Fig. 6) securing inner universal
joint cover. Slide cover clear of joint. Remove
four steel locknuts (2, Fig. 6) securing drive
shaft flange (3, Fig. 6) to brake disc.
Separate drive shaft from disc to enable shims
to be fitted.

NOTE: Addition of one shim, 0,5 mm (0.020
in) will alter camber position ¼°

Add or remove shims as required.
Replace drive shaft, cover, nipple and wheel.
Remove car from stands and re-check camber
angle

REAR HUB BEARING END-FLOAT

Check and adjust   64.15.13

Service tools: Hub remover JD 1D.
Thread protector JD 1C-7. Backlash
gauge JD 13A.

NOTE: End-float is controlled by a spacer
located next to the universal joint on the hub
shaft. Spacers are available in thickness from
2,77 mm (0.109 in) to 3,84 mm (0.151 in) in
0,076 mm (0.003 in) steps.
End-float is normally 0,026 to 0,076 mm
(0.001 to 0.003 in) and MUST be rectified if it
exceeds 0,127 mm (0.005 in) by changing the
spacer for a thicker one.

Checking

Raise car and place on stands.
Remove rear road wheel and tap hub towards
car.
Clamp tool JD 13A (1, Fig. 7) to hub carrier web,
as shown, so that stylus of dial gauge contacts
hub flange.
Note reading of dial gauge (2, Fig. 7).
Using two levers (3, Fig. 7) between hub and
hub carrier boss, press hub outwards. Take
care not to damage water thrower.
Note altered reading on dial gauge.

Fig. 7

NOTE: The difference between dial gauge
readings represents end-float of hub bearings.
If this exceeds 0,127 mm (0.005 in) refer to
'Adjusting' procedure.
Otherwise, remove tool and gauge and refit
road wheel

Adjusting

Remove split pin, nut and washer from end of
drive shaft.
Remove fulcrum shaft grease nipple from hub
carrier.
Place thread protector on end of drive shaft.
Fit hub puller JD 1D to rear hub and secure.
Withdraw hub and carrier from drive shaft and
remove hub puller and thread protector.
Remove spacer from drive shaft and measure
thickness with micrometer.

NOTE: A simple calculation will give the thickness of spacer required to reduce end-float to
specified 0,026 to 0.076 mm (0.001 to 0.003
in) i.e. If end-float measured above was 0,203
mm (0.007 in) a replacement spacer will need
to be 0,127 mm (0.005 in) thicker than that
removed to reduce end-float to 0,051 mm
(.002 in)

continued

64—3

As spacers are supplied in 0,075 mm (0.003 in) steps of thickness, a spacer 0,152 mm (0.006 in) thicker would be used, reducing end-float to 0,026 mm (0.001 in).

Clean dried Loctite from drive shaft splines. Place selected spacer on drive shaft.
Apply Loctite 'Stud Lock' to outer two thirds of drive shaft splines, using a small brush.
Enter drive shaft in hub and drift hub on to shaft.
Replace washer, tighten nut to figure quoted in data sheet and fit new split pin.
Replace grease nipple and re-check end-float.
Remove tool and gauge and refit road wheel.

REAR HUB AND CARRIER ASSEMBLY

Remove and refit   **64.15.01**

Including: WISHBONE OUTER FULCRUM BEARINGS—Remove and refit 64.35.16
See also REAR HUB AND CARRIER ASSY. OVERHAUL, operation 64.15.07

Service tools: Hub puller JD 1D. Dummy shaft JD 14.

Removing

Remove rear road wheel.
Place stand under rear of car.
Remove fulcrum shaft grease nipple (1, Fig. 8) from hub carrier.

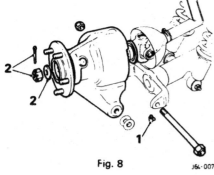

Fig. 8   J64·007

Withdraw split pin, remove castellated nut and plain washer (2, Fig. 8) from splined end of half-shaft and fit thread protector over end of shaft.

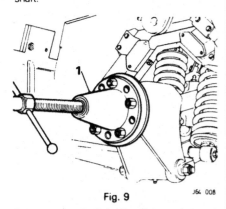

Fig. 9   J64·008

Fit hub puller, JD 1D (1, Fig. 9) to rear hub and secure. Withdraw hub and carrier from half

shaft. Remove hub puller from hub and carrier and recover thread protector.

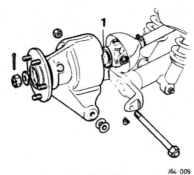

Fig. 10   J64·009

Recover spacer from half shaft (1, Fig. 10). Examine inner oil seal track and renew if necessary.

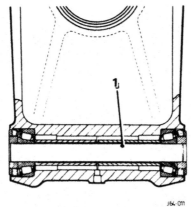

Fig. 11   J64·010

Remove one nut from outer wishbone fulcrum shaft and using a hide mallet, drift out shaft (1, Fig. 11). Remove hub and carrier assembly from car. Temporarily secure retaining washers and shims using adhesive tape.

Refitting

Fit dummy shaft tool number JD 14 (1, Fig. 12) to hub carrier fulcrum.

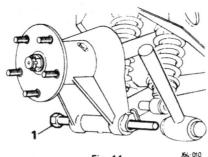

Fig. 12   J64·011

Fit hub carrier to wishbone, positioning shims removed between carrier and wishbone.
Replace outer wishbone fulcrum shaft, displacing dummy shaft.

Secure shaft with nut. Tighten to correct torque. Refit grease nipple.
If necessary fit oil seal track to half shaft splined flange. Refit spacer. Thoroughly clean and de-grease splines of half shaft and bore of hub.
Using a small brush sparingly apply Loctite 'Stud Lock' to outer two thirds of half shaft splines.
Assemble hub carrier to half shaft.
Fit washer and secure hub carrier assembly with castellated nut. Tighten to correct torque. Lock using new split pin.
Check, and if necessary, adjust hub bearing end-float.
Remove stands and refit the road wheel.

REAR ROAD SPRINGS

Remove and refit   **64.20.01**

Including: REAR HYDRAULIC DAMPERS

Remove and refit   **64.30.01**

Service tools: Handpress 47. Adaptor JD 11B.

Removing

NOTE: Rear springs can be removed with rear suspension fitted to car.

NOTE: Hydraulic dampers fitted to this car are of the gas pressurized type and therefore do not need to be exercised before installation.

Jack up car and remove rear road wheel.
Support rear of car on stands.
Place jack to support wishbone.

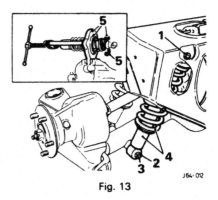

Fig. 13   J64·012

Remove self-locking nut and bolt (1, Fig. 13) securing top of hydraulic damper to suspension unit cross-beam.
Remove washers and nuts securing hydraulic dampers to wishbone.
Drift out damper mounting pin (2, Fig. 13).
Recover spacer at forward end of mounting pin tube (3, Fig. 13).
Withdraw hydraulic damper and road spring assembly (4, Fig. 13).
Using tools 47 and JD 11B (5, Fig. 13) compress road spring until collets and spring seat can be removed.
Release spring pressure and withdraw hydraulic damper from road spring.

Refitting

Replace spring on damper using tools 47 and JD 11B, insert unit, replace spacer and secure damper in position.
Tighten nuts (4 and 5, Fig. 13) to correct torque.
Replace road wheel.

BUMP STOP

Remove and refit   **64.30.15**

Removing

Remove rear road wheel.
Remove two self-locking nuts and washers and detach bump stop (1, Fig. 14).

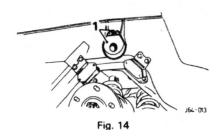

Fig. 14

Refitting

Reverse above operations, tightening nuts to correct torque.

REAR SUSPENSION UNIT

Remove and refit   **64.25.01**

Removing

Remove rear road wheels.
Place stands beneath car, forward of radius arm anchor points.
Release clamps (1 and 2, Fig. 15) securing intermediate exhaust pipes.

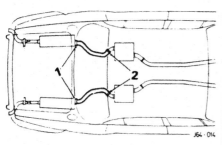

Fig. 15

Manoeuvre intermediate pipes from rear of suspension unit, after disengaging pipe mounting pin from rubber mounting.
Place suitably sized block of wood between each exhaust pipe trim and rear bumper to support rear silencer and tail pipe assembly in fitted position.

Remove special bolt and spring washer (1, Fig. 16) securing each radius arm safety strap to body.

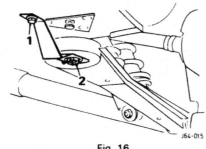

Fig. 16

Remove locking wire and bolts (2, Fig. 16) securing radius arms, remove safety straps.
Disconnect brake pipe hose from body mounting bracket, plug ends to prevent ingress of dirt.
Remove self-locking nuts and bolts securing propeller shaft rear flange to differential pinion flange.
Fully release handbrake.
Remove split pin, washer, and clevis pin securing handbrake cable to caliper actuating lever.
Slide protective rubber boot from brake outer cable.
Remove outer cable from trunnion on opposite lever.
Release outer brake cable from securing spring, secure cable away from suspension unit.
Position jack beneath tie plate of rear suspension unit.
Remove eight self-locking nuts and bolts, and four nuts securing mounting bracket to body (1, Fig. 17).

Fig. 17

Lower jack to remove suspension unit.

Refitting

Reverse operations for removal.

NOTE: Before refitting radius arms to body, it is advisable to wire brush spigot mounting and lightly smear it with waterproof grease. Wire lock radius arm bolt to safety strap.

Tighten attachments to correct torque figures. Bleed brakes. Adjust handbrake.

MOUNTING BRACKET

Remove and refit   **64.35.20**

Removing

Remove rear suspension unit.
Remove two self-locking nuts and bolts (1, Fig. 18) securing each mounting bracket to body.

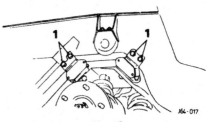

Fig. 18

Refitting

Fit new rear suspension rubber mountings to body with cut-away end of flange upwards.
Secure bracket using bolts and self-locking nuts. Tighten to correct torque figure.
Refit rear suspension unit.

WISHBONE

Remove and refit   **64.35.15**

Including: WISHBONE INNER FULCRUM BEARINGS—Remove and refit—64.35.16 and WISHBONE OIL SEALS—Remove and refit—64.35.17

Service tool: Dummy shaft JD 14

Removing

Remove rear road wheel
Support rear of car on stands forward of radius arms
Remove one self-locking nut from outer fulcrum shaft, drift out shaft (1, Fig. 19) and remove

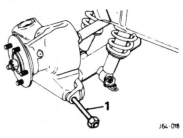

Fig. 19

Fit dummy shaft JD 14 to hub carrier assembly Retain shims and oil seal retaining washers at each side of fulcrum with adhesive tape.
Raise hub and drive shaft clear of wishbone and suspend with strong wire from cross beam

continued

64—5

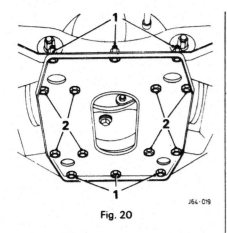

Fig. 20

Remove six bolts and nuts (1, Fig. 20) securing bottom tie-plate to cross-beam.

Remove locking wire and unscrew radius arm retaining bolt from body.

Detach forward end of radius arm from mounting on body.

Remove eight setscrews (2, Fig. 20) securing bottom tie-plate to inner fulcrum brackets.

Remove nuts and washers securing dampers to wishbone.

Drift out damper mounting pin and recover spacer.

Remove rear nut from inner fulcrum shaft, recover tie-down bracket.

Drift fulcrum shaft forward to free wishbone from inner fulcrum. Remove wishbone and radius arm.

Collect oil seals, distance washers and bearings.

Remove bolt securing radius arm to wishbone; discard tab washer.

Remove grease nipples from wishbone ends. Clean and inspect all parts.

Refitting

Smear needle bearing cage (1, Fig. 21) with grease and press into wishbone inner fulcrum boss, engraved face outwards.

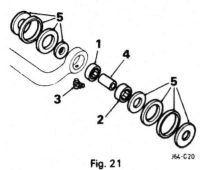

Fig. 21

From opposite end of boss, press in second needle bearing cage (2, Fig. 21) again with engraved face outwards.

Fit grease nipple (3, Fig. 21).

Insert bearing tube, (4, Fig. 21).

Repeat for other boss.

Attach radius arm to wishbone. Fit new tab washer and tighten nut to correct torque.

Smear four outer thrust washers, inner thrust washers, new oil seals and oil seal retainers (5, Fig. 21) with grease and place into position on wishbone.

Offer up wishbone to inner fulcrum mounting bracket with radius arm bracket towards front of suspension unit.

NOTE: Take great care not to displace any of the fulcrum bearing components.

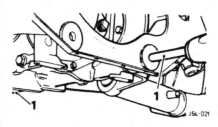

Fig. 22

Carefully enter dummy shaft (1, Fig. 22) tool JD 14 from each end to retain bearing assemblies and locate wishbone with mounting bracket.

Smear fulcrum shaft with grease and gently drift it through fulcrum to chase out dummy shafts.

NOTE: It is advisable to maintain a slight reaction pressure on dummy shafts as they emerge from fulcrum. This ensures that thrust washers are not knocked out of position. Should this happen, fulcrum shaft, dummy shaft and wishbone must be removed and installation operations repeated.

Fit self-locking nut to fulcrum shaft.

Tighten to correct torque.

Raise wishbone and replace damper mounting pin, spacer and tie-down bracket. Tighten nuts to correct torque.

Raise radius arm, clean and lightly grease spigot, replace bolt, tighten to correct torque and wire lock.

Remove wire suspending hubs assembly from cross-beam.

Remove adhesive tape attaching shims and washers to hub carrier, fit new seals, replace retainers and shims, and line up with wishbone.

Chase out dummy shaft with fulcrum shaft and tighten self-locking nuts to correct torque.

Replace bottom tie-plate and insert eight setscrews.

Replace six bolts and nuts and tighten all 14 bolts and setscrews to correct torque.

Replace road wheel, check camber angle and grease wishbone bearings.

WISHBONE BEARINGS

Remove and refit   **64.35.16**

Procedures for removal and refitting the wishbone outer fulcrum bearings are given in Rear hub and carrier assembly—remove and refit, see operation 64.15.01, and overhaul, see operation 64.15.07. The wishbone inner fulcrum bearings are covered in Wishbone—remove and refit, see operation—64.35.15.

WISHBONE OIL SEALS

Remove and refit   **64.35.17**

Follow procedure given under Wishbone—remove and refit, see operation 64.35.15.

REAR HUB OIL SEALS

Remove and refit   **64.15.15**

The degree of dismantling required to change rear hub oil seals is extensive; full rear hub overhaul procedure should therefore be carried out, see operation 64.15.07 and all oil seals, including outer wishbone fulcrum oil seals changed. Renew grease content of both hub and fulcrum bearing assemblies.

INNER FULCRUM BRACKET (ONE)

Remove and refit   **64.35.21**

Service tool: Dummy shaft JD 14

Removing

Remove adjacent rear road wheel.

Support rear of car on stands forward of radius arms.

Remove 14 bolts and setscrews securing bottom tie-plate to cross-beam and inner fulcrum brackets.

Detach forward end of radius arm from mounting on body.

Remove nuts and washers securing damper to wishbone.

Drift out damper mounting pin; recover spacer and tie-down bracket. Suspend hub and drive shaft assembly from cross-beam with strong wire.

Remove rear nut from inner fulcrum shaft.

Drift fulcrum shaft forward to free wishbone from inner fulcrum.

Collect oil seals, distance washers and bearings.

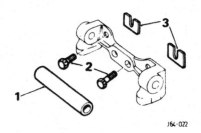

Fig. 23

Tap spacer tube (1, Fig. 23) from between lugs of fulcrum bracket.

Remove locking wire from two setscrews (2, Fig. 23) securing fulcrum bracket to final drive unit. Remove setscrews and withdraw fulcrum bracket, noting position and number of shims (3, Fig. 23) at each attachment point.

64—6

Refitting

Position fulcrum bracket against final drive unit and locate loosely with two setscrews.
Replace shims (3, Fig. 23) between bracket and final drive unit.
Tighten mounting setscrews to correct torque and wire lock.
Replace spacer tube between lugs of fulcrum bracket.
Clean, inspect and grease wishbone bearings, thrust washer etc. Refit with new oil seals.
Offer up wishbone to fulcrum bracket lugs and locate with dummy shafts (1, Fig. 24) tool number JD 14. Take great care not to displace any components during this operation.

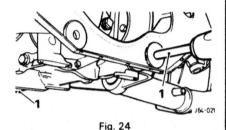

Fig. 24

Drift dummy shafts from fulcrum bracket with fulcrum shaft.
Restrain dummy shafts to prevent spacers or thrust washers dropping out of position.
Tighten fulcrum shaft nut to correct torque.
Remove wire suspending hub assembly from cross-beam.
Replace damper lower mounting shaft, refitting spacer and tie-down bracket.
Tighten nuts to correct torque.
Clean spigot on body, raise radius arm and replace bolt. Tighten to correct torque and wire-lock bolt.
Bolt anti-roll bar link to radius arm and tighten.
Replace bottom tie-plate and tighten bolts and setscrews to correct torque.
Replace road wheel.
Remove car from stands.

RADIUS ARM

Remove and refit   64.35.28

Removing

Jack up rear of car and support on stands forward of radius arm anchor points.
Remove rear road wheel.
Remove special bolt and spring washer (1, Fig. 25) securing safety strap to body.

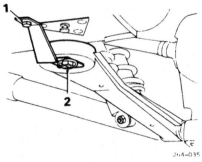

Fig. 25

Remove locking wire and bolt (2, Fig. 25) securing radius arm to body; remove safety strap.
Remove self-locking nut and flat washer (1, Fig. 26) securing forward damper assembly lower mounting pin.

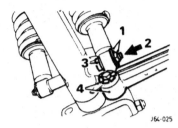

Fig. 26

Drift mounting pin to rear of wishbone clearing damper assembly mounting boss and spacer (2, Fig. 26).
Recover spacer (3, Fig. 26) and swing damper assembly to centre line of car.
Turn down tab washer and remove bolt (4, Fig. 26) securing radius arm to wishbone; remove radius arm.
Examine radius arm bushes and replace as necessary.

Refitting

NOTE: Prior to fitting radius arm to body spigot, wire brush spigot and smear with waterproof grease.

Reverse removal operations, tightening bolts and nuts to correct torque figures.
Renew locking wire and tab washer.

RADIUS ARM BUSHES

Remove and refit   64.35.29

Service tool: Mandrel JD 21

Removing — See Fig. 27

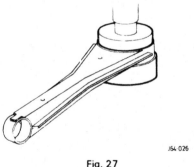

Fig. 27

Remove radius arm.
Use mandrel tool JD 21 and press front bush from housing.
Use mandrel tool JD 21 and press rear bush from housing.

Refitting

Press new bush into rear bush housing so that bush is central in radius arm.
Use mandrel and press new bush into front bush housing so that holes in bush rubber are in line with centre line of radius arm.
Press bush into radius arm until bush ring is flush with bush housing. When pressing bush, have small hole in bush core upwards.
Refit radius arm.

REAR HUB WHEEL STUDS

Remove and refit   64.15.26

Removing

Remove rear hub and carrier assembly
Support hub carrier and press out hub using hand press (1, Fig. 28) and suitable mandrel.

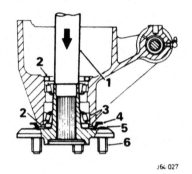

Fig. 28

Prise old oil seal (2, Fig. 28) from hub.
Draw outer bearing and oil seal track (3, Fig. 28) from hub.
Using a narrow, sharp cold chisel, open peening securing water thrower.
Remove thrower (4, Fig. 28).
Support hub, and file or grind staking from faulty stud/s (5, Fig. 28).
Unscrew stud/s (6, Fig. 28/1, Fig. 29) from hub flange

Refitting

Screw new stud/s into hub and stake in four places to back of flange (2, Fig. 29).

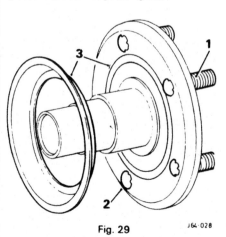

Fig. 29

continued

64—7

Fit water thrower to hub and use blunt cold chisel to peen over flange in three or four places (3, Fig. 29).

Press oil seal track and outer bearing race on to hub.

Press new outer and inner oil seals into hub.

Fit hub into hub carrier and pack with suitable grease.

Locate inner bearing over hub and press into position.

Refit rear hub and carrier assembly.

REAR SUSPENSION UNIT

Overhaul   64.25.06

The rear suspension unit is an assembly comprising individual units, the removal, refitting and overhaul of each being covered elsewhere in this Manual.

For this reason, an overhaul procedure is not given for the rear suspension unit assembly, although it is advisable to check all bushes, fulcrum bearings and oil seals for damage or leakage whenever the unit is removed from the car.

REAR HUB AND CARRIER ASSEMBLY

Overhaul   64.15.07
Including WISHBONE OUTER FULCRUM BEARINGS—Remove and refit 64.35.16 and REAR HUB OIL SEALS—Remove and refit 64.15.15.

Service tools: Master spacer JD 15. Dummy shaft JD 14. Press tool JD 16C. Hand press 47. Press tool JD 20A. Tool JD 20A-1. Adaptor JD 16C-1.

Dismantling

Remove rear hub and carrier assembly.

Prise out oil seal retainers (1, Fig. 30) from fulcrum shaft housing and remove seals, dummy shaft, bearings, distance tubes and shims (2, Fig. 30).

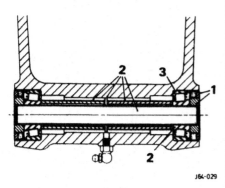

Fig. 30

Mount hub carrier in vice and drift out bearing cups (3, Fig. 30) from fulcrum shaft housing.

Transfer hub carrier to press and remove hub assembly from carrier.

Drift out inner hub bearing cup, with seal and bearing, from hub carrier.

Drift out outer bearing cup.

Fit hand press 47 with adaptors JD 16C-1 to hub and pull outer bearing from hub.

Remove oil seal track from hub shaft and clean and inspect all parts.

NOTE: When inspecting components, pay particular attention to oil seal tracks; a minute score can considerably shorten oil seal life. For further details on inspection of seals and bearings refer to 'General Fitting Instructions'.

Reassembling

Replace outer oil seal track (1, Fig. 31) on hub shaft.

Press outer bearing cone (2, Fig. 31) into position on hub shaft and grease bearing with 70 cc of Retinax 'A'.

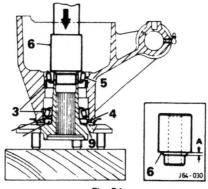

Fig. 31

Press outer and inner cups of bearings (3, Fig. 31) into hub carrier, using tool JD 20A with adaptor JD 20A-1.

Drift new outer oil seal (4, Fig. 31) into position in hub carrier and lower carrier on to hub shaft and outer bearing.

Place inner bearing (5, Fig. 31) into position for fitting.

Place master spacer JD 15 (6, Fig. 31) in position as shown and press bearing on to hub shaft.

Transfer hub and carrier assembly to vice, set up dial gauge (1, Fig. 32) and spacer (2, Fig. 32) JD 15 as shown and measure end-float, lifting carrier by using two screwdrivers (3, Fig. 32) as levers.

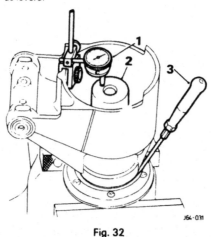

Fig. 32

Select spacer to be fitted on drive shaft.

NOTE: Master spacer has a diameter of length 'A' equivalent to a spacer of 3,81 mm (0.15 in). Calculate the spacer required to give end-float of 0,025 to 0,076 mm (0.001 to 0.003 in). Spacers are supplied in thicknesses of 2,77 to 3,84 mm (0.109 to 0.151 in) in steps of 0,076 mm (0.003 in) and are lettered A to R (less letters I, N and O).

SPACER LETTER	THICKNESS	
	mm	inches
A	2,77	0.109
B	2,85	0.112
C	2,92	0.115
D	3,00	0.118
E	3,07	0.121
F	3,15	0.124
G	3,23	0.127
H	3,30	0.130
J	3,38	0.133
K	3,45	0.136
L	3,53	0.139
M	3,61	0.142
P	3,68	0.145
Q	3,76	0.148
R	3,84	0.151

For example, assume end-float to be 0,66 mm (0.026 in). Subtract required nominal end-float of 0,050 mm (0.002 in) from measured end-float giving 0,61 mm (0.024 in). Since special collar is 3,81 mm (0.150 in) thick, the thickness of the spacer to be fitted will be 3,8 mm −0,61 mm, i.e. 3,20 mm (0.126 in). The nearest spacer is 3,23 mm (0.127 in) so letter G spacer should be fitted in place of special collar.

Remove adaptor and fit new inner bearing oil seal to hub carrier.

Fit fulcrum shaft bearing cups to hub carrier and insert one bearing.

Secure fulcrum shaft vertically in suitably protected jaws of vice and slide bearing in hub carrier over shaft.

Replace distance tubes and shims as removed in dismantling, adding 0,25 mm (0.010 in) extra shims. (One extra 0,076 mm (0.003 in) shim and one extra 0,178 mm (0.007 in) shim.

Fit second bearing over fulcrum shaft, remove hub assembly from vice and replace oil seal tracks outside bearings.

Place a large washer (1, Fig. 33) (e.g. inner fork thrust washer) next to one oil seal track.

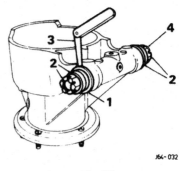

Fig. 33

Cover exposed plain length of fulcrum shaft with suitable temporary spacers, (2, Fig. 33) fit nuts and tighten to correct torque.

64—8

Apply pressure to fulcrum shaft at large washer end, turning it to settle taper rollers and using feeler gauge (3, Fig. 33) measure minimum distance between large washer and hub carrier.

Apply pressure to opposite end of fulcrum shaft (4, Fig. 33) and measure maximum distance between washer and hub carrier.

NOTE: End play of fulcrum shaft in hub carrier is now obtained by subtracting the minimum measurement from the maximum measurement.

This end play must be replaced by a pre-load of 0,05 mm (0.002 in) by removing shims, to a total thickness of 0,05 mm (0.002 in) more than the end play, from between spacer tubes: For example;

Assume end play found to be 0,25 mm (0.010 in).

Therefore shims to the value of 0,25 + 0,05 mm = 0,30 mm (0.010 + 0.002 in = 0.012 in) must be removed to give correct pre-load.

Release nut from large washer end of fulcrum shaft and detach spacers, washer, oil seal track and bearing.

Remove one spacer tube and extract shims to thickness established to give pre-load. Replace spacer tube, pack fulcrum shaft housing with grease and replace bearing and oil seal track.

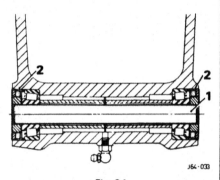

J64-033

Fig. 34

Push out fulcrum shaft by inserting dummy shaft (1, Fig. 34) and detach temporary spacers from fulcrum shaft. Check that oil seal tracks are in position.

Press new oil seals (2, Fig. 34) into fulcrum shaft housings and secure with oil seal retainers.

Replace rear hub and carrier assembly, see operation 64.15.01.

REAR SUSPENSION MOUNTINGS

Inspect   64.25.00

Drive the vehicle on to a ramp and position a ramp jack under the jacking point, in front of the rear radius arm body mounting.

Raise the ramp sufficiently to allow either the rear wheel to clear the ramp, or until the distance between the lower edge of the rear quarter valance and the ramp is 34 cm (13.5 in). **DO NOT** exceed this distance.

Visually inspect the condition of the rubber, and the rubber/metal bonding.

If the rubber shows signs of cracking, or there is unbonding of the rubber to a depth greater than 3,175 mm (0.125 in), then the mounting must be replaced.

If a visual inspection is not conclusive, insert a lever between the two 'V's of the mounting and apply pressure.

Check the rubber for cracking and the rubber/metal bonding.

Repeat the procedure for the other side.

DAMPER SAFETY   64.30.00

See page 60—10.

PAGE INTENTIONALLY LEFT BLANK

CONTENTS

continued

Contents—*continued*

DESCRIPTION

A common servo-assisted brake system is fitted to all Jaguar and Daimler Series III saloon cars. The fluid reservoir is integral with the master cylinder and is divided into two compartments, one supplying the front brakes and the other the rear brakes.

The two pipes from the master cylinder lead to each side of a Pressure Differential Warning Actuator (P.D.W.A.) in which a free piston, normally centrally located, is deflected to one side or the other if the pressure in one pipe differs from that in the second pipe.

In moving, the piston operates a switch which then completes the circuit to a warning light on the instrument panel.

This warning light must also illuminate when the ignition switch is in position 3 (Start), to provide a check that the warning circuit is operating satisfactorily.

Failure to do so indicates a bulb or circuit fault. If the light remains on when the ignition switch is returned to position 2 (Ignition), then a brake fault is indicated and the car MUST NOT be driven until the fault is corrected.

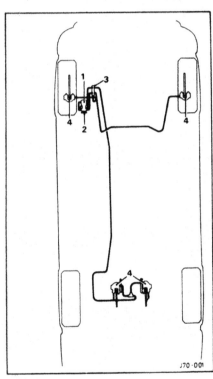

Fig. 1

KEY TO COMPONENT LOCATION

(See Fig. 1)

1. Brake fluid reservoir
2. Master cylinder
3. P.D.W.A. unit
4. Brake calipers

Two further pipes from the P.W.D.A. lead to the two front brakes and a third pipe connects with a T-piece mounted on the rear crossmember; another two pipes connect the T-piece with the two rear calipers, mounted on each side of the final drive unit.

Flexible hoses replace the pipes at each front caliper and a third hose is inserted between the front to rear pipe and the rear cross-beam.

A completely separate handbrake system operates small pads, at the rear discs, mechanically; self-adjusting mechanism maintains the correct clearance between released pads and discs and a manual adjustment is also provided. A switch mounted on the hand control completes a circuit to the handbrake warning lamp when the ignition is switched on and the handbrake is applied. It must extinguish when the handbrake is released or the ignition is switched off.

Operation of brake system (see Fig. 2)

On application of the brake pedal the servo unit, which is directly coupled to the master cylinder, transfers increased pedal pressure to the master cylinder primary piston 'A' causing the piston to move forward past the by-pass port 'P' to establish rear brake line pressure in chamber 'B'. Pressure from the primary cylinder return spring 'C' and rear brake line pressure force the secondary piston 'D' forward past the by-pass port 'P' to establish front brake line pressure in chamber 'E'.

Front and rear braking pressures enter the P.D.W.A. unit at ports 'F' and 'G', act on either end of the shuttle valve 'H' and travel to front and rear calipers via ports 'J' and 'K'. Should a fall in front or rear braking pressure occur the resultant pressure imbalance causes displacement of the shuttle valve, which in turn operates the switch 'L' and illuminates a warning light in the instrument panel. In order to reset the displaced shuttle valve the cause of fall in brake line pressure must first be established and rectified. During bleeding of the brake system which follows rectification the shuttle valve automatically resets, and extinguishes the warning light. Brake pressure entering the caliper 'M' forces the pistons 'T' out to act on the friction pads 'U' which in turn clamp the brake disc 'V'. On release of the brake pedal, brake line pressure collapses which allows the piston seals 'W' to retract the pistons into the caliper. Withdrawal of the pistons into the caliper is just sufficient for the friction pads to be

in a relaxed position away from the disc. This sequence provides automatic adjustment for brake pad lining wear.

Should the brake servo unit become inoperative front and rear braking systems will still operate but at a greatly reduced brake line pressure. A divided brake fluid reservoir 'R' ensures that in the event of fluid loss to front or rear brake systems one pair of brake calipers will at all times be operative. The fluid level indicator 'S' provides visual warning to the driver should the level of fluid in the reservoir fall to an unsatisfactory level.

1983 M.Y. SPECIFICATION
Brakes — All Models

The brake system pressure differential warning actuator (P.D.W.A.) unit has been deleted.

NOTE: This deletion in no way affects the performance of the braking system as the conventional split system is retained.

All steel brake pipes on 1983 model year cars will be plastic coated. This will improve the corrosion resistance of the pipe work.

Brake Pad Material Change — All Models

A semi metallic brake pad lining was introduced from:-

VIN 354035

Identification of semi metallic pads is by the friction material code FER 3401 printed on the rear face of the material adjacent to the pad batch number.

Semi metallic pads may be used in vehicle sets as a retrospective fit on Jaguar vehicles with 4 pot caliper front brakes.

WARNING: Under no circumstances should semi metallic and non semi metallic brake pads be mixed.
Brake pads must be used in vehicle sets only.

It is therefore necessary to check lining specification **on the complete vehicle** before replacing brake pads in axle sets to ensure that mixing does not occur.

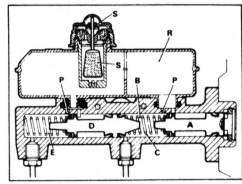
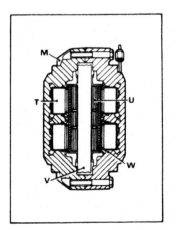
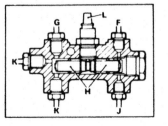

Fig. 2

70—3

Metrication

The examples shown in Figs. 3, 4 and 5 are intended as an aid to identification of brake components in metric form.

All metric pipe nuts, hose ends, unions and bleed screws are coloured black. The hexagon area of pipe nuts are indented with the letter 'M'.

Metric and U.N.F. pipe nuts are different in shape and the female nut is always used with a trumpet flared pipe, the male nut always having a convex flared pipe.

A = Metric   B = U.N.F.

Fig. 3

Hose ends differ slightly between metric and U.N.F.

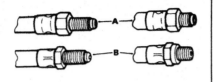

J70-004

A = Metric   B = U.N.F.

Fig. 4

Copper gaskets are not used with metric hose and a gap exists between the hose end and cylinder.

J70-003

A = Metric   B = U.N.F.

Fig. 5

Metrication does not apply to the following brake components.

1. Rear calipers.
2. Handbrake calipers.
3. Feed pipes from rear three-way connector to rear calipers.
4. Three-way connector.

DATA

Front brakes—make and type	Girling, ventilated disc
Rear brakes—make and type	Girling, inboard disc
Handbrake—type	Mechanical, operating on rear discs
Disc diameter—front	283,8 mm (11.175 in)
—rear	263,8 mm (10.385 in)
Disc thickness—front	24,0 mm (0.945 in)
—rear	Normal 12,7 mm (0.5 in)
	Min. permissible 11,43 mm (0.45 in)
Master cylinder bore diameter	23,8 mm (0.937 in)
Hydraulic fluid specification	Castrol Girling Code 1735 (SAE J1703)
Main brake friction pad specification	Ferodo 2430 (slotted)
Handbrake friction pad specification	Mintex M68/1
Servo unit make	Girling

70—4

TORQUE WRENCH SETTINGS

ITEM	DESCRIPTION	TIGHTENING TORQUE		
		Nm	kgf m	lbf ft
Pedal box to body	5/16 in U.N.F. bolt	14,9 to 17,6	1,53 to 1,79	11 to 13
Brake pedal pivot pin	3/8 in U.N.F. nut	19,0 to 24,4	1,94 to 2,48	14 to 18
Brake pedal lever shaft locking pin	1/4 in U.N.C. bolt	2,7 to 3,4	0,28 to 0,34	2 to 2.5
Brake reservoir to bracket	1/4 in U.N.F. nut	2,7 to 3,4	0,28 to 0,34	2 to 2.5
Hydraulic connections for 3/16 in pipes	U.N.F.	8,5 to 9,5	0,87 to 0,96	6.3 to 7
	M 12	16,3 to 19,0	1,66 to 1,94	12 to 14
	M 10 male	9,0 to 11,0	0,93 to 1,10	6.7 to 8
	M 10 female	11,0 to 13,5	1,10 to 1,38	8 to 10
Rear 3-way connection	1/4 in U.N.F. nut	8,1 to 9,5	0,83 to 0,96	6 to 7
Front and rear hoses to bracket	M 10 nut	13,6 to 16,3	1,40 to 1,65	10 to 12
Handbrake cable locknut	11/16 in X 16 U.N.F. nut	9,5 to 13,6	0,97 to 1,38	7 to 10
Handbrake switch locknut	1/4 in U.N.F. nut	4,7 to 6,1	0,48 to 0,62	3.5 to 4.5
Handbrake to body	1/4 in U.N.F. bolt	8,1 to 9,5	0,83 to 0,96	6 to 7
Relay lever pivot	3/8 in U.N.F. bolt	29,8 to 35,2	3,05 to 3,59	22 to 26
Fork end assembly	1/4 in U.N.F. nut	8,1 to 9,5	0,83 to 0,96	6 to 7
Cable guide	No. 10 U.N.F. bolt	5,4 to 6,1	0,48 to 0,62	4 to 4.5
Abutment to body	1/4 in U.N.F. bolt	8,1 to 9,5	0,83 to 0,96	6 to 7
Master cylinder to booster	M 10 nut	21,1 to 26,5	2,14 to 2,70	15.5 to 19.5
Booster to pedal box	M 8 nut	11,0 to 13,5	1,10 to 1,38	8 to 10
P.D.W.A. to body	1/4 in U.N.F. nut	8,1 to 9,5	0,83 to 0,96	6 to 7
Front double-end union to body	M 10 nut	13,6 to 16,3	1,40 to 1,65	10 to 12
Brake light switch to bracket	1/4 in U.N.F. bolt	4,7 to 6,1	0,48 to 0,62	3.5 to 4.5
Rear cable to relay lever	1/4 in U.N.F. nut	8,1 to 9,5	0,83 to 0,96	6 to 7
Brake cable support plate to body	No. 10 U.N.F. bolt	5,4 to 6,1	0,56 to 0,62	4 to 4.5
Cable guide to plate	No. 10 U.N.F. bolt	5,4 to 6,1	0,56 to 0,62	4 to 4.5
Front caliper to stub axle carrier	M 12 bolt	67,8 to 81,3	6,91 to 8,29	50 to 60
Disc shield and clamp to stub axle carrier	1/4 in U.N.F. nut	6,1 to 7,5	0,62 to 0,76	4.5 to 5.0
Rear caliper to drive unit flange	7/16 U.N.F. bolt	66,4 to 74,5	6,78 to 7,60	49 to 55
Wheels nuts	Special nuts—set spanner to	61	6,23	45

CLEANING SOLVENTS

WARNING: Never use methylated spirit (denatured alcohol) for cleaning purposes. Use only Castrol/Girling brake cleaning fluid.

Throughout the following operations absolute cleanliness must be observed to prevent grit or other foreign matter contaminating the brake system. If the system is to be flushed or cleaned through, only Girling brake cleaner must be used. Brake system components must be washed and all traces of cleaner removed before reassembly.

All brake system rubber components must be dipped in clean brake fluid and assembled using the fingers only.

BRAKE FLUID

WARNING: During operations which necessitate the handling of brake fluid, extreme care must be observed; brake fluid must not be allowed to contact the car paintwork. In instances where this has occurred the contaminated area must immediately be cleaned, using a clean cloth and white spirit. This should be followed by washing the area with clean water. Methylated spirit (denatured alcohol) must not be used to clean the contaminated area.

SYMPTOM AND DIAGNOSIS CHART FOR HYDRAULIC BRAKE SYSTEM

SYMPTOM	DIAGNOSIS	ACTION
Fade	Incorrect pads. Overloaded vehicle. Excessive braking. Old hydraulic fluid.	Replace the pads, decrease vehicle load or renew hydraulic fluid as necessary.
Spongy pedal	Air in system. Badly lined pads. Weak master cylinder mounting.	Check for air in the system, and bleed if necessary. Check the master cylinder mounting, pads and discs and replace as necessary.
Long pedal	Discs running out pushing pads back. Distorted damping shims. Misplaced dust covers.	Check that the disc run out does not exceed 0.004 in. (0,101 mm). Rotate the disc on the hub. Check the disc/hub mounting faces.
Brakes binding	Handbrake incorrectly adjusted. Seals swollen. Seized pistons. Servo faulty.	Check and adjust handbrake linkage. Check for seized pistons. Repair or replace as necessary. Refer to servo chart.
Hard pedal—poor braking	Incorrect pads. Glazed pads. Pads wet, greasy or not bedded correctly. Servo unit inoperative. Seized caliper pistons. Worn shock absorbers causing wheel bounce.	Replace the pads or if glazed, lightly rub down with rough sandpaper. Refer to Servo chart, if servo is faulty. Check caliper for damage and repair as necessary. Fit new shock absorbers.
Brakes pulling	Seized pistons. Variation in pads. Unsuitable tyres or pressures. Worn shock absorbers. Loose brakes. Greasy pads. Faulty discs, suspension or steering.	Check tyre pressures, seized pistons, greasy pads or loose brakes; then check suspension, steering and repair or replace as necessary. Fit new shock absorbers.
Fall in fluid level	Worn disc pads. External leak. Leak in servo unit.	Check the pads for wear and for hydraulic fluid leakage. Refer to Servo chart.
Disc brake squeal—pad rattle	Worn retaining pins. Worn discs. Worn pads. Broken anti-chatter spring.	Renew the retaining pins, or discs. Fit new pads, or anti-chatter spring.
Uneven or excessive pad wear	Disc corroded. Disc badly scored. Incorrect friction pads.	Check the disc for corrosion, or scoring and replace if necessary. Fit new pads with correct friction material.
Brake warning light illuminated	Fluid level low, combination valve or P.D.W.A. unit operated. Short in electrical warning circuit.	Top up reservoir. Check for leaks in system and pads for wear. Check electrical circuit.

BRAKE SYSTEM

Bleed—all round   70.25.02

Bleeding the brake system is not a routine maintenance operation and should only be necessary when air has contaminated the fluid or a part of the system has been disconnected.

Bleeding

Ensure fluid reservoir is topped up with fluid of correct specification.
Attach bleeder tube to left-hand rear bleed screw, immerse open end of tube in small jar partially filled with clean brake fluid.
Position gear selector in neutral and run engine at idling speed.
Slacken left-hand rear bleed screw.
Operate brake pedal through full stroke until fluid issuing from tube is free of air bubbles.

NOTE: The fluid level in reservoir must be checked at regular intervals and topped up as necessary.

Keep pedal fully depressed and close bleed screw.
Repeat above operations on right-hand rear brake.
Continue above operations on remaining front brakes.
Check tightness of all bleed screws and fit protective caps.
Top up reservoir as necessary.

CAUTION: Brake fluid emitted from system during above check must NOT be put back into system.

Apply normal working load to brake pedal for several minutes, if pedal moves or feels spongy further bleeding of system is required.
When pedal 'feel' is satisfactory release handbrake, brake warning light should extinguish. If warning light remains illuminated carry out the following operation:
Operate brake pedal applying heavy pedal pressure, warning light should extinguish; if light remains illuminated carry out P.D.W.A. check operation, see operation 70.25.08.

BRAKE SYSTEM

Drain and flush   70.25.17

Service tool: Brake piston retractor tool 64932392

Draining

Slacken all road wheel nuts.
Jack up front of car and place on stands.
Jack up rear of car and place on stands.
Remove all road wheels.
Attach bleeder tube to rear left-hand caliper bleed screw with open end of tube in suitable container.
Slacken bleed screw.
Operate brake pedal slowly through full stroke, until 'rear' brake section of fluid reservoir is drained and fluid ceases to issue from bleed tube.
Remove rear left-hand caliper friction pads, see operation 70.40.03.

WARNING: Do not operate brake pedal while friction pads are removed.

Using special tool 64932392, lever pistons into bores expelling remaining trapped fluid into container.

Replace friction pads.

NOTE: It is not necessary to replace retaining pins and clips at this time.

Close bleed screw.

Discard expelled fluid.

Repeat draining operations on right-hand rear and front calipers.

Flushing

Fill fluid reservoir with Castrol/Girling brake flushing fluid.

Attach bleeder tube to rear left-hand caliper bleed screw with open end of tube in container.

Slacken bleed screw.

Operate brake pedal slowly through full stroke, until clear flushing fluid issues from tube.

NOTE: The fluid level in the reservoir must be checked at regular intervals and topped up as necessary.

Closed bleed screw and operate pedal two or three times.

Repeat above bleed operations on remaining rear and front calipers.

Carry out draining operations on rear brake calipers.

Secure rear friction pads with retaining pins and clips. Repeat draining operations on front brake calipers.

Secure front friction pads with retaining pins, clips and anti-chatter springs.

Close bleed screws on front and rear calipers.

Discard expelled flushing fluid.

Refilling

Fill brake reservoir with new brake fluid of correct specification.

Bleed brakes see 70.25.02.

NOTE: Prior to closing bleed screw during the bleeding of each caliper, check that issuing brake fluid is completely free of flushing fluid.

Refit road wheels to car.

Remove stands.

PRESSURE DIFFERENTIAL WARNING ACTUATOR

Test   70.25.14

NOTE: Overhaul of the P.D.W.A. Unit is not possible, and the following test should be carried out at intervals detailed in the Maintenance Summary.

Operational check

Ensure car is adequately chocked.

Check brake fluid level and top-up if necessary. On cars with automatic transmission ensure gear selector lever is in 'N' neutral or 'P' (Park).

Check that with ignition on and handbrake applied 'Park Brake Warning' light is illuminated.

Run engine at idle speed and release handbrake.

Apply heavy foot pressure to brake pedal.

NOTE: The brake pedal should be fully depressed and kept fully applied throughout the following operations.

Release any brake caliper bleed nipple just sufficiently to allow fluid to be expelled, and ensure ejected fluid is collected in a jar or waste rag.

'Brake Warning' light should illuminate.

Close bleed nipple.

Release and re-apply foot pressure to brake pedal.

'Brake Warning' light should extinguish.

Switch off engine and apply handbrake.

Top-up brake fluid reservoir.

Should warning light fail to illuminate when fluid is released, repeat test operations.

A new P.D.W.A. unit is required if warning light fails to illuminate during repeat operation.

PRESSURE DIFFERENTIAL WARNING ACTUATOR

Check and reset   70.25.08

NOTE: Before commencing check and reset procedure ensure that car is adequately chocked and cars with automatic transmission have selector lever in 'P' or 'N' position.

Release handbrake: warning light should extinguish; if light remains illuminated carry out next operation.

Check brake reservoir fluid level, top up as necessary; if warning light remains illuminated, carry out remaining operation.

Disconnect electrical connector from P.D.W.A. Switch if warning light goes out P.D.W.A. has operated; if light remains illuminated check for 'short' in brake warning electrical circuit or a sticking reservoir fluid level switch.

NOTE: If P.D.W.A. unit has operated a major defect in the brake system is indicated.

Reset

Resetting of the P.D.W.A. unit is achieved automatically during bleeding of the brake system, which should only be carried out following rectification of defects that cause shuttle valve displacement.

BRAKE SERVO

Check and test procedure   70.50.05

The following tests on the vacuum system should only be carried out with the hydraulic braking system in a satisfactory condition.

Servo test and check

Jack up front of car and confirm one wheel turns freely. Start engine, allow vacuum to build up and apply brake pedal several times. It should be possible to rotate wheel immediately pedal is released. If brakes bind, a defect within the servo unit is indicated.

With engine running apply brake pedal several times and check operation of pedal. If response is sluggish, check condition of vacuum hoses and servo unit air filter.

Allow vacuum to build up, switch off engine and operate brake pedal, approximately two or three applications should be vacuum assisted; less indicates a leaking vacuum system or inoperative non-return valve.

Switch off engine and operate brake pedal several times to evacuate vacuum in system. Hold a light foot pressure on pedal and start engine. If servo is operating correctly, pedal will fall under existing foot pressure. If pedal remains stationary a leaking vacuum system is indicated.

HANDBRAKE CABLE

Adjust   70.35.10

The handbrake cable adjustment linkage is situated on the underside of the floor panel below the handbrake lever.

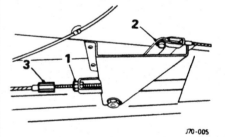

Fig. 6

To adjust, slacken the locknut (1, Fig. 6) at the forked end and remove the clevis pin (2, Fig. 6) securing the clevis to the handbrake lever.

Ensure that the levers at the calipers are in the 'Fully off' position by pressing towards the calipers.

Adjust the length of the cable by unscrewing the cable end (3, Fig. 6) to a point just short of where the caliper levers start to move.

Refit the clevis pin (2, Fig. 6) and tighten the locknut (1, Fig. 6).

Always use a new split pin to retain clevis pin. No attempt must be made to place the cable under tension otherwise handbrake may bind.

BRAKE PADS—REAR

Remove and refit   **70.40.03**

Service tool: Brake piston retractor tool
64932392

Removing

Jack up rear of car and place on stands, or raise
car on ramp.

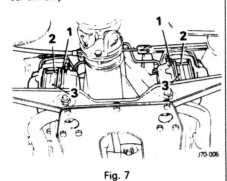

Fig. 7

Remove clips (1, Fig. 7) securing friction pad
mounting pins.
Remove mounting pins (2, Fig. 7).
Withdraw friction pads (3, Fig. 7).

Refitting

NOTE: It is advisable to reduce the level of
brake fluid in reservoir before fitting new pads.

If thickness of any pad is less than 4.0 mm (0.2
in) new pads MUST be fitted.
Using service tool 64932392 lever pistons into
cylinder bores. Fit new brake pads, locate with
mounting pins, ensure upper mounting pin
enters caliper from centre line of car and lower
mounting pin enters caliper from wheel side of
car.
Fit retaining clips to pad mounting pins.
Top up brake fluid reservoir.
Remove stands.
Run engine and apply brake pedal several times
until pedal feels solid.

BRAKE PADS—FRONT

Remove and refit   **70.40.02**

Service tool: Brake piston retractor tool
64932392

Removing

Remove road wheel.
Remove clips (1, Fig. 8) securing retaining pins.
Remove retaining pins (2, Fig. 8).
Recover anti-chatter springs (3, Fig. 8).
Withdraw worn pads (4, Fig. 8).

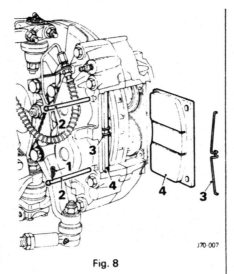

Fig. 8

Refitting

NOTE: It is advisable to reduce level of brake
fluid in reservoir before fitting new pads.

If thickness of any pad is less than 4 mm (0.2
in) new pads MUST be fitted.
Lever pistons into cylinder bores using service
tool 64932392.
Fit new brake pads to caliper.
Fit retaining pins.
Secure retaining pins with clips.
Fit anti-chatter springs.
Refit road wheel.
Top up brake fluid reservoir.
Run engine and apply brake pedal several times
until pedal feels solid.

HOSES

**General   fitting   and   removal
instructions**   **70.15.00**

Removing

Clean unions of hose to be removed.
Ensure pipe sealing plugs are at hand.
Fully release unions (1, Fig. 9) securing fluid
pipes to hose ends.

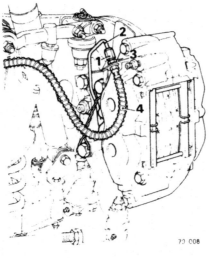

Fig. 9

Withdraw pipe unions (2, Fig. 9) from hose
ends, plug pipes to prevent loss of fluid and
ingress of dirt.
Remove locknuts (3, Fig. 9) securing hose ends
to mounting brackets.
Remove hose (4, Fig. 9) from car.

Inspection

After thoroughly cleaning hose examine for
any signs of deterioration or damage. If doubt
exists, a new hose must be fitted.
Thoroughly clean bore of hose by feeding compressed air into one end of hose.

Refitting

Reverse removal operations.
Bleed brakes, see operation 70.25.02.

PIPE

**General   fitting   and   removal
instructions**   **70.20.00**

Removing

Clean unions of pipe to be removed.
Ensure pipe sealing plugs are at hand.
Fully release pipe unions.
Withdraw pipe from car, plug open end of pipe
remaining on car.

Inspection

Thoroughly clean bore of pipe by feeding compressed air into one end.
After thoroughly cleaning pipe examine for any
sign of fracture or damage. If doubt exists, a
new pipe must be fitted.

DISC SHIELD—FRONT

Remove and refit   **70.10.18**

Removing

Remove road wheel.
Slacken upper bolt securing steering arm to
stub axle carrier.
Remove locking wire securing caliper mounting bolts.
Remove upper caliper mounting bolt.
Remove clips (1, Fig. 10) securing lower, secondary and main shield assemblies to lower
portion of stub axle carrier.
Withdraw lower and main shields (2, Fig. 10)
from disc assembly.
Remove brake feed pipe between flexible pipe
and caliper. Plug exposed ends to prevent
ingress of dirt and loss of fluid.

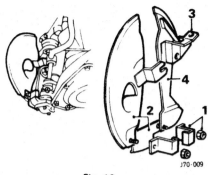

Fig. 10

Remove locknut (3, Fig. 10) securing brake hose union to secondary shield assembly; withdraw hose from securing bracket.
Withdraw shield (4, Fig. 10) from disc assembly.

Refitting

Reverse operations above, ensure brake hose is not twisted when securing to secondary shield bracket.
Fit new self-locking nuts to lower shield securing studs. Tighten steering arm bolt and caliper securing bolt to correct torque.
Refit road wheel.
Bleed brakes, see operation 70.25.02.

FRONT DISC

Remove and refit   70.10.10

Removing

Remove brake caliper friction pads (1, Fig. 11), see operation 70.40.02.
Remove front hub, see operation 60.25.01.
Remove locking wire (2, Fig. 11) from caliper mounting bolts.

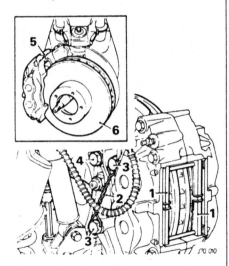

Fig. 11

Remove caliper mounting bolts (3, Fig. 11), recover and note position of shims located between steering arm and caliper.

Slacken bolt (4, Fig. 11) securing steering arm to hub carrier.
Gently easing caliper (5, Fig. 11) aside, remove disc (6, Fig. 11).

Inspection

Examine disc for cracks and heavy scoring; light scratches and scoring are not detrimental and may be ignored. If doubt exists a new disc should be fitted.

Refitting

If original disc is refitted reverse operations above and ensure caliper mounting bolts are tightened to the correct torque.
If new disc is fitted reverse operations above, ensuring mounting bolts are not wire locked.
Check gap between caliper abutments and disc face.
Gap on opposite sides of disc may differ by up to 0,25 mm (0.010 in) but gap on upper and lower abutment on same side of disc should be the same.
If disc is not central in caliper remove one caliper mounting bolt and add or withdraw shim required to centralize disc, refit caliper bolt.
Repeat above operation on remaining caliper mounting bolt.
Repeat gap check.
Tighten caliper mounting bolts to correct torque and wire lock.
Refit brake friction pads.

REAR DISCS

Remove and refit   70.10.11

Removing

Place car on ramp, remove road wheel adjacent to brake disc to be removed.
Place rear of car on stands.
Remove brake caliper, see operation 70.55.03.
Remove shock absorber lower fulcrum pin (1, Fig. 12), recover distance piece and washers.

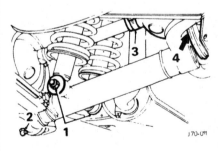

Fig. 12

Remove locking wire securing radius arm locking bolt (1, Fig. 13) and remove bolt.
Remove hub fulcrum shaft grease nipple (2, Fig. 12).
Place support blocks below hub.

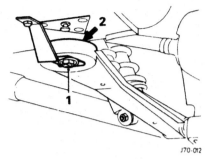

Fig. 13

Lower radius arm from spigot anchor point (2, Fig. 13).
Release clip (3, Fig. 12) securing inner universal joint cover, slide cover clear of joint.
Remove nuts securing universal joint to brake discs (4, Fig. 12).
Tap disc mounting bolts towards final drive unit.
Separate universal joint from brake disc, collect camber angle shims held on disc mounting bolts.
Jack up car sufficiently to allow removal of brake disc, lift out disc.

NOTE: Do not disturb shims mounted between final drive flange and brake disc.

Inspection

NOTE: The condition of discs are a vital factor in efficient functioning of the brakes.

Examine surface of disc, which should be smooth.
Scratches and light scoring are not detrimental after normal use.
Should doubt exist a new disc should be fitted.

Refitting

Locate new disc on mounting bolts, replace camber angle shims, fit universal joint over shims and tighten nuts to correct torque.
Check disc for run out, clamp dial test indicator to suspension unit cross-beam, position indicator rod against disc face and set reading to zero. Run out must not exceed 0,10 mm (0.004 in).
Offer brake caliper to mounting and secure with mounting bolts. Tighten to correct torque.
Check caliper centralization on brake disc. Dimensions between faces of disc and caliper abutments are to be equal within 0,25 mm (0.010 in). To adjust (if necessary) remove caliper and disc assembly, adding or withdrawing shims located between disc and axle unit output flange. Note thickness of shims added or withdrawn during this operation.

NOTE: On completion of centralization operation, (if necessary) add or withdraw a camber angle shim to size of centralization shim used in adjustment, e.g. if a 2,15 mm (0.06 in) shim was ADDED to centralization shims WITHDRAW same size shim from camber angle shims. If shims were WITHDRAWN in the centralization operation, ADD same size shim to camber angle shims. This operation corrects camber angle to that prior to the caliper centralization operation. *continued*

Replace inner universal joint cover.

NOTE: Prior to fitting radius arm to body spigot, wirebrush spigot and smear with grease.

Refit radius arm locking bolt.

Wire lock caliper mounting bolts.

NOTE: Before refitting brake friction pads check pads for wear. Minimum thickness 4.0 mm (0.2 in).

Fit brake friction pads to caliper.

Refit handbrake caliper.

Fit brake feed pipe to caliper, tighten connector at three way union.

Refit suspension unit tie plate.

Bleed brakes.

Refit road wheel.

Check and if necessary adjust camber angle.

THREE-WAY CONNECTOR— REAR

Remove and refit   **70.15.34**

Removing

Disconnect three feed pipe unions (1, Fig. 14) at connector, plug pipes to prevent loss of fluid and ingress of dirt.

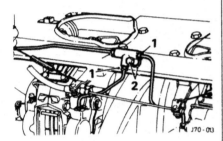

Fig. 14

Remove nut and bolt (2, Fig. 14) securing three-way connector to suspension unit, collect spacer and connector.

Refitting

Reverse removal operations, tightening nuts to correct torque and bleed system.

PRESSURE DIFFERENTIAL WARNING ACTUATOR

Remove and refit   **70.25.13**

Removing

Disconnect battery.

Remove air cleaner cover and element where necessary to improve access (on R.H.D. cars only).

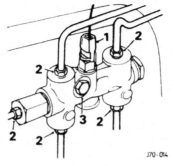

Fig. 15

Disconnect electrical lead (1, Fig. 15) from P.D.W.A. switch.

Disconnect all feed pipes (2, Fig. 15) from P.D.W.A. Plug pipes and P.D.W.A. unions to prevent loss of fluid and ingress of dirt.

Remove nut and bolt (3, Fig. 15) securing P.D.W.A. to wing valance.

Lift P.D.W.A. unit from car.

Refitting

Reverse operations above and bleed brakes.

TANDEM MASTER CYLINDER

Remove and refit   **70.30.08**

Removing

Disconnect battery.

Remove reservoir cap and switch assembly (1, Fig. 16).

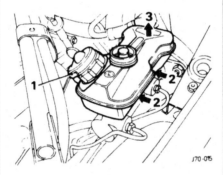

Fig. 16

Detach two spring clips and withdraw two retaining pins (2, Fig. 16).

Place suitable container in position to catch fluid.

Pull reservoir vertically away from master cylinder (3, Fig. 16).

Fit closing plugs to grommets in master cylinder ports.

NOTE: Before a master cylinder is removed from a direct acting servo it is imperative that the brake pedal is depressed and released at least 10 times. This is to ensure that no vacuum exists to operate the servo.

Operation of the servo when the master cylinder is not in place can cause its mechanism to travel past its normal limit. This can damage the servo beyond repair.

Disconnect master cylinder fluid delivery pipes, plug pipes to prevent ingress of dirt.

Remove nuts and washers securing master cylinder to servo unit.

Lift master cylinder from mounting studs.

Refitting

Fit replacement master cylinder over studs, replace washers and nuts, and tighten to correct torque.

Unplug delivery pipes and connect to master cylinder.

Prise grommets from master cylinder ports to reservoir.

Inspect ports for complete cleanliness and fit new grommets, lubricating them with brake fluid before insertion.

Press replacement reservoir into position.

Replace retaining pins and spring clips.

Fill reservoir to bottom of neck with recommended fluid (Castrol-Girling Universal Brake and Clutch Fluid).

Reconnect battery and bleed brakes.

FLUID RESERVOIR

Remove and refit   **70.30.16**

Removing

Disconnect battery.

Remove reservoir cap and switch assembly (1, Fig. 16).

Detach two spring clips and withdraw two retaining pins (2, Fig. 16).

Place suitable container in position to catch fluid.

Pull reservoir vertically away from master cylinder (3, Fig. 16).

Fit closing plugs to grommets in master cylinder ports.

Refitting

Prise grommets from master cylinder ports.

Inspect ports for complete cleanliness and fit new grommets, lubricating them with brake fluid before insertion.

Press replacement reservoir into position.

Replace retaining pins and spring clips.

Fill reservoir to bottom of neck with recommended fluid (Castrol-Girling Universal Brake and Clutch Fluid).

Reconnect battery.

Bleed brakes.

70—10

PEDAL BOX

Remove and refit   70.35.03

Removing

Disconnect battery.
Disconnect fluid delivery pipes from master cylinder, tape or plug pipes to prevent loss of fluid and ingress of dirt.
Peel cover from brake reservoir cap and disconnect leads from fluid level indicator switch.

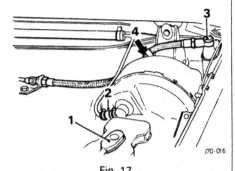

Fig. 17

Slacken clip (2, Fig. 17) securing brake vacuum hose to servo adaptor, slide hose from adaptor.

LEFT-HAND DRIVE CARS—Manual Transmission Only

Remove banjo bolt (3, Fig. 17) securing clutch slave cylinder hose to clutch master cylinder, recover copper washers and tape-up banjo union and master cylinder outlet.
Remove self-locking nut (4, Fig. 17) securing slave cylinder hose to pedal box; position hose clear of servo assembly.

RIGHT-HAND DRIVE CARS—Manual Transmission Only

Release nuts (1, Fig. 18) securing clutch feed pipe to master cylinder and slave cylinder hose, remove pipe from car. Tape-up open ends of pipe and master cylinder.

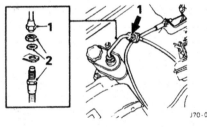

Fig. 18

Remove locknut (2, Fig. 18) securing slave cylinder hose to reservoir mounting bracket, disengage hose from bracket and tape-up open end of hose.
Remove self-locking nut (adjacent to clutch pedal housing) securing steering column lower mounting bracket to pedal box.

All Cars

Remove bolt, oval washer and spacer (1, Fig. 19) securing upper portion of pedal box to bulkhead.
Position driver's seat to rear as far as possible, remove seat cushion and lift out footwell carpets.
Remove brake stop light switch.

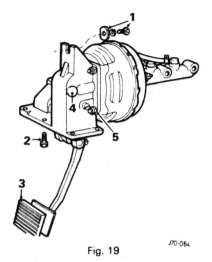

Fig. 19

Remove five bolts (2, Fig. 19) (right-hand drive cars), six bolts (left-hand drive cars), flat washers and spring washers securing pedal box base to bulkhead, recover clips retaining footwell noise absorbing mats.
Remove rubber pad (3, Fig. 19) from brake pedal.

Manual Transmission Cars Only

Remove nut and spring washer securing clutch pedal to operating lever, lift pedal from lever.

All Cars

Carefully raise servo unit, pedal box and master cylinder, draw complete assembly forward and lift from car.
Prise two rubber sealing plugs (4, Fig. 19) from sides of pedal box.
Remove split pin, washer and clevis pin securing brake pedal lever to servo operating rod.
Remove nuts (5, Fig. 19) securing pedal box to servo unit. Detach pedal box from servo unit.

Refitting

Reverse removal operations; fit new split pin to servo rod clevis pin.
Bleed clutch (manual transmission cars).
Bleed brakes.

HANDBRAKE LEVER ASSEMBLY

Remove and refit   70.35.08

Removing

Disconnect battery.
Disconnect handbrake operating cable (1, Fig. 20) at under floor lever.

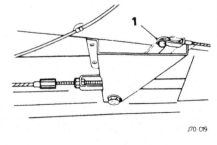

Fig. 20

Remove split pin, washer and clevis pin securing nylon roller to mounting bracket, withdraw roller.
Remove protective cover from nut securing nylon roller mounting bracket.
Remove nut securing roller mounting bracket.
Remove driver's side dash liner.
Remove steering column trim cover.

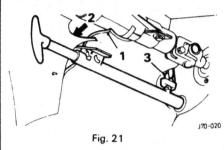

Fig. 21

Peel back trim (1, Fig. 21) covering handbrake mounting bracket securing bolts.
Remove bolts (2, Fig. 21) securing handbrake assembly to footwell side panel.
Noting terminal locations detach electrical leads (3, Fig. 21) from handbrake warning switch.

NOTE: If new handbrake assembly is to be fitted, remove warning switch from old handbrake.
Fit and adjust warning switch to new handbrake assembly.

Refitting

Reverse removal operations; fit new split pins to all clevis pins.

SERVO ASSEMBLY

Remove and refit   70.50.01

Removing

Remove pedal box.
Remove nuts securing master cylinder to servo unit.
Detach master cylinder and vacuum pipe support bracket from servo unit.
Prise vacuum pipe connector from servo, recover rubber sealing washer.

Refitting

Reverse above operations, fit new sealing rubber to vacuum pipe connector.

HANDBRAKE CABLE ASSEMBLY

Remove and refit   **70.35.16**

Removing

Set handbrake fully off.

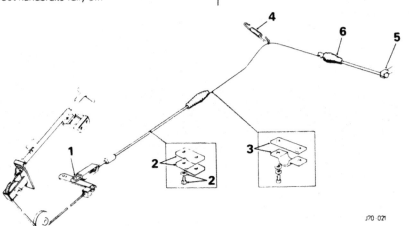

Fig. 22

Remove split pin, flat washer and clevis pin (1, Fig. 22) securing front yoke to lever.

Remove guide (2, Fig. 22) securing handbrake inner cable to underside of car body.

Remove guide (3, Fig. 22) securing outer cable to underside of car body.

Release guide spring (4, Fig. 22) from outer cable.

Remove split pin, flat washer and clevis pin (5, Fig. 22) securing rear yoke to handbrake caliper operating lever.

Slide rubber grommet (6, Fig. 22) clear of opposite handbrake lever, detach cable from lever.

Remove cable from car.

Refitting

Reverse removal operations, fit new split pins to clevis pins.

Check handbrake and adjust if necessary.

NON-RETURN VALVE

Remove and refit   **70.50.15**

Removing

Slacken clips securing vacuum hoses to non-return valve.

Pull hoses from non-return valve, lift valve from car.

Refitting

Prior to refitting, blow through valve to test one way action.

Ensuring arrow stamped on barrel of valve points away from manifold vacuum hose, fit valve to hoses.

Fully tighten hose securing clips.

FRONT CALIPER

Remove and refit   **70.55.02**

Removing

Slacken feed pipe union at caliper and disconnect feed pipe union (1, Fig. 23) at support bracket; plug pipe to prevent loss of fluid and ingress of dirt.

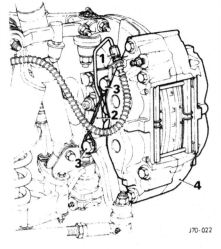

Fig. 23

Remove locking wire (2, Fig. 23) securing caliper mounting bolts.

CAUTION: Do not under any circumstances remove the four setbolts securing the two halves of caliper together.

Remove caliper mounting bolts (3, Fig. 23), note position and number of shims located between steering arm and caliper.

Withdraw caliper (4, Fig. 23) from disc.

Refitting

If original caliper is to be refitted, reverse removal operations, ensuring that shims are correctly replaced; if new caliper is fitted, carry out caliper/disc centralization.

Tighten mounting bolts to correct torque.

Bleed brakes.

REAR CALIPER

Remove and refit   **70.55.03**

Removing

Remove handbrake caliper.

Slacken caliper feed pipe union at three-way connector (1, Fig. 24).

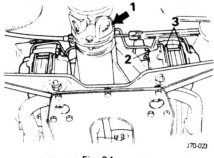

Fig. 24

Disconnect feed pipe at caliper (2, Fig. 24), swing pipe clear of caliper, plug holes to prevent ingress of dirt and loss of fluid.

Remove brake friction pads (3, Fig. 24).

Remove lock wire securing caliper mounting bolts.

CAUTION: Do not under any circumstances remove the four set bolts securing the two halves of caliper together.

Remove caliper mounting bolts.

Slide caliper around brake disc and withdraw through gap exposed by removal of tie plate.

Refitting

Offer caliper to mountings, fit mounting bolts and tighten to the correct torque.

Check that caliper is central of disc. Adjust as necessary, by adding or withdrawing brake disc shims.

NOTE: If adjustment is carried out camber angle must be checked as a final operation.

Wire lock caliper mounting bolts.

NOTE: Prior to fitting friction pads, check pads for wear, the minimum thickness being 4.0 mm (0.2 in)

Replace pads, feed pipe and handbrake caliper.

Bleed brakes.

70—12

HANDBRAKE MECHANISM

Remove and refit   70.55.04

Removing

Place car on ramp; remove nuts and bolts securing tie plate to suspension unit, lift off tie plate.
Ensure handbrake is fully off. Remove clevis pin securing handbrake cable to caliper operating lever.
Detach handbrake cable from remaining operating lever (1, Fig. 25).

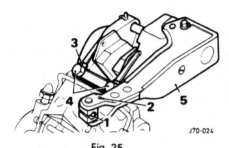

Fig. 25

Unclip return spring from handbrake operating lever (2, Fig. 25).
Bend back locking tabs (3, Fig. 25) securing handbrake caliper mounting bolts. Remove mounting bolts, tab washer and retraction lever (4, Fig. 25).
Slide caliper (5, Fig. 25) around brake disc and withdraw through gap exposed by removal of tie plate.

Refitting

If new pads are fitted, or mechanism overhauled, adjust caliper. Holding one pad carrier, rotate remaining one to give a dimension of 19,0 mm (0.75 in) between pad surfaces.
Refit caliper, mounting bolts and locking nuts. Operate actuating lever until adjuster ratchet ceases to click, this adjusts pads to correct clearance.
Reverse remaining removal operations.

HANDBRAKE PADS

Remove and refit   70.40.04

Removing

Remove handbrake caliper.
Remove nut and spring washer (1, Fig. 26) securing pads to brake pad carriers, remove pads (2, Fig. 26).

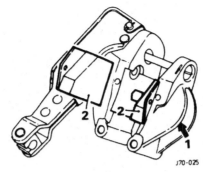

Fig. 26

Refitting

Holding one pad carrier, wind remaining one out two or three turns.
Fit new brake pads to carrier using new nut and spring washer.
Refit handbrake caliper.
Operate handbrake several times to adjust pads to correct clearance.

RESERVAC TANK (when fitted)

Remove and refit   70.50.04

Removing

Jack up car, support on stands, and remove right hand front wheel.
Remove horn relay (1, Fig. 27).

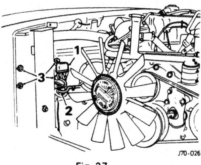

Fig. 27

Disconnect vacuum hose (2, Fig. 27) from reservac tank.
Remove nuts (3, Fig. 27) from securing straps, mounting reservac to wing valance.

Refitting

Reverse removal operations.

TANDEM MASTER CYLINDER

Overhaul   70.30.09

Remove master cylinder.

NOTE: Overhaul of the master cylinder should be carried out with the work area, tools and hands in a clean condition.

Dismantling

Using suitable screwdriver, lever sealing grommets (1, Fig. 28) from master cylinder.

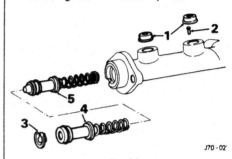

Fig. 28

Press primary piston into bore of cylinder and withdraw secondary piston stop pin (2, Fig. 28) from forward grommet housing.
Remove circlip (3, Fig. 28).
Tap flange end of cylinder on wooden block to remove primary piston and spring (4, Fig. 28), secondary piston and spring (5, Fig. 28).
It may prove necessary to feed compressed air into cylinder front delivery port.

NOTE: Once the piston assemblies are withdrawn the appropriate piston and spring must be kept together.
In the event of the springs being mixed, the secondary piston spring can be easily identified, it being slightly thicker and longer than the primary spring.

Remove spring, spring seat, recuperating seal and washer from secondary piston (1, Fig. 29).

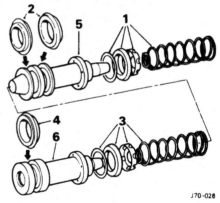

Fig. 29

Carefully prise seals (2, Fig. 29) from rear of secondary piston.
Remove spring, spring seat, recuperating seal and washer from primary piston (3, Fig. 29).
Carefully prise seal (4, Fig. 29) from rear of primary piston.
Discard all old seals and associated items that will be replaced by those contained within service kit.

continued

70—13

Inspection

Clean all parts with Girling cleaning fluid and dry with lint-free cloth.
Examine piston and bore of cylinder for visible score marks and corrosion.
If doubt exists as to condition of components, replace suspect item.

Reassembling

WARNING: To help prevent damage it is essential that generous amounts of clean brake fluid are used at all stages of seal assembly.

Carefully fit inner seal of secondary piston in locating groove, ensure seal lip faces forwards.
Fit remaining seal in locating groove, ensure seal lip faces towards primary piston, i.e. in opposite direction to seal.
Fit washer, recuperating seal, spring seat and spring over forward end of secondary piston.
Carefully fit rear seal of primary piston in locating groove, ensure seal lip faces forward, i.e. away from circlip.
Fit washer, recuperating seal, spring seat and spring over forward end of primary piston.
Generously lubricate bore of master cylinder with clean brake fluid.

WARNING: Adherence to the following instruction is vitally important. Failure to comply will result in damaged piston seals.

Secure master cylinder in vice and generously lubricate piston seals in new brake fluid. Offer secondary piston assembly (5, Fig. 29) to cylinder till recuperating seal rests centrally in mouth of cylinder. Ensuring seal is not trapped, slowly rotate and rock piston assembly whilst GENTLY introducing piston into cylinder bore. Once recuperating seal enters bore of cylinder SLOWLY push piston into bore in one continuous movement.
Repeat lubrication and insertion with primary piston and spring (6, Fig. 29).
Pressing piston into bore of cylinder, fit circlip (3, Fig. 28).
Press primary piston into bore of cylinder to full extent, fit secondary piston stop pin (2, Fig. 28).
Fit sealing grommets (1, Fig. 28), master cylinder, lubricating with brake fluid.
Refit master cylinder.

PEDAL BOX

Overhaul   70.35.04

Remove pedal box, see operation 70.35.03.

Dismantling

Carefully drift lower pivot shaft (1, Fig. 30) from pedal box, recover nylon washers from either side of lever boss (2, Fig. 30).

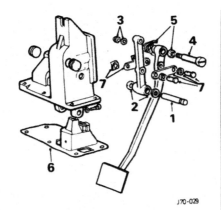

Fig. 30

Remove self-locking nut and flat washer (3, Fig. 30) securing pedal lever upper pivot shaft.
Using narrow drift, carefully remove upper pivot shaft (4, Fig. 30) from lever and pedal box.
Withdraw pedal lever assembly from box, recover nylon washers and return spring (5, Fig. 30).
Remove rubber boot (6, Fig. 30) by turning boot inside out and withdrawing over upper portion of levers.
Remove retaining clips, clevis pins and spring washers (7, Fig. 30) securing link arms to pedal levers.

Inspection

Clean all pedal lever components.
Examine pivot shafts, clevis pins, bushes and thrust washers for wear. Should doubt exist as to condition a new component must be fitted.

Reassembling

Slightly coat pivot shafts and thrust washers with grease.
Fit link arms to pedal lever, secure with clevis pins, spring washers and retaining clips (1, Fig. 31).

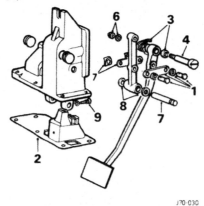

Fig. 31

Slide rubber boot (2, Fig. 31) over pedal levers, ensure that hole with side extensions fits over long pedal lever.
Position pedal lever return spring (3, Fig. 31) over extended boss of long lever, raise neck of rubber boot and locate spring hook over lever.

Position upper pivot shaft (4, Fig. 31) in one side of pedal box, enter shaft sufficient to allow nylon washer to locate on threaded portion of shaft.
Enter lever assembly into box, ensure return spring leg locates in guide channel.
Align pedal lever upper boss with upper shaft.
Enter shaft into boss, adjust nylon washer to locate over shaft.
Position second nylon washer between pedal box and extended boss of pedal lever.
Carefully push upper shaft fully home.
Position flat washer over shaft and secure with new locknut (6, Fig. 31).
Check operation of pedal lever, ensure lever operates freely.
Align small lever pivot boss with pedal box shaft mountings.
Ensuring that the groove in the lower pivot shaft aligns with the retaining pin locating hole, enter the shaft (7, Fig. 31) into the box.
Locate nylon washers (8, Fig. 31) on either side of lever boss and push pivot shaft fully home.
Align pivot shaft groove with retaining pin hole, test fit retaining pin (9, Fig. 31).
Check condition of servo/pedal box gasket and if necessary fit new gasket.
Refit pedal box.

SERVO ASSEMBLY

Overhaul   70.50.06

The servo assembly is a sealed unit and overhaul is not possible. Should the operation of the servo unit deteriorate to an extent where braking efficiency is affected, a replacement unit must be fitted.

BRAKE CALIPER—FRONT

Overhaul   70.55.13

Service tool: Piston clamp 18G 672

Remove front friction pads.
Remove front caliper.
Thoroughly clean caliper with Girling brake cleaner.

Dismantling

CAUTION: Under no circumstances must caliper halves be separated.

Remove spring clips (1, Fig. 32) securing piston dust covers.
Remove covers (2, Fig. 32) from pistons (3, Fig. 32).
Fit piston clamp to any half of caliper.
To expel pistons carefully feed compressed air into caliper fluid inlet port.
Remove pistons from caliper.

WARNING: Extreme care must be taken not to damage cylinder bore when extracting seals.

70—14

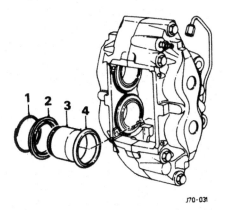

Fig. 32

Carefully prise seals (4, Fig. 32) from recess in cylinder wall.

Inspection

Using Girling brake cleaner thoroughly clean piston, cylinder bore and seal groove.
Examine piston and cylinder bore for signs of corrosion or scratches. Should doubt exist as to condition a new component must be fitted.

Assembling

Coat new seals in Girling brake disc lubricant.
Using fingers ONLY fit new seals (1, Fig. 33) to recess in cylinder bore.

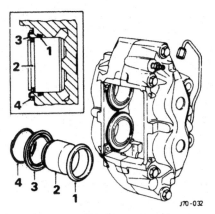

Fig. 33

Coat piston in clean disc brake lubricant.
Enter pistons (2, Fig. 33) into cylinder bores.
Fit new dust covers (3, Fig. 33) over pistons.
Push pistons fully home.
Locate dust cover over rim in caliper, secure with spring clips (4, Fig. 33).
Release piston clamp and fit to opposite half of caliper.
Repeat applicable operations on remaining two pistons.
Refit caliper to car.

BRAKE CALIPER—REAR

Overhaul   70.55.14

Service tool: Piston clamp 18G 672

Remove rear brake caliper, see operation 70.55.03.
Thoroughly clean caliper using Girling cleaning fluid.

Dismantling

CAUTION: Under no circumstances must the caliper halves be separated.

Fit piston clamp to retain one piston in location. Carefully feed compressed air into caliper fluid inlet port expelling one piston (3, Fig. 34).

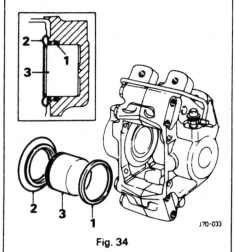

Fig. 34

Remove dust seal (2, Fig. 34) from piston and caliper cylinder bore.

WARNING: Extreme care must be taken not to damage the cylinder bore when extracting seal.

Carefully prise seal (1, Fig. 34) from recess in cylinder bore.

Inspection

Using Girling brake cleaner thoroughly clean piston, cylinder bore and seal recess.
Examine piston and cylinder for signs of corrosion or scratches. Should doubt exist as to condition, a new component must be fitted.

Assembly

Coat new seal with Girling disc brake lubricant.
Using 'fingers' ONLY fit new seal to recess in cylinder bore.
Locate dust cover in outer groove in cylinder bore.
Coat piston in clean disc brake lubricant.
Enter piston into cylinder bore through dust seal.
Locate dust seal into groove in piston.

Release piston clamp and fit to opposite side of caliper to press 'services' piston fully home.
Repeat applicable operations on remaining cylinder piston.
Remove piston clamp.
Refit rear brake caliper to car.

PAGE INTENTIONALLY LEFT BLANK

JAGUAR

Daimler

**Containing
Sections**

76 BODY

77 BODY PANEL REPAIRS

SERIES III
SERVICE MANUAL

INTRODUCTION

This Service Manual covers the Jaguar Series 3 and Daimler Series 3 range of vehicles. It is primarily designed to assist skilled technicians in the efficient repair and maintenance of Jaguar and Daimler vehicles.

Using the appropriate service tools and carrying out the procedures as detailed will enable the operations to be completed within the time stated in the 'Repair Operation Times'.

The Service Manual has been produced in 13 separate sections; this allows the information to be distributed throughout the specialist areas of the modern service facility.

A table of contents in section 1 lists the major components and systems together with the section and book numbers. The cover of each book depicts graphically and numerically the sections contained within that book. Each section starts with a list of operations in alphabetical order.

The title page of each book carries the part numbers required to order replacement books, binders or complete Service Manuals. This can be done through the normal channels.

Operation Numbering

A master index of numbered operations has been compiled for universal application to all vehicles manufactured by Jaguar Cars Ltd., and therefore, because of the different specifications of various models, continuity of the numbering sequence cannot be maintained throughout this manual.

Each operation described in this manual is allocated a number from the master index and cross-refers with an identical number in the 'Repair Operation Times'. The number consists of six digits arranged in three pairs.

Each operation is laid out in the sequence required to complete the operation in the minimum time, as specified in the 'Repair Operation Times'.

Service Tools

Where performance of an operation requires the use of a service tool, the tool number is quoted under the operation heading and is repeated in, following, the instruction involving its use. A list of all necessary tools is included in section 1, number 99.

References

References to the left- or right-hand side in the manual are made when viewing from the rear. With the engine and gearbox assembly removed the timing cover end of the engine is referred to as the front. A key to abbreviations and symbols is given in section 1, number 01.

REPAIRS AND REPLACEMENTS

When service parts are required it is essential that only genuine Jaguar/Daimler or Unipart replacements are used. Attention is particularly drawn to the following points concerning repairs and the fitting of replacement parts and accessories.

1.   Safety features embodied in the vehicle may be impaired if other than genuine parts are fitted. In certain territories, legislation prohibits the fitting of parts not to the vehicle manufacturer's specification.

2.   Torque wrench setting figures given in this Service Manual must be strictly adhered to.

3.   Locking devices, where specified, must be fitted. If the efficiency of a locking device is impaired during removal it must be replaced.

4.   Owners purchasing accessories while travelling abroad should ensure that the accessory and its fitted location on the vehicle conform to mandatory requirements existing in their country of origin.

5.   The vehicle warranty may be invalidated by the fitting of other than genuine Jaguar/Daimler or Unipart parts. All Jaguar/Daimler and Unipart replacements have the full backing of the factory warranty.

6.   Jaguar/Daimler Dealers are obliged to supply only genuine service parts.

SPECIFICATION

Purchasers are advised that the specification details set out in this Manual apply to a range of vehicles and not to any one. For the specification of a particular vehicle, purchasers should consult their Dealer.

The Manufacturers reserve the right to vary their specifications with or without notice, and at such times and in such manner as they think fit. Major as well as minor changes may be involved in accordance with the Manufacturer's policy of constant product improvement.

Whilst every effort is made to ensure the accuracy of the particulars contained in this Manual, neither the Manufacturer nor the Dealer, by whom this Manual is supplied, shall in any circumstances be held liable for any inaccuracy or the consequences thereof.

CONTENTS

continued

continued

76—2

ALIGNMENT CHECK

Service tool: Body alignment jig 700
Adaptors: J700-11; J700-18; J700-24; J700-35, J700-401; J700-402; J700-1148; S700-1111/2 J700-37

Data check   **76.10.01**

NOTE: The datum line is established by positioning the car (unladen, correct tyre pressures and fuel tanks full) on a flat surface and rolling the car forward approximately 12 m (40 ft). The datum line being 33,3 cm (13.12 in) above ground level at front and 33,8 cm (13.31 in) at rear, each measurement being taken through the centre line of wheel hubs.

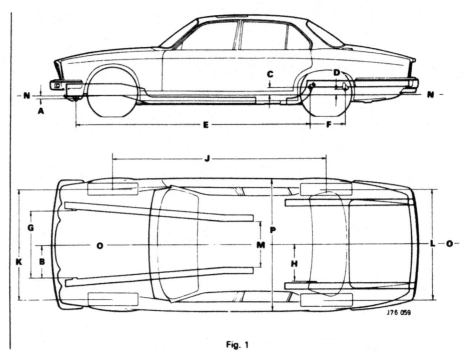

Fig. 1

SYMBOL	MEASUREMENT TAKEN FROM	cm	in
A	Front suspension mounting point to datum line	7,7	3.05
B	Inner face of front suspension mounting point to centre line of car	39,0	15.56
C	Rear suspension front lower mounting point to datum line	11,5	4.54
D	Rear suspension rear lower mounting point to datum line	11,0	4.34
E	Front suspension, front mounting point to rear suspension front lower mounting point	306,1	120.54
F	Rear suspension, front lower mounting point to rear suspension rear lower mounting point	33,05	13.06
G	Distance between inner faces of front suspension mounting points	79,4	31.12
H	Distance between inner face of rear suspension front mounting bracket and centre line of car	49,7	19.53
J	Wheelbase	288,5	112.87
K	Track (front)	147,0	58.0
L	Track (rear)	149,1	58.66
M	Distance between inner faces at rear of front chassis members	34,1	13.43
N	Horizontal datum line	—	—
O	Centre line of car	—	—
P	Overall width of car	176,3	69.6

SUN VISOR

Remove and refit   76.10.47

Removing

Disengage the visor from the retaining clip (1, Fig. 2).
Remove the screws (2, Fig. 2) securing the visor; withdraw the visor.

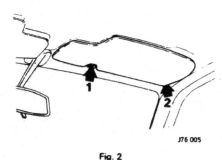

Fig. 2

Refitting

Place the visor in position and refit the retaining screws; engage the visor in the retaining clip.

INTERIOR MIRROR

Remove and refit   76.10.51

Removing

Grasp stem of mirror and pull rearwards to disengage retaining clip.

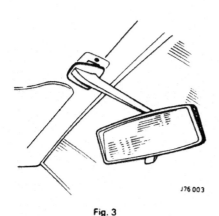

Fig. 3

Refitting

Position front of mirror stem in the mounting and strike underside of stem sharply with a rubber mallet to engage the retaining clip.

EXTERIOR MIRROR— MANUALLY OPERATED

Remove and refit   76.10.52

Removing

Adjust the mirror until access to the retaining screws is obtained.
Remove the two screws (1, Fig. 4) securing the adjusting lever surround to the door crash roll.
Partially withdraw the surround (2, Fig. 4) complete with operating lever away from the door crash roll.
Slacken the set screws (3, Fig. 4) securing the operating lever and withdraw lever from surround.
Remove the two screws (4, Fig. 4) securing the mirror to the door.

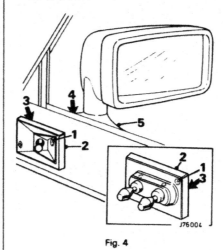

Fig. 4

Remove mirror and mounting pad (5, Fig. 4), carefully withdrawing the operating cable through the crash roll and door panel.

Refitting

Carefully feed the operating cable through the door panel and crash roll.
Refit the mirror and mounting pad.
Refit the lever to the surround and screw the assembly to the crash roll.
Test the mirror for correct operation.

EXTERIOR MIRROR— ELECTRICALLY OPERATED

Remove and refit   76.10.52

NOTE: Prior to carrying out this operation on Vanden Plas cars it will first be necessary to remove the door arm-rest and trim casing as described in operations 76.35.22 and 76.34.01.

Removing

Adjust the mirror until access to the retaining screws is obtained.
Disconnect the battery.
Remove the two screws (1, Fig. 4) securing the adjusting lever surround to the door crash roll (door pocket—Vanden Plas).
Partially withdraw the surround (2, Fig. 4) complete with operating levers and remove the setscrews (3, Fig. 4) securing the surround to the levers.
Remove the two screws (4, Fig. 4) securing the mirror to the door.

Vanden Plas only
Carefully feed operating levers into the door.

All Cars
Remove mirror and mounting pad (5, Fig. 4), carefully withdrawing the wiring harnesses and levers through the door panel.

Refitting

Carefully feed the operating levers and harnesses through the door panel and crash roll (door pocket—Vanden Plas).
Refit the mirror and mounting pad.
Refit the liners to the surround and screw the assembly to the crash roll/door pocket.

Vanden Plas only
Refit the door trim pad and arm-rest.

All Cars
Connect the battery and test mirror for correct operation.

FRONT TRIM CASING

Remove and refit   76.13.01

Removing

Remove the screws securing the tread plate (1, Fig. 5) to the sill; lift off the tread plate and packing piece.
Remove the underscuttle casing (2, Fig. 5) as described in operation 76.46.11.

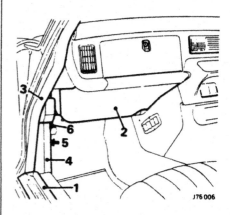

Fig. 5

Carefully prise approximately 200 mm (8.0 in) of draught welt (3, Fig. 5) off the flange adjacent to the trim casing.
Carefully peel edge of trim (4, Fig. 5) from tip of door aperture.
Remove two screws (5, Fig. 5) securing trim casing to side of footwell.
Disengage the casing from the air vent regulator control (6, Fig. 5) and withdraw casing from car.

Refitting

Coat lip of door aperture with suitable trim solution. Place trim casing in position and secure with two screws.
Fix edge of trim to lip of door aperture and clip draught welt to flange.
Refit the underscuttle casing, tread plate and packing piece.

'B' POST TRIM CASING—UPPER

Remove and refit   **76.13.08**

Removing

Prise the top edge of the plastic cover from the safety belt mounting; withdraw the cover (1, Fig. 6).
Remove the bolt, washers and spacer securing the safety belt mounting to the 'B' post.
Prise the interior light lens (2, Fig. 6) from the light fitting.
Starting at the bottom, carefully prise the trim casing from the 'B' post (3, Fig. 6).

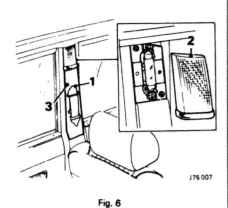

Fig. 6

Refitting

Ensure that the trim clips align with the holes in the 'B' post and refit the trim casing.
Clip the interior light lens into the light fitting.
Refit the safety belt mounting ensuring that the belt webbing is not kinked or twisted and refit the plastic cover.

'A' POST TRIM CASING AND CANT RAIL

Remove and refit   **76.13.10**

Removing

Remove two screws securing the escutcheon to the end of the crash roll; withdraw escutcheon (1, Fig. 7).
Prise draught welt away from the flange to gain access to the lower edge of the cant rail.
Carefully prise chrome finishers from ends of grab handle and remove the screws securing grab handle to cant rail (2, Fig. 7).
Remove screw and metal plate securing end of cant rail to body.
Working from rear of front of car, carefully prise off cant rail (3, Fig. 7).

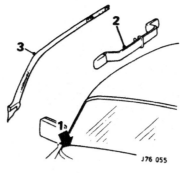

Fig. 7

Refitting

Check that trim clips and holes in body are in alignment and clip cant rail to body.
Refit screw and metal plate to secure end of cant rail.
Refit grab handle and chrome finishers.
Clip draught welt to flange and refit the escutcheon to the crash roll.

'B' POST TRIM CASING— LOWER

Remove and refit   **76.13.29**

Removing

Prise plastic cover (1, Fig. 8) off lower safety belt mounting bolt.
Remove the bolt, spacer and washer (2, Fig. 8) securing the belt mounting.
Prise the top edge of the plastic cover (3, Fig. 8) from the upper safety belt mounting; withdraw the cover.
Remove the bolt, washers and spacer securing the upper mounting to the 'B' post.
Prise the draught welt (4, Fig. 8) adjacent to the trim casing off the flange and remove the safety belt retaining strap (5, Fig. 8).

Starting from the bottom, prise the casing (6, Fig. 8) off the 'B' post.
Feed the safety belt through the slot and withdraw the casing.

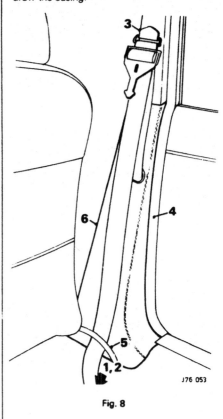

Fig. 8

Refitting

Ensuring that safety belt webbing is the correct way round, feed the belt through the slot in the trim casing.
Refit the trim casing and draught welt.
Attach the safety belt to the upper and lower mountings, refit the plastic covers and the retaining strap.

BONNET

Remove and refit   **76.16.01**

Removing

Place suitable protective material on the front bumper.
Disconnect the battery and the headlamp harnesses (1, Fig. 9) at the snap connectors.
Mark the relative positions of the bonnet and hinges.
Remove the nut and bolt (2, Fig. 9) securing the stay to the bonnet.

CAUTION: The bonnet must be adequately supported after removal of the stay.

Remove the bolts, spring and plain washers (3, Fig. 9) securing the bonnet to the hinge; lift off the bonnet.

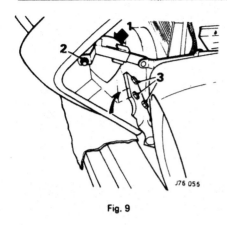

Fig. 9

Refitting

Position the bonnet on the hinges and fit but do not fully tighten the bolts, spring and plain washers.

Refit the bonnet stay and align the reference marks.

Tighten the securing bolts, close the bonnet and check fit of bonnet in aperture. If necessary, open the bonnet and reposition to obtain correct fit.

NOTE: The correct procedure for closing the bonnet is as follows:

Stand facing the front of the vehicle and grasp each end of the top of the radiator grille.

Lift front of bonnet smoothly; bonnet should now close. If difficulty is experienced however, reference should be made to operations 76.16.20 and 76.16.28.

Remove the protective covering from the front bumper.

Reconnect the headlamp harnesses and the battery; test the headlamps for correct operation.

BONNET HINGE

Remove and refit   **76.16.12**

Prior to carrying out this operation it will first be necessary to remove the bonnet and bonnet

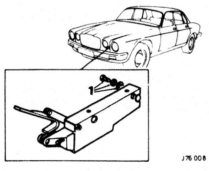

Fig. 10

assist spring(s) as detailed in operations 76.16.01 and 76.16.13.

Removing

Remove self-locking nuts, spacing washers and bolts (1, Fig. 10) securing the hinge; lift off the hinge.

Refitting

Place hinge in position and refit bolts, spacing washers and nuts.

Refit the bonnet assist spring(s) and the bonnet.

BONNET ASSIST SPRING

Remove and refit   **76.16.13**

Removing

Open the bonnet and place washers of suitable thickness between the spring coils (1, Fig. 11). Remove the bolt, spring and plain washer (2, Fig. 11) securing the spring retaining bracket to the right- or left-hand wing valance.

Remove the retaining bracket and disengage the spring from the lower bracket (3, Fig. 11). DO NOT remove the washers from the spring unless a new spring is to be fitted.

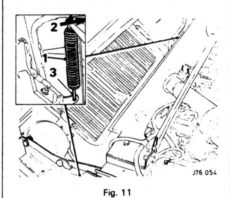

Fig. 11

Refitting

NOTE: If a new spring is to be fitted, it is advisable to pre-tension the spring by inserting washers of 1,6 mm (0.062 in) thickness between the coils of the spring.

Locate end of spring in lower bracket and refit the retaining bracket to the right-hand wing valance.

Remove the washers from the spring.

BONNET LOCK

Adjust   **76.16.20**

Slacken the locknut (1, Fig. 12) at the base of the striker peg (2, Fig. 12).

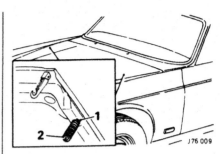

Fig. 12

Screw the peg in or out as required until, when closed, the bonnet is correctly positioned. Tighten the locknut and repeat for the other lock if necessary.

NOTE: The correct procedure for closing the bonnet is as follows:

Stand facing the front of the vehicle and grasp each end of the top of the radiator grille. Lift front of bonnet smoothly; bonnet should now close. If difficulty is experienced however, reference should be made to operations 76.16.20 and 76.16.28.

BONNET LOCK

Remove and refit   **76.16.21**

Removing

Slacken the clamp bolt (1, Fig. 13) securing the operating cable to the release lever on the bonnet lock platform.

Remove the bolts (2, Fig. 13), spring and plain washers securing the lock to the mounting bracket.

Disconnect the return spring from the release lever (3, Fig. 13) and withdraw the lock assembly.

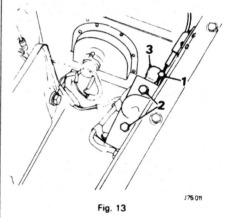

Fig. 13

Refitting

Position the lock under the mounting bracket and connect the return spring.

Bolt the lock to the mounting bracket and connect the operating cable to the release lever.

Check that when operating lever is pulled, the holes in the release lever and mounting plate are in alignment.

If holes do not align, refer to operation 76.16.28.

76—7

BONNET LOCK CONTROL CABLE

Adjust   **76.16.28**

Slacken the clamp bolt (1, Fig. 14) securing the operating cable to the release lever (2, Fig. 14) and push the lever forwards.
Tighten the clamp bolt and check the operation of the lock.

NOTE: A weak return spring will impair operation of the lock and if correct operation cannot be obtained by adjustment, the spring should be renewed.

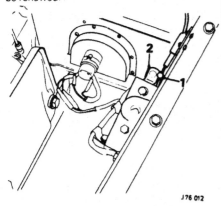

Fig. 14

After adjustment, check that when the operating lever is pulled, the holes in the release lever and mounting plate are in alignment; re-adjust as necessary.

BONNET LOCK CONTROL CABLE

Remove and refit   **76.16.29**

Removing

Slacken the clamp bolt (1, Fig. 15) securing the operating cable to the release lever on the bonnet lock platform. Repeat for other side.

Long operating cable only
Remove the cable bracket from the wing valance.

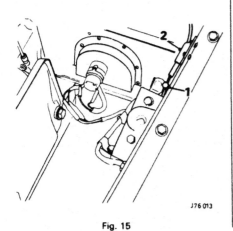

Fig. 15

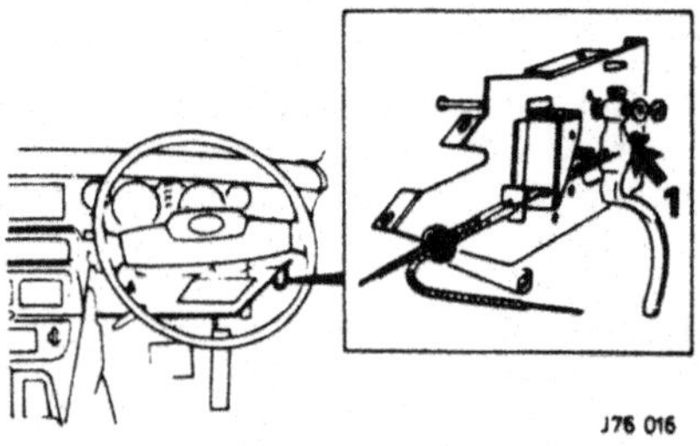

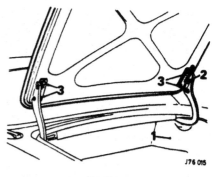

Fig. 16

Both cables

Withdraw the operating cable (1, Fig. 16) into the car; detach cables from lever.

Refitting

Ensure that clamping ends of operating cables are clean and that there are no loose strands of wire.
Feed cables through the operating lever and into the outer sleeves; pull cables taut and push operating lever forwards.

Long operating cable only
Refit the cable bracket to the wing valance.

Both cables
Connect the cables to the release levers, push the levers towards front of car and tighten the clamp bolts. Check that when operating lever is pulled, the holes in both release levers and mounting plate are in alignment. If holes do not align, refer to operation 76.16.28.

BONNET SAFETY CATCH

Remove and refit   **76.16.34**

Removing

Note fitted position of the catch return spring and remove the clevis pin retainer (1, Fig. 17). Withdraw the clevis pin (2, Fig. 17) followed by the safety catch (3, Fig. 17) return spring and washers.

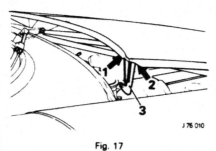

Fig. 17

Refitting

Locate the safety catch and spring in the attachment point; refit the clevis pin, washers and retainer.
Check that catch returns to the retaining position when released.

BOOT LID

Remove and refit   **76.19.01**

Removing

Disconnect the battery. Carefully prise the side trim casing from the boot and disconnect the harnesses at the snap connectors (1, Fig. 18). Attach strong string to the end of each harness, release each harness from the retaining clip (2, Fig. 18).
Carefully draw each harness through the grommets and detach the strings.
Mark the relative positions of the hinges to the boot lid mounting brackets, support the lid and remove the bolts, nuts, spring and plain washers (3, Fig. 18) securing the hinge to the brackets; lift off the lid.

Fig. 18

Refitting

Place boot lid in position and fit, but do not fully tighten, the retaining bolts.
Align reference marks and check that boot closes with 'push effort' only and is correctly positioned in the aperture.
Adjust boot lid if necessary by means of the slots in the hinge and mounting plates.
Tighten the securing bolts fully.
Attach each harness to the drawstring and carefully pull harness into position.
Clip harnesses to boot, remove the drawstring hinges and re-make the connections.
Re-connect the battery and check all rear lights for correct operation.
Refit the boot lid trim casing.

BOOT LID SEAL

Remove and refit   **76.19.06**

Removing

Remove the screws (1, Fig. 19) securing the sill cover-plate and ease seal off the flange.
Remove tape (2, Fig. 19) joining ends of seal and ease remainder of seal off the flange (3, Fig. 19).

76—8

Refitting

Position ends of seal in the centre of the boot sill and press approximately 15 cm (6.0 in) of each portion of seal on the lower flange.
Join ends of seal with adhesive tape.
Position seal equally around boot aperture and fit the corners of the seal to the flange.

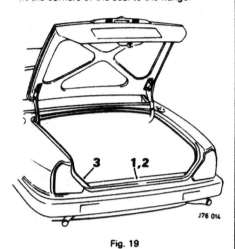

Fig. 19

Fit the remaining portion of the seal onto the flange taking care not to stretch the seal and ensuring that it is correctly bedded down.
Refit the screws to secure the sill cover-plate.
Cover the seal with french chalk and close boot. Check for transfer of chalk from seal to boot lid.
Where no transfer of chalk is evident, adjust the boot lid or striker, see operations 76.19.01. or 76.19.12.

BOOT LID HINGE

Remove and refit　　76.19.07

NOTE: Prior to removing the hinges, it will first be necessary to remove the boot lid as detailed in operation 76.19.01.

Removing

Remove four bolts, spring and plain washers securing the hinge to the body; withdraw the hinge.

Refitting

Place the hinge in position and secure with the four bolts, plain and spring washers.

BOOT LID LOCK

Remove and refit　　76.19.11

Removing

Release the clip (1, Fig. 20) securing the control link rod to the lock lever and detach the rod.
Remove the three screws (2, Fig. 20) securing the lock to the boot lid; withdraw the lock.

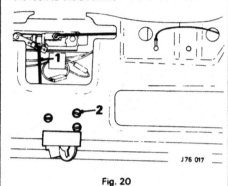

Fig. 20

Refitting

Position the lock in the boot lid and fit the securing screws.
Connect the control link rod to the lock lever and fit the retaining clip.
Check the lock for correct operation and that boot lid closes with 'push effort' only.
If boot does not close correctly, adjust the striker plate as detailed in operation 76.19.12.

BOOT LID LOCK STRIKER

Remove and refit　　76.19.12

Removing

Remove the screws securing the rear boot floor; lift out the floor.
Mark relative position (1, Fig. 21) of the striker to the clamp plate.
Slacken the bolts (2, Fig. 21) and remove the striker from the clamp plate.

Refitting

Position the striker in the clamp plate and check

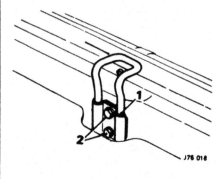

Fig. 21

that reference marks made during the dismantling procedure are in alignment.
Tighten the retaining bolts ensuring that the relative positions of striker and clamp plate remain unchanged.
Check that boot lid closes with 'push effort' only.
If boot does not close correctly, adjust the striker and re-check boot lid closure.
Refit the rear boot floor.

FRONT BUMPER

Remove and refit—European cars only　　76.22.08

Removing

Disconnect the battery.
Remove the nuts, spring and plain washers (1, Fig. 22) securing the chrome finisher to the side mounting brackets.
Prise up plastic covers (2, Fig. 22) located beneath each inner headlamp and remove the bolts, spring and plain washers (3, Fig. 22) securing the finisher to the inner mounting brackets; lift off finisher and recover upper apron.
Remove clips securing the rubber finishers (4, Fig. 22) to the bumper beam; withdraw the finishers.
Disconnect the light units by rotating the connector (5, Fig. 22) in an anti-clockwise direction.

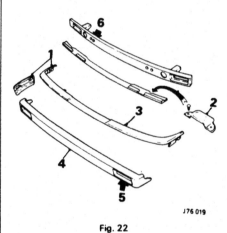

Fig. 22

Remove the bolts and spring washers (6, Fig. 22) securing the bumper beam to the mounting brackets; lift off the beam.

Refitting

Position the bumper beam on the mounting brackets and fit the retaining nuts and washers.
Connect the light units.
Refit the rubber and chrome finishers.
Connect the battery and check lights for correct operation.

76—9

FRONT BUMPER

Remove and refit—Non-European cars 76.22.08

Removing

Disconnect the battery.

Remove the nuts, spring and plain washers (1, Fig. 23) securing the chrome finisher to the side mounting brackets.

Prise up plastic covers (2, Fig. 23) located beneath each inner headlamp and remove the bolts, spring and plain washers (3, Fig. 23) securing the finisher to the inner mounting brackets; lift off finisher and recover upper apron.

Remove the bolts and washers (4, Fig. 23) securing the lower edge of rubber finisher to the energy absorbing beam and the trim clips (5, Fig. 23) securing the upper edge. Withdraw the finisher.

Remove the nuts and spring washers (6, Fig. 23) securing the side finishers to the mounting brackets; withdraw the finishers.

Disconnect the light units by rotating the connectors in an anti-clockwise direction.

Remove the nuts, bolts and washers (7, Fig. 23) securing the energy absorbing beam; lift off the beam.

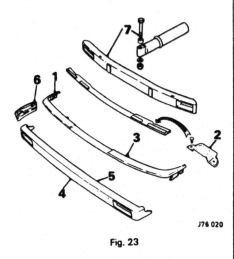

Fig. 23

J76 020

Refitting

Position beam on the energy absorbing struts, refit the nuts, bolts and washers.
Connect the light units.
Refit the rubber and chrome finishers.
Connect the battery and check lights for correct operation.

REAR BUMPER CENTRE SECTION

Remove and refit—All cars 76.22.12

Removing

On cars fitted with rear fog guard lights, disconnect the battery.

Remove clips (1, Fig. 24) securing rubber buffer (2, Fig. 24) and remove buffer.
Remove nuts and washers securing the rear beam (3, Fig. 24) to the body mounting brackets.
Remove the beam (4, Fig. 24).
Remove the nuts and washers securing rear blade to the side blades and the body (5, Fig. 24).
Remove the blade (6, Fig. 24) and recover the sealing strips.

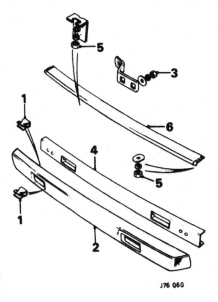

Fig. 24

J76 060

Refitting

Position rear beam on mounting brackets/ energy absorbing strut and fit retaining nuts and washers.
Conect fog guard lights (if fitted).
Refit rubber and chrome finishers ensuring that rubber sealing strips are interposed between centre and side finishers.
Connect the battery and check fog guard lights for correct operation.

REAR BUMPER SIDE SECTION

Remove and refit—All cars 76.22.13

Removing

Remove rear bumper beam as detailed in operation 76.22.12.
Remove the nuts and washers (1, Fig. 25) securing the rubber buffer (2, Fig. 25) to the quarter blade (3, Fig. 25).
Remove the nuts, washers and bolts (4, Fig. 25) securing the quarter blade to the body mounting brackets (5, Fig. 25).
Remove the blade (3, Fig. 25).

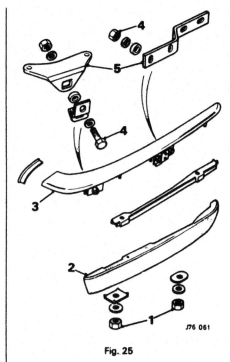

Fig. 25

J76 061

Refitting

Refit rubber and chrome finishers ensuring that rubber sealing strips are interposed between the side and centre chrome finishers.

ENERGY ABSORBING STRUT—FRONT

Remove and refit 76.22.31

Removing

Remove front energy absorbing beam.
Open bonnet and remove nut and flat washer (1, Fig. 26) securing strut to mounting tube.
Position energy absorbing beam mounting bolt (2, Fig. 26) in strut locating hole.
Gently tapping bolt head with hammer, remove strut from mounting tube.

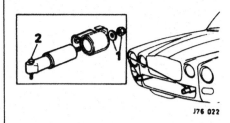

J76 022

Fig. 26

Inspection

Examine rubber sleeve in strut mounting tube for any signs of damage or deterioration. Reposition strut in mounting tube and check for any radial movement. If rubber sleeve is damaged or radial movement between strut and sleeve exists, a new rubber sleeve must be fitted.

Refitting

Place the beam mounting bolt in the strut locating hole. Position strut in the mounting and gently tap the bolt head until strut is correctly located in the mounting tube.
Refit the nut and flat washer.
Refit the energy absorbing beam.

ENERGY ABSORBING STRUT—REAR

Remove and refit   **76.22.32**

Removing

Remove rear energy absorbing beam.
Remove tail pipe and rear silencer.
Remove nut and plain washer (1, Fig. 27) securing strut to mounting tube.
Position energy absorbing beam mounting bolt (2, Fig. 27) in strut locating hole.
Gently tapping bolt head with hammer, remove strut from mounting tube.

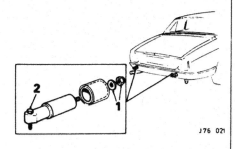

J76 021

Fig. 27

Inspection

Examine rubber sleeve in strut mounting tube for signs of damage or deterioration.
Reposition strut in mounting tube and check for any radial movement.
If rubber sleeve is damaged or radial play between strut and sleeve exists, a new sleeve must be fitted.

Refitting

Place the beam mounting belt in the strut locating hole.

Position strut in the mounting and gently tap the bolt head until strut is correctly located in the mounting tube.
Refit the nut and flat washer.
Refit the energy absorbing beam, tail pipe and rear silencer.

CONSOLE ASSEMBLY

Remove and refit   **76.25.01**

Removing

WARNING: Throughout the following operations it is imperative that the fitted positions of electrical harnesses and connections are noted prior to them being disconnected.

Disconnect the battery.
Remove the screws securing the ventilation louvres and side trim casings.
Pull each casing forward until it can be withdrawn.
Pull heater and ventilation knobs off the control spindles.
Remove threaded locking rings from heater and ventilation controls, withdraw panel sufficiently to gain access to centre parcel shelf securing screws; remove screws.

NOTE: Take care not to damage fibre optic elements.

Remove screws securing top of centre parcel shelf; withdraw shelf slightly and disconnect the sensor pipe.
Remove the cigar lighter and ashtrays.
Remove the screws securing the control escutcheon. Raise the escutcheon slightly and disconnect the cigar lighter, door lock and window switch harnesses. Lift off the escutcheon.
Remove the front seat cushions as described in operation 76.70.02.
Move both seats fully forwards.
Remove screws securing the rear window switch panel. Raise panel slightly and disconnect the wires from the switches and cigar lighter (where fitted). Remove the panel.
Remove the screws securing rear of the console to the transmission tunnel.
Disconnect the multi-plug connector at the rear of the console.
Raise rear of console and remove screws securing the wiring harness to the air duct.
Slide console towards rear of car until access to the electrical harness clipped to the front of the console is obtained. Release the harness from the clips.
Pass radio and ventilation panel through aperture in console at the same time sliding console away from the fascia.

CAUTION: Ensure that radio is adequately supported.

Disconnect the air ducting from the ventilation outlet.
Lift console over the transmission selector/gear lever.

Refitting

Position console over transmission selector/gear lever.
Connect air ducting to ventilation outlet.
Refit radio and panel.
Clip harness to front of console.
Slide console forwards until it is correctly positioned.
Raise rear of console slightly and attach the wiring harness to the air duct.
Connect the multi-plug and secure console to the transmission tunnel.
Connect rear window switches and cigar lighter (where fitted); refit the switch panel.
Refit the front seat cushions and move seats rearwards.
Connect window, door lock and cigar lighter harnesses; refit the control escutcheon.
Refit the centre parcel shelf, secure panel with locking rings.
Refit the heater and ventilation knobs.
Refit the side trim casings and ventilation louvres.
Connect the battery and test cigar lighter(s), window and door lock switches for correct operation.

CONSOLE SIDE CASING

Remove and refit   **76.25.02**

Removing

Remove two screws securing side casing and ventilation louvres (1, Fig. 28) slide casing towards front of car until it can be withdrawn.

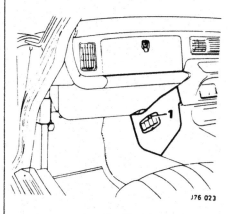

J76 023

Fig. 28

Refitting

Place casing towards front of footwell and slide casing rearwards until securing screw holes are in alignment; refit the ventilation louvre and securing screws.

AUTOMATIC TRANSMISSION SELECTOR QUADRANT

Remove and refit   **76.25.08**

Removing

Disconnect the battery.

Remove the screws securing the control escutcheon. Raise the escutcheon slightly and note the fitted position of the door lock, electric window and cigar lighter leads, disconnect the harnesses. Lift off the escutcheon.

Remove four nuts and washers securing quadrant cover to mounting plate (1, Fig. 29).

NOTE: Position of cable clips and electrical leads on quadrant cover mounting studs should be noted.

Detach cable feeding quadrant cover illumination bulb at snap connector.

Unscrew left- and right-hand sections of selector lever handle (2, Fig. 29).

Withdraw quadrant cover over selector lever (3, Fig. 29).

Noting location, detach electrical leads from reverse switch, inhibitor switch and seat belt warning switch (when fitted).

Remove screws securing fibre optic unit to bracket (4, Fig. 29).

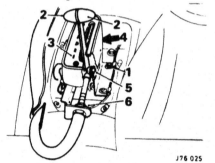

Fig. 29

Remove split pin and washer securing transmission operating cable to selector quadrant lever (5, Fig. 29), detach cable from mounting. Remove forward locknut securing operating cable to quadrant extension bracket (6, Fig. 29).

NOTE: Position of quadrant bracket on mounting studs should be marked for reference when refitting.

Remove three bolts and washers securing quadrant assembly to transmission tunnel cover.

Remove quadrant assembly from car.

Refitting

Place selector quadrant on transmission tunnel and fit the securing bolts.

Connect selector cable and check cable adjustment as detailed in operation 44.15.08.

Re-connect leads to starter inhibitor, reverse light and seat belt warning switches (when fitted).

Connect the quadrant illumination bulb.

Refit the quadrant cover, selector lever knob and control escutcheon.

Connect battery and test operation of cigar lighter, door lock and window switches.

FRONT DOOR

Remove and refit   **76.28.01**

Removing

Disconnect the battery.

Remove the door trim casing as detailed in operation 76.74.01 and the door pocket (Vanden Plas cars only), see operation 76.34.19.

If radio speaker is fitted, remove four screws securing speaker to door (1, Fig. 30). Noting position, detach leads from speaker unit, lift speaker from door—Not Vanden Plas cars.

Recover loom located in speaker mounting aperture.

Noting position of each electrical lead, detach leads from snap connectors.

Prise loom protective cover (2, Fig. 30) from forward face of door and 'A' post.

Withdraw loom and radio speaker cables through hole in forward face of door.

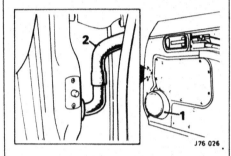

Fig. 30

Adequately supporting door, remove bolts securing door to hinges.

Remove door from hinges, recover packing pieces located between hinges and door.

Refitting

Fit bolts in hinges and place packing pieces over bolts, ensure door earthing strap is located behind one door securing bolt.

Fit door to hinges; do not fully tighten bolts.

Close door to correctly position and align with surrounding body.

Open door and fully tighten door mounting bolts.

Refit wiring loom, speaker cables and protective cover.

Refit radio speaker and door trim casing.

Connect the battery and test radio speaker, door lock and window switches for correct operation.

REAR DOOR

Remove and refit   **76.28.02**

Removing

Disconnect the battery and door trim casing as described in operation 76.34.04.

Locate cable loom inside door casing; noting fitted position, separate cables at snap connectors.

Prise loom protective cover from forward face of door.

Withdraw loom and radio speaker cables through hole in forward face of door.

Ensuring door is adequately supported, remove six bolts securing door to hinges.

Lift door from car.

Refitting

Fit bolts on hinges; ensure door earthing strap is located behind head of top inner hinge securing bolt.

Offer door to hinges, slightly tighten securing bolts.

Close door; ensure door fully closes and locks. Tighten door mounting bolts.

Refit wiring loom and speaker cables.

Insert loom cover into door panel.

Connect the battery, refit the door trim casing and radio speaker.

Check radio speaker, door lock and window switches for correct operation.

FRONT DOOR HINGES

Remove and refit   **76.28.42**

Removing

Remove door as detailed in operation 76.28.01.

Jack up front of car and position wheels on full left or right lock.

Remove five bolts and washers securing wheel arch diaphragm panel to wing and 'A' post, remove panel from car (1, Fig. 31).

Remove two bolts located inside wheel arch securing lower section of wing to sill (2, Fig. 31).

Remove two bolts between door hinges securing wing to 'A' post, recover door earthing strap fitted behind top bolt (3, Fig. 31).

Remove bolts, flat washers and spring washers securing top edge of wing to valance.

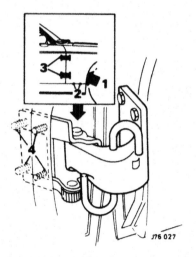

Fig. 31

76—12

Using suitable size wedge, separate lower portion of wing from body.
Remove eight bolts securing upper and lower hinges to 'A' post, lift hinges from car (4, Fig. 31).

Refitting

Coat mating faces of hinges with Bostik Sealant.
Refit hinges to body.
Bolt top edge of wing to valance.
Bolt wing to 'A' post and wheel arch.
Refit diaphragm panel, coat panel with underseal.
Refit the door.

REAR DOOR HINGES

Remove and refit   **76.28.43**

Removing

CAUTION: Throughout the following operation the door should be adequately supported in the closed position.

Remove bolts (1, Fig. 32) securing hinges to door and 'B—C' post, recover door earthing strap fitted to top hinge securing bolts.
Lift hinges (2, Fig. 32) from door.

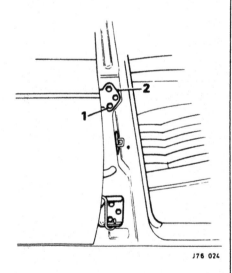

Fig. 32

Refitting

Coat mating faces of door hinges with Bostik Sealant.
Refit hinges and door.
Check that door closes correctly. If not, slacken hinge securing bolts, re-position door and re-tighten the bolts.

REAR DOOR GLASS

Remove and refit   **76.31.02**

Removing

Remove rear door trim casing as detailed in operation 76.34.03.
Prise chrome trim free from door glass frame.
Remove screw securing inner chrome trim to door glass frame, prise trim from frame (1, Fig. 34).

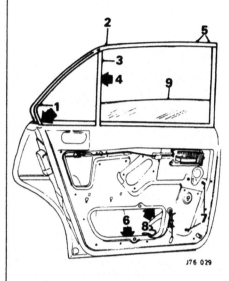

Fig. 34

Release rubber seal from door glass frame (2, Fig. 34).
Lower door glass and release upper portion of felt channel fitted to quarter-light (3, Fig. 34).
Remove screws exposed by removal of felt channel (4, Fig. 34).
Remove two screws adjacent to 'B-C' post securing vertical door glass frame to top glass frame and gently tap top glass frame free; lift frame from door (5, Fig. 34).
Remove screws securing glass buffer stop to door panel, lift buffer stop from door (6, Fig. 34).
Remove screw securing window lift mechanism to door panel (7, Fig. 34).
Disengage window lift arm from glass guide bracket (8, Fig. 34).
Withdraw glass from door (9, Fig. 34).
Remove guide bracket and seal from glass.

Refitting

Cut the Everseal strip (Part No. BD 47937) to make it 38 to 50 mm (1½ to 2 in) shorter than the bottom channel.
Thoroughly clean mating surfaces of channel, Everseal strip and door glass.
Fit the Everseal strip midway in the channel, i.e. with 19 to 25 mm (¾ to 1 in) between each end of the strip and the end of the channel.
Replace bottom channel, complete with strip, on door glass.

Fill the ends of the channel with Dow Corning Silastik 732 or a similar silicone sealant, using a hand-gunned cartridge. Allow time for sealant to cure before refitting door glass.
Locate new seal in correct position over glass.
Position lift arm guide bracket over seal; using mallet gently tap either side of guide until seal and guide are firmly secured to glass.
Refit guide bracket.
Position glass inside door.
Engage window lift arm in glass bracket.
Fit screw to secure lift mechanism to door panel.
Refit buffer stop.
Refit glass frame and felt channel.
Refit rubber seal and chrome trim.
Refit trim casing.

REAR DOOR QUARTER-LIGHT

Remove and refit   **76.31.31**

Removing

Remove rear door trim casing as detailed in operation 76.34.04.
Prise chrome trim free from quarter-light frame (1, Fig. 35).
Prise chrome beading from base of quarter-light (2, Fig. 35).
Remove screw securing inner chrome trim to door glass frame, prise trim from quarter-light frame (3, Fig. 35).

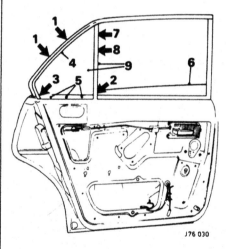

Fig. 35

Release section of door seal fitted to quarter-light frame (4, Fig. 35).
Remove three screws securing base of quarter-light to door (5, Fig. 35).
Lower door glass to full extent (6, Fig. 35).
Release upper portion of felt channel fitted to quarter-light (7, Fig. 35).
Remove screws exposed by removal of quarter-light channel (8, Fig. 35).
Prise chrome trim from quarter-light vertical post, lift quarter-light from door (9, Fig. 35).

76—13

Refitting

Position quarter-light in door.
Fit chrome trim to quarter-light vertical post.
Fit upper portion of channel to quarter-light and raise door glass.
Refit screws to secure quarter-light.
Refit door seal and chrome trim.
Using suitable sealing compound, seal area between base of quarter-light and chrome beading.

FRONT DOOR TRIM CASING

Remove and refit   76.34.01

Removing

Remove the arm-rest. For Vanden Plas see 76.34.22.

Carefully prise lower edge and sides of trim casing from door (1, Fig. 36).
Release upper edge of casing from crash roll (2, Fig. 37).

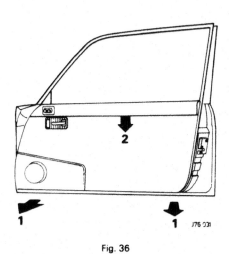

Fig. 36

Refitting

Align trim clips on casing and door.
Engage upper edge of casing with crash roll; refit the casing.
Refit the arm-rest.

REAR DOOR TRIM CASING

Remove and refit   76.34.04

Removing

Remove rear door arm-rest as detailed in operation 76.34.23.
Carefully prise lower edge and sides of trim casing from door.
Release upper edge of casing from crash roll.

Refitting

Align trim clips on casing and door.
Engage upper edge of casing with the door crash roll; refit the casing.
Refit the arm-rest.

DOOR CRASH ROLL

Remove and refit   76.34.17

Removing

Remove door trim casing as detailed in operations 76.34.01—Front or 76.34.04—Rear.
Remove screws securing mirror remote control operating lever surround (1, Fig. 37).
Withdraw surround slightly and remove setscrews securing control lever to surround (2, Fig. 37) (not Vanden Plas cars).
Unclip crash roll (3, Fig. 37) and lift it over the control lever assembly.

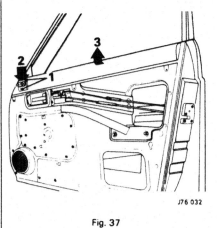

J76 032

Fig. 37

Refitting

Clip crash roll to door casing.
Refit remote control lever assembly and surround.
Refit door trim casing.
Test remote control mirror for correct operation.

DOOR POCKET

**Remove and refit — Vanden Plas only (early models)
Daimler (later models)   76.34.19**

Prior to carrying out this operation it will first be necessary to remove the arm-rest and door trim casing as described in operations 76.34.22 and 76.34.01.

Removing

Disconnect the battery.
Remove two screws securing the remote mirror control surround to the door pockets and partially withdraw the assembly until access to the lever locking setscrew is obtained.
Remove the setscrew and withdraw the surround.
Remove the screws securing the door pocket; withdraw the pocket slightly and disconnect the loudspeaker harness at the snap connectors.

Refitting

Connect the loudspeaker harness at the snap connectors and feed connectors back into the door casing.
Refit the door pockets.
Secure the remote mirror control to the surround and refit the surround.
Refit the door trim casing and arm-rest.
Reconnect the battery and check warning lamp and radio for correct operation.

FRONT DOOR ARM-REST

Remove and refit—Vanden Plas only   76.34.22

Removing

Disconnect the battery and remove the screw securing the warning lamp lens to the arm-rest.
Slide the lens rearwards and remove the warning lamp bulb (1, Fig. 38).
Remove the screw adjacent to the bulb holder securing the rear of the arm-rest to the door (2, Fig. 38).
Remove the screw from beneath front of arm-rest (3, Fig. 38) and slide top portion of arm-rest towards rear of door.
Remove screws securing arm-rest to door; withdraw arm-rest slightly.
Note fitted position of the two electrical leads and disconnect the leads at the snap connectors.

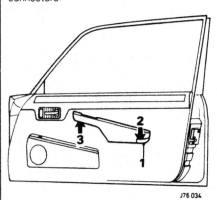

J76 034

Fig. 38

76—14

Refitting

Connect the warning lamp harness at the snap connectors and feed connectors back into the door casing.

Position arm-rest on door and secure with the self-tapping screws.

Refit top portion of arm-rest by sliding it forwards over the two raised screws.

Refit the screw to secure upper portion of arm-rest.

Refit the warning lamp bulb and lens.

Reconnect the battery and check the warning lamp for correct operation.

REAR DOOR ARM-REST

Remove and refit—Vanden Plas only   **76.34.23**

Removing

Disconnect the battery and remove the screw securing the warning lamp lens to the arm-rest. Slide the lens rearwards and remove the warning lamp bulb (1, Fig. 39).

Remove the screw adjacent to the bulb holder securing the rear of the arm-rest to the door (2, Fig. 39).

Remove the screw from beneath front of arm-rest (3, Fig. 39) and slide top portion of arm-rest towards rear of door.

Remove screws securing arm-rest to door; withdraw arm-rest carefully, ensuring that the warning lamp harness is not disconnected as the snap connectors are pulled through the grommet.

Note fitted positions of the warning lamp and loudspeaker wiring harnesses and disconnect the leads at the snap connectors.

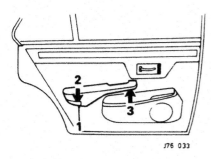

Fig. 39

Refitting

Connect the wiring harness at the snap connectors and ensuring that the grommet in the door casing is not displaced, feed snap connectors through grommet and into the door casing.

Refit the arm-rest to the door and secure with the self-tapping screws.

Refit top portion of arm-rest by sliding it forwards over the two raised screws.

Refit the screw to secure the upper portion of arm-rest.

Refit the warning lamp bulb and lens.
Reconnect the battery and check warning lamp and radio for correct operation.

DOOR LOCK

Adjust   **76.37.01**

WARNING: If any of the following symptoms become evident, immediate remedial action must be taken as outlined below:

A. Door fails to fully close.

B. Door fails to open on operation of inside handle.

C. Door opens upon initial movement of inside handle.

D. Door fails to lock upon operation of inside lock lever.

E. Door fails to open with inside lock lever in unlocked position.

1. Remove door trim casing as detailed in operations 76.34.01—Front, 76.34.04—Rear.

   NOTE: When symptoms A, B or C are evident, proceed as follows:

2. Squeeze inside handle link-rod spring connector and slightly operate handle, release spring connector. Close door and check for evidence of symptoms A, B or C.

3. Continue operation 2, adjusting link-rod to left or right of spring connector until door fully closes and opens. Check that inside handle opens door when handle is three-quarters operated.

   NOTE: If symptoms D or E are evident, proceed as follows:

4. Squeeze spring connector joining lock lever link-rods, slightly operate lock lever and release spring connector. Close door and check for evidence of symptoms D or E.

5. Continue operation 4, adjusting link-rod to left or right of spring connector until door locks with lever in rear position and opens with lever in forward position.

6. Refit door trim casing.

DOOR LOCK—FRONT

Remove and refit   **76.37.12**

Removing

Remove door trim casing as detailed in operation 76.34.01.

Ensure window is fully closed.

Release spring clip securing inside handle

remote control rod to latch lever mechanism, detach rod from lever (1, Fig. 40).

Release spring clip securing inside lock lever remote control rod to latch lever mechanism, detach rod from lever (2, Fig. 40).

Release spring clip securing outside door handle remote control rod to latch lever mechanism, detach rod from lever (3, Fig. 40).

Release spring clip securing key lock remote control rod to latch lever mechanism, detach rod from lever (4, Fig. 40).

Remove screw securing lower section of window channel to door casing.

Remove four screws securing latch outer unit and latch mechanism to door shut face, recover latch mechanism from behind window channel (5, Fig. 40).

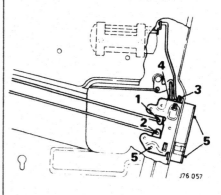

Fig. 40

Refitting

Check that inside lock lever and corresponding lever on latch mechanism are in forward position.

Ensure that latch outer unit is in open position. Offer latch mechanism and outer unit to door shut face, secure with Phillips-head screws.

Connect inside and outside handle/lock remote control rods to latch mechanism levers, secure with retaining clips.

Check operation of inside and outside door operating mechanism in 'lock' and 'unlocked' position, adjust as detailed in operation 76.37.01.

Secure lower section of window channel to door.

Refit door trim casing.

REAR DOOR LOCK

Remove and refit   **76.37.13**

Removing

Ensure that window is fully closed.

Remove rear door trim casing as detailed in operation 76.34.04.

Release spring clip securing inside handle remote control rod to latch lever mechanism, detach rod from door (1, Fig. 41).

Release spring clip securing inside lever lock remote control rod to latch lever mechanism, detach rod from lever (2, Fig. 41).

Prise child safety link from latch lever mechanism, withdraw operating link from door shut face (3, Fig. 41).

Release spring clip securing outside handle remote control rod to latch lever mechanism; detach rod from lever (4, Fig. 41).

Release spring clip securing solenoid remote control rod to latch lever mechanism, detach rod from lever (5, Fig. 41).

Remove four screws securing latch outer unit and latch mechanism to door shut face; recover latch mechanism from inside door (6, Fig. 41).

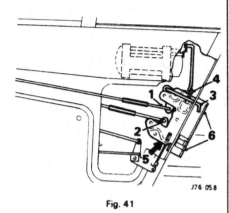

Fig. 41

Refitting

Check inside lock lever and corresponding lever on latch mechanism are in forward position.

Ensure latch outer unit is in open position.

Refit latch outer unit and mechanism to door shut face.

Connect solenoid control rod to lever.

Connect remote control rod to latch lever mechanism.

Refit child safety link and remote control mechanism.

Check door lock for correct operation in 'lock' and 'unlock' position. If adjustment is required, refer to operation 76.37.01.

Refit door trim casing.

FRONT DOOR LOCK STRIKER PLATE

Remove and refit	**76.37.23**

Removing

Remove the screws (1, Fig. 42) securing the access plate to the rear of 'B–C' post; withdraw the plate.

Remove the screws (2, Fig. 42) securing striker plate to 'B–C' post; lift striker plate clear of striker.

CAUTION: Hold rear of striker assembly to prevent any components falling inside the 'B–C' post.

Withdraw striker assembly through rear of 'B–C' post.

Remove all traces of sealing compound from striker plate and 'B–C' post.

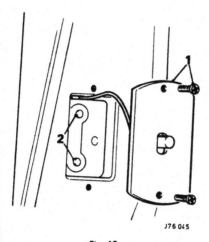

Fig. 42

Refitting

Coat rear of striker plate with suitable sealing compound.

Place striker assembly in position, refit plate and secure with the two screws; DO NOT tighten screws fully.

Close the door by pushing it firmly, open door carefully and ensuring that the striker and plate are not disturbed, tighten the striker plate securing screws.

Close door in the normal manner, door must close without undue effort and be correctly located in the aperture.

Refit the access plate to the rear of the 'BC' post.

Remove all traces of sealing compound from striker plate and 'B–C' post.

DOOR LOCK REMOTE CONTROL

Remove and refit	**76.37.31**

Removing

Remove the door inside handle as detailed in operation 76.58.18.

Release spring clip (1, Fig. 43) securing remote control link to door lock, detach control rod from lock lever.

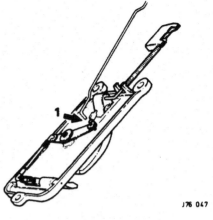

Fig. 43

Refitting

Refit remote control link and secure with spring clip.

Refit the door inside handle.

DOOR SEAL

Remove and refit	**76.40.01**

Removing

Pull seal from door channel and ensure that all traces of dirt are removed from the channel.

Refitting

Coat new seal and door channel with a solution of soft-soap.

Locate corners and ends of seal in the channel, DO NOT stretch the seal.

Locate remainder of seal in channel, clean off all traces of the soft-soap solution.

Ensure that seal is perfectly dry and dust inside face of seal with french chalk.

Close door firmly, open door and check that transfer of chalk from door seal to aperture has taken place.

Where no transfer of chalk is evident, either dress the channel or adjust the striker plate.

76—16

DRIP MOULDING BEADING

Remove and refit   **76.43.11**

Removing

Prise clip (1, Fig. 44) off beading.
Remove the Pop rivets securing the beading to the body flange, lift beading off the flange.

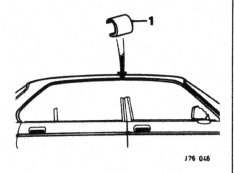

Fig. 44

Refitting

Lightly coat edge of beading with suitable sealing compound.
Locate beading on the body flange and secure with Pop rivets.
Refit the clip.
Remove all traces of sealing compound from beading and bodywork.

FASCIA PANEL

Remove and refit   **76.46.01**

Removing

Remove the crash roll (1, Fig. 45) as detailed in operation 76.46.04.
Remove the driver's underscuttle casing (2, Fig. 45) as detailed in operation 76.46.11.
Remove four screws securing fascia to screen rail (3, Fig. 45).
Remove two nuts and washers securing outer ends of fascia to lower mounting brackets (4, Fig. 45).
Pull off heater and ventilation control knobs and remove the two locking rings securing the radio panel (5, Fig. 45).
Withdraw radio panel (6, Fig. 45) forward sufficient to allow access to centre tray securing screws; ensure that radio is adequately supported. Care must be taken not to damage fibre optic elements.
Remove four screws securing centre shelf to console (7, Fig. 45).
Detach temperature air sensor pipe from centre parcel tray and position tray clear of fascia.
Remove two nuts, flat washers and spring washers securing fascia to heater/air conditioning unit.
Slacken clamp screws securing ignition and light switch shrouds.

Withdraw shrouds and mounting clamps from switches, detach fibre optic from rear of shrouds and switches.
Slacken steering column upper mounting bolts. Care must be taken not to fully remove bolts.
Remove three screws securing indicator switch assembly shroud, lift off shroud.
Ease fascia panel forward and disconnect electrical block connectors feeding instruments.
Disconnect speedometer cable from rear of speedometer.
Carefully lift fascia assembly from car. It should be noted that fascia air vent ducting is removed with fascia assembly.

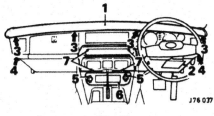

Fig. 45

Refitting

NOTE: For ease of refitting air vent ducts to demister outlets, slacken four nuts securing demister outlets to screen rail.

Position fascia in car and reconnect the speedometer and electrical harnesses.
Refit indicator switch shroud.
Tighten the upper steering column mounting bolts.
Refit ignition switch and light switch shrouds.
Refit nuts, plain and spring washers to secure fascia to heater/air conditioning unit.
Refit sensor pipe and centre parcel tray.
Refit radio panel, heater and ventilation knobs.
Fit nuts and washers to secure ends of fascia.
Fit screws to secure fascia to screen rail.
Refit underscuttle casing and crash roll.

FASCIA CRASH ROLL

Remove and refit   **76.46.04**

Removing

Disconnect the battery.
Prise demister air direction vents (1, Fig. 46) from crash roll.
Remove four screws (2, Fig. 46) securing front of crash roll to screen rail.
Prise map light (3, Fig. 46) from housing in crash roll.
Remove in-car sensor.
Detach Lucar connectors (4, Fig. 46) from map light.
Lift crash roll from car.

Refitting

Position crash roll on fascia.
Refit map light and in-car sensor.

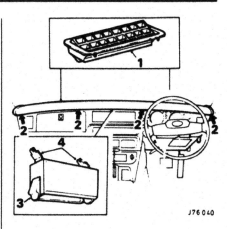

Fig. 46

Secure crash roll to fascia with four screws.
Push demister vents into crash roll.
Reconnect battery and test map light for correct operation.

PASSENGER'S UNDERSCUTTLE CASING

Remove and refit   **76.46.11**

Removing

Open glovebox (1, Fig. 47).
Remove two screws (2, Fig. 47) located adjacent to glovebox lid hinges securing underscuttle casing to fascia.
Remove two screws (3, Fig. 47) securing casing and quarter panel to fascia support bracket.
Manoeuvre underscuttle casing (4, Fig. 47) past footwell fresh air control, lift casing from car.
Remove quarter panel (5, Fig. 47) from car.

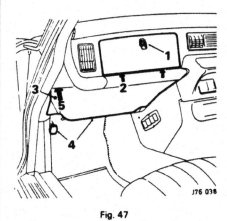

Fig. 47

Refitting

Refit quarter panel.
Manoeuvre underscuttle casing past fresh air control and secure casing to fascia support with two screws.
Refit screws adjacent to glovebox hinges; close glovebox lid

DRIVER'S UNDERSCUTTLE CASING

Remove and refit   **76.46.14**

Removing

Disconnect the battery.
Unscrew locking ring (1, Fig. 48) securing speedometer trip to underscuttle casing.
Remove two screws (2, Fig. 48) securing casing and quarter panel to fascia support bracket.
Lower top of casing sufficient to allow access to rheostat.
Noting fitted position, detach leads from rheostat (3, Fig. 48).
Withdraw underscuttle casing (4, Fig. 48) and quarter panel from car.

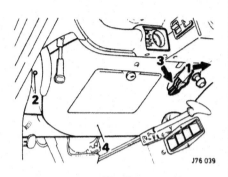

Fig. 48

Refitting

Place casing and quarter panel in car, feed speedometer trip through panel.
Reconnect the rheostat.
Secure casing and quarter panel with two screws.
Refit locking ring to secure speedometer trip cable to casing.
Reconnect the battery and check rheostat for correct operation.

GLOVEBOX LID AND LOCK

Remove and refit   **76.52.02**

Removing

Remove screws securing sliding stay to fascia frame.
Remove the screws securing the glovebox lid to the frame, withdraw the lid.
Remove the six screws (1, Fig. 49) securing the tray liner to the lid; lift off the liner.
Remove the two screws (2, Fig. 49) securing the lock retaining plate.
Unscrew the retaining ring (3, Fig. 49) and withdraw the lock, lid pull and mounting plate.

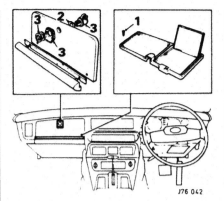

Fig. 49

Refitting

Refit the mounting plate, lid pull and lock; ensure that key aperture in lock is vertical and tighten the locking ring.
Refit the lid liner.
Place lid in position and tighten the securing screws.
Refit the sliding stay, check that lid closes properly and check lock for correct operation.

NOTE: Position of lid in fascia can be altered by repositioning the hinges on the fascia frame.

GLOVEBOX

Remove and refit   **76.52.03**

Prior to carrying out this operation it will be necessary to remove the underscuttle casing as detailed in operation 76.6.11.

Removing

Remove six screws (1, Fig. 50) securing glovebox to fascia.
Remove two screws (2, Fig. 50) securing sliding bracket to fascia.
Remove glovebox (3, Fig. 50) from rear of fascia through aperture exposed by removal of underscuttle casing.

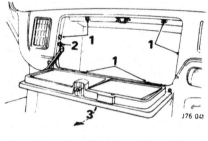

Fig. 50

Refitting

Insert glovebox into fascia through aperture in underscuttle casing.
Refit the securing screws and the sliding stay.
Refit the underscuttle casing.

RADIATOR GRILLE

Remove and refit   **76.55.03**

Removing

Remove the nuts, plain and spring washers securing the grille to the bonnet.
Withdraw grille from bonnet.

Refitting

Position grille in bonnet aperture. Ensuring that grille is centralized in aperture, refit the nuts, plain and spring washers.

DOOR OUTSIDE HANDLE

Remove and refit   **76.58.01**

Prior to carrying out this operation it will be necessary to remove the door trim casings as detailed in operations 76.34.01—Front or 76.34.04—Rear.

Removing

Ensure that door glass is fully closed.
Release spring clip (1, Fig. 51) securing link rod to latch lever mechanism; detach rod from lever.
Remove nuts and washers (2, Fig. 51) securing door handle surround retaining bracket (3, Fig. 51) to the door.
Withdraw surround and handle (4, Fig. 51); recover and discard the gasket.

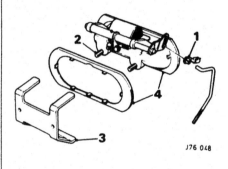

Fig. 51

Refitting

Position door handle and surround in door handle; use a new gasket.
Refit the retaining bracket.
Reconnect the link rod.
Check the door handle for correct operation and refit the door trim casing.

DOOR INSIDE HANDLE

Remove and refit   **76.58.18**

Prior to carrying out this operation it will first be necessary to remove the door crash roll as detailed in operation 76.34.17.

Removing

Disconnect the long section of outer link rod at the nylon connector (1, Fig. 52).
Remove screws (2, Fig. 52) securing inside handle to door casing.
Squeeze lower portion of link connector (3, Fig. 52) and slide rod and connector free of adjoining link.
Withdraw handle (4, Fig. 52) from door.

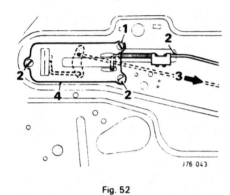

Fig. 52

Refitting

Ensure locking lever and corresponding lever on latch mechanism are in open position.
Refit handle to door.
Connect rear link.
Connect outer link at nylon connector.
Refit the door crash roll.

HEADLINING

Remove and refit   **76.64.01**

Removing

WARNING: This operation should not be attempted by persons known to be allergic to glass fibre (fibreglass). Should skin areas develop a rash or if itching occurs, wash affected area with water and seek medical advice immediately. Always wear gloves, face mask and goggles when handling headlining.

NOTE: A strip of Velcro approximately 30,4 cm (12 in) long and 5 cm (2 in) wide should be used to assist in removing and refitting of headlining.

Fig. 53

Remove 'A' post cant rail trim (1, Fig. 53) as detailed in operation 76.13.10.
Remove interior mirror as detailed in operation 76.10.51.
Remove sun visors (2, Fig. 53) as detailed in operation 76.10.47.
Prise back-light and windscreen upper trim panels free from roof rail (3, Fig. 53).
Attach Velcro strip to headlining.
Pull headlining forward and carefully disengage rear of headlining from locating recess.
Move headlining to right and disengage left-hand side of headlining from locating recess.
Move headlining to left, disengaging right-hand side of headlining from locating recess.
Pull headlining to rear and withdraw from car.

Refitting

CAUTION: Ensure that outer edge of headlining is of equal thickness. Thick sections must be trimmed with a sharp knife. Failure to observe this warning will result in extreme difficulty when refitting.

Fit rear right-hand corner of headlining in locating recess.
Position right-hand side of headlining in locating recess.
Attach Velcro strip to headlining.
Move headlining to rear and locate in recess.
Move headlining to left and locate in recess.
Move headlining forward and locate in screen rail.
Refit windscreen and back-light upper trim panels.
Refit sun visors, interior mirrors and cant rail trim.

CENTRE PARCEL SHELF

Remove and refit   **76.67.03**

Removing

Remove the clock (1, Fig. 54) as detailed in operation 76.67.03.
Pull off the heater and ventilation controls (2, Fig. 54).
Remove the threaded locking rings securing the radio panel.

Withdraw the panel (3, Fig. 54) slightly and remove parcel shelf securing screws (4, Fig. 54).
Remove screws (5, Fig. 54) securing upper portion of shelf to fascia.
Withdraw shelf slightly and detach air sensor pipe.

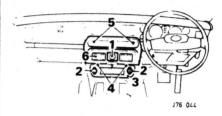

Fig. 54

Refitting

Attach air sensor pipe to parcel shelf.
Refit shelf and secure with four screws.
Refit the radio panel and control knobs.
Refit the clock.

REAR PARCEL SHELF

Remove and refit   **76.67.06**

Removing

Remove rear seat cushion and squab.
Carefully prise plastic escutcheon (1, Fig. 55) from rear of inertia mechanism.

CAUTION: Ensure that disengagement of retaining lugs is gradual and that escutcheon is not hinged too far forwards.

Remove bolt, spring washer, spacer and chrome washer (2, Fig. 55) securing inertia mechanism; lift mechanism clear of parcel shelf.
Remove inertia mechanism from opposite side of parcel shelf. Carefully prise rear parcel shelf (3, Fig. 55) away from panel.

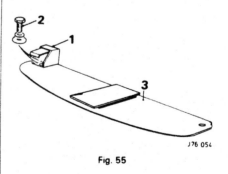

Fig. 55

Refitting

Clip parcel shelf to panel and refit the inertia reels. Road test car and check inertia mechanisms for correct operation.

76—19

FRONT ASHTRAY

Remove and refit   **76.67.13**

Removing

Open ashtray cover and withdraw ash container.
Remove two screws securing ash container holder to console.
Withdraw holder and securing bracket from console.

Refitting

Slightly secure bracket with one screw to holder unit.
Fit holder and bracket to console, turn bracket securing screw, do not fully tighten.
Align unsecured portion of bracket with hole in holder. Fit remaining bracket securing screw.
Fully tighten bracket securing screws.
Fit ash container to holder.

REAR ASHTRAY

Remove and refit   **76.67.14**

Removing

Open the ashtray.
Push the ashtray down against spring pressure and lift it out of the holder.

Refitting

Holding the ashtray in the horizontal position, i.e. open end facing away from the holder, push ashtray into holder against spring pressure, then raise ashtray into the open position.
Close the ashtray.

FRONT SEAT

Remove and refit   **76.70.01**

Removing

Cars fitted with seat belt warning and/or electric seat height adjustment—Disconnect the battery.
Remove Phillips head screw securing front of cushion to bracket, remove bracket from underside of cushion.
Position squab in reclining position.
Raise front of cushion and pull it forward. On cars fitted with seat belt warning and/or electric height adjustment, disconnect electrical connectors fitted to underside of cushion.
Lift cushion from seat frame.
Unlock seat runners, return springs (1, Fig. 56) from forward runner supports.

Remove two nuts, spring washers and spacers (2, Fig. 56) securing front runners to mounting brackets.
Slide seat forward to full extent.
Remove nuts and spring washers (3, Fig. 56) securing rear of runners to mounting bracket.
Remove seat assembly from car.

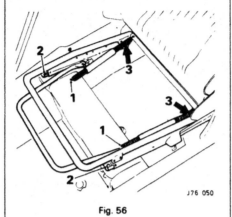

J76 050

Fig. 56

Refitting

Position seat in car and fit rear retaining nuts and washers.
Re-connect wiring harnesses (if fitted).
Fit front runner retaining nuts and washers.
Connect seat return springs.
Position cushion in seat frame.
Connect seat belt warning and/or electric height adjustment wiring harness.
Secure cushion to seat frame with bracket and screw.
Connect the battery and test seat belt warning and/or electric height adjustment for correct operation.

FRONT SEAT CUSHION

Remove and refit   **76.70.02**

Removing

Cars fitted with seat belt warning and/or electric seat height adjustment—Disconnect the battery.
Remove Phillips head screw securing front of cushion to bracket, remove bracket from underside of cushion.
Position squab in reclining position.
Raise front of cushion and pull it forward. On cars fitted with seat belt warning and/or electric height adjustment, disconnect electrical connectors fitted to underside of cushion.
Lift cushion from seat frame.

Refitting

Position cushion in seat frame.
Connect seat belt warning and/or electric height adjustment wiring harness.
Secure cushion to seat frame with bracket and screw.
Connect the battery and test seat belt warning and/or electric height adjustment for correct operation.

HEAD-REST

Fit   **76.70.29**

Remove head-rest guide blanking plug from front seat squab.
Locate head-rest slide in guide.
Adjust head-rest to required height.

REAR SEAT CUSHION

Remove and refit   **76.70.37**

Removing

Adjust front seats to fully forward position.
Remove screw either side of transmission tunnel securing cushion to seat pan cross-member.
Draw cushion forward and remove from car.

Refitting

Place cushion in seat pan and refit retaining screws.

REAR SEAT SQUAB

Remove and refit   **76.70.38**

Removing

Adjust front seats to fully forward position.
Remove screw either side of transmission tunnel securing cushion to seat pan cross-member.
Draw seat forward and remove from car.
Remove two bolts and shakeproof washers securing lower section of squab to rear of seat pan.
Push squab upwards and disengage rear of squab from retaining clips.
Remove squab from car.

Refitting

Position the squab over the retaining clips and push firmly downwards.
Refit the bolts and washers to secure lower portion of squab.
Refit the seat cushion.

REAR SEAT ARM-REST

Remove and refit   **76.70.39**

Removing

Adjust front seats to fully forward position.

76—20

Remove screw either side of transmission tunnel securing cushion to seat pan cross-member.
Draw seat forward and remove from car.
Remove two bolts and shakeproof washers securing lower section of squab to rear of seat pan.
Push squab upwards and disengage rear of squab from retaining clips.
Remove squab from car.
Remove four bolts and flat washers securing arm-rest to seat squab frame.
Remove six clips securing arm-rest trim to squab frame.
Withdraw arm-rest from squab.

Refitting

Position arm-rest in squab and refit the trim clips to secure trim to the frame.
Refit the bolts and washers to secure the arm-rest.
Position the squab over the retaining clips and push firmly downwards.
Refit the bolts and washers to secure lower portion of squab.
Refit the seat cushion.

FRONT SAFETY BELT

Remove and refit   **76.73.10**

Prior to carrying out this operation it will be necessary to remove the lower 'B' post trim casing as detailed in operation 76.13.29.

Removing

Remove the bolt, spring and plain washers (1, Fig. 57) securing the inertia reel mechanism to the 'B' post.
Prise plastic finisher from buckle assembly securing bolt.
Remove bolt, plain washer, anchor plate and spacer (2, Fig. 57) securing buckle assembly; withdraw assembly.

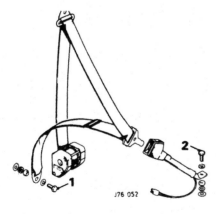

J76 052

Fig. 57

Refitting

Refit the inertia reel mechanism ensuring that it is in the vertical position.
Refit the lower 'B' post trim casing.
Smear threads of buckle assembly securing bolt with Bostik Sealant; refit buckle assembly.
Road test car and check inertia mechanism for correct operation.

REAR SAFETY BELT

Remove and refit   **76.73.18**

Removing

Slide front seats forward.
Remove screws securing rear seat cushion, draw cushion forward and remove from car.
Remove two bolts and shakeproof washers securing lower section of seat squabs to seat pan.
Push squab upwards and disengage rear of squab from retaining clips.
Carefully prise plastic escutcheon (1, Fig. 58) from rear of inertia mechanism.

CAUTION: Ensure that disengagement of retaining lugs is gradual and that escutcheon is not hinged too far forwards.

Remove bolt, spring washer, spacer and chrome washer (2, Fig. 58) securing inertia mechanism.
Remove bolts, plain washers and spacers securing lower mounting and buckle assemblies to the seat pan.

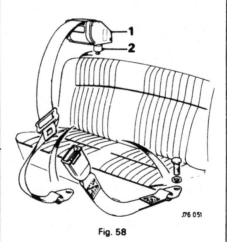

J76 051

Fig. 58

Refitting

Smear threads of lower mounting buckle assembly securing bolts with Bostik Sealant; refit buckle assembly.
Refit inertia mechanism, clip plastic escutcheon to reel holder.
Refit rear seat squab and cushion.
Road test car and check inertia mechanism for correct operation.

SILL TREAD PLATE

Remove and refit   **76.76.01**

Removing

Remove the screws securing the tread plate to the sill.
Lift off the tread plate and packing piece.

Refitting

Position packing piece and tread plate on sill and refit the retaining screws.

FRONT DOOR GLASS

Remove and refit   76.31.01

Removing

Open the bonnet and disconnect the battery.
Remove the door trim casing, as detailed in Operation 76.34.01, and the front door crash rail, as detailed in Operation 76.34.17.
Remove the door outer weather strip.

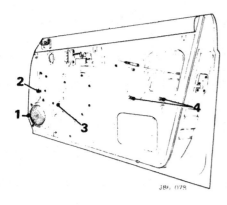

Fig. 59

Remove the door speaker (1, Fig. 59).
Remove the screws securing the window lift motor mounting plate (2, Fig. 59) and remove the stop peg (3, Fig. 59) from the mounting plate.
Remove the window lower channel securing bolts.
Remove the distance piece from the rear of the mounting plate.
Remove the regulator outer slide channel securing bolts (4, Fig. 59) and remove the channel.

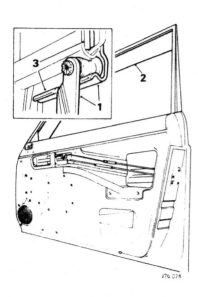

Fig. 60

Remove the motor from the mounting plate and disconnect the electrical feed cables.
Lower the motor to the bottom of the door.
Slide the door glass forward and disengage the lift motor operating arm from the guide channel (1, Fig. 60). Withdraw the glass (2, Fig. 60) from the door.
Remove the guide channel and seal (3, Fig. 60) from the door glass.

Refitting

Locate a new guide channel seal in position over the door glass.
Position the guide channel over the seal and gently tap either side of the guide until the seal and the guide are firmly secured to the door glass.
Refit the glass to the door, engage the lift motor operating arm with the guide channel.
Refit the motor to the mounting plate, reconnect the electrical feed cables.
Refit the outer slide channel and secure with the bolts.
Refit the distance piece to the rear of the mounting plate. Refit the window lower channel securing bolts.
Refit the stop peg to the mounting plate and refit the window lift motor mounting plate, secure with the screws.
Refit the door speaker, outer weather strip, front door crash rail, and door trim casing.
Reconnect battery and check operation of window lift mechanism.

WINDSCREEN — FRONT AND REAR

Remove and refit   76.81.01
                                        76.81.11

Description

Two different methods of direct glazing have been used on Series III Saloons.
The 'SOLBIT THERMO ELECTRICAL' method on the early cars and the 'BETASEAL' cold cure method on later cars, which is the only one now used as a service replacement.
The 'SOLBIT' method requires the use of an electrical transformer to heat wires embedded in the seal. The 'BETASEAL' method relies on the moisture in the air as a curing agent, the more humid the atmosphere the shorter the curing period.

Identification

To check which method of sealing has been used, remove the stainless steel finishers at each top corner of the screen. Carefully cut the seal and check for the end of the wire, if no wires are found, then the 'BETASEAL' method has been used.
Water leaks cannot be cured on screens employing the 'SOLBIT' method of sealing. The screen must be removed and refitted using the 'BETASEAL' process.

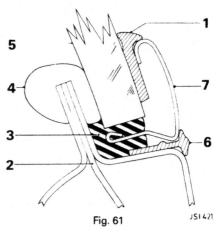

Fig. 61

1. Outer Plastic Finisher
2. Pillar
3. Solbit Sealer
4. Flange Finisher
5. Screen
6. Inner Plastic Finisher
7. Finisher

Removing

On screens fitted with the 'SOLBIT' process there are two methods of removal. One is by using a transformer to produce heat which softens the seal sufficiently for the screen to be pushed out. The other method which also is common to 'BETASEAL' is to cut through the seal using a cheese wire.

Method 1 — 'SOLBIT' only

Service Tool: Transformer, Churchill Tl Pt No MS 82.

Remove the windscreen wiper arm and blade assemblies.
Apply masking tape around the windscreen aperture paying particular attention to the top corner of the roof where the 'SOLBIT' wire ends are located.
Carefully remove the black plastic finishers by pulling away from the stainless steel trim.
Damaged plastic finishers must be renewed.
Remove and discard the inner flange rubber.
Pull the 'SOLBIT' heating wires clear of the windscreen, and connect the transformer leads to the bared heating wires. Ensure that the wires do not touch.
Set the transformers to No. 2 and switch on, allow ten minutes re-heat time at 24 volts, 11.5 amps to soften the seal.
Whilst the 'SOLBIT' is being heated, fit protective covers to the front seals, cover the centre console and front carpets with paper and mask the heater defrost vents with suitable tape.
Push the front seats fully back; place a board (or plank) between the B/C posts resting on the seats, to use as a secure backrest when pushing out the screen.
When the 'SOLBIT' has softened, ease the seal away from the outside of the glass into the aperture.
Push out the screen using the feet. Sit in each front seat alternately with the feet against the screen, and the back supported by the board (or plank).

76—22

An assistant is required outside the car to receive the screen and ease away the seal.

NOTE: If the screen is to be refitted, protect it from scratches by either wrapping rags around normal working footwear, or wearing soft soled shoes.

If the screen is to be replaced with a new one, carefully cut out the stainless steel trims.

If the screen is to be refitted, place on a cloth covered table. Using a sharp knife, carefully cut out the stainless steel trims and remove the 'SOLBIT' from the glass.

Clean the screen and store safely prior to refitting.

Removing

Method 2 — 'SOLBIT' or 'BETASEAL'

Service Tool: Cheese wire with handles.

The cheese wire is supplied in the 'BETASEAL' replacement kit. One end is connected to a piece of wooden dowel 150 × 20 mm (6 in × ¾ in) for use outside the car, and the other end to a hole drilled in the blade of an old screwdriver, for use inside the car. Proprietary handles such as Gas-ex may be used as an alternative to the above.

Pierce a hole through the seal at the top right-hand corner of the windscreen (Fig. 62). Thread the wire through to an assistant inside the car and connect each end to the handles (screwdriver inside the car).

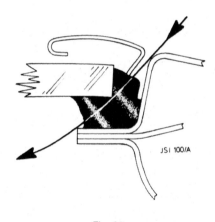

Fig. 62

Hold the outside handle approximately 150 mm (6 in) from the point where it is threaded through the screen and position the screwdriver a little distance from the same point (Fig. 63). Hold the wire taut, with the screwdriver handle close to the glass and the blade wedged into the seal for added purchase towards the inner handle, cutting with a narrow angle running parallel to the line of the seal. Reposition tne inner handle (screwdriver) and repeat the procedure. **DO NOT** use short fast strokes otherwise the wire will overheat and break. Use this method for the top and sides of the screen seal.

Because of the possibility of damaging the fascia when using the wire to cut the bottom of the screen seal, it is recommended that the lower seal is released by hinging the screen carefully backwards and forwards.

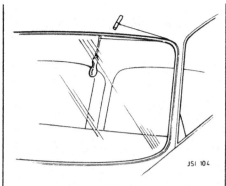

Fig. 63

If the screen is to be replaced with a new one, carefully cut out the stainless steel trims.

If the screen is to be refitted, place on a cloth covered table. Using a sharp knife carefully cut out the stainless steel trims and remove all traces of the old seal from the glass.

Body Preparation

Clean the screen aperture, any bare metal must be primed, before refitting the windscreen.

Prime using International Paints 'Double One' primer base reference number 6900 P 3000R1 and catalyst reference number 20007 0219. Mix equal quantities of primer base and catalyst, leave for 20 minutes before using. Allow between 1 to 2 hours drying time, depending on the ambient temperature.

Fitting the Windscreen

Service Tools: Rubber sucker glazing aids, Betaseal Kit.

Place a protective cover over the bonnet.

Position the support blocks, supplied in the kit, on the bottom of the windscreen aperture and rest the glass on them. Carefully centralize the glass in the aperture.

Stick two strips of masking tape, from the top of the glass, across the gap, to the body (Fig. 64). Mark the tape to facilitate correct location of the windscreen when finally fitting.

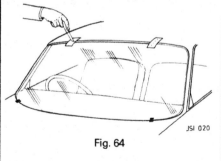

Fig. 64

Cut through the tape, between the glass and the body, and lift out the windscreen (Fig. 64).

Fit the inner rubber finisher (6, Fig. 61) to the aperture flange, with the joint at the centre of the top of the aperture.

If the original windscreen is to be re-used, it must be thoroughly cleaned and prepared using the Wipe No. 4, supplied in the kit. Wipe on using a lint free cloth and immediately wipe off with a clean dry cloth.

Remove any dust or dirt from the aperture flange with a clean dry cloth.

Shake well the two tins of primer. Apply the metal primer part number 435-46 to the flange. Apply the glass primer part number 84132-11, to a width of 10 mm, to the glass.

Allow ten minutes for the primer to dry.

Remove the bottom from the adhesive sealant cartridge.

Remove all the desiccant. If the desiccant is blue then the adhesive can be safely used, if it is pink then the shelf life of the adhesive has expired and it should be discarded and a new tube of adhesive used. Pierce the membrane, screw on the pre-cut nozzle and introduce the cartridge into the gun.

Run a continuous bead of adhesive sealant around the inside perimeter of the windscreen using the edge of the windscreen and the shape of the nozzle as a guide.

Position the support blocks on the bottom half of the aperture about 20 cm (8 in) from each corner. Fit the windscreen in the aperture, the use of rubber sucker glazing aids will greatly assist. Line up the marks of the adhesive tapes.

NOTE: Fit the windscreen within 10 minutes of applying the adhesive sealant.

Press gently all round the edge of the windscreen to ensure perfect adhesion of the adhesive sealant to the body.

Carry out a water leak test. If a leak is found, mark the spot and dry using compressed air. Squeeze out a small amount of adhesive sealant, and smooth into the affected area with a wet spatula. Carry out another water leak test and rectification (if required).

Offer up the stainless trims to the windscreen and adjust for the best fit.

Apply a bead of adhesive sealant to the space between the windscreen and the aperture. Fit the stainless trims and the outer plastic finisher, hold in place with masking tape.

Using a soft lead pencil mark around the inside of the windscreen against the flange finisher. This will cut through any excess adhesive sealant extruded during the fitting process. When cured this excess adhesive sealant can easily be peeled away from the windscreen. Any excess adhesive sealant on the outside of the vehicle can also be removed by this method.

When the stainless trims are firm, remove the masking tape and clean the windscreen. Fit the inner plastic finisher.

Refit the wiper arms and blades.

Leave the vehicle in a humid atmosphere for at least two hours, before driving.

SUNROOF MANUAL OPERATION

Where a sunroof motor has failed and the panel is stuck partially open, manual operation can be carried out by attaching a small handle (A, Fig. 65), supplied with the tool kit, to a shaft protruding from the base of the sunroof motor.
To gain access to the motor, remove boot front trim panel by releasing 2 quarter turn fasteners. (Details are given in the Drivers Handbook).

CAUTION: Where manual operation is to be carried out on a sunroof stuck in the FULLY OPEN or CLOSED position, it is important that the handle is rotated in the correct direction or damage to the motor wheelbox may result.

NOTE: Direction of rotation when viewing from UNDERNEATH the motor.

To open — rotate handle anti-clockwise.
To close — rotate handle clockwise (shown Fig. 65).

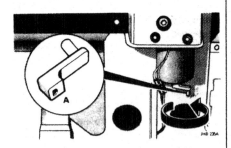

Fig. 65

If the sliding panel cannot be moved because the motor has seized, then the following emergency action can be taken.
Remove the rear seat cushion and squab, refer to operation 76.70.37/38.
Remove the two nuts securing the wheelbox cover, and remove the cover.
Remove the rack tubes from the wheelbox.
Grasp the sliding roof panel and move it in the desired direction.

SLIDING PANEL

Remove and refit   76.82.05

Open the sunroof panel 15 to 23 cm (6 to 9 in).
Remove the four screws from the front flange of the panel.
Move the sunroof to the closed position, lifting the front of the panel.
Lift the panel clear of the vehicle by pulling forward to release the two spring clips at the rear of the panel (Fig. 66).
To refit the panel reverse the above procedure.

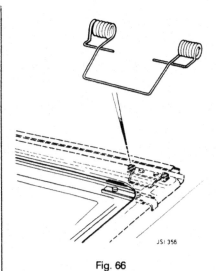

Fig. 66

SLIDING PANEL SEAL

Renew   76.82.15

Remove the sliding roof panel following the procedure detailed previously.
Remove the screws securing the two nylon lifting brackets and remove the brackets (A, Fig. 67).

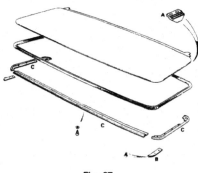

Fig. 67

Remove the screws securing the two wind deflector brackets and remove the brackets (B, Fig. 67).
Remove the screws and remove the seal retaining brackets (C, Fig. 67).
Remove the seal at the front and sides of the panel, and from the channel at the rear.
Apply soft soap to the seal channel at the rear of the panel.
Insert the new seal into the channel ensuring that it is fully seated.
Position the seal at the front and sides of the panel.
Refit the seal retaining brackets and secure with the screws.
Refit the sliding roof panel.

SLIDING ROOF PANEL RETAINING SPRING(S)

Renew   76.82.29

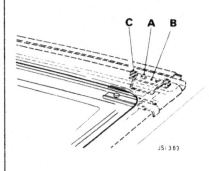

Fig. 68

Remove the sliding roof panel for access, refer to operation 76.82.05.
Fully close the under panel.
Slacken, but do not remove, the two nuts (A, Fig. 68) securing the spring retaining bracket (B, Fig. 68) sufficiently to allow the spring (C, Fig. 68) to be removed.

NOTE: The spring brackets are located at the rear of the sunroof aperture, between the undertray and the roof panel.

Fit the new spring; ensure that the bracket is correctly positioned before tightening the nuts.
Refit the sliding roof panel.

WIND DEFLECTOR

Renew   76.82.07

Open the sliding roof panel and mark the position of the wind deflector.
Undo and remove the two allen screws and remove the deflector.
If a new deflector is being fitted, position the screws in the mounting bracket prior to fitting to the vehicle.
Position the deflector to the marks previously made, fit but do not fully tighten the screws.
Operate the sliding roof panel to check that the wind deflector operates correctly.
Adjust as required and tighten the screws.

SLIDING PANEL

Adjust   76.82.04

The only adjustment possible on a fully trimmed vehicle is that required to raise or lower the rear edge of the panel.
To adjust the alignment of the sliding panel to roof profile refer to the 'adjusting copy' in the previous procedure.
To ensure correct centralisation of the sliding panel in the aperture, refer to the previous operation.

76—24

SLIDING ROOF RACK

Renew   76.82.42
                                         76.82.43

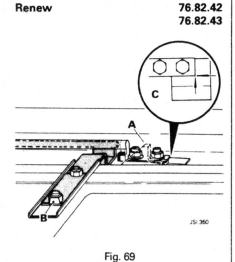

Fig. 69

Remove the roof sliding panel for access, refer to operation 76.82.05.
Fully close the under panel.
Remove the rear seat cushion and squab, refer to operation 76.70.37/38.
Remove the nuts securing the wheelbox cover and remove the cover.
Move the racks away from the housing.
Remove the black plastic lifting block (A, Fig. 69).
Bend back the lock tabs (B, Fig. 69) and remove the two nuts, lockplates, spring plates and rack mounting plate.
Mark the position of the rack stop (C, Fig. 69).
Remove the two nuts securing the rack stop and remove the stop from the rack tube.
Withdraw the rack from the tube and clear of the vehicle.

NOTE: Take care as the rack may be heavily greased.

Grease the rack as necessary and insert it into the tube. Ensure that the rack enters the second tube adjacent to the motor wheelbox.
Refit the rack stop and secure with the two nuts.
Refit the rack plate, spring plates, lockplates and secure with the two nuts. Bend up the locking tabs.
Refit the lifting block.
Fully close the under panel by hand ensuring that full travel of the sliding roof is obtained.
Refit the racks to the wheelbox housing. Fit the cover and secure with the nuts.
Operate the sunroof electrically to ensure that the fully open and closed positions can be obtained.
Refit the sliding roof panel.
Refit the seat squab and cushion.

SUNROOF MOTOR/WHEELBOX/DRIVE GEAR

Renew   76.82.45
                                         76.82.44

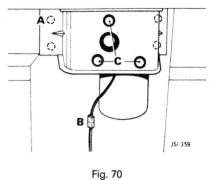

Fig. 70

Remove the rear seat cushion and squab, refer to operation 76.70.37/38.
Remove the two nuts securing the wheelbox cover and remove the cover.
Remove the racks from the housing.
Remove the four nuts securing the motor mounting bracket to the rear bulkhead (A, Fig. 70).
Open the boot lid and remove the front trim panel to gain access to the motor.
Disconnect the electrical harness (B, Fig. 70).
Remove the motor and mounting bracket assembly.
Remove the three hexagon headed screws securing the motor to the bracket (C, Fig. 70) and remove the motor.

MOTOR

Renew   86.76.01

Reverse instructions above.

WHEELBOX/DRIVE GEAR

Renew   76.82.44
                                         76.82.45

Remove the four screws securing the wheelbox to the motor (A, Fig. 71).
If the drive gear (B, Fig. 71) is to be renewed it should be done prior to the refitting of the wheelbox.
Refit or renew the wheelbox (C, Fig. 71) securing with the four screws.

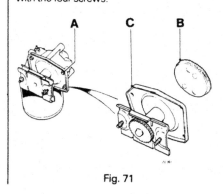

Fig. 71

SUNROOF ASSEMBLY

Renew   76.82.01

Remove the sun visors, interior mirror, reading lights (where fitted), passenger grab handles, roof aperture flange finisher and necessary door finishers, side cantrail trim rolls, and rear seat cushion and squab.
Move the rear seat belt inertia mechanism (where fitted) away from the rear panel shelf.
Remove the rear parcel shelf trim panel, rear quarter trim panels, headlining rear trim roll and headlining.
Cut the plastic straps securing the drain tubes and release the tubes.
Remove the wheelbox cover securing nuts and remove the cover.
Release the cable clips from the bulkhead and 'D' post.
Remove the racks from the wheelbox housing.
Tape the tubes together to prevent the possibility of grease marks.
Mark the position of the sunroof mounting brackets to the body and remove the setscrews.
Remove the nuts securing the brackets to the sunroof and remove the brackets.
Lower the sunroof assembly into the car. Rotate through 90 degrees and remove diagonally through the sunroof aperture.

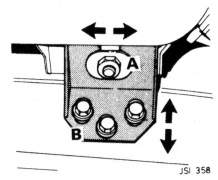

Fig. 72

Lower the sunroof, diagonally through the roof aperture, turn through 90 degrees and lift into position. Ensure that the inner seal is correctly fitted.
Fit the mounting brackets to the sunroof. Fit but do not tighten the securing nuts.
Fit but do nut fully tighten the setscrews securing the mounting brackets to the cantrail.
Reposition the rack tubes, fit the clips to the bulkhead and 'D' post. Fit but do not fully tighten the securing screws.
Ensure that the sunroof panel is fully closed and refit the rack cables. Refit the wheelbox cover and secure with the nuts.
Tighten the cable clip securing screws.
Reconnect the drain tubes and secure with the ratchet clips.
Refit the sliding roof panel.
Align the sliding panel to the roof profile and tighten the mounting bracket setscrews (B, Fig. 72).
Ensure that the sunroof is correctly aligned in the roof aperture and tighten the mounting bracket nuts (A, Fig. 72).
Reverse the remaining operations.

76——25

PAGE INTENTIONALLY LEFT BLANK

CONTENTS

BODY PANELS

Description   77.00.00

This section gives only body panel replacement details of use in repairing superficial damage. Repairing damage that may structurally alter the vehicle's driving geometry will require that the alignment check in Section 76 is carried out prior to and subsequent to repairs.

It is possible to carry out a repair using a variety of methods ranging from straightening procedures to the replacement of either individual parts or panel assemblies. The repairer is responsible for choice of repair method and this choice will normally be based on a balance between the economics of labour and material costs, and the available repair facilities.

It must be accepted that a repairer will choose the best and most economic repair he can, using the equipment available but, if a car is to be sold as new, the repairer must consider the legal implications of repair methods which differ from original production.

The instructions contained in this section are intended to assist skilled body repairers by explaining approved procedures for replacing panels so that a car body may be restored to a safe running condition. This does not necessarily mean that the car will be restored to new condition; repair facilities cannot always reproduce methods of construction used during production.

Damage may make it impossible or unnecessary to remove some of the mechanical and electrical components before carrying out a body repair, but when the components are being removed or refitted refer to the appropriate section for detailed instructions.

Legal requirements

'E' mark approved label

This label is attached to the L.H. valance. If it becomes detached or damaged, or if the valance is renewed, a new label should be ordered giving the vehicle chassis, commission body shell, and engine numbers. Attach the new label to the L.H. valance.

Preparation and techniques

To reduce the cost of repair, certain individual panels are available. The whole of each panel can be used but this may be found uneconomic due to the necessity for additional brackets, clips etc., and, in some cases, the complicated nature of the joints involved. The value of a separate panel is in the variety of ways with which it enables a repair to be made. With certain exceptions the panel can be cut at the most convenient point and only part of it need be used, leaving the remainder for possible future use. If damage is such that a complete new assembly is necessary, it is usually advisable to use the appropriate assembly rather than build it up from separate panels.

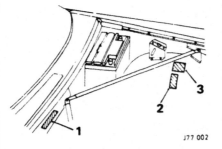

1. Chassis number-plate
2. 'E' mark label
3. · V I N Plate

Fig. 1

Types of weld

Spot weld (in this manual the term 'spot-weld' refers to resistance spot weld unless otherwise stated)—suitable for lap, double lap and flange joints; can be used in single or double (staggered) rows.

Single row—space the spot welds 15 to 25 mm (⅝ to 1 in) apart.

Double row—space the spot welds 22 to 31 mm (⅞ to 1¼ in) apart.

External examination gives little indication of the quality of a spot weld. Make a test joint using similar material and then split the test pieces apart. If the metal tears or the weld pulls a hole in one piece, the joint was satisfactory. Repeat this test each time the electrodes are re-dressed or changed and each time a change of metal gauge is encountered.

Fusion weld—suitable for butt and lap joints, and should be used where possible to reinforce corners and notches in flanges.

If it is necessary to fusion weld a flange joint, care must be taken to preserve the designed strength of the joint. A fusion weld along the toe of a flange is not generally acceptable unless the flange is cut back.

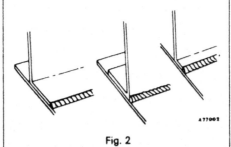

Fig. 2

NOT ACCEPTABLE   ACCEPTABLE

Plug weld—To make a plug weld, drill a 5 to 8 mm (³⁄₁₆ to ⁵⁄₁₆ in) hole through the accessible component and weld the components together through the hole.

To clamp the components together use drive screws at intervals and plug weld between them, then remove the drive screws and plug weld the remaining holes.

Types of joint

Butt joint

Lap joint

Double lap joint

Flange joint

Fig. 3

Removal of spot welded components

Centre punch each spot weld securing the component to be removed. Adjust a spot weld cutter so that it cuts just through the thickness of the material to be removed. Holding the cutter square to the material, cut through each spot weld.

If the new joint is to be made with spot welds, cut the old spot welds from the component which is to be discarded.

If the new joint is to be made with plug welds, cut the old spot welds from the component which is to be retained and use the holes for plug welding.

Preparation

Remove all traces of sealer from the area of the joint likely to be affected by heat. Clean, to bare metal, both sides of the welding areas on old and new panels.

Grind old welds smooth and dress the panels or flanges to ensure that the welding faces fit closely. Mask the welding areas and paint any areas which will be inaccessible after the panels are fitted. Remove the masking.

Where spot welding is to be used apply zinc-rich welding primer to both mating surfaces and spot weld while the primer is moist.

Finishing

Grind smooth the plug welds and butt welds. Fill and smooth the surface where necessary. Clean and repair for sealing and painting.

Sealing

After fitting the panel(s) seal the joints. Apply underseal where required.

THIS SECTION WAS COMPILED IN CONJUNCTION WITH THE MOTOR INSURANCE REPAIR RESEARCH CENTRE AT THATCHAM. JAGUAR CARS LTD. WISH TO ACKNOWLEDGE AND THANK THEM FOR THEIR CO-OPERATION AND ASSISTANCE GIVEN IN THIS PUBLICATION.

REPAIR NOTES

During repair, all old and new panel surfaces to be resistance spot welded together have the existing primer removed and are then treated with zinc-rich, weld-through primer to provide corrosion protection in the weld area.

The vehicle is undersealed in production. Jaguar Cars Ltd. recommend the use of 'Unipart' underseal material (Part No. GAC 1003) in repair.

A Welding Diagram and a Welding Table, which show the location and type of each welded joint, are included where applicable with each method description.

The weld nugget produced by the resistance spot welding equipment available to the motor vehicle repair trade is smaller than that produced by production equipment. In the Welding Tables, the expression single row of resistance spot welds' is used. This means that resistance spot welds should be spaced 16 mm (⅝ in) to 25 mm (1 in) apart which will usually mean that more resistance spot welds will be replaced in the repair joint than were removed from the factory joint.

To remove resistance spot welds, a resistance spot weld cutter such as the Dormer Roto-Bor or Sykes-Pickavant Zipcut should be used. If the new joint is to be MIG plug welded, the old resistance spot welds should be cut from the panel that is to be retained, whenever possible, and the holes used for plug welding. Alternatively, holes may be drilled for this purpose.

It must be emphazised that all safety precautions must be observed and protective equipment used when carrying out welding and grinding operations, etc.

SYMBOLS

The following symbols are used on the illustrations in this section to indicate cutting areas and types of weld required.

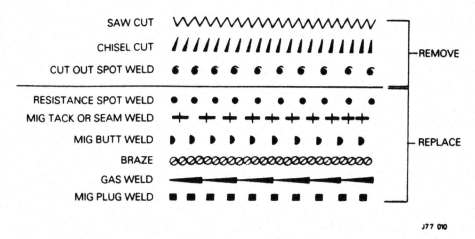

J77 010

Fig. 4

TOOLS AND EQUIPMENT

The tools used to carry out the repairs detailed in this section are listed below:

General equipment
Air line
Asbestos blankets
Axle stands

Fume extractor
Petrol storage unit
Trolley jack

Power tools and attachments
Air drill
Belt driven sander
Cengarette saw
Cone grinder 1 inch diameter
Grinderette

Spray guns
Rotary wire brush
Random orbital sander
Zipcut resistance spot weld cutters

Welding/heating equipment
ARO N179 spot welder
ARO arms 242A, 100737, 103402, 105010, 105492
Flat foot electrode
ARO electrode tip trimmer

MIG welder
Oxy-acetylene plant
Propane gas torch
Transformer

DOOR PANEL

Front 77.70.16
Rear 77.70.19

Remove and strip the door as detailed in Section 76.

Remove panel.

Grind off door-skin edges and MIG welds at window frame. Remove metal remnants. Separate and remove door-skin from frame.

Clean old and new panel joint edges. Expose resistance spot welds at upper stiffener on old panel. Centre-punch and cut out resistance spot welds. Separate and remove stiffener. Clean joint surfaces on stiffener and new panel for resistance spot welding. Apply weld-through primer to all surfaces to be resistance spot welded. Offer up stiffener to new panel, align and clamp in position. Resistance spot weld stiffener to new panel; fit anti-drum pad to inner surface of new panel.

Offer up new panel; align and clamp in position. Resistance spot weld new panel to frame, MIG weld new panel to window frame at either end. Turn over door-skin flanges, MIG weld at inner surfaces of lower corners and at upper joint; dress MIG welds.

Rebuild and refit door.

J77 005

Fig. 5

LOWER PANEL

Front 77.28.26

Disconnect battery. Remove flasher lamps, bumper side mounting bolts; horns; upper mounting bolt grommets R.H. and L.H., chrome finisher and plastic apron assembly; centre iron-to-bumper mounting bolts R.H. and L.H. and remove front bumper assembly; remove lower air intake grille and retaining clips. Jack up vehicle and place on axle stands. Remove eight mounting bolts from front wings R.H. and L.H. and at cross-member. Separate and remove panel and grommets from panel.

Refit grommets to panel. Offer up new panel, align, replace and tighten eight mounting bolts to cross-member and to front wings R.H. and L.H. Removal axle stands and lower vehicle.

Replace parts in reverse order of removal, reconnect battery, test those electrical items that have been removed and replaced.

J77 003

Fig. 6

LOWER PANEL

Rear 77.61.65

Disconnect battery and alternator. Remove spare wheel cover, spare wheel, fuel pump cover and rear boot trim assembly; scuff plate boot aperture weatherseal; tail lamp assemblies R.H. and L.H. and rear wiring loom; radio aerial cover-plate. Disconnect wiring. Remove aerial drive unit. Disconnect earth wiring and aerial socket. Remove aerial, separate aerial at lower joint, remove inner cable, reassemble unit and place aside. Remove upper finisher support brackets. Lay aside boot carpets. Remove data labels, boot lid striker, insulation R.H. and L.H., grommets, petrol tanks R.H. and L.H., vent cover trim and pipes R.H. and L.H., petrol pump assembly.

Protect vehicle, expose resistance spot welds at points 1 (inside boot), 2, 4, 5, 6, 7, and 8 in Welding Diagram. Centre punch and cut out, cut panel at point 'Z' and 'Y', R.H. and L.H., separate and remove bulk of panel and metal remnants. Remove solder and brazes at point 3, remove surplus material. Grind off and retain bumper mounting reinforcement plates.

Clean old and new panel joint edges. Apply weld-through primer to joint edges to be resistance spot welded.

Offer up new panel, align with boot lid and clamp in position. Resistance spot weld at points 2, 5, 6, 7 and 8. MIG plug weld at points 1 and 4. MIGtack weld at point 11. MIG weld at points 9 and 10, braze at point 3. Dress welds and brazes. Prepare and apply solder to rear wings at flanges above bumper mountings, shape and dress soldered joints. Apply weld-through primer to exposed surfaces. Apply joint sealant using applicator gun and tube to edges of new and existing panels. Apply underseal to boot floor and to wheel arches. Remove protective covering, axle stands and lower vehicle.

Replace parts in reverse order of removal, reconnect battery, alternator, test those mechanical and electrical items that have been removed and replaced.

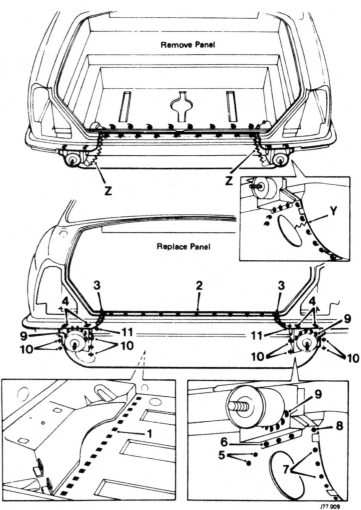

Fig. 7

NO.	LOCATION	FACTORY JOINT	REPAIR JOINT
1	To boot floor at front edge	15 resistance spot welds	15 MIG plug welds
2	To inner rear panel at boot drain channel	19 resistance spot welds	Single row of resistance spot welds ARO arms 242A
3	To rear wings R.H. and L.H. above flange	Braze each side	Braze each side
4	To rear wings R.H. and L.H. above bumper	1 resistance spot weld either side of mounting each side	1 MIG plug weld either side of mounting each side
5	To inner rear panel below bumper mountings R.H. and L.H.	2 resistance spot welds each side	2 resistance spot welds each side ARO arms 242A
6	To inner rear panel at bumper mountings R.H and L.H.	3 resistance spot welds each side	3 resistance spot welds each side ARO arms 242A
7	To inner lower rear wings R.H. and L.H.	6 resistance spot welds each side	Single row of resistance spot welds each side ARO arms 242A
8	To inner rear panel and inner lower rear wings R.H. and L.H.	1 resistance spot weld each side	1 resistance spot weld each side ARO arms 242A
9	To bumper mountings R.H. and L.H.	Continuous MIG weld each side	Continuous MIG weld each side
10	To bumper mountings R.H. and L.H. at edges	Continuous MIG weld run either side of each bumper mounting	Continuous MIG weld run either side of each bumper mounting
11	To rear wings R.H. and L.H. at inner corner of flanges	MIG tack weld each side	MIG tack weld each side

SILL PANEL 77.70.70

Disconnect battery and alternator. Remove rear seat cushion, squab and front seat cushion.

Disconnect seatbelt warning lamp wiring. Remove front seat frame, front and rear tread plates and clips; front and rear carpets and underfelts; upper and lower seat belt mountings; 'B' post front and rear aperture weatherseals/finishers; 'B' post courtesy lamp glass, 'B' post upper and lower trim sections, seat belt inertia reel. Release air volume control lever. Partially remove 'A' post weatherseal/finisher. Remove 'A' post lower trim section; inner sill carpet and underfelt. Disconnect and remove courtesy lamp switch; earth and wiring from 'A' post. Lay aside rear seat carpeting. Partially remove 'C' post aperture weatherseal/finisher and wheel arch lower trim. Remove rear wiring loom cover (L.H. only). Disconnect and lay aside radio aerial and wiring. Jack up vehicle, place on axle stands and remove front and rear road wheels and rear mud flap.

Remove front wing, see 77.28.29. Remove front door with hinges and rear door (see Section 76).

Protect vehicle interior, expose resistance spot welds at points 1, 2, 3, 4, 5, 6, 7 and 8 in Welding Diagram. Centre punch and cut out resistance spot welds. Cut sill panel and closing plate at points 'N' and 'O'. Separate and remove panels, remove metal remnants, including joint 9.

Clean old and new panel joint edges, drill holes in new panel for MIG plug welding at point 8 ahead of 'A' post. Clean joint edges on new rear closing plate. Apply weld-through primer to joint edges to be resistance spot welded.

Offer up new sill panel, align and clamp in position. Offer up front and rear doors, check alignment, remove doors. Resistance spot weld at points 1, 4, 7, MIG plug weld at points 5, 6 and 8. MIG tack weld at points 5 and 7. Dress MIG welds and resistance spot welds. Offer up rear closing plate, adjust. MIG tack weld at point 3. Resistance spot weld at points 2 and 3. Dress MIG welds and resistance spot welds. Prepare 'B' post and 'C' post joints. Apply solder to joints, shape and dress soldered joints. Apply joint sealant using applicator and tube to edges of new and existing panels. Remove protective covering. Replace front and rear road wheels, remove axle stands and lower vehicle.

Replace rear door, front door with hinges, replace front wing and adjust.

Replace parts in reverse order of removal, reconnect battery and alternator, test those mechanical and electrical items that have been removed and replaced, align headlamps if necessary.

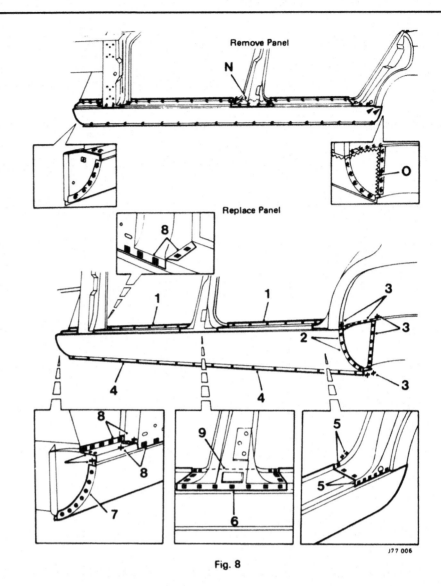

Fig. 8

NO.	LOCATION	FACTORY JOINT	REPAIR JOINT
1	To inner sill at upper flange at front and rear door aperture	42 resistance spot welds	Single row of resistance spot welds ARO arms 242A
2	To rear closing plate	7 resistance spot welds	Single row of resistance spot welds ARO arms 100737
3	Closing plate to outer wheelarch panel and chassis leg closing panel	10 resistance spot welds 3 MIG tack welds	Single row of resistance spot welds ARO arms 105492 Single row of reistance spot welds ARO arms 100737 4 MIG tack welds
4	To inner sill at lower flange	60 resistance spot welds 4 MIG tack welds	Single row of resistance spot welds ARO arms 103402
5	To base of 'C' post	10 resistance spot welds 3 MIG tack welds	10 MIG plug welds 3 MIG tack welds
6	To base of 'B' post and closing panel	17 resistance spot welds	17 MIG plug welds
7	To front wheel arch	9 resistance spot welds	2 single rows of resistance spot welds ARO arms 100737 1 MIG tack weld
8	To 'A' post	18 resistance spot welds	18 MIG plug welds
9	To inner sill, behind 'B' post inner closing panel	2 resistance spot welds 2 MIG tack welds	No access for welding See Repair Note 4, page 77—3

SILL PANEL—SECTION

Disconnect battery and alternator. Remove front seat cushion. Disconnect seat belt warning lamp. Remove front seat frame; front treadplate and retaining clips; front footwell carpet and underfelt. Release air volume control lever. Remove inner sill carpet section and underfelt. Jack up vehicle and place on axle stands. Remove front door, (see Section 76).

Protect vehicle interior, expose resistance spot welds at points 2 and 3 in Welding Diagram. Centre punch and cut out resistance spot welds. Cut panels at points 'P' and 'R', remove panel and metal remnants.

Clean old panel joint edges, cut a section from new panel to form approximate fit, clean new panel joint edges.

Offer up new panel section, align and clamp in position. Cut through old and new panels to form butt joints. Remove new panel section and metal remnants. Clean old and new panels at butt joints. Apply weld-through primer to joint edges to be resistance spot welded. Offer new panel, align and clamp in position. Offer up front door, check alignment and remove door. MIG butt weld and dress at points 1 and 4. Resistance spot weld at points 2 and 3. Prepare and apply solder at points 1 and 4, shape and dress soldered joints. Apply joint sealant using applicator gun and tube to edges of new and existing panels. Remove protective covering, and axle stands and lower vehicle.

Replace front door. Replace parts in reverse order of removal, reconnect battery and alternator, test those electrical items that have been removed and replaced.

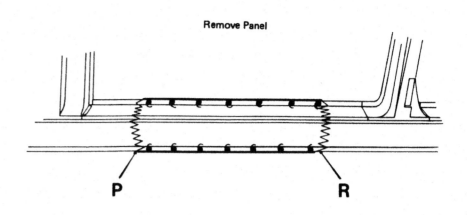

Remove Panel

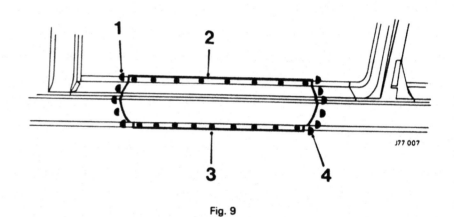

Replace Panel

Fig. 9

NO.	LOCATION	FACTORY JOINT	REPAIR JOINT
1	To existing panel at front end		Continuous MIG butt weld
2	To upper flange	11 resistance spot welds	Single row of resistance spot welds ARO arms 103402
3	To lower flange	17 resistance spot welds	Single row of resistance spot welds ARO arms 103402
4	To existing panel at rear end		Continuous MIG butt weld

WINGS

Front 77.28.29

Disconnect battery. Remove flasher lamps, bumper side mounting bolts, horns, upper mounting bolt grommets R.H. and L.H., chrome finisher and plastic apron assembly; centre fron-to-bumper mounting bolts R.H. and L.H. and remove front bumper assembly; remove outer headlamp bezel; wiring loom cover, fusebox (L.H. only), headlamp inner casing and tensioning spring. Pull aside wiring loom and disconnect from main loom. Remove headlamp casing with wiring and spire nuts. Remove flasher repeater assembly and grommet at flitch inside front of wing. Jack up vehicle, place on axle stands and remove front road wheel. Release front splashguard and remove rear splashguard and washers from wing, and bonnet counter-balancing spring.

Remove mounting bolts to flitch front and upper flanges, 'A' post, lower front panel and sill. Separate and remove wing.

Apply underseal to panel interior.

Offer up new panel, align, replace and tighten all mounting bolts. Re-secure front splashguard. Replace rear splashguard and front road wheel. Remove axle stands and lower vehicle. Replace parts in reverse order of removal except outer headlamp bezel. Reconnect battery, test those mechanical and electrical items that have been removed and replaced. Remove other headlamp bezel. Align headlamps. Replace headlamp bezels.

WINGS

Rear 77.70.67

Disconnect battery and alternator. Remove spare wheel cover, spare wheel, fuel pump cover and rear boot trim assembly, scuff plate, boot aperture weatherseal, radio aerial coverplate. Disconnect wiring. Remove aerial drive unit. Disconnect earth wiring and aerial socket. Remove aerial, separate aerial at lower joint, remove inner cable, re-assembly unit and place aside (L.H. only). Disconnect rear wiring loom and lay aside. Jack up vehicle and place on axle stands. Remove rear road wheel, petrol tanks R.H. and L.H., petrol pump assembly. Move aside boot courtesy lamp wiring and water drain tube. Remove breather pipes, rear seat cushion and squab, rear parcel shelf, rear inner and outer treadplates. Partially remove felt finisher at upper quarter. Release rear end of passenger grab handle. Remove upper quarter trim pad, rear screen lower padding. Disconnect and remove rear screen and finishers. Remove wheel arch trim. Lay aside rear seat cushion insulation felt and carpet. Remove wiring loom cover. Disconnect and lay aside wiring loom below squab. Remove rear retaining clips from treadplate, rear door striker plate, rear drip rail finisher, rear door impact buffer and boot lid.

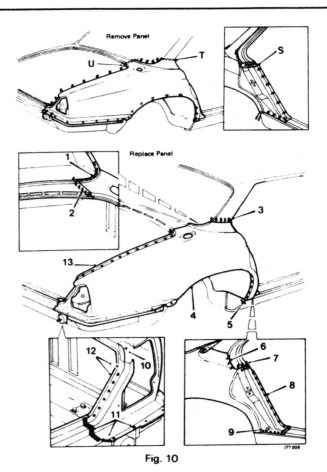

Fig. 10

NO.	LOCATION	FACTORY JOINT	REPAIR JOINT
1	To lower corner of screen aperture	13 resistance spot welds	Single row of resistance spot welds ARO arms 242A (modified) See Repair Note 7, page 77—3)
2	To rear screen panel	Continuous MIG weld	Continuous MIG weld
3	To upper quarter	Continuous MIG weld	Continuous MIG butt weld
4	To wheel arch flange	40 resistance spot welds	Single row of resistance spot welds ARO arms 105010
5	To rear of sill at wheel arch	2 resistance spot welds	1 X 20 mm MIG weld
6	To outer edge of door aperture at waist	3 MIG tack welds	3 MIG tack welds
7	To inner face of door aperture at waist	4 resistance spot welds MIG weld	4 MIG plug welds MIG weld
8	To 'D' post flange below waist	26 resistance spot welds	Single row of resistance spot welds ARO arms 242A
9	To sill	8 resistance spot welds	Single row of resistance spot welds ARO arms 242A 6 MIG plug welds
10	To inner rear wing inside tail lamp aperture	MIG weld	MIG weld
11	To bumper mounting and rear panel	2 resistance spot welds MIG tack weld Braze	2 resistance spot welds ARO arms 242A MIG tack weld Braze
12	To inner rear wing at drain channel lower section	6 resistance spot welds MIG weld	Single row of resistance spot welds ARO arms 242A MIG weld
13	To inner rear wing at drain channel	31 resistance spot welds	Single row of resistance spot welds ARO arms 242A

Protect vehicle, expose resistance spot welds at points 1, 4, 5, 7, 8, 9, 11 and 13 in Welding Diagram. Centre punch and cut out resistance spot welds. Remove solder and brazes at points 2 and 11. Cut panel at points 'S', 'T' and 'U'. Separate and remove bulk of panel. Remove metal remnants.

Clean old panel joint edges, cut new panel to form approximate fit.

Offer up new panel, align and clamp in position. Cut old and new panels to form butt joint at upper quarter. Remove new panel and metal remnants, clean old and new panel joints.

Apply weld-through primer to joint edges to be resistance spot welded. Apply joint sealant to outer edges of wheel arch. Offer up new panel, align and clamp in position. Replace boot lid hinge. Refit boot lid. Offer up rear screen, check alignment and remove screen, boot lid and hinge. MIG butt weld and dress at point 3. Resistance spot weld at points 1, 4, 8, 9, 11, 12 and 13. MIG weld at points 2, 5, 7, 10 and 12. MIG tack weld at points 6 and 11. Drill and MIG plug weld at points 7 and 9. Braze at point 11. Dress welds and braze. Prepare and apply solder to upper quarter, screen panel, sill and rear panel, inner face of door aperture at waist. Shape and dress soldered joints. Remove protective covering. Apply joint sealant using applicator gun and tube to edges of new and existing panels. Apply underseal. Replace road wheel, remove axle stands and lower vehicle. Replace boot lid. Replace parts in reverse order of removal, reconnect battery and alternator, test those mechanical and electrical items that have been removed and replaced and rear screen for water leaks.

Remove Panel

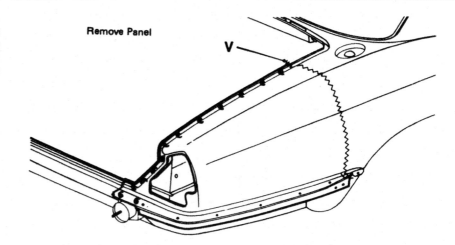

Replace Panel

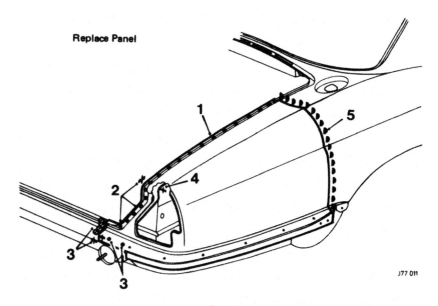

J77 011

Fig. 11

NO.	LOCATION	FACTORY JOINT	REPAIR JOINT
1	To inner rear wing at drain channel	31 resistance spot welds	Single row of resistance spot welds ARO arms 242A
2	To inner rear wing at drain channel section	6 resistance spot welds MIG weld	Single row of resistance spot welds ARO arms 242A MIG weld
3	To bumper mounting and rear panel	2 resistance spot welds MIG tack weld Braze	2 resistance spot welds ARO arms 242A MIG tack weld Braze
4	To inner rear wing inside tail lamp aperture	MIG weld	MIG weld
5	To existing panel		Continuous MIG butt weld

PAGE INTENTIONALLY LEFT BLANK

JAGUAR

Daimler

**Containing
Sections**

80 HEATING AND VENTILATION

82 AIR CONDITIONING

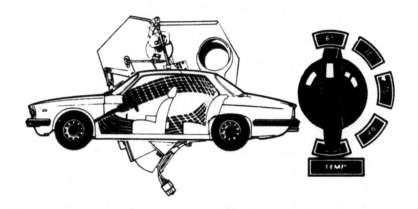

SERIES III
SERVICE MANUAL

INTRODUCTION

This Service Manual covers the Jaguar Series 3 and Daimler Series 3 range of vehicles. It is primarily designed to assist skilled technicians in the efficient repair and maintenance of Jaguar and Daimler vehicles.

Using the appropriate service tools and carrying out the procedures as detailed will enable the operations to be completed within the time stated in the 'Repair Operation Times'.

The Service Manual has been produced in 13 separate sections; this allows the information to be distributed throughout the specialist areas of the modern service facility.

A table of contents in section 1 lists the major components and systems together with the section and book numbers. The cover of each book depicts graphically and numerically the sections contained within that book. Each section starts with a list of operations in alphabetical order.

The title page of each book carries the part numbers required to order replacement books, binders or complete Service Manuals. This can be done through the normal channels.

Operation Numbering

A master index of numbered operations has been compiled for universal application to all vehicles manufactured by Jaguar Cars Ltd., and therefore, because of the different specifications of various models, continuity of the numbering sequence cannot be maintained throughout this manual.

Each operation described in this manual is allocated a number from the master index and cross-refers with an identical number in the 'Repair Operation Times'. The number consists of six digits arranged in three pairs.

Each operation is laid out in the sequence required to complete the operation in the minimum time, as specified in the 'Repair Operation Times'.

Service Tools

Where performance of an operation requires the use of a service tool, the tool number is quoted under the operation heading and is repeated in, following, the instruction involving its use. A list of all necessary tools is included in section 1, number 99.

References

References to the left- or right-hand side in the manual are made when viewing from the rear. With the engine and gearbox assembly removed the timing cover end of the engine is referred to as the front. A key to abbreviations and symbols is given in section 1, number 01.

REPAIRS AND REPLACEMENTS

When service parts are required it is essential that only genuine Jaguar/Daimler or Unipart replacements are used. Attention is particularly drawn to the following points concerning repairs and the fitting of replacement parts and accessories.

1.   Safety features embodied in the vehicle may be impaired if other than genuine parts are fitted. In certain territories, legislation prohibits the fitting of parts not to the vehicle manufacturer's specification.

2.   Torque wrench setting figures given in this Service Manual must be strictly adhered to.

3.   Locking devices, where specified, must be fitted. If the efficiency of a locking device is impaired during removal it must be replaced.

4.   Owners purchasing accessories while travelling abroad should ensure that the accessory and its fitted location on the vehicle conform to mandatory requirements existing in their country of origin.

5.   The vehicle warranty may be invalidated by the fitting of other than genuine Jaguar/Daimler or Unipart parts. All Jaguar/Daimler and Unipart replacements have the full backing of the factory warranty.

6.   Jaguar/Daimler Dealers are obliged to supply only genuine service parts.

SPECIFICATION

Purchasers are advised that the specification details set out in this Manual apply to a range of vehicles and not to any one. For the specification of a particular vehicle, purchasers should consult their Dealer.

The Manufacturers reserve the right to vary their specifications with or without notice, and at such times and in such manner as they think fit. Major as well as minor changes may be involved in accordance with the Manufacturer's policy of constant product improvement.

Whilst every effort is made to ensure the accuracy of the particulars contained in this Manual, neither the Manufacturer nor the Dealer, by whom this Manual is supplied, shall in any circumstances be held liable for any inaccuracy or the consequences thereof.

CONTENTS

80——1

HEATING AND VENTILATION SYSTEM (Non-Air Conditioned Cars)

Description   80.00.00

The car heating and ventilating system consists of selective ducting and a water-heated matrix through which fresh air can be forced, either by the passage of the car through the air or by twin, three-speed blower fans. The ducts channel air as required by the driver or passengers in front and rear compartments.

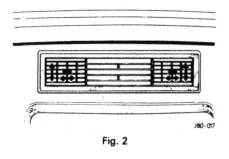

Fig. 1

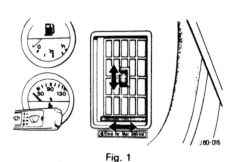

Fig. 2

Driver and Front Passenger Compartment (Fig. 1 and Fig. 2)

Face-level outlets (Fig. 1) at either end of the fascia may be opened or closed manually and adjusted for direction of delivery.

A face-level outlet (Fig. 2) is located in the centre of the fascia, the end sections of which can be adjusted for direction of delivery.

One outlet at each side of the centre console directs air into front footwells.

Windscreen

Non-adjustable vents, situated at the base of the windscreen, provide demisting and defrosting.

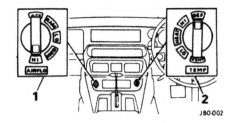

Fig. 3

Rear Passenger Compartment

Manually controlled louvred outlets (1, Fig. 3) direct air into each rear compartment footwell. A manually opened and closed directional outlet (2, Fig. 3) is located in the rear of the console.

Heater Controls (Fig. 4)

All heater controls are operated either by vacuum supplied by the engine or by mechanical linkage. With the engine switched off, a supply tank will provide sufficient vacuum for approximately six complete operations.

The control switches operate as follows:

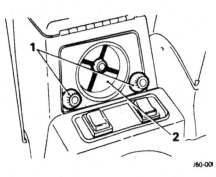

Fig. 4

Left-Hand Switch (Airflow symbol) (1, Fig. 4)

OFF

When the switch is set in this position the heating and ventilating system is inoperative.

RAM

When the switch is set in this position, air is forced into the car by its forward movement, then routed and heated as determined by the position of the right-hand switch, 'TEMP'.

LOW—MED—HIGH

When the switch is set to the 'HIGH' position, the blower fans rotate at a high speed to boost the air flow into the car. A resistor is switched into the blower fan circuit when the switch is moved to the 'MED' position therefore reducing the rotation speed of the fans. An additional resistor is switched in the fan circuit when the switch is moved to the 'LOW' position reducing the fan speed further.

The temperature of the air flow into the car is determined by the right hand 'TEMP' switch position.

Right-Hand Switch 'TEMP' (2, Fig. 4)

VENT

When the switch is set to this position, unheated fresh air is delivered from the face-level outlets across the fascia, at a delivery rate determined by the position of the left-hand switch. Individual outlets can be controlled as required. Movement of the knurled control knob beneath each of the side fascia outlets can be used to regulate airflow.

A small proportion of the airflow is bled to windscreen outlets for demisting.

LOW

When the switch is set to this position the hot water supply to the heater matrix is switched on and the centre fascia outlet is closed. A flap is positioned to deliver air at the minimum temperature. The airflow is distributed as follows:

a. Most of the air is delivered to the footwell outlets and the rear compartment.

b. A small proportion of the air is delivered to the fascia end outlets and to the windscreen.

DEF

When the switch is set to this position, air flow at maximum temperature is distributed 90% to windscreen and fascia end outlets and 10% to footwell and rear passenger compartment. The fascia end outlets may be aimed to defrost the side windows or closed to concentrate airflow at the windscreen.

Cold Weather

To obtain heating and demisting

a. Set the 'TEMP' control between 'LOW' and 'HIGH' to give the desired temperature, and allow a short period to elapse to permit the heater matrix to warm up.

b. Set the 'AIRFLOW' control to give the desired volume of air delivery.

c. Set the fascia end outlets as desired. For maximum demisting, close both outlets.

d. Set the rear compartment outlets as desired

To obtain rapid demisting or defrosting

a. Set the 'TEMP' control to 'DEF' and allow a short period to elapse to permit the heater matrix to warm up.

b. Close the fascia end outlets, or direct them to defrost the side windows as required.

c. Set the 'Airflow' control to 'HIGH'.

d. Close the rear compartment outlets.

Hot Weather

To obtain fresh air ventilation

a. Set the 'TEMP' control to 'VENT'.

b. Set the 'Airflow' control to give desired volume of air delivery.

c. Set the fascia end and centre outlets as desired.

d. Set the rear compartment outlets as desired.

To obtain rapid demisting

a. Set the 'TEMP' control to 'LOW'.

b. Set the 'Airflow' control to 'HIGH'.

c. Close the fascia end outlets, or direct the air flow to the side windows if desired.

d. Close the rear compartment outlets.

The air delivered to the fascia and windscreen although warm, is always cooler than the air delivered to the footwell. The volume of air to the windscreen may be increased by closing both fascia end outlets.

HIGH

The temperature of the air delivered is progressively increased to a maximum as the switch is rotated to 'HIGH'. Airflow from the fascia end and windscreen outlets is always cooler than that delivered to the footwell.

HEATER CONTROLS

Remove and refit   **80.10.02**

Removing

Disconnect the battery earth lead.
Remove the centre console as detailed in operation 76.25.01.
Remove two bolts, two nuts and associated shakeproof washers (1, Fig. 5) securing mounting plate to heater unit.
Remove three screws (2, Fig. 5) securing vacuum switches to mounting plate.
Note positions of vacuum pipes and disconnect from switches.
Remove circlips and locking rings (3, Fig. 5).
Remove mounting plate from studs.
Note position of cables and pipes on vacuum switch, and micro-switches before disconnecting.
To change micro-switch(es), remove secure screws and nuts as necessary.

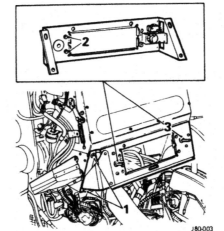

Fig. 5

NOTE: Ensure replacement switches are of correct pattern.

To change vacuum switch remove two screws securing mounting bracket.

Refitting

Refit mounting plate to studs.
Refit circlips and locking rings.
Reconnect the vacuum pipes to their correct positions on switches, and refit the three screws securing the vacuum switches to mounting plate.
Secure mounting plate to heater unit with the fixing nuts and bolts.
Refit the centre console.
Reconnect the battery.

HEATER TEMPERATURE CONTROL CABLE ASSEMBLY

Remove and refit   **80.10.05**

Removing

Disconnect the battery earth lead.
Remove the centre console as detailed in operation 76.25.01.
Remove right-hand dash liner as detailed in operation 76.25.02.
Remove nut and setscrew (1, Fig. 6) securing radio/heater controls mounting panel to heater unit R.H. side.
Remove four drive screws (2, Fig. 6) securing R.H. footwell outlet duct.
Remove three drive screws (3, Fig. 6) securing R.H. footwell and rear outlet assembly.

NOTE: One screw is located behind control mounting panel and will require use of a right-angle star-headed screwdriver.

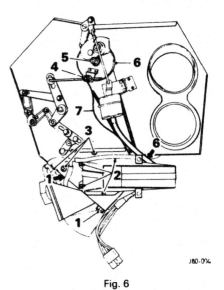

Fig. 6

Select 'VENT' position, loosen flap link operating rod locking nut (4, Fig. 6) on nylon wheel and cam assembly.
Remove nut and washer (5, Fig. 6) from the pivot of the nylon wheel and cam assembly.
Lift jockey pulleys against spring tension and remove main drive wheel (6, Fig. 6) from its fulcrum.
Ease radio/heater control panel and R.H. footwell outlet assembly away from heater unit.
Remove Bowden cable (7, Fig. 6) by releasing locking screw on driving bollard and removing nipples from main driving wheel.

continued

80—3

Refitting

Fit replacement cable to the pulley so that the cable is wound round the pulley 2½ times, i.e. when looking at the setscrew locking the pulley, three strands of wire should be seen. Ensure that at least two strands pass below the locking washer, but do not tighten at this stage. With temperature control knob in 10 o'clock position, and cable passing round jockey pulleys such that upper strand leaving bollard passes around forward pulley, stretch cable ends to fullest extent horizontally. Adjust cable until nipples are level with each other.

Tighten the locking screw, ensuring that the turns of cable are secured beneath the washer. Fit nipples into main drive wheel, ensuring cable ends do not cross.

Refit radio/heater control panel and R.H. footwell outlet assembly to heater unit.

Holding the wire taut, refit the main driving wheel.

NOTE: It may be necessary to lift the jockey pulleys to accomplish this. The upper cooling flap driving lever must also be pushed upwards to allow the wheel to be located on its shaft.

Rotate the main driving wheel and the right-hand control knob so that when the control knob is at heat position (9 o'clock) the main driving wheel is at the position shown.

Tighten the locking screw on the driving pulley. Reset flap operating mechanism as laid down in procedure for flap link adjustment in general section.

Refit and secure the right-hand footwell outlet duct.

Refit nut and screw securing radio/heater controls panel to heater unit.

Refit right-hand desk liner and the centre console.

Reconnect the battery.

HEATER WATER VALVE

Remove and refit   **80.10.16**

Removing

Drain coolant from system, see operation 26.10.01.

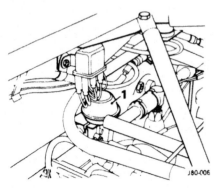

Fig. 7

NOTE: Conserve coolant if anti-freeze is in use.

Release hose clips and withdraw the hose from the unit.

Remove vacuum tube from connector and detach the unit (1, Fig. 7).

Refitting

Attach the unit and reconnect vacuum tube to the connector.

Refit hose and tighten the clip.

Refill the system with coolant.

NOTE: Water valves are sealed units and must be replaced if faulty.

AIR DIRECTION BOX REMOTE CONTROL

Remove and refit—Left- and Right-Hand   **80.10.31**

Removing

Withdraw two screws and one shrouded nut securing the parcel shelf.

Remove the shelf.

Withdraw two screws (1, Fig. 8) securing the control handle assembly.

Unclip operating arm (2, Fig. 8) from the control handle assembly.

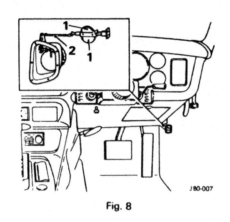

Fig. 8

Refitting

Reclip the operating arm to the control handle assembly.

Refit the two screws securing the control handle assembly.

Refit the shelf and secure with two screws and a shrouded nut.

AIR DIRECTION BOX

Remove and refit—Left- and Right-Hand   **80.10.32**

Removing

Remove the air direction box remote control, see operation 80.10.31.

Remove the lower body side front trim pad, see operation 76.13.01.

Withdraw five screws (1, Fig. 9) securing the air direction box.

Remove the air direction box (2, Fig. 9).

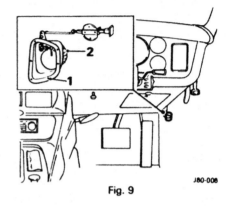

Fig. 9

Refitting

Refit the air direction box and secure with the five fixing screws.

Refit the lower body side front trim.

DEMISTER FLAP AND ACTUATOR ASSEMBLY

Remove and refit   **80.10.37**

Removing

Remove the crash roll, see operation 76.46.04.

Remove two nuts (1, Fig. 10) securing the assembly to screen rail.

Disconnect the plastic ducting (2, Fig. 10) from assembly.

Disconnect vaccum tube (3, Fig. 10) from the actuator.

Lift assembly (4, Fig. 10) away from screen rail.

80—4

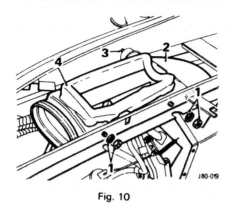

Fig. 10

Refitting

Locate assembly on to screen rail.
Reconnect vacuum tube and plastic ducting to the assembly.
Refit the two nuts to secure the assembly to the screen rail.
Refit the crash rail.

FLAP LINKAGE

Adjust   80.10.41

In order to obtain correct adjustment of the heater mechanism the following procedure should be adopted.
Turn temperature control knob (1, Fig. 11) to vent.
Slacken locking screws, 'A', 'B' and 'C'.
Rotate lever 'R' (2, Fig. 11) into fully clockwise position and hold in place using firm finger pressure. Tighten locking screw 'A'.
Press lever operating flap 'N' (3, Fig. 11) to fully clockwise position using finger pressure and tighten.
Turn temperature control knob to defrost. Using a screwdriver placed in slotted end of adjusting link (4, Fig. 11), apply pressure in order to push lever operating flap 'Q' into fully clockwise position. Tighten locking screw 'B'.
Check that detent loads at either ends of knob travel are acceptable. If not, some adjustment is possible by adjusting position of driving link pivot in lever 'R'. However, this should not normally be necessary.

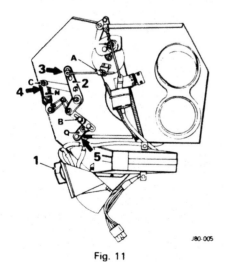

Fig. 11

The eccentric pivot on upper flap actuating cam is adjustable through about 180°.
This gives an adjustment of upper level temperature of 10°C in mid heat position.
Turning nut clockwise increases face-level temperature, turning it anti-clockwise reduces face-level temperature. With eccentric pivot in mid position and with R.H. knob in horizontal position, there should be a gap of about 6,35 mm (0.25 in) between flap and body of unit. This can only be checked with upper ducting removed.

DEMISTER DUCT OUTLETS

Remove and refit   80.15.02

Removing

Insert blade of narrow thin tool between edge of demister outlet grille and surround (1, Fig. 12). Carefully lever apart. Grille and surround are retained in place by nylon friction bushes (2, Fig. 12).

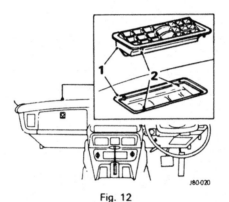

Fig. 12

Refitting

Place surround and grille in position and press firmly.

VENTILATOR (REAR)

Remove and refit   80.15.10

Removing

Lift the console glovebox lid and remove two screws (1, Fig. 13) securing lid retaining bar.
Withdraw the three screws (2, Fig. 13) securing hinge plate to glovebox.
Withdraw three screws (3, Fig. 13) securing glovebox liner.
Insert hand under glovebox liner and grip bayonet locking ring (4, Fig. 13) of air vent assembly. Exert pressure on front of vent assembly and rotate anti-clockwise until locking ring releases.
Remove air vent assembly (5, Fig. 13).

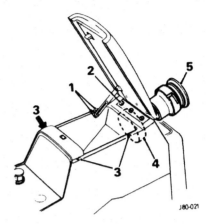

Fig. 13

Refitting

Refit the air vent assembly; secure by exerting pressure and rotating the locking ring until locked in position.
Fit the three screws to secure glovebox liner.
Fit the three screws securing the hinge plate to glovebox.
Lift the console glovebox lid and fit the two screws securing lid retaining bar.

VENTILATOR FASCIA OUTLETS

Remove and refit   Left   80.15.22
                            Right   80.15.23

Removing

Before carrying out the above operation it will be necessary to remove the fascia as detailed in operation 76.46.01.
Disconnect the battery earth lead.
Unclip outlet at rear of fascia.
Withdraw outlet assembly (1, Fig. 14) from ducting and fascia.

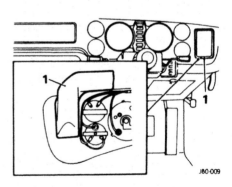

Fig. 14

Refitting

Insert the outlet assembly into ducting and fascia.
Reclip the outlet assembly.
Refit the fascia.
Reconnect the battery.

80—5

VENTILATOR FASCIA OUTLET (CENTRE)

Remove and refit   80.15.24

Removing

Before carrying out the above operations it will be necessary to remove the fascia as detailed in operation 76.46.01.
Disconnect the battery earth lead.
Withdraw the four retaining screws and remove the outlet assembly.

Refitting

Refit the outlet assembly and secure with the four retaining screws.
Refit the fascia.
Reconnect the battery earth lead.

FRESH AIR INTAKE

NOTE: With air conditioning fitted but inoperative, fresh air will not be available at fascia adjustable outlets with fans switched ON. Fascia outlets will only deliver air at the selected temperature.

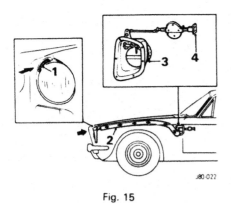

Fig. 15

An additional fresh air supply is available to driver and passenger. A grille located in the outer headlamp embellisher (1) admits air which is ducted via the wings (2) to outlets in the scuttle side panels (3) beneath the parcel tray. These outlets are controlled by a three-position lever marked 'PULL AIR' (4). The louvre outlets can be rotated to direct air as required.
Airflow will depend upon the speed at which the car is moving and position of selector level.

FRESH AIR INTAKE

Remove and refit Scuttle   80.15.29

Removing

Insert screwdriver under edge of intake and carefully lever away from nylon friction bush. Take care not to damage the paintwork.
Disconnect windscreen washer capillary tube from washer jet.

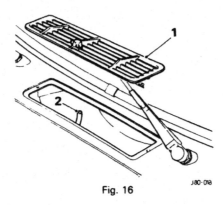

Fig. 16

Refitting

Reconnect the windscreen washer capillary tube from the washer jet and carefully replace the grille.

FRESH AIR INTAKE

Remove and refit   80.15.29

Removing

Remove the headlamp as detailed in operation 86.40.02.
Withdraw screw (1, Fig. 17) retaining intake grille.
Clear grille of road dirt, insects etc.

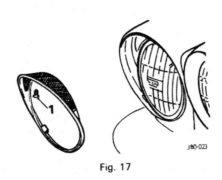

Fig. 17

Refitting

Refit headlamp embellisher and secure with retaining screw.

HEATER UNIT

Remove and refit   80.20.01

Removing

Disconnect the battery earth lead.
Drain the coolant from system.

NOTE: Conserve the coolant if anti-freeze is in use.

Remove the fascia crash roll, and fascia.
Remove the driver's and passenger's dash casings.
Remove the glove compartment liner.
Remove the centre parcel shelf and centre console assembly.
Disconnect the coolant hoses at heater matrix bulkhead connectors in engine compartment.

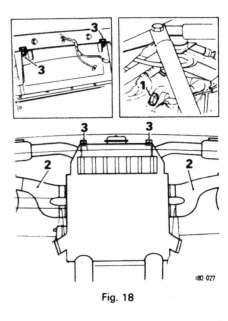

Fig. 18

NOTE: Retain the sponge collars from the stub pipes.

Remove the two nuts securing unit to the bulkhead (1, Fig. 18).
Locate the vacuum connectors and mark clearly before disconnecting.
Remove the flexible ducting from the heater unit (2, Fig. 18).
Disconnect the cable harness multi-pin connectors.
Remove the bolts securing the unit to the fascia rail. Ease the unit forward and lift from car (3, Fig. 18).

NOTE: Transmission selector should be in '1' position on automatic cars, or 4th, 2nd or Reverse gear on manual gearbox cars.
CAUTION: Great care must be exercised when lifting unit not to damage relay box. The unit must not be supported on these components.

Refitting

Offer unit up to mounting position and ease heater connectors through bulkhead apertures.

NOTE: Ensure sponge backing is in position.

Loosely fit retaining nuts, ensuring that pipes, speedometer cables and electrical harness are not trapped before tightening.
Refit the flexible ducting to the heater unit.
Reconnect the vacuum pipes as marked when dismantling.
Reconnect the electrical multi-pin connectors.
Ensure drain tubes from the unit are located through the grommets in side of transmission tunnel.
Refit the centre parcel tray.
Refit the glove compartment liner.
Refit the dash casings.
Refit the fascia and the fascia crash roll.
Reconnect the coolant hoses to the heater matrix bulkhead connectors in the engine compartment.

NOTE: Ensure sponge collars and metal washers are in place before connecting coolant hoses.

Refill with coolant.
Reconnect the battery earth lead.

HEATER MOTOR ASSEMBLY

Remove and refit
Right-Hand Unit   80.20.15

The blower fans are heavy duty motors with metal impellers attached. Speed variation is controlled by resistance units wired in series. Air flow control flaps are operated by a vacuum actuator mounted on the side of the inlet duct.

Removing

Disconnect the battery earth lead.
Remove the right-hand footwell trim pad, dash liner and console side pad as detailed in operation 76.46.11.
Remove the bulb failure unit from component panel.
Remove nuts securing component panel to blower assembly, and ease the panel clear.
Disconnect pliable trunking from the heater unit stub pipes.
Withdraw two screws securing fresh-air pull mounting bracket.
Remove two nuts retaining assembly from mounting posts.
Disconnect vacuum tube from actuator.
Disconnect electrical harness at snap connectors.
Ease fan motor assembly from car.

Refitting

Locate fan motor unit to its mounting positions.

Reconnect the electrical wiring harness.
Fit and tighten securing nuts.
Remove wedge holding the recirculation flap open.
Reconnect the pliable trunking to the stub pipes and the vacuum tube to the actuator.
Locate component panel to mounting studs and secure with securing nuts.
Refit the fresh-air pull mounting bracket.
Refit the bulb failure unit.
Refit the console side pad, dash liner and footwell trim pad.
Reconnect the battery earth lead.

NOTE: To refit assemblies successfully it is necessary to apply vacuum to the actuator, closing the top air flap. This simplifies insertion of the top flap and flange into its aperture and seal.

HEATER MOTOR ASSEMBLY

Remove and refit
Left-Hand Unit   80.20.15

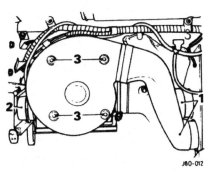

Fig. 19

Removing

Disconnect the battery earth lead.
Remove left-hand side footwell trim pad, dash liner, console trim pad, and glovebox as detailed in operation 76.46.11.
Remove nuts securing component panel to blower assembly, and ease the panel clear.
Disconnect the electrical feed to blower motor.
Disconnect the pliable trunking from the heater unit (1, Fig. 19), and the vacuum pipes from the actuator (2, Fig. 19).
Remove the motor assembly securing nuts and ease assembly from car (3, Fig. 19).

Refitting

Locate assembly to its mounting positions and secure with nuts.
Reconnect the pliable trunking and vacuum pipes.
Reconnect the electrical wiring harness.
Locate component panel to mounting studs and secure with the fixing nuts.
Refit the glovebox, dash liner, console trim pad, and footwell trim pad.
Reconnect the battery earth lead.

MOTOR RESISTANCE UNIT

Remove and refit
Left-Hand-Drive Cars   80.20.17

Removing

Disconnect the battery earth lead.
Remove the driver's side dash liner, and centre console side casing as detailed in operation 76.46.11.
Note position of cables at the resistance unit and disconnect (3, Fig. 20).
Withdraw the three retaining screws (1, Fig. 20) and remove resistance unit from the heater unit case (2, Fig. 10).

Refitting

Locate resistance unit into heater unit case and secure with the retaining screws.
Reconnect the electrical cables.
Refit the centre console side casing and dash liner.
Reconnect the battery earth lead.

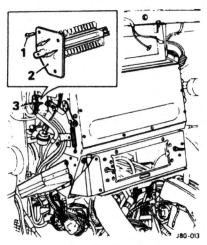

Fig. 20

MOTOR RESISTANCE UNIT

Remove and refit
Right-Hand-Drive Cars   80.20.17

Removing

Disconnect battery earth lead.
Remove glove compartment liner.
Note position of cables at the resistance unit and disconnect.
Withdraw the three retaining screws, and remove the resistance unit from the heater unit case.

Refitting

Locate resistance unit into heater unit case, and secure with the retaining screws.
Reconnect the electrical cables.
Refit the glove compartment liner.
Reconnect the battery earth lead.

continued

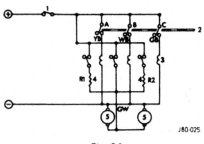

Fig. 21

KEY TO WIRING DIAGRAM

1   Ignition switch
2   Cam operated switches
3   Relays—motor speed
4   Resistors—motor speed
5   Fan motors

MOTOR RELAYS

Remove and refit   **80.20.19**

Removing

Disconnect the battery earth lead.
Remove the left-hand centre console side casing.
Withdraw the retaining screws and remove the footwell air outlet duct.
Note and mark the position of cables at the connectors on relay box, and remove the cables (1, Fig. 22).
Remove the nuts and washers securing the relay box, and remove relay box (2, Fig. 22).

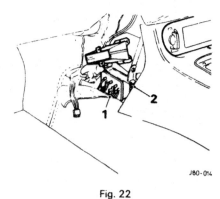

Fig. 22

Refitting

Fit and secure relay box with the retaining nuts and washers

NOTE: Ensure earth strap tag is replaced under relay box securing unit

Reconnect the electrical cables.
Refit the footwell air outlet duct, and left-hand centre console side casing.
Reconnect the battery earth lead.

80—8

BLOWER ASSEMBLY

Overhaul   **80.20.20**

Dismantling

Remove blower motor assembly as detailed in operation 80.25.13/14.
Pull down air recirculation flap for access to flap box securing screw, and remove screw.
Remove screws securing flap box at top of motor housing (1, Fig. 23).
Disconnect motor electrical connections (2, Fig. 23).
Remove the flap box.

NOTE: It is recommended at this stage that the positions of various components are marked either with paint or a scriber. This will facilitate reassembly.
One cable Lucar has a raised projection which matches the aperture in the motor casing. This ensures that the connections are replaced correctly and the rotation of the motor is not altered.
Remove the bolts securing the motor mounting bracket to fan housing (3, Fig. 23).
Remove the motor and fan assembly from the fan housing.
Remove the mounting bracket from the motor.
Using the appropriate Allen key, remove the impeller fan from the spindle.

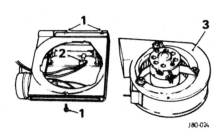

Fig. 23

Reassembling

Refit fan to the motor and secure to spindle.
Refit mounting bracket to motor.
Locate fan and mounting assembly into the fan housing
Fit and tighten bolts securing the assembly to fan housing.
Place flap box assembly to fan housing and reconnect electrical connections.
Fit and tighten screws securing the flap box to the housing.
Raise the recirculation flap, fit and tighten the remaining screw.
Refit the blower motor assembly.
Reconnect the battery

HEATER MATRIX

Remove and refit   **80.20.29**

Removing

Remove the heater unit as detailed in operation 80.20.01.
Using scriber or a thin brush and white paint mark the positions of all control rods, knobs and cams.
Disconnect tensioning springs from the heater matrix control flap operating arms.
Disconnect the operating rods.
Remove the two clips securing the inlet and outlet pipes to the heater unit case.
Withdraw six screws securing matrix cover-plate.
Withdraw one screw securing the cam and operating arm to footwell outlet flap shaft and remove arm.
Withdraw the heater matrix from side of heater unit with a steady straight pull. Care must be taken not to damage the inlet and outlet pipes.

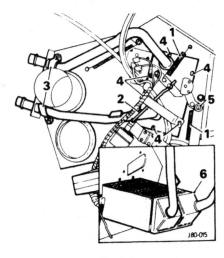

Fig. 24

Refitting

NOTE: Ensure that the sponge shock-absorbing pads are refitted correctly when replacing the matrix.
Refit the matrix into heater unit, taking care not to damage the inlet and outlet pipes.
Secure the cam and operating arm to footwell outlet flap shaft with the retaining screw.
Refit the matrix cover-plate and secure with the fixing screws.
Secure the inlet and outlet pipes to the heater unit with clips.
Reconnect the operating rods.
Reconnect the tensioning springs to the heater matrix control flap operating arms.
Refit the heater unit.

DEFROST AND DEMIST SYSTEM

Test   80.30.01

Purpose

To ensure that the heating system is functioning correctly in the 'defrost' mode, and that adequate airflow is maintained in the heat mode to ensure that the windscreen remains mist-free.

Method

a   Set L.H. control to fan speed 'High'.

b   Set R.H. control to 'Defrost'.

c   Close end of dash outlets.

d   Start engine and run for seven minutes at 1500 rev/min.

e   During the running period measure the airflow from each screen outlet using checking ducts and velometer. Ensure that the centre dash outlet is closed and that it seals satisfactorily. The velocity from the screen outlets should be:

7,62 m/s (1500 ft/min) (minimum)

f   Also during the running period turn the R.H. control to 'Heat' and open end of dash outlets. Using the screen outlet and end of dash checking ducts measure the resulting air velocity. These should be:

Minimum velocity

Screen	End of dash
2,29 m/s 450	3,30 m/s 650
ft/min	ft/min

g   At the end of seven minutes running at 1500 rev/min check that the water temperature gauge indicates 'Normal'. Using mercury in glass thermometers also check that the following minimum screen outlet temperatures are achieved.

Plenum Inlet		Screen Outlet (minimum)	
°C	°F	°C	°F
10	50	54	129.2
12	53.6	55	131
14	57.2	55.5	131.9
16	60.8	56.5	133.7
18	64.4	57	134.6
20	68	58	136.4
22	71.6	58.5	137.3
24	72.5	59.5	139.1

HEATER UNIT

Test   80.30.05

1. Warm up and heat pick-up on vent and water valve operation.

Turn the R.H. knob to 'Vent' and the L.H. knob to 'High'.

Start the engine and warm up, run at 1000 rev/min. In this condition the inlet flaps should be open and the centre outlet flap open.

With a thermometer placed in the air stream issuing from the centre vent, ensure that as the engine reaches normal operating temperatures, the air temperature does not rise above 5°C higher than it was in the engine cold state.

2. Defrost mode

Turn the R.H. knob to 'Defrost'.
The centre vent should close as should the upper mixing flap. The airflow to the footwell will be cut off apart from a small bleed.
At this point the defrost schedule can be operated if so desired. This will also check that the upper mixing flap is operating.

3. Fan speeds

Check that high, medium and low speeds can be obtained by rotating the L.H. knob.

4. Temperature range

By rotating the R.H. knob ensure that the air temperature changes between hot and ambient over the heating range.

5. Ram and off

On the road check that air flows from the vent when the L.H. knob is in the 'Ram' position, but is cut off in the 'Off' position.

Equipment required: 16 mm (⅝ in) bore hose at least 1,6 m (5 ft) long.
Water supply controlled by tap.
One 2 gallon or 10 litre capacity container.
Stop watch.

NOTE: All tests must be completed with the engine cold, i.e. with the thermostats closed. Should the engine temperature rise sufficiently to open the thermostats, the engine must be stopped and allowed to cool before the tests are continued.

1. Drain coolant; conserve for refill.

2. Disconnect hose from heater matrix outlet stub pipe (this hose connects to water pump intake). Plug open end of hose.

3. Connect 16 mm (⅝ in) bore hose to heater stub pipe and place other end in 10 litre or 2 gallon container.

4. Refill cooling system with water, leaving hose from supply tap in header tank.

5. Start engine, run at 1000 rev/min with 'defrost' selected on heater control. Adjust water supply to keep header tank filled.

6. When water from heater matrix is free from air, measure time required to fill the 10 litre or 2 gallon container. Stop engine. If the time to fill a 1 gallon container is more than 1 min. 11 secs, or for a 10 litre container more than 1 min. 18 secs, heater matrix is obstructed and must be cleared as detailed below.

7. Disconnect hose pipe from heater matrix output stub pipe, unplug car hose and refit to stub pipe.

8. Add one pint of Ferroclene to header tank, top-up system with water and replace both filler caps.

9. Start engine and run at 1000 rev/min for 15 minutes.

10. Stop engine and drain.
Continue flushing system for at least 30 minutes to remove all traces of Ferroclene which would otherwise cause internal corrosion.

11. Repeat operations 2 to 6 above. If necessary, repeat operations 7 to 10.

12. Refill, using coolant conserved in operation 1 above.

HEATING AND VENTILATING VACUUM SYSTEM

Description

The vacuum is supplied from the vacuum reservoir located in the engine compartment on the driver's side of the vehicle, adjacent to the brake servo.

Vacuum actuators operate the blower and centre flap ventilators, the flap in the screen vent, the rods connected to the upper cooling flap and the lower heater flap.

When the system is switched to 'VENT' the actuator on the right hand side of the heater unit operates to fully open the upper cooling flap. When 'LO' is selected a vacuum switch releases the holding vacuum and the flap actuating lever drops onto an operating cam. When 'VENT' is re-selected vacuum is re-applied and the flap re-opens.

The left hand actuator is operative in all positions except when in the defrost mode. In the positions the actuator is operative the lower heating flap is free to be controlled by a cam and peg on the right hand side of the heater unit.

The water valve is closed as vacuum is applied and no water flows through the heater matrix. When heat is selected (either high or low) the vacuum feed is removed from the water valve which opens to allow water to flow through the heater matrix.

80—9

VACUUM SYSTEM

Function

Air Flo Control: OFF
Temp Control: VENT

1. The vacuum switches on both controls are all on and will conduct vacuum.
2. The centre flap is opened as vacuum is applied.
3. The demist flaps are closed as vacuum is applied.
4. The blower motor casing air intake flaps are closed as vacuum is applied and no air transfer from the exterior to the interior of the vehicle can take place.
5. The right hand side vacuum actuator is operative. This operates to open the upper cooling flap.
6. The left hand side vacuum actuator is operative. The lower heating flap in this mode is controlled by a cam and peg on the right hand side of the heater unit. These operate the flap in all positions except defrost.
7. The water valve is closed as vacuum is applied and water will not circulate through the heater matrix.

Air Flo Control: RAM, LO, MED or HI
Temp Control: VENT

· The vacuum switches on the right hand control are all 'On' and conducting vacuum to the relevant units.
The units are:
1. The flaps in the screen vents.
2. The vaccum actuators on both sides of heater unit are operative.
3. The water valve is closed as vacuum is applied and water will not circulate through the heater matrix.
4. The centre flap is opened as vacuum is applied.
The vacuum switch on the left hand control is 'Off' and not conducting vacuum. The actuators on the blower motor casing are relaxed. The spring tension therefore opens the flaps to allow ambient air to the interior of the vehicle.

Air Flo Control: RAM, LO, MED or HI
Temp Control: LO—HI

1. The vacuum switch on the left hand control is 'Off' and not conducting vacuum. The actuators on the blower motor casing are relaxed. The spring tension therefore opens the flaps to allow ambient air to the interior of the vehicle.
2. The vacuum switches on the right hand are 'Off'.
3. Vacuum will be removed from the centre flap and the flap will close.
4. Vacuum will be removed from the right hand side actuator and the upper cooling flap will close to a position where the nylon disc and cam will take over the closing operation. The nylon disc is fitted with an

additional abutment rod and lever that holds the upper cooling flap cam follower firmly against the cam profile.
5. The vacuum applied to the water valve has been removed therefore the valve opens to allow water to circulate the heater matrix.

Air Flo Control: RAM, LO, MED or HI
Temp Control: DEF

1. In the 'DEF' mode vacuum is not applied to any of the actuators.
2. The centre flap is closed.
3. The vacuum actuator on the right hand side is inoperative and the upper cooling flap is closed.
4. The vacuum applied to the water valve has been removed therefore the valve opens to allow water to circulate the heater matrix.
5. The demist flaps to the screen are opened.
6. The vacuum actuator on the left hand side is inoperative and the lever attached to the lower heater flap is pushed upwards closing the flap. This overrides the action of the cam and peg on the right hand side of the lower heating pivot.

KEY TO VACUUM SYSTEM DIAGRAM

1. Demist flap actuator
2. Centre flap actuator
3. Actuator on the right hand side of heater unit
4. Actuator on the left hand side of heater unit
5. Switch on 'AIR FLO' control
6. Front switch on 'TEMP' control
7. Rear switch on 'TEMP' control
8. Blower flap actuator
9. To vacuum tank
10. To water valve actuator

HEATING AND VENTILATING VACUUM SYSTEM

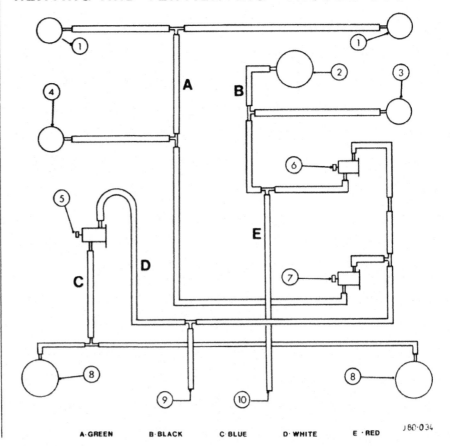

A · GREEN   B · BLACK   C · BLUE   D · WHITE   E · RED

J 80·034

80—10

CONTENTS

AIR CONDITIONING SYSTEM

CONTENTS

WARNING: EXTREME CARE SHOULD BE EXERCISED IN HANDLING THE REFRIGERANT. LIQUID REFRIGERANT AT ATMOSPHERIC PRESSURE BOILS AT −29°C (−20°F). SERIOUS DAMAGE OR BLINDNESS MAY OCCUR IF REFRIGERANT IS ALLOWED TO CONTACT THE EYES.
Goggles and gloves must be worn while working with Refrigerant.

FIRST AID: If refrigerant should contact the eyes or skin, splash the eyes or affected area with cold water for several minutes. Do not rub. As soon as possible thereafter, obtain treatment from a doctor or eye specialist.

SPECIAL TOOLS AND EQUIPMENT FOR SERVICING AIR CONDITIONING SYSTEM ON JAGUAR SERIES III

1 Pektron test unit
1 Charging station
1 Leak detector
1 Temperature test box
1 Compressor service tool kit
1 Setting jig for temperature differential control, 18G1363.
1 Voltmeter
1 Ohmmeter

TORQUE LEVELS FOR THE AIR CONDITIONING HOSE CONNECTIONS

Item	Nm	Kgf/m	lbf/ft
1. Compressor/Condenser (Compressor End)	40,67 to 47,45	4,15 to 4,84	30 to 35
2. Condenser/Compressor (Condenser End)	28,47 to 36,30	2,90 to 3,73	21 to 27
3. Condenser/Receiver Drier (Condenser End)	20,34 to 27,12	2,10 to 2,76	15 to 20
4. Receiver Drier/Condenser (Receiver Drier End)	40,67 to 47,45	4,15 to 4,84	30 to 35
5. Receiver Drier/Evaporator (Receiver Drier End)	40,67 to 47,45	4,15 to 4,84	30 to 35
6. Evaporator/Receiver Drier (Evaporator End)	14,91 to 17,62	1,52 to 1,80	11 to 13
7. Expansion Valve/Evaporator (Expansion Valve End)	20,34 to 27,12	2,10 to 2,76	15 to 20
8. Evaporator/Compressor (Evaporator End)	28,47 to 36,60	2,90 to 3,73	21 to 27
9. Compressor/Evaporator (Compressor End)	40,67 to 47,45	4,15 to 4,84	30 to 35

82—2

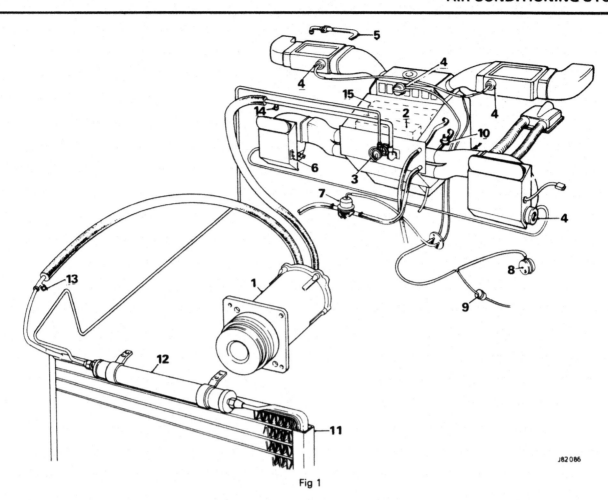

Fig 1

J82 086

KEY TO COMPONENTS (Fig. 1)

1. Compressor
2. Evaporator
3. Expansion valve
4. Vacuum valve
5. In-car sensor
6. Ambient temperature sensor
7. Water control valve
8. Vacuum reservoir
9. Non-return valve
10. Water valve temperature switch
11. Condenser
12. Receiver-drier
13. High pressure schrader valve
14. Low pressure schrader valve
15. Heater matrix

82—3

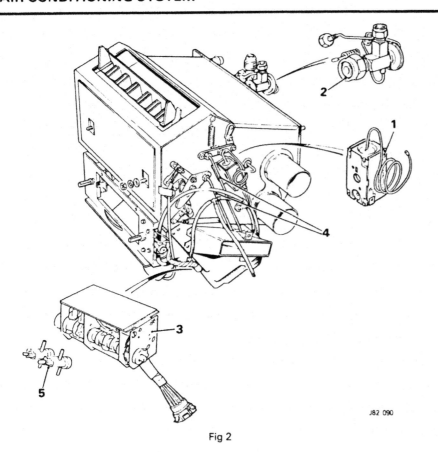

KEY TO COMPONENTS (Fig. 2)

1. Ranco thermostat
2. Expansion valve
3. Servo control unit
4. Control rod
5. Vacuum valve

J82 090

Fig 2

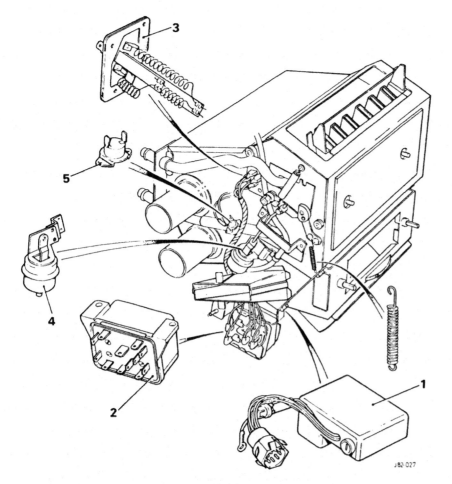

KEY TO COMPONENTS (Fig. 3)

1. Amplifier
2. Relays
3. Fan speed resistance
4. Vacuum actuator motor
5. Water thermostat

J82-027

Fig 3

82—4

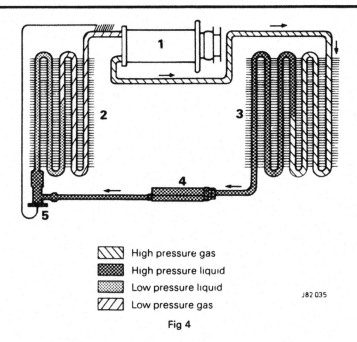

High pressure gas
High pressure liquid
Low pressure liquid
Low pressure gas

J82 035

Fig 4

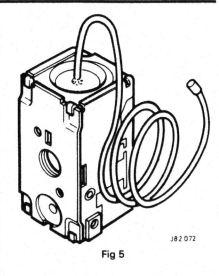

J82 072

Fig 5

The switch breaks the electric feed to the compressor magnetic clutch winding and the refrigeration cycle ceases. When the evaporator matrix temperature rises above 2°C (33.8°F) the thermostat switch closes and the refrigeration cycle re-starts.

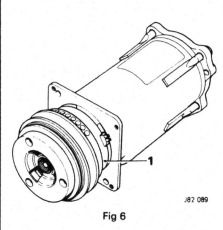

J82 089

Fig 6

The magnetic clutch coil is mounted on the end of the compressor (1, Fig. 6) and the electrical connections are made to the coil terminals. The clutch permits the compressor to be engaged or disengaged as required for the air conditioning operation. When current passes through the clutch coil, the armature clutch plate assembly, keyed to the compressor shaft, is drawn rearwards against the belt driven pulley that is free wheeling upon the same shaft. This locks pulley and armature plate together to drive the compressor. When current ceases to flow, springs in the armature plate draw the clutch face from the pulley. The compressor comes to rest and the pulley continues to free wheel.

REFRIGERATION CYCLE

Description   82.00.00

A belt-driven compressor (1, Fig. 4) draws in superheated refrigerant vapour at low pressure and compresses it.
The pressure forces the refrigerant round the refrigeration system.
The pressurized refrigerant is forced into a condenser (3, Fig. 4) located in front of the engine cooling radiator. The condenser is a matrix of tubes surrounded by fins. The refrigerant vapour travelling inside the tubes gives up its heat to the air-flow through the condenser. With the heat removed the vapour condenses to a cool liquid. The dimensions of the condenser determine that further heat transference occurs and the liquid becomes sub-cooled. Complete condensation has occurred.
The sub-cooled refrigerant still under pressure is forced into a receiver/drier (4, Fig. 4). The receiver/drier has several functions. It is a reservoir for the liquid; a filter to remove any particles which would contaminate the liquid; and it contains a quantity of molecular sieve desiccant to soak up any moisture in the liquid. Moisture would impair the efficiency of the refrigerant and cause damage at a later stage. The clean 'dry' liquid now passes into an expansion valve (5, Fig. 4) located at the inlet to the air conditioning unit. The liquid refrigerant is metered by the expansion valve so that the correct quantity is allowed to an evaporator matrix (2, Fig. 4) located in the air-conditioning unit. The metering orifice of the expansion valve is protected by a gauze filter located in the inlet union. The size of the metering orifice is controlled by the temperature sensed by a capillary at the evaporator outlet. If the temperature of the outlet pipe falls, the expansion valve closes to cut down the flow of refrigerant to the evaporator. As the temperature of the outlet

rises, a further quantity of refrigerant, metered by the expansion valve, enters the evaporator. The evaporator is a low pressure area so the refrigerant suddenly expands and the temperature drops. When the temperature falls below 0.6°C (33°F) it boils (i.e. vaporizes) and as any liquid requires a large amount of heat to change to vapour, the temperature of the evaporator matrix falls. Heat is taken from the air passing through the matrix on its way into the car.
Heat transfer continues until the vapour becomes low pressure super-heated vapour. The cycle recommences as the compressor draws in the super-heated low pressure vapour.

NOTE: Moisture from the cooled air passing over the fins of the evaporator condenses. The water is drained from the bottom of the evaporator by rubber tubes, and may form a pool of water under the vehicle when standing. This is normal and does not indicate a malfunction.

COMPONENT DESCRIPTION

RANCO THERMOSTAT

Ice formation on the evaporator fins due to moisture in the air is possible. Icing would damage the evaporator, so a thermostatic device to prevent this is fitted.
The Ranco thermostat (Fig. 5) is a temperature-operated switch which is normally closed in all functions and modes. It opens only when the temperature sensor capillary probe inserted in the evaporator matrix falls below 2°C (33.8°F).
It is important that the end of the capillary tube is inserted 10 cm and is in contact with the evaporator finning.

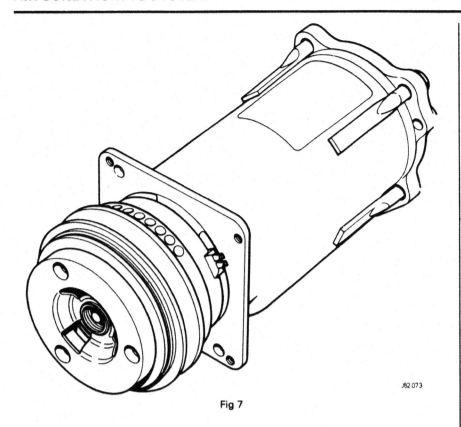

Fig 7

J82 073

COMPRESSOR

The compressor (Fig. 7) is a six-cylinder, reciprocating piston type of special design in which three sets of double acting pistons are actuated by a swash plate on the compressor shaft so that the pistons move back and forth in the cylinders as the shaft is rotated. There are in effect three independent cylinders at each end of the compressor and reed valves are provided for each cylinder at both ends of the compressor. Internal 'cross-over' passages for suction and discharge are provided within the compressor so that the high and low service fittings on the rear end of the compressor control refrigerant flow to and from all the cylinders. A gear type oil pump located in the rear head provides for compressor lubrication.

CONDENSER

The condenser (Fig. 8) consists of a refrigerant coil mounted in a series of thin cooling fins to provide a maximum of heat transfer in a minimum amount of space. It is usually mounted directly in front of the car radiator so that it receives the full flow of RAM AIR. Ram air is the air flow induced by the forward motion of the car and the suction of the cooling fan.

The condenser receives heat laden high pressure refrigerant vapour from the compressor.

The refrigerant enters the inlet at the top of the condenser as a high pressure very hot vapour and as this hot vapour passes down through the condenser coils, heat will follow its natural tendency and move from the hot refrigerant vapour into the cooler ram air as it flows across the condenser coils and fins.

When the refrigerant vapour reaches the temperature and pressure that will induce a change of state a large quantity of heat will be transferred to the outside air and the refrigerant will change from a high pressure HOT VAPOUR to a high pressure WARM LIQUID.

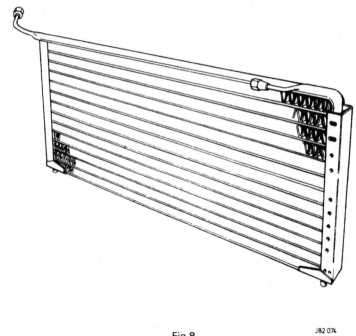

Fig 8

J82 074

82—6

SIGHT GLASS

The sight glass located on the output side of the receiver-drier through which the refrigerant flows is used to indicate the condition of the refrigerant charge. A clear sight glass (Fig. 9) normally indicates the system has a correct charge of refrigerant. It may also indicate the system has a complete lack of refrigerant; this will be accompanied by a lack of any cooling action by the evaporator. Also the system may be overcharged; this must be verified with test gauge readings.

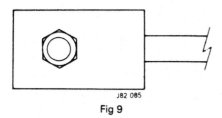

Fig 9

Foam or a constant stream of bubbles (Fig. 10) indicates the system does not contain sufficient refrigerant. Occasional bubbles when the system is first started is normal.

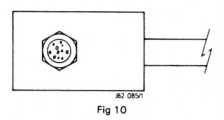

Fig 10

Foam or a heavy stream of bubbles (Fig. 11) indicates the refrigerant is very low.

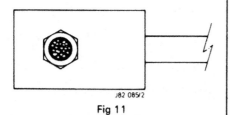

Fig 11

Oil streaks on the sight glass (Fig. 12) indicates a complete lack of refrigerant.

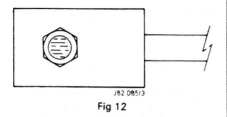

Fig 12

A cloudy sight glass (Fig. 13) indicates that the desiccant contained in the receiver-drier has broken down and is being circulated through the system.

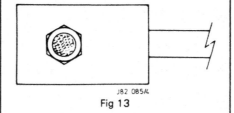

Fig 13

RECEIVER-DRIER

The receiver-drier (Fig. 14) is a storage tank which receives the high pressure warm refrigerant liquid from the condenser through an inlet line and delivers the refrigerant to the thermostatic expansion valve through the outlet line. The receiver-drier has two separate functions:

Acts as a storage tank for liquid refrigerant since the amount of refrigerant required by the evaporator varies widely under the different operating conditions.

Contains a filter and desiccant to remove and retain foreign particles and moisture from the refrigerant which would be harmful to the system if allowed to circulate with the refrigerant.

EVAPORATOR

The evaporator (Fig. 15) consists of a refrigerant coil mounted in a series of thin fins to provide a maximum amount of heat transfer in a mimimum amount of space. It is usually mounted in a housing under the cowl where warm air from the passenger compartment is blown across the coils and fins.

The evaporator receives refrigerant from the thermostatic expansion valve as a low pressure cold atomized liquid. As this cold liquid refrigerant passes through the evaporator coils, heat will follow its natural tendency and move from the warm air into the cooler refrigerant.

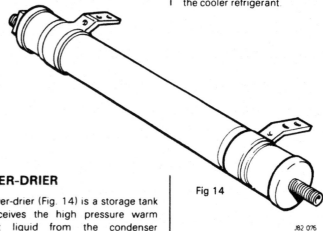

Fig 14

When the liquid refrigerant reaches a temperature and pressure that will induce a change of state, a large quantity of heat will move from the air into the refrigerant and the refrigerant will change from a low pressure COLD ATOMIZED LIQUID to a low pressure COLD VAPOUR.

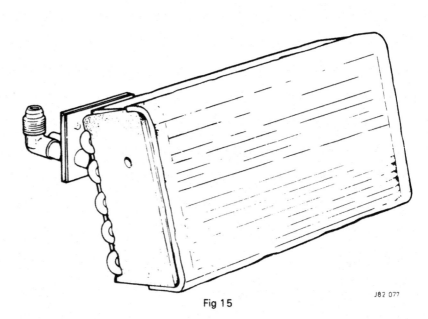

Fig 15

82—7

EXPANSION VALVE

The expansion valve (Fig. 16) is the dividing point between the high and low pressure sides of the system, and automatically meters the high pressure, high temperature liquid refrigerant through a small orifice, controlled by a metering valve, into the low presure, cold temperature side of the evaporator matrix. The refrigerant must be controlled to obtain the maximum cooling while assuring complete evaporation of the liquid refrigerant within the evaporator. To do this, the valve senses the outlet pipe temperature, the inlet pipe pressure, and increases or decreases the flow of refrigerant liquid to maintain the outlet temperature constant.

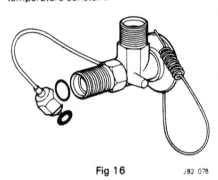

Fig 16   J82 078

The thermostatic expansion valve continually meters the exact amount of refrigerant required to supply some liquid refrigerant throughout the evaporator coil while ensuring that all of the refrigerant will be vapourized at the evaporator outlet. The refrigerant vapour then returns to the low (suction) side of the compressor.

AMPLIFIER

Automatic control is achieved by comparing car interior temperature and the temperature selected. This comparison provides an error signal to the air conditioning control unit, demanding an increase or decrease in car interior temperature. When the selected temperature is reached, the control unit will maintain it.

The error signal is detected across a Wheatstone Bridge circuit; two arms of which are fixed resistors, one arm contains the in-car thermistor and the fourth arm the temperature selection potentiometer. An error signal will be detected if car interior temperature is above or below that set on the temperature selection potentiometer. This signal is fed into the amplifier, (Fig. 17) amplified, and via relays, switches the servo motor to run clockwise or anti-clockwise. The position of the servo motor cam shaft directly determines the heating or cooling effect of the air conditioning system. Full heating and full cooling, are at opposite extremes of camshaft travel.

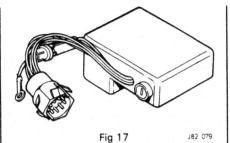

Fig 17   J82 079

The ambient thermistor in the Wheatstone Bridge circuit modifies the effect of the in-car thermistor. The result is a slightly colder interior temperature on hot days, and vice versa. A potentiometer driven by the servo motor is connected into the bridge circuit, modifying dynamic response. This provides control system damping, preventing excessive fluctuations in discharge air temperature.

SERVO CONTROL UNIT

The servo control unit (Fig. 18) is an electric servo motor and a reduction gearbox driving a camshaft. The camshaft controls seven functions:

1. Air discharge temperature — The camshaft moves blend flaps to vary air flow progressively from full cold to full heat. The cams are set to provide cooler air at head level, than to foot level, when the unit is in the low-medium heating mode. This prevents stuffiness at head level.
2. Fan speeds — The camshaft alters fan speed progressively to increase air flow at full cold or full heat positions. Four fan speeds are available on cooling, three on heating. On low heating or cooling the camshaft selects a low fan speed, preventing noise and excessive air movement.
3. Mode — The camshaft controls a vacuum switch so that the distribution of air in the car is automatically controlled by a vacuum operated flap. Cold air is distributed from the face level vents, and hot air is distributed mainly from foot level vents with a bleed of air from screen vents.

4. Fresh/Recirculated Air — To improve performance the camshaft selects recirculated air on maximum cooling. Fresh air is selected for all other requirements.
5. Water Valve — On maximum cold, the camshaft controls a second vacuum switch to switch off the water valve controlling flow through the heater block.
6. Water Thermostat — A thermostat is fitted to prevent the system operating until engine water is hot enough to produce warm air. When on cooling mode the camshaft overrides this switch, and allows the system to operate immediately.
7. Evaporator thermostat — A thermostat is fitted to prevent icing of the evaporator. Under conditions where icing would be impossible and maximum cooling performance is required, the thermostat is overriden by the camshaft.

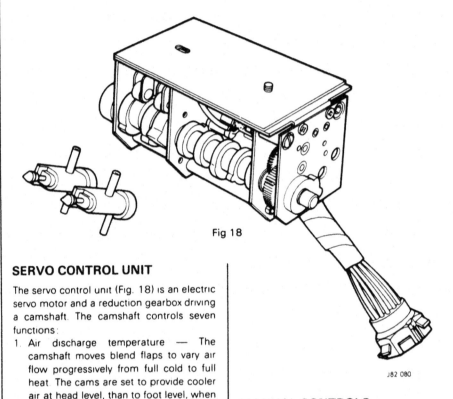

Fig 18

J82 080

MANUAL CONTROLS

Temperature Selector

The left hand control (1, Fig. 19) is the potentiometer to select the temperature from 18°C (65°F) to 29°C (85°F) that is to be maintained automatically in the car.

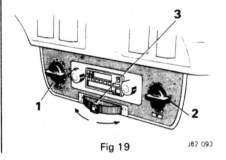

Fig 19   J82 093

MODE SWITCH

The right hand switch (2, Fig. 19) has five positions. When the switch is in the 'Off' position, the system is off and the fresh air intakes are closed. The 'Auto' position operates the system automatically. The high and low positions operate the fan high or low speed independently from that selected by the automatic control. The defrost position directs 90% of the air flow to the screen, closing the lower heater flap and opening the bleed flap to the screen outlets. At the same time, an additional resistor is switched into the Wheatstone Bridge circuit to ensure that the servo motor camshaft runs to full heat position.

Air Distribution Temperature Control

The thumbwheel (3, Fig. 19) can be used to alter the temperature of the air being distributed through the face level vents. It is most effective when the main controls are set at Auto and 75, and the system has been allowed to stabilise. To increase the temperature of the air being delivered through the vents, move the thumbwheel to the right; this will open the upper heater flap, allowing the increased air temperature to the face level vents. To decrease the air temperature, move the thumbwheel to the left; the upper flap will close and the air temperature to the vents will be lower.

METHOD OF TEMPERATURE VARIATION

Full Cooling

All air passes through the evaporator matrix in which the air is cooled and dehumidified. After leaving the evaporator, four blend flaps control the degree of heat added by the heater matrix. On maximum cooling, the cooler flaps are fully open and the heater flaps are fully closed. Cold air only flows into the car (Fig. 20). A larger area of the cooling matrix is exposed to the upper flap than is exposed to the lower outlets, and most of the cooling output is directed out through the centre face level grille.

A vacuum switch on the camshaft is closed so that the water valve closes to prevent hot water flowing to the heater matrix.

The water temperature thermostat is overridden in the cooling mode. (Water temperature thermostat prevents the fans operating before water reaches 40°C.)

The evaporator thermostat (Ranco) is overridden by the camshaft cam in this mode as normally full cooling is only required when ambient conditions would prevent the evaporator from icing up, i.e. hot days.

Full Heating

When full heating is selected the camshaft moves to the full heat position. The camshaft mechanically operates the four flaps in the air conditioning unit so that the upper and lower cooling flaps are fully closed preventing cold air reaching the car interior direct. The heater flaps are fully

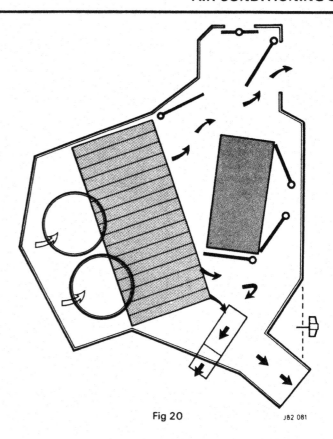

Fig 20   J82 081

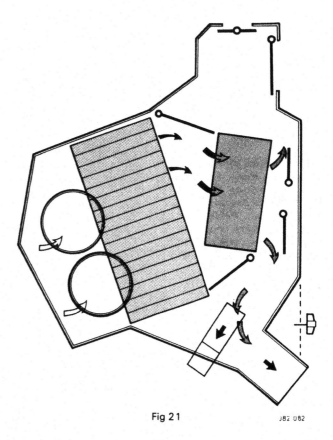

Fig 21   J82 082

open and the cool, de-humidified air blown through the evaporator now flows through the heater matrix and via the open heater flaps, to the screen rail end outlets and the front and rear footwells (Fig. 21).

The face level outlet is closed by the camshaft closing the vacuum switch so that

no hot air is delivered from the centre face level output. 90% of all air passing through the unit now passes out of the front and rear footwell outlets.

NOTE: Screen outlets are only open in defrost mode, although a slight air bleed is permitted for defrost purposes.

82—9

Air Blend

The system automatically maintains any temperature selected, irrespective of external ambient conditions by blending hot and cold air to maintain the temperature selected. Both heating and cooling flaps are progressively positioned so that the correct blend is obtained.

The illustration (Fig. 22) shows possible positions the flaps could adopt to give correct in-car temperature. It can be seen that both heating and cooling flaps are in operation.

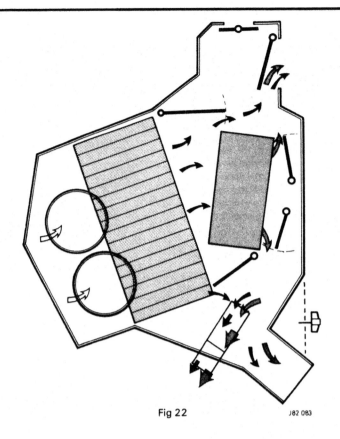

Fig 22   J82 083

Defrost

When defrost is selected the camshaft will travel to full heating. The vacuum switch on the right hand control will be closed to vacuum allowing the defrost flaps to open to pass air on to the windscreen. The left hand actuator will relax and allow the lower heating flap to close to direct 90% of all air through the unit to the windscreen (Fig. 23).

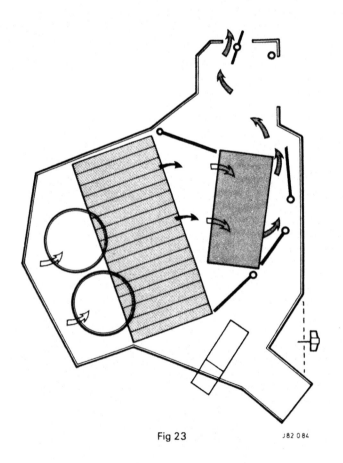

Fig 23   J82 084

82—10

GENERAL SECTION

This section contains safety precautions, general information, good practice and standards that must be followed when working upon the air conditioning system. A fault-finding and rectification section is included.

Safety precautions

The air conditioning equipment is manufactured for use only with Refrigerant 12 (dichlorodifluoromethane) and extreme care must be taken NEVER to use a methyl-chloride refrigerant.

The chemical reaction between methyl-chloride and the aluminium parts of the compressor will result in the formation of products which burn spontaneously on exposure to air, or decompose with violence in the presence of moisture. The suitable refrigerant is supplied under the following trade names.

Freon 12; Arcton 12; Isceon 12
or any refrigerant to specification 12.
Goggles and gloves must be worn while working with the refrigerant.

WARNING: EXTREME CARE SHOULD BE EXERCISED IN HANDLING THE REFRIGERANT. LIQUID REFRIGERANT AT ATMOSPHERIC PRESSURE BOILS AT −29°C (−20°F). SERIOUS DAMAGE OR BLINDNESS MAY OCCUR IF REFRIGERANT IS ALLOWED TO CONTACT THE EYES.

FIRST AID: If refrigerant should contact the eyes or skin, splash the eyes or affected area with cold water for several minutes. Do not rub. As soon as possible thereafter, obtain treatment from a doctor or eye specialist.

Good practice

1. The protective sealing plugs must remain in position on all replacement components and hoses until immediately before assembly.

2. Any part arriving for assembly without sealing plugs in position must be returned to the supplier as defective.

3. It is essential that a second backing spanner is always used when tightening all joints. This minimises distortion and strain on components or connecting pipes.

4. Components must not be lifted by connecting pipes, hoses or capillary tubes.

5. Care must be taken not to damage fins on condenser or evaporator matrices. Any damage must be rectified by the use of fin combs.

6. Before assembly of tube and hose joints, use a small amount of clean new refrigerant oil on the sealing seat.

7. Refrigerant oil for any purpose must be kept very clean and capped at all times. This will prevent the oil absorbing moisture.

8. Before assembly the condition of joints and flares must be examined. Dirt and even minor damage can cause leaks at the high pressure encountered in the system.

9. Dirty end fittings can only be cleaned using a cloth wetted with alcohol.

10. After removing sealing plugs and immediately before assembly, visually check the bore of pipes and components. Where ANY dirt or moisture is discovered, the part must be rejected.

11. All components must be allowed to reach room temperature before sealing plugs are removed. This prevents condensation should the component be cold initially.

12. Before finally tightening the hose connections ensure that the hose lies in the correct position, is not kinked or twisted, and will not be trapped by subsequent operations, e.g. closing bonnet, refitting bonnet.

13. Check that the hose is correctly fitted in clips or strapped to the sub-frame members.

14. The Frigidaire compressor must be stored horizontally and sump down. It must not be rotated before fitting and charging. Do not remove the shipping plate until immediately before assembly. Always use new 'O' ring seals beneath union housing plate, and in those pipe joints which incorporate them.

15. Components or hoses removed must be sealed immediately after removal.

16. After a system has been opened the receiver/drier must be renewed.

Before commencing checks, run the engine until normal running temperature is reached. This ensures that sufficient vacuum is available for tests. For cooling tests the engine must be running for the compressor clutch to operate.

SPECIAL TOOLS AND EQUIPMENT FOR SERVICING AIR CONDITIONING SYSTEM ON JAGUAR SERIES III

1 Pektron test unit
1 Charging station
1 Leak detector
1 Temperature test box
1 Compressor service tool kit
1 Setting jig for temperature differential control, 18G1363.
1 Voltmeter
1 Ohmmeter

The Pektron Climatic Control tester (Fig. 24) is recommended for testing the air conditioning electrical system.

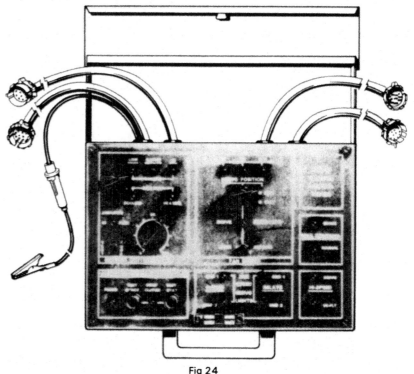

Fig 24

AIR CONDITIONING SYSTEM

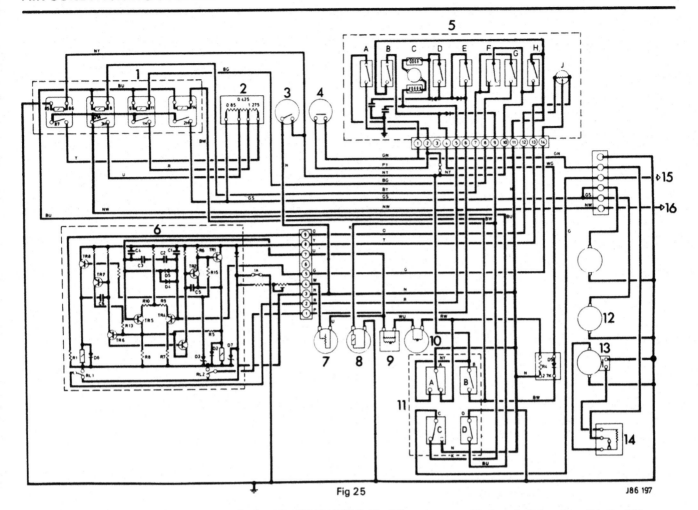

Fig 25

J86 197

KEY TO DIAGRAM

1. Blower motor relay
2. Blower motor resistor
3. Water temperature transmitter
4. Thermostat
5. Servo
6. Amplifier
7. Temperature selector
8. Vacuum valve
9. Ambient sensor
10. In-car sensor
11. Mode control switch
12. Blower motors
13. Compressor clutch
14. Thermal fuse
15. To fuse
16. To fuse

KEY TO SERVO UNIT (5, Fig. 25)

A   Thermo override
B   Recirc & Highspeed
C   Servo motor
D   Cool limit switch
E   Heat limit switch
F   Med 1 switch
G   Med 2 switch
H   Temperature bypass switch
J   Feedback potentiometer

Mode switch functions (11, Fig. 25)

Micro switch		Off	Lo	Auto	Hi	Def
A	Defrost	NC	NC	NC	NC	NO
B	High Speed	NO	NC	NO	NC	NC
C	On/Off	NO	NC	NC	NC	NC
D	Low Speed	NO	NO	NC	NC	NC

NC = Normally Closed
NO = Normally Open

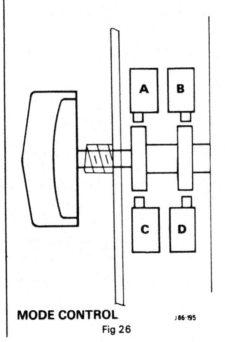

MODE CONTROL

Fig 26

J86-195

KEY TO MODE CONTROL

A   Defrost micro switch
B   High speed micro switch
C   Low speed micro switch
D   On/off micro switch

82—12

430

AIR CONDITIONING SERVO UNIT

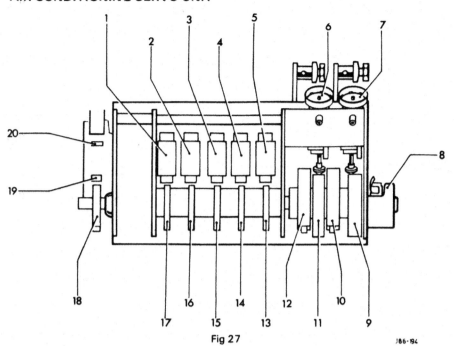

Fig 27   J86-194

KEY TO SERVO UNIT

1. Full cooling micro switch
2. Full heating micro switch
3. Med 1 micro switch
4. Med 2 micro switch
5. Temperature override micro switch
6. Water valve vacuum switch
7. Centre flap vacuum switch
8. Feedback potentiometer
9. Cam S9
10. Cam S8
11. Cam S7
12. Cam S6
13. Cam S5
14. Cam S4
15. Cam S3
16. Cam S2
17. Cam S1
18. Cam S10
19. Ranco override micro switch
20. Recirculate Hi Speed switch

Test Procedure

Allow coolant temperature to stabilize to ambient by not running the engine for at least two hours, and open all of the vehicle windows for this period.

Set the car mode control to off, and the temperature selector to approximately the ambient temperature in the vehicle. Ensure that the ignition is switched off, then disconnect the plug at the servo control unit. Insert the tester 15 way socket into the servo input and join the harness socket to the tester 15 way plug.

Disconnect the plug and socket at the amplifier. Insert the tester 12 way socket into the amplifier input, and join the harness to the tester 12 way plug. Connect the tester earth lead to a good earth on the vehicle. Carry out the following operations and note the effects.

ACTION	EFFECT	WHEN INCORRECT
A Switch on Car Ignition	'VAC SOLENOID MANUAL' will illuminate No other lights 'ON'	Check Ignition Supply. Fuse, etc Ensure that A/C Mode Control is 'OFF' Check Wiring to Vacuum Solenoid
B Start the Car Engine and switch car mode Control to LOW Then switch SERVO POSITION to HEAT and press the DRIVE CONTROL until the DRIVE INDICATOR goes out (Note It only comes ON when DRIVE CONTROL is Pressed)	1 The Fan Speed $\frac{1}{4}$, $\frac{1}{2}$ and $\frac{3}{4}$ lights should be ON for Servo Position	If the DRIVE INDICATOR did not light, switch SERVO POSITION to COOL and press the DRIVE CONTROL When this also does not light the DRIVE INDICATOR check the SERVO motor and servo components and wiring
	2 The vehicle cooling fans should be OFF	Ensure that the engine is not yet warmed up. then disconnect the water temperature switch in the car, and if fans continue to run suspect wiring and the Micro Switch Water Temp override in the Servo Control Unit (5, Fig 27).
	3 The VAC SOLENOID MANUAL lights should go out	Check Switch C in mode control unit (Fig 26) and wiring

82—13

ACTION	EFFECT	WHEN INCORRECT
C Run the car engine fast to warm up the cooling water to working temperature	1. The fans will start to run at low rate and the SERVO MED 1 light will operate (FAN SPEED SERVO LIGHT). The majority of air will be directed through the floor vents	Check water temperature switch Check low speed relay Check blower resistors R1 & 2 Check fans Check wiring.
	2. The compressor clutch will operate as indicated by RANCO COMP. CLUTCH light	(A) Check 10A fuse, which if faulty will be indicated by the RANCO FUSED light being ON (B) Check Ranco thermostat by shorting out at the component terminals and monitoring the COMP clutch light
D Switch the SERVO POSITION to COOL and press DRIVE CONTROL until '¾' light goes out then release.	MED 1 FAN SPEED SERVO light goes out.	Check MED 1 micro switch (3, Fig. 27) and wiring to SERVO Control Unit.
E Press DRIVE CONTROL until '½' light goes out then release	The air emission is evenly distributed between face level and floor vents	Check adjustment of blend flaps, or vacuum system
F Press DRIVE CONTROL until '¼' light goes out then release	MED 1 FAN SPEED SERVO light is 'ON'.	Check MED 1 micro switch (3, Fig. 27) and wiring to SERVO Control Unit.
G Press DRIVE CONTROL until DRIVE INDICATOR goes out, then release	HIGH SPEED SERVO light ON	Check HI-SPEED/RECIRC micro switch and wiring to SERVO Control Unit
	COMP. CLUTCH light stays on when TEST O'RIDE switch is pressed	Check ranco override micro switch (19, Fig. 27) and wiring to SERVO Control Unit.
	MED 2 FAN SPEED SERVO light is 'ON'	Check MED 2 Micro Switch (4, Fig. 27) and wiring to Servo Control Unit.
	VAC.-SOLENOID SERVO light 'ON'	Check Diode D3 in Servo control Unit harness
H Switch car mode control to AUTO. Drive servo to '¦' position by selecting DRIVE CONTROL until '¼' and '½' lights are 'ON'	This has given the cooling compressor the protection of its freezing sensing thermostat.	– – – – – – – – –
J Press MED 1 switch (FAN SPEED SERVO lights)	Car Fan Speed increases.	Check Main Relay. Check Resistor R3 Check Wiring
K Keeping MED 1 pressed, operate MED 2 (FAN SPEED SERVO light).	Car Fan Speed increases further	Check Main Relay Check Resistor R2 Check Wiring
L Release MED 1 and MED 2 switches. Select HI on car mode control.	Car fan speed increases to maximum	Check High Speed Micro Switch at mode control Check Main Relay Check Wiring
	Ensure D5-FLT does not light	Check Diode D5 in mode control harness Check Wiring
M Select AUTO on car mode control	To reduce fan speed to low rate	– – – – – – – – –

82—14

ACTION	EFFECT	WHEN INCORRECT
N Press TEST on AMPLIFIER fuse	AMPLIFIER Fuse light should be 'ON'. Feed to amplifier good.	Check feed to amplifier.
P Switch to AMPLIFIER on sensing Switching System (Tester) Rotate control 0-100 fully clockwise then fully anti-clockwise alternately.	Towards the '100' point HEATING light should come ON, then towards the '0' point COOLING light should come ON.	Check Wiring Replace Amplifier.
O Ensure that the car temperature setting control is at approximately the ambient temperature. Switch to SENSOR on Sensing Switching System (Tester). Monitor LOW, DATUM, and HI lights and adjust rotary control 0-100 until only DATUM is illuminated.	If it is not possible to 'balance' the DATUM light, then the ambient temperature may be incorrectly set on the vehicle temperature selector, or out of its range, or there is a fault in the sensors, wiring or Temperature Control. If OK proceed to Item R.	Check sensors and wiring. Check Micro Switch overriding sensing circuit in the mode control, and wiring. Check temperature SELECTOR and wiring.
R Increase or decrease the car TEMPERATURE SELECTOR by 5°F from its set point, whichever is convenient.	If increased the HI light will come ON in addition to the DATUM.	Check TEMPERATURE SELECTOR and wiring.
S Adjust the rotary 0-100 control to cancel the HI or LOW light obtained in Item R. Return the TEMPERATURE SELECTOR to its original point.	If decreased to its original point the LOW light will come ON in addition to the DATUM. If increased to its original point the HI light will come ON in addition to the DATUM.	Check TEMPERATURE SELECTOR and wiring.
T Adjust the rotary 0-100 control to cancel the HI or LOW light obtained in Item S. Switch the mode control from AUTO to DEF.	The HI light operates in addition to the DATUM.	Check Micro Switch override sensing circuit at mode control and resistance unit in mode control harness
U Select the OFF on the Mode control. Switch off the vehicle engine and ignition circuit.	All tester indicators are OFF.	Check vehicle ignition switch Check relays and wiring.
V Remove tester connectors and return the vehicle wiring and plugs and sockets to standard.	The complete system can now be tested following any corrective action taken as a result of the checks	Identify the problem area, and after carrying out the preliminary procedure of tester connection, repeat only the relevant parts of the schedule

Familiarity with the tester should be easily acquired, and then the Operator will find the flexibility of control offered by having access to test each sub-assembly will lead to quick identification of faults, and a system knowledge which allows him to extend this scope of the scheduled checks.

82—15

'IN-CAR' FAULT FINDING CHART

Equipment required

1. Voltmeter capable of covering 0 to 13 volts d.c
2. Continuity tester.
3. Ohmmeter capable of covering 0 to 20K ohms.
4. Vacuum gauges (not essential) to check vacuum level.

The battery should be disconnected whenever an electrical unit is being removed or refitted.

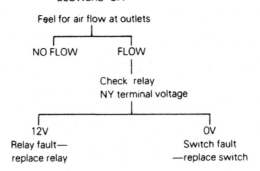

TEST 1   R.H. OFF   L.H. 75°

1. A

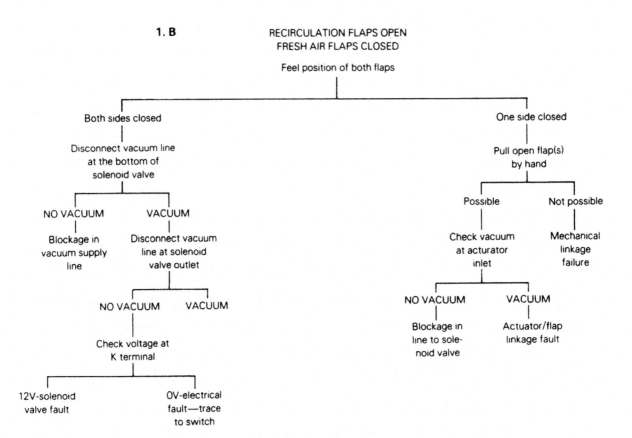

TEST 2   **R.H. 'DEFROST'**   **L.H. 75°**

BLOWERS TO HIGH SPEED

Listen to both sides

Check voltages at connectors
(each side)

BLOWER(S) OFF

0V

Voltage not present
Blower electrical
fault

Break in GS
line(s) relay
to blower
connections

Check voltage at triple
relay, GS lead and terminal

12V Switching OK

10V Blowers at Med. 2

5V Blowers on low speed

Blowers at low
speed

0V

Check voltage at NW lead
on relay

Check earth resistance
at BU lead

Relay

12V

0V

Check relay voltage
at NY lead

Electrical fault
in main supply

Low resistance

High resistance

Check voltage in
Relay lead BG

Harness breaks
in BU lead or
switch fault
in hand switch
D or bad earth

12V

0V

Check Relay earth resistance

Harness breaks
in NY lead or
switch fault

Low resistance

High resistance—earth
contact loose

0V—Relay fault
replace

12V

Fault in resistor
assembly or
connection to
harness—lead R

Check relay
Y terminal

Check
relay voltage
at BW lead

12V Resistor assembly
fault—check Y and GS
connections

0V Relay
fault—replace

0V

12V

Harness break in
BW line to hand
control

Relay fault—replace

2B   HOT AIR TO SCREEN

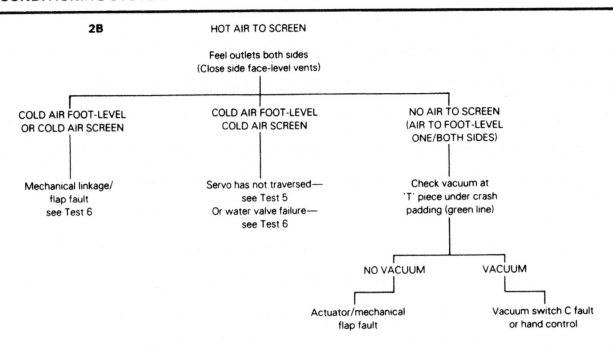

Feel outlets both sides
(Close side face-level vents)

COLD AIR FOOT-LEVEL OR COLD AIR SCREEN	COLD AIR FOOT-LEVEL COLD AIR SCREEN	NO AIR TO SCREEN (AIR TO FOOT-LEVEL ONE/BOTH SIDES)

Mechanical linkage/ flap fault see Test 6

Servo has not traversed— see Test 5 Or water valve failure— see Test 6

Check vacuum at 'T' piece under crash padding (green line)

NO VACUUM   VACUUM

Actuator/mechanical flap fault

Vacuum switch C fault or hand control

R.H. AUTO—HI   **L.H. HEATING MODE (HIGHER THAN AMBIENT)**

TEST 3
3A   BLOWER SPEED HIGH

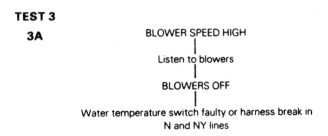

Listen to blowers

BLOWERS OFF

Water temperature switch faulty or harness break in
N and NY lines

3B   SCREEN FLAPS CLOSE
AIR TO FOOT-LEVEL

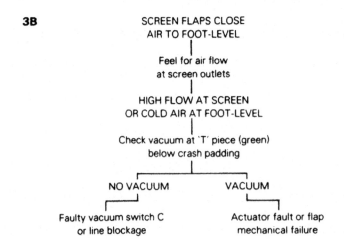

Feel for air flow
at screen outlets

HIGH FLOW AT SCREEN
OR COLD AIR AT FOOT-LEVEL

Check vacuum at 'T' piece (green)
below crash padding

NO VACUUM   VACUUM

Faulty vacuum switch C or line blockage

Actuator fault or flap mechanical failure

82—18

TEST 4   **R.H. AUTO—LOW**   **L.H. 85°**

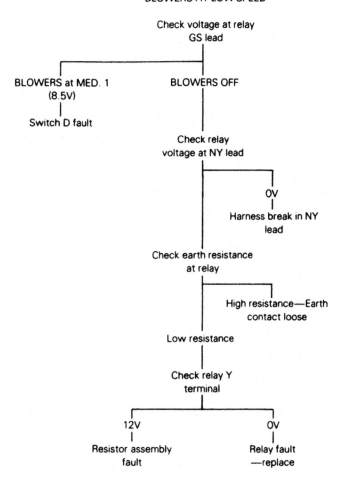

BLOWERS AT LOW SPEED

Check voltage at relay
GS lead

BLOWERS at MED. 1
(8.5V)

Switch D fault

BLOWERS OFF

Check relay
voltage at NY lead

0V

Harness break in NY
lead

Check earth resistance
at relay

High resistance—Earth
contact loose

Low resistance

Check relay Y
terminal

12V

Resistor assembly
fault

0V

Relay fault
—replace

TEST 5   **AMPLIFIER/SERVO RESPONSE**

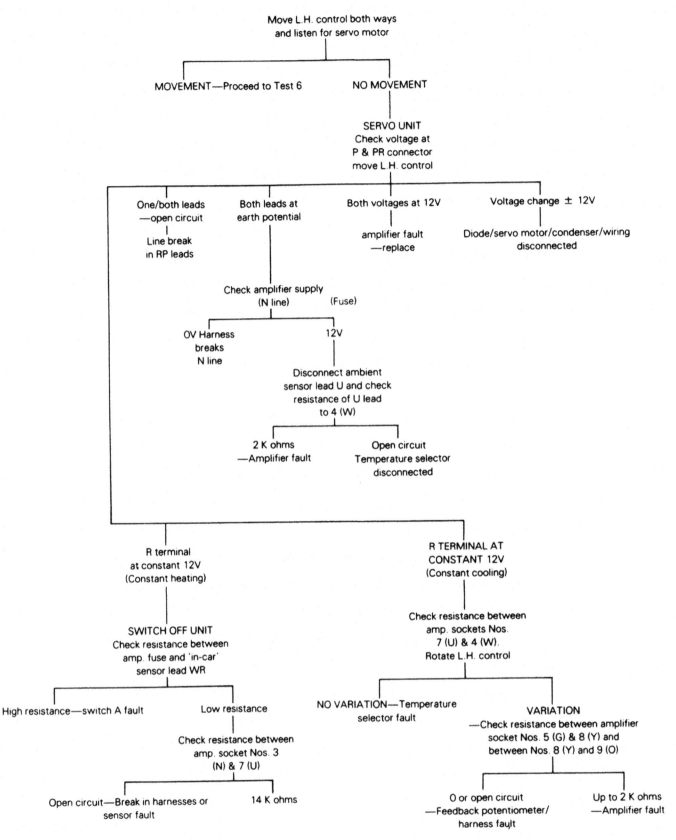

SERVO TRAVERSE

Move L.H. control both ways
and listen for servo motor

MOVEMENT—Proceed to Test 6   NO MOVEMENT

SERVO UNIT
Check voltage at
P & PR connector
move L.H. control

One/both leads —open circuit — Line break in RP leads

Both leads at earth potential

Both voltages at 12V — amplifier fault —replace

Voltage change ± 12V — Diode/servo motor/condenser/wiring disconnected

Check amplifier supply (N line)   (Fuse)

0V Harness breaks N line

12V — Disconnect ambient sensor lead U and check resistance of U lead to 4 (W)

2 K ohms —Amplifier fault

Open circuit Temperature selector disconnected

R terminal at constant 12V (Constant heating)

SWITCH OFF UNIT
Check resistance between amp. fuse and 'in-car' sensor lead WR

High resistance—switch A fault

Low resistance

Check resistance between amp. socket Nos. 3 (N) & 7 (U)

Open circuit—Break in harnesses or sensor fault

14 K ohms

R TERMINAL AT CONSTANT 12V (Constant cooling)

Check resistance between amp. sockets Nos. 7 (U) & 4 (W). Rotate L.H. control

NO VARIATION—Temperature selector fault

VARIATION —Check resistance between amplifier socket Nos. 5 (G) & 8 (Y) and between Nos. 8 (Y) and 9 (O)

0 or open circuit —Feedback potentiometer/ harness fault

Up to 2 K ohms —Amplifier fault

82—20

6.1   **AUTOMATIC FUNCTIONS**

LIMITED COOLING/HEATING

SERVO WILL NOT TRAVERSE

Could be damaged—check Test 5

6.2

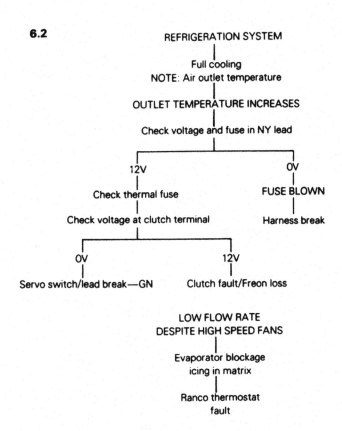

REFRIGERATION SYSTEM

Full cooling
NOTE: Air outlet temperature

OUTLET TEMPERATURE INCREASES

Check voltage and fuse in NY lead

12V	0V
Check thermal fuse	FUSE BLOWN
Check voltage at clutch terminal	Harness break

0V	12V
Servo switch/lead break—GN	Clutch fault/Freon loss

LOW FLOW RATE
DESPITE HIGH SPEED FANS

Evaporator blockage
icing in matrix

Ranco thermostat
fault

6.3   FRESH AIR/HIGH SPEED

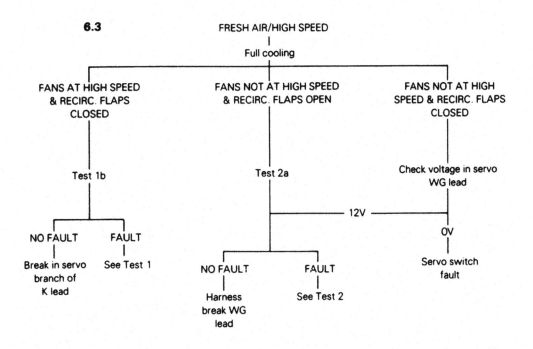

Full cooling

FANS AT HIGH SPEED
& RECIRC. FLAPS
CLOSED

FANS NOT AT HIGH SPEED
& RECIRC. FLAPS OPEN

FANS NOT AT HIGH
SPEED & RECIRC. FLAPS
CLOSED

Test 1b

Test 2a

Check voltage in servo
WG lead

12V

NO FAULT   FAULT

Break in servo
branch of
K lead

See Test 1

0V

NO FAULT   FAULT

Harness
break WG
lead

See Test 2

Servo switch
fault

82—21

6.4

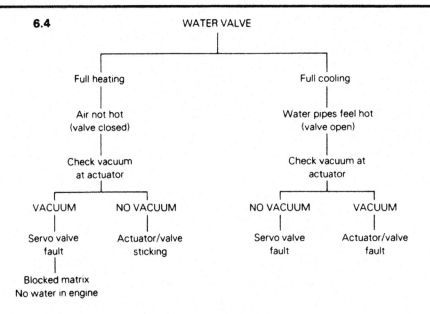

WATER VALVE

Full heating — Air not hot (valve closed) — Check vacuum at actuator
- VACUUM → Servo valve fault → Blocked matrix No water in engine
- NO VACUUM → Actuator/valve sticking

Full cooling — Water pipes feel hot (valve open) — Check vacuum at actuator
- NO VACUUM → Servo valve fault
- VACUUM → Actuator/valve fault

6.5

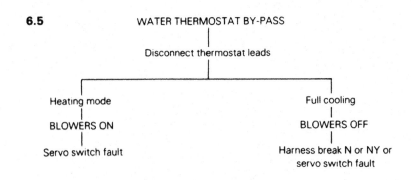

WATER THERMOSTAT BY-PASS

Disconnect thermostat leads

Heating mode — BLOWERS ON — Servo switch fault

Full cooling — BLOWERS OFF — Harness break N or NY or servo switch fault

6.6

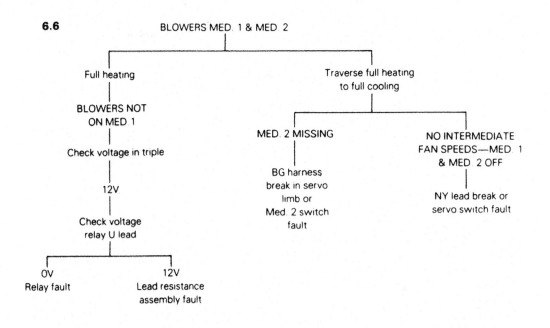

BLOWERS MED. 1 & MED. 2

Full heating — BLOWERS NOT ON MED. 1 — Check voltage in triple — 12V — Check voltage relay U lead
- 0V → Relay fault
- 12V → Lead resistance assembly fault

Traverse full heating to full cooling
- MED. 2 MISSING → BG harness break in servo limb or Med. 2 switch fault
- NO INTERMEDIATE FAN SPEEDS—MED. 1 & MED. 2 OFF → NY lead break or servo switch fault

82—22

6.7 FACE FLAP (MODE)

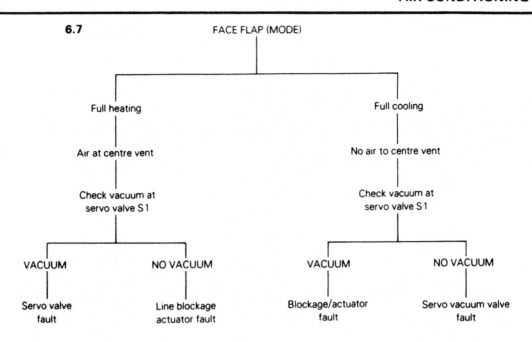

6.8 INCORRECT AIR TEMPERATURE AND AIR DISTRIBUTION

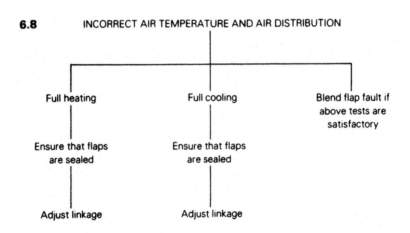

CHARGING AND TESTING EQUIPMENT

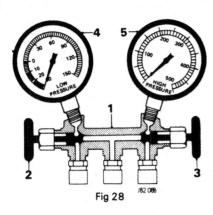

Fig 28   J82 086

The charging and testing equipment consists of a charging manifold (1, Fig. 28) fitted with two stop valves (2 & 3, Fig. 28). One compound gauge (4, Fig. 28) reading both vacuum and pressure, and it is connected to the suction side of the system. The other gauge is a high pressure gauge (5, Fig. 28) and is connected to the delivery side of the system.

WARNING: FOR SAFETY REASONS, THE ACCURACY OF BOTH GAUGES MUST BE CHECKED AT FREQUENT INTERVALS.

Gauge Manifold

The manifold is designed to control refrigerant flow. As shown in the following illustration, when the manifold test set is connected into the system, pressure is registered on both gauges at all times. During all tests, both the low and high side hand valves are in the closed position (turned inward until the valve is seated). Refrigerant will flow around the valve stem to the respective gauges and register the system low side pressure on the low side gauge, and the system high side pressure on the high side gauge. The hand valves isolate the low and high side from the central portion of the manifold.

Low Side Gauge

This gauge (4, Fig. 28) has a dial reading from 0 to 150 psi (pressure scale) in a clockwise direction, and from 0 to 30 inches of Mercury (vacuum scale) in a counter-clockwise direction. This low side gauge is called a Compound Gauge and has a dual purpose, to register both Pressure and Vacuum. This gauge is used to measure evaporator outlet pressure.

High Side Gauge

This gauge (5, Fig. 28) has a dial reading from 0 to 500 psi in a clockwise direction. The high side gauge is a Pressure gauge only.

A test hose connected to the fitting directly under the low side gauge is used to connect the low side of the test manifold into the low side of the system, and a similar connection is found on the high side.

Two hose connectors must be fitted with depressors to operate the schrader valves on the high and low pressure sides of the system.

CAUTION: Do not open the high side hand valve while the air conditioning system is in operation. Under no circumstances should this be done. If the high side hand valve should be opened while the system is operating, high pressure refrigerant will be forced through the high side gauge and to the refrigerant can if it is attached. This high pressure can rupture the can or possibly burst the fitting at the safety can valve, resulting in much damage (including physical injury).

With the engine switched off, remove the protective caps from the schrader valves. Ensure both high and low side hand valves are in the closed position. Connect the high pressure gauge hose to the high pressure schrader valve (1, Fig. 29) and connect the low pressure or compound valve hose to the low pressure schrader valve (2, Fig. 29).

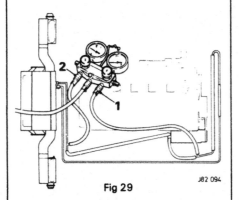

Fig 29   J82 094

PURGING TEST HOSES

Using System Refrigerant

Be sure high and low side hoses are properly connected to service valves (all hose connections tight).

Now, purge the high side test hose by opening the hand valve on the high side gauge for 3 - 5 seconds. This allows the system's refrigerant to force air through the test hoses and out of the centre service hose. Immediately close the high side gauge hand valve.

Purge the low side test hose in the same manner, using the hand valve of the low side gauge. Close hand valve after 3 - 5 seconds.

Stabilizing the System

The manifold gauge set is attached to the system, and the test hoses purged of air. You must now operate the system for a few minutes to stabilize all pressures and temperatures throughout the system in order to obtain accurate test gauge readings. Stabilize the system as follows:

Place all test hoses, gauge set and other equipment away from all engine moving parts. Also keep hoses from touching hot manifolds. Start the engine and adjust engine speed to fast idle.

Turn air conditioner controls to maximum cooling. Set blower fan on high speed.

Open doors and/or windows (to quickly eliminate interior heat).

Operate system under these conditions for 5 to 10 minutes and the system will be stabilized and ready for test readings.

Test Conditions

1. Use a large fan to substitute for normal ram air flow through the condenser.
2. Car adjusted to normal fast idle speed.
3. All conditions equivalent to 30 mph

TORQUE LEVELS FOR THE AIR CONDITIONING HOSE CONNECTIONS

Item	Nm	Kgf/m	lbf/ft
1. Compressor/Condenser (Compressor End)	40,67 to 47,45	4,15 to 4,84	30 to 35
2. Condenser/Compressor (Condenser End)	28,47 to 36,30	2,90 to 3,73	21 to 27
3. Condenser/Receiver Drier (Condenser End)	20,34 to 27,12	2,10 to 2,76	15 to 20
4. Receiver Drier/Condenser (Receiver Drier End)	40,67 to 47,45	4,15 to 4,84	30 to 35
5. Receiver Drier/Evaporator (Receiver Drier End)	40,67 to 47,45	4,15 to 4,84	30 to 35
6. Evaporator/Receiver Drier (Evaporator End)	14,91 to 17,62	1,52 to 1,80	11 to 13
7. Expansion Valve/Evaporator (Expansion Valve End)	20,34 to 27,12	2,10 to 2,76	15 to 20
8. Evaporator/Compressor (Evaporator End)	28,47 to 36,60	2,90 to 3,73	21 to 27
9. Compressor/Evaporator (Compressor End)	40,67 to 47,45	4,15 to 4,84	30 to 35

82—24

PRESSURE — TEMPERATURE RELATIONSHIP

NOTE: Pressures shown are under exact conditions (see Test Conditions below) and are not necessarily true for every car checked.

Ambient Temperature is given as the temperature of the air surrounding the condenser and is taken 2 inches in front of the condenser.

Ambient Temperature °F	High Pressure Gauge Reading
60	95-115
65	105-125
70	115-135
75	130-150
80	150-170
85	165-185
90	175-195
95	185-205
100	210-230
105	230-250
110	250-270
115	265-285
120	280-310

Low Pressure Gauge Reading	Evaporator Temperature °F
10	2
12	6
14	10
16	14
18	18
20	20
22	22
24	24
26	27
28	29
30	32
35	36
40	42
45	48
50	53
55	58
60	62
65	66
70	70

Normal operating ranges shown by dotted line boxes

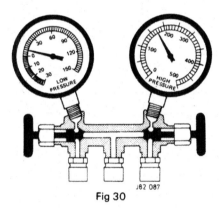

Fig 30

Complaint

Little or no cooling.

Condition

1. Low side gauge reading too low. Should be 15 - 30 psi.
2. High side gauge reading too low. Should be 185 - 205 psi at ambient temperature of 95°F.
3. Stream of bubbles evident in sight glass.
4. Discharge air from evaporator only slightly cool.

Diagnosis

System low on refrigerant. May be caused by small leak.

Correction

1. Leak test system.
2. Discharge refrigerant from system if necessary to replace units or lines.
3. Repair leaks.
4. Check compressor oil level. System may have lost oil due to leakage.
5. Evacuate system using vacuum pump.
6. Charge system with NEW Refrigerant.
7. Operate system and check performance.

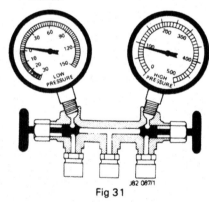

Fig 31

Complaint

Cooling is not adequate.

Condition

1. Low side gauge reading is very low. Should be 15 - 30 psi.
2. High side gauge reading very low. Should be 185 - 205 psi at ambient temperature of 95°F.
3. No liquid and no bubbles evident in sight glass.
4. Discharge air from evaporator is warm.

Diagnosis

System excessively low of refrigerant. Serious leak indicated.

Correction

1. Leak test system.

NOTE: Add partial refrigerant charge before leak testing to ensure a leak test indication. Leak test compressor seal area very carefully.

2. Discharge refrigerant from system.
3. Repair leaks.
4. Check compressor oil level. System may have lost oil due to leakage.
5. Evacuate system using vacuum pump.
6. Charge system with NEW Refrigerant.
7. Operate system and check performance.

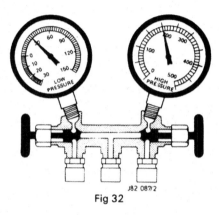

Fig 32

Complaint

Cooling is not adequate.

Condition

1. Low side gauge reading is constant and does not drop. Pressure should drop until compressor cycles (thermostat control).
2. High side gauge reading slightly high (or slightly lower especially if large fan used to substitute ram air): High side guage reading should be 185 - 205 psi at ambient temperature of 95°F.
3. Sight glass free of bubbles or only shows occasional bubble.
4. Discharge air from evaporator only slightly cool.

Diagnosis

Non condensables present in system. Air or moisture present instead of full refrigerant charge.

Correction

1. Leak test system.
Leak test compressor seal area very carefully.
2. Discharge refrigerant from system.
3. Repair leaks as located.
4. Replace receiver-drier. Drier probably saturated with moisture.
5. Check compressor oil level.
6. Evacuate system using vacuum pump.
7. Charge system with NEW Refrigerant 12.
8. Operate system and check performance.

82—25

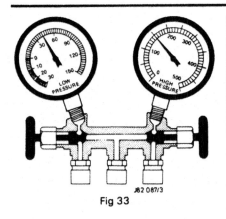

Fig 33

Complaint

Cooling is not adequate.

Condition

1. Low side gauge reading too high. Should be 15 - 30 psi.
2. High side gauge reading too low. Should be 185 - 205 psi at temperature of 95°F.
3. Sight glass free of bubbles (system is fully charged)
4. Discharge air from evaporator not sufficiently cool.

Diagnosis

Internal leak in compressor.

Correction

1. Discharge the system and replace compressor and receiver-drier.
2. Evacuate the system using a vacuum pump.
3. Charge the system with new refrigerant.
4. Operate system and check performance.

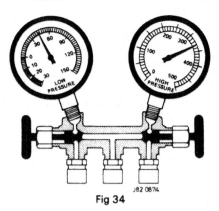

Fig 34

Complaint

Little or no coolant. Engine overheating may also be noted.

Condition

1. Low side gauge reading excessively high. Should be 15 - 30 psi.
2. High side gauge reading excessively high. Should be 185 - 205 psi at 95°F.
3. Bubbles may appear occasionally in sight glass. Liquid line very hot.
4. Discharge air from evaporator is warm.

Diagnosis

Improper condenser operation with lack of cooling caused by too high a high side pressure. System may have either normal or overcharge of refrigerant.

Correction

1. Check for loose or worn driver belts causing excessive compressor head pressures.
2. Inspect condenser for clogged air passages, bug screen, or other obstructions preventing air flow through condenser.
3. Inspect condenser mounting for proper radiator clearance.
4. Inspect clutch type fan for proper operation.
5. Inspect radiator pressure cap for correct type and proper operation.

After making the above checks:
Operate system and check performance.

If condition not corrected:

1. Inspect system for overcharge of refrigerant and correct as follows:
   (a) Discharge refrigerant until stream of bubbles appears in sight glass and both high and low gauge readings drop below normal.
   (b) Add new Refrigerant 12 until bubbles disappear and pressures are normal, then add $\frac{1}{4}$ - $\frac{1}{2}$ lb of additional refrigerant.
2. Operate system and check performance.

If gauge readings still too high:

1. Discharge system.
2. Remove and inspect condenser for oil clogging. Clean and flush condenser to ensure free passage of refrigerant or replace condenser.
3. Replace receiver-drier.
4. Evacuate system using vacuum pump.
5. Charge system with NEW Refrigerant 12.
6. Operate system and check performance.

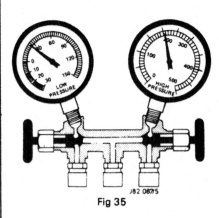

Fig 35

Complaint

Cooling is not adequate during hot part of day

NOTE: Cooling may be satisfactory during early morning or late evening hours but is not adequate during hot part of the day.

Condition

1. Low side gauge reading (15 - 30 psi) but may drop into vacuum during testing
2. High side gauge reading normal (205 psi at 95°F) but will drop when low side gauge reading drops into vacuum.
3. Sight glass may show tiny bubbles.
4. Discharge air from evaporator is sharp and cold but becomes warm when low side gauge reading drops into a vacuum.

Diagnosis

Excessive moisture in system. Desiccant agent saturated with moisture which is released during high ambient temperatures. Moisture collects and freezes in expansion valve and stops refrigerant flow.

Correction

1. Discharge refrigerant from system.
2. Replace receiver-drier.
3. Evacuate system with vacuum pump.
4. Charge system with NEW Refrigerant 12.
5. Operate system and check performance.

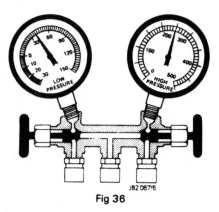

Fig 36

Complaint

Little or no cooling

Condition

1. Low side gauge reading too high. Should be 15 - 30 psi.
2. High side gauge reading too high. Should be 185 - 205 psi at ambient temperature of 95°F.
3. Occasional bubbles in sight glass.
4. Discharge air from evaporator is not cool.

Diagnosis

Air in system. Refrigerant contaminated by non-condensables (air and/or moisture).

Correction

1. Discharge refrigerant from system.
2. Replace receiver-drier which may be saturated with moisture.
3. Evacuate system using vacuum pump.
4. Charge system with NEW Refrigerant.
5. Operate system and check performance.

82—26

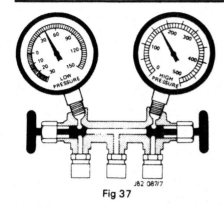

Fig 37

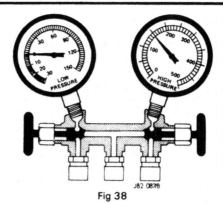

Fig 38

Complaint

Little or no cooling.

Condition

1. Low side gauge reading too high. Should be 15 - 30 psi.
2. High side gauge reading normal or slightly low. Should be 185 - 205 psi at an ambient temperature of 95°F.
3. Discharge air from evaporator warm.
4. Suction hose and evaporator show heavy sweating.

Diagnosis

Expansion valve allowing excessive flow of refrigerant through evaporator causing flooding of evaporator coils.

Testing

Check for expansion valve stuck open of incorrect mounting or temperature sensing bulb as follows:

(a) Set air conditioner for maximum cooling and operate the system.
(b) Spray liquid Refrigerant 12 on head of valve or capillary bulb, not low side gauge reading. Low side gauge should drop into a vacuum.
(c) If low side vacuum reading obtained, warm expansion valve diaphragm chamber with hand, then repeat test (step 'b').

Correction

1. If expansion valve test indicates valve operation is satisfactory, proceed as follows:
   (a) Clean contact surface of evaporator outlet pipe and temperature sensing bulb, clamp bulb securely in contact with pipe.
   (b) Operate system and check performance.
2. If expansion valve test indicates valve is defective, proceed as follows:
   (a) Discharge system.
   (b) Replace expansion valve.
   (c) Evacuate system using vacuum pump.
   (d) Charge system with NEW Refrigerant.
   (e) Operate system and check performance.

Complaint

Cooling is not adequate

Condition

1. Low side gauge reading too low (0 psi or a vacuum). Should be 15 - 30 psi.
2. High side gauge reading too low. Should be 185 - 205 psi at ambient temperature of 95°F.
3. Discharge air from evaporator only slightly cool.
4. Expansion valve inlet may show heavy sweating or frost.

Diagnosis

Expansion valve restricting refrigerant flow due to clogged screen, stuck valve, or temperature sensing bulb having lost its charge.

Testing

1. If expansion valve inlet is cool to touch, proceed as follows:
   (a) Set air conditioner for maximum cooling and operate the system.
   (b) Spray liquid Refrigerant 12 on head of valve of capillary bulb, note low side gauge reading. Low side gauge should drop into a vacuum.
   (c) If low side vacuum reading obtained, warm expansion valve diaphragm chamber with hand, then repeat test (step 'b').
   (d) If expansion valve test indicates valve operation is satisfactory, clean contact surface of evaporator outlet pipe and temperature sensing bulb, clamp bulb securely in contact with pipe. Proceed with correction procedure (below).
2. If expansion valve inlet shows sweating or frost proceed as follows:
   (a) Discharge system
   (b) Disconnect inlet at expansion valve, remove and inspect filter.
   (c) Clean and replace filter, reconnect inlet line.
   (d) Proceed with correction, procedure (below).
3. If expansion valve test (step '1' preceding) indicates valve is defective, proceed as follows:
   (a) Discharge system.
   (b) Replace expansion valve, then proceed with correction procedure.

Correction

1. After cleaning expansion valve screen, or replacing expansion valve if necessary, and properly mounting temperature sensing bulb on evaporator outlet pipe, proceed as follows:
   (a) Evacuate system using vacuum pump.
   (b) Charge system with NEW Refrigerant 12.
   (c) Operate system and check performance.

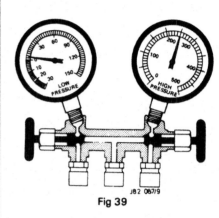

Fig 39

Complaint

Cooling is not adequate.

Condition

1. Low side gauge reading too low. Should be 15 - 30 psi.
2. High side gauge reading will build excessively high. Should be 185 - 205 psi at an ambient temperature of 95°F.

NOTE: An overcharged system, or a Condenser or receiver-drier that is too small, will cause high side gauge reading to be normal or excessively high.

3. Discharge air from evaporator only slightly cool.
4. Liquid line cool to the touch, line or receiver-drier may show heavy sweating or frost.

Diagnosis

Restriction in receiver-drier or liquid line with compressor removing refrigerant from evaporator faster than it can enter resulting in a 'starved' evaporator.

Correction

1. Discharge system.
2. Remove and replace receiver-drier, liquid lines, or other defective parts.
3. Evacuate system using vacuum pump.
4. Charge system with NEW Refrigerant 12.
5. Operate system and check performance.

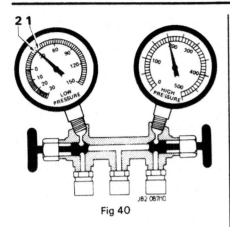

Fig 40

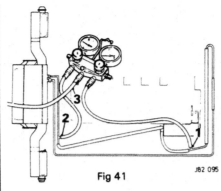

Fig 41

Complaint

Compressor cycles (cuts in and out) too rapidly. Compressor cycles on 34 psi (1, Fig. 40). Compressor cycles off 28 psi (2, Fig. 40).

Condition

1. Low side pressure cycle too high with insufficient range between OFF and ON. Cycle should be:
   Cycle 'Off' — 12 - 15 psi.
   Cycle 'On' — 36 - 39 psi.
   Cycle Range — 24 - 28 psi.
2. High side gauge reading Normal (200 psi). Should be 185 - 205 psi at ambient temperature of 95°F.

Diagnosis

Ranco thermostat faulty.

Correction

1. Stop car engine, turn air conditioning off and disconnect the battery.
2. Remove and discard old thermostatic switch, install new switch of same type
3. When installing new thermostatic switch, make certain that capillary tube installed in same position and to same depth in evaporator core as old switch tube

CAUTION: Do not kink or bend capillary tube too sharply — tube is gas filled.

Operate system and check performance of new thermostatic switch.

AIR CONDITIONING SYSTEM

Depressurise

Observe all safety precautions and do not smoke while carrying out the following procedure.

With the engine switched off, remove the protective caps from the schrader valves.

Connect the manifold gauge set with the red hose to the high pressure side (1, Fig 41) and the blue hose to the low pressure side (2, Fig 41).

Place the free end of the centre hose (3, Fig 41) into a suitable container. Slowly open the high or low side manifold hand valve and adjust the valve for a smooth refrigerant flow. Watch for any signs of escaping oil and adjust the hand valve so that no oil escapes. If oil is lost during the discharge, the compressor oil level will have to be checked and topped up.

As the discharge rate slows down, open the other manifold hand valve. Refrigerant will now flow from the high and low pressure sides of the system. Constantly adjust the hand valves to ensure that oil does not flow.

When a zero reading is shown on both the high and the low pressure gauges the system is discharged. Close both hand valves.

Evacuate

Once a system has been opened for repairs, or is found low of refrigerant, it must be fully evacuated with a vacuum pump to remove all traces of moisture before a new refrigerant charge is added.

Moisture may collect and freeze in the expansion valve which will block the refrigerant flow and stop the cooling action. Moisture will also react with Refrigerant 12 and cause corrosion of the small passages and orifices in the system.

The desiccant in the receiver-drier can absorb only a limited amount of moisture before it becomes saturated, therefore it is important to prevent moisture entering the system, and to remove any moisture which may have entered the system through a leak or an open connection.

Unwanted air and moisture are removed from the system by a vacuum pump. A vacuum pump is the only piece of equipment designed to lower the pressure sufficiently so that the moisture boiling temperature is reduced to a point where the water will vaporise and then can be evacuated from the system.

The compressor cannot be used as a vacuum pump because the refrigeration oil circulates with the refrigerant. The compressor depends to a large extent on the refrigerant distributing oil for lubrication and damage to the compressor may result due to lack of refrigerant which carries the oil for lubrication.

After the system has been fully discharged, and with the test gauge set still connected, attach the centre hose of the manifold gauge set, to the inlet fitting of the vacuum pump.

Open the low and high side manifold hand valves to their maximum positions.

Open the discharge valve on the vacuum pump or remove the dust cap on the discharge outlet whichever is appropriate.

Turn the vacuum pipe on, note the low side gauge to make certain that a vacuum is being created in the system by the vacuum pump.

From the time the lowest vacuum is attained, continue to operate the vacuum pump for a few minutes to be sure complete evacuation has been performed.

Close both gauge hand valves, turn off the vacuum pump, note the low side gauge reading. The gauge needle should remain stationary at the point where the pump was turned off. Should the gauge needle return towards zero a leak exists in the air conditioning system.

If a leak exists charge the system with R12 refrigerant, locate the leak with a leak detector, discharge the refrigerant from the system. Repair the leak and repeat the evacuation procedure.

If the gauge needle remains stationary and vacuum is maintained for 3 to 5 minutes, close both the high and low manifold hand valves, and disconnect the hose from the vacuum pump.

The air conditioning system is now ready for charging.

Flushing

If contamination of the expansion valve and associated pipeworks occurs it is essential that the whole of the air conditioning is fully flushed out using Freon 12, or other suitable charging gas.

Discharge the system.

Disconnect the inlet (low pressure) and the outlet (high pressure) pipes from the compressor.

Fit a suitable blanking plate over the end of the high pressure pipe and retain the plate with a suitable G clamp, also remove the schrader valve from the charging connection on the high pressure pipe.

Place the low pressure pipe into a suitable metal container and cover.

Disconnect the high pressure pipe from the expansion valve and carefully remove the conical filter, then reconnect the pipe on the expansion valve.

Carefully remove the thermal bulb coil attached to the evaporator outlet pipe and allow the thermal bulb to remain in the ambient air.

This will prevent the expansion valve closing when refrigerant is flushed through it.

Connect a suitable hose, from the liquid connection of a recommended refrigerant canister, to the charging connection on the high pressure pipe.

Open the canister (the pressure in the canister should be approximately 4.22 kgf/cm² (60 lbf/in²)) and allow the refrigerant to flush through the air conditioning system for approximately 30 seconds, or until a steady liquid flow is observed from the low pressure pipe.

Turn the refrigerant canister off and remove the connections.

IMPORTANT: On re-assembling the system. Fit a new receiver-drier.

Check the compressor oil level.

Thoroughly clean and refit the expansion valve filter.

Refit the thermal bulb on to the evaporator outlet pipe.

Refit the schrader valve into the high pressure pipe.

Refit all the pipe connections and recharge the system.

Charge

Charging the air conditioning system is the process of adding a specific quantity of refrigerant to the circuit. Before attempting the charging operation the system **must** have been evacuated and, if necessary, flushed through immediately beforehand. No delay between evacuation and charging procedures is permissible. The equipment should be fitted with a means of accurately weighing the refrigerant during the charging process. Great care must be taken to charge correctly, as undercharging will result in very inefficient operation, and overcharging will result in very high pressures and possible damage to components.

Evacuate the system with hoses (1 & 2, Fig. 42) connected as shown.

Connect the centre hose of the charging manifold (3, Fig. 42) to a supply of refrigerant. The supply available must be at least 3,3 kg (7.2 lb) weight.

Open the refrigerant supply valve.

Purge the centre hose by momentarily cracking the connection at the manifold block: retighten the connector.

Record the weight of refrigerant supply source. Open both valves on the charging manifold and allow the refrigerant source pressure to fill the vacuum in the system.

Between 0,23 kg and 0,45 kg ($\frac{1}{2}$ lb to 1 lb) weight will enter the system.

Record the quantity.

NOTE: The quantity drawn in will vary with ambient temperature.

Close the high pressure side valve on the manifold block.

Ensure that all is clear and start the vehicle engine. Run the engine at 1500 rev/min.

Set the air conditioning system blower speed control to **'Fast'**.

NOTE: This engages the compression clutch to start system circulation, and runs the blower motors at fast speed to heat the evaporator coil. Vapour will be turned to liquid in the condenser and stored in the receiver-drier.

Control the flow of refrigerant with the suction side valve on the charging manifold, and allow a total weight of 1,13 kg $\pm$ 0,028 kg ($2\frac{1}{2}$ lb $\pm$ 2 oz) refrigerant to enter system.

Close the suction side valve.

NOTE: Alternatively, observe the sight glass on receiver-drier until the sight glass clears, and no bubbles or foam are visible.

Re-open the suction valve for 2 to 5 minutes (2 minutes if the ambient temperature is low, 5 minutes if high).

This will allow an additional 0,11 kg ($\frac{1}{4}$ lb) of refrigerant to enter the system.

Run the system for 5 minutes, observing the sight glass.

If foaming is very slight, switch off the engine.

NOTE: It is normal for there to be slight foaming if the ambient air temperature is 21°C (70°F) or below.

Close the refrigerant supply valve, disconnect the hose.

Quickly disconnect the hoses from the schrader valves.

Fit protective sealing caps.

Switch on the engine and check the function of the air conditioning system.

Switch off the engine; flush the engine compartment and interior of the vehicle with shop compressed air line.

Conduct a leak test on the installation.

SUPERHEAT SWITCH AND THERMAL FUSE

Description

The superheat switch and a thermal fuse are included in the clutch circuit to provide a compressor protection system. This guards against low refrigerant charge and blockages causing extreme superheated inlet gas conditions and resulting compressor damage.

The superheat switch is located in the rear of the compressor in contact with the suction side gas, whose pressure drops and temperature rises with low refrigerant charge (ie Freon leak). This condition closes the superheat switch contacts.

The thermal fuse is a sealed unit containing a heater and meltable fuse. The superheat switch brings in the heater which melts the fuse and disconnects the compressor clutch and heater. The compressor stops and damage from insufficient lubrication will be avoided.

CAUTION: After a thermal fuse melt, establish and rectify the cause before replacing the thermal fuse unit complete.

Thermal fuse melt:

Temperature: 157 to 182°C (315 to 360°F)

Time: 2 minutes — 14V system voltage

     5.5 minutes — 11,5V system voltage

Heater resistance, cold: 8 to 10 ohms:

Air Conditioning Superheat Switch

Testing

If the refrigerant level is satisfactory and there is not a blockage in the air conditioning system but the thermal fuse persists in melting.

Carry out the following checks.

Test Procedure 'A' — for use with a cold engine and at ambient temperatures below 30°C (86°F).

Connect a test lamp in series with the superheat switch (Fig. 44).

NOTE: With the test lamp connected in the circuit it will prevent the thermal fuse from operating as a safety device therefore care should be taken when carrying out the test.

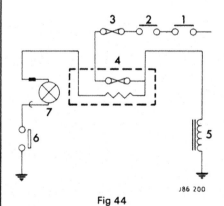

Fig 44

J86 200

KEY TO DIAGRAM (Fig. 44)

1. Air conditioning switch
2. Ambient switch
3. Compressor clutch fuse
4. Thermal fuse
5. Compressor clutch coil
6. Superheat switch
7. Test lamp

KEY TO DIAGRAM (Fig. 43)

1. To compressor clutch
2. Superheat switch
3. Thermal fuse
4. + Feed cable

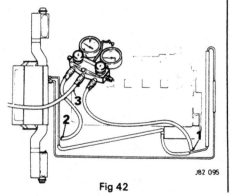

Fig 42

J82 095

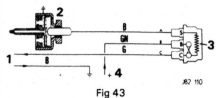

Fig 43

J82 110

82—29

With the ignition and air conditioning switched on

Ensure a serviceable thermal fuse is fitted.

Evacuate the air conditioning system and then close the taps.

The test lamp should not light. If the test lamp does light then follow test procedure 'B'.

With the lamp not illuminated start and run the engine at about 2000 rpm. After a few minutes the lamp should light. As soon as the test lamp lights, open the taps to allow refrigerant to charge into the system. As the air conditioning system becomes charged the lamp should go out.

If the above lamp functions do not occur, replace the superheat switch.

After checking remove the test lamp from the circuit and reconnect the superheat switch lead onto the terminal.

Operate and check the system.

Test Procedure B — for use with a hot engine or at ambient temperatures above 30°C (86°F).

Connect the test lamp in series with the superheat switch.

Switch the ignition and air conditioning on.

Ensure a serviceable thermal fuse is fitted.

Evacuate the air conditioning system and then close the taps.

The test lamp should light. (If the lamp does not light carry on checks as in Procedure 'A').

With the test lamp illuminated open the taps and allow refrigerant to charge the system. As the system becomes charged the test lamp should go out.

If the lamp functions do not occur, then replace the superheat switch.

After checking remove the test lamp and reconnect the superheat switch lead onto the terminal.

Operate and check the system.

SUPERHEAT SWITCH

Renew

Discharge system.

Disconnect harness connector from superheat switch.

Remove suction (low pressure) and out-put (high pressure) hoses.

Remove superheat switch retaining circlip and remove switch by pulling out of the compressor housing.

Remove the superheat switch 'O' ring located in the compressor housing.

Lightly lubricate the new 'O' ring seal and fit into compressor housing.

Locate the replacement superheat switch into the compressor housing and gently push switch into housing until seated.

Fit new circlip and secure.

Connect the suction (low pressure) and out put (high pressure) hoses to the compressor. Evacuate and recharge system and check system for leaks using suitable leak detection equipment.

COMPRESSOR

Remove and Refit

WARNING: BEFORE COMMENCING WORK, REFER TO THE GENERAL SECTION. DO NOT OPERATE THE COMPRESSOR UNTIL THE SYSTEM IS CORRECTLY CHARGED.

NOTE: Ensure that clean, dry male and female caps are to hand.

Disconnect the battery earth lead.

Depressurize the system.

On NAS vehicles, remove the air pump.

Note the position of the hoses.

Remove the clamping plate securing the high and low pressure hoses (1, Fig. 45). Displace the hoses (2, Fig. 45). Fit blanking caps to the hoses and the compressor.

Remove the superheat switch cable connector (3, Fig. 45).

Slacken the compressor front and rear pivot bolts (4, Fig. 45).

Slacken the adjusting link locking and adjusting nuts.

Remove the bolts securing the adjusting link and remove the link.

Displace the drive belt. Disconnect the clutch cable connector (5, Fig. 45).

Remove the nuts securing the cruise control actuator and displace the actuator unit.

Remove the compressor pivot bolts and displace the compressor.

Manoeuvre the compressor from the engine compartment, keeping it horizontal and the sump down.

If a new compressor is being fitted, remove the mounting brackets from the old compressor and fit to new unit.

On refitting, ensure that new 'O' sealing rings are fitted.

Ensure the compressor drive belt is adjusted to the correct tension.

Correct tension as follows:

A load of 2,9 kg (6.4 lb) must give a total belt deflection of 4,32 mm (0.17 in) when applied at mid-point of the belt.

Recharge the air conditioning system.

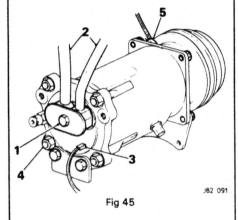

Fig 45

J82 091

CAUTION: After recharging, cycle the clutch in and out 10 times by selecting OFF-LOW, AUTO-OFF on the mode selector switch with the engine running. This ensures that the pulley face and the clutch plate are correctly bedded-in before a high demand is made upon them.

Check the system for correct operation.

Check the cruise control for correct operation.

COMPRESSOR OIL — CHECKING PROCEDURE

The following procedure should be adopted when checking the amount of oil in a compressor prior to its being fitted to a car:

1. Remove drain plug from compressor sump and drain oil into container having capacity of at least 285 cc (10 fl oz).

2. Remove pressure plate across inlet and outlet ports at rear of compressor: more oil may flow from sump plug hole.

3. With pressure plate still removed, set compressor on its rear end so that inlet and outlet ports are over container: slowly rotate drive plate through several revolutions both clockwise and anti-clockwise. Oil may flow from ports.

4. Measure quantity of oil drained out: make this up to 199 cc (7 fl oz) and re-fill compressor with this amount of 525 viscosity refrigerant oil.

If the compressor is not to be fitted immediately, it is important that the pressure plate be refitted over the ports and secured there, to prevent ingress of foreign matter.

Should it be suspected that the compressor oil level is low, on a car in service, the checking procedure detailed should be followed after the car engine has been run for at least 10 - 15 minutes with the air conditioning system switched on: this will cause the refrigerant oil to be returned to the compressor sump.

Should a new receiver-drier bottle, condenser or evaporator be fitted, without the car engine being run as above, immediately before dismantling, the following quantities of 525 viscosity refrigerant oil must be added to the system:

(a) For a new receiver-drier bottle — add 28 cc (1 fl oz).

(b) For a new condenser — add 85 cc (3 fl oz).

(c) For a new evaporator — add 85 cc (3 fl oz).

Additional oil is not needed after renewal of hose assemblies.

Oil may be added to the system either directly into the compressor or into the compressor charging port.

Compressor Servicing Procedure

To enable the servicing of the air conditioning compressor the following components are now available. The following servicing procedures should be adopted in the event of a malfunction of the compressor which involves any of the parts listed, as opposed to the replacement of the compressor unit.

Part Description

Pulley Bearing
Superheat Switch
Pressure Relief Valve
'O' Ring Suction Discharge Port
$\frac{1}{4}$ Pint 525 Viscosity Oil
Clutch Driver Assembly
Shaft Nut
Woodruff Key
Coil and Housing Clutch
Pulley Bearing Assembly
Retainer Ring Kit
Body of Compressor less Clutch, Pulley and Coil Housing Assembly
Shaft Kit for Seal
Bearing Retaining Ring

The specialist tool kit required to service the compressor unit in conjunction with the following procedures are available from KENT MOORE.

Tool Kit	10500
Hub Holding Tool	10418
Thin Walled Socket	10416

Tool Kit Contents

Pulley Extractor Kit
Pulley Bearing Remover and Installer Kit
Seal Assembly Remover and Installer
Hub Drive Plate Remover Kit
Hub and Drive Plate Assembly Installer
'O' Ring Remover
'O' Ring Installer
Snap Ring Installer
Ceramic Seal Remover and Installer, and Shaft
Seal Protector
Hub Holding Tool
Thin Walled Socket

When Servicing the compressor, remove only the necessary components that preliminary diagnosis indicates are in need of service.

Seven service operations may be performed on the GM 6 cylinder compressor.

(i) Replacement of compressor assembly.
(ii) Replacement of clutch drive and pulley assembly.
(iii) Replacement of pulley bearing.
(iv) Replacement of clutch coil and housing assembly.
(v) Replacement of shaft seal.
(vi) Replacement of superheat switch.
(vii) Replacement of compressor cylinder and shaft assembly (less clutch drive, coil housing and pulley).

General Instructions During Servicing Operations

(i) Discharge system prior to removal of compressor unit.

(ii) During removal, maintain the compressor positioned so that the sump is downward. Do not rotate compressor shaft.
(iii) If the compressor is being replaced due to a component failure within the main body of the compressor, the clutch coil housing and clutch plate drive and hub assembly must be removed from the original compressor unit and fitted to the replacement unit. This also applies when fitting a replacement compressor body.
(iv) If the original compressor is being reinstalled following servicing, replace with the right quantity of 525 viscosity oil.
(v) Discard 'O' rings from suction and discharge ports of compressor and replace and with new 'O' rings.
(vi) Install compressor and adjust drive belt tension to service manual specifications.
(vii) Lubricate 'O' rings with refrigerant oil and attach suction and discharge hose connections and retaining plate to compressor torque to 2,764 - 3,455 kgfm (20 - 25 ft lbs).

Replacement of Clutch Drive Plate and Hub Pulley, Clutch Coil and Housing Assemblies.

Discharge the system.
Remove the compressor from the engine.
Using suitable mounting jig or vice, secure compressor.
Holding the hub of the clutch drive plate with the hub holding tool. Using the thin walled $\frac{9}{16}$ in socket remove the shaft nut. Refer to Fig. 46.

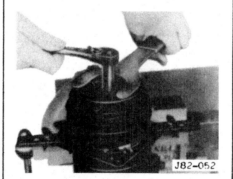

Fig 46

Screw the threaded hub puller to the hub. Hold the body of the hub puller with a suitable spanner, tighten centre screw of hub pulley (Fig. 47), until drive plate, hub and woodruff key can be removed (Fig. 48).

Fig 47

Fig 48

Using suitable circlip pliers remove the bearing to head retainer ring (Fig. 49).

Fig 49

82—31

449

Fig 50

Remove the absorbent felt sleeve retainer ring to enable the location of the pulley extraction tool.

Using the pulley extraction tool locate the puller pilot on hub of front head and remove the pulley assembly (Fig. 50).

NOTE: The next operation details removal of pulley bearing. DO NOT remove the pulley bearing unless it is to be replaced. Removal may cause the bearing to be damaged.

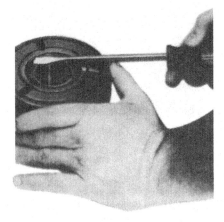

Fig 51

Fig 52

Remove bearing to pulley retaining ring with small screwdriver (Fig. 51). Drive out the bearing using bearing remover and handle (Fig. 52).

Fig 53

Mark position of the coil and housing assembly in relationship to the shell of the compressor. Remove the coil housing retainer ring using suitable circlip pliers (Fig. 53) and lift off the coil and housing assembly (Fig. 54).

Examine coil for loose or distorted terminals and cracked insulation. Check that the current consumption is 3.2 Amps at 12 volts. The resistance should be 3.75 Ohms at room temperature.

Fig 54

Reassemble coil and housing assembly by reversing the dismantling procedure. Be sure coil and housing assembly markings line up.

NOTE: If the pulley assembly is going to be reused, clean the friction surface with suitable solvent cleaner.

Fig 55

Drive the new bearing into the pulley assembly with the bearing installer and handle. The bearing installer will ride on the outer race of the bearing (Fig. 55).

Fig 56

Lock the bearing in position with the bearing to pulley retainer ring.

Press or tap the pulley assembly into the hub of front head using installer tool and handle (Fig 56).

Check the pulley for binding or roughness, and that the pulley rotates freely.

Using suitable circlip pliers lock pulley assembly in position with bearing to head retainer ring (flat side of retainer ring should face towards pulley).

Install square drive woodruff key in the key way of the clutch drive hub.

Wipe frictional surface of clutch plate and pulley clean. Using a suitable solvent.

Place clutch plate and hub assembly on shaft, aligning shaft key way with key in hub (refer to Fig. 48 dismantling procedure).

NOTE: The woodruff key is made with a slight curvature to help hold it in the plate hub during assembly.

IMPORTANT: To avoid damage to the compressor, undue force should not be applied to the hub or shaft. This could misplace axial plate on shaft, resulting in damage to the compressor.

Fig 57

Place spacer on hub. Thread clutch plate and hub assembly installer tool onto end of the shaft (Fig. 57).

Hold the head of the bolt and turn tool body several revolutions to press hub partially on shaft. Remove clutch plate and hub assembly installer and spacer.

Check alignment of woodruff key with key way in shaft. If alignment is correct, replace installer tool and continue to press hub into shaft until there is approximately 2,38 mm ($\frac{3}{32}$ in) air gap between the frictional surfaces of pulley and clutch plate. Remove installer tool and spacer.

Install a new shaft lock nut with the small diameter boss of the nut against the hub using a thin wall $\frac{7}{8}$ in socket. Hold clutch with holding tool and tighten nut to 2,07 kg/fm (15 ft/lbs), using a 3,455 kg/fm (25 ft/lbs) torque wrench. The air gap between the frictional surfaces of pulley and clutch plate should now be approximately 0,56 mm to 1,45 mm (0.022 in to 0.057 in).

Shaft Seal Leak Detection

A compressor shaft seal should not be changed because of an oil line on the underside of the bonnet. The seal is designed to seep some oil for lubrication purposes. Only change a shaft seal when a leak is detected by the following procedures:

Ensure there is refrigerant is in the system.
Turn off the engine.

Blow off compressor clutch area with compressed air. Blow out clutch vent holes to completely remove any freon and oil deposits.

Allow car to stand for 5 minutes, without operating compressor.

Rotate the compressor clutch drive plate by hand until one of the vent holes is at the lower side of drive plate. Using leak detector, sense through vent hole at lower side of drive plate only.

Some compression shaft seal leaks may be the result of misplacement of the axial plate on the compressor shaft. The mispositioning of the axial plate may be caused by improper procedures used during pulley and driven plate removal, undue force collisions, or dropping the compressor.

Replacement of Shaft Seal

Remove clutch driven plate and hub assembly as previously described.
Remove compressor absorbent felt retaining ring and felt sleeve.

Fig 58

Thoroughly clean the area inside the compressor neck surrounding the shaft, the exposed portion of the seat and the shaft itself of any dirt or foreign material. This is absolutely necessary to prevent any such material from getting into the compressor.
Remove the seal seat retaining circlip (Fig. 58) using suitable circlip pliers.

Fig 59

Remove the ceramic seal seat using the seal seat remover and installer tool (Fig. 59). Position tool into seal seat recess, grasp flange of shaft seal seat and pull straight out.

Fig 60

Using the seal remover and installer tool grip the seal by inserting the tool into the seal recess. Turning clockwise. Withdraw the tool and seal (Fig. 60).

Fig. 61

Remove the seal seat 'O' ring (Fig. 61) using the 'O' ring remover tool.

Recheck the inside of the compressor neck and the shaft. Be sure these areas are perfectly clean and free of burrs before installing new parts.

Coat shaft and 'O' ring with clean compressor 525 viscosity oil.

Fig 62

Place 'O' ring on 'O' ring installer (Fig. 62) and insert tool and 'O' ring into seal recess. Release 'O' ring by sliding down tool hook, and remove tool.

(Fig. 63) illustrates the tool being removed following 'O' ring installations.

Fig 63

Place the seal protective sleeve over the compressor shaft and fit new shaft seal. Gently twisting the tool clockwise to engage the seal housing flats onto the compressor shaft. Withdraw the tool by pressing downwards and twisting the tool anti-clockwise.

Coat the seal face of the new ceramic seal seat with clean 525 viscosity oil. Mount the seal seat on to the remover and installer tool and carefully guide the seal into the compressor neck gently twisting it into the 'O' ring seal.

Disengage and remove tool, and compressor shaft protective sleeve.

Install new circlip with the flat side against seal seat, and press home.

Install the new absorbent sleeve by rolling the material into the cylinder, overlapping the ends and slipping it into the compressor neck with the overlap at the top of the compressor. Using a small screwdriver or similar tool carefully spread the sleeve so that in its final position, the ends butt together at the top vertical centre line.

Install the new absorbent sleeve retainer so that its flange face will be against the front end of the sleeve, press and tap with a mallet setting the retaining ring and absorbent sleeve until the outer edge of the sleeve retainer is recessed approximately 0,8 mm ($\frac{1}{32}$ in) from the face of the compressor neck.

Lightly lubricate absorbent felt sleeve with 525 viscosity oil.

Refit clutch drive plate and hub assembly.

Check compressor oil level.

Refit compressor to vehicle, and connect the suction (low pressure) and discharge (high pressure) hoses using new 'O' ring seals. Prior to fitment of compressor drive belt, rotate the compressor drive plate clockwise several revolutions to prime lubrication pump.

Evacuate and recharge system.

NOTE: During charge procedure check compressor seals for leaks using suitable leak detection equipment.

Leak Test

A high proportion of all air conditioning work will consist of locating and repairing leaks. Many leaks will be located at points of connections and are caused by vibration. They may only require the retightening of a connection or clamp. Occasionally a hose will rub on a structural part of the vehicle and create a leak, or a hose will deteriorate and require a replacement. Any time the system requires more than $\frac{1}{2}$ lb of refrigerant after a period of operation, a leak is indicated which must be located and rectified.

The 'Robinair Robbitek 30001 Leak Detector' is designed for speedy detection of leaks. The leak detector is small and portable, and is battery operated. This instrument will indicate leaks electronically by sounding an alarm signal. Provision is made to plug in an earphone, which is useful in a noisy workshop; and it has the recommended sensitivity of 0,45 kg (1 lb) in 32 years.

FLAP LINKAGE

Adjust Air

Service Tools: 18G 1363, Setting Jig (Fig. 64)

Remove the console right hand panel and underscuttle trim panels to gain access to the air conditioning unit flap linkages. Note: On LH drive cars it is necessary to remove the glovebox compartment.

Remove the footwell outlet vent from the air conditioning unit.

Switch on the ignition, position the right hand control knob to 'DEF'. When the servo has reached its full heat position, switch off the ignition and disconnect the battery.

Disconnect the linkage rods (1, Fig. 66) from the servo lever connections.

Set the link bolt adjuster (2, Fig. 66) in its mid position.

Gently pull the wire link (3, Fig. 66) to detach it from the grommet in link (4, Fig. 66).

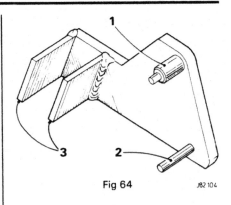

Fig 64   J82 104

Move the thumbwheel (Fig. 65), located in the radio console panel, fully to the right.

Using the jig setting tool 18G 1363, locate peg (1, Fig. 64) into the hole (7, Fig. 66) on the linkage protection bracket, and peg (2, Fig. 64) in the hole in linkage (4, Fig. 66), from which link (3, Fig. 66) was removed The parallel end guides on the setting jig tool (3, Fig. 64), should locate over the linkage assembly (8, Fig. 66) so that the linkage is in a straight line. If linkage (8, Fig. 66) is not in line adjust the distribution temperature control cable (9, Fig. 66), until the linkage is straight. Tighten the cable clamp (6, Fig. 66).

With the jig setting tool in position adjust the linkage (10, Fig. 66) until post (11, Fig. 66) is at the top of the slot.

Remove the jig setting tool.

Position the setbolt adjuster (12, Fig. 66) at its furthest point away from fulcrum (13, Fig. 66). Refit the link rod (3, Fig. 66) to linkage (4, Fig. 66).

Reconnect the servo linkage rods (1, Fig. 66) to the servo motor levers, ensure that the servo lever cam followers locate against the servo cams.

Reconnect the battery and switch on the ignition. Motor the system to the full cooling position.

Switch off the ignition.

Check that the linkage (14, Fig. 66) abuts against the snail cam (15, Fig. 66).

The lower heat flap should now be fully sealed; check by manually pushing the snail cam, no movement should be evident.

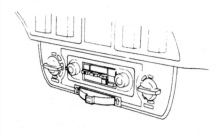

Fig 65   J82 105

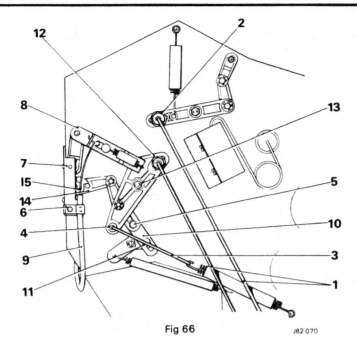

Fig 66   J82 070

If there is movement, switch on the ignition and motor the system to its full heat position, switch off the ignition. Slacken the set bolt adjuster (12, Fig. 66) and move it slightly towards the fulcrum point (13, Fig. 66). Reset the servo lever linkage rods (1, Fig. 66) so that the servo lever cam followers locate against the servo cam.

Switch on the ignition and motor the system to its full cooling position (AUTO 65). Check that linkage (14, Fig. 66) abuts against the snail cam (15, Fig. 66). Check manually by pressing the snail cam, if movement is evident, repeat the procedure in the previous paragraph.

If no movement is evident, then the lower heat flap is sealing correctly and the flap linkages and distribution temperature control are correctly set.

Ensure that all linkages and adjustments are secure.

Refit the footwell outlet vent, the underscuttle trim panels and console right hand side panel.

CONDENSER UNIT AND RECEIVER-DRIER

Renew

Before commencing this operation, ensure that suitable clean, dry sealing plugs and caps are to hand.

Disconnect the battery earth lead.

Depressurise the air conditioning system.

Remove the nuts and washers securing the fan cowl to the radiator (1, Fig. 67) top rail and pull the fan cowl clear of the mounting studs.

Disconnect the pipes from the receiver-drier (2, Fig. 67) and the pipe from the compressor to the condenser (3, Fig. 67). Fit blanking plugs to all the disconnected pipes to avoid contamination.

Remove the nuts and washers securing receiver-drier (4, Fig. 67).

Remove the receiver-drier (5, Fig. 67).

Note the connections and disconnect the cable harness to the ignition amplifier.

Remove the nuts and washers securing the condenser mounting bracket to the radiator top rail (6, Fig. 67).

Remove the four bolts and washers securing the radiator top rail to the wing valances (7, Fig. 67).

Ease the top rail clear of the condenser and lift the condenser clear of the car.

On refitting, reverse the above operations and fit a new receiver-drier.

NOTE: If the system is opened, even for a short time, the receiver-drier must be renewed. Do not remove the protective sealing caps from the new unit until it has been fitted and is ready for the pipes to be connected.

AMBIENT TEMPERATURE SENSOR

Renew

Disconnect the battery earth lead.

Remove the right hand underscuttle casing.

Remove the component panel securing screws and displace the component panel.

Note the position of the electrical connections and disconnect the cables from the sensor.

Remove the two screws securing the sensor and remove the sensor.

IN CAR TEMPERATURE SENSOR

Renew

Disconnect the battery earth lead.

Remove the screws securing the passengers underscuttle casing and remove the casing.

Remove the screws securing the glove box liner and the glove box latch. Remove the latch and carefully withdraw the liner.

Carefully manoeuvre the elbow hose from the sensor outlet.

Disconnect and remove the sensor assembly (1, Fig. 68) from the air pick-up tube (2, Fig. 68).

Remove the sensor assembly from the elbow hose (3, Fig. 68).

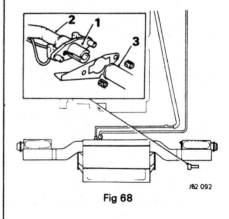

J82 092

Fig 68

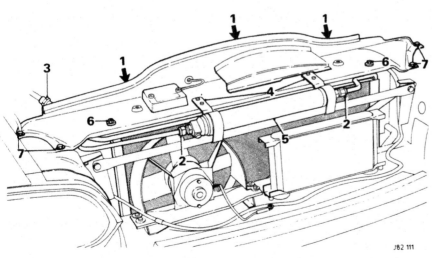

Fig 67   J82 111

TEMPERATURE SELECTOR

Renew

MODE SELECTOR

Renew

Disconnect the battery earth lead.

Carefully prise off the switch knobs from the temperature and fan controls.

Unscrew the fasteners from behind the control knobs and detach the control panel.

Disconnect the optical fibre elements, remove the control panel and the radio escutcheon assemblies.

Remove the right and left hand side pads.

Unscrew the gear selector control knob.

Remove the screws securing the switch panel to the centre console, ease the switch panel from the centre console, note the position of the wiring connectors, disconnect the connectors and remove the switch panel.

Remove the screws securing the front and rear ends of the console.

Displace the stop lamp bulb failure sensor and remove the console assembly.

Remove the bolts and washers securing the stays to the transmission tunnel (1, Fig. 69). Ease the stays aside to give access to the switch panel.

Remove the nuts and washers securing the switch panel to the left hand of the unit (2, Fig. 69).

Remove the screws securing the switch cover to the switch panel (3, Fig 69). Note the position and disconnect the vacuum pipes.

Remove the nut and washer securing the switch cover to unit at lower right hand side. Release the harness and remove the switch cover.

Remove the nut and washer securing the switch panel at the upper right hand side of the panel (5, Fig. 69).

Ease the panel clear of the mounting studs, remove the two screws securing the temperature selector (4, Fig 69), note the position of the cable connections, disconnect the cables at the connections (6, Fig 69) and remove the selector.

Note the position of and disconnect the cables from the mode selector micro-switches (1, Fig 70)

Note the position of the micro-switches, remove the two screws and nuts securing the switches (2, Fig 70).

Remove the switches and retain the distance pieces.

Remove the screws securing the vacuum switch mounting bracket (3, Fig. 70) and remove the vacuum switch assembly.

Remove the circlip securing the cam assembly and remove the cam assembly.

NOTE: Care must be taken to ensure that correct replacement parts are used, and that the items are replaced in the correct position.

When refitting the cams, ensure that the vacuum switch operating rod is pressed back to allow the camshaft into position.

THERMOSTAT

Renew

Disconnect the battery earth lead

Remove the right hand underscuttle casing and the right hand side casing.

On left hand drive cars remove the glove box liner

Remove the nut securing the thermostat to the bracket (1, Fig. 71).

Note the position of and disconnect the cables from the lucar connectors (2, Fig 71)

Carefully remove the thermostat by withdrawing the capillary tube from the air conditioning unit (3, Fig. 71).

NOTE: Ensure the replacement thermostat capillary tube is formed to the exact dimensions of the unserviceable unit, ensuring that the capillary tube makes contact with the evaporator matrix.

BLOWER MOTOR RESISTANCE UNIT

Renew

Disconnect the battery earth lead

On right hand drive cars, remove the left hand underscuttle casing and the glove box liner.

On left hand drive cars, remove the left hand underscuttle casing and the left hand side casing.

Note the position of and disconnect the cables from the resistance unit lucar connectors (1, Fig. 72).

Remove the screw securing the vacuum hose clip, move the hose to one side (2, Fig. 72).

Remove the screws securing the resistance unit and withdraw the unit from the air conditioning unit case (3, Fig. 72).

On refitting, ensure the cable connectors are secure and connected correctly.

WATER VALVE TEMPERATURE SWITCH

Renew

Disconnect the battery earth lead.

Remove the left hand underscuttle casing and the console side casing.

On right hand drive cars remove the glove box liner.

Disconnect the cables at the lucar connectors on the switch (1, Fig. 73).

Withdraw the securing screws and remove the switch (2, Fig. 73).

On refitting, ensure the connectors are clean and tight

Figs 69 — 73

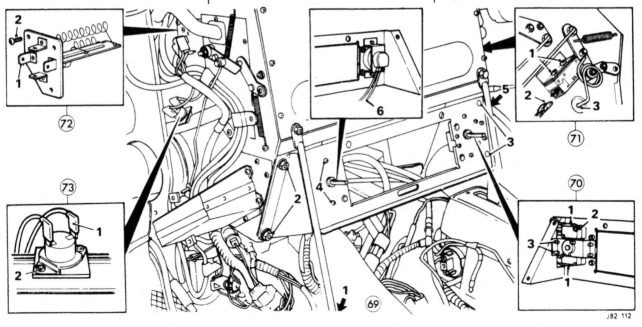

J82 112

BLOWER MOTOR RELAY

Renew

Disconnect the battery earth lead.
Remove the left hand console side casing.
Remove the screws securing the footwell air outlet duct and remove the duct.
Note the position of the cable connectors.
Disconnect the block connector, the lucars and the main feed cable from the relay (1, Fig. 74).
Remove the nuts securing the relay and remove the relay (2, Fig. 74).
On fitting replacement relay, ensure the cables are secure and connected correctly.

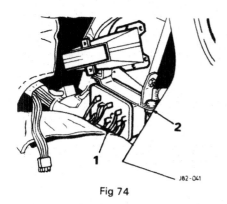

Fig 74

WATER VALVE

Renew

Remove the engine coolant filter and header tank caps, then open the radiator drain tap.
Allow the coolant to drain from the system.
Slacken the securing clip on the water valve to cylinder head hose and disconnect the water valve from the hose (1, Fig. 75).
Disconnect the vacuum hose from the water valve (2, Fig. 75).
Reposition the valve for access to the water valve to heater hose clip (3, Fig. 75).
Slacken the clip and remove the water valve.

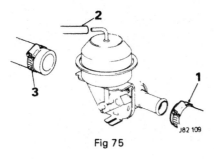

Fig 75

On refitting, ensure the cooling system is refilled with coolant to the correct specification.

THERMAL FUSE

Renew

Disconnect the cable block connector from the thermal fuse (1, Fig. 76) assembly located to the front of the right hand wing valance.
Remove the nut and screw securing the thermal fuse (2, Fig. 76).
Remove the thermal fuse.

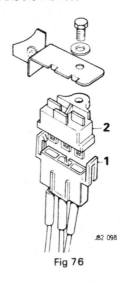

Fig 76

EXPANSION VALVE

Renew

Depressurize the air conditioning system.
Partially drain the engine coolant.
Disconnect the hose unions (1, Fig. 77) and seal with clean blanking caps.
Release the clip securing the water valve to the cylinder head hose, disconnect the water valve from the hose, and move the water valve clear of the expansion valve.
Remove the padding from the capillary tube (2, Fig. 77).
Disconnect the capillary tube at the union (3, Fig. 77).
Release the valve by unscrewing the union nut (4, Fig. 77).

NOTE: To avoid straining the joint or the pipe, ensure the valve is held firmly as the union is unscrewed.

Slacken the two screws securing the capillary tube clear of the clamp.
Remove the valve assembly carefully, manoeuvering the capillary tube clear of the clamp.
On fitting replacement unit, ensure new 'O' rings are fitted, the cooling system is refilled, and the air conditioning system is recharged.

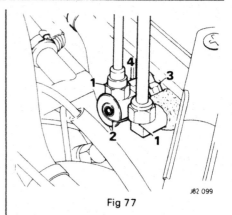

Fig 77

BLOWER ASSEMBLY

Remove and refit RH Unit

The blower fans are heavy duty motors with impellors attached. Speed is varied by controlled switching of resistances in series with the motors. The right hand unit has the ambient temperature sensor mounted in the inlet duct. Air flow control flaps are operated by a vacuum actuator situated in the side of the inlet duct.

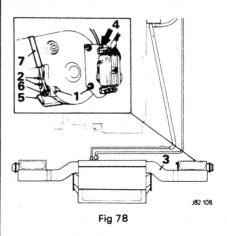

Fig 78

Disconnect the battery earth lead.
Remove the right hand underscuttle casing and right hand console casing.
On left hand drive cars, remove the glove box liner.
Remove the nuts securing the component panel to the blower (1, Fig. 78) assembly, secure the component panel clear for access to the blower assembly mounting bolts.
Disconnect the ambient temperature sensor leads at the lucar connectors (2, Fig. 78).
Disconnect the pliable trunking from the stub pipes on the side of the air conditioning unit (3, Fig. 78).
Disconnect the blower motor harness block connector.
Disconnect the vacuum pipe from the flap operating servo on blower assembly (4, Fig. 78).
Open the recirculation flap and fit a wedge to retain it in the open position (5, Fig. 78).
Remove the bolts securing blower assembly to mounting brackets (6, Fig. 78).
Ease the blower assembly from its location.
Remove the tape securing the ducting to the assembly (7, Fig. 78).

AIR CONDITIONING UNIT

Remove and refit

Removing

Disconnect the battery earth lead.

Withdraw the steering wheel and the adjuster assembly from the upper steering column.

Remove the left and right hand underscuttle casing.

Remove the instrument panel module and carefully remove switch panel.

Withdraw the air conditioning knobs from the air conditioning selector switches, remove the radio, remove the screws securing the facia and the console to the air conditioning unit.

Remove the glove box liner.

Slacken the nuts securing the top rear portion of the facia to the bulkhead, remove the bolts securing the sides of the facia to the bulkhead, remove the nut securing the main light switch, displace the switch and carefully remove the facia from the car.

Disconnect the air conditioning hoses at the bulkhead connectors to the expansion valve on the engine compartment (1, Fig. 79).

Disconnect the coolant hoses at the heater bulkhead connectors in the engine compartment.

Remove the nuts securing the air conditioning unit to the bulkhead (2, Fig. 79).

Unclip the main harness from the securing clips on the screen rail (3, Fig. 79).

Remove the bolts securing the demist duct support rail to the body mounting points and remove the support rail (4, Fig. 79).

Disconnect the pliable ducting between the air conditioning unit and the blower motors from the stub pipes (5, Fig. 79).

Remove the rear compartment ducts (6, Fig. 79).

Remove the nuts and bolts securing the unit support stays (7, Fig. 79); recover the stays.

Remove the automatic gearbox selector quadrant cover.

Remove the bolts securing the upper steering column to the mounting bracket; remove the spacers and the packing washers (8, Fig. 79).

Remove the bolts securing the earth leads and the support stays to the steering column mounting bracket. Retain the washers (9, Fig. 79).

Remove the bolt securing the mounting bracket to the screen rail (10, Fig. 79) and retain the bracket.

NOTE: To facilitate refitting, it is advised that the position of all the electrical multi-pin connectors are noted and marked. The position and the routes of all the vacuum pipes noted and marked.

Disconnect the blower motor flap vacuum pipes at the 'T' piece (11, Fig. 79), and the demister duct vacuum pipe at the servo (12, Fig. 79).

Disconnect the main panel harness electrical connectors and remove the harness from the securing clips.

Remove the nuts securing the air conditioning switch panel to the air conditioning unit (13, Fig. 79) and remove the screws securing the mode switch cover, retain the switch cover (14, Fig. 79).

Disconnect the mode switch vacuum pipes and the mode switch electrical connectors.

Disconnect the earth cable and the motor harness multi-pin at the air conditioning main harness.

Disconnect the remaining block connectors including the multi-pin connector of the windscreen wiper motor harness at the bulkhead.

Disconnect the ambient and in car sensors.

Ease the drain tubes clear of the grommets in the transmission tunnel, ease the main panel harness clear of the unit and ease the demist duct vane securing studs from the screen rail.

Retain the demist duct assembly.

Remove the screw securing the air conditioning unit to the top rail (15, Fig. 79). Manoeuvre the unit from its location taking great care to prevent damage to the unit or to the surrounding components.

With the unit on a workbench, remove the face level vent, the brackets and the demist duct assembly from the unit.

Refit by reversing the above procedure noting that the receiver-drier must be replaced.

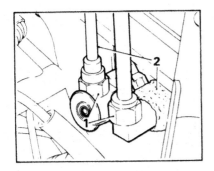
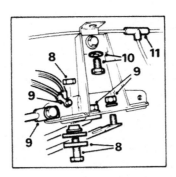
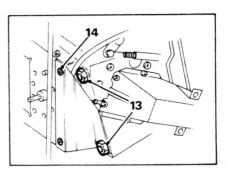

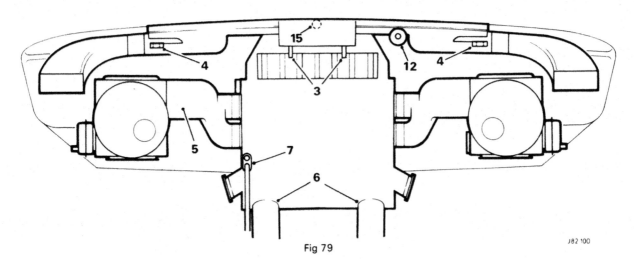

Fig 79

J82 100

BLOWER ASSEMBLY

Remove and refit LH Unit

Removing

Disconnect the battery earth lead.

Remove the left hand underscuttle casing and the left hand console casing.

On right hand drive cars, remove the glove box liner.

Remove the nuts securing the compartment panel (1, Fig. 80) to the blower motor assembly, ease the panel clear and secure for access to blower assembly (2, Fig. 80).

Disconnect the pliable ducting from the stub pipes at the side of the air conditioning unit (3, Fig. 80).

Disconnect the blower motor harness at the block connector.

Disconnect the vacuum pipe from the flap operating servo on the blower assembly (4, Fig. 80).

Open the recirculation flap in the base of the blower assembly and hold open with a suitable wedge (5, Fig. 80).

Remove the bolts securing the blower assembly to the mounting brackets, and ease the blower assembly from its location (6, Fig. 80).

Remove the tape securing the ducting to the assembly and remove the ducting (7, Fig. 80).

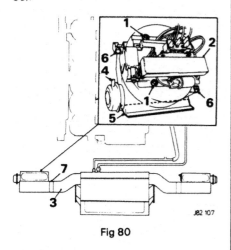

Fig 80

VENTILATORS

Remove and refit — Centre
Right hand
Left hand

Removing

For the centre and passengers side veneer panels, open the glove box for access. By using a suitable long thin-bladed instrument, carefully release the veneer panel, retaining clips, and remove the appropriate panel.

Withdraw the appropriate ventilator

HEATER MATRIX

Renew

With the air conditioning unit removed and located on a workbench, the heater matrix can be removed.

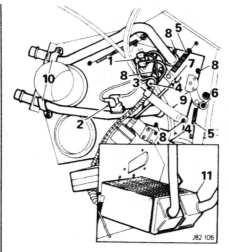

Fig 81

IMPORTANT: It is recommended that the positions of all the operating rods are marked with a scriber, or a similar methods.

Note and disconnect all the cables from the blower motor resistance unit (1, Fig. 81) and the water valve temperature switch (2, Fig. 81).

Remove the screws securing the cable harness clip and the bracket (3, Fig. 81).

Remove the screws securing the vacuum pipe clips (4, Fig. 81).

Disengage the return springs from the operating levers (5, Fig. 81), remove the screw securing the lower flap operating lever to flap hinge (6 Fig. 81) and remove the lever.

Slacken the screw securing the operating rod from the vacuum servo to the flap operating lever on the matrix cover (7, Fig. 81) and release the lever from the rod.

Remove the screws securing the matrix cover plate to the unit (8, Fig. 81).

Remove the screws securing the heater matrix pipes retaining bracket to unit and remove the bracket (9, Fig. 81).

Remove the pipe clips (10, Fig. 81).

With a straight pull, ease the matrix clear of the unit (11, Fig. 81).

Remove the sleeve from the top pipe, the cover plate and the water valve temperature switch from the lower pipe.

EVAPORATOR

Renew

With the air conditioning unit removed from the car and placed on a workbench.

Remove the screws securing the heater matrix pipe retaining bracket to the unit and remove the bracket.

Remove the screws securing the back plate to the unit, ease the rubber pad from the back plate (1, Fig 82), remove the screws securing the expansion valve mounting plate to the back plate (2, Fig. 82), and ease the back plate (3, Fig. 82) over the expansion valve.

NOTE: Take care to prevent damage to the capillary tube.

Remove the thermostat (4, Fig. 82) by disconnecting the cables and removing the fixing nut. Carefully ease the thermostat capillary tube from the air conditioning unit. Ease the evaporator clear of the air conditioning unit (5, Fig. 82).

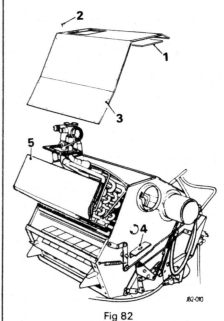

Fig 82

SERVO AND CONTROL UNIT

Remove and refit

Disconnect the battery earth lead.

Remove the RH console side casing.

Remove the RH footwell vent by withdrawing the four securing screws (1, Fig. 83).

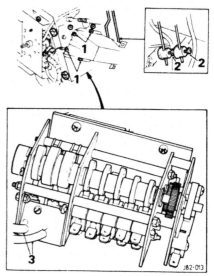

Fig 83

Disconnect the two flap operating rods from the cam followers, marking the rods to facilitate correct refitting (2, Fig. 83).

Mark the vacuum tubes for identification before disconnecting them from the vacuum switches (3, Fig. 83).

Disconnect the cable harness at the multi-pin plug and socket.

Remove the servo unit chrome dome nut and ease the servo clear of the unit.

Refit by reversing the above procedure.

82—39

SERVO AND CONTROL UNIT ASSEMBLY

Overhaul

CAUTION: No attempt must be made to dismantle the servo motor from the gearbox. 12 volts must never be applied direct to the motor connections. The motor will over-run the limit switches and could strip the gear assembly. Do not attempt to dismantle the camshaft assembly.

The servo and control unit must not be serviced under warranty.

Dismantling

To remove the Ranco thermostat and recirculation over-ride micro-switches, withdraw the two securing screws and take the switch from the end plate (1, Fig. 84).

The other micro-switches can now be removed by easing the friction washers from the ends of the micro-switch locating rods (2, Fig. 84). Push the rods through the micro-switch pack (3, Fig. 84) and ease the micro-switches from the assembly (4, Fig. 84).

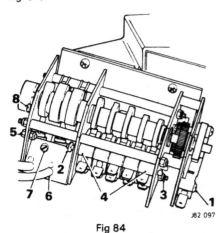

Fig 84

The vacuum switches can be removed by removing the two nuts and screws retaining the vacuum switch mounting bracket (5, Fig. 84). Pull the bracket from the assembly (6, Fig. 84). Remove the nut and screw clamping mounting plates together. Remove the plates to free the switches (7, Fig. 84).

The feedback potentiometer is removed by withdrawing the two securing screws (8, Fig. 84). Note the position of cables and unsolder.

Reassembling

Re-solder the cables to the potentiometer and secure with the two fixing screws.

Reposition the vacuum switches to the clamping plates. Fit the bracket to the assembly.

Secure with the nuts and screws.

Ease the micro-switch pack into the assembly.

Push the locating rods through the micro-switch pack and ease the friction washers onto the end of the rods.

Refit the Ranco thermostat and recirculation over-ride micro-switch with the two securing screws.

VACUUM SOLENOID

Renew

Remove the left hand console side pad (1, Fig. 85).

Remove the screws securing the footwell outlet vent to air conditioning unit and remove the vent.

Remove the nut securing the earth leads to the mounting bolt (2, Fig. 85).

Remove the nut and bolt securing the vacuum solenoid (3, Fig. 85).

Disconnect the vacuum pipes and electrical cables from the solenoid (4, Fig. 85).

Remove the vaccum solenoid.

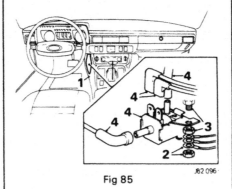

Fig 85

AMPLIFIER UNIT

Renew

Disconnect the battery.

Remove the left-hand console side panel.

Remove the screws securing the footwell vent to the air-conditioning unit and remove the duct (1, Fig. 86).

Remove the nut securing the blower motor relay to the mounting bracket on the air conditioning unit (2, Fig. 86).

Displace the vacuum solenoid from its location and swing aside (3, Fig. 86).

Disconnect the amplifier cable harness multi-pin plug and socket (4, Fig. 86).

Displace the amplifier from the spring clip under the unit and move the harness aside.

Remove the nylon strap securing the harnesses and remove the amplifier (5, Fig. 86).

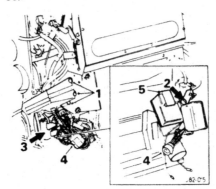

Fig 86

BLOWER ASSEMBLY

LH
Overhaul RH

NOTE: The blower assembly must not be dismantled under warranty.

Dismantling

Remove the three self tapping screws from the air intake casing (1, Fig. 87).

Part the air inlet casing (2, Fig. 87) from the motor assembly (3, Fig. 87) and disconnect electrical connections at the lucar connectors (4, Fig. 87).

NOTE: It is recommended at this stage that the positions of the various components are marked either with paint or a scriber. This will facilitate reassembly.

One cable Lucar has a raised projection which matches the aperture in the motor casing. This ensures that the connections are replaced correctly and that the rotation of the motor is not altered.

Remove the bolts securing the motor mounting bracket to the fan housing (5, Fig. 87).

Remove the motor and fan assembly from the fan housing.

Remove the mounting bracket from the motor.

Using the appropriate Allen key, remove the impeller fan from the spindle.

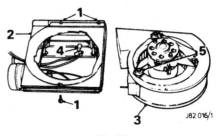

Fig 87

Reassembling

Refit the fan to the motor and secure it to the spindle.

Refit the mounting bracket to the motor.

Locate the fan and mounting assembly into the fan-housing.

Fit and tighten the bolts securing the assembly to the fan housing.

Place the flap box assembly to the fan housing and reconnect the electrical connections.

Fit and tighten the screws securing the flap box to the housing.

Raise the recirculation flap, fit and tighten the remaining screw.

Refit the blower motor assembly.

Reconnect the battery.

CHARGING VALVE CORE

Renew

A possible reason for very slow charging is a bent or damage schrader valve depressor. Do not attempt to straighten. The valve core must be replaced.

If excessive leakage is detected from the schrader valve cores at the rear of the compressor, use a soap solution to ensure that the valve core itself is at fault. If the valve core is leaking replace it by following this procedure.

Ensure replacement clean dry valve core is to hand before commencing operation.

Depressurize the system.

Remove the valve core using a schrader removing tool.

NOTE: Do not overtighten when refitting, then charge the system.

AIR CONDITIONING

Test operation

NOTE: During the following tests windows should be closed and footwell fresh air vents shut 'off'.

Warm the engine up and check operation of thermostatic cut-out and low speed over-ride. RH control to 'auto'.

With the engine cold, turn the LH knob to 'full heat'. Start the engine and run at 1000 rpm. If, after any previous running the camshaft has turned to the cold position, the servo will operate for a few seconds and then shut down. As the water temperature reaches 40°C the system will start up, the centre outlet will close if not already closed, and the fans will slip up to speed 2. This can be checked by turning the RH knob to low, when a drop in speed should be noticed.

Sequence of operation check. RH control to 'auto'

With the engine warm, turn the LH knob to 65° Operate the cigar lighter or other heat source and hold the heated unit about 1 in below the sensor inlet hole, which is situated below the centre parcel shelf. The unit should then go through the following sequence in approximately 20 seconds.

Blower speeds will drop to low.

Temperatures will decrease, the upper temperature dropping more quickly than the footwell temperature.

After approximately ten seconds the centre outlet flap will open.

Approximately one second after this the fan speeds will shift up to a medium 1.

A further one second later the fan speed will shift up to medium 2.

Another one second later the fan speeds will shift to maximum, at the same time the fresh air vents will close and the recirculating flaps will open. The rush of air into the air boxes will be felt along the bottom edge of the lower trim panels. Turn the RH knob to 'LOW' which should cause the fan speeds to drop. Return RH knob to auto setting

On some cars in which the servo action is

fairly fast the separation of the fan speeds may not be discernible.

Aspiration and intermediate position check

Remove the heat source from the sensor. Within ten seconds, depending upon ambient conditions, the unit should shift off recirculation and the blowers will drop to one of the intermediate speeds. This test can be carried out on the road since thermistor aspiration will be better and hence the test will be performed more quickly. In certain high ambient conditions the system will be reluctant to come off recirculation, in which case the intermediate modes can be checked by inching the servo through these positions. This is done by turning the LH knob slightly clockwise until the servo motor is heard to operate, and then returning it to a lower position to stop the servo motor at the desired position.

Defrost and fan vibration check

Turn the RH knob to defrost. The centre outlet flap should close and the screen outlets open. Air to the footwells should be cut off leaving air to the upper ducts only. The fans should shift to maximum speed and hot air should issue from the upper ducts. Fan vibration is best assessed under these conditions. Tests in accordance with the defrost schedule can be carried out at this point if desired.

Outlet vent valve check

Check that air can be cut off from the outer face-level vents by rotating the wheels beneath the outlets.

Settled mid-range and High speed over-ride check

Set the RH knob to 'Auto'. Set the LH knob to 75° and wait for the unit to settle. The fans should now be on low speed. Turn the RH knob to 'HIGH'. Maximum fan speeds should now be engaged.

DEFROST AND DEMIST TESTS

Purpose

To ascertain that the heating/air conditioning system is functioning correctly in the 'Defrost' mode, and that adequate airflow is maintained in the heat mode to ensure that the windscreen remains mist-free

Method

Set the LH control to '85°C'.
Set the RH control to 'Defrost'.
Close the end of dash outlets.
Start the engine and run it for seven minutes at 1500 rpm.
During the running period measure the air-flow from each screen outlet using checking ducts and velometer. Ensure that the centre dash outlet is closed and that it seals satisfactorily. The velocity from the screen outlets should be 1550 ft/min.
Also during the running period turn the RH

control to 'HIGH' and open the end of the dash outlets. Using the screen outlet and end of dash checking ducts measure the resulting air velocity. This should be:

Minimum velocity (ft/min)
Screen	End of dash
500	850

At the end of seven minutes running at 1500 rpm check that the water temperature gauge indicates 'Normal'. Using mercury in glass thermometers check that the following minimum screen outlet temperatures are achieved.

Plenum inlet		Screen outlet (minimum)	
°C	°F	°C	°F
10	50	54	129.2
12	53.6	55	131
14	57.2	55.5	131.9
16	60.8	56.5	133.7
18	64.4	57	134.6
20	68	58	136.4
22	71.6	58.5	137.3
24	75.2	59.5	139.1

Conclusions

If the above minimum requirements are met, then it can be assumed that:

(a) The thermostats are opening correctly.
(b) The water valve is opening fully.
(c) The flaps and linkages are correctly adjusted for the heating mode.
(d) The fans give adequate airflow at maximum speed.

If the above criteria are not met, the causes may be related to:

Thermostats

The water temperature guage will not achieve 'Normal' position within seven minutes and the air outlet temperature remains low. The thermostat(s) must be removed and checked for sticking open.

Water valve

The temperature gauge reads 'Normal' but the air outlet temperature remains low. Check that the vacuum-operated water valve is subjectd to at least 21,6 cmHg (8.5 inHg) of vacuum. If the valve is under adequate vacuum, change the valve. However, if the vacuum is low, check that the vacuum is being supplied to the whole system, that the water valve vacuum actuator is operational and that the water valve vacuum switch is operational. (See that the supply from the switch to valve is not pinched or trapped).

Flaps and linkages

Inadequate flap sealing will result in low air velocity at the screen outlets. Check that the centre facia flap closes fully on 'Defrost' and that only a small air bleed to the footwells occurs. These leaks can be detected by hand and may be rectified by adjusting the linkage. Excessive air-flow from the screen outlets in heat mode may be caused by the demist control flap sticking open.

Blowers

If following flap inspection the air flow is still low, investigations should be carried out into the blower assemblies. Check that full voltage is being received on maximum speed and that the units are correctly wired for rotation. If all is correct the only remaining procedure is to change the fan assembly.

NOTE: The engine must be running for this check.

Check that the compressor drive belt is correctly adjusted and is not slipping at higher engine speeds, at idle speed, or on sudden acceleration of the engine, with the compressor clutch speed.

Observe the sight glass on the receiver-drier and check for frothing or bubbles with engine running at 1000 rpm.

Slowly increase engine speed and repeat check at 1800 rpm.

NOTE: It is normal for there to be slight foaming if ambient air temperature is below 21°C (70°F).

Check for frosting on the connector union housing; the region around the suction part is normally cold, and slight frosting is permissible.

Check by feel along pipe lines for sudden temperature changes that would indicated blockage at that point.

Place a thermometer in the air outlet louvres.

Run the vehicle on the road and note the drop in temperature with air conditioning system switch on or off.

Ensure that the condenser matrix is free of mud, road dirt, leaves or insects that would prevent free air-flow. If necessary, clear the matrix.

If the foregoing checks are not met satisfactorily, refer to rectification and fault-finding procedures.

System check

The following check must be carried out to ensure that the system is basically functional. These checks may also be used to ensure satisfactory operation after any rectification has been done. If the system proves unsatisfactory in any way, refer to fault finding.

Check that blower fans are giving an air flow expected in relation to control switch position.

Check that air delivered is equal at both outlets.

Check that compressor clutch is operating correctly, engaging and releasing immediately control switch is set to an 'on' position.

NOTE: the engine must be running and the thermostat control set fully cool.

Check that the radiator cooling fan starts operating when the compressor clutch engages.

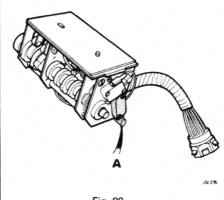

A

JSI 276

Fig. 88

Compressor thermal fuse

If problems are being encountered with the persistent failure of the air conditioning compressor thermal fuse and the normal test procedures cannot identify any obvious fault, then the following procedure should be carried out.

Step 1

Ensure that the valves of the charge station equipment are fully closed and connect them to the vehicle high and low pressure connections.

CAUTION: Observe all safety precautions as detailed in the Service Manual.

Run the engine at normal operating temperature, and select AUTO, 75°C; and allow the system to stabilise to ensure that the unit is neither on full cooling nor full heating mode. Adjust the engine speed to 1000 rev/min and note the readings on the gauges. The readings should be as follows:

The High Pressure gauge should indicate a pressure of between 10,5 and 15,8 kgf/cm² (150 to 225 lbf/in²).

The Low Pressure gauge should indicate a pressure not lower than 2,67 kgf/cm² (38 lbf/in²) when the compressor clutch engages, and not lower than 1,27 kgf/cm² (18 lbf/in²) when the compressor clutch disengages.

NOTE: Where higher ambient temperatures are encountered the high pressure readings may be greater than the above.

Ambient temperature is given as the temperature of the air surrounding the condensor and is taken 50,8 mm (2 in) in front of the condensor. Normal Ambient Temperature for the U.K. market is assumed to be between 5°C and 25°C (41°F to 77°F).

If the above is satisfactory proceed to Step 2.

If the low pressure reading drops below 1,27 kgf/cm² (18 lbf/in²) with the clutch still engaged, then the expansion valve is faulty.

Step 2

Increase the engine speed to 3 000 rev/min and note the reading on the low pressure gauge. The reading should be approximately 0,70 kgf/cm² (10 lbf/in²), at or just prior to, the disengagement of the compressor clutch. If the clutch fails to disengage and the pressure continues to drop to 0,35 kgf/cm² (5 lbf/in²) or below, then the expansion valve is faulty.

If the pressure remains at 0,70 kgf/cm² (10 lbf/in²) and the clutch cycle is correct, select low fan speed. Should the low pressure start to drop, carry out the modification detailed in Step 3.

Step 3

1. Disconnect the battery.
2. Remove the centre console right hand side trim panel to gain access to the air conditioning/heater unit.
3. Remove the plastic retaining plug from the black plastic cover surrounding the servo motor unit.
4. Carefully move aside the shield to gain access to the Ranco override micro switch, (A, Fig. 88).
5. Disconnect the green/brown (GN) lead and insulate.
6. Reverse procedure 1 to 4.

82—42

AIR CONDITIONING VACUUM SYSTEM

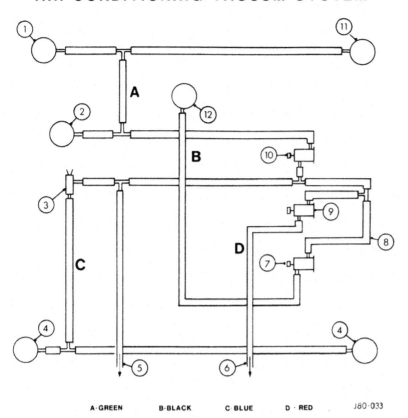

A·GREEN   B·BLACK   C·BLUE   D · RED   J80·033

KEY TO VACUUM SYSTEM DIAGRAM

1. Demist flap actuator (LH)
2. Lower heater flap actuator
3. Vacuum controlled solenoid
4. Blower case flap actuator
5. To vacuum supply
6. To water valve
7. Face level vacuum switch
8. Vacuum switches on servo unit
9. Water valve actuator
10. Screen vent actuator (for defrost only) on RH switch
11. Demist flap actuator (LH)
12. Face level front grille

VACUUM SYSTEM

Description

Off

When the system is in the off position, the engine is running and vacuum is available there is no heating or cooling effect from the system, but the following functions have however taken place.

1. The vacuum solenoid is energised so that air input flaps are closed to ambient air intake, i.e. it is in the recirculation mode.
2. The blower motors are switched off.
3. The compressor clutch is disconnected so that refrigeration does not take place.
4. Vacuum allows hot water to flow to the heater matrix, demist/defrost flaps open, the front face level grille flap closes and there is no output to the front or rear footwells.

Maximum cooling (Auto)

1. The centre face level flap opens by camshaft opening the vacuum switch.
2. Vacuum is applied to the water valve closing the valve thus preventing the flow of water to the heater matrix.
3. High speed recirculation switch is operated by the camshaft. A voltage is fed to the solenoid operated vacuum switch which applies vacuum to the fan motor flaps. The flaps move into a recirculating mode.
4. As the right hand control is at auto then vacuum will be applied to the screen flaps to keep them closed.

Maximum heating (Auto)

1. The camshaft now at full heating will close the vacuum switch to the centre flap which will relax to the closed position.
2. The camshaft will also have closed the vacuum switch controlling the water valve. The water valve opens to allow water to flow to the heater matrix.
3. The electrical supply to the solenoid vacuum switch is broken closing the vacuum switch. This action removes the vacuum supply to the blower motor casing flaps allowing ambient air to enter the car.
4. The screen flaps are kept closed and the lower heater flap is allowed to stay open by applying vacuum to their respective actuators.

Defrost

1. The camshaft will also have closed the vacuum switch controlling the water valve. The water valve opens to allow water to flow to the heater matrix.
2. No vacuum to the centre flap allowing the flap to close.
3. No vacuum to the screen vents allowing them to open, no vacuum to lower heater flap actuator closing the lower flap to allow 90% of air to the screen.
4. The electrical supply to the solenoid vacuum switch is broken closing the vacuum switch. This action removes the vacuum supply to the blower motor casing flaps allowing ambient air to enter the car.

NOTE: In the defrost position no vacuum is supplied to any actuator.

82——43

PAGE INTENTIONALLY LEFT BLANK

JAGUAR
Daimler

**Containing
Sections**

84 WIPERS AND WASHERS

86 ELECTRICAL

88 INSTRUMENTS

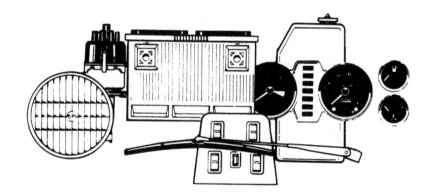

SERIES III
SERVICE MANUAL

INTRODUCTION

This Service Manual covers the Jaguar Series 3 and Daimler Series 3 range of vehicles. It is primarily designed to assist skilled technicians in the efficient repair and maintenance of Jaguar and Daimler vehicles.

Using the appropriate service tools and carrying out the procedures as detailed will enable the operations to be completed within the time stated in the 'Repair Operation Times'.

The Service Manual has been produced in 13 separate sections; this allows the information to be distributed throughout the specialist areas of the modern service facility.

A table of contents in section 1 lists the major components and systems together with the section and book numbers. The cover of each book depicts graphically and numerically the sections contained within that book. Each section starts with a list of operations in alphabetical order.

The title page of each book carries the part numbers required to order replacement books, binders or complete Service Manuals. This can be done through the normal channels.

Operation Numbering

A master index of numbered operations has been compiled for universal application to all vehicles manufactured by Jaguar Cars Ltd., and therefore, because of the different specifications of various models, continuity of the numbering sequence cannot be maintained throughout this manual.

Each operation described in this manual is allocated a number from the master index and cross-refers with an identical number in the 'Repair Operation Times'. The number consists of six digits arranged in three pairs.

Each operation is laid out in the sequence required to complete the operation in the minimum time, as specified in the 'Repair Operation Times'.

Service Tools

Where performance of an operation requires the use of a service tool, the tool number is quoted under the operation heading and is repeated in, following, the instruction involving its use. A list of all necessary tools is included in section 1, number 99.

References

References to the left- or right-hand side in the manual are made when viewing from the rear. With the engine and gearbox assembly removed the timing cover end of the engine is referred to as the front. A key to abbreviations and symbols is given in section 1, number 01.

REPAIRS AND REPLACEMENTS

When service parts are required it is essential that only genuine Jaguar/Daimler or Unipart replacements are used. Attention is particularly drawn to the following points concerning repairs and the fitting of replacement parts and accessories.

1.   Safety features embodied in the vehicle may be impaired if other than genuine parts are fitted. In certain territories, legislation prohibits the fitting of parts not to the vehicle manufacturer's specification.

2.   Torque wrench setting figures given in this Service Manual must be strictly adhered to.

3.   Locking devices, where specified, must be fitted. If the efficiency of a locking device is impaired during removal it must be replaced.

4.   Owners purchasing accessories while travelling abroad should ensure that the accessory and its fitted location on the vehicle conform to mandatory requirements existing in their country of origin.

5.   The vehicle warranty may be invalidated by the fitting of other than genuine Jaguar/Daimler or Unipart parts. All Jaguar/Daimler and Unipart replacements have the full backing of the factory warranty.

6.   Jaguar/Daimler Dealers are obliged to supply only genuine service parts.

SPECIFICATION

Purchasers are advised that the specification details set out in this Manual apply to a range of vehicles and not to any one. For the specification of a particular vehicle, purchasers should consult their Dealer.

The Manufacturers reserve the right to vary their specifications with or without notice, and at such times and in such manner as they think fit. Major as well as minor changes may be involved in accordance with the Manufacturer's policy of constant product improvement.

Whilst every effort is made to ensure the accuracy of the particulars contained in this Manual, neither the Manufacturer nor the Dealer, by whom this Manual is supplied, shall in any circumstances be held liable for any inaccuracy or the consequences thereof.

CONTENTS

WASHER RESERVOIR

Remove and refit	84.10.01
Bracket	84.10.02

Pull the plastic cap from the neck of the reservoir; (1, Fig. 1) withdraw the cap, feed the tube and filter complete from the reservoir.
Withdraw the reservoir from the bracket. The bracket is secured by two setscrews (2, Fig. 1).

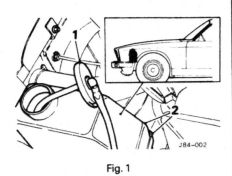

Fig. 1

Refitting is a reversal of the removal procedure.

NOTE: It is recommended that only soft water mixed with a proprietary cleaning fluid to the correct proportions is used when filling the washer system. This will minimize the formation of deposits that affect the performance of the system.

WASHER JETS

Remove and refit	84.10.09

Prise and raise the grille clear of the scuttle. Disconnect the washer tube from the jet assembly, then remove the grille from the car. Remove the washer jet butterfly nut and remove the jet from the grille (Fig. 2).

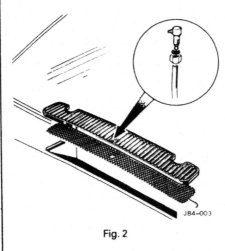

Fig. 2

After refitting operate the washers and adjust the jets.

WINDSCREEN WASHER PUMP

Remove and refit	84.10.21

Note the position of the leads, then disconnect the leads from the washer pump (1, Fig. 3).
Carefully prise the washer tube from the pump nozzles (2, Fig. 3).
Remove the screws securing the pump and tubing retaining clip to valance (3, Fig. 4) then withdraw the pump.

NOTE: Warming the tubing will facilitate refitting.

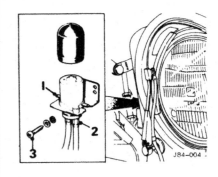

Fig. 3

WINDSCREEN WIPER ARM/ BLADES POSITION

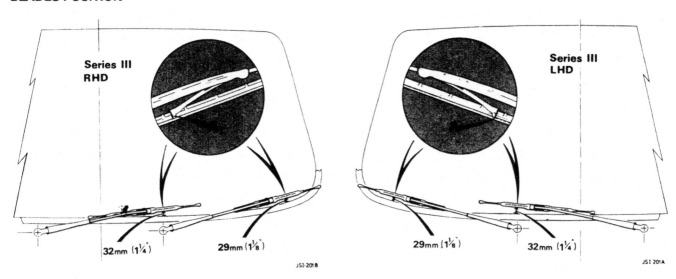

Fig. 4

WIPER ARMS

Remove and refit   **L.H.   84.15.02**
R.H.   84.15.03

Raise the plastic cover to expose the spindle nut (1, Fig. 5).
Note the position of the arm, then remove the nut.
Remove the arm and blade assembly.

When refitting, locate the arm and blade assembly to its noted position on the spindle.

Fig. 5

WIPER BLADES

Remove and refit   **84.15.05**

Raise the blade with one hand and with the thumb-nail of the other hand depress the spring clip (1, Fig. 6).
Press the wiper arm towards the windscreen to disengage the dimple from the blades (2, Fig. 6); slide the blade from the arm.

Press the blade straight onto the wiper arm until the dimple engages the spring clip to refit.

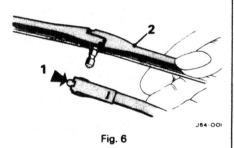

Fig. 6

WIPER MOTOR

Remove and refit   **84.15.12**

Disconnect and remove the battery.
Withdraw the wiper arms and blades from the spindles.

Remove the bonnet pull bracket nuts and bolts.
Remove the wiper motor cover.
Disconnect the cable rack conduit from the motor (1, Fig. 7).
Remove the two retaining nuts and washers from the motor clamp (2, Fig. 7).
Tilt the motor towards the engine and withdraw the cable connectors.
Remove the motor and drive as a complete assembly, drawing the rack drive from the conduit.

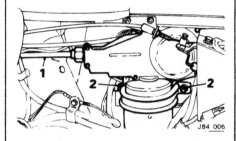

Fig. 7

When refitting, insert the rack into the conduit. It may be necessary to turn the wheelbase spindles to enable the rack to be pushed right home.

WIPER MOTOR GEAR ASSEMBLY

Remove and refit   **84.15.14**

Remove the wiper motor and rack drive cable.
Remove the circlip and washer on the gear assembly shaft (1, Fig. 8).
Mark and note the position of the gear assembly in relation to a chosen point on the housing and remove the gear (2, Fig. 8).

When refitting, ensure that the gear is to the position marked.

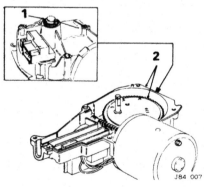

Fig. 8

WINDSCREEN WIPER RACK DRIVE

Remove and refit   **84.15.24**

Disconnect the battery.
Remove the wiper arm and blades.

Remove the bonnet-pull bracket nuts and bolts, and the wiper motor cover.
Remove the gear cover-plate by withdrawing the hexagon-head screws (1, Fig. 9).
Remove the link arm by removing the retaining clip and washer (2, Fig. 9).
Manoeuvre and withdraw the rack drive cable (3, Fig. 9).

To refit, grease and insert the rack into the tube, turning the wheelbox spindles to enable the rack to be just right home.
Align the rack with the link arm and fit the link arm. Continue to refit by reversing the above instructions.

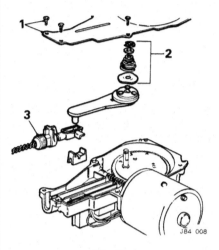

Fig. 9

WHEEL BOXES

Remove and refit

Disconnect and remove the battery.
Remove the wiper arm and blades.
Remove the screen rail fascia.
Remove the wiper motor.
Remove the demister flap/actuator assembly.
Remove the two nuts (1, Fig. 10) retaining the wheelbox backplate and release the drive conduit (2, Fig. 10).
Remove the nuts securing the wheelbox(es) to the scuttle and remove the chrome distance pieces and sealing rings (3, Fig. 10).
Remove the wheelboxes.

Reverse the above procedure to refit.

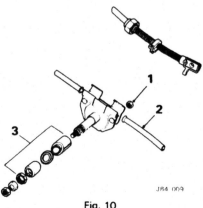

Fig. 10

84—3

WIPER MOTOR DELAY UNIT

Remove and refit   **84.15.36**

Remove the passenger's side dash casing.
The delay unit is retained in a socket behind the left-hand fusebox (1, Fig. 11).

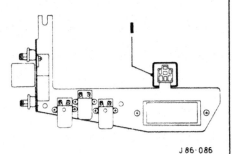

Fig. 11

WINDSCREEN WASHER/WIPER SWITCH

Remove and refit   **84.15.34**

Disconnect the battery.
Remove the driver's dash liner.
For access, remove the indicator switch.
Remove the upper shroud (1, Fig. 12).
Disconnect the wiper switch cable harness at the multi-pin connectors.
Remove the Spire nut from the switch spigot (2, Fig. 12).
Remove the two screws securing the wiper switch to assembly (3, Fig. 12) and remove switch.

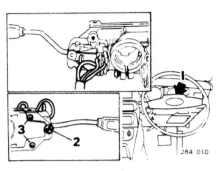

Fig. 12

Reverse the above procedure to refit.

HEADLAMP WASHER RESERVOIR

Remove and refit   **84.20.01**

NOTE: This reservoir supplies both windscreen and headlamp washing systems.

Raise the front of the car and place on stands.
Remove the L.H. front wheel.

Remove the three screws and detach the stoneguard; collect the sealing strips.
Slacken the hose clip securing the rubber elbow to filler neck (1, Fig. 13).
Remove the three screws securing the mounting strap assembly (2, Fig. 13), detach the mounting strap and lower the reservoir until the screws attaching the manifold assembly to the reservoir are accessible.
Remove the four screws securing the manifold assembly (3, Fig. 13), withdraw the reservoir from the pipes.

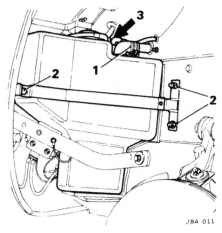

Fig. 13

Reverse the above procedure to refit.

HEADLAMP WIPER MOTOR

Left and Right Hand

Remove and refit   **84.25.12**

Disconnect the battery.
Remove the L.H. or R.H. cable harness cover.
Disconnect the tube from the washer reservoir filler cap (L.H. side).
Disconnect the cable block connector and reposition the tube and the cable block connector through the body grommets.
Turn the steering to full L.H. or R.H. lock.
Remove the wiper motor cable harness clip.
Displace the washer pump for access (L.H. side).

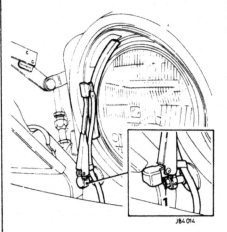

Fig. 14

Lift the wiper arm securing nut cover.
Remove the nut securing the wiper arm and remove the wiper arm (1, Fig. 14).
Slacken the wiper motor securing nut (1, Fig. 15) and remove the wiper motor.

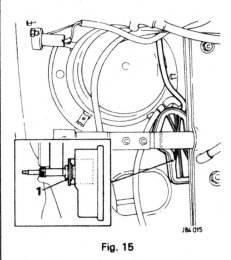

Fig. 15

Refitting is the reversal of the above procedure.

CONTENTS

CONTENTS

BATTERY

Description 86.15.00

The battery is a special high-performance type and is located in the engine compartment.

WARNING: The battery fitted to this vehicle has special topping-up facilities. When battery charging is carried out the vent cover should be left in position allowing gas to escape or flooding of electrolyte will result.

Data

Battery type: Lucas 12 volt 68 Ah Pacemaker CP 13/11.

BATTERY

Remove and refit 86.15.01

Ease back the battery terminal covers, slacken the pinch-bolts and disconnect the battery leads (1, Fig. 1).
Disconnect the snap connectors to the battery cooling fan (2, Fig. 1).
Slacken the retaining bolts (these are hinged and fixed to battery tray) (3, Fig. 1).
Withdraw the cooling inlet pipe from the grommet fixing (4, Fig. 1).
Release the positive battery lead from the clip on the cooling jacket (5, Fig. 1).
Ease the battery and cooling jacket forward until clear of the scuttle.
Lift the battery from the car.

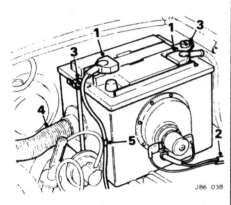

Fig. 1

To refit, reverse the above procedure.

BATTERY

Test 86.15.02

State of charge—S.G. readings

Lift the battery vent cover to one side.
Insert the hydrometer into each cell through the filling tube and note the readings (Fig. 2).

STATE OF CHARGE	SPECIFIC GRAVITY READINGS CORRECTED TO 60°F (15°C)	
	Climates normally below 77°F (25°C)	Climates normally above 77°F (25°C)
Fully charged	1.270 to 1.290	1.210 to 1.230
70% charged	1.230 to 1.250	1.170 to 1.190
Discharged	1.100 to 1.120	1.050 to 1.070

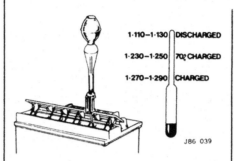

Fig. 2

Electrolyte temperature correction:
For every 18°F (10°C) below 60°F (15°C), subtract 0.007.
For every 18°F (10°C) above 60°F (15°C), add 0.007.

Heavy discharge test

This test should be carried out as a check to the battery condition. A heavy discharge tester applied to the battery terminals will determine whether the battery is capable of supplying the heavy currents required by the starter motor. With the discharge current set to 200 amps, observe the voltmeter reading during the battery discharge. If the voltmeter remains above 9.6 volts the battery is satisfactory.

BATTERY LEADS

Remove and refit
Positive	**86.15.17**
Negative	**86.15.19**
Battery Terminals	**86.15.20**

Ease back the plastic cover from the terminal on the battery post and slacken the clamp bolt. Remove the appropriate terminal from the battery post (1, Fig. 3).
Disconnect the positive lead from the terminal post located on the right-hand engine subframe member (2, Fig. 3).
Remove the negative lead from the bulkhead secured by two clips, setscrew and washer (3, Fig. 3).
When refitting, ensure that all connections are clean metal to metal.
Protect the battery terminal with a smear of petroleum jelly.
Tighten all fixings.

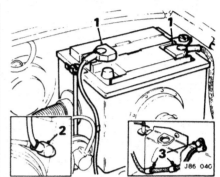

Fig. 3

The Freedom Battery

The freedom battery or the maintenance-free battery is what the name implies. When properly installed, no periodic maintenance is required.
A hydrometer is built into the cover, and has a glass rod which extends down into the electrolyte.
A 'cage' is attached to the lower end of the rod and a green ball is contained inside the cage. As the state of charge changes the green ball is free to move up and down inside the cage. When the state of charge is 65 % or greater, the green ball will rise and touch the bottom of the rod. A green dot will then appear when the hydrometer is observed.
When the state of charge is below 65 %, the green ball will move downwards and rest at the bottom of the cage. The hydrometer will then have a dark appearance and the green dot will have disappeared. A clear or light yellow appearance indicates the electrolyte level is low.
A cracked case, tipping the battery more than 45 degrees, or overcharging from the vehicle charging system or from an external source, can cause premature loss of electrolyte.

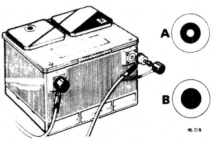

Fig. 4

86—3

ALTERNATOR

Description   86.10.00

The Lucas alternators—types 18ACR, 20ACR or 25ACR fitted according to specification of car, are high-output, three-phase machines which produce current at idling speed.

The heatsink, rectifier and terminal block assembly can be removed complete. There are six silicon diodes connected to form a full-wave rectifier bridge circuit, and three silicon diodes which supply current to the rotor winding. Individual diodes cannot be removed from the heatsink assemblies. Regulation is by a Lucas control unit mounted in the slip-ring end bracket. There is no provision for adjustment in service.

Individual connectors are used to connect external wiring to the alternator. The alternators main negative terminals are connected internally to the body of the machine.

Surge protection device

The surge protection device is a special avalanche diode, fitted to the outer face of the slip-ring end bracket (not to be confused with a suppression capacitor, similarly fitted in the end bracket). The avalanche diode is connected between terminal 'IND' and frame and its purpose is to protect the diode pack from damage by absorbing high transient voltages which could occur in the charging system due to faulty cable connections, or when certain switch devices are operated. (The surge protection device is intended to provide limited protection for the diode pack under normal working conditions and therefore the service precaution not to disconnect any of the charging system cables, particularly those at the battery, while the engine is running, should still be observed.)

Alternative high output alternators, the Motorola 9AR 2512P and 9AR 2533P are fitted to some later cars; instructions for their overhaul, which differ in some details from those for Lucas alternators, are given in the appropriate sections of the manual.

CAUTION: No part of the charging circuit should be connected or disconnected while the engine is running.

When using electric arc welding equipment in the vicinity of the engine take the following precautions to avoid damage to the semi-conductor devices used in the alternator and control box, and also the ignition system.

Disconnect the battery earthed lead.
Disconnect the alternator output cables.
Disconnect ignition and amplifier unit.

ALTERNATOR

Test in situ (Lucas alternators only)

Test equipment required: d.c. moving coil voltmeter, 0 to 20 volts; d.c. moving coil ammeter 5—0—100 amps; ohmmeter continuity tester.

Test 1

Remove the connectors from the alternator.
Switch the ignition on.
Connect the voltmeter between a good earth and each of the disconnected leads in turn (Fig. 5). The voltmeter should indicate battery voltage.
If the voltmeter indicates a zero reading when connected to the main output lead, check the wiring to the starter solenoid and battery.

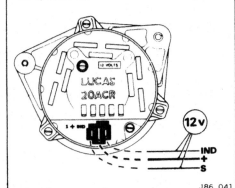

Test 1   J86 041

Fig. 5

If the voltmeter indicates a zero reading when connected to the 'IND' lead, check for earth or open-circuit between the warning light and the alternator connector. Check the warning light bulb and all connections to the warning light.
If the voltmeter indicates a zero reading when connected to the 'S' lead, check the wiring to the starter solenoid and battery.
A break in the sensing lead will result in the alternator not charging and the warning light not working.

Test 2

Refit the alternator connector.
Switch the ignition on.
Connect the voltmeter between a good earth and the 'IND' terminal (Fig. 6). The voltmeter should indicate approximately 2 volts.

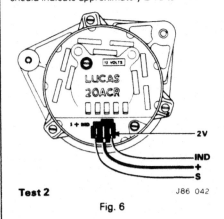

Test 2   J86 042

Fig. 6

If the voltmeter indicates a zero reading, the surge protection diode is suspect and should be checked.
If the voltmeter indicates battery voltage the brushes, rotor, or regulator are suspect.
Proceed to the next test.

Test 3

Connect the voltmeter between a good earth and the metal link on the regulator (Fig. 7). Switch the ignition on. The voltmeter should indicate approximately 0.5 volt. If 12 volts is indicated, the regulator is faulty.

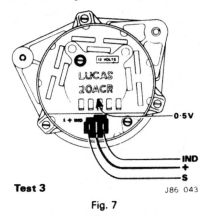

Test 3   J86 043

Fig. 7

If the reading is 0.5 volt but if a 12 volts was indicated on the previous test, check brushes, rotor and slip-rings.

NOTE: If the warning light operates with the ignition off but goes out when the ignition is switched on, check the voltage at the 'IND' terminal with the ignition switched 'off'. If battery voltage is indicated, the diode pack is faulty.

Test 4

Start and run the engine at a constant 2500 rev/min.

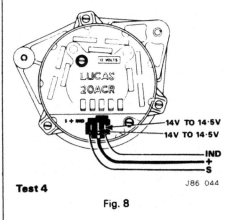

Test 4   J86 044

Fig. 8

Connect the voltmeter to a good earth and the 'IND' terminal; note the voltage. Connect the voltmeter to the main output terminal; the voltmeter readings should be the same (Fig. 8). If there is a difference of more than 0.5 volt, the diode pack is suspect.

Test 5

Connect the voltmeter between the battery insulated terminal and the alternator main output terminal (Fig. 9).
Start and run engine at approximately 2500 rev/min. The voltmeter should not exceed 0.5 volt.

86—4

If the voltmeter reading is higher than 0.5 volt, check the wiring from the alternator to the battery for loose or dirty connections.

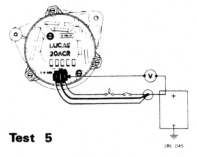

Test 5

Fig. 9

NOTE: The warning light glowing while the engine is running at normal charging speeds usually indicates a faulty diode pack or dirty or loose connections in the wiring from alternator to battery.

Test 6

Disconnect the battery earth lead.
Disconnect the alternator.
Connect an ammeter between the main output terminal or alternator and the disconnected output lead.
Connect a jumper lead between the 'IND' lead and 'IND' terminal (Fig. 10).
Re-connect the battery.
Switch on all load (except wipers) for one minute.

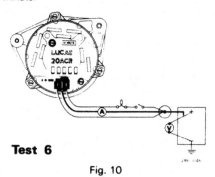

Test 6

Fig. 10

Start and run the engine at normal charging speed. The ammeter should indicate the maximum output for the alternator.
If the output is low, short the metal link on the regulator to earth with a jumper lead and repeat the test.
If maximum output is now indicated on the ammeter, the regulator is suspect.
Should the output still be low, the stator windings are suspect.
Disconnect the battery earth lead.
Connect the ammeter in series with the alternator main output cable and the starter solenoid.
Re-connect the battery.
Connect the voltmeter across the battery terminals.
Start and run engine at normal charging speed until the ammeter reads less than 10A.
The voltmeter should read 13.6 to 14.4 volts.
An incorrect reading indicates that the regulator is faulty.

ALTERNATOR

Test in situ (Motorola alternators) 86.10.01

Equipment required: Voltmeter and ammeter, field rheostat.

NOTE: Before commencing tests, ensure that the battery is fully charged. If not, disconnect the battery before recharging it.
Never disconnect the battery, alternator or regulator with the engine running.
Do not earth the field winding (terminal marked 'EX', connected to the regulator by a green lead).
On cars fitted with air-conditioning it is advisable to remove the alternator from the vehicle before carrying out tests 1 and 3 and to substitute bench tests 4, 5 and 6.
Always disconnect the battery when removing or refitting the alternator.

Test 1

Ignition switched off. Check of stator windings. Check voltage on one of the three phases of stator windings, accessible to a probe from voltmeter passing through ventilation hole as shown (Fig. 11).

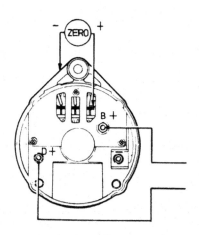

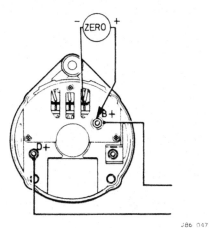

Fig. 11

Connect voltmeter first between the phase and earth, then between winding and positive terminal, observing correct polarity.
Indication of any reading other than zero on the voltmeter shows defective positive rectifier diode, necessitating changing of diode bridge.

Test 2

Ignition switched OFF. Check of battery connections. Check voltage at B+ terminal on alternator and at battery positive terminal (Fig. 12).

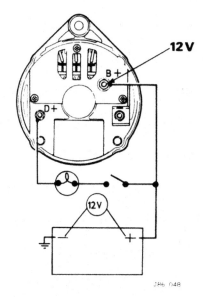

Fig. 12

Voltage should be the same at both points. If voltage at B+ terminal is lower than battery voltage, or fluctuates, check for broken wires, faulty connections or corroded terminals.

Test 3

Ignition on, engine not running. Check of field circuit.
Check voltage at slip-ring by touching probe of voltmeter on field terminal 'EX' (Fig. 13) with regulator attachment screws removed. If voltmeter reading is higher than 2 volts, field circuit is defective; remove brush holder by detaching green regulator lead from field terminal 'EX' and remove two setscrews, with washers securing brush holder to alternator. Check that brushes are free to slide, undamaged and not excessively worn; new brushes protrude by approximately 9 mm (0.35 in) from the brush holder, and complete brush holder must be renewed if either brush protrudes by less than 4 mm (0.15 in). Ensure that brush leads are not frayed and are securely attached to brushes, and that slip-rings are clean.

86—5

If voltmeter reads zero, check connections to regulator, ignition switch and ignition indicator lamp.

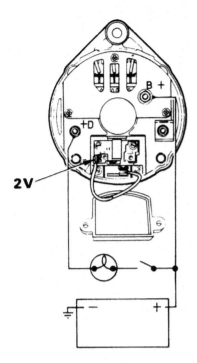

Fig. 13

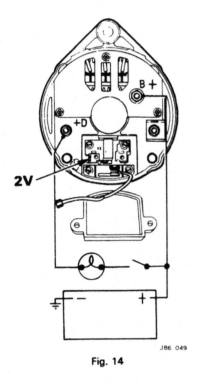

J86 049

Fig. 14

Also check regulator circuit by detaching its green lead from field EX terminal (Fig. 14) and measuring voltage across field windings, which should not exceed 2 volts. If this voltage is between 8 and 12 volts, alternator is defective. If correct, proceed to test 5.

Test 4

Ignition ON, engine running faster than idle. Further check field circuit.

If incorrect readings were obtained in Test 3, retest field circuit by disconnecting regulator from field terminal EX and connecting ammeter between this terminal and output terminal B + (Fig. 15). If meter indicates current less than 1 amp, recheck brushes, leads and slip rings.

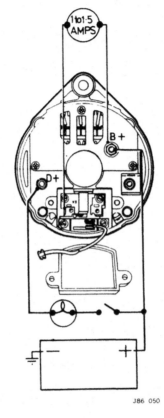

J86 050

Fig. 15

CAUTION: Use a field rheostat in series with ammeter, so that excessive current which could flow if the field is shorted will not damage ammeter.

Test 5

Ignition ON, engine running faster than idle. Check of output voltage.

Check voltage both at output terminal (B+) and at positive terminal of battery (Fig. 16). Correct voltage at both points is 14 2 volts ± 0.5 volts at 77°F (25°C).

If difference between battery voltage and voltage at B+ terminal is more than 0.3 volts, check wiring and terminals for corrosion or breaks.

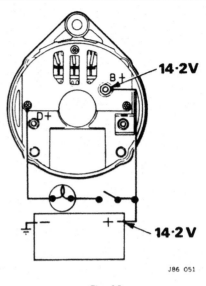

J86 051

Fig. 16

Test 6

Ignition on, engine running faster than idle. Check the voltage both at B+ and D+ terminals on the alternator (Fig. 17).

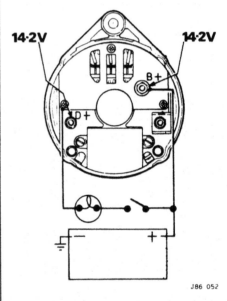

J86 052

Fig. 17

Voltage should be the same at both points. A difference of more than 0.5 volts between the B+ and D+ indicates a diode fault.

Test 7

Regulator field lead disconnected output terminal shorted to field terminal (Fig. 18), ignition on, engine running at fast idle.
Regulator and diodes check.
With alternator connected as specified above and shown in diagram (Fig. 18), check voltage between output terminal B+ and earth.

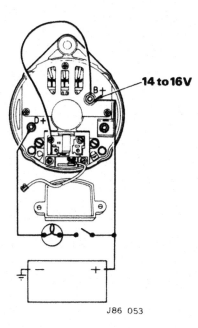

Fig. 18

If voltage rises to 14 to 16 volts in this test, but did not reach 14 volts in test 5, regulator is defective. Replace the regulator.
If output voltage does not rise and field circuit has been found satisfactory in tests 3 or 4, then either alternator stator or rectifier diodes are defective.

ALTERNATOR

Remove and refit (Lucas or Motorola)   **86.10.02**
6 cylinder

Disconnect the battery.

Slacken the alternator adjuster link arm locknut (on cars fitted with air conditioning this will be done from below the car).
Pivot the alternator towards the engine, and displace the drive belt from the pulley.
Remove the bolt securing the adjuster link to the alternator and swing the link clear of the alternator.
Disconnect the alternator cables.
Pivot the alternator away from the engine.
Withdraw the alternator mounting bolts.
Ease the alternator clear of the mounting bracket and remove from the engine compartment.

After refitting, adjust the link arm adjuster nut to correct belt tension. Deflection: 3,8 mm (0.15 in).

ALTERNATOR DRIVE BELT
6 cylinder

Remove and refit   **86.10.03**

Before removing the alternator drive belt it is necessary to remove the power steering pump drive belt (1, Fig. 19) and (if fitted) the air conditioning compressor drive belt (2, Fig. 19).
To remove the power steering pump belt slacken the two bolts securing the threaded adjuster link and trunnion, then slacken nut of pivot bolt and release locknut adjuster. Run the lower nut down and press the steering pump towards the engine.
With careful manoeuvring the belt can now be removed.
Slacken the two compressor mounting bolts. Slacken the compressor adjusting pivot arm locknut and adjust compressor as near to engine block as practicable without knocking the air conditioning hoses. The compressor drive belt can now be removed from beneath the car.
Slacken the alternator pivot bolts (3, Fig. 19), then slacken the locknut on adjuster link arm (4, Fig. 19).
Pivot the alternator (5, Fig. 19) towards the engine and remove the drive belt (6, Fig. 19).

Subsequent to refitting all belts must be tensioned correctly to avoid undue belt and component wear.

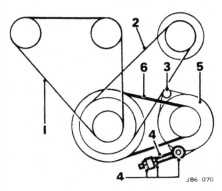

Fig. 19

ALTERNATOR DRIVE BELT

Remove and refit   **86.10.03**
12 cylinder

Remove the R.H. air cleaner. Remove the air conditioning compressor belt (1, Fig. 20), the power steering pump belt (2, Fig. 20) and the fan belt (3, Fig. 20). Slacken the alternator pivot bolts (4, Fig. 20) and the adjuster link pivot bolt (5, Fig. 20). Slacken the link arm

adjusting nut (6, Fig. 20) and pivot the alternator (7, Fig. 20) towards the engine until the belt can be removed.

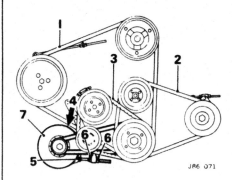

Fig. 20

ALTERNATOR DRIVE BELT

Adjustment (Lucas or Motorola)   **86.10.05**

Procedure for adjusting the alternator belt differs for air conditioned and non air conditioned cars.
The adjuster for air conditioned cars is only accessible from beneath the car.
In either case proceed as follows:
Slacken the nut or nuts of the alternator mounting pivot (two pivot bolts are fitted on air conditioned cars, one long bolt on the others).
Slacken the locknut and pivot bolts of adjuster and trunnion block.
Adjust belt tension by means of the adjusting link nut. Correct tension is as follows: A load of 1,5 kg (3.2 lb) must give a total belt deflection of 3,8 mm (0.15 in).
Tighten the locknut and all bolts.

ALTERNATOR

Remove and refit   **86.10.02**
12 cylinder

Disconnect the battery.
Remove the right-hand air cleaner.
Remove the air pump if fitted.
Slacken the nut securing the alternator.
Slacken the nut securing the alternator adjusting link.
Slacken the trunnion block to mounting bracket securing bolt.
Withdraw the electrical connector from the alternator.
Slacken the adjusting link lock nuts.
Ease the alternator drive belt off the alternator pulley.
Withdraw the alternator mounting bolt and the adjusting link bolt.
Remove the alternator complete from the engine compartment.
Refitting is the reversal of the above procedure.

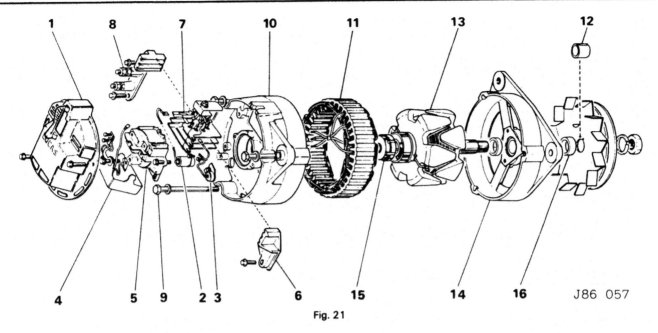

Fig. 21

Key to alternator
1. Moulded cover
2. Suppression capacitor
3. Surge diode
4. Regulator
5. Brush box assembly
6. Nylon damper block (rectifier plates)
7. Rectifier
8. Terminal assembly
9. Through-bolts
10. Slip-ring and bracket
11. Stator assembly
12. Shaft adaptor sleeve
13. Rotor assembly
14. Drive-end bracket
15. Slip-ring
16. Fan spacer

ALTERNATOR (Lucas)

Overhaul   86.10.08

NOTE: The alternator must not be dismantled under warranty.

Dismantling

The cover is removed by withdrawing the two retaining screws.
Withdraw the capacitor fixing screw, disconnect the lead from rectifier.
Remove the capacitor.
To remove the surge protection diode disconnect the diode lead from the brush box and the rectifier.
Withdraw the diode retaining screw and remove the diode.
Note the arrangement of the regulator brush box and other connections before disconnecting.
Remove the retaining screw and lift the regulator clear.
Remove the two screws securing the brush box assembly and remove the brush box.
The brushes, slip-ring and rotor can now be checked.

Rotor resistance

Connect an ohmmeter to the slip rings (Fig. 22).
Ohmmeter should register 3 to 3.5 ohms.

The slip-ring should be clean and smooth. Use extra fine sandpaper to rectify slight imperfections.

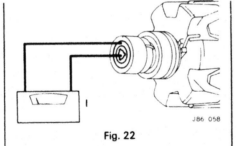

Fig. 22

Insulation test

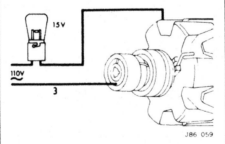

Fig. 23

Connect a test lamp to a slip ring and the rotor frame (Fig. 23).
The lamp should not light.

Diode testing

To remove the rectifier it is necessary to unsolder the stator cable ends from the rectifier.

Diode removal

Remove the terminal nut and damper blocks (when fitted), loosen the securing nuts and remove the rectifier.

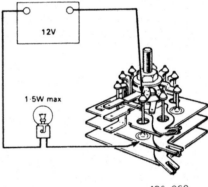

Fig. 24

Connect a battery lead in series with a test lamp to a diode plate.
Connect the other battery lead to each diode pin in turn (Fig. 24). Reverse the connections to plate and diode pins. The lamp should light in one direction only.
Should the lamp light in both directions, or not light at all, the diode is defective and a new rectifier pack should be fitted.

Stator insulator test

Remove the three through-bolts.
Mark the position of stator ring in the end brackets to ensure its correct assembly.
Separate the alternator into its three components: the slip-ring end bracket; the stator windings; the drive-end bracket rotor, fan and pulley.

86—8

Inspect the stator connections. Wires comprising each connection must be either soldered or twisted together before commencing the test.

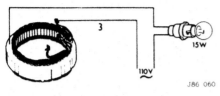

Fig. 25

Connect one side of the test lamp to the stator ring and the other side to one of the three connections (Fig. 25). The test lamp should not light.

To replace bearing.
Remove the fan and pulley.
Remove the Woodruff key and fan spacer.
Using a press, press the rotor shaft from the bearing.
Remove the bearing from the bracket.

Reassembling

Fit the rotor spacing collar on the rotor shaft.
Press the rotor shaft into the bearing.
Fit the fan spacer and Woodruff key.
Refit the fan and pulley.
Refit the stator winding and the slip-ring end bracket, using the marks to ensure correct position.

Fit and tighten the three through-bolts.
Loosely assemble the rectifier, the damper block and terminal assembly. Tighten the securing nut, tighten the terminal assembly screws and damper block screws.
Re-solder the stator connections.
Refit the brush box assembly and secure with the two retaining screws.
Refit the regulator and secure with the fixing screw. Re-connect the regulator leads, ensuring the correct arrangement.
Fit and secure the surge protection diode and re-connect lead to brush box assembly and rectifier.
Fit and secure the suppressor capacitor.
Refit and secure the moulded cover with two screws.

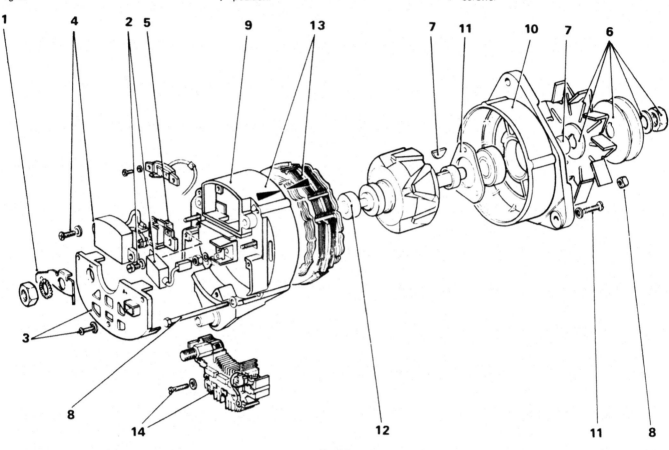

Fig. 26

J86 061

Key to alternator
1. Lucar connector blade
2. Capacitor and screw
3. Mould cover and screws
4. Regulator
5. Brush holders
6. Fan, pulley and pulley nut
7. Woodruff key and spacer
8. Through-bolts and nuts
9. Rear housing
10. Front housing
11. Bearing retaining plate
12. Rear bearing
13. Stator ring
14. Diode bridge and retaining screws

ALTERNATOR Motorola 9AR 2512P and 9AR 2533P

Overhaul 86.10.08

Dismantling

Detach nut, shakeproof washer and connector blade from B+ terminal at end cover (1, Fig. 26).
Remove setscrew and washer securing capacitor to alternator case, separate Lucar and detach the capacitor (2, Fig. 26).
Withdraw the three screws and remove the moulded rear cover (3, Fig. 26).
Remove the two setscrews and washers, identify the coding of wires, then separate the two Lucars and detach the regulator (4, Fig. 26).

Remove the two setscrews and washers and lift out the brush holder (5, Fig. 26).
Clamp the pulley, unscrew the pulley nut and remove the small washer, pulley fan and large washer from the alternator spindle (6, Fig. 26).
Extract the Woodruff key from the spindle and remove the spacer (7, Fig. 26).
Remove the four through-bolts; collect the washers and square trapped nuts (8, Fig. 26).
If the casing halves do not readily separate, clamp the alternator spindle in protected jaws of the vice and draw off the rear housing, with stator and diode bridge. The rear bearing will remain on the spindle.

CAUTION: Take care to avoid damage to the stator and windings by the rotor.

86—9

Remove the alternator spindle from the vice and draw off the front housing (9, Fig. 26).

Collect the short spacer adjacent to the rotor. If necessary remove the front bearing from the housing by withdrawing the three screws securing the retaining plate (11, Fig. 26) and pressing out the bearing.

If necessary, draw the rear bearing (12, Fig. 26) off the alternator spindle end.

Mark the position of the stator ring in the rear housing to ensure that it is correctly replaced (13, Fig. 26).

Unsolder the leads of the three-phase windings and D+ (red) lead from diode bridge.

CAUTION: Avoid transmitting excessive heat to the diodes by using long-nosed pliers to grip each terminal as the wire is unsoldered.

Withdraw the two setscrews and lift out the diode bridge (14, Fig. 26). Collect the washers.

Lift the housing off the stator, detach the two terminals from the housing and remove the D+ lead complete.

NOTE: To remove the diode bridge with a minimum of dismantling, remove the capacitor and moulded cover.

Unsolder the stator wire, withdraw the two setscrews and lift out the diode bridge.

Checking the brush holder

Touch each brush with test lead. The test lamp should not light (1, Fig. 27).

Connect the test leads on the field terminal and its corresponding brush (2, Fig. 27).

The lamp must light even when the brush is moved in its holder.

Transfer test leads to the negative terminal and the other brush (3, Fig. 27).

The lamp must light even when the brush is moved in its holder.

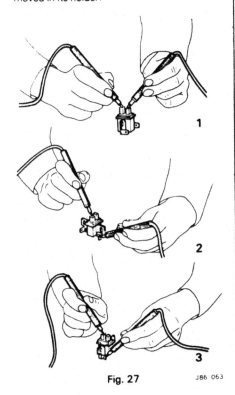

Fig. 27   J86 063

Checking the rotor

Connect ohmmeter leads to each slip-ring (Fig. 28).

The resistance should be between 3.8 and 5.2 ohms.

Connect the ohmmeter between a slip-ring and the alternator housing.

The reading should be infinity.

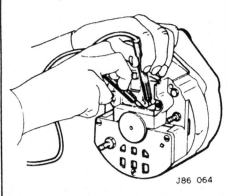

Fig. 28

Checking the stator

Inspect the windings for damage or overheating.

Check the stator insulation by connecting an ohmmeter between the alternator housing and each stator connection. The ohmmeter reading should be infinity.

Checking diodes

Positive diodes

Connect a battery lead to each phase terminal in turn, and the other battery lead in series with a test lamp to the B+ terminal.

Reverse the connections to the B+ terminal and the phase terminals (Fig. 29).

The lamp should light in one direction only.

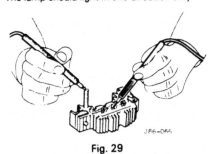

Fig. 29

Negative diodes

Connect one battery lead to the heatsink and the lead in series with the test lamp to each phase terminal in turn (Fig. 30).

Reverse the connections and the lamp should light in one direction only.

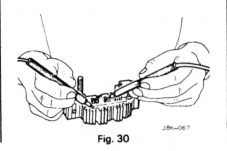

Fig. 30   J86-067

Checking the trio

Connect one battery lead to a phase terminal, the other lead in series with the test lamp to the other side of diode (Fig. 31). Reverse the connections and the lamp should light on one direction only.

Check the other two diodes in the same way. Should the lamp light in both directions, or not light at all, the diode under test is defective.

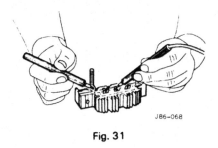

Fig. 31

Reassembling

Fit a new 'O' ring into the recess in the rear bearing housing.

Replace the D+ (red) lead assembly in the rear housing, securing it with two setscrews and washers at the Lucar carrier and bolt and nut at the D+ terminal. Thread the loose end of the lead through the hole below the D+ terminal.

Place the stator and coils in marked position with the three leads passing back through the housing. Rest the stator with the housing on top of it, on non-abrasive surface.

Lower the diode bridge, with terminals and capacitor fitted into position in housing with three leads passing through the gaps between the fins. Secure with two setscrews and washers, trapping capacitor connector under R.H. setscrew.

Using long-nosed pliers (as a thermal shunt) to grip each terminal in turn and prevent excess heat reaching the diode, solder the three-phase winding leads and D+ lead to the diode bridge. Do not overheat the diode bridge.

If required, press a new bearing onto the rear end of the rotor spindle.

Press the spindle and bearing into position in the rear housing.

Place the short spacer over the front end of spindle, ensuring that its larger inside diameter is next to the rotor.

If necessary, press a new front bearing into the front housing and secure with the retaining plate; apply Loctite to the screw threads and to the capped holes in the plate.

Press the front housing into position and insert the four through-bolts with plain washers under the heads.

Coat the threads of the through-bolts and trapped nuts with Loctite and tighten to 0,5 kgf m (3.6 lbf ft).

Place plain spacer over the spindle, insert the Woodruff key and replace large washer, fan, pulley, small washer and nut on spindle.

Tighten the nut to 4,0 kgf (29 lbf ft).

Refit the brush holder.

Reconnect the regulator wires to their correct positions and refit the regulator.

Refit the moulded cover, capacitor and the connector blade.

ELECTRICALLY OPERATED WINDOWS AND DOOR LOCKS

Description   86.25.00

The electrically operated door lock circuit comprises a solenoid which includes a capacitor and a resistor for each door, two relays and a thermal circuit breaker.

Operation

With the window lift master switch on, operation of any of the window switches will cause the associated window lift motor to run in the selected direction.

Fault conditions, i.e. sticking windows or overload, will result in excessive current consumption causing the thermal circuit breaker to operate.

The circuit breaker will reset after a short interval, allowing normal operations of the window lift motors to be resumed. If the condition persists, examination of the system is required.

The electric door lock circuit is activated from either of the front doors if the key is turned in either door lock.

All four door solenoids and the boot solenoid will lock, or all four doors will unlock, leaving the boot compartment solenoid in the lock position.

The two front interior tab locks will also operate all five solenoids into the locked position and all four door solenoids into the unlocked position.

Manual operation of the conventional door handles from inside the car will over-ride the door lock solenoid.

NOTE: Rapidly repeated operation of the door locks will result in an overload condition causing the thermal cut-out to operate, isolating the door lock solenoid circuit. A short wait is necessary before the thermal cut-out automatically resets.

WINDOW LIFT MOTOR—FRONT

Remove and refit   86.25.04

Removing

Disconnect the battery.
Remove the arm rest and door trim.
Remove the door speaker (1, Fig. 32).
Remove the screws securing the window lift motor mounting plate (2, Fig. 32) and remove the stop peg from the mounting plate (3, Fig. 32).
Remove the window lower channel securing bolts.

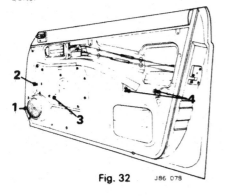

Fig. 32   J86 078

Remove the distance piece from the rear of the mounting plate.

Remove the regulator outer slide channel securing bolts and remove the channel (4, Fig. 32).

Remove the motor from the mounting plate. Disconnect the electrical feed cables.

Lower the motor to the bottom of the door.

Displace the felt from the lower window channel, and remove the lower channel.

Displace the glass from the regulator, raise the glass to the top of the door and secure the glass with tape.

Remove the regulator and motor assembly from the door.

Mark the position of the motor in relation to the regulator to facilitate the correct fitting of a new motor.

Remove the motor from the regulator.

Refitting is a reversal of the above procedure.

WINDOW LIFT MOTOR—REAR

Remove and refit   86.25.09

Remove the door casing and arm-rest.
Disconnect the battery.
Disconnect the cables from the motor at the plug and socket connection (1, Fig. 33).
Remove the four pan-headed setscrews and detach the regulator mechanism from the door panel (2, Fig. 33).

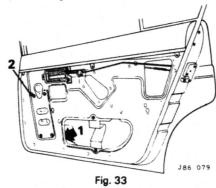

Fig. 33

Adjust the position of the door until the regulator arm can be removed from the channel.

Withdraw the regulator through the aperture in the door.

If it is necessary, remove the glass in order to withdraw the regulator.

Withdraw the three setscrews and washers and detach the motor from the regulator.

The motor is sealed during manufacture. Faulty units must be replaced, no service repair being possible.

Refitting is a reversal of the above procedure.

WINDOW LIFT SWITCHES

Remove and refit   86.25.07

To remove L.H. front (1), R.H. front (2), R.H. rear (3), L.H. rear (4) or the master window lift switch (5, Fig. 34).
Disconnect the battery.
Remove the screw securing the console.
Raise the cover and disconnect the cigar light cables (6, Fig. 34).

Tilt the control panel and disconnect the harness block connector from switch.

Depress the plastic lugs on the switch and remove the switch.

When refitting reverse the above procedure.

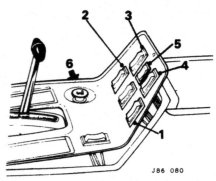

Fig. 34

REAR SWITCH PANEL WINDOW LIFT SWITCHES

Remove and refit   86.25.12

Disconnect the battery.
Lever the switch panel from the rear of the centre console (1, Fig. 35).
Disconnect the block connector.
Depress the plastic lugs on the switch and remove the switch.

When refitting reverse the above procedure.

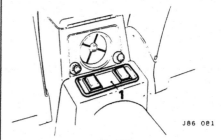

Fig. 35

WINDOW LIFT RELAY

Remove and refit   86.25.28

Disconnect the battery.
Remove the L.H. side dash casing.
Pull the relay/socket assembly from its mounting on the component panel and remove the relay (1, Fig. 36).

When refitting reverse the above procedure.

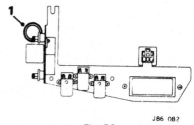

Fig. 36

86—11

CIRCUIT BREAKERS

Remove and refit   86.25.31

Disconnect the battery.
Remove the L.H. side dash casing.
Disconnect the cables from the circuit breaker.

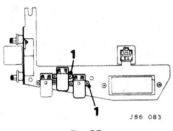

Fig. 37

Remove the screw securing the unit to the component panel and remove the unit (1, Fig. 37).

When refitting reverse the above procedure.

DOOR LOCK SOLENOIDS

Remove and refit   86.25.32

With the window closed, disconnect the battery.
Remove the door arm-rests and door trim.
Remove the rod from the lock and the anchor point on solenoid (1, Fig. 38).

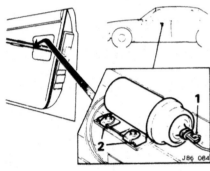

Fig. 38

Remove the bolts securing the solenoid (2, Fig. 38).
Disconnect the block connector from the cable harness and remove the solenoid.

When refitting reverse the above procedure.

DOOR LOCK SOLENOID RELAY—LEFT-HAND AND RIGHT-HAND SIDE

Remove and refit   86.25.33
                                86.25.34

Disconnect the battery.

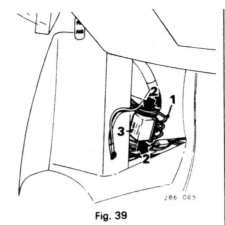

Fig. 39

Remove the R.H. or L.H. side footwell trim pad.
Identify and disconnect cables from the relay (1, Fig. 39).
Withdraw the screws securing the relay (2, Fig 39), retrieve the distance pieces and remove the relay (3, Fig. 39).

When refitting reverse the above procedure.

BOOT LID LOCK SOLENOID

Remove and refit   86.26.02

Disconnect the battery.
Open the luggage compartment.
Disconnect the solenoid multi-plug connector (1, Fig. 40).
Remove the solenoid securing bolts and disconnect the earth wire eyelet (2, Fig. 40).

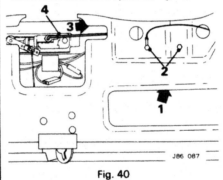

Fig. 40

Slacken the number-plate lamp securing nuts (3, Fig. 40) and withdraw the lamp as far as is necessary to allow the solenoid to be removed.
Remove the lock operating rod (4, Fig. 40).
Remove the solenoid.

Reverse the above procedure to refit.

HORNS

Description   86.30.00

Twin horns are fitted. Both horns operate simultaneously and are energised by a relay. The relay is connected to the battery through the ignition switch so that the horns will only operate with ignition switched on.

HORN-PUSH

Remove and refit   86.30.01

Disconnect the battery.
Slacken the steering-wheel adjusting nut, and pull the steering-wheel out to its maximum travel.
Remove the horn-push securing screws and remove the push from the steering wheel.

Reverse the above procedure to refit.

HORNS

Remove and refit   86.30.09

Disconnect the battery.
Disconnect the wiring at the Lucar connectors (1, Fig. 41).

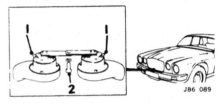

Fig. 41

Withdraw the retaining bolt and spacers (2, Fig. 41).
Remove the horns.

Reverse the above procedure to refit.

HORN RELAY

Remove and refit   86.30.18

Disconnect the battery.
Remove the relay cover.
Displace the fan motor relay for access.

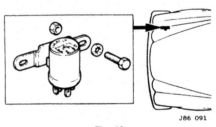

Fig. 42

Identify and disconnect the relay cables.
Remove the relay (Fig. 42).

After refitting, ensure that the cables are reconnected correctly. Refer to the wiring diagram if in doubt.

86—12

HORN RELAY CIRCUIT

Check in situ   86.30.17

Switch on the ignition.

NOTE: Avoid leaving the ignition on for extended periods.

With the ignition on a 12-volt test lamp connected between 'W1' and earth should light up.
If the lamp does not light, check fuse no. 1.
Test lamp on 'W2'. If test lamp fails to light, an unserviceable relay is indicated.
If the relay operates when horn-push is pressed a test lamp connected between 'C1' and earth should light up. Failure to do so indicates that relay contacts are inoperative or fuse No. 4 is unserviceable.
If checks 1 and 2 are satisfactory and horns do not operate, substitute a test lamp for each horn in turn. If the lamp lights, horn units are unserviceable. If the lamp does not light, further investigation of the horn harness will be required.

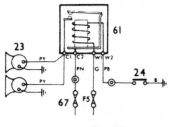

Fig. 43

HORN CIRCUIT CODE

23. Horns
24. Horn-push switch
61. Horn relay
67. Line fuse

HEADLAMP ASSEMBLY

Remove and refit

Headlamp rim finisher	86.40.01
Headlamp assembly (outer)	86.40.02
Headlamp assembly (inner)	86.40.03

Remove the top retaining screw and withdraw the headlight rim finisher, noting the retaining lug at the lower edge (1, Fig. 44).
Remove the three cross-headed screws and the headlight retaining rim (2, Fig. 44).

NOTE: On the inners the cross-headed screws require slackening only, the rim may be turned to remove. Do not turn the slot-headed screws as they are for headlamp alignment.

Withdraw the headlight and unplug the adaptor from the rear of the unit (3, Fig. 44).

When refitting, reverse the above procedure.

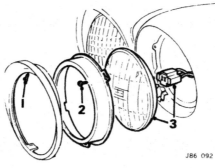

Fig. 44

HEADLAMP PILOT BULB

Remove and refit   86.40.11

Remove the outer headlight as previously described. Withdraw the pilot bulb holder with bulb from the fitting on the rear of the reflector (Fig. 45).
Remove the bulb.

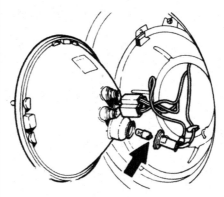

Fig. 45

Reverse the above procedure to refit.

HEADLIGHT ALIGNMENT
86.40.18

Headlight beam setting should only be carried out by qualified personnel, and with approved beam setting apparatus

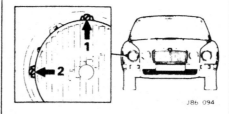

Fig. 46

Adjustment

Remove the headlight rim finisher.

Outer headlights.
Turn the top screw anti-clockwise to lower the beam, clockwise to raise the beam (1, Fig. 46).

Turn the side screw anti-clockwise to move the beam to the left, clockwise to move the beam to the right (2, Fig. 46).

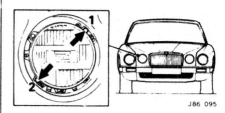

Fig. 47

Inner headlights
The adjustment screws are set diagonally opposite each other. The upper screw is for vertical alignment (1, Fig. 47), the lower screw is for horizontal alignment (2, Fig. 47).

CAUTION: Correct headlamp alignment is mandatory in certain countries.

FRONT FLASHER REPEATER ASSEMBLY

Remove and refit   86.40.53
Lens	86.40.51
Bulb	86.40.52

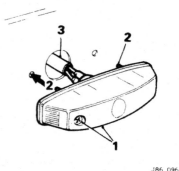

Fig. 48

Remove the retaining screw and detach the lens (1, Fig. 48).
Remove the bulb.
Remove the two nuts and lock washers from the captive retaining bolts (2, Fig. 48).
Disconnect the cables from the snap connectors (3, Fig. 48), check condition of seals while the assembly is removed from the car.

Reverse the above procedure to refit.

FRONT FLASHER ASSEMBLY

Remove and refit   86.40.42
Lens	86.40.40
Bulb	86.40.41

Disconnect the battery.
Remove the screws securing the lens assembly to the front bumper (1, Fig. 49).

Withdraw the assembly clear of the bumper for access. Rotate the assembly at the bulb holder and remove the lens assembly. Check condition of the seal.

Rotate the bulb holder anti-clockwise and withdraw it behind the bumper (2, Fig. 49).

Withdraw the bulb from the holder.

Remove the screw securing the fusebox to the front wing valance and ease the fusebox clear of the valance for access.

Disconnect the cables at the snap connectors. Attach a draw string to the end of the flasher lamp cables.

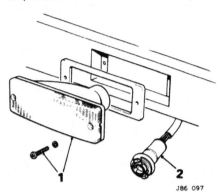

Fig. 49

Remove the plastic straps securing the harness to headlamp harness under the wing.

Remove the screws securing the flasher lamp assembly to the bumper, and withdraw the lamp with harness from its location.

Reverse the above procedure to refit.

SIDE MARKER ASSEMBLY

Remove and refit	86.40.64
	86.40.57
	86.40.58
	86.40.59
Bulb	86.40.62
Lens	86.40.63

Withdraw the crosshead retaining screw and remove the lens; note the retaining clip. Withdraw the bulb (1, Fig. 50).

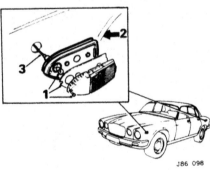

Fig. 50

Remove the retaining nuts and lock washers (2, Fig. 50).

Disconnect the cables from the snap connectors (3, Fig. 50).

Check the condition of seals while the assembly is removed from the car.

TAIL/STOP/FLASHER AND REVERSE LAMPS

Remove and refit	86.40.72
	86.40.73
	86.40.74

Remove the screws securing the lens, and detach the lens (1, Fig. 51).

Remove and check the sealing rubbers.

Remove the bulb (2, Fig. 51).

Remove the screw securing the assembly to the rear wing.

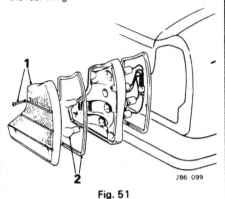

Fig. 51

Withdraw the assembly clear of the wing for access to the cable connections.

Disconnect the block and snap connectors and remove the assembly from the car.

NUMBER-PLATE LAMP ASSEMBLY

Remove and refit		86.40.86
	Lens	86.40.84
	Bulb	86.40.85

Remove the lens securing screws (1, Fig. 52). Ease the lens/lamp assembly from its location (2, Fig. 52).

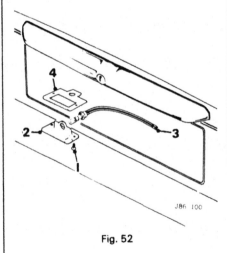

Fig. 52

Disconnect the cable snap connectors (3, Fig. 52).

Check the gasket while the assembly is removed from the car (4, Fig. 52).

NUMBER-PLATE LAMP ASSEMBLY HOUSING

Remove and refit	86.40.98

Open the boot lid, and release the solenoid operating rod from the clip. Withdraw the rod from the lock lever.

Remove the nuts, washers and shakeproof washers securing the number-plate lamp housing.

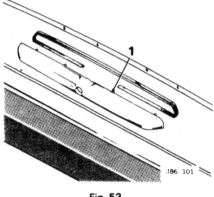

Fig. 53

Disconnect the number-plate lamp snap connectors and remove the assembly from the boot lid (Fig. 53).

Reverse the above operations.

REAR FOGLAMP ASSEMBLY

Remove and refit	86.40.99

Remove the rear lamp cluster for access.

Disconnect the fog lamp cables from the snap connectors and attach a draw-string to the cables.

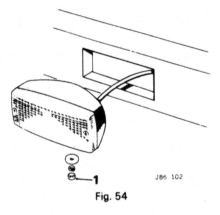

Fig. 54

Displace the rubber grommet from the body under the apron and withdraw the cables through the aperture.

Detach the draw-string from the cables.

Remove the nuts and washers securing the lamp assembly to the rear bumper (1, Fig. 54) and withdraw the lamp.

REAR FOG LAMP LENS AND BULB

Remove and refit **86.41.20**
86.41.21

Remove the screws securing the lens (1, Fig. 55) and remove the lens and bulb (2, Fig. 55).

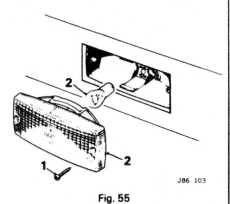

Fig. 55

FOG/SPOTLIGHT LENS UNIT AND BULB

Remove and refit **86.40.94**

Caution: Under no circumstances should bulbs in these units be touched with bare hands.

Disconnect the battery.

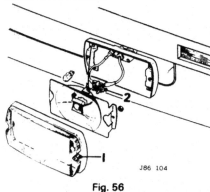

Fig. 56

Remove the two screws securing the light unit (1, Fig. 56).
Move the bulb retaining clip to one side and remove the bulb holder from the light unit (2, Fig. 56).
Using a cloth or glove, pull the bulb from the holder.
Remove the rubber retaining washers from the light unit retaining screws and separate the units.

FOG/SPOTLIGHT ASSEMBLY

Remove and refit **86.40.96**

Disconnect the battery.
Disconnect the cable at the snap connector.
Remove the shakeproof washers.
Remove the assembly.

DOOR POST LAMP ASSEMBLY AND BULB

Remove and refit **86.45.03**

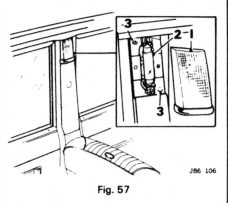

Fig. 57

Disconnect the battery.
Carefully lever the cover from the lamp (1, Fig. 57) and withdraw the festoon-type bulb from the holder (2, Fig. 57).
Withdraw the two retaining screws and lift the lamp from the post (3, Fig. 57).
Disconnect the cables from the snap connectors.

MAP LIGHT ASSEMBLY AND BULB

Remove and refit **86.45.09**

Withdraw the bulb holder by exerting pressure on the side clip and pulling the bulb holder downwards (1, Fig. 58).

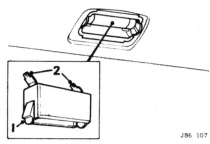

Fig. 58

Withdraw the festoon-type bulb.
Disconnect the cables from Lucar connectors and retain the lamp assembly (2, Fig. 58).

LUGGAGE COMPARTMENT LAMP ASSEMBLY AND BULB

Remove and refit **86.45.15**

Disconnect the battery.
The bulb is accessible through an aperture in the luggage compartment lid.

Carefully lever the lamp clear of the mounting plate on the boot lid.
Disconnect the cables and recover the lamp.

FIBRE OPTIC ILLUMINATION SYSTEM

Description

Consists of a centralized light source (Opticell) feeding localized illumination via fibre elements and diffuser lens units to specific areas. Control switches illuminated in this way are as follows:

1. Ignition switch (one element).

2. Lighting switch (one element).

3. Heater/air conditioning control switches (two elements to each control).

Failure of the light source will result in loss of illumination at all the above control units.

OPTICELL

Remove and refit **86.45.27**

Disconnect the battery.
Remove the centre console escutcheon and window lift switch panel.
Withdraw the two screws securing the Opticell to the transmssion selector quadrant (1, Fig. 59).

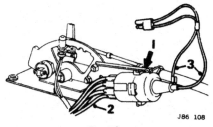

Fig. 59

Disconnect the fibre elements by pulling each one from the Opticell lens hood (2, Fig. 59).
Disconnect the cables (3, Fig. 59).

OPTICELL BULB

Remove and refit **86.45.28**

Disconnect the battery.
Remove the centre console escutcheon and window lift switch panel.
Pull the bulb holder from the Opticell reflector.
Withdraw the miniature bayonet capped bulb from the holder.

NOTE: Replace with a bulb of the correct size as necessary.

PANEL SWITCH ILLUMINATION BULB

Remove and refit   **86.45.31**

Disconnect the battery.
Carefully lever the sub panel assembly clear of the clock mounting panel.

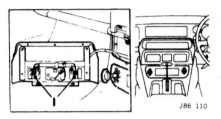

Fig. 60

Release the bulb holder from the lamp housing between the switches (1, Fig. 60), and remove the bulb from the holder.

TRANSMISSION INDICATOR BULB

Remove and refit   **86.45.40**

Remove the control knob from the selector lever (1, Fig. 61).
Prise the window lift switch panel and the escutcheon from the centre console.

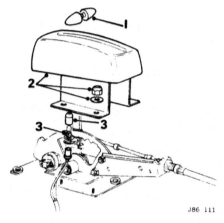

Fig. 61

Remove the four retaining nuts to release the transmission selector cover (2, Fig. 61).
Remove the bulb shroud and withdraw the bulb (3, Fig. 61).
Note: The bulbs used in this unit are of the capless design and only require a straight pull to remove them from the holder. Replace the bulb as necessary.

CIGAR LIGHTER ASSEMBLY

Remove and refit   **86.65.60**

Includes:
**Cigar lighter illumination
bulb—remove and refit**   **86.45.55**

Disconnect the battery.
Remove the centre console cover retaining screws and raise the cover for access (1, Fig. 62).
Press together the sides of the cigar lighter bulb holder (2, Fig 62) and remove from the cigar lighter.

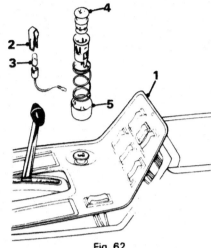

Fig. 62

Remove the bulb (3, Fig. 62)
Disconnect the cables from the cigar lighter.
Press the outer body of the cigar lighter towards the console panel and twist to release from the upper body and spring (4, Fig. 62)
Remove the outer body spring and upper body from the panel (5, Fig. 62).

REAR DOOR SPEAKER

Remove and refit   **86.50.14**

Includes:
**Rear door speaker grille
—remove and refit**   **86.50.08**

Remove the rear arm-rest.
Remove the nuts securing the speaker/grille assembly.
Remove the grille and speaker from the housing

FRONT DOOR SPEAKER

Remove and refit   **86.50.13**

Includes:
**Front door speaker grille
—remove and refit**   **86.50.09**
Remove the front door arm-rest and the front door lower trim panel.
Remove the screws securing the speaker assembly and lever carefully clear of adhesive on the door.
Disconnect the speaker wires and remove the nuts securing speaker grille assembly.
Remove the speaker and the grille.

AERIAL

Remove and refit   **86.50.21**

Removing

Disconnect the battery.
Remove the boot carpet, boot floor, spare wheel, petrol pump cover, and the boot side trim.
Remove the rear lamp assembly.
Disconnect the aerial lead from the aerial extension lead (1, Fig. 63).
Loosen the knurled nut at the top of the aerial shaft under the wing (2, Fig. 63).

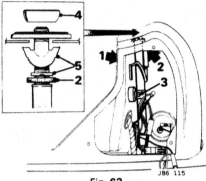

Fig. 63

Remove the bracket from the aerial shaft (3, Fig 63)
Remove the domed chromed nut from the top of the aerial (4, Fig. 63).
Withdraw the aerial down in to the wing retaining the distance pieces (5, Fig. 63).
Remove the aerial drive shroud from the rear of the boot (1, Fig 64).
Disconnect the aerial motor feed wires (2, Fig. 64).

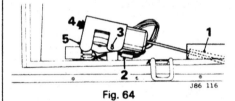

Fig. 64

Remove the bolt from the top of the aerial motor mounting bracket and tilt the assembly away from the rear of the boot (3, Fig. 64).
Remove the plastic drain tube from the bottom of the aerial motor (4, Fig. 64).
Remove the bracket from the aerial motor.
As the motor is withdrawn from the boot, guide the aerial drive and the aerial shaft through the rear of the body.

Refitting is the reversal of the above procedure.

AERIAL MOTOR RELAY

Remove and refit   **86.50.27**

Disconnect the battery.
Remove the boot carpet and floor.
Identify and disconnect the cables from the aerial relay.
Withdraw the relay from the mounting bracket.

REAR AERIAL OPERATING SWITCH

Remove and refit   **86.50.24**

Disconnect the battery.
Remove the centre console retaining screws and raise the console cover.
Disconnect the cables from the switch, depress the plastic lugs on the switch and withdraw the switch from the cover.

HEADLAMP RELAY

Remove and refit   **86.55.17**

Disconnect the battery.
Identify and disconnect the cables from the relay (1, Fig. 65).
Withdraw the bolts securing the relay to the wing valance (2, Fig. 65) and remove the relay.

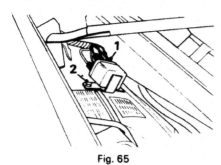

Fig. 65

HAZARD FLASHER UNIT

Remove and refit   **86.55.12**

Includes:

Heated rear window/back-light relay—remove and refit	**86.55.19**
Ignition load relay—remove and refit	**86.55.28**
Bulb failure indicator—remove and refit	**86.55.45**

Disconnect the battery.
Remove the screws securing the right-hand dash casing and remove the dash casing.
The hazard flasher (1, Fig. 66), heated rear back-light relay (2, Fig. 66), ignition load relay (3, Fig. 66), and the bulb failure indicator (4, Fig. 66) are now accessible.
Displace the flasher socket from the retaining bracket on the component panel, and withdraw flasher unit (1, Fig. 66) from the socket.
Withdraw the heated back-light relay and cable socket assembly from the bracket on the component panel; remove the relay (2, Fig. 66) from the cable socket.

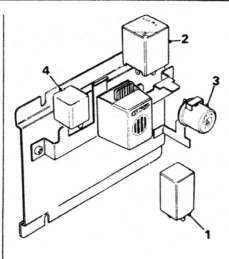

Fig. 66

Displace the ignition load relay and cable socket assembly from the component panel; remove the relay (3, Fig. 66) from the socket.
Remove the bulb failure unit and socket assembly from the bracket on the component panel; remove the unit (4, Fig. 66) from the socket.

STOP LIGHT AND REAR LAMP SENSOR UNITS

Remove and refit	**86.55.34**
	86.55.50

Remove the cover from the electronic control unit situated in the boot, for access to the sensors.
Identify and disconnect the cables from the appropriate sensor.
Withdraw the securing screws and remove the sensor from the mounting panel.

PARKING LAMP FAILURE SENSOR

Remove and refit   **86.55.22**

Also:

Low coolant warning control unit—remove and refit	**86.55.33**
Door, boot lock circuit breaker—remove and refit	**86.55.36**
Courtesy light delay unit—remove and refit	**86.55.49**

Removing

Disconnect the battery.
Remove the screws securing the left-hand-side dash casing and remove the casing.
The parking lamp failure sensor, low coolant warning control unit, door, boot lock circuit breaker, and the courtesy light delay unit are now accessible.

Identify and disconnect the cables from the parking lamp sensor unit.
Remove the nuts and screws securing the sensor unit to the component panel; remove the unit.
Remove the screw securing the coolant warning unit to the component panel.
Withdraw the screws securing the sensor unit to the component panel; remove the unit.
Remove the screws securing the coolant warning unit to the component panel.
Withdraw the screws securing the glovebox liner to the fascia, and ease the liner downwards for access to the warning unit multi-plug connector.
Disconnect the multi-plug connector from cable harness and remove the warning unit.
Disconnect the cables from the door lock circuit breaker.
Withdraw the drive screw securing the circuit breaker to the component panel and remove the unit.
Remove the courtesy delay unit and the cable socket assembly from the component panel, then withdraw the delay unit from the cable socket.

Refitting

Reverse the appropriate operations.

SEAT BELT SWITCH

Remove and refit	
Driver's buckle	**86.57.25**
Passenger's buckle	**86.57.27**

Disconnect the battery.
Adjust the seat to its full forward position.
Withdraw the screws securing the rear window switch panel and raise the panel clear of its location.
Remove the screw securing the console side panel and ease the panel clear for access to the switch block connector.
Disconnect the switch block connector front cable harness.
Withdraw the bolt securing the seat belt buckle and remove the buckle.

STARTER MOTOR—
6 cylinder

Remove and refit   **86.60.01**

Removing

Drive the car onto a ramp and disconnect the battery.
Remove the bolt securing the starter lead and the gearbox breather pipe to the bracket on the starter motor. Retrieve the distance piece from the bolt.
Displace the starter lead from the terminal post on the bulkhead.

Remove the top bolt securing the starter motor to the bell housing.
Raise the ramp.
Remove the lower securing bolt and ease the starter motor clear of the bell housing.
Retrieve the spigot plate from the bell housing.
Remove the starter lead from the starter solenoid and remove the bolt securing the bracket to the side of motor; remove the bracket.

Refitting

Refit the starter lead to the solenoid, and cover the terminal with the rubber boot.
Place the bracket in position. Fit and tighten the bolt to secure.
Place the spigot plate in position on the bell housing and position the starter motor.
Fit but do not tighten the lower securing bolt.
Fit and tighten the upper securing bolt and the lower bolt.
Fit the clip securing the breather pipe and the starter cable to the bracket on the motor.
Secure the cable to the terminal post on the bulkhead and refit the rubber boot over the post.
Reconnect the battery.

STARTER MOTOR
12 cylinder

Remove and refit   **86.60.01**

Removing

Disconnect the battery.
Loosen the two bolts from the steering column universal joints.
Disconnect the feed/return pipes from the power steering pump at the pinion housing and release the clip securing the pipes to the steering rack assembly.
Remove the lower steering column universal pinch bolt, and push the lower column upwards from the pinion housing.
Disconnect the steering tie rods.
Slacken the lower mounting bolts and remove the upper mounting bolt of the steering rack housing.
Remove the right hand exhaust front pipe and swing the steering rack assembly down to its furthest extent.
Disconnect the starter cables at the terminal post and the starter solenoid.

NOTE: Secure the cables loosely with wire or string to the top of the engine; this will facilitate feeding the cables back during the refitting operation.

Withdraw the starter mounting bolts.
Move the starter forward and rotate until the solenoid is in the underneath position, then ease the starter motor assembly down from the engine compartment.

After refitting, refill and bleed the power steering system.

STARTER SOLENOID

Remove and refit   **86.60.08**

Disconnect the battery.
Remove the starter motor, see operation 86.60.01.
Disconnect the starter lead from the solenoid.
Remove the nut securing the solenoid to the starter motor.
Remove the two fixing nuts and withdraw the solenoid from the bracket.
Retrieve the gasket and release plunger from the top of the drive engagement lever.

IGNITION/STARTER/STEERING LOCK SWITCH

Remove and refit   **86.65.03**

Disconnect the battery.
Slacken the ignition lock cover shroud screws and remove the shroud from the fibre optic (1, Fig. 67).

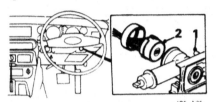

Fig. 67

Disconnect the switch multi-plug connector (2, Fig. 67).
Remove the switch to lock retaining screw, displace the plastic cover and remove the switch assembly.

STARTER MOTOR RELAY

Remove and refit   **86.55.05**

Disconnect the battery.
Identify and disconnect the relay cables (1, Fig. 68).

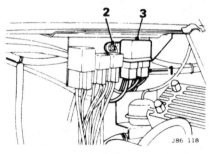

Fig. 68

Remove the nuts securing the relay to the mounting stud and remove the earth lead eyelet (2, Fig. 68).
Remove the relays (3, Fig. 68).

RHEOSTAT SWITCH

Remove and refit   **86.65.07**

Disconnect the battery.
Remove the right-hand dash casing.
Depress the spring stud and release the rheostat contact knob (1, Fig. 69).
Unscrew and remove the retaining ring (2, Fig. 69).

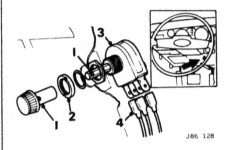

Fig. 69

Remove the rheostat and the adjusting nut (3, Fig. 69) from the switch strut.
Disconnect the cables at Lucar connections and withdraw switch (4, Fig. 69).

MASTER LIGHTING SWITCH

Remove and refit   **86.65.09**

Disconnect the battery.
Remove the driver's side dash liner.
Remove the screws securing the switch to the mounting bracket.

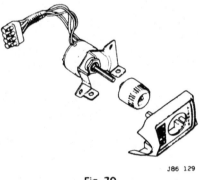

Fig. 70

Lower the switch and displace the fibre optic lead from the switch.
Disconnect the cable block connector from the harness and remove the switch assembly (Fig. 70).

86—18

DOOR PILLAR SWITCH

Remove and refit　　　　**86.65.15**

Disconnect the battery.
Remove the screw securing the switch to the pillar.

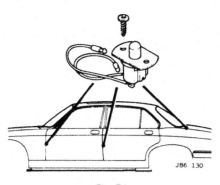

Fig. 71

Draw the switch clear of the pillar until the snap connector is accessible.
Disconnect the snap connector from the main harness and remove the switch (Fig. 71).

INTERIOR LIGHT SWITCH

Remove and refit　　　　**86.85.13**

Includes:
**Back-light heater switch
—remove and refit**　　　　**86.65.36**
**Fuel change over switch
—remove and refit**　　　　**86.65.39**
**Map light switch—
remove and refit**　　　　**86.65.43**

Disconnect the battery.
Lever the switch panel clear of the clock mounting panel.

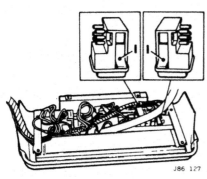

Fig. 72

Disconnect the multi-plug connector from the switch.
Depress the metal lugs (1, Fig. 72) securing the switch in the panel and push the switch clear.

LUGGAGE COMPARTMENT LIGHT SWITCH

Remove and refit　　　　**86.65.22**

Disconnect the battery.
Remove the screws securing the switch and displace the wire retainer pad.
Disconnect cables at snap connectors and remove the switch.

FUEL PUMP INERTIA CUT-OUT SWITCH

Reset　　　　**86.65.59**

An inertia switch is fitted in the electrical supply to the fuel pump. Should the car be subjected to a heavy impact, the switch opens, isolating the fuel pump, preventing fuel from being pumped in a potentially dangerous situation.
The pump is located on the passenger side 'A' post and is reset by pressing down the button located on top of the switch.

FUEL PUMP INERTIA CUT-OUT SWITCH

Remove and refit　　　　**86.65.58**

Disconnect the battery.
Remove the cover from the inertia switch (1, Fig. 73).

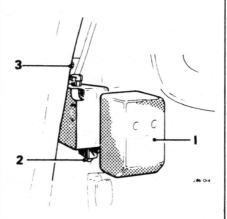

Fig. 73

Disconnect the cables from the switch (2, Fig. 73) and remove the screws securing the switch to the 'A' post (3, Fig. 73).
Remove the switch.

HANDBRAKE WARNING SWITCH

Remove and refit　　　　**86.65.45**

Disconnect the battery.
Remove the driver's side console side panel.
Remove the shroud and lay to one side (1, Fig. 74).
Pull back the gearbox cover carpet and remove the handbrake mounting bracket securing bolts.

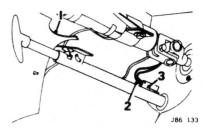

Fig. 74

Disconnect the cables from the switch (2, Fig. 74).
Ease the handbrake lever assembly clear of transmission tunnel for access.
Loosen the bolts securing the switch assembly to the mounting bracket (3, Fig. 74).
Retrieve the tapped plate and the switch assembly.

STOP LIGHT SWITCH

Remove and refit　　　　**86.65.51**

Disconnect the battery.
Remove the driver's side dash liner.

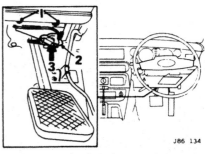

Fig. 75

Remove the bolts securing the switch mounting to the brake pedal housing (1, Fig. 75).
Lower the switch and bracket assembly.
Disconnect the switch cables from the block connector (2, Fig. 75).
Remove the switch to mounting bracket securing bolt, and remove the switch (3, Fig. 75).

86—19

COMBINED DIRECTION INDICATOR/HEADLIGHT/HORN SWITCH

Remove and refit	**86.65.55**
Hazard warning switch —remove and refit	**86.65.50**
Combined windscreen washer and wiper switch —remove and refit	**86.65.41**

Removing

Disconnect the battery.
Remove the driver's side dash liner.
Disconnect the switch cable multi-pin connector from the harness (1, Fig. 76).
Remove the lower shroud (2, Fig. 76).
Slacken the steering-wheel adjustment nut and pull the steering-wheel out to its limit.
Turn the wheel for access to the wheel slide grub screw; undo the locknut and remove the grub screw.
Turn the steering-wheel to the straight-ahead position, remove the ignition key to lock the steering wheel.
Remove the pinch-bolt securing the upper steering stub to the column.
Remove the steering-wheel and adjusting stub assembly.

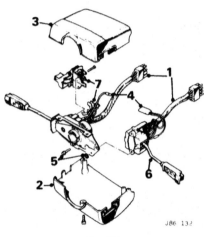

Fig. 76

Loosen the clamp screw securing the switch assembly to the column; slide the switch and upper shroud assembly clear of the column (3, Fig. 76).
Remove the upper shroud from the switch assembly and place the shroud to one side.
Disconnect the wiper switch earth cable from the snap connector (4, Fig. 76) and the cable harness multi-pin connector.
Remove the Spire nut and screws securing the wiper switch to the mounting plate (5, Fig. 76).
Remove the wiper switch and place to one side (6, Fig. 76).
Disconnect the cables from the hazard switch.
Withdraw the screws securing the switch to the assembly and remove the hazard switch (7, Fig. 76).

Caution: No attempt must be made to separate the direction indicator/headlight/flasher switch from the bracket. Faulty items are changed as complete assemblies.

Refitting

Reverse the above operations.

DRIVER'S SEAT ELECTRIC MOTOR

Remove and refit	**86.75.01**

Removing

Disconnect the battery.
Remove the front seat cushion and disconnect the electrical connection underneath the cushion.
Remove the front seat.
Remove the bolts securing the rise/fall mechanism to the mountings onto the floor, and remove the mechanism.
Mark the position of the motor on the mechanism.
Remove the bolts securing the motor to the frame and remove the motor.

To refit, reverse the above operations.

Sliding Roof Motor

Remove and refit	**86.76.01**

Removing

Disconnect the battery.
Remove the rear seat and the rear squab.
Remove the trim from the rear of the boot.
Remove the nuts securing the clamping plate.
Remove the four nuts securing the motor mounting bracket.
Disconnect the electrical feed cables at the snap connectors.
Remove the motor and bracket assembly.
Remove the motor from the bracket.

To refit, reverse the above procedure.

IGNITION SYSTEM—12 Cylinder

Description   86.36.00

The OPUS ignition system comprises:

A. Distributor
B. Amplifier unit
C. Ballast resistor
D. Ignition Coil

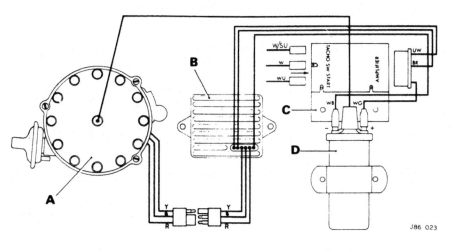

Fig. 77

The Distributor

The OPUS Distributor comprises:

1. Distributor cap rotor, timing rotor (and trigger) Japan and Australia only
2. Vacuum unit rod
3. Grommet
4. Pick-up module
5. Roll pin
6. Vacuum unit (retard/advance) Japan Australia—others
7. Retaining screws
8. Felt pad
9. Control spring
10. Centrifugal bub-weights
11. Distributor lead

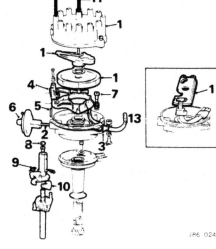

Fig. 78

The timing rotor and pick-up module, working in conjunction with a separate amplifier unit, replace the contact breaker and cam of a conventional distributor.

The timing rotor is a glass-filled nylon disc with small ferrite rods embedded into its outer edge, the number and spacing of the rods corresponding with the number of cylinders and firing angles of the engine.

An air gap (adjustable to specified limits) exists between the rotor and the ferrite core of the stationary pick-up module. The pick-up module assembly comprises a magnetically balanced small transformer with primary (input) and secondary (output) windings.

CAUTION: Magnetic balancing of the pick-up module. This unit is balanced during manufacture and the setting cannot alter in service. The sealed ferrite adjusting screw must not be disturbed.

Automatic control of ignition timing is provided by the vacuum unit which varies the static timing position of the pick-up module in relation to the ferrite rods in the timing rotor.

The distributor timing rotor and pick-up module generate an electronic timing signal, which is fed to the amplifier unit via external cables.

CAUTION: The length of this triple-core extruded-type cable must not be altered and the cables must not be separated or replaced by loose individual cables.

Amplifier unit—(B—Fig. 77)

This interprets the timing signals from the distributor. The power transistor incorporated in the printed circuit then functions as an electronic switch in the primary circuit of the ignition coil. The unit is connected to the ignition coil via a ballast resistor unit and external cables.

Ballast resistor unit—(C—Fig. 77)

An encapsulated assembly comprising three resistors in an aluminium heat-sink fixing bracket.

External wiring connects two of the resistors in series with the ignition coil primary winding. The third resistor unit is the drive for the power transistor in the amplifier unit.

Ignition coil—(D—Fig. 77)

The coil is mounted on the front of the throttle pedestal.

A specially designed, fluid-cooled, high-performance, ballast inition coil.

The coil terminals are marked '+' and '−' and have different types of Lucar connector to prevent incorrect cable connection.

CAUTION: The 'OPUS' coil is NOT interchangeable with any other type.

Operation

Normally when the engine is stationary, the distributor timing rotor will be in a position where none of its ferrite rods will be in proximity to the pick-up module.

When the ignition is switched on, a power transistor in the amplifier unit is in a conductive state and the ignition coil primary winding circuit is complete via the emitter/collector electrodes of the power transistor.

Simultaneously, a sinusoidal a.c. voltage is applied by the amplifier unit to the distributor pick-up module windings and a small residual a.c. voltage is produced at the pick-up secondary windings which at this stage is magnetically balanced. The voltage at the pick-up module secondary terminals is applied to the amplifier unit, but the residual voltage at this stage is insufficient to have any effect on transistor circuits which control the switching-off of the power transistor in the output stage of the amplifier unit.

When the engine is cranked, one of the ferrite rods in the rotor, now in proximity with the ferrite core of the module causes 'magnetic unbalancing' of the module core, resulting in an increase in the voltage at the module output terminals.

The voltage increases to maximum as the rotor rod traverses the centre and upper limbs of the module 'E' shaped core.

Maximum voltage is then applied to the amplifier unit, where it is rectified, the resulting (d.c.) voltage is then used to operate the transistor circuits which control the switching-off of the power transistor in the output stage. With the power transistor switched off, its emitter/collector electrodes cease to conduct and the coil primary winding is disconnected which causes a rapid collapse of the primary winding magnetic field through the secondary windings of the ignition coil, resulting in a high tension (h.t.) voltage being produced at the h.t. output terminal of the ignition coil.

DISTRIBUTOR

Remove and refit—Engine dismantling and reassembling   86.35.20

Removing

Remove the three captive screws and detach the distributor cover.

Disconnect the cable at the connecting plug (1, Fig. 79).

Disconnect the pipe from the vacuum retard unit (2, Fig. 79).

Release three Allen screws (3, Fig. 79), accessible through slots in the micro housing and withdraw the distributor.

Refitting

Rotate the engine until the mark 'A' etched on the crankshaft damper is in line with the 10° Federal B.T.D.C. mark on the timing plate.

CAUTION: No. 1 piston 'A' must be on firing stroke. Both inlet and exhaust valves in the cylinder will be closed and removal of the sparking plug will enable an observation to be made to ascertain that this is so. DO NOT rotate the engine backwards.

Rotate the distributor until No. 1 cylinder mark on the timing rotor is in alignment with the mark on the pick-up module.

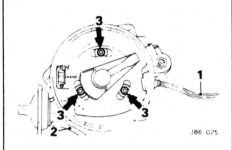

Fig. 79

When refitting, ensure that the marks on the timing rotor and pick-up module do not move out of alignment.
Check the ignition timing.

DISTRIBUTOR

Overhaul

Dismantling

Remove the distributor cover, electronic timing rotor, and trigger unit (1, Fig. 80)—Japan and Australia.

Lift the vacuum operating rod from peg on pick-up arm (2, Fig. 80).

Prise the cable grommet from the body of the distributor (3, Fig. 80).

Remove the pick-up arm bearing spring. Slide the pick-up arm sideways to disengage it from bearing. Lift from micro housing, drawing the cable in through the hole. Detach the pick-up module.

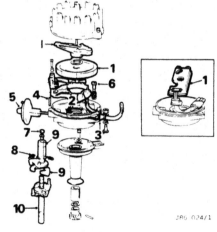

Fig. 80

Use a pin punch 1,85 mm (0.073 in) to tap out the roll-pin securing the vacuum unit in the micro housing (4, Fig. 80).

Withdraw the vacuum unit from the micro housing (5, Fig. 80).

Remove the three spring loaded screws and lift the micro housing from the distributor body (6, Fig. 80).

Extract the felt pad from the top of the rotor carrier shaft and release the screw (7, Fig. 80). Release the control springs from the fixing posts (8, Fig. 80).

Lift the rotor carrier shaft from the distributor shaft. Collect the centrifugal weights (9, Fig. 80).

Reassembling

Smear the centrifugal weights and rotor carrier pivot posts with either Rocol grease No. 30863 or Mobilgrease No. 2. Assemble the weights to the pivot posts.

Lubricate the bore of the rotor carrier shaft with clean engine oil and fit to distributor shaft. Retain with round-headed screw. Fit the oil pad.

Fit control springs.

NOTE: Ensure that the three socket-headed screws and plain washers are in place through slots in the distributor body base.

Liberally smear the auto advance mechanism with grease previously specified.

Fit the micro housing to the distributor body, ensuring that the micro adjustment eccentric peg engages in the slot.

Secure the micro housing to the body using screws, plain washers and springs. Tighten the screws to just short of coil binding.

Loosely secure pick-up module to the pick-up arm using two cheese-head screws, plain and spring washers.

Pass the pick-up module connector and cable out through the hole in the micro housing and locate the pick-up arm on the rotor carrier shaft.

Fit the bearing spring.

Engage the wide part of the cable grommet in the hole and prise into position.

Place the vacuum unit into position and secure with a new roll-pin.

Fit the vacuum operating rod to the peg on the pick-up arm.

Fit the electronic timing rotor and secure it using a wave washer and circlip.

Use feeler gauges to set the distance between the pick-up module 'E' core faces and timing rotor outer edge to 0,50 mm to 0,55 mm (0.020 in to 0.022 in).

Tighten both pick-up module securing screws.

Fit the trigger unit (Japan and Australia only).

Fit the rotor arm.

Fit the distributor.

'OPUS' IGNITION SYSTEM

Checking

Equipment required: D.C. moving-coil voltmeter, 0 to 20V scale; hydrometer; ohmmeter; h.t. jumper lead

Preliminary procedure
Battery Test   86.35.29/1

Heavy discharge test

This test should be carried out as a check to the battery condition. A heavy discharge tester applied to the battery terminals will determine whether the battery is capable of supplying the heavy currents required by the starter motor.

Specific gravity readings

Check the specific gravity of the electrolyte in each cell using a hydrometer. Lift the vent cover and tilt it to one side. Insert the hydrometer into each cell in turn through the filling tube and note the readings. A variation of more than 40 points (0.040) in any cell reading means the battery suspect. If necessary prove the battery by substitution.

Circuit test

Check the battery.

Disconnect the cable from the coil l.t. terminal marked '−'.

Connect the voltmeter (1, Fig. 81) between the battery earth and frame.

Operate the starter, check voltmeter reading which should not exceed 0.5 volt. Refit the coil cable.

If more than 0.5 volt is registered, rectify faulty connection between frame and battery.

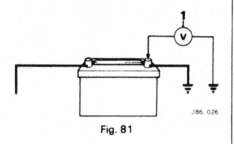

Fig. 81

Check for sparking

Disconnect the h.t. lead from the distributor cover and hold the free end approx. 6 mm (¼ in) from an unpainted part of the engine block. With ignition on crank the engine. Regular sparking should occur (Fig. 82).

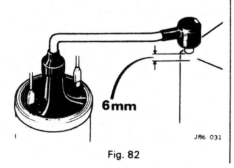

Fig. 82

NOTE: If no sparking occurs proceed to 86.35.29/3. If sparking occurs, check the following:
a. Distributor cover for cleanliness and cracks
b. H.T. cables
c. Rotor arm
d. Spark plugs
e. Fuel supply

Ballast resistor check   86.35.29/3

Withdraw the socket from the amplifier side of the ballast resistor (1, Fig. 83).

Connect the voltmeter between battery earth and each terminal of the ballast resistor amplifier output in turn (2, Fig. 83).

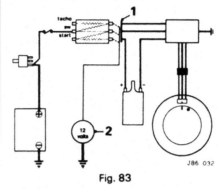

Fig. 83

CAUTION: Voltmeter test lead must not come into contact with the ballast resistor housing.

With ignition on, meter should read battery voltage.

NOTE: If satisfactory, proceed to 86.35.29/4.

If no reading is obtained check supply to 'SW' terminal. Trace the circuit back through the ignition switch.

Coil voltage check   86.35.29/4

Reconnect the socket to the amplifier side of the ballast resistor.

Disconnect the amplifier/distributor socket (1, Fig. 84).

Connect the voltmeter between battery earth and '+' terminal on the coil (2, Fig. 84).

With ignition on, the reading should be 4 to 6 volts. The coil resistance is 0.8 to 1.0 ohm (3, Fig. 84).

NOTE: High reading indicates a faulty coil or amplifier.

No reading, check supply to '+' terminal on coil.

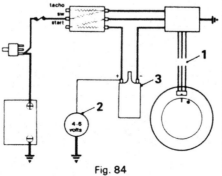

Fig. 84

Coil Primary Winding Check
86.35.29/5

Disconnect the lead at '−' terminal on the h.t. coil (1, Fig. 85), then connect a voltmeter between the '−' terminal and earth (2, Fig. 85). With ignition on the meter should read battery voltage.

NOTE: No reading, replace the h.t. coil.

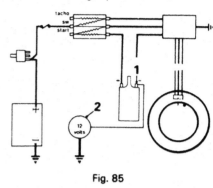

Fig. 85

Amplifier volts drop

Reconnect the lead to the '−' terminal on the coil (1, Fig. 86).

Connect the voltmeter between the coil '−' terminal and the battery earth (2, Fig. 86).

With ignition on, meter should read 0 to 2 volts.

NOTE: High reading battery voltage, replace amplifier. High reading between 2 volts and battery voltage, check for earth fault.

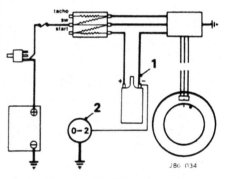

Fig. 86

Distributor pick-up module

a. Primary (input) winding resistance (measured between the centre terminal and the outer terminal with red cable): 2.5 ohms nominal at 20°C (1, Fig. 87).

b. Secondary (output) winding resistance (measured between centre terminal and outer terminal with yellow cable): 0.9 ohm nominal at 20°C (2, Fig. 87).

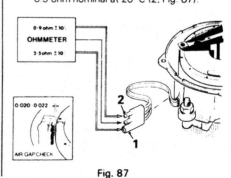

Fig. 87

IGNITION TIMING

Check   86.35.29/7

'P' System. Digital fuel injection (Retrospective from 1980 MY)
Series III RHD VIN No. 310613.
LHD 310676. XJS RHD VIN No. 104146
LHD 104236
Ensure the engine is at its normal operating temperature.
Disconnect the vacuum pipe. Run the engine at 3000 rev/min. Check the timing with a stroboscope, adjust the timing to 24° B.T.D.C.
Non Digital system. 'D' system (Japan and Australia). Set the engine idle speed at 750 rev/min.
Disconnect the vacuum pipe. Check the timing with a stroboscope and adjust the timing to 10° B.T.D.C.
Tighten the locknut.

AMPLIFIER UNIT

Remove and refit   86.35.30

Disconnect the battery.
Withdraw the unit cable plug from the ballast resistor assembly (1, Fig. 88).
Disconnect the plug adaptor between the distributor and amplifier unit line (2, Fig. 88).
Remove the two screws and washers (3, Fig. 88).
Remove the amplifier unit (4, Fig. 88) from the cross-member (5, Fig. 88).

Reverse the procedure above to refit.

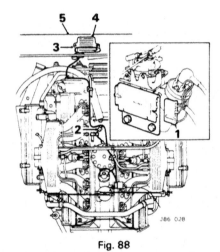

Fig. 88

COIL

Remove and refit   86.35.32

Disconnect the battery earth lead.
Disconnect the h.t. lead (1, Fig. 89).
Disconnect the l.t. leads at Lucars on the coil (2, Fig. 89).
Remove the bolts and shakeproof washers securing the coil to the throttle pedestal (3, Fig. 89).
Remove the coil from its location (4, Fig. 89).

Reverse the above operations to refit.

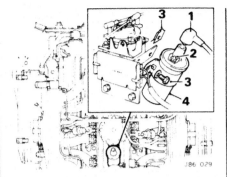

Fig. 89

BALLAST RESISTOR

Removing   86.35.33

Disconnect the battery earth lead.
Disconnect the block connectors at the ballast resistor (1, Fig. 90).
Disconnect the No. 5 injector electrical connector (for access only).
Disconnect the throttle operating rod at the bell-crank on the induction manifold and swing it aside (2, Fig. 90).
Remove the bolts and shakeproof washers securing ballast resistor to the throttle pedestal (3, Fig. 90).
Manoeuvre the resistor clear of its location.

Reverse the above operations to refit.

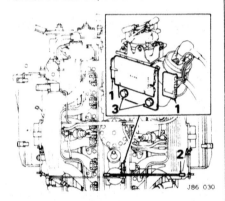

Fig. 90

BALLAST RESISTOR/ STARTER RELAY

Remove and refit   86.35.34

Disconnect the battery.
Note the connections and pull the connectors from the relay.
Release the two setscrews securing the relay and recover the plain washers and spring washers.

Reverse the above operations to refit ensuring that the earth tag is fitted beneath the lower screw.

BALLAST RESISTOR/ STARTER RELAY

Test in situ   86.35.35

If the starter motor does not operate when the ignition key is turned initially, check as follows:

Pull the cable from the connectors 'C1', 'C2', and 'C4' on the relay and short them together (Fig. 91). The starter motor should operate, which shows the relay is at fault. If the starter does not operate, either there is no supply in (brown cable +ve) or the starter motor is at fault.

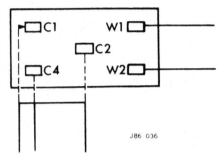

Fig. 91

IGNITION PROTECTION RELAY

Remove and refit   86.35.36

Disconnect the battery.
Remove the driver's side dash liner.
Remove the direction/hazard warning flasher unit by lifting out of the connector block (1, Fig. 92).
Remove the four nuts securing the fusebox mounting panel and ease the panel down to its full extent (2, Fig. 92).
Remove two screws, nuts and shakeproof washers securing the relay to the mounting bracket.
Note carefully the position of cables.
Disconnect the cables at the Lucar connectors.

Reverse the above operations to refit.

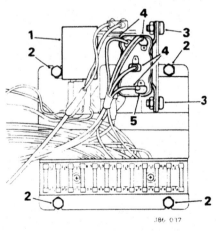

Fig. 92

86—24

Lucas constant energy ignition

A Lucas Constant Energy Ignition System fitted to XJ 4.2 E.F.I. Models on Series III. The new ignition system operates by maintaining the energy stored in the coil at a constant level, allowing the output voltage to remain constant over a wide range of engine speeds. The power dissipated in both the coil and module compared with equivalent constant dwell systems is greatly reduced.

Constant energy system component description

Amplifier AB 14

The amplifier (1, Fig. 93) consists of a solid state electronic module housed in an aluminium case with two pre-wired leads (2, Fig. 93) which connect to the low tension terminals on the ignition coil.

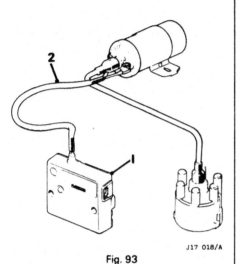

Fig. 93

Connection from the distributor pick-up module is made by an assembly of two leads (1, Fig. 94) inside a screening braid which plugs into a socket on the amplifier side. The amplifier mounting as shown in (2, Fig. 94).

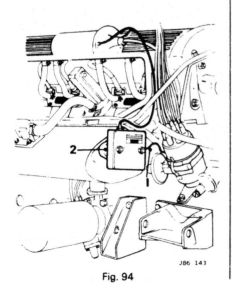

Fig. 94

Distributor (45 DM)

The distributor incorporates a standard automatic advance system, anti-flash shield (1, Fig. 95), rotor arm, and cover (2, Fig. 95). The previous pick-up and module assembly is replaced by a reluctor and pick-up module (3, Fig. 95). The reluctor is a gear-like component (with as many teeth as there are cylinders) which is mounted on the distributor drive shaft.

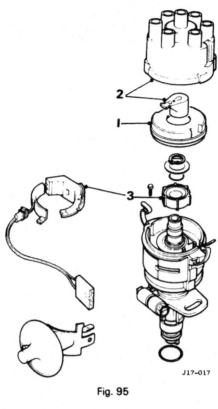

Fig. 95

The pick-up module consists of a winding around a pole-piece attached to a permanent magnet.
The distributor is pre-wired with two leads terminating in a moulded two-pin inhibited connector, which plugs into the amplifier previously described.

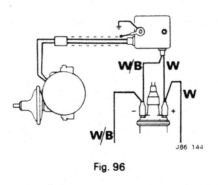

Fig. 96

During normal service the air gap between the reluctor and the pick-up module does not alter and will only require re-setting if it has been tampered with. If it is necessary to adjust the gap, then it should be set such that the minimum clearance between the pick-up and the

reluctor teeth is not less than 0,20 mm (0.008 in). The gap should not be set wider than 0,35 mm (0.014 in).

The air gap is measured between a reluctor tooth and the pick-up module (1, Fig. 97) and should be checked with a plastic feeler gauge. The use of a metal feeler gauge may result in a misleading gauge reading due to the pick-up module contacts being magnetic. However, their use will not affect the electrical operation of the pick-up module.

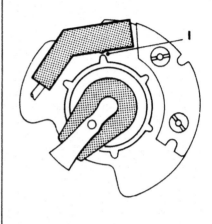

Fig. 97

When the reluctor tooth passes across the pick-up limb, the magnetic field strength around the pick-up winding is intensified, creating a voltage in the winding. The rise and fall of this voltage is sensed by the amplifier and is used to trigger the output stage of the amplifier, which in turn switches on and off the current flowing in the primary winding of the HT coil. A 6 volt HT coil is used in this system. There is no separate ballast resistor in the circuit. The amplifier controls the maximum current flowing in the primary circuit.

CONSTANT ENERGY IGNITION TEST

Test 1

Check the battery. A heavy discharge test will determine whether the battery is capable of supplying the heavy currents required by the starter motor.

Check the specific gravity of the electrolyte in each cell. A variation of (0.040) in any cell means the battery is suspect.

Test 2

Check for HT spark. Remove the HT lead from the centre of the distributor cap and hold the lead approximately 6 mm (0.25 in) from the engine (Fig. 98). Crank the engine. If a good spark is obtained, check the HT leads, spark plugs, distributor cap, and rotor.

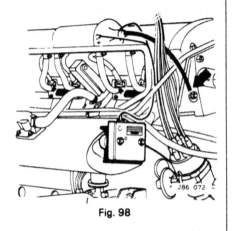

Fig. 98

Test 3

With ignition switched on, the voltage at the HT coil positive terminal (Fig. 99) should be 12 volts. If the voltage is less than 11 volts check wiring to/from the ignition switch.

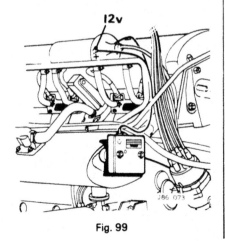

Fig. 99

Test 4

With ignition switched on the voltage at the negative terminal of HT coil should be 12 volts (Fig. 100).

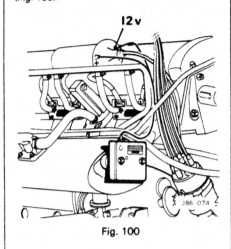

Fig. 100

If a zero reading is obtained, disconnect the lead to the amplifier from the negative terminal of the HT coil (Fig. 101).

If the voltage is zero, a faulty HT coil is indicated.

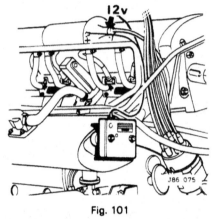

Fig. 101

A 12 volt reading indicates a faulty amplifier.

Test 5

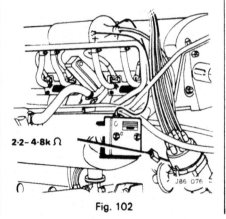

Fig. 102

Disconnect the distributor pick-up leads from the amplifier, and measure the resistance of the pick-up coil. The resistance should be 2.2 to 4.8 ohms (Fig. 102).

Test 6

Connect a test lamp to the negative terminal of the HT coil and earth. Crank the engine. The lamp should dim and flicker slightly (Fig. 103).

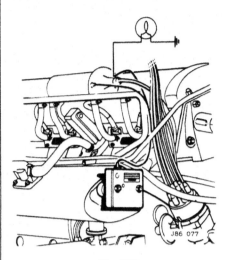

Fig. 103

86—26

IGNITION COIL

Remove and refit 86.35.32

Disconnect the battery.
Remove the bolts securing the HT coil.
Note the position of the cables and disconnect the cables.
Withdraw the HT lead.
Remove the coil.
Reverse the above procedure to refit.

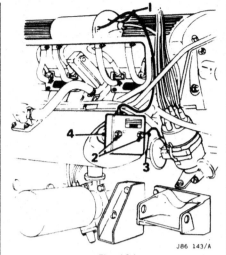

Fig. 104

J86 143/A

IGNITION TIMING

Static Check 86.35.15

Remove the distributor cap and anti-flash shield.
Rotate the engine until the rotor arm approaches No. 6 cylinder segment in the distributor cap.
Slowly rotate the engine until the ignition timing scale on the crankshaft damper is at the appropriate number of degrees at the pointer on the lower L.H. side of the timing chain cover.
4.2 Litre 'H' or 'S' compression ratio, 6 B.T.D.C.
3.4 Litre 'H' compression ratio, 8 B.T.D.C.
Slacken the distributor pinch-bolt and rotate the distributor body so that the pick-up is lined up with the nearest reluctor tooth.
Switch on the ignition.
Position the end of the distributor centre HT cable approximately 6 mm (¼ in) from a good earth point on the engine.
Turn the distributor body slowly until a spark between the HT lead and earth occurs.
Repeat the operation as a check.
Switch off the ignition.
Tighten the distributor pinch-bolt, refit the anti-flash shield and the distributor cap.
Refit the centre HT lead to the distributor cap.

AMPLIFIER UNIT

Remove and refit 86.35.30

Removing

Disconnect the battery.
Remove the air cleaner.
Remove the plastic cover from the HT coil and disconnect the two amplifier leads from the coil (1, Fig. 104).
Remove the two amplifier securing bolts (2, Fig. 104).
Disconnect the distributor pick-up leads (3, Fig. 104) and withdraw the amplifier (4, Fig. 104).
To refit, reverse the above procedure.

ELECTRONIC SPEEDOMETER WIRING CIRCUIT

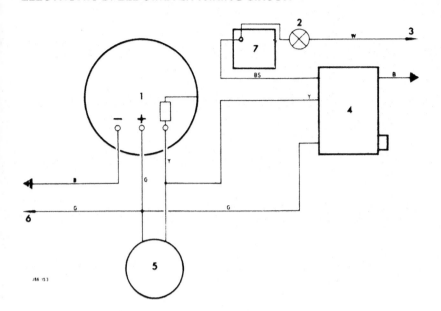

KEY TO DIAGRAM

1. Speedometer
2. Oxygen sensor warning light (USA only)
3. Feed to ignition switch
4. Service interval counter (SIC) (USA only)
5. Speed transducer
6. Feed to fuse
7. Warning light bulb failure unit

COLOUR CODE

G	Green
Y	Yellow
B	Black
BS	Black/Slate

Fig. 105

ELECTRONIC SPEEDOMETER

Description

The two major parts of the system are, an electronic speedometer head and an 8 pole transducer which is situated in the automatic/ manual transmission unit in place of the conventional angle drive.

The electronic speedometer operates in a similar way to integrated circuit tachometers.

It should be noted that:

Due to the nature of the instrument a slight flickering of the speedometer pointer may be noticeable at below 15 km/h (10 mph).

The control for resetting the odometer is situated in the speedometer facia and is operated by depressing the control button.

The cause(s) of faults which result in incorrect operation are best diagnosed by substitution, having first checked for continuity of wiring/ connectors and that battery voltage is supplied to both instrument and transducer. Ensure that earth connections are clean and tight. A fault diagnosis chart is given opposite to assist:

FAULT DIAGNOSIS

Apparent Fault	Probable Cause	Remedy
No reading on Speedometer	Defective Transducer	Substitute Transducer
	Defective Speedometer	Substitute Speedometer
	Defective Wiring	Check continuity of wiring with multimeter, check the positive supply connected to both speedometer and transducer.
Incorrect Speedo Reading	Defective Speedometer	Substitute Speedometer
	Defective Transducer	Substitute Transducer
	Ratio between idle and transducer driven gear incorrect	Check for discrepancy in gear ratios by undoing the knurled collar holding the transducer to the output/drive gear from the gearbox and marking the square drive end. Observe that for every six revolutions of the road wheels the square drive turns $7\frac{1}{2}$ revolutions.
Pointer does not always return to Zero when the vehicle is stationary	Transducer Fault	Substitute Transducer
Excessive needle flicker up to 30 km/h (20 mph) and an odometer count when stationary	Transducer Fault	Substitute Transducer
Needle flicker when brake and trafficator used	Transducer Fault	Substitute Transducer
Various speed indications or needle deflection to max speed-when stationary	Transducer Fault	Substitute Transducer

86—28

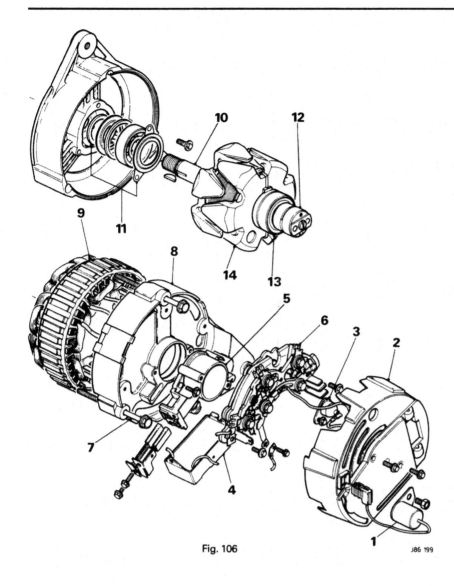

Fig. 106   J86 199

ALTERNATOR

Description   86.10.00

The A133 alternator is a three phase machine with a delta wound stator, twelve pole rotor, full wave rectification and a 15TR voltage regulator. The alternator is machine sensed with an externally fitted radio suppression capacitor.

Operation

The rotor and stator windings generate a three phase alternating current which is rectified to a direct current suitable for charging the battery. The electronic voltage regulator unit controls the alternator output voltage by high frequency switching of the rotor field circuit.

Specification

Voltage	12 volts
Maximum rev/min	15,000 rev/min
Maximum Output	75 amps
Regulated Voltage	13.6 to 14.4 volts
Rotor Resistance	2,46 ohms
Stator Winding Resistance per phase	0.144 ohms
Maximum Brush Length	20 mm (0.79 ins)
Minimum Brush Length	10 mm (0.39 ins)
Warning Lamp Bulb	2.2 watts

The 'on the vehicle' testing procedures are the same as the ACR range of alternators.

KEY TO ALTERNATOR

1. Capacitor
2. Cover
3. Surge Protective Diode
4. Regulator
5. Brush Box Assembly
6. Rectifier Pack
7. Through Bolts
8. Slip-ring End Bracket
9. Stator
10. Rotor Shaft
11. Bearing Kit
12. Slip-ring
13. Slip-ring End Bearing
14. Rotor

Alternator   86.10.08

Dismantle.

Disconnect the capacitor Lucas connector.

Remove the capacitor securing screw and remove the capacitor (1, Fig. 106).

Remove the two screws securing the cover and remove the cover (2, Fig. 106).

Remove the surge protection diode (3, Fig. 106). Note the arrangement of the regulator leads, disconnect the leads and remove the regulator (4, Fig. 106).

Remove the two screws securing the brush box assembly and remove the brush box (5, Fig. 106).

Apply a hot iron to the stator lead terminal tags on the rectifier pack and prise out the stator leads when the solder melts.

Remove the remaining two screws securing the rectifier pack assembly (6, Fig. 106) and lift the pack from the slip-ring end bracket (8, Fig. 106).

Remove the three through bolts (7, Fig. 106) and lift the slip-ring end bracket (8, Fig. 106) from the stator (9, Fig. 106) using a mallet if necessary.

Note the position of the stator leads relative to the alternator fixing lugs, and then lift the stator (9, Fig. 106) from the drive end bracket.

Remove the shaft nut, washer, pulley, cooling fan, woodruff key and spacers from the rotor shaft (10, Fig. 106).

Press the rotor shaft from the drive end bearing (11, Fig. 106).

To replace the slip-ring end bearing (13, Fig. 106) unsolder the outer and inner slip-rings (12, Fig. 106) then prise the slip-rings gently off the rotor shaft.

Using a suitable extractor withdraw the bearing from the rotor shaft.

NOTE: Care should be taken not to damage the insulation on the rotor leads when removing or refitting the slip-rings. Use a resin covered solder ensuring a build-up of solder does not occur on the upper face of the inner slip-ring.

Check all the components using normal procedures. Referring to the resistance values and brush lengths as detailed.

Re-assembly is the reversal of the dismantling procedure ensuring the brushes move freely in the brush box, also ensure the slip-rings are clean and smooth.

KIEKERT CENTRAL LOCKING SYSTEM

Description   86.25.00

The central door locking system fitted FROM 1986 MY vehicles incorporates a control module fitted in the driver's door and lock operating motors in the passenger doors. The control module is connected to the driver's door lock mechanism by mechanical linkage and is activated by the locking flap or the door key. The passenger doors and the boot lid are fitted with the motors which are connected to the locking mechanism by mechanical linkage. The motors are activated by voltage signals from the control module to lock or unlock. The motor fitted to the boot lid will lock electrically, but is inhibited from unlocking by the mechanical linkage. The boot lid is unlocked by using the boot lock key.

All the doors can be locked or unlocked from the drivers door either by using the door key or by operating the door locking flap from the inside of the vehicle. The front passenger door can be unlocked and locked with the door key without any of the other locks operating.

The driver's door control module and the lock motors are mounted on brackets welded to door intrusion rails as is the lock solenoid. The boot lock motor is mounted on the lid inner panel adjacent to the lock mechanism.

DOOR LOCK CONTROL MODULE

Renew   86.25.03

Remove the door trim casing (Operation No. 76.74.01).

With the door glass in the fully closed position, remove the adhesive tape securing the control module harness to the door interior, and disconnect the control module block connector from the door harness.

Remove the two setscrews securing the control module assembly to the bracket on the intrusion member, release the locking link from the module and remove from the door.

Separate the control module from the mounting bracket by removing the two self tapping screws.

To fit a new control module reverse operations 2 to 4. **Do not fully tighten the setscrews at this stage.**

DOOR LOCK CONTROL MODULE

Adjust   86.25.04

Remove the 'A' post lower trim panel, driver's side. (76.13.22).

Locate the door harness multiplug connector within the 'A' post with orange/red and orange/green leads. Disconnect the connector.

Connect a test lamp across the connector terminals on the door harness side.

Set the outer door lock to **full closed** position. Set the door lock inner flap to **full locked** position.

Move the control module by hand fully towards the lock assembly, then carefully move the module slowly in the opposite direction until the test light flashes momentarily. The module should now be positioned correctly, tighten the setscrews.

To check the setting move the door lock inner flap slowly to the unlock position. If the setting is correct the lamp will flash momentarily just before the flap reaches full travel. When the flap is moved back towards the lock position, the lamp will flash again just before the flap reaches full travel.

Disconnect the test lamp and reconnect the harness block connector.

Operate the outer door handle to release the latch.

Close the door and recheck the operation of **all** doors using the key in the driver's door lock.

Refit trim panels to 'A' post and door.

CAUTION: Should it be necessary to connect an independent battery feed to the control module whilst in situ, the following connections must be **observed:**

Positive feed to purple wire.
Negative feed to black wire.

A wrong connection can destroy the control module and it is recommended that this operation is carried out with the unit removed from the vehicle.

FRONT PASSENGER DOOR LOCK MOTOR

Renew   86.25.46

REAR DOOR LOCK MOTOR

Renew   86.25.47

Remove door trim casing (76.74.01 Front Door) (76.34.04 Rear Door).

With the door glass in the fully closed position disconnect the door lock motor block connector from the door harness.

NOTE: It may be necessary to remove the plastic strap from around the harness for access.

Remove two setscrews securing the lock motor assembly to the mounting plate on the intrusion member, release the locking link from the motor and remove the motor assembly from the door. Separate the motor from its mounting bracket by removing two self tapping screws.

To fit a new motor unit, reverse operations 2 to 4. **Do not fully tighten the setscrews at this stage.**

FRONT PASSENGER DOOR LOCK MOTOR

Adjust   86.25.51

Set the door lock to the **full closed** position. Slide the lock motor assembly **towards** the door lockface to take up **all** free movement, tighten the setscrews.

Operate the exterior door handle, close door.

Check the setting by operating with the key from the driver's door.

REAR DOOR LOCK MOTOR

Adjust   86.25.52

Set the door outer lock to the **full closed** position.

Slide the lock motor assembly **away** from the door lockface to take up **all** free movement, tighten the setscrews.

Operate the exterior door handle, close door.

Check the setting by operating with the key from the driver's door.

BOOT LID LOCK MOTOR

Renew   86.25.49

Disconnect the lock motor block connector from the boot lid harness.

Remove the two setscrews securing the lock motor assembly to the boot lid inner panel. Release the locking link from the motor and remove the motor assembly from the boot lid. Separate the motor from its mounting bracket.

To fit a new boot lock, reverse operations 1 to 3. **Do not fully tighten the setscrews at this stage.**

BOOT LID LOCK MOTOR

Adjust 86.25.53

Ensure that latch is in the unlocked position.
Slide the motor assembly towards the latch to take up all free movement, tighten the setscrews.
Close the boot lid and check the setting by locking with the key from the driver's door.

Fault Finding — All Locks Inoperative

Check the fuse, mounted above the passenger's side fuse box.
Fuse intact — check battery supply to 'A' post block connector at purple wire.
Feed established — check battery supply to control unit at the block connector inside the door (see caution).
Feed established — reconnect the connector inside the door, connect a test lamp across the door harness connector located in the 'A' post as previously described, and operate the door lock. If the lamp does not light momentarily when operating the door lock, change the control unit.

Passenger Door Motor or Boot Motor Inoperative

Check the system with the test lamp connected across the cable harness block connectors.
If the test lamp lights momentarily when operating the driver's door lock at a motor block connector, change the motor.

HIGH MOUNTED STOP LAMP BULB

Renew 86.41.02

Depress the two catches situated on the lower face of the cover (1, Fig. 107) and remove the cover (2, Fig. 107).
Turn and twist the relevent bulb holder (3, Fig. 107) and pull the bulb to remove.
Fit the replacement bulb and reverse the removal procedure to refit.

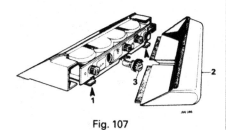

Fig. 107

HIGH MOUNTED STOP LAMP

Renew 86.41.01

Depress the two catches situated on the lower face of the cover (1, Fig. 108) and remove the cover (2, Fig. 108).
Disconnect the harness (3, Fig. 108) from the lamp assembly and slide the holder assembly (4, Fig. 108) off the brackets attached to the rear screen.
Reverse the removal procedure to refit the replacement lamp assembly.

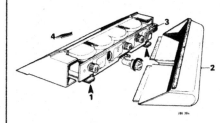

Fig. 108

DISTRIBUTOR BREATHER OUTLET TUBE

Renew 86.35.25

Remove the auxiliary air valve elbow, slide the clip (1, Fig. 109) up the tube (2, Fig. 109) situated on top of the distributor cap, pull the tube from the connector. Remove the plastic right angled adaptor from the tube.
Fit the connector to the replacement tube, transfer the clip and feed back under the manifold, push the tube onto the connector on the distributor cap and secure with the clip.
Push the plastic right angled adaptor back into the elbow and refit the auxiliary air valve elbow.

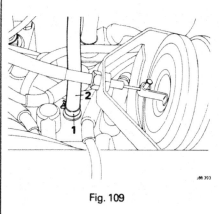

Fig. 109

DISTRIBUTOR CAP

Renew 86.35.11

Disconnect the king lead from the cap.
Slacken the cruise control cable solderless nipple (1, Fig. 110), disconnect the inner cable (2, Fig. 110) from the actuator (3, Fig. 110) and collect the nipple.
Remove the cruise control cable bracket securing bolts, compress the actuator bellows (4, Fig. 110), displace the bracket (5, Fig. 110) and place the assembly to one side.

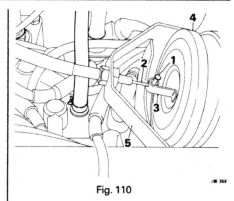

Fig. 110

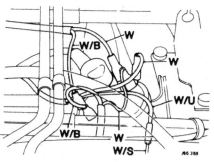

Fig. 111

Note the position of the high tension leads (Fig. 111) relative to the cap and disconnect.
Slide the upper (outlet) breather tube securing clip back along the tube and remove the tube.
Slacken the distributor cap securing screws and lift the cap for access to the clip securing the lower breather tube.
Slide the clip back along the tube, remove the tube, lift off the cap and discard the gasket.
Reverse the removal procedure ensuring that the replacement gasket is seated correctly.

IGNITION COIL

Renew 86.35.32

Disconnect the king lead from the cap.
Note the position of the low tension leads relative to the ignition coil (Fig. 111).
Remove the bolts securing the ignition coil to the pedestal and lift out the ignition coil assembly.
Remove the nuts securing the male lucar terminals to the low tension connector posts (treble to positive post).
Discard the ignition coil and king lead assembly.
Place the insulation sleeve (1, Fig. 112) over the king lead mounting post (2, Fig. 112), fit the

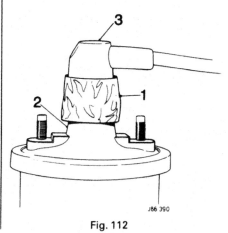

Fig. 112

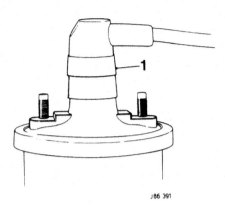

J86 391

Fig. 113

replacement king lead (3, Fig. 112) to the ignition coil ensuring that the lead will face the front of the engine when the coil is fitted.

Place the sleeve over the king lead connecting plug and using an electrical heat gun apply heat to the sleeve until traces of the adhesive are visible at the top and bottom of the sleeve, when shrunk (1, Fig. 113) the lead should be securely attached to the ignition coil.

Reverse the remaining removal procedure to refit the ignition coil.

DISTRIBUTOR BREATHER FILTER

Renew   **86.35.23**

Displace the ratchet strap (1, Fig. 114) away from the filter. Slide the pipe securing clip (1, Fig. 114) up the vacuum hose and pull the filter (3, Fig. 114) from the hose (4, Fig. 114).

Reverse the removal procedure to refit the replacement filter ensuring that the arrow on the filter faces towards the engine.

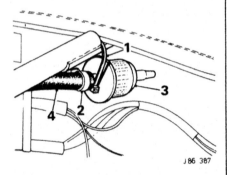

J 86 387

Fig. 114

DISTRIBUTOR BREATHER INLET TUBE

Renew   **86.35.24**

Remove the distributor cap, displace the clip (1, Fig. 115) up the tube (2, Fig. 115) and remove the tube from the cap.

Cut the ratchet straps (3, Fig. 115), push the clip securing the filter up the tube and remove the filter (4, Fig. 115).

Transfer the clips to the replacement tube, fit the filter to the tube ensuring that the arrow is pointing towards the engine and secure with the clip.

Feed the tube back to the distributor cap, fit the tube to the cap and secure with the clip.

Refit the distributor cap and secure the tube to the wing tie bar ensuring that the tube is not compressed with the ratchet straps.

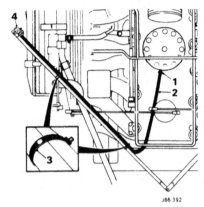

J86 392

Fig. 115

CONTENTS

CLOCK

Remove and refit　　　　**88.15.07**

Disconnect the battery.
Lever the clock from the aperture.
Pull the clock illumination bulb holder from the back of the clock.
Note the position of the Lucar connectors and disconnect the cables.

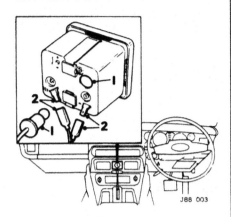

Fig. 1

OIL PRESSURE TRANSMITTER

Remove and refit　　　　**88.25.07**

Disconnect the battery.
Disconnect the cable from the connector on top of the transmitter (1).
Remove the transmitter, located on the oil filter head on 6 cylinder models (2, Fig. 2), and on the manifold on 12-cylinder models (2, Fig. 3).

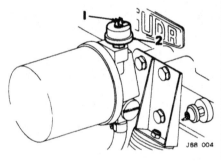

Fig. 2

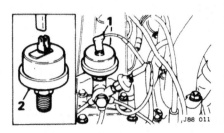

Fig. 3

OIL PRESSURE WARNING SWITCH

Remove and refit　　　　**88.25.08**

Disconnect the battery.
Disconnect the cable from the connector on top of the switch (1).
Withdraw the switch from the cylinder block on 6 cylinder models (2, Fig. 4), and the manifold on 12 cylinder models (2, Fig. 5).

CAUTION: When refitting, care must be taken not to overtighten the switch, torque figure 4 to 5,5 Nm (3 to 4 lb ft), or the oil pressure transmitter.

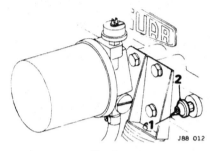

Fig. 4

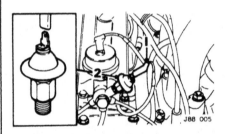

Fig. 5

COOLANT TEMPERATURE TRANSMITTER

Remove and refit　　　　**88.25.20**

Disconnect the battery.
Remove the remote header tank cap to depressurize the cooling system.

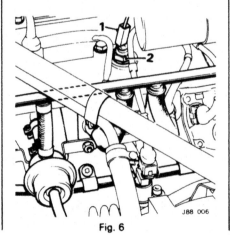

Fig. 6

WARNING: Only remove the cap when the engine is cold.

Disconnect the connector on top of the transmitter (1), and withdraw the transmitter (2, Fig. 6). 6 cylinder cars or (1, Fig. 7) 12 cylinder cars.

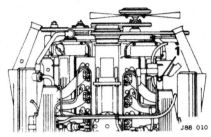

Fig. 7

Refitting

Reverse the above procedure.

FUEL TANK UNIT

Remove and refit　　　　**88.25.32**

Disconnect the battery.
Raise the rear of the car and drain the fuel tank.
Remove the wheel.
On later cars remove the rear lamp assembly for access.
Remove the cover-plate and disconnect the Lucar connections (1, Figs. 8 or 9).
Using tool No. 18G 1001, rotate the locking ring anti-clockwise to clear the lugs in the tank. Remove the locking ring and withdraw the tank unit (2, Figs. 8 or 9).
WARNING: Tank unit seal should be replaced with a new seal every time this operation is carried out.

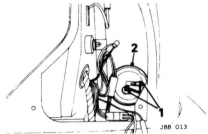

Fig. 8

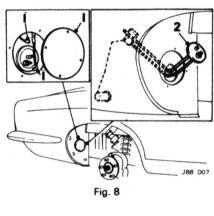

Fig. 9

88—2

SPEEDOMETER

Remove and refit	**88.30.01**

Includes:

Speedometer illumination bulb—remove and refit	**86.45.49**
Flasher indicator bulb— remove and refit	**86.45.63**
Ignition low charge indicator bulb—remove and refit	**86.45.64**
Fuel gauge—remove and refit	**88.25.26**
Fuel gauge illumination bulb—remove and refit	**86.45.52**
Temperature gauge— remove and refit	**88.25.14**
Temperature gauge illumination bulb— remove and refit	**86.45.51**

Removing

Disconnect the battery.
Press the speedometer (1, Fig. 10) in towards the fascia and rotate in a clockwise direction for right-hand drive cars and anti-clockwise for left-hand drive cars, until the instrument releases from the locking tabs. Withdraw speedometer from the fascia (1, Fig. 11).
Note the positions of the cables and disconnect from the Lucar connectors at the back of the instrument (2, Fig. 11).
Unscrew the speedometer drive cable and turn the trip reset connector anti-clockwise until it releases, then pull it off.

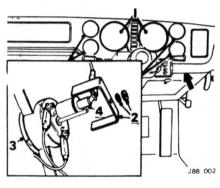

Fig. 10

Withdraw the speedometer illumination bulb, the flasher indicator bulb, and the ignition low charge indicator bulb (3, Fig. 11).

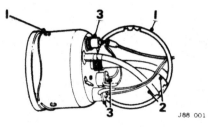

Fig. 11

With the speedometer removed, the fuel gauge retaining bracket nut (2, Fig. 10) can be removed and the indicator (3, Fig. 10) withdrawn from the fascia.
Remove the fuel gauge illumination bulb holder and remove the bulb (4, Fig. 10).
The temperature gauge can also be removed by removing the retaining bracket nut and withdrawing the indicator from the fascia.
Remove the temperature gauge illumination bulb holder and remove the bulb.

Refitting

Reverse the above operations.

SPEEDOMETER TRIP RESET

Remove and refit	**88.30.02**

Disconnect the battery.
Remove the retaining ring from the speedometer trip reset knob, located in the driver's side dash casing.
Press the speedometer in towards the fascia, rotate anti-clockwise and release it from the fascia.
NOTE: When refitting the speedometer trip reset, it is advisable to remove the fuse block access panel, to assist in the location of the lower end of the reset cable through the mounting bracket.

SPEEDOMETER CABLE ASSEMBLY

Remove and refit	**88.30.06**

Disconnect the battery.
Press the speedometer in towards the fascia; rotate and release it from the fascia.
Disconnect the cable at the angle drive (1, Fig. 12).
Attach a draw-string to the end of the cable.
Raise the car.
Undo the knurled nut securing the speedometer cable to the angle drive on the gearbox.
Displace the grommet from the transmission tunnel and feed the cable into the car.
Withdraw the cable (2, Fig. 12) from the instrument into the footwell, remove the draw-string.

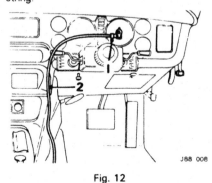

Fig. 12

Refitting

Feed the cable through the hole in the transmission tunnel and replace the grommet.

Reconnect the cable to the angle dive and tighten the knurled nut to secure.
Attach the draw-string to the instrument end of the cable and draw the cable up to the rear of the speedometer.
Reconnect the cable to the angle drive on the speedometer.
Detach the draw-string.
Refit the speedometer.
Reconnect the battery.

SPEEDOMETER CABLE—INNER

Remove and refit	**88.30.07**

Removing

Disconnect the battery.
Remove the speedometer.
Remove the inner cable.
If the cable is broken, the gearbox end will have to be disconnected to allow the other half to be relieved.

Refitting

Reverse the above operations. Lubricate the cable before refitting.
NOTE: (a) Lubrication should not be excessive; oil should never be used. Use only T.S.D. 119 or equivalent.
(b) The inner cable should only project by 9,52 mm (⅜in) from the outer casing at the instrument end to ensure correct engagement at the point of drive.

SPEEDOMETER RIGHT ANGLE DRIVE—INSTRUMENT

Remove and refit	**88.30.15**

Removing

Disconnect the battery.
Remove the speedometer.
Unscrew the knurled retaining ring and withdraw the drive.

Refitting

Reverse the above procedure.

SPEEDOMETER RIGHT ANGLE DRIVE—GEARBOX

Remove and refit   **88.30.16**

Removing

Disconnect the speedometer drive cable.
Remove the right angle drive by unscrewing the knurled retaining ring nut.

Refitting

Reverse the above procedure.

TACHOMETER

Remove and refit   **88.30.21**

Includes:

Tachometer illumination bulb—remove and refit	**86.45.53**
Oil gauge—remove and refit	**88.25.01**
Oil gauge illumination bulb—remove and refit	**86.45.50**
Heated back-light warning lamp bulb—remove and refit	**86.45.82**
Warning lamp cluster—remove and refit	**86.45.62**
Battery condition indicator—remove and refit	**88.10.07**
Battery condition indicator bulb—remove and refit	**86.45.56**

Removing

Disconnect the battery.
Press the tachometer (1, Fig. 13) in towards the fascia and rotate in a clockwise direction for right-hand drive cars and anti-clockwise for left-hand drive cars, until the instrument releases from the locking tabs. Withdraw the tachometer from the fascia (1, Fig. 14).

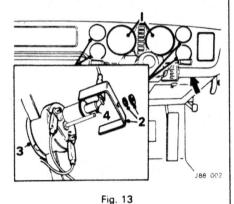

Fig. 13

Lever the warning lamp cluster lens from the assembly and working through the tachometer aperture, disconnect the warning lamp cluster harness block connector.
Bend back the clip securing the cluster harness at rear of the fascia.
Remove the cluster securing screws and withdraw the unit from the fascia.

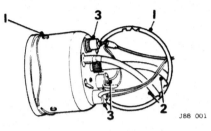

Fig. 14

Note the position of the cables and disconnect the Lucar connectors at the back of the instrument (2, Fig. 14).
Withdraw the bulb holder from the instrument and remove the bulb (3, Fig. 14).
Remove the heated back-light bulb holder and withdraw the bulb.
With the tachometer removed, the oil gauge retaining bracket nut (2, Fig. 13) can be removed and the gauge withdrawn from the fascia (3, Fig. 13).
Remove the oil gauge illumination bulb holder (4, Fig. 13) from the gauge and withdraw the bulb.
The battery condition indicator can also be removed by removing the retaining bracket nut and withdrawing the indicator from the fascia.
Disconnect the cables at the Lucar connectors.
Remove the battery condition indicator illumination bulb holder and remove the bulb.

88—4

ELECTRICAL DATA CHART

6 cyl (later type)

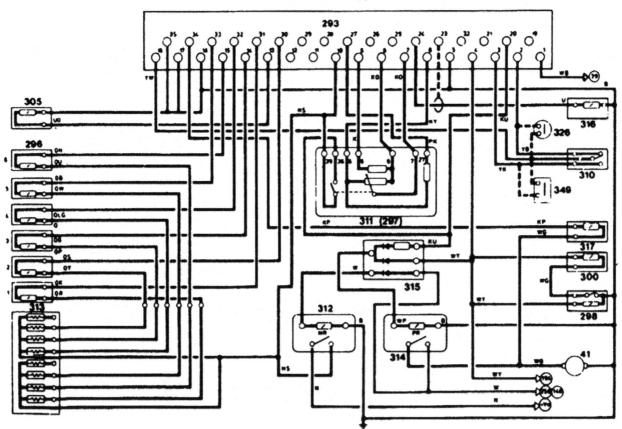

12 cyl
DIGITAL FUEL INJECTION

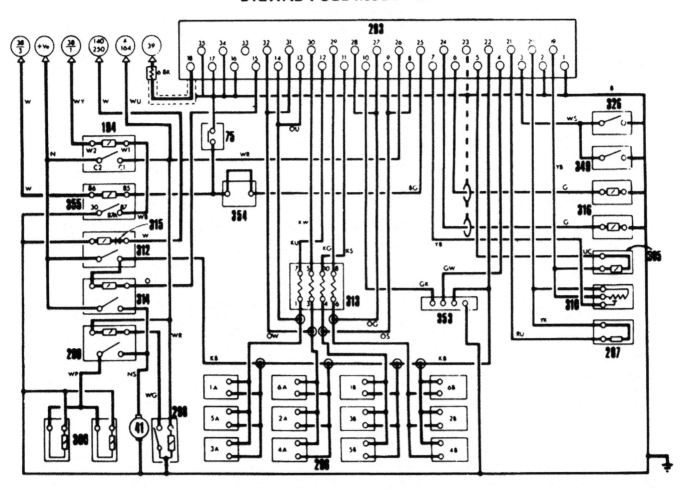

3·4 IGN & FUEL SYSTEM

VACUUM DELAY TIMER

KICK DOWN INHIBIT/SPEED CONTROL
(Alternative Circuit)

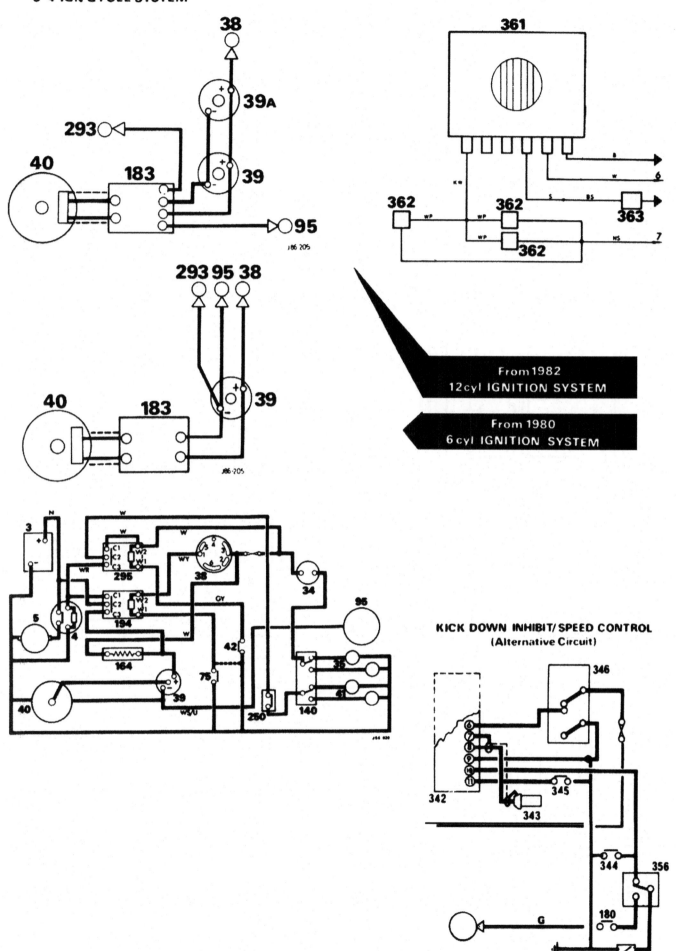

From 1982
12 cyl IGNITION SYSTEM

From 1980
6 cyl IGNITION SYSTEM

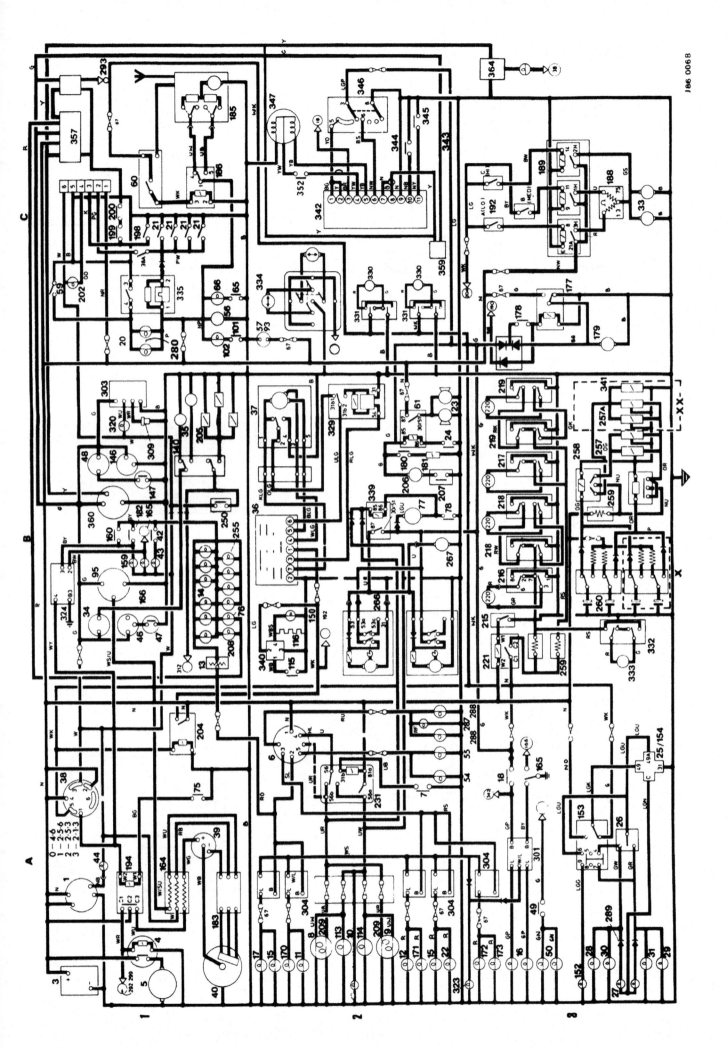

J86 006 B

508

KEY TO WIRING DIAGRAMS

No.	Description	Grid ref.
1	Alternator	A1
3	Battery	A1
4	Starter solenoid	C1
5	Starter motor	A1
6	Master lighting switch	C1
7	Headlamp flash switch	A2
8	Headlamp beam RH	A2
9	Headlamp beam LH	A2
10	Main beam warning light	A2
11	RH side lamp	A2
12	LH side lamp	A2
13	Panel lamp rheostat	B1
14	Panel lamps	B1
15	Number plate illumination lamp(s)	A2
16	Stop lamp(s)	A3
17	Tail lamp RH	A2
18	Stop lamp switch	A3
19	Fuse box(es) (not shown)	—
20	Puddle light(s)	A2
21	Door switch	C1
22	Tail lamp LH	A2
23	Horns	B2
24	Horn push	B2
25	Flasher unit (part of 154)	A3
26	Direction indicator switch	A3
27	Direction indicator warning lights	A3
28	RH front flasher	A3
29	LH front flasher	A3
30	RH rear flasher	A3
31	LH rear flasher	A3
33	Blower motors	C3
34	Fuel gauge	B1
35	Fuel gauge tank unit	B1
36	Windscreen wiper switch	B2
37	Windscreen wiper motor	B2
38	Ignition/starter switch	A1
38A	Key switch (part of 38)	A1
39	Ignition coil	A1
39A	Auxiliary coil 12 cyl.	A1
40	Distributor	—
41	Fuel pump	B2
42	Oil pressure switch	B2
43	Oil pressure warning light	B2
44	Ignition warning light	A1
46	Coolant temperature gauge	B1
47	Water temperature transmitter	B1
48	Oil pressure gauge	B1
49	Reverse lamp switch	A3
50	Reverse lamp(s)	A3
54	Fog lamp RH	A2
55	Fog lamp LH	A2
56	Clock (where fitted)	C1

No.	Description	Grid ref.
57	Cigar lighter socket	C1
59	Interior light switch	C1
60	Radio	C1
61	Horn relay	B2
65	Boot light switch	C1
66	Boot light	C1
67	Line fuse	A2
75	Automatic gearbox safety switch	A1
76	Automatic gearbox selector lamp	B1
77	Windscreen washer pump	B2
78	Windscreen washer switch	B2
93	Charging and inspection lamp socket	C2
95	Tachometer	B1
101	Map light switch	C1
102	Map light	A2
111	Rear passenger lamps	A3
112	Drivers lamp	A2
113	Headlamp inner RH	A3
114	Headlamp inner LH	C1
115	Rear window demist switch	C1
116	Rear window demist unit	A2
140	Fuel changeover switch	B2
146	Battery condition indicator	B2
147	Oil pressure transmitter	A3
150	Rear window demister warning light	A3
152	Hazard warning light	A3
153	Hazard warning switch	A3
154	Hazard warning flasher unit	A3
159	Brake fluid level warning light	A3
160	Brake differential pressure switch	A3
164	Ballast resistor	B1
165	Handbrake switch	B1
166	Handbrake warning light	B1
170	Side markers RH front	B2
171	Side markers LH front	B2
172	Side markers RH rear	A2
173	Side markers LH rear	A2
174	Radiator cooling fan diode(s)	A3
177	Radiator cooling fan relay	C3
178	Radiator cooling thermostat (in pump)	C3
179	Radiator cooling fan motor	C3
180	Kickdown switch	B2
181	Kickdown solenoid	A1
182	Brake fluid level switch	B1
183	Ignition amplifier	B1
185	Aerial motor	A1
186	Aerial motor relay	C1
188	Resistor	C1
189	Blower speed relay	C3
190	Compressor clutch	C3
191	Thermostat	C1

No.	Description	Grid ref.
192	Control switch	A1
194	Starter solenoid/ballast coil relay	A1
198	Seat belt switch-driver	C1
199	Seat belt switch-passenger } Non	C1
200	Seat switch-passenger } Fed.	C1
202	Seat belt warning light	C1
204	Ignition protection relay	A1
205	Fuel solenoid valves	B1
206	Battery cooling fan	B2
207	Battery cooling fan otterstat	B2
208	Cigar lighter illumination	B1
209	Headlamp dip beam RH and LH	A2
215	Window lift master switch	B3
216	Window lift switch RH front	B3
217	Window lift switch LH front	B3
218	Window lift switch RH rear	B3
219	Window lift switch LH rear	B3
220	Window lift motor(s)	B3
221	Window lift relay	B3
231	Headlamp relay	A2
231A	Headlamp inhibit relay (XJS only)	
250	Inertia switch	B1
255	Fibre optics illumination bulb	B1
257	Door lock solenoid	
257A	Rear door lock solenoid	
258	Door lock solenoid relay	B3
259	Thermal circuit breaker	B3
260	Door lock switch	B3
261	Amplifier	B1
262	Servo	B1
263	Vacuum valve	A1
264	In car sensor	A3
265	Ambient sensor	B1
266	Headlamp wiper motor	B2
267	Headlamp wash motor	B2
280	Roof lamps	A3
287	Fog guard warning light	A2
288	Fog guard lamp	A2
289	Direction indicator blocking diode	A3
290	Seat belt logic unit (Federal)	C1
291	EGR control unit	
292	Fuel injection amplifier	C3
293	Fuel injection control unit (ECU)	C3
296	Fuel injectors	B2
297	Air temperature sensor	B2
298	Thermotime switch	B1
299	Cold start relay	A1
300	Cold start injector	C1
301	Stop lamp failure sensor	C1
303	Low coolant control unit	C3
304	Park lamp failure sensor	C3
305	Coolant temperature sensor	

No.	Description	Grid ref.
306	Trigger unit	
307	EGR valve	
308	EGR thermo switch	B1
309	Low coolant sensor	
310	Throttle switch	
312	Main relay	
313	Power resistor	
314	Fuel pump relay	
315	Blocking diode (part of 312)	
316	Oxygen sensor	
318	Manifold pressure sensor	
320	Low coolant warning light	B1
323	Lamp failure warning light	A3
324	Invertor	B1
326	Full throttle switch	
327	Temperature selector	
329	Timer Relay — wipers	B2
330	Seat adjust motor	C2
331	Seat adjuster switch	C2
332	Sliding roof switch	B3
333	Sliding roof motor	B3
334	Electric door mirror	C2
335	Interior lamp delay up to 1983	C1
339	Headlamp wiper relay	B2
340	Heated back-light delay (XJS only)	B2
341	Boot lock solenoid (not applicable to XJS)	
342	Speed control unit	C2
344	Inhibit switch (see 356)	C2
345	Set switch	C2
346	Switch control unit	C2
347	Actuator	C2
349	Throttle micro-switch	
350	Over-temperature switch	
351	Thermal fuse	
352	Speed control brake switch	C2
353	Feedback monitor socket	
354	Feedback disable socket	
355	Feedback relay	
356	Kickdown/Speed control Inhibit switch	C2
357	Trip computer	C1
358	Interface unit (where fitted)	C1
359	Pulse generator	C2
360	Speedometer (electronic)	B1
361	Vacuum timer relay	
362	Solenoid valves	
363	Coolant temperature switch	
364	Service interval counter (NAS)	
365	Purge valve	

X   Circuit in box up to 1983 Model year

XX   Circuit in box not XJS

AIR CONDITIONING

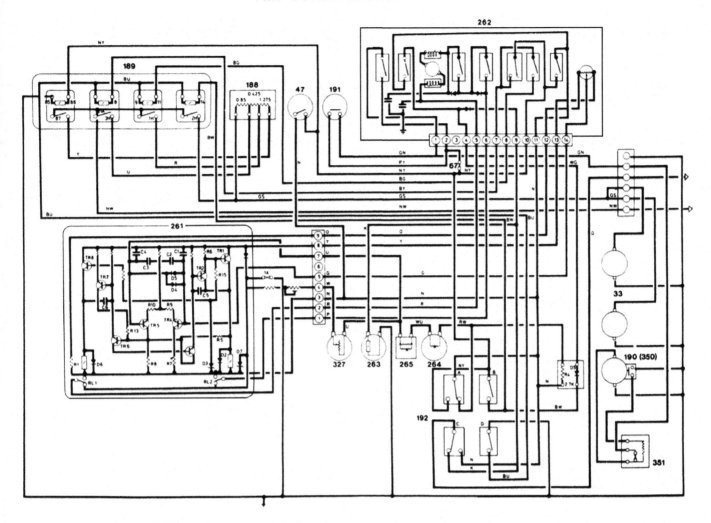

VACUUM DELAY TIMER
North American

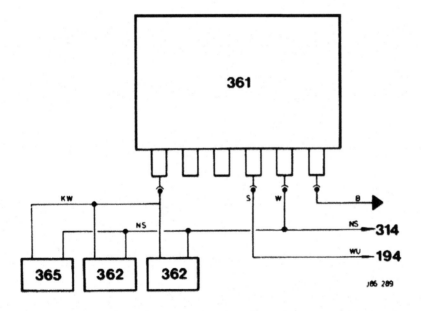

J86 289

CABLE COLOUR CODE

When a cable has two colour code
letters, the first denotes the Main
Colour and the second the Tracer
Colour.

N. Brown — Positive Cable
B. Black — Negative cable
W. White
K. Pink   Ignition switch controlled
G. Green
R. Red   Y. Yellow   O. Orange   S. Slate   L. Light   U. Blue

SYMBOLS USED

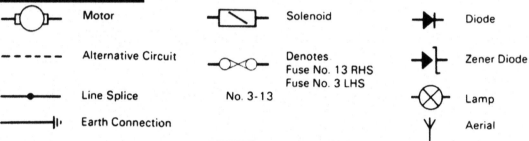

Motor	Solenoid	Diode
Alternative Circuit	Denotes Fuse No. 13 RHS Fuse No. 3 LHS	Zener Diode
Line Splice	No. 3-13	Lamp
Earth Connection		Aerial
Resistor	Reed Switch	
Potentiometer	Transistor	

BULB CHART

	WATTS	LUCAS PART NO.	UNIPART NO.	NOTES
Headlamps —				
LH Traffic Markets —				
— Tungsten — Outer	60/45	54529739	GLU 136	XJ 3.4 Std only. Sealed beam light unit
— Inner	50	54529740	GLU 134	XJ 3.4 Std. only. Sealed beam light unit
— Halogen — Outer	60/55	472	GLB 472	H4 base
— Inner	55	448	GLB 448	H1 base
RH Traffic Markets —				
Normal — Halogen — Outer	60/65	472	GLB 472	H4 base
— Inner	55	448	GLB 448	H1 base
France — Halogen — Outer	60/55	475	GLB 476	Yellow bulb H4 base
— Inner	45/40	411	GLB 411	Yellow bulb The 40 watt filament is not used
USA — Tungsten — Outer	37.5/60			Sealed beam light unit
— Inner	50			Sealed beam light unit
Front Parking Lamp	4	233	GLB 233	Not USA Headlamp pilot
Front Flasher Lamp	21	382	GLB 382	Not USA
Front Parking and Flasher Lamp	5/21	380	GLB 380	USA only
Front Fog Lamp — Cibie	55	—	GLB 212	H2 base
Flasher Repeater	4	233	GLB 233	Not USA
Front Marker Lamp	4	233	GLB 233	USA only
Rear Marker Lamp	4	233	GLB 233	USA only
Rear Door Guard Lamp	5	989	GLB 989	
Stop Lamp	21	382	GLB 382	
Tail Lamp	5	207	GLB 207	
Rear Flasher Lamp	21	382	GLB 382	
Reverse Lamp	21	382	GLB 382	
Plate Illumination Lamp	4	233	GLB 233	
Rear Fog Lamp	21	382	GLB 382	Not USA
Instrument Illumination	2.2	987	GLB 987	
Warning Light — Cluster	1.2	286	GLB 286	
— LH Turn Signal	3	504	GLB 504	
— Heated Backlight	2.8	650	GLB 650	24 volt bulb
— Bulb Failure	2.2	987	GLB 987	
— RH Turn Signal	3	504	GLB 504	
— Rectangular Unit	2	281	GLB 281	Special markets only
Map Lamp	6	254	GLB 254	
Clock Illumination	2.2	987	GLB 987	
Switch Panel Illumination	1.2	—	GLB 284	
Automatic Selector Illumination	2.2	987	GLB 987	
Cigarette Lighter Illumination	2	—	GLB 288	
Fibre Optic Lamp	6	254	GLB 254	
Interior Lamp	5	989	GLB 989	
Reading Lamp	4	233	GLB 233	
Luggage Boot Lamp	5	239	GLB 239	

HEADLAMP FUSE BOX

	PROTECTED CIRCUIT	FUSE CAPACITY	UNIPART NUMBER
1	RADIATOR COOLING FAN (WHERE FITTED) 12 CYLINDER 6 CYLINDER	8/15A 10/20A	GFS 415 GFS 420
2	RH DIP	10/20A	GFS 420
3	RH MAIN	17/35A	GFS 435
4	LH DIP	10/20A	GFS 420
5	LH MAIN	17/35A	GFS 435

IN LINE FUSES

PROTECTED CIRCUIT	FUSE	UNIPART No.	LOCATION
Horn	15A	GFS 415	Adjacent to servo RH cars To the battery LH cars
Cigar Lighter	20A	GFS 420	Behind RH front console side casing
Electric Seat Adjustment	30A	GFS 430	Under carpet below LH side of console in front of seat
Air conditioning Amplifier	3A	GFS 43	Behind LH front console side casing
RH Tail lamp and No. plate lamp (Red lead with black ring) LH Tail lamp and No. plate lamp (Red lead with yellow ring Side marker (lamps (where fitted) Red lead	3A	GFS 43	In the luggage compartment behind the trim below the parcel shelf
Radio cassette	2A	GFS 42	Behind the radio

MAIN FUSE BOX L.H. Stg. up to 1983 models

	PROTECTED CIRCUIT	FUSE CAPACITY	UNIPART NUMBER
1	FOG LAMPS	20A	GFS 420
2	HAZARD WARNING SEAT BELT LOGIC UNIT	15A	GFS 415
3	MAP AND INTERIOR LAMPS, CLOCKS, AERIAL, CIGAR LIGHTER	15A	GFS 415
4	PANEL INSTRUMENTS, REVERSE LAMPS, LOW COOLANT SENSOR and WARNING LIGHT	15A	GFS 415
5	HEATED REAR SCREEN	35A	GFS 435
6	WINDSCREEN WIPERS	35A	GFS 435
7	—	—	—
8	PANEL ILLUMINATION	15A	GFS 415
9	FOG REAR GUARD LAMPS	10A	GFS 410
10	DIRECTION INDICATORS	15A	GFS 415
11	BATTERY COOLING FAN, HORN RELAY WINDINGS RADIATOR AUXILIARY FAN, RELAY WINDINGS, WINDSCREEN WASHERS, STOP LAMPS, SERVICE INTERVAL COUNTER (AMERICA ONLY)	35A	GFS 435
12	CRUISE CONTROL	2A	GFS 42

MAIN FUSE BOX L.H. Stg. from 1983 models

	PROTECTED CIRCUIT	FUSE CAPACITY	UNIPART NUMBER
1	FOG LAMPS	20A	GFS 420
2	HAZARD WARNING, SEAT BELT LOGIC UNIT	15A	GFS 415
3	MAP AND INTERIOR LAMPS, CLOCK, AERIAL, CIGAR LIGHTER	15A	GFS 415
4	PANEL INSTRUMENTS, REVERSE LAMPS, LOW COOLANT SENSOR and WARNING LIGHT	15A	GFS 415
5	HEATED REAR SCREEN	35A	GFS 435
6	WINDSCREEN WIPERS	35A	GFS 435
7	TRIP COMPUTER	2A	GFS 42
8	PANEL, CIGAR LIGHTER AND GLOVE BOX ILLUMINATION	15A	GFS 415
9	FOG REAR GUARD LAMPS	10A	GFS 410
10	DIRECTION INDICATORS	15A	GFS 415
11	AUTOMATIC TRANSMISSION KICK DOWN SOLENOID, HORN RELAY WINDINGS RADIATOR AUXILIARY FAN, RELAY WINDINGS, WINDSCREEN WASHERS, STOP LAMPS, SERVICE INTERVAL COUNTER (AMERICA ONLY) HEADLAMP WASH/WIPE (WHERE FITTED)	35A	GFS 435
12	CRUISE CONTROL	2A	GFS 42

AUXILIARY FUSE BOX R.H. Stg. up to 1983 models

	PROTECTED CIRCUIT	FUSE CAPACITY	UNIPART NUMBER
13	MAP AND INTERIOR LAMPS, CLOCK, AERIAL, CIGAR LIGHTER	15A	GFS 415
14	DOOR LOCK RELAY, ELECTRIC DOOR MIRROR, DOOR LAMPS	5A	GFS 45
15	FOG LAMPS	20A	GFS 420
16	—		—
17	FRONT PARKING LAMPS	3A	GFS 43

AUXILIARY FUSE BOX L.H. Stg. up to 1983 models

	PROTECTED CIRCUIT	FUSE CAPACITY	UNIPART NUMBER
13	AIR CONDITIONING, RELAY AND CLUTCH	15A	GFS 415
14	FRONT PARKING LAMPS	3A	GFS 43
15	ANTI RUN-ON VALVE 3.4 CARS ONLY	10A	GFS410
16	AIR CONDITIONING OR HEATER MOTORS	50A	GFS 450
17	DOOR LOCK RELAY, ELECTRIC DOOR MIRRORS, DOOR LIGHTS	3A	GFS 43

MAIN FUSE BOX R.H. Stg. up to 1983 models

	PROTECTED CIRCUIT	FUSE CAPACITY	UNIPART NUMBER
1	ANTI RUN-ON VALVE 3.4 CARS ONLY	10A	GFS 410
2	HAZARD WARNING	15A	GFS 415
3	AIR CONDITIONING OR HEATER MOTORS	50A	GFS 450
4	PANEL INSTRUMENTS, REVERSE LAMPS, LOW COOLANT SENSOR and WARNING LIGHT	15A	GFS 415
5	HEATED REAR SCREEN	35A	GFS 435
6	AIR CONDITIONING RELAY AND CLUTCH	15A	GFS 415
7	WINDSCREEN WIPERS	35A	GFS 435
8	PANEL ILLUMINATION	15A	GFS 415
9	FOG REAR GUARD LAMPS	10A	GFS 410
10	DIRECTION INDICATORS	15A	GFS 415
11	BATTERY COOLING FAN, HORN RELAY WINDINGS, RADIATOR AUXILIARY FAN RELAY, SCREEN WASHERS, STOP LAMPS, SERVICE INTERVAL COUNTER (AMERICA ONLY)	35A	GFS 435
12	CRUISE CONTROL	2A	GFS 42

MAIN FUSE BOX R.H. Stg. from 1983 models

	PROTECTED CIRCUIT	FUSE CAPACITY	UNIPART NUMBER
1	ANTI RUN-ON VALVE 3.4 CARS ONLY	10A	GFS 410
2	HAZARD WARNING	15A	GFS 415
3	AIR CONDITIONING OR HEATER MOTORS	50A	GFS 450
4	PANEL INSTRUMENTS, REVERSE LAMPS, LOW COOLANT SENSOR and WARNING LIGHT	15A	GFS 415
5	HEATED REAR SCREEN	35A	GFS 435
6	AIR CONDITIONING RELAY AND CLUTCH	15A	GFS 415
7	WINDSCREEN WIPERS	35A	GFS 435
8	PANEL, CIGAR LIGHTER AND GLOVE BOX ILLUMINATION	15A	GFS 415
9	FOG REAR GUARD LAMPS	10A	GFS 410
10	DIRECTION INDICATORS	15A	GFS 415
11	AUTOMATIC TRANSMISSION KICK DOWN SOLENOID, HORN RELAY WINDINGS, RADIATOR AUXILIARY FAN RELAY, WINDSCREEN WASHERS, STOP LAMPS, SERVICE INTERVAL COUNTER (AMERICA ONLY) HEADLAMP WASH/WIPE (WHERE FITTED)	35A	GFS 435
12	CRUISE CONTROL	2A	GFS 42